Name and Type of Organization as Focus Illustration of Each Chapter

Chapter Title	Focus Company	Type of Organization	Managerial Focus	Contrast Companies
8. Operational Assets—Property, Plant and Equipment; Natural Resources; and Intangibles	***Delta Air Lines***	Major international air carrier	Planning productive capacity	*AMAX Gold, Inc.* *General Electric* *Sony*
9. Measuring and Reporting Liabilities	***General Mills***	Manufacturer of popular food items	Capital structure	*Toyota* *Washington Post* *Ford*
10. Measuring and Reporting Bonds	***Showboat, Inc.***	Operator of gambling casinos and hotels	Long-term debt financing	*Sears, Roebuck* *Southwestern Bell* *Eastman Kodak* *Halliburton*
11. Measuring and Reporting Owners' Equity	***Wal-Mart***	Retail industry	Corporate ownership	*Greyhound Lines, Inc.* *Chrysler* *Bally Manufacturing*
12. Measuring and Reporting Investments in Other Corporations	***American Brands***	Global consumer products holding company	Strategic investment in other companies	*Chiquita Brands* *Delta Air Lines* *Lands' End*
13. Statement of Cash Flows	***Home Shopping Network***	Retail sales	Management of cash	*USAir* *Pep Boys*
14. Using and Interpreting Financial Statements	***Home Depot***	Home improvement retailers	Financial statement analysis	*Lowe's* *Hechinger* *Grossman's*

FINANCIAL ACCOUNTING

THE IRWIN SERIES IN UNDERGRADUATE ACCOUNTING

Bernstein
Financial Statement Analysis: Theory, Application and Interpretation
Fifth Edition

Bernstein and Maksy
Cases in Financial Statement Reporting and Analysis
Second Edition

Boatsman, Griffin, Vickrey and Williams
Advanced Accounting
Seventh Edition

Boockholdt
Accounting Information Systems
Fourth Edition

Booker, Caldwell, Gallbreath, and Rand
Ready Slides
Ready Shows
Ready Notes
Power Point Classroom Presentation Products

Carse and Slater
Payroll Accounting
1996 Edition

Danos and Imhoff
Introduction to Financial Accounting
Second Edition

Dyckman, Dukes and Davis
Intermediate Accounting
Third Edition

Edwards, Hermanson and Maher
Principles of Financial and Managerial Accounting
Revised Edition

Engler, Bernstein and Lambert
Advanced Accounting
Third Edition

Engstrom and Hay
Essentials of Accounting for Governmental and Not-for-Profit Organizations
Fourth Edition

Engstrom and Hay
Essentials of Governmental Accounting for Public Administrators

Epstein and Spalding
The Accountant's Guide to Legal Liability and Ethics

Ferris
Financial Accounting and Corporate Reporting: A Casebook
Fourth Edition

Garrison and Noreen
Managerial Accounting
Seventh Edition

Hay and Wilson
Accounting for Governmental and Nonprofit Entities
Tenth Edition

Hermanson and Edwards
Financial Accounting: A Business Perspective
Sixth Edition

Hermanson, Edwards and Maher
Accounting: A Business Perspective
Sixth Edition

Hermanson and Walker
Computerized Accounting with Peachtree Complete® Accounting, Version 8.0

Hoyle
Advanced Accounting
Fourth Edition

Koerber
College Accounting
Revised Edition

Larson and Miller
Financial Accounting
Sixth Edition

Larson
Fundamental Accounting Principles
Fourteenth Edition

Larson, Spoede and Miller
Fundamentals of Financial and Managerial Accounting

Libby, Libby and Short
Financial Accounting

Maher and Deakin
Cost Accounting
Fourth Edition

Mansuetti and Weidkamp
Introductory/Intermediate Practice Set Series
Fourth Edition

Marshall and McManus
Accounting: What the Numbers Mean
Third Edition

Miller, Redding and Bahnson
The FASB: The People, the Process and the Politics
Third Edition

Morris
Short Audit Case
Seventh Edition

Mueller, Gernon and Meek
Accounting: An International Perspective
Third Edition

Pasewark and Louwers
Real World Accounting Series
Athletronics, Inc.
Shoe Business, Inc.
Understanding Corporate Annual Reports

Pany and Whittington
Auditing

Peters and Peters
College Accounting
Second Edition

Pratt and Kulsrud
Corporate, Partnership, Estate and Gift Taxation, 1996 Edition

Pratt and Kulsrud
Federal Taxation, 1996 Edition

Pratt and Kulsrud
Individual Taxation, 1996 Edition

Rayburn
Cost Accounting: Using a Cost Management Approach
Sixth Edition

Robertson
Auditing
Eighth Edition

Schrader
College Accounting: A Small Business Approach
Second Edition

Van Breda and Hendriksen
Accounting Theory
Sixth Edition

Whittington and Pany
Principles of Auditing
Eleventh Edition

Yacht
Computer Accounting with Peachtree® for Microsoft® Windows® Release 3.0

Yacht and Terry
Computer Accounting for Microsoft® Windows®

FINANCIAL ACCOUNTING

Robert Libby
Cornell University

Patricia A. Libby
Ithaca College

Daniel G. Short
Miami University

IRWIN

Chicago • Bogotá • Boston • Buenos Aires • Caracas
London • Madrid • Mexico City • Sydney • Toronto

Irwin Book Team

Publisher:	Mike W. Junior
Sponsoring editor:	Mark Pfaltzgraff
Editoral assistant:	Ted Brown
Marketing manager:	Heather L. Woods
Project editor:	Mary Conzachi
Production supervisor:	Dina L. Treadaway
Designer:	Larry J. Cope
Cover designer:	Annette Rapier; AM Design/Larry Cope
Assistant manager, graphics:	Charlene R. Perez
Compositor:	Precision Graphic Services, Inc.
Typeface:	10.5/12 Palatino
Printer:	Von Hoffmann Press, Inc.

Times Mirror
Higher Education Group

Library of Congress Cataloging-in-Publication Data

Libby, Robert.
Financial accounting / Robert Libby, Patricia A. Libby, Daniel G. Short.
p. cm. — (The Irwin series in undergraduate accounting)
Includes indes.
ISBN 0-256-16053-8
1. Accounting. 2. Corporations—Accounting. 3. Financial statements. I. Libby, Patricia A. II. Short, Daniel G. III. Title. IV. Series.
HF5635.L684 1996
657—dc20 95–36377

Printed in the United States of America
1 2 3 4 5 6 7 8 9 0 VH 2 1 0 9 8 7 6 5

To our parents:
Herman and Doris Hargenrater
Oscar and Selma Libby
Bob and Mary Ann Short

and our daughters:
Laura Libby
Heather and Jenni Short

About the Authors

Robert Libby is the David A. Thomas Professor of Management at the Johnson Graduate School of Management at Cornell University. Bob teaches the introductory financial accounting course. He previously taught at the University of Illinois, Pennsylvania State University, the University of Texas, the University of Chicago, and the University of Michigan. He received his B.S. from Pennsylvania State University and his M.A.S. and Ph.D. from the University of Illinois; he is also a CPA. Bob is a widely published author specializing in behavioral accounting. His prior text, *Accounting and Human Information Processing* (Prentice Hall, 1981), was awarded the AICPA/AAA Notable Contributions to the Accounting Literature Award. He has published numerous articles in the *Journal of Accounting Research, The Accounting Review, Accounting, Organizations, and Society,* and other accounting journals. He is an active member of the American Accounting Association and the American Institute of CPAs, and is a member of the editorial boards of the *Journal of Accounting Research; The Accounting Review; Accounting; Organizations, and Society; Journal of Accounting Literature;* and *Journal of Behavioral Decision Making.*

Patricia Libby is Associate Professor of Accounting at Ithaca College where she teaches the undergraduate financial accounting course. She previously taught graduate and undergraduate financial accounting at Eastern Michigan University and the University of Texas. Before entering academe, she was an auditor with Price Waterhouse and a financial administrator at the University of Chicago. She received her B.S. from Pennsylvania State University, M.B.A. from DePaul University, and Ph.D. from the University of Michigan; she is also a CPA. Pat conducts research on how to use cases in the introductory course and in other parts of the accounting curriculum. She has published articles in *The Accounting Review, Issues in Accounting Education,* and *The Michigan CPA.* She also conducts seminars nationally on active learning strategies, including cooperative learning methods, and is the chair of the Collaborative Learning at Ithaca College faculty support group.

Dan Short is Dean of the Richard T. Farmer School of Business at Miami University. Previously, Dan was dean of the College of Business at Kansas State University and before that associate dean at the University of Texas at Austin, where he taught the undergraduate and graduate financial accounting courses. He also taught at the University of Chicago. He received his undergraduate degree from Boston University and his M.B.A. and Ph.D. from the University of Michigan. Dan has won numerous awards for his outstanding teaching abilities and has published articles in *The Accounting Review,* the *Journal of Accounting Research, The Wall Street Journal,* and other business journals. He has worked with a large number of Fortune 500 companies, commercial banks, and investment banks to develop and teach executive education courses on the effective use of accounting information.

Instructor Summary: Why This Book?

We wrote this book in the belief that the subject, financial accounting, is inherently interesting, but financial accounting textbooks often are not. Furthermore, the typical texts do not demonstrate that accounting is an exciting major field or important to future careers in marketing, finance, and other areas of management. As a consequence, we approached the writing of this text with **career relevance** as our guide to selection of material and the need to **engage the student** as our guide to style and pedagogy. Our experience, probably similar to yours, suggests that if we fail to engage students, many of them will ignore the text as a worthwhile course resource. In every aspect of writing and designing this book, we have been mindful of this challenge to capture the students' interest; based on what our reviewers and the students who've read and class-tested the manuscript have told us, we've succeeded.

We have met this challenge by

1. *Integrating real-world business and accounting practices by building each chapter around the operations and financial statements of its own "focus company" (e.g., Harley-Davidson in Chapter 7) through which the key concepts in the chapter material are examined.* Learning accounting and financial reporting in real business contexts naturally creates interest for students, demonstrates career relevance, and illustrates management and external uses of financial statements. This can't be accomplished effectively by inserting disjointed vignettes or colorful short features into a traditional preparer-oriented text. We wrote our chapters from scratch around our realistic focus companies, and our financial analysis, international, and ethics features are integrated into the chapters.
2. *Choosing material for its managerial significance and relevance to using real financial statements.* Actual company practices and decisions made by our focus companies and "contrast companies" illustrate the variety in real-world situations. More importantly, they guided our choice of material toward that which would be more interesting and relevant to users of financial statements in finance, marketing, and management, as well as to future accountants. Chapter 5, which illustrates the complete financial reporting process in the information environment of modern financial markets, is unique.
3. *Choosing examples and explaining material in a manner appropriate for the introductory student.* To ensure accessibility of the material, we employ a building block approach; we carefully cover the basics before we address more complex issues. As the students' sophistication develops throughout the term, so does the sophistication of the focus company and contrasting company illustrations. Smaller, single industry companies with simple operations, capital structures, and disclosures were selected for the early chapters. The examples increase in sophistication as a student's knowledge grows, both within chapters (e.g., Chapter 7's coverage of LIFO) and between chapters (e.g., Chapter 1 versus Chapter 5 versus Chapter 14).
4. *Including active-learning features that engage the student, provide interactive feedback, and promote critical thinking skills.* Our unique Self-Study Quizzes reinforce key concepts and provide important feedback before students move to the next part of each chapter. Many of the quizzes and end-of-chapter materials rely on real statements and require students to make judgments, search for additional information, and think backward from outputs to inputs, thereby giving students exposure to and practice managerial thinking.

Preface

We wrote this book in the belief that the subject, financial accounting, is inherently interesting, but financial accounting textbooks often are not. Furthermore, the typical texts do not demonstrate that accounting is an exciting major field or important to future careers in marketing, finance, and other areas of management. As a consequence, we approached the writing of this text with **career relevance** as our guide to selection of material and the need to **engage the student** as our guide to style and pedagogy. Our experience, probably similar to yours, suggests that if we fail to engage students, many of them will ignore the text as a worthwhile course resource. In every aspect of writing and designing this book we have been mindful of this challenge to capture the students' interest; based on what our reviewers and the students who've read and class-tested the manuscript have told us, we've succeeded. However, in the final analysis it is you and your students who will determine the true worth of our efforts.

This text is aimed at students with career interests in marketing, finance, banking, manufacturing, and human resources, as well as accounting, but with no prior exposure to accounting and financial statements, and often little exposure to the business world. We have carefully designed the scope and depth of the text so that most or all of it can be covered in a single term.

GOALS OF TEXT

To truly engage readers and stimulate their interest in the subject matter is an obvious, yet often overlooked, goal of a textbook. Only you can tell us if we've succeeded in **motivating the reader** and **increasing concept retention** where so many others haven't. Again, our reviewers and students think so, and if you and your classes are at all like them, investing the time to read a chapter, we believe, will ultimately make a big difference to you and your students! Other key goals we had in mind when writing the text were

- To convey the importance of financial accounting and financial statements to managers.
- To help students learn how investing, financing, and operating decisions of different **real** merchandising, manufacturing, and service businesses are reflected in their **financial statements**.
- To help students understand how these statements are used in **real business decisions**.
- To encourage and develop critical thinking by incorporating a strong decision-making orientation.

Besides meeting our overall objective of stimulating an interest in the subject matter to improve learning, these goals are in accordance with the recommendations of the Accounting Education Change Commission **to teach students more effectively the relevance and use of accounting information**.

DEVELOPMENT STORY

Meeting the ever-changing needs of instructors and students, many of which are driven by continued change in the accounting profession and the dynamic business environment of the 1990s, requires input from many people. The development process that provided that input to this project was extensive and, we believe, instrumental in making this text and package truly market-driven. In virtually every instance where preferences were at stake, we deferred to the suggestions of our colleagues and their students. In our acknowledgments we will attempt to thank everyone involved, but first we wanted to provide a brief overview of the market-driven process that guided the development of this book.

Exhibit A

HARLEY-DAVIDSON, INC.
CONSOLIDATED BALANCE SHEET

(In thousands, except per share amounts)

December 31	1993
Assets	
Current assets:	
Cash and cash equivalents	$44,122
Accounts receivable, net of allowance for doubtful accounts	93,178
Inventories	94,428
Total Current Assets	265,465

HARLEY-DAVIDSON, INC.
CONSOLIDATED STATEMENT OF INCOME

(In thousands, except per share amounts)

Year ended December 31	1993
Net sales	$1,105,284
Cost of goods sold	808,871
Gross profit	296,413

As we wrote the first draft, we had 15 accounting educators provide detailed chapter-by-chapter feedback on the entire first draft manuscript. We then had a between-drafts reviewer conference, where seven of our reviewers discussed in detail their recommendations and preferences for treatment of different topics. While this gave us a strong focus and direction for writing the second draft, we did not stop asking for input and advice from you. Twenty individuals gave us additional detailed information on a chapter-by-chapter basis as they read from our second draft manuscript. At this point, over 60 students who read from chapters of our book completed questionnaires that allowed us to directly incorporate student feedback as well. We were able to use all of this extensive and extremely helpful input in shaping a final draft that we feel best meets the needs of our intended audience.

The tremendous feedback provided by this process helped us develop the numerous differences and advantages we believe distinguish our text and allow us to meet our goals. The four features listed below are ones that you have told us are the most important.

WHAT'S DIFFERENT AND WHY: KEY FEATURES

1. *Integration of real-world business and accounting practices into the material by building each chapter around the operations and financial statements of an interesting "focus company" (e.g., Harley-Davidson, see Exhibit A).*

The major topics of each chapter are integrated around a single focus company, its operations, and its financial statements and related disclosures. Focus companies were selected from Forbes' Best Small Companies in America as well as the Fortune 1,000. They include well-known and exciting companies such as Timberland, Harley-Davidson, Callaway Golf, Sbarro Restaurants, Showboat, and Delta Air Lines. Each accounting and reporting issue raised is discussed in the context of the focus company and its financial statements and other disclosures. In addition, each chapter emphasizes a different aspect of management, including marketing strategy, human resources, financing strategy, manufacturing, corporate communication, and mergers and acquisitions. (See the inside front cover for a listing.) This directly demonstrates the relevance of the material to a variety of future careers. Integration as opposed to add-on, disjointed vignettes distinguishes our approach from that of other texts; it is also the key to demonstrating career relevance and conveying the excitement of real accounting and reporting problems. For example, in Chapters 2–4 typical transactions from Sbarro, Inc., a family-style Italian restaurant chain, are shown to demonstrate this firm's investing, financing, and operating decisions.

We also regularly integrate "contrast company" examples where appropriate to illustrate the variety in real-world practices, and the effect of a company's particular circumstances on its accounting and reporting practices. Our selection of focus and contrast companies provides the proper balance of merchandising, manufacturing, and service companies.

For example, Harley-Davidson is the focus company for Chapter 7, "Measuring Inventory and Cost of Goods Sold." We first examine the inventory accounting issues faced by Harley's motorcycle and motorclothes product lines to demonstrate differences between inventory accounting for manufacturing and merchandising operations. We then focus on its growing manufacturing operations where Harley faces rising costs and compare it to three contrast companies that face very different inventory accounting issues: Deere & Co., which is a shrinking manufacturer; Compaq Computer which is a declining-cost manufacturer; and the housing division of Asahi Chemicals (of Japan), which produces valuable, distinguishable inventory items.

FINANCIAL ANALYSIS

Judging Advertising Strategy Based on the 10-K

In its description of the business included in the 10-K, Callaway discloses that it spent approximately $6.5 million, $10.7 million, and $21 million on advertising and promotional expenditures over the last three years. The difference between these three numbers and those disclosed on the schedule of advertising costs printed above is the amount spent each year on promotional and endorsement-related expenditures including compensation to professional golfers.

While both numbers have been rising along with sales, Callaway increased its spending on promotional and endorsement-related expenditures in the current year at a much faster rate than spending on other types of advertising. Promotional activities grew in one year from 22% [($10.7 – $8.4) ÷ $10.7] to 30% [($21.0 – $14.8) ÷ $21.0] of the total advertising and promotion budget. This increasing emphasis on professional endorsements represents a change in strategy for Callaway which is probably related to its new product introductions planned for the coming year.

By the time students complete the semester, they have examined a wide variety of company situations and real financial disclosures. Just as important, these examples are appropriate for the introductory student. For example, in Chapter 5, where we discuss the communication of accounting information using Callaway Golf as the focus company, we take time to define acronyms such as CEO and CFO and terms like institutional investor to be sure that the introductory student has an understanding of common business terminology. The reviewers of our text have unanimously endorsed our superior use of real company examples and believe as we do that they will maintain students' interest in the material.

2. *Material selected for its managerial significance and its relevance to understanding and using real company financial statements—a true user orientation.*

The material included in this text was selected for its relevance to understanding real companies, financial statements and real management decisions. Unrealistic topics and practices have been eliminated. For example, LIFO applied on a perpetual basis was eliminated because it is rarely used in practice. Further, in keeping with the financial statement focus of the text, pure recordkeeping functions have been included in appendixes or reserved for future coursework. We replace these topics with often-omitted material that is fundamental to understanding financial statements. By eliminating the recordkeeping emphasis, we can use basic transaction analysis, journal entries, and T-accounts to provide the structure for understanding the interplay between management decisions and financial statements and the analysis of financial statements. We demonstrate how this structure is as important to future financial statement users as it is to accountants.

An equal part of this feature is the integration of discussions of the decisions made by management and financial statement users in our focus and contrasting companies. Our financial analysis features, shown above, along with the international and ethics features, relate directly to the decisions faced by managers and financial statement users at our focus and contrasting companies. For example, the focus company in Chapter 5, "The Communication of Accounting Information," is Callaway Golf. Here we trace the decisions of Ely Callaway (chairman and CEO), Carol Kerley (CFO) and her accounting staff, as well as the auditors at Price Waterhouse, bankers at First Interstate Bank of California, investment bankers at Merrill Lynch, and the managers at Sumitomo Corporation (which exports and sells Callaway's golf clubs in Japan), as Callaway develops the necessary financial statements and related reports needed to obtain both private and public financing for the growing company. This decision-making focus encourages and develops critical thinking. At the same time, we cover the highly technical requirements for financial reporting format and content within a context that literally makes some of the most technical accounting material come alive. As a consequence, students will better remember the technical material and better understand its importance.

3. *Choosing examples and explaining material in a manner appropriate for the introductory student.*

The pace, depth of coverage, and level of difficulty of the material and examples are carefully matched to the needs and abilities of introductory students. To ensure accessibility of the material, we employ a building block approach; we carefully cover the basics before we address more complex issues. As the students' sophistication develops throughout the term, so does the sophistication of the focus company and contrasting company illustrations. Smaller, single industry companies with simple operations, capital structures, and disclosures were selected for the early chapters. The examples increase in sophistication as a student's knowledge grows, both within chapters (e.g., Chapter 7's coverage of LIFO) and between chapters (e.g., Chapter 1 versus Chapter 5 versus Chapter 14).

The technical material is conveyed with clear step-by-step presentations within the realistic examples. For example, Chapters 2, 3, and 4 follow Sbarro, Inc. (a chain of Italian fast-food restaurants) through each step of the basic accounting process, ensuring that students are prepared for the later material. The emphasis on contrasting company practices is conveyed through side-by-side illustrations that punctuate the effects of differences in financial statement presentations and accounting methods. Numerous exhibits and other visual aids are included to enhance comprehension and learning (see Exhibit B). To further increase comprehension, we define unfamiliar terminology (including terms that develop general business knowledge rather than strictly accounting terminology) within the text material, in marginal definitions, and in a glossary of key terms at the end of the book. We also list key terms with page references at the end of each chapter.

Exhibit B

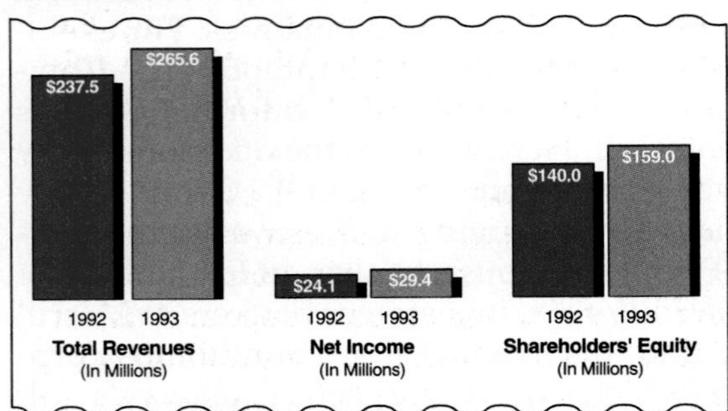

Sbarro also uses graphs to communicate key financial data.

4. *Active-learning features engage the student, provide interactive feedback, and promote critical thinking skills.*

Active learning creates attention and promotes retention. The integration of technical material in the real-world context produces major advantages here. A unique feature, Self-Study Quizzes (see Exhibit C), stops the student at strategic points throughout each chapter to make sure that key points are well understood. These quizzes reinforce key points and help students avoid reading the text in the same fashion as they do a novel; to understand accounting, students must be able to work with the numbers. Students who class-tested the book commented that in anticipation of a quiz, they think about what they are reading, which improves learning. The quizzes often require that students prepare or use financial statement disclosures based on actual companies to reinforce the usefulness of what they are learning. For example, in Chapter 5 students actually determine whether Callaway's senior management had earned their bonuses. The quizzes are part of our integrative approach. These are followed by Demonstra-tion Cases presented at the end of the chapter. Students who have carefully worked with these two types of learning aids are ready to work the end-of-chapter homework assignments.

Exhibit C

Self-Study Quiz

Callaway executives will receive bonuses if sales growth and pretax earnings as a percent of sales meet or exceed target amounts (35.1 % and 21.1%, respectively). Use Exhibit 5–5 to see if Callaway executives earned their bonuses in the most recent year.

Computations:

____

____

____

____

Discuss why Callaway might choose to pay executives based on performance and why they use the same accounting numbers used in reports to shareholders to measure the executives' performance.

The material within chapters is followed by an extensive selection of end-of-chapter questions, exercises, problems, and cases that examine single concepts or integrate multiple concepts presented in the chapter. To maintain the real-world flavor of the chapter material, they are often based on other real domestic and international companies, and require analysis as well as conceptual thought, and calculation as well as written communication. Assignments suitable for individual or group written projects and oral presentations are included in strategic locations.

TREATMENT OF DIFFICULT TOPICS

Among the myriad of topics that are covered in an introductory financial accounting course, a number were identified by our reviewers as difficult ones for students to comprehend. A listing of some of these follows along with a brief discussion of some strengths of our approach to these areas:

- **Bonds:** Our primary coverage of bonds, in Chapter 10, begins with a strong discussion of the uses and nature of bonds, presented in context with the Showboat, Inc., company example. This allows students to understand the relevance of this material better. At one point in the chapter, KC Southern's amortization policy is contrasted with Showboat's to point out a financial analyst's potential interpretation of the two policies.
- **Time Value of Money:** Our reviewers clearly feel that a key strength of our discussion of the time value of money (Chapter 9) is the practical illustration of its applications to accounting through short cases with General Mills, Inc., as the focus company.
- **Inventory:** We clearly took a user-oriented approach to the discussion of this material in Chapter 7 with a goal of providing an understanding of what accountants do with inventory and why. Throughout the entire chapter the focus is on the key concepts of inventory valuation and their effects on financial statements without placing undue emphasis on recordkeeping.
- **Adjusting Entries:** Again, we start with a premise that students will better understand the *how* behind this concept if we first illustrate through a real-company example *why* adjusting entries are necessary. To an introductory student, adjusting entries are often not intuitive and our reviewers unanimously endorsed our walk-through of the Sbarro, Inc., analysis as an effective tool for presenting this hard-to-grasp concept.

KEY FEATURES IN EACH CHAPTER

Chapter 1: Financial Statements and Business Decisions

- Students are introduced immediately to the four basic financial statements through the use of an interesting company example, based on an actual case. At the same time, interindustry differences in financial reporting are illustrated to begin building critical thinking skills for the student.
- Financial Analysis discussions are introduced throughout this chapter (and then carried through all chapters) to show students how useful accounting knowledge can be in making economic decisions.

Chapter 2: The Accounting Model and Transaction Analysis

- Exhibit 2–1 illustrates a unique presentation of the Conceptual Framework that becomes the building block for the transaction analysis approach to follow.
- Balance sheet concepts are examined and reinforced before the income statement concepts are presented in Chapter 3.
- As an active-learning feature for better comprehension, students must complete the transaction analysis illustration following the process discussed in the chapter.
- Debit-credit and T-account concepts are presented clearly in context with the ongoing Sbarro, Inc., focus company case. Students thus see the relevance and use of these often confusing procedural topics.
- Financial Analysis discussions emphasize financing and investing decisions.

Chapter 3: Income Measurement and Operating Decisions

- Income statement concepts and their relationships to balance sheet concepts are examined and reinforced in their own separate chapter.
- Transaction Analysis model as illustrated through the Sbarro, Inc., example is continued to allow students to build upon concepts presented in Chapter 2.
- Financial Analysis discussions emphasize operating decisions.
- Strong conceptual development of the principles related to revenue recognition and the matching concept are introduced in this chapter, including a conceptual discussion of accruals and deferrals. Timelines are presented as useful analytical tools for providing visual representations of transactions or series of transactions.

Chapter 4: The Adjustment Process and Financial Statement Preparation

- After first showing students the *why* behind adjusting entries, we show them the *how* through a consistent three-step process that can be applied to analyze any situation requiring an adjusting journal entry. The focus is on understanding versus rote memorization.

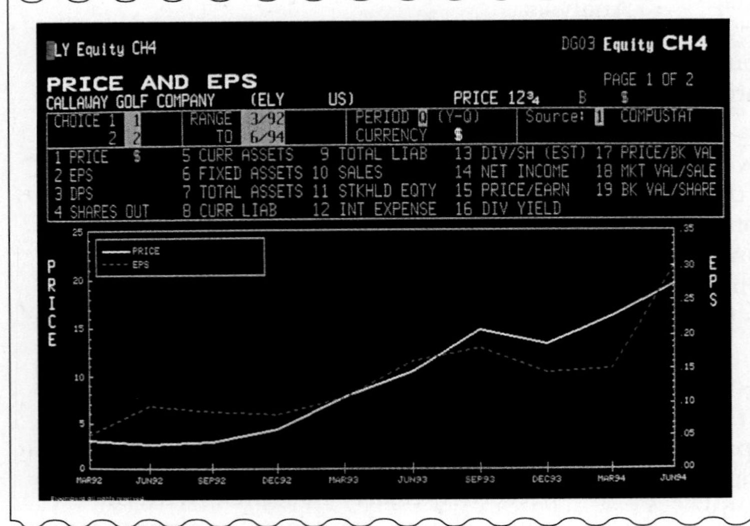

- The statement of cash flows, its importance and where it comes from, is discussed here so that students can keep cash effects in mind through later chapters without being overburdened with technical details.
- Formal recordkeeping formats and reversing entries are included as optional chapter supplements.

Chapter 5: The Communication of Accounting Information

- This unique chapter clearly and concisely presents how financial statements are disseminated and used, emphasizing not just the output, but the people and process involved. Exhibits 5–1 and 5–2 are truly innovative (5–2 is shown above).
- Through a presentation of financial information sources, electronic information services, and actual reports used by companies, we help the students redefine the uses behind the process presented in the previous three chapters.
- An often overlooked item, footnotes to financial statements, which were first presented in Chapter 1, are discussed in greater detail here with actual corporate examples used to illustrate these important components of the reporting process.

Chapter 6: Accounting for Sales Revenue, Cash, and Receivables

- To improve student understanding, receivable issues are linked with revenue recognition.
- Issues related to discounts, returns, and bad debts are presented as part of marketing strategy and financial management at Timberland, Inc., not as pure recordkeeping functions.
- The concept of bad debt expense is presented clearly with an emphasis on analyzing the effects of this expense on actual financial statements; students work with actual statements and footnotes.
- Recognizing revenue in unusual circumstances is covered at a level appropriate for the introductory student.

Chapter 7: Measuring Inventory and Cost of Goods Sold

- The influence of choice of inventory method on financial statement information is presented through examples of choices facing Harley-Davidson, Inc., a company with which most students can readily identify.
- Harley-Davidson's inventory method choices are compared to those of other companies in different circumstances.
- In the discussion of periodic versus perpetual inventory systems, the focus is on the usefulness of perpetual inventory systems for managerial decisions rather than heavy coverage of recordkeeping.

Chapter 8: Operational Assets—Property, Plant, and Equipment; Natural Resources; and Intangibles

- The depreciation methods are presented in a decision-making framework that minimizes procedure and emphasizes how methods are chosen.

- The discussion of residual value and estimated useful life is strengthened by the continued use of examples from Delta Air Lines, Inc.
- The chapter develops student interest in a potentially dry topic by showing how planning productive capacity is an essential management responsibility.

Exhibit D

Real World Excerpt
Wal-Mart Stores, Inc.
Dividend Declaration

Dateline: Bentonville, Ark., June 2, 1994

The Board of Directors of Wal-Mart Stores, Inc. today declared a quarterly cash dividend on common stock of four-and-one-quarter cents ($0.0425) a share, payable July 8, 1994, to shareholders of record June 13, 1994.

Chapter 9: Measuring and Reporting Liabilities

- As in other chapters, ratios (e.g., current ratio) are discussed as the accounts used in computations are covered, allowing students to more clearly see the linkages and understand the importance of ratio analysis.
- Topics were selected based on a review of hundreds of financial statements. To provide relevance, students are exposed to liabilities that they will see on most statements. Complex issues are introduced without excessive details.

Chapter 10: Measuring and Reporting Bonds

- Student interest is maintained by following an actual bond issuance for Showboat, Inc., from the prospectus stage through sale, concluding with a vote by bondholders to amend bond covenants.
- Based on reviewer feedback, material was added on bond investments held to maturity, which briefly illustrates why certain companies choose this as an investment strategy and how they report it in their financial statements. By combining bond liabilities and bond investments, students develop a better understanding of these instruments.

Chapter 11: Measuring and Reporting Owners' Equity

- Through the primary use of examples from Wal-Mart, a corporate success story all students can appreciate and understand, the focus is on comprehending the relationships among dividends, cash, and retained earnings. Students are shown real-world examples such as notice of an annual meeting, a vote to amend a corporate charter, a dividend declaration (see Exhibit D), and a stock repurchase.
- Material on initial public offerings (IPOs) is presented here with a discussion of the reasons why a company might want to go public and examples of formerly small start-up operations that are now corporate giants (e.g., Dell Computers and Microsoft, Inc.).

Chapter 12: Measuring and Reporting Investments in Other Corporations

- By illustrating actual examples from American Brands, McDermott Corporation, and others, the student is shown the strategies behind a company's decision to invest in other companies.
- As in other chapters, the approach focuses on presenting the business environment that drives transactions and then developing the accounting treatments necessary to capture and present properly the information in financial statements.
- The chapter discussion uses a modular approach that permits the instructor to cover as much or as little of intercorporate investments as is deemed appropriate.

Chapter 13: Statement of Cash Flows

- Financial Analysis sections, a feature that appears in all chapters, are inserted frequently here to show the use and importance of cash flow so students are able to view the statement of cash flows as an analytical tool to help convey new information about a company.
- A spreadsheet approach is utilized to show in a more intuitive way how the statement of cash flows can be prepared. The indirect method, the one most com-

monly used in actual practice, is presented first and with greater emphasis.

- The chapter effectively bridges from a simplified example used to introduce concepts to the actual statement of cash flows for Home Shopping Network to illustrate how concepts are applied in practice.

Chapter 14: Using and Interpreting Financial Statements

- Financial ratios are used to compare Home Depot with leading competitors Grossman's, Hechinger, and Lowe's to illustrate the uses and potential shortcomings of ratio analysis.
- To increase understanding of actual practices, students are briefly introduced to how information is used in an efficient market.
- Financial analysis is integrated with Home Depot's business strategy and operating decisions to allow students to see the types of strategic and other decisions facing business managers.

END-OF-CHAPTER MATERIAL

For success in the business world in general and in accounting, students must possess strong written and oral communication skills and be able to deal with ambiguity, solve unstructured problems, gather information from human and electronic sources, use critical thinking skills to make good judgments, and work effectively in groups. The AECC and the Big 6 firms stress a broad liberal arts foundation with an understanding of business and organizations as being more important than specific accounting or auditing knowledge. We have responded to these needs by framing each chapter in a business setting so as to enhance students' understanding of accounting in the context of various businesses. Although the material within the chapters provides varied resources for students to use in developing the necessary skills, we have also included numerous end-of-chapter items that (1) incorporate a writing component, (2) drill students on key concepts, (3) require students to search for information by contacting companies, searching libraries, and utilizing computerized services (see especially Chapter 5), (4) require students to make judgments without having access to additional information, often necessitating thinking backward from outputs to inputs, and (5) can be structured by the instructor as group learning experiences.

The end-of-chapter material consists of four types of items: questions, exercises, problems, and cases. The questions and exercises usually cover single topics and require less time and effort to complete than the problems and cases that typically integrate more than one concept and require more analytical and critical-thinking skills. The material follows the topical coverage as outlined in the chapter, includes multiple items on each topic, and moves from easy to more challenging with very challenging items noted. We carry through the user orientation in the end-of-chapter material by including examples from small business settings, problems that deal with real financial statement excerpts, international company examples (see Exhibit E), and ethical issues examples. To allow maximum instructor flexibility and ample student practice, each of the key topics is covered by at least two items (i.e. questions, exercises, problems, and cases).

Exhibit E

C5–4 An International Perspective **Grand Metropolitan**

Grand Metropolitan is a major international company that is located in London. A recent annual report contained the following information concerning its accounting policies.

Accounting convention:
The financial statements of the group are prepared under the historical cost convention. They have been drawn up to comply in all material respects with U.K. statements of standard accounting practice in force at the relevant time.

UNIQUE, REAL-WORLD OFFERING

Financial Accounting, *The Wall Street Journal Edition*, (ISBN: 0-256-21586-3). The price of this version of the text includes a 10-week subscription to *The Wall Street Journal*, the leading business daily newspaper. The *Journal*'s coverage of accounting, financial, and general business topics, both domestic and global, is unparalleled by any other business periodical. Your Irwin sales representative can provide you more information on this unique offering.

SUPPLEMENTS FOR THE INSTRUCTOR

Instructor's Resource Guide, by Betty McMechen (Mesa State College), contains the following items by chapter to provide additional support for the instructor: Chapter Outline, Chapter Summary, Chapter Lecture Notes (cross-referenced to Learning Objectives), Problem Assignment Grid, Guide to Other Chapter Features, Supplemental Enrichment Activities (**including suggestions for group or collaborative exercises for both inside and outside the classroom**), Suggested Reading List, and Transparency Masters. In addition an electronic version of this manual is available.

Solutions Manual, prepared by the textbook authors and carefully reviewed for accuracy by outside sources, contains solutions to all assignment material and is available in electronic format as well.

Solutions Transparencies are set in large, boldface type to maximize their effectiveness in large classrooms.

Ready Shows, Ready Slides are teaching enhancement packages prepared by Jon A. Booker, Charles W. Caldwell, Susan C. Galbreath, and Richard S. Rand, all of Tennessee Technological University.

Ready Shows. This is a package of multimedia lecture enhancement aids that uses PowerPoint® software to illustrate chapter concepts.

Ready Slides. These selected four-color teaching transparencies are printed from the PowerPoint® Ready Shows. (See also "Ready Notes" under Student Supplements.)

Test Bank, by Harry Dickenson (University of Richmond), contains multiple-choice, true-false, matching and completion questions, and short problems requiring analysis and written answers. The testing material is coded by type of question and level of difficulty.

Computest is a computerized version of the manual testbank for more efficient use, available in Macintosh, Windows, or DOS versions. The extensive features of this test generator program include random question selection based on the user's specification of learning objectives, type of question, and level of difficulty.

Teletest allows users to call a toll-free number, specify the content of desired exams, and have a laser-printed copy of the exams mailed to them.

Lecture Enhancement Video Series are short, action-oriented videos that provide the impetus for lively classroom discussion. The *Financial Accounting Video Library* includes videos with the Financial Accounting Standards Board, Ben & Jerry's, and a video with Art Wyatt discussing the impact of the International Accounting Standards Committee.

SUPPLEMENTS FOR THE STUDENT

Study Guide, by Patricia Doherty (Boston University), contains a number of useful references for the student. Each chapter includes Overview of Chapter, Restatement of Learning Objectives, Chapter Outline, Questions and Exercises (multiple-choice, true-false, matching, short answer, and group exercises), and a word search puzzle of key terms to build critical thinking skills.

Active Learning Workbook: Student Learning Tools, by Barbara Chiappetta (Nassua Community College) contains material for students' use in an active learning environment. It is designed to facilitate a concept approach with a user emphasis and the development of interpersonal skills. The Introduction is aimed at motivating the student to participate by developing an understanding of the need for and the value of active learning. Functional aspects of learning teams are explained, and forms for team use are provided. The material is divided into three sections: class activities, team presentation assignments, and writing assignments. For instructors who address procedural issues, accounting forms (journal paper, two- and three-column paper, and T-accounts) are provided for reproduction.

Ready Notes is a booklet of Ready Show screen printouts that enables students to take notes during Ready Show or Ready Slide presentations.

Room Zoom: The CPA Source Disc is a multimedia, interactive CD-ROM that provides an exciting guide to a CPA career. Students will be able to experience a day in the life of a CPA, review salary statistics, learn about scholarships and internships, understand the technology inherent in the profession, learn about the CPA exam, and much more. Available to your students for a nominal charge when purchased with *Financial Accounting* from Irwin, this innovative technology component would also be perfect for the first day of class.

Working Papers, selected and prepared by the authors, contain all the forms necessary for completing the end-of-chapter materials.

IEM: Iowa Electronics Market is the first ever Introductory Accounting product offered via the Internet, by Joyce Berg, Robert Forsythe, and Tom Rietz (all of the University of Iowa). This fully interactive, real-time experience allows your students to explore accounting issues beyond just the numbers. Contact your Irwin sales representative for more information on this innovative offering.

Real-World Accounting Series are practice sets from Timothy Louwers and William Pasewark, both of the University of Houston, that offer students hands-on experience in analyzing and understanding corporate annual reports. They are intended to show the big picture at the end of the accounting process, thereby emphasizing interpretation and analysis rather than preparation of financial statements.

Athletronics, Inc. This practice set emphasizes the effect of generally accepted accounting principles on decisions based on accounting data. The student is required to perform financial analysis on the data contained in the manual.

Shoe Business, Inc. This humorous yet serious practice set focuses on the frequent overemphasis of bottom-line net income by investors. The student is led through extensive analysis of footnote disclosures, financial ratios, and bankruptcy prediction models.

Understanding Corporate Annual Reports. This practice set contains instructions for obtaining an annual report from a publicly traded corporation and performing analysis on that report.

GLAS (General Ledger Applications Software) is a revised package containing most of the features of commercial accounting software, yet easily used by students with little or no computer background. A large number of problem assignments are preloaded on the package, and it can also be used to solve any problem that calls for journal entries. Both DOS and Windows versions are available.

SPATS (Spreadsheet Applications Template Software) includes Lotus 1-2-3 (or the equivalent) templates for selected problems and exercises from the text. The templates gradually become more complex, requiring students to build a variety of formulas. "What if" questions are added to show the power of spreadsheets and a simple tutorial is included. Instructors may request a free master template for students to use or copy, or students may purchase shrinkwrapped versions for a nominal fee. Both DOS and Windows versions are available.

Tutorial Software provides multiple-choice, true-false, journal entry review, and glossary review questions that can be randomly accessed by students. Explanations of right and wrong answers are provided and scores are tallied. Instructors may request a free master template for students to use or copy, or students may purchase shrinkwrapped versions for a nominal fee. Both DOS and Windows versions are available.

Computerized and Multimedia Practice Sets. Computerized practice sets by Leland Mansuetti and Keith Weildkamp (both of Sierra College) are available in DOS and Windows formats. In addition, multimedia versions incorporating sound and video into our best-selling practice set series add excitement to the learning process.

ACKNOWLEDGMENTS

Writing a successful text requires a team effort, and we have enjoyed working with excellent teammates. Throughout the process of writing this text, many people stepped forward with tremendous efforts that allowed us to accomplish our stated goals. We would like to recognize the sincere and devoted efforts of the many people who added their input to the process of developing this text. As stated above in the Development Story section, we received invaluable advice and suggestions during the manuscript development process. For this assistance, we thank the following colleagues:

D'Arcy Becker, *University of New Mexico*
Linda Bell, *William Jewell College*
Wayne Boutell, *University of California at Berkeley*
Patricia Doherty, *Boston University*
Allan Drebin, *Northwestern University*
Marie Dubke, *University of Memphis*
Gary Fish, *Illinois State University*
Paul Frishkoff, *University of Oregon*

Flora Guidry, *University of New Hampshire*
Marcia Halvorsen, *University of Cincinnati*
Leon Hanouille, *Syracuse University*
Peggy Hite, *Indiana University*
David Hoffman, *University of North Carolina at Chapel Hill*
Kathy Horton, *University of Illinois at Chicago*
Sharon Jackson, *Auburn University at Montgomery*
Naida Kaen, *University of New Hampshire*
Sue Kattelus, *Eastern Michigan University*
Jim Kurtenbach, *Iowa State University*
David Lavin, *Florida International University*
Joan Luft, *Michigan State University*
Betty McMechen, *Mesa State College*
Greg Merrill, *California State University at Fullerton*
Brian Nagle, *Duquesne University*
Ron Pawliczek, *Boston College*
Don Putnam, *California State University Polytechnic at Pomona*
Michael Ruble, *Western Washington University*
Mary Alice Seville, *Oregon State University*
Wayne Shaw, *University of Colorado at Boulder*
Ken Smith, *Idaho State University*
Ralph Spanswick, *California State University at Los Angeles*
Kevin Stocks, *Brigham Young University*
Kathryn Sullivan, *George Washington University*
Michael Welker, *Drexel University*
T. Sterling Wetzel, *Oklahoma State University*
William Zorr, *University of Wisconsin–Oshkosh*

In addition, we are deeply indebted to the following individuals who helped develop, critique, and shape the extensive ancillary package: Jon Booker, Tennessee Technological University; Charles Caldwell, Tennessee Technological University; Harry Dickenson, University of Richmond; Patricia Doherty, Boston University; Jeannie Folk, College of DuPage; Susan Galbreath, Tennessee Technological University; Leland Mansuetti, Sierra College; Betty McMechen, Mesa State College; Richard Rand, Tennessee Technological University; Barbara Schnathorst, The Write Solution, Inc.; Jack Terry, ComSource, Inc.; and Keith Weidkamp, Sierra College.

We also received invaluable input and support from numerous colleagues and associates, in particular: William Wright, University of California at Irvine; Marge Hubbard, Kristina Szafara, Steve Gallucci, and Carol Marquardt, all of Cornell University; and Susan Dahl, Kansas State University. Furthermore, we appreciate the additional comments, suggestions, and support of our students and our colleagues at Cornell University, Ithaca College, and Kansas State University.

Finally, the extraordinary efforts of a talented group of individuals at Irwin made all of this come together. We would especially like to thank our sponsoring editor, Mark Pfaltzgraff, for championing this project from first draft manuscript stage to a finished product; Jeff Shelstad for encouraging us to begin the project in the first place and providing input and support along the way; creative marketing ideas and support from our marketing manager, Heather Woods; Larry Cope, Michael Warrell, and Keith McPherson for outstanding design work; Kim Meriwether, our desktop publishing champion; Mary Conzachi and Rita McMullen, our tireless project editors; our production editor, Dina Treadaway; and Glenn Turner and the staff at Burrston House, for outstanding marketing research support and feedback. Throughout the project various members of Irwin's editorial management team, in particular, Mike Junior, John Black, and Merrily Mazza were always available to provide guidance, direction, and additional support.

Robert Libby
Patricia A. Libby
Daniel G. Short

Contents in Brief

Contents

CHAPTER 4
The Adjustment Process and Financial Statement Presentation

CHAPTER 5
The Communication of Accounting Information 242

FINANCIAL ACCOUNTING

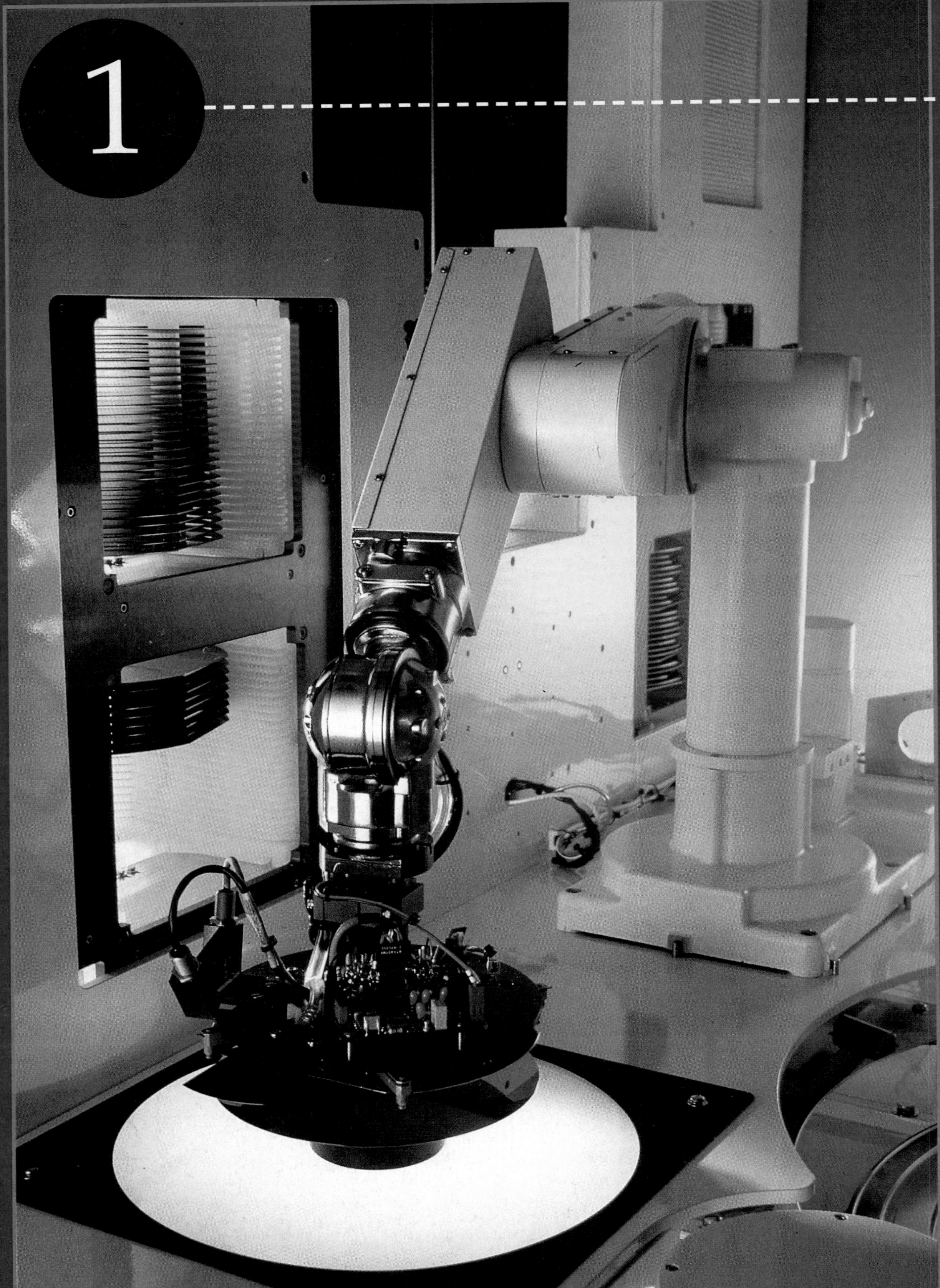
1

FINANCIAL STATEMENTS AND BUSINESS DECISIONS

Business people need financial information to make rational economic decisions. Investors and creditors need financial information before they provide cash to a business. A primary source of financial information is the organization's financial statements. The primary purposes of this chapter are to describe how the results of business operations are reflected in the numbers in the basic financial statements and how the statements are used, and to introduce the parties involved in the accounting communication process.

LEARNING OBJECTIVES

After studying this chapter, you should be able to:

1. **Recognize the information conveyed in the four basic financial statements and how it is used by different decision makers (investors, creditors, and managers).** *7*
2. **Identify the role of generally accepted accounting principles (GAAP) in determining the content of financial statements.** *21*
3. **Distinguish the roles of managers and auditors in the accounting communication process.** *25*
4. **Appreciate the importance of ethics, reputation, and legal liability in accounting.** *27*

Management Decision Setting
MAXIDRIVE CORPORATION

An Acquisition Gone Wrong*

In January, Exeter Investors purchased Maxidrive Corp., a fast-growing manufacturer of personal computer disk drives, for $32 million. The price Exeter paid was decided by considering the value of the economic resources owned by Maxidrive, its debts to others, its ability to sell goods for more than the cost to produce them, and its ability to generate the cash necessary to pay its current bills. Much of this assessment was based on financial information provided by Maxidrive to Exeter. This financial information was presented in the form of *financial statements*. By July, Exeter

discovered a variety of problems both in the operations of Maxidrive and in the financial statements that Maxidrive had provided to them. It now appeared that Maxidrive was worth only about half of what Exeter had paid. Further, Maxidrive did not have enough cash to pay its debt to the American Bank. In response, Exeter filed a lawsuit against the prior owners and others responsible for Maxidrive's financial statements to recover the overpayment.

THE OBJECTIVES OF *FINANCIAL ACCOUNTING*

Determining the price Exeter paid for Maxidrive is typical of the economic decisions that are made based on financial statements. Businesses use financial statements as the primary means to communicate financial information to parties outside the organization. The purpose of this text is to help you develop the ability to read and interpret financial statements of business organizations and understand the system that produces those statements. This book is aimed at two groups of readers: *future managers*, who will need to interpret and use financial statement information in business decisions, and *future accountants*, who will prepare financial statements for these managers. It provides future managers with a firm basis for using financial statement information in their careers in marketing, finance, banking, manufacturing, personnel, sales, information systems, or other areas of management, and future accountants with a solid foundation for further professional study.

Both managers and accountants must understand *financial statements* (what the statements tell you and what they do not tell you about a business enterprise), *business operations*, and *the use of financial statements in decision making* to successfully perform their duties. As a consequence, we integrate actual business practice in our discussions starting with Chapter 1. We will examine the fundamentals of financial accounting in a variety of business contexts relevant to your future careers. Each chapter's material is integrated around a "focus company" (in this chapter, Maxidrive). The focus companies are drawn from 12 different industries, providing you with a broad spectrum of experience with realistic business and financial accounting practices. Where appropriate, the focus company's operations and financial statements are then compared to "contrast companies." When you complete this book, you will be able to read and understand financial statements of real companies.

How seasoned managers use financial statements in modern businesses has guided our selection of learning objectives and content. At the same time, our teaching approach recognizes that students using this book have no prior exposure to accounting and financial statements, and often little exposure to the

*The Maxidrive case is a realistic representation of an actual case of fraud. No names in the case are real. The actual fraud is discussed in the epilogue to the chapter.

business world. The book is also aimed at helping you "learn how to learn" by teaching efficient and effective approaches for learning the material.

We start this process with a brief but comprehensive overview of the four basic financial statements and the people and organizations involved in their preparation and use. This overview provides you with a context in which you can learn the more detailed material that is presented in the following chapters. We begin the overview by returning to our discussion of the Maxidrive acquisition, in particular to how two primary users of the statements, investors (owners) and creditors (lenders), relied on each of Maxidrive's four basic financial statements in their ill-fated decisions to buy and lend money to Maxidrive. Later in the chapter, we will begin to discuss a broader range of uses of financial statement data in marketing, management, personnel, and other business contexts.

BUSINESS BACKGROUND

Understanding the Players

Maxidrive was founded by two engineers who had formerly worked for General Data, then a manufacturer of large computers. Predicting the rise in demand for personal computers with a hard disk drive, they started a company specializing in the manufacture of this important computer component (now called Maxidrive Corp.). To start the enterprise, the founders invested a major portion of their own savings, becoming the sole owners of Maxidrive. As is common in new businesses, the founders also functioned as the managers of the business (they were *owner-managers*).

The founders soon discovered that they needed additional money to develop the business. Based on the recommendation of a close friend, they turned to American Bank to borrow money. While Maxidrive has borrowed from others over the years, American Bank continued to lend to Maxidrive as the need arose, becoming its largest lender, or *creditor*. Early last year, one of the founders of the business became gravely ill. This event, plus the stresses of operating in their highly competitive industry, led the founders to search for a buyer for their company. In January of this year, they struck a deal for the sale of the company to the company's new *owners*, Exeter Investors, a small group of wealthy private investors. Both founders retired and a new manager was hired to run Maxidrive for the new owners. The new *manager* had formerly worked for another company owned by Exeter but was not an owner of the company.

Owners (often called *investors* or *stockholders*), whether they are groups such as Exeter who recently bought all of Maxidrive Corp. or individuals who buy small percentages of large corporations, make their purchases with two sources of possible gain in mind: selling them in the future at a higher price than they paid and/or receiving a portion of what the company earns in the form of cash payments called *dividends*. As the Maxidrive case suggests, not all stock increases in value and not all companies have sufficient cash to pay dividends. *Creditors*, whether they are individuals, business organizations, or financial institutions such as banks, lend money to a company for a specific length of time and hope to gain by charging interest on the money they lend. As American Bank, Maxidrive's major creditor, has learned, not all borrowers are able to repay their debts.

Understanding the Business Operations

To understand any company's financial statements, you must first understand its operations. As noted above, Maxidrive designs and manufactures hard disk drives for personal computers. The major parts that go into the drive include the disks on which information is stored, the motors that spin the disks, the heads that read and write to the disks, and the computer chips which control the operations of the drive. Maxidrive purchases the disks and motors from other companies, referred to as *suppliers*. It designs and manufactures the heads and chips and then assembles the drives. Maxidrive does not sell disk drives directly to the public. Instead, its *customers* are computer manufacturers such as IBM and Apple Computer, which install the drives in machines they sell to retailers (businesses that sell to consumers) such as Computerland. Thus, Maxidrive is a supplier to IBM and Apple.

The hard disk drive business is very competitive. Maxidrive competes with other much larger drive companies by investing a great deal of money in developing new and improved drives and by using robots in its factory to keep labor costs low and ensure product quality. Among the employees working for Maxidrive are 36 engineers and technical staff who work in research and development to develop new disk drives.

Accounting is a system that collects and processes (analyzes, measures, and records) financial information about an organization and reports that information to decision makers.

Like all businesses, Maxidrive has an **accounting** system that collects and processes (analyzes, measures, and records) financial information about an organization and reports that information to decision makers. Reports produced by this system are used both by Maxidrive's managers (often called *internal decision makers*) and by parties outside the firm such as investors like the managers at Exeter Investors and the loan officer at American Bank (often called *external decision makers*). The two parts of the accounting system are outlined in Exhibit 1–1. Internal managers typically require continuous detailed information because they must plan and manage the day-to-day operations of the organization. Developing accounting information for internal decision makers is called *management accounting* and is the subject of a separate accounting course. The focus of this text is accounting for external decision makers, called *financial accounting*, and the four basic financial statements and related disclosures that are the output of that system.

To determine the type of information reported in each statement, we will now examine the financial statements that Maxidrive's former owner-managers presented to Exeter. Then we will test what you have learned by trying to correct the errors in each of the statements and discuss the implications of the errors on the value of Maxidrive. Finally, we will discuss the ethical and legal responsibilities of various parties for those errors.

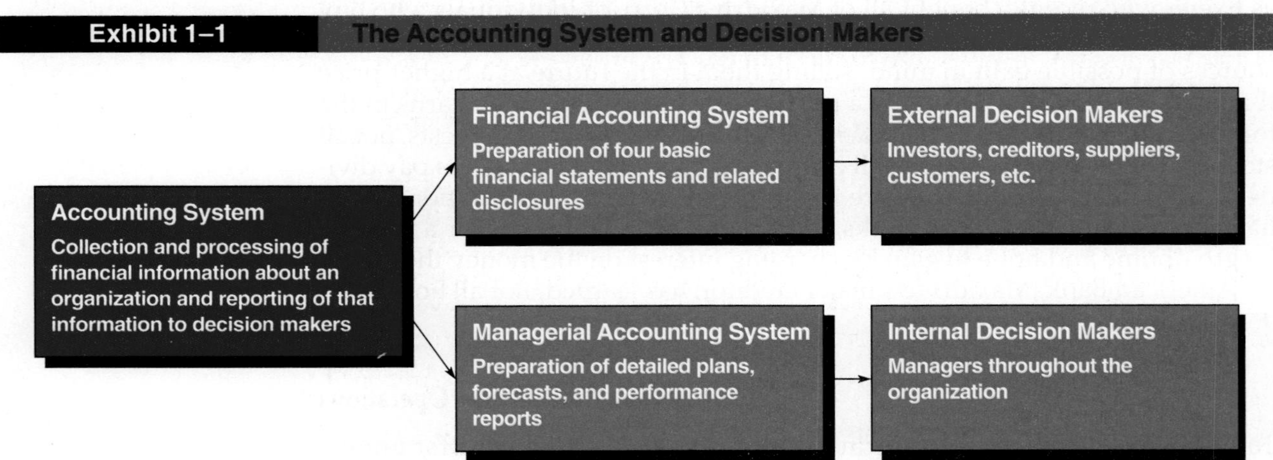

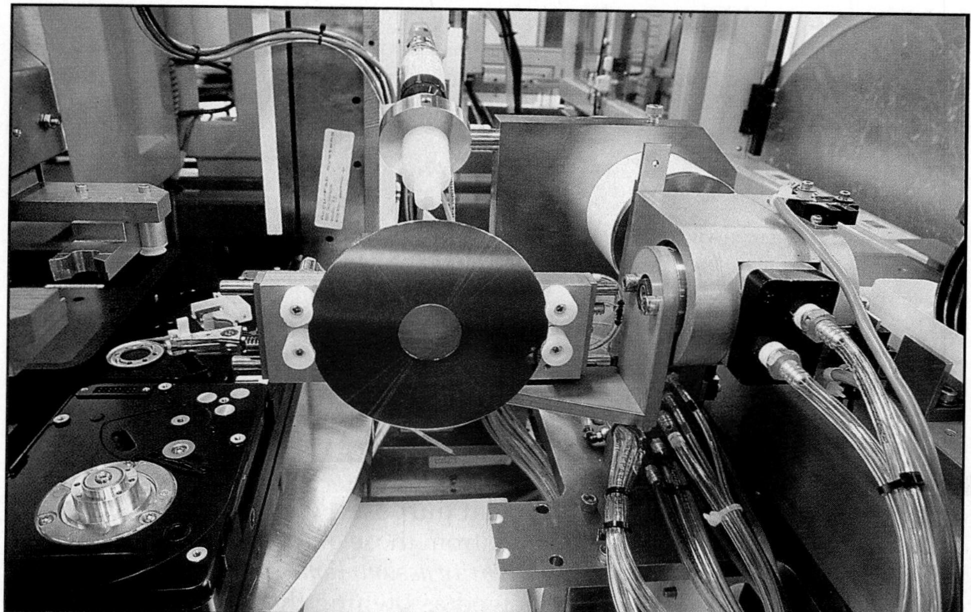

Hard disk drive production requires the precision, quality control, and efficiency of a modern manufacturing environment.

REFLECTING BUSINESS OPERATIONS IN FINANCIAL STATEMENTS

Learning Objective 1
Recognize the information conveyed in the four basic financial statements and how it is used by different decision makers (investors, creditors, and managers).

Both Exeter Investors (Maxidrive's new owner) and American Bank (Maxidrive's largest creditor) used Maxidrive's financial statements to learn more about the company before making their purchase and lending decisions. In doing so, Exeter and American Bank assumed the statements accurately represented Maxidrive's financial condition. However, as they soon learned and now have claimed in their lawsuits, the statements were in error. Maxidrive had (*a*) on its *balance sheet,* overstated the economic resources it owned and understated its obligations to others; (*b*) on its *income statement,* overstated its ability to sell goods for more than the costs to produce and sell them; and (*c*) on its *cash flow statement,* overstated its ability to generate from those sales the cash necessary to meet its current debts. These three financial statements and the *retained earnings statement* are the four basic statements normally prepared by profit-making organizations for external reporting to owners, potential investors, creditors, and other decision makers.

The four basic statements summarize the financial activities of the business. They can be prepared at any point in time (such as the end of the year, quarter, or month) and can apply to any time span (such as one year, one quarter, or one month). Like most companies, Maxidrive prepares financial statements for investors and creditors at the end of each quarter (known as *quarterly reports*) and at the end of the year (known as *annual reports*).

To understand how Exeter Investors used financial statements in its decision and how it was misled, we must first understand what specific information is presented in the four basic financial statements for a company like Maxidrive. Basic to this process is an emphasis on learning *definitions* of key business and accounting terms that we rely on throughout the book and key *relationships* among the terms used in financial statements. As is common with other professions, the terminology of accounting is technical because precision is essential. During this overview, we will provide general definitions of these key terms, and then for certain key accounting terms, we will add more detail to the definitions in later chapters. Even so, we will be presenting many new business and financial statement terms in the next section. To be sure that you understand each definition, we will review the key terminology at the end of the chapter. If you are unsure of the definitions of other terms, please refer to the glossary at the back of the book.

The Balance Sheet

We can learn a great deal about what the balance sheet reports just by reading the statement from the top. The balance sheet of Maxidrive Corp., presented by its former owners to Exeter Investors, is presented in Exhibit 1–2. Notice that the *heading* specifically identifies four significant items related to the statement:

(1) the name of the entity **Maxidrive Corp.**

An **accounting entity** is the organization for which financial data are to be collected.

Accounting requires a precise definition of the specific organization for which financial data are to be collected. When the organization is defined, it is called an **accounting entity**. For measurement purposes, the resources, debts, and activities of the entity are kept separate from those of the owners and other entities. This focus is called the *separate-entity assumption.*[1] The business entity itself, not the business owners, is viewed as owning the economic resources used by it and as owing its debts.

A **balance sheet (statement of financial position)** reports the financial position (assets, liabilities, and stockholders' equity) of an accounting entity at a point in time.

(2) the title of the statement **Balance Sheet**

The purpose of the **balance sheet** is to report the financial position (assets, liabilities, and stockholders' equity) of an accounting entity at a point in time. Therefore, the balance sheet is sometimes called the **statement of financial**

Exhibit 1–2 **Balance Sheet**

MAXIDRIVE CORP. **Balance Sheet** **At December 31, 19A** **(in thousands of dollars)**			*name of the entity* *title of the statement* *specific date of the statement* *unit of measure*
Assets			
Cash		$ 4,895	*the amount of cash in the company's bank accounts*
Accounts receivable		5,714	*amounts owed by customers from prior sales*
Inventories		8,517	*parts and completed but unsold disk drives*
Plant and equipment		7,154	*factories and production machinery*
Land		981	*land on which the factories are built*
Total assets		$27,261	
Liabilities			
Accounts payable	$7,156		*amounts owed to suppliers for prior purchases*
Notes payable	9,000		*amounts owed on written debt contracts*
Total liabilities		$16,156	
Stockholders' Equity			
Contributed capital	$2,000		*amounts invested in the business by stockholders*
Retained earnings	9,105		*past earnings not distributed to stockholders*
Total stockholders' equity		11,105	
Total liabilities and stockholders' equity		$27,261	

The footnotes are an integral part of these financial statements.

[1]The separate-entity assumption is used for all types of business entities (corporations as well as sole proprietorships and partnerships, which we discuss later in the chapter).

position. The meaning of financial position will become more evident when we read the body of the statement.

(3) the specific date of the statement	**At December 31, 19A**

The heading of each statement indicates the *time dimension* of the report. The balance sheet is like a financial snapshot indicating financial position *at a specific point in time*—in this case, December 31, 19A—which is stated clearly on the balance sheet. Note that this book often uses the convention "19A" for the first year, "19B" for the second, and so forth. Thus, the sequence of years 19A, 19B, and 19C can be thought of as equivalent to any three-year sequence such as 1995, 1996, and 1997.

(4) unit of measure	**(in thousands of dollars)**

Companies normally prepare reports denominated in the major currency of the country in which they are located, in this case U.S. dollars. Similarly, Canadian companies would report in Canadian dollars and Mexican companies in pesos. Medium-sized companies such as Maxidrive and much larger companies such as Wal-Mart often report in thousands of dollars; that is, the last three digits are rounded to the nearest thousand. As a result, the listing of "Cash $4,895" actually means $4,895,000. After the statement heading, the three elements reported on a balance sheet are listed—assets, liabilities, and stockholders' equity.

Assets

Maxidrive lists five items under the category Assets:

Cash	$4,895	*the amount of cash in the company's bank accounts*
Accounts receivable	5,714	*amounts owed by customers from prior sales*
Inventories	8,517	*parts and completed but unsold disk drives*
Plant and equipment	7,154	*factories and production machinery*
Land	981	*land on which the factories are built*

The exact items listed as assets on a company's balance sheet will depend on the nature of its operations. The five items listed by Maxidrive are the economic resources needed to manufacture and sell disk drives to companies such as IBM. Each of these economic resources is expected to provide future benefits to the firm. To prepare to manufacture the drives, Maxidrive first needed *cash* to purchase *land* on which it built factories and installed production machinery (*plant and equipment*). After completing its production facility, Maxidrive began purchasing parts and producing disk drives, which gave rise to the balance assigned to *inventories*. When Maxidrive sells its disk drives to IBM and Apple Computer, it sells them on credit and receives promises to pay called *accounts receivable*, which are collected in cash later. Maxidrive lists as cash the amount of cash in its bank accounts on the balance sheet date, which it will use to pay its own bills. These items that are called *assets* are the probable (expected) future economic benefits owned by the entity as a result of past transactions.

Every asset is initially measured on the balance sheet on the basis of the total cost incurred to acquire it. For example, the balance sheet for Maxidrive reports "Land, $981"; this is the amount paid (in thousands) for the land when it was acquired. Even if the market value of the land increases, the balance sheet will report the land at its *original acquisition cost* (this is called the *cost principle*). Balance sheets *do not purport to show the current market value* of the assets listed. If Maxidrive attempted to sell the land, it might receive more or less than the amount listed.

FINANCIAL ANALYSIS

Interpreting Assets on the Balance Sheet

Assessment of Maxidrive's assets was important to its creditor, American Bank, and to its prospective investor, Exeter, because assets provide a basis for judging whether sufficient resources are available to operate the company. Assets are also important because they could be sold for cash in the event Maxidrive goes out of business. However, as indicated above, if the assets were sold, there is no assurance that the amount listed on the balance sheet would be the amount received from the sale. Some unsophisticated users of financial statements do not understand this point and can easily misinterpret the financial position of a business.

Liabilities and Stockholders' Equity

Basic accounting equation (balance sheet equation): Assets = Liabilities + Stockholders' Equity.

Maxidrive's balance sheet next lists its liabilities and stockholders' equity. They are the sources of financing, or claims against the company's economic resources. Financing provided by creditors creates a liability. Financing provided by owners creates owners' equity. Since Maxidrive is a corporation, its owners' equity is designated as *stockholders' equity.*[2] Since the acquisition of each asset must have a source of financing, a company's assets must, by definition, always be equal to the company's liabilities and stockholders' equity. This **basic accounting equation**, often called the **balance sheet equation**, is restated below:

Assets	=	Liabilities + Stockholders' Equity
Economic resources		*Sources of financing for the economic resources*
(e.g., cash, inventory, etc.)		Liabilities: *from creditors*
		Stockholders' Equity: *from stockholders*

The basic accounting equation shows what is meant when we refer to the company's *financial position,* the economic resources the company owns and the sources of financing for those resources.

Under the category Liabilities, Maxidrive lists two items:

Accounts payable	$7,156	*amounts owed to suppliers for prior purchases*
Notes payable	9,000	*amounts owed on written debt contracts*

Liabilities are probable (expected) debts or obligations of the entity that result from past transactions and will be paid with assets or services in the future. They arise primarily from the *purchase of goods or services* on credit and through *cash borrowings* to finance the business.

Many businesses purchase goods and services from their suppliers on credit that does not involve a formal written contract (a note). For example, for the disk drives it produces, Maxidrive purchases electric motors from Magnalite, Inc. This transaction creates a liability known as *accounts payable.* Since there is no formal written contract, such purchases are often described as being on "open account." The amount of accounts payable listed by Maxidrive includes all of its debts to suppliers on open account.

Business entities often borrow money, primarily from lending institutions such as banks, by entering into a formal written debt contract. In this case, a liability called *notes payable* is created. A note payable specifies an amount to be re-

[2]A *corporation* is a business that is incorporated under the laws of a particular state. The owners are called *stockholders* or *shareholders*. Ownership is represented by shares of capital stock that usually can be bought and sold freely. The corporation operates as a separate legal entity, separate and apart from its owners. The stockholders enjoy limited liability; they are liable for the debts of the corporation only to the extent of their investments. Chapter Supplement A discusses forms of ownership in more detail.

paid, a definite maturity or payment date, and the rate of interest charged by the lender. The amount listed as Maxidrive's notes payable ($9,000,000) is owed to American Bank, is due in five years, and also requires a yearly (annual) interest payment of 5% of the debt every December 31 (5% × $9,000,000 = $450,000).

FINANCIAL ANALYSIS

Interpreting Liabilities on the Balance Sheet

Maxidrive's existing debts were relevant to American Bank's decision to lend money to Maxidrive because these existing creditors share American Bank's claim against Maxidrive's assets. If a business does not pay its creditors, the law may give the creditors the right to force the sale of assets sufficient to meet their claims. If Maxidrive does not find another source of funds to pay its debts, American Bank and its other creditors will likely take this action. Exeter Investors was also interested in information concerning Maxidrive's debts because of its concern for whether the company had sufficient sources of cash to pay its debts.

Stockholders' Equity

Stockholders' equity indicates the amount of financing provided by owners of the business and operations. Stockholders' equity comes from two sources: (1) *contributed capital*, the investment of cash and other assets in the business by the owners, and (2) *retained earnings*, the amount of accumulated earnings kept in the business and thus not distributed to owners in the form of dividends.

In Exhibit 1–2, the Stockholders' Equity section reports the following:

Contributed capital	$2,000	*amounts invested in the business by stockholders*
Retained earnings	9,105	*past earnings not distributed to stockholders*

The two founding stockholders of Maxidrive invested a total of $2,000,000 in the business. Each stockholder received 10,000 shares of capital stock (20,000 shares in total). They invested an average price of $100 per share ($2,000,000 ÷ 20,000 shares). It should be noted that the amounts in contributed capital on Maxidrive's balance sheet did not change when the two founding stockholders sold their shares to Exeter Investors since the transaction did not involve an additional contribution of cash or other assets to Maxidrive. This transaction, which took place between Maxidrive's original owners and Exeter, occurred outside of the accounting entity Maxidrive, and thus was not recorded by its accounting system.

The accumulated amount of earnings (or losses incurred) less all dividends paid to the stockholders since formation of the corporation is reported as *retained earnings*. Thus, retained earnings includes the portion of earnings not distributed to owners. The computation is reported on the retained earnings statement discussed later. Total stockholders' equity of $11,105,000 equals the sum of the original owners' investment ($2,000,000) plus the retained earnings ($9,105,000).

FINANCIAL ANALYSIS

Interpreting Shareholders' Equity on the Balance Sheet

The basic accounting equation (Assets = Liabilities + Stockholders' Equity) shows that stockholders' equity is equal to total assets minus total liabilities of the business. Stockholders' equity sometimes is called *net worth*. The amount of total stockholders' equity or net worth of Maxidrive is important to American Bank because creditors' claims legally come first before those of owners. As a consequence, if Maxidrive went out of business and its assets were sold, the proceeds of that sale would have to be used to pay back creditors such as American Bank before the owners receive any money. Thus, stockholders' equity is considered a "cushion" that protects creditors should the entity go out of business. When Exeter Investors was considering buying Maxidrive, it also looked at stockholders' equity. However, recall that the amount recorded on the balance sheet for assets (called the *book value*) *does not necessarily correspond to the current prices for those assets* (called *market value*), which may be greater than or less than the reported amounts. As a consequence, Exeter knew that the amount of stockholders' equity did not represent the market value of the company as a whole to its owners.

A Note on Format

A few additional formatting conventions are worth noting here. Assets are listed on the balance sheet by ease of conversion to cash. Liabilities are listed by their maturity (due date). Most financial statements include the monetary unit sign (in the U.S., the $) before the first dollar amount in a group of items (e.g., the cash amount in the assets) that will be combined in an arithmetic process (added or subtracted). Also, it is common to place a single underline below the last item in a group (e.g., land). A dollar sign is also placed before group totals (e.g., total assets). The same conventions are followed in all four basic financial statements. We will discuss alternative balance sheet formats in more detail in Chapter 5.

Self-Study Quiz*

1. Maxidrive's *assets* are listed in one section and *liabilities* and *stockholders' equity* in another. Notice that the two sections balance in conformity with the basic accounting equation. In the following chapters, you will learn that the basic accounting equation is the basic building block for the entire accounting process. Your task here is to verify that the stockholders' equity of $11,105,000 is correct using the numbers for assets and liabilities presented in Exhibit 1–2 and the basic accounting equation in the form:

Assets – Liabilities = Stockholders' Equity

2. Accounts receivable are amounts owed to the company by customers from prior sales and accounts payable are amounts owed to suppliers on open account. One way a supplier might estimate Maxidrive's ability to pay its accounts payable is to make the following calculation. If Maxidrive used all of the cash available on December 31, 19A to pay some of its accounts payable, how much of its accounts receivable would it need to collect to have enough cash to pay the remaining amount of accounts payable? Use the balances presented in Exhibit 1–2 and the following structure to compute your answer.

	Accounts payable on December 31, 19A	________
–	Cash on December 31, 19A	________
=	Collections of accounts receivable necessary to pay remaining balance	________

Compare this amount to its accounts receivable on December 31, 19A. What does this simplified cash flow analysis say about the likelihood that the suppliers will be paid? ____________________

*If you do not wish to keep this book as part of your professional library, we recommend that you write your answers on a separate piece of paper.

3. Learning which items belong in each of the balance sheet categories is an important first step in understanding their meaning. Mark each balance sheet item in the following list as an asset (A), liability (L), or stockholders' equity (SE), without referring to Exhibit 1–2.

L	Accounts payable	A	Inventories
A	Accounts receivable	A	Land
A	Cash	L	Notes payable
SE	Contributed capital	SE	Retained earnings
A	Plant and equipment		

After you have completed your answers, check them with the solutions presented at the bottom of this page.*

The Income Statement

A quick reading of Maxidrive's income statement also indicates a great deal about its purpose and content. The income statement of Maxidrive Corp. is presented in Exhibit 1–3. The heading of the income statement again specifically identifies the name of the entity, the title of the report, and unit of measure used in the statement. However, unlike the Balance Sheet, which reports as of a certain date, the income statement reports for a specified period of time (for the year ended December 31, 19A). The time period covered by the financial statements (one year in this case) is called an **accounting period**.

The **accounting period** is the time period covered by the financial statements.

The **income statement (statement of income, statement of earnings, or statement of operations)** reports the accountant's primary measure of performance of a business, the revenues less the expenses of the accounting period. The term *profit* is used widely in our language for this measure of performance, but accountants prefer to use the technical terms *net income* or *net earnings*.

The **income statement (statement of income, statement of earnings, statement of operations)** reports the revenues less the expenses of the accounting period.

Income Statement **Exhibit 1–3**

MAXIDRIVE CORP.
Income Statement
For the Year Ended December 31, 19A
(in thousands of dollars)

name of the entity
title of the statement
accounting period
unit of measure

Revenues:			
Sales revenue	$37,436		*revenue earned from sale of disk drives*
Total revenues		$37,436	
Expenses:			
Cost of goods sold expense	$26,980		*cost to produce disk drives sold*
Selling, general and administrative expense	3,624		*operating expenses not directly related to production*
Research and development expense	1,982		*expenses incurred to develop new products*
Interest expense	450		*cost of using borrowed funds*
Total expenses		33,036	
Pretax income		$ 4,400	
Income tax expense		1,100	*income taxes on period's pretax income*
Net income		$ 3,300	

The footnotes are an integral part of these financial statements.

*1. Assets ($27,261,000) – Liabilities ($16,156,000) = Stockholders' Equity ($11,105,000). 2. $7,156,000 – $4,895,000 = $2,261,000. This is less than half of accounts receivable, indicating a high likelihood of payment. 3. L, A, A, SE, A, A, A, L, SE.

Maxidrive's net income measures its success in selling disk drives for more than it cost them to generate those sales.

Notice that Maxidrive's income statement has three major captions: *revenues, expenses,* and *net income.*[3] The income statement equation that describes their relationships is:

Net Income = Revenues – Expenses

Revenues

Revenues are earned from the sale of goods or services to customers (in Maxidrive's case, its sale of disk drives) and are defined as inflows of net assets (assets less liabilities) from ongoing operations (sales to customers). Revenues are normally reported on the income statement when the goods or services are sold to the customer who has either paid for them or promised to pay in the future. When a business sells goods or renders services, it may receive cash immediately. However, this is a rare occurrence with the exception of retail stores like Wal-Mart or McDonald's. Goods or services are normally sold on credit. When Maxidrive sells its disk drives to IBM and Apple Computer, it receives a promise of future payment called an *account receivable,* which is collected in cash later. In either case, the business recognizes total sales (cash and credit) as revenue for the period. *The period in which a revenue is recognized is the period in which goods and services are sold, not necessarily the period in which cash is received.* Revenue is measured in dollars as the bargained cash-equivalent price agreed on by the two parties to the transaction. Various terms are used in financial statements to describe different sources of revenue (e.g., provision of services, sale of goods, rental of property, etc.). Maxidrive lists only one, *sales revenue,* for disk drives delivered to customers.

Expenses

Maxidrive lists five items as expenses on its income statement. *Expenses* represent the dollar amount of resources used up by the entity to earn revenues during a period of time. Expenses are defined as the outflows of net assets from ongoing operations. *Cost of goods sold expense* is the total cost to Maxidrive to produce the disk drives delivered to customers during the year, including the costs of parts used in production, wages paid to the factory workers, and even a portion of the cost of the factories and equipment used to produce the goods that were sold (called depreciation). *Selling, general and administrative expense* includes a wide variety of expenses, such as the salaries of management, sales staff, the internal company accountants, and other general costs of operating the company not directly related to production.

Maxidrive is a high technology company and must constantly spend money developing new products to keep ahead of competitors. These costs are listed as *research and development expense.* Maxidrive also reported *interest expense* for one year on the $9,000,000, 5% note payable to American Bank ($9,000,000 × 5% = $450,000) which was outstanding for all of 19A. Finally, as a corporation, Maxidrive must pay income tax at a 25% rate on pretax income.[4] Therefore, Maxidrive incurred *income tax expense* of $1,100,000 (pretax income of $4,400,000 × 25%).

---

[3]Other less commonly occurring elements of the income statement are discussed in later chapters.

[4]Federal tax rates for corporations actually ranged from 15% to 35% at the time this book was written. State and local governments may levy additional taxes on corporate income resulting in a higher total income tax rate.

Expenses may require the immediate payment of cash, a payment of cash in a later period, or use of some other resource such as an inventory item, which may have been bought and paid for in a previous period. For accounting purposes, *the period in which an expense is reported on the income statement is the period in which goods and services are used to earn revenues, not necessarily the period in which cash is paid for the expense item*. The expense reported in one accounting period may be paid for in another accounting period.

Net Income

Net income or net earnings (often called *profit* or *the bottom line* by nonaccountants) is the excess of total revenues over total expenses. If the total expenses exceed the total revenues, a net loss is reported. (Net losses are normally noted by brackets around the income figure.) When revenues and expenses are equal for the period, the business has operated at break even.

FINANCIAL ANALYSIS

Analyzing the Income Statement: Beyond the Bottom Line

Investors such as Exeter and creditors such as American Bank closely monitor a firm's net income because it indicates the ability to sell goods and services for more than they cost to produce and deliver. The details of the statement are also important. For example, Maxidrive had to sell over $37 million worth of disk drives to make just over $3 million. The disk drive industry is very competitive. If Maxidrive is forced to match a competitor that lowers prices just 10%, or if Maxidrive needs to triple research and development to catch up to a competitor's innovative new product, its net income could easily turn into a net loss.

Self-Study Quiz

1. During the period 19A, Maxidrive delivered disk drives to customers for which the customers paid or promised to pay in the future amounts totaling $37,436,000. During the same period, it collected $33,563,000 in cash from its customers. Without referring to Exhibit 1–3, indicate which of the two numbers will show up on Maxidrive's income statement as *sales revenue* for 19A. Why did you select your answer? ______________________

____

2. During the period 19A, Maxidrive *produced* disk drives with a total cost of production of $27,130,000. During the same period, it *delivered* to customers disk drives that had cost a total of $26,980,000 to produce. Without referring to Exhibit 1–3, indicate which of the two numbers will show up on Maxidrive's income statement as *cost of goods sold expense* for 19A? Why did you select your answer? ______________________

____

After you have completed your answers, check them with the solutions presented at the bottom of this page.*

* 1. Sales revenue would be recognized in the amount of $37,436,000 because sales revenue is normally reported on the income statement when the goods or services have been delivered to the customer who has either paid *or* promised to pay for them in the future. 2. Cost of goods sold expense would be $26,980,000 because expenses are the dollar amount of resources used up to earn revenues during the period. Only those disk drives delivered to customers are used up. Those disk drives still on hand are part of the asset inventory.

Statement of Retained Earnings

The **statement of retained earnings** reports how net income and the distribution of dividends affected the financial position of the company during the accounting period.

The **statement of retained earnings** reports how net income and the distribution of dividends affected the financial position of the company during the accounting period. As we discussed in our look at the balance sheet, there are two major causes of changes in retained earnings. The earning of net income during the year increases the balance of retained earnings, showing the relationship of the income statement to the balance sheet. The declaration of dividends to the stockholders decreases retained earnings.[5] The retained earnings equation which describes these relationships is:

Ending Retained Earnings =
Beginning Retained Earnings + Net Income – Dividends

Maxidrive prepares a separate statement of retained earnings, shown in Exhibit 1–4, which explains changes to the retained earnings balance that occurred during the year. Other corporations report these changes at the end of the income statement or in a more general statement of stockholders' equity which we discuss in Chapter 4. Like the income statement, the statement of retained earnings reports for a specified period of time (the accounting period), which in this case is one year. It begins with Maxidrive's beginning of the year *retained earnings*. The current year's *net income* reported on the income statement is added and the current year's *dividends* are subtracted from this amount.

During 19A, Maxidrive earned $3,300,000, as shown on the income statement (Exhibit 1–3). This amount was added to the beginning-of-the-year retained earnings in computing end-of-the-year retained earnings. A cash *dividend* pays an equal amount for each share of stock outstanding. During 19A, Maxidrive declared and paid a total of $1,000,000 in dividends to its two original stockholders. This amount was subtracted in computing end-of-the-year retained earnings on the balance sheet. The ending retained earnings amount is the same as that reported in Exhibit 1–2 on the Maxidrive Balance Sheet.

FINANCIAL ANALYSIS

Interpreting Retained Earnings

Reinvestment of earnings or retained earnings is an important source of financing for Maxidrive, representing more than one-third of its financing. Creditors such as American Bank closely monitor a firm's retained earnings statement because it indicates Maxidrive's policy on dividend payments to the stockholders. This is important to American Bank because every dollar Maxidrive pays to stockholders as dividends is not available to be used to pay back its debt to American Bank or the interest on that debt.

Statement of Cash Flows

Maxidrive's statement of cash flows is presented in Exhibit 1–5. As discussed earlier in this chapter, reported revenues do not always equal cash collected from customers because some sales may be on credit. Also, expenses reported on the income statement may not be equal to the cash paid out during the period because expenses may be incurred in one period and paid for in another. As a result, net income (revenues minus expenses) is usually *not* the amount of cash received minus the amount paid out during the period. In fact, many successful companies may earn large amounts of income and still have to borrow more money from the bank because they do not have sufficient cash to meet their other obligations. Because the income statement does not provide any

[5]Net losses are subtracted. The complete process of declaring and paying dividends is discussed in a later chapter.

Statement of Retained Earnings — **Exhibit 1–4**

MAXIDRIVE CORP. Statement of Retained Earnings For the Year Ended December 31, 19A (in thousands of dollars)		*name of the entity* *title of the statement* *accounting period* *unit of measure*
Retained earnings, January 1, 19A	$ 6,805	*last period's ending retained earnings*
Net income for 19A	3,300	*net income reported on the income statement*
Dividends for 19A	(1,000)	*dividends declared during the period*
Retained earnings, December 31, 19A	$ 9,105	*ending retained earnings on the balance sheet*
The footnotes are an integral part of these financial statements.		

information concerning cash flows, accountants prepare the **statement of cash flows** to report inflows and outflows of cash in the categories of operations, investing, and financing. Like the income statement, the cash flow statement reports for a specified period of time (the accounting period), which in this case is one year. Many bankers consider this the most important statement they use to estimate whether companies can afford to pay their debts.

The **statement of cash flows** reports inflows and outflows of cash during the accounting period in the categories of operations, investing, and financing.

The statement divides Maxidrive's cash inflows and outflows (receipts and payments) into the three primary categories of cash flows in a typical business. *Cash flows from operating activities* are cash flows directly related to earning income (normal business activity including *interest* paid and *income taxes* paid). For example, when IBM, Apple Computer, and other *customers* pay Maxidrive for disk drives that have previously been delivered, the amounts collected are listed as cash collected from customers. When Maxidrive pays salaries to its 36 *employees* involved in research and development or pays bills received from its parts *suppliers,* the amounts are included in cash paid to suppliers and employees. Alternative ways to present cash flows from operations are discussed in Chapter 5.

Cash flows from investing activities include cash flows that are related to the acquisition or sale of productive assets used by the company. This year,

Statement of Cash Flows — **Exhibit 1–5**

MAXIDRIVE CORP. Statement of Cash Flows For the Year Ended December 31, 19A (in thousands of dollars)			*name of the entity* *title of the statement* *accounting period* *unit of measure*
Cash flows from operating activities:			*directly related to earning income*
Cash collected from customers	$33,563		
Cash paid to suppliers and employees	(30,854)		
Cash paid for interest	(450)		
Cash paid for taxes	(1,190)		
Net cash flow from operating activities		$1,069	
Cash flows from investing activities:			*purchase/sale of productive assets*
Cash paid to purchase manufacturing equipment	$ (1,625)		
Net cash flow from investing activities		(1,625)	
Cash flows from financing activities:			*from investors and creditors*
Cash received from bank loan	$ 1,400		
Cash paid for dividends	(1,000)		
Net cash flow from financing activities		400	
Net decrease in cash during the year		$ (156)	*change in cash during the period*
Cash at beginning of year		5,021	*last period's ending cash balance*
Cash at end of year		$4,865	*ending cash on the balance sheet*
The footnotes are an integral part of these financial statements.			

Maxidrive only had one cash outflow from investing activities, the *purchase of additional manufacturing equipment* to meet growing demand for its products. *Cash flows from financing activities* are directly related to the financing of the enterprise itself. They involve receipt or payment of money to investors and creditors (except for suppliers). This year, Maxidrive *borrowed* an additional $1,400,000 from the bank to purchase most of the new manufacturing equipment. It also paid out $1,000,000 in *dividends* to the founding stockholders before the company was sold.

FINANCIAL ANALYSIS

Interpreting the Cash Flow Statement

Many analysts believe the statement of cash flows is particularly useful for predicting future cash flows that may be available for payment of debt to creditors and dividends to investors. Each section provides analysts with important information. Bankers often consider the operating activities section most important because it indicates the company's ability to generate cash from sales to meet current cash needs. Any amount left over can be used to pay back the bank debt or expand the company.

Stockholders will only invest in a company they believe will eventually generate more cash from operations than it uses because only this cash is available to pay dividends in the long run. The investing section tells us that Maxidrive is making heavy investments in new manufacturing capacity to meet the increasing demand for its products. This is a good sign if demand continues to increase. However, as the financing section indicates, if Maxidrive is not able to sell more drives, it may have trouble meeting the payments that the new bank debt will require.

Self-Study Quiz

1. During the period 19A, Maxidrive delivered disk drives to customers for which the customers paid or promised to pay in the future amounts totaling $37,436,000. During the same period, it collected $33,563,000 in cash from its customers. Without referring to Exhibit 1–5, indicate which of the two numbers will show up on Maxidrive's cash flow statement for 19A. ____________

2. Learning which items belong in each cash flow statement category is an important first step in understanding their meaning. Mark each item in the following list as a cash flow from operating activities (O), investing activities (I), or financing activities (F), without referring to Exhibit 1–5. Also, place brackets around the letter if it is a cash outflow and no brackets if it is a cash inflow.

_______ Cash paid for dividends
_______ Cash paid for interest
_______ Cash received from bank loan
_______ Cash paid for taxes
_______ Cash paid to purchase manufacturing equipment
_______ Cash paid to suppliers and employees
_______ Cash collected from customers

After you have completed your answers, check them with the solutions presented at the bottom of this page.*

---

* 1. $33,563,000 would be recognized on the cash flow statement because this number represents the actual cash collected from customers related to current and prior years' sales. 2. (F), (O), F, (O), (I), (O), O.

Footnotes

At the bottom of each of Maxidrive's four basic financial statements stands the inscription: *The footnotes are an integral part of these financial statements.* This is the accounting equivalent of the Surgeon General's warning on the side of a package of cigarettes. It warns users that failure to read the **footnotes** (or **notes**) to these financial statements will result in an incomplete picture of the company's financial health. Footnotes provide supplemental information about the financial condition of a company, without which the financial statements cannot be fully understood.

Footnotes (notes) provide supplemental information about the financial condition of a company, without which the financial statements cannot be fully understood.

There are three basic types of footnotes. The first type provides descriptions of the accounting rules applied in the company's statements. The second presents additional detail about a line on the financial statements. For example, Maxidrive's inventory footnote indicates the amount of parts, drives under construction, and finished disk drives included in its total inventory amount listed on the balance sheet. The third type of footnote presents additional financial disclosures about items not listed on the statements themselves. For example, Maxidrive leases one of its production facilities; terms of the lease are disclosed in a footnote. We will discuss many footnote disclosures throughout the book because understanding their content is critical to understanding the company.

FINANCIAL ANALYSIS

Management Uses of Financial Statements

In our discussion of financial analysis thus far, we have focused on the perspectives of *investors* and *creditors.* In addition, managers within the firm often make direct use of financial statements. For example, Maxidrive's *marketing managers* and *credit managers* use customers' financial statements to decide whether to extend them credit for their purchases of disk drives. Maxidrive's *purchasing managers* use potential parts suppliers' financial statements to judge whether the suppliers have the resources necessary to meet Maxidrive's current demand for parts and to invest in the development of new parts in the future. Both the *employees' union* and Maxidrive's *human resource managers* use Maxidrive's financial statements as a basis for contract negotiations, to determine what pay rates the company can afford. The net income figure even serves as a basis to pay *bonuses* not only to management but to all employees through the profit sharing plan. Regardless of the functional area of management in which you are employed, you will *use* financial statement data. You will also be *evaluated* based on the impact of your decisions on your company's financial statement data. Learning financial accounting now will benefit you in the future.

THE FRAUD

Correcting the Errors

We will next look at the errors Exeter Investors later found in Maxidrive's statements to see if we have learned enough to make the necessary corrections. Then we will discuss the responsibilities of various parties in the financial reporting process for the information in these financial statements. The article that began the chapter continues as follows:

> **Maxidrive Corp.**
> Among Exeter's claims are that:
> 1. Disk drives available for sale (part of inventories) included $1 million of obsolete drives that could not be sold and must be scrapped.

2. Reported sales to customers (and accounts receivable) for last year included $700,000 of overstatements. Maxidrive had cut the price of a certain type of disk drive by 40%. But Maxidrive personnel had created fake customer bills (called *invoices)* with the old higher prices to support these sales amounts.
3. Maxidrive had included in the amounts collectible from customers for last year's sales (accounts receivable) $500,000 owed by now bankrupt companies.

These three items together significantly overstate on the balance sheet the economic resources owned by Maxidrive (its assets) and overstate on the income statement Maxidrive's ability to sell goods for more than the cost of production.

For purposes of our discussion, we will focus on the above effects on the income statement because these effects were most relevant to Exeter Investors' evaluation of Maxidrive. The simplest way to determine the effects of these three errors on the income statement is to use the income statement equation we have just examined in this chapter. As we indicated earlier, one of the keys to understanding financial statements is to learn the elements of each of the basic financial statements and their relationships, which are represented in the basic equations. The top line in Exhibit 1–6 presents the income statement equation, followed by the amounts reported in Maxidrive's 19A income statement. Below them is listed each of the three errors that were subsequently discovered and the correction necessary to eliminate the effect of each error.

Correcting the three errors, in total, reduces pretax income to $2,200,000. After we subtract 25% for income tax expense, we are left with a corrected net income equal to $1,650,000, just *half* of the amount initially reported by Maxidrive.

Determining the Purchase Price for Maxidrive

Even at this early stage of your study of accounting, we can provide some examples of the process Exeter Investors went through to determine the price they were willing to pay for Maxidrive Corp. As indicated at the beginning of the chapter, this is a particularly interesting case for analysis because Exeter Investors have claimed that the financial statements they used to estimate the value of Maxidrive were in error. The price Exeter paid was decided by considering a variety of factors including the value of the economic resources owned by Maxidrive, its debts to others, its ability to sell goods for more than their production cost, and its ability to generate the cash necessary to pay its

Exhibit 1–6 **Correction of the Income Statement Amounts (In thousands of dollars)**

	Revenues	–	Expenses	=	Pretax Income
As presented on Maxidrive's 19A Income Statement	$37,436		$33,036		$4,400
1. Record expense for scrapping obsolete inventory.			1,000		(1,000)
2. Reduce sales revenue by amount of overstatement.	(700)				(700)
3. Record expense for uncollectible accounts.			500		(500)
After correction of errors	$36,736		$34,536		$2,200

Item 1: Since the obsolete inventory items are held for sale, but now have no value, their cost should be added to this year's expenses. Accordingly, expenses should increase by $1,000,000.
Item 2: Item two involved recording the sales price of a certain type of disk drive at too high an amount, and thus total sales revenue is too high. Its correction requires a reduction of $700,000 of revenues.
Item 3: The $500,000 of accounts receivable which will not be paid (bad debts) are no longer an asset or economic resource of Maxidrive. Like the first item, this is an added expense of $500,000.

current bills. As we have now learned, these factors are the subject matter of financial statements: balance sheet, income statement, and cash flow statement.

Maxidrive's current and prior years' income statements played a particularly important part in Exeter's evaluation. Prior years' income statements (which were not presented to you) indicated that the company had earned income every year since its founding, except for the first year of operations. Many new companies do not become profitable this quickly. Further, both sales revenue and net income had been rising rapidly every year. One method for estimating the value of a company is with a *price/earnings multiplier* (purchase price ÷ current earnings). A key to Exeter's decision was the fact that other companies in the same industry with similar performance and growth were selling for 12 times their current year's earnings. Accordingly, the opportunity to buy Maxidrive for 10 times its current earnings seemed like an excellent one, particularly since economic forecasts suggested that the next five years would see continuing growth and profitability for disk drive manufacturers. The key calculation that determined the price Exeter paid was:

$$\text{Purchase Price} = 10 \times \text{Net Income}$$
$$\$33{,}000{,}000 = 10 \times \$3{,}300{,}000$$

The number 10 in the formula is called the *price/earnings multiplier*. Using the same formula, the corrected net income figure would suggest a much lower price for Maxidrive.

$$\$16{,}500{,}000 = 10 \times \$1{,}650{,}000$$

A difficult part of this analysis is deciding what price/earnings multiplier is appropriate for this situation. Exeter carefully considered this issue, and their analysis involved more than this simple formula. However, it provides a very real first approximation of their loss—a $16.5 million overpayment. This is the amount Exeter hopes to recover from those responsible for the fraudulent financial statements they relied on in their analysis.

RESPONSIBILITIES FOR THE ACCOUNTING COMMUNICATION PROCESS

Learning Objective 2
Identify the role of generally accepted accounting principles (GAAP) in determining the content of financial statements.

Effective communication means that the recipient understands what the sender intends to convey. Communication involves problems in understanding the words, symbols, and sounds used by the parties involved. Accounting uses words and symbols to communicate financial information that is relevant to decision makers. For the decision makers at Exeter to use the information in Maxidrive's financial statements effectively, they had to understand what information each of the statements conveys. This is why we began our discussion with the content of the four basic financial statements. Yet, the fraud suggests that this understanding is not sufficient.

The decision makers also needed to understand the *measurement rules* applied in computing the numbers on the statements and they needed to know that the numbers in the statements represented what was claimed. The first point is a simple one in concept: a swim coach would never try to evaluate a swimmer's time in the 100 freestyle without first asking if the time was for a race in meters or in yards. Likewise, a decision maker should never attempt to use accounting information without first understanding the measurement rules that were used to develop the information. These measurement rules are called **generally accepted accounting principles**, or **GAAP**. The second point is equally important in concept: numbers that do

Generally accepted accounting principles (GAAP) are the measurement rules used to develop the information in financial statements.

not represent what they claim to are meaningless. For example, if the balance sheet lists $2,000,000 for a factory that does not exist, that part of the statement does not convey useful information. However, actually developing a system of measurement rules for complex business transactions (GAAP) and a system for assuring that statements fairly represent what they claim (called *auditing*) is much more complicated, as the Maxidrive fraud suggests.

Generally Accepted Accounting Principles

How Are Generally Accepted Accounting Principles Determined?

As the above discussion suggests, we must understand the measurement rules used to develop the information in the statements to understand the numbers in the statements. The accounting system that we use today has a long history. Its foundations are normally traced back to the works of an Italian monk and mathematician, Fr. Luca Pacioli, in 1494, who described an approach developed by Italian merchants to account for their activities as owner-managers of business ventures. While many others had written works on accounting after Pacioli, prior to 1933 financial reporting practices were largely determined by each company's management. Thus there was little uniformity in practice among companies.

The Securities Act of 1933 and The Securities Exchange Act of 1934 were passed into law by the U.S. Congress in response to the dramatic stock market decline of 1929. Part of these securities acts created the **Securities and Exchange Commission (SEC)** as part of the Department of the Treasury, and gave it broad powers to determine the financial statements that companies must provide to stockholders and the measurement rules that must be applied in producing those statements. Contrary to popular belief, these rules are different from those that companies follow when filing their income tax returns. We discuss these differences further in later chapters.

The **Securities and Exchange Commission (SEC)** is the U.S. government agency that determines the financial statements that public companies must provide to stockholders and the measurement rules that must be used in producing those statements.

Since its establishment, the SEC has worked with organizations of professional accountants to establish groups that are given the primary responsibilities to work out the detailed rules that become generally accepted accounting principles. The name of the current group that has this responsibility is the **Financial Accounting Standards Board (FASB)**. The Board has seven full-time voting members and a permanent staff who consider the appropriate financial reporting responses to ever-changing business practices. As of the date of publication of this book, the official pronouncements of the FASB (*Financial Accounting Standards*) and its predecessors total more than 2,500 pages of very fine print. Such detail is made necessary by the enormous diversity and complexity of current business practices.

The **Financial Accounting Standards Board (FASB)** is the private sector body given the primary responsibility to work out the detailed rules that become generally accepted accounting principles.

Stock of *privately held* corporations such as Maxidrive is owned by small groups of individuals and is not available for sale to the public at large. Like all prospective purchasers of shares of privately held companies, Exeter had to negotiate directly with the current owners to arrange the purchase. The stock of some corporations such as Maxidrive's largest customers, Apple Computer and IBM, and other well-known companies such as General Motors, Wal-Mart, and McDonald's, is *publicly traded*; that is, it can be bought and sold by investors on established stock exchanges (organized markets for stocks) such as the New York Stock Exchange. The SEC sets additional financial reporting requirements that only publicly traded companies must follow. We will introduce some of these additional requirements later in the book.

It is not necessary for most managers to learn all of the details included in these standards. Our approach is to focus on those details that have the *greatest*

U.S. corporations spend over $8.5 billion communicating through annual reports, according to Michigan consultant Sid Cato, who publishes a monthly newsletter on the topic.

impact on the numbers presented in financial statements and are appropriate for a course at this level.

Why Do Managers, Accountants, and Users Care What Is Generally Accepted?

One thing that you can be sure of is that the determination of what is included in generally accepted accounting principles (GAAP) is of great interest to the companies that must prepare the statements, to auditors, and to the readers of the statements. *Companies and their managers and owners* are most directly affected by the information presented in the statements and for that reason express the most interest. Companies incur the cost of preparing the statements and bear the major economic consequences of their publication. These economic consequences include, among others, *potential*

1. Effects on the selling price of a company's stock.
2. Effects on the amount of bonuses received by management and employees.
3. Loss of competitive advantage over other companies.

Recall that the amount Exeter was willing to pay the prior owners for Maxidrive was determined in part by net income computed under GAAP. This presents the possibility that changes in GAAP can affect the price buyers are willing to pay for companies, to either the benefit or the detriment of the prior owners. The business press often suggests this possibility. For example, in a recent *Wall Street Journal* article, the chief financial officer of Lotus Development (the producer of the popular computer program 1-2-3) and other managers suggested that a proposed change in accounting methods to record management pay would lower their stock price. Others have suggested that this same rule change will make it more difficult for entrepreneurs of high-technology companies such as Maxidrive to sell their companies. Regardless of the validity of these claims, the owners and managers (whose obligation it is to make money for owners) would be concerned by these occurrences.

Another source of interest in the nature of GAAP is the fact that managers and other employees often receive part of their pay based on reaching stated targets for net income and are thus directly concerned with how net income is computed. For example, *USA Today* cited how the Chairman of Ford Motor Company did not receive his annual bonus one year because of a slump in auto sales.

Managers and owners are also often concerned that publishing more information in financial statements will disclose the details of their successes and failures, which will help other similar companies compete with them. Claims are even made that more detailed U.S. accounting requirements make it more difficult for U.S. companies to compete with international competitors that operate in countries with less revealing accounting rules.

As a consequence of these and other concerns, changes in GAAP are actively debated, and use of political muscle and lobbying often takes place. For example, owners and managers who were concerned about a proposed change in accounting for management pay let their elected representatives in government know about their concerns. In response, numerous senators and the Secretary of the Treasury sent letters to the FASB opposing this proposed change in GAAP. The result was a modification of the proposal which was reported in the following *Accounting Today* headline:

Real World Excerpt
Accounting Today

Politics kills FASB stock options plan

Norwalk, Conn. - Ending a decade of study and more than two years of increasingly acrimonious opposition, the Financial Accounting Standards Board has dropped its plan forcing companies to charge executive stock options against earnings.

SOURCE: *Accounting Today*, January 2–15, 1995, p. 1.

AN INTERNATIONAL PERSPECTIVE

Are Generally Accepted Accounting Principles Similar in Other Countries?

While business people compete in a single global economy, different sets of generally accepted accounting principles have developed within particular countries. Differences in political, cultural, and economic histories have produced a great number of cross-national differences in practice. These differences can have dramatic effects on the numbers presented in the financial statements. For example, Daimler-Benz, the manufacturer of Mercedes Benz automobiles, recently began preparing two sets of financial statements for the same accounting period, one using German standards and one using U.S. standards. *The Wall Street Journal* reported that:

Real World Excerpt
The Wall Street Journal

Daimler-Benz Reports First Ever Loss, Reflecting New Accounting . . .

Stuttgart, Germany—Daimler-Benz AG, bound by a new set of strict U.S. disclosure rules, was forced to report its first loss since World War II.

The loss wouldn't have appeared in the German auto concern's six month profit and loss account without the stringent standards imposed by the U.S. Securities and Exchange Commission,

Daimler officials said . . . Daimler swung to a 949 million mark ($592 million) group net loss under the U.S. system in the first half . . . Under Germany's less transparent rules, the company showed a small profit. . .

SOURCE: *The Wall Street Journal*, September 20, 1993, p. A10.

Efforts are being made by the International Accounting Standards Board and others to eliminate these differences. But, for now, managers and users of financial statements who cross national borders must be aware of the specific nature of these reporting differences to interpret financial statements successfully. While our primary focus is on U.S. GAAP, we will briefly discuss practice in other countries where appropriate.

Management Responsibility and the Demand for Auditing

Learning Objective 3
Distinguish the roles of managers and auditors in the accounting communication process.

The owners and managers of Exeter were well aware of the details of U.S. GAAP, but they were still misled. While the measurement rules Maxidrive had used to produce its financial statements were consistent with GAAP, the underlying figures in the accounting system were fictitious; that is, they did not fairly represent reality. Any measurement system applied to underlying facts that do not match reality will produce unrepresentative measures. Before financial statement readers even consider what GAAP have been used to prepare the statements about to be analyzed, they must consider what assurance they have that the statements fairly represent what is claimed. Who is responsible for the numbers in Maxidrive's financial statements? Two documents taken from Maxidrive's annual report provide us with much of the answer to this question.

The **report of management** indicates management's primary responsibility for financial statement information and the steps to ensure the accuracy of the company's records.

The **report of management**, shown in Exhibit 1–7, makes two points clear. First, primary responsibility for the information in the financial statements lies with management, as represented by the highest officer of the company and the highest officer involved with the financial side of the company. Second, the managers take three important steps to ensure the accuracy of the company's records: (1) they maintain a system of controls over both the records and assets of the company; (2) they hire outside independent audi-

Report of Management **Exhibit 1–7**

Report of Management

The management of Maxidrive is responsible for preparing the financial statements and other information contained in this annual report. Management believes that the financial statements fairly reflect, in all material respects, the form and substance of events and transactions and that the financial statements present the Company's financial position and results of operations in conformity with generally accepted accounting principles. Management has included in the Company's financial statements amounts that are based on informed judgments and estimates, which it believes are reasonable under the circumstances.

Maxidrive maintains a system of internal accounting policies, procedures and controls intended to provide reasonable assurance, at appropriate cost, that transactions are processed in accordance with Company authorization and are properly recorded and reported in the financial statements, and that assets are adequately safeguarded.

Smith and Walker, CPAs, the Company's independent auditing firm, audits the Company's financial statements in accordance with generally accepted auditing standards, which provide the basis of its report on the financial statements.

The Board of Directors of the Company has an Audit Committee composed of nonmanagement directors. The Committee meets with financial management and the independent auditors to review internal accounting controls and accounting, auditing, and financial reporting matters. In addition, Smith and Walker, CPAs, has full and free access to the Audit Committee, without management present, to discuss the results of its audits, the adequacy of the company's internal accounting controls, and the quality of its financial reporting.

Harold T. West
President and Chairman of the Board

Robert P. Malony
Chief Financial Officer

tors to verify the fairness of the statement presentations; and (3) they have a committee of the board of directors whose job it is to review these other two safeguards. These safeguards have failed in the case of Maxidrive, and those primarily responsible, whether directly involved or not, are listed in the report of management.

The **report of independent accountants (audit report)** describes the auditors' opinion of the fairness of the financial statement presentations and the evidence gathered to support that opinion.

The role of the independent auditor is described in more detail in the second report (Exhibit 1–8), the **report of independent accountants** or **audit report**, which describes their opinion of the fairness of the financial statement presentations and the evidence gathered to support that opinion. An accountant may be licensed as a *Certified Public Accountant*, or *CPA*. This designation is granted only on completion of requirements specified by each state. While other accountants can offer various accounting services to the public, only a licensed CPA can issue an audit report. In this role, accountants are known as *independent CPAs* (or independent accountants) because they have certain responsibilities that extend to the general public in addition to those to the specific business that pays for the services. Independent CPAs, although paid by their clients, are not employees of their clients. Independence has important implications for the legal liability of CPA firms such as Smith and Walker, the CPAs who audited Maxidrive's statements, when financial statements prove to be in error. We discuss these implications in the next section.

An **audit** is an examination of the financial reports to assure that they represent what they claim and conform with generally accepted accounting principles.

An **audit** involves an examination of the financial reports (prepared by the management of the entity) to assure that they represent what they claim and conform with generally accepted accounting principles (GAAP). In performing an audit, the independent CPA examines the underlying transactions, including the collection, classification, and assembly of the financial data incorporated in the financial reports. To appreciate the magnitude of these responsibilities, consider the enormous number of transactions involving a major enterprise such as General Motors—billions of dollars each year. However, the CPA does not examine each of these transactions; rather, professional approaches are used to ascertain beyond reasonable doubt that transactions were measured and reported properly. There are many unintentional and, as we have learned in the Maxidrive case, intentional opportunities to prepare misleading financial reports. The audit function performed by an independent CPA is the best protection available to the public. However, when

Exhibit 1–8 **Report of Independent Accountants**

Report of Independent Accountants

To the Stockholders and Board of Directors of Maxidrive Corp.

We have audited the accompanying balance sheet of Maxidrive Corp. as of December 31, 19A, and the related statements of income, shareholders' equity and cash flows for the period ended December 31, 19A. These financial statements are the responsibility of the Company's management. Our responsibility is to express an opinion on these financial statements based on our audits.

We conducted our audits in accordance with generally accepted auditing standards. Those standards require that we plan and perform the audit to obtain reasonable assurance about whether the financial statements are free of material misstatement. An audit includes examining, on a test basis, evidence supporting the amounts and disclosures in the financial statements. An audit also includes assessing the accounting principles used and significant estimates made by management, as well as evaluating the overall financial statement presentation. We believe that our audits provide a reasonable basis for our opinion.

In our opinion, the financial statements referred to above present fairly, in all material respects, the financial position of Maxidrive Corp. at December 31, 19A, and the results of its operations and its cash flows for the period ended December 31, 19A, in conformity with generally accepted accounting principles.

Smith and Walker, CPAs

that protection fails, the independent CPA is often found liable for losses incurred by those who rely on the statements.

Ethics, Reputation, and Legal Liability

Learning Objective 4
Appreciate the importance of ethics, reputation, and legal liability in accounting.

If financial statements are to be of any value to decision makers, users must have confidence in the fairness of the information. These users will have greater confidence in the information if they know that the people who were associated with auditing the financial statements were required to meet professional standards of ethics and competence.

The American Institute of Certified Public Accountants (AICPA) requires all of its members to adhere to a professional code of ethics. These broad principles are supported by specific rules that govern the performance of audits by members of the AICPA. Failure to comply with the rules of conduct can result in serious professional penalties. The AICPA can suspend members for up to two years and, in serious cases, permanently expel members. State boards can suspend or revoke a CPA's license to practice. However, the potential economic effects of damage to reputation and malpractice liability provide even stronger incentives to abide by professional standards.

CPAs' reputations for honesty and competence are their most important assets. Remember that the purpose of an audit is to add credibility to the numbers presented by management on financial statements. An audit by a CPA whose reputation for competence or honesty has been tarnished will not provide that added credibility. If the Smith and Walker firm is found to be either negligent or dishonest in the audit of Maxidrive, American Bank and other lenders will refuse to lend money based on statements that firm has audited, and the firm's other clients will quickly choose new auditors. Financial statement fraud is a fairly rare event, due in part to the diligent efforts of practicing CPAs. In fact, many such frauds are first identified in the course of the annual audit. However, even the most diligent audit may not immediately uncover the results of fraud involving collusion of the top officers of a corporation, such as occurred here.

We noted above that the independence of CPAs has important implications for their liability in cases of malpractice. In case of malpractice, physicians are subject to potential lawsuits only from the patient involved (and the patient's family). In contrast, in case of malpractice in the audit function, the independent CPA is subject to potential liability that may extend to all parties (whether known to the CPA or not) who have suffered loss because of reliance on financial statements examined by the CPA. Even if Smith and Walker was unaware that Exeter was using the statements as input to their decision to buy Maxidrive, if the CPAs' failure to detect the errors in the statements was a result of their malpractice, they could be liable for Exeter's loss.

As a result of the fraud, Maxidrive filed for bankruptcy, and will likely be sold in an attempt to pay off creditors. Exeter Investors and American Bank claimed losses of $16.5 million and $9 million, respectively, in a civil law suit brought against the officers of Maxidrive for having "perpetrated a massive fraud" and against the auditors for "overlooking the errors" in the audit.[6] Exeter and American Bank have also asked for punitive damages for gross negligence. The president and the chief financial officer of Maxidrive are also under indictment by a federal grand jury for three counts of criminal securities fraud for which they face possible fines and prison terms.

---

[6]Even some accountants are confused about the auditor's responsibility to detect fraud. Statement on Auditing Standards No. 53, *The Auditor's Responsibility to Detect and Report Errors and Irregularities*, requires that auditors design tests to assure detection of fraud that materially affects financial statements. However, the statement notes that no audit can guarantee the discovery of sophisticated collusive fraud.

EPILOGUE

Though financial statement fraud is a fairly rare event, the misrepresentations in Maxidrive's statements aptly illustrate the importance of fairly presented financial statements to investors and creditors, and the crucial importance of the public accounting profession in ensuring the integrity of the financial reporting system. As noted at the beginning of the chapter, Maxidrive is not a real company but is based on a real company where a similar fraud was perpetrated.[7] The focus companies and contrasting examples in the remaining chapters are *real* companies except where indicated.

Maxidrive is loosely based on the infamous MiniScribe fraud. Further, the size of the real fraud was more than *10 times* as great as in the fictional case, as were the losses incurred and the lawsuits which followed. (Many of the numbers in the financial statements are simply one-tenth the amounts presented in MiniScribe's fraudulent statements.) The nature of the fraud was also quite similar. At MiniScribe, sales revenue was overstated by transferring nonexistent inventory between two of MiniScribe's own facilities and creating phony documents to make it look like the inventory was transferred to customers. MiniScribe even packaged *bricks* as finished products, shipped them to distributors, and counted them as sold. Cost of goods sold was understated by activities such as counting scrap parts and damaged drives as usable inventory. Further, members of management even broke into the auditors' locked trunks to change numbers on their audit papers. As a consequence, MiniScribe reported net income of $31 million which was subsequently shown to be $9 million. Prior years' statements contained similar errors. MiniScribe's investors and creditors filed lawsuits asking for over $1 billion in damages. Actual damages in the hundreds of millions were paid. Both the chairman and the chief financial officer of MiniScribe were convicted of federal securities and wire fraud charges and sentenced to jail. While most managers and owners act in an honest and responsible fashion, this incident is a stark reminder of the economic consequences of lack of fair presentation in financial reports. Sales revenue and inventory frauds to this day are the most frequently occurring financial statement frauds.[8]

DEMONSTRATION CASE

At the end of most chapters, one or more demonstration cases are presented. These cases provide an overview of the primary issues discussed in the chapter. Each demonstration case is followed by a recommended solution. You should read the case carefully, and then prepare your own solution before you study the recommended solution. This self-evaluation is highly recommended.

The introductory case presented below will start you thinking in financial statement terms of some of the resource inflows and outflows of a business.

ABC Service Corporation was organized by Able, Baker, and Cain on January 1, 19A. On that date, the investors exchanged $36,000 cash for all of the stock of the company. On the same day, the corporation borrowed $10,000 from a local bank and signed a three-year, 15% note payable. The interest is payable each December 31. On January 1, 19A, the corporation purchased service supplies for $20,000 cash. Operations started immediately.

---

[7]None of the names of individuals in the case are real.

[8]*Fraud Survey Results 1993*, KPMG Peat Marwick, 1993

At the end of 19A, the corporation had completed the following additional business transactions (summarized):

a. Performed services and billed customers for $100,500, of which $94,500 was collected in cash by year-end.
b. Used up $5,000 of service supplies while rendering services.
c. Paid $54,000 cash for other service expenses.
d. Paid $1,500 in annual interest expense on the note payable.
e. Paid all income taxes in cash to the Internal Revenue Service (IRS). (The income tax rate was 20%.)

Required:

Complete the following two 19A financial statements by entering the correct amounts. The suggested solution follows the blank statements.

ABC SERVICE CORPORATION
Income Statement
______(date)
(in dollars)

			Computation
Revenues:			
Service revenue		$	
Expenses:			
Service expenses	$		
Interest expense			
Total expenses			
Pretax income		$	
Income tax expense			
Net Income		$	

ABC SERVICE CORPORATION
Balance Sheet
______(date)
(in dollars)

			Computation
Assets			
Cash		$	
Accounts receivable			
Service supplies			
Total assets		$	
Liabilities			
Note payable (15%)	$		
Total liabilities		$	
Stockholders' equity			
Contributed capital	$		
Retained earnings			
Total stockholders' equity		$	
Total liabilities and stockholders' equity		$	

SUGGESTED SOLUTION

ABC SERVICE CORPORATION
Income Statement
For the Year Ended December 31, 19A
(in dollars)

			Computation
Revenues:			
Service revenue		$100,500	Given (cash & on open account)
Expenses:			
Service expenses	$59,000		$54,000 cash + 5,000 supplies
Interest expense	1,500		$10,000 x 15%
Total expenses		60,500	
Pretax income		$ 40,000	
Income tax expense		8,000	$40,000 x 20%
Net Income		$ 32,000	

ABC SERVICE CORPORATION
Balance Sheet
at December 31, 19A
(in dollars)

			Computation
Assets			
Cash		$57,000	$36,000 + $10,000 + $94,500 – $54,000 – $1,500 – $8,000 – $20,000
Accounts receivable		6,000	$100,500 – $94,500
Service supplies		15,000	$20,000 – $5,000
Total assets		$78,000	
Liabilities			
Note payable (15%)	$10,000		Given, bank loan
Total liabilities		$10,000	
Stockholders' equity			
Contributed capital	$36,000		Given
Retained earnings	32,000		From income statement
Total stockholders' equity		68,000	
Total liabilities and stockholders' equity		$78,000	

SUMMARY

The four basic financial statements are the balance sheet, the income statement, the statement of cash flows, and the statement of retained earnings.

The *balance sheet* is a statement of financial position that reports dollar amounts for the assets, liabilities, and stockholders' equity at a specific point in time.

The *income statement* is a statement of operations that reports revenues, expenses, and net income for a stated period of time.

The *statement of cash flows* reports inflows and outflows of cash for a specific period of time.

The *statement of retained earnings* explains changes to the retained earnings balance that occurred during the reporting period.

The financial statements and the parties to the accounting communication process were illustrated in the context of the purchase of a disk drive company that published fraudulent financial statements. In the next four chapters, we will look more closely at the process of preparing financial statements and their use in business decision making. You will learn to analyze business transactions using the basic accounting equations to determine exactly how the results of your future business decisions will be reflected in financial statements. You will also begin learning how to examine other companies' financial statements to draw inferences about the quality of the decisions their managers made. This is the heart of financial statement analysis. The accounting equation for the balance sheet, *Assets = Liabilities + Stockholders' Equity,* is the foundation for the entire accounting process and the understanding of financial statements.

Chapter Supplement A

Types of Business Entities

This textbook emphasizes *accounting for profit-making business entities.* There are three main types of business entities—sole proprietorship, partnership, and corporation. A *sole proprietorship* is an unincorporated business owned by one person. This type of business entity is usually small in size and is common in the service, retailing, and farming industries. Often the owner is the manager. Legally the business and the owner are not separate entities. However, accounting views the business as a separate entity that must be accounted for separately from its owner.

A *partnership* is an unincorporated business that is owned by two or more persons known as *partners.* Some partnerships are large in size (e.g., international public accounting firms and law firms). The agreements between the owners are specified in a partnership contract. This contract deals with such matters as division of income each reporting period and distribution of resources of the business upon termination of its operations. A partnership is not legally separate from its owners. Legally each partner in a general partnership is responsible for the debts of the business (each general partner has *unlimited liability*). However, the partnership is a separate business entity to be accounted for separately from its several owners.

A *corporation* is a business that is incorporated under the laws of a particular state. The owners are called *stockholders* or *shareholders.* Ownership is represented by shares of capital stock that usually can be bought and sold freely. When an approved application for incorporation is filed by the organizers, the state issues a charter. This charter gives the corporation the right to operate as a separate legal entity, separate and apart from its owners. The stockholders enjoy *limited liability.* Stockholders are liable for the debts of the corporation only to the extent of their investments. The corporate charter specifies the types and amounts of capital stock that can be issued. Most states require a minimum of two or three stockholders and a minimum amount of resources to be contributed at the time of organization. The stockholders elect a governing board of directors, which in turn employs managers and exercises general supervision of the corporation. Accounting also views the corporation as a separate business entity that must be accounted for separately from its owners.

In terms of economic importance, the corporation is the dominant form of business organization in the United States. This dominance is caused by the many advantages of the corporate form: *(a)* limited liability for the stockholders, *(b)* continuity of life, *(c)* ease in transferring ownership (stock), and *(d)* opportunities to raise large amounts of money by selling shares to a large number of people. The primary disadvantage of a corporation is that its income may be subject to double taxation (corporate income is taxed when earned and then again when it is distributed to stockholders as dividends). In this textbook, we emphasize the corporate form of business. Nevertheless, the accounting concepts and procedures that we discuss also apply to other types of businesses.

Chapter Supplement B

Employment in the Accounting Profession Today

Since 1900, accounting has attained the stature of such professions as law, medicine, engineering, and architecture. As with all recognized professions, accounting is subject to professional competence requirements, is dedicated to service to the public, requires a high level of academic study, and rests on a common body of knowledge. An accountant may be licensed as a Certified Public Accountant, or CPA. This designation is granted only on completion of requirements specified by the state from which the license will be granted. Although the CPA requirements vary among states, they include a college degree with a specified number of accounting courses, good character, one to five years of professional experience, and successful completion of a professional examination. The CPA examination, scheduled in each state simultaneously on a semiannual basis, is prepared by the American Institute of Certified Public Accountants.

Accountants (including CPAs) commonly are engaged in professional practice or are employed by businesses, government entities, nonprofit organizations, and so on. Accountants employed in these activities may take and pass a professional examination to become a Certified Management Accountant, or CMA (the CMA examination is administered by the Institute of Management Accountants), or a Certified Internal Auditor, or CIA (the CIA examination is administered by the Institute of Internal Auditors).

Practice of Public Accounting

Although an individual may practice public accounting, usually two or more individuals organize an accounting firm in the form of a partnership (in some states, incorporation is permitted). Accounting firms vary in size from a one-person office, to regional firms, to the Big Six firms (Arthur Andersen & Co., Coopers and Lybrand, Deloitte & Touche, Ernst & Young, KPMG Peat Marwick, and Price Waterhouse), which have hundreds of offices located worldwide. Accounting firms usually render three types of services: auditing, management consulting services, and tax services.

Auditing

The most important service performed by the CPA in public practice is *auditing,* the attest function. The purpose of an audit is to lend credibility to the financial reports; that is, to assure that they fairly represent what they claim. An audit involves an examination of the financial reports (prepared by the management of the entity) to assure that they conform with generally accepted accounting principles (GAAP).

Management Consulting Services

Many independent CPA firms offer *management consulting services*. These services usually are accounting based and encompass such activities as the design and installation of accounting, data processing, and profit-planning and control (budget) systems; financial advice; forecasting; inventory controls; cost-effectiveness studies; and operational analysis. This facet of public CPA practice is growing rapidly.

Tax Services

CPAs in public practice usually provide income tax services to their clients. These services include both tax planning as a part of the decision-making process and determination of the income tax liability (reported on the annual income tax return). Because of the increasing complexity of state and federal tax laws, a high level of competence is required, which can be provided by CPAs specializing in taxation. The CPA's involvement in tax planning often is quite significant. Most major business decisions have significant tax impacts; in fact, tax-planning considerations often govern certain business decisions.

Employment by Organizations

Many accountants, including CPAs, CMAs, and CIAs, are employed by profit-making and nonprofit organizations. An organization, depending on its size and complexity, may employ from a few to hundreds of accountants. In a business enterprise, the chief financial officer (usually a vice president or controller) is a member of the management team. This responsibility usually entails a wide range of management, financial, and accounting duties.

In a business entity, accountants typically are engaged in a wide variety of activities, such as general management, general accounting, cost accounting, profit planning and control (budgeting), internal auditing, and computerized data processing. A primary function of the accountants in organizations is to provide data that are useful for internal managerial decision making and for controlling operations. Also, the functions of external reporting, tax planning, control of assets, and a host of related responsibilities normally are performed by accountants in industry.

Employment in the Public and Not-for-Profit Sector

The vast and complex operations of governmental units, from the local to the international level, create a need for accountants. The same holds true for other not-for-profit organizations such as hospitals and universities. Accountants employed in the public and not-for-profit sector perform functions similar to those performed by their counterparts in private organizations. Also, the General Accounting Office (GAO) and the regulatory agencies, such as the Securities and Exchange Commission (SEC) and Federal Communications Commission (FCC), use the services of accountants in carrying out their regulatory duties.

KEY TERMS

Accounting A system that collects and processes (analyzes, measures, and records) financial information about an organization and reports that information to decision makers. *6*

Accounting Entity The organization for which financial data are to be collected (separate and distinct from its owners). *8*

Accounting Period The time period covered by the financial statements. *13*

Audit An examination of the financial reports to assure that they represent what they claim and conform with generally accepted accounting principles. *26*

Balance Sheet (Statement of Financial Position) A statement that reports the financial position (assets, liabilities, and stockholders' equity) of an accounting entity at a point in time. *8*

Basic Accounting Equation (Balance Sheet Equation) Assets = Liabilities + Stockholders' Equity. *10*

Financial Accounting Standards Board (FASB) The private sector body given the primary responsibility to work out the detailed rules that become generally accepted accounting principles. *22*

Footnotes (Notes) Supplemental information about the financial condition of a company, without which the financial statements cannot be fully understood. *19*

Generally Accepted Accounting Principles (GAAP) The measurement rules used to develop the information in financial statements. *21*

Income Statement (Statement of Income, Statement of Earnings, or Statement of Operations) A statement that reports the revenues less the expenses of the accounting period. *13*

Report of Independent Accountants (Audit Report) A report that describes the auditors' opinion of the fairness of the financial statement presentations and the evidence gathered to support that opinion. *26*

Report of Management A report that indicates management's primary responsibility for financial statement information and the steps taken to ensure the accuracy of the company's records. *25*

Securities and Exchange Commission (SEC) The U.S. government agency that determines the financial statements that public companies must provide to stockholders and the measurement rules that must be used in producing those statements. *22*

Statement of Cash Flows A statement that reports inflows and outflows of cash during the accounting period in the categories of operations, investing, and financing. *17*

Statement of Retained Earnings A statement that reports how net income and the distribution of dividends affected the financial position of the company during the accounting period. *16*

QUESTIONS

1. Define accounting.
2. Briefly distinguish financial accounting from managerial accounting.
3. The accounting process generates financial reports for both internal and external users. Identify some of the groups of users.
4. Briefly distinguish investors from creditors.
5. What is an accounting entity? Why is a business treated as a separate entity for accounting purposes?
6. Briefly explain the importance of assets and liabilities to the decisions of investors and creditors.
7. Financial statements are the end products of the accounting process. Explain.
8. Define *communication.*
9. Complete the following:

Name of Statement	Alternative Title
a. Income statement	*a.* __________
b. Balance sheet	*b.* __________
c. Audit report	*c.* __________

10. What information should be included in the heading of each of the three primary financial statements?

11. Explain why the income statement and the statement of cash flows are dated "For the Year Ended December 31, 19X," whereas the balance sheet is dated "At December 31, 19X."
12. Define *revenue.*
13. Define *expense.*
14. Briefly define the following: *net income, net loss,* and *break even.*
15. What are the purposes of *(a)* the income statement, *(b)* the balance sheet, *(c)* the statement of cash flows, and *(d)* the statement of retained earnings?
16. Explain the accounting equation for the income statement. What are the three major items reported on the income statement?
17. Explain the accounting equation for the balance sheet. Define the three major components reported on the balance sheet.
18. Explain the accounting equation for the statement of cash flows. Explain the three major components reported on the statement.
19. Explain the accounting equation for the statement of retained earnings. Explain the four major items reported on the statement of retained earnings.
20. What are the two primary sources of stockholders' equity in a business?
21. Financial statements discussed in this chapter are aimed at *external* users. Briefly explain how *internal* company managers in different functional areas (e.g., marketing, purchasing, human resources) might use financial statement information.
22. Briefly describe how accounting measurement rules (generally accepted accounting principles) are determined in the United States.
23. Briefly describe why managers and owners care what measurement methods are generally accepted.
24. Briefly explain the responsibility of company management and the independent auditors in the accounting communication process.
25. (Supplement A) Briefly differentiate between a sole proprietorship, a partnership, and a corporation.
26. (Supplement B) List and briefly explain the three primary services provided by CPAs in public practice.

EXERCISES

E1–1 Identifying Important Accounting Abbreviations

Below is a list of important abbreviations used in the chapter. These abbreviations also are used widely in business. For each abbreviation give the full designation. The first one is an example.

	Abbreviation	Full Designation
______	(1) CPA	Certified Public Accountant
______	(2) GAAP	______
______	(3) CMA	______
______	(4) AICPA	______
______	(5) SEC	______
______	(6) FASB	______

E1–2 Matching Definitions with Terms or Abbreviations

Match each definition with its related term or abbreviation by entering the appropriate letter in the space provided.

Term or Abbreviation		Definition
________ (1)	SEC	A. A system that collects and processes financial information about an organization and reports that information to decision makers.
________ (2)	Auditing	B. Measurement of information about an entity in the monetary unit—dollars or other national currency.
________ (3)	Sole proprietorship	C. An unincorporated business owned by two or more persons.
________ (4)	Corporation	D. The organization for which financial data are to be collected (separate and distinct from its owners).
________ (5)	Accounting	E. An incorporated entity that issues shares of stock as evidence of ownership.
________ (6)	Separate entity	F. Initial recording of financial statement elements at acquisition cost.
________ (7)	Audit report	G. An examination of the financial reports to assure that they represent what they claim and conform with generally accepted accounting principles.
________ (8)	Cost principle	H. Certified Public Accountant.
________ (9)	Partnership	I. An unincorporated business owned by one person.
________ (10)	AICPA	J. A report that describes the auditors' opinion of the fairness of the financial statement presentations and the evidence gathered to support that opinion.
________ (11)	FASB	K. Securities and Exchange Commission.
________ (12)	CPA	L. Financial Accounting Standards Board.
________ (13)	Unit of measure	M. Company that can be bought and sold by investors on established stock exchanges.
________ (14)	GAAP	N. Generally accepted accounting principles.
________ (15)	Publicly traded	O. American Institute of Certified Public Accountants.

Procter & Gamble

E1–3 Assigning Financial Statement Items to Financial Statement Categories

According to its annual report, "Procter & Gamble markets a broad range of laundry, cleaning, paper, beauty care, health care, food and beverage products in more than 140 countries around the world, with leading brands including Tide, Ariel, Crest, Crisco, Vicks and Max Factor." Listed below are items taken from its recent balance sheet and income statement. Note that different companies use slightly different titles for the same item. Mark each item in the following list as an asset (A), liability (L), or stockholders' equity (SE) that would appear on the balance sheet or a revenue (R) or expense (E) that would appear on the income statement.

________	Accounts payable	________	Land
________	Accounts receivable	________	Marketing, administrative, and other operating expenses
________	Cash and cash equivalents		
________	Cost of products sold	________	Long-term debt
________	Property, plant, and equipment	________	Net sales
________	Income taxes	________	Notes payable
________	Interest expense	________	Retained earnings
________	Inventories	________	Taxes payable

Tootsie Roll

E1–4 Assigning Financial Statement Items to Financial Statement Categories

Tootsie Roll Industries is engaged in the manufacture and sale of candy. Major products include: Tootsie Roll, Tootsie Roll Pops, Tootsie Pop Drops, Tootsie Flavor Rolls, Charms, and Blow-Pop lollipops. The following items were listed on Tootsie Roll's recent income statement and balance sheet. Mark each item from the balance sheet as an asset (A), liability (L), or shareholders' equity (SE) and each item from the income statement as a revenue (R) or expense (E).

________	Accounts payable	________	Buildings
________	Accounts receivable	________	Cash and cash equivalents

________	Cost of goods sold	________	Land
________	Distribution and warehousing	________	Machinery and equipment
________	Dividends payable	________	Marketing, selling, and advertising
________	General and administrative	________	Net sales
________	Income taxes payable	________	Notes payable to banks
________	Inventories	________	Provision for income taxes*
________	Investments	________	Retained earnings

*In the United States, "provision for income taxes" is most often used as a synonym for "income tax expense."

E1–5 *Using the Income Statement and Balance Sheet Equations*

Review the chapter explanations of the income statement and the balance sheet equations. Apply these equations in each independent case below to compute the two missing amounts for each case. Assume it is the end of 19A, the first full year of operations for the company.

Independent Cases	Total Revenues	Total Assets	Total Expenses	Total Liabilities	Net Income (Loss)	Stockholders' Equity
A	$100,000	$150,000	$82,000	$70,000	$	$
B		112,000	80,000		12,000	60,000
C	80,000	104,000	86,000	26,000		
D	50,000			22,000	13,000	77,000
E			81,000	73,000	(6,000)	28,000

E1–6 *Analyzing an Income Statement*

Pest Away Corporation was organized by three individuals on January 1, 19A, to provide insect extermination services. At the end of 19A, the following income statement was prepared:

PEST AWAY CORPORATION
Income Statement
For the Year Ended December 31, 19A

Revenues:		
Service revenue (cash)	$192,000	
Service revenue (credit)	24,000	
Total revenues		$216,000
Expenses:		
Salaries expense	$ 76,000	
Rent expense	21,000	
Utilities expense	12,000	
Advertising expense	14,000	
Supplies expense	25,000	
Interest expense	8,000	
Total expenses		156,000
Pretax income		$ 60,000
Income tax expense		21,000
Net income		$ 39,000

Required:

1. What was the average monthly revenue amount?
2. What was the monthly rent amount?
3. Explain why supplies are reported as an expense.
4. Explain why interest is reported as an expense.
5. What was the average income tax rate for Pest Away Corporation?
6. Can you determine how much cash the company had on December 31, 19A? Explain.

E1–7 Preparing a Simple Income Statement

Assume you are the owner of The Collegiate Shop, which specializes in items that interest students. At the end of January 19A, you find that (for January only):

a. Sales, per the cash register tapes, of $120,000, plus one sale on credit (a special situation) of $1,000.
b. With the help of a friend (who majored in accounting), you determined that all of the goods sold during January had cost $40,000 to purchase.
c. During the month, according to the checkbook, you paid $38,000 for salaries, rent, supplies, advertising, and other expenses; however, you have not yet paid the $600 monthly utilities for January on the store and fixtures.

Required:

On the basis of the data given, what was the amount of income for January (disregard income taxes)? Show computations. (Hint: A convenient form to use would have the following major side captions: revenue from sales, expenses, and the difference—net income.)

Compaq Computer

E1–8 Matching Cash Flow Statement Items to Categories

Compaq Computer is a leading designer and manufacturer of personal computers. The following items were taken from its recent cash flow statement. Note that different companies use slightly different titles for the same item. Without referring to Exhibit 1–5, mark each item in the list as a cash flow from operating activities (O), investing activities (I), or financing activities (F). Also, place brackets around the letter if it is a cash outflow and no brackets if it is a cash inflow.

_______ Cash paid to suppliers and employees
_______ Cash received from customers
_______ Income taxes paid
_______ Interest and dividends received
_______ Interest paid
_______ Proceeds from sale of investment in Conner Peripherals, Inc.
_______ Purchases of property, plant, and equipment
_______ Repayment of borrowings

E1–9 Analyzing Cash Inflow from Operations

Paul's Painters, a service organization, prepared the following special report for the month of January 19A:

Service Revenue, Expenses, and Income

Service revenue:		
Cash services (per cash register tape)	$105,000	
Credit services (per charge bills; not yet collected by end of January)	30,500	
		$135,500
Expenses:		
Salaries and wages expense (paid by check)	$ 50,000	
Salary for January not yet paid	3,000	
Supplies used (taken from stock, purchased for cash during December)	2,000	
Estimated cost of using company-owned truck for the month (depreciation)	500	
Other expenses (paid by check)	26,000	81,500
Pretax income		$ 54,000
Income tax expense (not yet paid)		13,500
Income for January		$ 40,500

Required:

1. The owner (who knows little about the financial part of the business) asked you to compute the amount that cash increased in January 19A from the operations of the company. You decided to prepare a detailed report for the owner with the following major side captions: cash inflows (collections), cash outflows (payments), and the difference—net increase (or decrease) in cash.
2. What was the average income tax rate?
3. See if you can reconcile the difference—net increase (or decrease) in cash—you computed in (1) with the income for January 19A.

E1–10 Preparing a Simple Income Statement

Wal-Mart

Wal-Mart Stores, Inc., is the largest retail chain in the United States, operating over 2,000 stores. Its recent quarterly income statement contained the following items (in thousands). Solve for the missing amounts and prepare a condensed income statement for the quarter ended October 31, 19A.

Cost of sales	$16,200,873
Interest costs	184,190
Net income	?
Net sales	20,417,717
Operating, selling and general and administrative expenses	3,340,263
Provision for income taxes*	339,422
Rental and other income	235,116
Total costs and expenses	?
Total revenues	?
Pretax income	?

*In the United States, "provision for income taxes" is a common synonym for "income tax expense."

E1–11 Preparing a Condensed Balance Sheet

Honda Motor Co.

Established less than 50 years ago, Honda Motor Co., Ltd. of Japan is a leading international manufacturer of automobiles and the largest manufacturer of motorcycles in the world. As a Japanese company, it follows Japanese GAAP and reports its financial statements in millions of Yen (the sign for Yen is ¥). Its recent condensed balance sheet contained the following items (in millions). Solve for the missing amounts and prepare a condensed balance sheet as of March 31, 19A.

Cash and cash equivalents	¥ 150,554
Contributed capital	281,208
Current liabilities	1,308,748
Inventories	606,689
Investments	212,294
Long-term debt	569,479
Net property, plant, and equipment	1,008,196
Other assets	213,845
Other liabilities	94,485
Retained earnings	755,419
Total assets	?
Total liabilities and stockholders' equity	?
Trade accounts, notes, and other receivables	817,761

E1–12 Preparing a Simple Income Statement and Balance Sheet

Clay Corporation was organized by five individuals on January 1, 19A. At the end of January 19A, the following monthly financial data are available:

Total revenues	$130,000
Total expenses (excluding income taxes)	80,000
Cash balance, January 31, 19A	30,000
Receivables from customers (all considered collectible)	15,000
Merchandise inventory (by inventory count at cost)	42,000

Payables to suppliers for merchandise purchased from them (will be paid during February 19A)	11,000
Contributed capital (2,600 shares)	26,000
No dividends were declared or paid during 19A.	

Assume a 30% tax rate on the income of this corporation; the income taxes will be paid during the first quarter of 19B.

Required:

Complete the following two statements:

CLAY CORPORATION
Income Statement
For the Month of January 19A

Total revenues	$ ______
Less: Total expenses (excluding income tax)	______
Pretax income	______
Less: Income tax expense	______
Net income	$ ______

CLAY CORPORATION
Balance Sheet
At January 31, 19A

Assets		
Cash		$ ______
Receivables from customers		______
Merchandise inventory		______
Total assets		$ ______
Liabilities		
Payables to suppliers		$ ______
Income taxes payable		______
Total liabilities		$ ______
Stockholders' equity		
Contributed capital	$ ______	
Retained earnings	______	
Total liabilities and stockholders' equity		$ ______

E1–13 Completing a Simple Balance Sheet

Read More Store was organized as a corporation by Terry Lloyd and Joan Lopez; each contributed $50,000 cash to start the business. Each received 4,000 shares of common stock. The store completed its first year of operations on December 31, 19A. On that date, the following financial items for the year were determined: December 31, 19A, cash on hand and in the bank, $48,900; December 31, 19A, amounts due from customers from sales of books, $26,000; unused portion of store and office equipment, $48,000; December 31, 19A, amounts owed to publishers for books purchased, $8,000; and a note payable, 12%, one-year, dated July 1, 19A, to a local bank for $2,000. No dividends were declared or paid to the stockholders during the year.

Required:

1. Complete the following balance sheet as of the end of 19A.
2. What was the amount of net income for the year?
3. Show how the $120 liability for interest payable was computed. Why is it shown as a liability on this date?

____
____
____

Assets		Liabilities		
Cash	$ _____	Accounts payable	$ _____	
Accounts receivable	_____	Note payable	_____	
Store and office equipment	_____	Interest payable	120	
		Total liabilities		$ _____
		Stockholders' Equity		
		Contributed capital	$ _____	
		Retained earnings	12,780	
		Total stockholders' equity		_____
Total assets	$ _____	Total liabilities and stockholders' equity		$ _____

E1–14 Preparing a Simple Statement of Cash Flows

NITSU Manufacturing Corporation is preparing the annual financial statements for the stockholders. A statement of cash flows must be prepared. The following data on cash flows were developed for the entire year ended December 31, 19D: cash inflow from operating revenues, $270,000; cash expended for operating expenses, $180,000; sale of unissued NITSU stock for cash, $30,000; cash dividends declared and paid to stockholders during the year, $22,000; and payments on long-term notes payable, $80,000. During the year, a tract of land was sold for $15,000 cash (which was the same price that NITSU had paid for the land in 19C), and $38,000 cash was expended for two new machines. The machines were used in the factory. The beginning of the year cash balance was $63,000.

Required:

Prepare the statement of cash flows for 19D. Follow the format illustrated in the chapter.

E1–15 Completing a Simple Income Statement

Home Realty, Incorporated has been operating for five years and is owned by three investors. J. Doe owns 60% of the total outstanding stock of 9,000 shares and is the managing executive in charge. On December 31, 19C, the following financial items for the entire year were determined: commissions earned and collected in cash, $150,000, plus $16,000 uncollected; rental service fees earned and collected, $20,000; salaries expense paid, $62,000; commissions expense paid, $35,000; payroll taxes paid, $2,500; rent paid, $2,200 (not including December rent yet to be paid); utilities expense paid, $1,000; promotion and advertising paid, $8,000; and miscellaneous expenses paid, $500. There were no other unpaid expenses at December 31. Home Realty rents its office space but owns the furniture therein. The furniture cost $6,000 when acquired. The portion used this period (called depreciation) was $600. The average income tax rate for this corporation is 25%. Also during the year, the company paid the owners "out of profit" cash dividends amounting to $12,000. Complete the following income statement:

____

____

____

Revenues:		
Commissions earned	$____	
Rental service fees	____	
Total revenues		$____
Expenses:		
Salaries expense	$____	
Commission expense	____	
Payroll tax expense	____	
Rent expense	____	
Utilities expense	____	
Promotion and advertising expense	____	
Miscellaneous expenses	____	
Depreciation expense	____	
Total expenses (excluding income taxes)		____
Pretax income		$____
Income tax expense		____
Net income		$55,500

E1–16 Applying the Balance Sheet Equation

On June 1, 19F, Bland Corporation prepared a balance sheet just prior to going out of business. The balance sheet totals showed the following:

Assets (no cash)	$90,000
Liabilities	50,000
Stockholders' equity	40,000

Shortly thereafter, all of the assets were sold for cash.

Required:

1. How would the balance sheet appear immediately after the sale of the assets for cash for each of the following cases? Use the format given below.

		Balances Immediately after Sale				
	Cash Received for the Assets	Assets	–	Liabilities	=	Stockholders' Equity
Case A	$90,000	$____		$____		$____
Case B	80,000	$____		$____		$____
Case C	100,000	$____		$____		$____

2. How should the cash be distributed in each separate case? (Hint: Creditors must be paid in full before owners receive any payment.) Use the format given below.

	To Creditors	To Stockholders	Total
Case A	$____	$____	$____
Case B	$____	$____	$____
Case C	$____	$____	$____

PROBLEMS

P1–1 Analyzing Transactions

Below are listed five transactions completed by Soloman Company during the year 19A:

a. Sold services for cash, $55,000.

b. Purchased a microcomputer for use in performing the accounting function of the company: cost, $8,000; paid cash.

c. Paid salaries, $30,000 cash.

d. Borrowed $15,000 cash on a 15% interest-bearing note.

e. The owner of Soloman Company purchased a special pickup for his personal use: cost, $18,000 paid cash from his personal funds.

Required:

Complete the tabulation given below. Indicate the effects (in dollars) of each of the above transactions on the balance sheet, income statement, and statement of cash flows of Soloman Company. Consider only the effects on the date the transactions were completed. Provide explanatory comments to support your response for each transaction. Use "+" for increase and "–" for decrease on the income statement and balance sheet.

	Transaction				
Financial Statements	**(*a*)**	**(*b*)**	**(*c*)**	**(*d*)**	**(*e*)**
Income statement Revenues Expenses					
Balance sheet Assets Liabilities Stockholders' equity					
Statement of cash flows Cash inflow Cash outflow					
Explanations					

P1–2 *Analyzing Data to Support a Loan Application*

On January 1, 19A, three individuals organized West Company as a corporation. Each individual invested $10,000 cash in the business. On December 31, 19A, they prepared a list of resources owned (assets) and a list of the debts (liabilities) to support a company loan request for $70,000 submitted to a local bank. None of the three investors had studied accounting. The two lists prepared were as follows:

Company resources:	
Cash	$ 12,000
Service supplies inventory (on hand)	7,000
Service trucks (four practically new)	68,000
Personal residences of organizers (three houses)	190,000
Service equipment used in the business (practically new)	30,000
Bills due from customers (for services already completed)	15,000
Total	$322,000
Company obligations:	
Unpaid wages to employees	$ 19,000
Unpaid taxes	8,000
Owed to suppliers	10,000
Owed on service trucks and equipment (to a finance company)	50,000
Loan from organizer	10,000
Total	$ 97,000

Required:

1. If you were advising the local bank about the two lists, what issues would you raise? Explain the basis for each question and include any recommendations that you have (consider the fact that the company is considered to be separate from the owners).
2. In view of your response to (1), what do you think the amount of *net resources* (i.e., assets minus liabilities) of the company would be? Show your computations.

P1–3 *Comparing Income with Cash Flow*

New Delivery Company was organized on January 1, 19A. At the end of the first quarter (three months) of operations, the owner prepared a summary of its operations as shown in the first row of the following tabulation:

	Computation of	
Summary of Transactions	**Income**	**Cash**
1. Services performed for customers, $66,000, of which one-sixth remained uncollected at the end of the quarter.	+$66,000	+$55,000
2. Cash borrowed from the local bank, $30,000 (one-year note).		
3. Small service truck purchased for use in the business: cost, $9,000; paid 30% down, balance on credit.		
4. Expenses, $36,000, of which one-sixth remained unpaid at the end of the quarter.		
5. Service supplies purchased for use in the business, $3,000, of which one-fourth remained unpaid (on credit) at the end of the quarter. Also, one-fifth of these supplies were unused (still on hand) at the end of the quarter.		
6. Wages earned by employees, $21,000, of which one-half remained unpaid at the end of the quarter.		
Based only on the above transactions, compute the following for the quarter: Income (or loss) Cash inflow (or outflow)		

Required:

1. For each of the six transactions given in the tabulation above, enter what you consider the correct amounts. Enter a zero when appropriate. The first transaction is illustrated.
2. For each transaction, explain the basis for your dollar responses.

P1–4 *Preparing a Simple Income Statement and Balance Sheet*

Assume you are president of Nuclear Company. At the end of the first year (December 31, 19A) of operations, the following financial data are available for the company:

Cash	$ 25,000
Receivables from customers (all considered collectible)	12,000
Inventory of merchandise (based on physical count and priced at cost)	90,000
Equipment owned, at cost less used portion	45,000
Note payable, one year, 14% annual interest, owed to the bank (dated July 1, 19A)	30,000
Interest payable on the note through December 31, 19A (due to be paid to the bank on June 30, 19B; $30,000 x 14% x 6/12)	2,100
Salary payable for 19A (on December 31, 19A, this was owed to an employee who was away because of an emergency; will return around January 10, 19B, at which time the payment will be made)	2,000
Total sales revenue	140,000
Expenses, including the cost of the merchandise sold (excluding income taxes at a 30% rate; the taxes will be paid during the first quarter of 19B)	89,100
Contributed capital, 7,000 shares outstanding	87,000
No dividends were declared or paid during 19A.	

Required: (show computations)

1. Prepare a summarized income statement for the year 19A.
2. Prepare a balance sheet at December 31, 19A.

P1–5 *Analyzing a Student's Business and Preparing a Simple Income Statement*

During the summer between her junior and senior years, Susan Irwin needed to earn sufficient money for the coming academic year. Unable to obtain a job with a reasonable salary, she decided to try the lawn-care business for three months. After a survey of the market potential, Susan bought a used pickup truck on June 1 for $1,500. On each door she painted "Susan's Lawn Service, Phone 471-4487." Also, she spent $900 for mowers, trimmers, and tools. To acquire these items she borrowed $2,500 cash on a note at 12% interest per annum, payable at the end of the three months (ending August 31).

At the end of the summer, Susan realized that she had done a lot of work, and her bank account looked good. This fact prompted her to become concerned about how much profit the business had earned.

A review of the check stubs showed the following: Deposits in the bank of collections from customers totaled $12,600. The following checks were written: gas, oil, and lubrication, $920; pickup repairs, $210; mower repair, $75; miscellaneous supplies used, $80; helpers, $4,500; payroll taxes, $175; payment for assistance in preparing payroll tax forms, $25; insurance, $125, telephone, $110; and $2,575 to pay off the note including interest (on August 31). A notebook kept in the pickup, plus some unpaid bills, reflected that customers still owed her $800 for lawn services rendered and that she owed $200 for gas and oil (credit card charges). She estimated that the depreciation for use of the truck and the other equipment for three months amounted to $500.

Required:

1. Prepare a quarterly income statement for Susan's Lawn Service for the months June, July, and August 19A. Use the following main captions: revenues from services, expenses, and net income. Because this is a sole proprietorship, the company will not be subject to income tax.
2. Do you see a need for one or more additional financial reports for this company for 19A and thereafter? Explain.

P1–6 *Analyzing a Student's Business and Preparing a Simple Income Statement*

Upon graduation from high school, John Abel immediately accepted a job as an electrician's assistant for a large local electrical repair company. After three years of hard work, John received an electrician's license and decided to start his own business. He had saved $12,000, which he invested in the business. First, he transferred this amount from his savings account to a business bank account for Abel Electric Repair Company, Incorporated. His lawyer had advised him to start as a corporation. He then purchased a used panel truck for $9,000 cash and secondhand tools for $1,500; rented space in a small building; inserted an ad in the local paper; and opened the doors on October 1, 19A. Immediately, John was very busy; after one month, he employed an assistant.

Although John knew practically nothing about the financial side of the business, he realized that a number of reports were required and that costs and collections had to be controlled carefully. At the end of the year, prompted in part by concern about his income tax situation (previously he only had to report salary), John recognized the need for financial statements. His wife, Jane, developed some financial statements for the business. On December 31, 19A, with the help of a friend, she gathered the following data for the three months just ended. Deposits in the bank account of collections for electric repair services totaled $32,000. The following checks were written: electrician's assistant, $8,500; payroll taxes, $175; supplies purchased and used on jobs, $9,500; oil, gas, and maintenance on truck, $1,200; insurance, $700; rent, $500; utilities and telephone, $825; and miscellaneous expenses (including advertising), $600. Also, there were uncollected bills to customers for electric repair services amounting to $3,000. The rent for December amounting to $200 had not been paid. The average income tax rate is 30%. The depreciation on the truck and tools due to use during the three months was estimated by John to be $1,200.

Required:

1. Prepare a quarterly income statement for Abel Electric Repair for the three months October–December 19A. Use the following main captions: revenue from services, expenses, pretax income, and net income.
2. Do you think that John may have a need for one or more additional financial reports for 19A and thereafter? Explain.

CASES

C1–1 *Analyzing the Assets and Liabilities of a Business*

Elizabeth Watkins owns and operates Liz's Boutique (a sole proprietorship). An employee prepares a financial report for the business at each year-end. This report lists all of the resources (assets) owned by Watkins, including such personal items as the home owned and occupied by Watkins. It also lists all of the debts of the business, but not the personal debts of Watkins.

Required:

1. From the accounting point of view, in what ways do you disagree with what is being included in and excluded from the report of business assets and liabilities?
2. Upon questioning, Watkins responded, "Don't worry about it, we use it only to support a loan from the bank." How would you respond to this comment?

C1–2 *Deciding about a Proposed Audit*

You are one of three partners who own and operate Mary's Maid Service. The company has been operating for seven years. One of the other partners has always prepared the company's annual financial statements. Recently you proposed that the statements be audited each year because it would benefit the partners and preclude possible disagreements about the division of profits. The partner who prepares the statements proposed that his Uncle Ray, who has a lot of financial experience, can do the job and at little cost. Your other partner remained silent.

Required:

1. What position would you take on the proposal? Justify your response.
2. What would you strongly recommend? Give the basis for your recommendation.

C1–3 *Identifying and Correcting Deficiencies in an Income Statement and Balance Sheet*

Performance Corporation was organized on January 1, 19A. At the end of 19A, the company had not yet employed an accountant. However, an employee who was "good with numbers" prepared the following statements at that date:

PERFORMANCE CORPORATION
December 31, 19A

Income from sales of merchandise	$175,000
Total amount paid for goods sold during 19A	(90,000)
Selling costs	(25,000)
Depreciation (on service vehicles used)	(10,000)
Income from services rendered	52,000
Salaries and wages paid	(62,000)

PERFORMANCE CORPORATION
December 31, 19A

Resources:		
Cash		$ 32,000
Merchandise inventory (held for resale)		42,000
Service vehicles		50,000
Retained earnings (profit earned in 19A)		30,000
Grand total		$154,000
Debts:		
Payables to suppliers		$ 22,000
Note owed to bank		25,000
Due from customers		13,000
Total		$ 60,000
Supplies on hand (to be used in rendering services)	$15,000	
Accumulated depreciation* (on service vehicles)	10,000	
Contributed capital, 6,500 shares	65,000	
Total		90,000
Grand total		$150,000

*Accumulated depreciation represents the used portion of the asset and should be subtracted from the asset balance.

Required:

1. List all the deficiencies that you can identify in the above statements. Give a brief explanation of each one.
2. Prepare a proper income statement (correct net income is $30,000) and balance sheet (correct total assets are $142,000).

C1–4 Ethics and Auditor Responsibilities

A key factor that an auditor provides is independence. The *AICPA Code of Professional Conduct* states that "a member in public practice should be independent in fact and appearance when providing auditing and other attestation service."

Required:

Do you consider the following circumstances to suggest a lack of independence? Justify your position. (Use your imagination. Specific answers are not provided in the chapter.)

1. Jack Jones is a partner with a large audit firm and is assigned to the Ford audit. Mr. Jones owns 10 shares of Ford.
2. Jane Winkler has invested in a mutual fund company that owns 500,000 shares of Sears stock. She is the auditor of Sears.
3. Bob Franklin is a clerk/typist who works on the audit of AT&T. He has just inherited 50,000 shares of AT&T stock. (Bob enjoys his work and plans to continue despite his new wealth.)
4. Nancy Sodoma worked on weekends as the controller for a small business that a friend started. Nancy quit the job in midyear and has no association with the company. Nancy works full time with a large CPA firm and has been assigned to do the audit of her friend's business.
5. Mark Jacobs borrowed $100,000 for a home mortgage from the First City National Bank. The mortgage was granted on normal credit terms. Mark is the partner in charge of the First City audit.

C1–5 Financial Statement Analysis

Toys "Я" Us

Refer to the financial statements of Toys "Я" Us in Appendix B at the end of this book.

Required:

1. What is the amount of net income for the current year?
2. What amount of revenue was earned in the current year?
3. How much long-term debt does the company have at the end of the current year?

4. By what amount did cash and cash equivalents* change during the year?
5. Who is auditor for the company?

*Cash equivalents are short-term investments readily convertible to cash whose value is unlikely to change.

Toys "Я" Us

C1–6 Financial Statement Analysis

Refer to the financial statements of Toys "Я" Us in Appendix B at the end of this book.

Required:

Read the annual report. Look at the income statement, balance sheet, and cash flow statement closely and attempt to infer what kinds of information they report. Then, answer the following questions based on the report.

1. What types of products does it sell?
2. Did the chief executive officer (CEO) think that the company had a good year?
3. On what day of the year does its fiscal year end?
4. For how many years does it present complete:
   a. Balance sheets?
   b. Income statements?
   c. Cash flow statements?
5. Are its financial statements audited by independent CPAs? How do you know?
6. Did its total assets increase or decrease over the last year?
7. What was the ending balance of inventories?
8. Write out its basic accounting (balance sheet) equation in dollars at year-end.

2

THE ACCOUNTING MODEL AND TRANSACTION ANALYSIS

In Chapter 1, we studied the basic financial statements that communicate financial information to external users. Chapters 2, 3, and 4 provide a more detailed look at the financial statements and examine how the accounting function translates data about business transactions into these statements. Learning how to translate back and forth between business transactions and financial statements is the key to the use of financial statements in planning and decision making. The purpose of Chapter 2 is to begin our discussions of how the accounting function collects data about business transactions and processes the data to provide the periodic financial statements, with emphasis on the balance sheet. To accomplish this purpose, the chapter discusses key accounting concepts, the accounting model, transaction analysis, and analytical tools. We will examine typical business activities of an actual service-oriented company to demonstrate the concepts in Chapters 2, 3, and 4.

LEARNING OBJECTIVES

After studying this chapter, you should be able to:

1. **Define the objective of financial reporting, the elements of the balance sheet, and the related key accounting assumptions and principles.** *53*
2. **Identify what constitutes a business transaction.** *57*
3. **Define an account and identify common balance sheet account titles used in business.** *59*
4. **Apply transaction analysis to analyze simple business transactions in terms of the accounting model: Assets = Liabilities + Stockholders' Equity.** *60*
5. **Record the results of transaction analysis using two basic tools: (*a*) journal entries and (*b*) T-accounts.** *66*
6. **Prepare a simple balance sheet.** *74*

Management Decision Setting

SBARRO, INC.

Tops in the Italian Fast-Food Sector

Americans appear to love Italian food and the Sbarro family, headed by brothers Mario Sbarro (Chairman of the Board) and Anthony Sbarro (President and Chief Operating Officer), seems to have carved out its own niche in the highly competitive restaurant business. Sbarro remains one of only 13 companies that appear on both the 1989 and 1994 Forbes' 200 Best Small Companies in America lists.*

Incorporated in 1977, Sbarro develops and operates or franchises a national chain of family-style Italian restaurants located mostly in shopping malls.† The restaurants feature popular freshly prepared Italian foods including pizza, pasta, and hot and cold Italian entrees, salads, and desserts. Most of the restaurants serve the food cafeteria style. Sbarro has over 750 restaurants in 48 states, Washington, D. C., Puerto Rico, Canada, Great Britain, Australia, Belgium, Kuwait, Qatar, Saudi Arabia, Chile, and the Philippines, with plans for continued rapid expansion. Approximately three-fourths of the restaurants are company-owned, and one-fourth are franchises (owned by others who pay fees to Sbarro for various services Sbarro provides to them).

Sbarro has experienced continuing growth as indicated in its balance sheets presented for two recent years (in thousands of dollars):‡

	Assets	=	Liabilities	+	Stockholders' Equity
1/3/93	$183,000	=	$43,000	+	$140,000
1/2/94	207,700	=	48,700	+	159,000
Change	+ $ 24,700	=	+ $ 5,700	+	$ 19,000

*See *Forbes*, November 7, 1994.

†For stock price information, Sbarro is listed on the New York Stock Exchange under the symbol SBA.

‡These totals are rounded amounts from the actual financial statements for the respective years. Amounts used in illustrations throughout Chapters 2, 3, and 4 are realistic estimates of actual monthly amounts which are not publicly available.

BUSINESS BACKGROUND

To understand the meaning of these amounts for Sbarro, we must answer the following questions:

1. What business activities cause changes in balance sheet amounts from one period to the next?
2. How do specific activities affect each of the balances?
3. How do companies keep track of these balance sheet amounts?

Once we have answered these questions, we will be able to perform two key analytical tasks. First, we will be able to predict the effects of our business decisions on the firm's financial statements. Second, we will be able to use financial statements of other companies to identify and evaluate activities other managers engaged in during a past period. These latter inferences are a key to *financial statement analysis*.

In this chapter, we will focus on typical asset acquisition activities (often called *investing activities*) that Sbarro engages in, along with the related *financing activities* such as borrowing funds from creditors and receiving funds from investors to acquire the assets. Activities affecting only balance sheet amounts will be examined; operating activities affecting both income statement and balance sheet amounts are discussed in Chapters 3 and 4. This simplification is to aid your understanding. Let us begin our answers to the three questions by a return to the basic concepts introduced in Chapter 1.

OVERVIEW OF THE CONCEPTUAL FRAMEWORK

Learning Objective 1
Define the objective of financial reporting, the elements of the balance sheet, and the related key accounting assumptions and principles.

Many key accounting terms and concepts were defined in Chapter 1. These are part of a framework of accounting theory developed over many years and synthesized by the Financial Accounting Standards Board in a series of publications called *FASB Statements of Financial Accounting Concepts*. These Statements make up the conceptual framework of accounting which is outlined in Exhibit 2–1 and will be discussed in each of the next four chapters. In the exhibit in each chapter, terms and concepts emphasized in the current chapter are indicated in bold white print and concepts emphasized in prior chapters are indicated in bold black print. This pyramid will be used to organize the concepts and terms. An understanding of the accounting concepts will be helpful as you study. It is much easier to learn and remember how the accounting process works if you know why it works a certain way. A clear understanding will also help you in future chapters as we examine more complex business activities.

Concepts Emphasized in Chapter 2

Objective of Financial Reporting

The top of the pyramid in Exhibit 2–1 indicates the **primary objective of external financial reporting** which guides the remaining sections of the conceptual framework. The primary objective of financial accounting is to provide useful economic information about a business to help external parties, primarily investors and creditors, make sound financial decisions. The users of accounting information are identified as *decision makers*. These decision makers are defined in the conceptual framework as average, prudent investors, creditors, and experts who provide financial advice. They are expected to have a reasonable understanding of accounting concepts and procedures (this may be one of the reasons you are studying accounting). Of course, as we discussed in Chapter 1, many other groups, such as suppliers and customers, also use external financial statements. Usually, users are interested in information to assist them in projecting future cash inflows and outflows of a business.

The **primary objective of external financial reporting** is to provide useful economic information about a business to help external parties make sound financial decisions.

Underlying Assumptions of Accounting

The assumptions of accounting are primarily based on the business environment in which accounting operates. They reflect the scope of accounting and the expectations that set certain limits on the way accounting information is reported. Three of these assumptions were discussed in Chapter 1. Under the **separate-entity assumption**, each business must be accounted for as an individual organization, separate and apart from its owners, all other persons, and other entities. Under the **unit-of-measure assumption**, each business entity will account for and report its financial results primarily in terms of the national monetary unit (dollars in the U.S., yen in Japan, francs in France, etc.).

The **separate-entity assumption** requires business transactions to be separate from the transactions of the owners.

The **unit-of-measure assumption** requires accounting information to be measured and reported in the national monetary unit.

For accounting purposes, a business is normally assumed to stay in business long enough to meet contractual commitments and plans. This **continuity assumption** is sometimes called the *going-concern assumption* because we expect a business to continue to operate into the foreseeable future. Violation of this assumption means that assets and liabilities can be valued and reported on the balance sheet as if the company were to be liquidated (that is, discontinued with all assets sold and all debts paid). In all future chapters, unless indicated otherwise, we will assume businesses meet the continuity assumption.

Under the **continuity assumption**, businesses are assumed to continue to operate into the foreseeable future.

Exhibit 2–1 Financial Accounting and Reporting Conceptual Framework

Primary Objective of External Financial Reporting

To provide useful economic information to external users for decision making (for assessing future cash flows) [Ch.2]

Qualitative Characteristics of Information

[Ch. 5]

Overall: Information should be

Cost-beneficial Benefits of accounting and reporting should exceed costs.

Primary:

Relevance Information influences decisions; it is timely and has predictive and feedback value.

Reliability Information is accurate, unbiased, and verifiable.

Secondary:

Comparability Information can be compared to other businesses.

Consistency Information can be compared across time.

Elements of Financial Statements

Assets Probable future economic benefits owned by the entity from past transactions. [Ch. 2]

Liabilities Debts or obligations from past transactions to be paid with assets or services. [Ch. 2]

Stockholders' Equity Financing provided by owners and operations. [Ch. 2]

Revenues Inflows of net assets (assets minus liabilities) from ongoing operations. [Ch. 3]

Expenses Outflows of net assets (assets minus liabilities) from ongoing operations. [Ch. 3]

Gains Inflows of net assets from peripheral transactions. [Ch. 3]

Losses Outflows of net assets from peripheral transactions. [Ch. 3]

Assumptions

1. **Separate-entity** Transactions of the business are separate from transactions of the owners. [Ch. 2]
2. **Unit-of-measure** Accounting measurements will be in the national monetary unit. [Ch. 2]
3. **Continuity** The entity will not go out of business in the near future. [Ch. 2]
4. *Time-period* The long life of a company can be reported over a series of shorter time periods. [Ch. 3]

Principles

1. **Cost** Cash-equivalent cost given up is the basis for initial recording of elements. [Ch. 2 and 3]
2. *Revenue* Record revenues when earned and measurable (an exchange has taken place, the earnings process is nearly complete, and collection is probable). [Ch. 3]
3. *Matching* Record expenses when incurred in earning revenue. [Ch. 3]
4. *Full-disclosure* Disclose relevant economic information. [Ch. 5]

Constraints

[Ch. 5]

1. *Materiality* Relatively small amounts not likely to influence decisions are to be recorded in the most cost-beneficial way.
2. *Cost-benefit* Benefits of recording and reporting information should outweigh costs.
3. *Conservatism* Exercise care not to overstate assets and revenues or understate liabilities and expenses.
4. *Industry peculiarities* Differences in accounting and reporting for certain items are permitted if there is a clear precedent in the industry.

Elements of the Balance Sheet

As discussed in Chapter 1, assets, liabilities, and shareholders' equity are the key elements of the balance sheet. Let's review the definitions.

Assets are probable future economic benefits owned by the entity as a result of past transactions. For illustration purposes, the balance sheet of Sbarro, Inc., has been simplified in Exhibit 2–2, with amounts rounded to the nearest hundred thousand dollars. Notice that Sbarro's year ends on the Sunday closest to December 31; the choice of year-ends will be discussed in the next chapter. As indicated in Sbarro's simplified balance sheet in Exhibit 2–2, Sbarro's assets include cash, marketable securities (stocks and bonds purchased by Sbarro as investments of excess cash), receivables (due from franchisees[1] and others on account), inventories (of food, beverages, and paper supplies), prepaid expenses (such as rent paid by Sbarro in advance of the use of mall space), and property and equipment. The other assets category includes a number of assets with smaller balances which total the amount presented. Assets are usually listed on the balance sheet in order of liquidity (how soon an asset can be turned into cash).

Assets are probable future economic benefits owned by the entity as a result of past transactions.

Liabilities are probable debts or obligations of the entity as a result of past transactions which will be paid with assets or services. Those entities that a company owes money to are called *creditors*. Creditors usually receive payment of the amount owed and sometimes interest on those amounts. The balance sheet of Sbarro includes six liabilities: accounts payable, accrued expenses payable, dividends payable, income taxes payable, deferred income, and deferred income taxes. Accrued expenses payable is actually a summary of several liabilities related to payroll, rent, and other obligations. Dividends payable is the amount due to stockholders as a distribution of company earnings based on the board of directors' authorization. They become a liability until paid. These and other liabilities will be discussed in subsequent chapters. Liabilities are listed on the balance sheet in order of maturity (how soon a liability is to be paid).

Liabilities are probable debts or obligations of the entity as a result of past transactions which will be paid with assets or services.

Stockholders' equity (owners' equity or **shareholders' equity)** is the financing provided by the owners and the operations of the business. **Contributed capital** results from owners providing cash (and sometimes other assets) to the

Stockholders' equity (owners' equity or **shareholders' equity)** is the financing provided by the owners and the operations of the business.

Contributed capital results from owners providing cash (and sometimes other assets) to the business.

Most of the Sbarro restaurants serve food cafeteria-style. This one is buffet-style.

[1]Franchises are contracts in which a franchisor provides rights to franchisees to sell or distribute a specific line of products or provide a particular service. The franchisees in return usually pay initial fees to obtain the franchise and make annual payments to receive ongoing services from the franchisor (such as accounting, advertising, and training). When franchisees owe the annual payments, the franchisor records the receivable. Examples of franchises include Holiday Inn, McDonald's, Dairy Queen, and National Football League teams.

Exhibit 2–2 **Balance Sheet**

SBARRO, INC. AND SUBSIDIARIES*
Balance Sheets
at January 2, 1994 and January 3, 1993
(in thousands of dollars)

	January 2, 1994	January 3, 1993
Assets		
Cash	$ 33,300	$ 61,900
Marketable securities	37,200	0
Receivables (franchise fees and other)	1,300	1,000
Inventories	2,500	2,200
Prepaid expenses	1,500	1,500
Property and equipment	128,700	113,500
Other assets	3,200	2,900
Total assets	**$207,700**	**$183,000**
Liabilities		
Accounts payable	$ 4,500	$ 4,000
Accrued expenses payable (rent, payroll, and other)	18,400	16,600
Dividend payable	2,700	0
Income taxes payable	4,600	4,400
Deferred income	400	100
Deferred income taxes	18,100	17,900
Total liabilities	$ 48,700	$ 43,000
Stockholders' Equity		
Contributed capital	$ 29,700	$ 29,200
Retained earnings	129,300	110,800
Total stockholders' equity	159,000	140,000
Total liabilities and stockholders' equity	**$207,700**	**$183,000**

*A subsidiary is a company owned by another company which controls more than 50% of the voting stock of the subsidiary.

business. When this occurs, we often say that owners invest in the business, or the company sells or issues its stock to owners. The investors in Sbarro, Inc., are the members of the Sbarro family, who own approximately 44% of the company, and corporate employees and the general public, who together own the rest of the company. Owners invest (or buy stock) in a company in the hope of receiving two types of cash flows: dividends, which are a distribution of a company's earnings (a return on the shareholders' investment), and capital gains, which result from selling their stock in the company for more than they paid. Earnings that are not distributed to the owners and are reinvested in the business by management are called **retained earnings.**[2] A look at Sbarro's balance sheet (Exhibit 2–2) indicates that Sbarro's growth has been predominantly financed by the substantial reinvestment of earnings in the business; 81% of Sbarro's stockholders' equity is retained earnings ($129,300 retained earnings ÷ $159,000 total stockholders' equity).

Retained earnings are the cumulative earnings of a company that are not distributed to the owners and are reinvested in the business.

FINANCIAL ANALYSIS

Financing Strategies

Sbarro's approach to financing involves relatively little borrowing and a great deal of stockholders' equity with heavy reinvestment of earnings. In fact, total debt at January 2, 1994, is only

[2]Retained earnings can only increase from profitable operations. In addition, as we will learn in Chapter 3, a company's annual income from operations is usually not equal to the net cash flows for the year.

23% ($48,700 ÷ $207,700) of Sbarro's total financing. Debt financing (also called *leverage*) is considered more risky than financing with stockholders' equity because the interest payments on debt must be made every period (they are legal obligations), whereas dividends on stock can be postponed if Sbarro has a bad year. Robert Morris Associates Annual Statement Studies for the same year indicates that the average fast-food restaurant chain is financed 79% with debt. This suggests that Sbarro is following a less risky (more conservative) strategy than other companies in its industry. A low ratio makes sense given that Sbarro typically rents mall space instead of constructing new buildings financed by borrowings as some other fast-food companies do. When comparing companies to an industry average, differences in business strategy such as this should be considered. A significantly different value for one company may or may not suggest that the company is being overly risky or conservative in its financing.

Basic Accounting Principle

The **cost principle** states that the cash-equivalent cost needed to acquire the asset (the historical cost) should be used for initially recognizing (recording) all financial statement elements. Under the cost principle, cost is measured on the date of the transaction as the cash paid plus the current dollar value of all noncash considerations (any assets, privileges, or rights) also given in the exchange. For example, if you trade your computer plus cash for a new car, the cost of the new car is equal to the cash paid plus the market value of the computer.

The **cost principle** requires assets to be recorded at the cash-equivalent cost, which on the date of the transaction is cash paid plus the current dollar value of all noncash considerations also given in the exchange.

Now that we have reviewed several of the basic accounting concepts and terms, we need to understand the economic activities of a business that result in changes in amounts reported in financial statements and the process used in generating the financial statements.

WHAT BUSINESS ACTIVITIES CAUSE CHANGES IN FINANCIAL STATEMENT AMOUNTS?

Nature of Business Transactions

Learning Objective 2
Identify what constitutes a business transaction.

Accounting focuses on certain events, though not all events, that have an economic impact on the entity. Those events that are recorded as a part of the accounting process are called **transactions**. The first step in translating the results of business events to financial statement numbers is determining which events are and are not reflected in the statements. Note that the above definitions of assets and liabilities indicate that only economic resources and debts *resulting from past transactions* are recorded on the balance sheet. A broad definition of transactions includes two types:

A **transaction** is (1) an *exchange* between a business and one or more external parties or (2) a measurable event internal to a business, such as *adjustments* for the use of assets in operations.

QUESTION OF ETHICS

Environmental Liabilities

Due to changing legal requirements and concerns for social responsibility, companies are facing significant pressure to disclose environmental liabilities, such as the cleanup of hazardous waste sites. However, in a recent survey of 523 companies, 62% indicated "they have known environmental exposures that haven't been recorded in their financial statements."* By definition, liabilities are recorded when they are probable; they also need to be reasonably estimable. Determining the amounts and likelihood of environmental obligations can be very difficult. Given the growing magnitude of these issues, the accounting profession, led by the Financial Accounting Standards Board, will need to address the challenge.

*L. Berten, "SEC Rule Forces More Disclosure," *The Wall Street Journal*, December 13, 1993, p. B1.

1. External events: *exchanges* of assets and liabilities between the business and one or more other parties. Examples include the purchase of a machine, the sale of merchandise, the borrowing of cash, and the investment in the business by the owners. These types of transactions will be discussed in this chapter as they affect the balance sheet elements and in Chapter 3 as they affect income statement elements.
2. Internal events: certain events that are not exchanges between the business and other parties but have a direct and measurable effect on the accounting entity. Examples include losses due to fire or other natural disasters and *adjustments* such as those to record the use of property, plant, and equipment in operations and the incurrence of interest expense on money that was borrowed. Adjustments will be discussed in Chapter 4.

Throughout this textbook, the word *transaction* will be used in the broad sense to include both types of events.

At the same time, some important events that have an economic impact on the company are not reflected in Sbarro's statements. In most cases, the signing of a contract, where no cash, goods, services, or property have yet changed hands, is not considered to be a transaction because it only involves the exchange of promises, not assets or liabilities. For example, if Sbarro hires a new district manager and signs an employment contract, there is no transaction from an accounting perspective because there has been no exchange of assets or liabilities. Each party to the contract has made promises (the manager agrees to work; Sbarro agrees to pay in exchange for the manager's work). However, for each day the new manager works, the exchange of services by the employee results in a transaction that Sbarro must record (as an obligation to pay the manager's salary).

FINANCIAL ANALYSIS

Unrecorded but Valuable Assets

Managers and analysts use the balance sheet as a basis for managing the firm's assets and for valuing the firm. At the same time, they recognize that often a firm's most valuable assets are not even listed on the balance sheet (they have no "book value").* One such asset is a firm's trademark or brand name. For example, *Financial World* estimated that the Budweiser brand name is worth $10 billion to its owner, Anheuser-Busch. However, its book value is zero because it was developed internally over time (created through research, development, and advertising); there was *no identifiable exchange transaction* (it was not purchased). Many valuable intangible assets, such as trademarks, patents, and copyrights that are developed inside the firm, have no book value.

This same asset recognition rule (that assets are recorded at cost based on an exchange with an external party) suggests the circumstances in which trademarks and brand names *will* be reported on the balance sheet. As in the Budweiser example, a look at General Electric's balance sheet will reveal no listing for the GE trademark. Again, this trademark was developed internally. However, GE recently sold its television business to a French company, Thomson SA, which is the world's largest producer of televisions. Since the Thomson brand name has no value in the United States, it also purchased the right to use GE's trademark for 10 years at a cost of 250 million French francs (approximately $50 million). Thomson's balance sheet lists GE's trademark, which was initially recorded at its acquisition cost of 250 million francs.

* "Book value" is the amount reported on the balance sheet which is usually an asset's original acquisition cost minus amounts used in past operations.

Accounts

Learning Objective 3
Define an account and identify common balance sheet account titles used in business.

An **account** is a standardized format used by organizations to accumulate the dollar effects of transactions on each financial statement item.

An **account** is a standardized format used by organizations to accumulate the dollar effects of transactions on each financial statement item. The resulting balances are kept separate for financial statement purposes. Each company must establish a chart of accounts to facilitate recording transactions. A chart of accounts is the listing of all the account names, usually organized by financial statement element. That is, asset accounts are listed first (such as Cash, Inventory, Accounts Receivable, Equipment, and Land) followed by liability accounts (such as Accounts Payable, Notes Payable, and Taxes Payable), stockholders' equity accounts (Contributed Capital and Retained Earnings), revenue accounts (such as Sales Revenue), and expense accounts (such as Payroll Expense). The account names listed here are quite common and will be used by most companies.

The accounts you see in the financial statements are actually summations (or aggregations) of a number of more detailed accounts in a company's accounting system. For example, Sbarro keeps separate inventory accounts for paper supplies, food, and beverages, but combines them as Inventories on the balance sheet. Since our aim is to understand financial statements, we will focus on aggregated accounts as presented in the statements.

Every company will have a different chart of accounts, depending on the nature of the business activities. For example, a small lawn-care service may have an asset account called Lawn Mowing Equipment, but it is unlikely that General Motors would need such an account. These differences will become more apparent as we examine the balance sheets of many various companies.

AN INTERNATIONAL PERSPECTIVE

Understanding the Meaning of Account Titles in Foreign Financial Statements

Chapter 1 states that differences in the political, cultural, and economic environment of other countries have produced significant variation in accounting and reporting rules. Foreign companies' account titles often use different words with the same meanings as common U.S. account titles. Some use additional accounts for financial statement items not normally reported under U.S. accounting rules. For example, the Australian company, The News Corporation Limited, headed by K. Rupert Murdoch, follows A-GAAP (Australian Generally Accepted Accounting Principles). The principal activities of the group of corporations making up The News Corporation Limited include printing and publishing of newspapers and magazines, television broadcasting, film production and distribution, motion picture studio operations, and book publishing. U.S. corporations included in the news group include Fox Broadcasting Company and Twentieth Century Fox Film Corporation. The titles of asset accounts in a recent financial report are similar to those used by U.S. companies, but the liabilities and stockholders' equity account titles are different:

Australian Accounts	U.S. Equivalents
Liabilities:	
Borrowings	similar to Notes and Bonds Payable
Creditors	relates to what is owed to suppliers and others, similar to Accounts Payable
Provision	a summary of payables for income tax, dividends, payroll, and other liabilities
Shareholders' Equity:	
Share Capital	similar to Contributed Capital
Reserves	a summary of a variety of other stockholders' equity accounts, many which will be covered in future chapters
Retained Profits	similar to Retained Earnings.

Because each company has a different chart of accounts, you should not try to memorize a typical chart of accounts. When you prepare homework problems, either you will be given the account names used by the company or you should select appropriate descriptive names. Once a name is selected for an account, the exact name must be used in all transactions that affect the account.

HOW DO TRANSACTIONS AFFECT ACCOUNTS?

Learning Objective 4
Apply transaction analysis to analyze simple business transactions in terms of the accounting model: Assets = Liabilities + Stockholders' Equity.

Managers make business decisions that often result in transactions affecting financial statements. Typical decisions are to expand the number of stores, advertise a new product, change employee benefit packages, and invest excess cash. Keeping a historical record (like a diary of important events) allows managers to evaluate the effects of past decisions and plan future business activities. In planning, managers are interested in how the implementation of their plans (their decisions) will be reflected on the financial statements. For example, the decision to purchase additional inventory for cash in anticipation of a major sales initiative increases the inventory and decreases cash. If the demand for the inventory does not occur, a lower cash balance reduces the company's flexibility and ability to pay other obligations. Business decisions often involve an element of risk which should be assessed. Therefore, it is necessary for business managers to understand how transactions impact the accounts on the financial statements. The process for determining the effect of transactions is called *transaction analysis* and is discussed below.

Transaction Analysis

Transaction analysis is the process of studying a transaction to determine its economic effect on the business in terms of the accounting equation.

Transaction analysis is the process of studying a transaction to determine its economic effect on the entity in terms of the accounting equation. We will outline the process in this section of the chapter and create a visual tool representing the process (the transaction analysis model). The basic accounting equation and two principles are the foundation for the transaction analysis model. You will recall from Chapter 1 that the basic accounting equation for a business organized as a corporation is as follows:

One of Sbarro's business decisions is where to locate new restaurants, such as at this busy downtown site.

Assets (A) = Liabilities (L) + Stockholders' Equity (SE)

The two principles underlying the transaction analysis process are:

1. Every transaction affects at least two accounts (duality of effects); it is critical to identify correctly the accounts affected and the direction of the effect (increase or decrease).
2. The accounting equation must remain in balance after each transaction.

Success at performing transaction analysis depends on your clear understanding of how the transaction analysis model is constructed based on these concepts. Study this material well. You should not move on to a new concept until you understand and can apply all prior concepts. Now let's create the transaction analysis model from these basic principles.

Duality of Effects

The first concept is that every transaction has *at least two effects* on the basic accounting equation. This is known as the *duality of effects*. (It is from this duality concept that we have developed what is known as the *double-entry system* of recordkeeping.) Most transactions with external parties involve an *exchange* where the business entity both gives up something and receives something in return. For example, suppose that Sbarro purchased some paper napkins inventory for cash.

Transaction (1)	**Sbarro Received**	**Sbarro Gave Up**
Purchased paper napkins for cash	Inventory	Cash

In analyzing this transaction, we determined that the appropriate accounts affected were Inventory and Cash. Identifying the appropriate accounts affected and the direction of the effect on each are critical in transaction analysis. In the exchange, Sbarro received inventory (an increase in an asset) and gave up cash in return (a decrease in an asset).

As we discussed in Chapter 1, however, most inventory is purchased on credit (money is owed to suppliers). In this case, Sbarro would engage in *two* transactions: (1) a purchase of an asset on credit and (2) an eventual payment. In the first, it would receive inventory (an increase in an asset) and in return give a promise to pay later called *accounts payable* (an increase in a liability). In the second, Sbarro would eliminate (receive back) its promise to pay, accounts payable, (a decrease in a liability) and give up cash (a decrease in an asset).

Transactions (2)	**Sbarro Received (eliminated)**	**Sbarro Gave Up**
Purchased paper napkins on credit	Inventory	Accounts payable
Paid accounts payable	Accounts payable	Cash

As noted earlier, not all important business activities result in a transaction that affects the financial statements. Most importantly, the signing of a contract involving the exchange of two promises to perform does not result in an accounting transaction that is recorded. For example, consider the case where Sbarro and Xerox sign an agreement where Xerox promises to provide repair service on Sbarro's copy machines at a price of $50 for each visit during the next year and Sbarro promises to pay for the service when provided by Xerox. No accounting transaction has taken place here because Sbarro and Xerox have only exchanged promises. However, any time Xerox provides service, a transaction occurs since service has been exchanged for a promise to pay.

Similarly, if Sbarro sent an order to its paper supplier for more napkins and the supplier accepted the order which will be filled next week, no transaction has taken place for accounting purposes. Only two promises have been exchanged. From the supplier's perspective, the same holds true. No transaction has taken place, so the supplier's financial statements are unaffected. However, as soon as the goods are shipped to Sbarro, the supplier has given up inventory in exchange for a promise from Sbarro to pay for the goods, while Sbarro has exchanged its promise to pay for the goods that are received as ordered. Now *one promise* has been exchanged for *goods*, so a transaction has taken place, and both Sbarro's and the supplier's statements will be affected.

Maintain the Accounting Equation

The accounting equation must remain in balance after each transaction. Total assets must equal total liabilities and stockholders' equity. If all of the correct accounts have been identified, and the appropriate direction of the effect on accounts has been identified, and the appropriate direction of the effect on each account has been determined, the equation should remain in balance. Therefore, in performing the transaction analysis process, you should complete the following steps in this order:

1. **Identify the accounts affected** (by name), making sure the duality principle is met (at least two accounts change). Also, classify each account as an asset (A), liability (L), or stockholders' equity (SE) account.
2. **Determine the effect on each account** [amount of increase (+) or decrease (-) on A, L, and/or SE].
3. **Determine that the accounting equation (A = L + SE) remains in balance.**

Let us consider typical transactions of Sbarro, Inc., and most other businesses, as examples to illustrate the use of this process. As we stated above, only transactions affecting balance sheet accounts will be presented in this chapter. Assume Sbarro has the following transactions during January 1994 (the month following the balance sheet in Exhibit 2–2). The month will end on the Sunday closest to January 31, which will be January 30. Remember that all amounts are in thousands of dollars:

Transaction (A) Sbarro issues $200 of additional common stock to new investors for cash.

1. Identify at least two accounts affected.	*Cash (A) and Contributed Capital (SE).*
2. Determine the effect on each account.	*Cash (A) increases by $200; Contributed Capital (SE) increases by $200.*
3. Is the accounting equation in balance?	*Yes. There is a $200 increase on the left side of the equation and a $200 increase on the right side of the equation.*

	Assets	=	Liabilities	+	Stockholders' Equity
	Cash		Notes Payable		Contributed Capital
(A)	+ 200	=			+ 200

Transaction (B) The Company borrows $1,000 from its local bank, signing a promissory note to be paid in one year.

1. Identify at least two accounts affected. — *Cash (A) and Notes Payable (L).* Notes Payable is the name of the account that represents a signed promise to pay.
2. Determine the effect on each account. — *Cash (A) increases by $1,000; Notes Payable (L) increases by $1,000.*
3. Is the accounting equation in balance? — *Yes. There is a $1,000 increase on the left side of the equation and a $1,000 increase on the right side of the equation.*

	Assets	=	Liabilities	+	Stockholders' Equity
	Cash		Notes Payable		Contributed Capital
(A)	+ 200	=			+ 200
(B)	+ 1,000	=	+ 1,000		
Balances	+ 1,200	=	+ 1,000		+ 200
Cumulative Effect	**+1,200**	=	**+1,200**		

Transactions (A) and (B) are financing transactions. Companies that need cash, for example, to buy or build additional facilities as part of their plans for growth, will often seek funds by selling stock to investors (as in Transaction A) or borrowing from creditors, usually banks (as in Transaction B). Operating transactions also affect cash available to the business; this type of transaction will be discussed in Chapter 3.

Transaction (C) Sbarro acquires $70 in paper supplies, paying cash to its suppliers.

1. Identify at least two accounts affected. — *Inventory (A) and Cash (A).*
2. Determine the effect on each account. — *Inventory (A) increases by $70; Cash (A) decreases by $70.*
3. Is the accounting equation in balance? — *Yes. The equation balances remain the same because assets increase and decrease by the same amount.*

	Assets		=	Liabilities	+	Stockholders' Equity
	Cash	Inventory		Notes Payable		Contributed Capital
(A)	+ 200		=			+ 200
(B)	+ 1,000		=	+ 1,000		
(C)	− 70	+ 70				
Balances	+ 1,130	+ 70	=	+ 1,000		+ 200
Cumulative Effect		**+1,200**	=	**+1,200**		

Transaction (D) Sbarro opens a new restaurant and purchases $600 in equipment (primarily ovens and refrigeration equipment), paying $100 in

cash with the rest due in six months on a promissory note to the equipment manufacturer.

1. Identify at least two accounts affected. — *Equipment (A), Cash (A), and Notes Payable (L).* Notice that three accounts were affected.
2. Determine the effect on each account. — *Equipment (A) increases by $600; Cash (A) decreases by $100; Notes Payable (L) increases by $500.* This transaction is more complex. The equipment is acquired by giving up an asset and also promising to pay.
3. Is the equation in balance? — *Yes. There is a $500 net increase on the left side (+$600 – $100) and a $500 increase on the right side of the equation.*

	Assets			=	Liabilities	+	Stockholders' Equity
	Cash	Inventory	Equipment		Notes Payable		Contributed Capital
(A)	+ 200			=			+ 200
(B)	+ 1,000			=	+ 1,000		
(C)	− 70	+ 70					
(D)	− 100		+ 600		+ 500		
Balances	+ 1,030	+ 70	+ 600	=	+ 1,500		+ 200
Cumulative Effect			**+1,700**	**=**	**+1,700**		

Transaction (E) Sbarro acquires $300 in food and beverage supplies on credit.

1. Identify at least two accounts affected. — *Inventory (A) and Accounts Payable (L).*
2. Determine the effect on each account. — *Inventory (A) increases by $300; Accounts Payable (L) increases by $300.*
3. Is the accounting equation in balance? — *Yes. There is a $300 increase on the left side of the equation and a $300 increase on the right side.*

	Assets			=	Liabilities		+	Stockholders' Equity
	Cash	Inventory	Equipment		Accounts Payable	Notes Payable		Contributed Capital
(A)	+ 200			=				+ 200
(B)	+ 1,000			=		+ 1,000		
(C)	− 70	+ 70						
(D)	− 100		+ 600			+ 500		
(E)		+ 300			+ 300			
Balances	+ 1,030	+ 370	+ 600	=	+ 300	+ 1,500		+ 200
Cumulative Effect			**+2,000**	**=**	**+2,000**			

For Transaction (F), the analysis is performed below; however, the effects are listed below the summary of the effects of Transactions (A) through (E) in the chart at the end of the Self-Study Quiz. For Transactions (G) through (J), space is left on the chart for your answers to the quiz which follows Transaction (F).

Transaction (F) Sbarro lends $40 to a franchisee who signed a note agreeing to repay the loan in one month.

1. Identify at least two accounts affected.	*Notes Receivable (A) and Cash (A).*
2. Determine the effect on each account.	*Notes Receivable (A) increases by $40; Cash (A) decreases by $40.*
3. Is the accounting equation in balance?	*Yes. The equation remains the same because assets increase and decrease by the same amount.*

Self-Study Quiz

The most effective way to develop your transaction analysis skills is to practice with many transactions. Therefore, beginning with the balances generated in (A) through (E) with (F) added, complete the transaction analysis steps and following chart for Transactions (G) through (J). The key is repeating the three steps until they become a natural part of your thought process:

Transaction (G) Sbarro pays $200 cash on its accounts payable to suppliers.

1. Identify at least two accounts affected.	(A) Cash + AC Pay (L)
2. Determine the effects on each account.	Cash (−) and Accts (−)
3. Is the accounting equation in balance?	Y

Transaction (H) Sbarro collects $40 cash on the note receivable from the franchisee.

1. Identify at least two accounts affected.	Cash Note Rec
2. Determine the effects on each account.	Cash + −
3. Is the accounting equation in balance?	Y

Transaction (I) Sbarro paid $300 on the promissory note with the local bank.

1. Identify at least two accounts affected.	Note Pay (L) Cash (A)
2. Determine the effects on each account.	− −
3. Is the accounting equation in balance?	Y

Transaction (J) Sbarro purchased $250 of new tables and chairs (equipment), paying $90 in cash and the rest on account (owed to the furniture manufacturer in 60 days).

1. Identify at least two accounts affected.
2. Determine the effects on each account.
3. Is the accounting equation in balance?

Complete the following chart.

	Assets				=	Liabilities		+	Stockholders' Equity
	Cash	Notes Receivable	Inventory	Equipment		Accounts Payable	Notes Payable		Contributed Capital
(A) to (E)	+ 1,030	+ 0	+ 370	+ 600	=	+ 300	+ 1,500		+ 200
(F)	− 40	+ 40							
(G)									
(H)									
(I)									
(J)									
Balances					=				
Cumulative Effect					=				

After you have completed the schedule, check your solution with the answers in the footnote at the bottom of the page.*

HOW DO COMPANIES KEEP TRACK OF ACCOUNT BALANCES?

Learning Objective 5
Record the results of transaction analysis using two basic tools: (*a*) journal entries and (*b*) T-accounts.

Because companies have significantly more transactions every day than those illustrated above, recording transaction effects and keeping track of account balances in the manner used in the above illustration is impractical for most organizations. We will now expand the transaction analysis model and develop two very important tools that aid in reflecting the results of transaction analysis and performing other financial analysis tasks: journal entries and T-accounts.

These analytical tools are more efficient mechanisms for reflecting the effects of transactions and for determining account balances for financial statement preparation. These efficiencies are important from the standpoint of accounting systems design. As future business managers, you should develop your understanding and use of these tools in financial analysis. For those studying accounting, this knowledge is the foundation for understanding the accounting system and future coursework. After we learn to perform transaction analysis using these tools, we will illustrate their use in financial analysis.

*(G) Accounts Payable - $200; Cash -$200.
(H) Cash +$40; Notes Receivable - $40.
(I) Notes Payable - $300; Cash - $300.
(J) Equipment + $250; Cash -$90; Accounts Payable +$160.
Assets ($1,660) = Liabilities ($1,460) + Stockholders' Equity ($200)
If your answers did not agree with ours, we recommend that you go back to each transaction to make sure that you have completed each of the three steps for each transaction.

The Direction of Transaction Effects

As discussed above, assets, liabilities, and stockholders' equity account balances increase and decrease from the effects of transactions. To learn how to reflect the effects efficiently, the transaction analysis model first needs to be structured in a manner that shows the *direction* of the effects. This direction rule is critical for construction of the model as a tool for transaction analysis. As you can see in the following model, the word "Increase" *is written on the left when we are on the left side of the accounting equation and on the right when we are on the right side of the accounting equation.* The transaction analysis model is as follows:

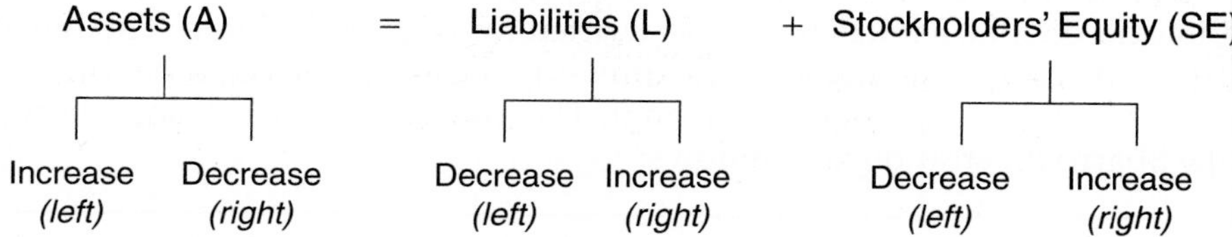

As we illustrated earlier for Transactions (A) through (J), each account (such as Cash and Accounts Payable) in each of these categories can be increased (+) or decreased (–) by transactions, and each account has a balance.

The Debit-Credit Framework

The concepts of debit and credit are now added to the model. **Debit** means the left side of an account and **credit** means the right. For each element of the model, we substitute the term *debit* for left and the term *credit* for right. The transaction analysis model now is as follows:

Debit means the left side of an account; **credit** means the right side of an account.

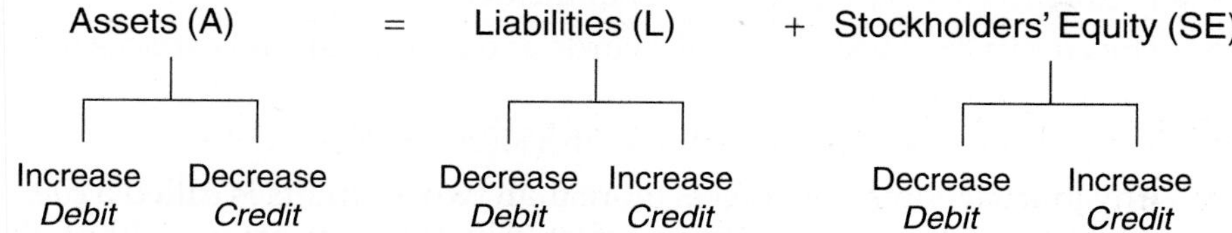

From this model, we can also observe the following:

- Asset accounts have debit balances (their positive, or increase, side).
- Liabilities and stockholders' equity accounts have credit balances (their positive, or increase, side).

As you are learning to perform transaction analysis, you should refer to this model often until you can construct it on your own without assistance. We will be building on this model in Chapter 3 when we add transactions affecting operations.

Many students have trouble with accounting because they forget that the only meaning for debit is the left side of an account and the only meaning for credit is the right side of an account. Perhaps someone once told you that you were a credit to your school or your family. As a result, you may think that there is "goodness" attached to credits and perhaps a "badness" attached to debits. Such is not the case. Just remember that *debit means left* and *credit means right.*

It should also be easy to remember which accounts debits increase and which accounts credits increase. A debit (left) increases asset accounts because assets are on the left side of the accounting model (A = L + SE). A credit (right) increases liability and stockholders' equity accounts because they are on the right side of the accounting model.

If the correct accounts and effects have been identified through the transaction analysis, the accounting equation will remain in balance. What will also be true is that *the total dollar value of all debits will equal the total dollar value of all credits* in a transaction. Therefore, this equality check (debits = credits) should be added to the transaction analysis process.

Analytical Tool: The Journal Entry

A **journal entry** is an accounting method for expressing the effects of a transaction on accounts in a debits-equal-credits format.

In a bookkeeping system, transactions are initially recorded in chronological order in a *journal*. After analyzing the business documents that describe a transaction, the accountant prepares the formal entry in the journal. Using debits and credits, a journal entry is written for each transaction. The **journal entry** is an accounting method for expressing the effects of a transaction on accounts in a debits-equal-credits format. The journal entry for Transaction (D) in the Sbarro illustration is as follows:

		Debit	Credit
(date or reference)	Equipment (A)	600	
	Cash (A)		100
	Notes payable (L)		500

Notice the following:

- It is useful to include a date or some form of reference for each transaction.
- The debits are written first (on top).
- The credits are written below all of the debits.
- The credits are indented (both words and amounts) a few spaces to the right below the debits.
- Total debits ($600) equal total credits ($100 + $500).
- Any journal entry that affects more than two accounts is called a *compound entry*. Three accounts are affected by this transaction. Although this and Transaction (J) are the only transactions in the above illustration that require a compound entry, many transactions in future chapters will require recording a compound journal entry.

While you are learning to perform transaction analysis, use the symbols A, L, and SE next to each account title, as is done in the above journal entry, including all homework problems at least in Chapters 2, 3, and 4. Specifically identifying accounts as assets (A), liabilities (L), or stockholders' equity (SE) will make using the transaction analysis model clearer and journal entries easier.

We have found that many students try to memorize journal entries without understanding or using the transaction analysis model. The task becomes increasingly more difficult as new detailed transactions are presented in subsequent chapters. However, *memorizing, understanding, and using the transaction analysis model* presented above and *following the three steps in the transaction analysis process* will work for any transaction, including those in future chapters.

Analytical Tool: The T-Account

After the journal entries have been recorded, the bookkeeper posts (transfers) the dollar amounts to each account that was affected by the transaction to determine account balances. As a group, the accounts are called a *ledger*. In a

T-Accounts Illustrated **Exhibit 2–3**

Cash (A)

	Increase (debit)		Decrease (credit)		
	Beginning balance	33,300			
+1,240	(A)	200	(C)	70	−800
	(B)	1,000	(D)	100	
	(H)	40	(F)	40	
			(G)	200	
			(I)	300	
			(J)	90	
	Ending balance	33,740			

Accounts Payable (L)

	Decrease (debit)		Increase (credit)		
			Beginning balance	4,500	
−200	(G)	200	(E)	300	+460
			(J)	160	
			Ending balance	4,760	

manual accounting system used by some small organizations, the ledger is often a three-ring binder with a separate page for each account. In a computerized system, accounts are stored on a disk.

Journal entries by themselves do not provide balances in accounts. One very useful tool for summarizing transaction effects and determining balances for individual accounts is called a **T-account**, which is a simplified representation of a ledger account. The T-accounts for the Cash and Accounts Payable accounts for Sbarro, Inc., based on the above transactions are presented in Exhibit 2–3. Notice that, for Cash which is classified as an asset, increases are on the left and decreases are on the right side of the T-account. However, for Accounts Payable, increases are on the right and decreases are on the left since the account is a liability.

The **T-account** is a tool for summarizing transaction effects for each account, determining balances, and drawing inferences about a company's activities.

T-accounts can be written as equations that yield balances for financial statement purposes:

		Cash	Accounts Payable
	Beginning Balance	33,300	4,500
+	All effects on the increase side	+ 1,240	+ 460
−	All effects on the decrease side	− 800	− 200
	Ending Balance	33,740	4,760

Handwritten or manually maintained accounts in the T-account format shown here may be used in small businesses. Computerized systems retain the concept of the account, but not the T-account format.

The words *debit* and *credit* are used as verbs, nouns, and adjectives. For example, we can say that: (1) Sbarro's Cash account was debited (verb) when stock was issued to investors; (2) to credit (verb) an account means to put the amount on the right side of the T-account; (3) a debit (noun) is the left side of an account; and (4) Notes Payable is a credit account (adjective). These terms will be used instead of left and right throughout the rest of the textbook. The next section is an illustration of the steps you should follow in using the model to record the effects of transactions in journal entries and determine account balances by using T-accounts.

TRANSACTION ANALYSIS ILLUSTRATED

The typical monthly transactions of Sbarro, Inc., presented above will be used to demonstrate transaction analysis and the use of journal entries and T-accounts. We analyze each transaction, checking that the accounting equation remains in balance and debits equal credits. In the T-accounts, located together at the end of the illustration, the amounts from Sbarro's January 2,

1994, balance sheet have been inserted as the beginning balances in each account. After reviewing or preparing each journal entry, trace the effects to the appropriate T-accounts using the transaction letters as a reference. The first transaction has been highlighted for you.

You should study this illustration carefully (including the explanations of transaction analysis). Careful study of the illustration is *essential* to the understanding of (a) the accounting model, (b) transaction analysis, (c) recording the dual effects of each transaction, and (d) the dual-balancing system. The most effective way to learn these critical concepts which affect material throughout the rest of the text is to practice, practice, practice.

(A) Sbarro sells $200 in additional stock to new investors.

Transaction Analysis	Journal Entry
Cash (A) increases by $200; to increase assets, debit the account. Stock certificates were issued, which means Contributed Capital (SE) increases by $200; to increase stockholders' equity, credit the account.	**Transaction (A)** — **Debit** / **Credit** Cash (A) — 200 Contributed capital (SE) — 200
Is the Accounting Equation in Balance?	Debits = Credits
Assets on the left side of the equation increase by $200; stockholders' equity on the right increases by $200. The equation is in balance.	These effects were posted to the appropriate T-accounts at the end of the illustration. To post, transfer the debit or credit amount on each line to the appropriate T-account indicated to accumulate balances for each account. For example, the $200 debit is listed in the debit column of the Cash T-account.

(B) The Company borrows $1,000 from its local bank, signing a promissory note to be paid in one year.

Transaction Analysis	Journal Entry
Cash increases by $1,000. Cash is an asset; to increase assets, debit the account. Notes Payable increases by $1,000. Notes Payable is a liability; to increase a liability, credit the account.	**Transaction (B)** — **Debit** / **Credit** Cash (A) — 1,000 Notes payable (L) — 1,000
Is the Accounting Equation in Balance?	Debits = Credits
Assets on the left side of the equation increase by $1,000; liabilities on the right increase by $1,000. The equation is in balance.	These effects were posted to the appropriate T-accounts at the end of the illustration.

(C) Sbarro acquires $70 in paper supplies, paying cash to its suppliers.

Transaction Analysis	Journal Entry
Supplies inventory increases by $70. Inventory is an asset; to increase an asset, debit the account. The Cash account decreases by $70. Cash is an asset; to decrease assets, credit the account.	**Transaction (C)** — **Debit** / **Credit** Inventory (A) — 70 Cash (A) — 70
Is the Accounting Equation in Balance?	Debits = Credits
Assets increase and decrease by the same amount. The equation remains in balance.	These effects were posted to the appropriate T-accounts at the end of the illustration.

(D) Sbarro opens a new restaurant and purchases $600 in equipment (primarily ovens and refrigeration equipment), paying $100 in cash with the rest due in six months on a promissory note to the equipment manufacturer.

Transaction Analysis	Journal Entry
Equipment increases by $600. Equipment is an asset; to increase an asset, debit the account. Cash decreases by $100. Cash is an asset; to decrease assets, credit the account. Notes Payable is increased by $500. Notes Payable is a liability; to increase a liability, credit the account.	**Transaction (D)** — **Debit** / **Credit** Equipment (A) 600 Cash (A) 100 Notes payable (L) 500
Is the Accounting Equation in Balance?	Debits = Credits
Assets on the left side of the equation increase by $500 ($600 – $100); liabilities on the right side increase by $500. The equation is in balance.	This compound entry balances with $600 on the debit side and $600 on the credit side. These effects were posted to the appropriate T-accounts at the end of the illustration.

(E) Sbarro acquires $300 in food and beverage supplies on credit to its suppliers.

Transaction Analysis	Journal Entry
Supplies inventory increases by $300. Inventory is an asset; to increase an asset, debit the account. Accounts Payable increases by $300. Accounts Payable is a liability; to increase a liability, credit the account.	**Transaction (E)** — **Debit** / **Credit** Inventory (A) 300 Accounts payable (L) 300
Is the Accounting Equation in Balance?	Debits = Credits
Assets on the left side of the equation increase by $300; liabilities on the right increase by $300. The equation is in balance.	These effects were posted to the appropriate T-accounts at the end of the illustration.

(F) Sbarro lends $40 to a franchisee who signed a note agreeing to repay the loan in one month.

Transaction Analysis	Journal Entry
Notes Receivable increases by $40. Notes Receivable is an asset; to increase an asset, debit the account. Cash decreases by $40. Cash is an asset; to decrease assets, credit the account.	**Transaction (F)** — **Debit** / **Credit** Notes receivable (A) 40 Cash (A) 40
Is the Accounting Equation in Balance?	Debits = Credits
Assets increase and decrease by the same amount. The equation is in balance.	These effects were posted to the appropriate T-accounts at the end of the illustration.

Self-Study Quiz

For Transactions (G) through (J), fill in the missing information, including postings to T-accounts. When completed, you can check your answers with the solution at the end of the illustration:

(G) Sbarro pays $200 cash on its accounts payable to suppliers.

Transaction Analysis	Journal Entry
Accounts Payable decreases by $200. Accounts Payable is a liability; to decrease a liability, debit the account. Cash also decreases by $200. Cash is an asset; to decrease assets, credit the account.	**Transaction (G)** **Debit** **Credit** Accts Pay (L) 200 Cash (A) 200
Is the Accounting Equation in Balance?	**Debits = Credits**
Assets on the left side of the equation decrease by $200; liabilities on the right decrease by $200. The equation is in balance.	These effects were posted to the appropriate T-accounts at the end of the illustration.

(H) Sbarro collects on the note receivable from the franchisee.

Transaction Analysis	Journal Entry
Cash increase by 40. Notes Rec dec. by 40. Cash is asset to increase, debit. Notes R is an asset to decrease, credit.	**Transaction (H)** **Debit** **Credit** Cash (A) 40 Notes receivable (A) 40
Is the Accounting Equation in Balance?	**Debits = Credits**
Assets increase and decrease by the same amount. The equation is in balance.	

Cash
40 | 40

NR
40 | 40

(I) Sbarro pays $300 on the promissory note with the local bank.

Transaction Analysis	Journal Entry
Notes Payable decreases by $300. Notes Payable is a liability; to decrease a liability, debit the account. Cash decreases by $300. Cash is an asset; to decrease assets, credit the account.	**Transaction (I)** **Debit** **Credit**
Is the Accounting Equation in Balance?	**Debits = Credits**
	These effects were posted to the appropriate T-accounts at the end of the illustration.

(J) Sbarro purchases $250 of new tables and chairs (equipment), paying $90 in cash and the rest on account.

Transaction Analysis	Journal Entry
Equipment increases by $250. Equipment is an asset; to increase an asset, debit the account. Cash decreases by $90. Cash is an asset; to decrease assets, credit the account. Accounts Payable increases by $160. Accounts Payable is a liability; to increase a liability, credit the account.	**Transaction (J)** **Debit** **Credit**
Is the Accounting Equation in Balance?	**Debits = Credits**
Assets on the left side of the equation increase by $160; liabilities on the right increase by $160. The equation is in balance.	

The following is a chart of the T-accounts that changed during the period because of the above transactions. The balances of all other accounts remained the same. The January 2, 1994, balances from Sbarro's balance sheet have been included as the beginning balances:

Cash (A)

Debit (Inc.)		Credit (Dec.)	
Beg. Bal.	33,300	(C)	70
(A)	200	(D)	100
(B)	1,000	(F)	40
(H)		(G)	200
		(I)	300
		(J)	
End. Bal.	33,740		

Receivables (Notes and other) (A)

Debit (Inc.)		Credit (Dec.)	
Beg. Bal.	1,300		
(F)	40	(H)	
End. Bal.	1,300		

Inventory (A)

Debit (Inc.)		Credit (Dec.)
Beg. Bal.	2,500	
(C)	70	
(E)	300	
End. Bal.	2,870	

Equipment (A)

Debit (Inc.)		Credit (Dec.)
Beg. Bal.	128,700	
(D)	600	
(J)		
End. Bal.	129,550	

Accounts Payable (L)

Debit (Dec.)		Credit (Inc.)	
		Beg. Bal.	4,500
(G)	200	(E)	300
		(J)	
		End. Bal.	4,760

Notes Payable (L)

Debit (Dec.)		Credit (Inc.)	
		Beg. Bal.	0
(I)	300	(B)	1,000
		(D)	500
		End. Bal.	1,200

Contributed Capital (SE)

Debit (Dec.)	Credit (Inc.)	
	Beg. Bal.	29,700
	(A)	200
	End. Bal.	29,900

You can verify that you posted the entries properly by adding the increase side and subtracting the decrease side, then comparing your answer to the ending balance given in each of the T-accounts. You can check your answers with the solutions at the bottom of this page.*

FINANCIAL ANALYSIS

Inferring Business Activities from T-Accounts

T-accounts are useful primarily for instructional purposes and as a financial analysis tool. There will be many cases in which we use the T-account tool to determine what transactions a company engaged in during a period. For example, the primary transactions affecting accounts payable for a period are purchases of assets on account and cash payments to suppliers. If we know the beginning and ending balances of accounts payable and all of the amounts that were purchased on credit during a period, we can determine the amount of cash paid. The T-account will include the following:

---

*(G) Journal Entry:

	Debit	Credit
Accounts payable (L)	200	
Cash (A)		200

(H) Transaction Analysis: Cash increases by $40. Cash is an asset; to increase assets, debit the account. Notes Receivable decreases by $40. Notes Receivable is an asset; to decrease an asset, credit the account.
Debits = Credits: Post each line to appropriate T-account.

(I) Is the Accounting Equation in Balance? Assets on the left side of the equation decrease by $300 ; liabilities on the right decrease by $300. The equation is in balance.
Journal Entry:

	Debit	Credit
Notes payable (L)	300	
Cash (A)		300

(J) Journal Entry:

	Debit	Credit
Equipment (A)	250	
Accounts payable (L)		160
Cash (A)		90

Debits = Credits: This is another compound entry with three accounts affected by the transaction. Debits are $250 and the credits are $250. Post each line to the appropriate T-account.

Accounts Payable (L)

Debit (Dec.)		Credit (Inc.)	
		Beginning balance	600
Cash payments	?	Purchases on account	1,500
		Ending Balance	300

SOLUTION:

Beg. balance +	Purchases –	Cash payments =	Ending balance
$600 +	$1,500 –	Cash payments =	$ 300
	$2,100 –	Cash payments =	300
		Cash payments =	$1,800

BALANCE SHEET PREPARATION

Learning Objective 6
Prepare a simple balance sheet.

It is possible to prepare a balance sheet at any point in time from the balances in the accounts. The date January 30, 1994, is the Sunday closest to the end of the month. Using the new balances shown in the T-accounts in the preceding Sbarro illustration plus the original balances in the accounts that did not change, the balance sheet in Exhibit 2–4 compares the account balances at January 30, 1994, with those at January 2, 1994. Notice that when multiple periods are presented, the most recent balance sheet amounts are usually listed on the left, though this may vary.

Exhibit 2–4 Balance Sheet

SBARRO INC. AND SUBSIDIARIES
Balance Sheets
at January 30, 1994 and January 2, 1994
(in thousands of dollars)

	January 30, 1994	January 2, 1994
Assets		
Cash	$ 33,740	$ 33,300
Marketable securities	37,200	37,200
Receivables (franchise fees and other)	1,300	1,300
Inventories	2,870	2,500
Prepaid expenses	1,500	1,500
Property and equipment	129,550	128,700
Other assets	3,200	3,200
Total assets	**$209,360**	**$207,700**
Liabilities		
Notes payable	$ 1,200	$ 0
Accounts payable	4,760	4,500
Accrued expenses payable, (rent, payroll, and other)	18,400	18,400
Dividend payable	2,700	2,700
Income taxes payable	4,600	4,600
Deferred income	400	400
Deferred income taxes	18,100	18,100
Total liabilities	$ 50,160	$ 48,700
Stockholders' Equity		
Contributed capital	$ 29,900	$ 29,700
Retained earnings	129,300	129,300
Total stockholders' equity	159,200	159,000
Total liabilities and stockholders' equity	**$209,360**	**$207,700**

At the beginning of the chapter, we presented the changes in Sbarro's balance sheets from the beginning of the year (January 3, 1993) to the end of the year (January 2, 1994). We questioned what made the accounts change and what the process was for reflecting the changes. Now we can see that the accounts have changed again in one month:

	Total Assets	=	Total Liabilities	+	Stockholders' Equity
1/2/94	$207,700	=	$ 48,700	+	$159,000
1/30/94	209,360	=	50,160	+	159,200
Change	+$ 1,660	=	+$ 1,460	+	$ 200

In this chapter, all of the additional changes were the result of transactions that involved the acquisition and sale of assets and borrowing and lending activities (including collecting on debts of others and paying back debts to others) and issuance of stock. You may have noticed that there were no transactions resulting in revenues or expenses for the Company. This chapter focused on balance sheet transactions; Chapter 3 will focus on analyzing transactions affecting operations. Because no operating activities occurred (e.g., selling food, paying employees), several accounts did not change, including retained earnings in the stockholders' equity section of the balance sheet.

FINANCIAL ANALYSIS

Comparing Companies in the Same Industry

One of the important uses of balance sheet information is to compare companies' financing and investing strategies (other analyses will be discussed in future chapters). For example, let's compare Sbarro, Inc., to another company in the restaurant industry, Ryan's Family Steak Houses, Inc. Both companies were incorporated in the same year and own (versus franchise) the majority of their restaurants (75% for Sbarro and 82% for Ryan's). However, they have undertaken different financing and investing strategies. The following chart reflects the differences:

	Sbarro, Inc.	Ryan's Family Steak Houses, Inc.
Investing: % of property, plant, and equipment to total assets	62%	96%
Financing: % of total debt to total liabilities and stockholders' equity	23%	28%

Their investment strategies have been different. The most dramatic difference is in the amount of property and equipment. Sbarro has 62% of its total assets in property and equipment ($128,770 property and equipment ÷ $207,700 total assets at 1/2/94), whereas Ryan's has 96% of its total assets in property and equipment. This appears reasonable because, unlike Sbarro which primarily leases space in shopping malls across the country, Ryan's constructs its own buildings. Such an investment strategy often requires a different financing strategy, usually involving increased borrowing. Much of the financing for Ryan's heavier investment in land, buildings, and equipment comes from borrowing through notes payable, which Sbarro does not do, and issuing more stock to shareholders than Sbarro does.

SOME MISCONCEPTIONS

Some people confuse bookkeeping with accounting. In effect, they confuse a part of accounting with the whole. Bookkeeping involves the routine, clerical part of accounting and requires only minimal knowledge of accounting. A bookkeeper may record the repetitive and uncomplicated transactions in most businesses and may maintain the simple records of a small business. In contrast, the accountant is a highly trained professional, competent in the design of information systems, analysis of complex transactions, interpretation of financial data, financial reporting, auditing, taxation, and management consulting.

Another prevalent misconception is that all transactions are subject to precise and objective measurement and that the accounting results reported in the financial statements are exactly what happened that period. In reality, accounting numbers are influenced by estimates, as will be illustrated in subsequent chapters. Some people believe that financial statements report the market value of the entity (including its assets), but they do not. To understand and interpret financial statements, the user must be aware of their limitations as well as their usefulness. One should understand what the financial statements do and do not try to accomplish.

Finally, financial statements are often thought to be inflexible because of their quantitative nature. As you study accounting, you will learn that it requires considerable *professional judgment* on the part of the accountant to capture the economic essence of complex transactions. Accounting is stimulating intellectually; it is not a cut-and-dried subject. It calls on your intelligence, analytical ability, creativity, and judgment. Accounting is a communication process involving an audience (users) with a wide diversity of knowledge, interest, and capabilities; therefore, it will call on your ability as a communicator. The language of accounting uses concisely written phrases and symbols to convey information about the resource flows measured for specific organizations.

To understand financial statements, you must have a certain level of knowledge of the concepts and the measurement procedures used in the accounting process. You should learn what accounting is really like and appreciate the reasons for using certain procedures. This level of knowledge cannot be gained by reading a list of the concepts and a list of the misconceptions. Neither can a generalized discussion of the subject matter suffice. A certain amount of involvement, primarily problem solving (similar to the requirement in mathematics courses), is essential in the study of accounting focused on the needs of the user. Therefore, we provide problems aimed at the desirable knowledge level for the user as well as the preparer of financial statements.

DEMONSTRATION CASE

On April 1, 1995, three ambitious college students started the Terrific Lawn Maintenance Corporation. Completed transactions (summarized) through April 30, 1995, for Terrific Lawn Maintenance Corporation were:

(a.) Issued $9,000 of common stock in total to the three investors in exchange for cash. Each investor received 500 shares of stock (totalling 1,500 issued shares).

(b.) Acquired rakes and other handtools (equipment), $600; paid $200 cash and the balance on account with the hardware store.

(c.) Ordered three lawn mowers and two edgers from XYZ Lawn Supply, Inc., for $4,000.

(d.) Purchased 4 acres of land for a future building site of a new storage garage. Paid cash, $5,000.

(e.) Received the mowers and edgers that had been ordered, agreeing to pay XYZ Lawn Supply in full in 30 days.

(f.) Sold one acre of land to the city for a park. The city will pay Terrific Lawn Maintenance Corp. $1,250 by the end of the month.

(g.) Paid $700 owed on account to suppliers (XYZ and the hardware store).

(h.) Collected cash on account owed by the city.

Required:

1. Set up T-accounts for Cash, Accounts Receivable (from the city), Lawn Equipment (for hand tools and mowing equipment), Land, Accounts Payable (to suppliers), and Contributed Capital. Beginning balances are $0; indicate these beginning balances in the T-accounts.

   Analyze each transaction using the three steps outlined in the chapter.

   Prepare journal entries in chronological order.

   Enter the effects of the transactions on the accounting model in the appropriate T-accounts. Identify each amount with its letter given above.

2. Use the amounts in the T-accounts developed in Requirement 1 to prepare a balance sheet for Terrific Lawn Maintenance Corporation at April 30, 1995. The April 30, 1995, balance sheet requires use of the account balances for all assets, liabilities, and stockholders' equity.

   The transaction analysis model is presented for your use:

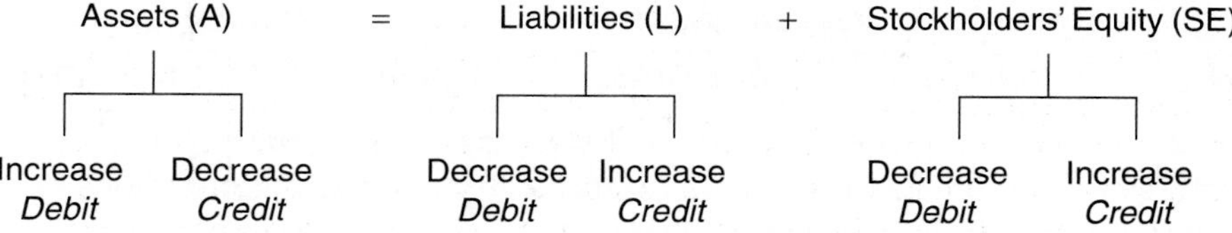

Now, you can check your answers with the solution to these requirements shown below.

SUGGESTED SOLUTION

1. Transaction analysis, journal entries, and T-accounts:

	Transaction Analysis	Journal Entry
(a.)	Cash (A) increases $9,000; Contributed Capital (SE) increases $9,000. Accounting equation in balance? Yes. Assets increase by $9,000; stockholders' equity increases by $9,000.	**Debit Credit** Cash (A) 9,000 Contributed capital (SE) 9,000 Debits = Credits; posted to appropriate T-accounts.
(b.)	Equipment (A) increases $600; Cash (A) decreases $200; Accounts Payable (L) increases $400. Accounting equation in balance? Yes. Assets increase by a net of $400 ($600 – $200); liabilities increase by $400.	Equipment (A) 600 Cash (A) 200 Accounts payable (L) 400 Debits = Credits; posted to appropriate T-accounts.
(c.)	No accounts are affected. **This is not an accounting transaction; no exchange takes place.**	
(d.)	Land (A) increases $5,000; Cash (A) decreases $5,000. Accounting equation in balance? Yes. Assets increase and decrease by the same amount.	Land (A) 5,000 Cash (A) 5,000 Debits = Credits; posted to appropriate T-accounts.
(e.)	Equipment (A) increases $4,000; Accounts Payable (L) increases $4,000. Accounting equation in balance? Yes. Assets increase by $4,000; liabilities increase by $4,000.	Equipment (A) 4,000 Accounts payable (L) 4,000 Debits = Credits; posted to appropriate T-accounts.

	Transaction Analysis	Journal Entry
(f.)	Accounts Receivable (A) increases $1,250; Land (A) decreases $1,250. Accounting equation in balance? Yes. Assets increase and decrease by the same amount.	**Debit** **Credit** Accounts receivable (A) 1,250 Land (A) 1,250 Debits = Credits; posted to appropriate T-accounts.
(g.)	Accounts Payable (L) decreases $700; Cash (A) decreases $700. Accounting equation in balance? Yes. Assets decrease by $700; liabilities decrease by $700.	Accounts payable (L) 700 Cash (A) 700 Debits = Credits; posted to appropriate T-accounts.
(h.)	Cash (A) increases $1,250; Accounts Receivable (A) decreases $1,250. Accounting equation in balance? Yes. Assets increase and decrease by the same amount.	Cash (A) 1,250 Accounts receivable (A) 1,250 Debits = Credits; posted to appropriate T-accounts.

Cash (A)

Debit (Inc.)		**Credit (Dec.)**	
Beg. bal.	0		
(a)	9,000	*(b)*	200
(h)	1,250	*(d)*	5,000
		(g)	700
End. bal.	4,350		

Accounts Receivable (A)

Debit (Inc.)		**Credit (Dec.)**	
Beg. bal.	0		
(f)	1,250	*(h)*	1,250
End. bal.	0		

Equipment (A)

Debit (Inc.)		**Credit (Dec.)**
Beg. bal.	0	
(b)	600	
(e)	4,000	
End. bal.	4,600	

Land (A)

Debit (Inc.)		**Credit (Dec.)**	
Beg. bal.	0		
(d)	5,000	*(f)*	1,250
End. bal.	3,750		

Accounts Payable (L)

Debit (Dec.)		**Credit (Inc.)**	
		Beg. bal.	0
(g)	700	*(b)*	400
		(e)	4,000
		End. bal.	3,700

Contributed Capital (SE)

Debit (Dec.)	**Credit (Inc.)**	
	Beg. bal.	0
	(a)	9,000
	End. bal.	9,000

2. Balance sheet:

TERRIFIC LAWN MAINTENANCE CORPORATION
Balance Sheet
At April 30, 1995

Assets		**Liabilities**	
Cash	$ 4,350	Accounts payable	$ 3,700
Equipment	4,600		
Land	3,750		
		Stockholders' Equity	
		Contributed capital	9,000
		Total liabilities and	
Total assets	$12,700	stockholders' equity	$12,700

Two balance sheet forms: **Report form** assets on top; liabilities and stockholders' equity on the bottom; **Account form** assets on the left; liabilities and stockholders' equity on the right.

Notice that balance sheets presented earlier in the text have listed assets on the top and liabilities and stockholders' equity on the bottom. This is called the **report form**. Preparing a balance sheet with assets on the left side and liabilities and stockholders' equity on the right side, such as above, is called the **account form**. Both are used in practice.

SUMMARY

This chapter reviewed the parts of the conceptual framework relevant to the balance sheet (the objective of external financial reporting, definitions of balance sheet elements, and the cost principle). This chapter then discussed the accounting model and illustrated its application in the accounting system for a business. For accounting purposes, transactions were defined as (*a*) exchanges of assets and liabilities between the business and other individuals and organizations, and (*b*) certain events that do not occur between the business and other parties but exert a direct effect on the entity (such as, recording adjustments to reflect the use of equipment in operations).

Application of the accounting model—Assets = Liabilities + Stockholders' Equity—was illustrated for Sbarro, Inc. The application involved (*a*) transaction analysis, (*b*) journal entries, and (*c*) the accounts (T-account format). Each transaction causes at least two different accounts to be affected in terms of the accounting model. The model often is referred to as a double-entry system because each transaction has a dual effect. The process used in transaction analysis involves (1) identifying the accounts affected and classifying each as an asset, liability, or stockholders' equity account, (2) determining the effect on each of the accounts, and (3) determining that the accounting equation remains in balance.

The transaction analysis model (built on the accounting model) and the mechanics of the debit-credit concept in T-account format can be summarized as follows:

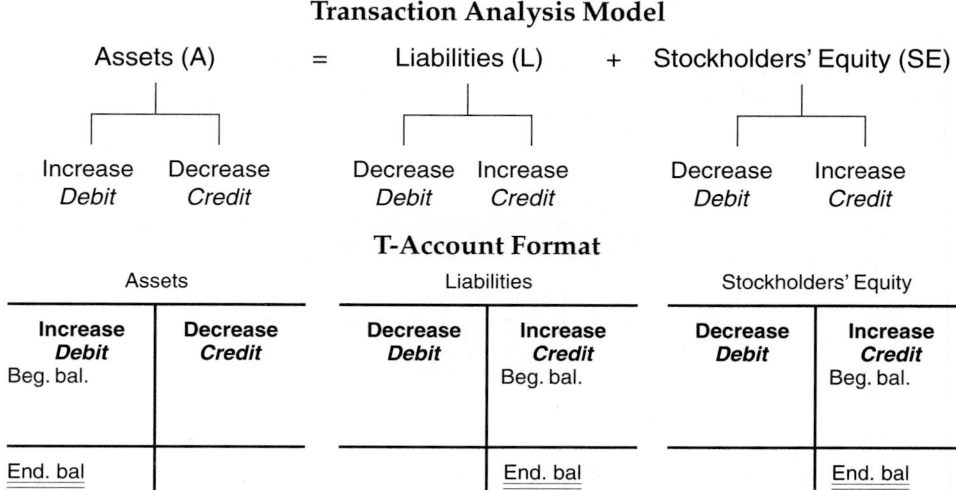

KEY TERMS

Account A standardized format used by organizations to accumulate the dollar effects of transactions on each financial statement item. *59*

Assets Probable future economic benefits owned by the entity as a result of past transactions. *55*

Continuity Assumption Businesses are assumed to continue to operate into the foreseeable future. *53*

Contributed Capital Results from owners providing cash (and sometimes other assets) to the business. *55*

Cost Principle An accounting assumption that requires assets to be recorded at the cash-equivalent cost, which on the date of the transaction is cash paid plus the current dollar value of all noncash considerations also given in the exchange. *57*

Debits and Credits Debit is the name for the left side of an account. Debits represent increases in assets and decreases in liabilities and stockholders' equity. Credit is the name for the right side of an account. Credits represent decreases in assets and increases in liabilities and stockholders' equity. *67*

Journal Entry An accounting method for expressing the effects of a transaction on accounts in a debits-equal-credits format. *68*

Liabilities Probable debts or obligations of the entity as a result of past transactions which will be paid with assets or services. *55*

Primary Objective of External Financial Reporting To provide useful economic information about a business to help external parties make sound financial decisions. *53*

Retained Earnings Cumulative earnings of a company that are not distributed to the owners and are reinvested in the business. *56*

Report and Account Forms These are two common balance sheet preparation forms. The report form lists assets on the top and liabilities and stockholders' equity on the bottom. The account form list assets on the left side and liabilities and stockholders' equity accounts on the right side. *78*

Separate-Entity Assumption Business transactions are separate from the transactions of the owners. *53*

Stockholders' Equity (Owners' Equity or Shareholders' Equity) The financing provided by the owners and the operations of the business. *55*

T-accounts An analytical tool for summarizing transaction effects for each account, determining balances for financial statement preparation, and drawing inferences about a company's activities. *69*

Transaction (1) An exchange between a business and one or more external parties, such as borrowing money from a bank, or (2) a measurable event internal to a business, such as adjustments for the use of assets in operations. *57*

Transaction Analysis The process of studying a transaction to determine its economic effect on the business in terms of the accounting equation: Assets = Liabilities + Stockholders' Equity. *60*

Unit-of-Measure Assumption Accounting information will be measured and reported in the national monetary unit. *53*

QUESTIONS

1. What is the primary objective of financial reporting for external users?
2. Give the accounting model and define each category.
3. Define a business transaction in the broad sense and give an example of the two different kinds of transactions.
4. Explain what the separate-entity assumption means in accounting.
5. Explain what the unit-of-measure assumption means in accounting.
6. Explain what the continuity assumption means in accounting.
7. Explain what the cost principle means in accounting.
8. What are the owners of a business organized as a corporation called? What is the basis for this name?
9. At December 31, 19A (end of year 1), the accounting model for THIS Company showed the following: stockholders' equity, $90,000; and liabilities, $30,000.
   a. Show how THIS Company stands in terms of the accounting model.
   b. Show the summarized balance sheet.
10. For accounting purposes, what is an account? Explain why accounts are used in an accounting system.
11. Explain what *debit* and *credit* mean.
12. What two equalities in accounting must be maintained in transaction analysis?
13. Briefly explain what is meant by transaction analysis. What are the three steps in transaction analysis?

14. Complete the following table by entering either the word *debit* or *credit* in each column.

Item	Increase	Decrease
Assets		
Liabilities		
Stockholders' Equity		

15. Complete the following table by entering either the word *increases* or *decreases* in each column.

Item	Debit	Credit
Assets		
Liabilities		
Stockholders' Equity		

16. What is a T-account? What is its purpose?
17. What is a journal entry?
18. Assume you and a friend started a new business called Dos Amigos Corporation. Each of you invested $5,000 in cash for equal shares of stock. Give the effect of this transaction on the company in terms of:

    a. The accounting model.

    b. A journal entry.

    c. The T-accounts.

EXERCISES

E2–1 Matching Definitions with Terms

Match each definition with its related term by entering the appropriate letter in the space provided.

	Term		Definition
________ (1)	Separate-entity assumption	A.	= Liabilities + Stockholders' Equity.
________ (2)	Cost principle	B.	Reports assets, liabilities, and stockholders' equity.
________ (3)	Credits	C.	Accounts for a business separate from its owners.
________ (4)	Assets	D.	Increase assets; decrease liabilities and stockholders' equity.
________ (5)	Transaction	E.	An exchange between an entity and other parties.
________ (6)	Continuity assumption	F.	Businesses will operate into the foreseeable future.
________ (7)	T-account	G.	Decrease assets; increase liabilities and stockholders' equity.
________ (8)	Balance sheet	H.	Assets should be recorded at cash-equivalent cost.
________ (9)	Debits	I.	A standardized format used to accumulate data about each item reported on financial statements.

E2–2 Identifying Asset Accounts

Assets are probable future economic benefits owned by an entity as a result of past transactions (cash, goods, or services must be exchanged). Following the cost principle, the initial valuation of assets is the cash-equivalent cost (the amount of cash and other assets needed to acquire the asset).

Required:

Using the above definition and valuation rule, indicate whether or not the following events would result in recording an asset on the balance sheet. If an asset would be recorded, indicate an appropriate account title and amount.

Event	Does an Asset Result?	Account Title	Amount
1. A company orders and receives 10 personal computers for office use for which it promises to pay $25,000 within three months.	Y	Equipment	25,000
2. A company purchases a new delivery truck which has a list, or sticker, price of $24,000 for $21,000 cash.	✓	Vehicle	21,000
3. A women's clothing retailer orders 1,000 fall blouses for $18 each for future delivery. The terms require payment within 30 days of delivery. Answer from the standpoint of the retailer.	No	—	—
4. The manufacturer of women's blouses receives the written order described in (3) above. Answer from the standpoint of the manufacturer.	No	—	—
5. A manufacturing company signs a contract for the construction of a new warehouse for $500,000. At the signing, the company writes a check for $50,000 as a deposit on the future construction.	Yes	Building	50,000
6. A publishing firm purchases the copyright (an intangible asset) to a manuscript for an introductory accounting text from the author for $40,000.	Yes	Copyright	40,000
7. A manufacturing firm pays its marketing staff $100,000 to produce an advertising campaign for a new product.	[illegible] Y	Expense (prepaid)	100,000
8. A company purchases 100 shares of Apple Computer common stock for $5,000 cash.	✓	Marketable	5,000

E2–3 *Identifying Asset Accounts*

Assets are probable future economic benefits owned by an entity as a result of past transactions (cash, goods, or services must be exchanged). Following the cost principle, the initial valuation of assets is the cash-equivalent cost (the amount of cash and other assets needed to acquire the asset).

Required:

Using the above definition and valuation rule, indicate whether or not the following events would result in recording an asset on the balance sheet. If an asset would be recorded, indicate an appropriate account title and amount.

Event	Does an Asset Result?	Account Title	Amount
1. A company purchases a piece of land for $50,000 cash. An appraiser for the buyer valued the land at $52,500.			
2. A new company is formed and sells 100 shares of stock for $12 per share to investors.			

Event	Does an Asset Result?	Account Title	Amount
3. A manufacturing company purchases the patent on a new digital satellite system for television reception for $500,000 cash and a $400,000 note payable due in one year at 10% annual interest.			
4. The accountant for a well-known snowboard manufacturing company feels that the company has accumulated $800,000 in goodwill over the 10 years it has been in business. The company has never been sold in the marketplace.			
5. A local construction company receives a delivery of $5,000 of lumber. Terms indicate that payment will be due within 60 days of delivery.			
6. An insurance company receives $1,200 from a customer for coverage for next year. Answer from the insurance company's point of view.			
7. Answer (6) above from the customer's point of view.			
8. A local company is a sole proprietorship (one owner), and the owner buys a car for $10,000 for personal use. Answer from the company's point of view.			

E2–4 Identifying Liability Accounts

Liabilities are probable debts or obligations of an entity as a result of past transactions (the receipt of cash, goods, or services) that will be paid with assets or services. The general rule for initial valuation is the cash-equivalent cost (what you could pay it off for today in cash, goods, or services).

Required:

Using the above definition and valuation rule, indicate whether or not the following events would result in recording a liability on the balance sheet. If a liability would be recorded, indicate an appropriate account title and amount.

Event	Does a Liability Result?	Account Title	Amount
1. A company orders and receives 10 personal computers for office use for which it promises to pay $25,000 within three months.	Yes	Accounts Payable	25K
2. A company signs a note and receives a $10,000 loan from the bank, which it agrees to pay back in one year with 10% interest.	✓	Notes Payable	10K
3. A women's clothing retailer orders 1,000 fall blouses for $18 each for future delivery. The terms require payment within 30 days of delivery. Answer from the standpoint of the retailer.	No	—	—
4. The manufacturer of women's blouses receives the written order described in (3) above. Answer from the standpoint of the manufacturer.	No	—	—

Event	Does a Liability Result?	Account Title	Amount
5. A manufacturing company signs a contract for the construction of a new warehouse for $500,000. At the signing, the company writes a check for $50,000 as a deposit on the future construction.			
6. Answer (5) from the standpoint of the construction company.			
7. A publishing firm uses $1,000 worth of electricity and natural gas for which it has not yet been billed.			
8. Apple Computer issues 100 shares of its common stock for $5,000 cash.			

E2–5 *Identifying Liability Accounts*

Liabilities are probable debts or obligations of an entity as a result of past transactions (the receipt of cash, goods, or services) that will be paid with assets or services. The general rule for initial valuation is the cash-equivalent cost, (what you could pay it off for today in cash, goods, or services).

Required:

Using the above definition and valuation rule, indicate whether or not the following events would result in recording a liability on the balance sheet. If a liability would be recorded, indicate an appropriate account title and amount.

Event	Does a Liability Result?	Account Title	Amount
1. A local construction company places a $5,000 order for lumber to be received next week. The terms indicate payment is due within 60 days of delivery.			
2. The company in (1) above receives the lumber today.			
3. A company signs a six-month note for a $1,000 loan on 6/30/19A to be paid back on 12/31/19A with 10% annual interest. Answer for the 6/30/19A date.			
4. A company pays $1,500 on its accounts payable.			
5. A retail company orders and receives $1,000 of merchandise inventory on accounts payable.			
6. A landlord receives $12,000 from the local bookstore for rent for the next 12 months. Answer from the landlord's point of view.			
7. A local business receives its telephone bill for $200 for the past month. The bill is not yet due nor has it been paid.			
8. An airline receives $800 from you for a ticket purchased in advance to go to Honolulu next month. Answer from the airline's point of view.			

E2–6 *Identifying Accounts and Their Usual Balances (Debit versus Credit)*

As described in a recent annual report, Polaroid Corporation designs, manufactures, and markets worldwide a variety of products primarily in instant image recording fields, including instant photographic cameras and films, electronic imaging recording devices, conventional films, and light polarizing filters and lenses. For each of the following accounts from Polaroid's recent balance sheet, complete the chart below by indicating whether the account is categorized as an asset (A), liability (L), or stockholders' equity (SE), and whether the account usually has a debit or credit balance.

Account	Balance Sheet Categorization	Debit or Credit
a. Land		
b. Retained earnings		
c. Notes payable		
d. Prepaid expenses		
e. Investments		
f. Contributed capital		
g. Machinery and equipment		
h. Accounts payable		
i. Short-term investments		
j. Federal, state, and foreign taxes		

E2–7 Applying Transaction Analysis

Complete the following tabulation by indicating the amount and direction of the effect of each transaction (+ or –):

Transaction	Assets	Liabilities	Stockholders' Equity
a. Investment of cash by organizers, $20,000			
b. Borrowed cash from a bank, $6,000			
c. Purchased $12,000 in inventory on account			
d. Loaned $300 to an employee			
e. Paid bank $6,000 (amount borrowed in *(b)* above)			
f. Purchased $8,000 equipment, paying $1,000 in cash and the rest on account			
Ending balances			

E 2–8 Applying Transaction Analysis

Wagner Service Company, Inc., was organized by Julie Wagner and five other investors.

Required:

1. Using the three-step transaction analysis process outlined in the text [(1) identify accounts affected, (2) determine the effect and amount on each account, and (3) determine that the accounting equation remains in balance], perform transaction analysis on each of the following transactions for Wagner Service Company. A sample transaction is provided.

	Transaction	Accounts Affected	Effect on Each Account	Equation in Balance?
a.	The investors paid in $60,000 cash to start the business. Each one was issued 1,000 shares of capital stock.	Cash (A) Contributed Capital (SE)	+ 60,000 + 60,000	A $60,000 = L $0 + SE $60,000

	Transaction	Accounts Affected	Effect on Each Account	Equation in Balance?
b.	Equipment for use in the business was purchased at a cost of $12,000; one quarter was paid in cash, and the balance is due in six months.	Equip Cash Accts. Pay	12,000 3000 9000	
c.	Signed an agreement with a cleaning service to pay $120 per week to them for cleaning the corporate offices.	~~Supp~~ Labor Payable	120/wk 120/wk	
d.	Purchased $2,000 of office supplies on account.	Supplies Accts. Pay	2000 2000	
e.	$4,000 in cash was collected from customers in advance for services to be performed by Wagner Service Company (an unearned revenue).	Cash Unearned Rev.	4000 4000	
f.	Paid cash, $2,000, on accounts payable.	Accts. Pay Cash	2000 2000	
g.	Julie Wagner borrowed $10,000 for personal use from a local bank and signed a one-year, 10% note for that amount.			

2. Explain your response to Transaction *c.*

E2–9 Matching Definitions with Terms

Match each definition with its related term by entering the appropriate letter in the space provided.

	Term		Definition
________ (1)	Journal entry	A.	Accounting model.
________ (2)	Note payable	B.	Four periodic financial statements.
________ (3)	Assets = Liabilities + Stockholders' Equity	C.	The two equalities in accounting that aid in providing accuracy.
________ (4)	Assets	D.	The results of transaction analysis in accounting format.
________ (5)	Duality	E.	The account that is credited when money is borrowed from a bank.
________ (6)	A = L + SE, and Debits = Credits	F.	Probable future economic benefits owned by an entity.
________ (7)	Income statement, balance sheet, statement of retained earnings, and statement of cash flows	G.	Cumulative earnings of a company that are not distributed to the owners.
________ (8)	Liabilities	H.	Every transaction has at least two effects.
________ (9)	Retained earnings	I.	Probable debts or obligations to be paid with assets or services.

E2–10 Understanding Effects of Transactions on Balance Sheet Accounts

During its first week of operations, January 1-7, Nervegna Retail Company completed eight transactions with the dollar effects indicated in the following schedule:

Accounts	Dollar Effect of Each of the Eight Transactions								Ending Balance
	1	2	3	4	5	6	7	8	
Cash	$12,000	$50,000	$(4,000)	$(3,000)	$(7,000)	$(8,000)	$(9,000)	$2,000	$33,000
Note receivable				3,000				(2,000)	1,000
Inventory						59,000			59,000
Store fixtures					7,000				7,000
Land			12,000						12,000
Accounts payable						51,000	(9,000)		42,000
Note payable		50,000	8,000						58,000
Contributed capital	12,000								12,000

Required:

1. Write a brief explanation of Transactions 1 through 8. The effects of each transaction are listed above. Explain any assumptions that you made.
2. Complete the following tabulation after the eight transactions:

Balance Sheet Summary:

Total assets	________
Total liabilities	________
Total stockholders' equity	________

E 2–11 *Understanding Effects of Transactions on Balance Sheet Accounts*

During its first month of operations, Morehouse Retail Company completed seven transactions with the dollar effects indicated in the following schedule:

Accounts	Dollar Effect of Each of the Seven Transactions							Ending Balance
	1	2	3	4	5	6	7	
Cash	$50,000	$(2,000)	$(500)		$(2,000)	$(450)	$200	$45,250
Note receivable			500				(200)	300
Inventory				$2,000				2,000
Truck		10,000						10,000
Accounts payable				2,000	(2,000)			0
Note payable		8,000				(450)		7,550
Contributed capital	50,000							50,000

Required:

1. Give the journal entry for Transactions 1 through 7, and give a brief explanation for each. Explain any assumptions that you made.
2. Complete the following tabulation after the seven transactions:

Balance Sheet Summary:

Total assets	________
Total liabilities	________
Total stockholders' equity	________

E2–12 *Preparing Simple Journal Entries*

Perform transaction analysis for each of the following six transactions. Based on your analysis, prepare journal entries for each (be sure to categorize each account as an asset (A), liability (L), or stockholders' equity (SE)).

a. Example: Three investors who own Boyce Corporation each invested $20,000 additional cash.

Cash (A) ($20,000 × 3)	60,000	
Contributed capital (SE)		60,000

b. Borrowed $6,000 cash and signed a 12% note.

c. Purchased $10,000 in equipment, paying $8,000 in cash and the rest on account.

d. Ordered $16,000 in inventory.

e. Paid off $2,000 on accounts payable.

f. Collected $1,000 on accounts receivable.

g. Received the inventory ordered in *(d)* above; it will be paid next month.

E2–13 *Applying Transaction Analysis*

Complete the following tabulation by indicating the amount and direction of the effect of each transaction (+ or –):

Transaction	Assets	Liabilities	Stockholders' Equity
a. Investment of cash by organizers, $55,000.			
b. Purchased $13,500 in inventory on account.			
c. Loaned $300 to an employee.			
d. Purchased a truck; paid $1,000 cash and signed a note for $9,000.			
e. Paid $2,000 on account from *(b)* above.			
f. Received $500 from a customer for services to be rendered next month.			
Ending balances			

E2–14 *Applying Transaction Analysis*

Complete the following tabulation by indicating the amount and direction of the effect of each transaction (+ or –):

Transaction	Assets	Liabilities	Stockholders' Equity
a. Investment of cash by organizers, $80,000.			
b. Borrowed $25,000 from the bank and signed a note payable due in one year with 10% annual interest.			
c. Purchased $12,000 in inventory for $5,000 cash and the remainder on account.			
d. Received $200 from a customer for services to be rendered next month.			
e. Prepaid next month's rent of $2,000.			
f. Paid the balance due on account from *(c)* above.			
Ending balances			

E2–15 *Using T-Accounts; Summarizing the Results*

Hudnell Company has been operating one year (19A). At the start of 19B, its T-account balances were:

Assets:

Cash		Accounts Receivable		Land	
5,000		2,000		4,000	

Liabilities:

Accounts Payable	
	300

Note Payable	
	400

Income Taxes Payable	
	200

Stockholders' equity:

Contributed Capital	
	10,100

Required:

1. Using the data from the above T-accounts, amounts for the following on January 1, 19B, were:

   Assets $________ = Liabilities $________ + Stockholders' Equity $________.
2. Enter the following 19B transactions in the T-accounts:
   a. Paid the income tax.
   b. Collected the accounts receivable.
   c. Paid the accounts payable.
   d. Sold one-fourth of the land for $1,000 in cash.
   e. Borrowed $1,600 at 6% from the bank (signing a note).
3. Using the data from the above T-accounts, amounts for the following on December 31, 19B, were:

   Assets $________ = Liabilities $________ + Stockholders' Equity $________.

E 2–16 *Preparing the Balance Sheet*

From the ending balances in the T-accounts in E 2–15, prepare a balance sheet for December 31, 19B, in good form.

E 2–17 *Using T-Accounts; Summarizing the Results*

Rossetter Delivery Company, Inc., was organized and issued 10,000 shares of its capital stock for $40,000 cash. The following transactions occurred during year 19E:

a. Received the cash from the organizers, $40,000.
b. Collected $20,000 cash in advance for future services (an unearned income account).
c. Purchased supplies for $2,000 on account.
d. Bought two used delivery trucks for operating purposes at the start of the year at a cost of $10,000 each; paid $3,000 cash and signed a promissory note due in three years for the rest.
e. Paid $3,000 cash to a truck repair shop for a new motor for one of the trucks. (Hint: Increase the account you used to record the purchase of the trucks.)
f. Traded the other truck and $6,000 cash for a new one.
g. Stockholder Nancy Rossetter paid $22,000 cash for a vacant lot (land) for her personal use.

Required:

Set up appropriate T-accounts with beginning balances of $0 for Cash, Supplies, Equipment, Accounts Payable, Notes Payable, Unearned Service Fees, and Contributed Capital.

Record in them the dual effects on the accounting model of each of the above transactions that should be recorded by Rossetter Delivery Company. Identify the amounts with the letters starting with (*a*).

E2–18 Preparing the Balance Sheet

Use the balances of the completed T-accounts in E2–17 to prepare a balance sheet in good form.

E2–19 Identifying Typical Activities in Accounts

The following T-accounts indicate the effects of normal business transactions:

Equipment

	Debit	Credit
1/1	300	
	250	?
12/31	450	

Accounts Receivable

	Debit	Credit
1/1	75	
	?	290
12/31	50	

Income Taxes Payable

Debit		Credit
	1/1	130
?		170
	12/31	180

Required:

1. For each T-account, compute the missing amounts.
2. For each T-account, describe the typical transactions that affect each account.

Hilton Hotels

E2–20 Analyzing Transactions and Preparing Journal Entries

Hilton Hotels Corporation constructs, operates, and franchises domestic and international hotel and hotel-casino properties. Information from the company's December 31, 1992, statement of cash flows indicates the following investing and financing activities during 1992 (simplified):

	In Millions
Investing Activities:	
a. Purchase and renovation of properties	$274.5
b. Purchase of investments	282.2
c. Receipt of notes receivable	5.4
d. Sale of property (assume sold at cost)	4.7
Financing Activities:	
e. Additional borrowings from banks	438.5
f. Payment of debt	32.2
g. Issuance of stock	2.9

Required:

1. For each activity, identify the accounts that were affected and the direction of the effect (increase +, or decrease –).
2. Prepare journal entries for each activity. Indicate whether (1) the debits equal the credits and (2) the accounting equation remains in balance after each entry.

Walt Disney

E2–21 Analyzing Transactions and Preparing Journal Entries

The Walt Disney Company owns and operates theme parks and destinations resorts, produces live-action and animated films, and licenses the Walt Disney name and characters for consumer products. Information from the company's September 30, 1993, statement of cash flows indicates the following investing and financing activities during 1993 (simplified):

	In Millions
Investing Activities:	
a. Expansion of theme parks and resort properties	$ 794.7
b. Investment in films	1,264.6
c. Advance to Euro Disney	140.1
d. Other investments (net)	461.3

Financing Activities:	In Millions
e. Borrowings	1,256.0
f. Reduction of borrowings	(1,119.2)
g. Repurchase of capital stock	(31.6)
h. Payment of cash dividends	(128.6)
i. Other loans	136.1

Required:

1. Prepare journal entries for each activity. State the effect (increase +, or decrease –) on each account balance after the account name in your journal entry.
2. Calculate the net inflow or outflow of cash as a result of the financing and investing activities, respectively.

E2–22 *Understanding the Effects of Transactions on Balance Sheet Accounts*

The Kraham and Staff Furniture Repair Service, a company with two stockholders, began operations on June 1, 19A. The following T-accounts indicate the activities for the month of June:

Cash

	Debit		Credit
a.	17,000	*b.*	10,000
f.	500	*d.*	1,500
g.	800	*e.*	1,000

Notes Receivable

	Debit		Credit
d.	1,500	*f.*	500

Parts Inventory

	Debit		Credit
c.	2,200		

Tools and Equipment

	Debit		Credit
a.	3,000	*g.*	800

Building

	Debit		Credit
b.	50,000		

Accounts Payable

	Debit		Credit
e.	1,000	*c.*	2,200

Notes Payable

	Debit		Credit
		b.	40,000

Contributed Capital

	Debit		Credit
		a.	20,000

Required:

Explain Transactions *a* through *g*, which gave rise to the entries in the T-accounts.

E2–23 *Preparing the Balance Sheet*

Ben & Jerry's

Ben & Jerry's Homemade, Inc., based in Vermont, produces Ben & Jerry's super premium ice cream, lowfat frozen yogurt, and ice cream novelties. These products are marketed through supermarkets, grocery stores, convenience stores, and restaurants. The company also franchises Ben & Jerry's ice cream scoop shops. The following list shows the accounts and balances from the company's December 26, 1992, annual report. The accounts, although not necessarily listed in good order, have normal debit and credit balances. Some of the information has been simplified.

Investments	$25,200,000	Prepaid expenses	$ 208,996
Bonds and leases payable	3,269,080	Accounts receivable	8,849,326
Retained earnings	18,579,709	Property, plant and equipment	26,737,425
Inventories	17,089,857	Net deferred income tax (an asset)*	411,000
Cash and cash equivalents	7,356,133	Accounts payable and accrued expenses	16,858,919
Contributed capital	48,180,107		
Income taxes receivable	306,193	Other assets	728,885

*Represents future lower taxes due to differences between tax accounting rules and financial accounting rules.

Required:

1. Prepare a balance sheet in good form for Ben & Jerry's at December 26, 1992.
2. Compute the ratio for Ben & Jerry's total debt to total debt and stockholders' equity.
3. What does this ratio indicate?

Walt Disney

E2–24 *Preparing the Balance Sheet*

The Walt Disney Company's balance sheet accounts as of September 30, 1993 (the end of its fiscal year) are shown below. The accounts have normal debit and credit balances; however, the accounts are not listed in good order. Some of the information has been simplified for this exercise. The amounts are stated in millions.

Short-term investment	$1,888.5	Accounts payable	$2,530.1
Income taxes payable	291.0	Cash	363.0
Attractions, buildings, and equipment	5,133.9	Borrowings	2,385.8
Unearned royalties	840.7	Retained earnings	4,869.8
Receivables	1,390.3	Deferred taxes payable	673.0
Land	94.3	Merchandise inventory	608.9
Contributed capital	160.7	Films in progress (an asset)	1,360.9
		Other assets	911.3

Required:

1. Prepare a balance sheet in good form for the Walt Disney Company at September 30, 1993.
2. Calculate the ratio for Walt Disney's total debt to total debt and stockholders' equity.

PROBLEMS

P2–1 *Analyzing Transactions and Recording Transaction Effects*

Metzger Home Healthcare Services was organized on January 1, 19A, by four friends. Each organizer invested $10,000 in the company and, in turn, was issued 8,000 shares of stock. To date, they are the only stockholders. During the first month (January, 19A), the company completed the following six transactions:

a. Collected a total of $40,000 from the organizers and, in turn, issued the shares of stock.

b. Purchased a building for $65,000, equipment for $16,000, and three acres of land for $12,000; paid $13,000 in cash, with the balance due in 15 years on a 10% mortgage payable to the local bank. (Hint: Five different accounts are affected.)

c. One stockholder reported to the company that 500 shares of his Metzger stock had been sold and transferred to another stockholder for a cash consideration of $5,000.

d. Purchased supplies for $3,000 on account.

e. Sold one acre of land for $4,000 in cash.

f. Loaned one of the shareholders $5,000 for moving costs, receiving a signed note due in one year from the shareholder.

Required:

1. Was Metzger Home Healthcare Services organized as a sole proprietorship, a partnership, or a corporation? Explain the basis for your answer.
2. During the first month, the records of the company were inadequate. You were asked to prepare the summary of transactions given above. To develop a quick assessment of their economic effects on Metzger Home Healthcare Services, you have decided to complete the tabulation that follows and to use plus (+) for increases and minus (–) for decreases for each account. The first transaction is used as an example.

Accounts	Dollar Effect of Each of the Six Transactions						Ending Balance
	a	b	c	d	e	f	
Cash	+$40,000	$	$	$	$	$	$
Note receivable							
Supplies							
Land							
Building							
Equipment							
Accounts payable							
Mortgage payable							
Contributed capital	+ 40,000						

3. Did you include the transaction between the two stockholders in the above tabulation? Why?
4. Based only on the completed tabulation above, provide the following amounts (show computations):
   a. Total assets at the end of the month.
   b. Total liabilities at the end of the month.
   c. Total shareholders' equity at the end of the month.
   d. Cash balance at the end of the month.

P2–2 *Classifying Accounts as Assets, Liabilities, and Stockholders' Equity and Their Normal Balances (Debit versus Credit)*

Listed below are several of the accounts of the Bannister Industrial Corporation:

a. Cash.
b. Accounts receivable.
c. Contributed capital.
d. Bonds payable.
e. Insurance premium paid in advance of use.
f. Investments, long term.
g. Machinery and equipment.
h. Patents (an intangible asset).
i. Property taxes payable.
j. Land, plant site (in use).
k. Accounts payable.
l. Supplies inventory (held for use as needed).
m. Note payable, short term.
n. Retained earnings.
o. Investments, short term.
p. Certificates of deposit (CDs) held (investments).
q. Income taxes payable.
r. Land held for future plant site.
s. Wages payable.
t. Merchandise inventory (held for resale).

Complete a tabulation similar to the following. Enter two checkmarks for each account listed above, one for the type of account and one for its usual balance. Account *a* is used as an example.

Account	Type of Account			Usual Balance	
	Asset	Liability	Stockholders' Equity	Debit	Credit
a.	√			√	

P2–3 *Classifying Accounts as Assets, Liabilities, and Stockholders' Equity and Their Normal Balances (Debit versus Credit)*

Listed below are several of the accounts of the Bennett Corporation:

a. Cash.
b. Accounts payable.
c. Retained earnings.
d. Goodwill.*
e. Prepaid rent.
f. Investments.
g. Notes payable.
h. Notes receivable.

* An intangible asset resulting from purchasing another company.

i. Petty cash.
j. Wages payable.
k. Buildings.
l. Land (store parking lot).
m. Merchandise inventory.
n. Supplies inventory (unused).
o. Utilities payable.
p. Accounts receivable.
q. Income taxes payable.
r. Contributed capital.

Complete a tabulation similar to the following. Enter two checkmarks for each account listed above, one for the type of account and one for its usual balance. Account *a* is used as an example.

	Type of Account			Usual Balance	
Account	**Asset**	**Liability**	**Stockholders' Equity**	**Debit**	**Credit**
a.	√			√	

P2–4 *Analyzing and Recording Transactions and Summarizing Transaction Effects*

Carey Plastics Company has been operating for three years. At the end of 19C, the accounting records reflected assets of $320,000 and liabilities of $120,000. During the year 19D, the following summarized transactions were completed:

a. Purchased equipment that cost $30,000; paid $10,000 cash, and the balance is due next year.

b. Issued an additional 2,000 shares of capital stock for $20,000 cash.

c. Collected $12,000 on accounts receivable.

d. Purchased $15,000 in investments.

e. Paid $15,000 on accounts payable.

f. Borrowed $20,000 cash on a 10% interest-bearing note from a local bank (on December 31, 19D); payable June 30, 19E.

g. Purchased a patent (an intangible asset) for $6,000.

h. Built an addition to the factory for $42,000 in cash.

i. Hired a new president at the end of the year. The contract was for $85,000 per year plus options to purchase company stock at a set price based on company performance.

j. Returned defective supplies to the manufacturer, receiving a cash refund of $2,000.

Required:

1. Enter each of the above transactions in the following schedule. The first transaction is used as an example.

	Assets		Liabilities		Stockholders' Equity	
Transaction	***Debit***	***Credit***	***Debit***	***Credit***	***Debit***	***Credit***
Balances, January 1, 19D	$320,000			$120,000		$200,000
a. Equipment purchase	30,000	10,000		20,000		
b.						
Etc.						

2. Respond to the following:
   a. Why were two credits entered in the above schedule for Transaction (*a*)?
   b. Complete the following at the end of 19D:

Balance sheet:

Assets	$ ________
Liabilities	$ ________
Stockholders' equity	$ ________

3. Explain your response to Transaction *i.*

P2–5 *Analyzing and Recording Transactions and Summarizing Transaction Effects*

Alex Incorporated is a small manufacturing company that makes model trains to sell to toy stores and has a small service department that repairs customers' trains for a fee. The company has been in business for five years. At the end of the most recent year, 19E, the accounting records reflected total assets of $500,000 and total liabilities of $200,000. During the current year, 19F, the following summarized transactions were completed:

a. Issued an additional 10,000 shares of capital stock for $100,000 cash.

b. Borrowed $120,000 cash from the bank and signed a note with terms of 12% annual interest with principal and interest due in a lump sum in two years.

c. Built an addition on the factory for $200,000 and paid cash to the contractor.

d. Purchased equipment for the new addition for $30,000 cash.

e. Received $85,000 on accounts receivable.

f. Returned a $3,000 piece of equipment, from *(d)* above, because it proved to be defective.

g. Paid $48,000 on accounts payable.

h. Purchased a delivery truck for $10,000; paid $5,000 cash and the remainder on a note payable.

i. Loaned the company president, Alex Ross, $2,000 cash. Mr. Ross signed a note with terms showing the principal plus 10% annual interest due in one year.

j. A stockholder sold $5,000 of his capital stock in Alex Incorporated to his neighbor.

k. Received $250 cash from a customer, Mr. Harold, for services to be provided at the beginning of 19G.

Required:

1. Enter each of the above transactions in the following schedule. The first transaction is used as an example.

Transaction	Assets		Liabilities		Stockholders' Equity	
	Debit	***Credit***	***Debit***	***Credit***	***Debit***	***Credit***
Balances, January 1, 19F	$500,000			$200,000		$300,000
a. Issued stock	100,000					100,000
b.						
Etc.						

2. Complete the following at the end of 19F:

Balance sheet:

Assets	$ ________
Liabilities	$ ________
Stockholders' equity	$ ________

3. Explain your response to Transaction *j.*

Foster's Brewing

P2–6 Analyzing Transactions and Preparing Journal Entries, T-Accounts, and the Balance Sheet—A Challenging Problem

Foster's Brewing Group Limited is an Australian corporation that brews beer including the popular Foster's and Molson brands and markets its products around the world. Shown below is Foster's June 30, 1994, balance sheet.

FOSTER'S BREWING GROUP LIMITED AND CONTROLLED ENTITIES
Balance Sheet at 30 June 1994
(in millions of Australian dollars)

Assets	
Cash	$ 106.6
Receivables	1,129.8
Inventories	227.1
Investments	1,198.2
Property, plant and equipment	2,030.3
Intangibles	717.8
Other assets	893.9
Total assets	6,303.7
Liabilities	
Creditors	928.9
Borrowings	1,958.9
Provisions *	596.6
Total liabilities	3,484.4
Net assets	$2,819.3
Shareholders' equity	
Share capital	3,267.4
Reserves	882.6
Accumulated losses	(1,362.8)
Outside equity interest in controlled entities†	32.1
Total shareholders' equity	$2,819.3

*Includes dividends payable, taxes payable, amounts owed to employees for wages earned and pension plans.

†100% of the assets and liabilities of controlled entities are included; however, not all controlled entities are owned at 100% (say 80% ownership). This account represents the minority ownership of outside parties (the amount not owned by Foster's).

Assume the following transactions occurred in July 1994:

a. Received $822.3 on receivables owed by customers.
b. Paid $134.1 in dividends owed to shareholders.
c. Paid $59.7 cash for income taxes owed.
d. Paid suppliers $657.7 cash.
e. Purchased inventories of $443.1 on account.
f. Issued additional shares of stock for $850.3 in cash.
g. Repaid $150.0 of borrowings to banks.
h. Purchased property, plant and equipment; paid $161.1 in cash and $479.4 with additional bank loans.
i. Acquired additional investments; paid $48.3 in cash.
j. Sold additional shares of stock for $352.8 in cash.

Required:

1. Analyze each transaction by identifying the accounts affected, the direction of the effects, and the impact on the accounting equation.
2. Prepare a journal entry for each transaction.

3. Create T-accounts for each balance sheet account and include the June 30, 1994, balances. Post each journal entry to the appropriate T-accounts.
4. Prepare a balance sheet from the T-account ending balances for Foster's at July 31, 1994, based on the above transactions.
5. Explain the meaning of "Accumulated losses."

CASES

C2–1 Inspection of a Balance Sheet to Evaluate Its Reliability

A. Smith asked a local bank for a $50,000 loan to expand his small company. The bank asked A. Smith to submit a financial statement of the business to supplement the loan application. Smith prepared the balance sheet shown below.

Balance Sheet
June 30, 19F

Assets:	
Cash and CDs (investments)	$ 9,000
Inventory	30,000
Equipment	46,000
Personal residence (monthly payments, $2,800)	300,000
Remaining assets	20,000
Total assets	$405,000
Liabilities:	
Short-term debt to suppliers	$ 62,000
Long-term debt on equipment	38,000
Total debt	100,000
Stockholders' equity, A. Smith	305,000
Total liabilities and stockholders' equity	$405,000

Required:

The balance sheet has several flaws; however, there is at least one major deficiency. Identify it and explain its significance.

C2–2 Analytical Case

Your best friend from home writes you a letter about an investment opportunity that has come her way. A company is raising money by issuing shares of stock and wants your friend to invest $20,000 (her recent inheritance from her great aunt's estate). Your friend has never invested in a company before and, knowing you are taking an accounting class, asks that you look over the balance sheet and send her some advice. An *unaudited* balance sheet, in only moderately good form, is enclosed with the letter:

DEWEY, CHEETUM AND HOWE, INC.
Balance Sheet
For the year ending December 31, 1995

Accounts receivable	$ 8,000
Cash	1,000
Inventory	8,000
Furniture and fixtures	52,000
Delivery truck (net)	12,000
Buildings (estimated market value)	98,000
Total assets	$179,000
Accounts payable	$ 16,000
Payroll taxes payable	13,000
Notes payable	15,000
Mortgage payable	50,000
Total liabilities	$ 94,000
Contributed capital	$ 80,000
Retained earnings	5,000
Total stockholders' equity	$ 85,000

There is only one footnote, and it states that the building was purchased for $65,000, has been depreciated by $5,000 on the books, and still carries a mortgage (shown in the liability section). The footnote further states that, in the opinion of the company president, the building is "easily worth $98,000."

Required:

1. Draft a new balance sheet for your friend, correcting any errors you note. (If any of the account balances need to be corrected, you may need to adjust the retained earnings balance correspondingly.) If no errors or omissions exist, state so.
2. Write a letter to your friend explaining the changes you made to the balance sheet, if any, and offer your comments on the company's apparent financial condition. Suggest other information your friend might want to review before coming to a final decision on whether to invest.

Leslie Fay

C2–3 Ethical Considerations

In 1993, Leslie Fay Companies, manufacturer of women's apparel, filed for Chapter 11 bankruptcy protection shortly after a scandal erupted over fraudulent accounting information. As reported in *The Wall Street Journal* (March 28, 1995, p. B1, B16), the company's audit committee report sharply criticized top management, suggesting that "it would have been difficult for senior management not to spot the extensive inventory and sales fraud." There were numerous ways in which Leslie Fay committed the fraud, according to the report: To boost sales and lower costs, midlevel company officials forged inventory tags, ignored expected inventory shrinkage, multiplied the value of items in inventory, improperly inflated sales, and made up phantom inventory. These officials also constantly altered records to meet sales targets. In March 1995, Leslie Fay's independent auditors, BDO Seidman, filed charges against Leslie Fay management, suggesting a cause of the fraudulent activity was due to senior management's adoption of unrealistic budgets: ". . . senior management created an environment which encouraged and rewarded the cooking of Leslie Fay's books and records" (*The Wall Street Journal,* March 29, 1995).

Required:

1. Describe the parties that were harmed or helped in this fraud.
2. Explain how adopting unrealistic budgets may have contributed to the fraud.
3. Why do you think the independent auditor filed charges against its former client?

Marvel Comics

C2–4 Financial Statement Analysis

Refer to the balance sheet of the Marvel Entertainment Group (producer of Marvel Comics) on the next page and answer the following questions:

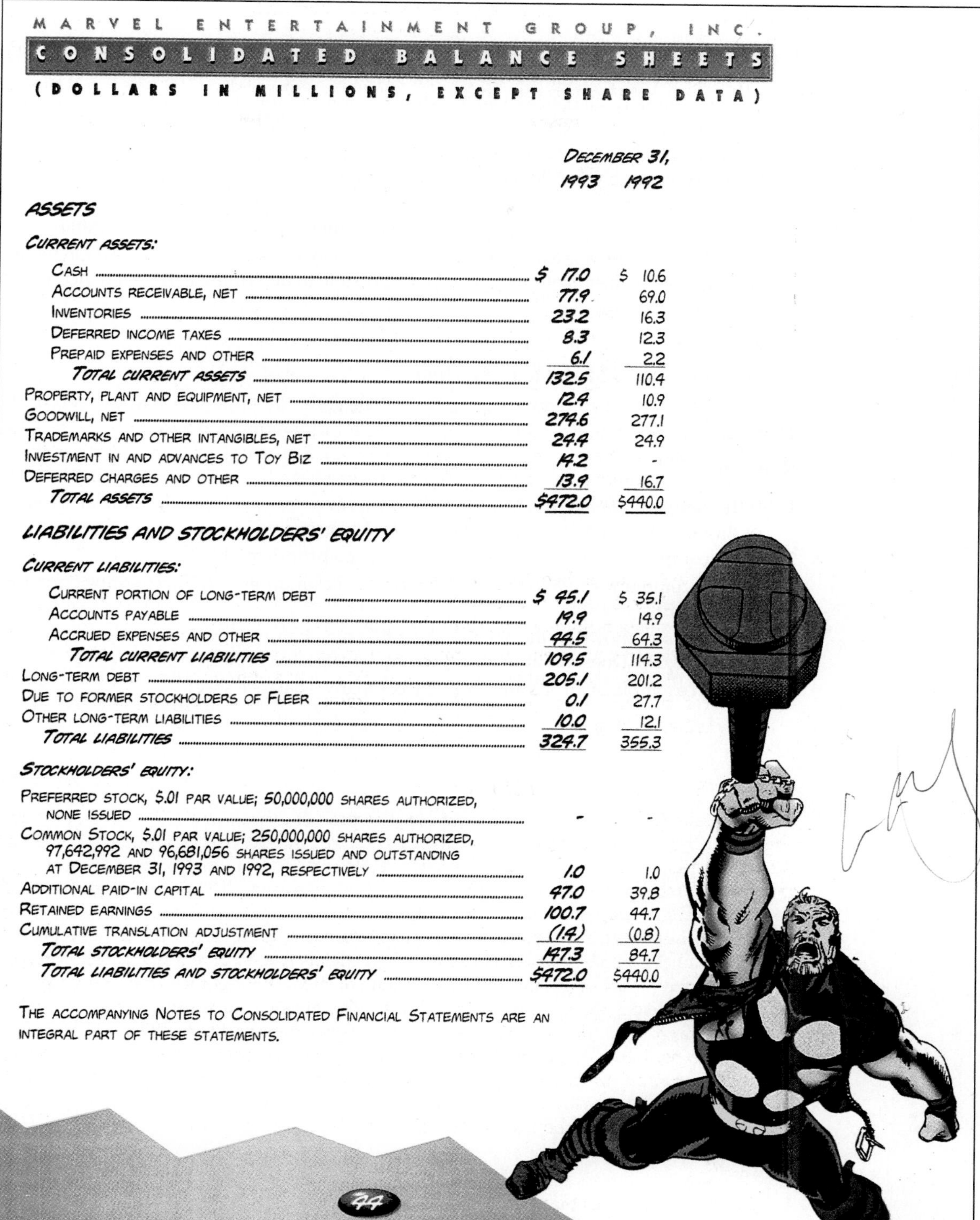

MARVEL ENTERTAINMENT GROUP, INC.

CONSOLIDATED BALANCE SHEETS

(DOLLARS IN MILLIONS, EXCEPT SHARE DATA)

	December 31, 1993	December 31, 1992
ASSETS		
Current assets:		
Cash	$ 17.0	$ 10.6
Accounts receivable, net	77.9	69.0
Inventories	23.2	16.3
Deferred income taxes	8.3	12.3
Prepaid expenses and other	6.1	2.2
Total current assets	132.5	110.4
Property, plant and equipment, net	12.4	10.9
Goodwill, net	274.6	277.1
Trademarks and other intangibles, net	24.4	24.9
Investment in and advances to Toy Biz	14.2	-
Deferred charges and other	13.9	16.7
Total assets	$472.0	$440.0
LIABILITIES AND STOCKHOLDERS' EQUITY		
Current liabilities:		
Current portion of long-term debt	$ 45.1	$ 35.1
Accounts payable	19.9	14.9
Accrued expenses and other	44.5	64.3
Total current liabilities	109.5	114.3
Long-term debt	205.1	201.2
Due to former stockholders of Fleer	0.1	27.7
Other long-term liabilities	10.0	12.1
Total liabilities	324.7	355.3
Stockholders' equity:		
Preferred stock, $.01 par value; 50,000,000 shares authorized, none issued	-	-
Common Stock, $.01 par value; 250,000,000 shares authorized, 97,642,992 and 96,681,056 shares issued and outstanding at December 31, 1993 and 1992, respectively	1.0	1.0
Additional paid-in capital	47.0	39.8
Retained earnings	100.7	44.7
Cumulative translation adjustment	(1.4)	(0.8)
Total stockholders' equity	147.3	84.7
Total liabilities and stockholders' equity	$472.0	$440.0

The accompanying Notes to Consolidated Financial Statements are an integral part of these statements.

44

Required:

1. Is the Marvel Entertainment Group a corporation, sole proprietorship, or partnership? Explain the basis of your answer.
2. Use the company's balance sheet to determine the amounts in the accounting equation (A = L + SE).
3. Calculate the company's ratio of total debt to total debt and stockholders' equity. Interpret the ratio you calculated. What other information would make your interpretation more useful?
4. Give the journal entry the company will make when it pays its accounts payable.
5. Does the company appear to have been profitable over its years in business? On what account are you basing your answer? If impossible to determine without an income statement, state so.

Toys "Я" Us

C2–5 Financial Statement Analysis

Refer to the financial statements of Toys "Я" Us given in Appendix B at the end of the book.

Required:

1. If the company repaid in cash all of its short-term notes payable to the bank at the end of the current year, what journal entry would be prepared?
2. Is the company a corporation, a partnership, or a proprietorship?
3. Use the company's balance sheet to determine the amounts in the accounting equation (A = L + SE).
4. The company shows on the balance sheet that merchandise inventories are worth $1,777,569,000. Does this amount represent the expected selling price?
5. Give an example of an account from the company's balance sheet.

3
sbarro Express
Pizza

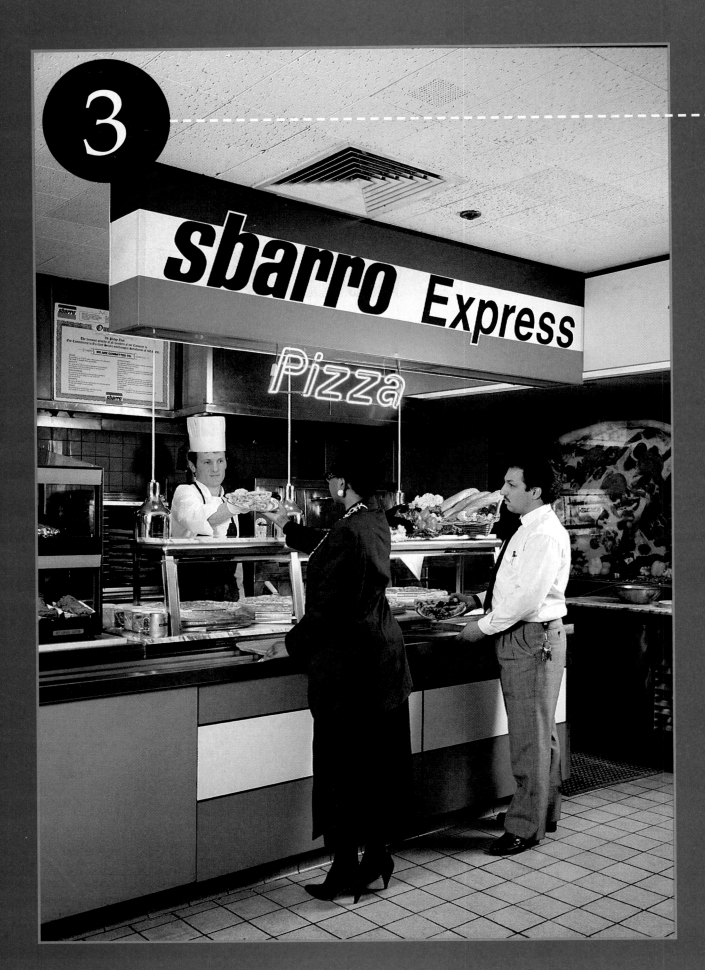

INCOME MEASUREMENT AND OPERATING DECISIONS

In Chapter 2, we discussed the fundamental accounting model and transaction analysis. Journal entries and T-accounts were used to record the results of transaction analysis for investing and financing decisions that affect balance sheet accounts. In this chapter, we continue our detailed look at financial statements and in particular the income statement. The purpose of this chapter is to build on your knowledge by discussing concepts for the measurement of revenues and expenses and by illustrating transaction analysis for operating decisions.

LEARNING OBJECTIVES

After studying this chapter, you should be able to:

1. **Understand the time-period assumption and the elements of the income statement.** ***105***
2. **Explain a typical business operating cycle.** ***109***
3. **Explain the cash basis and accrual basis of accounting.** ***111***
4. **Apply the revenue, matching, and cost principles to determine the timing and amount of revenue and expense recognition.** ***111***
5. **Explain the phases in the accounting cycle and how the differences between the operating cycle and accounting cycle affect the income measurement process.** ***116***
6. **Apply transaction analysis to examine and record the effects of operating activities on the financial statements.** ***117***
7. **Prepare a simple income statement.** ***132***

Management Decision Setting
SBARRO, INC.

People Are a Key to Profits

As stated in a recent annual report:

> THE MISSION OF SBARRO, INC. is to deliver high quality, affordably priced Italian food products to a wide range of consumers.
>
> We will serve our guests in attractive, distinctively designed, strategically located restaurants, wherever the demand for our products exists.
>
> We are committed to excellent service, dedicated to achieving Company objectives and maintaining profitability through the pride and commitment to excellence by our people.
>
> We create new guests through entrepreneurial-minded people who operate their restaurants with the Sbarro passion for guest satisfaction and maximum profit.

Based on this mission, Sbarro has opened restaurants across the United States in shopping malls and airports and more recently in foreign countries and nontraditional sites such as universities, hospitals, large chain stores, and Yankee Stadium (". . . wherever the demand for our products exists"). Sbarro relies on its people, mentioned twice in the mission statement, to accomplish its goals, including profit maximization. A primary goal over the past decade has been to realize systemwide sales of $500 million by the mid-1990s from franchised and company-owned restaurants. However, Sbarro recently ignored its stated tie between its people and profitability.

Forbes recently reported that Sbarro added a new organizational level of regional and district managers to manage its growth.* Instead of promoting qualified people from within the Company, the Sbarro family decided to recruit managers from bigger fast-food chains who would add broader industry and managerial experience to their talent pool. How will Sbarro and investors know if this strategy of hiring outside managers is working?

*R. La Franco, "Promote from within," *Forbes*, February 28, 1994, pp. 86–87.

BUSINESS BACKGROUND

To reach its long-range sales target, Sbarro must develop goals, plans (expectations), strategies, and measurable indicators of progress toward its goals. Companies such as Sbarro plan their companywide operations in terms of the elements of the income statement (specific revenues and expenses). Financial analysts also develop their own set of expectations about Sbarro's future performance. The published income statement provides the primary basis for comparing these plans or projections to actual results of operations. We will discuss these comparisons and the stock market's reactions to Sbarro's results throughout this chapter as we learn about income determination and income statement preparation. To understand how business plans and the results of operations are reflected on the income statement, we need to answer the following questions:

1. What business activities affect the income statement?
2. How are each of these activities measured?
3. How are these activities reported on the income statement?

In this chapter, we will focus on Sbarro's operating activities which involve the sale of food to the public and the sale of goods and services to the owners of franchised restaurants. The results of these activities are reported on its income statement. First we will discuss relevant accounting terms and concepts related to income measurement and reporting. Then we will expand the transaction analysis model outlined in Chapter 2 to incorporate operating activities. Finally, we will create an income statement from the operating activities.

RETURN TO THE CONCEPTUAL FRAMEWORK

Learning Objective 1
Understand the time-period assumption and the elements of the income statement.

The accounting conceptual framework initially outlined in Chapter 2 is presented again in Exhibit 3–1. The concepts relevant to the income statement will be reviewed as they apply to Sbarro, Inc. Concepts and terms in Exhibit 3–1 that are emphasized in this chapter are indicated in bold white print and concepts emphasized in prior chapters are indicated in bold black print.

Concepts Emphasized in Chapter 3

Underlying Assumption of Accounting

In Chapter 2, we examined the separate-entity, unit-of-measure, and continuity assumptions. The remaining accounting assumption, **the time-period assumption,** is directly relevant to the income statement. It recognizes that decision makers require periodic information about the financial condition and performance of a business. Most businesses exist for several years, decades, and even centuries. To meet decision makers' needs for periodic information, we assume the long life of a company can be reported in shorter time periods, usually months, quarters, and years. In addition to the audited annual statements, most businesses prepare quarterly financial statements (also known as *interim reports* covering a three-month period) for external users. Publicly traded companies are required to do so by the Securities and Exchange Commission.

The **time-period assumption** indicates that the long life of a company can be reported in shorter time periods.

The annual accounting period does not have to conform to the calendar year. In a recent survey of 600 companies, 239 (nearly 40%) did not use a December 31 year-end.[1] In addition, 123 companies (nearly 20%) chose a fiscal year defined, for example, as the last Saturday of the month or the Saturday closest to the end of the month, which results in financial information in some years covering 52 weeks and in other years 53 weeks. Sbarro, Inc. defines its fiscal year-end as the Sunday nearest December 31. For example, Sbarro's 1994 year ended on Sunday, January 2.

Furthermore, many companies use a natural business year-end, which occurs at the lowest point in their annual business cycle. Retail stores, for example, tend to experience much seasonal fluctuation in business activity, with the holiday shopping period in November and December and merchandise returns in January being the highest level of activity followed immediately by the lowest level of activity. They often use a January 31 year-end. The following is a sample of well-known companies and their year-end dates:

Company	Industry	Year-End
Campbell Soup Company	Foods	Sunday nearest July 31
USAir Group, Inc.	Airline	December 31
Federal Express	Delivery	May 31
Honda Motor Co., Ltd.	Automobile	March 31
Wendy's International, Inc.	Fast Food	Sunday nearest December 31
McDonald's Corporation	Fast Food	December 31
Kmart Corporation	Retail	Last Wednesday in January
Dayton Hudson Corp.	Retail	Sunday nearest January 31
Woolworth Corporation	Retail	Last Saturday in January except European and Mexican operations which end December 31

While the time-period assumption may appear to be of little consequence at first glance, many of the most difficult accounting problems we examine in this book involve issues in assigning business activities to time periods.

[1]American Institute of Certified Public Accountants, Inc., *Accounting Trends and Techniques*, 47th ed. (New York, New York: AICPA, 1993), pp. 28–29.

Exhibit 3–1 Financial Accounting and Reporting Conceptual Framework

Primary Objective of External Financial Reporting

To provide useful economic information to external users for decision making (for assessing future cash flows) [Ch.2]

Qualitative Characteristics of Information

[Ch. 5]

Overall: Information should be

Cost-beneficial Benefits of accounting and reporting should exceed costs.

Primary:

Relevance Information influences decisions; it is timely and has predictive and feedback value.

Reliability Information is accurate, unbiased, and verifiable.

Secondary:

Comparability Information can be compared to other businesses.

Consistency Information can be compared across time.

Elements of Financial Statements

Assets Probable future economic benefits owned by the entity from past transactions. [Ch. 2]

Liabilities Debts or obligations from past transactions to be paid with assets or services. [Ch. 2]

Stockholders' Equity Financing provided by owners and operations. [Ch. 2]

Revenues Inflows of net assets (assets minus liabilities) from ongoing operations. [Ch. 3]

Expenses Outflows of net assets (assets minus liabilities) from ongoing operations. [Ch. 3]

Gains Inflows of net assets from peripheral transactions. [Ch. 3]

Losses Outflows of net assets from peripheral transactions. [Ch. 3]

Assumptions

1. **Separate-entity** Transactions of the business are separate from transactions of the owners. [Ch. 2]
2. **Unit-of-measure** Accounting measurements will be in the national monetary unit. [Ch. 2]
3. **Continuity** The entity will not go out of business in the near future. [Ch. 2]
4. **Time-period** The long life of a company can be reported over a series of shorter time periods. [Ch. 3]

Principles

1. **Cost** Cash-equivalent cost given up is the basis for initial recording of elements. [Ch. 2 and 3]
2. **Revenue** Record revenues when earned and measurable (an exchange has taken place, the earnings process is nearly complete, and collection is probable). [Ch. 3]
3. **Matching** Record expenses when incurred in earning revenue. [Ch. 3]
4. *Full-disclosure* Disclose relevant economic information. [Ch. 5]

Constraints

[Ch. 5]

1. *Materiality* Relatively small amounts not likely to influence decisions are to be recorded in the most cost-beneficial way.
2. *Cost-benefit* Benefits of recording and reporting information should outweigh costs.
3. *Conservatism* Exercise care not to overstate assets and revenues or understate liabilities and expenses.
4. *Industry peculiarities* Differences in accounting and reporting for certain items are permitted if there is a clear precedent in the industry.

Elements of the Income Statement

A recent income statement for Sbarro, Inc., is presented in Exhibit 3–2. For purposes in this chapter, the income statement has been simplified by rounding the dollar amounts.[2] In addition, only one year's income statement is presented here. Publicly traded companies such as Sbarro are required to present three years of income information to help users assess trends over time.

Revenues are inflows of net assets (increases in assets and/or reductions of liabilities) from ongoing operations.[3] This means that when a revenue occurs, assets (usually cash or receivables) increase or liabilities (usually deferred or unearned revenue) decrease. Sbarro's income statement in Exhibit 3–2 indicates that restaurant sales revenue is Sbarro's largest category of revenues. These revenues are recognized when Sbarro's company-owned restaurants provide food service for which they usually receive cash immediately. Sbarro also has contractual arrangements with its franchisees (owners of franchised restaurants) from which Sbarro earns two kinds of revenues: (1) initial franchise fees for opening each new franchised restaurant and (2) royalties based on a percentage of revenues earned by each franchised restaurant. These two revenues are combined in the account Franchise Related Income. Interest income represents the amount of interest earned on investments (marketable securities). The last revenue listed on the income statement, other income, is a summary of several small income sources, including gains and losses which are defined below.

Revenues are inflows of net assets (increases in assets and/or reductions in liabilities) from ongoing operations.

Expenses are outflows of net assets (decreases in assets and/or increases in liabilities) from ongoing operations. This means that when an expense occurs, assets (such as inventory and equipment) decrease or are used up or liabilities (such as salaries payable) increase resulting from the generation of revenues. Sbarro's three largest expenses are:

Expenses are outflows of net assets (decreases in assets and/or increases in liabilities) from ongoing operations.

1. The cost of food and paper products, from using inventories of these items.
2. Payroll and other employee benefits, a restaurant operating expense primarily paid directly in cash to employees.
3. Occupancy and other expenses, primarily rent paid to shopping mall owners.

Sbarro's mission to locate restaurants where demand exists includes places such as universities (Adelphi University), interstate service plazas, and airports.

[2] As another simplification, the Other Income account is listed in Exhibit 3–2 under revenues, but Sbarro actually reports the account as a negative amount at the end of the costs and expenses section.

[3] Net assets are total assets minus total liabilities.

Exhibit 3–2 **Income Statement**

SBARRO, INC. AND SUBSIDIARIES
Statement of Income
For the Year Ended January 2, 1994
(In thousands of dollars, except for per share data)

Revenues:		
Restaurant sales		$259,200
Franchise related income		4,800
Interest income		1,600
Other income		1,200
Total revenues		266,800
Costs and expenses:		
Cost of food and paper products		55,400
Restaurant operating expenses:		
Payroll and other employee benefits	$64,700	
Occupancy and other expenses	68,200	132,900
Depreciation and amortization		18,600
General and administrative		12,900
Total costs and expenses		219,800
Income before income taxes and cumulative effect of change in accounting method		47,000
Income taxes		18,600
Income before cumulative effect of accounting change		28,400
Cumulative effect of change in method of accounting for income taxes		1,000
Net income		$ 29,400
Earnings per share		$2.17

Depreciation and amortization expense is the portion of the cost of long-lived assets such as property and equipment and intangibles such as the costs of new restaurant openings which were used in the period to generate revenue. The general and administrative expense category includes the overall business expenses, such as salary of the president and other officers, advertising costs, office supplies, and insurance. We noted in Chapter 2 that Sbarro is not financed with short- or long-term debt. If Sbarro had debt, interest expense would also be reported separately on the income statement.

Income taxes is the last expense listed. All profit-making corporations are required to compute income taxes owed to federal, state, and foreign governments. Though we will add further detail in Chapter 9, income tax expense is calculated as a percentage of the difference between revenues and expenses determined by applying IRS tax rates. Using the information in Sbarro's income statement in Exhibit 3–2, we can determine Sbarro's effective income tax rate for taxes owed to federal, state, and foreign governments as follows:

Effective tax rate = $18,600 income taxes ÷
$47,000 income before income taxes = 39.6%

Gains are inflows of net assets from peripheral transactions.

Gains are inflows of net assets from peripheral transactions. Therefore gains, like revenues, result in increases in assets or decreases in liabilities, or both. Peripheral transactions are those activities that create net asset inflows or outflows but are not related to the central operations of the business. If, for example, Sbarro sells an oven (equipment) at a price of $2,500, but the equipment is recorded in Sbarro's accounts at $2,000, a gain (not a revenue) of $500 will result. Sbarro is not in the business of selling its equipment; the equipment sale is a peripheral transaction due to an investing activity.

Losses are outflows of net assets from peripheral transactions.

Losses are outflows of net assets from peripheral transactions. If equipment with a recorded value of $2,800 is sold for $2,500, Sbarro would recognize a loss of $300 on the sale. In Sbarro's income statement in Exhibit 3–2, no gains or losses are reported separately. As noted above, most companies, including Sbarro, combine small gains and losses in the other income category on the income statement. We will present the transaction analysis for gains and losses in future chapters dealing with the valuation and disposition of specific assets and liabilities.

There is one last item on the income statement in Exhibit 3–2 that impacts net income, Cumulative Effect of Change in Method of Accounting for Income Taxes. It exists, if, for example, the Deferred Taxes Liability account showed a $3,000 balance under the old method, but should be $2,000 under the new method; the $1,000 difference is the cumulative effect of the change in method. This is an example of one of the gains and losses from special situations, such as discontinuing a segment of the business, natural disasters, or changing detailed accounting principles, which may be listed after income tax expense. These items require separate emphasis on the income statement and in the notes to the statements. We will discuss and illustrate reporting these special situations in Chapter 5.

Basic Accounting Principles Affecting Income Determination

The basic principles of accounting are important because they provide the conceptual guidelines for measuring, recording, and reporting business transactions. Three of the principles apply to income determination:

1. The revenue principle.
2. The matching principle.
3. The cost principle.

These principles need to be understood clearly. We will discuss and illustrate these concepts in the next section of the chapter.

INCOME MEASUREMENT

To understand how to apply the principles listed above, it is first necessary to understand the operating cycle (also called the *cash-to-cash cycle*) for a typical business.

The Operating Cycle

Learning Objective 2
Explain a typical business operating cycle.

Exhibit 3–3 presents a typical operating cycle in the form of a timeline. In simple terms, the long-term objective for any business is to turn cash into more cash. The **operating cycle** is the time it takes for a company to purchase goods or services from suppliers, sell goods or services to customers, and collect cash from customers. A merchandiser or manufacturer (1) purchases or manufactures and stocks the inventory; (2) pays cash to suppliers; (3) sells the product on credit (hopefully at a price exceeding costs); and (4) finally receives cash from the customer. Thus, cash is turned into more cash. For ongoing businesses, additional inventory is purchased or produced and the cycle is repeated.

The **operating cycle** is the time it takes for a company to purchase goods or services from suppliers, sell goods and services to customers, and collect cash from customers.

For service companies, the operating cycle is similar. While there is no need to spend cash on a product, other relevant costs are incurred in providing the service, such as rent, the use of necessary supplies and equipment, and employee wages. Then, the service is provided on credit at a price exceeding costs. Finally, the cash is received from the customer.

In the example in Exhibit 3–3, $10,000 was expended and $17,000 was received for a net increase in cash of $7,000. The net increase can be used to buy

Exhibit 3–3 **A Typical Business Operating Cycle (or Cash-to-Cash Cycle)**

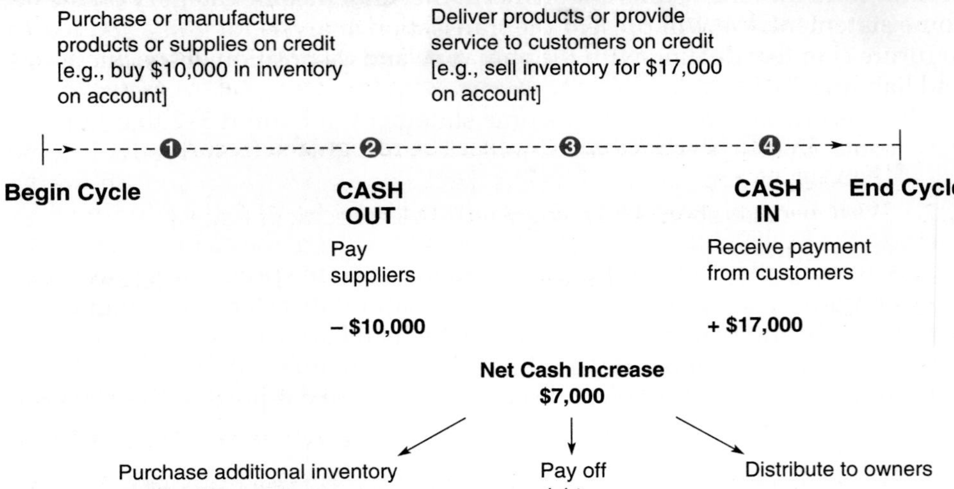

additional assets (resources for the business), pay off debt, and/or be distributed to owners. Although the cash increase of $7,000 is the result of completing the operating cycle, we will learn in this chapter and Chapter 4 that different portions of the $7,000 may be reported in different time periods (e.g., $3,000 this year and $4,000 next year) because the company's accounting period ends at a point other than the end of the operating cycle.

The length of time for a company's operating cycle depends on the nature of its business. For Sbarro, the cycle should be shorter than for a company producing consumer products such as refrigerators or clothing. Shortening the operating cycle by creating incentives to encourage customers to pay faster or to shorten the time between purchase or manufacture of goods to sale of goods to customers reduces costs and improves the company's financial position.

Although Exhibit 3–3 presents a typical operating cycle, it is important to note that there are many instances where cash is received (point 4) or paid (point 2) at other times. For example, companies that sell magazine subscriptions receive cash from customers well *before* any product is delivered. Also, insurance premiums are usually paid *before* companies are covered for risk of loss, but utility bills usually are received for payment *after* the company has used the utilities. Also, in the case of Sbarro, cash is received from customers at the point of sale (point 3).

FINANCIAL ANALYSIS

Short-Term Debt Financing and the Operating Cycle

From the timing of the cash outflows and inflows in Exhibit 3–3, we can see that for most businesses there is often a need for short-term borrowing to pay suppliers and employees until cash is received from customers. That is, a cash outflow occurs before a cash inflow, causing companies to seek short-term financing. Then when cash is received from customers, the liability is paid off. In addition, if a company plans to grow, say to sell twice as many goods as in the prior period, there may not have been enough cash collected from the prior period's customers to purchase the amount of inventory needed in the next period. Sources of financing include suppliers through accounts payable and financial institutions (banks and commercial credit companies) through notes payable. Short- and long-term debt financing will be discussed in Chapters 9 and 10.

Notice in Exhibit 3–3 that the typical earnings process involves four basic activities or transactions that take place in sequence over time. Timelines similar to the one in Exhibit 3–3 that list activities, dates, and amounts are useful tools to illustrate the income recognition issues discussed below. Timelines will help you focus on the two primary questions for income measurement:

1. *When* should revenues and expenses be recognized (recorded)? [Timing issues]
2. *What amounts* should be recognized? [Measurement issues]

We will answer these as we discuss the principles relating to the accrual basis of accounting.

Accrual Basis of Accounting

Cash versus Accrual Basis

Learning Objective 3
Explain the cash basis and accrual basis of accounting.

Most of you determine your personal financial position by the cash balance in your bank account. Your financial performance is measured as the difference between your cash balance at the beginning of the period and the balance at the end of the period (that is, whether you end up with more or less cash). If you have a higher cash balance, cash receipts exceeded cash disbursements for the period. Measuring income in this manner is called **cash basis accounting.** Using this system, revenues are recorded when cash is received and expenses are recorded when cash is paid, regardless of when the revenues are earned and expenses are incurred (due to actions causing outflow of resources to generate revenues).

Cash basis accounting records revenues when cash is received and expenses when cash is paid.

Many small retailers, medical offices, and other small businesses use the cash basis of accounting. However, it is not considered appropriate for preparing income statements and balance sheets for external financial reporting purposes for two main reasons. First, except for transactions involving cash, no assets or liabilities are recorded; therefore, a complete financial position is not available for analysis. In addition, cash basis net income, which is the difference between cash receipts and disbursements, can be manipulated. For example, a company using the cash basis can report higher net income simply by postponing certain payments until the next period. Since financial statements created under the cash basis of accounting normally postpone or accelerate recognition of revenues and expenses long before or after goods and services are produced and delivered, these statements are less relevant to external decision makers.

In contrast to cash basis accounting, **accrual basis accounting** is required by generally accepted accounting principles for financial reporting purposes. This means that assets, liabilities, revenues, and expenses should be recognized when the transaction that caused them is complete or nearly complete, not necessarily when cash is received or paid. However, cash flow information is important for estimating whether companies can afford to pay their debts. In fact, this information is reported on a separate statement, the statement of cash flows, which is very important in financial statement analysis. The statement of cash flows will be discussed in detail in Chapter 13. The two basic accounting principles that determine when revenues and expenses are to be recorded under the accrual basis of accounting are the revenue principle and the matching principle.

Accrual basis accounting requires recording revenues when earned and expenses when incurred, regardless of the timing of cash receipts or payments.

Learning Objective 4
Apply the revenue, matching, and cost principles to determine the timing and amount of revenue and expense recognition.

Timing of Revenues: The Revenue Principle

The **revenue principle** states that revenues are recognized when the earnings process is nearly complete, an exchange has taken place, and collection is probable.

Under the **revenue principle,** three conditions normally must be met for revenue to be recognized. If *any* of the following conditions are *not* met, revenue normally is *not* considered recognized and cannot be recorded.

1. *The earnings process is complete or nearly complete.* This means that the company has performed or substantially performed the promised acts (provided goods or services).
2. *An exchange transaction takes place.* In exchange for the company's performance, the customer provides cash or a promise to pay cash (a receivable).
3. *Collection is reasonably assured.* As discussed in greater depth in Chapter 6, companies establish credit policies to reduce the risk of extending credit to customers who fail to pay. On the date of a sale on credit, assuming the credit policies have been followed, collection is usually considered reasonably probable. We will learn in Chapter 6 that, even with strong credit policies, companies need to evaluate the likelihood that some accounts will not be collected. Probable bad debts will need to be estimated.

In practice, these conditions are met for most businesses at the point of delivery of goods or services. In Exhibit 3–3, revenue would usually be recorded on the date of delivery (point 3). For sales of magazine subscriptions, even though cash is received, revenue is not recorded until the magazines are delivered. Instead, since the earnings process is not complete, the initial cash transaction results in a liability (deferred or unearned revenue account that represents the amount of goods or services owed to the customers or a refund due if they cancel their orders) until delivery. As stated before, revenue is recorded according to the revenue principle when the three conditions are met, *regardless of when cash is received.*

As is typical in the fast-food industry, Sbarro receives nearly 98% of its revenues in cash at the time of sale of food products to customers. Thus, points 3 and 4 in the operating cycle occur on the same day. Sbarro also sells franchises where cash is received from new franchisees *before* Sbarro provides start-up services to them. When the services are provided, Sbarro earns and records revenues. Franchisees must also pay royalties to Sbarro based on a percentage of their sales revenues. Sbarro receives cash *after* it earns royalty revenue. Companies usually disclose their revenue recognition practices in a footnote to the financial statements. The following excerpt from Sbarro's Footnote 1 describes how they recognize these two forms of franchise related income:

Real World Excerpt

Sbarro, Inc.
Annual Report

Notes To Consolidated Financial Statements

Sbarro, Inc. and Subsidiaries

1. SUMMARY OF SIGNIFICANT ACCOUNTING POLICIES

...

Franchise related income

Initial franchise fees are recorded as income as restaurants are opened by the franchisees and all services have been substantially performed by the Company. . . . Royalties and other fees from franchisees are accrued as earned . . .

...

These practices follow the conditions of the revenue principle discussed above. We will discuss in Chapter 6 special generally accepted practices applied in certain circumstances where one of the conditions is not met (such as, accounting for revenue under long-term construction contracts before the projects are completed).

Timing of Expenses: The Matching Principle

The **matching principle** requires that expenses be recorded when incurred in earning revenue.

Resources that are used to earn revenues are called *expenses*. The **matching principle** requires that when the period's revenues are properly recognized in conformity with the revenue principle, all of the resources consumed in earning those revenues should be recorded in that same period, *regardless of when cash is paid.* When Sbarro records total restaurant sales revenue for the period, all of the related expenses (such as the cost of food and paper products from inventories, payroll expense, and occupancy expense) used to generate the revenues should also be recorded. The expense should be matched with revenues for the same period.

Just as in the case of revenues and cash receipts, expenses and cash outlays are not necessarily recorded on the same date. For example, the acquisition of, and sometimes the cash outlay for, food and paper product supplies occurs *prior* to their use. However, they are recorded as inventory, an asset, when purchased and are not expensed as the cost of food and paper products until they are used. Similarly, companies usually pay for rent in *advance* of using the property and record the cash outlay in an asset account, Prepaid Expense, that represents future benefits to the company. The asset is allocated over time to occupancy expense as it is used. In addition, a part of the cost of long-lived assets, such as equipment that is used in operations, needs to be matched with the revenues generated by their use in a period. The used portion of the assets is allocated to depreciation expense. In other cases, resources are used to generate revenues prior to the cash outlay. For Sbarro, payroll expense represents the amount earned by managers and employees who prepare and serve the food and is an expense of that period. Cash is usually paid to employees *after* the point when they provide their services. However, expense should be recorded when the service is provided.

Amount of Revenues and Expenses: The Cost Principle

In Chapter 2, we defined the cost principle as the requirement that financial statement elements be recorded at the cash-equivalent price on the date of the transaction. We apply this same principle to revenue and expense recognition. By definition, revenues are inflows of net assets. Since assets are recorded on the balance sheet at the cash or cash-equivalent price, revenues are measured at the cash or cash-equivalent value of the assets to be received from customers. Similarly, since expenses are expired assets, they are measured at the cash or cash-equivalent purchase price (cost) of the assets expended.

Analytical Tool: Timeline

We indicated earlier that timelines are useful tools. In determining how much revenue or expense to record in a particular period, a **timeline** is often helpful in providing a visual representation of a transaction or series of transactions. Timelines indicate relevant activities, dates, and amounts. Learning to construct and use timelines will help you in determining the appropriate timing and amounts to be recognized for transactions in this and several future chapters.

A **timeline** is a visual representation of a series of business activities, listing dates and amounts over time.

To illustrate the use of timelines, consider a transaction in which a company provides a service to a customer on May 23 with $300 cash payment in full made by the customer on June 16. On the date the service is provided, the earnings process is complete, an exchange transaction of service for a promise to pay has taken place, and the cash collection is reasonably assured. Therefore, as indicated on the timeline, $300 is recognized as revenue in May, not in June when the cash is collected from the customer. The name of the revenue account would be Service Revenue.

QUESTION OF ETHICS

Management's Incentives to Violate the Revenue Recognition Principle

In two recent articles, *The Wall Street Journal* reported:

Tech Concerns Fudge Figures To Buoy Stocks

More small technology companies are pumping up their sales and earnings through aggressive and sometimes questionable accounting to help inflate their stock prices, accountants say.

SOURCE: L. Berton, *The Wall Street Journal,* May 19, 1994, p. B1.

Three Kurzweil Officials Quit, Fourth Fired After Sales Inquiry; Stock Plunges

Kurzweil Applied Intelligence Inc. said three top managers resigned and a fourth was fired following the discovery that "a number of significant" sales had been booked as revenues before actually being completed. The company's stock price plunged nearly 40%.

SOURCE: S. Stecklow, *The Wall Street Journal,* May 24, 1994, p. B6.

These headlines refer to companies in the very competitive computer industry. They suggest that when companies experience financial difficulty, some managers attempt to improve the picture painted in the financial statements by violating revenue recognition rules. The hope is to fool investors so that much-needed funds can be raised through the stock market. Mentioned in the first article is Kendall Square Research Corp., maker of supercomputers, which ". . . has acknowledged that it counted as sales numerous computers that customers apparently couldn't pay for." This violates the condition, collection should be reasonably assured. The second article indicates that Kurzweil, a software manufacturer, recorded revenues before the earnings process was complete, thus violating the first condition. The importance of revenue recognition and earnings to the value of a company's stock is emphasized by the dramatic drop in share price often experienced when the discovery of such improprieties is announced.

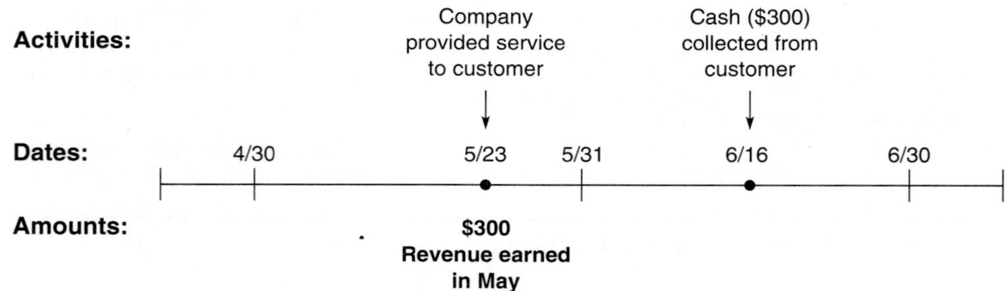

Self-Study Quiz

This self-study quiz will allow you to practice applying the revenue recognition and matching principles under accrual accounting. We recommend that you refer back to the three revenue recognition criteria and the description of the matching principle presented earlier as you answer each question.

The following transactions are a sample of typical monthly operating activities of Sbarro, Inc. In each, indicate the *amount,* if any, of revenue or expense that Sbarro recognizes during January and the *title* of the revenue or expense account. It is important to complete this quiz now to make sure you can apply these principles. You should refer to the Sbarro income statement presented in Exhibit 3–2 for examples of account titles. A partially completed timeline is provided for your use. List activities and amounts on the timeline to assist you with your answer.

	Amount of Revenue or Expense Sbarro Recognizes in January	Revenue or Expense Account Title
1. In January, Sbarro's company-owned restaurants sold food to customers for $24,000 in cash. December January February		
2. Sbarro is entitled to royalties from franchisees based on a percentage of their gross revenues. In January, franchisees report that based on January's gross revenues, they owe Sbarro $500 which they will pay to Sbarro in February. December January February		
3. A mall department store paid Sbarro a $30 deposit in January in exchange for Sbarro's promise to provide food for an employee party in February. December January February		
4. An oven in a company-owned restaurant was repaired in January. The bill for $50 was received and paid by Sbarro in January. December January February		
5. Bills for $60 were received in February from electric and gas companies for utility usage by Sbarro company-owned restaurants in January. December January February		
6. In December, Sbarro paid $5,000 to mall owners to rent mall space in January. December January February		
7. Sbarro received $700 in cash for royalties from franchisees in January based on the franchisees' December revenues. December January February		
8. In January, Sbarro received and paid suppliers $120 cash for paper products that will be used in February. December January February		

After you have completed the quiz, check your solution with the answers in the footnote at the bottom of this page.*

*1. $24,000 Restaurant Sales Revenue.
2. $ 500 Franchise Related Income
3. $ 0 Not a revenue in January, but will be recorded as a revenue in February when the service is provided.
4. $ 50 Repair Expense (part of occupancy and other expenses).
5. $ 60 Utility Expense (part of occupancy and other expenses).
6. $ 5,000 Occupancy Expense.
7. $ 0 Not a revenue in January, but was a December revenue when earned.
8. $ 0 Not an expense in January, but will be expensed in February when used.

The Accounting Cycle

Learning Objective 5
Explain the phases in the accounting cycle and how the differences between the operating cycle and accounting cycle affect the income measurement process.

Measuring a company's financial performance and financial position requires establishing a distinct accounting period, usually a month, quarter, or year. We know from Exhibit 3–3 that the operating cycle involves both cash inflows and outflows and a series of revenues and expenses which are recognized according to the revenue recognition and matching principles of accrual accounting. *Often, revenue and expense recognition dates do not coincide with cash flow dates. Further, the operating cycle may extend over more than one accounting period.* To understand the impact of these timing issues, let's return to our definitions of the two types of business transactions discussed in Chapter 2 and examine when and how these transactions are accounted for in typical accounting systems.

Transactions of the first type are exchanges of assets and liabilities between the business and one or more other parties. The second type of transaction includes certain events that do not result in an actual exchange between the business and other parties but do have a direct and measurable effect on the accounting entity, particularly for revenue and expense recognition. This second type of transaction is based on either (1) past business activities where the passage of time causes revenues to be earned or expenses to be incurred (such as recognition of interest revenue on a note receivable or depreciation accumulated on the equipment used during the period) or (2) reasonable estimates (such as the amount of utilities used during the period). These transactions are normally recorded at the end of the accounting period and are called *adjusting entries.*

Phases in the Accounting Cycle

The **accounting cycle** is the recordkeeping process used during and at the end of the accounting period that results in financial statements.

The recordkeeping process used during and at the end of the accounting period that results in the preparation of financial statements is often referred to as the **accounting cycle**. Exhibit 3–4 highlights the fundamental steps in the accounting cycle. (A more detailed description of the formal recordkeeping process is provided in Chapter 4, Supplements A, B, and C.) The exhibit indicates two separate phases. Phase 1 includes the analysis and recording of the first type of transactions, those based on exchanges with external parties *during* the accounting period. Sbarro's investing and financing transactions that we presented in Chapter 2 occurred in Phase 1. Sbarro's operating activities to be discussed in this chapter also occur during Phase 1. We will learn to recognize which of the Phase 1 transactions will require adjusting entries in Phase 2.

The second phase includes all of the activities at the *end* of the accounting period to update account balances for proper revenue and expense recognition (the adjustment process), to prepare financial statements, and to prepare the records for the beginning of the next period of activity. These steps are discussed in Chapter 4. We briefly note in Exhibit 3–4 that organizations maintain two basic types of accounting records (or books): a general journal, which is a formal listing of each journal entry in chronological order, and a general ledger, in which each page resembles a more detailed T-account. Though some small businesses maintain manual records, computer technology has become so inexpensive and easy to use that most companies have computerized accounting systems. However, even sophisticated computerized accounting systems still produce records similar in form to the basic general journal and general ledger. The accounting concepts employed remain the same, whether a manual or computerized recordkeeping system is used.

Many students confuse the accounting cycle and the business operating cycle. Remember that the timing of the operating cycle is determined by the

Fundamental Steps in the Accounting Cycle **Exhibit 3–4**

START OF ACCOUNTING PERIOD

Phase 1:
During the Accounting Period
(discussed in Chapters 2 and 3)

Perform **transaction analysis** based on a review of source documents from each transaction
↓
Record **journal entries** for each transaction (in chronological order in the general journal)
↓
Post amounts to the general ledger (pages are similar to **T-accounts**)
↓

Phase 2:
At the End of the Accounting Period
(discussed in Chapter 4)

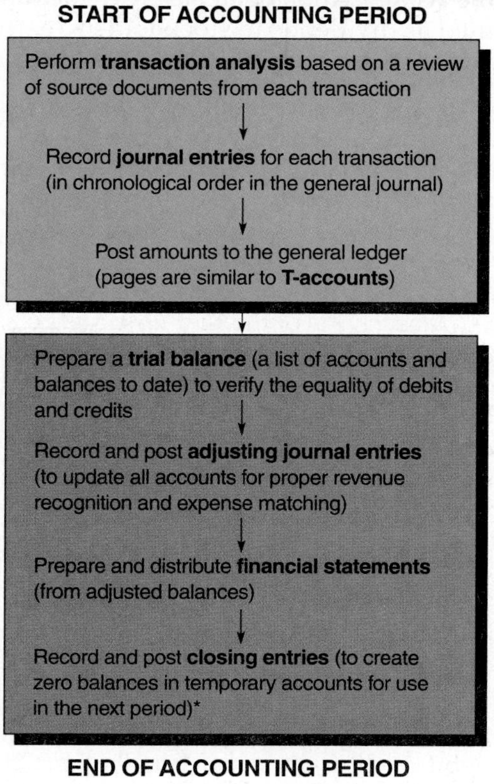

Prepare a **trial balance** (a list of accounts and balances to date) to verify the equality of debits and credits
↓
Record and post **adjusting journal entries** (to update all accounts for proper revenue recognition and expense matching)
↓
Prepare and distribute **financial statements** (from adjusted balances)
↓
Record and post **closing entries** (to create zero balances in temporary accounts for use in the next period)*

END OF ACCOUNTING PERIOD

*Temporary accounts are those that accumulate balances for the period. They are revenue, expense, and dividends declared accounts.

nature of the business. It may be short or long and represents the time it takes a company to turn cash into more cash. The accounting cycle coincides with the accounting period, usually a month, quarter, or year, which is similar across all companies.

COMPLETION OF THE TRANSACTION ANALYSIS MODEL

Learning Objective 6
Apply transaction analysis to analyze and record the effects of operating activities on the financial statements.

Now that we have indicated what business activities affect the income statement and how they are measured, we need to complete the transaction analysis model to show how these business activities are recorded in the accounting system and reflected in the financial statements. Only investing and financing activities affecting assets, liabilities, and contributed capital were presented in Chapter 2. We will now expand the transaction analysis model to include transactions involving revenues and expenses (from operating activities), gains and losses (from investing and financing activities), and the distribution of earnings to investors known as dividends (an additional financing activity). The model as we left it in Chapter 2 is presented below:

Assets (A)		=	Liabilities (L)		+	Stockholders' Equity (SE)	
Increase	Decrease		Decrease	Increase		Decrease	Increase
Debit	*Credit*		*Debit*	*Credit*		*Debit*	*Credit*

To begin, we need to add detail to the stockholders' equity element of the equation. Recall from Chapter 1 that stockholders' equity consists of contributed capital and retained earnings. The Retained Earnings account is the accumulation of all past revenues and expenses minus any income distributed as dividends to stockholders (earnings not retained in the business). By adding these concepts, the transaction analysis model becomes:

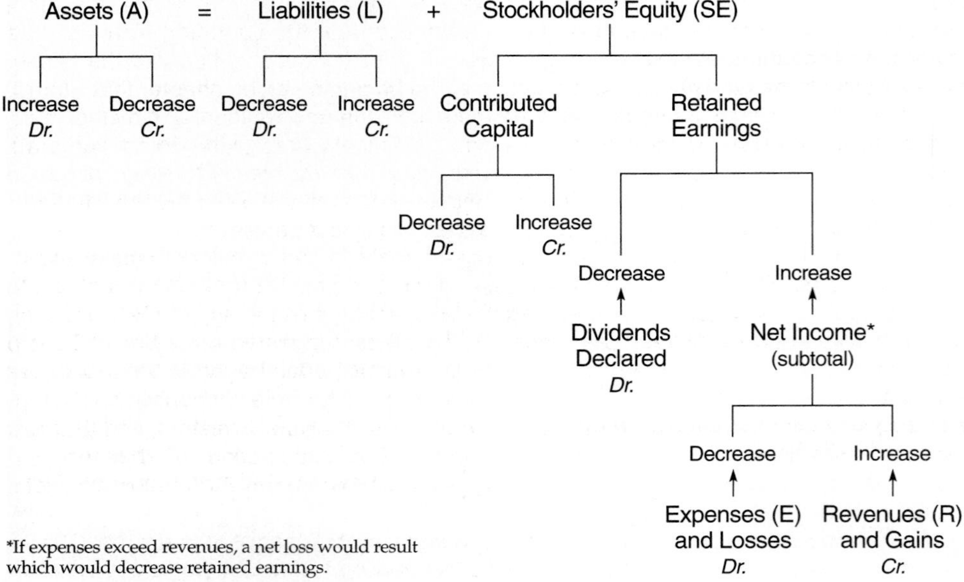

*If expenses exceed revenues, a net loss would result which would decrease retained earnings.

In constructing this complete model, we maintained the direction rule and debit-credit framework described in Chapter 2:

- For direction, the word *Increase* is written on the left when we are on the left side of the equation and the word *Increase* is written on the right when we are on the right side of the equation at each level.
- Debits are written on the left side of each element and credits are written on the right. However, we have used abbreviations. *Debit* becomes *Dr.* and *credit* becomes *Cr.* These abbreviations are often used when writing journal entries.

Retained Earnings increases by the net income of the period when income is positive and decreases when a net loss is reported. Retained Earnings also decreases when dividends are declared as a distribution of the earnings to shareholders. As we will illustrate below, the title Dividends Declared is the name of the account used by many companies when their boards of directors authorize a dividend distribution. However, net income is not an account name, but is a subtotal of various revenues, expenses, gains, and losses.

Before we illustrate the use of the transaction analysis model for these new elements, it is important to emphasize the following. The word *increase* is written above revenues because these accounts increase retained earnings. The word *decrease* is written above expenses and dividends declared because these accounts decrease retained earnings. However, since retained earnings is on the right side of the equation, to increase an expense and thus decrease net income, the expense account needs to be debited, as does dividends declared. Therefore, *revenues normally have credit balances, and expenses and dividends declared normally have debit balances.* A company that has revenues exceeding expenses will report positive net income. However, if expenses exceed revenues, the company will report a net loss.

FINANCIAL ANALYSIS

The Feedback Value of Accounting Information

A net loss does not have to occur for a company to recognize that it is experiencing difficulty. Any unexpected variance in actual performance from the operating plan, such as lower than expected quarterly earnings, should trigger an investigation into the cause. Recall from the management decision setting at the beginning of the chapter that Sbarro, Inc., made the decision to hire outside managers to fill the new regional and district manager positions. However, many of these outsiders soon tried to change the Sbarro corporate culture. Morale among the restaurant managers sagged and company earnings began to fall below expectations. Sbarro was not meeting its stated mission of "...maintaining profitability through the pride and commitment to excellence by our people."

Accounting information is used by stock market analysts and investors to make investment decisions. These buy-and-sell decisions affect the price of a company's stock. In Sbarro's case, the stock price reached a high of $50 per share by the end of 1991. However, during the first quarter of 1992, as reports in the press suggested problems at Sbarro restaurants due primarily to the hiring decision, the stock price began to fall to $38 per share by early May. When Sbarro's actual first quarter earnings were announced on May 12, the stock price fell 11 points to $27 per share in one day. Analysts, investors, and Sbarro's management noticed the marked decline in earnings from expectations. *Forbes* reported that "in the first quarter of 1992 the company's earnings came in 33% below analysts' expectations."[4]

This is a clear example of how corporate decisions affect financial data and how the information is used by internal and external users. Accounting information has a pervasive effect on all forms of corporate decision making, as well as on the economic decisions made by investors and creditors.

Transaction Analysis Rules

As discussed in Chapter 2, (1) every transaction affects at least two accounts (the duality rule), and (2) the accounting equation must remain in balance after each transaction (the equality rule). Since revenues are defined as inflows of net assets, then by definition to record a revenue (a credit), an asset or liability is usually debited. In like manner, when recording an expense (a debit), an asset or liability is usually credited. Revenues and expenses normally are not recorded in the same journal entry.

Revenue and Expense Recognition Entries

Under accrual accounting, revenues should be recorded when earned and expenses should be recorded when incurred. However, many students find this concept difficult to apply because the cash receipt or payment date does not necessarily coincide with the revenue or expense recognition date. To help you understand the timing of revenue and expense recognition, we will discuss four basic types of entries and illustrate these first with a simple fictitious company and then with Sbarro, Inc. The four types of revenue and expense recognition entries are:

1. Cash receipt or payment coinciding with revenue or expense recognition.
2. Promise to pay coinciding with revenue or expense recognition.

[4] R. La Franco, "Promote from within," *Forbes*, February 28, 1994, pp.86–87.

3. Cash receipt or payment occurring after revenue and expense recognition (accruals).
4. Cash receipt or payment occurring before revenue and expense recognition (deferrals).

Assume that Al's Auto Repair Shop provides (1) repair and maintenance service for individual customers who pay cash on the date of service and (2) routine repairs and maintenance of taxis under a contract with a taxi cab company which is billed at the end of the month for the month's repairs. We will use R for revenue and E for expense to identify the type of account used in each entry.

Cash Coincides with Recognition

The clearest income recognition transactions are when the cash receipt *coincides* with the completion of the earnings process or cash payment *coincides* with the expense matching process. This type of transaction is represented in the following timeline:

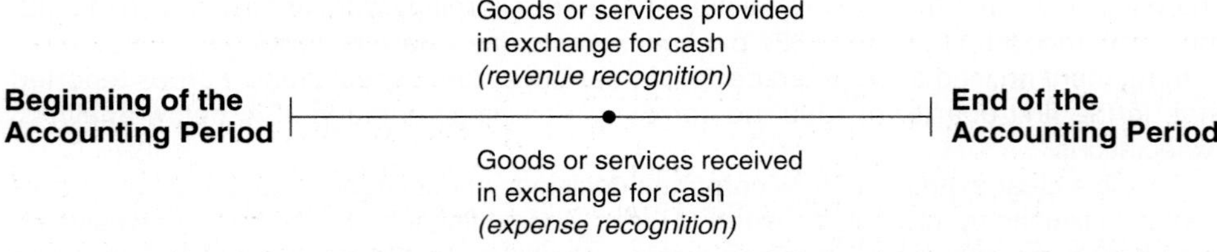

Transaction	Journal Entry		
On March 5, a customer brings in her car for minor repairs. She picks up her car the same day and pays the auto repair shop $75.		**Debit**	**Credit**
	Cash (A)	75	
	Repair service revenue (R)		75

Cash is received and revenue is earned on the same day. Assets on the left side of the accounting equation increase by $75 and revenues on the right side of the accounting equation increase by $75. Debits equal credits; the accounting equation is in balance. No adjustment will be necessary at the end of the period because revenue has been properly recorded in full in the current period when earned.

Transaction	Journal Entry		
On March 7, a local heating company made a service call to Al's Auto Repair Shop to fix a broken furnace. Al, the owner, wrote a check that day for $160 to pay for the furnace repairs.		**Debit**	**Credit**
	Furnace repairs expense (E)	160	
	Cash (A)		160

An expense for the service received is incurred and cash is paid on the same day. Expenses on the right side of the accounting equation increase by $160 and assets on the left side of the accounting equation decrease by $160. Debits equal credits; the accounting equation is in balance. No adjustment will be necessary at the end of the period because expense has been properly recorded in full in the current period when incurred.

Promise to Pay Coincides with Recognition

Revenue and expense are also recorded when a promise to pay is received from the customer at the completion or near completion of the earnings process or at the completion of the expense matching process. A second transaction to record cash received or paid is made *after* the revenue or expense recognition entry. These transactions are represented in the following timeline:

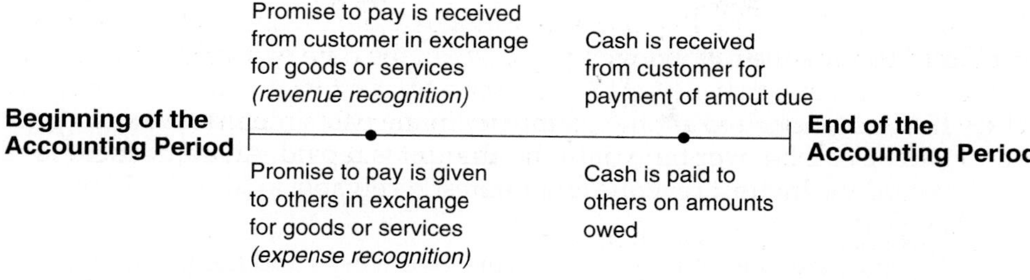

Transaction	Journal Entry		
A taxi cab was repaired on March 14 for $620. The amount will be added to the cab company's bill.		**Debit**	**Credit**
	Accounts receivable (A)	620	
	Repair service revenue (R)		620

A receivable is recorded and revenue is recognized on the date of service. Receivables on the left side of the accounting equation increase by $620 and revenue on the right side of the accounting equation increases by $620. Debits equal credits; the accounting equation is in balance. No adjustment will be necessary at the end of the period because revenue has been properly recorded in full in the current period. A second transaction when the cab company pays its bill will be recorded at a later date (debit Cash (A), $620, and credit Accounts Receivable (A), $620).

Transaction	Journal Entry		
Al uses the local copy center to design and print coupons for a discount on an oil change. The copy center will bill Al for the cost of $32.		**Debit**	**Credit**
	Printing expense (E)	32	
	Accounts payable (L)		32

The expense is incurred for the service received from the copy center in exchange for Al's promise to pay. Expenses on the right side of the accounting equation increase by $32 and liabilities on the right side of the accounting equation increase by $32. Debits equal credits; the accounting equation is in balance. No adjustment will be necessary at the end of the period because expense has been properly recorded in full in the current period when incurred. A second transaction for the payment of cash will be recorded at a later date (debit Accounts Payable (L), $32, and credit Cash (A), $32).

The third and fourth types of revenue and expense recognition transactions involve evaluating a past business activity or transaction to determine if the *passage of time* results in earning revenues or incurring expenses. If so, adjusting entries are needed at the end of the accounting period to reflect the proper amount of revenue or expense in the current period. However, the two types differ based on when cash is received or paid.

Accruals

If cash will be received or paid *after* the end of the accounting period for revenues or expenses that have been earned or incurred but not recorded during the accounting period, an adjusting entry is necessary. This third type of transaction is known as an *accrual*.

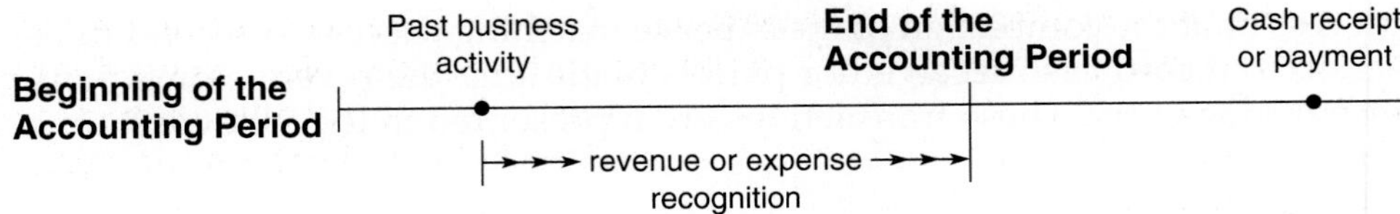

Examples include the following:

- If Al lent money to another company in the past, interest revenue will be earned over time until the amount is repaid. An adjustment to record the interest revenue and interest receivable in March will be needed.
- If wages are paid to employees every two weeks and the next pay period covers one week in March and one week in April, the March amount will need to be recorded in March as wages expense and wages payable.

The process for computing and recording adjusting entries for accruals will be discussed in Chapter 4.

Deferrals

If cash is received or paid *before* completion of the revenue recognition process or expense matching process, the related revenues may have been earned or expenses incurred by the end of the accounting period. If so, an adjusting entry is necessary to record revenues and expenses in the proper period. The original entry creates an asset or liability account that is known as a *deferral.* Usually liabilities (unearned revenues) and assets (prepaid expenses, supplies, and long-lived assets used in operations) are recorded when cash is received or paid.

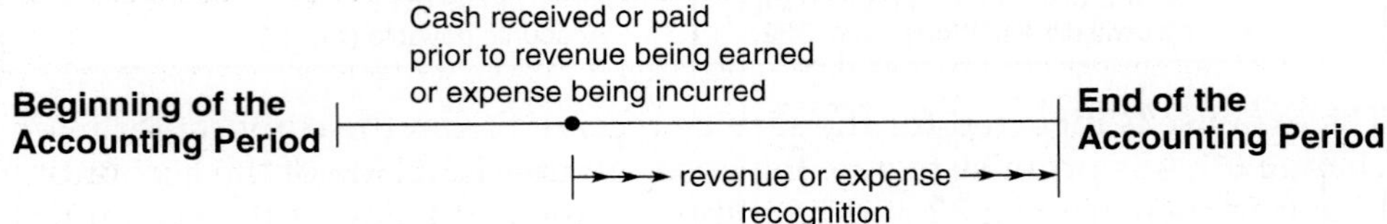

Examples include the following:

- If the auto repair shop purchases a three-year insurance policy (an increase in the asset Prepaid Insurance), by the end of the accounting period a portion of the insurance has been used up (an increase in Insurance Expense and a decrease in Prepaid Insurance).
- If a customer gives Al money to store and maintain a car while the customer is out of the country for a year (an increase in the liability Unearned Service Revenue), by the end of the accounting period a portion of the revenue has been earned (an increase in Service Revenue and a decrease in Unearned Service Revenue).

The process for computing and recording adjusting entries for deferrals will be discussed in Chapter 4.

In summary, the first two types of transactions result in revenues and expenses being recorded *during* the accounting period (Phase 1 of the accounting cycle). The last two types of transactions, accruals and deferrals, result in revenues and expenses being recorded *at the end* of the accounting period through adjusting entries (Phase 2 of the accounting cycle). Now, as we did in Chapter 2, we will present an illustration of the transaction analysis steps you should follow to record the effects of transactions in journal entries and determine account balances by using T-accounts.

TRANSACTION ANALYSIS ILLUSTRATED

We will follow the same process used in Chapter 2 to examine the effects of typical simplified income related transactions of Sbarro, Inc. You will recall that transaction analysis requires identifying the two or more accounts affected, determining the direction and amount of the effect, and maintaining the accounting model's equality. Based on the analysis, a journal entry can be prepared (verifying that debits equal credits) and amounts can be posted to the appropriate T-accounts. In this illustration, we will also identify entries or business activities that will require an adjusting entry at the end of the period.

As we emphasized in Chapter 2, refer to the transaction analysis model until you can construct it on your own without assistance. You should also study this illustration carefully to make sure that you understand the impact of operating activities on the balance sheet and income statement. We will begin with Sbarro's January 30, 1994, balance sheet constructed at the end of Chapter 2, which included the effects of the typical investing and financing transactions illustrated in that chapter but ignored any operating activities for the month. We will use the account titles listed in that balance sheet and those shown on the income statement in Exhibit 3–2 as we analyze operating activities and additional financing and investing activities. All amounts are in thousands of dollars.

(A) During the first half of January, Sbarro's company-owned restaurants sold food to customers for $12,000 in cash.

Transaction Analysis	Journal Entry
Cash increases by $12,000. Cash is an asset; to increase an asset, debit the account. Restaurant Sales Revenue increases by $12,000. Restaurant Sales Revenue is a revenue which increases retained earnings; to increase a revenue, credit the account.	**Transaction (A)** — **Debit** / **Credit** Cash (A) — 12,000 Restaurant sales revenue (R) — 12,000
Is the Accounting Equation in Balance?	Debits = Credits
Assets on the left side of the equation increase by $12,000; stockholders' equity through retained earnings on the right side increases by $12,000. The equation is in balance.	These effects were posted to the appropriate T-accounts at the end of the illustration.
Will an Adjusting Entry Be Necessary at Month-End?	
Since the recognition of revenue coincides with the cash receipt date and the revenue is properly recorded in the correct period, no adjusting entry will be necessary.	

(B) Sbarro is entitled to royalties from franchisees based on a percentage of their weekly revenues. Near the end of January, franchisees reported that they owe Sbarro $500 based on the first three weeks of January's revenues. They will pay the royalties in early February.

Transaction Analysis	Journal Entry
Receivables increases by $500. Receivables is an asset account; to increase an asset, debit the account. Franchise Related Income increases by $500. Franchise Related Income is a revenue; to increase a revenue which increases retained earnings, credit the account.	**Transaction (B)** **Debit** **Credit** Receivables (A) 500 Franchise related income (R)[5] 500
Is the Accounting Equation in Balance?	Debits = Credits
Assets on the left side of the equation increase by $500; stockholders' equity through retained earnings on the right side increases by $500. The equation is in balance.	These effects were posted to the appropriate T-accounts at the end of the illustration.
Will an Adjusting Entry Be Necessary at Month-End?	
Since the date of recognition of revenue coincides with the receipt of the promise to pay and the revenue is properly recorded in the correct period, no adjusting entry is necessary. However, there is one more week of January revenue which is not yet recorded. An adjusting entry for the final week's revenue accrual will be necessary at the end of the month.	

(C) A mall department store paid Sbarro a $30 deposit in January in exchange for Sbarro's promise to provide food for an employee party in February.

Transaction Analysis	Journal Entry
Cash increases by $30. Cash is an asset; to increase an asset; debit the account. Deferred Income (also known as *unearned* or *deferred revenue*) increases by $30. Deferred Income is a liability; to increase a liability, credit the account.	**Transaction (C)** **Debit** **Credit** Cash (A) 30 Deferred income (L) 30
Is the Accounting Equation in Balance?	Debits = Credits
Assets on the left side of the equation increase by $30; stockholders' equity through retained earnings on the right side increases by $30. The equation is in balance.	These effects were posted to the appropriate T-accounts at the end of the illustration.
Will an Adjusting Entry Be Necessary at Month-End?	
The Deferred Income account postpones revenue recognition until revenue is earned. Since the earnings process will not be complete until February, no adjusting entry will be necessary in January. Revenues have been properly deferred until the following month.	

[5]Franchise Related Income is the revenue account title used by Sbarro. The word *income* is often used in subtotals, though here it refers to a revenue account.

(D) Several ovens in company-owned restaurants were repaired in January. Bills for $50 were received and paid by Sbarro in January.

Transaction Analysis	Journal Entry
Repair Expense (included in Occupancy and Other Expenses on the income statement) increases by $50. To increase an expense (which decreases retained earnings), debit the account. Cash decreases by $50. Cash is an asset; to decrease an asset, credit the account.	**Transaction (D)** **Debit** **Credit** Repair expense - occupancy and other (E) 50 Cash (A) 50
Is the Accounting Equation in Balance?	Debits = Credits
Assets on the left side of the equation decrease by $50; stockholders' equity through retained earnings on the right side decreases by $50. The equation is in balance.	These effects were posted to the appropriate T-accounts at the end of the illustration.
Will an Adjusting Entry Be Necessary at Month-End?	
Since the recognition of expense coincides with the cash payment date and is matched in the period the ovens are used to generate revenues, no adjusting entry will be necessary. The expense is properly recorded in the correct month.	

(E) Bills totaling $60 were received in late January from electric and gas companies for utility usage by Sbarro company-owned restaurants for the first half of January. The bills were paid in January when received.

Transaction Analysis	Journal Entry
Utilities Expense (included in Occupancy and Other Expenses on the income statement) increases by $60. To increase an expense (which decreases retained earnings), debit the account. Cash decreases by $60. Cash is an asset; to decrease an asset, credit the account.	**Transaction (E)** **Debit** **Credit** Utilities expense - occupancy and other (E) 60 Cash (A) 60
Is the Accounting Equation in Balance?	Debits = Credits
Assets on the left side of the equation decrease by $60; stockholders' equity through retained earnings on the right side decreases by $60. The equation is in balance.	These effects were posted to the appropriate T-accounts at the end of the illustration.
Will an Adjusting Entry Be Necessary at Month-End?	
Since the recognition of expense coincides with the cash payment date and the expense is properly recorded in the correct period, no adjusting entry will be necessary. However, there are two more weeks of utility usage that are not recorded and will require an adjusting entry for the expense accrual at the end of the month.	

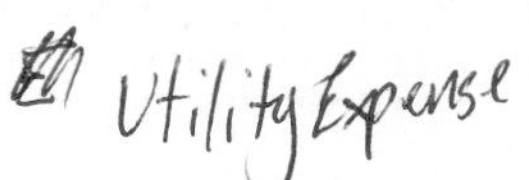

(F) At the beginning of January, Sbarro paid $12,600 to mall owners to rent mall space in January, February, and March.

Transaction Analysis	Journal Entry
Since the rent is for future periods, Prepaid Expenses for rent increases by $12,600. Prepaid Expenses is an asset; to increase an asset, debit the account. Cash decreases by $12,600. Cash is an asset; to decrease an asset, credit the account.	**Transaction (F)** — **Debit** / **Credit** Prepaid expenses (A) — 12,600 Cash (A) — 12,600
Is the Accounting Equation in Balance?	**Debits = Credits**
Assets on the left side of the equation decrease and increase by $12,600. The equation is in balance.	These effects were posted to the appropriate T-accounts at the end of the illustration.
Will an Adjusting Entry Be Necessary at Month-End?	
The Prepaid Expense account is a deferral representing a right to use mall space in the future. As each day passes, the company uses mall space. Therefore, an adjusting entry will be necessary to recognize January rent expense.	

(G) Sbarro paid $2,800 in wages to employees for working the first two weeks of the month.

Transaction Analysis	Journal Entry
Wages Expense (included in Payroll and Other Employee Benefits on the income statement) increases by $2,800. To increase an expense (which decreases retained earnings), debit the account. Cash decreases by $2,800. Cash is an asset; to decrease an asset, credit the account.	**Transaction (G)** — **Debit** / **Credit** Wages expense - payroll and other (E) — 2,800 Cash (A) — 2,800
Is the Accounting Equation in Balance?	**Debits = Credits**
Assets on the left side of the equation decrease by $2,800; stockholders' equity through retained earnings on the right side decreases by $2,800. The equation is in balance.	These effects were posted to the appropriate T-accounts at the end of the illustration.
Will an Adjusting Entry Be Necessary at Month-End?	
Since the expense has been properly recorded in the correct period, no adjusting entry will be necessary. The employees have worked; the expense is incurred. However, there are two more weeks in January that have not been recorded and an adjusting entry may be needed for the remaining wage expense accrual.	

(H) In January, Sbarro purchased $120 of paper products from suppliers. Sbarro paid $80 in cash and the rest was on account.

Transaction Analysis	Journal Entry
Inventory of food and paper supplies increases by $120. Inventory is an asset; to increase an asset, debit the account. Cash decreases by $80. Cash is an asset; to decrease an asset, credit the account. Accounts Payable increases by $40. Accounts Payable is a liability; to increase a liability, credit the account.	**Transaction (H)** — **Debit** / **Credit** Inventory (A) — 120 Cash (A) — 80 Accounts payable (L) — 40
Is the Accounting Equation in Balance?	**Debits = Credits**
Assets on the left side of the equation increase by $40 ($120 – $80); liabilities on the right side increase by $40. The equation is in balance.	The effects of this compound entry were posted to the appropriate T-accounts at the end of the illustration.
Will an Adjusting Entry Be Necessary at Month-End?	
As the inventory is used over time in generating revenues, the cost of the used up inventory will need to be matched with revenues in the proper period. An adjusting entry will need to be made at the end of the month for the cost of the used inventory.	

(I) In January, Sbarro's board of directors declared a $2,000 cash dividend to be paid to stockholders in March. Dividends are a return of assets to owners (a share in profits). Often, as in this Sbarro example, there is a delay between the decision to return assets to the owners and the actual writing of the checks. Therefore, this entry increases the account Dividends Declared, which reduces Retained Earnings (the account in which profits are accumulated), and increases the liability, Dividends Payable.

Transaction Analysis	Journal Entry
Dividends Declared increases by $2,000. To increase Dividends Declared (which decreases retained earnings), debit the account. Dividends Payable increases by $2,000. Dividends Payable is a liability; to increase a liability, credit the account.	**Transaction (I)** — **Debit** / **Credit** Dividends declared (reduces RE) — 2,000 Dividends payable (L) — 2,000
Is the Accounting Equation in Balance?	**Debits = Credits**
Liabilities on the right side of the equation increase by $2,000; stockholders' equity through retained earnings on the right side decreases by $2,000. The equation is in balance.	These effects were posted to the appropriate T-accounts at the end of the illustration.
Will an Adjusting Entry Be Necessary at Month-End?	
Declaring dividends is a financing decision, not an operating activity. No revenue or expense recognition is involved; therefore, no adjusting entry will be needed.	

(J) Sbarro's company-owned restaurants received $2,100 in fresh fruits and vegetables from local grocers who bill Sbarro for the delivered goods. These food products are used immediately.

Transaction Analysis	Journal Entry
Cost of Food and Paper Products increases by $2,100. Cost of Food and Paper Products is an expense; to increase an expense (which decreases retained earnings), debit the account. Accounts Payable increases by $2,100. Accounts Payable is a liability; to increase a liability, credit the account.	**Transaction (J)** **Debit** **Credit** Cost of food and paper products (E) 2,100 Accounts payable (L) 2,100
Is the Accounting Equation in Balance?	Debits = Credits
Liabilities on the right side of the equation increase by $2,100; stockholders' equity through retained earnings on the right side decreases by $2,100. The equation is in balance.	These effects were posted to the appropriate T-accounts at the end of the illustration.
Will an Adjusting Entry Be Necessary at Month-End?	
Since the food will be used immediately in generating revenues, the expense (cost of food and paper products) is properly recorded in the correct period. The company's promise to pay coincides with the expense recognition. No adjusting entry will be necessary.	

(K) In January, Sbarro paid the $4,600 income taxes due to the federal, state, and foreign governments as reported on the January 2, 1994, balance sheet.

Transaction Analysis	Journal Entry
Income Taxes Payable decreases by $4,600. Income Taxes Payable is a liability; to decrease a liability, debit the account. Cash decreases by $4,600. Cash is an asset; to decrease an asset, credit the account.	**Transaction (K)** **Debit** **Credit** Income taxes payable (L) 4,600 Cash (A) 4,600
Is the Accounting Equation in Balance?	Debits = Credits
Assets on the left side of the equation decrease by $4,600; liabilities on the right side decrease by $4,600. The equation is in balance.	These effects were posted to the appropriate T-accounts at the end of the illustration.
Will an Adjusting Entry Be Necessary at Month-End?	
The income taxes payable was created by the prior month's adjusting entry to record income tax expense in December. The expense was properly recorded in December. An adjusting entry to accrue the income tax expense for January will need to be made at the end of the month.	

Self-Study Quiz

For transactions (L) through (O), fill in the missing information. Be sure to post journal entries to the T-accounts at the end of the illustration. When completed, you can check your answers with the solution at the end of the illustration:

(L) In the second half of January, Sbarro sold food to customers for $11,800 in cash.

Transaction Analysis	Journal Entry
	Transaction (L) **Debit** **Credit** Cash (A) 11,800 Restaurant sales revenue (R) 11,800
Is the Accounting Equation in Balance?	Debits = Credits
Assets on the left side of the equation increase by $11,800; stockholders' equity through retained earnings on the right side increases by $11,800. The equation is in balance.	
Will an Adjusting Entry Be Necessary at Month-End?	
Since the recognition of revenue coincides with the cash receipt date, the revenue is properly recorded in the correct period. No adjusting entry will be necessary.	

(M) Sbarro paid $2,500 in cash as wages to employees who worked the second two weeks of January.

Transaction Analysis	Journal Entry
Wages Expense increases by $2,500. To increase an expense (which decreases retained earnings), debit the account. Cash decreases by $2,500. Cash is an asset; to decrease an asset, credit the account.	**Transaction (M)** **Debit** **Credit** Wages (E) 2500 Cash (A) 2500
Is the Accounting Equation in Balance?	Debits = Credits
	These effects were posted to the appropriate T-accounts at the end of the illustration.
Will an Adjusting Entry Be Necessary at Month-End?	
Transactions (G) and (M) result in four weeks of wages expense being recorded in January. An adjusting entry may be necessary at the end of the month to accrue additional expense if there are any more days worked by employees during January that are not paid until February.	

(N) Near the end of January, Sbarro purchased insurance for $600 cash to cover potential property loss in February through July.

Transaction Analysis	Journal Entry		
	Transaction (N) Insurance (E) Cash (A)	**Debit** 600	**Credit** 600
Is the Accounting Equation in Balance?	Debits = Credits		
Assets on the left side of the equation increase and decrease by $600. The equation is in balance.	These effects were posted to the appropriate T-accounts at the end of the illustration.		
Will an Adjusting Entry Be Necessary at Month-End?			

(O) In late January, Sbarro received bills totaling $130 from the telephone companies servicing the company-owned restaurants in January. Sbarro will pay the bills during the first week of February.

Transaction Analysis	Journal Entry		
Utilities Expense (included in Occupancy and Other Expenses on the income statement) increases by $130. To increase an expense (which decreases retained earnings), debit the account. Accounts Payable increases by $130. Accounts Payable is a liability; to increase a liability, credit the account.	**Transaction (O)** Utilities expense - occupancy and other (E) Accounts payable (L)	**Debit** 130	**Credit** 130
Is the Accounting Equation in Balance?	Debits = Credits		
Will an Adjusting Entry Be Necessary at Month-End?			

T-Accounts

In the T-accounts, the asterisk (*) indicates the balance in the account at January 30 (the Sunday closest to the end of the month) after the investing and financing transactions in Chapter 2. The transactions in January from this chapter are referenced (A) through (O).

ASSETS

Cash

	Debit (Inc.)		Credit (Dec.)
*	33,740	(D)	50
(A)	12,000	(E)	60
(C)	30	(F)	12,600
(L)		(G)	2,800
		(H)	80
		(K)	4,600
		(M)	2,500
		(N)	600
End. Bal.	34,280		

Marketable Securities

	Debit (Inc.)		Credit (Dec.)
*	37,200		
End. Bal.	37,200		

Receivables

	Debit (Inc.)		Credit (Dec.)
*	1,300		
(B)	500		
End. Bal.	1,800		

Inventory

	Debit (Inc.)		Credit (Dec.)
*	2,870		
(H)	120		
End. Bal.	2,990		

Prepaid Expenses

	Debit (Inc.)		Credit (Dec.)
*	1,500		
(F)	12,600		
(N)	600		
End. Bal.	14,700		

Property and Equipment

	Debit (Inc.)		Credit (Dec.)
*	129,550		
End. Bal.	129,550		

Other Assets

	Debit (Inc.)		Credit (Dec.)
*	3,200		
End. Bal.	3,200		

LIABILITIES

Notes Payable

	Debit (Dec.)		Credit (Inc.)
		*	1,200
		End. Bal.	1,200

Accounts Payable

	Debit (Dec.)		Credit (Inc.)
		*	4,760
		(H)	40
		(J)	2,100
		(O)	
		End. Bal.	7,030

Accrued Expenses Payable

	Debit (Dec.)		Credit (Inc.)
		*	18,400
		End. Bal.	18,400

Dividends Payable

	Debit (Dec.)		Credit (Inc.)
		*	2,700
		(I)	2,000
		End. Bal.	4,700

Income Taxes Payable

	Debit (Dec.)		Credit (Inc.)
(K)	4,600	*	4,600
		End. Bal.	0

Deferred Income

	Debit (Dec.)		Credit (Inc.)
		*	400
		(C)	30
		End. Bal.	430

Deferred Income Taxes

	Debit (Dec.)		Credit (Inc.)
		*	18,100
		End. Bal.	18,100

STOCKHOLDERS' EQUITY

Contributed Capital

	Debit (Dec.)		Credit (Inc.)
		*	29,900
		End. Bal.	29,900

Retained Earnings

	Debit (Dec.)		Credit (Inc.)
		*	129,300
		End. Bal.	?

DIVIDENDS

Dividends Declared

	Debit (Inc.)		Credit (Dec.)
*	0		
(I)	2,000		
End. Bal.	2,000		

EXPENSES

Cost of Food and Paper Products

	Debit (Inc.)		Credit (Dec.)
*	0		
(J)	2,100		
End. Bal.	2,100		

Wages Expense

	Debit (Inc.)		Credit (Dec.)
*	0		
(G)	2,800		
(M)	2,500		
End. Bal.	5,300		

Utilities Expense

	Debit (Inc.)		Credit (Dec.)
*	0		
(E)	60		
(O)			
End. Bal.	190		

Repair Expense

	Debit (Inc.)		Credit (Dec.)
*	0		
(D)	50		
End. Bal.	50		

REVENUES

Restaurant Sales Revenue

	Debit (Dec.)		Credit (Inc.)
		*	0
		(A)	12,000
		(L)	
		End. Bal.	23,800

Franchise Related Income

	Debit (Dec.)		Credit (Inc.)
		*	0
		(B)	500
		End. Bal.	500

In Chapter 4, we will discuss the process for updating the Retained Earnings account to reflect the effects of revenues, expenses, and dividends declared. However, we can calculate the ending Retained Earnings balance from the information in the T-accounts:

Ending retained earnings	=	Beginning retained earnings	+	Net income	– Dividends declared
Ending retained earnings	=	Beginning retained earnings	+	(Revenues – Expenses)	– Dividends declared
Ending retained earnings	=	$129,300	+	(24,300 – 7,640)	– 2,000
Ending retained earnings	=	$143,960			

You may check your answers with the solutions at the bottom of the page.*

INCOME STATEMENT PREPARATION

Learning Objective 7
Prepare a simple income statement.

Based on the January transactions that have been posted in the T-accounts, we can prepare an income statement reflecting operating activities in January. However, the statement is called *unadjusted* because no adjusting entries have been recorded. Therefore, the revenue and expense accounts are not up-to-date. For example, many large expenses are not yet included, especially the cost of food and paper products used in January and depreciation on equipment used during the month. You will also notice that we have not calculated income taxes. Because this statement is unadjusted, the amount of taxes due is not yet determinable. These statements do not at this point reflect generally accepted accounting principles based on accrual accounting. We will adjust the accounts and prepare complete statements in Chapter 4.

*(L) Transaction Analysis: Cash increases by $11,800. Cash is an asset; to increase an asset, debit the account. Restaurant Sales Revenue increases by $11,800. To increase a revenue (which increases retained earnings), credit the account.

Debits = Credits: Post each line to the appropriate T-account.

(M) Journal Entry: Wages expense—payroll and other (E) 2,500
Cash (A) 2,500

Is the Accounting Equation in Balance? Assets on the left side of the equation decrease by $2,500; stockholders' equity through retained earnings on the right side decreases by $2,500. The equation is in balance.

(N) Transaction Analysis: Prepaid Expense for insurance increases by $600. Prepaid Expense is an asset; to increase an asset, debit the account. Cash decreases by $600. Cash is an asset; to decrease an asset, credit the account.

Journal Entry: Prepaid expense (A) 600
Cash (A) 600

Will an Adjusting Entry Be Necessary at Month-End? The Prepaid Expense account represents a deferral of expense until used. Since the insurance does not cover January, no adjusting entry is needed.

(O) Is the Accounting Equation in Balance? Liabilities on the right side of the equation increase by $130; stockholders' equity through retained earnings on the right side of the equation decreases by $130. The equation remains in balance.

Debits = Credits: Post each line to the appropriate T-account.

Will an Adjusting Entry Be Necessary at Month-End? Since the expense is properly recorded in January as incurred and the promise to pay coincides with expense recognition, no adjusting entry is necessary.

SBARRO, INC. AND SUBSIDIARIES
Statement of Income (unadjusted)
For the Period Ended January 30, 1994
(in thousands of dollars)

Revenues:			
Restaurant sales		$23,800	
Franchise related income		500	
Total revenues			$24,300
Costs and expenses:			
Cost of food and paper products		2,100	
Restaurant operating expenses:			
Payroll and other employee benefits (wages)	$5,300		
Occupancy and other expenses (utilities and repairs)	240	5,540	
Total costs and expenses			7,640
Net Income			$16,660

AN INTERNATIONAL PERSPECTIVE

Reporting Financial Information by Geographic Segments

Many companies, especially very large companies, operate in multiple geographic segments. These types of companies are often called *multinationals.* The simple income statement presented above based on aggregated data may not prove as useful to investors seeking to assess possible risks and returns from companies operating in foreign markets. Therefore, additional summary information about geographic segments is provided in footnotes to the financial statements. For example, an excerpt from a recent annual report of General Motors Corporation follows:

Real World Excerpt

General Motors Corporation Annual Report

NOTE 19. Segment Reporting
Geographic Segments

Net Sales and Revenues *(Dollars in millions)*	United States	Other North America	Europe	Latin America	All Other	Total
1993	99,573.2	8,203.5	24,140.1	4,838.8	1,463.9	138,219.5
1992	90,243.5	8,550.2	28,437.2	3,461.9	1,549.4	132,242.2
1991	84,025.7	9,414.7	25,027.9	2,679.9	1,960.6	123,108.8

In addition, they report net income, total assets, net assets, and the average number of employees for the same segments. For companies operating in multiple industries, summary financial information is also provided by major industrial segment. For General Motors, the major segments are automotive products, financing and insurance operations, and other products.

Returning to our Sbarro illustration, we can also prepare a revised unadjusted balance sheet that incorporates the effects of the operating activities discussed here. Again, the balance sheet reflects all investing, financing, and operating transactions as of January 30 (Sbarro's month-end). However, it is called unadjusted because no adjusting entries have been recorded. Notice the balance in Retained Earnings is now the sum of its beginning balance ($129,300) plus the partial net income ($16,660) minus Dividends Declared ($2,000). Revenue, expense, and dividend amounts are not included on the balance sheet directly, but are summarized in Retained Earnings. We will explore the relationships among each of the financial statements in the next chapter.

SBARRO, INC. AND SUBSIDIARIES
Balance Sheet (unadjusted)
at January 30, 1994
(in thousands of dollars)

Assets	
Cash	$ 34,280
Marketable securities	37,200
Receivables (franchise fees and other)	1,800
Inventory	2,990
Prepaid expenses	14,700
Property and equipment	129,550
Other assets	3,200
Total assets	**$223,720**
Liabilities	
Notes payable	$ 1,200
Accounts payable	7,030
Accrued expenses payable (rent, payroll, and other)	18,400
Dividends payable	4,700
Income taxes payable	0
Deferred income	430
Deferred income taxes	18,100
Total liabilities	$ 49,860
Stockholders' Equity	
Contributed Capital	$ 29,900
Retained earnings	143,960
Total stockholders' equity	173,860
Total liabilities and stockholders' equity	**$223,720**

EPILOGUE

We noted earlier that Sbarro saw dramatic drops in earnings compared to expectations after hiring outside managers. According to *Forbes*, "Fortunately, the brothers had seen and corrected their mistake before it could do irreparable damage."[6] In the Spring of 1992, they fired 14 of the 20 new managers and promoted long-term Sbarro employees to the regional and district managerial positions, people who knew the products and had the entrepreneurial talent to "...operate their restaurants with the Sbarro passion for guest satisfaction and maximum profit" (from the mission statement). Within six months, sales and earnings were again meeting growth expectations and the stock price rose to more normal levels.

FINANCIAL ANALYSIS

Company Wins Workers' Loyalty by Opening Its Books

We saw throughout the chapter how Sbarro came to realize the tremendous value of a loyal workforce in reaching corporate goals. A growing number of companies are developing innovative programs to build employee loyalty and improve their financial performance. One such pioneering human resource development effort is occurring at Springfield ReManufacturing Corporation (SRC), an engine rebuilder in Missouri.

Until 1983, the company, then a division of International Harvester, was considered poorly managed with deep worker distrust. Thirteen managers, who recognized that employees were a key to improved plant operations, purchased the division. They immediately instituted several employee incentives, including an employee stock ownership plan and expanded

[6] R. La Franco, "Promote from within," *Forbes*, February 28, 1994, pp. 86–87.

bonus program. Even more radical was the decision to distribute on a weekly basis *all* company financial information to the employees and to help them learn how to evaluate the information. As noted in *The Wall Street Journal*, "SRC employees, who also own 31% of the company, clearly have responded positively to this strategy, known as 'open-book management.'" In part due to this disclosure policy, SRC escaped ruin and is reporting record growth. According to company officials, "the more (employees) learned, the more they could do. We matched up higher levels of thinking with higher levels of performance." In addition, "every employee knows that if the value of the company increases, so does the value of their shares." Loyalty among the employees to the company is markedly strong. *The Wall Street Journal* reported that, "while SRC workers obviously value their big stock holding, they maintain that *it's even more important to understand the company's numbers* (emphasis added)."

SOURCE: T. L. O'Brien, *The Wall Street Journal*, December 20, 1993, pp. B1–2.

DEMONSTRATION CASE

This case is a continuation of the Terrific Lawn Maintenance Corporation originally introduced in Chapter 2. The company was established with supplies, property, and equipment purchased ready for business. The balance sheet at April 30, 1995, based on investing and financing activities is as follows:

TERRIFIC LAWN MAINTENANCE CORPORATION
Balance Sheet
At April 30, 1995

Assets		**Liabilities**	
Cash	$ 4,350	Accounts Payable	$ 3,700
Lawn Equipment	4,600	Total Liabilities	$ 3,700
Land	3,750		
		Stockholders' Equity	
		Contributed Capital	$ 9,000
Total Assets	$12,700	Total Liabilities and Stockholders' Equity	$12,700

The following completed activities occurred during April, 1995:

a. Purchased gasoline for mowers and edgers for $90 in cash at a local gas station. Terrific Lawn also established an account with the gas station owner to purchase gas in the future on account to be billed and paid monthly. Gasoline is used very quickly.

b. In early April, the city paid Terrific Lawn $1,600 cash in advance for lawn maintenance service for April through July, $400 each month.

c. Mowed lawns for residential customers who are billed every two weeks. A total of $5,200 of service was billed in April.

d. Residential customers paid $3,500 on their accounts.

e. Paid the balance due of $3,700 on account to XYZ Lawn Supply, Inc., and the hardware store.

f. Paid wages every two weeks. Total cash paid in April was $3,900.

g. Purchased and used additional gasoline of $320 on account in April.

h. In early April, purchased insurance costing $300 covering six months, April through September.

i. Declared a $100 dividend for each of the three owners to be paid in May ($100 × 3 = $300).

Required:

1. *a.* On a separate sheet of paper, set up T-accounts for Cash, Accounts Receivable, Lawn Equipment, Land, Prepaid Expenses, Accounts Payable, Dividends Payable, Unearned Revenue (same as deferred revenue), Contributed Capital, Retained Earnings, Mowing Service Revenue, Fuel Expense, Wages Expense, and Dividends Declared. Beginning balances for balance sheet accounts should be taken from the balance sheet presented above. Beginning balances for operating and dividends declared accounts are $0. Indicate these balances on the T-accounts.
   b. Analyze each transaction using the three steps outlined in Chapter 2 and indicate if an adjusting entry will be necessary. Please refer to the complete transaction analysis model presented in this chapter.
   c. On a separate sheet of paper, prepare journal entries in chronological order.
   d. Enter the effects on the accounting model in the appropriate T-accounts. Identify each amount with its letter given above.
   e. Compute balances in each of the T-accounts.
2. Use the amounts in the T-accounts developed in requirement 1 to prepare an unadjusted income statement and unadjusted balance sheet for Terrific Lawn Maintenance Corporation at April 30, 1995. Adjustments will be recorded in Chapter 4. To calculate the balance sheet amount for retained earnings, use the following formula:

	Beginning balance in Retained Earnings
+	Net income (revenues – expenses)
–	Dividends declared
	Ending balance in Retained Earnings

Now, you can check your answers to these requirements with the solution shown below.

SUGGESTED SOLUTION

1. Transaction analysis, journal entries, and T-accounts:

	Transaction Analysis	Journal Entry
(a)	Fuel Expense (E) increases $90 (and decreases retained earnings); debit the account. Cash (A) decreases $90; credit the account. Accounting Equation in Balance? Assets decrease by $90 and stockholders' equity through retained earnings decreases by $90. Will an Adjusting Entry Be Necessary? Since fuel is used quickly and is recorded in the proper month, no adjusting entry will be necessary.	**Debit Credit** Fuel expense (E) 90 Cash (A) 90 Debits = Credits? Yes; posted to appropriate T-accounts.
(b)	Cash (A) increases $1,600; Unearned Revenue (L) increases $1,600. Accounting Equation in Balance? Assets increase by $1,600; liabilities increase by $1,600. Will an Adjusting Entry Be Necessary? As Terrific mows lawns for the city in April, the company will earn revenue. The Unearned Revenue account is a deferral of revenue until earned. An adjusting entry will be necessary.	**Debit Credit** Cash (A) 1,600 Unearned revenue (L) 1,600 Debits = Credits? Yes; posted to appropriate T-accounts.

	Transaction Analysis	Journal Entry
(c)	Accounts Receivable (A) increases $5,200; Mowing Service Revenue (R) increases $5,200 (which increases retained earnings). Accounting Equation in Balance? Assets increase by $5,200; stockholders' equity through retained earnings increases by $5,200. Will an Adjusting Entry Be Necessary? The customers' promises to pay coincide with revenue recognition. Revenue is properly recorded in April; no adjusting entry will be necessary.	**Debit Credit** Accounts receivable (A) 5,200 Mowing service revenue (R) 5,200 Debits = Credits? Yes; posted to appropriate T-accounts.
(d)	Cash (A) increases $3,500; Accounts Receivable (A) decreases $3,500. Accounting Equation in Balance? Assets increase and decrease by the same amount. Will an Adjusting Entry Be Necessary? The revenue has already been recorded. No revenue is generated when customers pay bills. No adjusting entry will be necessary.	**Debit Credit** Cash (A) 3,500 Accounts receivable (A) 3,500 Debits = Credits? Yes; posted to appropriate T-accounts.
(e)	Accounts Payable (L) decreases $3,700; Cash (A) decreases $3,700. Accounting Equation in Balance? Assets decrease by $3,700; liabilities decrease by $3,700. Will an Adjusting Entry Be Necessary? This is a payment of an obligation. No adjusting entry is necessary.	**Debit Credit** Accounts payable (L) 3,700 Cash (A) 3,700 Debits = Credits? Yes; posted to appropriate T-accounts.
(f)	Wages Expense (E) increases $3,900 (which decreases retained earnings); Cash (A) decreases $3,900. Accounting Equation in Balance? Yes. Stockholders' equity through retained earnings decreases by $3,900; assets decrease by $3,900. Will an Adjusting Entry Be Necessary? The cash payment coincides with the expense recognition. Expense is properly recorded in April. No adjusting entry will be necessary.	**Debit Credit** Wages expense (E) 3,900 Cash (A) 3,900 Debits = Credits? Yes; posted to appropriate T-accounts.
(g)	Fuel Expense (E) increases by $320 (which decreases retained earnings); Accounts Payable (L) increases by $320. Accounting Equation in Balance? Stockholders' equity through retained earnings decreases by $320; liabilities increase by $320. Will an Adjusting Entry Be Necessary? Since fuel is used quickly and is recorded in the proper month, no adjusting entry will be necessary.	**Debit Credit** Fuel expense (E) 320 Accounts payable (L) 320 Debits = Credits? Yes; posted to appropriate T-accounts.
(h)	Prepaid Expenses for insurance (A) increases by $300; Cash (A) decreases by $300. Accounting Equation in Balance? Assets increase and decrease by the same amount. Will an Adjusting Entry Be Necessary? By the end of the month, $50 of insurance expense will have been used. An adjusting entry will be necessary to reduce prepaid expenses and increase insurance expense.	**Debit Credit** Prepaid expenses (A) 300 Cash (A) 300 Debits = Credits? Yes; posted to appropriate T-accounts.

	Transaction Analysis	Journal Entry
(*i*)	Dividends Declared (SE) increases by $300; Dividends Payable (L) increases by $300. Accounting Equation in Balance? Yes. Stockholders' equity through retained earnings decreases by $300; liabilities increase by $300. Will an Adjusting Entry Be Necessary? This is a financing, not operating, activity. No adjusting entry will be necessary.	**Debit** **Credit** Dividends declared (reduces SE) 300 Dividends payable (L) 300 Debits = Credits? Yes; posted to appropriate T-accounts.

T-accounts

ASSETS

Cash

Debit (Inc.)		Credit (Dec.)	
Beg. Bal.	4,350	(*a*)	90
(*b*)	1,600	(*e*)	3,700
(*d*)	3,500	(*f*)	3,900
		(*h*)	300
End. Bal.	1,460		

Accounts Receivable

Debit (Inc.)		Credit (Dec.)	
Beg. Bal.	0	(*d*)	3,500
(*c*)	5,200		
End. Bal.	1,700		

Prepaid Expenses

Debit (Inc.)		Credit (Dec.)	
Beg. Bal.	0		
(*h*)	300		
End. Bal.	300		

Lawn Equipment

Debit (Inc.)		Credit (Dec.)	
Beg. Bal.	4,600		
End. Bal.	4,600		

Land

Debit (Inc.)		Credit (Dec.)	
Beg. Bal.	3,750		
End. Bal.	3,750		

LIABILITIES

Accounts Payable

Debit (Dec.)		Credit (Inc.)	
(*e*)	3,700	Beg. Bal.	3,700
		(*g*)	320
		End. Bal.	320

Dividends Payable

Debit (Dec.)		Credit (Inc.)	
		Beg. Bal.	0
		(*i*)	300
		End. Bal.	300

Unearned Revenue

Debit (Dec.)		Credit (Inc.)	
		Beg. Bal.	0
		(*b*)	1,600
		End. Bal.	1,600

DIVIDENDS

Dividends Declared

Debit (Inc.)		Credit (Dec.)	
Beg. Bal.	0		
(*i*)	300		
End. Bal.	300		

STOCKHOLDERS' EQUITY

Contributed Capital

Debit (Dec.)		Credit (Inc.)	
		Beg. Bal.	9,000
		End. Bal.	9,000

Retained Earnings

Debit (Dec.)		Credit (Inc.)	
		Beg. Bal.	0
Will decrease from dividends		Will increase from net income	
		End. Bal.	

REVENUES

Mowing Service Revenue

Debit (Dec.)		Credit (Inc.)	
		Beg. Bal.	0
		(*c*)	5,200
		End. Bal.	5,200

EXPENSES

Fuel Expense

Debit (Inc.)		Credit (Dec.)	
Beg. Bal.	0		
(*a*)	90		
(*g*)	320		
End. Bal.	410		

Wages Expense

Debit (Inc.)		Credit (Dec.)	
Beg. Bal.	0		
(*f*)	3,900		
End. Bal.	3,900		

2. Income statement and balance sheet:

TERRIFIC LAWN MAINTENANCE CORPORATION
Income Statement (unadjusted)
For the period ended April 30, 1995

Revenues:		
Mowing service revenue		$5,200
Expenses:		
Fuel expense	410	
Wages expense	3,900	
Total expenses		4,310
Net income		$ 890

TERRIFIC LAWN MAINTENANCE CORPORATION
Balance Sheet (unadjusted)
At April 30, 1995

Assets		**Liabilities**	
Cash	$ 1,460	Accounts Payable	$ 320
Accounts Receivable	1,700	Dividends Payable	300
Prepaid Expenses	300	Unearned Revenue	1,600
Lawn Equipment	4,600	Total Liabilities	$ 2,220
Land	3,750		
		Stockholders' Equity	
		Contributed Capital	$ 9,000
		Retained Earnings	590*
		Total Stockholders' Equity	$ 9,590
Total Assets	$11,810	Total Liabilities and Stockholders' Equity	$11,810

*Retained Earnings is calculated as follows:

	Beginning balance	$ 0
+	Net income	890
−	Dividends declared	(300)
	Ending balance	$ 590

SUMMARY

This chapter discussed the accounting concepts relevant to income determination: the time-period assumption, definitions for the income statement elements (revenues, expenses, gains, and losses), the revenue principle, the matching principle, and the cost principle. These accounting principles are defined in accordance with the accrual basis of accounting which requires revenues to be recorded when earned and expenses to be recorded when incurred in generating revenues during the period.

The operating and accounting cycles were discussed as they apply to income measurement. The operating cycle is the span of time it takes a company to acquire goods or services, sell them to customers, and receive cash from customers. The cycle varies by company. The accounting cycle is the recordkeeping process used during the accounting period (usually a month, quarter, or year) which results in financial statements.

The transaction model introduced in Chapter 2 was completed by adding revenues (gains), expenses (losses), and dividends declared. Application of the income recognition rules combined with the complete transaction analysis model was illustrated for Sbarro, Inc., continuing the illustration in Chapter 2. In addition to the transaction analysis steps discussed in Chapter 2, the need for an adjusting entry based on the transaction was determined. Transactions where cash is received before the revenue is earned or paid before the expense is incurred often result in adjusting entries at the end of the period to record income in the proper period. Transactions where revenues have been earned or expenses have been incurred but are not yet recorded by the end of the accounting period will also require an adjusting entry.

Based on the balances in the T-accounts in the illustration, an unadjusted income statement and unadjusted balance sheet were prepared. These statements will be used in the next chapter which presents the second phase of the accounting process that takes place at the end of the accounting period.

KEY TERMS

Accounting Cycle The recordkeeping process used during and at the end of the accounting period that results in the preparation of financial statements. *116*

Accrual Basis Accounting Revenues are recorded when earned and expenses when incurred, regardless of when the related cash is received or paid. *111*

Cash Basis Accounting Revenues are recorded when cash is received and expenses are recorded when cash is paid, regardless of when the revenues are earned or expenses are incurred. Cash basis accounting is not appropriate for preparing financial statements for external users. *111*

Expenses Expenses are outflows of net assets (decreases in assets and/or increases in liabilities) from ongoing operations. *107*

Gains Gains are inflows of net assets (total assets minus total liabilities) from peripheral transactions. *108*

Losses Losses are outflows of net assets from peripheral transactions. *108*

Matching Principle Expenses are recognized (recorded) when incurred in earning revenue. *112*

Operating Cycle The time it takes for a company to purchase goods or services from suppliers, sell goods or services to customers, and collect cash from customers. It is also known as the *cash-to-cash cycle. 109*

Revenues Revenues are inflows of net assets (increases in assets and/or reductions of liabilities) from ongoing operations. *107*

Revenue Principle Revenues are recognized (recorded) when the earnings process is nearly complete, an exchange has taken place, and collection is probable. *111*

Time-Period Assumption The long life of a company can be reported in shorter time periods, usually months, quarters, and years. *105*

Timeline A visual representation of a series of business activities, listing dates and amounts over time. *113*

QUESTIONS

1. Explain what the time-period assumption means in accounting.
2. Indicate the income statement equation and define each element.
3. Explain the difference between:
   a. Revenues and gains.
   b. Expenses and losses.
4. Assume your personal finances currently consist of assets, $40,000, and debts, $15,000. You borrow $12,000 to buy a car and receive $120 in interest on your savings account for the year. Show how your personal financial condition will change in terms of the accounting model.
5. Big Company paid principal and interest on a note to the bank. Show how this transaction would affect the accounting model (use + for increase, – for decrease, and NE for no effect).
6. Explain a typical business operating cycle.
7. Define accrual accounting. Contrast it with cash basis accounting.
8. What three conditions normally must be met for revenue to be recognized under the accrual basis of accounting?

9. Explain the matching principle.
10. Describe the accounting cycle. List the sequence of activities in each phase of the cycle.
11. Explain why stockholders' equity is increased by revenues and decreased by expenses.
12. Explain why revenues are recorded as credits and expenses as debits.
13. Demonstrate the dual effect on the accounting model of (*a*) a cash sale of services for $2,000 and (*b*) a cash payment of $700 for office rent for the business.
14. Create a transaction for each of the following situations:
    a. Revenue is recognized before cash is received during the accounting cycle.
    b. Expense is recognized after cash is paid.
    c. Revenue is recognized before cash is received in the next accounting cycle.
    d. Expense is recognized before cash is paid.
    e. Revenue is recognized after cash is received.
15. Complete the following matrix by entering either debit or credit in each cell:

Item	Increase	Decrease
Revenues		
Dividends declared		
Losses		
Gains		
Expenses		

16. Complete the following matrix by entering either increases or decreases in each cell:

Item	Debit	Credit
Revenues		
Dividends declared		
Losses		
Gains		
Expenses		

17. Complete the following tabulation, indicating the amount and effect ("+" for increase and "–" for decrease) of each transaction:

Transaction	Assets	Liabilities	Stockholders' Equity	Revenues	Expenses	Net Income
a. Investment of cash by organizers, $20,000						
b. Borrowed cash, $6,000						
c. Performed legal services for cash, $12,000						
d. Paid expenses, $3,000 cash						
e. Purchased equipment, $8,000 cash						
Ending balances						

18. For each of the following transactions, indicate whether an adjusting entry will be needed at the end of the accounting period and why or why not:

Transaction	Need an Adjusting Entry?	Why or Why Not?
a. Received a utility bill covering utility usage for the first three weeks of the month.		
b. Paid off a six-month bank loan (principal and interest).		
c. Sold merchandise to customers for cash.		
d. Purchased a large machine at the beginning of the year, paying half with cash and borrowing the other half from a bank to be paid back in five years.		
e. Received cash in advance from a company renting an office in your building; the rent covers the next six months.		

EXERCISES

E3–1 Matching Definitions with Terms

Match each definition with its related term by entering the appropriate letter in the space provided.

Term

_______ (1) Losses

_______ (2) Matching principle

_______ (3) Revenues

_______ (4) Time-period assumption

_______ (5) Cost principle

_______ (6) Expenses

_______ (7) Gains

_______ (8) Revenue principle

Definition

A. Outflows of net assets from ongoing operations.
B. The cash-equivalent cost given up is the basis for initially recording assets, liabilities, revenues and expenses.
C. Outflows of net assets from peripheral transactions.
D. Record revenues when earned and measurable (an exchange takes place, the earnings process is nearly complete, and collection is probable).
E. Inflows of net assets from ongoing operations.
F. Record expenses when incurred in earning revenue.
G. The long life of a company can be reported in shorter time periods.
H. Inflows of net assets from peripheral transactions.

E3–2 Identifying Revenue Accounts

Revenues are normally recognized when the earnings process is nearly complete, a transaction has taken place, and collection is reasonably assured. The amount recorded is the cash-equivalent sales price.

Required:

Using the above definition and valuation rules, indicate whether or not each of the following events would result in recording a revenue on the income statement for the month indicated. If a revenue would be recorded, indicate an appropriate account title and amount. Use the following headings:

Event	Does a Revenue Result?	Account Title	Amount

1. In February, a customer orders and receives 10 personal computers from Gateway 2000; the customer promises to pay $25,000 within three months.
2. In March, Sam Shell Dodge sells a delivery truck with a list, or "sticker," price of $24,000 for $21,000 cash.
3. In April, Hudson's Department Store orders 1,000 men's shirts from Arrow Shirt Company for $18 each for future delivery. The terms require payment in full within 30 days of delivery. Answer from the standpoint of the manufacturer.
4. In May, Arrow Shirt Company completes production of the shirts described in (3) above. Answer from the standpoint of the manufacturer.
5. In May, Arrow Shirt Company delivers the order described in (3) above. Answer from the standpoint of the manufacturer.
6. In June, Arrow receives payment from Hudson's for the order described in (3) above. Answer from the standpoint of the manufacturer.
7. In December, a customer purchases a ticket from American Airlines for $500 cash to travel the following January.
8. In October, General Motors issues $26 million in new common stock.
9. In May, Penn State University receives $20,000,000 cash for 80,000 five-game season football tickets.
10. In September, the first game referred to in (9) above is played.
11. In November, Turner Construction Company signs a contract with a customer for the construction of a new $500,000 warehouse. At the signing, Turner receives a check for $50,000 as a deposit on the future construction.

E3–3 *Identifying Revenue Accounts*

Revenues are normally recognized when the earnings process is nearly complete, a transaction has taken place, and collection is reasonably assured. The amount recorded is the cash-equivalent sales price.

Required:

Using the above definition and valuation rules, indicate whether each of the following events would result in recording a revenue on the income statement for the months indicated. If a revenue would be recorded, indicate an appropriate account title and amount. Use the following headings:

Event	Does a Revenue Result?	Account Title	Amount

1. Staples, an office supply store, sells a computer desk with a list price of $700 for $425 cash.
2. A local car dealer sells a used car for $5,000 cash. The salesperson will receive a $500 commission for the sale.
3. (Answer 3, 4, 5, and 6 from the Roth Company point of view.) Ford Motor Company orders three tons of aluminum from the Roth Company. Ford is quoted a price of $2,000 per ton.
4. Roth Company produces three tons of aluminum to be shipped next week to Ford Motor Company.
5. Three tons of aluminum are delivered today to Ford by the Roth Company. Payment is due within 45 days after delivery.

6. Thirty-five days after delivery, Ford pays Roth in full for the shipment.
7. Nationwide Insurance Company receives a $1,200 check for a fire insurance policy. The policy covers the current month and the next 11 months.
8. On 7/1/19A, a bank lends $1,000 to a company. The loan carries a 12% annual interest rate, and the principal and interest are due in a lump sum on 6/30/19B. Today is 12/31/19A and the bank is preparing its year-end financial reports. Answer from the standpoint of the bank.
9. Sears, a retail store, sells a $100 lamp to a customer who charges the sale on his store credit card.
10. A popular ski magazine company receives a total of $1,800 today from subscribers. The subscriptions will begin in the next fiscal year.

E3–4 *Identifying Expense Accounts*

Revenues are normally recognized when goods or services have been provided and payment or promise of payment has been received. Expense recognition is guided by an attempt to match the costs associated with the generation of those revenues to the same time period.

Required:

Using the above expense recognition rule, indicate the amount of expense (if any) that will be recognized on each company's income statement for the month of February as a result of each of the following events. Use the following headings:

Event	Does an Expense Result?	Account Title	Amount

1. On February 8, Gateway 2000 pays its computer service technicians $90,000 in salary for the two weeks ended February 7.
2. On January 2, Turner Construction Company pays $4,500 in worker's compensation insurance for the first three months of the year.
3. During February, Richard D. Irwin publishing company uses $1,000 worth of electricity and natural gas in its headquarters building for which it has not yet been billed.
4. On February 9, Arrow Shirt Company completes production of 1,000 men's shirts ordered by Hudson's Department Store at a cost of $9 each. Answer from the standpoint of the manufacturer.
5. On February 14, Arrow Shirt Company delivers the order described in (4) above. Answer from the standpoint of the manufacturer.
6. On February 28, Arrow receives payment in cash for the order described in (4) above. Answer from the standpoint of the manufacturer.
7. On February 2, Sam Shell Dodge pays its salespersons $3,500 in commissions related to January automobile sales.
8. On February 28, Sam Shell Dodge determines that it will pay its salespersons $4,200 in commissions related to February sales. The payment will be made on March 3.
9. On February 28, a new grill is installed at a McDonald's Restaurant. On the same day, payment of $12,000 is made in cash.
10. On February 15, the University of Florida orders 60,000 season football tickets from its printer and pays $6,000 in advance for the custom printing. (The first game is played in September.)
11. On February 1, Pyramid Mall had janitorial supplies costing $1,000 in storage. An additional $600 worth of supplies was purchased during February. At the end of February, $900 worth of janitorial supplies remained in storage.

E3–5 *Identifying Expense Accounts*

Revenues are normally recognized when goods or services have been provided and payment or promise of payment has been received. Expense recognition is guided by an attempt to match the costs associated with the generation of revenues in the period in which the earning process occurs.

Required:

Using the above expense recognition rule, indicate the amount of expense (if any) that will be recognized on each company's income statement as a result of each of the following events. Use the following headings:

Event	Does an Expense Result?	Account Title	Amount

1. On January 1, the campus bookstore orders 500 accounting texts for the spring semester. The store is quoted a cost of $50 per book.
2. On January 10, the campus bookstore receives 500 accounting texts at a cost of $50 each. The terms indicate that payment is due within 30 days of delivery.
3. During the last week of January, 450 accounting texts are sold to students at a sales price of $60 each.
4. A Colorado State University employee works eight hours, at $15 per hour, on June 30. The university's fiscal year ends on June 30; however, payday is not until July 3. Answer from the university's point of view.
5. On January 2, 19B, Amber Incorporated purchased a delivery van for $12,000 cash. The van will be used for five years and is expected to have a $2,000 residual value. Answer for the year 19B.
6. Wang Company paid $3,600 for a fire insurance policy. The policy covers the current month and the next 11 months. Answer from Wang's point of view.
7. Amber Incorporated has its delivery van repaired for $280 and charges the amount on account.
8. Rob & Company had a beginning supply inventory of $500, purchased $250 of supplies with cash during the period, and had an ending supply inventory on 12/31/19B of $400.
9. Ziegler Company, a farm equipment company, receives its phone bill for $230. The bill has not been paid to date.

10. Spina Company receives and pays a $1,500 invoice from a consulting firm for services rendered in the current period.
11. Falkowski's Tax Company pays a $600 invoice from a consulting firm for services rendered and recorded in the prior fiscal year.

E3–6 Matching Definitions with Terms

Match each definition with its related term by entering the appropriate letter in the space provided.

Term

________ (1) Cash basis accounting

________ (2) Deferred revenue

________ (3) Operating cycle

________ (4) Ending retained earnings = Beginning retained earnings + Net income – Dividends declared

________ (5) Accounting cycle

________ (6) Accrual basis accounting

________ (7) Net assets

________ (8) Revenue – Expenses = Net income

Definition

A. A liability account used to record cash received before revenues have been earned; the account may need to be adjusted at the end of the accounting cycle to reflect the amount of revenues earned during the period.
B. The recordkeeping process used during and at the end of the accounting period that results in financial statements.
C. Record revenues when earned and expenses when incurred.
D. The time it takes to purchase goods or services from suppliers, sell goods or services to customers, and collect cash from customers.
E. Total assets minus total liabilities.
F. Record revenues when received and expenses when paid.
G. The income statement equation.
H. The retained earnings equation.

E3–7 Performing Transaction Analysis: Nonquantitative

For each transaction given below, indicate the effect on assets, liabilities, and stockholders' equity by entering a plus for increase and a minus for decrease.

		Effect on		
	Transactions	**Assets**	**Liabilities**	**Stockholders' Equity**
a.	Issued stock to organizers for cash (example).	+		+
b.	Borrowed cash from local bank.			
c.	Purchased equipment on credit.			
d.	Earned revenue, collected cash.			
e.	Incurred expenses, on credit.			
f.	Earned revenue, on credit.			
g.	Paid cash on account.			
h.	Incurred expenses, paid cash.			
i.	Earned revenue, collected three-fourths in cash, balance on credit.			
j.	Theft of $100 cash.			
k.	Declared and paid cash dividends.			
l.	Collected cash from customers on account.			
m.	Incurred expenses, paid four-fifths in cash, balance on credit.			
n.	Paid income tax expense for the period.			

E3–8 Performing Transaction Analysis: Nonquantitative Using Debit-Credit Framework

The 12 transactions given below were completed by TNT Cleaning Service Company during the year 1996:

a. The organizers paid cash and in turn received 10,000 shares of stock.
b. TNT Cleaning borrowed cash from the local bank.
c. TNT Cleaning purchased a company van, paid three-fourths in cash with the balance due in six months.
d. Revenues earned, collected cash in full.
e. Expenses incurred, paid cash in full.
f. Revenues earned, on credit.
g. Expenses incurred, on credit.
h. Declared and paid a cash dividend to stockholders.
i. Collected half of the amount on credit in (*f*).
j. Paid all of the credit amount in (*g*).
k. A spare tire was stolen from the company van, not insured.
l. Sold the van at the end of the year for more than the company paid.

Required:

For each transaction given above, enter in the table below the abbreviations Dr (for debit) and Cr (for credit) to reflect the increases and decreases in the balance sheet and income statement accounts listed. Transaction (*a*) is used as an example.

	Transaction											
	a	*b*	*c*	*d*	*e*	*f*	*g*	*h*	*i*	*j*	*k*	*l*
Assets	Dr											
Liabilities												
Contributed Capital	Cr											
Dividends Declared												
Revenues												
Gains												
Expenses												
Losses												

E3–9 Using the Accounting Model—Personal Financial Transactions

You finished college and began working for Murphy Services Company. At the start of the first month, your financial situation was as shown in the following schedule. You are to complete the schedule by recording your transactions for the first month, summarized in the first column, and indicating your ending financial position on the last line.

Transaction	Assets	Liabilities	Owner's Equity
a. Beginning financial position (personal items, including your rather used auto).	$4,000	$800	$3,200
b. Borrowed $1,500 to get through the first month.			
c. Paid rent on apartment, $700.			
d. Paid utility deposits, $250.			
e. Personal expenses: food, cleaning, etc., $800.			
f. Auto payment, $450 (including $350 interest).			
g. Trip to visit a special person, $400.			
h. Received a gift from your family, $200 cash.			
i. You gave your date a special present, $100.			
j. You received your first paycheck (net of deductions), $2,100.			
Your ending financial position			

E3–10 Performing Transaction Analysis

Sysco

Sysco, formed in 1969, is America's largest marketer and distributor of food service products, serving nearly a quarter million restaurants, hotels, schools, hospitals, and other institutions. The following summarized transactions are typical of those that occurred in a recent year.

a. Borrowed $80 million from a bank, signing a short-term note.
b. Provided $10.02 billion in service to customers during the year, with $9.5 billion on account and the rest received in cash.
c. Purchased plant and equipment for $127.9 million in cash.
d. Purchased $8.268 billion inventory on account.
e. Paid payroll, $1.02 billion during the year.
f. Customers paid $410 million on account.
g. Purchased and used fuel of $400 million in delivery vehicles during the year (paid for in cash).
h. Declared and paid $48.8 million in dividends for the year.
i. Paid $8.2 billion cash on accounts payable.
j. Incurred $20 million in utility usage during the year; paid $15 million in cash and the rest on account.

Required:

For each of the transactions:

1. Perform transaction analysis as outlined in the chapter.
2. Prepare journal entries.
3. Determine if the accounting equation remains in balance and debits equal credits.
4. Determine if an adjusting entry will be needed at the end of the accounting cycle.

E3–11 Performing Transaction Analysis

Greek Peak

Greek Peak Incorporated is a ski resort in upstate New York. The company sells lift tickets, ski lessons, and ski equipment. It operates several restaurants and rents townhouses to vacationing skiers. The following hypothetical December transactions are typical of those that occur at the resort.

a. On December 1, borrowed $500,000 from the bank with a six-month note at 12% annual interest to finance the beginning of the new season. The principal and interest are due on the maturity date.
b. Purchased a new snow plow for $20,000 cash on December 1. The plow is estimated to have a five-year life and a $5,000 residual value.

c. Purchased and received $10,000 of ski equipment on account to sell in the ski shop.
d. Incurred $22,000 in routine maintenance expenses for the chair lifts; paid cash.
e. Sold $72,000 of season passes and received cash.
f. Sold daily lift passes for a total of $76,000 in cash.
g. Sold a pair of skis for $350 on account. (The cost of the pair was $250.)
h. Received a $320 deposit on a townhouse to be rented for five days in January.
i. Paid half the charges incurred on account in (*c*).
j. Received $200 on account from the customer in (*g*).
k. Paid $108,000 in wages to employees for the month of December.

Required:

1. Prepare journal entries for each transaction.
2. Determine whether the debits equal the credits.
3. Determine whether the accounting equation is still in balance.
4. Assume Greek Peak had a $1,200 balance in Accounts Receivable at the beginning of the year. Determine the ending balance in the Accounts Receivable account. Show your work in T-account format.

E3–12 *Analyzing the Effect of Transactions on Financial Statement Elements*

For each of the transactions given below, indicate the effect on assets, liabilities, stockholders' equity, revenues, expenses, and net income by entering a plus (+) for increase, a minus (–) for decrease, and NE for no effect. An example is provided.

	Transactions	Assets	Liabilities	Stockholders' Equity	Revenues	Expenses	Net Income
	Provided services to customers on account.	+	NE	+	+	NE	+
a.	Incurred expenses on credit.						
b.	Declared and paid cash dividends.						
c.	Collected cash on account.						
d.	Incurred expenses, paid part cash and part on credit.						
e.	Borrowed cash from bank.						
f.	Purchased equipment on credit.						
g.	Paid cash on account.						
h.	Issued additional stock.						

E3–13 *Analyzing the Effect of Transactions on Financial Statement Elements*

For each of the transactions given below, indicate the effect on assets, liabilities, stockholders' equity, revenues, expenses, and net income by entering a plus (+) for increase, a minus (–) for decrease, and NE for no effect. An example is provided.

	Transactions	Assets	Liabilities	Stockholders' Equity	Revenues	Expenses	Net Income
	Received the property tax bill. It has not yet been paid.	NE	+	–	NE	+	–
a.	Purchased equipment on account.						
b.	Sold services on account.						
c.	Issued additional stock for cash.						
d.	Paid the property tax bill shown in the example above.						
e.	Declared and paid cash dividends.						
f.	Received cash from a customer on an account receivable.						
g.	Recognized the depreciation on equipment.						
h.	Paid next year's rent in advance.						

E3–14 Preparing Journal Entries

The Lustig-Liebman Air Transport Service has been in operation for three years. Perform transaction analysis for each of the following transactions during the first week in February. Based on your analysis, prepare journal entries for each. Be sure to categorize each account as an asset (A), liability (L), stockholders' equity (SE), revenue (R), or expense (E).

Example:

February 1 Cargo was flown from Chicago to Denver. The customer was billed $1,600.

2/1 An asset (Accounts Receivable) increases by $1,600; to increase an asset, debit the account. A revenue (Transport Revenue) increases by $1,600; to increase a revenue (which increases stockholders' equity through retained earnings), credit the account.

	Debit	Credit
Accounts receivable (A)	1,600	
Transport revenue (R)		1,600

February 1	Lustig-Liebman paid $200 for rent of hangar space in February.
February 2	Fuel costing $450 was purchased on account for the next flight to Dallas.
February 2	A customer paid Lustig-Liebman $800 to ship several items to Philadelphia next month.
February 3	Cargo was flown from Denver to Dallas; the customer paid $900 for the air transport.
February 4	The pilot was paid $1,200 in wages for flying in January.
February 4	Lustig-Liebman paid $60 for an advertisement in the local paper to run on February 7.
February 5	Cargo for two customers was flown from Dallas to Albuquerque for $1,700; one customer paid $500 cash and the other asked to be billed.
February 6	Spare parts for the planes costing $1,350 were purchased on account.
February 7	Lustig-Liebman declared a $200 cash dividend to be paid in March.

E3–15 Preparing Journal Entries

Brian Brent organized a new company called CollegeCaps. The company operates a small store in an area mall and specializes in baseball-type hats with logos printed on them. Brian, who is never without a cap, feels that his target market is college students. You have been hired to record the transactions occurring in the first two weeks of operation.

Required:

Perform transaction analysis for each of the following transactions during March. Based on your analysis, prepare journal entries for each transaction. Be sure to categorize each account as an asset (A), liability (L), stockholders' equity (SE), revenue (R), or expense (E).

Example:

March 1	One thousand shares of capital stock were issued for $30 per share.

3/1 An asset (Cash) increased by $30,000; debit the account. A stockholders' equity account (Contributed Capital) increased by $30,000; credit the account.

Cash (A)	30,000	
Contributed capital (SE)		30,000

March 1	Borrowed $50,000 from the bank to provide additional working capital to begin operations. The interest rate is 14% annually; principal and interest are due in 24 months.
March 1	Paid $1,200 for the current month's rent and another $1,200 for next month's rent.
March 1	Paid $2,400 for a one-year fire insurance policy.
March 3	Purchased furniture and fixtures for the store for $15,000 on account. The amount is due within 30 days.
March 4	Purchased a supply of University of Iowa and Iowa State University baseball caps for the store for $1,800 cash.
March 5	Placed advertisements in local college newspapers for a total of $250 cash.
March 9	Total sales of caps amounted to $400, half of which was charged on account. The cost of the caps sold was $150.
March 10	Full payment was made for the furniture and fixtures purchased on account on March 3.
March 14	Received $50 from a customer on account.

E3–16 *Preparing Journal Entries*

Rhonda Bennett is the president of ServicePro, Inc., a company that provides temporary employees for not-for-profit companies. ServicePro has been operating for five years and revenues are increasing with each passing year. You have been hired to help Rhonda with the recordkeeping for ServicePro.

Required:

Perform transaction analysis for each of the following transactions during September. Based on your analysis, prepare journal entries for each transaction. Be sure to categorize each account as an asset (A), liability (L), stockholders' equity (SE), revenue (R), or expense (E).

Example:

April 2	Purchased office supplies for $500 on account.

4/2 An asset (Office Supplies Inventory) increased by $500; debit the account. A liability (Accounts Payable) increased; credit the account.

Office supplies inventory (A)	500	
Accounts payable (L)		500

April 3	Received the telephone bill for $245.
April 5	Billed United Way $1,950 for temporary services provided.
April 8	Paid $250 for supplies purchased and recorded on account last period.
April 8	Placed an advertisement in the local paper for $400 cash.
April 9	Purchased a new computer for the office costing $2,300 cash.
April 10	Paid employee wages of $1,200. Of this amount, $200 had been earned and recorded in the prior period.
April 11	Received $1,000 on account from United Way.
April 12	Purchased land as the site of a future office for $10,000. Paid $2,000 down and signed a note payable for the balance. The note is due in five years and has an annual interest rate of 10%.
April 13	Issued 2,000 additional shares of capital stock for $40 per share in anticipation of building a new office.
April 14	Billed Family & Children's Service $2,000 for services rendered.

E3–17 Using T-Accounts

Hamilton Piano Rebuilding Company has been operating for one year (19A). At the start of 19B, its income statement accounts had zero balances and its balance sheet account balances were as follows:

Cash	$ 6,000	Accounts Payable	8,000
Accounts Receivable	25,000	Deferred Revenue (deposits)	3,200
Supplies	1,200	Note Payable (due in three years with	
Equipment	8,000	12% annual interest due annually)	40,000
Land	6,000	Contributed Capital	8,000
Building	22,000	Retained Earnings	9,000

Required:

1. Create T-accounts for the balance sheet accounts above and for these additional accounts: Rebuilding Fees Revenue, Rent Revenue, Wages Expense, Utilities Expense, and Dividends Declared.
2. Enter the following January, 19B, transactions in the T-accounts, using the letter of each transaction as the reference:
   a. Hamilton received a $500 deposit from a customer who wanted her piano rebuilt.
   b. Hamilton rented a part of the building to a bicycle repair shop; $300 was received for rent in January.
   c. Hamilton delivered 10 rebuilt pianos to customers who paid $14,500 in cash.
   d. Customers paid $6,000 on their accounts.
   e. An electric and gas utility bill for $350 was received, but will be paid in February.
   f. Hamilton ordered $800 in supplies.
   g. $1,700 on account was paid in January.
   h. Mr. Hamilton, the major shareholder, brought a $600 tool (equipment) from home to use in the business.
   i. Hamilton paid $10,000 in wages to employees in January.
   j. A $3,000 dividend was declared and paid.
   k. The supplies in *(f)* above were received and paid for in cash.
3. Using the data from the T-accounts, amounts for the following on January 31, 19B, were:

   Revenues, $ ________ – Expenses, $ ________ = Net Income, $ ________

   Assets, $ ________ = Liabilities, $ ________ + Stockholders' Equity, $ ________
4. What would net income be if Hamilton used the cash basis of accounting?

E3–18 Preparing an Income Statement and Balance Sheet

Use the ending balances in the T-accounts in E3–17 to complete the following.

1. Prepare an unadjusted income statement for January 31, 19B, in good form.
2. Compute the January 31, 19B, ending balance in Retained Earnings.
3. Prepare an unadjusted balance sheet for January 31, 19B, in good form.

E3–19 Using T-Accounts to Summarize Transactions

Vivianne Macedo and Stephanie Meltzer had been operating a catering business, Traveling Gourmet, for several years. In March 19C, the partners were planning to expand by opening a retail sales shop and decided to form the business as a corporation called The Traveling Gourmet, Inc. The following transactions occurred in March 19C:

a. Each of the two shareholders contributed $10,000 to form the corporation, along with $2,000 in accounts receivable, $5,300 in equipment, a van (equipment) appraised at fair market value of $13,000, and $1,200 in supplies.

b. Vivianne and Stephanie found a vacant store for sale in a good location. In March, the business purchased the building for $60,000 with a $9,000 cash down-payment and a mortgage from a local bank for the rest.

c. The company borrowed $25,000 from the local bank on a 10%, one-year note and immediately purchased $15,000 of equipment (refrigerated display cases, cabinets, tables, and chairs) and renovated and decorated the new store for $10,000 (added to the cost of the building).

d. Food and paper supplies costing $8,830 were purchased for cash and used in March.

e. Vivianne and Stephanie made and sold food at the retail store for $10,900 in cash.

f. Four parties were catered in March for $3,200; $1,500 was billed and the rest was received in cash.

g. A $320 telephone bill for March was received in March but not paid.

h. The Traveling Gourmet paid $63 in gas for the van in March.

i. The company paid $5,080 in wages to employees in March.

j. Each of the owners received a $300 dividend from the corporation.

Required:

1. Set up appropriate T-accounts for Cash, Accounts Receivable, Supplies, Equipment, Building, Accounts Payable, Note Payable, Mortgage Payable, Contributed Capital, Dividends Declared, Food Sales Revenue, Catering Sales Revenue, Cost of Food and Paper Products, Utilities Expense, Wages Expense, and Gasoline Expense.
2. Record in the T-accounts the effects of each transaction for The Traveling Gourmet, Inc., in March. Identify the amounts with the letters starting with (*a*).
3. Indicate which of the transactions will require adjusting entries at the end of the month.

E3–20 Preparing an Income Statement and a Balance Sheet

Use the balances in the completed T-accounts in E3–19 to respond to the following:

1. Prepare an unadjusted income statement in good form for the month of March 19C.
2. Prepare an unadjusted balance sheet in good form for the end of March 19C.
3. How did you compute the amount in Retained Earnings?
4. What do you think about the success of this company based on the results of the first month of operation?

E3–21 Using T-Accounts to Summarize Transactions

Tracey Malloy, a connoisseur of fine chocolate, opened Tracey's Treats in Collegetown on February 1, 19A. The shop specializes in a selection of gourmet chocolate candies and a line of gourmet ice cream. You have been hired to maintain the financial records for the store. The following transactions occurred in February 19A, the first month of operations.

a. Four shareholders contributed a total of $16,000 to form the corporation.

b. Three months' store rent was paid at $800 per month (for February, March, and April).

c. Supplies were purchased for $300 cash.

d. Candy was purchased and received for $5,000, on account, due in 60 days.

e. The company negotiated a $10,000 loan at the bank, at 12% annual interest. The principal and interest are due in a lump sum in two years.

f. The company used the money from (*e*) to purchase a computer for $2,500 (for recordkeeping and inventory tracking) and the balance for furniture and fixtures for the store.

g. A grand opening advertisement was placed in the local paper for $425 cash.

h. Sales on Valentine's Day totaled $1,800; $1,525 was in cash and the rest on accounts receivable. The cost of the candy sold was $1,000.

i. A $500 payment was made on accounts payable.

j. Employee wages of $420 were incurred and paid.

k. Accounts receivable of $50 were collected from customers.

l. A repair was made on one of the display cases for $118 cash.

m. Cash sales of $2,000 were made during the rest of the month. The cost of the goods sold was $1,100.

Required:

1. Set up appropriate T-accounts for Cash, Accounts Receivable, Supplies, Merchandise Inventory, Prepaid Rent, Equipment, Furniture and Fixtures, Accounts Payable, Notes Payable, Contributed Capital, Sales Revenue, Cost of Goods Sold (Expense), Advertising Expense, Wage Expense, and Repair Expense.
2. Record in the T-accounts the effects of each transaction for Tracey's Treats in February. Identify the transactions in the accounts with the letters beginning with (*a*).
3. Show the unadjusted ending balances in the T-accounts.
4. Indicate which of the transactions will require adjusting entries at the end of the month (for simplicity, do not record the entries).

E3–22 Preparing an Income Statement and Balance Sheet

Use the balances in the completed T-accounts in E3–21 to respond to the following:

1. Prepare an unadjusted income statement in good form for the month of February, 19A.
2. Prepare an unadjusted balance sheet in good form as of the end of February, 19A.
3. Write a short memo to Tracey offering your opinion on the results of operations during the first month of business.

E3–23 Preparing an Income Statement

Snapple Beverage Corp.

In June 1993, Snapple Beverage Corporation purchased Mr. Natural, Inc., Snapple's distributor for New York City and Westchester County, New York. Included in Snapple's 1993 annual report is the December 31, 1993, Statement of Operations for Mr. Natural for the six months since the acquisition. Below are listed the accounts and balances from the annual report. The accounts are not necessarily listed in good order and have normal debit and credit balances:

Interest expense	$ 643,423	Income tax expense	$1,555,619
Goodwill amortization expense*	305,700	Promotion and marketing expense	261,947
Advertising expense	832,489	Professional fees expense	342,075
Net revenues	36,481,638	Other income	133,744
Interest income	35,674	Payroll expense	1,410,642
Other expenses	867,284	Repairs and maintenance expense	243,149
Cost of sales (products sold)	28,605,529	Depreciation and amortization expense*	156,132

*Goodwill (an intangible) results from purchasing another company at a price above book value. The amount is recorded as an asset and the cost is allocated over several years. The allocated amount of an intangible asset is called amortization expense.

Required:

Prepare a statement of operations (income statement) in good form for Mr. Natural, Inc., for the six months ended December 31, 1993.

PROBLEMS

P3–1 *Multiple Choice*

1. At the end of the accounting period, Lublin Corporation owed $800 in property taxes that had not been recorded or paid. The adjusting entry should include
   a. A debit to an expense account and a credit to an asset account.
   b. A credit to a liability account and a debit to an expense account.
   c. A credit to a liability account and a debit to an asset account.
   d. A credit to an expense account and a debit to a liability account.
   e. None of the above; the answer is ______________.
2. On April 1, 19B, the Supply Inventory account correctly showed a beginning balance of $400. During April, $300 of supplies were purchased for cash. At the end of April, $325 of supplies remained unused. The April 19B income statement should show a supply expense of
   a. $0
   b. $300
   c. $325
   d. $400
   e. None of the above; the answer is ______________.
3. Hubbert Company failed to make an adjusting entry to recognize accrued wages payable. The omission would cause
   a. An overstatement of assets and an understatement of net income.
   b. An understatement of assets and an overstatement of net income.
   c. An understatement of liabilities and an overstatement of net income.
   d. An understatement of liabilities and no effect on net income.
   e. None of the above; the answer is ______________.
4. The accounting concept that states that transactions of the business should be kept separate from the transactions of the owner is the
   a. Matching principle.
   b. Conservatism constraint.
   c. Full-disclosure principle.
   d. Separate-entity assumption.
   e. Two of the above are true; ________ and ________.
5. The revenue principle states that, for revenue to be recognized (recorded), the following conditions must be met:
   a. The earnings process is complete or nearly complete.
   b. An exchange transaction takes place.
   c. Cash is collected.
   d. All of the above are true.
   e. Only two of the above are true; ________ and ________.

P3–2 *Analyzing and Recording Transactions*

Listed below is a series of accounts for Dinjian Corporation, which has been operating for three years. These accounts are listed and numbered for identification. Below the accounts is a series of transactions. For each transaction, indicate the account(s) that should be debited and credited by entering the appropriate account number(s) to the right of each transaction. If no journal entry is needed, write *none* after the trasaction. The first transaction is used as an example.

Account No.	Account Title	Account No.	Account Title
1	Cash	9	Wages Payable
2	Accounts Receivable	10	Income Taxes Payable
3	Supplies Inventory on Hand	11	Contributed Capital
4	Prepaid Expense	12	Retained Earnings
5	Equipment	13	Service Revenue
6	Patents	14	Operating Expenses
7	Accounts Payable	15	Income Tax Expense
8	Note Payable	16	None of the above

Transactions	Debit	Credit
a. Example: Purchased equipment for use in the business; paid one-third cash and gave a note payable for the balance.	5	1, 8
b. Investment of cash in the business; stock was issued.	______	______
c. Paid cash for salaries and wages.	______	______
d. Collected cash for services performed this period.	______	______
e. Collected cash for services performed last period.	______	______
f. Performed services this period on credit.	______	______
g. Paid operating expenses incurred this period.	______	______
h. Paid cash for operating expenses incurred last period.	______	______
i. Incurred operating expenses this period, to be paid next period.	______	______
j. Purchased supplies for inventory to be used later; paid cash.	______	______
k. Used some of the supplies from inventory for operations.	______	______
l. Purchased a patent (an intangible); paid cash.	______	______
m. Made a payment on the equipment note in (*a*); the payment was part principal and part interest expense.	______	______
n. Collected cash on accounts receivable for services previously performed.	______	______
o. Paid cash on accounts payable for expenses previously incurred.	______	______
p. Paid three-fourths of the income tax expense for the year; the balance to be paid next period.	______	______
q. On the last day of current period, paid cash for an insurance policy covering the next two years.	______	______

P3–3 *Analyzing and Recording Transactions*

Listed below is a series of accounts for Ortiz & Ortiz, Incorporated. The company has been operating for two years. The accounts are listed and numbered for identification. Below the accounts is a series of transactions. For each transaction, indicate the account(s) that should be debited and credited by entering the appropriate account number(s) to the right of each transaction. If no journal entry is needed, write *none* after the transaction. The first transaction is given as an example.

Account No.	Account Title	Account No.	Account Title
1	Cash	9	Wages Payable
2	Accounts Receivable	10	Income Taxes Payable
3	Supplies Inventory	11	Contributed Capital
4	Prepaid Expense	12	Retained Earnings
5	Buildings	13	Service Revenue
6	Land	14	Operating Expenses
7	Accounts Payable	15	Income Tax Expense
8	Mortgage Payable	16	Dividends Declared

Transactions	Debit	Credit
a. Example: Investment of cash in the business this period; stock was issued.	1	11
b. Performed services this period on credit.	______	______
c. Purchased (but did not use) supplies this period on credit.	______	______
d. Prepaid a fire insurance policy this period to cover the next 12 months.	______	______

Transactions	Debit	Credit
e. Purchased a building this period with a 20% cash down payment and a mortgage loan for the balance.	______	______
f. Collected cash this year for services rendered and recorded in the prior year.	______	______
g. Paid cash this period for wages earned and recorded last period.	______	______
h. Paid cash for operating expenses charged on accounts payable in the prior period.	______	______
i. Paid cash for operating expenses charged on accounts payable in the current period.	______	______
j. Incurred and recorded operating expenses on credit to be paid next period.	______	______
k. Collected cash at the point of sale for services rendered.	______	______
l. Used supplies from inventory to clean the offices.	______	______
m. Recorded income taxes for this period to be paid at the beginning of the next period.	______	______
n. Declared and paid a cash dividend this period.	______	______
o. Made a payment on the building; the payment was part principal repayment and part interest.	______	______
p. This period a shareholder sold some shares of her stock to another person for an amount above the original issuance price.	______	______

Cedar Fair

P3–4 Performing Transaction Analysis, Preparing Journal Entries, and Posting to T-Accounts

Cedar Fair, L. P. (Limited Partnership) owns and operates three seasonal amusement parks: Cedar Point in Ohio, Valleyfair near Minneapolis/St. Paul, and Dorney Park and Wildwater Kingdom near Allentown, Pennsylvania. Below are summarized transactions similar to those that occurred in a recent year (19A):

a. Guests at the parks paid $89,664,000 cash in admissions.

b. The primary operating expenses (such as employee wages, utilities, and repairs and maintenance) for the year 19A were $66,347,000 with $60,200,000 paid in cash and the rest on account.

c. Interest paid on long-term debt was $6,601,000.

d. The parks sell food and merchandise and operate games. The cash received in 19A for these combined activities was $77,934,000.

e. The cost of products sold during the year was $19,525,000.

f. Cedar Fair purchased and built additional buildings, rides, and equipment during 19A, paying $23,813,000 in cash.

g. The most significant assets for the company are land, buildings, rides, and equipment. Therefore, a large expense for Cedar Fair is depreciation expense. In 19A, the amount was $14,473,000 (credit Accumulated Depreciation which will reduce the asset account).

h. Guests may stay at accommodations owned by the company at the three parks. In 19A, Accommodations Revenue was $11,345,000; $11,010,000 was paid by the guests in cash and the rest was on account.

i. Cedar Fair paid $2,900,000 on notes payable.

j. The company purchased $19,100,000 in food and merchandise inventory for the year, paying $18,000,000 in cash and the rest on account.

k. The selling, general, and administrative expenses (those not classified as operating expenses, such as the president's salary and advertising for the parks) for 19A were $21,118,000. $19,500,000 was paid in cash and the rest was on account.

l. Cedar Fair paid $8,600,000 on accounts payable during the year.

Required:

1. For each of the above transactions, perform transaction analysis following the illustration in the chapter.
2. Prepare journal entries for each of the transactions.
3. Create T-accounts for the income statement accounts only and post the income statement effects of each of the transactions. Determine ending balances.

P3–5 Preparing an Income Statement

Use the balances of the completed T-accounts in P3–4 to prepare in good form an unadjusted income statement for Cedar Fair at December 31, 19A.

P3–6 Performing Transaction Analysis, Preparing Journal Entries, and Posting to T-Accounts

Green Stables, Inc., is a company in Philadelphia that provides stables, care for animals, and grounds for riding and showing horses. You have been hired to assist Jennifer Dembeck, the chief financial officer, in the accounting office. The following transactions for April 19C are provided for your review.

a. The company provided animal care services, all on credit, for $5,260. The company rented stables to customers who cared for their animals and was paid cash of $3,200. Use one revenue account.

b. $1,100 was collected on a note receivable from a customer who previously purchased riding equipment. Of the amount collected, $100 was interest.

c. Straw (a supply inventory) was purchased on account for $3,210. (This was added to the $1,400 of straw already on hand in the barn.)

d. Utilities for the month totaled $845 and were paid in cash as incurred.

e. A customer paid $1,500 to board her horse for April, May, and June.

f. A small barn was built for $42,000. The company paid half the amount in cash and signed a three-year note payable for the balance on April 1, 19C. The note carries an annual interest rate of 12%; the principal is due on the maturity date and an interest payment is due at the end of each month.

g. $3,210 was paid on accounts payable for a previous purchase of straw.

h. $50,000 was received from customers on accounts receivable.

i. Wages expense of $2,600 was incurred and paid.

j. Dividends of $5,000 were declared and paid.

k. $3,600 was paid for property insurance. The policy runs from 4/1/19C to 3/31/19D.

l. An interest payment of $210 was made for the note in (*f*) for April.

m. An inventory count indicated that $925 of straw remained unused at the end of the month.

Required:

1. For each of the above transactions, perform transaction analysis as illustrated in the chapter.
2. Prepare journal entries for each transaction. If a transaction does not require a journal entry, state so.
3. Create T-accounts for the income statement accounts only and post the income statement effects of each transaction. Determine and label the ending balances.

P3–7 Preparing an Income Statement

Use the balances of the completed T-accounts in P3–6 to prepare an unadjusted income statement in good form for Green Stables, Inc., for the month ending April 30, 19C.

Federal Express

P3–8 *Preparing T-Accounts, an Income Statement, and a Balance Sheet*

Below are several May 31 account balances (in thousands of dollars) from a recent annual report of Federal Express Corporation, followed by several typical transactions. The business is described in the annual report as follows:

> Federal Express Corporation offers a wide range of express services for the time-definite transportation of goods and documents throughout the world using an extensive fleet of aircraft and vehicles and leading-edge information technologies.

Account	Balance	Account	Balance
Flight and ground equipment	$3,476,268	Contributed capital	$ 701,866
Retained earnings	969,515	Receivables	922,727
Accounts payable	554,111	Other assets	1,010,953
Prepaid expenses	63,573	Cash	155,456
Accrued expenses payable	761,357	Spare parts, supplies, and fuel	164,087
Notes payable	2,016,076	Deferred income taxes (credit)	72,479
Other liabilities	717,660		

These accounts are not necessarily in good order and have normal debit or credit balances.

June transactions:

a. Provided delivery service to customers, receiving $600,000 in accounts receivable and $50,000 in cash.

b. Purchased new equipment costing $68,000 on account.

c. Paid $62,000 cash to rent equipment and aircraft, with $54,000 for June rental and the rest for rent in July and August.

d. Spent $33,000 cash to maintain and repair facilities and equipment in June.

e. Collected $302,000 from customers on account.

f. Borrowed $75,000 by signing a note.

g. Issued additional stock for $20,000.

h. Paid employees $317,000 in June.

i. Purchased for cash and used $41,000 in fuel for the aircraft and equipment.

j. Paid $32,000 on accounts payable.

k. Ordered $6,000 in spare parts and supplies.

Required:

1. Prepare T-accounts for May 31 from the above list; enter the respective balances. You will need additional T-accounts for income statement accounts; enter $0 balances.
2. For each transaction, record the effects in the T-accounts. Label each using the letter of the transaction.
3. Prepare an unadjusted income statement and unadjusted balance sheet in good form.

Exxon Corp.

P3–9 *Preparing T-Accounts, an Income Statement, and a Balance Sheet*

Below are the summary account balances from the December 31, 1994, balance sheet of the Exxon Corporation. The accounts are followed by a list of hypothetical transactions for the month of January 1995. The following accounts are shown in millions of dollars.

Cash	$ 1,157	Marketable Securities	$ 618
Notes Payable	3,858	Accounts Payable	13,391
Accounts Receivable	8,073	Income Tax Payable	2,244
Inventories	5,541	Prepaid Expenses	1,071
Other Debt	30,954	Investments	5,394
Property & Equipment, Net	63,425	Intangibles, Net	2,583
Shareholders' Equity	37,415		

The accounts have normal debit or credit balances, but they are not necessarily listed in good order.

January transactions:

a. Purchased new equipment costing $150 million on account.

b. Received $500 million on accounts receivable.

c. Received and paid the telephone bills for $1 million.

d. Sales to customers on account were $5 million. Cost of sales was $1 million.

e. Paid employees $1 million for wages earned in January.

f. Paid half of the income taxes payable.

g. Purchased supplies inventory for $23 million on account.

h. Prepaid rent for February for a warehouse for $12 million.

i. Paid $10 million of other debt and $11 million in interest on the debt.

j. Purchased a patent (an intangible asset) for $8 million cash.

Required:

1. Prepare T-accounts for January 31, 1995, from the above account balances. Make additional T-accounts for the revenues and expenses and enter $0 for the beginning balances.
2. For each transaction, record the effects in the T-accounts. Label each using the letter of the transaction.
3. Prepare an unadjusted income statement and unadjusted balance sheet in good form.

CASES

C3–1 *Analyzing and Restating an Income Statement that Has Major Deficiencies: A Challenging Case*

Tom Martinez started and operated a small service company during 19A. At the end of the year, he prepared the following statement based on information stored in a large filing cabinet:

MARTINEZ COMPANY
Profit for 19A

Service fees income collected during 19A		$75,000
Cash dividends received		10,000
Total		$85,000
Expense for operations paid during 19A	$52,000	
Cash stolen	500	
Supplies purchased for use on service jobs (cash paid)	1,200	
Total		53,700
Profit		$31,300

Below is a summary of completed transactions:

a. Service fees earned during 19A, $87,000.

b. The cash dividends received were on shares of ABC Industrial stock purchased by Tom Martinez six years earlier.

c. Expenses incurred during 19A, $61,000.

d. Supplies on hand (unused) at the end of 19A, $700.

Required:

1. Did Martinez prepare the above statement on a cash basis or an accrual basis? Explain how you can tell. Which basis should be used? Explain why.

2. Revise the above statement to make it consistent with proper accounting and reporting. Explain (using footnotes) the reason for each change that you make.

C3–2 *Challenging Analytical Case Related to Application of the Accounting Model*

Wilsey Painting Service Company was organized during January 19A by three individuals. On January 20, 19A, the company issued 5,000 shares of stock to each of its organizers. Below is a schedule of the cumulative account balances immediately after each of the first 10 transactions.

Accounts	Cumulative Balances									
	a	*b*	*c*	*d*	*e*	*f*	*g*	*h*	*i*	*j*
Cash	$75,000	$70,000	$85,000	$71,000	$61,000	$61,000	$57,000	$46,000	$41,000	$57,000
Accounts Receivable			12,000	12,000	12,000	26,000	26,000	26,000	26,000	10,000
Office Fixtures		20,000	20,000	20,000	20,000	20,000	20,000	20,000	20,000	20,000
Land				18,000	18,000	18,000	18,000	18,000	18,000	18,000
Accounts Payable					3,000	3,000	3,000	10,000	5,000	5,000
Note Payable		15,000	15,000	19,000	19,000	19,000	19,000	19,000	19,000	19,000
Contributed Capital	75,000	75,000	75,000	75,000	75,000	75,000	75,000	75,000	75,000	75,000
Retained Earnings										
Dividends Declared							4,000	4,000	4,000	4,000
Paint Revenue			27,000	27,000	27,000	41,000	41,000	41,000	41,000	41,000
Supplies Expense					5,000	5,000	5,000	8,000	8,000	8,000
Wages Expense					8,000	8,000	8,000	23,000	23,000	23,000

Required:

1. Analyze the changes in the above schedule for each transaction; then explain the transaction. Transactions *(a)* and *(b)* are examples:
   a. Cash increased $75,000, and contributed capital (stockholders' equity) increased $75,000. Therefore, transaction (*a*) was an issuance of the capital stock of the corporation for $75,000 cash.
   b. Cash decreased $5,000, office fixtures (an asset) increased $20,000, and note payable (a liability) increased $15,000. Therefore, transaction (*b*) was a purchase of office fixtures that cost $20,000. Payment was made as follows: cash, $5,000; note payable, $15,000.
2. Based only on the above schedule (disregarding your response to requirement 1) respond to the following after transaction (*j*):

Income statement:	
Revenues	$
Expenses	______
Net income	$______
Balance sheet:	
Assets	$
Liabilities	______
Stockholders' equity	$______

C3–3 *An Ethical Dilemma*

Ray Ramsay is the manager of an upstate New York regional office for an insurance company. As the regional manager, his compensation package comprises a base salary, commissions, and a bonus when the region sells new policies in excess of its quota. Mr. Ramsay has been under enormous pressure lately, stemming largely from two factors. First, he is experiencing a mounting personal debt due to a family member's illness. Second, compounding his worries, the region's sales of new policies have dipped below the normal quota for the first time in years.

You have been working for Mr. Ramsay for two years, and like everyone else in the office, you consider yourself lucky to work for such a supportive boss. You also feel great sympathy for his personal problems over the last few months. In your position as accountant for the regional office, you are only too aware of the drop in new policy sales and the impact this will have on the manager's bonus. While you are working late at year-end, Mr. Ramsay stops by your office.

Mr. Ramsay asks you to change the manner in which you have accounted for a new property insurance policy for a large local business. A check for the premium, substantial in amount, came in the mail on December 31, the last day of the reporting year. The premium covers a period beginning on January 5. You deposited the check and correctly debited cash and credited a *revenue collected in advance* account. Mr. Ramsay says, "Hey, we have the money this year, so why not count the revenue this year. I never did understand why you accountants are so picky about these things anyway. I'd like you to change the way you have recorded the transaction. I want you to credit a *revenue* account. And anyway, I've done favors for you in the past, and I am asking for such a small thing in return." With that, Mr. Ramsay leaves for the day.

Required:

How should you handle this situation? What are the ethical implications of Mr. Ramsay's request? Who are the parties that would be helped or harmed if you complied with the request? If you fail to comply with his request, how will you explain your position to Mr. Ramsay in the morning?

C3–4 International Financial Statements: A Challenging Case

Volkswagen

Your cousin, an engineering major, has inherited some money and wants to invest in an auto company. She has never taken an accounting course and has asked you to help her compare a United States automaker's financial statements to a German automaker's financial statements. Your cousin has given you the income statement, asset section of the balance sheet, and audit opinion for Volkswagen for 1992.

Required:

Review the following excerpts of Volkswagen's financial statements. Write a letter to your cousin explaining the similarities and the dissimilarities you would expect to find if you compared Volkswagen's statements to a company in the United States. Offer your opinion on whether you would expect the underlying accounting principles of the two countries to be similar or dissimilar. On what are you basing your opinion?

Audit certificate

"The consolidated financial statements, which we have audited in accordance with professional standards, comply with the German legal provisions. With due regard to the generally accepted accounting principles, the consolidated financial statements give a true and fair view of the Group's assets, liabilities, financial position and profit or loss. The Group management report is consistent with the consolidated financial statements."

Hanover, February 24, 1993

C&L TREUARBEIT
DEUTSCHE REVISION
Aktiengesellschaft

Statement of Earnings of the Volkswagen Group for the Fiscal Year Ended December 31, 1992—DM million—

	Note	1992	1991
Sales	(13)	**85,403**	**76,315**
Cost of sales		79,155	69,472
Gross profit		**+ 6,248**	**+ 6,843**
Selling and distribution expenses		5,661	5,414
General administration expenses		2,316	2,185
Other operating income	(14)	4,246	4,406
Other operating expenses	(15)	2,634	3,104
Results from participations	(16)	+ 55	+ 97
Interest results	(17)	+ 739	+ 1,228
Write-down of financial assets and securities classified as current assets		75	86
Results from ordinary business activities		**+ 602**	**+ 1,785**
Taxes on income		455	671
Net earnings	(18)	**147**	**1,114**

Balance Sheet of the Volkswagen Group, December 31, 1992—DM million—

Assets	Note	Dec. 31, 1992	Dec. 31, 1991
Fixed assets	(1)		
Intangible assets		631	372
Tangible assets		24,050	21,126
Financial assets		2,747	2,655
Leasing and rental assets		7,393	6,293
		34,821	**30,446**
Current assets			
Inventories	(2)	9,736	9,049
Receivables and other assets	(3)	21,065	18,675
Securities	(4)	1,497	2,329
Cash on hand, deposits at German Federal Bank and postal giro balances, cash in banks		7,836	9,255
		40,134	**39,308**
Prepaid and deferred charges	(5)	**329**	**336**
Balance-sheet total		**75,284**	**70,090**

Toys "Я" Us

C3–5 Financial Statement Analysis

Refer to the January 29, 1994 financial statements of Toys "Я" Us given in Appendix B at the end of the book.

Required:

1. State the amount of the largest expense on the 1994 income statement and describe the transaction represented by the expense.
2. Give the journal entry for interest expense for the year ended January 29, 1994 (for this question, assume the amount has not yet been paid).
3. Assuming all net sales are on credit, how much cash did Toys "Я" Us collect from customers? (Hint: Use a T-account of accounts receivable to infer collection.)
4. A shareholder has complained that "more dividends should be paid because the company had net earnings of $482,953,000. Since this amount is all cash, more of it should go to the owners." Explain why the shareholder's assumption that earnings equal net cash inflow is valid. If you feel the assumption is not valid, state so and support your position concisely.
5. Describe and contrast the purpose of an income statement versus a balance sheet.

4

THE ADJUSTMENT PROCESS AND FINANCIAL STATEMENT PREPARATION

Chapters 2 and 3 introduced you to the fundamental accounting model and transaction analysis. The chapters also discussed the use of journal entries and T-accounts to record the results of transaction analysis for operating, investing, and financing activities during the accounting period. In this chapter, we will build on your knowledge and discuss the income determination activities at the end of the accounting period: the adjustment process, preparation of financial statements, and the closing process. For those wanting information on formal recordkeeping procedures in the accounting cycle, supplements to the chapter are included.

LEARNING OBJECTIVES

After studying this chapter, you should be able to:

1. **Explain the purpose of a trial balance and construct one from T-account balances.** *168*
2. **Analyze deferrals and accruals at the end of the period and determine the adjustments necessary to update accounts for proper matching of revenues and expenses.** *170*
3. **Prepare a complete set of financial statements: income statement, statement of stockholders' equity, balance sheet, and statement of cash flows.** *183*
4. **Explain the closing process and prepare closing entries.** *188*
5. **(Supplement A) Utilize a formal general journal and general ledger format in preparing journal entries and accumulating account balances.** *197*
6. **(Supplement B) Construct a year-end worksheet that includes a trial balance, adjustments, and amounts for the income statement and balance sheet.** *199*
7. **(Supplement C) Explain and prepare reversing entries.** *203*

Management Decision Setting

SBARRO, INC.

The Busiest Time of the Fiscal Year

As indicated in a recent annual report, "the Company's business is subject to seasonal fluctuations, the effects of weather and economic conditions. Earnings have been highest in its fourth fiscal quarter due primarily to increased [sales] volume in shopping malls during the holiday shopping season . . ." These differences in volume are borne out by the accompanying graph of quarterly sales.

For Sbarro, the fourth and first quarters are the busiest from an operating standpoint. The end of the fourth quarter and beginning of the first quarter also mark the busiest and most critical times from an accounting standpoint—the time when revenues and expenses are adjusted, financial statements are prepared, and the books are closed. It is also the point at which the external auditors complete their work and issue their opinion on the fairness of the financial statements and the company makes the statements available to external users.

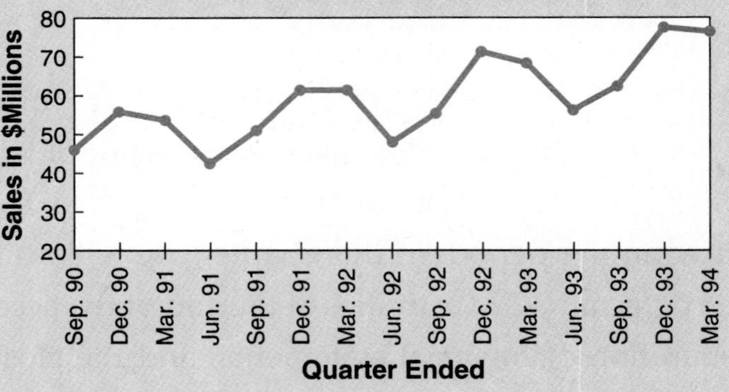

BUSINESS BACKGROUND

In Chapter 3 we noted that Sbarro, like all well-managed companies, organizes its accounting system with recordkeeping efficiency in mind. As a consequence, it usually records external transactions when the business documents supporting those transactions are processed. For example, the sale of food would be recorded at the end of each day based on the daily cash register total. When the end of the accounting period falls at a point other than the end of the operating cycle, the revenue and expense accounts may not be fully up-to-date following accrual accounting principles. That is, some revenues and expenses and the related changes in assets and liabilities may not be properly recorded in the correct accounting period. As a consequence, adjustments or corrections are necessary.

This problem is particularly acute in the case of internal activities that do not result in an actual exchange between the business and other parties but have a direct and measurable effect on the business entity. These internal transactions, introduced in Chapter 3, include

- *Accruals* Revenues that have been earned or expenses that have been incurred by the end of the period but have not been recorded and no cash has been received or paid.
- *Deferrals* Receipts of assets or payments of cash in advance of the related revenue or expense recognition.

Exhibit 4–1 presents the fundamental steps in the accounting cycle. Phase 1 of the accounting cycle involves analyzing and recording transactions that occur during the accounting period. In this chapter, we examine the end-of-period steps in Phase 2 that focus primarily on adjustments relating to accruals and deferrals. Why do we need to understand the steps in the second phase of the accounting cycle? Income measurement would be incomplete without an updating of accounts to ensure proper revenue recognition and expense matching for the period (the adjustment process).

Unlike the fairly routine entries based on supporting documentation during the accounting period, *knowledge* and *judgment* are primary inputs in determining end-of-period adjustments to revenues and expenses. As such, the accounts most subject to year-end adjustment are of considerable interest to external users of the financial statements. Analysts recognize that management's judgment plays the greatest role in determining year-end adjustments and that these judgments may provide important signals of management's expectations for the future. At the same time, analysts recognize that these adjustments are thus most subject to error and manipulation. Therefore, adjustments also receive significant scrutiny by auditors. You must understand the mechanics of the adjustment process before you can understand the information adjustments contain and the errors that can occur.

After these adjustments are determined, financial statements can be prepared. (Many businesses use accounting worksheets, described in Chapter Supplement B, to speed up the production of financial statements.) In addition, certain accounts, such as revenues and expenses, need to be prepared for the beginning of the next accounting period. This step is called the *closing process*.

Fundamental Steps in the Accounting Cycle **Exhibit 4–1**

START OF ACCOUNTING PERIOD

Phase 1:
During the Accounting Period
(discussed in Chapters 2 and 3)

Phase 2:
At the End of the Accounting Period
(discussed in Chapter 4)

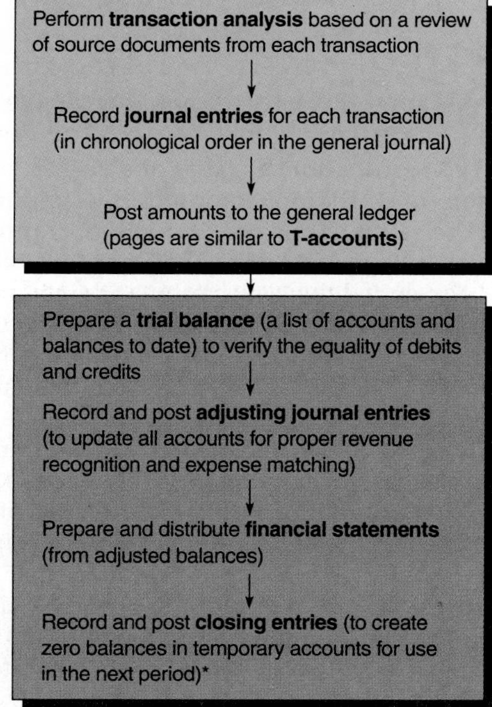

Perform **transaction analysis** based on a review of source documents from each transaction
Record **journal entries** for each transaction (in chronological order in the general journal)
Post amounts to the general ledger (pages are similar to **T-accounts**)
Prepare a **trial balance** (a list of accounts and balances to date) to verify the equality of debits and credits
Record and post **adjusting journal entries** (to update all accounts for proper revenue recognition and expense matching)
Prepare and distribute **financial statements** (from adjusted balances)
Record and post **closing entries** (to create zero balances in temporary accounts for use in the next period)*

END OF ACCOUNTING PERIOD

*Temporary accounts are those that accumulate balances for the period. They are revenue, expense, and dividends declared accounts.

You must understand these steps before you can fully understand the process of communicating accounting information to users which we will discuss in Chapter 5. In this chapter, we will emphasize the use of the same analytical tools employed in Chapters 2 and 3 (T-accounts, journal entries, and timelines) to understand how adjustments are analyzed and entries prepared.

THE TRIAL BALANCE

Learning Objective 1
Explain the purpose of a trial balance and construct one from T-account balances.

A **trial balance** is a listing of all accounts with their balances to provide a check on the equality of the debits and credits.

The first step normally taken at the end of the accounting period is to create a **trial balance**, also known as an *unadjusted trial balance*. A trial balance is a listing of individual accounts, usually in financial statement order, with their ending debit or credit balances. Using two columns, debit balances are indicated in the left column and credit balances are indicated in the right column. Then the two columns are totaled to provide *a check on the equality of the debits and credits*. In fact, that is all that the trial balance reflects. Many types of errors may still have been made even though debits equal credits:

- Wrong accounts may have been used in journal entries.
- Wrong but equal amounts may have been used in journal entries.
- Wrong accounts may have been posted from correct journal entries.
- Wrong but equal amounts may have been posted from correct journal entries.

The trial balance will not indicate a problem due to these errors. However, if the two columns are not equal, errors have occurred in one or more of the following:

- In preparing journal entries where debits do not equal credits.
- In posting the correct dollar effects of transactions from the journal entry to the ledger.
- In computing ending balances in accounts.
- In copying ending balances in the ledger to the trial balance.

These errors can be traced and should be corrected before moving to the next step. Even though computerized accounting systems should reduce some of these potential errors, the use of improper accounts or equal but incorrect amounts in transaction analysis may still occur.

We ended the last chapter with incomplete, unadjusted financial statements for Sbarro, Inc., because several internal transactions relating to revenue and expense items had not been recorded in the proper period. The unadjusted balances in the Chapter 3 T-accounts are listed in the trial balance in Exhibit 4–2. A trial balance is a schedule prepared for internal purposes and is not considered a financial statement for external users. However, the schedule should be clearly labeled for future reference as in Exhibit 4–2.

You will notice in Exhibit 4–2 that the balance in Retained Earnings is the amount at the beginning of the period since net income and dividend amounts have not been formally entered into that account through journal entries. These entries, as part of the closing process, will be discussed later in the chapter.

You will also notice that the Equipment account is stated at original cost of \$204,350 in the trial balance but was stated at \$129,550 (original cost minus the portion allocated to past operations) in the T-accounts in prior chapters. For long-lived assets such as equipment used in operations, individual account

Trial Balance for Sbarro, Inc. **Exhibit 4–2**

SBARRO, INC. AND SUBSIDIARIES Unadjusted Trial Balance At January 30, 1994	Debit	Credit
Cash	$ 34,280	
Marketable securities	37,200	
Receivables (from franchisees and others)	1,800	
Inventory (supplies of food and paper products)	2,990	
Prepaid expenses	14,700	
Equipment	204,350	
Accumulated depreciation—equipment		$ 74,800
Other assets	3,200	
Notes payable		1,200
Accounts payable		7,030
Accrued expenses payable (rent, payroll, and other)		18,400
Dividends payable		4,700
Deferred income (unearned revenue)		430
Deferred income taxes		18,100
Contributed capital		29,900
Retained earnings		129,300
Restaurant sales revenue		23,800
Franchise related income		500
Cost of food and paper products	2,100	
Wages expense	5,300	
Utilities expense	190	
Repairs expense	50	
Dividends declared	2,000	
Totals	$308,160	$308,160

balances remain at original cost to preserve the historical information. To reflect the used-up portion of the assets' cost, a **contra-asset**, or offset, account is created. Any contra account is directly related to another account but has the opposite balance. For equipment, the contra-asset is called Accumulated Depreciation—Equipment. It has a credit balance. We will discuss many contra accounts in other chapters and will designate contra accounts with an X in front of the type of account to which it is related (e.g., Accumulated Depreciation (XA) for contra-asset).

A **contra account** is an account that is an offset to, or reduction of, the primary account.

The difference between an asset's acquisition cost and accumulated depreciation is called **book value (net book value or carrying value)**. The book value does not represent the current market value of the asset because accounting for depreciation is a cost allocation process rather than a market valuation process (discussed later in the chapter). Sbarro, like many other companies, subtracts the balance in Accumulated Depreciation from the cost in the Equipment account, reporting the net amount on the balance sheet. The balance of each individual account is disclosed in a footnote to the financial statements. The note disclosure from a recent Sbarro annual report is as follows:

Book value (net book value, carrying value) of an asset is the difference between an asset's acquisition cost and accumulated depreciation, its related contra account.

Real World Excerpt

Sbarro, Inc.
Annual Report

Notes To Consolidated Financial Statements

3. PROPERTY AND EQUIPMENT[1]	Sbarro, Inc. and Subsidiaries (In thousands)	
	January 2, 1994	January 3, 1993
Leasehold improvements	$127,202	$104,509
Furniture, fixtures and equipment	73,162	59,310
Construction-in-progress	3,090	7,965
	203,454	171,784
Less accumulated depreciation and amortization	74,801	58,285
	$128,653	$113,499

ADJUSTING ENTRIES

Learning Objective 2
Analyze deferrals and accruals at the end of the period and determine the adjustments necessary to update accounts for proper matching of revenues and expenses.

Adjusting entries are entries necessary at the end of the accounting period to measure income properly, correct errors, and provide for adequate valuation of balance sheet accounts.

We learned in the last chapter that under accrual accounting, revenues are recorded when earned and expenses are matched with the related revenues in the same period. Operating income for a period of time, therefore, is determined by measuring *all* revenues and expenses of that period. Often **adjusting entries** are necessary at the end of the accounting period to meet this objective. We also learned in the last chapter to identify when an account may need to be adjusted at the end of the accounting period. In reality, nearly all asset and liability accounts will need to be analyzed and adjusted at year-end to measure income properly, correct errors, and provide for adequate valuation of accounts on the balance sheet. We will introduce the adjustment process in this chapter for common adjusting entries. You will learn about additional adjustments in future chapters, most of which relate to the valuation of specific accounts such as accounts receivable and corrections of errors.

You will recall that the two types of internal transactions requiring adjustment are deferrals and accruals:

1. **Deferrals** Previously recorded assets, liabilities, revenues, or expenses that need to be adjusted at the end of the period to reflect earned revenues or incurred expenses. Examples are:
   a. Insurance premium paid in advance of coverage:
   a deferred (or prepaid) expense (A)
   b. Rent collected in advance of occupancy by tenant:
   a deferred (or unearned) revenue (L)
2. **Accruals** Revenues that have been earned and expenses that have been incurred by the end of the current accounting period but will be collected or paid in a future accounting period. Examples are:
   a. Services performed in advance of collection:
   an accrued revenue (a receivable) (A)
   b. Wages earned by employees but not yet paid:
   an accrued expense (a payable) (L)

[1]Leasehold improvements are modifications to leased property (property that is being rented), such as installing new plumbing or flooring or replacing an existing elevator or roof. These expenditures are assets because they have use beyond the current accounting period. Construction-in-progress is the accumulated costs to date for the construction of buildings and equipment that are not yet ready for use. In addition, the total amounts in the footnote do not exactly match with the property and equipment amounts indicated on Sbarro's balance sheets in Exhibit 2–2 because the amounts in the exhibit were rounded for simplification.

The process for determining the proper adjusting entry in each case is slightly more complex for deferrals than accruals. The three primary tools used in the process are T-accounts, timelines, and journal entries. We will begin with deferrals.

Deferrals

Since deferral accounts result from recording a transaction during the accounting period, you must analyze how the original entry was recorded before you can determine the appropriate adjustment. A simple example will illustrate this point. Let's assume that a dental office has a fiscal year that ends on December 31. The dentist maintains her accounting records on an accrual basis. At the end of the year, she identifies two items that require adjustment: (1) professional liability insurance paid for in the past that provides for insurance coverage in the future and (2) unearned dental fees she received in advance from local businesses to provide dental care to their employees in the future. Insurance coverage and dental services are assumed to occur evenly over time unless otherwise indicated.

On November 15, she paid $1,800 for insurance for six months of coverage (from November 15 to May 15 of next year). This results in $300 coverage each full month. By December 31, the dentist will have received one and one-half months of coverage ($450). Therefore, for the current year, the amount of insurance expense should be $450 with $1,350 in the Prepaid Insurance (A) account on the balance sheet. However, performing this level of analysis each time an entry is made is cumbersome. It is easier for organizations to make a simple journal entry when cash is paid without anticipating the year-end balances, then adjust accounts at the end of the period. Therefore on November 15, there are two ways this payment could have been recorded initially:

Original Entry Option 1:		
Prepaid insurance expense (A)	1,800	
Cash (A)		1,800

Original Entry Option 2:		
Insurance expense (E)	1,800	
Cash (A)		1,800

Option 1 is more consistent with accrual accounting because on November 15, the amount paid represents future benefits (insurance coverage) to the dental office. This is the definition of an asset. However, payments are often recorded as expenses on the payment date (option 2) to simplify recordkeeping since they are frequently incurred by the end of the accounting period. When the full amount is not completely incurred, an adjustment is necessary.

The same process to determine the appropriate adjustment should now be followed for either of these possible original entries:

Step 1. Create two T-accounts for each option: one for a balance sheet account and one for its related expense. One of the accounts for each option is from the original entry. Fill in the unadjusted amounts from the original entries (❶ in the T-accounts).

Step 2. Determine the amounts needed as ending balances in each of the accounts (consider using a timeline). Fill in the desired ending balances in the T-accounts (❷ in the T-account).

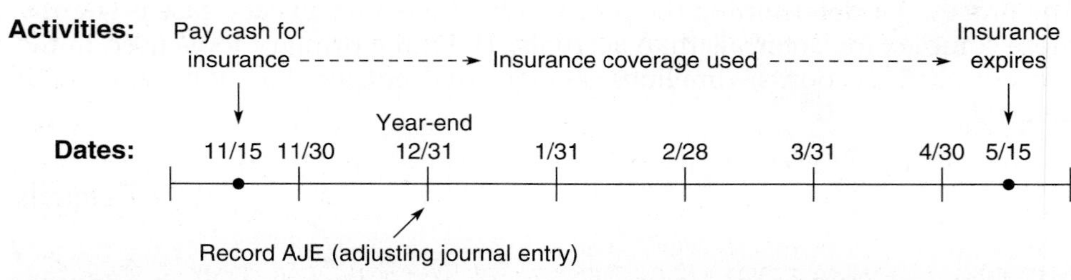

Amounts: $1,800 for 6 months = $300 per month. By December 31, insurance for one and one-half months has been used; $450 should be the ending balance in insurance expense. The remaining $1,350 ($1,800 – $450) represents four and one-half months of future insurance coverage (an asset) on December 31.

Step 3. The amounts needed to convert from the original entry to the appropriate ending balances create *the required* adjusting journal entry (AJE). Prepare and post the entry in the T-accounts.

If Original Entry Option 1 is recorded:

Prepaid Insurance Expense (A)			Insurance Expense (E)	
❶ 1,800			0	
	AJE 450		AJE 450	
❷ 1,350			❷ 450	

or

If Original Entry Option 2 is recorded:

Prepaid Insurance Expense (A)			Insurance Expense (E)	
0			❶ 1,800	
AJE 1,350				AJE 1,350
❷ 1,350			❷ 450	

Adjusting Entry for Option 1:

Insurance expense (E)	450	
Prepaid insurance expense (A)		450

Adjusting Entry for Option 2:

Prepaid insurance expense (A)	1,350	
Insurance expense (E)		1,350

Regardless of which account was debited in the original entry, the same correct ending balances in Prepaid Insurance Expense and Insurance Expense result. However, the adjusting entry that is required is different.

Now we will consider the second situation where on December 1, the dental office accepted a $2,400 payment from local businesses to provide dental care to their employees over the next three months. There are two ways this receipt could have been recorded initially :

Original Entry Option 1:

Cash (A)	2,400	
Unearned dental fees (L)		2,400

or

Original Entry Option 2:

Cash (A)	2,400	
Dental fee revenue (R)		2,400

As before, option 1 appears more consistent with accrual accounting because the amount received on December 1 represents what the dental office owes to clients in the future. Cash was received prior to the delivery of services. This is a liability since either the cash received must be returned or the services must be delivered in the future. However, receipts may be recorded as revenues on the cash receipt date (option 2). When the full amount is not earned in the period, an adjustment is necessary.

The process to determine the adjustment will now be followed for both of these possible original entries:

Step 1. Create two T-accounts for each option: one for a balance sheet account and one for its related revenue. One of the accounts for each option is from the original entry. Fill in the unadjusted balances from the original entries (❶ in the T-account).

Step 2. Determine the amounts needed as ending balances (consider using a timeline). Fill in the ending balances in the T-accounts (❷ in the T-account).

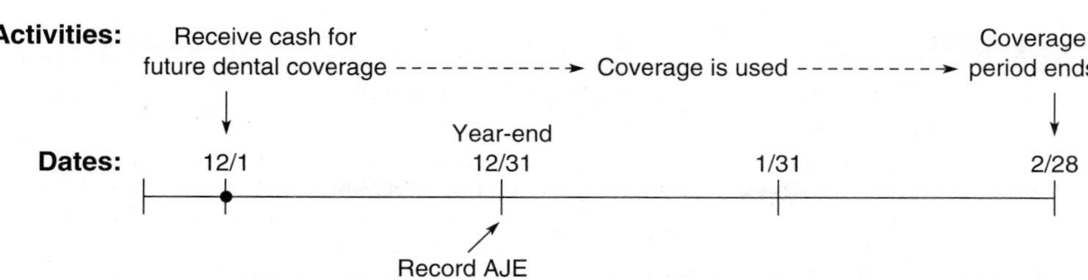

Amounts: $2,400 for 3 months = $800 per month. From December 1 to December 31, one month of dental service has been provided; $800 × 1 month = $800 dental fee revenue. The remainder of $1,600 ($2,400 – $800) represents future dental service owed to businesses (a liability).

Step 3. The amounts needed to convert from the original entry to the appropriate ending balances create the required adjusting journal entry. Prepare and post the entry in the T-accounts.

If Original Entry Option 1 is recorded:

Unearned Dental Fees (L)				Dental Fee Revenue (R)			
		❶	2,400				0
AJE	**800**					**AJE**	**800**
		❷	1,600			❷	800

or

If Original Entry Option 2 is recorded:

Unearned Dental Fees (L)				Dental Fee Revenue (R)			
			0			❶	2,400
		AJE	**1,600**	**AJE**	**1,600**		
		❷	1,600			❷	800

Adjusting Entry 1:

Unearned dental fees (L)	800	
Dental fee revenue (R)		800

Adjusting Entry 2:

Dental fee revenue (R)	1,600	
Unearned dental fees (L)		1,600

As before, regardless of which original entry was made, the same correct ending balances in Unearned Dental Fees and Dental Fee Revenue result after the adjusting entry. However, the adjusting entry is different in each case.

Accruals

Accruals occur when the company has undertaken activities that result in earning revenues or incurring expenses where no cash has been exchanged and no source document reflecting the earning of the revenue or incurring of the expense has been given or received by the end of the accounting period. Unlike deferrals, no original entry has been recorded. Therefore, the process for adjusting the accounts is simpler. Here we compute the amount to be recorded directly.

Let us continue our example of the adjustment process for the dental office. Two activities that normally require an accrued expense and an accrued revenue adjustment are wages to employees and interest on a loan to an employee.

Assume that all employees are paid $3,000 biweekly. Payment for 10 working days is made on the second Friday. The last payment for the year was on Friday, December 27. The employees continued to work through December 31, the end of the accounting period, but they will not be paid until January 10. The unadjusted balance in the Wages Expense account is $75,000.

Step 1. Create appropriate T-accounts. An expense and a payable will be created. Fill in the unadjusted balances (❶ in the T-account).

Step 2. Determine the amount to be accrued (consider using a timeline). Unlike deferrals, no ending balance is determined in this step for accruals. Therefore, the T-account does not reflect ending balances for step 2.

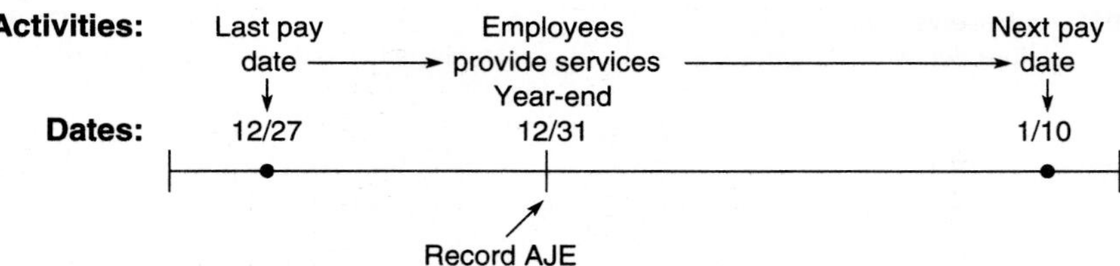

Amounts: $3,000 for 10 working days = $300 per working day. Assume there are two weekend days and two working days from December 28 through December 31; $300 × 2 working days = $600 to be recorded as wages expense in the current period.

Step 3. Prepare and post the adjusting journal entry in the T-accounts (determined in step 2).

Wages expense (E)	600	
Wages payable (L)		600

Wages Payable (L)			Wages Expense (E)		
		0	❶	75,000	
	AJE	**600**	**AJE**	**600**	
		600		75,600	

Since no entry related to the $600 expense had been recorded in the past, the adjusting entry increases an expense and increases a payable by the computed amount.

As a second example, the dental office loaned $2,000 to an employee on September 1 for which the employee signed a note. The note principal along with interest at a 12% annual rate is to be repaid in six months. Interest is the cost of borrowing money. As each day passes, more interest is owed. By the end of the year, four months have passed, so the dental office has earned four months of interest revenue for which it will not be paid until March 1.

Step 1. Create appropriate T-accounts. A revenue and a receivable will be created. Fill in the unadjusted balances (❶ in the T-account).

Step 2. Determine the amount to be accrued (consider using a timeline). Unlike deferrals, no ending balance is determined in this step for accruals. Therefore, the T-account does not reflect ending balances for step 2.

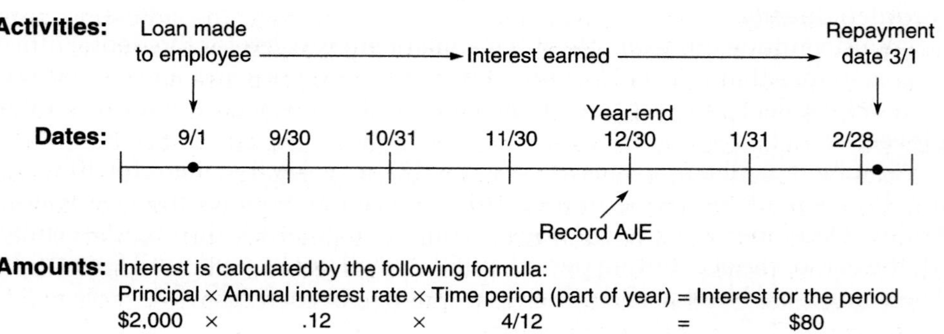

Step 3. Prepare and post the adjusting journal entry in the T-accounts (determined in step 2).

Interest receivable (A)	80	
Interest revenue (R)		80

Sbarro considers its flagship product, the Sbarro pizza, its "Best Pie Chart."

Interest Receivable (A)				Interest Revenue (R)	
	0			❶	0
AJE	**80**			AJE	**80**
	80				80

Since the accrued revenue has not yet been recorded, the adjusting entry increases a receivable and increases a revenue by the computed amount.

In summary, since no prior entry has been made, expense accruals *increase* an expense and a payable and revenue accruals *increase* a revenue and a receivable. As a consequence, we directly compute the amount of the needed adjustment. However, deferred accounts already exist at the end of the accounting period from a prior entry. Either a revenue, expense, asset, or liability is overstated and must be *decreased,* while its related account is understated and must be *increased.* Here we compute the corrected ending balance in the account and adjust the balances to that number. In each case, two tools will be quite useful: T-accounts and timelines.

These adjusting entries are recorded in the journal and posted to the T-accounts. When completed, the adjusted balances are used to prepare financial statements, which is the next step of the accounting cycle. Before we illustrate a complete set of financial statements, we need to adjust the accounts of Sbarro, Inc., at the end of the month. You will recall from Chapter 3 that Sbarro's policy for fiscal year-end is the Sunday closest to the end of the month. Therefore, we will adjust the accounts on January 30, the Sunday closest to month-end.[2] Companies can choose fiscal periods other than actual month-ends and financial statements can cover different accounting periods (month, quarter, or year).

FINANCIAL ANALYSIS

Accruals and Deferrals: The Keys to Financial Reporting Strategy

Most of the deferrals and accruals discussed in this chapter, such as the allocation of prepaid insurance or determination of accrued interest revenue, involve direct calculations and little judgment on the part of the company's accountants. In later chapters, we will discuss many other adjustments that involve difficult and complex estimates about the future. These include, for example, estimates of customers' ability to make payments to the company on account, the useful lives of new machines, and future amounts that a company may owe on warranties on products sold in the past. Each of these estimates, and many others, can have significant effects on the stream of net earnings that companies report over time.

When analysts attempt to value firms based on their balance sheet and income statement data, they also evaluate the estimates that form the basis for accruals and deferrals. Those firms that make relatively pessimistic estimates that reduce current income are judged to follow conservative financial reporting strategies, and their reports of performance are given more credence by experienced analysts. The earnings numbers reported by these companies are often said to be of "higher quality" because they are less influenced by management's natural optimism. However, firms that consistently make optimistic estimates that result in reporting higher net income are judged to be aggressive. These companies' operating performance is judged to be of lower quality by analysts.

ADJUSTING ENTRIES ILLUSTRATED

We illustrate common adjusting entries by updating the accounts of Sbarro, Inc., based on the account balances and transactions in Chapters 2 and 3. As we review Sbarro's trial balance in Exhibit 4–2, we can identify several deferral accounts that will need to be analyzed and may need to be adjusted:

Prepaid Expenses (e.g., rent and insurance) All or a portion may have been used by month-end.

Inventory of Supplies and Equipment A portion of each has been used during the month.

Deferred Income All or a portion may have been earned by month-end.

In addition, we can see that several accruals need to be recorded for activities that have generated unrecorded revenues or expenses:

Marketable Securities An investment in stocks and bonds usually produces investment income (dividends on stocks and interest on bonds).

Receivables Franchisees may owe additional royalties to Sbarro that should be recognized as revenue by January 30.

Notes Payable Sbarro would normally owe interest on any borrowed funds that should be recognized as an expense and interest payable.

Accrued Expenses Payable Any rent due to mall owners, wages due to employees, and amounts due for utilities not yet due by or billed to Sbarro will need to be recorded as expenses.

Income Taxes Payable Income tax expense will need to be recorded for the period.

[2] Adjusting entries may be prepared monthly, quarterly and/or annually to ensure that proper amounts are included on the financial reports presented to external users.

The process we use will include the three steps outlined above for deferrals and the three steps for accruals. You should study the following illustration carefully to understand the steps in the adjustment process, paying close attention to the computation of the amounts in the adjustment and the effects on the T-account balances. First, we will adjust the deferrals, then the accruals.

Deferrals

We will adjust the following deferral accounts identified above: *Prepaid Expenses* for rent and insurance, *Inventory* of food and paper product supplies, *Equipment* used during the month, and *Deferred Income* for unearned revenue.

A. Prepaid Expenses of $14,700 include a $12,600 payment made in early January for the rental of mall space at several malls for the three-month period from January through March. (The remaining $2,100 in Prepaid Expenses is for prepaid insurance discussed in the next transaction.)

Step 1: Create T-accounts based on the original entry.

Step 2: Determine the appropriate ending balances: $12,600 for 3 months = $4,200 per month. At the end of January, one month has passed and two months remain. Prepaid expenses ending balance = $14,700 – 4,200 = $10,500.

Prepaid Expenses (A)

Debit	Credit
14,700	
	AJE 4,200
10,500	

Rent Expense (occupancy and other) (E)

Debit	Credit
0	
AJE 4,200	
4,200	

Step 3: Determine, prepare, and post the adjusting entry:

	Debit	Credit
Rent expense—occupancy and other (E)	4,200	
Prepaid expenses (A)		4,200

The words *occupancy and other* added after Rent Expense represent the categorization of rent expense on Sbarro's income statement. Many accounts of similar nature are often aggregated or combined in the financial statements. In this case, rent expense that Sbarro categorizes as Occupancy and Other Expenses relates to operating the Company-owned restaurants. We will need to know this categorization when we prepare the financial statements. We will see in the next analysis that expenses for operations are often separated from expenses not directly related to operations, such as rent for administrative offices and salaries of the employees working in the offices.

B. In addition to the January rent expense in (A), the $10,500 that remains in Prepaid Expenses also includes $2,100 for insurance for January paid last year. Two-thirds of the amount relates to restaurants (operations) and one-third covers property at Sbarro headquarters. Expenses related to the headquarters are categorized as general and administrative expense on the income statement.

Step 1: Create T-accounts based on the original entry.

Step 2: Determine the appropriate ending balances: $2,100 is given as expense for January; $1,400 (two-thirds) is for operations and $700 (one-third) is a general and administrative expense.

Prepaid Expenses (A)

Debit	Credit
10,500	
	AJE 2,100
8,400	

Insurance Expense (occupancy and other) (E)

Debit	Credit
0	
AJE 1,400	
1,400	

Insurance Expense (general and administrative) (E)

Debit	Credit
0	
AJE 700	
700	

Step 3: Determine, prepare, and post the adjusting entry:

	Debit	Credit
Insurance expense—occupancy and other (E)	1,400	
Insurance expense—general and administrative (E)	700	
Prepaid expenses (A)		2,100

C. Equipment with a cost of $204,350 and accumulated depreciation of $74,800 has an estimated useful life of eight years and an estimated residual value of $12,350.

When long-lived assets are used over time, we say they are *depreciated* (for tangible assets such as plant and equipment) or *amortized* (for intangible assets such as patents on inventions). The accounting process of depreciation and amortization involves the systematic and rational allocation of the cost of an operational asset over its useful life to the periods in which the asset is used to generate revenues. This accounting concept of depreciation and amortization does not necessarily match the change in the market value of the asset and thus differs from the layperson's usage in the statement that a new car "depreciates" when it is driven off the dealer's lot.

Depreciation and amortization will be discussed in much greater detail in Chapter 8. To simplify matters until we reach that chapter, we will assume that long-lived assets used in operations provide benefits to the company evenly over time. Therefore, they are depreciated or amortized in equal amounts each period. This is known as the *straight-line* method. Depreciation for each period is computed under the straight-line method using the following formula:

(Cost − residual value) ÷ Useful life =
Depreciation or amortization expense for the period

Residual value is the estimated sales price or scrap value of the asset at the end of its useful life to the company. Intangible assets do not usually have a residual value at the end of their useful lives. However, plant and equipment often do. When the amount of depreciation is computed for a year (quarter or month), the useful life should be stated in the same time units (years, quarters, or months).

Step 1: Create T-accounts based on the original entry.

Step 2: Determine the appropriate ending balances:
(Cost − residual value) ÷ Useful life = Depreciation expense ($204,350 − $12,350) ÷ 96 months = $2,000 depreciation expense per month.

Step 3: Determine, prepare, and post the adjusting entry:

Accumulated Depreciation—equipment (XA)			Depreciation Expense (E)	
		74,800	0	
	AJE	2,000	AJE 2,000	
		76,800	2,000	

Depreciation expense (E)	2,000	
Accumulated depreciation—equipment (XA)		2,000

D. On January 30, the managers at the Company-owned restaurants counted $2,670 in food and paper products supplies inventory on hand. The rest was used during January.

Step 1: Create T-accounts based on the original entry.

Step 2: Determine the appropriate ending balances:
Purchases of supplies inventory during the period were recorded in the Inventory account. Therefore, the unadjusted balance of $2,990 in the account represents all food and paper products available for use in the period. Since the managers counted $2,670 on hand, $320 must have been used during the period and should be expensed. This concept can be written in a formula:

Beginning inventory balance	$2,500
+ Purchases during the period	+ 490
Amount available for use	2,990
− Ending balance (counted at the end)	−2,670
Amount used during the period	$ 320

Step 3: Determine, prepare, and post the adjusting entry:

Inventory (A)			Cost of Food and Paper Products (E)	
2,990			2,100	
	AJE	320	AJE 320	
2,670			2,420	

Cost of food and paper products (E)	320	
Inventory (A)		320

Self-Study Quiz

To practice the steps and tools used in the adjustment process for deferrals, fill in the missing information for the next adjustment.

E. Deferred Income of $430 includes $150 paid in advance by customers in December for services rendered by Sbarro in January. The remaining $280 relates to services to be rendered after January.

Step 1: Create T-accounts based on the original entry.

Step 2: Determine the appropriate ending balances:

Step 3: Determine, prepare, and post the adjusting entry:

Deffered Income (L)			Restaurant Sales Revenue (R)	
	430			23,800
AJE 150				AJE 150
	280			23,950

Deferred income (L)	150	
Rest Sales Rev (R)		150

You can check your answers with the solution in the footnote at the bottom of this page.*

Accruals

Now we will prepare adjusting entries for accruals, those earned revenues and incurred expenses that are not yet recorded. From the trial balance, we identified investment income on marketable securities, interest expense on borrowed funds, rent due to mall owners, wages due to employees, and amounts due for utilities not yet billed to Sbarro. The last three items are part of the Accrued Expenses Payable account. Since we have identified potential accruals, we will use the adjustment process described earlier in the chapter for determining the proper adjusting entry in each case.

F. Sbarro invested in marketable debt securities that pay interest revenue. We will assume that these investments, which have a principal balance of $37,200 listed in the trial balance, pay 5% annual interest, but no cash for interest earned was received in January. Therefore, interest revenue needs to be accrued for January.

Step 1: Create T-accounts based on the original entry.

Step 2: Determine the amount to be accrued:

Principal x Annual interest rate x Time period (part of year) = Interest for the period

$37,200 x .05 x 1/12 = $155 for the month

Step 3: Prepare and post the adjusting entry:

Interest Receivable (A)			Interest Revenue (R)	
0				0
AJE 155				**AJE 155**
155				155

Interest receivable (A)	155	
Interest revenue (R)		155

*E. The amount of the adjustment is given as $150 additional revenue. The adjusting entry is:

Deferred income (L)	150	
Restaurant sales revenue (R)		150

Deferred Income (L)			Restaurant Sales Revenue (R)	
	430			23,800
AJE 150				**AJE 150**
	280			23,950

G. The January rental fee for Sbarro's leased headquarters building is $90 which will be paid in February.

Step 1: Create T-accounts based on the original entry.

Step 2: Determine the amount to be accrued:
The amount for unrecorded rent expense for use of the headquarters building in January is given as $90. Such expenses are categorized as general and administrative.

Step 3: Prepare and post the adjusting entry :

Accrued Expenses Payable (L)		Rent Expense (general and administrative) (E)	
	18,400	0	
	AJE **90**	AJE **90**	
	18,490	90	

Rent expense—general and administrative (E)	90	
Accrued expenses payable (L)		90

H. Sbarro received a utility bill on February 2 that included $65 for eight days of electric and gas usage at Company-owned restaurants during January.

Most companies cannot adjust and issue financial statements on the last day of the accounting period because more time is needed for analysis of necessary adjustments, preparation of financial statements, and completion of an audit. Therefore, it is possible to receive bills early in the next period relating to the prior period and make appropriate adjustments. If such a bill was not available, Sbarro would estimate the amount owed.

Step 1: Create T-accounts based on the original entry.

Step 2: Determine the amount to be accrued:
The amount to be accrued as Utilities Expense is given as $65.

Step 3: Prepare and post the adjusting entry:

Accrued Expenses Payable (L)		Utility Expense (occupancy and other) (E)	
	18,490	190	
	AJE **65**	AJE **65**	
	18,555	255	

Utilities expense—occupancy and other (E)	65	
Accrued expenses payable (L)		65

Self-Study Quiz

Now complete the next two accruals, following the steps in the adjustment process illustrated above.

I. Employees in Company-owned restaurants are paid every two weeks on Fridays. The last payday was January 21. Employees earned an additional $600 between January 21 and January 30.

Step 1: Create T-accounts based on the original entry.

Step 2: Determine the amount to be accrued:

Step 3: Prepare and post the adjusting entry:

Accrued Expenses Payable (L)		Wages Exp	
	18555	5,300	
	AJE 600	AJE 600	
	19,155	5,900	

Wages Exp		
Accrued expenses payable (L)		600

J. Sbarro owes interest expense on the $1,200 note. Both principal and interest will be paid together when the note is due. Therefore, interest must be accrued over time until paid. The annual interest rate on the note is 10%. Interest is accrued for January (one month).

Step 1: Create T-accounts based on the original entry.

Step 2: Determine the amount to be accrued:

1200 x .10 x

Step 3: Prepare and post the adjusting entry:

Interest Payable (L)		Int. Exp (L)	
		0	
	AJE 10	AJE 10	
	10	10	

Interest expense (E)	10	
____________		10

You can check your answers with the solution in the footnote at the bottom of this page.*

K. The final adjusting journal entry is to record the accrual of state, federal, and foreign government income taxes due (an unrecorded expense). We will use a 40% income tax rate.

Step 1: Create T-accounts based on the original entry.

Step 2: Determine the amount to be accrued:

All revenues	$24,605
− All expenses	− 17,025
Income before taxes	7,580
× 40% tax rate	× .40
Income tax expense	$ 3,032

Income Taxes Payable (L)

		0
	AJE	**3,032**
		3,032

Income Tax Expense (E)

	0	
AJE	**3,032**	
	3,032	

Step 3: Prepare and post the adjusting entry:

Income tax expense (E)	3,032	
Income taxes payable (L)		3,032

Exhibit 4–3 now shows the adjusted trial balance which was constructed by adding all of the adjustments made in Transactions A through K to the appropriate account balances in the unadjusted trial balance in Exhibit 4–2. Any new accounts created during the adjustment process are included. From this group of adjusted balances, we can prepare a complete set of accrual-based financial statements at the end of the accounting period (January 30).

FINANCIAL ANALYSIS

End-of-Period Adjustments and Auditing

Since end-of-period adjustments are the most complex portion of the annual recordkeeping process, they are prone to error. As noted in Chapter 1, external auditors (independent CPAs) examine the company's records on a test, or sample, basis. To maximize the chance of catching any errors significant enough to affect users' decisions, they allocate more of

---

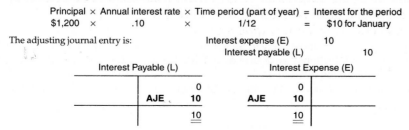

*I. The amount of the accrual is given as $600. The adjusting journal entry is:

Wages expense (E)	600	
Accrued expenses payable (L)		600

Accrued Expenses Payable (L)

		18,555
	AJE	**600**
		19,155

Wages Expense (E)

	5,300	
AJE	**600**	
	5,900	

J. The formula to compute interest is:

Principal × Annual interest rate × Time period (part of year) = Interest for the period
$1,200 × .10 × 1/12 = $10 for January

The adjusting journal entry is:

Interest expense (E)	10	
Interest payable (L)		10

Interest Payable (L)

		0
	AJE	**10**
		10

Interest Expense (E)

	0	
AJE	**10**	
	10	

Exhibit 4–3 **Adjusted Trial Balance for Sbarro, Inc.**

SBARRO, INC. AND SUBSIDIARIES Adjusted Trial Balance At January 30, 1994		
	Debit	**Credit**
Cash	$ 34,280	
Marketable securities	37,200	
Receivables (from franchisees and others)	1,800	
Interest receivable	155	
Inventory (supplies of food and paper products)	2,670	
Prepaid expenses	8,400	
Equipment	204,350	
Accumulated depreciation—equipment		$ 76,800
Other assets	3,200	
Notes payable		1,200
Accounts payable		7,030
Accrued expenses payable (rent, payroll, and other)		19,155
Interest payable		10
Dividends payable		4,700
Income taxes payable		3,032
Deferred income (unearned revenue)		280
Deferred income taxes		18,100
Contributed capital		29,900
Retained earnings		129,300
Restaurant sales revenue		23,950
Franchise related income		500
Interest revenue		155
Cost of food and paper products	2,420	
Wages expense	5,900	
Rent expense (occupancy and other)	4,200	
Utilities expense (occupancy and other)	255	
Repairs expense (occupancy and other)	50	
Insurance expense (occupancy and other)	1,400	
Depreciation expense	2,000	
Rent expense (general and administrative)	90	
Insurance expense (general and administrative)	700	
Interest expense	10	
Income tax expense	3,032	
Dividends declared	2,000	
Totals	$314,112	$314,112

their testing to transactions most likely to be in error. A number of accounting research studies have documented the most error-prone transactions for medium-sized manufacturing companies.[3] End-of-period accrual errors such as "failure to provide adequate product warranty liability," "failure to include items that should be accrued," and "end-of-period transac-

[3] J. R. Coakley and J. K. Loebbecke, "The Expectation of Accounting Errors in Medium-Sized Manufacturing Firms," *Advances in Accounting*, Vol. 2 (1985), pp. 199–245.

tions recorded in the wrong period (called *cut-off errors*)" are in the top category and thus receive a great deal of attention from the auditors.

FINANCIAL STATEMENT PREPARATION

Learning Objective 3
Prepare a complete set of financial statements: income statement, statement of stockholders' equity, balance sheet, and statement of cash flows.

The next step of the accounting cycle is preparation of a complete set of financial statements:

- *Income statement.*
- *Statement of retained earnings* (reports how net income and the distribution of dividends affected retained earnings of the company).

  or

  Statement of stockholders' equity (includes the same information as the statement of retained earnings plus a description of the activities that changed contributed capital for the period, primarily stock issuances and stock repurchases).[4]
- *Balance sheet.*
- *Statement of cash flows.*

Since the statement of stockholders' equity provides greater disclosure, we will prepare this statement. First, we will illustrate the relationships between the statements, that is, how the numbers in one statement flow into the next statement.

The transaction analysis model developed in Chapter 3 is reprinted in Exhibit 4–4. It illustrates how information flows from the income statement to the

Transaction Analysis Model **Exhibit 4–4**

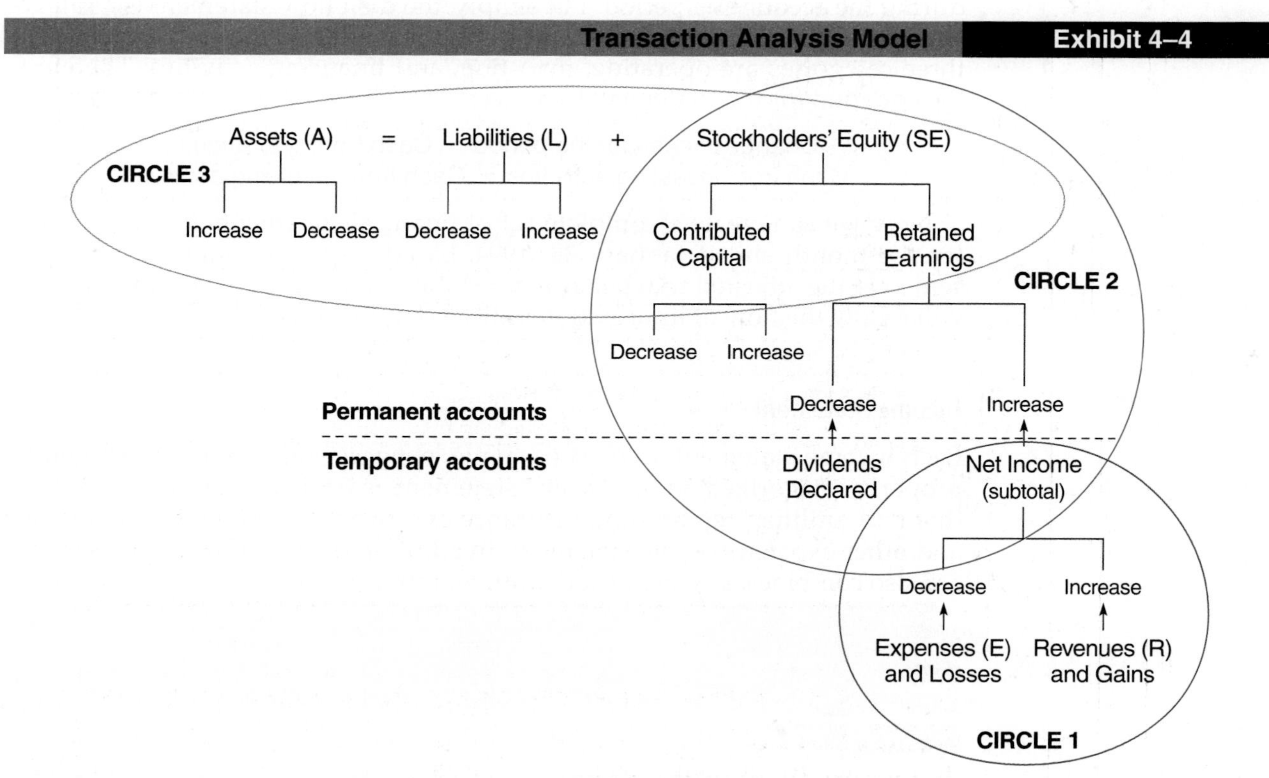

[4] Other complex transactions such as stock dividends, which are also reported on this statement, are discussed in Chapter 11.

statement of stockholders' equity to the balance sheet. The portions of the model that relate to these three statements are indicated by overlapping circles.

Circle 1 highlights the information used on the income statement which can be represented by the income statement equation:

Net income = (Revenues + Gains) − (Expenses + Losses)

Circle 2 highlights the components of the statement of stockholders' equity. Net income and dividends affect retained earnings, a component of stockholders' equity. These changes can be represented by the retained earnings equation:

Ending retained earnings = Beginning retained earnings + Net income − Dividends

Notice that net income from the first equation is included in the second equation. Stock issuances and repurchases (discussed in more detail in Chapter 11) can be represented by a similar equation:

Ending contributed capital = Beginning contributed capital + Stock issuances − Stock repurchases

The changes in retained earnings and contributed capital during the period are normally represented as separate columns on the statement of stockholders' equity. Then, the ending balances in retained earnings, contributed capital, and total stockholders' equity are included in the balance sheet (Circle 3). These relationships are represented in the balance sheet equation:

Assets = Liabilities + Stockholders' Equity

The fourth and final statement of cash flows explains the difference between the ending and beginning balances in the Cash account on the balance sheet during the accounting period. Put simply, the cash flow statement is a categorized listing of all transactions of the period that affected the cash account. The three categories are operating, investing, and financing activities. Therefore, the equation for this statement becomes:

Change in cash for the period = Cash from operations ± Cash from investing activities ± Cash from financing activities

Now we can create a complete set of financial statements for Sbarro, Inc., for the month ended January 30, 1994, based on the account balances presented in the adjusted trial balance in Exhibit 4–3 and the above equations. We will follow the flow of information indicated in Exhibit 4–4.

Income Statement

Each income statement account (revenue, expense, gain, and loss) should be properly categorized on the income statement as presented on page 185. Note that rent, utilities, repairs, and insurance expense are combined as occupancy and other expenses on the statement. In addition, rent and insurance expense are also combined as general and administrative expenses.

This statement based on adjusted balances more closely resembles the actual Sbarro annual income statement presented at the beginning of Chapter 3 in Exhibit 3–2 except for two items: (1) the amounts are for one month only and (2) Sbarro does not have any interest expense since it does not have any notes payable. Actual income statements prepared for external parties, as you may recall, are normally prepared quarterly and annually (presenting three years of data), though we have simplified this requirement in this chapter.

Earnings per share (EPS) is also reported on the income statement or in the notes to the statements. For companies like Sbarro, Inc., which have simple

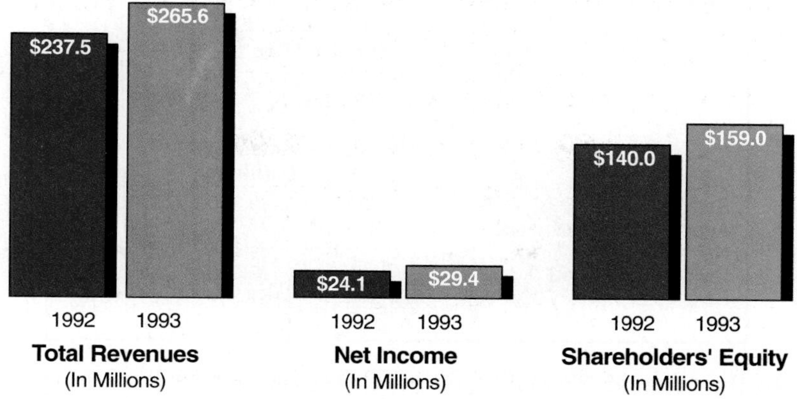

Sbarro also uses graphs to communicate key financial data.

capital structures (no other debt or equity securities that could potentially increase the number of shares of stock outstanding), earnings per share is computed as follows:

$$\text{EPS} = \text{Net income} \div \text{Weighted-average number of shares of stock outstanding during the period}$$

The calculation of the denominator is complex and is covered in other accounting courses. Based on the actual Sbarro annual report for 1994, the weighted-average number of shares of stock outstanding was approximately 13,548,000. For simplicity, we can use this same denominator in the computations of the earnings per share shown on the income statement.

$$\$4{,}548{,}000 \div 13{,}548{,}000 = \$.34 \text{ per share (rounded)}$$

Additional EPS disclosures will be discussed in Chapter 5.

Statement of Stockholders' Equity

The final total from the income statement, net income, is carried forward to the retained earnings portion of the statement of stockholders' (or shareholders')

SBARRO, INC. AND SUBSIDIARIES
Income Statement
For the Month Ended January 30, 1994
(in thousands of dollars)

Revenues:		
Restaurant sales		$23,950
Franchise related income		500
Interest revenue		155
Total revenues		24,605
Costs and expenses:		
Cost of food and paper products		2,420
Restaurant operating expenses:		
Payroll and other employee benefits (wages)	$5,900	
Occupancy and other expenses (rent, utilities, repairs and insurance)	5,905	11,805
Depreciation expense		2,000
General and administrative expense (rent and insurance)		790
Total costs and expenses		17,015
Income before interest and income taxes		7,590
Interest expense		10
Income after interest and before income taxes		7,580
Income taxes		3,032
Net Income		$ 4,548
Earnings per share		$ .34

SBARRO INC. AND SUBSIDIARIES
Statement of Shareholders' Equity
For the Month Ended January 30, 1994
(in thousands of dollars)

	Contributed Capital	Retained Earnings	Total
Balance at January 2, 1994	$29,700	$129,300	$159,000
Additional stock issuance	200		200
Net income		4,548	4,548
Dividends declared		(2,000)	(2,000)
Balance at January 30, 1994	$29,900	$131,848	$161,748

equity. To this, the additional elements of the statement are added from the trial balance.

Transactions from prior chapters are also included in the statement above: Dividends declared (Chapter 3) and an additional stock issuance (Chapter 2).

Balance Sheet

The ending balances in the shareholders' equity accounts are then carried to the balance sheet with the remaining assets and liabilities taken from the trial balance.

The balances for contributed capital and retained earnings from the statement of shareholders' equity flow into the balance sheet. You will notice that the contra-asset account, Accumulated Depreciation, has been subtracted from the Equipment account to reflect net book value (or carrying value) at month-end for balance sheet purposes. Detailed information on the cost of the equipment and the balance in the Accumulated Depreciation account could be

SBARRO INC. AND SUBSIDIARIES
Balance Sheets
At January 30, 1994 and January 2, 1994
(in thousands of dollars)

	January 30, 1994	January 2, 1994
Assets		
Cash	$ 34,280	$ 33,300
Marketable securities	37,200	37,200
Receivables (franchise fees, interest, and other)	1,955	1,300
Inventory	2,670	2,500
Prepaid expenses	8,400	1,500
Equipment (net of accumulated depreciation of $76,800 on January 30, 1994, and $74,800 on January 2, 1994)	127,550	128,700
Other assets	3,200	3,200
Total assets	$215,255	$207,700
Liabilities		
Notes payable	$ 1,200	0
Accounts payable	7,030	4,500
Accrued expenses payable (rent, payroll, and other)	19,155	18,400
Interest payable	10	0
Dividends payable	4,700	2,700
Income taxes payable	3,032	4,600
Deferred income	280	400
Deferred income taxes	18,100	18,100
Total liabilities	53,507	48,700
Stockholders' Equity		
Contributed Capital	29,900	29,700
Retained Earnings	131,848	129,300
Total stockholders' equity	161,748	159,000
Total liabilities and stockholders' equity	$215,255	$207,700

provided in footnotes to the statements. You will also notice that three accounts did not change during the month (Marketable Securities, Other Assets, and Deferred Income Taxes). There were no transactions affecting these accounts.

Statement of Cash Flows

We stated above that the statement of cash flows describes the changes in cash for the period and categorizes the changes into operating, investing, and financing activities. In concept, preparation of the cash flow statement is straightforward. You need to follow two steps:

1. Identify all transactions where the cash account was debited (increased) or credited (decreased). For our purposes in this chapter, we analyzed the cash transactions listed in Chapters 2 and 3 to construct the following statement.
2. Each time cash was increased or decreased, categorize the inflow or outflow as one of the three types of activities.

Operating activities are those involving the sale of services or goods (products) to customers, including the payment of interest on debt and income taxes. *Investing activities* are those involving the purchase and sale of long-term investments, loans to others (e.g., employees, subsidiaries, franchisees), and the purchase and sale of long-term assets (such as equipment, land, and patents). *Financing activities* are those involving issuing or borrowing and repaying debt, issuing and repurchasing stock, and paying dividends.

While this method will suffice for our simple example, due to the volume of transactions occurring in most organizations, other techniques are necessary to construct the statement. They will be described in Chapter 13. In addition, most companies use a different format for reporting the operating activities section of the statement. The format we have shown is known as the *direct method;* most companies use the *indirect method.* This, too, will be discussed in Chapter 13.

You can see that the statement on page 188 ties to the balance sheet. The beginning cash balance for the month ($33,300) and the ending cash balance for the month ($34,280) on the balance sheet are the same as those reported on the statement of cash flows. Information is provided on how Sbarro acquired and spent cash during the month.

FINANCIAL ANALYSIS

Cash Flow from Operations, Net Income, and Financial Analysis

Many standard financial analysis texts warn analysts to be on the lookout for unusual deferrals and accruals when they attempt to predict future periods' earnings. They often suggest that wide disparities between net income and cash flow from operations is a useful warning sign. For example, Bernstein suggests that:

> Analysts prefer to relate CFO (cash flow from operations) to reported net income as a check on the quality of that income. Some analysts believe that the higher the ratio of CFO to net income, the higher the quality of that income. Put another way, a company with a high level of net income and a low cash flow may be using income recognition or expense accrual criteria that are suspect.[5]

---

[5]L. Bernstein, *Financial Statement Analysis* (Burr Ridge, IL: Richard D. Irwin, 1993), p. 461.

SBARRO INC. AND SUBSIDIARIES
Statement of Cash Flows
For the Month Ended January 30, 1994
(in thousands of dollars)

Operating activities:	
Cash inflows:	
From customers	$23,830
From franchisees	0
From investments	0
Cash outflows:	
To suppliers	(13,660)
To employees	(5,300)
For income taxes	(4,600)
For interest	0
Net cash provided by operating activities	270
Investing activities:	
Cash inflows:	
Repayment of loan by employee	40
Cash outflows:	
Purchase of equipment	(190)
Loan to employee	(40)
Net cash used in investing activities	(190)
Financing activities:	
Cash inflows:	
Proceeds from bank borrowing	1,000
Additional stock issuance	200
Cash outflows:	
Repayment of bank note	(300)
Payment of dividends	0
Net cash provided by financing activities	900
Increase in cash	$ 980
Cash at the beginning of the month	33,300
Cash at the end of the month	$34,280

THE CLOSING PROCESS

Learning Objective 4
Explain the closing process and prepare closing entries.

You will notice in Exhibit 4–4 that a dashed line has been drawn that separates income statement accounts (revenues, expenses, gains, and losses) and dividends declared from the balance sheet accounts (assets, liabilities, and stockholders' equity). The balance sheet accounts are updated continuously throughout the accounting period, and the ending balance for the current period becomes the beginning account balance for the next. These accounts are *not* closed (cleared out to a zero balance) periodically; therefore, they are often called **permanent** or **real accounts**. To illustrate, the ending cash balance of one accounting period must be the beginning cash balance of the next accounting period. The only time a permanent account has a zero balance is when the item represented is no longer owned or owed.

Permanent (real) accounts are the balance sheet accounts that carry their ending balances into the next accounting period.

In contrast, revenue, expense, gain, loss, and dividends declared accounts are often called **temporary**, or **nominal accounts** because they are used to accumulate data for the *current accounting period only*. At the end of each period, their balances are transferred, or closed, to the Retained Earnings account. This periodic clearing out of the balances of the income statement and dividends declared accounts into Retained Earnings is done by using closing entries.

Temporary (nominal) accounts are income statement and dividends declared accounts that are closed at the end of the accounting period.

The process of recording **closing entries** to transfer the balances of all temporary accounts to retained earnings is only a clerical phase. Closing entries have two purposes: (1) to transfer net income or loss and dividends declared to retained earnings and (2) to establish a zero balance in each of the temporary accounts to start the accumulation in the next accounting period. Accounts with credit balances are closed by debiting the total amount; accounts with debit balances are closed by crediting the total amount. For income

Closing entries are made at the end of the accounting period to transfer net income or loss and dividends declared to retained earnings and to establish a zero balance in each of the temporary accounts.

QUESTION OF ETHICS

Incentives, Accruals, and Ethics

We noted in Chapter 1 that owners and managers of companies are most directly affected by the information presented in financial statements. If the financial performance and condition of the company appears strong, the company's stock price rises. Shareholders usually receive dividends and have gains on their investment value. Managers often receive bonuses based on the strength of a company's financial performance, and many in top management are compensated with options to buy their company's stock at prices below market. The higher the market value, the more compensation they earn. When actual performance lags behind expectations, managers and owners may be tempted to manipulate accruals and deferrals to make up part of the difference. For example, managers may record cash received in advance of being earned as revenue in the current period or may fail to accrue certain expenses at year-end.

There is evidence from studies of large samples of companies that some do engage in such behavior. This research is borne out by enforcement actions of the Securities and Exchange Commission against companies and sometimes against their auditors. These SEC enforcement actions most often relate to accrual of revenue and receivables that should be deferred to future periods.* In many of these cases, the firms involved, their managers, and their auditors are penalized for such actions. Further, owners suffer because the company's stock price reacts negatively to news of an SEC investigation.

*E. H. Feroz, K. Park, and V. S. Pastena, "The Financial and Market Effects of the SEC's Accounting and Auditing Enforcement Releases," *Journal of Accounting Research* (Supplement 1991), pp. 107–142.

statement accounts, the other half of the entry is often made to a special temporary summary account, called **Income Summary** (although companies may close income statement accounts directly to Retained Earnings). Income Summary is also closed to Retained Earnings, as is Dividends Declared which is not part of income determination. In this way, the income statement accounts and the Dividends Declared accounts are again ready for their temporary accumulation function for the next period.

Income Summary is a temporary account used only during the closing process to facilitate closing revenues and expenses.

Referring to Exhibit 4–4, the process involves closing the lowest level of accounts in the model to the next higher level until a permanent account (Retained Earnings) is reached. Therefore, there are four types of closing entries:

1. Close all revenues and gains (credit-balance income statement accounts) to Income Summary (a new temporary account used only for closing).
2. Close all expenses and losses (debit-balance income statement accounts) to Income Summary.
3. Close Income Summary, which reflects net income or loss for the period, to Retained Earnings (a permanent account).
4. Close Dividends Declared (an account with a debit balance) to Retained Earnings (a permanent account).

Closing entries are dated the last day of the accounting period, entered in the usual debits-equal-credits format (in the journal), and immediately posted to the ledger (or T-accounts). We will illustrate the closing process by preparing and posting the closing entries for Sbarro, Inc., at January 30, 1994, though most companies close their records only at the end of the fiscal year. The amounts are taken from the adjusted trial balance in Exhibit 4–3. The T-accounts following the entries reflect the flow of the amounts into the permanent account, Retained Earnings. Closing entries are referenced with CE. Also, for illustrative purposes, only summary T-accounts for revenues, expenses, gains, and losses are shown. Normally, each account would be closed.

1. Close revenues and gains to Income Summary:

	Debit	Credit
Restaurant sales revenue	23,950	
Franchise related income	500	
Interest revenue	155	
Income summary		24,605

2. Close expenses and losses to Income Summary:

	Debit	Credit
Income summary	20,057	
Cost of food and paper products		2,420
Wages expense		5,900
Rent expense (occupancy and other)		4,200
Utilities expense (occupancy and other)		255
Repairs expense (occupancy and other)		50
Insurance expense (occupancy and other)		1,400
Depreciation expense		2,000
Rent expense (general and administrative)		90
Insurance expense (general and administrative)		700
Interest expense		10
Income tax expense		3,032

3. Close Income Summary to Retained Earnings:

	Debit	Credit
Income summary	4,548	
Retained earnings		4,548

4. Close Dividends Declared to Retained Earnings:

	Debit	Credit
Retained earnings	2,000	
Dividends declared		2,000

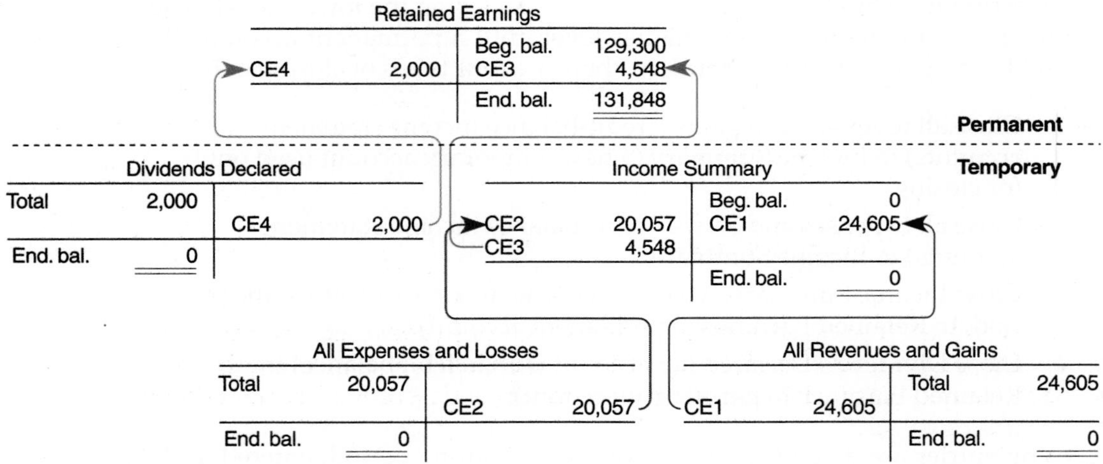

A **post-closing trial balance** should be prepared as the last step of the accounting cycle to check that debits equal credits and all temporary accounts have been closed.

After the closing process is completed, all of the income statement and dividends declared accounts have a zero balance. These accounts are then ready for the recording of revenues and expenses and dividends in the new accounting period. The ending balance in Retained Earnings now is up-to-date (matches the amount on the balance sheet) and is carried forward as the beginning balance for the next period. As the last step of the accounting information processing cycle, a **post-closing trial balance** should be prepared as a check that debits equal credits and all temporary accounts have been closed.

THE ACCOUNTING CYCLE AND COMMUNICATION PROCESS

While the preparation of statements and the closing of the books represents the final stage of the formal recordkeeping process, it represents only the beginning of the formal process of communicating financial statement information to external users. In the next chapter we take a closer look at the preparation of financial statements and related disclosures that appear in a company's annual report, quarterly reports, and for public companies, additional reports filed with the Securities and Exchange Commission. We also examine the process by which this and related information is disseminated to professional analysts, investors, and the public.

DEMONSTRATION CASE

We take our final look at the accounting activities of Terrific Lawn Maintenance Corporation by illustrating the activities at the end of the accounting cycle: the adjustment process, financial statement preparation, and the closing process. Chapter 2 presented investing and financing activities and Chapter 3 presented operating activities. However, no adjustments had been made to the accounts to reflect all revenues earned and expenses incurred in April. The trial balance for Terrific on April 30, 1995, based on the unadjusted balances in Chapter 3 is as follows:

TERRIFIC LAWN MAINTENANCE CORPORATION
Unadjusted Trial Balance
At April 30, 1995

	Debit	Credit
Cash	1,460	
Accounts receivable	1,700	
Prepaid expenses	300	
Lawn equipment	4,600	
Land	3,750	
Accounts payable		320
Dividends payable		300
Unearned revenue		1,600
Contributed capital		9,000
Retained earnings		0
Mowing service revenue		5,200
Fuel expense	410	
Wages expense	3,900	
Dividends declared	300	
Totals	16,420	16,420

In reviewing the trial balance, three deferral accounts (unearned revenue, prepaid expenses, and equipment) may need to be adjusted and additional accruals may be necessary. The following information is determined at the end of the accounting cycle:

Deferrals:

a. Unearned revenue received from the city at the beginning of April has been partially earned by the end of April.

b. Prepaid expense for insurance has been partially used in April.

c. Mowers and edgers (equipment) have been used and need to be depreciated. Mowers and edgers have a total cost of $4,000 and an estimated useful life of 10 years; rakes and hand tools have a total cost of $600 and an estimated useful life of 5 years. No residual value is expected.

Accruals:

d. Wages have been paid through April 28. Wages earned in April by the employees but not yet paid accrue at $130 per day.

e. An extra telephone line was installed in April. The telephone bill for $37 with hookup and usage charges was received on May 4.

f. The estimated income tax rate for Terrific is 35% for state and federal income taxes.

Required:

1. *a.* Set up T-accounts and their balances for Prepaid Expenses, Accumulated Depreciation, Unearned Revenue, Accrued Expenses Payable, Income Taxes Payable, Retained Earnings, Mowing Service Revenue, Insurance Expense, Depreciation Expense, Fuel Expense, Wages Expense, Utilities Expense, Income Tax Expense, Dividends Declared, and Income Summary. Insert the unadjusted balances from the trial balance presented above. The Income Summary has a $0 balance.
   b. Analyze each deferral and each accrual using the three steps outlined in this chapter. Post the effects to the T-accounts. Compute ending balances.
   c. Prepare an adjusted trial balance for April 30, 1995.
2. Use the amounts on the adjusted trial balance from requirement 1 to prepare an income statement, statement of stockholders' equity, balance sheet, and statement of cash flows for the month ended April 30, 1995. For the statement of cash flows, review all cash transactions in Chapters 2 and 3, categorizing them as operating, investing, or financing cash flows.
3. Prepare closing entries for April 30, 1995. Post these to the T-accounts in requirement 1.

Now, you can check your answers with the following solution to these requirements.

SUGGESTED SOLUTION

1. Analysis of deferrals and accruals, adjusting entries, and adjusted trial balance:
   a. Create T-accounts.
   T-accounts used to facilitate the analysis are located together after the following analysis of deferrals and accruals.

	b. Analyze each deferral (by determining ending balances) and each accrual (by determining necessary adjustments).	Prepare and post adjusting entries.		
a.	The city paid $1,600 for mowing service for April through July. One-fourth of the deferred amount has been earned by the end of April. This is a deferral where the original entry was to Unearned Revenue (L). The balance in the liability account should be $1,200 with $400 shown as revenue for April.	Unearned revenue (L) Mowing service revenue (R)	400	 400
b.	The $300 paid in April for six months of insurance coverage was originally recorded as a deferral in the Prepaid Expenses account. One-sixth ($50) of the insurance has now been used and $250 remains prepaid.	Insurance expense (E) Prepaid expenses (A)	50	 50
c.	Long-lived assets have been used in the generation of revenues; therefore, a part needs to be expensed. The straight-line formula to calculate periodic depreciation is: (Cost – residual value) ÷ useful life Mowers: ($4,000 – 0) ÷ 120 months = $33 per month Tools: ($600 – 0) ÷ 60 months = $10 per month.	Depreciation expense (E) Accumulated depreciation (XA)	43	 43
d.	Two additional days of wages have been earned by the employees at $130 per day. $130 x 2 days = $260 is the amount of wages expense and accrued expenses payable.	Wages expense (E) Accrued expenses payable (L)	260	 260

e.	An adjustment is necessary to record the telephone expenses for April that were not known until early May. The amount of $37 is given.	Utilities expense (E) 37 Accrued expenses payable (L) 37
f.	Income taxes are estimated to be 35% of net income on the accrual basis. Total Revenues $5,600 – Total expenses – 4,700 ($410 + 4,160 + 37 + 50 + 43) Income before taxes 900 × 35% × .35 Tax expense $ 315	Income tax expense (E) 315 Income tax payable (L) 315

T-Accounts Affected by Adjusting and Closing Entries

Balance Sheet (permanent) Accounts:

Prepaid Expenses (A)

Unadj. bal.	300		
		AJE(*b*)	50
End. bal.	250		

Accumulated Depreciation (XA)

		Unadj. bal.	0
		AJE(*c*)	43
		End. bal.	43

Unearned Revenue (L)

		Unadj. bal.	1,600
AJE(*a*)	400		
		End. bal.	1,200

Accrued Expenses Payable (L)

		Unadj. bal.	0
		AJE(*d*)	260
		AJE(*e*)	37
		End. bal.	297

Income Tax Payable (L)

		Unadj. bal.	0
		AJE(*f*)	315
		End. bal.	315

Retained Earnings (SE)

		Beg. bal.	0
CE(4)	300	CE(3)	585
		End. bal.	285

Temporary Accounts:

Dividends Declared

Bal.	300		
		CE(4)	300
Closed Bal.	0		

Mowing Service Revenue (R)

		Unadj. bal.	5,200
		AJE(*a*)	400
		End. bal.	5,600
CE(1)	5,600		
		Closed bal.	0

Income Summary

		Beg. bal.	0
CE(2)	5,015	CE(1)	5,600
		End. bal.	585
CE(3)	585		
		Closed. bal.	0

Fuel Expense (E)

Unadj. bal.	410		
End. bal.	410		
		CE(2)	410
Closed Bal.	0		

Insurance Expense (E)

Unadj. bal.	0		
AJE(*b*)	50		
End. bal.	50		
		CE(2)	50
Closed bal.	0		

Utilities Expense (E)

Unadj. bal.	0		
AJE(*e*)	37		
End. bal.	37		
		CE(2)	37
Closed. bal.	0		

Depreciation Expense (E)

Unadj. bal.	0		
AJE(*c*)	43		
End. bal.	43		
		CE(2)	43
Closed Bal.	0		

Wages Expense (E)

Unadj. bal.	3,900		
AJE(*d*)	260		
End. bal.	4,160		
		CE(2)	4,160
Closed bal.	0		

Income Tax Expense (E)

Unadj. bal.	0		
AJE(*f*)	315		
End. bal.	315		
		CE(2)	315
Closed. bal.	0		

c.

TERRIFIC LAWN MAINTENANCE CORPORATION
Adjusted Trial Balance
At April 30, 1995

	Debit	Credit
Cash	1,460	
Accounts receivable	1,700	
Prepaid expenses	250	
Lawn equipment	4,600	
Accumulated depreciation		43
Land	3,750	
Accounts payable		320
Accrued expenses payable		297
Dividends payable		300
Unearned revenue		1,200
Income taxes payable		315
Contributed capital		9,000
Retained earnings		0
Mowing service revenue		5,600
Fuel expense	410	
Wages expense	4,160	
Utilities expense	37	
Insurance expense	50	
Depreciation expense	43	
Income tax expense	315	
Dividends declared	300	
Totals	17,075	17,075

2. Financial statements

TERRIFIC LAWN MAINTENANCE CORPORATION
Income Statement
For the Period Ended April 30, 1995

Revenues:	
Mowing service revenue	$5,600
Expenses:	
Wages expense	$4,160
Fuel expense	410
Insurance expense	50
Utility expense	37
Depreciation expense	43
Total expenses	$4,700
Income before income taxes	$ 900
Income tax expense	315
Net income	$ 585
Earnings per share	$ .39

As indicated in Chapter 2, a total of 1,500 shares of stock was originally issued to the three owners. EPS is calculated as:

$585 net income ÷ 1,500 shares = $.39 per share

TERRIFIC LAWN MAINTENANCE CORPORATION
Statement of Shareholders' Equity
For the Period Ended April 30, 1995

	Contributed Capital	Retained Earnings	Total
Beginning balances, April 1, 1995	$ 0	$ 0	$ 0
Stock issuance	9,000		9,000
Net income		585	585
Dividends declared		(300)	(300)
Ending balances, April 30, 1995	$9,000	$ 285	$9,285

The amount for net income ($585) flows from the income statement into the statement of shareholders' equity as an increase in retained earnings.

TERRIFIC LAWN MAINTENANCE CORPORATION
Balance Sheet
At April 30, 1995

Assets			**Liabilities**	
Cash		$ 1,460	Accounts payable	$ 320
Accounts receivable		1,700	Dividends payable	300
Prepaid expenses		250	Unearned revenue	1,200
Lawn equipment	$4,600		Accrued expenses payable	297
Accumulated depreciation	(43)	4,557	Income taxes payable	315
Land		3,750	Total Liabilities	$ 2,432
			Stockholders' Equity	
			Contributed capital	$ 9,000
			Retained earnings	285
			Total stockholders' equity	9,285
Total Assets		$11,717	Total Liabilities and Stockholders' Equity	$11,717

TERRIFIC LAWN MAINTENANCE CORPORATION
Statement of Cash Flows
For the Month Ended April 30, 1995

			Transaction Categories
Operating activities:			
Cash inflows:			
From customers		$5,100	Ch3b, $1,600; Ch3d, $3,500.
Cash outflows:			
To suppliers	$(4,790)		Ch2g, $700; Ch3a, $90; Ch3e, $3,700; Ch3h, $300.
To employees	(3,900)	(8,690)	Ch.3f, $3,900
Net cash used in operating activities		$(3,590)	
Investing activities:			
Cash inflows:			
Sale of land to city		1,250	Ch.2h, $1,250.
Cash outflows:			
Purchase of equipment	$ (200)		Ch.2b, $200.
Purchase of land	(5,000)	(5,200)	Ch.2d, $5,000.
Net cash used in investing activities		$(3,950)	
Financing activities:			
Cash inflows:			
Issuance of stock		9,000	Ch.2a, $9,000
Net cash provided by financing activities		$9,000	
Net increase in cash		1,460	
Beginning cash balance, 4/1/95		0	
Ending cash balance, 4/30/95		$1,460	

The ending cash balance on the statement of cash flows agrees with the ending cash balance on the balance sheet. The statement of cash flows reconciles the changes in cash for the month. You will notice that Terrific Lawn Maintenance Corporation did not increase cash from operations. This is quite typical of new companies which often must undertake substantial financing and investing activities early in the start-up of the company. In the long run, though, companies need to be able to realize positive cash flows from operations to remain in business.

3. Closing entries
   a. The four basic closing entries follow:
      (1.) Close revenues and gains to Income Summary:

Mowing service revenue (R)	5,600	
Income summary		5,600

      (2.) Close expenses and losses to Income Summary:

Income summary	5,015	
Wages expense (E)		4,160
Fuel expense (E)		410
Insurance expense (E)		50
Utility expense (E)		37
Depreciation expense (E)		43
Income tax expense (E)		315

(3.) Close Income Summary to Retained Earnings:

Income summary	585	
Retained earnings (SE)		585

(4.) Close Dividends Declared to Retained Earnings:

Retained earnings	300	
Dividends declared		300

b. These entries have been posted to the T-accounts in requirement 1. All temporary accounts now have zero balances to begin accumulating amounts for May activities.

SUMMARY

An accounting system is designed to collect, process, and report financial information. During each period, an accounting information processing cycle starts with data collection and ends with preparing the required financial statements and closing the temporary accounts. The phases of the cycle were summarized in Exhibit 4–1.

The accounting model that was described in Chapters 2 and 3 provides the basic framework for transaction analysis. The dual effect of each transaction can be stated in terms of its impact on assets, liabilities, and shareholders' equity. These effects are first recorded in the journal and then posted to a ledger (T-accounts) which includes a separate account for each type of asset, liability, shareholders' equity, revenue, and expense. At the end of the accounting period, accrual and deferral accounts have to be updated to reflect that revenues have been earned and properly matched with their related expenses in the current period according to accrual accounting principles. Adjusting entries are prepared and posted to the ledger (T-accounts) to record the effects of these events. At this point, the financial statements are prepared.

The statements relate to each other. Net income from the income statement is included on the statement of shareholders' equity which lists activities for the period in retained earnings and contributed capital. Then the ending balances on the statement of shareholders' equity are included on the balance sheet (stockholders' equity section). Finally, the Cash account on the balance sheet is analyzed on the statement of cash flows. The activities that generated or used cash during the period are categorized by type of activity—operating, investing, and financing.

Revenue, expense, and dividends declared accounts reflect activities for only a single accounting period. At the beginning of each new period, their balances must be zero. Therefore, closing entries are recorded at the end of each period to return the balances of all revenue, expense, and dividend declared accounts to zero and to transfer their balances to Retained Earnings. The balance sheet accounts are never closed. A post-closing trial balance should be prepared as a check for recording accuracy as the last step of the accounting information processing cycle.

Chapter Supplement A

The Formal Recordkeeping System

For those interested in a deeper understanding of the formal records used in the accounting system, the following discussion describes and illustrates the use of the General Journal and General Ledger during the accounting period.

Learning Objective 5
Utilize a formal general journal and general ledger format in preparing journal entries and accumulating account balances.

General Journal

After transaction analysis, the economic effects of each transaction are formally entered into the accounting system in a record known as the **journal** (or general journal). The effects of each transaction are recorded in journal entries in chronological order (i.e., in order of date of occurrence). Typically, the effects of transaction analysis are recorded first in the journal. Thus, the general journal is referred to as *the book of original entry*. The journal is the only place in the accounting system where the economic effects of each transaction are linked physically and recorded chronologically. In most businesses, the formal records have been computerized. For educational purposes, it is easier to understand the formal records if we illustrate them in a manual system.

A **journal** is the record that lists chronologically the effects of transactions.

You will recall from Chapter 2 that journal entries prepared as analytical tools include a date, the account(s) to be debited on the top, and the account(s) to be credited on the bottom and indented to the right. Formal journal entries also include an explanation of the transaction with sufficient detail for tracing the entry to the source documents (to provide an **audit trail** for future reference) and the account, or reference, number from the company's chart of accounts. Exhibit 4–5 illustrates the first two transactions for Terrific Lawn Maintenance Corporation (from the Demonstration Case in Chapter 2).

An **audit trail** is the referencing system with sufficiently detailed explanations necessary for tracing an entry back to its source documents.

General Ledger

In Chapters 2 through 4, we illustrated the use of T-accounts as tools to reflect the effects of transactions for each account and to accumulate balances.

Illustration of the Journal — **Exhibit 4–5**

GENERAL JOURNAL

Page 1

Date	Account Titles and Explanation	Posted Ref.	Debit	Credit
4/1/95	Cash	101	9,000	
	Contributed capital	301		9,000
	Issued 1,500 shares of stock to investors (names).			
4/3/95	Equipment	110	600	
	Cash	101		200
	Accounts payable	201		400
	Purchased hand tools (supplier and invoice data			
	indicated), paying part in cash (check number			
	indicated) and			
	part on account.			

A **ledger** contains all of the individual accounts for revenues, expenses, assets, liabilities, and stockholders' equity.

Collectively, these individual T-accounts resemble pages from the second formal record known as the **ledger,** or general ledger. The ledger may take on many forms. Handwritten accounting systems may use a loose-leaf ledger—one page for each account. With a computerized accounting system, the ledger is kept on electronic storage devices, but there are still individual accounts maintained. Each account is identified by a descriptive name and an assigned number (e.g., Cash, 101; Accounts Payable, 201; and Sales Revenue, 401).

The ledger contains information that was initially recorded in the journal and then transferred to the appropriate accounts in the ledger. The transfer of information from the journal to the ledger is called *posting.* This transfer from the chronological arrangement in the journal to the account format in the ledger is important because the ledger reflects the data classified as assets, liabilities, owners' equity, revenues, and expenses. This reclassification of the data facilitates the subsequent preparation of financial statements.

The economic data concerning transactions end up in the ledger; therefore, it has been called the *book of final entry.* Exhibit 4–6 shows a page from the ledger of Terrific Lawn Maintenance Corporation in columnar format. The T-account concept is maintained with a running balance added.

Usually a business of the size of a doctor's office or local retail shop will record the transactions in the journal each day and post to the ledger less frequently, say, every few days. Of course, the timing of these activities varies with the data processing system used and the complexity of the entity. In many computerized systems, the transactions can be posted instantaneously into the ledger when recorded in the journal. Many affordable computerized accounting software packages are available for small businesses.

To post to the ledger, the debits and credits shown in the journal entries are transferred directly as debits and credits to the appropriate accounts in the ledger. Both the journal and the ledger have a Posted Reference column for cross-reference between these two records. When posting has occurred, the appropriate reference is indicated in each formal record. In the journal, the

Exhibit 4–6 Illustration of a Ledger Account in Columnar Format

GENERAL LEDGER

Account Title Cash — Account Number 101

Date	Explanation	Posted Ref.	Debit	Credit	Balance
4/1/95	Investments by owners	1	9,000		9,000
4/3/95	Hand tools purchased	1		200	8,800
4/4/95	Land purchased	1		5,000	3,800
4/5/95	Fuel purchased	1		90	3,710
4/6/95	Revenue in advance	2	1,600		5,310
4/10/95	Collection from customers	2	3,500		8,810
4/11/95	Suppliers paid	2		700	8,110
4/14/95	Wages paid	3		1,950	6,160
4/21/95	Suppliers paid	3		3,700	2,460
4/26/95	Purchased insurance	3		300	2,160
4/28/95	Wages paid	4		1,950	210
4/29/95	Collection from city	4	1,250		1,460

numbers in the Posted Reference column indicate the ledger account to which the dollar amounts were posted. In the ledger account, the numbers in the Posted Reference column indicate the journal page from which the dollar amounts were posted. Reference numbers are used in the posting phase (*a*) to indicate that posting has been done and (*b*) to provide an *audit trail*.

Chapter Supplement B

Accounting Worksheets

Learning Objective 6
Construct a year-end worksheet that includes a trial balance, adjustments, and amounts for the income statement and balance sheet.

At the end of the accounting period, an accounting worksheet may be prepared. The worksheet is prepared before the adjusting and closing entries are recorded. The completed worksheet provides all the data needed to complete the remaining end-of-period steps by bringing together in one place, in an orderly way, (1) the unadjusted trial balance, (2) amounts for adjusting entries, (3) the income statement, (4) the statement of retained earnings, and (5) the balance sheet. Closing entries can also be prepared from the information provided on the worksheet.

Illustration

A simplified case for High-Rise Apartments, Inc., will be used to illustrate preparation of a worksheet at the end of the accounting period. To make the illustration easier, two exhibits are given:

Exhibit 4–7 Worksheet format with the unadjusted trial balance and adjusting entry amounts.

Exhibit 4–8 Completed worksheet with the income statement, statement of retained earnings, and balance sheet.

The sequential steps used to develop the worksheet are:

Step 1. Set up the worksheet format by entering the appropriate column headings. This step is shown in Exhibit 4–7. The left column shows the account titles (taken directly from the ledger). There are six separate pairs of debit-credit money columns. Notice that the last three pairs of debit-credit columns show the data for the financial statements.

Step 2. Enter the unadjusted trial balance as of the end of the accounting period directly from the ledger into the first pair of debit-credit columns. When all the current entries for the period, excluding the adjusting entries, have been recorded in the journal and posted to the ledger, the amounts for the unadjusted trial balance columns are the balances of the respective ledger accounts. Before going to the next step, the equality of the debits and credits should be tested by totaling each column ($491,460). Adding a column is called *footing*. When a worksheet is used, there is no need to develop a separate unadjusted trial balance because it can be developed on the worksheet.

Step 3. The second pair of debit-credit columns, headed Adjusting Entries, is completed by developing and then entering the amounts of the adjusting entries directly on the worksheet. The adjustments for High-Rise Apartments shown in Exhibit 4–7 were entered for illustration purposes. Review each entry to be sure that you can explain why it was recorded. To facilitate examination (for potential errors), the adjusting entries usually are coded on the worksheet as illustrated in Exhibit 4–7. Some of the adjusting entries may need one or more

Exhibit 4–7 Worksheet Format with Unadjusted Trial Balance and Adjusting Entry Amounts Already Entered

HIGH-RISE APARTMENTS, INC.
Worksheet for the Year Ended December 31, 19B

	Unadjusted Trial Balance		Adjusting Entries		Adjusted Trial Balance		Financial Statements					
							Income Statement		Retained Earnings		Balance Sheet	
Account Titles	Debit	Credit	Debit	Credit	Debit	Credit	Debit	Credit	Debit	Credit	Debit	Credit
Cash	12,297											
Prepaid insurance	2,400			(*c*) 1,200								
Inventory of maintenance supplies	600			(*e*) 400								
Land	25,000											
Apartment building	360,000											
Accumulated depreciation, building		10,000		(*d*) 10,000								
Note payable, long-term		30,000										
Mortgage payable, long-term		238,037										
Contributed capital		55,000										
Retained earnings, Jan. 1, 19B		29,960										
Dividends declared and paid	12,000											
Rent revenue		128,463	(*a*) 500	(*b*) 600								
Advertising expense	500											
Maintenance expense	3,000		(*e*) 400									
Salary expense	17,400		(*f*) 900									
Interest expense	19,563		(*g*) 600									
Utilities expense	34,500											
Miscellaneous expenses	4,200											
Rent collected in advance				(*a*) 500								
Insurance expense			(*c*) 1,200									
Depreciation expense			(*d*) 10,000									
Salaries payable				(*f*) 900								
Interest payable				(*g*) 600								
Rent revenue receivable			(*b*) 600									
	491,460	491,460	14,200	14,200								

(*a*) $500 rent collected, not yet earned.
(*b*) Rent earned, not yet collected, $600.
(*c*) Used $1,200 of insurance.
(*d*) Annual depreciation of buildings, $10,000.
(*e*) Used $400 of maintenance supplies.
(*f*) Accrued wages, $900.
(*g*) Accrued $600 interest on note payable.

account titles in addition to those of the original trial balance listing (see last five account titles in Exhibit 4–7). After the adjusting entries are completed on the worksheet, the equality of debits and credits for those amounts is checked by totaling the two columns ($14,200 each).

The remaining steps to complete the worksheet are shown in the last six columns in Exhibit 4–8. These steps are:

Step 4. The pair of debit-credit columns headed Adjusted Trial Balance is completed. Although not essential, this pair of columns helps to assure accuracy. The adjusted trial balance is the line-by-line combined amounts of the unadjusted trial balance, plus or minus the amounts entered as adjusting entries in the second pair of columns. For example, the Rent Revenue account shows a $128,463 credit balance under Unadjusted Trial Balance. To this amount is added the credit amount, $600, minus the debit amount, $500, for a combined amount of $128,563, which is entered as a credit under Adjusted Trial Balance. (Adding across such as this is called *cross-footing*.) For those accounts that were not affected by the adjusting entries, the unadjusted trial balance amount is carried directly across to the Adjusted Trial Balance column. After each line has been completed, the equality of the debits and credits under Adjusted Trial Balance is checked (column totals, $503,560).

Step 5. The amount on each line, under Adjusted Trial Balance, is extended horizontally across the worksheet and entered under the heading for the financial statement on which it must be reported (income statement, retained earnings, or balance sheet). Debit amounts are carried across as debits, and credit amounts are carried across as credits.

You can see that (1) each amount extended across was entered under only one of the six remaining columns, and (2) debits remain debits and credits remain credits in the extending process.

Step 6. At this point, the two Income Statement columns are summed (subtotals). The difference between these two subtotals is the pretax income (or loss). Income tax expense then is computed by multiplying this difference by the tax rate. In Exhibit 4–8, the computation was (revenues of $128,563 – pretax expenses of $92,263) × tax rate of 20% = $7,260. The adjusting entry for income tax then was entered at the bottom of the worksheet. Income tax expense and income taxes payable now can be extended horizontally to the Income Statement and Balance Sheet columns. Net income is entered as a balancing debit amount in the Income Statement column and as a credit in the Retained Earnings column. This represents the entry in the closing process that results in a debit to Income Summary and a credit to Retained Earnings. A net loss would appear as a credit in the Income Statement column and as a debit in the Retained Earnings column.

Step 7. The two Retained Earnings columns are summed. The difference is the ending balance of retained earnings. This balance amount is entered as a balancing debit amount under Retained Earnings and also as a balancing credit amount under Balance Sheet (i.e., an increase to owners' equity). At this point, the two Balance Sheet columns should sum to equal amounts. The continuous checking of the equality of debits and credits in each pair of debit-credit columns helps to assure the correctness of the worksheet. However, the balancing feature alone does not assure that the worksheet has no errors. For example, if an expense amount (a debit) were extended to either the Retained

Exhibit 4–8 **Accounting Worksheet Completed**

HIGH-RISE APARTMENTS, INC.
Worksheet for the Year Ended December 31, 19B

							Financial Statements					
	Unadjusted Trial Balance		Adjusting Entries		Adjusted Trial Balance		Income Statement		Retained Earnings		Balance Sheet	
Account Titles	Debit	Credit	Debit	Credit	Debit	Credit	Debit	Credit	Debit	Credit	Debit	Credit
Cash	12,297				12,297						12,297	
Prepaid insurance	2,400			(*c*) 1,200	1,200						1,200	
Inventory of maintenance supplies	600			(*e*) 400	200						200	
Land	25,000				25,000						25,000	
Apartment building	360,000				360,000						360,000	
Accumulated depreciation, building		10,000		(*d*) 10,000		20,000						20,000
Note payable, long-term		30,000				30,000						30,000
Mortgage payable, long-term		238,037				238,037						238,037
Contributed capital		55,000				55,000						55,000
Retained earnings, Jan. 1, 19B		29,960				29,960				29,960		
Dividends declared and paid	12,000				12,000				12,000			
Rent revenue		128,463	(*a*) 500	(*b*) 600		128,563		128,563				
Advertising expense	500				500		500					
Maintenance expense	3,000		(*e*) 400		3,400		3,400					
Salary expense	17,400		(*f*) 900		18,300		18,300					
Interest expense	19,563		(*g*) 600		20,163		20,163					
Utilities expense	34,500				34,500		34,500					
Miscellaneous expenses	4,200				4,200		4,200					
Rent collected in advance				(*a*) 500		500						500
Insurance expense			(*c*) 1,200		1,200		1,200					
Depreciation expense			(*d*) 10,000		10,000		10,000					
Salaries payable				(*f*) 900		900						900
Interest payable				(*g*) 600		600						600
Rent revenue receivable			(*b*) 600		600						600	
	491,460	491,460	14,200	14,200	503,560	503,560	92,263	128,563				
Income tax expense			(*h*) 7,260				7,260					
Income tax payable				(*h*) 7,260								7,260
Net income							29,040			29,040		
(*a*) $500 rent collected, not yet earned.	(*e*) Used $400 of maintenance supplies.						128,563	128,563	12,000	59,000		
(*b*) Rent earned, not yet collected, $600.	(*f*) Accrued wages, $900.								47,000			47,000
(*c*) Used $1,200 of insurance.	(*g*) Accrued $600 interest on note payable.								59,000	59,000		
(*d*) Annual depreciation of buildings, $10,000.	(*h*) Income tax ($29,040 pretax income × 20% rate).											399,297

Earnings debit column or to the Balance Sheet debit column, the worksheet would balance in all respects; however, at least two columns would have one or more errors. Therefore, special care must be used in selecting the appropriate debit-credit columns during the horizontal extension process.

Financial statements for High-Rise Apartments can be prepared directly from the completed worksheet in Exhibit 4–8.

Chapter Supplement C

Reversing Entries

Learning Objective 7
Explain and prepare reversing entries.

Reversing entries are optional entries made at the start of the next accounting period to reverse the effects of certain adjusting entries.

Some accountants add an optional phase to the accounting cycle, called **reversing entries**. Reversing entries are given this name because they reverse at the start of the next accounting period, the effects of certain adjusting entries made at the end of the previous period. They are used for the sole purpose of facilitating certain subsequent entries in the accounts. Due to the rather continuous nature of the operating cycle, certain revenues and expenses are recorded routinely as such. When the end of the accounting period falls between the points for earning or incurring revenues or expenses and the cash receipt or payment dates, assets (such as Prepaid Rent Expense) and liabilities (such as Wages Payable) are created in the adjustment process. If reversing entries are not employed on the first day of the next accounting period, then the routine entry will cause an error in recognizing revenues and expenses properly in the next period. Let's look at an example.

Let's assume that the Day Company, which has a fiscal year ending on December 31, records payroll every two weeks using the following entry:

Wages expense (E)	8,400	
Cash (A)		8,400

If the last payday was December 22, an adjustment will be necessary to record an additional nine days of wages expense in the current period, though payment will be made in the following period.

Activities:

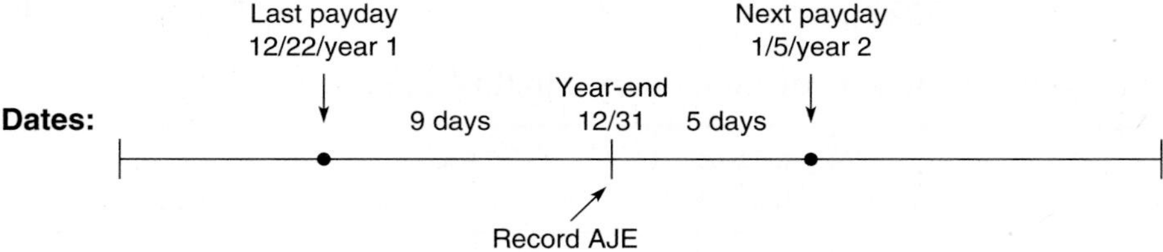

Amounts: $8,400 ÷ 14 days = $600 per day
Wages Expense, Year 1: 9 days × $600 = $5,400
Wages Expense, Year 2: 5 days × $600 = $3,000

The adjusting entry at December 31 will be

Wages expense (E)	5,400	
Wages payable (L)		5,400

The adjusting entry is posted to the appropriate T-accounts. Then the records are closed for Year 1, resulting in the following balances (the unadjusted balance in wages expense is assumed to be $200,000):

Wages Expense (E)		Wages Payable (L)	
Unadj. bal. 200,000			Unadj. bal. 0
AJE 5,400			AJE 5,400
	CE 205,400		
Closed bal. 0			End. bal. 5,400

If no reversing entry is made at the beginning of the accounting period, on January 5 the payroll system will record a routine journal entry for $8,400 as wages expense in Year 2 (credit to Cash). However, only $3,000 was incurred by the company in Year 2. In addition, the Wages Payable account is not reduced, even though it was paid off on January 5. Both the expense and the liability are overstated in Year 2:

IN ERROR

Wages Expense (E)		Wages Payable (L)	
Year 1			Year 1
Unadj. bal. 200,000			Unadj. bal. 0
AJE 5,400			AJE 5,400
	CE 205,400		
Closed bal. 0			End. bal. 5,400
Year 2			Year 2
January 5 8,400			
End. bal. 8,400			End. bal. 5,400

If a reversing entry (RE) is made on January 1, the balances after the reversing entry will reflect no liability and a negative amount in Wages Expense. Then when the January payroll entry is made, the correct balance in Wages Expense will result for Year 2:

CORRECT

Wages Expense (E)		Wages Payable (L)	
Year 1			Year 1
Unadj. bal. 200,000			Unadj. bal. 0
AJE 5,400			AJE 5,400
	CE 205,400		
Closed bal. 0			End. bal. 5,400
Year 2			Year 2
	RE 5,400	RE 5,400	
January 5 8,400			
End. bal. 3,000			End. bal. 0

The reversing entry made on January 1 in this example is

Wages payable (L)	5,400	
Wages expense (E)		5,400

If reversing entries are not used, the only way to avoid the error is to monitor and manually record payroll on January 5 as follows:

Wages payable (L)	5,400	
Wages expense (E)	3,000	
Cash (A)		8,400

Therefore, either reversing entries are used or numerous transactions will need to be monitored throughout the next accounting period to make manual entries to avoid any overstatement errors. The reversing-entry option is used in most companies, whether the system is manual or computerized.

Not all adjusting entries should be reversed. Those that can be reversed are:

- All adjusting entries related to accruals.
- Only adjusting entries for deferrals that created (or increased) an asset or liability account as part of the adjusting process.

To illustrate reversing entries, let's assume the following December 31 year-end adjustments for an orthodontist's office:

a. Earned $1,200 interest on investments which will be received next month. This is an accrual at year-end.

b. Estimated $430 in utility usage for the current month which will be paid next month. This is an accrual at year-end.

c. Depreciated office equipment costing $130,000 with an estimated residual value of $20,000 and an estimated useful life of 10 years. This is a deferral which was originally recorded in an asset account. Depreciation expense is $11,000 for the year [($130,000 cost − $20,000 residual value) ÷ 10 years].

d. Paid $30,000 in insurance on August 1 for one year of coverage. The account Insurance Expense was debited on August 1. This is a deferral. By December 31, five months of coverage ($30,000 ÷ 12 = $2,500 per month × 5 months = $12,500 insurance expense) has been used. Insurance Expense is overstated by $17,500 ($30,000 − $12,500) and Prepaid Insurance representing seven months of future coverage is understated by the same amount.

e. Received $24,000 cash on November 1 for annual rent from businesses leasing other floors of the office building. The account Rent Revenue was credited on November 1. This is a deferral. By December 31, only two months of rent revenue ($24,000 ÷ 12 months = $2,000 per month × 2 months = $4,000) has been earned. Rent Revenue is overstated by $20,000 ($24,000 − $4,000); Unearned Rent Revenue is understated by the same amount.

f. Received $870 cash in advance of dental services on December 1. Half of the services were performed by December 31. The liability account Fees Collected in Advance was credited on December 1. This is a deferral. By December 31, $435 (half of $870) is earned and $435 remains a liability to be paid in services in the future. The liability account is overstated and the Fees Revenue account is understated by the same amount.

Adjusting Entry			Is a Reversing Entry Possible?		
a. Interest receivable (A)	1,200		This is an accrual. Accruals can be reversed.		
Interest revenue (R)		1,200	Interest revenue (R)	1,200	
			Interest receivable (A)		1,200
			When the cash is received, credit Interest Revenue.		
b. Utilities expense (E)	430		This is an accrual. Accruals can be reversed.		
Accrued utilities payable (L)		430	Accrued utilities payable (L)	430	
			Utilities expense (E)		430
			When the cash is paid, debit Utilities Expense.		
c. Depreciation expense (E)	11,000		This is an adjustment of a deferral. The adjusting entry decreases an asset account. To reverse this would reflect that no depreciation has been recorded on the equipment. Do not reverse the adjusting entry.		
Accumulated depreciation (XA)		11,000			

Adjusting Entry			Is a Reversing Entry Possible?
d. Prepaid insurance (A) Insurance expense (E)	17,500	 17,500	This is an adjustment of a deferral. The adjusting entry created an asset account. To reverse this would reflect $17,500 in insurance expense for the next year and an elimination of the asset account. Since this is the desired effect, a reversing entry can be made. Insurance expense (E) 17,500 Prepaid insurance (A) 17,500
e. Rent revenue (R) Unearned rent revenue (L)	20,000	 20,000	This is an adjustment of a deferral. The adjusting entry created a liability account. To reverse this would reflect $20,000 in rent revenue for the next year and an elimination of the liability account. Since this is the desired effect, a reversing entry can be made. Unearned rent revenue (L) 20,000 Rent revenue (R) 20,000
f. Fees collected in advance Fees revenue	435	 435	This is an adjustment of a deferral. The adjusting entry decreases a liability account. To reverse this would reflect that service is due on all the fees collected in advance. Do not reverse the adjusting entry.

As indicated, the first two adjusting entries are accruals. They can be reversed since the cash receipt or payment is in the future. The last four adjusting entries adjust deferral accounts. Entries *c* and *f* were initially recorded as assets or liabilities. To reverse these would result in an error by increasing the amount of the asset and liability that has already been used up or earned. Entries *d* and *e* increased assets or liabilities. A reversal of the adjusting entry in the next period would (1) eliminate the asset or liability account as if it were earned or used up by the end of the next year and (2) reflect the appropriate amount of expense or revenue in the next period. These can be reversed.

Reversing entries allow routine recording of events during the next period so that special adjustments only have to be made during the year-end process. Perhaps the most compelling reason for reversing entries is to increase the likelihood that the effects of certain adjusting entries will not be overlooked when recording the next related transaction in the following period.

KEY TERMS

Accruals Revenues that have been earned and expenses that have been incurred by the end of the current accounting period but that will not be collected or paid until a future accounting period. *170*

Adjusting Entries End-of-period entries necessary to measure income properly, correct errors, and provide for adequate valuation of balance sheet accounts. *170*

Audit Trail The referencing system with sufficiently detailed explanations necessary for tracing an entry back to its source documents. *197*

Book Value (Net Book Value, Carrying Value) The difference between an asset's acquisition cost and accumulated depreciation, its related contra account. *169*

Closing Entries Made at the end of the accounting period to transfer net income or loss and dividends declared to retained earnings and to establish a zero balance in each of the temporary accounts. *188*

Contra Account An account that is an offset to, or reduction of, the primary account. *169*

Deferrals Previously recorded assets, liabilities, revenues, or expenses that need to be adjusted at the end of the period to reflect earned revenues or incurred expenses. *170*

Income Summary A temporary account used only during the closing process to facilitate the closing of revenues and expenses; it is closed to Retained Earnings. *189*

Journal A record that lists chronologically the effects of transactions; the book of original entry. *197*

Ledger Contains all of the individual accounts for revenues, expenses, assets, liabilities, and stockholders' equity; the book of final entry. *198*

Permanent (Real) Accounts The balance sheet accounts that carry their ending balances into the next accounting period. Permanent accounts are not closed at the end of the period. *188*

Post-Closing Trial Balance Should be prepared as the last step in the accounting cycle to check that debits equal credits and all temporary accounts have been closed. *190*

Reversing Entries Optional entries made at the start of the next accounting period to reverse the effects of certain adjusting entries; facilitates subsequent entries and simplifies the bookkeeping function. *203*

Temporary (Nominal) Accounts Income statement and dividends declared accounts that are closed at the end of the accounting period. *188*

Trial Balance A listing of all accounts with their balances to provide a check on the equality of the debits and credits. The unadjusted trial balance does not include the effects of the adjusting entries. *168*

QUESTIONS

1. Explain the accounting information processing cycle.
2. Identify, in sequence, the phases of the accounting information processing cycle.
3. What is a trial balance? What is its purpose?
4. Briefly explain adjusting entries. List the two types of adjusting entries. Give examples of each type.
5. XYZ Company collected $900 rent for the period December 1, 19A, to March 1, 19B. The $900 was credited to Rent Revenue Collected in Advance on December 1, 19A. Give the adjusting entry required on December 31, 19A (end of the accounting period).
6. On December 31, 19B, Company J recorded the following adjusting entry:

Rent revenue receivable	600	
Rent revenue		600

   Explain the situation that caused this entry and give the subsequent related entry.
7. On July 1, 19A, R Company paid a two-year insurance premium of $300 and debited Prepaid Insurance for that amount. Assuming the accounting period ends in December, give the adjusting entries that should be made at the end of 19A, 19B, and 19C.
8. Explain estimated residual value. Why is it important in measuring depreciation expense?
9. What is a contra-asset? Give an example of a contra-asset.
10. Explain why adjusting entries are entered in the journal on the last day of the accounting period and then are posted to the ledger.
11. Explain how the financial statements relate to each other.
12. What is the equation for each of the following statements:
   (*a*) Income statement (*b*) Balance sheet (*c*) Statement of cash flows, and (*d*) Statement of stockholders' equity?
13. How is earnings per share computed?
14. The Baker Company reported net income of $1,142,400 for the year. There were 420,000 shares of stock outstanding all year. Calculate earnings per share for the year.
15. Contrast an unadjusted trial balance with an adjusted trial balance. What is the purpose of each?
16. What is the purpose of closing entries? Why are they recorded in the journal and posted to the ledger?
17. Differentiate among (*a*) permanent, (*b*) temporary, (*c*) real, and (*d*) nominal accounts.
18. Why are the income statement accounts closed but the balance sheet accounts are not?

19. What is a post-closing trial balance? Is it a useful part of the accounting information processing cycle? Explain.
20. (Supplement A) What is (*a*) the book of original entry and (*b*) the book of final entry?
21. (Supplement A) Define the journal. What is its purpose?
22. (Supplement A) Define the ledger. What is its purpose?
23. (Supplement A) What is an audit trail?
24. (Supplement B) What is the basic purpose of the worksheet?
25. (Supplement B) Why are adjusting entries entered on the worksheet?
26. (Supplement B) Why are adjusting entries recorded in the journal and posted to the ledger even though they are entered on the worksheet?
27. (Supplement C) What are reversing entries? When are reversing entries useful?
28. (Supplement C) Give one example of (*a*) an adjusting entry that should be reversed and (*b*) one that should not be reversed.

EXERCISES

E4–1 Matching Definitions with Terms

Below are terms related to adjusting entries. Match each definition with its related term. There will be two answers for each term.

Terms

1. Accrued expense
2. Deferred expense
3. Accrued revenue
4. Deferred revenue

Definitions

_______ A. A revenue not yet earned; collected in advance.

_______ B. Office supplies on hand; will be used next accounting period.

_______ C. Rent revenue collected; not yet earned.

_______ D. Rent not yet collected; already earned.

_______ E. An expense incurred; not yet paid or recorded.

_______ F. A revenue earned; not yet collected.

_______ G. An expense not yet incurred; paid in advance.

_______ H. Property taxes incurred; not yet paid.

E4–2 Matching Transactions with Terms

Match each transaction with its related term.

Terms

_______ 1. Deferred revenue

_______ 2. Accrued revenue

_______ 3. Deferred expense

_______ 4. Accrued expense

Transactions

A. At the end of the year, wages payable of $3,600 had not been recorded or paid.
B. Supplies for office use were purchased during the year for $500, and $100 of the office supplies remained on hand (unused) at year-end.
C. Interest of $250 on a note receivable was earned at year-end, although collection of the interest is not due until the following year.
D. At the end of the year, service revenue of $2,000 was collected in cash but was not yet earned.

E4–3 Making Two Simple Adjusting Entries

Evans Company has completed its first year of operations on December 31, 19A. All of the 19A entries have been recorded, except for the following:

a. At year-end, employees have earned wages of $6,000. These wages will be paid on the next payroll date, January 6, 19B.

b. At year-end, interest revenue of $3,000 has been earned by the company. The cash will be collected March 1, 19B.

Required:

1. What is the annual reporting period for this company?
2. Give the required adjusting entry for transactions (*a*) and (*b*) above. Give appropriate dates and write a brief explanation of each entry.

E4–4 Identifying Adjusting Entries from Unadjusted Trial Balance

Procter & Gamble

As stated in its annual report, "Procter & Gamble markets a broad range of laundry, cleaning, paper, beauty care, health care, food and beverage products in more than 140 countries around the world, with leading brands including Tide, Ariel, Crest, Crisco, Vicks and Max Factor." P&G employs 96,500 people worldwide. Below is a trial balance listing accounts used by P&G. Assume the balances are unadjusted at the end of a recent fiscal year ended June 30.

PROCTER & GAMBLE COMPANY AND SUBSIDIARIES
Unadjusted Trial Balance
At June 30, 19A
(millions of dollars)

	Debit	Credit
Cash	2,373	
Marketable securities	283	
Accounts receivable	3,115	
Inventories	2,877	
Prepaid expenses	624	
Property, plant, and equipment	15,896	
Accumulated depreciation		5,872
Goodwill and other intangible assets	4,510	
Accumulated amortization*		756
Other assets	2,485	
Accounts payable		3,264
Accrued liabilities		2,961
Taxes payable		0
Long-term debt		6,355
Other liabilities		3,683
Contributed capital		3,186
Retained earnings		3,587
Sales		30,296
Cost of products sold	17,355	
Marketing, administrative, and other operating expenses	9,361	
Interest expense	482	
Other income		248
Income tax expense	0	
Dividends declared	847	
	60,208	60,208

*Accumulated amortization is similar to accumulated depreciation. It is a contra-asset that represents the portion of the intangible assets' cost that has been used in past operations.

Required:

1. Based on the information in the unadjusted trial balance, list the deferrals that may need to be adjusted at June 30 and the related account for each (no computations are necessary).
2. Based on the information in the unadjusted trial balance, list the accruals that may need to be recorded at June 30 and the related account for each (no computations are necessary).

E4–5 Preparing a Trial Balance

Latta Marketing Consultants, Inc., provides marketing research for clients in the retail industry. The company had the following unadjusted balances at September 30, 19A:

Account	Debit	Credit	Account	Debit	Credit	Account	Debit	Credit
Dividends Declared	25,000		Accumulated Depreciation		18,100	Accrued Expenses Payable		25,650
Cash	173,000		General and Administrative Expense	320,050		Supplies Inventory	12,200	
Wages and Benefits Expense	1,590,000		Prepaid Expenses	10,200		Interest Expense	17,200	
Accounts Receivable	225,400		Consulting Fees Earned		2,564,200	Retained Earnings		170,510
Income Taxes Payable		2,030	Travel Expense	23,990		Building and Equipment	323,040	
Utilities Expense	25,230		Gain on Sale of Land		5,000	Unearned Consulting Fees		32,500
Investment Income		10,800	Accounts Payable		86,830	Land	60,000	
Other Operating Expenses	188,000		Contributed Capital		233,370	Professional Development Expense	18,600	
Notes Payable		160,000	Rent Expense (on leased computers)	152,080		Investments	145,000	

Required:

Prepare in good form an unadjusted trial balance for Latta Marketing Consultants, Inc., at September 30, 19A.

E4–6 Effects of Three Adjusting Entries on the Income Statement and Balance Sheet

Oklahoma Company started operations on January 1, 19A. It is now December 31, 19A, end of the annual accounting period. The part-time bookkeeper needs your help to analyze the following three transactions:

a. On January 1, 19A, the company purchased a special machine for a cash cost of $12,000 (debited to the machine account). The machine has an estimated useful life of 10 years and no residual value.

b. During 19A, the company purchased office supplies that cost $1,400. At the end of 19A, office supplies of $400 remained on hand.

c. On July 1, 19A, the company paid cash of $400 for a two-year premium on an insurance policy on the machine that begins coverage on July 1, 19A.

Required:

Complete the following schedule of the amounts that should be reported for 19A:

Selected Balance Sheet Amounts at December 31, 19A:	**Amount to Be Reported**
Assets:	
Machine	$ ______
Accumulated depreciation	______
Carrying value of machine	______
Office supplies inventory	______
Prepaid insurance	______
Selected Income Statement Amounts for the Year Ended December 31, 19A:	
Expenses:	
Depreciation expense	$ ______
Office supplies expense	______
Insurance expense	______

E4–7 Recording Seven Typical Adjusting Entries

Crawford's Department Store is completing the accounting process for the year just ended, December 31, 19B. The transactions during 19B have been journalized and posted. The following data with respect to adjusting entries are available:

a. Office supplies inventory at January 1, 19B, was $250. Office supplies purchased and debited to Office Supplies Inventory during the year amounted to $600. The year-end inventory showed $300 of supplies on hand.

b. Wages earned during December 19B, unpaid and unrecorded at December 31, 19B, amounted to $2,700. The last payroll was December 28; the next payroll will be January 6, 19C.

c. Three-fourths of the basement of the store is rented for $1,100 per month to another merchant, M. Riesman. Riesman sells compatible, but not competitive, merchandise. On November 1, 19B, the store collected six months' rent in advance from Riesman in the amount of $6,600, which was credited in full to Rent Revenue when collected.

d. The remaining basement space is rented to Rita's Specialty Shop for $520 per month, payable monthly. On December 31, 19B, the rent for November and December 19B was not collected or recorded. Collection is expected January 10, 19C.

e. Delivery equipment that cost $30,000 was being used by the store. The equipment was estimated to have a useful life of four years and a residual value at the end of the four years of $6,000. Assume depreciation for a full year for 19B. The asset will be depreciated evenly over its useful life.

f. On July 1, 19B, a two-year insurance premium amounting to $3,000 was paid in cash and debited in full to Prepaid Insurance. Coverage began on July 1, 19B.

g. Crawford's operates an alteration shop to meet its own needs. Also, the shop does alterations for M. Riesman. At the end of December 31, 19B, M. Riesman had not paid for alterations completed amounting to $750. This amount has not been recorded as Alteration Shop Revenue. Collection is expected during January 19C.

Required:

1. Identify each of the above transactions as either creating a deferral account during the year to be adjusted at the end of the year or creating an accrual account at the end of the year.
2. Give the adjusting entry for each situation that should be recorded for Crawford's Department Store at December 31, 19B.

E4–8 Adjusting Entries for Interest on Two Notes Receivable

Note A: On April 1, 19B, Samrick Corporation received a $10,000, 10% note from a customer in settlement of a $10,000 open account receivable. According to the terms, the principal of the note, plus interest, is payable at the end of 12 months. The annual accounting period for Samrick ends on December 31, 19B.

Required:

1. Give the journal entry for Samrick for receipt of the note on April 1, 19B.
2. Give the adjusting entry required on December 31, 19B.
3. Give the journal entry on the date of collection, March 31, 19C, for the principal and interest.

Note B: On August 1, 19B, to meet a cash shortage, Samrick Corporation obtained a $20,000, 12% loan from a local bank. The principal of the note plus interest expense is payable at the end of 12 months.

Required:

4. Give the journal entry for Samrick on the date of the loan, August 1, 19B.
5. Give the adjusting entry required on December 31, 19B.
6. Give the journal entry on the date of payment, July 31, 19C.

E4–9 Adjusting Entries for Prepaid Insurance—Two Cases

Jenson Company is making adjusting entries for the year ended December 31, 19B. In developing information for the adjusting entries, the accountant learned that on September 1, 19B, a two-year insurance premium of $7,200 was paid for coverage beginning on that date.

Required:

1. What amount should be reported on the 19B income statement for insurance expense?
2. What amount should be reported on the December 31, 19B, balance sheet for prepaid insurance?
3. Give the adjusting entry at December 31, 19B, under each of two cases:
   Case 1 Assume that when the premium was paid on September 1, 19B, the bookkeeper debited the full amount to Prepaid Insurance.
   Case 2 Assume that when the premium was paid on September 1, 19B, the bookkeeper debited the full amount to Insurance Expense.
   (Hint: In Case 2 be sure that after the adjusting entry, you end with the same amount in the Prepaid Insurance account as in Case 1.)

E4–10 Adjusting Entries for Unearned Subscriptions—Two Cases

Weld News Company is making adjusting entries for the year ended March 31, 19C. In developing information for the adjusting entries, the controller learned that on September 1, 19B, $18,000 cash was received from customers for three-year magazine subscriptions beginning on that date. The magazines are published and mailed to customers monthly.

Required:

1. What amount should be reported on the 19C income statement for subscription revenue?
2. What amount should be reported on the March 31, 19C, balance sheet for unearned subscription revenue?
3. Give the adjusting entry at March 31, 19C, under each of two cases:
   Case 1 Assume that when the subscriptions were received on September 1, 19B, the bookkeeper debited the full amount to Unearned Subscriptions Revenue.

Case 2 Assume that when the subscriptions were received on September 1, 19B, the bookkeeper debited the full amount to Subscriptions Revenue.
(Hint: In Case 2 be sure that after the adjusting entry, you end with the same amount in the Unearned Subscriptions Revenue account as in Case 1.)

E4–11 Adjusting Entry for Supplies Inventory

Collens Company uses a large amount of shipping supplies that are purchased in large volume, stored, and used as needed. At December 31, 19B, the following data relating to shipping supplies were obtained from the records and supporting documents:

Shipping supplies on hand, January 1, 19B	$15,000
Purchases of shipping supplies during 19B	72,000
Shipping supplies on hand, per inventory December 31, 19B	11,000

Required:

1. What amount should be reported on the 19B income statement for shipping supplies expense?
2. What amount should be reported on the December 31, 19B, balance sheet for shipping supplies inventory?
3. Give the adjusting entry at December 31, 19B, assuming the purchases of shipping supplies were debited in full to Shipping Supplies Inventory ($72,000).
4. What adjusting entry would you make assuming the bookkeeper debited Shipping Supplies Expense for the $72,000? [Hint: In solving (3) and (4), be sure that each solution ends up with the same amount remaining in the Shipping Supplies Inventory account.]

E4–12 Identifying Transactions

Deere & Company

Deere & Company is the world's leading producer of agricultural equipment, a leading supplier of a broad range of industrial equipment for construction, forestry, and public works, a producer and marketer of a broad line of lawn and grounds care equipment, and a provider of credit, managed health care plans, and insurance products for businesses and the general public. The following information was from a recent annual report (in millions of dollars):

Income Taxes Payable			
		Beg. bal.	71
a	?	*b*	332
		End. bal.	80

Dividends Payable			
		Beg. bal.	43
c	?	*d*	176
		End. bal.	48

Interest Payable			
		Beg. bal.	45
e	297	*f*	?
		End. bal.	51

Required:

1. Identify the nature of the transaction indicated for each of the lettered transactions (*a*) to (*f*).
2. For transactions (*a*), (*c*), and (*f*), compute the amount.

E4–13 Analyzing the Effects of Errors on Financial Statement Items

Campbell and Long, Inc., publishers of movie and song trivia books, made the following errors in adjusting the accounts at year-end (December 31):

a. Did not record depreciation on the equipment costing $130,000 ($30,000 residual value, 10-year useful life).

b. Failed to adjust the Unearned Revenue account to reflect that $3,000 was earned by the end of the year.

c. Recorded a full year of accrued interest expense on a $15,000, 12% note payable which was only outstanding since November 1.

d. Failed to adjust Insurance Expense to reflect that $400 related to future insurance coverage.

e. Did not accrue $750 owed to the company by another company renting part of the building as a storage facility.

Required:

1. For each of the errors, prepare the adjusting journal entry that should have been made at year-end.
2. Using the following headings, indicate the effect of (+ for overstated, – for understated, and NE for no effect) and the amount of the effect for each of the errors.

Error	Assets	Liabilities	Stockholders' Equity	Revenues	Expenses	Net Income

E4–14 *Correcting Income Statement and Balance Sheet Amounts for the Effects of Three Adjusting Entries*

On December 31, 19B, Cohen and Company prepared an income statement and balance sheet and failed to take into account four adjusting entries. The income statement, prepared on this incorrect basis, reflected income before income taxes of $30,000. The balance sheet (before the effect of income taxes) reflected total assets, $90,000; total liabilities, $40,000; and stockholders' equity, $50,000. The data for the four adjusting entries were:

a. Depreciation was not recorded for the year on equipment that cost $85,000; estimated useful life, 10 years, and residual value, $5,000.

b. Wages amounting to $17,000 for the last three days of December 19B were not paid and not recorded (the next payroll will be on January 10, 19C).

c. Rent revenue of $4,800 was collected on December 1, 19B, for office space for the period December 1, 19B, to February 28, 19C. The $4,800 was credited in full to Rent Revenue when collected.

d. Income taxes were not recorded. The income tax rate for the company is 30%.

Required:

Complete the following tabulation to correct the financial statements for the effects of the four errors (indicate deductions with parentheses):

Items	Net Income	Total Assets	Total Liabilities	Stockholders' Equity
Balances reported	$30,000	$90,000	$40,000	$50,000
Effects of depreciation				
Effects of wages				
Effects of rent revenue				
Adjusted balances				
Effect of income taxes				
Correct balances				

E4–15 *Preparing Correct Income Statement to Include Effects of Seven Adjusting Entries and Giving Adjusting Entries*

Barton, Inc., completed its first year of operations on December 31, 19A. Because this is the end of the annual accounting period, the company bookkeeper prepared the following tentative income statement:

Income Statement, 19A

Rental revenue		$114,000
Expenses:		
Salaries and wages expense	$28,500	
Maintenance expense	12,000	
Rent expense (on location)	9,000	
Utilities expense	4,000	
Gas and oil expense	3,000	
Miscellaneous expenses (items not listed above)	1,000	
Total expenses		57,500
Income		$ 56,500

An independent CPA reviewed the income statement and developed additional data as follows:

a. Wages for the last three days of December amounting to $310 were not recorded or paid (disregard payroll taxes).

b. The telephone bill for December 19A amounting to $400 has not been recorded or paid.

c. Depreciation on rental autos, amounting to $23,000 for 19A, was not recorded.

d. Interest on a $20,000, one-year, 10% note payable dated October 1, 19A, was not recorded. The 10% interest is payable on the maturity date of the note.

e. Rental revenue includes $4,000 rental revenue for the month of January 19B.

f. Maintenance expense includes $1,000, which is the cost of maintenance supplies still on hand (per inventory) at December 31, 19A. These supplies will be used in 19B.

g. The income tax expense is $7,000. Payment of income tax will be made in 19B.

Required:

1. Give the adjusting entry at December 31, 19A, for each of the additional data items. If none is required, explain why.
2. Prepare a correct income statement for 19A, assuming 7,000 shares of stock are outstanding. Show computations.

E4–16 Preparing Three Adjusting Entries and Recasting the Income Statement and Balance Sheet

On December 31, 19C, the bookkeeper for Mesley Company prepared the income statement and balance sheet summarized below but neglected to consider three of the adjusting entries.

	As Prepared	Effects of Adjusting Entries	Corrected Amounts
Income statement:			
Revenues	$98,000		
Expenses	(72,000)		
Income tax expense			
Net income	$26,000		
Balance Sheet:			
Assets			
Cash	$20,000		
Accounts receivable	22,000		
Rent receivable			
Equipment*	50,000		
Accumulated depreciation	(10,000)		
	$82,000		
Liabilities			
Accounts payable	$10,000		
Income taxes payable			
Stockholders' Equity			
Contributed capital	40,000		
Retained earnings	32,000		
	$82,000		

*Acquired January 1, 19A, 10-year life, no residual value; straight-line depreciation.

Data on the three adjusting entries:

a. Depreciation on the equipment was not recorded for 19C.

b. Rent revenue earned of $2,000 for December 19C was neither collected nor recorded.

c. Income tax expense for 19C was not paid or recorded. The amount was $6,900.

Required:

1. Prepare the three adjusting entries that were omitted. Use the account titles given above.
2. Complete the two columns to the right in the above tabulation to show the correct amounts on the income statement and balance sheet.

E4–17 Preparing Four Adjusting Entries

Cayuga Company prepared the following unadjusted trial balance at the end of the accounting year, December 31, 19A (the first year of operations). To simplify the case, the amounts given are in thousands of dollars.

Account Titles	Debit	Credit
Cash	$ 38	
Accounts receivable	9	
Prepaid insurance	6	
Machinery (10-year life, no residual value)	80	
Accumulated depreciation		$ 8
Accounts payable		9
Wages payable		

Income taxes payable		
Contributed capital (4,000 shares)		68
Retained earnings		
Dividends declared and paid during 19A	4	
Revenues (not detailed)		84
Expenses (not detailed)	32	
Totals	$169	$169

Other data not yet recorded at December 31, 19A:

a. Insurance expired during 19A, $5.
b. Depreciation expense for 19A, $4.
c. Wages payable, $7.
d. Income tax expense, $9.

Required:

Give the adjusting entries for 19A.

E4–18 Prepare Financial Statements

Using the adjusted balances in E4–17, complete the income statement, statement of stockholders' equity, and balance sheet given below for 19A.

Income Statement
For the Year Ended December 31, 19A

Revenues (not detailed)	$ ______
Expenses (not detailed)	______
Pretax income	______
Income tax expense	______
Net income	$ ______
EPS	$ ______

Statement of Stockholders' Equity
For the Year Ended December 31, 19A

	Contributed Capital	Retained Earnings	Total Stockholders' Equity
Beginning balances, 1/1/19A	$ ______	$ ______	$ ______
Stock issuance	______	______	______
Net income	______	______	______
Dividends declared	______	______	______
Ending balances, 12/31/19A	$ ______	$ ______	$ ______

Balance Sheet
December 31, 19A

Assets		**Liabilities**	
Cash	$ ______	Accounts payable	$ ______
Accounts receivable	______	Wages payable	______
Prepaid insurance	______	Income taxes payable	______
Machinery	______	Total liabilities	$ ______
Accumulated depreciation	______		
		Stockholders' Equity	
		Contributed capital	______
	______	Retained earnings	______
Total assets	$ ______	Total liabilities and stockholders' equity	$ ______

E4–19 Preparing Closing Entries

Using the adjusted balances in E4–17, give the closing entries for 19A.

E4–20 Recording Adjusting Entries

For each of the following 10 independent situations, give the journal entry by entering the appropriate code(s) and amount(s).

Codes	Accounts	Codes	Accounts
A	Cash	K	Interest revenue
B	Office supplies inventory	L	Wage expense
C	Revenue receivable	M	Depreciation expense
D	Office equipment	N	Interest expense
E	Accumulated depreciation	O	Supplies expense
F	Note payable	P	Contributed capital
G	Wages payable	Q	Retained earnings
H	Interest payable	R	Dividends declared
I	Service revenue collected in advance	S	Income summary
J	Service revenue	X	None of the above

	Independent Situations	Debit		Credit	
		Code	Amount	Code	Amount
a.	Accrued wages, unrecorded and unpaid at year-end, $400 (example).	L	400	G	400
b.	Service revenue collected earlier and recorded as revenue but not yet earned, $800.				
c.	Dividends declared and paid during year; debited to Dividends Declared account, $900. Give year-end entry.				
d.	Depreciation expense for year not yet recorded, $1,000.				
e.	Balance at year-end in Service Revenue account, $62,000. Give the closing entry at year-end.				
f.	Service revenue earned but not yet collected at year-end, $600.				
g.	Balance at year-end in Interest Revenue account, $420. Give the closing entry at year-end.				
h.	Office Supplies Inventory account at year-end, $400; inventory of supplies on hand at year-end, $150.				
i.	At year-end, interest on note payable not yet recorded or paid, $220.				
j.	Balance at year-end in Income Summary account after all revenue and expense accounts have been closed, $7,800 (credit).				

E4–21 (Supplement A) Journalizing and Computing Account Balances

On January 1, 19A, Hamilton and Dyson organized the Tennis Company, Inc. The completed transactions from January 1, 19A, through February 3, 19A, can be summarized as follows:

Jan. 1 Cash invested by the organizers: Hamilton, $40,000 (for 4,000 shares) and Dyson, $30,000 (for 3,000 shares).

3 Paid monthly rent, $2,000.

15 Purchased equipment that cost $28,000 for use in the business; paid $4,000 down and signed a 10% note payable for the balance. Monthly payments made up of part principal and part interest are to be paid on the note.

30 Paid cash for operating expenses amounting to $25,000; in addition, operating expenses of $6,000 were incurred on credit.

30 Service fees earned amounted to $60,000, of which $48,000 was collected and the balance was on credit.

Feb. 1 Collected $8,000 on account for services performed in January and originally recorded as an account receivable and service revenue.

2 Paid $2,000 on the operating expenses incurred in January and originally recorded as an account payable and operating expenses.

3 Paid the first installment of $750 on the equipment note, including $200 interest expense.

Required:

1. Analyze and journalize each of the above transactions in proper general journal format.
2. Create general ledger pages and post each entry to the ledger.
3. Compute the following:
   a. Cash balance at February 3, 19A.
   b. Pretax income for the period January 1, 19A, through February 3, 19A.

E4–22 *(Supplement A) Writing Journal Entries from T-Accounts*

The following T-accounts for Seattle Service Company, Inc., show six different transactions (entries). Create a general journal and prepare a journal entry in good form for each transaction. Write a complete description of each one. (Hint: Notice that some transactions have two debits or two credits.)

Cash

(*a*)	60,000	(*c*)	10,000
(*b*)	30,000	(*e*)	2,000
(*d*)	3,000	(*f*)	7,000

Accounts Receivable

(*b*)	4,000	(*d*)	3,000

Equipment

(*f*)	25,000		

Accounts Payable

(*e*)	2,000	(*c*)	3,000

Note Payable

		(*f*)	18,000

Contributed Capital (6,000 shares)

		(*a*)	60,000

Service Revenue

		(*b*)	34,000

Operating Expenses

(*c*)	13,000		

E4–23 *(Supplement B) Identifying Adjusting Entries by Comparing Unadjusted and Adjusted Trial Balances*

Scoones Company is in the process of completing the information processing cycle at the end of the accounting year, December 31, 19B. The worksheet and financial statements have been prepared. The next step is to journalize the adjusting entries. The following two trial balances were taken directly from the completed worksheet.

	December 31, 19B			
	Unadjusted Trial Balance		Adjusted Trial Balance	
Account Titles	**Debit**	**Credit**	**Debit**	**Credit**
a. Cash	$ 9,300		$ 9,300	
b. Accounts receivable			500	
c. Prepaid insurance	2,000		1,350	
d. Equipment	120,000		120,000	
e. Accumulated depreciation		$ 22,000		$ 25,000
f. Income taxes payable				4,100
g. Contributed capital		50,000		50,000
h. Retained earnings, January 1, 19B		26,300		26,300
i. Service revenue		51,000		51,500
j. Salary expense	18,000		18,000	
k. Depreciation expense			3,000	
l. Insurance expense			650	
m. Income tax expense			4,100	
	$149,300	$149,300	$156,900	$156,900

Required:

By examining the amounts in each trial balance, reconstruct the adjusting entries that were made between the unadjusted trial balance and the adjusted trial balance. Give an explanation of each adjusting entry.

E4–24 *(Supplement B) Completing a Worksheet Starting with an Unadjusted Trial Balance*

Fairbanks Company is completing the annual accounting information processing cycle at December 31, 19B. The worksheet, as shown below, has been started (to simplify, amounts given are in thousands of dollars).

Account No.	Account Titles	Unadjusted Trial Balance Debit	Unadjusted Trial Balance Credit
101	Cash	$ 28	$
102	Accounts receivable	40	
103	Inventory	21	
104	Prepaid insurance	4	
110	Equipment (10-year life, no residual value)	80	
111	Accumulated depreciation, equipment		8
119	Accounts payable		12
120	Wages payable		
121	Income taxes payable		
122	Revenue collected in advance		
123	Note payable, long-term (10% interest due each December 31)		25
130	Contributed capital		77
140	Retained earnings		22
141	Dividends declared	10	
145	Revenues		108
146	Expenses	69	
147	Income tax expense		
		$252	$252

Data not yet recorded for 19B:

a. Insurance expense, $2.

b. Depreciation expense, $8.

c. Wages earned by employees; not yet paid, $1.

d. Revenue collected by Morgan; not yet earned, $4.

e. Income tax rate, 25%.

(Note: No accrued interest is recorded because interest is paid on each December 31.)

Required:

Complete the worksheet in every respect (you may use account numbers instead of account titles). Set up additional column headings for Adjusting Entries, Adjusted Trial Balance, Income Statement, Retained Earnings, and Balance Sheet. Record all revenues and expenses except income tax in the two accounts given (145 and 146).

E4–25 *(Supplement B) Completing a Worksheet Starting with an Unadjusted Trial Balance*

Ricci Corporation, a small company, is completing the annual accounting information processing cycle at December 31, 19B. The worksheet, prior to the adjusting entries, has been started as follows:

Account Titles	Unadjusted Trial Balance Debit	Credit
Cash	$ 16,000	
Accounts receivable	8,000	
Equipment	20,000	
Accumulated depreciation		$ 5,000
Other assets	38,000	
Accounts payable		7,000
Note payable, long-term		8,000
Contributed capital		36,000
Retained earnings		10,000
Revenues		50,000
Expenses	34,000	
	$116,000	$116,000
Income tax expense		
Income taxes payable		
Net income		

Data not yet recorded for 19B:

a. Depreciation expense, $3,000.

b. Income tax rate, 30%.

Required:

Complete the worksheet in all respects, including a legend explaining the adjustments. Set up additional column headings for Adjusting Entries, Adjusted Trial Balance, Income Statement, Retained Earnings, and Balance Sheet.

E4–26 (Supplement C) Determining When to Use a Reversing Entry

Canadian Company has completed the accounting information processing cycle for the year ended December 31, 19A. Reversing entries are under consideration on January 1, 19B, for two different adjusting entries made on December 31, 19A. For case purposes, the relevant data are given in T-accounts:

Prepaid Insurance

Debit		Credit	
1/1/19A Balance	400	(*a*) 12/31/19A Adj. entry	200

Insurance Expense

Debit		Credit	
(*a*) 12/31/19A Adj. entry	200	(*c*) 12/31/19A Closing entry	200

Accrued Wages Payable

Debit		Credit	
		(*b*) 12/31/19A Adj. entry	2,000

Wages Expense

Debit		Credit	
Paid during 19A	20,000	(*d*) 12/31/19A Closing entry	22,000
(*b*) 12/31/19A Adj. entry	2,000		

Income Summary

Debit		Credit	
12/31/19A Closing entries		12/31/19A	
(*c*)	200	Closed to Retained Earnings	22,200
(*d*)	22,000		

Required:

Would a reversing entry on January 1, 19B, facilitate the next related entry for (*a*) Prepaid Insurance and (*b*) Accrued Wages Payable? Explain why.

PROBLEMS

P4–1 *Preparing Four Simple Adjusting Entries*

The annual accounting year used by McCain Company ends on December 31. It is December 31, 19X, and all of the 19X entries have been made except the following adjusting entries:

a. On September 1, 19X, McCain collected six months' rent of $4,800 on storage space. At that date, McCain debited Cash and credited Rent Revenue for $4,800.

b. The company earned service revenue of $3,000 on a special job that was completed December 29, 19X. Collection will be made during January 19Y; no entry has been recorded.

c. On November 1, 19X, McCain paid a one-year premium for property insurance, $4,200, for coverage starting on that date. Cash was credited and Insurance Expense was debited for this amount.

d. At December 31, 19X, wages earned by employees not yet paid, $1,100. The employees will be paid on the next payroll date, January 15, 19Y.

Required:

Give the adjusting entry required for each transaction. Provide a brief explanation for each entry.

P4–2 *Preparing Four Types of Adjusting Entries*

DeWitt Company started operations on September 1, 19A. It is now August 31, 19C, end of its second year of operations. All entries for the annual accounting period have been journalized and posted to the ledger accounts. The following end-of-year entries are to be recorded:

a. Service revenue collected in advance, $2,200. On August 15, 19C, the company debited Cash and credited Service Revenue for this amount. The services will be performed during September 19C.

b. Revenue earned but not yet collected or recorded, $6,000. The company completed a large service job, which passed inspection on August 31, 19C. Collection is expected on September 6, 19C.

c. Expense paid in advance, $2,500. The company purchased service supplies on August 1, 19C, at which time Supplies Expense was debited and Cash credited for this amount. At August 31, 19C, one-half of these supplies were on hand (will be used later on other jobs).

d. Expense incurred but not yet paid or recorded. The company used the consulting services of an engineer during the last two weeks of August 19C. The services have been performed, and the company expects to pay the $800 billing on September 15, 19C.

Required:

1. What is the accounting (i.e., reporting) year for this company? What accounting assumption supports your answer?
2. Prepare the required adjusting entry for each situation, including a brief explanation of each entry.
3. Explain the effect on net income if these entries are not made on August 31, 19C (disregard income tax).

P4–3 *Preparing Six Adjusting Entries and Related Balance Sheet Classifications*

Johnston Company is preparing the adjusting entries for the year ended December 31, 19B. On that date, the bookkeeper for the company assembled the following data:

a. On December 31, 19B, salaries earned by employees but not yet paid or recorded, $4,000.

b. Depreciation must be recognized on a service truck that cost $12,000 on July 1, 19B (estimated useful life is six years with no residual value).

c. Cash of $1,500 was collected on December 28, 19B, for services to be rendered during 19C (Service Revenue was credited).

d. On December 27, 19B, the company received a tax bill of $300 from the city for 19B property taxes on land that is payable during January 19C.

e. On July 1, 19B, the company paid $900 cash for a two-year insurance policy on the service truck (*b* above). Prepaid Insurance was debited.

f. On October 1, 19B, the company borrowed $10,000 from a local bank and signed a 12% note for that amount. The principal and interest are payable on maturity date, September 30, 19C.

Required:

1. The bookkeeper has asked you to assist in preparing the adjusting entries at December 31, 19B. For each situation above, give the adjusting entry and a brief explanation. If none is required, explain why.
2. Based on your entries given in requirement (1), complete the following schedule to reflect the amounts and balance sheet classifications:

Item	Accounts	19B Amount	Balance Sheet Classification (One Check on Each Line) Assets	Liabilities	Stockholders' Equity
a	Salaries payable	$ ______	______	______	______
b	Accumulated depreciation	______	______	______	______
c	Revenue collected in advance	______	______	______	______
d	Property taxes payable	______	______	______	______
e	Prepaid insurance	______	______	______	______
f	Interest payable	______	______	______	______

P4–4 *Preparing Eight Adjusting Entries and Recomputing Income to Include Their Effects*

Handy Haulers Company is at the end of its accounting year, December 31, 19B. The following data that must be considered were developed from the company's records and related documents:

a. On July 1, 19B, a three-year insurance premium on equipment in the amount of $1,200 was paid and debited in full to Insurance Expense on that date. Coverage began on July 1.

b. During 19B, office supplies amounting to $800 were purchased for cash and debited in full to Supplies Inventory. At the end of 19A, the inventory count of supplies remaining on hand (unused) showed $200. The inventory of supplies on hand at December 31, 19B, showed $300.

c. On December 31, 19B, Bert's Garage completed repairs on one of the company's trucks at a cost of $800, the amount is not yet recorded and by agreement will be paid during January 19C.

d. In December 19B, a tax bill for $1,600 on land owned during 19B was received from the city. The taxes, which have not been recorded, are due and will be paid on February 15, 19C.

e. On December 31, 19B, the company completed a contract for an out-of-state company. The bill was for $8,000 payable within 30 days. No cash has been collected, and no journal entry has been made for this transaction.

f. On July 1, 19B, the company purchased a new hauling van at a cash cost of $23,600. The estimated useful life of the van was 10 years, with an estimated residual value of $1,600. No depreciation has been recorded for 19B (compute depreciation for six months in 19B).

g. On October 1, 19B, the company borrowed $10,000 from the local bank on a one-year, 12% note payable. The principal plus interest is payable at the end of 12 months.

h. The income before any of the adjustments or income taxes was $30,000. The company's federal income tax rate is 30%. Compute adjusted income based on (*a*) through (*g*) to determine income tax expense.

Required:

Give the adjusting entry required on December 31, 19B, related to each of the above transactions. Give a brief explanation with each entry.

P4–5 *Computing Income Statement Amounts for Three Items and Identifying Any Adjusting Entries*

The following information was provided by the records of Collegetown Apartments (a corporation) at the end of the annual fiscal period, December 31, 19B:

Revenue:	
a. Rent revenue collected in cash during 19B for occupancy in 19B (credited to Rent Revenue)	$512,000
b. Rent revenue earned for occupancy in December 19B; will not be collected until 19C	16,000
c. In December 19B, collected rent revenue in advance for January 19C (credited to Rent Revenue)	12,000
Salary expense:	
d. Cash payment made in January 19B for employee salaries earned in December 19A	4,000
e. Salaries incurred and paid during 19B (debited to Salary Expense)	62,000
f. Salaries earned by employees during December 19B; will not be paid until January 19C	3,000
g. Cash advance to employees in December 19B for salaries that will be earned in January 19C (debited to Receivable from Employees)	1,500
Supplies used:	
h. Maintenance supplies inventory on January 1, 19B (balance on hand)	3,000
i. Maintenance supplies purchased for cash during 19B (debited to Maintenance Supplies Inventory when purchased)	8,000
j. Maintenance supplies inventory on December 31, 19B	1,700

Required:

1. In conformity with the revenue and matching principles, compute the amounts that should be reported on Collegetown's 19B income statement for
   a. Rent revenue
   b. Salary expense
   c. Maintenance supplies expense
   Show computations.
2. Check the items that would need an adjusting entry at the end of 19B and indicate whether the checked item is an accrual or deferral:

	Need Adjusting Entry? Yes/No	If So, Accrual or Deferral?		Need Adjusting Entry? Yes/No	If So, Accrual or Deferral?
a.	________	________	*f.*	________	________
b.	________	________	*g.*	________	________
c.	________	________	*h.*	________	________
d.	________	________	*i.*	________	________
e.	________	________	*j.*	________	________

P4–6 *Determining the Effect of Five Adjusting Entries on the Income Statement*

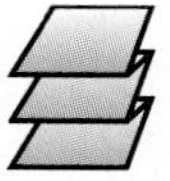

Alabama Air Company has completed its annual financial statements for the year ended December 31, 19C. The income statement (summarized) reflected the following:

Revenues:	
Service revenue	$ 98,200
Rental revenue (office space)	4,000
Total revenues	102,200
Expenses:	
Salaries and wages expense	46,000
Service supplies used	2,800
Depreciation expense	3,000
Maintenance of equipment	2,050
Rent expense (service building)	6,800
Oil and gas for equipment	2,200
Insurance expense	400
Utilities expense	800
Other expenses	7,700
Total expenses	71,750
Net income	$ 30,450

The company is a partnership; therefore, it does not pay income taxes. An audit of the records and financial statements by a CPA revealed that the following items were not considered:

a. Service revenue of $850 earned but not collected on December 31, 19C, was not included in the $98,200 on the income statement.

b. The $2,800 of service supplies used included $400 of service supplies still on hand in the supplies storeroom on December 31, 19C.

c. Rent revenue of $100 that was collected in advance and not yet earned by December 31, 19C, was included in the $4,000 on the income statement.

d. A property tax bill of $600 for 19C was received during December 19C but will be paid during January 19D (not included in the above amounts on the income statement).

e. A two-year insurance premium of $800 was paid on July 1, 19B; no premiums were paid in 19C.

Required:

1. Recast the above income statement to include, exclude, or omit each of the items identified by the CPA. Use a format similar to the following:

Items	Amounts as Reported	Corrections	Amounts that Should Be Reported

2. The owner of the company asked you to explain the following:
   a. The insurance premium was paid in 19B; therefore, why was insurance expense reported in 19C?
   b. Although the company paid no cash for depreciation expense, $3,000 was included in 19C as expense. Why was this so?

P4–7 *Determining the Effects of Six Entries on the Income Statement and Balance Sheet*

It is December 31, 19B, end of the annual accounting period for Clinton Company. Below are listed six independent transactions (summarized) that affected the company during 19B.

Required:

Analyze the transactions as to their effects on the balance sheet and income statement for 19B as indicated.

a. On January 1, 19A, the company purchased a machine that cost $30,000 cash (estimated useful life six years and no residual value).

1. Show how the machine should be reported on the 19B balance sheet.
2. Show how the 19B income statement should report the effects of the machine usage.

b. On September 1, 19B, the company signed a $9,000, one-year, 12% note payable. The principal plus interest is payable on maturity date.
1. Show how the liability should be reported on the 19B balance sheet.
2. Show how the effects of the note should be reported on the 19B income statement.

c. During 19B, service revenues of $80,000 were collected, of which $20,000 was collected in advance.
1. Show how the $20,000 should be reported on the 19B balance sheet.
2. Show how the 19B income statement should report the effects of the transaction.

d. In 19B, expenses paid in cash amounted to $50,000, of which $5,000 was paid for expenses yet to be incurred (prepaid).
1. Show how the 19B balance sheet should report the $5,000.
2. Show how the income statement should report this situation.

e. In 19B, $95,000 cash revenues were collected; and in addition, revenues of $10,000 were on credit.
1. Show how the $10,000 should be reported on the 19B balance sheet.
2. Show how the 19B income statement should report the revenues.

f. In 19B, expenses amounting to $70,000 were paid in cash; in addition, expenses of $6,000 were on credit.
1. Show how the $6,000 should be reported on the 19B balance sheet.
2. Show how the expenses should be reported on the 19B income statement.

P4–8 *Analysis—Comparing Two Sets of Account Balances to Determine What Adjusting Entries Were Made*

Hourigan Company is completing the information processing cycle at the end of its fiscal year, December 31, 19B. Following are the correct balances at December 31, 19B, for the accounts both before and after the adjusting entries for 19B.

	Account Balance, December 31, 19B			
	Before Adjusting Entries		After Adjusting Entries	
Items	Debit	Credit	Debit	Credit
a. Cash	$ 9,000		$ 9,000	
b. Service revenue receivable			400	
c. Prepaid insurance	600		400	
d. Operational assets	120,200		120,200	
e. Accumulated depreciation, equipment		$31,500		$40,000
f. Income taxes payable				4,700
g. Contributed capital		80,000		80,000
h. Retained earnings, January 1, 19B		14,000		14,000
i. Service revenue		46,000		46,400
j. Salary expense	41,700		41,700	
k. Depreciation expense			8,500	
l. Insurance expense			200	
m. Income tax expense			4,700	
	$171,500	$171,500	$185,100	$185,100

Required:

1. Compare the amounts in the columns before and after the adjusting entries to reconstruct the adjusting entries that were made in 19B. Provide an explanation of each.
2. Compute the amount of income assuming (*a*) it is based on the amounts before adjusting entries and (*b*) it is based on the amounts after adjusting entries. Which income amount is correct? Explain why.

P4–9 *Computing Effects of Adjusting Entries on the Balance Sheet and Income Statement in Two Consecutive Years*

On January 1, 19A, four persons organized Atlantic Company. The company has been operating for two years, 19A and 19B. Given below are data relating to six selected transactions that affect both years. The annual accounting period ends December 31.

a. On January 1, 19A, the company purchased a computer for use in the business at a cash cost of $22,500. The computer has an estimated useful life of five years and no residual value. It will be depreciated on a straight-line basis.

b. On July 1, 19A, the company borrowed $15,000 cash from City Bank and signed a one-year, 10% interest-bearing note. The interest and principal are payable on June 30, 19B.

c. The company owns its office building. On October 1, 19A, the company leased some of its office space to A. B. Jones for $7,200 per year. Jones paid this amount in full on October 1, 19A, and expects to use the space for one year only. The company increased (debited) Cash for $7,200 and increased (credited) Rent Revenue for $7,200 on October 1, 19A.

d. Office supplies were purchased for use in the business. Cash was decreased (credited), and Office Supplies Inventory was increased (debited). The unused supplies at each year-end are determined by inventory count. The amounts were:

Year	Purchased	Year-End Inventory
19A	$600	$200
19B	400	100

e. Wages are paid by the company at the end of each two weeks. The last payroll date in December usually is four days before December 31. Therefore, at each year-end, unpaid wages exist that are paid in cash on the first payroll date in the next year. The wages paid in cash and the wages incurred but not yet paid or recorded at each year-end were:

Year	Wages Paid in Cash during the Year	Wages Unpaid and Unrecorded at Dec. 31
19A	$35,000	$ 400
19B	41,000	4,000

f. On July 1, 19A, the company paid a two-year insurance premium of $360 on the computer. At that date, the company increased (debited) an asset account, Prepaid Insurance, and decreased (credited) Cash, $360.

Required:

Complete the following schedule for 19A and 19B by entering the amounts that should be reported on the financial statements of Atlantic Company. Show computations.

	19A	19B
Balance sheet:		
Assets		
Computer	$ ______	$ ______
Less: Accumulated depreciation	______	______
Carrying value	______	______
Office supplies inventory	______	______
Prepaid insurance	______	______
Liabilities		
Note payable, City Bank	______	______
Interest payable	______	______
Rent revenue collected in advance	______	______
Wages payable	______	______

Income statement:		
Rent revenue	$ ________	$ ________
Depreciation expense	________	________
Interest expense	________	________
Office supplies expense	________	________
Wage expense	________	________
Insurance expense	________	________

P4–10 *Preparing an Income Statement and Balance Sheet from an Unadjusted Trial Balance and Including the Effects of Five Adjusting Entries*

Crabbe and Sons, Inc., a small service company, keeps its records without the help of an accountant. After much effort, an outside accountant prepared the following unadjusted trial balance as of the end of the annual accounting period, December 31, 19D:

Account Titles	Debit	Credit
Cash	$ 60,000	
Accounts receivable	13,000	
Service supplies inventory	800	
Prepaid insurance	1,000	
Service trucks (5-year life, no residual value)	20,000	
Accumulated depreciation, service trucks		$ 12,000
Other assets	11,200	
Accounts payable		3,000
Wages payable		
Income taxes payable		
Note payable (3 years; 10% each December 31)		20,000
Contributed capital (5,000 shares outstanding)		28,200
Retained earnings		10,500
Dividends declared	3,000	
Service revenue		77,000
Remaining expenses (not detailed)*	41,700	
Income tax expense		
Totals	$150,700	$150,700

*Excludes income tax expense.

Data not yet recorded at December 31, 19D:

a. The supplies inventory count on December 31, 19D, reflected $300 remaining on hand; to be used in 19E.

b. Insurance expired during 19D, $500.

c. Depreciation expense for 19D, $4,000.

d. Wages earned by employees not yet paid on December 31, 19D, $900.

e. Income tax expense was $7,350.

Required:

1. Give the 19D adjusting entries. (Hint: Journalize the above five data items.)
2. Complete the financial statements given below (show computations) for 19D to include the effects of the five transactions listed above.
3. Give the 19D closing entries.

Income Statement
For the Year Ended December 31, 19D

Service revenue		$ ________
Supplies expense	$ ________	
Insurance expense	________	
Depreciation expense	________	
Wages expense	________	
Remaining expenses (not detailed)	________	
Total expenses		________
Pretax income		________
Income tax expense		________
Net income		$ ________
EPS		$ ________

Balance Sheet
At December 31, 19D

Assets		**Liabilities**	
Cash	$ ______	Accounts payable	$ ______
Accounts receivable	______	Wages payable	______
Service supplies inventory	______	Income taxes payable	______
Prepaid insurance	______	Note payable, long-term	______
Service trucks	______	Total liabilities	______
Accumulated depreciation	______	**Stockholders' Equity**	
Other assets (not detailed)	______	Contributed capital	______
		Retained earnings	______
		Total stockholders' equity	______
Total assets	$ ______	Total liabilities and stockholders' equity	$ ______

P4–11 *Using the T-Account Balances to Explain the Adjusting Entries Recorded, Prepare the Closing Entries, and Answer Three Analytical Questions*

The T-accounts of Longhorn Company at the end of the third year of operations, December 31, 19C (prior to the closing entries), were as shown below. The 19C adjusting entries are identified by letters.

Cash

Debit		Credit	
Bal.	20,000		

Inventory, Maintenance Supplies

Debit		Credit	
Bal.	500	*(a)*	300

Service Equipment

Debit		Credit	
1/1/19A	90,000		

Accumulated Depreciation, Service Equipment

Debit		Credit	
		Bal.	18,000
		(d)	9,000

Remaining Assets

Debit		Credit	
Bal.	42,500		

Note Payable 8%

Debit		Credit	
		1/1/19B	10,000

Interest Payable

Debit		Credit	
		(b)	800

Income Taxes Payable

Debit		Credit	
		(f)	13,020

Wages Payable

Debit		Credit	
		(e)	500

Revenue Collected in Advance

Debit		Credit	
		(c)	6,000

Contributed Capital (8,000 shares)

Debit		Credit	
		Bal.	56,000

Retained Earnings

Debit		Credit	
		Bal.	9,000

Service Revenue

Debit		Credit	
(c)	6,000	Bal.	220,000

Expenses

Debit		Credit	
Bal.	160,000		
(a)	300		
(b)	800		
(d)	9,000		
(e)	500		
(f)	13,020		

Required:

1. Develop three 19C trial balances of Longhorn Company using the following format:

Account	Unadjusted Trial Balance		Adjusted Trial Balance		Post-Closing Trial Balance	
	Debit	Credit	Debit	Credit	Debit	Credit

2. Write an explanation for each adjusting entry for 19C.
3. Give the closing journal entries.
4. What was the apparent useful life of the service equipment? What assumptions must you make to answer this question?
5. What was the average income tax rate for 19C?
6. What was the average issue (sale) price per share of the capital stock?

P4–12 *Comprehensive Review Problem: From Transaction Analysis to Preparation of Financial Statements (See Chapters 2, 3, and 4)*

Herman's Service Company (a corporation) began operations on January 1, 19A. The annual reporting period ends December 31. The trial balance on January 1, 19B, was as follows (rounded to thousands to simplify):

Account No.	Account Titles	Debit	Credit
01	Cash	$ 3	
02	Accounts receivable	5	
03	Service supplies inventory	12	
04	Land		
05	Equipment	60	
06	Accumulated depreciation (equipment)		$ 6
07	Remaining assets (not detailed to simplify)	4	
11	Accounts payable		5
12	Notes payable		
13	Wages payable		
14	Interest payable		
15	Income taxes payable		
21	Contributed capital (65,000 shares)		65
31	Retained earnings		8
35	Service revenue		
40	Depreciation expense		
41	Income tax expense		
42	Interest expense		
43	Remaining expenses (not detailed to simplify)		
50	Income summary		
	Totals	$84	$84

Transactions during 19B (summarized in thousands of dollars) were:

a. Borrowed $10 cash on a 12% note payable, dated March 1, 19B.

b. Purchased land for future building site, paid cash, $9.

c. Revenues for 19B, $160, including $40 on credit.

d. Sold 3,000 additional shares of capital stock for $1 cash per share.

e. Remaining expenses for 19B, $85, including $15 on credit.

f. Collected accounts receivable, $24.

g. Purchased additional assets, $10 cash (debit Remaining Assets).

h. Accounts payable paid, $13.

i. Purchased service supplies for future use, $18 (debit to Account No. 3).

j. Signed a $25 service contract to start February 1, 19C.

k. Declared and paid cash dividend, $17. (The accountant decided to debit Account No. 31 rather than a special account.)

Data for adjusting entries:

l. Service supplies inventory counted on December 31, 19B, $14 (debit Remaining Expenses).

m. Equipment, useful life 10 years (no residual or scrap value).

n. Accrued interest on notes payable (to be computed).

o. Wages earned since the December 24 payroll; not yet paid, $12.

p. Income tax expense was $8, payable in 19C.

Required:

1. Analyze and journalize each of the 11 transactions.
2. Set up the 20 T-accounts and post the entries.

3. Journalize and post the adjusting entries.
4. Prepare an income statement, statement of stockholders' equity, balance sheet, and statement of cash flows.
5. Journalize and post the closing entries.
6. Prepare a post-closing trial balance.

P4–13 Comprehensive Problem: Preparing Six Adjusting Entries and Recasting the Income Statement and Balance Sheet

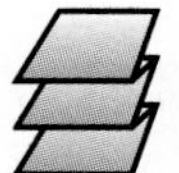

Meadville Corporation has been in operation since January 1, 19A. It is now December 31, 19A, the end of the annual accounting period. The company has not done well financially during the first year, although revenue has been fairly good. The three stockholders manage the company, but they have not given much attention to recordkeeping. In view of a serious cash shortage, they asked a local bank for a $20,000 loan. The bank requested a complete set of financial statements. The following 19A annual financial statements were prepared by a clerk and then were given to the bank.

MEADVILLE CORPORATION
December 31, 19A

Income Statement

Transportation revenue	$85,000
Expenses:	
Salaries expense	17,000
Maintenance expense	12,000
Other expenses	22,000
Total expenses	51,000
Net income	$34,000

MEADVILLE CORPORATION
December 31, 19A

Balance Sheet

Assets	
Cash	$ 2,000
Receivables	3,000
Inventory of maintenance supplies	6,000
Equipment	40,000
Remaining assets	27,000
Total assets	$78,000
Liabilities	
Accounts payable	$ 9,000
Stockholders' Equity	
Contributed capital	35,000
Retained earnings	34,000
Total liabilities and stockholders' equity	$78,000

After briefly reviewing the statements and "looking into the situation," the bank requested that the statements be redone (with some expert help) to "incorporate depreciation, accruals, inventory counts, income taxes, and so on." As a result of a review of the records and supporting documents, the following additional information was developed:

a. The inventory of maintenance supplies of $6,000 shown on the balance sheet has not been adjusted for supplies used during 19A. An inventory count of the maintenance supplies on hand (unused) on December 31, 19A, showed $1,800. Supplies used were debited to Maintenance Expense.

b. The insurance premium paid in 19A was for years 19A and 19B; therefore, the prepaid insurance at December 31, 19A, amounted to $2,000. The total insurance premium was debited in full to Other Expenses when paid in 19A.

c. The equipment cost $40,000 when purchased January 1, 19A. It had an estimated useful life of five years (no residual value). No depreciation has been recorded for 19A.

d. Unpaid (and unrecorded) salaries at December 31, 19A, amounted to $2,200.

e. At December 31, 19A, hauling revenue collected in advance amounted to $7,000. This amount was credited in full to Transportation Revenue when the cash was collected earlier during 19A.

f. Income tax expense was $3,650 (the tax rate is 25%).

Required:

1. Give the six adjusting entries required on December 31, 19A, based on the above additional information.
2. Recast the above statements after taking into account the adjusting entries. You do not need to use classifications on the statements. Suggested form for the solution:

Items	Amounts Reported	Changes		Correct Amounts
		Plus	Minus	
(List here each item from the two statements)				

3. Omission of the adjusting entries caused:
   a. Net income to be overstated or understated (select one) by $ ________.
   b. Total assets on the balance sheet to be overstated or understated (select one) by $ ________.
4. Write a brief, nontechnical report to the bank explaining the causes of these differences.

P4–14 *(Supplement A) Completing the First Four Steps of the Accounting Information Processing Cycle*

Four Seasons Company, Inc., was started on January 1, 19A. During the first year ended December 31, 19A (end of the accounting period), the following summarized entries were completed:

Date	Transaction
a.	Issued 30,000 shares of its common stock for $80,000 cash.
b.	Purchased equipment for use in operations that cost $50,000 cash. Estimated life, 10 years.
c.	Borrowed $40,000 cash on a long-term note payable (10% interest).
d.	Revenues earned, $102,000, of which $8,000 was on credit (not yet collected at year-end).
e.	Expenses incurred (including interest on the note payable), $70,000, of which $8,000 was on credit (not yet paid at year-end).
f.	Paid cash dividend, $7,000. (Hint: Debit Retained Earnings.)
g.	Recorded depreciation expense. Assume no income tax.

Required:

Process the above transactions through the accounting information processing cycle by steps as follows:

Step 1. Analyze: Write your analysis of each transaction in terms of Assets = Liabilities + Stockholders' Equity, and Debits = Credits (as discussed in Chapters 2 and 3).

Step 2. Journalize each transaction: Start your general journal with page 1. Use the date letters for identification of transactions.

Step 3. Post to the ledger: Set up the following ledger accounts and account numbers: Cash, 101; Accounts Receivable, 102; Equipment, 105; Accumulated Depreciation, 106; Accounts Payable, 201; Note Payable, Long-Term, 205; Contributed Capital, 301; Retained Earnings, 303; Revenues, 310; and Expenses, 315. Post the journal entries to the ledger accounts (as you complete each journal entry or after the last journal entry).

Step 4 Prepare a trial balance.

P4–15 (Supplement B) Completing a Worksheet Starting with the Adjusted Trial Balance, Computing the Amounts for the Adjusting Entries, and Giving the Closing Entries

Anderson Corporation has partially completed the following worksheet for the year ended December 31, 19E:

Account Titles	Unadjusted Trial Balance		Adjusting Entries	
	Debit	Credit	Debit	Credit
Cash	33,000			
Accounts receivable	22,000			
Supplies inventory	1,200			(a) 600
Interest receivable			(b) 300	
Long-term note receivable (10%; dated September 1, 19E)	9,000			
Equipment (8-year life, no residual value)	80,000			
Accumulated depreciation		35,000		(c) 10,000
Accounts payable		10,000		
Note payable, short-term (12%; dated July 1, 19E)		12,000		
Interest payable				(d) 720
Income taxes payable				(e) 3,620
Contributed capital		35,000		
Retained earnings		20,000		
Service revenue		72,000		
Interest revenue				(b) 300
Expenses (not detailed)	38,800		(a) 600	
Depreciation expense			(c) 10,000	
Interest expense			(d) 720	
Income tax expense			(e) 3,620	
Totals	184,000	184,000	15,240	15,240

Required:

1. Use additional columns for Adjusted Trial Balance, Income Statement, Retained Earnings, and Balance Sheet; and complete the worksheet.
2. Show how the following adjusting entry amounts were computed: (*a*) \$600, (*b*) \$300, (*c*) \$10,000, (*d*) \$720.
3. Give the closing entries.
4. Why are the adjusting and closing entries journalized and posted?

P4–16 *(Supplement B) Comprehensive Worksheet Problem—Starting with an Unadjusted Trial Balance and Ending with the Closing Entries*

Marine Pool Service & Repair, Inc., has been in operation for several years. Revenues have increased gradually from both the pool cleaning and repair services. The annual financial statements prepared in the past have not conformed to GAAP. The newly employed president decided that a balance sheet, income statement, and statement of retained earnings would be prepared in conformity with GAAP. The first step was to employ a full-time bookkeeper and engage a local CPA firm. It is now December 31, 19C, the end of the current accounting year. The bookkeeper has developed a trial balance from the ledger. A member of the staff of the CPA firm will advise and assist the bookkeeper in completing the accounting information processing cycle for the first time. The unadjusted trial balance at December 31, 19C, is shown below.

MARINE POOL SERVICE & REPAIR, INC.
Unadjusted Trial Balance
December 31, 19C

Debits		Credits	
Cash	$ 27,500	Accumulated depreciation	$ 24,000
Accounts receivable	2,080	Accounts payable	8,000
Office supplies inventory	170	Wages payable	
Prepaid insurance	800	Interest payable	
Land for future building site (not in use)	5,000	Revenue collected in advance	
Equipment	72,000	Income taxes payable	
Remaining assets (not detailed)	22,000	Note payable (12%)	20,000
Salary expense	60,000	Contributed capital (25,000 shares)	25,000
Advertising expense	2,000	Retained earnings, January 1, 19C	12,800
Utilities expense	1,400	Repair revenue	72,000
Maintenance expense	3,200	Cleaning revenue	38,000
Miscellaneous expenses	650		
Insurance expense			
Wage expense			
Depreciation expense			
Interest expense			
Income tax expense			
Dividends declared	3,000		
	$199,800		$199,800

Examination of the records and related documents provided the following additional information that should be considered for adjusting entries:

a. A physical count of office supplies inventory at December 31, 19C, reflected $70 on hand. Office supplies used are a miscellaneous expense. Office supplies purchased during 19C were debited to this inventory account.

b. On July 1, 19C, a two-year insurance premium was paid amounting to $800; it was debited to Prepaid Insurance.

c. The equipment cost $72,000 when acquired. Annual depreciation expense is $12,000.

d. Unpaid and unrecorded wages earned by employees at December 31, 19C, amounted to $900.

e. The $20,000 note payable was signed on October 1, 19C, for a 12% bank loan; principal and interest are due at the end of 12 months from that date.

f. Cleaning revenue collected and recorded as earned before December 31, 19C, included $150 collected in advance from three customers for cleanings to be done in January, 19D. (Hint: Reduce Cleaning Revenue.)

g. Gasoline, oil, and fuel purchased for the vehicles and used during the last two weeks of December 19C amounting to $200 have not been paid for or recorded (this is considered maintenance expense).

h. The average income tax rate is 20%, which produces income tax expense of $5,720.

Required:

1. Enter the unadjusted trial balance on a worksheet; then, based on the above data, enter the adjusting entries. Complete the worksheet.

2. Using the worksheet, prepare an income statement (use two captions: Revenues and Expenses), statement of retained earnings, and balance sheet.
3. Using the worksheet, prepare the 19C adjusting entries in journal form.
4. Using the worksheet, prepare the 19C closing entries in journal form.

P4–17 (Supplement C) Selecting Adjusting Entries that Often Are Reversed

Global Corporation has completed all information processing including the annual financial statements at December 31, 19D. The adjusting entries recorded at that date were as follows:

	Debit	Credit
a. Insurance expense	250	
Prepaid insurance		250
b. Interest receivable	400	
Interest revenue		400
c. Supplies expense	90	
Supplies inventory		90
d. Depreciation expense	3,000	
Accumulated depreciation		3,000
e. Wage expense	700	
Wages payable		700
f. Interest expense	600	
Interest payable		600
g. Income tax expense	5,500	
Income taxes payable		5,500

Required:

For each of the above adjusting entries indicate whether it usually would be reversed. Give the reversing entry in each instance (if none, so state) and explain the basis for your response.

CASES

C4–1 Analyzing Four Transactions of a Real Estate Company that Involve Adjusting Entries

Seneca Land Company, a closely held corporation, invests in commercial rental properties. Seneca's annual accounting period ends on December 31. At the end of each year, numerous adjusting entries must be made because many transactions completed during current and prior years have economic effects on the financial statements of the current and future years. This case is concerned with four transactions that have been selected for your analysis. Assume the current year is 19D.

Transaction A:

On July 1, 19A, the company purchased office equipment costing $14,000 for use in the business. The company estimates that the equipment will have a useful life of 10 years and no residual value.

a. Over how many accounting periods will this transaction directly affect the financial statements of Seneca? Explain.

b. Assuming straight-line depreciation, how much depreciation expense should be reported on the 19A and 19B income statements?

c. How should the office equipment be reported on the 19C balance sheet?

d. Would an adjusting entry be made by Seneca at the end of each year during the life of the equipment? Explain your answer.

Transaction B:

On September 1, 19D, Seneca collected $24,000 rent on office space. This amount represented the monthly rent in advance for the six-month period, September 1, 19D, through February 28, 19E. Rent Revenue was increased (credited) and Cash was increased (debited) for $24,000.

a. Over how many accounting periods will this transaction affect the financial statements of Seneca? Explain.

b. How much rent revenue on this office space should Seneca report on the 19D income statement? Explain.

c. Did this transaction create a liability for Seneca as of the end of 19D? Explain. If yes, how much?

d. Should an adjusting entry be made by Seneca on December 31, 19D? Explain why. If your answer is yes, give the adjusting entry.

Transaction C:

On December 31, 19D, Seneca owed employees unpaid and unrecorded wages of $7,500 because the payroll was paid on December 27 and between this day and year-end, employees worked three more days in December 19D. The next payroll date is January 5, 19E.

a. Over how many accounting periods would this transaction affect the financial statements of Seneca? Explain.

b. How would this $7,500 affect the 19D income statement and balance sheet of Seneca?

c. Should an adjusting entry be made by Seneca on December 31, 19D? Explain why. If your answer is yes, give the adjusting entry.

Transaction D:

On January 1, 19D, Seneca agreed to supervise the planning and subdivision of a large tract of land for a customer—J. Ray. This service job, to be performed by Seneca, involved four separate phases. By December 31, 19D, three phases had been completed to the satisfaction of Ray. The remaining phase will be done during 19E. The total price for the four phases (agreed on in advance by both parties) was $60,000. Each phase involves about the same amount of services. On December 31, 19D, no cash had been collected by Seneca for the services already performed.

a. Should Seneca record any service revenue on this job for 19D? Explain why. If yes, how much?

b. If your answer to (*a*) is yes, should Seneca make an adjusting entry on December 31, 19D? If yes, give the entry. Explain.

c. What entry will be made by Seneca when the last phase is completed, assuming the full contract price is collected on completion date, February 15, 19E?

C4–2 *Analyzing How Alternative Ways of Recording a Transaction Affect Adjusting Entries*

General situation: On December 1, 19A, Aniello Massa collected $6,000 cash for office space rented to an outsider. The rent was collected for the period December 1, 19A, through March 31, 19B. The annual accounting period ends on December 31.

Required:

1. How much of the $6,000 should Massa report as revenue on the 19A annual income statement? How much of it should be reported as revenue on the 19B income statement?
2. What is the amount of rent revenue collected in advance as of December 31, 19A? How should Massa report this amount on the 19A financial statements?
3. On December 1, 19A, Massa could have recorded the $6,000 collection in one of three different ways as follows:

Approach A:		
Cash	6,000	
Rent revenue		6,000
Approach B:		
Cash	6,000	
Rent revenue collected in advance		6,000
Approach C:		
Cash	6,000	
Rent revenue		1,500
Rent revenue collected in advance		4,500

For each approach, give the appropriate adjusting entry (in journal form) at December 31, 19A. If no adjusting entry is required, explain why.

4. Do you believe one of the approaches shown above is better than the other two? Which one? Explain.

C4–3 Identifying and Correcting Several Accounting Errors

The bookkeeper of Austin Company prepared the following trial balance at December 31, 19B:

Account Titles	Debit	Credit
Notes receivable	$ 6,000	
Supplies inventory		$ 300
Accounts payable	600	
Land	14,000	
Contributed capital		22,000
Cash	5,045	
Interest revenue	300	
Note payable		4,000
Operating expenses	21,000	
Interest expense		600
Other assets	9,583	
Service revenue		29,583
Totals	$56,483	$56,483

An independent CPA (auditor) casually inspected the trial balance and saw that it had several errors.

Required:

Draft a correct trial balance and explain any errors that you discover. All of the dollar amounts are correct except "Other assets."

C4–4 A Complex Situation that Requires Technical Analysis of an Income Statement: Challenging

Cathy Webking, a local attorney, decided to sell her practice and retire. She has had discussions with an attorney from another state who wants to relocate. The discussions are at the complex stage of agreeing on a price. Among the important factors have been the financial statements of Webking's practice. Webking's secretary, under her direction, maintained the records. Each year they developed a Statement of Profits on a cash basis from the incomplete records maintained, and no balance sheet was prepared. Upon request, Webking provided the other attorney with the following statements for 1996 prepared by her secretary:

C. WEBKING
Statement of Profits
1996

Legal fees collected		$115,000
Expenses paid:		
Rent for office space	$13,000	
Utilities expense	360	
Telephone expense	2,200	
Office salaries expense	22,000	
Office supplies expense	900	
Miscellaneous expenses	2,400	
Total expenses		40,860
Profit for the year		$ 74,140

Upon agreement of the parties, you ıave been asked to examine the financial figures for 1996. The other attorney said: "I question the figures because, among other things, they appear to be on a 100% cash basis." Your investigations revealed the following additional data at December 31, 1996:

a. Of the $115,000 legal fees collected in 1996, $32,000 was for services performed prior to 1996.

b. At the end of 1996, legal fees of $9,000 for services performed during the year were uncollected.

c. Office equipment owned and used by Webking cost $5,000 and had an estimated useful life of 10 years.

d. An inventory of office supplies at December 31, 1996, reflected $200 worth of items purchased during the year that were still on hand. Also, the records for 1995 indicate that the supplies on hand at the end of that year were about $125.

e. At the end of 1996, a secretary whose salary is $18,000 per year had not been paid for December because of a long trip that extended to January 15, 1997.

f. The phone bill for December 1996, amounting to $1,400, was not paid until January 11, 1997.

g. The office rent paid of $13,000 was for 13 months (it included the rent for January 1997).

Required:

1. On the basis of the above information, prepare a correct income statement for 1996. Show your computations for any amounts changed from those in the statement prepared by Webking's secretary. (Suggested solution format with four-column headings: Items; Cash Basis per Webking Statement, $; Explanation of Changes; and Corrected Basis, $.)
2. Write a comment to support your schedule prepared in (1). The purpose should be to explain the reasons for your changes and to suggest other important items that should be considered in the pricing decision.

Scott Paper Company

C4–5 Analyzing the Fiscal Year for an Actual Company

An annual report for Scott Paper Company, the world's largest manufacturer and marketer of sanitary tissue products including Scott facial tissues, Baby Fresh wipes, and Scott towels, included the following note:

1. Accounting Policies

Fiscal Year End

The Company's fiscal year ends on the last Saturday in December, which results in a 52- or 53-week year. Fiscal year 1994 consisted of 53 weeks while fiscal years 1993 and 1992 consisted of 52 weeks. To facilitate prompt reporting of Scott's financial results, the financial statements of most of the international subsidiaries and affiliates are based on the twelve months ending November 30.

Required:

1. Why would a company want to use a fiscal year of variable length?
2. As an analyst, would the fiscal year policy of Scott Paper Company have any impact on your work?

C4–6 *Analytical—Preparing Adjusting and Closing Entries by Analyzing Unadjusted and Adjusted Trial Balances; Answering 10 Analytical Questions*

Rowland Company was organized on January 1, 19A. At the end of the first year of operations, December 31, 19A, the bookkeeper prepared the following two trial balances (amounts in thousands of dollars):

Account No.	Account Titles	Unadjusted Trial Balance		Adjusted Trial Balance	
		Debit	Credit	Debit	Credit
11	Cash	$ 40	$	$ 40	$
12	Accounts receivable	17		17	
13	Prepaid insurance	2		1	
14	Rent receivable			2	
15	Operational assets	46		46	
16	Accumulated depreciation, operational assets				11
17	Other assets	6		6	
18	Accounts payable		27		27
19	Wages payable				3
20	Income taxes payable				5
21	Rent revenue collected in advance				4
22	Note payable (10%; dated January 1, 19A)		20		20
23	Contributed capital (1,000 shares)		30		30
24	Retained earnings				
25	Dividends declared	3		3	
26	Revenues (total)		105		103
27	Expenses (total including interest)	68		83	
28	Income tax expense			5	
	Totals	$182	$182	$203	$203

Required:

1. Based on inspection of the two trial balances, give the 19A adjusting entries developed by the bookkeeper (provide brief explanations).
2. Based on the above data, give the 19A closing entries with brief explanations.
3. Answer the following questions (show computations):
   a. How many shares of stock were outstanding at year-end?
   b. What was the estimated useful life of the operational assets assuming a $2,000 residual value and a purchase date of 1/1/19A?
   c. What was the amount of interest expense that was included in the total expenses?
   d. What was the balance of Retained Earnings on December 31, 19A?
   e. What was the average income tax rate?
   f. How would the two accounts—Rent Receivable and Rent Revenue Collected in Advance—be reported on the balance sheet?
   g. Explain why cash increased by $40,000 during the year even though net income was very low comparatively.
   h. What was the amount of EPS for 19A?

i. What was the average selling price of the shares?

j. When was the insurance premium paid and over what period of time did the coverage extend?

Hershey Foods Corporation

C4–7 The Matching Concept for an Actual Company

A recent annual report for Hershey Foods Corporation contained the following information:

Supplemental Income Statement Information

Supplemental income statement information is provided in the table below. These costs are expensed in the year incurred.

For the Years Ended December 31 (in thousands of dollars)	Current Year	Previous Year
Promotion	$256,237	$230,187
Advertising	121,182	99,082
Maintenance and repairs	58,842	54,377
Depreciation expense	54,543	43,721
Rent expense	20,033	17,618
Research and development	16,094	15,695

Required:

1. What types of costs are included in the following categories: promotion, advertising, maintenance and repairs, research and development?
2. In your judgment, should any of these costs have been recorded as an asset and allocated over several accounting periods?

Toys "Я" Us

C4–8 Financial Statement Analysis

Refer to the financial statements of Toys "Я" Us given in Appendix B at the end of this book.

Required:

1. Give examples of business documents that are analyzed by the company's accountants to record sales transactions.
2. How should the company record the payment of $500 on account by one of its credit customers?
3. How should the company record the purchase of $8,000 of inventory on credit from one of its suppliers?
4. Does the collection of an account receivable by the company affect its total assets?
5. When does the company's fiscal year end?
6. What company accounts would not appear on a post-closing trial balance?
7. Give the closing entry for Prepaid Expenses.

5

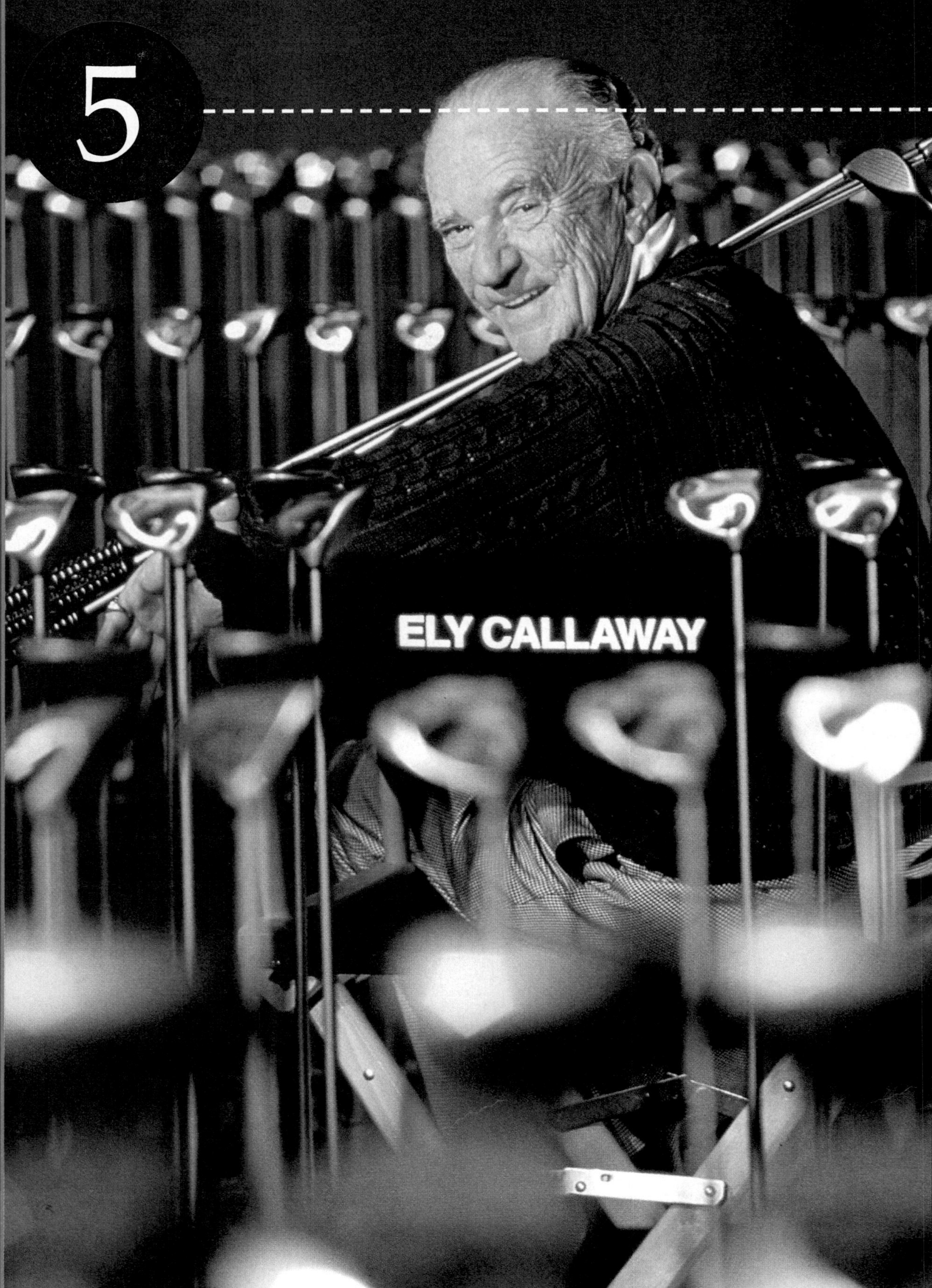

THE COMMUNICATION OF ACCOUNTING INFORMATION

Chapter 4 discussed the important portions of the accounting process that take place at the end of the year. These included the adjustment process, preparation of the four basic financial statements, and the closing process which prepares the records for the next accounting period. However, this end to the internal portions of the accounting process is just the beginning of the process of communicating accounting information to external users. In this chapter, we discuss the important players in this communication process, the many statement format choices available, the additional note disclosures that are required for both private and public companies, and the process, manner, and timing of the transmission of this information to users. At the same time we discuss common uses of the information in investment analysis, debt contracts, and management compensation decisions. These discussions will help you consolidate much of what you have learned about the financial reporting process from prior chapters. It will also preview many of the important issues we will address later in the book.

LEARNING OBJECTIVES

After studying this chapter, you should be able to:

1. **Recognize the people involved in the accounting communication process (managers, auditors, information intermediaries, government regulators, and users), their roles in the process, and the guidance they receive from legal and professional standards.** ***245***
2. **Understand the principles and constraints that guide management and the FASB in deciding what financial information should be reported.** ***252***
3. **Analyze the different financial statement and disclosure formats used by companies in practice.** ***255***
4. **Identify the steps in the accounting communication process, including issuance of press releases, annual reports, quarterly reports, and SEC filings, and the role of electronic information services in this process.** ***270***

Management Decision Setting

CALLAWAY GOLF

Clear Communication with Customers and Financial Statement Users Is a Hallmark of Callaway's Success

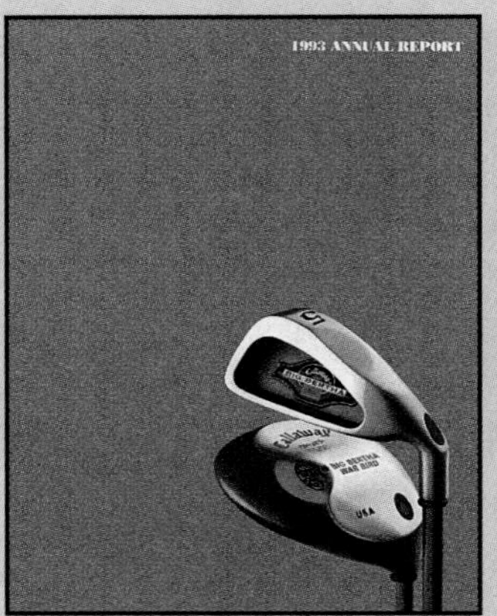

In just 10 years, Ely [pronounced EE-lee] Callaway took a small manufacturer of specialty golf clubs with $500,000 in annual sales and built it into an industry leader with sales of over $250 million. Callaway attributes this success to the innovative Big Bertha oversized clubs, created by a team of aerospace and metallurgical engineers, that make the game easier to learn and play. Both touring pros and average golfers including Bill Clinton and George Bush carry a Big Bertha driver in their golf bags. But industry insiders attribute an equal portion of Ely Callaway's success to his marketing skills. He spends hours each day talking to the pros who use his clubs at televised events and the dealers who sell his clubs. He even writes much of the Company's ad copy.

He and his CFO (chief financial officer), Carol Kerley, applied that same personal marketing touch to the financial side of the business when they persuaded managers of the General Electric Pension Fund to invest $10 million in the company to provide capital that fueled its initial growth in 1989. The same enthusiasm and clear approach to communication were apparent in the Company's initial public offering (first stock issuance to the public, or IPO) in 1992. The CFO and her accounting staff worked tirelessly with the company's outside auditors, Price Waterhouse, and its investment bankers, Merrill Lynch, to prepare the detailed financial information necessary for the IPO. Callaway had prepared audited statements in the past. Now as a publicly traded company, it is required to provide even more information in regular filings with the Securities and Exchange Commission.

Clear communication with Callaway's four customer groups—professional endorsers, dealers, golfing consumers, and investors and other users of financial statements—continues to be a hallmark of its business strategy. This approach has met with success in each case. Callaway drivers are now the most popular on the Senior and Ladies PGA tours and second in the regular PGA tour, and Callaway is the fastest growing golfing equipment company in the world. The stock market has rewarded these operating successes and its financial communication strategy with a *quintupling* of its stock price over the first two years following the IPO. Marketing the company can be as important as marketing quality products.

BUSINESS BACKGROUND

Callaway Golf Company designs, manufactures, and markets high-quality innovative golf clubs that sell at premium prices. Its Big Bertha oversized stainless steel woods and irons account for most of its sales. These clubs are judged by many to be the "friendliest" in the game because they are less sensitive to off-center hits. The company manufactures its metal woods and irons in its new Carlsbad, California, factories using clubheads supplied by Cast Alloys and Coastcast Corporation, shafts supplied by Aldila, True Temper, and Unifiber, and grips supplied by other independent vendors. The clubs are sold primarily at high-end pro shops. Callaway invests considerable amounts in research and development and is known for introducing new innovative products long before the end of its existing products' life cycles. While they are *manufacturers* of golf clubs, they also sell other golf-related equipment, including balls, bags, and headcovers, that is manufactured by others. Thus, they are *merchandisers* for this other equipment.

Successful companies such as Callaway learn to match their financial reporting strategies to their business strategies. Marketing and communication are fundamental to both strategies. While Callaway has a company policy of never publicly predicting future sales or financial results, it values integrity in the communication of financial results as much as it does in its relationships with suppliers, customers, and employees. It deals honestly and candidly with the financial press, financial analysts, and the investing public. Also, to its credit, the financial statements and related disclosures provided in its annual report are a model of clarity and include important details often left out of the reports of others. Callaway's management believes that such an approach eases the company's access to capital from lenders and investors. This approach lowers the costs of borrowing (interest rates) and lowers investors' perceptions of the riskiness of Callaway's stock. These policies, the fact that the Company has recently changed from private to public financing, and its astonishing business success make Callaway Golf an excellent example through which we can complete our discussion of the accounting communication process.

Chapters 2 through 4 focused on the mechanics of preparing the income statement, balance sheet, statement of stockholders' equity, and cash flow statement. In this chapter, we will discuss the principles guiding the exact statement formats and additional disclosures provided in annual reports and related reports. We will also focus on the sequential process that conveys accounting information to statement users during a typical year, as well as the people involved in that process.

PLAYERS IN THE ACCOUNTING COMMUNICATION PROCESS

Learning Objective 1
Recognize the people involved in the accounting communication process, their roles in the process, and the guidance they receive from legal and professional standards.

Exhibit 5–1 summarizes the accounting communication process in terms of the people involved, their roles in the process, and the guidance they receive from legal and professional standards.

Managers (CEO, CFO, and Accounting Staff)

As noted in Chapter 1, the primary responsibility for the information in Callaway's financial statements and related disclosures lies with management as represented by the highest officer in the company, often called the *chairman and chief executive officer* (CEO) and the highest officer associated with the financial and accounting side of the business, often called the *chief financial officer* (CFO). These two officers normally sign the statement of management responsibility (as also discussed in Chapter 1), if one is included in the annual report. For public companies, the same officers sign the principal reports filed with the SEC. At Callaway, Ely Callaway, chairman and CEO, and Carol Kerley, CFO, had that responsibility at the time of Callaway's initial public offering (IPO). They were responsible for the conformance of the statements and related disclosures with GAAP (generally accepted accounting principles). Though their legal responsibility is smaller, the *accounting staff* who actually prepare the details of the reports also have professional responsibility for the accuracy of this information. Their professional success in the future depends heavily on their reputations for honesty and competence.

Auditors

Even before Callaway Golf first issued stock to the public, the company submitted its statements for verification by a team of independent auditors, or CPAs, who conduct their examinations in conformance with generally accepted auditing standards (GAAS). While publicly traded companies are required by the SEC to have their statements audited by CPAs, many privately owned companies also have their statements audited to add credibility to the statements and meet agreements with lenders and private investors who are not actively involved in management of the companies. Callaway Golf was initially financed through investments by Mr. Callaway and some of his close friends and loans from financial institutions (e.g., banks and commercial

Exhibit 5–1 The Accounting Communication Process

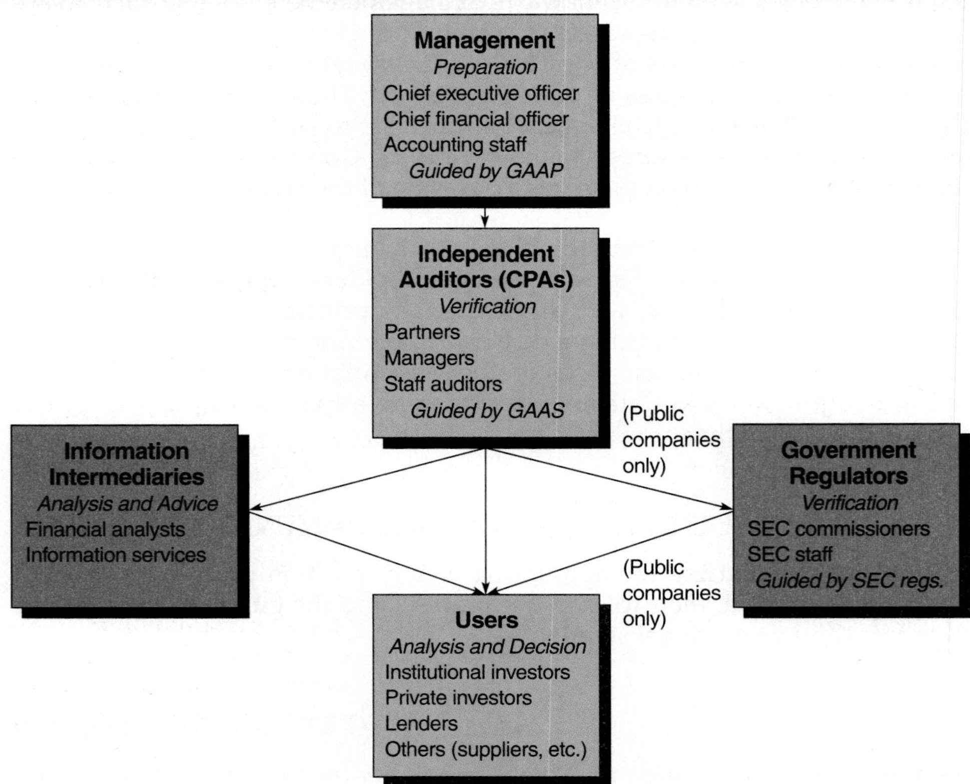

finance companies). By subjecting the company's statements to independent verification, Callaway reduced the risk to the private investors and financial institutions that the company's condition was not as represented in the statements. As a consequence, rational investors and lenders should lower the rate of return (interest) they charge for providing capital.

Price Waterhouse (which along with KPMG Peat Marwick, Arthur Andersen and Co., Ernst & Young, Deloitte & Touche, and Coopers and Lybrand make up what are referred to as the "Big 6" CPA firms) is currently Callaway Golf's auditor. Each of these firms employs thousands of CPAs in offices scattered throughout the world. They audit the great majority of publicly traded companies and many privately held companies. Some public companies and most private companies are audited by CPA firms of smaller size. A few well-known companies and their auditors are listed below.

Company	Industry	Auditor
The Boeing Company	Aircraft	Deloitte & Touche
Hilton Hotels Corporation	Hotels	Arthur Andersen & Co.
Honda Motor Co. Ltd. (Japan)	Automobiles	KPMG Peat Marwick
John Labatt Limited (Canada)	Beer	Ernst & Young
Wendy's	Fast food	Coopers & Lybrand

An **unqualified**, or **clean**, **audit opinion** states that the financial statements are fair presentations in all material respects in conformity with GAAP.

As we discussed in Chapter 1, by signing an **unqualified**, or **clean**, **audit opinion**, the CPA firm assumes financial responsibility for the fairness of the financial statements and related presentations. Much of the evidence that the auditors gather to support their opinion is collected throughout the year. However, the busiest time for most auditors is the end of the reporting period when they apply final tests to the records and examine the final statements and other disclosures. Financial reporting standards set by the SEC and FASB, combined with the independent examination provided by CPAs and the legal liability that they assume, add significant credibility to a company's financial statements and related disclosures.

Carol Kerley, Callaway's CFO at the time of the initial public offering, was a senior manager with Price Waterhouse before she moved to Callaway Golf. Companies often hire financial managers from their CPA firms because of their broad financial experience as well as their specific company knowledge gained during prior years' audits.

Information Intermediaries: Analysts and Information Services

The Role of Financial Analysts

Students often view the communication process between companies and financial statement users as involving a simple process of mailing the report to individual shareholders who read the reports and then make investment decisions based on what they have learned. This simple picture is far from today's reality. Now sophisticated *financial analysts* use modern information technology to gather and analyze information. They receive accounting reports and other information about the company from electronic information services (discussed below). They also gather information through personal phone conversations with company executives and visits to company facilities. They then combine the results of these analyses with information about competitors, the overall economy, and even population trends to make predictions of future earnings and stock price. These predictions form the basis of their buy, hold, or sell recommendations for a company's stock.

Analysts often work in the research departments of brokerage and investment banking houses such as Merrill Lynch, mutual fund companies such as Fidelity Investments,[1] and investment advisory services such as Value Line that sell their advice to others. Individual analysts often specialize in particular industries (such as sporting goods or energy companies) and in particular companies. For example, Eric Katzman at Merrill Lynch and Arda Minocherhomjee of William Blair and Co. (both brokerage and investment banking companies) are among those who follow Callaway Golf. Together with other analysts at their firms, they write reports that analyze the company's future prospects.

Analysts' reports normally include the analysts' estimate or forecast of future quarterly and annual earnings per share for the company.[2] In making these **earnings forecasts**, the analysts rely heavily on their knowledge of the way the accounting system translates business events into the numbers on a company's financial statements.[3] This knowledge includes an understanding of the alternative accounting methods available to companies to account for different transactions and specialized industry practices that may be applied to a particular industry. We discuss both of these issues later in this chapter. Their employers either use the reports directly or sell them to other investors. As a consequence, the analyst is transferring his or her knowledge of accounting, the company, and the industry to others who lack this expertise. Many believe that decisions made based on analysts' advice cause stock market prices

Earnings forecasts are predictions of earnings for future accounting periods.

[1]Individuals buy shares in mutual fund companies which invest that money in the stocks and bonds of various companies.

[2]For further discussion of analysts' forecasts, see K. Schipper, "Analysts' Forecasts," *Accounting Horizons,* December 1991, pp. 105–121.

[3]See G. J. Previts, R. J. Bricker, T. R. Robinson, and S. J. Young, "A Content Analysis of Sell-Side Financial Analyst Reports," *Accounting Horizons,* June 1994, pp. 55–70.

QUESTION OF ETHICS

It Pays to Be a Wary Investor

Recent events on Wall Street suggest that savvy investors should apply a healthy dose of skepticism along with their accounting knowledge when reading or listening to investment advice. Alleged ethical lapses, questionable business practices, and illegal activity by representatives of some of the largest, most highly respected brokerage and investment banking houses have recently made the news. These activities include the rigging of prices in securities auctions, excess trading of customers' accounts to generate higher commissions, insider trading, the sale of securities without full disclosure of their risks, and executing trades for some customers at more advantageous prices than others. While most analysts, brokers, and investment bankers act in an honest and ethical fashion, they earn profits by charging commissions on securities transactions. When brokers let their need to earn commissions cloud their investment advice, it can lead to unethical behavior.

to react quickly to accounting information announcements. A quick, unbiased reaction to information is called *market efficiency* in finance.

It is highly unlikely that unsophisticated investors can glean more information from financial statements than has already been learned by the sophisticated analysts. However, careful analysis does not lead all analysts to the same conclusions. These differences of opinion are reflected in the earnings forecasts and stock recommendations for Callaway by four groups of analysts listed on the Bloomberg Business News service at the time this chapter was written.

Real World Excerpt
Bloomberg Business News

Company: CALLAWAY GOLF

Firm	Stock Recommendation	Earnings Forecast for 12/94	Earnings Forecast for 12/95
Cruttendon & Co	Accumulate	1.75	2.25
Raymond James	Strong buy	1.80	2.30
William Blair	Outperformance	1.80	2.25
Wheat First/Butcher	Hold	1.83	2.20

The information services discussed in the next section allow investors to monitor the recommendations of a variety of analysts.

Information Services

Financial analysts obtain much of the information they use from the wide variety of electronic information services available today. These services are normally either available on-line (via modem or computer networks) or on CD-ROM (compact disk, read-only memory). Some of the services provide specialized information. For example, I/B/E/S, Inc., provides consensus (average) and analyst-by-analyst earnings forecasts for over 11,700 domestic and foreign companies. Analysts from over 480 research departments contribute earnings forecasts to the service.

Some services provide access to financial statement and related information. The NEXIS service is a major source of financial statement information. The service provides full-text versions of annual reports and SEC filings, which we describe below, via modem. They also allow users to search the database by key words, including various terms in financial statements. Companies can actually file SEC forms electronically with EDGAR (Electronic Data Gathering and Retrieval Service), sponsored by the SEC, Mead Data, and New

York University. Then this information is available to users through EDGAR within 24 hours of filing with the Commission, long before it is available through the mail in hard-copy form. Many of the financial statement examples used in this book were downloaded (electronically copied) from different services.

More general information services include the Dow Jones News Retrieval Service and Bloomberg Financial Markets and Commodities News. Dow Jones provides access via modem to news stories about companies taken from publications and news wires owned by Dow Jones (e.g., *The Wall Street Journal*) and to current and historical stock price information (among other information). Many company press releases, including the initial announcements of annual and quarterly financial results, are available from this service. This information is again available electronically through the information service long before shareholders and others receive the hard-copy reports. The Bloomberg service provides an even wider spectrum of information including stock prices, news stories, press releases, financial statement information, earnings forecasts, general economic news, and much more. It also provides the ability to combine these sources of information in sophisticated analyses. The graph presented in Exhibit 5–2 plots Callaway's quarterly price per share and earnings per share over 10 quarters (2½ years). The graph was printed directly from a Bloomberg terminal. Listed above the graph are other financial statement and price statistics that can be directly plotted on the Bloomberg terminal.

Price and Earnings per Share Graph from Bloomberg Terminal **Exhibit 5–2**

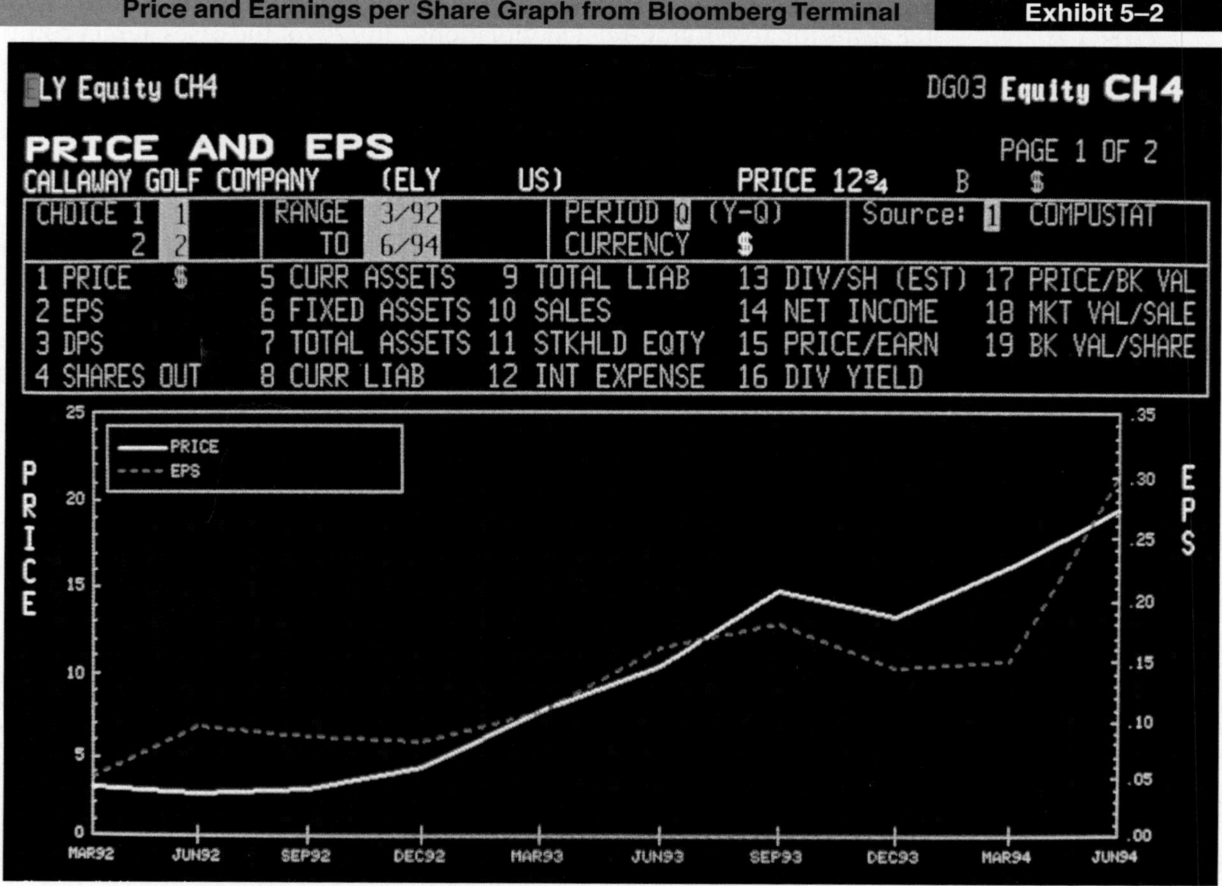

FINANCIAL ANALYSIS

Information Services: Uses in Marketing, Classwork, and Job Search

Information services have become the primary tools used not only by sophisticated analysts but by marketing strategists for analysis of competing firms. Sales representatives also use the services for analysis of potential customers. These analyses allow the sales representative to determine which customers have growing needs for their products and which have the financial strength necessary to qualify for credit. Such companies are the most profitable targets for the sales representative's efforts.

The information services are an important source of information for student term papers and even for students' job searches. Potential employers expect top job applicants to be knowledgeable about their company before an interview. We suggest that you contact the business or reference librarian at your college or university library or visit a local brokerage house to learn more about these modern electronic information services and the usage fees they charge.

Government Regulators

The *Securities and Exchange Commission (SEC)* sets additional reporting standards for firms with publicly traded debt or equity securities. We discuss these requirements later in the chapter and throughout the text where relevant. The SEC staff reviews these reports for compliance with their standards and investigates and punishes violators of their regulations. Research indicates that during a recent seven-year period, the SEC brought enforcement actions against 188 firms for accounting-related violations.[4] In 72% of the cases, target companies fired or forced the resignation of top managers, and in 81% of the cases, the shareholders subsequently sued the companies. The companies' auditors were also penalized in 42% of the cases.

Users: Institutional and Private Investors, Creditors, and Others

Institutional investors are managers of pension, mutual, endowment, and other funds that invest on the behalf of others.

Institutional investors include the managers of private pension funds (associated with unions and employees of specific companies), public pension funds (for state and municipal employees), mutual funds, and endowment, charitable foundation, and trust funds (such as the endowment of your college or university). These institutional stockholders usually employ their own analysts and also make use of the information intermediaries discussed above. Institutional shareholders such as these control the majority of publicly traded shares of U.S. companies. For example, at the time this book was written, three institutional investors together owned over 16% of Callaway's outstanding stock:

Institution	Approximate Ownership
Investors Research	2.5 million shares
Fidelity Investments	1.5 million shares
Smith Barney Shearson	1.5 million shares

Twenty-seven other institutional investors such as Mellon Bank, Bankers Trust, and the New York State Teachers' Retirement Fund owned between 119,000 and 1.5 million shares each. Most small investors own stock in companies such as Callaway Golf *indirectly* through mutual and pension funds such as these.

[4] These statistics are reported in E. H. Feroz, K. Parke, and V. S. Pastena, "The Financial and Market Effects of the SEC's Accounting and Auditing Enforcement Releases," *Journal of Accounting Research* (Supplement 1991), pp. 107–142.

QUESTION OF ETHICS

Conflicting Interests of Managers, Stockholders, and Creditors

The economic interests of managers, stockholders, and creditors often are different. For example, paying dividends to stockholders benefits the stockholders but leaves less money available to pay creditors, and refurnishing the offices occupied by managers benefits the managers but leaves less money to pay dividends. Expectations of ethical conduct and mutual trust play a major role in keeping these differing interests in check.

Accounting and financial statements also play a major role in enforcing these relationships of trust. Later in the chapter we will discuss how compliance with agreements between managers and stockholders and between stockholders and creditors are monitored with financial statement data.* When the U.S. negotiates arms treaties with other countries, "trust but verify" is a common rule that is followed. Applying the same rule in business practice is prudent.

*Research that examines the use of accounting in contracting is called *agency theory*.

Private investors include large individual investors such as Ely Callaway and his friends who invested directly in Callaway Golf before it became a public company and smaller retail investors who, like most individuals, buy a small number of shares of publicly traded companies through brokers such as Merrill Lynch. Retail investors normally lack the expertise to understand financial statements and the resources to gather other important data efficiently. As a consequence, they often rely on the advice of information intermediaries or turn their money over to the management of mutual and pension funds (institutional investors).

Private investors include individuals who purchase shares in companies.

Lenders, or **creditors**, include suppliers, banks, commercial credit companies, and other financial institutions that lend money to companies. Lending officers and financial analysts in these organizations use these same public sources of information in their analyses. In addition, when companies borrow money from financial institutions, they often agree to provide additional financial information (e.g., monthly statements) as part of the lending contract. Lenders are often the primary external user group for financial statements of private companies. Individuals and mutual funds also become creditors when they buy publicly traded bonds and debentures issued by a company.[5]

Lenders (creditors) include suppliers and financial institutions that lend money to companies.

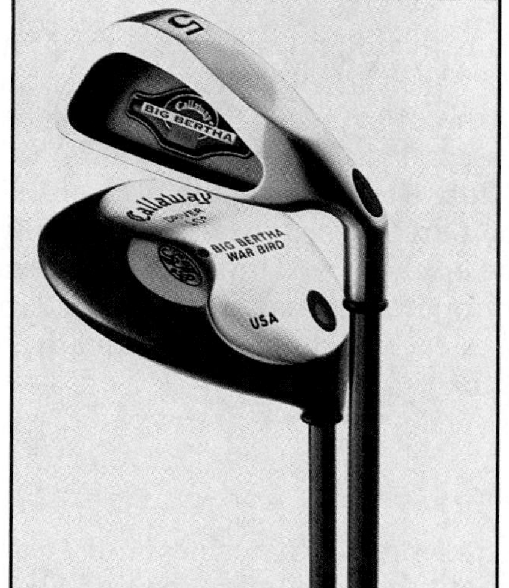

Key to investor evaluations of Callaway's stock is their successful new product development efforts.

[5]Debentures are debt securities not secured with specific collateral (no specific assets are pledged as security for the debt). Bonds are normally secured by specific collateral such as investments in stock of other companies.

As noted in Chapter 1, these same financial statements play an important role in the relationships between customers and suppliers. Customers evaluate the financial health of suppliers to determine if they will be able to provide a reliable, up-to-date source of supply. Suppliers evaluate their customers to estimate customers' future needs and ability to pay their debts to the supplier. Competitors also attempt to learn useful information about a company from its statements. The potential loss of competitive advantage is one of the costs to the preparer of public financial disclosures. Other uses of financial statement information in labor-management relations and in government regulation were discussed in Chapter 1.

GUIDING PRINCIPLES FOR COMMUNICATING USEFUL INFORMATION: THE REMAINING PARTS OF THE CONCEPTUAL FRAMEWORK

Learning Objective 2
Understand the principles and constraints that guide management and the FASB in deciding what financial information should be reported.

Now that we know who the players are in communicating accounting information to users external to the company, we need to complete our understanding of the conceptual framework by examining the concepts that guide the quality of the information being reported. The portions of the framework that we discuss here are highlighted in Exhibit 5–3 in bold, white print.

Qualitative Characteristics of Financial Information

External decision makers expect financial information in reports to be *useful* to them in making their resource allocation decisions. To satisfy this primary objective of financial reporting, the Financial Accounting Standards Board (FASB) determined that several characteristics should guide management and the FASB in deciding what financial information should be reported.

Relevant information can influence a decision; it is timely and has predictive and/or feedback value.

Reliable information is accurate, unbiased, and verifiable.

The two *primary qualitative characteristics* that useful information should possess are *relevance* and *reliability*. **Relevant information** is capable of influencing decisions. If the information is provided in a timely fashion and allows users to assess past activities (feedback value) and/or predict future activities (predictive value), it is relevant. **Reliable information** must be accurate, unbiased, and verifiable (independent parties can agree on the nature of the transaction and amount).

Comparable information can be compared across businesses.

Consistent information can be compared over time.

If the information is relevant and reliable, accounting information should also possess the *secondary qualitative characteristics* of comparability and consistency. **Comparable information** means that users can compare financial information across businesses. This normally requires that similar accounting methods are applied. **Consistent information** means that within a company, information can be compared over time. This normally requires that similar accounting methods be applied over time. These secondary qualitative characteristics are of lesser importance than relevance and reliability. However, information that possesses each of these four qualitative characteristics will be useful to decision makers.

Full-Disclosure Principle

The **full-disclosure principle** requires disclosure of all relevant economic information of the business.

The periodic financial statements of a business must clearly report all required relevant information about the economic affairs of a business. This is the **full-disclosure principle**, and it requires *(a)* a complete set of financial statements and *(b)* notes to the financial statements to explain accounting policy choices, elaborate on the "numbers," and provide information on other items with financial implications, such as pending lawsuits.

Financial Accounting and Reporting Conceptual Framework — Exhibit 5–3

Primary Objective of External Financial Reporting

To provide economic information to external users for decision making (for assessing future cash flows) [Ch.2]

Qualitative Characteristics of Information

[Ch. 5]

Overall: Information should be

Cost-beneficial Benefits of accounting and reporting should exceed costs.

Primary:

Relevance Information influences decisions; it is timely and has predictive and feedback value.

Reliability Information is accurate, unbiased, and verifiable.

Secondary:

Comparability Information can be compared to other businesses.

Consistency Information can be compared across time.

Elements of Financial Statements

Assets Probable future economic benefits owned by the entity from past transactions. [Ch. 2]

Liabilities Debts or obligations from past transactions to be paid with assets or services. [Ch. 2]

Stockholders' Equity Financing provided by owners and operations. [Ch. 2]

Revenues Inflows of net assets (assets minus liabilities) from ongoing operations. [Ch. 3]

Expenses Outflows of net assets (assets minus liabilities) from ongoing operations. [Ch. 3]

Gains Inflows of net assets from peripheral transactions. [Ch. 3]

Losses Outflows of net assets from peripheral transactions. [Ch. 3]

Assumptions

1. **Separate-entity** Transactions of the business are separate from transactions of owners. [Ch. 2]
2. **Unit-of-measure** Accounting measurements will be in the national monetary unit. [Ch. 2]
3. **Continuity** The entity will not go out of business in the near future. [Ch. 2]
4. **Time-period** The long life of a company can be reported over a series of shorter time periods. [Ch. 3]

Principles

1. **Cost** Cash-equivalent cost given up is the basis for initial recording of elements. [Ch. 2 and 3]
2. **Revenue** Record revenues when earned and measurable (an exchange has taken place, the earnings process is nearly complete, and collection is probable). [Ch. 3]
3. **Matching** Record expenses when incurred in earning revenue. [Ch. 3]
4. Full-disclosure Disclose relevant economic information. [Ch. 5]

Constraints

[Ch. 5]

1. Materiality Relatively small amounts not likely to influence decisions are to be recorded in the most cost-beneficial way.
2. Cost-benefit Benefits of recording and reporting information should outweigh costs.
3. Conservatism Exercise care not to overstate assets and revenues or understate liabilities and expenses.
4. Industry peculiarities Differences in accounting and reporting for certain items are permitted if there is a clear precedent in the industry.

Constraints of Accounting

Constraints of accounting measurement provide practical guidelines to reduce the *volume* and *cost* of reporting accounting information without reducing its value to decision makers. The constraints are *materiality, cost-benefit, conservatism,* and *industry practices.*

Materiality Constraint

Although items and amounts that are of low significance must be accounted for, they do not have to conform precisely to specified accounting guidelines or be separately reported if they would not influence reasonable decisions. Accountants usually designate such items and amounts as immaterial. Measurement of **materiality** is often very subjective.

Material amounts are amounts that are large enough to influence a user's decision.

Cost-Benefit Constraint

The **cost-benefit constraint** suggests that the benefits of accounting for and reporting information should outweigh the costs.

The benefits that decision makers gain from accounting information should be greater than the cost of providing that information. This **cost-benefit constraint** recognizes that it is costly to produce and report accounting information. These costs include the costs of preparation *and* the loss of competitive advantage through disclosure of what had been secret information. Disclosure of information, the benefits of which do not outweigh the costs, would clearly be uneconomical; however, measurement of benefits is difficult.

As an example of the application of both the materiality and cost-benefit constraints, consider the purchase of a few electric pencil sharpeners. They could be accounted for as equipment since they will benefit the company over several years. However, equipment is depreciated over time as it is used in operations. The effort of keeping track of the cost and depreciation for the minor purchase for years into the future exceeds the usefulness of the information; it is too costly. In this case, the pencil sharpeners can be expensed immediately instead of being recorded as a long-lived asset and depreciated. The amounts are also immaterial (that is, they will not affect a user's decision).

Conservatism Constraint

Conservatism suggests that care should be taken not to overstate assets and revenues or understate liabilities and expenses.

The **conservatism constraint** requires that special care be taken to avoid *(a)* overstating assets and revenues and *(b)* understating liabilities and expenses. This guideline attempts to offset managers' natural optimism about their business operations which sometimes creeps into financial reports they prepare. This constraint produces more conservative income statement and balance sheet amounts. When companies have choices in accounting methods and one choice does not dominate the others, the conservative approach is to choose the alternative with the least positive effect on net income. We will learn more about accounting method alternatives later in this chapter and throughout the rest of the text.

Industry Peculiarities

The final guideline relates to differences due to long-standing and accepted accounting and reporting practices in various industries. For example, public utilities (an industry regulated by government) often present balance sheet information in what appears to be upside-down order. That is, property, plant, and equipment are listed first, followed by the more liquid assets (cash, accounts receivable, and supplies). In like manner, the long-term debt which is often issued to finance the building of the property, plant, and equipment is listed first in the liabilities section, followed by the shorter-term liabilities. The reason for the presentation is that regulatory commissions in many states require this format from public utilities. Property, plant, and equipment and its related long-term debt are the most significant items on the balance sheet of a public utility and are the primary items of interest to regulatory commissions that approve rates charged by the utilities to customers.

Self-Study Quiz

Match the players involved in the accounting communication process with their roles or the guiding principles for communicating information with their definitions.

1. Relevant information	*a.* Managers primarily responsible for accounting information.
2. CEO and CFO	*b.* Independent parties who verify financial statements.
3. Financial analysts	*c.* Information that influences users' decisions.
4. Auditors	*d.* Only information that provides benefits in excess of costs should be reported.
5. Cost-benefit constraint	*e.* Avoid overstating assets and revenues and understating expenses and liabilities.
6. Conservatism	*f.* Individuals who analyze financial information and provide advice.

After you have completed the quiz, check your answers with the solutions presented in the footnote at the bottom of this page.*

A CLOSER LOOK AT FINANCIAL STATEMENT FORMATS

Learning Objective 3
Analyze the different financial statement and disclosure formats used by companies in practice.

We already know that the financial data contained in accounting reports are important factors in decisions made by investors, creditors, and analysts. To make financial statements more useful to decision makers, specific *classifications* of information are included on the statements.

There are a variety of classifications used in practice. You should not be confused when you notice different formats used by different companies. You will find that each format is consistent with the principles discussed in this text. The following is a discussion of these classified financial statements.

A Classified Balance Sheet

The December 31, 1993, balance sheet for Callaway Golf is presented in Exhibit 5–4. First, notice the title of the statement—Consolidated Balance Sheet. *Consolidated* means that the accounts of Callaway and the accounts of its wholly owned subsidiary, Callaway Golf (UK) Limited, have been added together through a consolidation process that results in a single number being reported for each item. (We discuss the consolidation process further in

*1*c*, 2*a*, 3*f*, 4*b*, 5*d*, 6*e*.

Current assets are assets that will be turned into cash or expire (be used up) within the longer of one year or the operating cycle.

Current liabilities are obligations to be paid with current assets, normally within one year.

Chapter 12.) In addition, some companies choose to call the balance sheet the *Statement of Financial Position* or *Statement of Financial Condition*.

Callaway's balance sheet is shown in the report format (assets listed first, then liabilities and shareholders' equity accounts underneath in one column). Another common way to display the balance sheet data is in account format (assets on the left side and liabilities and shareholders' equity on the right).

Callaway's balance sheet is also classified. That is, assets and liabilities are listed in a particular order and are separated into current and noncurrent classifications. **Current assets** are defined as those that will be turned into cash or expire (be used up) within one year or by the end of the operating cycle, whichever is longer. In Chapter 3, we noted that the operating, or cash-to-cash, cycle varies by company, and may be longer than one year. **Current liabilities**

Exhibit 5–4 **Balance Sheet of Callaway Golf***

Callaway® GOLF

Consolidated Balance Sheet

(in thousands)	**December 31,**	
	1993	**1992**
ASSETS		
Current assets:		
Cash and cash equivalents	$ 48,996	$20,019
Accounts receivable, net	17,546	11,302
Inventories, net	29,029	15,285
Deferred taxes	13,859	7,315
Other current assets	2,036	1,263
Total current assets	111,466	55,184
Property, plant and equipment, net	30,661	12,757
Other assets	2,233	996
	$144,360	$68,937
LIABILITIES AND SHAREHOLDERS' EQUITY		
Current Liabilities:		
Accounts payable and accrued expenses	$ 11,949	$ 6,915
Accrued compensation and benefits	6,104	2,344
Accrued warranty	9,730	4,617
Income taxes payable		1,945
Total current liabilities	27,783	15,821
Long-term debt		3,366
Shareholders' equity:		
Common Stock, $.01 par value, 60,000,000 shares authorized, 16,897,608 and 14,115,360 issued and outstanding at December 31, 1993 and 1992 (Notes 5 and 11)	169	140
Paid-in-capital	57,807	31,948
Retained earnings	58,601	17,662
Total shareholders' equity	116,577	49,750
	$144,360	$68,937

See accompanying notes to consolidated financial statements.

*Callaway Golf Company has granted permission to use its logo, but it has not reviewed, approved, or endorsed the content of the text.

are defined as those obligations that will be paid with current assets, normally within one year. Typically a balance sheet is classified as follows:

A. Assets (by order of liquidity):
   1. Current assets (short term):
      a. Cash and cash equivalents
      b. Short-term investments
      c. Accounts receivable
      d. Inventory
      e. Prepaid expenses (i.e., expenses paid in advance of use)
      f. Other current assets
   2. Noncurrent assets:
      a. Long-term investments
      b. Operational assets (property, plant, and equipment)— at cost less accumulated depreciation
      c. Intangible assets
      d. Deferred charges (long-term prepayments)
      e. Other (miscellaneous) assets
         Total assets
B. Liabilities (by order of time to maturity):
   1. Current liabilities (short-term):
      a. Accounts payable
      b. Accrued expenses payable
      c. Other short-term liabilities
   2. Long-term liabilities
      a. Bonds payable
      b. Lease obligations
         Total liabilities
C. Stockholders' equity (by source):
   1. Contributed capital (by owners)
   2. Retained earnings (accumulated earnings minus accumulated dividends declared)
         Total stockholders' equity
         Total liabilities and stockholders' equity

It should be emphasized again that each financial statement item is a combination of a number of accounts used in the company's accounting system. Under current assets, Callaway does not separately report any short-term investments or prepaid expenses. Any such amounts would be included and combined in Other Current Assets. However, the company does include Deferred Taxes in the current asset section. Deferred taxes, depending on the circumstances, can be listed in any of four places on the balance sheet: as a current asset, current liability, noncurrent asset, or noncurrent liability. The Deferred Taxes account represents the amount of income taxes that will most likely be paid or saved in the future based on differences in the application of tax laws and GAAP for recognizing revenues and expenses in the current period. If the amount is an asset (either current or noncurrent), then future tax benefits (reductions) are expected. If the amount is a current or noncurrent liability, then future tax payments are expected.

After the current asset section, *long-term investments* are reported. They include assets that are not used in operating the business. Examples include investments in real estate and stocks and bonds of other companies. This classification may include cash set aside in special funds (such as savings accounts) for use for a specified long-term purpose. Callaway does not separately report any long-term investments.

Operational assets are often called *fixed assets* or *property, plant, and equipment.* This group includes tangible assets that were acquired for use in operating the business rather than for resale as inventory items or held as investments. The assets included are buildings; land on which the buildings sit; and equipment, tools, furniture, and fixtures used in operating the business. Operational assets, with the exception of land, are depreciated as they are used. Their initial cost is apportioned to expense over their estimated useful lives. As we discussed in Chapter 4, this apportionment of cost is called *depreciation*. Land is not depreciated because it does not wear out like machinery, buildings, and equipment. The amount of depreciation computed for each period is reported on the income statement as depreciation expense. The accumulated amount of depreciation expense for all past periods is deducted from the initial cost of the asset to derive the *book*, or *carrying, value* reported on the balance sheet (cost − accumulated depreciation). To illustrate, assume that Callaway purchased a new computer system for $22,000. It had an estimated useful life of five years. Depreciation expense is computed as $22,000 ÷ 5 years = $4,400 per year. The balance sheets developed during the five-year period would report the following, probably in a footnote to the financial statements:

	19A	19B	19C	19D	19E
Computer system (at cost)	$22,000	$22,000	$22,000	$22,000	$22,000
Less: Accumulated depreciation	4,400	8,800	13,200	17,600	22,000
Book, or carrying, value	$17,600	$13,200	$ 8,800	$ 4,400	$ 0

Intangible assets have no physical existence and have a long life. Their value is derived from the *legal rights* and *privileges* that accompany ownership. Examples are patents, trademarks, copyrights, franchises, and goodwill from purchasing other companies. Intangible assets usually are not acquired for resale but rather are directly related to the operations of the business. Although no intangible assets are separately reported in the financial statements, Callaway has at least 26 trademarks for its products and advertising slogans and numerous patents. As we discussed in Chapter 2, internally developed intangible assets often are not reflected on the balance sheets of companies because there is no identifiable transaction; only those that are material and purchased from others are included. Yet the value of these unrecorded internally developed intangible assets is significant.

Deferred charges are long-term prepayments for goods and services that are expected to help generate revenue in the future. They are often included in the classification "Other assets." Prepaid expenses and deferred charges are similar. The term *prepaid expense* is used typically for items classified as *current* assets; *deferred charges* is used for items classified as *noncurrent* assets.

Current liabilities are expected to be paid out of the current assets listed on the same balance sheet normally within the coming year. Current liabilities include accounts payable, short-term notes payable, wages payable, income taxes payable, and other expenses incurred (used) but not yet paid. Callaway combines Accounts Payable and Accrued Expenses Payable, and also lists Accrued Compensation and Benefits, Accrued Warranty, and Income Taxes Payable. As discussed in Chapters 3 and 4, accrued liabilities are obligations arising from expenses incurred in the current period that will be billed and paid for in the future.

Callaway's substantial investment in its diverse group of employees is not directly recognized as an asset on the balance sheet.

Long-term liabilities are the other debts of a company that are not classified as current liabilities. Long-term liabilities have maturities that extend beyond one year from the balance sheet date. Examples include long-term bank loans, bond liabilities, mortgages, pension liabilities, and lease obligations. In 1993, Callaway's balance sheet showed that the long-term debt outstanding at the end of 1992 was eliminated during 1993. A footnote disclosed that the bonds (8% convertible subordinated bonds) were converted by the bondholders into shares of Callaway stock during 1993.

Stockholders' equity represents the residual claim of the owners (i.e., A – L = SE). This claim results from the initial contributions of the stockholders (contributed capital) plus retained earnings, which is the accumulated earnings of the company less the accumulated dividends declared. Retained earnings represents the amount of earnings that has been left in the company for growth. Typically long-time successful companies have grown more from resources generated by operating activities than from additional contributions by investors for capital stock.

Until this chapter, we have identified the financing by investors as contributed capital. In practice, this account is often shown as two accounts: Common Stock and Contributed Capital in Excess of Par. Each share of common stock usually has a nominal (low) **par value** printed on the face of the certificate. Par value is a legal amount per share established by the board of directors; par value has *no* relationship to the market price of the stock. Its significance is that it establishes the minimum amount that a stockholder must contribute. Callaway's common stock has a par value of $.01 per share while the 1,039,000 shares were sold in its 1992 initial public offering at a market price of $15.84 per share (net of issuance costs).[6] When a corporation issues capital stock at net market value, the amount is recorded in part as Common Stock (number of shares × par value per share) and the excess as Capital in Excess of Par (also called Additional Paid-in Capital, Contributed Capital in Excess of Par, or Paid-in Capital, which is used by Callaway). The journal entry to record Callaway's 1992 initial public offering is:

Par value is a legal amount per share established by the board of directors; it establishes the minimum amount a stockholder must contribute and has no relationship to the market price of the stock.

Cash ($15.84 × 1,039,000 shares)	16,457,760	
Common stock ($.01 per share × 1,039,000 shares)		10,390
Paid-in capital ($16,457,760 – 10,390)		16,447,370

[6] These numbers are rounded.

The face of Callaway's balance sheet (as is common for most companies) discloses information on the number of shares the company is authorized to issue (60 million), the number of shares issued to investors (16,897,608 at the end of 1993), and the number of shares outstanding that remain on the open market (not repurchased by the company). Since the number issued and outstanding is the same for Callaway, no common stock repurchases existed at the end of 1993. When there are authorized but unissued shares, additional issuances in the future do not need to be approved by shareholders. Additional discussion of accounting and reporting issues for owners' equity is presented in Chapter 11.

FINANCIAL ANALYSIS

Liquidity, Current Ratio, and Debt Contracts

Liquidity refers to a company's ability to meet its current maturing debts. Tests of liquidity focus on the relationship between current assets and current liabilities:

Working capital = Current assets − Current liabilities
Current ratio = Current assets ÷ Current liabilities

They measure the cushion of working capital that is maintained to allow for the unevenness in the flow of funds through the working capital accounts. For example, a current ratio of 2 means that the company has $2 of current assets for every $1 of current liabilities. Even if for a short period the current assets turn into cash half as quickly as the current liabilities come due, the company should have sufficient cash to pay its debts.

When firms borrow money, they agree to make specific payments of interest and principal in the future. To provide protection for the creditors, they also often agree to other restrictions on their activities. For example, Callaway has a $20 million line of credit with its bank, First Interstate Bank of California, at an interest rate equal to the prime rate. This line of credit is not secured by specific assets of the company as collateral. However, as part of the agreement with the bank, Callaway agrees to maintain a minimum specified current ratio. Maintaining this level of the ratio assures the bank that the company has sufficient liquid assets, after the payment of other current liabilities, to pay its debt.

Classified Income Statements

Callaway Golf's 1993 Consolidated Statement of Income is reprinted for you in Exhibit 5–5. Other common titles include *Statement of Earnings* and *Statement of Operations*. Income statements have up to five major sections:

A. Continuing operations
B. Discontinued operations
C. Extraordinary items
D. Cumulative effect of changes in accounting methods

   Net income (sum of A, B, C, and D)

E. Earnings per share

All companies' income statements will have sections A (continuing operations) and E (earnings per share). Depending on their particular circumstances, one or more of sections B, C, and D will be reported. The amounts for section A and any of B, C, or D that are reported are summed to equal bottom line *Net Income*. We will first focus on the most common and important section, *continuing operations*.

Income Statement of Callaway Golf **Exhibit 5–5**

Consolidated Statement of Income

(in thousands, except per share data)	**Year Ended December 31,**					
	1993		**1992**		**1991**	
Net sales	$254,645	100%	$132,058	100%	$54,753	100%
Cost of goods sold	115,458	45%	62,970	48%	26,175	48%
Gross profit	139,187	55%	69,088	52%	28,578	52%
Selling expenses	38,485	15%	19,810	15%	11,342	21%
General and administrative expenses	28,633	11%	14,990	11%	5,622	10%
Research and development costs	3,653	1%	1,585	1%	845	2%
Income from operations	68,416	27%	32,703	25%	10,769	20%
Other income (expense)						
Interest income (expense), net	1,024		403		(163)	
Other income, net	160		69		165	
Income before income taxes and cumulative effect of accounting change	69,600	27%	33,175	25%	10,771	20%
Provision for income taxes	28,396		13,895		4,355	
Income before cumulative effect of accounting change	41,204	16%	19,280	15%	6,416	12%
Cumulative effect of accounting change	1,658					
Net income	$ 42,862	17%	$ 19,280	15%	$ 6,416	12%
Earnings per common share:						
Primary						
Income before cumulative effect of accounting change	$2.39		$1.28		$0..48	
Cumulative effect of accounting change	.10					
Net income	$2.49		$1.28		$0.48	
Fully diluted						
Income before cumulative effect of accounting change	$2.34		$1.13		$0.43	
Cumulative effect of accounting change	.09					
Net income	$2.43		$1.13		$0.43	
Common equivalent shares:						
Primary	17,241		15,080		13,444	
Fully diluted	17,630		17,256		15,348	

See accompanying notes to consolidated financial statements.

Continuing Operations

This first section of an income statement presents the results of continuing operations. Companies such as Callaway that do not have any discontinued operations (discussed below) do not title this section separately. However, this section can be presented using one of three common formats:

1. Single-step.
2. Multiple-step with operating costs and expenses deducted from sales to show operating income as a subtotal.

3. Multiple-step with cost of goods sold deducted from sales to show gross margin (or gross profit) as a subtotal and then other operating expenses deducted to show operating income as a second subtotal.

Callaway's income statement follows the third format with a subtotal for gross profit and a subtotal for income from operations before adding or subtracting other income, gains, expenses, and losses. In prior chapters, however, we illustrated a simplified format known as the *single-step* format in which all revenue, income, and gains were listed first, then all costs, expenses, and losses were subtracted. About one-third of the companies in a recent survey used the single-step approach.[7] In Exhibit 5–6, we reorder the accounts in Callaway's income statement to show you how the same 1993 data would be displayed using the single-step format. We also present the same information using the second approach (*multiple step, one subtotal*) in which only one subtotal for operating income is presented followed by other income, gains, expenses, and losses, and the third approach (*multiple step, two subtotals*).

There is no difference in the individual revenue, expense, gain, and loss items reported using the three formats. The differences between them relate only to the use of categories and subtotals, which are highlighted by shading in Exhibit 5–6. The primary difference between the single-step and two multiple-step approaches is the subtotal *Income from operations* separating items relating to normal operations from those relating to peripheral activities of the company, such as earning interest on investments and incurring losses on sales of fixed assets. The primary difference between the two multiple-step approaches is the significance placed on relating sales to the cost of goods sold to report the subtotal *Gross profit* before reporting the remaining operating items.

We will now describe the various accounts and subtotals on an income statement constructed using the *multiple-step, two-subtotal format*. *Net sales* are gross sales minus any discounts, returns, and allowances during the period. These latter items are discussed in Chapter 6.

Exhibit 5–6 **Alternative Income Statement Formats for Continuing Operations**

Single Step

Net sales	$254,645
Interest income, net	1,024
Other income, net	160
Total revenues	255,829
Cost of goods sold	115,458
Selling expenses	38,485
General and administrative expenses	28,633
Research and development costs	3,653
Total expenses	186,229
Income before income taxes and cumulative effect of accounting change	69,600
Provision for income taxes	28,396
Income before cumulative effect of accounting change	41,204
Cumulative effect of an accounting change	1,658
Net Income	$42,862

Multiple Step (one subtotal)

Net sales	$254,645
Cost of goods sold	115,458
Selling expenses	38,485
General and administrative expenses	28,633
Research and development costs	3,653
Income from operations	68,416
Other income (expense):	
Interest income (expense), net	1,024
Other income, net	160
Income before income taxes and cumulative effect of accounting change	69,600
Provision for income taxes	28,396
Income before cumulative effect of accounting change	41,204
Cumulative effect of an accounting change	1,658
Net Income	$42,862

Multiple Step (two subtotals)

Net sales	$254,645
Cost of goods sold	115,458
Gross profit	139,187
Selling expenses	38,485
General and administrative expenses	28,633
Research and development costs	3,653
Income from operations	68,416
Other income (expense):	
Interest income (expense), net	1,024
Other income, net	160
Income before income taxes and cumulative effect of accounting change	69,600
Provision for income taxes	28,396
Income before cumulative effect of accounting change	41,204
Cumulative effect of an accounting change	1,658
Net Income	$42,862

[7]American Institute of Certified Public Accountants, *Accounting Trends & Techniques*, 1993.

Cost of goods sold is the cost of inventory sold by a merchandiser (a company that buys products from manufacturers for resale) or a manufacturer (a company that produces goods for sale to wholesalers or retail merchandisers). For example, assume Callaway sold golf club inventory costing $90,000 to Sumitomo Corporation (which exports and sells Callaway's golf clubs in Japan) for $200,000 on account. The journal entries would be as follows:

Accounts receivable	200,000	
Sales revenue		200,000
To reflect the earning of revenue in exchange for a promise to pay from the customer.		
Cost of goods sold	90,000	
Inventory		90,000
To reflect the use of inventory to generate revenues in the period.*		

*This example illustrates a perpetual inventory system. Alternative systems are illustrated in Chapter 7.

Any inventory that is purchased or produced but not sold during the period is included in the inventory on the balance sheet. We presented a similar illustration in Chapter 4 when we discussed the amount of food, beverage, and paper products Sbarro, Inc., had on hand at the end of the accounting period that was included on the balance sheet. Anything purchased for the period that was not on hand at the end was accounted for as the cost of food and paper products on the income statement. We will present additional discussion of accounting for sales and cost of goods sold for merchandising and manufacturing companies in Chapters 6 and 7.

Gross margin, or **gross profit**, is a subtotal, not an account. It is the difference between *net sales* and *cost of goods sold*. You may hear of gross profit being discussed in terms of a percentage. The formula for calculating the gross profit (to sales) percentage is:

Gross margin, or **gross profit,** is net sales less cost of goods sold.

Gross profit to sales percentage = Gross profit ÷ Net sales

Notice in Exhibit 5–5 that Callaway also reports income statement line items as a percentage of net sales, including the gross profit percentage of 55% in 1993. Most companies do not report these percentages which are often called *common-sized income statements*. However, many analysts compute these common-sized statements as a first step in analysis because they ease year-to-year comparisons. For example, in Callaway's income statement in Exhibit 5–5, you can easily see that gross profit percentages improved between 1992 and 1993 (that is, they increased from 52% in 1992 to 55% in 1993). This resulted from increases in sales of higher margin products.

Operating expenses are the usual expenses that are incurred in operating a business during an accounting period. Often they are classified between selling expense and general and administrative expense. *Selling expense* includes all amounts incurred during the period in performing sales activities, such as salaries of salespeople. *General and administrative expense* includes the overall business expenses, such as the salary of the president. Callaway also adds a line for research and development expenses that represent about 5% of all operating expenses. Differences in the specific expense and revenue categories reported are common depending on the nature of each company and industry. Another subtotal is computed after subtracting operating expenses from gross profit—**income from operations** (also called **operating income**).

Income from operations (**operating income**) equals net sales less cost of goods sold and other operating expenses.

Nonoperating (other) items are income, expenses, gains, and losses which are not considered as resulting from the central operations of the business but are not unusual or infrequent in nature. Examples are interest income, interest expense, and gains and losses on the sale of fixed assets. Interest expense on debt is sometimes combined (netted) with interest revenue so that only a single

Income before income taxes (pretax earnings) is revenues minus all expenses except income tax expense.

amount is reported. These nonoperating items are added to or subtracted from income from operations to obtain **income before income taxes**, which is also called **pretax earnings**.

FINANCIAL ANALYSIS

Accounting-Based Executive Bonuses

Callaway Golf believes in tying executives' compensation to the performance of the company as measured by accounting numbers. Callaway pays its five executive officers bonuses of up to 200% of base salary if sales growth and pretax earnings as a percentage of sales (computed below) meet or exceed target amounts.

	Targets
Sales growth % = (Current year sales − Last year sales) ÷ Last year sales	35.1%
Pretax earnings % = Pretax earnings ÷ Net sales	21.1%

Meeting these goals in the current year would result in bonuses ranging from $400,000 to $700,000 for each of the five executive officers.

Self-Study Quiz

Callaway executives will receive bonuses if sales growth and pretax earnings as a percent of sales meet or exceed target amounts (35.1 % and 21.1%, respectively). Use Exhibit 5–5 to see if Callaway executives earned their bonuses in the most recent year.

Computations:

____

____

____

____

Discuss why Callaway might choose to pay executives based on performance and why they use the same accounting numbers used in reports to shareholders to measure the executives' performance.

____

____

____

____

Now check your answers to those in the footnote at the bottom of the page*

Discontinued Operations

Discontinued operations result from the disposal of a major segment of the business and are reported net of income tax effects.

Any company that plans to dispose of a major segment of its business or customer line needs to present separate information on the income statement accompanied by disposal details written in a footnote. **Discontinued operations** can result from abandoning or selling the major segment. Any operating income generated by the discontinued segment is disclosed separately from any gain or

---

*Sales growth % = (254,645 − 132,058) ÷ 132,058 = 92.8% versus 35.1% target.
Pretax earnings % = 69,600 ÷ 254,645 = 27.3% versus 21.1% target.
They earned their bonuses. The company believes in aligning the interests of the shareholders with the interests of the managers. In addition, the numbers in the annual report to shareholders have been independently verified by the auditors.

loss on the disposal (the difference between the cost of the net assets being disposed of and the sale price or the abandonment costs). The disclosure of each can be in a footnote or on the face of the income statement. Each line is to be reported net of the income tax effects. Separate reporting informs users that these results of discontinued operations are less useful as predictors of the company's future.

An example of a partial income statement that includes discontinued operations is presented in Exhibit 5–7 for Tenneco Inc., a major industrial conglomerate involved in natural gas transportation and marketing; farm and construction equipment; automotive parts; ship design, construction, and repair; packaging; and chemicals. The footnote accompanying the income statement reported that during 1992 Tenneco sold two segments—its minerals and pulp chemicals operations.

Extraordinary Items

Extraordinary items are gains or losses incurred by the company that are considered both unusual in nature and infrequent in occurrence. Examples include losses suffered from natural disasters such as floods and hurricanes in geographic areas where such disasters rarely occur. These items must be separately reported on the income statement net of income tax effects. Separate reporting informs decision makers that the items are not likely to recur and for that reason are less relevant to predicting the company's future. Footnote disclosure is needed to explain the nature of the extraordinary item. In the same year as it listed discontinued operations, Tenneco Inc. also reported extraordinary losses due to the early retirement of long-term debt (Exhibit 5–7). Accounting for early retirement of debt is discussed in Chapter 10.

Extraordinary items are gains and losses that are both unusual in nature and infrequent in occurrence; they are reported net of tax on the income statement.

Cumulative Effects of Changes in Accounting Methods

The fourth section of the income statement reflects the income statement effects of any adjustment made to balance sheet accounts because of changing to a different acceptable accounting method. These amounts are called **cumulative effects of changes in accounting methods**. The goal is to determine what the balance sheet amount should be as if the new accounting method had always been applied, net of any tax effects. Often these changes are required by new pronouncements made by the FASB. At other times, corporate management determines that a change to an alternative accounting method is necessary due to changes in business activities. Changing accounting principles, however, violates the qualitative characteristic of information related to consistent application of methods over time. Therefore, footnote disclosure to explain the nature and effects of the change is necessary.

Cumulative effects of changes in accounting methods are the effects of adjustments made to balance sheet accounts when applying different accounting principles.

Partial Income Statements for Tenneco Inc. **Exhibit 5–7**

Real World Excerpt

Tenneco Inc. Annual Report

STATEMENTS OF INCOME (LOSS)

Tenneco Inc. and Consolidated Subsidiaries			
Years Ended December 31 (Millions Except Share Amounts)	**1993**	1992	1991
Income (loss) from continuing operations	**451**	(683)	(692)
Income (loss) from discontinued operations, net of income tax	**- - -**	71	(40)
Income (loss) before extraordinary loss	**451**	(612)	(732)
Extraordinary loss, net of income tax	**(25)**	(12)	- - -
Income (loss) before cumulative effect of changes in accounting principles	**426**	(624)	(732)
Cumulative effect of changes in accounting principles, net of income tax	**- - -**	(699)	- - -
Net income (loss)	**426**	(1,323)	(732)

In 1993, Callaway adopted a change in accounting for deferred income taxes as required by the FASB, resulting in an increase in deferred taxes on the balance sheet of $1,658,000 with the cumulative effect of the change reflected on the income statement, net of income taxes, in Exhibit 5–5. We can see in Exhibit 5–7 that Tenneco Inc. also reported the cumulative effect of a change in accounting principles in 1992. Tenneco adopted two different FASB pronouncements (one relating to deferred taxes and one relating to accounting for benefits to retired employees). These are shown net of the income tax effect and are appropriately disclosed in footnotes. The effects of accounting methods changes are separated because they are normally not directly relevant to predicting the company's future.

Finally, we come to "the bottom line," net income. However, an income statement is not complete without including earnings per share information for corporations.

Earnings Per Share

As we discussed in Chapter 4, simple computations for earnings per share (EPS) are as follows:

$$\text{EPS} = \frac{\text{Net income available to common shareholders}}{\text{Weighted-average number of common shares outstanding during the reporting period}}$$

However, as you can see in Exhibit 5–5, Callaway's disclosure of EPS takes up more room on the page than the income statement. Three factors impact the amount of EPS disclosure to be shown.

First, any company that has a complex capital structure (that is, debt or equity securities convertible into common stock or a stock option plan) needs to compute the effect of these items as if they had been converted at the beginning of the period, or when initially issued if during the current reporting period. These items are considered potentially dilutive in that they are likely to reduce EPS for common shareholders when the debt is converted or options are exercised by the holders. Thus, Callaway, which has a complex capital structure (convertible debt and a stock option plan), lists both *Primary EPS* and *Fully Diluted EPS.* The computation of these amounts is beyond the scope of this text and is usually presented in advanced coursework for accounting majors.

The second factor that adds complexity to EPS disclosure results from including any section on the income statement for discontinued operations, extraordinary items, or cumulative effect of changes in accounting methods. These same sections must be displayed in EPS. You can see in Exhibit 5–5 that Callaway shows Primary EPS broken down into a line for EPS before cumulative effect and also a line for the cumulative effect to obtain EPS based on net income. The same is true for Fully Diluted EPS.

A Note on Taxes

One of the features of the five sections of the income statement is that each section shows the amount of income tax expense related to that section. This is known as *intraperiod income tax allocation*. Items presented after continuing operations are reported net of the tax effect. For example, a $1,000 extraordinary loss is reported as $600 ($1,000 – 400 tax effect).

Before income from continuing operations is computed, the *provision (expense) for income taxes* is calculated and subtracted. For Callaway Golf, income tax expense is approximately 40% of pretax income from operations. Income tax expense is incurred by a corporation but not by a sole proprietorship or partnership. Income taxes are payable each year (part in advance in quarterly estimates).

Statement of Cash Flows Classifications

We have introduced the statement of cash flow classifications in prior chapters. They are:

A. Cash Flows from Operating Activities. This section reports cash flows associated with earning income.
B. Cash Flows from Investing Activities. Cash flows in this section are associated with buying and selling productive assets (other than inventory) and investments in other companies.
C. Cash Flows from Financing Activities. These cash flows are related to financing the business through debt and equity issuances and payments or repurchases.

Callaway's 1993 Consolidated Statement of Cash Flows is presented in Exhibit 5–8. It follows the sections indicated above. The first section (cash from operations) can be illustrated using either the *direct* or *indirect* method. For Callaway, the first section (cash flows from operating activities) is reported using the indirect method as a reconciliation of net income on an accrual basis to cash flows from operations. This more common format is different from the presentation made in the statement prepared for Sbarro at the end of Chapter 4 that was constructed using the direct method. Both formats will be discussed in detail in Chapter 13.

Notes to Financial Statements

The numbers reported on the various financial statements provide important information to decision makers, but most users require additional details to facilitate their analysis. All financial reports include additional information in notes that follow the statements. Callaway's 1993 footnotes are categorized below by type of footnote (key accounting policies, additional detail supporting reported numbers, and relevant financial information not disclosed on the statements). Examples are provided.

Descriptions of Accounting Rules Applied in the Company's Statements

The first note is typically a summary of significant accounting policies. As you will see in your study of subsequent chapters, generally accepted accounting principles (GAAP) permit companies to select alternative methods for measuring the effects of transactions. The summary of significant accounting policies tells the user which accounting methods have been adopted by the company. It is impossible to analyze a company's financial results effectively without first understanding the various accounting methods that have been used. The policy for accounting for property, plant, and equipment is as follows:

Note 1
THE COMPANY AND SIGNIFICANT ACCOUNTING POLICIES
PROPERTY, PLANT AND EQUIPMENT
Property, plant and equipment are stated at cost less accumulated depreciation. Depreciation is computed using the straight-line method over estimated useful lives of five to fifteen years. Repairs and maintenance costs are charged to expense as incurred.

Real World Excerpt
Callaway Golf Annual Report

Exhibit 5–8 **Cash Flow Statement of Callaway Golf**

Callaway® GOLF

Consolidated Statement of Cash Flows

(in thousands)	Year Ended December 31,		
	1993	**1992**	**1991**
Cash flows from operating activities:			
Net income	$42,862	$19,280	$6,416
Adjustments to reconcile net income to net cash provided by operating activities:			
Depreciation	3,016	1,372	633
Non-cash compensation	5,486	1,501	1,075
Increase (decrease) in cash resulting from changes in:			
Accounts receivable, net	(6,271)	(5,205)	(3,989)
Inventories, net	(13,771)	(4,097)	(2,660)
Deferred taxes	(6,544)	(5,042)	(1,808)
Other assets	(2,019)	(933)	(893)
Accounts payable and accrued expenses	5,055	1,189	3,326
Accrued compensation and benefits	2,009	1,387	671
Accrued warranty	5,114	3,316	1,074
Income taxes payable	(1,945)	782	1,163
Net cash provided by operating activities	32,992	13,550	5,008
Cash flows from investing activities:			
Capital expenditures	(20,939)	(11,370)	(1,540)
Sale of fixed assets	17	3	4
Net cash used in investing activities	(20,922)	(11,367)	(1,536)
Cash flows from financing activities:			
Repayments on note payable			(1,000)
Issuance of long-term debt			1,416
Issuance of common stock	5,603	16,461	
Retirement of common stock	(336)	(5,000)	
Retirement of stock options			(32)
Tax benefit from exercise of stock options	13,261	1,197	
Dividends paid	(1,591)		
Net cash provided by financing activities	16,937	12,658	384
Effect of exchange rate changes on cash	(30)		
Net increase in cash and cash equivalents	28,977	14,841	3,856
Cash and cash equivalents at beginning of year	20,019	5,178	1,322
Cash and cash equivalents at end of year	$48,996	$20,019	$5,178

See accompanying notes to consolidated financial statements.

FINANCIAL ANALYSIS

Alternative Accounting Methods and GAAP

Many people are under a misimpression concerning the nature of the rules that make up generally accepted accounting principles (GAAP)—that GAAP permits only one accounting method to be used for the computation of each value on the financial statements (e.g., inventory). Actually, GAAP often allows selection of an accounting method from a menu of acceptable methods. This permits a company to choose the methods that most closely reflect its particular economic circumstances (economic reality). However, this adds an additional complexity to the financial statement users' task—they must also understand how the company's choice of accounting methods will affect its financial statement presentations. For example, before analyzing two companies' statements prepared using different accounting methods, one company's statements must be converted to the other's methods to make them comparable. Otherwise the reader would be in a situation analogous to comparing distances in kilometers and miles without conversion to a common scale. In later chapters, we will focus on developing the ability to make these conversions.

Additional Detail Supporting Reported Numbers

Note 2	Selected Financial Statement Information
Note 4	Long-Term Debt
Note 5	Common and Preferred Stock
Note 8	Income Taxes
Note 9	Sales Information
Note 10	Supplemental Statement of Cash Flows Information

The second category of notes provides supplemental information concerning the data shown on the financial statements. Among other information, these notes may show revenues broken out by geographic region or line of business, descriptions of unusual transactions, and expanded detail concerning a specific classification. For example, Callaway provides detail on cash; accounts receivable; inventory; property, plant and equipment; accounts payable and accrued expenses; and accrued compensation and benefits in Note 2. Note 9, which follows, shows sales information by geographic region:

Real World Excerpt

Callaway Golf Annual Report

Note 9
SALES INFORMATION

The Company is engaged in domestic and international sales through distributors located within the following geographic areas:

(in thousands)	**Year Ended December 31,**		
	1993	**1992**	**1991**
United States	$188,099	$102,323	$44,896
Japan	30,975	11,890	5,451
All others—individually less than 5% of net sales	35,571	17,845	4,406
	$254,645	$132,058	$54,753

Relevant Financial Information Not Disclosed on the Statements

Note 3	Bank Line of Credit
Note 6	Stock Options and Rights
Note 7	Benefit Plan
Note 11	Subsequent Event

The final category includes information that impacts the company financially but is not specifically indicated on the statements. Examples include information on stock option plans, legal matters, and any material event that occurs subsequent to year-end but before the financial statements are published. Note 3 is as follows:

Real World Excerpt

Callaway Golf Annual Report

Note 3

BANK LINE OF CREDIT

In November 1993, the Company renegotiated its bank line of credit. The credit line was increased to $20,000,000 with an interest rate equal to the bank's prime rate. The interest rate at December 31, 1993 was 6.0%. The line of credit has been primarily utilized to support the issuance of letters of credit of which there were $1,491,000 outstanding at December 31, 1993, reducing the amount available under the Company's line of credit to $18,509,000.

The line of credit is unsecured and is subject to renewal on December 1, 1994. The line requires Callaway to maintain certain financial ratios, including current and debt to equity ratios. The Company is also subject to other restrictive covenants under the terms of the credit agreement.

THE DISCLOSURE PROCESS

Learning Objective 4
Identify the steps in the accounting communication process including issuance of press releases, annual reports, quarterly reports, and SEC filings, and the role of electronic information services in this process.

As noted in our discussion of information services and information intermediaries, the accounting communication process includes more steps and participants than one would envision in a world where annual and quarterly reports were simply mailed to shareholders.

Press Releases

A **press release** is a written public news announcement that is normally distributed to major news services.

Callaway and most public companies announce quarterly and annual earnings through a **press release** as soon as the verified figures (audited for annual and reviewed for quarterly earnings) are available to provide timely information to external users and limit the possibility of selective leakage of information. Callaway normally issues its earnings press releases within four weeks of the end of the accounting period. The announcements are sent via fax to the major print and electronic news services including Dow Jones, the PR Newswire, and Bloomberg Business News, where they are made immediately available to subscribers. The first page of a typical quarterly press release for Callaway is reprinted in Exhibit 5–9. It includes key financial figures and management's discussion of the results. Attached to the release are condensed income statements and balance sheets (unaudited) which will be included in the formal quarterly report to shareholders, mailed after the press release.

For actively traded stocks such as Callaway Golf, most of the stock market reaction (stock price increases and decreases from investor trading) to the news in the press release usually occurs quickly. Recall that a number of analysts follow Callaway and regularly predict the company's earnings. When the actual earnings are published, the market reacts *not* to the amount of earnings, but to the difference between expectations of earnings and actual earnings. This amount is called *unexpected earnings.* For example, the Bloomberg News Service recently reported the following:

Real World Excerpt

Bloomberg Business News

Callaway Golf Stock Climbs 7% on 4th-Qtr Earnings Rise

Carlsbad, Calif., Jan. 27 (Bloomberg)—Callaway Golf Co. shares finished 7% higher today after the company said fourth-quarter earnings more than doubled . . .

Fourth-quarter earnings rose to $10.3 million, or 58 cents a share . . .

The results were above the predictions of Merrill Lynch & Co. analyst Eric Katzman, who was estimating earnings of 49 cents a share.

Compared to Katzman's estimate, unexpected earnings were plus 9 cents per share.

Earnings Press Release for Callaway Golf Company **Exhibit 5–9**

CALLAWAY GOLF COMPANY REPORTS SALES AND EARNINGS UP 93 PERCENT AND 114 PERCENT, RESPECTIVELY

CARLSBAD, Calif., Jan. 27—Callaway Golf Company (NYSE: ELY) had income (before the cumulative effect of accounting change) for the year ended Dec. 31, 1993, of $41.2 million ($2.34 per share fully diluted), an increase of 114 percent, as compared with the $19.3 million ($1.13 per share fully diluted) reported for 1992. Sales increased 93 percent to $254.6 million over the previous year's sales of $132.1 million, it was announced today by Ely Callaway, chairman and chief executive officer, and Donald H. Dye, president and chief operating officer.

Net sales for the three months ended Dec. 31, 1993, were $68.2 million, up 86 percent from sales of $36.7 million for the comparable period in 1992. For the three months ended Dec. 31, 1993, net income was $10.3 million, or $.58 per share fully diluted, up 101 percent from the $5.1 million, or $.30 per share fully diluted, for the comparable period a year ago.

The 1993 gross margin was 55 percent compared to 52 percent in 1992. The increase is due, in part, to reduced provision requirements for obsolete inventory and warranty. The gross margin was also positively affected by an increase in the sales of Big Bertha® metal woods which provide a higher margin, offset partially by increased material costs and a provision for possible future returns resulting from current sales.

Callaway went on to say: "Our continued increase in volume and profits was attributable to increased customer demand for Callaway's "Big Bertha®" drivers and fairway woods, in particular the No. 7 Wood, and Heaven Wood™, the Divine Nine™ Wood, and the company's S_2H_2® irons.

"At the PGA Merchandise Show in Orlando, FL, this week, we anticipate announcing some new products for 1994. We believe that there will be significant pressure on the company to predict the impact these new products will have on our financial performance, and that security analysts who follow the company may offer their own opinions on that subject. We remind our shareholders and others interested in the company that Callaway Golf does not make such predictions."

2285 Rutherford Road • Carlsbad, CA 92008-8815
Telephone: (619) 931-1771 • Outside California (800) 228-2767
FAX: (619) 931-9539

Companies like Callaway issue press releases concerning other important events such as new product announcements, new appointments of officers and members of the board of directors, and new endorsement contracts with professional golfers. News services also gather information about Callaway from other sources. The stock market often appears to react to some of these important announcements. For example, Bloomberg recently reported the following:

Real World Excerpt
Bloomberg Business News

Callaway Shares Rise After Spokesman Wins Pro-Am

New York, Feb. 7 (Bloomberg)—The shares of golf-club maker Callaway Golf Co. rose 6.6% today after Callaway's celebrity spokesman Johnny Miller won a California golf tournament yesterday . . . marking the 46-year-old golfer's first win in seven years.

This was the first tournament where Miller had used Callaway's new Big Bertha irons. Presumably, the stock market inferred that this would provide an impetus for future sales of the new product.

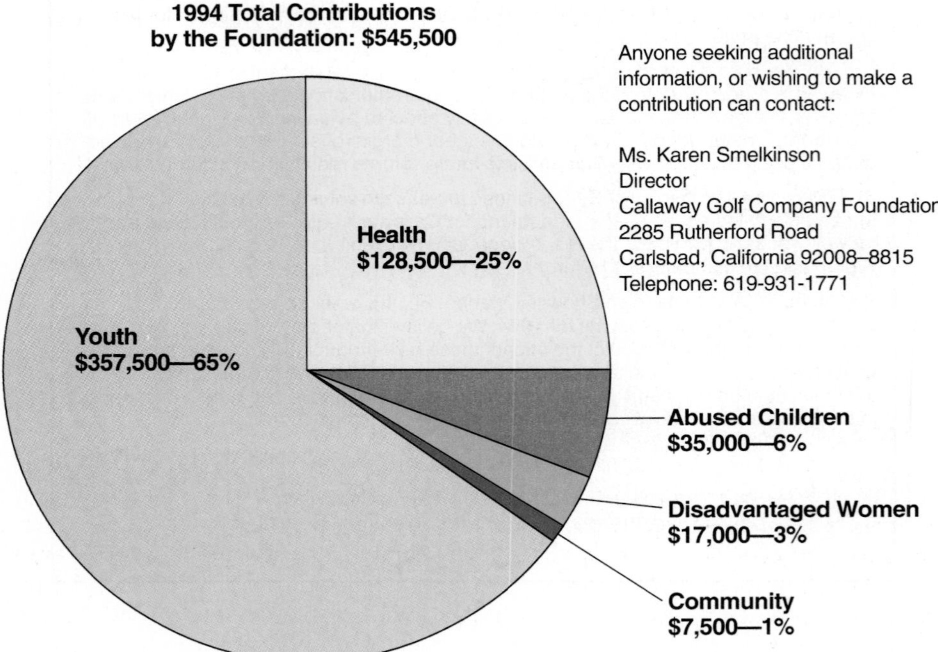

Anyone seeking additional information, or wishing to make a contribution can contact:

Ms. Karen Smelkinson
Director
Callaway Golf Company Foundation
2285 Rutherford Road
Carlsbad, California 92008–8815
Telephone: 619-931-1771

Callaway's annual report also discusses the activities of its charitable foundation which focuses on youth and health issues.

Press releases related to annual earnings and quarterly earnings often precede the issuance of the quarterly or annual report by 15 to 45 days. This time is necessary to prepare the additional detail and to print and distribute those reports.

Annual Reports

For privately held companies, *annual reports* are relatively simple affairs photocopied on white bond paper. They normally include only

1. Four basic financial statements: income statement, stockholders' equity or retained earnings statement, cash flow statement, and balance sheet.
2. Related footnotes or notes as described above.
3. Report of independent accountants (auditor's opinion).

The annual reports of public companies are significantly more elaborate, both because of additional SEC reporting requirements imposed on these companies, and the fact that many companies use their annual reports as public relations tools to communicate nonaccounting information to shareholders, customers, the press, and others.

The annual reports of public companies are normally split into two sections: The first, "nonfinancial," section usually includes a letter to stockholders from the chairman and CEO, descriptions of the company's management philosophy, products, its successes (and occasionally its failures), and exciting prospects and challenges for the future. Beautiful photographs of products, facilities, and personnel are often included. The second, "financial," section, which is often printed on a different color of paper to make it easy to find, includes the core of the report. The SEC sets minimum disclosure standards for the financial section of the annual reports of public companies. The principal components of the financial section include

1. Summarized financial data for a five- or ten-year period.
2. Management's Discussion and Analysis of Financial Condition and Results of Operations.
3. The four basic financial statements.
4. Footnotes (Notes).
5. Report of Independent Accountants (Auditor's Opinion) and sometimes the Report of Management Responsibility.
6. Recent stock price information.
7. Summaries of the unaudited quarterly financial data (described below).
8. Listings of directors and officers of the company and relevant addresses.

The order of these components varies.

Most of these elements except for the Management Discussion and Analysis have been discussed earlier in the chapter. This element includes management's discussion and explanation of key figures on the financial statements and future risks the company faces. For example, in a recent annual report, Callaway explained a 93% increase in sales over the prior year as being "attributable to a continued increase in unit sales of Big Bertha Metal Woods in both domestic and foreign markets." This increase in sales of the oversized woods, along with relatively stable sales of normal-sized irons may have provided the impetus for the development of Callaway's new oversized Big Bertha irons.

Future risks faced by the company are also discussed. For example, the report notes that

Real World Excerpt

Callaway Golf Annual Report

> a significant portion of the Company's Big Bertha® Metal Wood heads is presently produced by only a single foundry. If the ability to produce Big Bertha® heads was substantially interfered with at this foundry, the Company could be materially adversely affected.

A complete annual report from Toys "Я" Us, which includes all of these sections, is reprinted in Appendix B at the end of this book.

Quarterly Reports

Quarterly reports normally begin with a short letter to shareholders. This is followed by a condensed income statement for the quarter, which often shows less detail than the annual income statement, and a condensed balance sheet dated at the end of the quarter (e.g., March 31 for the first quarter). These condensed financial statements are not audited and are so marked *unaudited*. Also, the cash flow statement, statement of stockholders' equity (or retained earnings statement), and notes to the financial statements are often not included. Private companies also normally prepare quarterly reports for lenders. These reports are usually similar to the ones prepared by public companies. Callaway's quarterly reports are issued about five weeks after the end of each quarter.

SEC Reports—10-K, 10-Q, 8-K

Public companies must also file periodic reports with the SEC. They include the annual report on Form 10-K, quarterly reports on Form 10-Q, and current event reports on Form 8-K. These reports are normally referred to by number (for example, the "10-K"). The SEC requires that the 10-K be filed within 90 days of the fiscal year-end and the 10-Q be filed within 45 days of the end of quarter. In general, the 10-K and 10-Q present all the information in the annual and quarterly reports, respectively, along with additional management discussion and several required schedules.

Form 10-K Annual Report

The **Form 10-K** is the annual report that publicly traded companies must file with the SEC.

In the **Form 10-K**, companies provide a more detailed description of the business including items such as their products, product development, sales and marketing, manufacturing, and competitors. For example, Callaway states:

Real World Excerpt

Callaway Golf Form 10-K

> The Company believes that its principal competitors include Karsten Manufacturing Corporation (Ping), Tommy Armour Golf Company and Cobra Golf Incorporated, with respect to its irons, and Taylor Made Golf Company and Yonex, with respect to its metal woods.

They also list properties owned and leased, any legal proceedings they are involved in, and significant contracts that the company has signed. This last point is particularly important given that, as we emphasized in Chapter 2, many important contracts between the company and other parties such as key employees, distributors, and others represent important economic assets and/or liabilities to the company. However, they are not included on the balance sheet. That is, they have no *book value*. For example, Callaway's 10-K lists employment contracts between Callaway Golf and Richard Helmstetter, the genius behind Callaway's research and product development group. This "human asset" is of tremendous economic value to the company but is not listed as an asset on its balance sheet.

Exhibit 5–10 Advertising Cost Schedule from Form 10-K

Real World Excerpt

Callaway Golf Form 10-K

CALLAWAY GOLF COMPANY
CONSOLIDATED SUPPLEMENTARY INCOME STATEMENT INFORMATION

Column A Item	Column B Charged to Costs and Expenses (in thousands)
Advertising costs (1)	
Year ended December 31, 1991	$4,853
Year ended December 31, 1992	$8,351
Year ended December 31, 1993	$14,761

(1) Includes costs related to print, television and other advertising media.

The 10-K also provides more detailed schedules concerning various figures on the income statement and balance sheet including bad debts, warranties, inventories, and advertising. For example, Callaway reports more detailed information about advertising costs in a schedule reprinted in Exhibit 5–10. This information is useful to analysts who can judge changes in Callaway's advertising and promotion strategy based on this and other numbers reported on the 10-K. We will discuss these disclosures in more detail in later chapters starting with the Chapter 6 discussion of bad debts.

FINANCIAL ANALYSIS

Judging Advertising Strategy Based on the 10-K

In its description of the business included in the 10-K, Callaway discloses that it spent approximately \$6.5 million, \$10.7 million, and \$21 million on advertising and promotional expenditures over the last three years. The difference between these three numbers and those disclosed on the schedule of advertising costs printed above is the amount spent each year on promotional and endorsement-related expenditures including compensation to professional golfers.

While both numbers have been rising along with sales, Callaway increased its spending on promotional and endorsement-related expenditures in the current year at a much faster rate than spending on other types of advertising. Promotional activities grew in one year from 22% [(\$10.7 – \$8.4) ÷ \$10.7] to 30% [(\$21.0 – \$14.8) ÷ \$21.0] of the total advertising and promotion budget. This increasing emphasis on professional endorsements represents a change in strategy for Callaway which is probably related to its new product introductions planned for the coming year.

Form 10-Q Quarterly Report

The **Form 10-Q** report includes all the information included in the quarterly report to shareholders, along with a statement of shareholders' equity and a cash flow statement for the quarter, a variety of footnotes, and a management discussion. The amount of information disclosed in the 10-Q is very close to that included in the annual report to shareholders but less than that required by the Form 10-K. Like the quarterly report to shareholders, the information in the 10-Q is unaudited.

Form 10-Q is the quarterly report that publicly traded companies must file with the SEC.

Form 8-K Current Report

The **Form 8-K** Current Report is used to report any material event important to investors that has not been previously reported in the 10-Q or 10-K. It normally must be filed within 15 days of any event specified in the form. An example of an event requiring submission of a Form 8-K is a change of auditors.

Form 8-K is used by publicly traded companies to disclose any material event not previously reported that is important to investors.

EPILOGUE

As noted earlier, Callaway is well known for introducing innovative new products long before the end of existing products' life cycles. The year 1994 was no exception with the introduction of Big Bertha® Irons in April. Some analysts questioned whether Callaway could successfully penetrate this highly competitive market with a new product. However, these questions were answered directly in its January 25, 1995, press release announcing for 1994 an annual sales increase of 76% and an annual earnings increase of 89%. Importantly, Callaway made an additional voluntary disclosure to put any rumors to rest concerning its new product: "Sales of the Big Bertha® Irons for the last eight months of the year were \$82.0 million. Shipments of the irons began in late April." Such detailed product line disclosures are not required by generally accepted accounting principles but are consistent with Callaway's clear and forthright approach to communicating with users of financial statements.

DEMONSTRATION CASE

Microsoft Corporation

Complete the following requirements before proceeding to the suggested solution. Microsoft Corporation, developer of a broad line of computer software including the DOS and Windows operating systems and Word (word processing) and Excel (spreadsheet) programs, is now the largest computer-related company in the world. Presented below is a listing of the financial statement items and amounts adapted from Microsoft's 1993 income statement and balance sheet. These items have normal debit and credit balances and are reported in millions of dollars. There were 303 million weighted-average number of shares of stock outstanding for 1993. The company closes its books on June 30.

Accounts payable	$ 239	Net revenues	$3,753
Accounts receivable	338	Other current assets	95
Accrued compensation	86	Other current liabilities	111
Cash and short-term investments	2,290	Other revenues and expenses (debit balance)	7
Common stock and paid-in-capital	1,086	Other noncurrent assets	88
Cost of goods sold	633	Property, plant, and equipment (net)	867
General and administrative	119	Provision for income taxes	448
Income taxes payable	127	Research and development	470
Interest income (net)	82	Retained earnings	2,156
Inventories	127	Sales and marketing	1,205

Required:

Prepare in good form a multiple-step income statement (showing both gross profit and operating income) and a classified balance sheet for the year.

SUGGESTED SOLUTION:

MICROSOFT CORPORATION
Income Statement
For the period ended June 30, 1993
(in millions)

Net revenues	$3,753
Cost of goods sold	633
Gross profit	3,120
Operating expenses:	
Research and development	470
Sales and marketing	1,205
General and administrative	119
Total operating expenses	1,794
Operating income	**1,326**
Nonoperating income and expenses:	
Interest income (net)	82
Other revenues and expenses	(7)
Income before income taxes	1,401
Provision for income taxes	448
Net income	**$ 953**
Earnings per share	**$ 3.15**

MICROSOFT CORPORATION
Balance Sheet
June 30, 1993
(in millions)

Assets	
Current assets	
Cash and short-term investments	$2,290
Accounts receivable	338
Inventories	127
Other current assets	95
Total current assets	2,850
Noncurrent assets	
Property, plant, and equipment (net)	867
Other noncurrent assets	88
Total assets	$3,805
Liabilities	
Current liabilities	
Accounts payable	$ 239
Accrued compensation	86
Income taxes payable	127
Other current liabilities	111
Total current liabilities	563
Noncurrent liabilities	0
Stockholders' equity	
Common stock and paid-in-capital	1,086
Retained earnings	2,156
Total stockholders' equity	3,242
Total liabilities and stockholders' equity	$3,805

SUMMARY

Company managers, auditors, government regulators, and information intermediaries including analysts and information services are the key players in the communication of accounting information. Management of the reporting company must decide on the appropriate format (categories) and level of detail to be presented in their financial statements. They must also provide extensive additional disclosures in the notes to financial statements. The conceptual framework of accounting, in particular the qualitative characteristics of financial statements and constraints, provide guidance in this process. Financial statement announcements from public companies are usually first transmitted to users through electronic information services. These include earnings press releases, annual and quarterly reports, and the more detailed reports required by the SEC. Analysts play a major role in making this and other information available to average investors through their stock recommendations and earnings forecasts. These analysts consider the company's selection from the alternative measurement rules available under GAAP in making their assessments. A major focus of future chapters, which analyze each element of the financial statements, will be the financial statement effects of these alternative methods.

KEY TERMS

Comparable Information Information that can be compared across businesses. 252

Conservatism Care should be taken not to overstate assets and revenues or understate liabilities and expenses. 254

Consistent Information Information that can be compared over time. 252

Cost-Benefit Constraint The benefits of accounting for and reporting information should outweigh the costs. 254

Cumulative Effects of Changes in Accounting Methods Amount reflected on the income statement for adjustments made to balance sheet accounts when applying different accounting principles. *265*

Current Assets Assets that will be turned into cash or expire (be used up) within the longer of one year or the operating cycle. *256*

Current Liabilities Obligations to be paid with current assets normally within one year. *256*

Discontinued Operations Results from the disposal of a major segment of the business; reported net of income tax effects. *264*

Earnings Forecasts Predictions of earnings for future accounting periods. *247*

Extraordinary Items Gains and losses that are both unusual in nature and infrequent in occurrence; they are reported net of tax on the income statement. *265*

Form 8-K The report used by publicly traded companies to disclose any material event not previously reported that is important to investors. *275*

Form 10-K The annual report that publicly traded companies must file with the SEC. *274*

Form 10-Q The quarterly report that publicly traded companies must file with the SEC. *275*

Full-Disclosure Principle The requirement to disclose all relevant economic information of the business. *252*

Gross Margin (gross profit) Net sales less cost of goods sold. *263*

Income before Income Taxes (Pretax Earnings) Revenues less all expenses except income tax expense. *264*

Income from Operations (Operating Income) Net sales less cost of goods sold and other operating expenses. *263*

Institutional Investors Managers of pension, mutual, endowment, and other funds that invest on the behalf of others. *250*

Lenders (Creditors) Suppliers and financial institutions that lend money to companies. *251*

Material Amounts Amounts large enough to influence a user's decision. *254*

Par Value A legal amount per share established by the board of directors; it establishes the minimum amount a stockholder must contribute and has no relationship to the market price of the stock. *259*

Press Release A written public news announcement that is normally distributed to major news services. *270*

Private Investors Individuals who purchase shares in companies. *251*

Relevant Information Information that can influence a decision; it is timely and has predictive and/or feedback value. *252*

Reliable Information Information that is accurate, unbiased, and verifiable. *252*

Unqualified Audit Opinion (Clean Audit Opinion) Auditors' statement that the financial statements are fair presentations in all material respects in conformity with GAAP. *246*

QUESTIONS

1. Describe the roles and responsibilities of management and independent auditors in the financial reporting process.
2. Define the following three users of financial accounting disclosures and the relationships among them: Financial analysts, private investors, and institutional investors.
3. Briefly describe the role of information services in the communication of financial information.
4. Briefly explain why a conceptual framework of accounting is important.
5. Explain why information must be relevant and reliable to be useful.
6. Briefly explain the cost-benefit constraint.
7. The two secondary characteristics of accounting information involve what two comparisons?

8. What are the two primary characteristics of accounting information? Briefly explain each.
9. List the six categories that constitute the conceptual framework of accounting. Briefly explain each.
10. List and briefly explain the four accounting constraints.
11. Explain the basic difference between accrual basis accounting and cash basis accounting.
12. What basis of accounting is required by GAAP on the *(a)* income statement, *(b)* balance sheet, and *(c)* statement of cash flows?
13. What is the primary purpose of the classifications of the information presented on financial statements?
14. What are the five major classifications on the income statement?
15. Define extraordinary items. Why should they be reported separately on the income statement?
16. List the six major classifications reported on a balance sheet.
17. Briefly define *(a)* current assets, *(b)* current liabilities, *(c)* working capital, and *(d)* current ratio.
18. For operational assets, as reported on the balance sheet, explain *(a)* cost, *(b)* accumulated depreciation, *(c)* book value, and *(d)* carrying value.
19. Briefly explain the major classifications of stockholders' equity for a corporation.
20. What are the three major classifications on a statement of cash flows?
21. List the four elements reported on the income statement. Explain the primary difference between revenues and gains and expenses and losses.
22. What are the three major categories of notes or footnotes presented in annual reports? Cite an example of each.
23. Briefly explain the normal sequence and form of financial reports produced by private companies in a typical year.
24. Briefly explain the normal sequence and form of financial reports produced by public companies in a typical year.

EXERCISES

E5–1 Matching Players in the Accounting Communication Process with Their Definitions

Match each player with the related definition by entering the appropriate letter in the space provided.

Players

_________ (1) SEC

_________ (2) Independent auditors

_________ (3) Institutional investors

_________ (4) CEO and CFO

_________ (5) Creditors

_________ (6) Financial analysts

_________ (7) Private investors

_________ (8) Information services

Definitions

A. Advisors who analyze financial and other economic information to form forecasts and stock recommendations.
B. Financial institutions and suppliers who lend money to the company.
C. Chief executive officer and chief financial officer who have primary responsibility for the information presented in financial statements.
D. Independent CPAs who examine financial statements and attest to their fairness.
E. Securities and Exchange Commission, which regulates financial disclosure requirements.
F. Companies that gather, combine, and transmit (paper and electronic) financial and related information from various sources.
G. Individuals who purchase shares in companies.
H. Managers of pension, mutual, and endowment funds that invest on the behalf of others.

E5–2 Matching Definitions with Terms from the Conceptual Framework

Match each definition with its related term by entering the appropriate letter in the space provided.

Terms

_________ (1) Users

_________ (2) Cost-benefit constraint

_________ (3) Secondary qualities

_________ (4) Objective of financial reporting

_________ (5) Immaterial amounts

_________ (6) Primary qualities

Definitions

A. Consistency with prior periods and comparability with other entities.
B. Provide economic information useful to external decision makers.
C. Decision makers who need financial information.
D. Relevance to decisions and reliability.
E. Amounts not large enough to influence important decisions.
F. Cost of developing and reporting should be less than the use value to decision makers.

E5–3 Matching Definitions with Terms from the Conceptual Framework

Match each definition with its related term by entering the appropriate letter in the space provided.

Terms

_________ (1) Primary users of financial statements

_________ (2) Broad objective of financial reporting

_________ (3) Qualitative characteristics of financial statements

_________ (4) Implementation assumptions

_________ (5) Elements of financial statements

_________ (6) Implementation principles

_________ (7) Exceptions to implementation principles

_________ (8) Detailed accounting practices and procedures

_________ (9) None of the above

Definitions

A. To prepare the income tax return of the business.
B. Separate entity, continuity, time period, and unit of measure.
C. Guidelines to apply the assumptions and principles.
D. To provide economic information that is useful in making decisions.
E. Relevance and reliability.
F. Investors, creditors, and those who advise and represent them (decision makers).
G. Materiality, cost-benefit, conservatism, industry peculiarities.
H. Assets, liabilities, owners' equity, revenues, expenses, gains, and losses.
I. Revenue, cost, matching, full disclosure.

E5–4 Matching Financial Statements with the Elements of Financial Statements

Match each financial statement with the items presented on it by entering the appropriate letter in the space provided.

Elements of Financial Statements

_________ (1) Liabilities

_________ (2) Cash from operating activities

_________ (3) Losses

_________ (4) Assets

_________ (5) Revenues

_________ (6) Cash from financing activities

_________ (7) Gains

_________ (8) Owners' equity

_________ (9) Expenses

_________ (10) Assets owned by a stockholder

Financial Statements

A. Income statement
B. Balance sheet
C. Cash flow statement
D. None of the above

E5–5 *Matching Definitions with Elements of Financial Statements*

Match each element to its related definition by entering the appropriate letter in the space provided.

Elements

Income statement:

_________ (1) Revenues

_________ (2) Expenses

_________ (3) Gains

_________ (4) Losses

Balance sheet:

_________ (5) Assets

_________ (6) Liabilities

_________ (7) Owners' equity

Definitions

A. Cash received during the accounting period.
B. Debts or obligations from past transactions to be paid with assets or services.
C. Increase in net assets from peripheral transactions.
D. Outflow of net assets from ongoing operations.
E. Financing provided by owners and operations.
F. Inflow of net assets from major ongoing operations.
G. Cash paid out during the period.
H. Probable future economic benefits; owned by the entity from past transactions.
I. Decrease in net assets from peripheral transactions.

E5–6 *Matching Definitions with Income Statement-Related Terms*

Below are terms related to the income statement. Match each definition with its related term by entering the appropriate letter in the space provided.

Terms

_________ (1) Cost of goods sold

_________ (2) Interest expense

_________ (3) Extraordinary items

_________ (4) Service revenue

_________ (5) Income tax expense on operations

_________ (6) Income before extraordinary items

_________ (7) Net income

_________ (8) Gross margin on sales

_________ (9) EPS

_________ (10) Operating expenses

_________ (11) Pretax income from operations

Definitions

A. Sales revenue minus cost of goods sold.
B. Items that are both unusual and infrequent.
C. Sales of services for cash or on credit.
D. Revenues + Gains – Expenses – Losses including effects of discontinued operations, extraordinary items, and cumulative effects of accounting changes (if any).
E. Amount of resources used to purchase or produce the goods that were sold during the reporting period.
F. Income tax on revenues minus operating expenses.
G. Cost of money (borrowing) over time.
H. Net income divided by average shares outstanding.
I. Income before unusual and infrequent items and the related income tax.
J. Total expenses directly related to operations.
K. Income before all income tax and before discontinued operations, extraordinary items, and cumulative effects of accounting changes (if any).
L. None of the above.

E5–7 *Ordering the Classifications on a Typical Balance Sheet*

Following is a list of classifications on the balance sheet. Number them in the order in which they normally appear on a balance sheet.

No.	Title
_________	Current liabilities
_________	Long-term liabilities
_________	Long-term investments
_________	Intangible assets
_________	Operational assets (property, plant, and equipment)
_________	Current assets
_________	Retained earnings
_________	Contributed capital
_________	Other noncurrent assets
_________	Deferred charges

E5–8 Matching Definitions with Information Releases Made by Public Companies

Below are the titles of various information releases. Match each definition with the related release by entering the appropriate letter in the space provided.

Information Release	Definition
________ (1) Annual report	A. Written public news announcement that is normally distributed to major news services.
________ (2) Form 8-K	B. Report containing the four basic statements for the year, related notes, and often statements by management and auditors.
________ (3) Press release	C. Brief unaudited report for quarter normally containing summary income statement and balance sheet (unaudited).
________ (4) Form 10-Q	D. Annual report filed by public companies with the SEC that contains additional detailed financial information.
________ (5) Quarterly report	E. Quarterly report filed by public companies with the SEC that contains additional unaudited financial information.
________ (6) Form 10-K	F. Report of special events (e.g., auditor changes, mergers) filed by public companies with the SEC.

E5–9 Matching Information Items to Financial Reports

Below are information items included in various financial reports. Match each information item with the report(s) where it would most likely be found by entering the appropriate letter(s) in the space provided.

Information Item	Report
________ (1) Summarized financial data for 5- or 10-year period.	A. Annual report
________ (2) Initial announcement of quarterly earnings.	B. Form 8-K
________ (3) Announcement of a change in auditors.	C. Press release
________ (4) Complete quarterly income statement, balance sheet, and cash flow statement.	D. Form 10-Q
________ (5) The four basic financial statements for the year.	E. Quarterly report
________ (6) Summarized income statement information for the quarter.	F. Form 10-K
________ (7) Detailed discussion of the company's competition.	G. None of the above
________ (8) Notes to financial statements.	
________ (9) A description of those responsible for the financial statements.	
________ (10) Initial announcement of hiring of new vice president for sales.	

E5–10 Reporting Operational Assets on the Balance Sheet

On January 1, 19B, Laura Anne's Bakery purchased a new oven for $6,800. It was expected that the oven would be used for four years and then would be sold for $2,000 on January 1, 19F. Prepare a schedule showing the amounts that would be reported on the balance sheets prepared at the end of 19B, 19C, 19D, and 19E for the oven (at cost), accumulated depreciation, and net book value.

E5–11 Recording Stock Issuances with Par Value and Reporting Stockholders' Equity

On February 17, 19A, Cayuga Kennels was organized to provide temporary care for dogs and cats of vacationing owners. The two founders contributed a total of $30,000 in exchange for 10,000 shares of $.01 par value stock. During 19A, Cayuga Kennels earned net income of $18,000 and paid no dividends.

Required:

1. Prepare the journal entry required to record the stock issuance on February 17, 19A. Write a brief explanation of the entry.
2. Prepare the stockholders' equity section of Cayuga Kennels' balance sheet at December 31, 19A.

E5–12 Recording Stock Issuances with Par Value

Ben & Jerry's

In a recent year, Ben & Jerry's Homemade, Inc., maker of Ben & Jerry's ice cream and frozen yogurt, issued 12,000 shares of its $.033 par value stock for $96,000 (these numbers are rounded). These additional shares were issued under a stock purchase plan available to current shareholders that allows them to purchase additional newly issued shares directly from Ben & Jerry's without paying a brokerage commission. Prepare the journal entry required to record the stock issuance.

E5–13 Recording Stock Issuances with Par Value

PolyGram Group

PolyGram Group, a Dutch company, is one of the three largest recorded music companies in the world. Its popular artists include Bryan Adams, Sting, U2, The Scorpions, Def Leppard, and many others. Its financial statements are denominated in Netherlands Guilders (symbol "NLG"). To help finance its recent purchase of the legendary Motown recording label (Temptations, Boyz II Men), PolyGram issued 10 million additional shares (par value per share NLG 0.50) for NLG 599 million. Prepare the journal entry required to record the stock issuance.

E5–14 Interpreting Changes in Stockholders' Equity

Callaway Golf

Callaway Golf recently reported the following December 31 balances in its stockholders' equity accounts (in thousands):

	Current Year	Prior Year
Common stock	$ 169	$ 140
Paid-in capital	57,807	31,948
Retained earnings	58,601	17,662
Total shareholders' equity	$116,577	$ 49,750

During the current year, Callaway reported net income of $42,862. Assume that the only two other transactions that affected stockholders' equity during the current year were a single stock issuance and a single cash dividend which was declared and paid during the current year.

Required:

Recreate the two journal entries reflecting the stock issuance and dividend.

E5–15 Preparing a Classified Balance Sheet

Compaq Computer

Compaq Computer Corporation began as the first manufacturer of portable computers compatible with the MS-DOS operating system. These sewing machine-sized computers found their most important market niche with independent CPAs for whom portability was a must. Today, Compaq is the leading manufacturer of computers compatible with the MS-DOS and Windows operating systems. Compaq sells a wide variety of desktop, portable, and home computers, as well as powerful servers that run business networks. Presented below are the items listed on its recent balance sheet (in millions) presented in alphabetical order:

Accounts payable	$ 637
Accounts receivable, net	1,377
Cash and cash equivalents	627
Common stock and capital in excess of par value	586
Deferred income taxes (noncurrent)	186 credit
Income taxes payable	69
Inventories	1,123
Other current liabilities	538
Other noncurrent assets	14
Prepaid expenses	164
Property, plant, and equipment, less accumulated depreciation	779
Retained earnings	2,068

Required:

Prepare a classified consolidated balance sheet for Compaq for the current year (ended December 31, 19A) using the categories presented in the chapter.

Marvel Entertainment Group

E5–16 Preparing a Classified Balance Sheet (Challenging)

Marvel Entertainment Group is a leading entertainment company aimed at the youth market. Its products include Marvel Comics (X-Men, Captain America, Spider Man, Fantastic Four) and Fleer sports picture trading cards (baseball, basketball, hockey, football). Marvel is 80% owned by billionaire Ronald O. Perelman; the remaining 20% of the stock is publicly traded on the New York Stock Exchange under the symbol MRV. Presented below are the items listed on its recent balance sheet (in millions) presented in alphabetical order:

Accounts payable	19.9
Accounts receivable, net	77.9
Accrued expenses and other	44.5
Additional paid-in capital	47.0
Cash	17.0
Common stock, $ .01 par value; 250,000,000 shares authorized, 97,642,992 shares issued and outstanding at December 31, 19A	1.0
Current portion of long-term debt	45.1
Deferred charges and other (noncurrent)	13.9
Deferred income taxes (current)	8.3 debit
Due to former stockholders of Fleer (long-term)	0.1
Goodwill, net	274.6
Inventories	23.2
Investment in and advances to Toy Biz	14.2
Long-term debt	205.1
Other long-term liabilities	10.0
Prepaid expenses and other	6.1
Property, plant and equipment, net	12.4
Retained earnings (including cumulative translation adjustment)	99.3
Trademarks and other intangibles, net	24.4

Required:

1. Prepare a classified consolidated balance sheet for Marvel Entertainment for the current year (ended December 31, 19A) using the categories presented in the chapter.
2. Four of the items end in the term *net*. Explain what this term means in each case.

E5–17 Analyzing Income Statement Relationships

Supply the missing dollar amounts for the 19B income statement of Ultimate Style Company for each of the following independent cases:

	Case A	**Case B**	**Case C**	**Case D**	**Case E**
Sales revenue	$900	$700	$410	$?	$?
Selling expense	?	150	80	400	250
Cost of goods sold	?	380	?	500	310
Income tax expense	?	30	20	40	30
Gross margin	400	?	?	?	440
Pretax income	200	90	?	190	?
Administrative expense	150	?	60	100	80
Net income	170	?	50	?	80

E5–18 Preparing a Multiple-Step Income Statement Using the Gross Margin Ratio

The following data were taken from the records of Village Corporation at December 31, 19B:

Gross margin (35% ratio)	$24,500
Selling (distribution) expense	8,000
Administrative expense	?
Pretax income	12,000
Income tax rate	30%
Shares of stock outstanding	3,000

Required:

Prepare a complete multiple-step income statement for the company (showing both gross profit and income from operations). Show all computations. (Hint: Set up the side captions starting with sales revenue and ending with earnings per share; rely on the percentages given.)

E5–19 Preparing Single- and Multiple-Step Income Statements Using the Gross Margin Ratio

The following data were taken from the records of Kimberly Appliances, Incorporated, at December 31, 19D:

Sales revenue `	$120,000
Administrative expense	10,000
Selling (distribution) expense	18,000
Income tax rate	25%
Gross margin ratio	40%
Shares of stock outstanding	2,000

Required:

1. Prepare a complete single-step income statement for the company. Show all computations. (Hint: Set up side captions starting with sales revenue and ending with earnings per share; rely on the percentages given.)
2. Prepare a complete multiple-step income statement for the company (showing both gross profit and income from operations).

E5–20 Understanding The Wall Street Journal *Earnings Digest*

Callaway Golf

For many public companies, *The Wall Street Journal* prints summary information from quarterly earnings announcements in its "Digest of Earnings Reports" on the day after the announcement. Printed below is the information reported in *The Wall Street Journal* "Digest" for Callaway Golf's recent fourth quarter.

CALLAWAY GOLF CO. (N)

Quar Dec 31:	1994	1993
Sales	$115,180,000	$68,248,000
Net income	19,526,000	10,334,000
Avg shares	36,530,000	a35,802,000
Shr earns (primary)		
Net income	.53	a.29
Year:		
Sales	448,729,000	254,645,000
Income	78,022,000	41,204,000
Acctg adj	....	b1,658,000
Net income	78,022,000	42,862,000
Avg shares	36,552,000	a34,482,000
Shr earns (primary):		
Income	2.13	a1.19
Net income	2.13	a1.24
Shr earns (fully diluted):		
Income	2.13	a1.17
Net Income	2.13	a1.22

a-Adjusted for a two-for-one stock split paid in March 1994.
b-Cumulative effect on prior periods of an accounting change.

Required:

Using this information and the Callaway financial statements presented in the chapter, answer the following questions.

1. Match the common abbreviations used in the digest with the five major sections of the income statement presented in the chapter by placing the appropriate letter in front of each abbreviation.

Abbreviation	Income Statement Section
________ (1) Acctg adj	A. Continuing operations
________ (2) Extrd chg	B. Discontinued operations
________ (3) Inco dis op	C. Extraordinary items
________ (4) Inco cnt op	D. Cumulative effect of changes in accounting methods
________ (5) Shr earns	E. Earnings per share
________ (6) Extrd credit	

2. What accounts for the difference between the two earnings per share (primary) numbers reported for 1993?

E5–21 *Understanding an Income Statement with Extraordinary Items*

The following data were taken from the year-end records of Southmost Company. You are to fill in all of the missing amounts. Show computations.

	Independent Cases	
Income Statement Items	**Case A**	**Case B**
Gross sales revenue	$160,000	$232,000
Sales returns and allowances	?	18,000
Net sales revenue	?	?
Cost of goods sold	(68%) ?	?
Gross margin on sales	?	(30%) ?
Operating expenses	18,500	?
Pretax income	?	20,000
Income tax expense (20%)	?	?
Income before extraordinary items	?	?
Extraordinary items	(gain) 10,000	(loss) 2,000
Less: Income tax (20%)	?	?
Net income	?	?
EPS (10,000 shares)	3.00	?

E5–22 Completing a Partial Income Statement with Income Tax and an Extraordinary Loss

Skylark Corporation (common stock, 10,000 shares outstanding) is preparing the income statement for the year ended December 31, 19D. The pretax operating income was $200,000, and there was a $50,000 pretax loss in earthquake damages to one of the plants (properly classified as an extraordinary item). Total tax expense is $45,000 on the basis of a 30% tax rate on operations and on the earthquake loss.

Required:

1. Complete the following income statement:

   (Already completed to here)
   Pretax operating income
   Less: Income tax
   Income before extraordinary items:
   Extraordinary loss
   Less: Income tax
   Net income
   Earnings per share

2. Why is the income tax of $45,000 separated into two parts?

E5–23 Preparing a Single-Step Income Statement with Discontinued Operations and Cumulative Effects of Accounting Changes (Challenging)

Adolph Coors Company

Adolph Coors Company, established in 1873, is the third-largest brewer of beer in the United States. Its products include Coors, Coors LIGHT, ZIMA, and many other malt beverages. Recently, Coors discontinued its ceramics, aluminum, packaging, and technology-based developmental businesses. In the same year, it reported two changes in accounting methods mandated by the FASB. The items reported on its income statement for that year (ended December 26, 19A) are presented below (in thousands) in alphabetical order:

Cost of goods sold	1,035,544
Cumulative effect of change in accounting for income taxes	30,500
Cumulative effect of change in accounting for postretirement benefits (net of tax)	(38,800)
Income tax expense	22,900
Interest expense	16,014
Interest income	255
Marketing, general and administrative	429,573
Miscellaneous income—net	1,087
Net loss from discontinued operations	29,415
Net sales	1,550,788
Research and project development	12,370

Required:

Using appropriate headings and subtotals, prepare a single-step consolidated income statement for the company starting with the caption "Net sales," ending with the caption "Net income (loss)."

E5–24 Preparing a Multiple-Step Income Statement (both formats) with Discontinued Operations and Cumulative Effects of Accounting Changes (Challenging)

Adolph Coors Company

Use the listing of Adolph Coors Company's income statement information presented in the above exercise to complete this exercise.

Required:

1. Using appropriate headings and subtotals, prepare a multiple-step consolidated income statement using the one-subtotal and two-subtotal formats presented in the chapter. Both versions of the income statement should start with the caption "Net sales" and end with the caption "Net income (loss)."

2. What information does each of the multiple-step formats emphasize that the single-step income statement does not?

E5–25 *Preparing a Simple Statement of Cash Flows*

At the end of the annual reporting period, December 31, 19B, the records of Pluto Company showed the following:

a. Cash account: beginning balance, $40,000; ending balance, $27,000.

b. From the income statement:

(1)	Cash revenues	$190,000
(2)	Cash expenses	144,000

c. From the balance sheet:

(1) Additional capital stock sold: common stock, par $10; sold 3,000 shares at $12 per share.

(2) Borrowed cash on a long-term note, $20,000.

(3) Purchased equipment for use in the business: paid cash, $80,000.

(4) Paid a long-term note, $12,000.

(5) Declared and paid a cash dividend, $15,000.

(6) Purchased land for employee parking lot, $8,000.

Required:

Prepare the 19B statement of cash flows for Pluto Company using the direct method as discussed in Chapter 4.

PROBLEMS

P5–1 *Matching Definitions with Balance Sheet-Related Terms*

Below are terms related to the balance sheet. Match each definition with its related term by entering the appropriate letter in the space provided.

Terms

_______ (1) Retained earnings
_______ (2) Current liabilities
_______ (3) Liquidity
_______ (4) Contra-asset account
_______ (5) Accumulated depreciation
_______ (6) Intangible assets
_______ (7) Other assets
_______ (8) Shares outstanding
_______ (9) Normal operating cycle
_______ (10) Book value
_______ (11) Working capital
_______ (12) Liabilities
_______ (13) Operational assets
_______ (14) Shareholders' equity
_______ (15) Current assets
_______ (16) Assets
_______ (17) Long-term liabilities

Definitions

A. A miscellaneous category of assets.
B. Current assets minus current liabilities.
C. Total assets minus total liabilities.
D. Nearness of assets to cash (in time).
E. Assets expected to be collected in cash within one year or operating cycle, if longer.
F. Same as carrying value; cost less accumulated depreciation to date.
G. Accumulated earnings minus accumulated dividends.
H. Asset offset account (subtracted from asset).
I. Balance of the Common Stock account divided by the par value per share.
J. Assets that do not have physical substance.
K. Probable future economic benefits owned by the entity from past transactions.
L. Liabilities expected to be paid out of current assets normally within the next year.
M. The average cash-to-cash time involved in the operations of the business.
N. Sum of the annual depreciation expense on an asset from its acquisition to the current date.
O. All liabilities not classified as current liabilities.
P. Property, plant, and equipment.
Q. Debts or obligations from past transactions to be paid with assets or services.
R. None of the above.

P5–2 *Matching Transactions with Concepts*

Below are listed the concepts of accounting. Match each transaction with its related concept by entering the appropriate letter in the space provided. Use one letter for each blank.

Concepts:

_________ (1) Users of financial statements

_________ (2) Objective of financial statements

Qualitative Characteristics:

_________ (3) Relevance

_________ (4) Reliability

Implementation Assumptions:

_________ (5) Separate entity

_________ (6) Continuity

_________ (7) Unit of measure

_________ (8) Time period

Elements of Financial Statements:

_________ (9) Revenues

_________ (10) Expenses

_________ (11) Gains

_________ (12) Losses

_________ (13) Assets

_________ (14) Liabilities

_________ (15) Stockholders' equity

Implementation Principles:

_________ (16) Cost

_________ (17) Revenue

_________ (18) Matching

_________ (19) Full disclosure

Constraints of Accounting:

_________ (20) Materiality threshold

_________ (21) Cost-benefit constraint

_________ (22) Conservatism constraint

_________ (23) Industry peculiarities

Transactions

A. Recorded a $1,000 sale of merchandise on credit.
B. Counted (inventoried) the unsold items at the end of the period and valued them in dollars.
C. Acquired a vehicle for use in operating the business.
D. Reported the amount of depreciation expense because it likely will affect important decisions of statement users.
E. Identified as the investors, creditors, and others interested in the business.
F. Used special accounting approaches because of the uniqueness of the industry.
G. Sold and issued bonds payable of $1 million.
H. Paid a contractor for an addition to the building with $10,000 cash and $20,000 market value of the stock of the company ($30,000 was deemed to be the cash equivalent price).
I. Engaged an outside independent CPA to audit the financial statements.
J. Sold merchandise and services for cash and on credit during the year; then determined the cost of those goods sold and the cost of rendering those services.
K. Established an accounting policy that sales revenue shall be recognized only when ownership to the goods sold passes to the customer.
L. To design and prepare the financial statements to assist the users in making decisions.
M. Established a policy not to include in the financial statements the personal financial affairs of the owners of the business.
N. Sold an asset at a loss that was a peripheral or incidental transaction.
O. The user value of a special financial report exceeds the cost of preparing it.
P. Valued an asset, such as inventory, at less than its purchase cost because the replacement cost is less.
Q. Dated the income statement "For the Year Ended December 31, 19B."
R. Used services from outsiders—paid cash for some and the remainder on credit.
S. Acquired an asset (a pencil sharpener that will have a useful life of five years) and recorded it as an expense when purchased for $1.99.
T. Disclosed in the financial statements all relevant financial information about the business; necessitated the use of notes to the financial statements.
U. Sold an asset at a gain that was a peripheral or incidental transaction.
V. Assets of $500,000 – Liabilities of $300,000 = Stockholders' Equity of $200,000.
W. Accounting and reporting assumes a "going concern."

P5–3 *Preparing a Balance Sheet and Analyzing Some of Its Parts*

King Jewelers is developing the annual financial statements for 19C. The following amounts were correct at December 31, 19C: cash, $42,000; accounts receivable, $51,300; merchandise inventory, $110,000; prepaid insurance, $800; investment in stock of Z corporation (long-term), $26,000; store equipment, $48,000; used store equipment held for disposal, $7,000; accumulated depreciation, store equipment, $9,600; accounts payable, $42,000; long-term note payable, $30,000; income taxes payable, $7,000; retained earnings, $86,500; and common stock, 100,000 shares outstanding, par $1 per share (originally sold and issued at $1.10 per share).

Required:

1. Based on the above data, prepare a 19C balance sheet. Use the following major captions (list the individual items under these captions):
   Assets: Current assets, Long-term investments, Operational assets, and Other assets.
   Liabilities: Current liabilities and Long-term liabilities.
   Stockholders' equity: Contributed capital and Retained earnings.
2. What is the book or carrying value of the
   a. Inventory?
   b. Accounts receivable?
   c. Store equipment?
   d. Note payable (long-term)?
   Explain what these values mean.
3. What is the amount of working capital?

P5–4 *Reporting Building, Land, and Depreciation Expense*

Stewart Company is preparing the balance sheet at December 31, 19X. The following assets are to be reported:

a. Building, purchased 15 years ago (counting 19X): original cost, $450,000; estimated useful life, 25 years from date of purchase; and no residual value.

b. Land, purchased 15 years ago (counting 19X): original cost, $70,000.

Required:

1. Show how the two assets should be reported on the balance sheet. What is the total book value of these operational assets?
2. What amount of depreciation expense should be reported on the 19X income statement? Show computations.

P5–5 *Preparing the Stockholders' Equity Section of a Balance Sheet*

At the end of the 19A annual reporting period, the balance sheet of Mesa Corporation showed the following:

MESA CORPORATION
Balance Sheet
At December 31, 19A

Stockholders' Equity	
Contributed capital:	
Common stock (par $10, 7,000 shares)	$ 70,000
Contributed capital in excess of par	10,000
Total contributed capital	$ 80,000
Retained earnings:	
Ending balance	50,000
Total stockholders' equity	$130,000

During 19B, the following selected transactions (summarized) were completed:

a. Sold and issued 1,000 shares of common stock at $15 cash per share (at year-end).

b. Net income, $40,000.

c. Declared and paid a cash dividend on the beginning shares outstanding of $3 per share.

Required:

1. Prepare the stockholders' equity section of the balance sheet at December 31, 19B.
2. Give the journal entry to record the sale and issuance of the 1,000 shares of common stock.

P5–6 Completing an Income Statement with Income Tax, Extraordinary Gain, and EPS

Jetton Company, Inc., was organized on January 1, 19A. On that date, a total of 10,000 shares of common stock was issued to three owners for $125,000 cash.

At the end of the first year, December 31, 19A, the company records showed the following:

a. Merchandise sold: for cash, $225,000; on credit, $35,000.
b. Interest on debt, $2,000, paid in cash.
c. Salaries and wages paid in cash, $60,000.
d. Other operating expenses, $7,000, incurred (used) but not yet paid.
e. Cost of the merchandise sold, $110,000.
f. Services sold (all for cash), $15,000.
g. Extraordinary gain, $10,000 (subject to income tax).
h. Average corporate income tax rate on all items, 25%.

Required:

1. Complete the following income statement for the year, 19A:

Revenues
Expenses:
  Cost of goods sold
  Operating expenses
  Interest expense
Pretax income from operations
  Income tax expense
Income before extraordinary item
Extraordinary gain
  Less: Income tax
Net income
EPS

2. What was the total amount of income tax for 19A?
3. Explain why the cash paid by the organizers is not considered to be revenue.

P5–7 Preparing Both an Income Statement and Balance Sheet from a Trial Balance

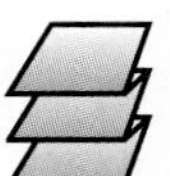

Thomas Real Estate Company (organized as a corporation on April 1, 19A) has completed the accounting cycle for the second year, ended March 31, 19C. Thomas also has completed a correct trial balance as follows:

THOMAS REAL ESTATE COMPANY
Trial Balance
At March 31, 19C

Account Titles	Debit	Credit
Cash	$ 53,000	
Accounts receivable	44,800	
Office supplies inventory	300	
Automobiles (company cars)	30,000	
Accumulated depreciation, automobiles		$ 10,000
Office equipment	3,000	
Accumulated depreciation, office equipment		1,000
Accounts payable		20,250
Income taxes payable		0
Salaries and commissions payable		1,500
Note payable, long-term		30,000
Capital stock (par $1; 30,000 shares)		30,000
Contributed capital in excess of par		5,000
Retained earnings (on April 1, 19B)		7,350
Dividends declared and paid during the current year	8,000	
Sales commissions earned		77,000

Management fees earned		13,000
Operating expenses (detail omitted to conserve your time)	48,000	
Depreciation expense (on autos and including $500 on office equipment)	5,500	
Interest expense	2,500	
Income tax expense (not yet computed)		
Totals	$195,100	$195,100

Required:

1. Complete the financial statements, as follows:
   a. Income statement for the reporting year ended March 31, 19C. Include income tax expense, assuming a 30% tax rate. Use the following major captions: Revenues, Expenses, Pretax income, Income tax, Net income, and EPS (list each item under these captions).
   b. Balance sheet at the end of the reporting year, March 31, 19C. Include (1) income taxes for the current year in income taxes payable and (2) dividends in retained earnings. Use the captions that follow (list each item under these captions).

Assets
Current assets
Operational assets

Liabilities
Current liabilities
Long-term liabilities

Stockholders' Equity
Contributed capital
Retained earnings

2. Give the journal entry to record income taxes for the year (not yet paid).

P5–8 Preparing a Simple Statement of Cash Flows

Blackwell Corporation is preparing its annual financial statements at December 31, 19A. The following cash flow data have been determined to be correct for 19A:

a. Sales and service revenues, $270,000, including $32,000 on credit and not yet collected.
b. Expenses, $247,000, including $15,000 noncash items.
c. Borrowed cash, $25,000, on a three-year note payable (10% interest payable each year-end). The note was dated December 31, 19A.
d. Purchased a new delivery truck for $12,000 cash.
e. Issued stock for $22,000 cash.
f. Purchased a tract of land for a future building site that cost $36,000; paid cash.
g. Cash account: balance, January 1, 19A, $36,000; and balance, December 31, 19A, $41,000.

Required:

Prepare the 19A statement of cash flows for Blackwell Corporation. The section reporting cash flows from operations should indicate revenues received in cash and expenses paid in cash (the direct method).

P5–9 A Challenging Analysis of the Amounts on an Income Statement

Below is a partially completed income statement of Reginold Corporation for the year ended December 31, 19B.

Items	Other Data	Amounts	
Net sales revenue			$260,000
Cost of goods sold			
Gross margin on sales	Gross margin as percent of sales, 35%		
Expenses:			
Selling expense			
General and administrative expense		$28,000	
Interest expense		4,000	
Total expenses			
Pretax income			
Income tax on operations			
Income before extraordinary items:			
Extraordinary gain		12,000	
Income tax effect			
Net extraordinary gain			
Net income			
EPS (on common stock):			
Income before extraordinary gain			1.20
Extraordinary gain			
Net income			

Required:

Based on the data given above, and assuming (1) a 20% income tax rate on all items and (2) 25,000 common shares outstanding, complete the above income statement. Show all computations.

CASES

C5–1 *Analyzing Financial Statements*

The amounts listed below were selected from the annual financial statements for Genesis Corporation at December 31, 19C (end of the third year of operations):

From the 19C income statement:	
Sales revenue	$275,000
Cost of goods sold	(170,000)
All other expenses (including income tax)	(95,000)
Net income	$ 10,000
From the December 31, 19C, balance sheet:	
Current assets	$ 90,000
All other assets	212,000
Total assets	$302,000
Current liabilities	$ 40,000
Long-term liabilities	66,000
Capital stock (par $10)	100,000
Contributed capital in excess of par	16,000
Retained earnings	80,000
Total liabilities and stockholders' equity	$302,000

Required:

Analyze the data on the 19C financial statements of Genesis by answering the questions that follow. Show computations.

1. What was the gross margin on sales?
2. What was the amount of EPS?
3. What was the amount of working capital?

4. If the income tax rate was 25%, what was the amount of pretax income?
5. What was the average sales price per share of the capital stock?
6. Assuming no dividends were declared or paid during 19C, what was the beginning balance (January 1, 19C) of retained earnings?

C5–2 *Analyzing Some Simple Errors to Determine the Effects of Each on Income, Assets, and Liabilities*

Megan Company (not a corporation) was careless about its financial records during its first year of operations, 19A. It is December 31, 19A, end of the annual accounting period. An outside CPA examined the records and discovered numerous errors. All of those errors are described below. Assume each error is independent of the others.

Required:

Analyze each error and indicate its effect on 19A and 19B income, assets, and liabilities if not corrected. Do not assume any other errors. Use these codes to indicate the effect of each dollar amount: O = Overstated, U = Understated, and N = No effect. Write an explanation of your analysis of each transaction to support your response.

	Effect On					
	Net Income		Assets		Liabilities	
Independent Errors	19A	19B	19A	19B	19A	19B
a. Depreciation expense for 19A, not recorded in 19A, $950.	O $950	N	O $950	O $950	N	N
b. Wages earned by employees during 19A not recorded or paid in 19A but will be paid in 19B, $500.						
c. Revenue earned during 19A but not collected or recorded until 19B, $600.						
d. Amount paid in 19A and recorded as expense in 19A but not an expense until 19B, $200.						
e. Revenue collected in 19A and recorded as revenue in 19A but not earned until 19B, $900.						
f. Sale of services and cash collected in 19A. Recorded as a debit to Cash and as a credit to Accounts Receivable, $300.						
g. On December 31, 19A, bought land on credit for $8,000, not recorded until payment was made on February 1, 19B.						

Following is a sample explanation of analysis of errors if not corrected, using the first error as an example:

a. Failure to record depreciation in 19A caused depreciation expense to be too low; therefore, income was overstated by $950. Also, accumulated depreciation is too low by $950, which causes assets to be overstated by $950 until the error is corrected.

Grand Metropolitan

C5–3 *An International Perspective: A Challenging Case*

As the economy becomes more international in scope, users of financial statements may be expected to analyze companies that are not incorporated in the United States. Grand Metropolitan is a major world corporation that is located in London. It owns many familiar U.S. businesses such as the Pillsbury Company, Burger King, and Häagen-Dazs ice cream.

Required:

Based on the concepts presented in this book, explain the meaning of the various account classifications shown on the portion of the Grand Metropolitan Annual Report presented below. (Note: There are five reserve accounts. The middle three relate to topics that are discussed in advanced accounting courses.)

GRAND METROPOLITAN
Consolidated Balance Sheet
At 30th September, 19B

		19B		19A	
	Notes	**£m**	**£m**	**£m**	**£m**
Fixed assets:					
Intangible assets	11		2,652		588
Tangible assets	12		3,839		3,280
Investments	13		144		206
			6,635		4,074
Current assets:					
Stocks	14	1,269		761	
Debtors	15	1,451		873	
Cash at bank and in hand		215		138	
		2,935		1,772	
Creditors—Due within one year:					
Borrowings	17	(362)		(187)	
Other creditors	19	(2,316)		(1,301)	
		(2,678)		(1,488)	
Net current assets	15		257		284
Total assets less current liabilities			6,892		4,358
Creditors—Due after more than one year:					
Borrowings	17	(3,494)		(702)	
Other creditors	20	(231)		(163)	
			(3,725)		(865)
Provisions for liabilities and charges	21		(325)		(55)
			2,842		3,438
Capital and reserves:					
Called up share capital	22		506		443
Reserves:	23				
Share premium account		436		7	
Revaluation reserve		(944)		649	
Special reserve		—		282	
Related companies' reserves		10		16	
Profit and loss account		2,802		2,010	
			2,304		2,964
			2,810		3,407
Minority interests			32		31
			2,842		3,438

C5–4 An International Perspective

Grand Metropolitan

Grand Metropolitan is a major international company that is located in London. A recent annual report contained the following information concerning its accounting policies.

> **Accounting convention:**
> The financial statements of the group are prepared under the historical cost convention. They have been drawn up to comply in all material respects with U.K. statements of standard accounting practice in force at the relevant time.

Required:

Discuss how this accounting convention compares with accounting conventions in this country.

C5–5 Annual Report Format and Earnings Announcement Project

Using local library resources and company provided information, your task is to understand the formats used for financial statements and notes in an annual report and to track the stock-price reaction to the most recent annual earnings announcement for a public company. Your instructor may assign a particular company for you to analyze, or you may choose one of the focus companies in this text, a competitor company in the same industry, or a company in which you have career-related interests.

Required:

1. Contact the investor relations department of the company and obtain a copy of the most recent annual report. Alternatively, if your instructor so assigns, look in *The Wall Street Journal* stock price listings and select one company marked with the "♣" symbol. Call *The Wall Street Journal* Annual Reports Service at 1-800-654-2582 (check a recent issue to see if the number has been changed) and request a copy of the most recent annual report for the selected company. (At publication time, this service was free.)
   a. Describe the formats used to present the balance sheet and the income statement.
   b. Describe the information contained in one footnote that describes an accounting rule applied in the company's statements, one footnote that presents additional detail about a reported financial statement number, and one footnote that reports financial statement information not listed in the statements.
2. Using *The Wall Street Journal* Index or Dow Jones News Retrieval Service (or an instructor assigned resource), find one article reporting the company's annual earnings announcement. Using *The Wall Street Journal* or another newspaper, locate the stock price listing for the company.
   a. Prepare a graph of the closing stock price for your company for the date of the earnings announcement and the five days preceding and following the announcement.
   b. Describe the apparent effect of the announcement on the company's stock price.
   c. Describe any explanations for the reported earnings or the stock price changes provided in the press article and whether you find the explanations convincing.

C5–6 News Announcement, Financial Reporting, and Analysis Project (Extended)

Using local library resources and company provided information, your task is to track the information announcement process for a public company for a three-month period following its most recent year-end. Your instructor may assign a particular company for you to analyze or you may choose one of the focus companies in this text, a competitor in the same industry, or a company in which you have career-related interests.

Required:

1. **Gathering the Necessary Information**
   a. Contact the investor relations department of the company and obtain copies of the most recent annual report, Form 10-K, and earnings press release for the fourth quarter of the year in question.
   b. Using *The Wall Street Journal* Index or Dow Jones News Retrieval Service (or instructor-assigned resource), find one article reporting the company's annual earnings and one article reporting a nonearnings-related significant event that took place during the three-month period.
   c. Using *The Wall Street Journal* or another newspaper, prepare a graph of the closing stock price for your company for the date of each news article selected in part *b* and the five days preceding and following the two news events.
2. **Analyzing the Information Announcements**
   a. Based on the annual report and Form 10-K, determine the company's principal lines of business and major competitors.
   b. Determine the format used by the company to prepare its income statements and balance sheets in the annual report.
   c. Find one financial statement-related schedule that is included in the Form 10-K but not in the annual report (see for example, the advertising schedule presented in the chapter).
   d. Using a computerized spreadsheet program (Lotus, Excel, etc.), graph the stock price information gathered related to each of the selected news announcements.
   e. Compare the earnings per share, gross margin percentage, and current ratio for the chosen year to the preceding year.

3. Presenting the Results of Your Analysis

Prepare a written report including the following components:

a. A brief description of the company and its operations and competitors.

b. The formats used in the income statement and balance sheet and an example of additional information provided in the Form 10-K.

c. The two selected important news announcements, the apparent effect on the company's stock price, and any explanations for the reported events or the stock price changes provided in the press articles.

d. A summary of your comparative analysis of the company's performance and liquidity based on the company's earnings per share, gross margin percentage, and current ratio.

C5–7 *Financial Statement Analysis* — **Toys "Я" Us**

Refer to the financial statements of Toys "Я" Us given in Appendix B at the end of this book.

The full-disclosure principle requires companies to present all relevant economic information. The following questions illustrate the types of information that you can find in the financial statements. (Hint: Use the notes.)

Required:

1. What was the highest stock price for the company during 1993?
2. How much land did the company own at the end of the current year?
3. What was rent expense for the current year?
4. How much of the company's sales were earned in foreign locations during the current year?
5. In what season does the company generate the most sales activity?

C5–8 *Financial Statement Analysis* — **Toys "Я" Us**

Refer to the financial statements of Toys "Я" Us given in Appendix B at the end of this book.

Required:

1. Compute working capital and the current ratio for the current year and prior year. Has liquidity increased or decreased during the current year?
2. Compute the gross margin percentage for the current year and prior year. Has the gross margin percentage improved during the current year? Does management provide any explanation for the change?

6

ACCOUNTING FOR SALES REVENUE, CASH, AND RECEIVABLES

In this chapter, we begin our in-depth discussion of the financial statements. We will begin with two of the most liquid assets, cash and accounts receivable, and transactions that involve revenue, adjustments to revenues, and certain selling expenses that relate to recording cash and accounts receivable. Accuracy in revenue recognition and the related recognition of cost of goods sold (discussed in the next chapter) are thought by many analysts and the SEC to be the most important determinants of the accuracy and thus the usefulness of financial statement presentations. We also introduce concepts related to the management and control of cash and receivables, which is a critical business function. A detailed understanding of these topics is crucial to future managers, accountants, and financial analysts.

LEARNING OBJECTIVES

After studying this chapter, you should be able to:

1. **Apply the revenue principle to determine the appropriate time to record sales revenue for typical retailers, wholesalers, and manufacturers.** ***302***
2. **Determine the appropriate amount to report as net sales when there are cash sales, credit card sales, credit sales (and sales discounts), and sales returns.** ***302***
3. **Estimate, account for, and report the effects of uncollectible accounts receivable (bad debts) on the financial statements.** ***309***
4. **Apply the revenue principle to special circumstances including deferred revenues, installment sales, and long-term construction and service contracts.** ***316***
5. **Report, control, and safeguard cash.** ***320***

Management Decision Setting

THE TIMBERLAND COMPANY

Timberland Footwear—"Virtually waterproof, bunion-proof, and wearout-proof"

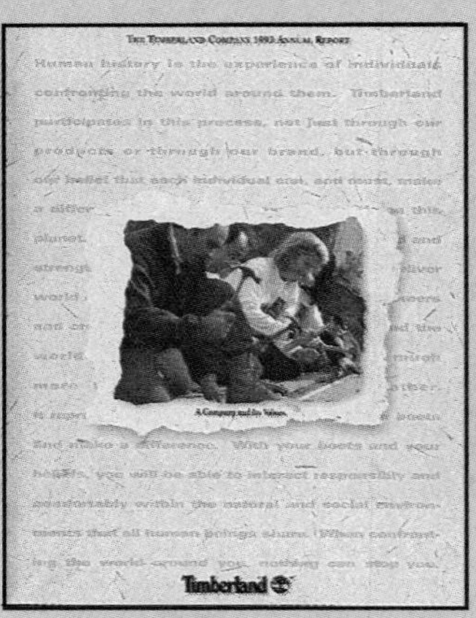

Initially aimed at outdoorsmen including hunters and hikers, Timberland's premium boots, casual shoes, boat shoes and sandals are now as popular on the streets of New York City as they are on the 1,000 mile Iditarod Sled Dog Race in Alaska. Its footwear is sold through quality department, retail, and specialty stores in more than 50 countries and through company-owned outlet stores in the United States. An emphasis on handsewn, high-quality construction, classic styling, and protection from the elements has led to dramatic gains in revenues and profits for Timberland during the 1990s, along with dramatic changes in its stock price. Unlike many shoe companies, it has accomplished this feat while keeping the majority of its manufacturing facilities in the United States.

Though it is a publicly traded company with sales of over $400 million, Timberland is also a family operation. Sidney Swartz and his son Jeffrey are the top two officers of the company and their family interests own about two-thirds of the company's stock. In the past, a key to Timberland's success has been maintaining higher prices and higher gross margin on sales than many of its competitors, such as Wolverine Worldwide and Rocky Shoes and Boots. However, it has now changed marketing strategies, *lowering prices and increasing advertising expenses in an attempt to boost sales.* Can it increase net income while making less money on each sale? For this strategy to be successful, the resulting increase in sales volume has to offset the decrease in gross margin on each sale and the increase in advertising. The big question is: Can expanding the Company's exposure and providing better customer value lead to greater success for Timberland?

BUSINESS BACKGROUND

The answer to the question regarding Timberland's success can be found in the comparative statements of income of The Timberland Company for the current and prior year presented in Exhibit 6–1. Following the multiple-step format for the income statement (with two subtotals as discussed in Chapter 5), Net Sales is first reported and Cost of Goods Sold (an expense) is set out separately from the remaining expenses. Similar account titles sometimes used are Cost of Sales and Cost of Products Sold. Notice that the income statement then shows *gross profit* (*gross margin*), which is net sales revenue minus cost of goods sold.

A quick answer to our strategic question can be given by computing the gross profit ratio (gross profit ÷ sales revenue) for the current and prior years.

Current year: $152,707,000 ÷ $418,918,000 = 36.45%
Prior year: $107,858,000 ÷ $291,368,000 = 37.02%

Even though the gross profit ratio has dropped and selling expenses have risen by 44.5% [($82,585 – $57,145) ÷ $57,145], the dramatic 43.8% increase in net sales [($418,918 – $291,368) ÷ $291,368] has boosted net income to record levels. A more detailed answer to our strategic question requires an understanding of how net sales and cost of goods sold are determined. In this chapter, we will focus on the transactions that affect *net sales* (and some selling expenses) on the income statement and *cash* and *accounts receivable* on the balance sheet. In the next chapter, we will discuss transactions related to cost of goods sold on the income statement and inventories on the balance sheet.

Cash, accounts receivable, and inventories are important from the standpoint of cash management and the prevention of fraud. As we discuss later

Statements of Income* **Exhibit 6–1**

The Timberland Company

CONSOLIDATED STATEMENTS OF INCOME
For the Years Ended December 31, 1993 and 1992
(Amounts in Thousands, Except Per Share Data)

	1993	1992
Net sales	$418,918	$291,368
Cost of goods sold	266,211	183,510
Gross profit	152,707	107,858
Operating expenses		
Selling	82,585	57,145
General and administrative	28,956	24,194
Amortization of goodwill	774	677
Total operating expenses	112,315	82,016
Operating income	40,392	25,842
Other expenses (income)		
Interest expense	6,252	5,528
Other, net	17	1,315
Total other expense	6,269	6,843
Income before income taxes	34,123	18,999
Provision for income taxes	11,602	6,080
Net income	$22,521	$12,919
Earnings per share	$2.01	$1.18
Weighted average shares and share equivalents outstanding	11,206	10,922

The accompanying notes are an integral part of these consolidated financial statements.

*Note that all of the account titles, formats, and amounts are taken directly from Timberland's annual report to shareholders.

in this chapter and in Chapter 7, the primary source of operating cash for most organizations is the collection of accounts receivable, and a primary use is payments for inventories. As a consequence, careful management of receivables and inventory can be the key to avoiding a business failure driven by cash shortages. Since misappropriation of funds is the most common form of fraud, appropriate internal controls on cash are also critical to management.

Lenders, shareholders, and analysts also carefully monitor these accounts because of their importance as predictors of the future success of companies. Their importance is supported by the fact that the majority of shareholder lawsuits and SEC Enforcement Actions against companies for misleading financial statements relate to these accounts. We will discuss an example of actual misleading statements later in the chapter.

Timberland is a particularly useful example for discussing recognition of revenue because it sells footwear to two different kinds of customers. It sells most of its footwear to other *businesses* (retailers) including large department stores such as Kaufmann's, specialty retail chains such as American Eagle Outfitters, and independent retail stores, which then sell the goods to consumers. However, Timberland also operates its own factory outlet stores that sell footwear directly to *consumers.* Some business practices differ between sales to businesses and consumers and as a result, create accounting issues that are specific to one type of customer or the other. Since most companies sell to either businesses or consumers, you will be able to apply what you have learned about Timberland to understand many different companies' statements.

ACCOUNTING FOR SALES REVENUE

Learning Objective 1
Apply the revenue principle to determine the appropriate time to record sales revenue for typical retailers, wholesalers, and manufacturers.

As indicated in Chapter 3, the *revenue principle* requires that revenues be recorded when earned (an exchange has taken place, the earnings process is nearly complete, and collection is probable). In most cases, these criteria are met when the goods pass from the seller to the buyer; the seller of goods records sales revenue on that date. Service companies most often record sales revenue when services have been provided to the buyer. The specific revenue recognition rule followed by a company will be disclosed in the footnote to its financial statements entitled Summary of Significant Accounting Policies. In that note, Timberland reports the following:

Real World Excerpt
The Timberland Company Annual Report

NOTES TO CONSOLIDATED FINANCIAL STATEMENTS
1. SUMMARY OF SIGNIFICANT ACCOUNTING POLICIES
. . .
Recognition of Revenue
Revenue is recognized upon shipment of products to customers.

Timberland's recognition rule is the one that is most commonly used by manufacturers, wholesalers, and retailers. In a manual accounting system, revenue would be recognized when a shipping report is filed. In a computerized system, the bar codes on the inventory labels attached to each container of goods are read when they are loaded. At this point, the shipment is automatically matched to the sales reports and revenue is recorded.

Many companies recognize revenue at shipment regardless of whether title passes at shipment or delivery.[1] This common practice is usually employed because it is easier to keep track of shipments than deliveries to customers. As long as the rule is applied *consistently*, recording sales revenue on the *shipping date* versus the *delivery date* usually has little effect on the financial statements. *Both* revenue recognition points meet the criterion that the "earnings process is *nearly* complete" and thus are in accordance with GAAP, regardless of whether title passes at shipment or delivery. Other revenue recognition rules which are used in special circumstances are discussed later in the chapter.

The *cash equivalent* sales price is the appropriate measure of the *amount* of revenue that should be recorded. Both the form of payment (cash, credit card, or credit) and returns and allowances affect the amount recorded as *net sales* on the income statement. If the sale involves the trade-in of a noncash asset (such as the trade-in of an old car for a new car), the amount of revenue is the cash equivalent of the goods received or given up, whichever is the more clearly determinable.

Learning Objective 2
Determine the appropriate amount to report as net sales when there are cash sales, credit card sales, credit sales (and sales discounts), and sales returns.

Cash Sales

In Timberland's factory stores, many of the sales to consumers are for cash. If the sale is for cash (or check), the amount of revenue to be recorded is simply the amount of cash received. If such cash sales at one factory store amounted to $2,000 for January 2, Timberland would record the following entry:

[1]The point where title (ownership) changes hands is determined by the shipping terms in the sales contract. When goods are shipped "F.O.B. shipping point," title changes hands at shipment and the buyer normally pays for shipping. When thay are shipped"F.O.B. destination," title changes hands on delivery and the seller normally pays for shipping. Auditors expend a great deal of effort ensuring that revenue recognition rules are applied consistently and revenues are recognized in the proper period.

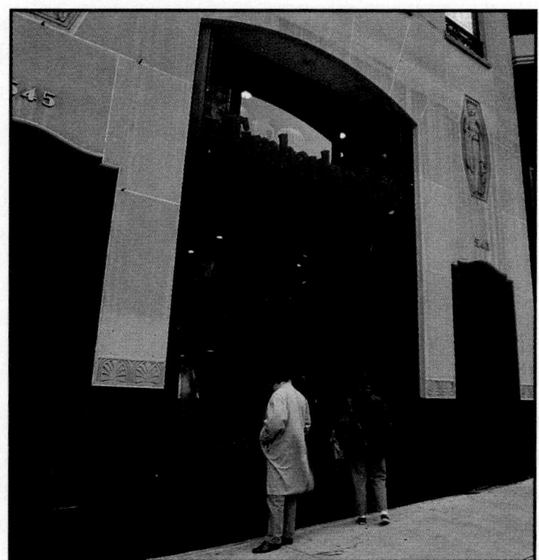

Timberland specialty stores, such as the North Michigan Avenue store in Chicago, are part of Timberland's overall marketing strategy.

Jan. 2	Cash (A)	2,000	
	Sales revenue (R)		2,000

Timberland keeps track of the sales revenues of its various factory outlets separately and uses information concerning sales revenue for each store for a variety of purposes. For example, an increase in the sales volume in the Lake George, New York, store may indicate a need to assign additional salespeople to work there. A very small portion of Timberland's sales to other businesses are transacted for cash. In these cases, Timberland makes the same journal entry it would for a cash sale to a consumer.

Credit Card Sales

Many consumers use credit cards (mainly VISA, MasterCard, and American Express) to pay for purchases. Timberland accepts these three credit cards as payment at its factory stores for a variety of reasons. First, it believes that offering this service will increase the number of people who will shop at its factory stores. Second, Timberland avoids the costs of providing credit directly to consumers (recordkeeping and bad debts, discussed later). Third, accepting credit cards instead of checks avoids losses due to bad checks written by dishonest consumers. The credit card company (e.g., VISA) absorbs any losses from fraudulent credit card sales as long as Timberland follows the credit card company's verification procedure. Finally, Timberland receives its money faster than it would if it provided credit directly to consumers. It can deposit credit card receipts directly to its bank account.

The credit card company charges a fee for the service it provides. For example, when Timberland deposits its credit card receipts in the bank, it might only receive credit for an amount equal to 98% of the sales price. The credit card company is charging a 2% fee (the **credit card discount)** for its service. If credit card sales were $3,000 at the same store for January 2, Timberland would record the following entry.

A **credit card discount** is the fee charged by the credit card company for services.

Jan. 2	Cash (A)	2,940	
	Credit card discounts (XR or E)	60	
	Sales revenue (R)		3,000

Credit Card Discounts may be reported as *(a)* a *contra revenue account* and thus a deduction in the computation of *net sales* or *(b)* an addition to *selling expenses*. In either case, it would reduce net income by the same amount. Recall from Chapter 4 that a *contra account* is an account, related to a primary account, that is an offset (or reduction) to the primary account. Thus a contra revenue account reduces the related revenue. Credit Card Discounts treated as a contra revenue account is a deduction from Sales Revenue in the computation of Net Sales reported on the income statement.

Credit Sales

Most of Timberland's noncash sales are credit sales to businesses on open account; that is, there is no formal written promissory note indicating the amount owed to Timberland by the customer. In the case of a sale of $1,000 worth of footwear to a retailer, the following journal entry would be made:

Jan. 2	Accounts receivable (A)	1,000	
	Sales revenue (R)		1,000

Credit Sales and Sales Discounts

When Timberland sells footwear to retailers on credit, credit terms are printed on each sales document and invoice (bill) sent to the customer. Often, credit terms are abbreviated using symbols. For example, if the full price is due within 30 days of the invoice date, the credit terms would be noted as "n/30." Here, the "n" means the sales amount "net" of or less any sales returns. The terms "10, EOM," mean the full price is due not later than 10 days after the end of the month (EOM) in which the sale was made.

A **sales** (or **cash**) **discount** is a cash discount offered to encourage prompt payment of an account receivable.

In other cases, a **sales discount** (often called a *cash discount*) is granted to the purchaser to encourage early payment. For example, let's assume that Timberland offers standard credit terms of "2/10, n/30," which means that the customer may deduct 2% from the invoice price if cash payment is made within 10 days from the date of sale. However, if cash payment is not made within the 10-day discount period, the full sales price (less any returns) is due within a maximum of 30 days from date of sale.

Timberland offers this sales discount to give its customers an incentive for fast payment of the accounts receivable. This benefits Timberland because prompt receipt of cash from customers reduces the necessity to borrow money from Morgan Guaranty Trust (and its other banks) to meet operating needs. Also, if a customer pays Timberland's bills earlier than the bills from other suppliers, it decreases the chances that the customer will run out of funds before Timberland's bill is paid.

Usually customers will pay within the discount period because the savings are substantial. With terms 2/10, n/30, 2% is saved by paying 20 days early (the 10th day instead of the 30th), which is approximately 37% annual interest. This annual interest rate is obtained by first computing the interest rate for the discount period. When the 2% discount is taken, the customer pays only 98% of the gross sales price. Thus, the interest rate for the 20 day discount period is:

(Amount saved ÷ Amount paid) = Interest rate for 20 days
(2% of the bill ÷ 98% of the bill) = 2.04% for 20 days

The annual interest rate is then computed in the following manner:

Interest rate for 20 days × (365 days ÷ 20 days) = Annual interest rate
2.04% × (365 days ÷ 20 days) = 37.23% Annual interest

Credit customers would save a great deal even if they had to borrow cash from a bank at 15% to take advantage of cash discounts. Normally, the bank's interest rate is less than the high interest rate associated with failing to take cash discounts.

Companies commonly record sales discounts using the gross method where sales revenue is recorded without deducting the sales discount.[2] The following journal entry would be made for a $1,000 sale with terms 2/10, n/30:

Jan. 18	Accounts receivable (A)	1,000	
	Sales revenue (R)		1,000

The entry at collection will depend on whether or not the payment is made within the discount period. If payment is made *within* the discount period (the usual case) with terms 2/10, n/30 ($1,000 × 0.98 = $980), the following entry would be made:

Jan. 27	Cash (A)	980	
	Sales discounts (XR or E)	20	
	Accounts receivable (A)		1,000

Alternatively, if payment is made *after* the discount period (the unusual case), the following entry will be made:

Feb. 17	Cash (A)	1,000	
	Accounts receivable (A)		1,000

The Sales Discounts account may be reported as *(a)* a *contra revenue account* and thus a deduction in the computation of *net sales* or *(b)* a component of *selling expenses*. Note that both the purpose of sales discounts and the accounting for sales discounts are very similar to the purpose of and the accounting for credit card discounts. They both provide an attractive service to customers while promoting faster receipt of cash, reducing recordkeeping costs, and minimizing bad debts. Both sales discounts and credit card discounts are reported as either contra revenues or expenses on the income statement.

It is important not to confuse a cash discount with a **trade discount.** A trade discount is sometimes used by vendors for quoting sales prices; the list or printed catalog price *less* the trade discount is the sales price. For example, an item may be quoted at $10 per unit subject to a 20% trade discount on orders of 100 units or more; thus the price for the large order would be $8 per unit. Similarly, the price on a slow-moving product line can be lowered simply by increasing the trade discount. Sales revenue should always be recorded net of trade discounts.

A **trade discount** is a discount that is deducted from list price to derive the actual sales price.

Sales Returns and Allowances

For Timberland, prompt delivery of exactly what the customer ordered is a key to maintaining good relations with the retailers to whom they sell. Delivery of incorrect or damaged merchandise may cost the retailer sales and can destroy these relationships. When this occurs, the customers have a right to return unsatisfactory or damaged merchandise and receive a refund or an adjustment to their bill.

Although the Sales account could be debited (reduced) to record these reductions in sales, a separate account called **Sales Returns and Allowances** is

Sales Returns and Allowances is a contra revenue account used to record return of or allowances for unsatisfactory goods.

[2]We use this method in all examples in this text. Some companies use the alternative net method, where sales revenue is recorded after deducting the amount of the cash discount. Since the choice of method has little effect on the financial statements, discussion of this method is left for an advanced course.

QUESTION OF ETHICS

Stretching Out the Payables

Hoffa Shoes has been incurring significant interest charges (12%) on short-term borrowing from its bank.* Hoffa normally purchased shoes from suppliers on terms 1/10, n/30. Since the annual rate of interest earned by taking the discount was 18.43% computed as follows:

(Amount saved/Amount paid) = Interest rate for 20 days
(1% ÷ 99%) = 1.01% for 20 days,
Interest rate for 20 days ×
(365 days ÷ 20 days) = Annual interest rate
1.01% × (365 days ÷ 20 days) = 18.43% annual interest,

Hoffa's policy had been to take all purchase discounts even if it had to borrow at 12% to make the early payment. They reasoned that they earned 6.43% more than they paid in interest (18.43% – 12%).

A new employee suggested a new plan. Records indicated that, even though the terms of Hoffa's agreement with their suppliers (1/10, n/30) required payment of the full amount within a maximum of 30 days, the suppliers would not complain as long as payment was made within 55 days of the purchase, since they normally did not send out a second bill until 60 days after the purchase. She reasoned that Hoffa would be better off forgoing the discount and paying on the 55th day after the purchase. She argued that since Hoffa would now be paying in 55 days instead of 10 days of the purchase, not taking the discount would be borrowing for *45* days, not the 20 days used in the former analysis. The analysis supporting the proposal is as follows:

(1% ÷ 99%) = 1.01% for *45* days
Interest rate for *45* days ×
(365 days ÷ *45* days) = Annual interest rate
1.01% × (365 days ÷ *45* days) = 8.19% annual interest.

In effect, her plan allows Hoffa to borrow from suppliers at 8.19% instead of the bank's rate of 12%, saving 3.81%. When she presented this plan to the management for discussion, the purchasing manager agreed with the arithmetic presented but objected nonetheless. Since the plan violated its agreement with suppliers, the purchasing manager thought it was unethical. Many ethical dilemmas in business involve trade-offs between monetary benefits and potential violations of moral values.

*Hoffa Shoes is a fictitious company, but this dilemma is faced by most companies.

often used. This account has an important purpose because it informs Timberland's management of the volume of returns and allowances, and thus provides a measure of the quality of service provided to customers. The Sales Returns and Allowances account is a *contra revenue account;* therefore, it is a deduction from gross sales revenue. Assume that Fontana Shoes of Ithaca, NY, bought 40 pairs of hiking boots from Timberland for $2,000 on account. On the date of sale, Timberland would make the following journal entry:

Aug. 31	Accounts receivable (A)	2,000	
	Sales revenue (R)		2,000

Before paying for the boots, Fontana discovered that 10 pairs of boots were not the color ordered and they returned them to Timberland. On that date Timberland would record:

Sept. 10	Sales returns and allowances (XR)	500	
	Accounts receivable (A)*		500

*If payment had already been made, cash would be credited if a check was sent to Fontana Shoes.

Reporting Net Sales

On the books of the company, sales returns and allowances, sales discounts, and credit card discounts are accounted for separately to allow monitoring of the costs of the related activities (returns of incorrect or damaged merchandise, offering sales discounts, allowing use of credit cards, respectively). The amount of net sales reported on the income statement is computed in the following manner:

Sales revenue
Less: Sales returns and allowances
Sales discounts (if treated as a contra revenue)
Credit card discounts (if treated as a contra revenue)

Net sales (reported on the income statement)

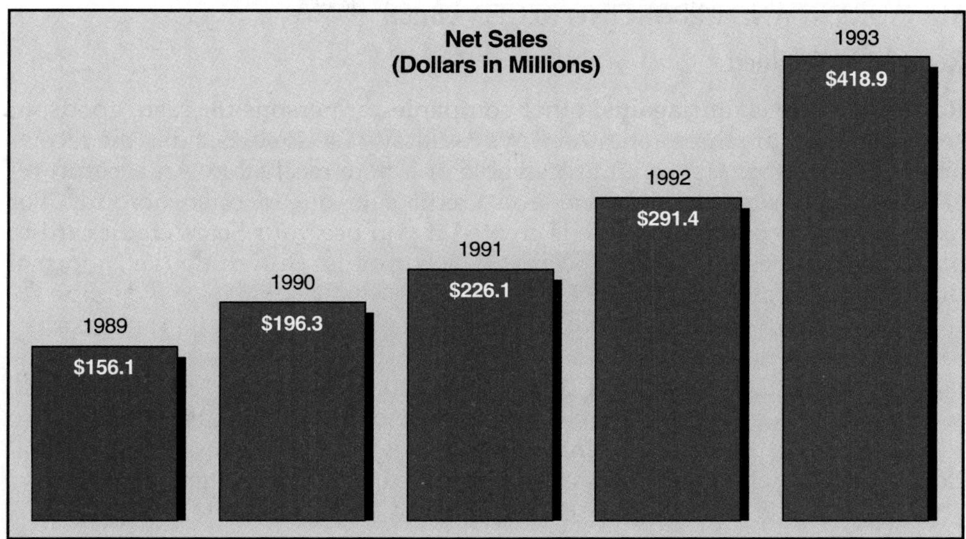

Real World Excerpt

The Timberland Company Annual Report

Graphics are often used to highlight key figures in the management discussion and analysis section of the annual report.

FINANCIAL ANALYSIS

Contra Revenues and Evaluating Gross Profit

The computation of net sales is rarely reported on the financial statements. Note that if sales discounts and credit card discounts are recorded as contra revenues, net sales is reduced, and thus both gross profit (and the gross profit percentage) and operating income are *reduced*. However, if they are treated as selling expenses, operating income is reduced, but gross profit is *unaffected*. Comparisons of gross profit percentages between firms using the alternative treatments can be distorted by this difference.

Self-Study Quiz

1. Assume that Timberland sold $2,000 worth of footwear to Mast Shoe Stores of Ann Arbor, Michigan, with terms 1/10, n/30, and recorded the transaction using the gross method. Ten days after the delivery of the footwear, Mast paid the $1,980 amount (purchase price less the discount). What journal entry would Timberland record for the collection of Mast's receivable?

Cash 1980
Sales Dis. 20
Accts Rec 2000

2. Assume that Fast Shoes of Tuscaloosa, Alabama, returns $500 of footwear which they had purchased on account but not paid for. What journal entry would Timberland record for the sales return?

Sales Returns & All. 500
Accts Rec 500

After you have completed your answers, check them with the solutions presented in the footnote at the bottom of this page.*

MEASURING AND REPORTING RECEIVABLES

Receivables Defined

Accounts receivable (trade receivables, receivables) are open accounts owed to the business by trade customers.

Notes receivable are written promises that require another party to pay the business under specified conditions (amount, time, interest).

Receivables are claims against other companies or persons for cash, goods, or services. There are three common ways to classify receivables. First, the receivable may be either an account receivable or a note receivable. An **account receivable** is created when there is a credit sale on an open account. For example, an account receivable is created if you use your Sears credit card to buy a new television. A **note receivable** is a promise in writing (i.e., a formal document) to pay (1) a specified sum of money on demand or at a definite future date known as the *maturity date* and (2) specified interest at one or more future dates. A note often involves two distinctly different amounts: (1) *principal,* which is the amount that the interest rate is based on, and (2) *interest,* which is the specified amount charged for use of the principal. The notes also require periodic recording of interest revenue. We will discuss the computation of interest when we discuss notes payable in a later chapter.

Second, receivables may be classified as trade or nontrade receivables. A *trade receivable* is created in the normal course of business whenever there is a sale of merchandise or services on credit. A *nontrade receivable* arises from transactions other than the normal sale of merchandise or services. For example, if Timberland loaned money to a new vice president for international operations to help finance a home at the new job location, it would be classified as a nontrade receivable. Third, in a classified balance sheet, receivables are also classified as either *current* or *noncurrent* (short-term or long-term) depending on when the cash is expected to be collected.

Like many companies, Timberland reports only one type of receivable account, Accounts Receivable from customers (trade receivables), and classifies the asset as a current asset (short term) because the accounts receivable are all due to be paid within one year. Companies also keep separate records (subsidiary records) for each customer to provide a basis for billing. Recall that Timberland was willing to pay a credit card discount fee to allow customers at the factory outlet stores to use credit cards because it would draw more customers to the stores. Similarly, Timberland allows its business customers (the retail stores that buy and then resell its footwear) to purchase goods on open account because they believe that providing this service will result in greater sales to this type of customer.

Like the case of the credit card fee, there is also a cost to providing this service to business customers. Timberland must pay to maintain a billing system and face the fact that not all customers will pay their debts. Further, from the financial statement user's perspective, inadequate accounting for bad debts can lead to highly misleading financial statements. From the reporting corporation's view, such misleading statements can lead to legal actions. For example, *The Wall Street Journal* reported the following:

Real World Excerpt
The Wall Street Journal

T2 Medical Discloses SEC Investigation Relating to Two Earnings Restatements

ALPHARETTA, Ga. – **T2 Medical** Inc. disclosed that the Securities and Exchange Commission is investigating events surrounding the company's restatement of two quarterly earnings announcements...

*1. Dr. Cash (A) 1,980; Dr. Sales discount (XR or E) 20; Cr. Accounts receivable (A) 2,000.
2. Dr. Sales returns and allowances (XR) 500; Cr. Accounts receivable (A) 500.

Last August, T2 Medical (pronounced T-squared) restated its earnings sharply downward for the first and second quarters of its 1993 fiscal year after the company said it discovered "accounting irregularities and errors." The original disclosure of accounting problems was accompanied by the resignation of T2 Medical's chief executive officer...

The earnings restatements stemmed largely from inadequate provisions for "doubtful accounts...."

SOURCE: *The Wall Street Journal*, January 7, 1994, p. A2.

Accounting for Bad Debts

Learning Objective 3
Estimate, account for, and report the effects of uncollectible accounts receivable (bad debts) on the financial statements.

Businesses that extend credit know that there will be a certain amount of bad debts on credit sales. In fact, an extremely low rate of bad debts may not be good because it may indicate too tight of a credit policy. If the credit policy is too restrictive, many good credit customers may be turned away, causing a loss of sales volume. The decision to loosen credit policies should be determined based on the *trade-off* between profits on additional sales and any additional bad debts. Bad debts can be thought of as a necessary expense associated with generating credit sales. Steps firms can take to limit bad debts are discussed at the end of this section.

Bad debt expense (doubtful accounts expense, uncollectible accounts expense, provision for uncollectible accounts) is the expense associated with estimated uncollectible accounts receivable. In conformity with the matching principle, bad debt expense should be recorded (matched) in the *same* accounting period in which the sales related to the uncollectible account were made rather than in the year that the seller learns that the customer is unable to pay. A well-managed company like Timberland sells only to customers it believes will pay their bills, based on the information available at the time of sale. However, it is inevitable that some customers will prove unable to pay their debts. Further, Timberland may not learn that any particular customers will not pay until the *next* accounting period.

Bad debt expense (doubtful accounts expense, uncollectible accounts expense, provision for uncollectible accounts) is the expense associated with estimated uncollectible accounts receivable.

Timberland resolves this problem and satisfies the matching principle by using the **allowance method** to measure bad debt expense. There is no way of knowing in advance which individual customers will not pay. Therefore, the allowance method is based on *estimates* of the expected amount of bad debts. There are two primary steps in employing the allowance method: (1) the adjusting entry to record bad debt expense estimates and (2) writing off specific accounts determined to be uncollectible during the period.

The **allowance method** bases bad debt expense on an estimate of uncollectible accounts.

Recording Bad Debt Expense Estimates

The bad debt estimate is recorded by an *adjusting journal entry at the end of the accounting period*. For the year ended December 31, 1993, Timberland estimated bad debt expense to be $1,131,000 and made the following adjusting entry on December 31:

Bad debt expense (E)	1,131,000	
Allowance for doubtful accounts (XA)		1,131,000

Bad Debt Expense of $1,131,000 would be reported on the current year's income statement. It would normally be included in the category "Selling" on Timberland's income statement (see Exhibit 6–1). It would be matched with the related sales revenue for the current year, the year in which the credit was granted. The Bad Debt Expense account is closed at the end of each accounting period along with the other expense accounts. The credit in the above journal entry was made to a *contra asset account* called **Allowance for Doubtful**

Allowance for Doubtful Accounts (Allowance for Bad Debts, Allowance for Uncollectible Accounts) is a contra asset account containing the estimated uncollectible accounts receivable.

Accounts (also called **Allowance for Bad Debts** or **Allowance for Uncollectible Accounts**). Accounts Receivable cannot be credited because there is no way to know which account receivable is involved. As a contra asset, the balance in Allowance for Doubtful Accounts is *always* subtracted from the balance of Accounts Receivable. Thus, it is treated exactly like the first contra asset we discussed in Chapter 4, Accumulated Depreciation. The balance in an account with the contra account subtracted is normally reported on the balance sheet with the term *net* following the account title.

Allowance for Doubtful Accounts has a cumulative credit balance. It is not closed at the end of the accounting period because it is a balance sheet account. The balance of the allowance account is an approximation of the total amount of the accounts receivable that is estimated to be uncollectible. The balances of Accounts Receivable less the allowance account measures the *estimated net realizable value* (or how much Timberland expects to collect) of accounts receivable. As we noted in earlier chapters, the balance in a balance sheet account less the balance in the related contra account is called the *net book value* or *book value*, in this case, of accounts receivable.

Writing Off Specific Accounts Determined to Be Uncollectible

When a specific customer's account receivable is determined to be uncollectible (e.g., due to bankruptcy), the amount should be removed from the Accounts Receivable account with an offsetting reduction of the Allowance account. Write-offs of bad debts are recorded through *journal entries made throughout the year*. Suppose that Timberland had sold $200,000 of footwear to a regional retail chain which was properly credited to Sales Revenue and debited to Accounts Receivable. On January 30, Timberland learned that the retail chain had filed for bankruptcy and would never be able to pay its debt. The journal entry to record the *write-off on January 30*, is:

	Debit	Credit
Allowance for doubtful accounts (XA)	200,000	
Accounts receivable (A)		200,000

Notice that the above journal entry *did not affect any income statement accounts*. It did not record a bad debt expense because the estimated expense was recorded with an adjusting entry in the period of sale and the related allowance account was established. Also, the entry did not change the *net realizable value* (book value) of Accounts Receivable since the decrease in the asset account (Accounts Receivable) was offset by the decrease in the contra asset account (Allowance for Doubtful Accounts).

Write-offs of bad debts involve debiting the Allowance account. Since bad debts are written off continuously throughout the year, the preadjustment balance of the Allowance for Doubtful Accounts account can be a debit or a credit. During the remainder of the year, Timberland wrote off approximately an additional $1,838,000. The entries for these *write-offs during the year* are summarized in the following journal entry:

	Debit	Credit
Allowance for doubtful accounts (XA)	1,838,000	
Accounts receivable (A)		1,838,000

Reinstatement of Accounts Previously Written Off

When a customer makes a payment after an account has been written off, the journal entry to write off the account is reversed and the collection of cash recorded. Assume on June 1 of the current year, that a retail store paid $100,000 on the account that was written off in a previous period. The entries to reinstate the account (which maintains a complete credit history for the customer) and to collect the account are:

Accounts receivable (A)	100,000	
Allowance for doubtful accounts (XA)		100,000
Cash (A)	100,000	
Accounts receivable (A)		100,000

As noted earlier in the chapter, to aid billing and collection, the accounting system keeps track of each customer's receivables separately in what is called a *subsidiary account* (or *subsidiary ledger account*).

Actual Write-Offs Compared with Estimates

The amount of uncollectible accounts actually written off seldom will equal the estimated amount previously recorded. This situation will be resolved when the next adjusting entry is made at the end of the accounting period. When estimates are found to be incorrect, financial statement values for *prior* annual accounting periods are not corrected.

Summary of the Accounting Process

Timberland's complete 1993 accounting process for bad debts can now be summarized in terms of the changes in Accounts Receivable and the Allowance for Doubtful Accounts:

Accounts Receivable (A)			
Beginning balance	......		
Sales on account	......	Collections on account	.....
Reinstatements	100,000	Write-offs	2,038,000
Ending balance	......		

Allowance for Doubtful Accounts (XA)			
		Beginning Balance	1,821,000
Write-offs*	2,038,000	Bad debt adjustment	1,131,000
		Reinstatements	100,000
		Ending balance	1,014,000

*Timberland only reports write-offs net of reinstatements. The $100,000 reinstatement is included for purposes of this illustration only and may not match actual reinstatements during 1993.

FINANCIAL ANALYSIS

Evaluating the Collectibility of Receivables

The receivables turnover ratio measures the effectiveness of credit granting and collection activities. It is computed as follows:

$$\text{Receivables turnover} = \frac{\text{Net credit sales}}{\text{Average net trade accounts receivable}}$$

[Use the net sales amount if net credit sales is not available.The average net trade accounts receivable is normally computed as the beginning balance plus ending balance divided by 2.]

It reflects how many times trade receivables were recorded, collected, then recorded again during the period. Granting credit to poor credit risks and using ineffective collection methods will cause this ratio to be low. Since differences across industries in the manner in which customer purchases are financed cause dramatic differences in the ratio, a particular firm's ratio should only be compared with other firms in the same industry or with prior years' figures for the same firm. Timberland's receivables turnover ratios for 1992 and 1993 were 5.70 and 5.69, respectively. This indicates that Timberland's goal of increased sales was not accomplished by providing credit to customers less likely to pay their debts; it has maintained the collectibility of its receivables.

Exhibit 6–2 **Accounts Receivable on the Balance Sheet**

The Timberland Company

CONSOLIDATED BALANCE SHEETS
As of December 31, 1993 and 1992
(Dollars in Thousands)

Assets	**1993**	**1992**
Current assets		
Cash and equivalents	$3,281	$1,220
Accounts receivable, net of allowance for doubtful accounts of $1,014 in 1993 and $1,821 in 1992	93,226	54,141
Inventories	111,380	70,542
. . . . . .	. . . . .	. . . . .

Reporting Accounts Receivable and Bad Debts

In Exhibit 6–2, Timberland reports accounts receivable, net of allowance for doubtful accounts of $93,226 and $54,141 and also indicates the amount of the allowance for each year.

The amounts of bad debt expense included in selling expenses on the income statement and accounts receivable written off for the period are normally not disclosed in the annual report. However, these amounts are reported on a schedule that publicly traded companies include in their Annual Report Form 10-K filed with the SEC (discussed in Chapter 5). Exhibit 6–3 presents this schedule from Timberland's 1993 filing. Write-offs are reported on Timberland's 10-K net of (less) reinstatements of previously written-off accounts.

Methods for Estimating Bad Debts

The bad debt expense amount recorded in the end-of-period adjusting entry is estimated in each accounting period often based on either (1) the total credit sales for the period or (2) an aging of accounts receivable.

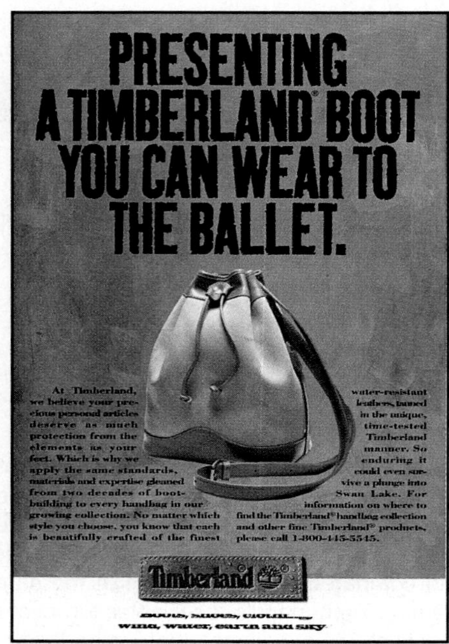

Sales growth relies in part on new products that are based on successful product concepts from Timberland's footwear line.

Accounts Receivable Valuation Schedule (Form 10-K) **Exhibit 6–3**

Schedule VIII

THE TIMBERLAND COMPANY
Valuation and Qualifying Accounts
(in Thousands)

Description	Balance at Beginning of Period	Additions: Charged to Costs and Expenses	Additions: Charged to Other Accounts	Deductions: Net Write-Offs	Balance at End of Period
Allowance for doubtful accounts:					
Year ended:					
December 31, 1993	$1,821	$1,131		$1,938	$1,014
December 31, 1992	1,675	1,374		1,228	1,821
December 31, 1991	904	1,107		336	1,675

Percentage of Credit Sales

Many companies make their estimates using the **percentage of credit sales method**, which bases bad debt expense on the historical percentage of credit sales that result in bad debts. The average percentage of credit sales that result in bad debts can be computed by dividing total bad debt losses by total *credit* sales. A company that has been operating for some years has sufficient experience to project probable future bad debt losses. For example, assume that Rogers and Lambert (a hypothetical company) had experienced the following in three recent years:

Percentage of credit sales method bases bad debt expense on the historical percentage of credit sales that result in bad debts.

Year	Bad Debt Losses	Credit Sales
19A	$ 900	$ 190,000
19B	1,200	220,000
19C	1,400	290,000
Total	$3,500	$700,000

$3,500 ÷ $700,000 = 0.5% average loss rate for the three-year period 19A–19C.

If net credit sales in the current year were approximately $268,000, and the company used this method, they would record bad debt expense (and allowance for doubtful accounts) of $268,000 × .5% = $1,340 in the current year. New companies often rely on the experience of similar companies that have been operating for a number of years. Usually a company will adjust the historical average loss rate to reflect future expectations. For example, if retail sales were rising, the company might decrease its rate to 0.4%, reasoning that fewer of its business customers (retailers) will become bankrupt.

FINANCIAL ANALYSIS

Judging the Appropriateness of Bad Debt Estimates

Without access to detailed information concerning any changes in customer mix and credit terms, an outside financial analyst would have little basis for judging the appropriateness of the current period's bad debt estimates. For example, in the case of T2 Medical discussed in *The Wall Street Journal* article reprinted earlier in the chapter, the company had increased its recognized bad debt expense from 5.4% of sales in the prior year to 6.5% of sales in recognition of an increase in the risk of bad debts. However, after the accounting irregularities were investigated, it was determined that the appropriate bad debt rate was 11% of sales. While the financial community expected an increase in the bad debt rate, a doubling of the rate surprised most analysts because they were not aware of the dramatic changes in the company's credit sales policies.

Aging of Accounts Receivable

Aging of accounts receivable method estimates uncollectible accounts based on the age of each account receivable.

As an alternative to the percentage-of-credit-sales method, many companies use the age that accounts receivable have been outstanding to estimate bad debt expense. This is called the **aging of accounts receivable method**. Usually, older accounts receivable are less likely to be collectible. For example, a receivable due in 30 days that has not been paid after 60 days is more likely to be collected, on average, than a similar receivable that still remains unpaid after 120 days.

Based on its prior experience, the company could estimate what portion of receivables of different ages will not be paid. Suppose that Rogers and Lambert split its receivables into five age categories, as presented in Exhibit 6–4. Management of the company might then *estimate* the following probable bad debt loss rates; not yet due, 1%; 1 to 30 days past due, 3%; 31 to 60 days, 6%; 61 to 90 days, 10%; over 90 days, 25%. The total of the amounts estimated to be uncollectible under the aging method is the balance that *should be* in the allowance for doubtful accounts at the end of the period. This is called the *estimated balance.*

The approach to recording bad debt expense using the aging method is different from that for the percentage of credit sales method. Recall that using the percentage of credit sales, we *directly computed* the amount to be recorded as bad debt expense for the period in the adjusting journal entry. Alternatively, when using the aging method, we are computing the *final ending balance* we would like to have in the allowance for doubtful accounts after we make the necessary entry. Thus, the *difference* between the actual balance in the account and the estimated balance is recorded as the adjusting entry for bad debt expense for the period.

The amount of bad debt expense for the period is the difference between the estimated uncollectible accounts (calculated above) and the balance of the allowance for doubtful accounts at the end of the period *before the adjusting entry* has been made.

Exhibit 6–4 Aging Schedule

ROGERS AND LAMBERT
Aging Analysis of Accounts Receivable,
December 31, 19A

Customer	Not Yet Due	1–30 Days Past Due	31–60 Days Past Due	61–90 Days Past Due	Over 90 Days Past Due	Total
Adams, Inc.	$ 600					$ 600
Baker Stores	300	$ 900	$ 100			1,300
Cox Co.			400	$ 900	$ 100	1,400
Zoe Stores	2,000		1,000			3,000
Total	$17,200	$12,000	$8,000	$1,200	$1,600	$40,000
× Estimated % uncollectible	1%	3%	6%	10%	25%	
Estimated uncollectible accounts	$ 172	$ 360	$ 480	$ 120	$ 400	$ 1,532

Computation:

Estimated balance (from aging schedule)	$1,532
Current balance (preadjustment balance from ledger account)	188
Bad debt expense to be recorded for the current year (solve)	$1,344

This computation can also be illustrated in T-account form. The current credit balance in the allowance, before the end-of-period adjustment, is $188. We insert the new ending balance from the aging schedule, and then solve for the current amount of bad debt expense.

Allowance for Doubtful Accounts (XA)

Debit	Credit	
	Unadjusted bal.	188
	Bad debt expense (*solve*)	1,344
	Estimated bal. (*from aging*)	1,532

The end-of-period adjusting entry to Bad Debt Expense and Allowance for Doubtful Accounts would be made on December 31 for $1,344.

While the percentage-of-credit-sales method focuses on an income statement valuation (bad debt expense matched to the period's sales), the aging method focuses on a balance sheet valuation (estimated net realizable value of accounts receivable). Both methods are acceptable under GAAP and are widely used in practice.

FINANCIAL ANALYSIS

Sales versus Collections—The Marketing/Financial Management Conflict

Inc. Magazine reports that many managers of sales- and marketing-oriented companies fall into the trap of saying "get the sales now; work on collecting the receivables later." The article points out that these companies that emphasize sales without monitoring the collection of credit sales will soon find much of their current assets tied up in accounts receivable. Accounts receivable are good only if they can be collected in a short time.

"Cash is a necessity for service companies so they can pay their employees. Cash is also necessary to manufacturing companies so they can pay for their raw materials as well as pay their employees. The primary source of cash for a business is sales. Therefore, companies that make credit sales must ensure the collection of the amounts customers owe them—their accounts receivable. Collection of accounts receivable depends upon the creditworthiness of the customer owing for credit sales."[3] They recommend that companies minimize bad debts by following two procedures that involve a joint effort by the marketing and finance departments:

1. Establish the credit history of customers before allowing customers to charge their purchases. The savings from checking potential clients' credit history can be measured as the amount saved from fewer bad debts less the cost of the credit searches on potential customers.
2. Age accounts receivable periodically. Customers with overdue payments can then be contacted to encourage payment and future sales can be made to them only on a cash basis.

Self-Study Quiz

In an earlier year, Timberland's Form 10-K reported beginning and ending balances in the Allowance for Doubtful Accounts of $723 and $904, respectively. They also reported that write-offs of bad debts amounted to $648 (all numbers

[3]Jill Andresky Fraser, *Inc. Magazine*, June 1990, pp. 58–60.

in $000). Assuming that no previously written-off accounts had been collected (there were no reinstatements), what amount did they record as bad debt expense for the period? (*Solution approach:* Use the Allowance for Doubtful Accounts T-account to solve for the missing value.)

Allowance for Doubtful Accounts (XA)

After you complete your answer, check it with the solution presented in the footnote at the bottom of this page.*

APPLYING THE REVENUE PRINCIPLE IN SPECIAL CIRCUMSTANCES

Learning Objective 4
Apply the revenue principle to special circumstances including deferred revenues, installment sales, and long-term construction and service contracts.

The revenue principle was introduced in Chapter 3. As noted earlier, application of this principle in the case of Timberland and similar companies was fairly straightforward. Such companies record revenue when goods or services are shipped or delivered. We will now expand our discussion of the revenue principle and see how it is applied in business practice by companies other than typical manufacturers, wholesalers, and retailers.

Delayed Revenue Recognition

Recall that, to record revenue, (1) an exchange must take place, (2) the earnings process must be nearly complete, and (3) collection must be probable. If one of the criteria has not been satisfied when an exchange takes place, the recording of revenue must be delayed until all the criteria have been met. This normally occurs in two situations: when cash is collected before goods are delivered and when cash collection is highly uncertain.

Deferred Revenues

As discussed in Chapter 4, companies that collect cash before they deliver goods or services must delay revenue recognition and record deferred revenues. When *Time* magazine collects cash in advance for a one-year subscription, no revenue is recorded since the earnings process related to each portion of the subscription is not "nearly complete" until each magazine is delivered. Time Warner (which owns Time, Inc.) reports the following revenue recognition rule for magazine subscriptions:

Real World Excerpt

Time Warner Annual Report

Time Warner Inc.
NOTES TO CONSOLIDATED FINANCIAL STATEMENTS
1. SUMMARY OF SIGNIFICANT ACCOUNTING POLICIES
... The unearned portion of paid magazine subscriptions is deferred until magazines are delivered to subscribers. Upon each delivery, a proportionate share of the gross subscription price is included in revenues.

Assume that on July 31, 19A, Time Warner collected $120,000 for magazine subscriptions that would be delivered during the period August 1, 19A, to

* Allowance for Doubtful Accounts (XA)

		Beginning balance	723
Write-offs	648	Bad debt expense (*solve*)	**829**
		Ending balance	904

Beginning + Bad debt expense − Write-offs = Ending; $723 + X − 648 = $904; X = $829.

July 31, 19B. On July 31, 19A, Time Warner has received the cash (and therefore satisfied the first and third revenue recognition criteria), but the earnings process is not nearly complete (the second criterion is not met). Following the above recognition rule, Time Warner would record the following entry.

Cash (A)	120,000	
Unearned revenue (L)		120,000

Unearned revenue is reported on the balance sheet as a liability because Time Warner has an obligation to perform a future service or return the cash to its customers.

On December 31, 19A (the end of the fiscal year), Time Warner must make an adjusting entry to record the amount of revenue that was earned from delivering magazines to these customers from August through December (5 months) in the amount of $50,000 ($\$120,000 \times 5/12$).

Unearned revenue (L)	50,000	
Sales revenue (R)		50,000

On the December 31, 19A, balance sheet, Time Warner would show $70,000 of unearned revenue related to the magazines that will be delivered during 19B. The $70,000 will be recognized as sales revenue in 19B after the magazines have been delivered to the subscribers.

It should be noted that other industries besides magazine publishing must use delayed revenue recognition. For example, Southwest Airlines Co. often sells tickets to passengers weeks, and sometimes months, before the actual air travel takes place. Their annual report contains the following note:

Real World Excerpt

Southwest Airlines Annual Report

SOUTHWEST AIRLINES CO.
NOTES TO CONSOLIDATED FINANCIAL STATEMENTS

1. SUMMARY OF SIGNIFICANT ACCOUNTING POLICIES

. . .

Revenue recognition Passenger revenue is recognized when the transportation is provided. Tickets sold but not yet used are included in "Air traffic liability."

The accounting for Southwest's unearned revenue would be very similar to the publishing example.

FINANCIAL ANALYSIS

Marketing, Promotional Fares, and Revenue Recognition in the Airline Industry

Air traffic liability is a significant current liability on Southwest's balance sheet, totaling in the $10s of millions. Many airlines conduct special marketing programs where they offer summer vacationers special rates if they will buy their tickets during the winter. By reading the above note, an analyst would know that if Southwest offered a special promotion, it would not affect Southwest's net income until the passengers actually flew. Until then, the amounts would be included in air traffic liability.

Installment Method

Failure to meet the third revenue recognition criterion (collection must be probable) is a second situation where revenue recognition is delayed until after an initial exchange. When there is a great deal of uncertainty concerning the

The **installment method** recognizes revenue on the basis of cash collection after the delivery of goods.

collectibility of the sales price, revenue recognition is postponed until *cash is collected from the customer*. This revenue recognition method, called the **installment method**, is considered to be a very conservative method since it postpones revenue recognition, sometimes long after goods are delivered. The most common application is in certain types of *real estate transactions* where payment is made over a multiyear period, and a large proportion of customers stop making payments long before the final payment is due. Certain types of expensive equipment, such as supercomputers, are sometimes sold under contracts where payment is made over a multiyear period and the customers have the right to return the equipment and cease making payments if they are dissatisfied. The installment method is also appropriate here. Application of this specialized revenue recognition method is discussed in Intermediate Accounting.

Exceptions to the Revenue Recognition Criteria

Long-Term Construction Contracts

An important exception to the usual criteria exists for companies involved in long-term construction projects such as building an office complex for a large corporation. These projects may take a number of years to complete. As a result, if the company recorded no revenue or expenses directly related to the project during the years that it worked on the project and then recorded a massive amount of revenue in the year that it delivered the product to the customer, the financial statements would not accurately represent the economic activities of the firm. This method of accounting is often referred to as the *completed contract method.*

The **percentage-of-completion method** records revenue based on the percentage of work completed during the accounting period.

The **completed-contract method** records revenue when the completed product is delivered to the customer.

In order to deal with this unique problem for long-term construction projects, many companies use the **percentage-of-completion method,** which records revenue based on the percentage of work completed during the accounting period instead of the **completed-contract method,** which records revenue when the completed product is delivered to the customer.

Under the percentage-of-completion method, revenues are based on the amount of work done each year. Typically, the amount of work accomplished each year is measured by the *percentage of total cost* that was incurred during the year. For example, assume that the total contract price was $50 million and the total cost for construction was $40 million. In 19A, the construction company spent $10 million, which was 25% of the contract cost ($10 million ÷ $40 million).[4] This percentage of completion is then multiplied by the total contract revenue to determine the amount of revenue to be reported in 19A (25% × $50,000,000 = $12,500,000).

The amount of expense reported each year is the actual cost incurred ($10,000,000 in 19A), and the amount of income is simply the difference between revenue and expense ($12,500,000 − $10,000,000 = $2,500,000 in 19A). It is important to note that the total revenue, expenses, and income for the two methods over the life of the contract are exactly the same. The methods differ only in terms of the accounting periods in which the various revenues and expenses are reported (their timing). Percentage of completion recognizes income throughout the contract period; completed contract recognizes income only in the year of completion.

Notice that the percentage-of-completion method does not completely satisfy the second revenue recognition criterion because revenue is reported before the earnings process is complete. However, it is the preferred method in cases such as this because the completed-contract method makes it appear

[4]Cost overruns (underruns), which did not occur in this simple example, create additional accounting problems.

that the contractor was not able to generate any profits for the initial years of the contract and then it became very profitable in the final year. In reality, the company was active in all years. Thus, the percentage-of-completion method better represents this type of underlying economic activity.

Companies may use the percentage-of-completion method where progress toward completion and costs to complete the contract can be reasonably estimated and they have a firm contract that guarantees payment in order to satisfy the cash collectibility revenue recognition criterion. In a recent survey of 600 companies,[5] 134 companies were involved in long-term construction contracts. Only 5 used the completed-contract method. The remaining firms used the percentage-of-completion or a closely related method.

Service Contracts

Service companies that provide services over more than one accounting period often follow revenue recognition policies similar to those followed for long-term construction contracts. They may record revenue after all services have been provided (after the contract is completed) or recognize revenue from the completed portion of the services. Since the individual size of the contracts involved is often small (compared to construction contracts), and companies often are engaged in many service contracts with different beginning and ending dates, the distortion caused by the completed-contract method is usually smaller than in the case of long-term construction contracts. Yet, many service companies, such as Federal Express which provides air delivery service, employ the percentage-of-completion revenue recognition policy as indicated in the following note:

Real World Excerpt

Federal Express Annual Report

Federal Express Corporation and Subsidiaries
Notes to Consolidated Financial Statements

NOTE 1. SUMMARY OF SIGNIFICANT ACCOUNTING POLICIES

Revenue recognition. Revenue is generally recognized upon delivery of shipments. For shipments in transit, revenue is recorded based on the percentage of service completed.

For the services in progress at the end of the accounting period, Federal Express uses the percentage-of-completion method for revenue recognition, recognizing only a percentage of the revenues and related costs of providing the services based on the degree of completion of the service. This method is also called the *proportional performance* method. This form of revenue recognition is very similar to Time Warner's accounting for its subscription contracts and McDermott's accounting for its construction contracts. Each company recognizes revenues and expenses related to the *completed portion* of their contract with the customer. The major difference is that Time Warner is paid for the magazine subscriptions in advance, McDermott receives progress payments throughout the contract period, and Federal Express receives payment from its business customers after it completes provision of the service.

FINANCIAL ANALYSIS

Revenue Recognition and Financial Statement Analysis

Financial analysts cannot evaluate the income earned by a company if they do not understand how the revenue recognition criteria were applied by the company. As a result, all

[5] *Accounting Trends and Techniques* (New York: AICPA) 1993.

companies disclose any special revenue recognition issues in the notes to their financial statements. For example, General Motors' annual report states:

Real World Excerpt

General Motors Annual Report

> Certain sales under long-term contracts, primarily in the defense business, are recorded using the percentage-of-completion (cost-to-cost) method of accounting. Under this method, sales are recorded equivalent to costs incurred plus a portion of the profit expected to be realized on the contract, determined based on the ratio of costs incurred to estimated total costs at completion.

This succinct explanation of the percentage-of-completion method is an adequate explanation for someone who has read this chapter, but it is doubtful that someone who has not studied accounting would understand its meaning. This is an excellent example of why careful study of accounting is important even if you do not major in accounting.

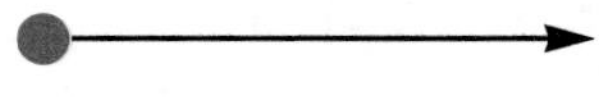

Self-Study Quiz

Assume that (1) Federal Express had shipments in transit involving fees totaling $20 million on December 31 of the current year; (2) none of the fees had been collected; and (3) on average, the shipments in transit were 60% completed.

a. What amount related to the shipments in transit would be recognized as revenue in the current year using the revenue recognition rule indicated in its footnote printed above?

b. What asset(s) would be affected by the recording of revenue from the shipments in transit (accounts and amounts)?

After you complete your answer, check it with the solution presented in the footnote at the bottom of this page.*

REPORTING AND SAFEGUARDING CASH

Cash and Cash Equivalents Defined

Learning Objective 5
Report, control, and safeguard cash.

Cash is money or any instrument that banks will accept for deposit and immediate credit to the depositor's account, such as a check, money order, or bank draft.

Cash equivalents are short-term investments with original maturities of three months or less that are readily convertible to cash and whose value is unlikely to change.

Cash is defined as money or any instrument that banks will accept for deposit and immediate credit to the depositor's account, such as a check, money order, or bank draft. Cash excludes such items as notes receivable, IOUs, and postage stamps (a prepaid expense). Cash usually is divided into three categories: cash on hand, cash deposited in banks, and other instruments that meet the definition of cash.

FASB Statement 95 defines **cash equivalents** as investments with original maturities of three months or less that are readily convertible to cash and whose value is unlikely to change (that is, are not sensitive to interest rate changes). Typical instruments included as cash equivalents are bank certificates of deposit and treasury bills that the U.S. government issues to finance its activities.

All cash accounts and cash equivalents are usually combined as one amount for financial reporting purposes, even though a company may have several bank accounts and several types of cash equivalents. Timberland reports a single account, Cash and Equivalents. It also reports that the book values of cash equivalents on the balance sheet equal their fair market value, which we should expect given the nature of the instruments included as cash equivalents (investments whose value is unlikely to change).

**a.* Delivery revenue would be recorded for $12,000,000. *b.* Accounts Receivable would increase by $12,000,000.

Many businesses receive a large amount of cash, checks, and credit card receipts from their customers each day. Cash can be spent by anyone, so management must develop procedures to safeguard the cash that is used in the business. Effective cash management involves more than protecting cash from theft, fraud, or loss through carelessness. Other cash management responsibilities are:

1. Accurate accounting so that reports of cash flows and balances may be prepared.
2. Control to assure that enough cash is on hand to meet *(a)* current operating needs, *(b)* maturing liabilities, and *(c)* unexpected emergencies.
3. Preventing excess amounts of idle cash from accumulating. Idle cash earns no revenue; therefore, it is often invested in securities to earn a revenue (return) pending future need for the cash.

Internal Control of Cash

Internal controls refers to policies and procedures that are designed to properly account for and safeguard all of the assets of the enterprise and ensure the accuracy of financial records. Internal control procedures should extend to all assets—cash, receivables, investments, operational assets, and so on. Controls that ensure the accuracy of the financial records are designed to prevent inadvertent errors and fraud like that described in the Maxidrive example discussed in Chapter 1.

Internal controls are policies and procedures designed to safeguard the assets of the business and ensure the accuracy of financial records.

Because cash is the asset most vulnerable to theft and fraud, a significant number of internal control procedures should focus on cash. You have already observed internal control procedures for cash, although you may not have known it at the time. At most movie theaters, one employee sells tickets and another employee collects the tickets. It would be less expensive to have one employee do both jobs, but it would also be easier for that single employee to steal cash and admit a patron without issuing a ticket. If different employees perform the tasks, a successful theft requires participation of both.

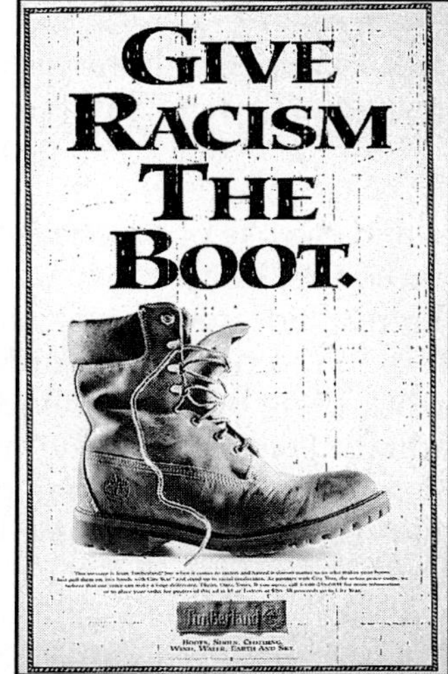

Timberland also reports on its Give Racism the Boot and City Year corporate responsibility efforts in its annual report.

QUESTION OF ETHICS

Ethics and the Need for Internal Control

Some people are bothered by the recommendation that all well-run companies should have strong internal control procedures. These people believe that control procedures suggest that the management of the company does not trust its employees. While the vast majority of employees are trustworthy, it is an unfortunate fact of life that employee theft costs businesses billions of dollars each year. Interviews with convicted felons indicate that in many cases they stole from their employers because they thought that it was easy and that no one cared (internal control procedures were not present).

Many companies give their employees a formal code of ethics that includes high standards of behavior in dealing with customers, suppliers, fellow employees, and the assets of the company. While each employee is ultimately responsible for his or her own ethical behavior, internal control procedures can be thought of as important value statements from management.

Effective internal control of cash should include:

1. Separation of duties.
   a. Complete separation of the jobs of receiving cash and disbursing cash.
   b. Complete separation of the procedures of accounting for cash receipts and cash disbursements.
   c. Complete separation of the physical handling of cash and all phases of the accounting function.
2. Responsibilities assigned to individuals.
   a. Require that all cash receipts be deposited in a bank daily. Keep any cash on hand (e.g., petty cash discussed in Chapter Supplement B) under strict control.
   b. Require separate approval of the purchases and other expenditures and separate approval of the actual cash payments. Prenumbered checks should be used. Special care must be taken with payments by electronic funds transfers since no controlled documents (checks) are processed by the bank.
   c. Assign the cash payment approval and the actual check signing or electronic funds transfer transmittal responsibilities to different individuals.
   d. Require monthly reconciliation of bank accounts with the cash accounts on the company's books (discussed in detail in Chapter Supplement A).

The separation of individual responsibilities and the use of prescribed policies and procedures are important phases in the control of cash. Separation of duties deters theft because collusion would be needed among two or more persons to steal cash and then conceal the theft in the accounting records. Prescribed procedures are designed so that the work done by one individual is checked by the results reported by other individuals. For example, the amount of cash collected at the cash register by the sales clerk can be compared with the amount of cash deposited at the bank by another employee. Reconciliation of the cash accounts to the bank statements, which is discussed in the chapter supplement, provides a further control on deposits.

All cash disbursements should be made with prenumbered checks. If prenumbered checks are not used, an employee could easily write a check to a friend and not record it. Cash payments should involve separate responsibilities for (1) payment approvals, (2) check preparation, and (3) check signing. When procedures similar to these are followed, it is difficult to conceal a fraudulent cash disbursement without the collusion of two or more persons. Again, the bank reconciliation provides an additional control on disbursements. The level of internal control, which is reviewed by the outside independent auditor, increases the reliability of the financial statements of the business.

DEMONSTRATION CASE A

(Complete the requirements before proceeding to the suggested solutions.)

Wholesale Warehouse Stores sold $950,000 in merchandise during 19C, $400,000 of which was on credit with terms 2/10, n/30. On December 31, 19C, the accounts receivable balance was $80,000 and the allowance for doubtful accounts was $3,000 (credit balance).

Required:

1. Assume that during 19C, payment on a credit sale of $2,000 was received on the ninth day after the sale. Record the receipt of payment for this sale. (Wholesale uses the gross method of accounting for sales discounts.)
2. Assume that Wholesale uses the percentage-of-sales method for estimating bad debt expense and that they estimate that 2% of credit sales will produce bad debts. Record bad debt expense for 19C.
3. Assume that Wholesale uses the aging-of-accounts method and they estimate that $10,000 worth of current accounts are uncollectible. Record bad debt expense for 19C.

SUGGESTED SOLUTION

1. Using the gross method, any sales (cash) discounts taken by customers are recorded as sales discounts which may be treated as a *contra revenue* or an *expense* on the income statement.

Cash (A)	1,960	
Sales discounts (E or XR)	40	
Accounts receivable (A)		2,000

2. The percentage estimate of bad debts should be applied to credit sales. Cash sales never produce bad debts.

Bad debt expense (E) (2% × $400,000)	8,000	
Allowance for doubtful accounts (XA)		8,000

3. The entry made when using the aging-of-accounts method is the estimated balance minus the unadjusted balance.

Bad debt expense (E) ($10,000 − $3,000)	7,000	
Allowance for doubtful accounts (XA)		7,000

SUMMARY

This chapter discussed measuring, recording, and reporting of revenues, cash, and receivables on the financial statements. Revenue recognition policies are widely recognized as one of the most important determinants of the fair presentation of financial statements. For most merchandisers and manufacturers, the appropriate revenue recognition point is the time of shipment or delivery of goods. For service companies, it is the time services are provided. Important issues facing these companies are proper recording of credit card and sales discounts, sales returns and allowances, and bad debt expense. Other companies, particularly those with long-term contracts, use special practices such as the percentage-of-completion method. Accurate comparisons between firms can only be made if differences in revenue recognition policies do not significantly affect the statements.

Cash is the most liquid of all assets, flowing continually into and out of a business. As a result, cash presents some of the most critical control problems facing the managers. Also, management of cash may be of critical importance to decision makers who must have cash available to meet current needs, yet must avoid excess amounts of idle cash which produces no revenue.

Chapter Supplement A

Reconciliation of the Cash Accounts and the Bank Statements

Bank Statements to Depositors

A **bank statement** is a monthly report from a bank that shows deposits recorded, checks cleared, other debits and credits, and a running bank balance.

Proper use of the bank accounts of a business can be an important internal control procedure for cash. Each month, the bank provides the depositor (the company) with a **bank statement** that lists (1) each deposit recorded by the bank during the period, (2) each check cleared by the bank during the period, and (3) the balance in the depositor's account. The bank statement also shows the bank charges or deductions (such as service charges) made directly to the depositor's account by the bank. The bank statement may include copies of the deposit slips and all checks that cleared through the bank during the period covered by the statement, though this practice is declining because it increases the bank's processing costs. A typical bank statement (excluding the deposit slips and canceled checks) is shown in Exhibit 6–5.

Exhibit 6–5 lists three items that need explanation. Notice that on June 20, listed under Checks and Debits, there is a deduction for $18 coded *NC*.[6] A check for $18 was received from a customer, R. Smith, and deposited by J. Doe Company with its bank, the Texas Commerce Bank. The bank processed the check through banking channels to Smith's bank. Smith's account did not have sufficient funds to cover it; therefore, Smith's bank returned it to the Texas Commerce Bank which then charged it back to J. Doe Company. This type of check often is called an *NSF check* (not sufficient funds). The NSF check is now a receivable; consequently, J. Doe Company must make an entry to debit Receivables (R. Smith) and credit Cash for the $18.

Notice the $6 listed on June 30 under Checks and Debits and coded *SC*. This is the code for bank service charges. The bank statement included a memo by the bank explaining this service charge (which was not documented by a check). J. Doe Company must make an entry to reflect this $6 decrease in the bank balance as a debit to an appropriate expense account, such as Bank Service Expense, and a credit to Cash.

Notice the $100 listed on June 12 under Deposits and the code *CM* for credit memo. The bank collected a note receivable owned by Doe and increased the

[6] These codes vary among banks.

Example of a Bank Statement **Exhibit 6–5**

Texas Commerce Bank
Austin
NATIONAL ASSOCIATION

7TH & LAVACA
AUSTIN, TEXAS 78789
PHONE: 512/476-6611

ACCOUNT NUMBER	STATEMENT DATE	PAGE NO.
877-95861	6-30-96	1

J. Doe Company
1000 Blank Road
Austin, Texas 78703

STATEMENT OF ACCOUNT
Please examine statement and checks promptly. If no error is reported within ten days, the account will be considered correct. Please report change of address.
For questions or problems call TCB-Austin's Hotline—476-6100

ON THIS DATE	YOUR BALANCE WAS	DEPOSITS ADDED NO.	DEPOSITS ADDED AMOUNT	CHECKS AND DEBITS SUBTRACTED NO.	CHECKS AND DEBITS SUBTRACTED AMOUNT	SERVICE COST	RESULTING BALANCE
6–1–96	7,762,40	5	4,050,00	23	3,490,20	6,00	8,322,20

CHECKS AND DEBITS			DEPOSITS	DATE	DAILY BALANCE
				6–1–96	7 762 40
			3 000 00	6–2–96	10 762 40
500 00				6–4–96	10 262 40
55 00	5 00	40 00		6–5–96	10 162 40
100 00			500 00	6–8–96	10 562 40
8 20	16 50	160 00		6–10–96	10 377 70
2 150 00	10 00		*100 00CM	6–12–96	8 317 70
7 50	15 30			6–16–96	8 294 90
35 00	1 50		150 00	6–17–96	8 408 40
40 20	15 00	6 00		6–18–96	8 347 20
*18 00NC				6–20–96	8 329 20
125 50	80 00	2 00		6–21–96	8 121 70
18 90			300 00	6–24–96	8 402 80
7 52	19 60			6–27–96	8 375 68
15 00	32 48			6–28–96	8 328 20
*6 00SC				6–30–96	8 322 20

Code:
CM–Credit Memo—Customer note collected
NC–Not sufficient funds
SC–Service charge

MEMBER F.D.I.C. IMPORTANT: SEE REVERSE SIDE OF STATEMENT

depositor account of J. Doe Company. The bank service charge (SC) included the collection service cost. J. Doe Company must record the collection by making an entry to debit Cash and credit Note Receivable for the $100 (assume interest on the note had been recorded).

Bank Reconciliation

A **bank reconciliation** is the process of comparing (reconciling) the ending cash balance in the company's records and the ending cash balance reported by the bank on the monthly bank statement. A bank reconciliation should be completed for each separate checking account (i.e., for each bank statement received from each bank) at the end of each month.

A **bank reconciliation** is the process of verifying the accuracy of both the bank statement and the cash accounts of a business.

Usually, the ending cash balance as shown on the bank statement does not agree with the ending cash balance shown by the related cash ledger account on the books of the depositor. For example, the cash ledger account of J. Doe Company showed the following at the end of June (Doe has only one checking account):

Cash			
June 1 balance	7,010.00	June checks written	3,800.00
June deposits	5,750.00		
Ending balance	8,960.00		

The $8,322.20 ending cash balance shown on the bank statement (Exhibit 6–5) is different from the $8,960.00 ending book balance of cash shown on the books of the J. Doe Company. This difference exists because (1) some transactions affecting cash were recorded in the books of depositor Doe but were not shown on the bank statement and (2) some transactions were shown on the bank statement but had not been recorded in the books of the depositor, Doe. The most common causes of differences between the ending bank balance and the ending book balance of cash are as follows:

1. **Outstanding checks** Checks written by the depositor and recorded in the depositor's ledger as credits to the cash account. These checks have not cleared the bank (they are not shown on the bank statement as a deduction from the bank balance). The outstanding checks are identified by comparing the canceled checks that the bank returned with the record of checks (such as check stubs or a journal) maintained by the depositor.
2. **Deposits in transit** Deposits sent to the bank by the depositor and recorded in the depositor's ledger as debits to the cash account. These deposits have not been recorded by the bank (they are not shown on the bank statement as an increase in the bank balance). Deposits in transit usually happen when deposits are made one or two days before the close of the period covered by the bank statement. Deposits in transit are determined by comparing the deposits listed on the bank statement with the copies of the deposit slips retained by the depositor or other company records.
3. **Bank service charges** An expense for bank services; listed on the bank statement. This expense must be recorded in the depositor's ledger by making a debit to an appropriate expense account, such as bank service expense, and a credit to cash.
4. **NSF checks** A "bad check" that was deposited and must be deducted from the depositor's account. The depositor must make a journal entry to debit accounts receivable and credit cash.
5. **Credit memo** A note receivable collected by the bank for the depositor. It is recorded by making a debit to cash and a credit to notes receivable.
6. **Errors** Both the bank and the depositor may make errors, especially when the volume of cash transactions is large.

Bank Reconciliation Illustrated

A bank reconciliation should be made by the depositor immediately after each bank statement is received. A bank reconciliation is an important element of internal control and is needed for accounting purposes. The bank reconciliation for the month of June prepared by J. Doe Company to reconcile the ending bank balance (Exhibit 6–5, $8,322.20) with the ending book balance ($8,960) is shown in Exhibit 6–6. On the completed reconciliation, Exhibit 6–6, the correct cash balance is $9,045. This balance is different from both the reported bank and book balances before the reconciliation.

The format of a bank reconciliation can vary. A simple and flexible one uses a balancing format with the Depositor's Books and the Bank Statement identified separately. This format starts with two different amounts: (1) the ending balance per books and (2) the ending balance per bank statement. Space is provided for additions to and subtractions from each balance so that the last line shows the same correct cash balance (for the bank and the books). This correct balance is the amount that should be shown in the cash account after the reconciliation. In this example, it is also the correct amount of cash that should be reported on the balance sheet (J. Doe Company has only one checking account and no cash on hand). J. Doe Company followed these steps in preparing the bank reconciliation:

1. **Identify the outstanding checks.** A comparison of the canceled checks returned by the bank with the company's records of all checks drawn showed the following checks still outstanding (not cleared) at the end of June:

Check No.	Amount
101	$ 145.00
123	815.00
131	117.20
Total	$1,077.20

   This total was entered on the reconciliation as a deduction from the bank account. These checks will be deducted by the bank when they clear the bank.

2. **Identify the deposits in transit.** A comparison of the deposit slips on hand with those listed on the bank statement revealed that a deposit made on June 30 for $1,800 was not listed on the bank statement. This amount was entered on the reconciliation as an addition to the bank account. It will be added by the bank when the deposit is recorded by the bank.

Bank Reconciliation Illustrated **Exhibit 6–6**

J. DOE COMPANY
Bank Reconciliation
For the Month Ending June 30, 1996

Depositor's Books			Bank Statement	
Ending cash balance per books		$8,960.00	Ending cash balance per bank statement	$8,322.20
Additions:			Additions:	
Proceeds of customer note collected by bank		100.00	Deposit in transit	1,800.00
Error in recording check No. 137		9.00		
		9,069.00		10,122.20
Deductions:			Deductions:	
NSF check of R. Smith	$18.00		Outstanding checks	1,077.20
Bank service charges	6.00	24.00		
Ending correct cash balance		$9,045.00	Ending correct cash balance	$9,045.00

3. **Record bank charges and credits:**
   a. Proceeds of note collected, $100—entered on the bank reconciliation as an addition to the book balance; it already has been included in the bank balance. A journal entry is needed to debit Cash and credit Note Receivable.
   b. NSF check of R. Smith, $18—entered on the bank reconciliation as a deduction from the book balance; it has been deducted from the bank statement balance. A journal entry is needed to credit Cash and to debit Accounts Receivable.
   c. Bank service charges, $6—entered on the bank reconciliation as a deduction from the book balance; it has been deducted from the bank balance. A journal entry is needed to credit Cash and to debit an expense account, Bank Service Expense.
4. **Determine the impact of errors.** At this point, J. Doe Company found that the reconciliation did not balance by $9. Because this amount is divisible by 9, they suspected a transposition. (A transposition, such as writing 27 for 72, always will cause an error that is exactly divisible by 9.) Upon checking the journal entries made during the month, they found that a check was written for $56 to pay an account payable. The check was recorded in the company's accounts as $65. The incorrect entry made was a debit to Accounts Payable and a credit to Cash for $65 (instead of $56). Therefore, $9 (i.e., $65 – $56) must be added to the book cash balance on the reconciliation; the bank cleared the check for the correct amount, $56. The following correcting entry must be made in the accounts: Cash, debit $9; Accounts Payable, credit $9.

Note in Exhibit 6–6 that the Depositor's Books and the Bank Statement parts of the bank reconciliation now agree at a correct cash balance of $9,045. This amount will be reported as cash on a balance sheet prepared at the end of the period. If the company had petty cash or cash on hand for making change, it would be added to the $9,045, and the total would be reported on the balance sheet.

A bank reconciliation as shown in Exhibit 6–6 accomplishes two major objectives:

1. Checks the accuracy of the bank balance and the company cash records, which involves development of the correct cash balance. The correct cash balance (plus petty cash and cash on hand, if any) is the amount of cash that is reported on the balance sheet.
2. Identifies any previously unrecorded transactions or changes that are necessary to cause the company's Cash account(s) to show the correct cash balance. These transactions or changes need journal entries. The explanations given above of the development of the bank reconciliation of J. Doe Company cite such transactions and changes. Therefore, the following journal entries based on the Depositor's Books side of the bank reconciliation (Exhibit 6–6), must be entered into the company's records.

Accounts of J. Doe Company

	Debit	Credit
a. Cash (A)	100	
Note receivable (A)		100
To record note collected by bank.		

b. Accounts receivable (A)	18	
Cash (A)		18
To record NSF check..		
c. Bank service expense (E)	6	
Cash (A)		6
To record service fees charged by bank.		
d. Cash (A)	9	
Accounts payable (L)		9
To correct error made in recording a check payable to a creditor.		

Cash account of J. Doe Company:

The cash account prior to reconciliation was given earlier in this chapter. After the above journal entries are posted, the cash account is as follows:

Cash (after Recording Results of Bank Reconciliation)

June 1 Balance	7,010.00	June Checks written	3,800.00
June Deposits	5,750.00	June 30 NSF check*	18.00
June 30 Note collected*	100.00	June 30 Bank service charge*	6.00
June 30 Correcting entry*	9.00		
Correct cash balance	$9,045.00		

*Based on the bank reconciliation.

Notice that all of the additions and deductions on the Depositor's Books side of the reconciliation need journal entries to update the cash account. The additions and deductions on the Bank Statement side do not need journal entries because they will work out automatically when they clear the bank. The cash amount reported on the balance sheet and reflected in the Cash account will be the correct cash balance only if the proper journal entries are made after the bank reconciliation is completed.

DEMONSTRATION CASE B

(Complete the requirements before proceeding to the suggested solution that follows.)

Heather Ann Long, a freshman at a large state university, has just received her first checking account statement. This was her first chance to attempt a bank reconciliation. She had the following information to work with:

Bank balance, September 1	$1,150
Deposits during September	650
Checks cleared during September	900
Bank service charge	25
Bank balance, October 1	875

Heather was surprised that her deposit of $50 that was made on September 29 had not been posted to her account and was pleased that her rent check of $200 had not cleared her account. Her checkbook balance was $750.

Required:

1. Complete Heather's bank reconciliation.
2. Why is it important for individuals such as Heather and businesses to do a bank reconciliation each month?

SUGGESTED SOLUTION

1. Heather's bank reconciliation:

Heather's Books		Bank Statement	
October 1 cash balance	$750	October 1 cash balance	$875
Additions:		Additions:	
None		Deposit in transit	50
Deductions:		Deductions:	
Bank service charge	(25)	Outstanding check	(200)
Correct cash balance	$725	Correct cash balance	$725

2. Bank statements, whether personal or business, should be reconciled each month. This process will help ensure that a correct balance is reflected in the customer's books. Failure to reconcile a bank statement will increase the chance that an error will not be discovered and may result in bad checks being written. Businesses must reconcile their bank statements for an additional reason: the correct balance that is calculated during reconciliation is recorded on the balance sheet.

Chapter Supplement B

Petty Cash

A petty cash fund is established to avoid the inconvenience and cost of writing checks for the many small payments that occur daily in some businesses. To establish a petty cash fund, a check should be written for the estimated amount needed to meet the expected payments, say, for an average month. The check, made payable to "Petty Cash," is cashed. The money is kept in a safe place under the direct control of a designated individual known as the custodian.

The custodian should keep a perpetual record of all disbursements and the amount of cash on hand. No entry is made in the regular ledger accounts at the time each payment is made from the petty cash fund. Instead, the custodian keeps a separate petty cash record in which each disbursement is recorded when made. This record is supported by documentation, such as a signed bill, voucher, or receipt for each payment made. As an internal control feature, occasional surprise audits of the fund and the records of disbursements should be conducted. Borrowing from the fund by the custodian or others should not be allowed. Careless handling of petty cash often leads to theft.

When the amount of cash held by the custodian gets low, and at the end of each accounting period, the fund should be reimbursed (or replenished) with an amount of cash sufficient to restore it to the original amount. Reimbursement is made by having the custodian submit the petty cash record and the supporting documents to the accountants. On the basis of these records, a check to "Petty Cash" is written for the amount of cash needed for replenishment, which is the same as the sum of the expenditures reported by the custodian. The check is cashed, and the money is given to the custodian, which increases the cash held by the custodian to the original amount. A journal entry is made to credit Cash for the amount of the check and to debit expenses. The petty cash documents turned in by the custodian provide the underlying support for this journal entry.

KEY TERMS

Accounts Receivable (**trade receivables** or **receivables**) Open accounts owed to the business by trade customers. *308*

Aging of Accounts Receivable Method Estimates uncollectible accounts based on the age of each account receivable. *314*

Allowance for Doubtful Accounts Contra asset account containing the estimated uncollectible accounts receivable; also called allowance for bad debts or allowance for uncollectible accounts. *309*

Allowance Method Method that bases bad debt expense on an estimate of uncollectible accounts. *309*

Bad Debt Expense (**doubtful accounts expense, uncollectible accounts expense,** or **provision for uncollectible accounts**) Expense associated with estimated uncollectible accounts receivable. *309*

Bank Reconciliation Process of verifying the accuracy of both the bank statement and the cash accounts of the business. *325*

Bank Statement Monthly report from a bank that shows deposits recorded, checks cleared, other debits and credits, and a running bank balance. *324*

Cash Money and any instrument that banks will accept for deposit and immediate credit to the depositor's account, such as a check, money order, or bank draft. *320*

Cash Equivalents Short-term investments with original maturities of three months or less that are readily convertible to cash and whose value is unlikely to change. *320*

Completed-Contract Method Records revenue when the completed product is delivered to the customer. *318*

Credit Card Discount Fee charged by the credit card company for services. *303*

Installment Method Recognizes revenue on the basis of cash collection after the delivery of goods. *318*

Internal Controls Policies and procedures designed to safeguard the assets of the business and ensure the accuracy of financial records. *321*

Note Receivable A written promise that requires another party to pay the business under specified conditions (amount, time, interest). *308*

Percentage-of-Completion Method Records revenue based on the percentage of work completed during the accounting period. *318*

Percentage of Credit Sales Method Bases bad debt expense on the historical percentage of credit sales that result in bad debts. *313*

Sales (or Cash) Discount Cash discount offered to encourage prompt payment of an account receivable. *304*

Sales Returns and Allowances A contra revenue account used to record return of or allowances for unsatisfactory goods. *305*

Trade Discount A discount that is deducted from list price to derive the actual sales price. *305*

QUESTIONS

1. Explain the difference between sales revenue and net sales.
2. What is gross profit or gross margin on sales? How is the gross profit ratio computed? In your explanation, assume that net sales revenue was $100,000 and cost of goods sold was $60,000.
3. What is a credit card discount? How does it affect amounts reported on the income statement?
4. What is a sales discount? Use 1/10, n/30 in your explanation.
5. When merchandise invoiced at $2,000 is sold on terms 2/10, n/30, the seller must make the following entry:

   Accounts receivable
   Sales revenue

   What amounts should be used in this entry under the gross method of recording sales discounts? If the buyer pays within the discount period, how will amounts on the income statement be affected?
6. A sale is made for $700; terms are 2/10, n/30. At what amount should the sale be recorded under the gross method of recording sales discounts? Give the required entry with an explanation. Also, give the collection entry assuming it is during the discount period.

7. What is the distinction between sales allowances and sales discounts?
8. Differentiate accounts receivable from notes receivable.
9. Which basic accounting principle is the allowance method of accounting for bad debts designed to satisfy?
10. Using the allowance method, is bad debt expense recognized in *(a)* the period in which sales related to the uncollectible were made, *(b)* the period in which the seller learns that the customer is unable to pay?
11. What is the effect of the write-off of bad debts (using the allowance method) on *(a)* net income and *(b)* accounts receivable, net?
12. Why are the revenue recognition criteria important?
13. What are the three revenue recognition criteria?
14. When should a company report revenue if it has not completed its earnings process but has collected all of the cash related to earning the revenue?
15. Under what circumstances would the following journal entry be made?

Cash	75,000	
Unearned revenue		75,000

16. When is it appropriate to use the percentage-of-completion method?
17. How is the percentage that is complete determined under the percentage-of-completion method?
18. If an airline sells tickets months before a passenger flies and collects cash at the point of sale, when should it record revenue?
19. If a company defers revenue to a subsequent accounting period because it has not yet earned the revenue, how should it account for the expenses that are related to earning the revenue?
20. Define cash and cash equivalents in the context of accounting and indicate the types of items that should be included and excluded.
21. Summarize the primary characteristics of an effective internal control system for cash.
22. Why should cash-handling and cash-recording activities be separated? How is this separation accomplished?
23. (Based on Supplement A) What are the purposes of a bank reconciliation? What balances are reconciled?
24. (Based on Supplement A) Briefly explain how the total amount of cash reported on the balance sheet is computed.
25. (Based on Supplement B) What is the purpose of petty cash? How is it related to the regular cash account?

EXERCISES

E6–1 Analyzing Income Statement Relationships

Supply the missing dollar amounts for the 19B income statement of Rockland Shoe Company for each of the following independent cases:

	Case A	Case B	Case C	Case D	Case E
Sales revenue	$900	$700	$410	$?	$?
Selling expense	?	150	80	400	250
Cost of goods sold	?	380	?	500	310
Income tax expense	?	30	20	40	30
Gross margin	400	?	?	?	440
Pretax income	200	90	?	190	?
Administrative expense	150	?	60	100	80
Net income	170	?	50	?	80

E6–2 *Preparing Single- and Multiple-Step Income Statements Using the Gross Margin Ratio*

The following data were taken from the records of Gonzales Electronics, Incorporated, at December 31, 19D:

Sales revenue	$120,000
Administrative expense	10,000
Selling (distribution) expense	18,000
Income tax rate	25%
Gross margin ratio	40%
Shares of stock outstanding	2,000

Required:

1. Prepare a complete single-step income statement for the company. Show all computations. (Hint: Set up side captions starting with sales revenue and ending with earnings per share; rely on the percentages given.)
2. Prepare a complete multiple-step income statement for the company (showing both gross profit and income from operations).

E6–3 *Preparing a Multiple-Step Income Statement*

The following data were taken from the records of Leung Enterprises Corporation at December 31, 19B:

Gross margin (35% ratio)	$24,500
Selling (distribution) expense	8,000
Administrative expense	?
Pretax income	12,000
Income tax rate, 30%	
Shares of stock outstanding	3,000

Required:

Prepare a complete multiple-step income statement for the company (showing both gross profit and income from operations). Show all computations. (Hint: Set up the side captions starting with sales revenue and ending with earnings per share; rely on the percentages given.)

E6–4 *Preparing a Multiple-Step Income Statement and Analyzing Gross Margin*

The following data were taken from the records of Roberts Corporation on December 31, 19B:

Sales of merchandise for cash	$110,000
Sales of merchandise for credit	252,000
Sales returns and allowances	12,000
Selling expense	70,000
Cost of goods sold	224,000
Administrative expense	32,000
Items not included in above amounts:	
Estimated bad debt loss, 1% of credit sales.	
Average income tax rate, 25%.	
Number of shares of common stock outstanding, 9,000.	

Required:

1. Based on the above data, prepare a multiple-step income statement (showing both gross profit and income from operations). There were no extraordinary items. Include a Percentage Analysis column.
2. How much was the gross margin? What was the gross margin ratio? Explain what these two amounts mean.

E6–5 Preparing a Multiple-Step Income Statement and Analyzing Gross Margin

The following summarized data were provided by the records of Slate, Incorporated, for the year ended December 31, 19B:

Sales of merchandise for cash	$220,000
Sales of merchandise on credit	32,000
Cost of goods sold	147,000
Selling expense	40,200
Administrative expense	19,000
Sales returns and allowances	7,000
Items not included in above amounts:	
Estimated bad debt loss, 2.5% of credit sales.	
Average income tax rate, 30%.	
Number of shares of common stock outstanding, 5,000.	

Required:

1. Based on the above data, prepare a multiple-step income statement (showing both gross profit and income from operations). Include a Percentage Analysis column.
2. What was the amount of gross margin? What was the gross margin ratio? Explain.

E6–6 Recording Credit Sales and Sales Discounts

During the months of January and February, Bronze Corporation sold goods to three customers. The sequence of events was as follows:

Jan.	6	Sold goods for $1,000 to S. Green and billed that amount subject to terms 2/10, n/30.
	6	Sold goods to M. Munoz for $800 and billed that amount subject to terms 2/10, n/30.
	14	Collected cash due from S. Green.
Feb	2	Collected cash due from M. Munoz.
	28	Sold goods for $500 to R. Reynolds and billed that amount subject to terms 2/10, n/45.

Required:

1. Give the appropriate journal entry for each date. Do not record cost of goods sold.
2. Assuming that sales discounts is treated as a contra revenue, compute net sales for the two months ended February 28.

E6–7 Recording Credit Sales, Sales Discounts, and Credit Card Sales

The following transactions were selected from the records of Evergreen Company:

July	12	Sold merchandise to Customer R who charged the $1,000 purchase on his VISA credit card. VISA charges Evergreen a 2% credit card fee.
	15	Sold merchandise to Customer S at an invoice price of $5,000; terms 3/10, n/30.
	20	Sold merchandise to Customer T at an invoice price of $3,000; terms 3/10, n/30.
	23	Collected payment from Customer S from July 15 sale.
Aug.	25	Collected payment from Customer T from July 20 sale.

Required:

Give the appropriate journal entry for each of the above transactions. Do not record cost of goods sold.

E6–8 Recording Credit Sales, Sales Discounts, Sales Returns, and Credit Card Sales

The following transactions were selected from among those completed by Hailey Retailers in 19B:

Nov.	20	Sold two items of merchandise to Customer B who charged the $400 sales price on her VISA credit card. VISA charges Hailey a 2% credit card fee.
	25	Sold 20 items of merchandise to Customer C at an invoice price of $4,000 (total); terms 3/10, n/30.

	28	Sold 10 items of merchandise to Customer D at an invoice price of $6,000 (total); terms 3/10, n/30.
	30	Customer D returned one of the items purchased on the 28th; the item was defective, and credit was given to the customer.
Dec.	6	Customer D paid the account balance in full.
	30	Customer C paid in full for the invoice of November 25, 19B.

Required:

1. Give the appropriate journal entry for each of the above transactions assuming the company records sales revenue under the gross method. Do not record cost of goods sold.
2. Assume that sales discounts and credit card discounts are treated as contra revenues; compute net sales for the two months ended December 31, 19B.

E6–9 Determining the Annual Interest Rate Implicit in a Sales Discount

Laura's Landscaping bills customers subject to terms 3/10, n/60.

Required:

1. Compute the annual interest rate implicit in the sales discount.
2. If his bank charges 15% interest, should the customer borrow from the bank so that he can take advantage of the discount? Explain your recommendation.

E6–10 Accounting for Bad Debts Using the Allowance Method

Connor Company started business on January 1, 19A. During the year 19A, the company's records indicated the following:

Sales on cash basis	$400,000
Sales on credit basis	150,000
Collections on accounts receivable	100,000

The manager of the company is concerned about accounting for the bad debts. At December 31, 19A, although no accounts were considered bad, several customers were considerably overdue in paying their accounts. A friend of the manager suggested a 1% bad debt rate on sales, which the manager decided to use at the start.

Required:

1. You have been employed on a part-time basis to assist with the recordkeeping for the company. The manager told you to set up bad debt expense of $5,500. Give the required entry.
2. You are concerned about how the $5,500 was determined. The manager told you it was from another manager "who knew his business" and used 1% of sales. Do you agree with the estimate of bad debts? If you disagree, give the correct entry and explain the basis for your choice.
3. Show how the various accounts related to credit sales should be shown on the December 31, 19A, income statement and balance sheet.

E6–11 Analyzing and Evaluating a Bad Debt Estimate

During 19G, Martin's Camera Shop had sales revenue of $170,000, of which $85,000 was on credit. At the start of 19G, accounts receivable showed a $10,000 debit balance, and the allowance for doubtful accounts showed an $800 credit balance. Collections of accounts receivable during 19G amounted to $68,000.

Data during 19G:

a. On December 31, 19G, an account receivable (J. Doe) of $1,500 from a prior year was determined to be uncollectible; therefore, it was written off immediately as a bad debt.

b. On December 31, 19G, on the basis of experience, a decision was made to continue the accounting policy of basing estimated bad debt losses on 2% of credit sales for the year.

Required:

1. Give the required journal entries for the two items on December 31, 19G (end of the accounting period).
2. Show how the amounts related to accounts receivable and bad debt expense would be reported on the income statement and balance sheet for 19G. Disregard income tax considerations.
3. On the basis of the data available, does the 2% rate appear to be reasonable? Explain.

Sears

E6–12 Analyzing the Impact of Uncollectible Accounts

A recent annual report for Sears contained the following information at the end of their fiscal year:

	Year 1	Year 2
Accounts receivable	$7,022,075,000	$7,336,308,000
Allowance for doubtful accounts	(86,605,000)	(96,989,000)
	$6,935,470,000	$7,239,319,000

A footnote to the financial statements disclosed that uncollectible accounts amounting to $55,000,000 were written off as bad during year 1 and $69,000,000 during year 2. Assume that the tax rate for Sears was 30%.

Required:

1. Determine the bad debt expense for year 2 based on the facts given above.
2. Working capital is defined as current assets minus current liabilities. How was Sears's working capital affected by the write-off of $69,000,000 in uncollectible accounts during year 2? What impact did the recording of bad debt expense have on working capital in year 2?
3. How was net income affected by the $69,000,000 write-off during year 2? What impact did the recording of bad debt expense have on net income for year 2?

Federal Express

E6–13 Analyzing the Write-Off of Bad Accounts

A recent annual report for Federal Express contained the following data:

	(In thousands)	
	Current Year	Previous Year
Accounts receivable	$1,034,608	$805,495
Less: Allowance for doubtful accounts	36,800	38,225
Net accounts receivable	$ 997,808	$767,270
Bad debt expense	55,147	31,388

Required:

Determine the amount of accounts receivable that were actually written off during the current year.

Daimler-Benz

E6–14 Analyzing the Impact of Uncollectible Accounts

Daimler-Benz AG is the largest industrial group in Germany. Best known as the manufacturer of Mercedes-Benz cars and trucks, it also manufactures products in the fields of rail systems, aerospace, propulsion, defense, and information technology. In its recent filings pursuant to its listing on the New York Stock Exchange, it disclosed the following information concerning its allowance for doubtful accounts (in millions of German marks denoted DM):

Balance at Beginning of Period	Charged to Costs and Expenses	Amounts Written Off	Balance at End of Period
1,933	92	(52)	1,973

Required:

1. Record summary journal entries related to bad debts for the current year.
2. If Daimler-Benz had written off an additional DM 10 million of accounts receivable during the period, how would receivables, net, and net income have been affected? Explain why.

E6–15 Drawing Financial Statement Inferences: Credit Sales and Bad Debts

Microsoft

Microsoft develops, produces, and markets a wide range of computer software including the DOS and Windows operating systems. On a recent balance sheet, Microsoft reported the following information about net sales revenue and accounts receivable.

	19B	19A
Accounts receivable, net of allowances of \$76 and \$57	\$ 338	\$ 270
Net revenues	3,753	2,759

According to its Form 10-K, Microsoft recorded bad debt expense of \$47 and did not reinstate any previously written-off accounts during 19B.

Required:

1. What amount of bad debts was written off during 19B?
2. Assuming that all of Microsoft's sales during the period were on open account, solve for cash collected from customers for 19B.

E6–16 Calculating Income Using the Percentage-of-Completion Method

The Jackson Construction Company entered into a long-term construction contract with the federal government to build a special landing strip at an Air Force base in Rapid City, South Dakota. The project took three years and cost the government \$12 million. Jackson spent the following amounts each year: 19A, \$2 million; 19B, \$5 million; 19C, \$3 million. The company uses the percentage-of-completion method. Cost estimates equaled actual costs.

Required:

Determine the amount of net income Jackson can report each year for this project.

E6–17 Determining Income Using the Percentage-of-Completion Method

The Marine Division of General Construction signed a contract with the U.S. Navy to build a large aircraft carrier with several complex computer control systems. The Marine Division spent the following amounts each year: 19A, \$10 million; 19B, \$5 million; 19C, \$20 million; 19D, \$5 million. The division expected to make \$10 million on this contract. The Division uses the percentage-of-completion method. Cost estimates equaled actual costs.

Required:

Determine the amount of revenue, expenses, and net income that the Marine Division would report each year for this project.

E6–18 Accounting for Unearned Revenue

The Dallas Evening News ran a special promotion for their customers that gave them a 20% discount if they signed a contract for a one-year subscription and paid in advance. On

September 1, 19A, the *News* collected $72,000 and immediately began supplying customers with newspapers.

Required:

1. What journal entry should be recorded by *The Dallas Evening News* on September 1, 19A?
2. What journal entry, if any, should be recorded on December 31, 19A (the end of the fiscal year for *The Dallas Evening News*)?
3. Should any journal entries be made during 19B related to this transaction? If yes, show the entry and the date.

E6–19 Accounting for Revenue before It Is Earned

On April 1, 19A, Trump Airline sold $75,000 worth of tickets to a university that planned to sponsor a trip for a large group of college students to travel to several museums on the East coast. The trip took place during the summer and was completed on August 15, 19A.

Required:

1. What journal entry would be recorded by Trump on April 1, 19A?
2. What journal entry would be recorded on August 15, 19A?
3. What type of account is Unearned Revenue? On which financial statement is it reported?

E6–20 Applying the Revenue Principle

At what point should revenue be recognized in each of the following independent cases?

Case A. For Christmas presents, McDonald's restaurant sells coupon books for $10. Each of the $1 coupons may be used in the restaurant any time during the following 12 months. The customer must pay cash when the coupon book is purchased.

Case B. Howard Land Development Corporation sold a lot to Quality Builders to construct a new home. The price of the lot was $50,000. Quality made a down payment of $100 and agreed to pay the balance in six months. After making the sale, Howard learned that Quality Builders often entered into these agreements but refused to pay the balance if they did not find a customer who wanted a house built on the lot.

Case C. In 19A, Smilor Construction Company started a long-term construction project to build a large office complex. The project was completed in 19C. At the end of 19C, Smilor had not yet sold the project because they were asking top dollar for the office space. They were very confident that they could sell the building for their asking price because there was a serious shortage of office space in the area.

Case D. Chrysler Corporation has always recorded revenue at the point of sale. Recently, they have extended their warranties to cover all repairs for a period of seven years. One young accountant with the company now questions whether Chrysler has completed its earning process when it sells the cars. She suggests that the warranty obligation for seven years means that a significant amount of additional work must be performed in the future.

E6–21 Reporting Cash and Cash Equivalents When There Are Several Bank Accounts

Strake Corporation has manufacturing facilities in several cities and has cash on hand at several locations as well as in several bank accounts. The general ledger at the end of 19A showed the following accounts: Petty Cash—Home Office, $700; City Bank—Home Office,

$58,600; Cash Held for Making Change, $300 (included in the regular cash account balance); Petty Cash—Location A, $100; National Bank—Location A, $3,350; Petty Cash—Location B, $200; Southwest Bank—Location B, $785; Petty Cash—Location C, $200; State Bank—Location C, $965; Metropolitan Bank—3-month Certificate of Deposit, $5,800; and Southwest Bank–6-month Certificate of Deposit, $850.

The bank balances given represent the current cash balances as reflected on the bank reconciliations.

Required:

What cash and cash equivalents amount should be reported on the company's 19A balance sheet? Explain the basis for your decisions on any questionable items.

E6–22 (Supplement A) Bank Reconciliation, Entries, and Reporting

Jones Company has the June 30, 19B, bank statement and the June ledger accounts for cash, which are summarized below:

Bank Statement

	Checks	Deposits	Balance
Balance, June 1, 19B			$ 7,200
Deposits during June		$17,000	24,200
Checks cleared through June	$18,100		6,100
Bank service charges	50		6,050
Balance, June 30, 19B			6,050

Cash

June 1	Balance	6,800	June	Checks written	18,400
June	Deposits	19,000			

Petty Cash

June 30 Balance	300	

Required:

1. Reconcile the bank account. A comparison of the checks written with the checks that have cleared the bank shows outstanding checks of $700. Some of the checks that cleared in June were written prior to June. There were no deposits in transit carried over from May, but there is a deposit in transit at the end of June.
2. Give any journal entries that should be made as a result of the bank reconciliation.
3. What is the balance in the cash account after the reconciliation entries?
4. What is the total amount of cash that should be reported on the balance sheet at June 30?

E6–23 (Supplement A) Bank Reconciliation, Entries, and Reporting

The September 30, 19D, bank statement for Russell Company and the September ledger accounts for cash are summarized below:

Bank Statement

	Checks	Deposits	Balance
Balance, September 1, 19D			$ 6,300
Deposits recorded during September		$27,000	33,300
Checks cleared during September	$28,500		4,800
NSF checks—Betty Brown	150		4,650
Bank service charges	50		4,600
Balance, September 30, 19D			4,600

Cash

Sept. 1	Balance	6,300	Sept.	Checks written	28,600
Sept.	Deposits	28,000			

Petty Cash		
Sept. 30 Balance	400	

There were no outstanding checks and no deposits in transit carried over from August; however, there are deposits in transit and checks outstanding at the end of September.

Required:

1. Reconcile the bank account.
2. Give any journal entries that should be made as the result of the bank reconciliation.
3. What should the balance in the cash account be after the reconciliation entries?
4. What total amount of cash should the company report on the September 30 balance sheet?

E6–24 (Supplement A) Bank Reconciliation

The March 31, 19C, bank statement for State Company and the March ledger accounts for cash are summarized below:

Bank Statement	Checks	Deposits	Balance
Balance, March 1, 19C			$10,650
Deposits during March		$29,000	39,650
Notes collected for depositor (including $100 interest)		980	40,630
Checks cleared during March	$32,200		8,430
Bank service charges	25		8,405
Balance, March 31, 19C			8,405

Cash					
Mar. 1	Balance	10,100	Mar.	Checks written	32,500
Mar.	Deposits	31,000			

Petty Cash		
Mar. 31 Balance	200	

A comparison of March deposits recorded on the company's books with deposits on the bank statement showed deposits in transit of $2,000. Outstanding checks at the end of March were determined to be $850.

Required:

1. Prepare a bank reconciliation for March. The bank figures have been verified as correct.
2. Give any journal entries that should be made by the company based on the reconciliation.
3. What amount should be shown as the ending balance in the Cash account after the reconciliation entries? What total amount of cash should be reported on the company's balance sheet at the end of March?

E6–25 (Supplement B) Accounting and Reporting Petty Cash

On January 1, 19B, Italy Company established a petty cash fund of $300 by writing a check to Petty Cash. The fund was assigned to J. Walton, an employee, to administer as custodian. At the end of January, $58 cash remained in the fund. Signed receipts existed for the following petty cash expenditures during January: postage, $48; office supplies, $52; transportation, $88; newspapers, $34; and miscellaneous (coffee for the office), $20.

Required:

1. Give the journal entry to establish the petty cash fund on January 1, 19B.
2. Give the journal entry to replenish the fund on January 31, 19B.

3. What balance would be shown in the Petty Cash account in the ledger at January 31? Explain.
4. How would petty cash be reported on the balance sheet at January 31, 19B?
5. Explain how the petty cash fund affected the January 19B income statement.
6. Assume it is January 5, 19C, and the management has decided to decrease the petty cash fund to $200. Give the required journal entry.

PROBLEMS

P6–1 Understanding the Income Statement

The following data were taken from the year-end records of Nomura Export Company. You are to fill in all of the missing amounts. Show computations.

	Independent Cases	
Income Statement Items	**Case A**	**Case B**
Gross sales revenue	$160,000	$232,000
Sales returns and allowances	?	18,000
Net sales revenue	?	?
Cost of goods sold	(68%)?	?
Gross margin on sales	?	(30%)?
Operating expenses	18,500	?
Pretax income	?	20,000
Income tax expense (20%)	?	?
Income before extraordinary items	?	?
Extraordinary items	10,000 (gain)	2,000 (loss)
Less: Income tax (20%)	?	?
Net income	?	?
EPS (10,000 shares)	3.00	?

P6–2 Preparing a Multiple-Step Income Statement

Builders Company, Inc., sells heavy construction equipment. There are 10,000 shares of capital stock outstanding. The annual fiscal period ends on December 31. The following condensed trial balance was taken from the general ledger on December 31, 19D:

Account Titles	**Debit**	**Credit**
Cash	$ 42,000	
Accounts receivable	18,000	
Inventory, ending	65,000	
Operational assets	50,000	
Accumulated depreciation		$ 21,000
Liabilities		30,000
Capital stock		90,000
Retained earnings, January 1, 19D		11,600
Sales revenue		182,000
Sales returns and allowances	7,000	
Cost of goods sold	98,000	
Selling expense	17,000	
Administrative expense	18,000	
Interest expense	2,000	
Extraordinary loss, unusual and infrequent storm damage	8,000	
Income tax expense*	9,600	
Totals	$334,600	$334,600

*Assume a 30% average tax rate on both operations and the extraordinary loss.

Required:

Prepare a multiple-step income statement (showing both gross profit and income from operations).

P6–3 *Preparing and Analyzing a Multiple-Step Income Statement*

Big Tommy Corporation is a local grocery store organized seven years ago as a corporation. At that time, common stock totaling 6,000 shares was issued to the three organizers. The store is in an excellent location, and sales have increased each year. At the end of 19G, the bookkeeper prepared the following statement (assume all amounts are correct; note the inappropriate terminology and format):

BIG TOMMY CORPORATION
Profit and Loss
December 31, 19G

	Debit	Credit
Sales		$420,000
Cost of goods sold	$279,000	
Sales returns and allowances	10,000	
Selling expense	58,000	
Administrative and general expense	16,000	
Interest expense	1,000	
Extraordinary loss	6,000	
Income tax expense (on operations, $16,800 less $1,800 saved on the extraordinary loss)	15,000	
Net profit	35,000	
Totals	$420,000	$420,000

Required:

Prepare a multiple-step income statement (showing both gross profit and income from operations). Assume an average 30% income tax rate.

P6–4 *Recording Sales, Returns, and Bad Debts*

The data below were selected from the records of May Company for the year ended December 31, 19C.

Balances January 1, 19C:	
Accounts receivable (various customers)	$102,000
Allowance for doubtful accounts	6,000

In the order given below, except for cash sales, sold merchandise and made collections on credit terms 2/10, n/30 (assume a unit sales price of $500 in all transactions and use the gross method to record sales revenue).

Transactions during 19C:

a. Sold merchandise for cash, $228,000.

b. Sold merchandise to R. Jones; invoice price, $12,000.

c. Sold merchandise to K. Black; invoice price, $26,000.

d. Two days after purchase date, R. Jones returned one of the units purchased in *(b)* above and received account credit.

e. Sold merchandise to B. Sears; invoice price, $24,000.

f. R. Jones paid his account in full within the discount period.

g. Collected $98,000 cash from customer sales on credit in prior year, all within the discount periods.

h. K. Black paid the invoice in *(c)* above within the discount period.

i. Sold merchandise to R. Roy; invoice price, $17,000.

j. Three days after paying the account in full, K. Black returned seven defective units and received a cash refund.

k. After the discount period, collected $7,000 cash on an account receivable on sales in a prior year.

l. The company wrote off a 19A account of $2,900 after deciding that the amount would never be collected.

m. The estimated bad debt rate used by the company was 1% of credit sales net of returns.

Required:

1. Give the journal entries for the above transactions, including the write-off of the uncollectible account and the adjusting entry for estimated bad debts. Do not record cost of goods sold. Show computations for each entry.
2. Show how the accounts related to the above sale and collection activities should be reported on the 19C income statement. (Treat sales discounts as a contra revenue.)

P6–5 *Interpreting Disclosure of Allowance for Doubtful Accounts*

Kimberly-Clark

Kimberly-Clark manufactures and markets a variety of paper and synthetic fiber products, the best known of which is Kleenex tissues. It recently disclosed the following information concerning the allowance for doubtful accounts on its Form 10-K Annual Report submitted to the Securities and Exchange Commission.

Schedule VIII

VALUATION AND QUALIFYING ACCOUNTS
FOR THE YEARS ENDED DECEMBER 31, 19C, 19B, AND 19A
(Millions of dollars)

Description: Allowances for Doubtful Accounts	Balance at Beginning of Period	Charged to Costs and Expenses	Charged to Other Accounts[a]	Write-Offs	Balance at End of Period
December 31, 19C	$8.2	$4.5	$.2	$ 2.7	$10.2
December 31, 19B	7.1	4.8	—	(?)	8.2
December 31, 19A	6.4	(?)	.2	3.3	7.1

[a] Primarily bad debt recoveries

Required:

1. Record summary journal entries related to bad debts for 19C.
2. Supply the missing dollar amounts noted by (?) for 19A and 19B.

P6–6 *Determining Bad Debt Expense Based on Aging Analysis*

Green Pastures Equipment Company uses the aging approach to estimate bad debt expense at the end of each accounting year. Credit sales occur frequently on terms n/60. The balance of each account receivable is aged on the basis of three time periods as follows: *(a)* not yet due, *(b)* up to one year past due, and *(c)* more than one year past due. Experience has shown that for each age group the average loss rate on the amount of the receivable at year-end due to uncollectability is *(a)* 1%, *(b)* 5%, and *(c)* 30%.

At December 31, 19F (end of the current accounting year), the accounts receivable balance was $41,000 and the allowance for doubtful accounts balance was $1,020 (credit). To simplify, only five customer accounts are used; the details of each on December 31, 19F, follow:

B. Brown—Account Receivable

Date	Explanation	Debit	Credit	Balance
3/11/19E	Sale	14,000		14,000
6/30/19E	Collection		5,000	9,000
1/31/19F	Collection		4,000	5,000

D. Donalds—Account Receivable

Date	Explanation	Debit	Credit	Balance
2/28/19F	Sale	22,000		22,000
4/15/19F	Collection		10,000	12,000
11/30/19F	Collection		8,000	4,000

N. Napier—Account Receivable

Date	Explanation	Debit	Credit	Balance
11/30/19F	Sale	9,000		9,000
12/15/19F	Collection		2,000	7,000

S. Strothers—Account Receivable

3/2/19D	Sale	5,000		5,000
4/15/19D	Collection		5,000	–0–
9/1/19E	Sale	10,000		10,000
10/15/19E	Collection		8,000	2,000
2/1/19F	Sale	19,000		21,000
3/1/19F	Collection		5,000	16,000
12/31/19F	Sale	3,000		19,000

T. Thomas—Account Receivable

12/30/19F	Sale	6,000		6,000

Required:

1. Set up an aging analysis schedule and complete it.
2. Compute the estimated uncollectible amount for each age category and in total.
3. Give the adjusting entry for bad debt expense at December 31, 19F.
4. Show how the amounts related to accounts receivable should be presented on the 19F income statement and balance sheet.

P6–7 Accounting for Unearned Revenue

Innovative Ideas, Incorporated, developed a unique service for busy people. The Christmas holiday is a traditional time for parties, with the largest often being a New Year's celebration. Unfortunately, most people have to return to work the next day and are in no mood to clean up after the festivities. Innovative Ideas uses college students who are on Christmas break to clean homes during the first week of January. These same students spend the last two weeks of December going door to door to sell the services. In December 19A, Innovative sold $25,000 worth of cleaning contracts and paid the sales force $5,000 in commissions. In January 19B, the company performed the cleaning services and paid the students an additional $7,500 for their work. After the work was completed, the company collected cash from their customers.

Required:

1. Prepare journal entries for each of the transactions listed above.
2. What amount of net income (or loss) should Innovative report each year?
3. What journal entries would be different if Innovative Ideas collected cash from the customers in December when they signed the cleaning contracts? How would this affect the net income or loss that is reported each year?

P6–8 Accounting for Revenue before It Is Earned

Trans America Airways sold $100,000 worth of tickets during December 19A for travel that will take place during January 19B. The company collected cash for the tickets at the time of sale. Trans America paid $15,000 in commissions to travel agents in December. Customers completed $95,000 worth of travel during January but inclement weather in Detroit forced the cancellation of several flights. Trans America refunded fares to the affected passengers.

Required:

1. Prepare all necessary journal entries for 19A and 19B to record these events.
2. Determine the net income for Trans America for 19A and 19B assuming that there were no revenues and expenses other than the ones mentioned in the case.

P6–9 Analyzing Internal Control

Cripple Creek Company has one trusted employee who, as the owner said, "handles all of the bookkeeping and paperwork for the company." This employee also is responsible for counting, verifying, and recording cash receipts and payments, such as making the weekly bank deposit, preparing checks for major expenditures (signed by the owner), making small expenditures from the cash register for daily expenses, and collecting accounts receivable. The owners asked the local bank for a $20,000 loan. The bank asked that an audit be performed covering the year just ended. The independent auditor (a local CPA), in a private conference with the owner, presented some evidence of the following activities of the trusted employee during the past year:

a. Cash sales sometimes were not entered in the cash register, and the trusted employee pocketed approximately $50 per month.

b. Cash taken from the cash register (and pocketed by the trusted employee) was replaced with expense memos with fictitious signatures (approximately $12 per day).

c. A $300 collection on an account receivable of a valued out-of-town customer was pocketed by the trusted employee and was covered by making a $300 entry as a debit to sales returns and a credit to accounts receivable.

d. An $800 collection on an account receivable from a local customer was pocketed by the trusted employee and was covered by making an $800 entry as a debit to allowance for doubtful accounts and a credit to accounts receivable.

Required:

1. What was the approximate amount stolen during the past year?
2. What would be your recommendations to the owner?

P6–10 *(Supplement A) Preparing a Bank Reconciliation and Related Journal Entries*

The bookkeeper at Hopkins Company has not reconciled the bank statement with the cash account, saying, "I don't have time." You have been asked to prepare a reconciliation and review the procedures with the bookkeeper.

The April 30, 19D, bank statement and the April ledger accounts for cash showed the following (summarized):

Bank Statement

	Checks	Deposits	Balance
Balance, April 1, 19D			$25,850
Deposits during April		$36,000	61,850
Notes collected for depositor (including $70 interest)		1,070	62,920
Checks cleared during April	$44,200		18,720
NSF check—A. B. Wright	140		18,580
Bank service charges	50		18,530
Balance, April 30, 19D			18,530

Cash

Apr. 1	Balance	23,250	Apr.	Checks written	43,800
Apr.	Deposits	42,000			

Petty Cash

Apr. 31 Balance	100	

A comparison of checks written before and during April with the checks cleared through the bank showed outstanding checks at the end of April of $2,200. No deposits in transit were carried over from March, but there was a deposit in transit at the end of April.

Required:

1. Prepare a detailed bank reconciliation for April.
2. Give any required journal entries as a result of the reconciliation. Why are they necessary?

3. What were the balances in the cash accounts in the ledger on May 1, 19D?
4. What total amount of cash should be reported on the balance sheet at the end of April?

P6–11 *(Supplement A) Computing Outstanding Checks and Deposits in Transit and Preparing a Bank Reconciliation and Journal Entries*

The August 19B bank statement for Martha Company and the August 19B ledger accounts for cash are given below:

Bank Statement

Date		Checks	Deposits	Balance
Aug.	1			$17,470
	2	$ 300		17,170
	3		$12,000	29,170
	4	400		28,770
	5	250		28,520
	9	900		27,620
	10	300		27,320
	15		4,000	31,320
	21	400		30,920
	24	21,000		9,920
	25		7,000	16,920
	30	800		16,120
	30		2,180*	18,300
	31	100†		18,200

*$2,000 note collected plus interest.
†Bank service charge.

Cash

		Checks written:	
Aug. 1 Balance	16,520		
Deposits		Aug. 2	300
Aug. 2	12,000	4	900
12	4,000	15	290
24	7,000	17	550
31	5,000	18	800
		18	400
		23	21,000

Petty Cash

Aug. 31 Balance	200		

Outstanding checks at the end of July were $250, $400, and $300. There were no deposits in transit at the end of July.

Required:

1. Compute the deposits in transit at the end of August.
2. Compute the outstanding checks at the end of August.
3. Prepare a bank reconciliation for August.
4. Give any journal entries that should be made as a result of the bank reconciliation by the company. Why are they necessary?
5. After the reconciliation journal entries are posted, what balances would be reflected in the cash accounts in the ledger?
6. What total amount of cash should be reported on the August 31, 19B, balance sheet?

P6–12 *(Supplement A) Computing Outstanding Checks and Deposits in Transit and Preparing a Bank Reconciliation*

The December 31, 19B, bank statement for Packer Company and the December 19B ledger accounts for cash are given below.

Bank Statement

Date		Checks	Deposits	Balance
Dec.	1			$48,000
	2	$400; 300	$17,000	64,300
	4	7,000; 90		57,210
	6	120; 180; 1,600		55,310
	11	500; 1,200; 70	28,000	81,540
	13	480; 700; 1,900		78,460
	17	12,000; 8,000		58,460
	23	60; 23,500	36,000	70,900
	26	900; 2,650		67,350
	28	2,200; 5,200		59,950
	30	17,000; 1,890; 300*	19,000	59,760
	31	1,650; 1,350; 150†	5,250‡	61,860

*NSF check, J. Left, a customer.
†Bank service charge.
‡Note collected, principal, $5,000 plus interest.

Cash

		Checks written during December:		
Dec. 1 Balance	64,100			
Deposits		60	5,000	2,650
Dec. 11	28,000	17,000	5,200	1,650
23	36,000	700	1,890	2,200
30	19,000	3,300	1,600	7,000
31	13,000	1,350	120	300
		180	90	480
		12,000	23,500	8,000
		70	500	1,900
		900	1,200	

Petty Cash

Dec. 31 Balance	300	

The November 19B bank reconciliation showed the following: correct cash balance at November 30, $62,300; deposits in transit on November 30, $17,000; and outstanding checks on November 30, $400 + $500 = $900.

Required:

1. Compute the deposits in transit December 31, 19B.
2. Compute the outstanding checks at December 31, 19B.
3. Prepare a bank reconciliation at December 31, 19B.
4. Give any journal entries that should be made as a result of the bank reconciliation made by the company. Why are they necessary?
5. After the reconciliation journal entries, what balances would be reflected in the cash accounts in the ledger?
6. What total amount of cash should be reported on the December 31, 19B, balance sheet?

CASES

C6–1 Analyzing and Evaluating Internal Controls

Lane Manufacturing Company is a relatively small local business that specializes in the repair and renovation of antique furniture. The owner is an expert craftsman. Although a number of skilled workers are employed, there is always a large backlog of work to be done. A long-time employee, who serves as clerk-bookkeeper, handles cash receipts, keeps the records, and writes checks for disbursements. The checks are signed by the owner. Small amounts are paid in cash by the clerk-bookkeeper, subject to a month-end review by the owner. Approximately 80 regular customers regularly are extended credit that typically amounts to less than $1,000. Although credit losses are small, in recent years the bookkeeper had established an allowance for doubtful accounts, and all write-offs were made at year-end. During January 19E (the current year), the owner decided to start construction as soon as possible of a building for the business that would provide many advantages over the presently rented space and would have space usable for expansion of facilities. As a part of the considerations in financing, the financing institution asked for 19D audited financial statements. The company statements never had been audited. Early in the audit, the independent CPA found numerous errors and one combination of amounts, in particular, that caused concern.

There was some evidence that a $2,500 job completed by Lane had been recorded as a receivable (from a new customer) on July 15, 19D. The receivable was credited for a $2,500 cash collection a few days later. The new account never was active again. The auditor also observed that shortly thereafter three write-offs of Accounts Receivable balances had been made to Allowance for Doubtful Accounts as follows: Jones, $800; Blake, $750; and Sellers, $950—all of whom were known as regular customers. These write-offs drew the attention of the auditor.

Required:

1. What caused the CPA to be concerned? Explain. Should the CPA report the suspicions to the owner?
2. What recommendations would you make in respect to internal control procedures for this company?

UPS, Federal Express, Airborne

C6–2 Alternative Recognition Points and Financial Statement Analysis

UPS, Federal Express, and Airborne are three of the major players in the highly competitive package delivery industry. Comparability is a key qualitative characteristic of accounting numbers that allows analysts to compare similar companies. However, the revenue recognition footnotes of the three competitors reveal three different revenue recognition points for package delivery revenue: package delivery, percentage of service completed, and package pickup. These points correspond to the end, continuous recognition, and the beginning of the earnings process.

United Parcel Service of America, Inc.
Revenue is recognized upon delivery of a package.

Federal Express Corporation
Revenue is generally recognized upon delivery of shipments. For shipments in transit, revenue is recorded based on the percentage of service completed.

Airborne Freight Corp.
Domestic revenues and most domestic operating expenses are recognized when shipments are picked up from the customer....

However, the Airborne footnote goes on to say: "The net revenue resulting from existing recognition policies does not materially differ from that which would be recognized on a delivery date basis."

Required:

1. Do you believe that the difference between Airborne's and UPS's revenue recognition policies materially affect their reported earnings? Why or why not?
2. Assume that all three companies pick up packages from customers and receive payment of $1 million for services each day of the year, and that each package takes two days to deliver. What would each company's service revenue be for a year given their stated revenue recognition policy?
3. Given your answers to question 2, under what conditions would that answer change?
4. Which revenue recognition rule do you prefer? Why?

Foster's Brewing

C6–3 Financial Statement Analysis and Bad Debt Disclosure

Foster's Brewing controls over 50% of the beer market in Australia, and owns 40% of Molson Breweries of Canada and 100% of Courage Limited of the United Kingdom. As an Australian company, it follows Australian GAAP and uses Australian accounting terminology. In the footnotes to its recent annual report, it discloses the following information on receivables (all numbers are reported in thousands of Australian dollars):

Note 3: Receivables	**19B**	**19A**
Current		
Trade debtors	792,193	999,159
Provision for doubtful debts	(121,449)	(238,110)
Other debtors	192,330	130,288
Provision for doubtful debts	(384)	(2,464)
Non-current		
Trade debtors	164,808	200,893
Other debtors	15,094	16,068
Provision for doubtful debts	(7,920)	(7,400)

Note 15: Operation Profit	**19B**	**19A**
Amounts set aside to provisions for		
Doubtful debts—trade debtors	(21,143)	(53,492)
Doubtful debts—other debtors	(228)	(2,570)

Required:

1. The account titles used by Foster's are different from those normally used by U.S. companies. What account titles do they use in place of Allowance for Doubtful Accounts and Bad Debts Expense?
2. Sales on account for 19B were $9,978,875. Compute the accounts receivable—trade debtors turnover ratio for 19B (ignore uncollectible accounts).
3. Compute Provision for Doubtful Debts as a percentage of current receivables separately for receivables from trade debtors and receivables from others. Explain why these percentages might be different.
4. What was the total amount of receivables written off in 19B?

C6–4 Financial Statement Analysis

Toys "Я" Us

Refer to the financial statements of Toys "Я" Us given in Appendix B at the end of this book.

Required:

1. How much cash and cash equivalents does the company hold at the end of the current year?
2. The company does not report bad debt expense on the income statement. Explain why.
3. Compare the company's accounts and other receivables as a percentage of total assets to that of Timberland (see Exhibit 6–2) which has total assets of $290,611,000. Explain the differences in these percentages.

C6–5 Financial Statement Analysis

Toys "Я" Us

Refer to the financial statements of Toys "Я" Us given in Appendix B at the end of this book.

Required:

1. What does the company disclose about the market value of its cash and cash equivalents? Would you expect this statement to be true given the securities included in cash equivalents?
2. The company does not report allowance for doubtful accounts on the balance sheet or in the footnotes. Explain why.
3. Compare the company's gross profit percentage to that of Timberland (see Exhibit 6–1). What might cause the difference?

7

MEASURING INVENTORY AND COST OF GOODS SOLD

Closely related to recording revenue is recording the cost of what was sold. This chapter focuses on transactions related to inventory and cost of goods sold. This topic is important because cost of goods sold has a major impact on a company's gross profit and net income, which are closely watched by investors, analysts, and other users of financial statements. Increasing emphases on quality, productivity, and cost have further focused production managers' attention on cost of goods sold and inventory. Since inventory cost figures play a major role in product introduction and pricing decisions, they are also important to marketing and general managers. Finally, since inventory accounting has a major effect on many companies' tax liabilities, this is an important place to introduce the effect of taxation on management decision making and financial reporting.

LEARNING OBJECTIVES

After studying this chapter, you should be able to:

Management Decision Setting

HARLEY-DAVIDSON, INC.

From Turmoil to Triumph as a World-Class Manufacturer

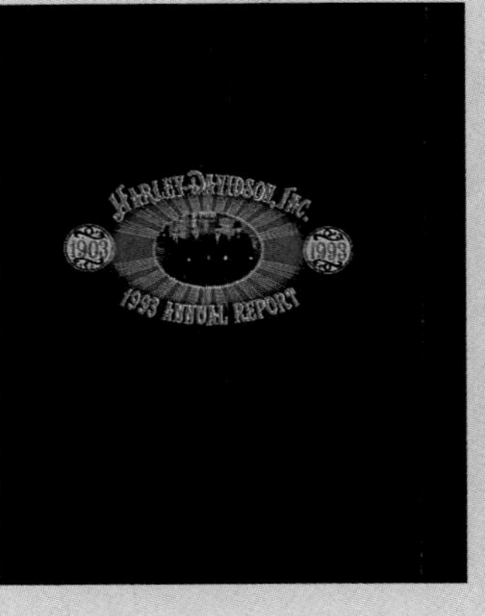

Written off in the early 1980s as unable to compete with its more reliable Japanese rivals, Harley-Davidson now controls nearly two-thirds of the U.S. market for superheavyweight motorcycles. The Milwaukee-based company has more than doubled motorcycle production in the last decade, has dramatically expanded its riding and fashion apparel sales, and even sells 30 percent of its bikes overseas. The Harley-Davidson eagle trademark was once known best as a popular request in tattoo parlors. Now over $1 million worth of neckties emblazoned with its trademarks are sold each year. The stunning popularity of its products across the tattoo and necktie sets is the net result of involved employees working in teams to make Harley-Davidson a world-class manufacturer of motorcycles in terms of inventory quality and costs. While significant investments have been made in new plant, the company also focuses on empowering, educating, and training both salaried and unionized employees to achieve personal growth, improvements in inventory quality, and reductions in the components of inventory cost: raw materials, labor, and overhead. While Harley-Davidson does not manufacture the apparel it sells, it does work closely with apparel suppliers to maximize quality and minimize inventory costs. The provision of accurate and timely inventory accounting information is a key to many of these efforts. Furthermore, in a typical year, selection of appropriate accounting methods for inventory saves Harley-Davidson over $500,000 in income taxes.

However, competition in the industry remains fierce, and the domestic market for superheavyweight bikes is growing slowly. Its major competitors, Honda and Suzuki, also have more financial and marketing resources available. Continuous improvement in manufacturing and inventory management will be necessary for the Harley-Davidson eagle to continue its rise.

BUSINESS BACKGROUND

Concerns about the cost and quality of inventory face all modern manufacturers and merchandisers and turn our attention to *cost of goods sold* on the income statement and *inventory* on the balance sheet. Exhibit 7–1 presents the relevant excerpts from Harley-Davidson's financial statements that present these accounts. Cost of goods sold is subtracted from net sales to produce gross profit on its multiple-step income statement. (The multiple-step format is discussed in Chapter 5.) Inventory is a current asset on the balance sheet. It is reported below cash and accounts receivable because it is less liquid than those two current assets.

Harley-Davidson's successful management of production, cost of goods sold, and inventory requires a joint effort by human resource managers, engineers and production managers, marketing managers, and accounting and financial managers. It is truly a multidisciplinary task. The primary goals of inventory management are to have sufficient quantities of high-quality inventory available to serve customers' needs while minimizing the costs of carrying inventory (production, storage, obsolescence, financing, etc.). For example, purchasing or producing too *few* units of a hot-selling item causes stock-outs that mean lost sales revenue and decreases in customer satisfaction. Purchasing too *many* units of a slow-selling apparel item increases the storage costs and interest costs on short-term borrowings to finance the inventory purchases, and may even lead to losses if the merchandise cannot be sold at normal prices.

To meet these inventory management goals, marketing, financial, and production managers must work together to forecast customer demand for different motorcycle models or apparel items and provide feedback so that production or purchasing adjustments can be made. Production, human resource, and purchasing managers must also work on controlling the cost of goods sold to improve gross profit margin. Towards the end of the chapter, we

Balance Sheet and Income Statement Excerpts **Exhibit 7–1**

HARLEY-DAVIDSON, INC. CONSOLIDATED BALANCE SHEET *(In thousands, except per share amounts)*	
December 31	**1993**
Assets	
Current assets:	
Cash and cash equivalents	$44,122
Accounts receivable, net of allowance for doubtful accounts	93,178
Inventories	94,428
Total Current Assets	265,465

HARLEY-DAVIDSON, INC. CONSOLIDATED STATEMENT OF INCOME *(In thousands, except per share amounts)*	
Year ended December 31	**1993**
Net sales	$1,105,284
Cost of goods sold	808,871
Gross profit	296,413

discuss how faulty inventory purchasing decisions can even affect Harley's income tax liability. As a consequence, managers, investors, and financial analysts emphasize cost of goods sold and inventory because they are such important determinants of a company's success.

The accounting system plays three roles in the inventory management process. First, the system must provide accurate information necessary for preparation of periodic financial statements and reports to tax authorities.[1] Second, it must provide up-to-date information on inventory quantities and costs to facilitate ordering and manufacturing decisions. Third, since inventories are subject to theft and other forms of misuse, the system must also provide the information necessary to help protect these important assets. We will first discuss the important choices management must make in the financial and tax reporting process. We will then briefly discuss how accounting systems are organized to keep track of inventory quantities and costs for decision making and control. This topic will be the principal subject matter of your managerial accounting course.

Harley's successful production and inventory management strategy and its mix of product lines make it a particularly good example for this chapter. The organization of Harley-Davidson's Motorcycle Division is illustrated in Exhibit 7–2. Though best known as a *manufacturer* of motorcycles, Harley also purchases and resells completed products such as its popular line of Motorclothes™ apparel. In the second case, it acts as a *wholesaler,* or middleman. Both the motorcycle and Motorclothes™ product lines are sold to the public through a network of independent dealers who are the *retailers* for the products. From an accounting standpoint, these independent dealers are Harley-Davidson's customers. The inventory accounting problems faced by wholesalers and retailers (both often called *merchandisers*) are similar and will be covered by

[1]As we discuss later, tax reports often differ from the statements prepared for other external users.

Exhibit 7–2 Harley-Davidson Motorcycle Division Product Lines

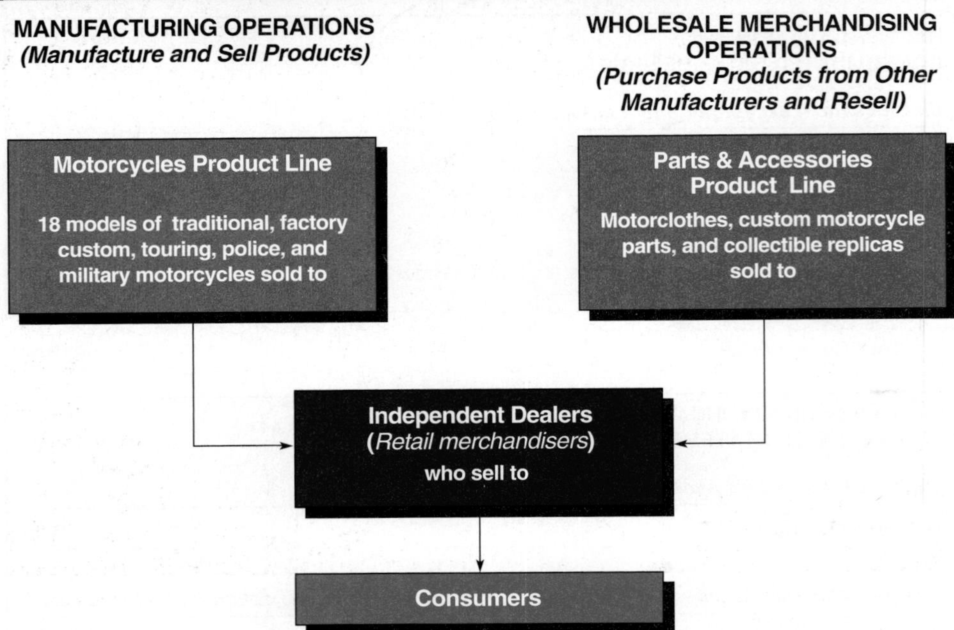

discussing the Motorclothes™ line. The additional complexities faced by manufacturers will be discussed in the context of the motorcycle product line.[2] We will also illustrate the application of these same inventory accounting principles to other companies that face different economic circumstances.

NATURE OF INVENTORY AND COST OF GOODS SOLD

Items Included in Inventory

Learning Objective 1
Apply the cost principle to identify the amounts that should be included in inventory and the matching principle to determine cost of goods sold for typical retailers, wholesalers, and manufacturers.

Inventory is tangible property that is held for sale in the normal course of business or will be used in producing goods or services for sale.

Merchandise inventory includes goods held for resale in the ordinary course of business.

Raw materials inventory includes items acquired for the purpose of processing into finished goods.

Inventory is tangible property that (1) is held for sale in the normal course of business or (2) will be used in producing goods or services for sale. Inventory is reported on the balance sheet as a current asset because it usually will be used or converted into cash within one year or within the next operating cycle of the business, whichever is longer. The kinds of inventory normally held depend on the characteristics of the business. Merchandisers (wholesale or retail businesses) hold the following:

> **Merchandise inventory** Goods (or merchandise) held for resale in the normal course of business. The goods usually are acquired in a finished condition and are ready for sale without further processing.

For Harley-Davidson, merchandise inventory includes the Motorclothes™ line and other parts and accessories it purchases for sale to its independent dealers.

Manufacturing businesses hold the following:

> **Raw materials inventory** Items acquired by purchase, growth (such as food products), or extraction (natural resources) for processing into finished goods. Such items are included in raw materials inventory until used, at which point they become part of work in process inventory.

[2]Harley-Davidson also manufactures recreational vehicles and commercial vehicles.

The success of Harley-Davidson's 90th anniversary motorcycle caravan demonstrates the intense loyalty of its customers.

Work in process inventory Goods in the process of being manufactured but not yet completed. When completed, work in process inventory becomes finished goods inventory.

Finished goods inventory Goods manufactured by the business, completed and ready for sale.

Inventories related to Harley-Davidson's motorcycle manufacturing operations are recorded in these accounts.

Work in process inventory includes goods in the process of being manufactured.

Finished goods inventory includes manufactured goods that are completed and ready for sale.

Inventory Cost

Goods in inventory are recorded in conformity with the *cost principle.* The primary basis of accounting for inventory is cash equivalent cost, which is the price paid or consideration given to acquire an asset. Inventory cost includes, in principle, the sum of the applicable expenditures and charges directly or indirectly incurred in bringing an article to usable or salable condition and location.

When Harley-Davidson purchases raw materials for the motorcycle line and merchandise inventory for the Motorclothes™ line, it follows similar accounting practices. Theoretically, the amount recorded for purchase of raw materials or merchandise should include the invoice price and indirect expenditures related to the purchase, such as freight charges to deliver the items to its warehouses (freight-in) and inspection and preparation costs. In general, the company should cease accumulating costs of purchases when the raw materials are *ready for use* or when the merchandise inventory is in a condition and location *ready for shipment* to the dealers. Any additional costs related to selling the merchandise inventory to the dealers, such as marketing department salaries and dealer training sessions, should be included in Selling, General, and Administrative Expenses of the period of sale to the dealers since they are incurred after the inventory is ready for use in the normal course of business.

FINANCIAL ANALYSIS

Applying the Materiality Constraint in Practice

Incidental costs such as inspection and preparation costs often are not *material in amount* (see the discussion of the materiality constraint in the Chapter 5 discussion of the Conceptual Framework of Accounting) and do not have to be assigned to the inventory cost. Thus, for practical reasons, many companies use the *invoice price,* less returns and discounts, to assign a unit cost to raw materials or merchandise and record the other indirect expenditures as a separate cost that is reported as an expense. Invoice price may or may not include transportation charges for shipment to the warehouse, freight-in.

Inventory Flows

The flow of inventory costs for merchandisers, both wholesalers and retailers, is relatively simple, as shown in Exhibit 7–3. When merchandise is purchased, the merchandise inventory is increased. When the goods are sold, cost of goods sold is increased and the merchandise inventory is decreased.

The flow of inventory costs in a manufacturing environment is diagrammed in Exhibit 7–3. For Harley-Davidson's motorcycle manufacturing operations, the flow of inventory costs is more complex. First raw materials must be purchased. These raw materials include steel and aluminum castings, forgings, sheet, and bars and certain motorcycle component parts including carburetors, batteries, and tires, which are produced by its small network of suppliers. When used, the cost of each material is removed from the raw

Exhibit 7–3 Flows of Inventory Costs

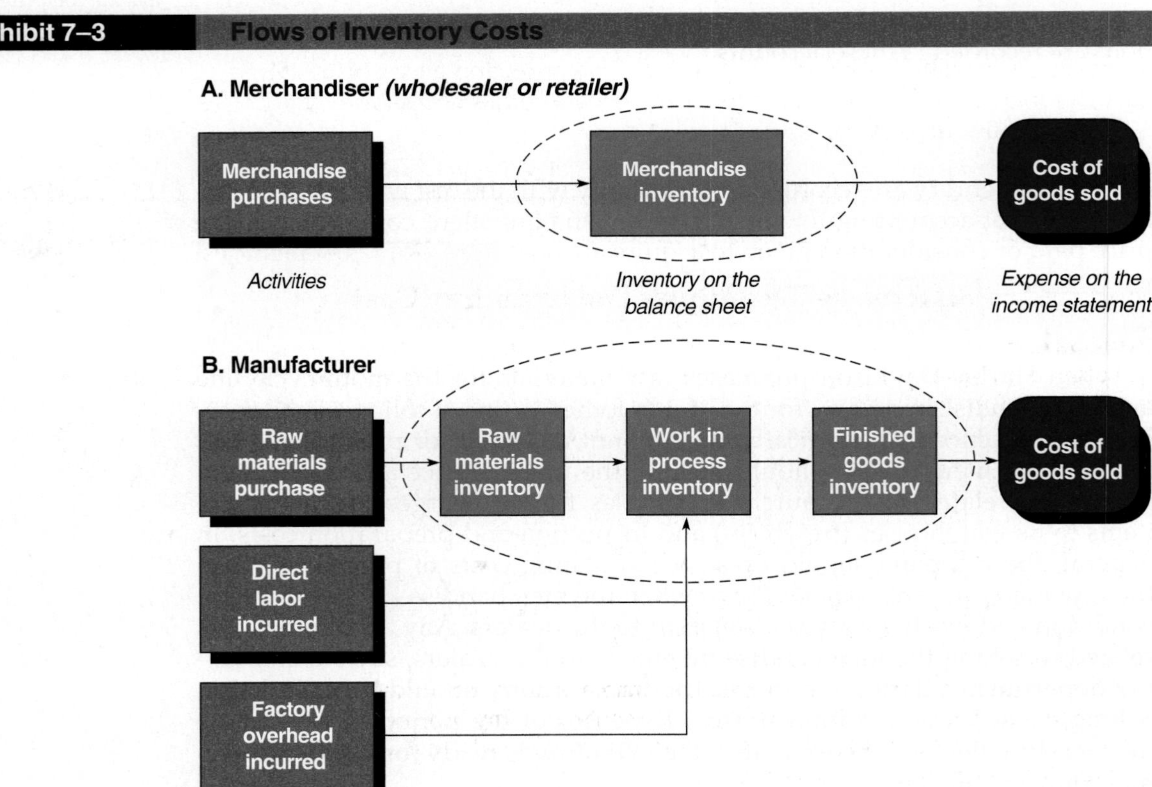

materials inventory account and added to the work in process inventory account, along with two other components of manufacturing costs.

Direct labor and factory overhead costs are also added to the work in process inventory when incurred in the manufacturing process. **Direct labor** cost represents the earnings of employees who work directly on the products being manufactured. **Factory overhead** costs include all manufacturing costs that are not raw material or direct labor costs. For example, the salary of the factory supervisor and the cost of heat, light, and power to operate the factory are included in factory overhead. When the motorcycles are completed and ready for sale, the related amounts in work in process inventory are transferred to finished goods inventory. When the finished goods are sold, cost of goods sold is increased and the finished goods inventory is decreased.

Direct labor is the earnings of employees who work directly on the products being manufactured.

Factory overhead costs are manufacturing costs that are not raw material or direct labor costs.

Note from the exhibit that for *both* merchandisers and manufacturers, there are three stages to inventory cost flows. The first involves purchasing and/or production activities. In the second, these activities result in additions to inventory accounts on the balance sheet. At the third stage, the time of sale, these inventory amounts become cost of goods sold expense on the income statement.

Harley-Davidson's recent inventory footnote reports the following:

Real World Excerpt

Harley-Davidson, Inc.
Annual Report

HARLEY-DAVIDSON, INC.
NOTES TO CONSOLIDATED FINANCIAL STATEMENTS

2. ADDITIONAL CASH FLOW AND BALANCE SHEET INFORMATION
(In thousands)

Raw materials and work in process	$43,885
Finished goods	41,973
Parts and accessories	30,635*

*These don't add up to the balance reported in Exhibit 7–1 because they do not include the "LIFO adjustment" discussed later.

Harley-Davidson combines the raw materials and work in process. Other companies separate these two components. The parts and accessories category includes purchased parts and Motorclothes™ and other accessories that make up merchandise inventory.

FINANCIAL ANALYSIS

Modern Manufacturing Techniques and Inventory Costs

The flows of inventory costs diagrammed in Exhibit 7–3 represent the keys to manufacturing cost and quality control. Since the company must pay to finance and store raw materials and purchased parts, minimizing these inventories in keeping with projected manufacturing demand is the first key to the process. This requires that Harley-Davidson work closely with its suppliers in design, production, and delivery of manufactured parts and in planning raw materials deliveries; the related techniques are often called *just-in-time inventory.* Review and redesign of manufacturing operations and worker training and involvement programs are the keys to minimizing direct labor and factory overhead costs. New product designs are often aimed at reducing manufacturing complexity which leads to higher product quality and reduced scrap and rework costs. For example, at its new Sportster assembly line in York, Pennsylvania, three-person teams are responsible for assembly of a complete vehicle which has resulted in both cost and quality improvements.

Harley-Davidson's management accounting system is designed to monitor the success of these changes and provide information to allow continuous improvements in these manufacturing efforts. Issues faced in the design of such systems are the subject matter of management accounting and cost accounting courses.

Nature of Cost of Goods Sold

Cost of goods sold (CGS) is a major expense item for most nonservice businesses and is directly related to sales revenue. The amount of sales revenue during an accounting period is the number of units sold multiplied by the sales price. Cost of goods sold is the same number of units multiplied by their unit costs; it includes the cost of all merchandise and finished goods sold during the period. The measurement of cost of goods sold is an excellent example of the application of the matching principle.

The flow of inventory costs from merchandise inventory to cost of goods sold for the merchandiser and from finished goods inventory to cost of goods sold for the manufacturer involves similar processes. In both cases, Harley-Davidson starts each accounting period with a stock of inventory on hand for sale to the dealers called the *beginning inventory* (BI). The merchandise and finished goods on hand at the end of an accounting period are called the *ending inventory* (EI). The ending inventory for one accounting period automatically becomes the beginning inventory for the next period.

Goods available for sale is the sum of beginning inventory and purchases (or transfers to finished goods) for the period.

During the accounting period, the beginning inventory is increased by the purchase of more merchandise or the transfer of work in process to finished goods. The sum of the beginning inventory and the *purchases* of merchandise or *transfers* of work in process to finished goods during the period (P) represents the **goods available for sale** (GAS) during that period. Typically, not all of the goods available for sale are sold, so there is an ending inventory for the period. From these relationships, we can compute cost of goods sold as follows:

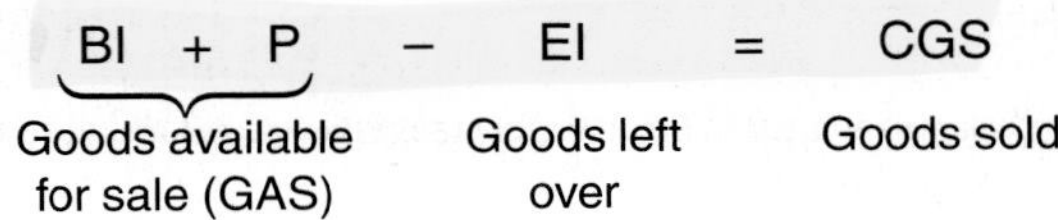

Cost of goods sold equation: BI + P − EI = CGS

Later in the chapter, this **cost of goods sold equation** will serve as a basic tool for analyzing the effects of inventory errors and different accounting methods on the financial statements. To illustrate the relationships represented by the equation for merchandise inventory, assume that for the Motorclothes™ line, Harley-Davidson reported cost of goods sold of $60,000, which was computed as follows:

Beginning inventory (January 1, 19F)	$40,000
Add: Purchases of merchandise during 19F	+ 55,000
Goods available for sale	$95,000
Deduct: Ending inventory (December 31, 19F)	− 35,000
Cost of goods sold	$60,000

Similarly, for finished goods inventory, assume that for the motorcycle product line, Harley-Davidson reported cost of goods sold of $700,000, which was computed as follows:

Beginning finished goods inventory (January 1, 19F)	$500,000
Add: Transfers from work in process during 19F	+ 650,000
Goods available for sale	$1,150,000
Deduct: Ending finished goods inventory (December 31, 19F)	− 450,000
Cost of goods sold	$700,000

These same relationships can be represented in the merchandise inventory and finished goods inventory T-accounts as follows:

Merchandise Inventory*			
Beginning inventory	$40,000		
Add: Purchases	55,000	*Deduct: Cost of goods sold*	60,000
Ending inventory	$35,000		

Finished Goods Inventory			
Beginning inventory	$500,000		
Add: Transfers	650,000	*Deduct: Cost of goods sold*	700,000
Ending inventory	$450,000		

*At this point in the course, most students have learned how to identify assets, liabilities, stockholders' equity, revenues, and expenses. As such, we will stop noting account types with letter designations from this point forward. You may wish to continue using the designations if they still seem helpful.

FINANCIAL ANALYSIS

Gross Profit Comparisons

Analysts often calculate an amount called *gross profit* or *gross margin on sales,* which is the difference between net sales revenue and cost of goods sold. This amount is reported on the multiple-step format of the income statement (see Exhibit 7–1). Gross profit reflects the total amount of markup on all goods sold during the period. It can be expressed as a dollar amount or as a ratio called the *gross margin ratio.* The gross margin ratio is calculated as gross margin ÷ net sales revenue. Harley-Davidson's gross margin for the current year was $296,413,000; its ratio was 26.8% ($296,413,000 ÷ $1,105,284,000).

Analysts use the gross margin ratio to compare *similar* companies and to compare the operations of the *same* company over time. Using similar companies for comparison is important because companies in different industries often have highly different gross margins. For example, Harley-Davidson produces both motorcycles and motorhomes. Though they are related industries, in a recent year the gross margin was 30.4% on motorcycle sales but only 16.4% on motorhome sales.

If either Harley-Davidson's gross margin changed or a major competitor reported a much different gross margin, analysts would attempt to determine the cause of the difference. For example, Harley-Davidson recently opened new production facilities which will increase production volume and decrease costs in the future. However, start-up costs at these new facilities reduced the gross margin on motorcycles in the short run. This suggests that even a short-term decline in gross margin is not always bad news. This example illustrates how analysts can use accounting information to gain additional insight into the operations and competitiveness of a company.

Errors in Measuring Ending Inventory

Learning Objective 2
Measure the effects of inventory errors on financial statements.

As the cost of goods sold equation indicates, a direct relationship exists between ending inventory and cost of goods sold because items not in the ending inventory are assumed to have been sold. Thus, the measurement of ending inventory affects both the balance sheet (assets) and the income statement (cost of goods sold, gross profit, and net income). The measurement of ending inventory affects not only the net income for that period but also the net income for the *next accounting period.* This two-period effect occurs because the ending inventory for one period is the beginning inventory for the next accounting period.

The Wall Street Journal recently reported that greeting card maker Gibson Greetings had overstated its current year profits by 20% because one division had overstated ending inventory for the year.[3] You can compute the effects of

[3]*The Wall Street Journal,* July 5, 1994, p. A4.

the error on both the current year's and next year's pretax profits using the cost of goods sold equation. Assume that ending inventory is overstated by $10,000 due to a clerical error, and it is not discovered the next year. It would have the following effects:

Current year

BI	+	P	–	EI	=	CGS
				Overstated $10,000		Understated $10,000

Thus, income before taxes would be *overstated* by $10,000 in the current year. Since the current year's ending inventory becomes the next year's beginning inventory, it would have the following effects next year:

Next year

BI	+	P	–	EI	=	CGS
Overstated $10,000						Overstated $10,000

Income before taxes would be *understated* by the same amount in the next year. Each of these errors would flow into retained earnings such that at the end of the current year, retained earnings would be overstated by $10,000 (less the related income tax expense). This error would be offset in the next year and retained earnings and inventory at the end of next year would be correct.

In this example, we assumed that the overstatement of ending inventory was inadvertent, the result of a clerical error. However, as we noted in Chapter 6, inventory fraud is one of the two most common forms of financial statement fraud. It occurred in the Maxidrive case discussed in Chapter 1 as well as in the real MiniScribe fraud. The problem is sufficiently severe that *The Wall Street Journal* recently reported the following:

Real World Excerpt
The Wall Street Journal

Convenient Fiction
Inventory Chicanery Tempts More Firms, Fools More Auditors
A Quick Way to Pad Profits, It Is Often Revealed Only When Concern Collapses

* * * * *

When companies are desperate to stay afloat, inventory fraud is the easiest way to produce instant profits and dress up the balance sheet . . .

Even auditors at the top accounting firms are often fooled.

SOURCE: *The Wall Street Journal,* December 14, 1992, p. A1.

Self-Study Quiz

Assume the following facts for Harley-Davidson's Motorclothes™ Leather Baseball Jacket product line for the year 19F:

Beginning inventory 500 units at unit cost of $75.
Ending inventory 600 units at unit cost of $75.
Sales 1,100 units at a sales price of $100 (cost per unit $75).

1. Using the cost of goods sold equation, compute the dollar amount of purchases of Leather Baseball Jackets for the period.

BI + P – EI = CGS

2. Prepare the first three lines of a multiple-step income statement (showing gross profit) for the Leather Baseball Jacket line for the year 19F.

BI

EI

NS

After you have completed your answers, check them with the solutions presented in the footnote at the bottom of this page.*

INVENTORY COSTING METHODS

Learning Objective 3
Use the four inventory costing methods to determine the appropriate amounts to report as inventory and cost of goods sold.

In the Motorclothes™ example presented in the self-study quiz, the cost of all units of the Leather Baseball Jackets was the same—$75. If inventory costs normally did not change, this would be the end of our discussion of inventory costs. However, we are all aware that the prices of most goods often change. The costs of many manufactured items such as automobiles and motorcycles have risen in recent years, though only at a moderate rate. However, in other industries, such as computers, costs of production (and retail prices) have dropped dramatically.

When inventory costs have changed, the determination of which inventory items will be treated as sold and which as still remaining in ending inventory can turn profits into losses (and vice versa) and cause companies to pay or save hundreds of millions in taxes. Before we examine these complexities, we will use a simple example to discuss the mechanics of each accepted method for determining which goods will be treated as sold. We will then look at which methods Harley-Davidson and other companies use and discuss the bases for their choices. Do not let the simplicity of our example mislead you. As you will see, the results of this example generalize broadly to actual company practices. The example is based on the following data. New Company began operations on January 1, 19A.

The following events took place during 19A:

Jan.	15	Purchased 1 unit of product A at $1
April	2	Purchased 1 unit of product A at $3
June	27	Purchased 1 unit of product A at $5
Nov.	5	Sold 2 units for $7 each.

Note that inventory costs are rising rapidly! On November 5, two units are sold for $7 each; revenues of $14 would be recorded. What amount would be recorded as cost of goods sold? The answer would depend on which specific goods are assumed sold. There are four generally accepted inventory costing methods available for doing so:

1. First-in, first-out (FIFO).
2. Last-in, first-out (LIFO).
3. Weighted average.
4. Specific identification.

---

*1.

BI	+	P	−	EI	=	CGS
37,500	+	P	−	45,000	=	82,500
				P	=	90,000

2.

Net sales	$110,000
Cost of goods sold	82,500
Gross profit	$ 27,000

The four inventory costing methods are *alternative allocation methods* for assigning the total dollar amount of goods available for sale (BI + P) between (*a*) ending inventory (reported as an asset at the end of the period) and (*b*) cost of goods sold (reported as an expense of the period). It is important to note at this point that the choice among the four inventory costing methods is *not* based on the physical flow of goods on and off the shelves. For example, the actual physical flow of goods at a supermarket is first-in, first-out (FIFO). However, a supermarket can use LIFO or any of the inventory costing methods to report cost of goods sold and inventory in its financial statments. Generally accepted accounting principles (GAAP) require only that the inventory costing method used be rational and systematic. Since they need not follow the actual physical flow of inventory, they are often called *cost flow assumptions.*

A useful visual learning tool for representing inventory cost flows is a bin, or container. The different inventory costing methods can then be visualized as flows of inventory in and out of the various bins. We will use this concept to illustrate inventory flow throughout the following sections.

First-In, First-Out Inventory Costing Method

The **first-in, first-out method (FIFO)** assumes that the oldest units (the first costs in) are the first units sold.

The **first-in, first-out method**, frequently called **FIFO**, assumes that the oldest units (the first costs in) are the first units sold (the first costs out). Under FIFO, cost of goods sold and ending inventory are computed as if the flows in and out of the FIFO inventory bin in Exhibit 7–4 had taken place. First, each purchase is treated as if it was deposited in the bin from the top in sequence (one unit each at $1, $3, and $5). Each good sold is then removed from the *bottom* in sequence (one unit at $1 and one at $3); *first in is first out*. These goods totaling $4 become cost of goods sold (CGS). The remaining unit ($5) becomes ending inventory. These financial statement effects are summarized in Exhibit 7–5. If there were any goods in beginning inventory, they would be treated as if they were sold first. Then the units from the first purchase are sold next, and so on until the units left in the ending inventory all come from the most recent purchases. FIFO allocates the *oldest* unit costs to *cost of goods sold* and the *most recent* unit costs to the *ending inventory*.

Exhibit 7–4 FIFO and LIFO Inventory Flows—New Company, Year 1

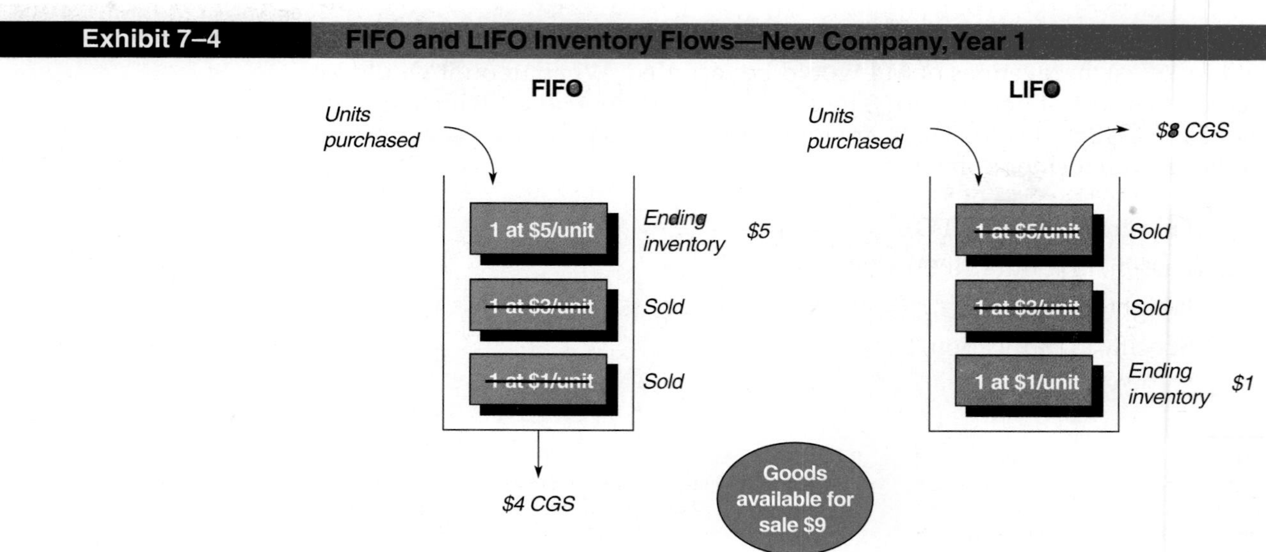

Last-In, First-Out Inventory Costing Method

The **last-in, first-out method,** often called **LIFO,** assumes that the most recently acquired goods are sold first. This method can be visualized as involving a LIFO inventory bin such as that presented in Exhibit 7–4. As in the case of the FIFO bin, each purchase is treated as if it was deposited in the bin from the top in sequence ($1, $3, $5). However, unlike the FIFO case, each good sold is then removed from the *top* in sequence ($5, $3). These goods totaling $8 become cost of goods sold (CGS). The remaining unit ($1) becomes ending inventory. These financial statement effects are summarized in Exhibit 7–5.

The **last-in, first-out method (LIFO)** assumes that the most recently acquired units are sold first.

If there were any goods in beginning inventory, they would be treated as if they were sold last. The units from the last purchase are always sold first, and so on until the units left in the ending inventory all come from the oldest purchases. Therefore, the unit costs of the beginning inventory and the earlier purchases remain in the ending inventory. LIFO allocates the *most recent* unit costs to *cost of goods sold* and the *oldest* unit costs to the *ending inventory.* The LIFO flow assumption is the exact opposite of the FIFO flow assumption.

Weighted-Average Inventory Costing Method

The **weighted-average method** requires computation of the weighted-average unit cost of the goods available for sale.[4] The computed unit cost is multiplied by the number of units in inventory to derive the total cost of ending inventory. Cost of goods sold is determined by subtracting the ending inventory amount from the amount of goods available for sale. For the New Company data, the weighted-average cost is computed as:

The **weighted-average method** uses the weighted-average unit cost of the goods available for sale for both cost of goods sold and ending inventory.

Number of units	×	Unit cost	=	Total cost
1		$1		$1
1		3		3
1		5		5
3				$9

Exhibit 7–5 Financial Statement Effects of Inventory Costing Methods

	FIFO	LIFO	Weighted Average
Cost of goods sold calculation:			
Beginning inventory	$0	$0	$0
Add: Purchases	9	9	9
Goods available for sale	$9	$9	$9
Deduct: Ending inventory	5	1	3
Cost of goods sold	$4	$8	$6
Effect on the income statement:			
Sales	$14	$14	$14
Cost of goods sold	4	8	6
Gross profit	$10	$ 6	$ 8
Effect on the balance sheet:			
Inventory	$ 5	$ 1	$ 3

[4] A weighted-average unit cost rather than a simple average of the unit costs must be used. In most cases a simple average would be incorrect because it does not consider the number of units at each unit cost. For example, if one unit was purchased at $1, one unit at $3, and *two* units at $5, the average cost would be $3.50 ([$1 + $3 + $5 + $5] ÷ 4 units).

$$\text{Average cost} = \frac{\text{Cost of goods available for sale}}{\text{Number of units available for sale}}$$

$$\text{Average cost} = \frac{\$9}{3\text{ units}} = \$3\text{ per unit}$$

In these circumstances, cost of goods sold and ending inventory would be assigned the same weighted average cost per unit of $3. Cost of goods sold would be $6 for two units sold and ending inventory would be $3 for one unit. These financial statement effects are summarized in Exhibit 7–5.

Specific Identification Inventory Costing Method

The **specific identification method** identifies the cost of the specific item that was sold.

When the **specific identification method** is used, the cost of each item sold is individually identified and recorded as cost of goods sold. This method requires keeping track of the purchase cost of each item. This is done by either (1) coding the purchase cost on each unit before placing it in stock or (2) keeping a separate record of the unit and identifying it with a serial number. In the New Company example, any two of the three items could have been sold, and the cost of those two items would become cost of goods sold. The cost of the remaining item would be ending inventory.

Given the way in which some inventory accounting systems are organized (discussed later in this chapter), the specific identification method is impractical when large numbers of different items are stocked. On the other hand, when there are expensive items such as automobiles at a dealership or fine jewelry, this method is appropriate because each item tends to be different from the other items. The method may be manipulated when the units are *identical* because one can affect the cost of goods sold and the ending inventory accounts by picking and choosing from among the several available unit costs, even though the goods are identical in other respects.

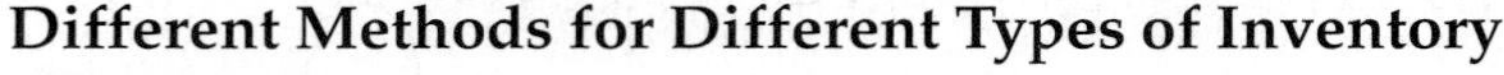

AN INTERNATIONAL PERSPECTIVE

Different Methods for Different Types of Inventory

Asahi Chemical Industry Co., Ltd. is a major Japanese manufacturer of chemicals, plastics, fibers and textiles, and housing and construction materials. Most of its inventories are accounted for by using average cost which is very common in Japan. However, its housing and construction materials division also constructs and sells homes. It accounts for both residential lots and dwellings under construction, which are *expensive, distinguishable items*, by using specific identification.

Comparison of the Inventory Costing Methods

Each of the four alternative inventory costing methods is in conformity with GAAP and the tax law. However, each method may produce significantly different income and asset (ending inventory) amounts. To illustrate this difference, the comparative results for New Company using FIFO, LIFO, and weighted average are presented in Exhibit 7–5. Notice that the difference in the *gross margin* among each of the methods is the same as the difference in the *ending inventory* amounts. The method that gives the highest ending inventory amount also gives the highest gross margin and income amounts and vice versa. The weighted-average cost method will give income and inventory amounts that are between the FIFO and LIFO extremes.

Note in the comparison above that unit costs were increasing. When unit costs are *rising, LIFO* produces *lower income* and a *lower inventory valuation* than FIFO. Even though we may be experiencing general inflation, some companies' costs decline. When unit costs are *declining, LIFO* produces *higher income* and *higher inventory valuation* than FIFO. These effects occur because LIFO will cause the new unit costs to be reflected in cost of goods sold on the income statement, which is a realistic measurement of the current cost of items that were sold, whereas FIFO will cause the older unit costs to be reflected in cost of goods sold on the income statement. In contrast, on the balance sheet, the ending inventory amount under LIFO is based on the oldest unit costs, which may be an unrealistic valuation, whereas FIFO ending inventory is a realistic measurement of their current cost.

Which allocation method should be used in which circumstances? Our current system allows selection among the alternative methods for financial statements and a second selection for tax purposes. As we will discuss below, a particular company's choice will depend on management's incentives, the tax law, and the reporting company's particular economic circumstances. Because of the potential effects on reported performance and tax payments, an understanding of these choices is important to all managers and financial statement users.

Again, it is important to remember that regardless of the physical flow of goods, a company can use any of the inventory costing methods. Furthermore, a company is not required to use the same inventory costing method for all inventory items, and no particular justification is needed for the selection of one or more of the acceptable methods. As was the case in the Asahi Chemical example discussed above, Harley-Davidson and most large companies use different inventory methods for different inventory items.

To enhance comparability, accounting rules require companies to apply their accounting methods on a consistent basis. A company is not permitted to use LIFO one period, FIFO the next, and then go back to LIFO. A change in method is allowed only if the change will improve the measurement of financial results and financial position. Changing from one inventory costing method to another is a significant event. Such a change requires full disclosure about the reason for the change and the accounting effects.

ALTERNATIVE INVENTORY COSTING METHODS IN PRACTICE

Choosing Inventory Costing Methods

Learning Objective 4
Decide when the use of different inventory costing methods is beneficial to a company.

Accounting Trends and Techniques reported that while 358 (60%) of the 600 companies surveyed reported using LIFO, only 23 (4%) use LIFO for all inventories.[5] This raises an important question: What motivates companies to choose different inventory costing methods? Our discussion in Chapter 5 suggests that management should choose the method allowed by GAAP that most closely reflects its economic circumstances for its external financial statements (book purposes). Management must also make a second choice of accounting method to use on its tax return (tax purposes). The choice from among the acceptable methods for use on the company's tax return should be the one that allows payment of the least amount of taxes as late as possible—the "least-latest rule."

A business typically may use one set of accounting procedures for external financial statements and a different set of procedures for preparing the tax

[5] *Accounting Trends and Techniques* (New York: AICPA, 1993).

return. However, the choice of inventory costing methods is a special case because of what is called the *LIFO conformity rule.* If LIFO is used on the income tax return, it must also be used to calculate inventory and cost of goods sold for the financial statements.[6] Since LIFO often minimizes taxes, the LIFO conformity rule leads many companies to adopt LIFO for *both* tax and financial reporting purposes. For most companies facing rising costs of inventory, LIFO is used for U.S. inventories. For inventory located in countries that do not allow LIFO for tax purposes or that do not have a LIFO conformity rule, FIFO or weighted average are mostly used. Similarly, when costs are falling, FIFO or weighted average are most often used. Since most companies in the same industry face similar cost structures, clusters of companies in the same industries often choose the same accounting method.

AN INTERNATIONAL PERSPECTIVE

LIFO and International Comparisons

The methods of accounting for inventories discussed in this chapter are used in most major industrialized countries. There are several countries where the LIFO method is not generally used. In England, for example, LIFO is not acceptable for tax purposes, and it is not widely used in financial reporting. LIFO is also not used in Australia and Hong Kong but may be used in Singapore only if the difference between LIFO and FIFO is reported. These differences can create comparability problems when one attempts to compare companies across international borders. For example, General Motors, Chrysler, and Ford use LIFO to value U.S. inventories and Honda (of Japan) and Daimler-Benz (maker of Mercedes-Benz of Germany) use FIFO.

The income tax effects associated with LIFO and FIFO for companies facing rising costs can be illustrated by continuing our simple New Company example. Using the data from Exhibit 7–5 and assuming that expenses other than cost of goods sold were $2 and the tax rate was 25%, the following differences in taxes would result.

	Inventory Costing Method	
	FIFO	**LIFO**
Sales revenue	$14	$14
Cost of goods sold	4	8
Gross margin	$10	$ 6
Other expenses	2	2
Pretax income	$ 8	$ 4
Income tax expense (.25 × pretax income)	2	1
Net income	$ 6	$ 3

In this situation, cost of goods sold and pretax income were different by $4, which was caused by the differences between the FIFO and LIFO methods. Costs were rising, and there was a significant difference between the old and new unit costs. When multiplied by the 25% income tax rate, the $4 difference in pretax income generates cash tax savings of $1. It is important to remember that this choice is independent of the actual physical flow of goods. This example illustrates the primary motivations for the choice of LIFO. In an inflationary world, most companies face cost increases. In the United States, the tax

[6]Note that LIFO can be used for financial statement purposes along with FIFO or weighted average for tax purposes. However, this is rarely done.

QUESTION OF ETHICS

LIFO and Conflicts between Managers' and Owners' Interests

As discussed earlier in this chapter, the selection of an inventory method can have significant effects on financial statements. Company managers may have incentives to select a particular method that may not be consistent with the objectives of the owners. For example, the use of LIFO during a period of rising prices may be in the best interests of the owners because LIFO often reduces the tax liability of the company. On the other hand, managers may prefer FIFO because it typically results in higher profits and the compensation of most managers is affected by reported profits.

A well-designed compensation scheme should reward managers for acting in the best interests of the owners, but unfortunately this is not always the case. Clearly, a manager who selects an accounting method that is not optimal for the company, solely in order to increase his or her compensation, has engaged in questionable ethical behavior.

benefit in such circumstances plus the LIFO conformity rule explain widespread use of the method.

This simple example illustrates the computations necessary to determine the tax savings but may not indicate the magnitude of the effect often faced in practice. Harley-Davidson is a fairly typical "mixed" LIFO company. The $94 million in inventory reported in Exhibit 7–1 included U.S. motorcycle and new transportation vehicle inventories of $78 million at LIFO. As we will compute in the next section, Harley saved $651,000 in taxes in 1993 alone. They have saved a total of approximately $8 million in taxes from the date they adopted the LIFO method through 1993. This is a significant benefit to Harley. Harley does not use LIFO for its non-U.S. motorcycle inventory either because LIFO is not acceptable for tax purposes or there is no LIFO conformity rule in those countries.

In theory, LIFO cannot provide permanent tax savings because (*a*) when inventory levels drop or (*b*) costs drop, the income effect reverses and the income taxes deferred will have to be paid. The economic advantage of deferring income taxes in such situations is due to the fact that interest can be earned on the money that otherwise would be paid as taxes for the current year. However, much of this amount is postponed for a very long period, and some is never paid because of accumulated losses preceding the end of the company's life.

Alternatively, many high-technology companies are facing declining costs. In such circumstances, the FIFO method, in which the oldest, most expensive goods become cost of goods sold, produces the largest cost of goods sold, the lowest gross profit, and thus the lowest income tax liability. For example, Apple Computer, Compaq Computer, and Microsoft all account for inventories at FIFO.

Alternative Inventory Costing Methods and Financial Statement Analysis

Learning Objective 5
Analyze financial statements prepared using different inventory costing methods.

Critics of GAAP charge that the existence of alternative accounting methods is inconsistent with the *comparability* characteristic of useful information. This quality is needed so that analysts can compare information for a company with that of other companies for the same time period. These types of comparisons are more difficult if different accounting methods are used, since one company's statements must be converted to a comparable basis *before* meaningful comparisons can be made. However, careful readers of this text will be able to make many of the necessary adjustments.

Converting cost of goods sold and income before taxes from one inventory costing method to another is eased by the requirement that public companies using LIFO also report beginning and ending inventory on a FIFO, average cost, or related method basis in the notes if the LIFO and FIFO vaues are materially different. We can use this information along with the cost of goods sold equation to convert cost of goods sold and income before taxes to the FIFO basis. This process is similar to the manner in which we corrected errors in inventory earlier in this chapter. Recall that the cost of goods sold equation is:

$$BI + P - EI = CGS$$

Recall further that the choice of a cost flow assumption affects how goods available for sale are allocated to ending inventory and cost of goods sold. It does not affect the recording of purchases. Since last year's ending inventory is this year's beginning inventory, beginning inventory is also affected by the choice of a cost flow assumption. As a consequence, we can compute the effects of the *difference* in cost flow assumptions on cost of goods sold in the following manner:

$$\Delta BI - \Delta EI = \Delta CGS$$

Difference in beginning inventory (LIFO to FIFO)
Less: Difference in ending inventory (LIFO to FIFO)
Difference in cost of goods sold (LIFO to FIFO)

LIFO Reserve is a contra-asset for the excess of FIFO over LIFO inventory.

Harley-Davidson provides a typical disclosure of the differences between LIFO and FIFO values for beginning and ending inventory. The difference between its inventory valued using FIFO and LIFO is labeled "Excess of FIFO over LIFO inventory." This amount is often referred to as the **LIFO Reserve.** Companies that use a LIFO reserve keep their inventory account during the accounting period using FIFO (or possibly average cost). At the end of the year, they convert the balances in inventory and cost of goods sold to LIFO through an adjusting entry to the LIFO Reserve, which is a contra-asset to the Inventory account. The approach taken is very similar to that used when adjusting the Allowance for Doubtful Accounts employing the aging method (discussed in Chapter 6).

Real World Excerpt

Harley-Davidson, Inc.
Annual Report

HARLEY-DAVIDSON, INC.
NOTES TO CONSOLIDATED FINANCIAL STATEMENTS

2. ADDITIONAL CASH FLOW AND BALANCE SHEET INFORMATION
(In thousands)

Inventories:	**1993**	**1992**
Components at . . . FIFO	$116,493	$127,080
Excess of FIFO over LIFO inventories	22,065	20,397
	$ 94,428	$106,683

LIFO Reserve (→ Excess of FIFO over LIFO inventories)

Inventory at LIFO reported on the balance sheet (→ $106,683)

The LIFO Reserve provides the needed information for the conversion. Using the above formula, we can compute the difference in cost of goods sold for the current year when we convert from LIFO to FIFO (a *decrease* of $1,668). Since cost of goods sold decreases pretax income, the conversion's effect on pretax income is the opposite—an *increase* of $1,668. To compute the tax savings (postponement) from using LIFO instead of FIFO for the current year, multiply this increase by Harley's 39% total income tax rate which yields approximately $651.

Difference in beginning inventory (LIFO to FIFO)	$20,397 ← *Beginning LIFO Reserve*
Less: Difference in ending inventory (LIFO to FIFO)	22,065 ← *Ending LIFO Reserve*
Difference in cost of goods sold (LIFO to FIFO)	($1,668)
Difference in pretax income (LIFO to FIFO)	$ 1,668
Difference in taxes (LIFO to FIFO) (39% × 1,668)	$ 651

Because no inventory costing method can be considered best, the accounting profession has been unwilling to require all companies to follow a single method. As a result, users of financial statements must be knowledgeable about alternative accounting methods and how they affect statements. Users must be certain that their decisions are based on real differences and not artificial differences created by alternative accounting methods. Remember that the choice of inventory costing method does not affect the physical attributes or economic value of the inventory.

LIFO and Financial Statement Analysis

Analysts often use the inventory turnover ratio to measure the liquidity (nearness to cash) of the inventory. The computation is as follows:

$$\text{Inventory turnover} = \frac{\text{Cost of goods sold}}{\text{Average inventory [(beginning + ending)} \div 2]}$$

It reflects the relationship of the inventory to the volume of goods sold during the period. Higher inventory turnover indicates that inventory is turned into cash more quickly. It is also considered to be a measure of the efficiency of using inventory because it relates the cost of goods sold to the average amount of inventory kept on hand to generate those sales (higher ratio means greater efficiency). However, for many LIFO companies this measure can be deceptive. Consider Deere & Co., manufacturer of John Deere farm, lawn, and construction equipment. Its inventory footnote lists the following values:

Real World Excerpt

Deere & Company Annual Report

DEERE & COMPANY
NOTES TO CONSOLIDATED FINANCIAL STATEMENTS

INVENTORIES
[in millions]

	1993	1992	
Raw materials and supplies	$192	$213	
Work-in-process	295	377	
Finished machines and parts	919	979	← Inventory at FIFO
Total FIFO value	1,406	1,569	
Adjustment to LIFO basis	942	1,044	← LIFO Reserve
Inventories	$464	$525	← Inventory at LIFO

John Deere's cost of goods sold for 1993 was $5,374.6 million. If the ratio is computed using the reported LIFO inventory values for the denominator of the ratio, it would be:

$$\text{Inventory turnover} = \frac{\$5{,}374.6}{(\$464 + \$525) \div 2} = 10.9$$

Using the more current FIFO inventory values, it would be:

$$\text{Inventory turnover} = \frac{\$5{,}374.6}{(\$1{,}406 + \$1{,}569) \div 2} = 3.6$$

Note that the FIFO inventory values are three times the LIFO values; the ratio is 1/3 the amount. Since the LIFO values for cost of goods sold on the *income statement* and the FIFO inventory numbers on the *balance sheet* are closer to current prices, they are normally thought to be the most appropriate numerator and denominator, respectively, for use in this ratio. The LIFO beginning and ending inventory numbers are artificially small because they reflect old lower costs. Thus, the numerator in the first calculation does not relate in a meaningful way to the denominator.

LIFO Liquidations

A **LIFO liquidation** is a sale of a lower-cost inventory item from beginning LIFO inventory.

When a LIFO company sells more inventory than it purchases or manufactures, items from beginning inventory become part of cost of goods sold. This is called a **LIFO liquidation.** For companies facing rising inventory costs, these items in beginning inventory have lower costs which produce a higher gross margin when they are sold. (People often call items purchased at the same price *LIFO layers.*) We illustrate this process by continuing our simple New Company example into its second year.

In its first year of operation, units were purchased for $1, $3, and $5 in sequence and the $5 and $3 units were sold under LIFO, leaving the $1 unit in ending inventory. These events were represented using a LIFO inventory bin in Exhibit 7–4. We continue this illustration in Exhibit 7–6. The ending inventory from year 1 becomes the beginning inventory for year 2. In part A of the exhibit, we assume that in year 2 New Company purchased *two* additional units at $6 each, the sales price has been raised to $8, and three units are sold. Using LIFO, these two new $6 units and the old $1 unit would become cost of goods sold. Given that revenue is $8 per unit, the gross margin on the newly purchased units would be 2 units × $2 = $4. Since the cost of the old unit is only $1, the gross margin on this one unit is $7 ($8 – $1) instead of $2, raising total gross profit to $11. This calculation is presented below the inventory bin.

Now assume instead, as we do in part B of Exhibit 7–6, that New Company actually purchased a total of *three* inventory units at the current $6 price before year-end. Now only the three recently purchased $6 inventory items become

Exhibit 7–6 **Inventory Flows—New Company, Year 2**

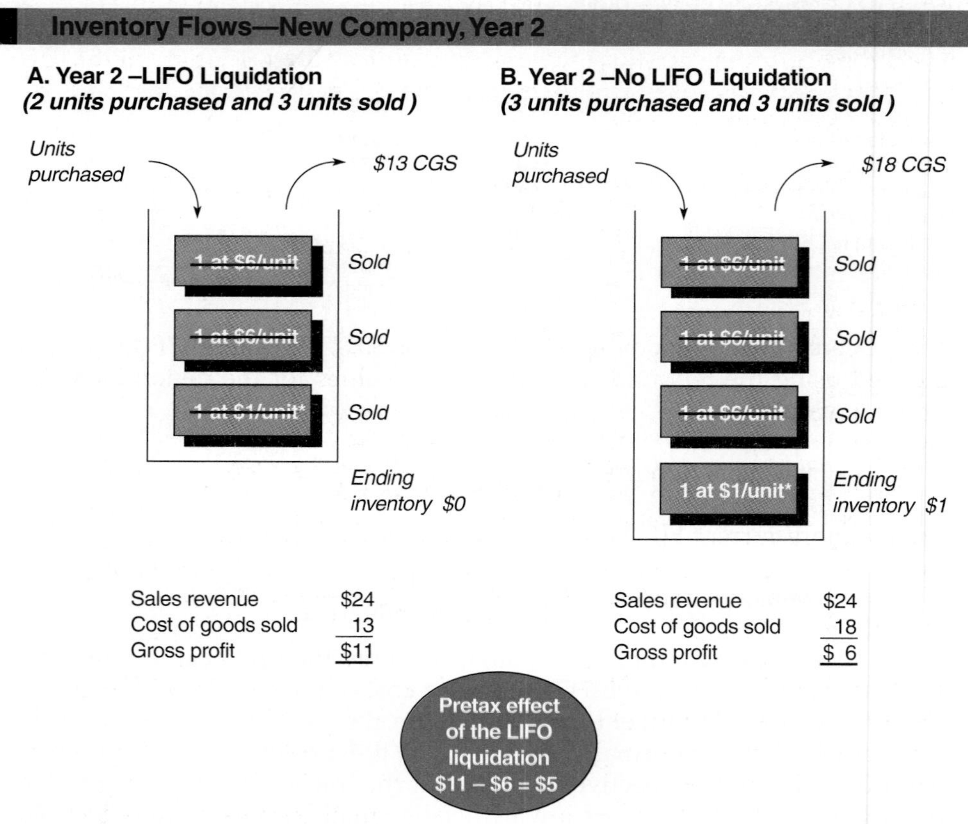

*Beginning inventory = Ending inventory from year 1

part of cost of goods sold, and the old $1 item from beginning inventory becomes ending inventory. Compared to part A, cost of goods sold is increased by $5 to $18 and gross profit and income before taxes are decreased by $5. This $5 change is the *pretax effect of the LIFO liquidation* which took place in part A. Given the assumed tax rate of 25%, taxes paid are $1.25 (.25 × $5) lower in this second situation. This will occur even if the purchase takes place *after* the sale of the third item because the tax law allows LIFO to be applied *as if* all purchases during an accounting period take place before any sales and cost of goods sold are recorded. Because of this feature, temporary LIFO liquidations can be eliminated by purchasing additional inventory before year-end. Most companies apply LIFO in this manner.

LIFO Liquidations and Financial Statement Analysis

Over the past decade, Deere & Company has faced declining demand and increasing competition in most major segments of its business which reduces the inventory quantities necessary to meet customers' needs. It has also instituted modern manufacturing techniques that further decrease inventory levels. Deere, a long-time LIFO user, has experienced continuing LIFO liquidations over this period. Companies must disclose the effects of LIFO liquidations in the footnotes when they are material, as Deere has done (see the excerpt that follows the next paragraph). The second paragraph of the note explains the effect. The last sentence lists the pretax (after-tax) effects of the liquidations.

Over the past three years, LIFO liquidations have increased Deere's reported income before taxes by a total of $244 million ($51 + $65 + $128). (These numbers are the equivalent of the $5 effect of the liquidation computed in the New Company example.) To compute pretax income as if the liquidations had not taken place (as if current year's production was large enough so that no items from beginning inventory were sold), simply subtract the LIFO liquidation effect from pretax income.

Pretax income (reported on the income statements)	$290
Less: Pretax effect of LIFO liquidations (from footnote)	244
Pretax income on LIFO basis as if no liquidations	$ 46

Real World Excerpt

Deere & Company Annual Report

DEERE & COMPANY
NOTES TO CONSOLIDATED FINANCIAL STATEMENTS

INVENTORIES

Substantially all inventories owned by Deere & Company and, its United States equipment subsidiaries are valued at cost on the "last-in, first-out" (LIFO) method . . .

Under the LIFO inventory method, cost of goods sold ordinarily reflects current production costs thus providing a matching of current costs and current revenues in the income statement. However when LIFO-valued inventories decline, as they did in 1993 and 1992, lower costs that prevailed in prior years are matched against current year revenues, resulting in higher reported net income. Benefits from the reduction of LIFO inventories totaled $51 million ($33 million or $ .43 per share after income taxes) in 1993, $65 million ($43 million or $ .56 per share after income taxes) in 1992 and $128 million ($84 million or $1.11 per share after income taxes) in 1991.

Pretax (after-tax) effects of LIFO liquidations

Fully 84% ($244 ÷ $290) of Deere's reported pretax profit over the three years is the result of LIFO liquidations. Since the $46 million pretax profit figure reflects Deere's current costs of production, educated analysts use this figure when comparing Deere's performance to that of other LIFO companies. It is important to emphasize that these numbers still are on a *LIFO* basis but are prepared *as if no liquidation took place.*

FINANCIAL ANALYSIS

Inventory Management and LIFO Liquidations

Several research studies have documented the year-end inventory purchasing decisions of firms that use LIFO.[7] Many firms avoid LIFO liquidations and the accompanying increase in tax expense by purchasing sufficient quantities of inventory at year-end to ensure that ending inventory quantities are greater than or equal to beginning inventory quantities. While this practice increases the costs of carrying inventory (storage, financing, etc.), for these firms, the taxes saved exceed these amounts.

As noted earlier in the chapter, Harley-Davidson and many other firms have moved to more efficient just-in-time inventory techniques that greatly reduce the amount of inventory manufacturers keep on hand. When managers compare the savings in carrying costs against the costs of implementing the new system (new computers, training, etc.), they must also consider the added taxes they may pay if they account for the inventory using the LIFO method. When the company switches to the new just-in-time system, ending inventory quantity will normally decline below beginning inventory quantity, causing a LIFO liquidation and a one-time increase in taxes. This cost should be considered when deciding whether to adopt the new system. In this case the tax law provides an incentive for U.S. companies *not* to become more efficient.

Self-Study Quiz

1. Deere & Company reported pretax earnings of $272.3 million in 1993. Using the information in the inventory footnote on page *369*, convert pretax earnings from a LIFO to a FIFO basis.

Difference in beginning inventory (LIFO to FIFO)	________
Less: Difference in ending inventory (LIFO to FIFO)	________
Difference in cost of goods sold	________
Pretax income (LIFO)	________
Difference in Pretax Income (LIFO to FIFO)	________
Pretax income (FIFO)	________

Note that in this case, the LIFO liquidation increased pretax earnings to such an extent that pretax income under LIFO is actually higher than under FIFO. Had the liquidation not taken place, the opposite would have occurred.

2. Assume that OLD Company has employed the LIFO method for the past 20 years. Its beginning inventory and purchases for 19B included:

Beginning inventory	10 units @ $ 6 each
Purchases January	5 units @ $10 each
Purchases November	5 units @ $12 each.

During 19B, 15 units were sold for $20 each and other operating expenses totaled $100.

a. Compute cost of goods sold and pretax income for 19B.

____

____

b. Now assume that OLD Company was able to purchase an additional 5 units at $12 each on December 31. Compute cost of goods sold and pretax income for 19B.

____

[7] M. Frankel and R. Trezevant, "The Year-End LIFO Inventory Purchasing Decision: An Empirical Test," *The Accounting Review* (April 1994), pp. 382–98.

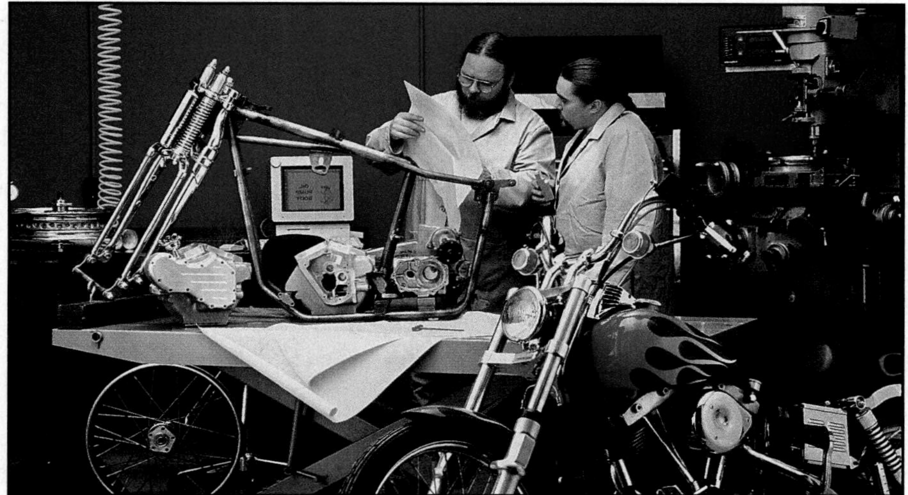

Engineering and design are key first steps in quality manufacturing.

c. Explain how LIFO causes this difference in your answers to parts *a* and *b*.

After you have completed your answers, check them with the solutions presented in the footnote at the bottom of this page.*

VALUATION AT LOWER OF COST OR MARKET

Learning Objective 6
Apply the lower-of-cost-or-market (LCM) rule.

Inventories should be measured at their purchase cost in conformity with the cost principle. However, when the goods remaining in ending inventory can be replaced with identical goods at a lower cost, the lower cost should be used as the inventory valuation. Also, damaged, obsolete, and deteriorated items in inventory should be assigned a unit cost that represents their current estimated net realizable value if that is below cost. This rule is known as measuring inventories at the **lower of cost or market (LCM).**

Lower of cost or market (LCM) is a valuation method departing from the cost principle that serves to recognize a loss when replacement cost or net realizable value drops below cost.

It is a departure from the cost principle because of the conservatism constraint (see Chapter 5) that requires special care to avoid overstating assets and income. It is particularly important for two types of companies: (1) high-technology companies such as Compaq Computer and Apple Computer who manufacture goods for which the cost of production and the selling price are declining and (2) companies such as The GAP or The Limited that sell seasonal goods such as clothing, the value of which drops dramatically at the end of each selling season (fall or spring).

Replacement cost is the current purchase price for identical goods.

For companies like Compaq Computer, under LCM, a "holding" loss is recognized in the period in which the **replacement cost** of an item dropped,

*1.

Difference in beginning inventory	$1,044	Pretax income (LIFO)	$272.3
Less: Difference in ending inventory	942	Difference in pretax income	(102.0)
Difference in cost of goods sold	102	Pretax income (FIFO)	$170.3

2.

	BI	+	P	−	EI	=	CGS	Sales	−	CGS	−	Operating exp.	=	Pretax income
a.	$60	+	$110	−	$30	=	$140	$300	−	$140	−	$100	=	$60
b.	$60	+	$170	−	$60	=	$170	$300	−	$170	−	$100	=	$30

c. Under LIFO, inventory most recently purchased is assumed sold. In part *a,* lower cost units from beginning inventory were assumed sold. In part *b,* puchases were sufficient such that no items from beginning inventory were sold.

rather than in the period in which the item is sold. The holding loss is the difference between purchase cost and the subsequent lower replacement cost and is added to the cost of goods sold of the period. To illustrate, assume that Compaq Computer has 1,000 Pentium microprocessor chips in the 19B ending inventory. The chips were bought for $250 each. At the end of the year, the same chips can be purchased for $200. The 1,000 chips should be recorded in the ending inventory at the lower of cost ($250) or current market ($200). Under LCM, the ending inventory should be reduced to $200 per unit. Compaq would make the following journal entry to record the write-down:

Cost of Goods Sold	50,000	
Inventory*		50,000

*Some companies credit a contra-asset to inventory called a *reserve* which is adjusted at the end of each accounting period.

Several effects are caused by using a replacement cost of $200 instead of the original purchase cost of $250. By recording the chips in ending inventory at $50 per unit below their purchase cost, 19B pretax income will be $50,000 less (1,000 × $50) than it would have been had they been recorded in the inventory at $250 per unit. This $50,000 loss in the value of the inventory (the holding loss) was due to a decline in the replacement cost. Pretax income is reduced by $50,000 in the period in which the replacement cost dropped (19B) rather than in the next period (19C) when the chips will be used in the production of computers and sold. As a consequence, LCM transfers the added expense from the period of sale (19C) back to the current period (19B). Since the cost of goods sold for period 19B is *increased* by $50,000 and the cost of goods sold for 19C is *decreased* by $50,000, the total cost of goods sold expense (and net income before taxes) for the two periods (19B and 19C) combined do not change. On the balance sheet, the $50,000 loss in 19B reduces the amount of inventory that is reported on December 31, 19B.

In contrast, if the replacement cost had increased to $300 each, the company would have experienced an economic holding gain. Recognition of holding gains is not permitted by GAAP (except for certain marketable securities discussed in Chapter 12) because revenue and gains are normally recognized only at the date of sale.

Net realizable value is the expected sales price less selling costs (e.g., repair and disposal costs).

In the case of seasonal goods such as clothing, obsolete goods, or damaged goods, if the sales price less selling costs (or **net realizable value**) drops below cost, this difference is subtracted from ending inventory and added to cost of goods sold of the period. This has the same effects on current and future periods' financial statements as the write-down to replacement cost.

Under Generally Accepted Accounting Principles in the United States, the lower of cost or market rule can be applied to inventories the cost of which is determined using any of the four acceptable inventory costing methods. Note that in the two footnote examples below, both Harley-Davidson, which is a mixed LIFO company, and Compaq Computer, which is a FIFO company, report use of lower of cost or market for financial statement purposes. For tax purposes, the lower of cost or market calculations may be applied with all inventory costing methods except LIFO.

Real World Excerpt

Harley-Davidson, Inc. Annual Report

HARLEY-DAVIDSON, INC.
NOTES TO CONSOLIDATED FINANCIAL STATEMENTS

1. SUMMARY OF SIGNIFICANT ACCOUNTING POLICIES

Inventories – Inventories are valued at lower of cost or market. Motorcycle and transportation vehicle inventories located in the United States are valued using the last-in, first-out (LIFO) method. Other inventories, . . . , are valued at the lower of cost or market using the first-in, first-out (FIFO) method.

Real World Excerpt

Compaq Computer Annual Report

Notes to Consolidated Financial Statements
Compaq Computer Corporation
Note 1 - Description of Business and Significant Accounting Policies:
Inventories – Inventories are stated at the lower of cost or market, cost being determined on a first-in, first-out basis.

KEEPING TRACK OF INVENTORY QUANTITIES AND COSTS

Learning Objective 7
Keep track of inventory quantities and amounts in different circumstances.

To compute cost of goods sold, three amounts must be known: (1) beginning inventory, (2) purchases of merchandise (or transfers to finished goods) during the period, and (3) ending inventory. To simplify the discussion of how accounting systems keep track of these amounts, we will focus this discussion on the Motorclothes™ line for which Harley-Davidson is a wholesaler. Though the same general principles apply, the more complex details of manufacturing accounting systems are discussed in management accounting and cost accounting courses.

As noted earlier, the beginning inventory of one accounting period is the ending inventory of the previous period. The amount of purchases for the period is always accumulated in the accounting system. The amount of the ending inventory can be determined by using one of two different inventory systems: the periodic or perpetual inventory systems.

Periodic Inventory System

In a **periodic inventory system,** ending inventory and cost of goods sold are determined at the end of the accounting period based on a physical count.

Under the **periodic inventory system,** no up-to-date record of inventory is maintained during the year. An actual physical count of the goods remaining on hand is required at the *end of each period*. The number of units of each type of merchandise on hand is multiplied by their unit cost to compute the dollar amount of the ending inventory. Cost of goods sold is calculated using the cost of goods sold equation as follows:

$$\text{Beginning inventory} + \text{Purchases} - \text{Ending inventory} = \text{Cost of goods sold}$$

Thus, the amount of inventory is not known until the end of the period, when the inventory count is done. Also, the amount of cost of goods sold cannot be determined reliably until the inventory count is done. Companies using a periodic system must estimate the amount of inventory on hand.[8]

In the past, the primary reason for using the periodic inventory system was its low cost. Before affordable computers and bar code readers were available, the expense and difficulty associated with attempting to keep track of the number of units sold and the cost of each purchase and sale for thousands of items was very high. For example, in many retail stores, no record was made at the cash register of the cost and quantity of each item sold. As a consequence, only the total sales price was entered at the time of sale (for example, at an old-style cash register still used in some small retail businesses). The primary disadvantage of a periodic inventory system is the lack of inventory information. Managers are not provided with any information concerning low stock or overstocked situations. Most modern companies could not survive without this information. As noted at the beginning of the chapter, cost and quality pressures brought on by increasing competition, combined with

[8]Methods for estimating inventory and cost of goods sold are discussed in intermediate accounting texts and courses.

dramatic declines in the cost of computers, have made sophisticated perpetual inventory systems a minimum requirement at all but the smallest companies.

Perpetual Inventory System

In a **perpetual inventory system,** a detailed inventory record is maintained recording each purchase and sale during the accounting period.

A **perpetual inventory system** involves the maintenance of up-to-date inventory records in the accounting system during the period. For each type of merchandise stocked, a detailed record is maintained that shows (*a*) units and cost of the beginning inventory, (*b*) units and cost of each purchase, (*c*) units and cost of the goods for each sale, and (*d*) the units and cost of the goods on hand at any point in time. This up-to-date record is maintained on a transaction-by-transaction basis throughout the period. In a complete perpetual inventory system, the inventory record gives both the amount of ending inventory and the cost of goods sold amount at any point in time. Under this system, a physical count must be performed from time to time to assure accurate records in case errors or theft of inventory occur.

This system typically involves a computer system. Whether the accounting system is manual or computerized, the data that are recorded and reported are the same. The maintenance of a separate inventory record for each type of good stocked on a transaction-by-transaction basis usually is necessary for purchasing, manufacturing, and distribution decisions. A company such as Harley-Davidson relies heavily on this system and even shares some of this information electronically with its suppliers.

In a perpetual inventory system, purchase transactions are directly recorded in Inventory instead of a Purchases account. In addition, when each sale is recorded, a companion cost of goods sold entry is also made. As a result, information on cost of goods sold and ending inventory is available on a continuous (perpetual) basis.

Comparison of Periodic and Perpetual Systems

The differences between the periodic and perpetual inventory systems can be summarized using the basic inventory equation:

Periodic system:

Model:	Beginning inventory	+	Purchases of the period	−	Ending inventory	=	Cost of goods sold
	↓		↓		↓		↓
Source:	Carried over from prior period		Accumulated in the Purchases account		Measured at end of period by physical inventory count		Computed as a residual amount

Perpetual system:

Model:	Beginning inventory	+	Purchases of the period	−	Cost of goods sold	=	Ending inventory
	↓		↓		↓		↓
Source:	Carried over from prior period		Accumulated in the Inventory account		Measured at every sale based on perpetual record		Perpetual record updated at every sale

Assume, for this illustration only, that Harley-Davidson stocks and sells only one item, its Eagle Harness Boots, and that only the following events occur in 19F:

Jan. 1 Beginning inventory: 800 units, at unit cost of $50.
April 14 Purchased: 1,100 additional units, at unit cost of $50.
Nov. 30 Sold: 1,300 units, at unit sales price of $83.
Dec. 29 Return sale: 100 units (returned to stock and refunded sales price).

In the two types of inventory systems, the following sequential steps would take place:

Periodic Records	**Perpetual Records**

1. Record all purchases in an account called *Purchases.*
 	
April 14, 19F:
Purchases (1,100 units at $50) 55,000
  Accounts payable (or Cash) 55,000
	1. Record all purchases in the *Inventory* account and in a detailed perpetual inventory record.
	
	April 14, 19F:
	Inventory (1,100 units at $50)* 55,000
	  Accounts payable (or Cash) 55,000
	
	*Also entered in the detailed perpetual inventory record as 1,100 Harness Boots at $50 each.

2. Record all sales in a Sales Revenue account.
 	
November 30, 19F:
Accounts receivable (or Cash) 107,900
  Sales revenue (1,300 units at $83) 107,900
	2. Record all sales in the Sales Revenue account and record the cost of goods sold.
	
	November 30, 19F:
	Accounts receivable (or Cash) 107,900
	  Sales revenue (1,300 units at $83) 107,900
	Cost of goods sold 65,000
	  Inventory (1,300 units at $50)* 65,000
	
	*Also entered in the perpetual inventory record as a reduction of 1,300 units at $50 each.

3. Record all sales returns.
 	
December 29, 19F:
Sales returns and allowances (100 units at $83) 8,300
  Accounts receivable (or Cash) 8,300
	3. Record all sales returns and related inventory.
	
	December 29, 19F:
	Sales returns and allowances (100 units at $83) 8,300
	  Accounts receivable (or Cash) 8,300
	Inventory (100 units at $50) 5,000*
	  Cost of goods sold 5,000
	
	*This amount is also restored to the perpetual inventory record.

4. At end of period:
 	
a. Count the number of units on hand.
b. Compute the dollar valuation of the ending inventory.
c. Compute and record the cost of goods sold.
 	
Beginning inventory (last period's ending) $40,000
Add purchases (balance in the Purchases account) 55,000
  $95,000
Deduct ending inventory (physical count —700 units at $50) 35,000
Cost of goods sold $60,000
 	
December 31, 19F:
Transfer beginning inventory and purchases (GAS) to cost of goods sold:
 	
Cost of goods sold 95,000
  Inventory (beginning) 40,000
  Purchases 55,000
 	
Subtract the ending inventory amount from the cost of goods sold to complete its computation and establish the ending inventory balance:
 	
Inventory (ending) 35,000
  Cost of goods sold 35,000
	4. Use cost of goods sold and inventory amounts. At the end of the accounting period, the balance in the Cost of Goods Sold account is the amount of that expense reported on the income statement. It is not necessary to compute cost of goods sold because under the perpetual inventory system the Cost of Goods Sold account is up-to-date. Also, the Inventory account shows the ending inventory amount reported on the balance sheet. The sum of all the inventory balances in the various perpetual inventory records should equal the balance in the Inventory account in the ledger at any point in time. A physical inventory count is still necessary to assess the accuracy of the perpetual records and assess theft and other forms of misuse (called *shrinkage*).
	
	No entry

Perpetual Inventory Records in Practice

The decision to use a perpetual versus a periodic inventory system is based primarily on management's need for timely information for use in operating decisions and on the cost of the perpetual system. Further, the specific manner in which the perpetual system is designed will also be determined with these trade-offs in mind. Many inventory ordering and production decisions require only exact information on inventory quantities, and not costs. For example, at Harley-Davidson's Sportster™ assembly line in York, Pennsylvania, a bar code reader is used to keep track of each bike, which provides the needed information to schedule further purchases, production, and delivery of raw materials. This same information is necessary to provide up-to-date information for estimating delivery dates for finished motorcycles. If during testing of the completed motorcycles, problems are identified with a part such as a carburetor, the system provides the information necessary to track those problems back to the specific lot of purchased carburetors. Harley-Davidson can replace the defective carburetors before the motorcycles are delivered to customers and then work with the supplier to correct the problem. Note that the information necessary for efficient management of inventory, providing delivery information to dealers, and quality control did *not* require exact cost information.

Systems that do keep track of the costs of individual items or lots normally do so on a FIFO, estimated average (or standard) cost basis, or for distinguishable high-value items using specific identification. Perpetual records are rarely kept on a LIFO basis for two reasons: (1) it is more complex and costly to do so, and (2) doing so often causes LIFO liquidations which can increase tax payments. The conversion to LIFO is made as an adjusting entry.

Additional Issues in Measuring Purchases

Purchase Returns and Allowances

Goods purchased may be returned to the vendor if they do not meet specifications, arrive in damaged condition, or otherwise are unsatisfactory. When the goods are returned or when the vendor makes an allowance because of the circumstances, the effect on the cost of purchases must be measured. The purchaser normally will receive a cash refund or a reduction in the liability to the vendor when there is a return. Assume Harley-Davidson returned unsatisfactory Harness Boots that cost $1,000 to a supplier. The return would be recorded by Harley-Davidson as follows:

Accounts payable (or Cash)	1,000	
Purchase returns and allowances*		1,000

*Inventory is credited when the perpetual inventory system is used.

Purchase Returns and Allowances is a deduction from the cost of purchases associated with unsatisfactory goods.

Purchase Returns and Allowances are accounted for as a deduction from the cost of purchases.

Purchase Discounts

A **purchase discount** is a cash discount received for prompt payment of an account payable.

Cash discounts must be accounted for by both the seller and the buyer (accounting by the seller was discussed in Chapter 6). When merchandise is bought on credit, terms such as 2/10, n/30, sometimes are specified. This means that if payment is made within 10 days from date of purchase, a 2% cash discount is granted, known as the **purchase discount**. If payment is not made within the discount period, then the full invoice cost is due 30 days after purchase. Assume on January 17, Harley-Davidson bought goods that had a $1,000 invoice price with terms 2/10, n/30. Assuming they use the gross method discussed in Chapter 6, the purchase should be recorded as follows:

Date of purchase:

Jan. 17	Purchases*	1,000	
	Accounts payable		1,000

*Inventory is debited when a perpetual inventory system is used.

Date of payment, within the discount period:

Jan. 26	Accounts payable	1,000	
	Purchase discounts		20
	Cash		980

If for any reason Harley-Davidson did not pay within the 10-day discount period, the following entry would be needed:

Feb. 1	Accounts payable	1,000	
	Cash		1,000

The **Purchase Discounts account** is a deduction from the cost of purchases in the calculation of cost of goods sold for discounts taken.

Purchase Discounts should be reported as a deduction from the cost of purchases in the calculation of cost of goods sold.

DEMONSTRATION CASE A

(Complete the requirements before proceeding to the suggested solution that follows.)

Metal Products, Incorporated, has been operating for three years as a distributor of a line of metal products. It is now the end of 19C, and for the first time the company will undergo an audit by an independent CPA. The company uses a *periodic* inventory system. The annual income statements (note which column is the current year) prepared by the company were:

	For the Year Ended December 31			
	19B		19C	
Sales revenue		$750,000		$800,000
Cost of goods sold:				
Beginning inventory	45,000		40,000	
Add purchases	460,000		484,000	
Goods available for sale	505,000		524,000	
Less ending inventory	40,000		60,000	
Cost of goods sold		465,000		464,000
Gross margin on sales		285,000		336,000
Operating expenses		275,000		306,000
Pretax income		10,000		30,000
Income tax expense (20%)		2,000		6,000
Net income		$ 8,000		$ 24,000

During the early stages of the audit, the independent CPA discovered that the ending inventory for 19B was understated by $15,000.

Required:

1. Based on the above income statement amounts, compute the gross margin ratio on sales for each year. Do the results suggest an inventory error? Explain.
2. Correct and reconstruct the two income statements.
3. Answer the following questions:
   a. What are the correct gross margin ratios?
   b. What effect did the $15,000 understatement of the ending inventory have on 19B pretax income? Explain.
   c. What effect did the inventory error have on the 19C pretax income? Explain.
   d. How did the inventory error affect income tax expense?

SUGGESTED SOLUTION

1. Gross margin ratios as reported:

19B: $285,000 ÷ $750,000 = 0.38
19C: $336,000 ÷ $800,000 = 0.42

The change in the gross margin ratio from 0.38 to 0.42 suggests the possibility of an inventory error in the absence of any other explanation.

2. Income Statements Corrected:

	For the Year Ended December 31			
	19B		19C	
Sales revenue		$750,000		$800,000
Cost of goods sold:				
Beginning inventory	45,000		55,000*	
Add purchases	460,000		484,000	
Goods available for sale	505,000		539,000	
Less ending inventory	55,000*		60,000	
Cost of goods sold		450,000		479,000
Gross margin on sales		300,000		321,000
Operating expenses		275,000		306,000
Pretax income		25,000		15,000
Income tax expense (20%)		5,000		3,000
Net income		$ 20,000		$ 12,000

*Increased by $15,000.

3. *a.* Correct gross margin ratios:

19B: $300,000 ÷ $750,000 = 0.400
19C: $321,000 ÷ $800,000 = 0.401

The inventory error of $15,000 was responsible for the difference in the gross margin ratios reflected in requirement 1. The error in the 19B ending inventory affected gross margin for both 19B and 19C—in the opposite direction but by the same amount, $15,000.

b. Effect on pretax income in 19B: Ending inventory *understatement* ($15,000) caused an *understatement* of pretax income by the same amount.

c. Effect on pretax income in 19C: Beginning inventory *understatement* (by the same $15,000 since the inventory amount is carried over from the prior period) caused an *overstatement* of pretax income by the same amount.

d. Total income tax expense for 19B and 19C combined was the same ($8,000) regardless of the error. However, there was a shift of $3,000 ($15,000 × 20%) income tax expense from 19B to 19C.

Observation: An ending inventory error in one year affects pretax income by the amount of the error and in the next year affects pretax income again by the same amount but in the opposite direction.

DEMONSTRATION CASE B

(Complete the requirements before proceeding to the suggested solution that follows.)

This case reviews a periodic inventory system assuming the LIFO inventory costing method is applied.

Balent Appliances distributes a number of high-cost household appliances. One product, microwave ovens, has been selected for case purposes. Assume the following summarized transactions were completed during the accounting period in the order given below (assume all transactions are cash):

	Units	Unit Cost
a. Beginning inventory	11	$200
b. Purchases	9	220
c. Purchase returns (damaged in shipment)	1	220
d. Sales (selling price, $420)	8	?
e. Sales returns (can be resold as new)	1	220

Required:

1. Compute the following amounts assuming application of the LIFO inventory costing method:

	Ending Inventory		Cost of Goods Sold	
	Units	Dollars	Units	Dollars
LIFO (costed at end of period)				

2. Give the indicated journal entries for transactions (*b*) through (*e*).

SUGGESTED SOLUTION

1.

	Ending Inventory		Cost of Goods Sold	
	Units	Dollars	Units	Dollars
LIFO (costed at end of the period)	12	$2,420	7	$1,540

Computations:

Goods available for sale = Beginning inventory + (Purchases − Purchase returns)
= (11 units × $200 = $2,200) + (8 units × $220 = $1,760)
= $3,960

LIFO inventory (costed at end of period):

Ending inventory: (11 units × $200 = $2,200) + (1 unit × $220 = $220) = $2,420.
Cost of goods sold: (Goods available, $3,960) − (Ending inventory, $2,420) = $1,540.

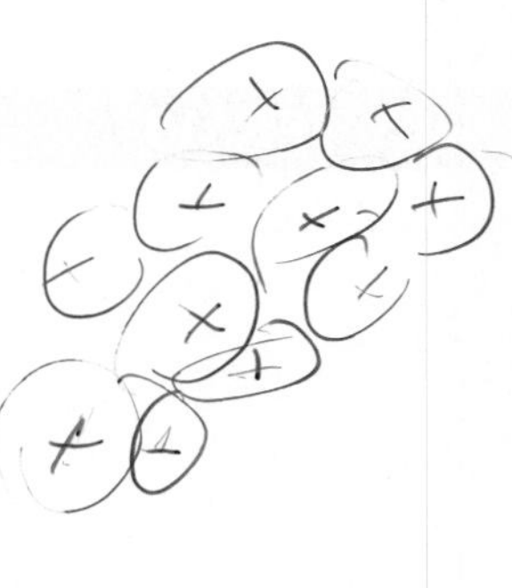

2. Journal Entries:

b. Purchases:

	Debit	Credit
Purchases	1,980	
Cash (9 × $220)		1,980

c. Purchase returns:

	Debit	Credit
Cash	220	
Purchase returns		220

d. Sales:

	Debit	Credit
Cash (8 × $420)	3,360	
Sales revenue		3,360

e. Sales returns:

	Debit	Credit
Sales returns	420	
Cash (1 × $420)		420

SUMMARY

Costs flow into inventory when goods are purchased or manufactured and flow out (as an expense) when the goods are sold or disposed of otherwise. In conformity with the matching principle, the total cost of the goods sold during the period must be matched with the sales revenue earned during the period. Cost of goods sold measures the cost of inventory that was sold while sales revenue measures the selling price of the same inventory. When cost of goods sold is deducted from sales revenue for the period, the difference is called *gross profit* or *gross margin on sales.* From this amount, the remaining expenses must be deducted to derive income.

This chapter focused on the problem of measuring cost of goods sold and ending inventory when unit costs change during the period. Inventory should include all the items held for resale that the entity owns. When there are different unit cost amounts, a rational and systematic method must be used to allocate costs to the units remaining in inventory and to the units sold. The chapter discussed four different inventory costing methods and their applications in different economic circumstances. The methods discussed were FIFO, LIFO, weighted-average cost, and specific identification. Each of the inventory costing methods is in conformity with GAAP. The selection of a method of inventory costing is important because it will affect reported income, income tax expense (and hence cash flow), and the inventory valuation reported on the balance sheet. In a period of rising prices, FIFO normally results in a higher income than does LIFO; in a period of falling prices, the opposite result occurs. Public companies using LIFO provide footnote disclosures that allow conversion of inventory and cost of goods sold to FIFO amounts and the elimination of the effects of any LIFO liquidations.

Ending inventory should be measured on the basis of the lower of actual cost or replacement cost (LCM basis) which can have a major effect on the statements of companies facing declining costs. Also, damaged, obsolete, and deteriorated items in inventory should be assigned a unit cost that represents their current estimated net realizable value if that is below cost.

Two inventory systems were discussed for keeping track of the ending inventory and cost of goods sold for the period: (1) the perpetual inventory system, which is based on the maintenance of detailed and continuous inventory records for each kind of inventory stocked; and (2) the periodic inventory system, which is based on a physical inventory count of ending inventory and the costing of those goods to determine the proper amounts for cost of goods sold and ending inventory.

KEY TERMS

Cost of Goods Sold Equation BI + P – EI = CGS *358*

Direct Labor The earnings of employees who work directly on the products being manufactured. *357*

Factory Overhead Manufacturing costs that are not raw material or direct labor costs. *357*

Finished Goods Inventory Manufactured goods that are completed and ready for sale. *355*

First-In, First-Out (FIFO) Method Inventory costing method that assumes the oldest units are the first units sold. *362*

Goods Available for Sale The sum of beginning inventory and purchases (or transfers to finished goods) for the period. *358*

Inventory Tangible property that is held for sale in the normal course of business or will be used in producing goods or services for sale. *354*

Last-In, First-Out (LIFO) Method Inventory costing method that assumes the most recently acquired units are sold first. 363

LIFO Liquidation A sale of a lower-cost inventory item from beginning LIFO inventory. 370

LIFO Reserve A contra-asset for the excess of FIFO over LIFO inventory. 368

Lower of Cost or Market (LCM) Valuation method departing from cost principle that serves to recognize a loss when replacement cost or net realizable value drops below cost. 373

Merchandise Inventory Goods held for resale in the ordinary course of business. 354

Net Realizable Value The expected sales price less selling costs (e.g., repair and disposal costs). 374

Periodic Inventory System Ending inventory and cost of goods sold are determined at the end of the accounting period based on a physical inventory count. 375

Perpetual Inventory System A detailed inventory record is maintained recording each purchase and sale during the accounting period. 376

Purchase Discount Cash discount received for prompt payment of an account payable. 378

Purchase Discounts Account A deduction from the cost of purchases in the calculation of cost of goods sold for discounts taken. 379

Purchase Returns and Allowances A deduction from the cost of purchases associated with unsatisfactory goods. 378

Raw Materials Inventory Items acquired for the purpose of processing into finished goods. 354

Replacement Cost The current purchase price for identical goods. 373

Specific Identification Method Inventory costing method that identifies the cost of the specific item that was sold. 364

Weighted-Average Method Inventory costing method that uses the weighted-average unit cost of the goods available for sale for both cost of goods sold and ending inventory. 363

Work in Process Inventory Goods in the process of being manufactured. 355

QUESTIONS

1. Match the type of inventory with the type of business in the following matrix:

	Type of Business	
Type of Inventory	**Merchandising**	**Manufacturing**
Merchandise		
Finished goods		
Work in process		
Raw materials		

2. Why is inventory an important item to both internal (management) and external users of financial statements?
3. What are the general guidelines for deciding which items should be included in inventory?
4. Define goods available for sale. How does it differ from cost of goods sold?
5. Define beginning inventory and ending inventory.
6. In measuring cost of goods sold and inventory, why is passage of ownership an important issue? When does ownership to goods usually pass? Explain.
7. Explain the application of the cost principle to an item in the ending inventory.
8. Assume the 19A ending inventory was understated by $100,000. Explain how this error would affect the 19A and 19B pretax income amounts. What would be the effects if the 19A ending inventory were overstated by $100,000 instead of understated?

9. The chapter discussed four inventory costing methods. List the four methods and briefly explain each.
10. Explain how income can be manipulated when the specific identification inventory costing method is used.
11. Contrast the effects of LIFO versus FIFO on reported assets (i.e., the ending inventory) when (*a*) prices are rising and (*b*) prices are falling.
12. Contrast the income statement effect of LIFO versus FIFO (i.e., on pretax income) when (*a*) prices are rising and (*b*) prices are falling.
13. Contrast the effects of LIFO versus FIFO on cash outflow and inflow.
14. Explain briefly the application of the LCM concept to the ending inventory and its effect on the income statement and balance sheet when market is lower than cost.
15. When should net realizable value be used in costing an item in the ending inventory?
16. Briefly explain the comparability quality. How might it relate to the inventory costing methods?
17. When a perpetual inventory system is used, unit costs of the items sold are known at the date of each sale. In contrast, when a periodic inventory system is used, unit costs are known only at the end of the accounting period. Why are these statements correct?
18. The periodic inventory calculation is BI + P – EI = CGS. The perpetual inventory calculation is BI + P – CGS = EI. Explain the significance of the difference between these two calculations.
19. What accounts are debited and credited for a purchase of goods for resale (*a*) when a perpetual inventory system is used and (*b*) when a periodic inventory system is used?
20. What accounts are debited and credited for a sale of goods on credit (*a*) when a perpetual inventory system is used and (*b*) when a periodic inventory system is used?

EXERCISES

E7–1 Analyzing Income Statement Relationships

Supply the missing dollar amounts for the 19B income statement of Lewis Retailers for each of the following independent cases:

Cases	Sales Revenue	Beginning Inventory	Purchases	Total Available	Ending Inventory	Cost of Goods Sold	Gross Margin	Expenses	Pretax Income or (Loss)
A	$ 650	$100	$700	$?	$500	$?	$?	$200	$?
B	900	200	800	?	?	?	?	150	0
C	?	150	?	?	300	200	400	100	?
D	800	?	600	?	250	?	?	250	100
E	1,000	?	900	1,100	?	?	500	?	(50)

E7–2 Finding Missing Amounts Based on Income Statement Relationships

Supply the missing dollar amounts for the 19D income statement of Travis Company for each of the following independent cases:

	Case A	Case B	Case C
Sales revenue	$8,000	$ 6,000	$?
Sales returns and allowances	150	?	275
Net sales revenue	?	?	5,920
Beginning inventory	11,000	6,500	4,000
Purchases	5,000	?	9,420
Transportation-in	?	120	170
Purchase returns	350	600	?
Goods available for sale	?	14,790	13,370
Ending inventory	10,000	10,740	?
Cost of goods sold	?	?	5,400
Gross margin	?	1,450	?
Expenses	1,300	?	520
Pretax income	800	(500)	-0-

E7–3 *Correcting Costs Included in the Cost of Purchases for a Merchandiser*

Elite Apparel purchased 80 new shirts and recorded a total cost of $3,140 determined as follows:

Invoice cost	$2,600
Less: Cash discount 3% taken	
Shipping charges	165
Import taxes and duties	115
Interest paid in advance (10%) on $2,600 borrowed to finance the purchase	260
	$3,140

Required:

Make the needed corrections in the above calculation. Give the journal entry(s) to record this purchase in the correct amount assuming a periodic inventory system. Show computations.

E7–4 *Costs Included in the Cost of Inventories for a Manufacturer*

Operating costs incurred by a manufacturing company become either (*a*) part of the cost of inventory to be expensed as cost of goods sold at the time the finished goods are sold or (*b*) expenses at the time they are incurred. Indicate whether each of the following costs belongs in category (*a*) or (*b*).

	(*a*) Part of Inventory	(*b*) Expense as Incurred
1. Wages of factory workers		
2. Sales salaries		
3. Costs of raw materials purchased		
4. Heat, light, and power for the factory building		
5. Heat, light, and power for the headquarters office building		

E7–5 *Using the Cost of Goods Sold Equation to Estimate Purchases*

J. C. Penney

J. C. Penney Company, Inc., is a major retailer with department stores in all 50 states. The dominant portion of the company's business consists of providing merchandise and services to consumers through department stores that include catalog departments. In a recent annual report, J. C. Penney reported cost of goods sold was $10,969 million, ending inventory for the current year was $3,062 million, and ending inventory for the previous year was $2,969 million.

Required:

Is it possible to develop a reasonable estimate of the merchandise purchases for the year? If yes, prepare the estimate; if not, explain why.

GAP, Inc.

E7–6 Analyzing Merchandise Purchases

The Gap, Inc., is a specialty retailer that operates stores selling clothes under the trade names Gap, GapKids, BabyGap, and Banana Republic. Assume that you are employed as a stock analyst and your boss has just completed a review of the new Gap annual report. She provided you with her notes, but they are missing some information that you need. Her notes show that the ending inventory for Gap in the current year was $243,482,000 and in the previous year was $193,268,000. Net sales for the current year were $1,586,596,000. Gross margin was $540,360,000; net income was $97,628,000. For your analysis, you determine that you need to know the amount of purchases for the year and cost of goods sold.

Required:

Do you need to ask your boss for her copy of the annual report, or can you develop the information from her notes? Explain and show calculations.

E7–7 Analyzing the Impact of an Inventory Error

Dallas Corporation prepared the following two income statements (simplified for illustrative purposes):

	First Quarter 19B		Second Quarter 19B	
Sales revenue		$15,000		$18,000
Cost of goods sold:				
Beginning inventory	$ 3,000		$ 4,000	
Purchases	7,000		12,000	
Goods available for sale	10,000		16,000	
Ending inventory	4,000		9,000	
Cost of goods sold		6,000		7,000
Gross margin		9,000		11,000
Expenses		5,000		6,000
Pretax income		$ 4,000		$ 5,000

During the third quarter it was discovered that the ending inventory for the first quarter should have been $4,400.

Required:

1. What effect did this error have on the combined pretax income of the two quarters? Explain.
2. Did this error affect the EPS amounts for each quarter (see Chapter 5 discussion of EPS)? Explain.
3. Prepare corrected income statements for each quarter.
4. Set up a schedule that reflects the comparative effects of the correct and incorrect amounts.

E7–8 Analyzing the Effects of an Error in Recording Purchases

Garraway Ski Company had mistakenly recorded purchases of inventory on account received during the last week of December 19A as purchases during January of 19B (this is called a *purchases cutoff error*). Garraway uses a periodic inventory system and ending inventory was correctly counted and reported each year. Assuming that no correction was made in 19A or 19B, indicate whether each of the following financial statement amounts will be understated, overstated, or correct.

1. Net Income for 19A.
2. Net Income for 19B.
3. Retained Earnings for December 31, 19A.
4. Retained Earnings for December 31, 19B.

E7–9 Analyzing the Effect of an Inventory Error Disclosed in an Actual Note to a Financial Statement

Lafayette Radio Electronics

Several years ago, the financial statements of Lafayette Radio Electronics Corporation contained the following footnote:

> Subsequent to the issuance of its financial statements the company discovered a computational error in the amount of $1,046,000 in the calculation of its year-end inventory which resulted in an overstatement of ending inventory.

Assume that Lafayette reported an incorrect net income amount of $3,101,000 for the year in which the error occurred and that the income tax rate is 40%.

Required:

1. Compute the amount of net income that Lafayette should report after correcting the inventory error. Show computations.
2. Assume that the inventory error was not discovered. Identify the financial statement accounts that would have been incorrect for the year the error occurred and for the subsequent year. State whether each account was understated or overstated.

E7–10 Using the Four Inventory Methods

The records at the end of January 19B for All Star Company showed the following for a particular kind of merchandise:

Transactions	Units	Total Cost
Inventory, December 31, 19A	19	$266
Purchase, January 9, 19B	25	375
Sale, January 11, 19B (at $38 per unit)	40	
Purchase, January 20, 19B	50	800
Sale, January 27, 19B (at $39 per unit)	28	

Required:

Assuming a periodic inventory system, compute the amount of (*a*) goods available for sale, (*b*) ending inventory, and (*c*) cost of goods sold at January 31, 19B, under each of the following inventory costing methods (show computations and round to the nearest dollar):

1. Weighted-average cost.
2. First-in, first-out.
3. Last-in, first-out.
4. Specific identification (assume the sale on January 11 was identified with the purchase of January 9, and any excess identified with the beginning inventory; the sale of January 27 was identified with the purchase of January 20).

E7–11 Comparing Alternative Inventory Methods

Lunar Company uses a periodic inventory system. At the end of the annual accounting period, December 31, 19B, the accounting records provided the following information for Product 2:

Transactions	Units	Unit Cost
1. Inventory, December 31, 19A	3,000	$12
For the year 19B:		
2. Purchase, April 11	9,000	$10
3. Sale, May 1 ($40 each)	5,000	
4. Purchase, June 1	8,000	$13
5. Sale, July 3 ($40 each)	6,000	
6. Operating expenses (excluding income tax expense), $195,000.		

Required:

1. Prepare a separate income statement through pretax income that details cost of goods sold for:
   a. Case A: Weighted average.
   b. Case B: FIFO.
   c. Case C: LIFO.
   d. Case D: Specific identification assuming two-fifths of the first sale was selected from the beginning inventory and three-fifths was selected from the items purchased on April 11, 19B. The second sale was selected from the purchase of June 1, 19B.

   For each case, show the computation of the ending inventory. (Hint: Set up adjacent columns for each case.)
2. Compare the pretax income and the ending inventory amounts among the four cases. Explain the similarities and differences.

*E7–12 Comparing LIFO and FIFO**

The records at the end of January 19B for All Star Company showed the following for a particular kind of merchandise:

Transactions	Units	Total Cost
Inventory, December 31, 19A	19	$266
Purchase, January 9, 19B	25	375
Sale, January 11, 19B (at $38 per unit)	40	
Purchase, January 20, 19B	50	800
Sale, January 27, 19B (at $39 per unit)	28	

Assume cash transactions and a periodic inventory system.

Required:

1. Compute (*a*) goods available for sale, (*b*) cost of goods sold, and (*c*) ending inventory for Case A, FIFO, and Case B, LIFO.
2. In parallel columns, give the journal entries for each purchase and sale transaction, assuming a periodic inventory system is used for each case. Set up captions as follows:

	FIFO		LIFO	
Accounts	Debit	Credit	Debit	Credit

3. Prepare an income statement through gross margin and explain why the FIFO and LIFO ending inventory, cost of goods sold, and gross margin amounts are different.
4. Which inventory costing method may be preferred for income tax purposes? Explain.

*Uses data from E7–10.

E7–13 Comparing Cash Flow and Income Effects of LIFO and FIFO

During January 19B, Camry Company reported sales revenue of $370,000 for the one item stocked. The inventory for December 31, 19A, showed 9,000 units on hand with a cost of

$189,000. During January 19B, two purchases of the item were made: the first was for 6,000 units at $22 per unit, and the second was for 4,850 units at $23 each. The periodic inventory count reflected 10,600 units remaining on hand on January 31, 19B. Total operating expense for the month was $97,000.

Required:

1. On the basis of the above information, complete the 19B summary income statements under FIFO and LIFO. Use a single list of side captions, including computation of cost of goods sold. Set up three separate column headings as follows: Units, FIFO, and LIFO. Show your computations of the ending inventory.
2. Which method gives the higher pretax income? Why?
3. Which method gives the more favorable cash flow effects? By how much, assuming a 30% tax rate?

E7–14 Comparing Alternative Inventory Methods Using the Periodic Inventory System

Courtney Company uses a periodic inventory system. Data for 19B: beginning merchandise inventory (December 31, 19A), 2,000 units at $35; purchases, 8,000 units at $38; expenses (excluding income taxes), $142,000; ending inventory per physical count at December 31, 19B, 1,800 units; sales price per unit, $70; and average income tax rate, 30%.

Required:

1. Prepare income statements under the FIFO, LIFO, and weighted-average costing methods. Use a format similar to the following:

		Inventory Costing Method		
			Weighted	
Income Statement	**Units**	**FIFO**	**LIFO**	**Average**
Sales revenue		$	$	$
Cost of goods sold:				
Beginning inventory				
Purchases				
Goods available for sale				
Ending inventory				
Cost of goods sold				
Gross margin				
Expenses				
Pretax income				
Income tax expense				
Net income				

2. Between FIFO and LIFO, which method is preferable in terms of (*a*) net income and (*b*) cash flow? Explain.
3. What would be your answer to requirement 2 assuming prices were falling? Explain.

E7–15 Analyzing Cash Flow Effects of Alternative Inventory Methods

Following is partial information for the income statement of Timber Company under three different inventory costing methods assuming a periodic inventory system:

	FIFO	LIFO	Weighted Average
Unit sales price, $50			
Cost of goods sold:			
Beginning inventory (330 units)	$11,220	$11,220	$11,220
Purchases (475 units)	17,100	17,100	17,100
Goods available for sale			
Ending inventory (510 units)			
Cost of goods sold			
Expenses, $1,600			

Required:

1. Compute cost of goods sold under the FIFO, LIFO, and weighted-average inventory costing methods.
2. Prepare an income statement through pretax income for each method.
3. Rank the three methods in order of favorable cash flow and explain the basis for your ranking.

Ford Motor Company

E7–16 Adjustment of Inventory from LIFO to FIFO

The following note was contained in a recent Ford Motor Company annual report:

Inventory Valuation—Automotive. Inventories are stated at the lower of cost or market. The cost of most US inventories is determined by the last-in, first-out ("LIFO") method. The cost of the remaining inventories is determined substantially by the first-in, first-out ("FIFO") method.

If FIFO were the only method of inventory accounting used by the company, inventories would have been $1,235 million higher than reported this year and $1,246 million higher than reported last year.

The major classes of inventory for the company's Automotive business segment at December 31 were as follows:

	Inventory (in $ millions)	
	Current Year	**Previous Year**
Finished products	$3,413.8	$3,226.7
Raw material and work in process	2,983.9	2,981.6
Supplies	419.1	429.9
Total	$6,816.8	$6,638.2

Required:

1. Determine the ending inventory that would have been reported in the current year if Ford had used only FIFO.
2. The cost of goods sold reported by Ford for the current year was $74,315 million. Determine the cost of goods sold that would have been reported if Ford had used only FIFO for both years.

Chrysler Corporation

E7–17 Adjustment of Inventory from LIFO to FIFO

The following note was contained in a recent Chrysler Corporation annual report:

Inventories

Inventories are valued at the lower of cost or market. The cost of approximately 44 percent and 50 percent of inventories for the current and previous years, respectively, is determined on a Last-In, First-Out (LIFO) basis. The balance of inventory cost is determined on a First-In, First-Out (FIFO) basis.

Inventories and Cost of Sales

Inventories are summarized by major classification as follows (in $ millions):

	Current Year	**Previous Year**
Finished products, including service parts	$1,145	$ 972
Raw materials, finished production parts and supplies	985	1,165
Vehicles held for short-term lease	760	336
Total	$2,890	$2,473

Inventories valued on the LIFO basis would have been $160 million and $123 million higher than reported had they been valued on the FIFO basis at December 31 of the current year and previous year, respectively.

Total automotive manufacturing cost of sales aggregated $27.2 billion and $26.3 billion for the current year and previous year, respectively.

Required:

1. Determine the ending inventory that would have been reported in the current year if Chrysler had used only FIFO.
2. Determine the cost of goods sold that would have been reported if Chrysler had used only FIFO for both years.

E7–18 *Analyzing the Effects of a Reduction in the Amount of LIFO Inventory*

Standard Oil

An annual report of Standard Oil Company (Indiana) contained the following footnote:

> During this year and last year, the company reduced certain inventory quantities that were valued at lower LIFO costs prevailing in prior years. The effect of these reductions was to increase aftertax earnings this year by $71 million, or $0.24 per share, and $74 million, or a $0.25 per share last year.

Required:

1. Explain why the reduction in inventory quantity increased after-tax earnings (net income) for Standard Oil.
2. If Standard Oil had used FIFO, would the reductions in inventory quantity during the two years have increased after-tax earnings? Explain.

E7–19 *Alternative Applications of LCM*

Peterson Company is preparing the annual financial statements dated December 31, 19B. Ending inventory information about the five major items stocked for regular sale is:

	Ending Inventory, 19B		
Item	Quantity on Hand	Unit Cost When Acquired (FIFO)	Replacement Cost (Market) at Year-End
A	50	$15	$13
B	75	40	40
C	10	50	52
D	30	30	30
E	400	8	6

Required:

1. Compute the valuation that should be used for the 19B ending inventory using the LCM rule applied on an item-by-item basis. (Hint: Set up columns for Item, Quantity, Total Cost, Total Market, and LCM Valuation).
2. Compute the valuation of ending inventory using the LCM rule applied to total cost and total market value of the inventory.
3. Which method, 1 or 2, is preferable? Why?

E7–20 *Accounting for Sales and Purchases Using the Periodic Inventory System*

The following transactions involving Collegiate Book Store were selected from the records of January 19B:

a. Sales: cash, $175,000; and on credit, $28,000 (terms n/45).

b. Some of the merchandise sold on credit in (*a*) was subsequently returned for credit, $2,000.

c. Purchases: cash, $60,000; and on credit, $12,000 (terms n/60).

d. Some of the merchandise purchased was subsequently returned for credit, $800.

e. Shipping costs paid in cash on the merchandise purchased, $700 (debit Transportation-In).

Required:

1. Give the journal entry that would be made for each transaction, assuming the company uses a periodic inventory system.
2. Prepare an income statement for January 19B through the caption "Gross margin on sales" and show the details of cost of goods sold. The December 31, 19A, inventory of merchandise was $120,000, and the physical inventory count of merchandise taken on January 31, 19B, amounted to $90,000.

E7–21 *Accounting for Sales and Purchases under the Perpetual Inventory System*

O'Shea Company uses a perpetual inventory system that provides amounts for the period for (*a*) cost of goods sold and (*b*) ending inventory. Physical inventory counts are made from time to time to verify the perpetual inventory records. On December 31, 19B, the end of the accounting year, the perpetual inventory record for Item 18 showed the following (summarized):

	Units	Unit Cost	Total Cost
Beginning inventory	400	$3	$1,200
Purchases during the period	800	3	2,400
Sales during the period (sales price $5)	600		

Required:

1. Give the journal entry to record the purchase of 800 units for cash during the period.
2. Give the journal entry to record the sales for cash during the period.
3. Assume a physical inventory count was made after the above transactions, showing 595 units of Item 18 on hand. Give any journal entry required.
4. Give the following amounts for 19B related to Item 18:
   a. Ending inventory units ________ $ ________
   b. Cost of goods sold units ________ $ ________
   c. Shrinkage loss units ________ $ ________
5. As a manager, what would you investigate in this situation? How?

E7–22 *Comparing the Periodic and Perpetual Inventory Systems*

During 19B, Ward Corporation's records reflected the following for one product stocked:

a. Beginning inventory	1,500 units, unit cost $10
b. Purchases	2,000 units, unit cost $10
c. Sales	1,800 units, unit sales price $15
d. Purchase returns	25 units, for $10 per unit refund from the supplier
e. Sales returns	10 units, for $15 per unit refund to the customer

Required:

1. All transactions were in cash; give the journal entries for the above transactions assuming (*a*) Case A, perpetual inventory system, and (*b*) Case B, periodic inventory system.
2. How would the amount of cost of goods sold be determined in each case?
3. Would you expect the cost of goods sold amount to be the same for Case A as for Case B? Why?

E7–23 *Recording Sales and Purchases Using the Gross Method*

The Cycle Shop sells merchandise on credit terms of 2/10, n/30. A sale invoiced at $800 was made to Missy Clemons on February 1, 19B. The company uses the gross method of recording sales discounts.

Required:

1. Give the journal entry to record the credit sale.
2. Give the journal entry assuming the account was collected in full on February 9, 19B.
3. Give the journal entry assuming, instead, the account was collected in full on March 2, 19B.

On March 4, 19B, the company purchased bicycles and accessories from a supplier on credit, invoiced at $8,000; the terms were 1/15, n/30. The company uses the gross method to record purchases.

Required:

4. Give the journal entry to record the purchase on credit. Assume the periodic inventory system.
5. Give the journal entry assuming the account was paid in full on March 12, 19B.
6. Give the journal entry assuming, instead, the account was paid in full on March 28, 19B.

PROBLEMS

P7–1 Analyzing Possible Inventory Errors

Reggie Company has just completed a physical inventory count at year-end, December 31, 19B. Only the items on the shelves, in storage, and in the receiving area were counted and costed on a FIFO basis. The inventory amounted to $70,000. During the audit, the independent CPA developed the following additional information:

a. Goods costing $500 were being used by a customer on a trial basis and were excluded from the inventory count at December 31, 19B.

b. Goods in transit on December 31, 19B, from a supplier, with terms FOB destination, cost $600. Because these goods had not arrived, they were excluded from the physical inventory count.

c. On December 31, 19B, goods in transit to customers, with terms FOB shipping point, amounted to $1,000 (expected delivery date January 10, 19C). Because the goods had been shipped, they were excluded from the physical inventory count.

d. On December 28, 19B, a customer purchased goods for cash amounting to $2,000 and left them "for pickup on January 3, 19C." Reggie Company had paid $1,200 for the goods and because they were on hand, included the latter amount in the physical inventory count.

e. On the date of the inventory, the company received notice from a supplier that goods ordered earlier, at a cost of $2,200, had been delivered to the transportation company on December 27, 19B; the terms were FOB shipping point. Because the shipment had not arrived by December 31, 19B, it was excluded from the physical inventory.

f. On December 31, 19B, the company shipped $950 worth of goods to a customer, FOB destination. The goods are expected to arrive at their destination no earlier than January 8, 19C. Because the goods were not on hand, they were not included in the physical inventory count.

g. One of the items sold by the company has such a low volume that the management planned to drop it last year. To induce Reggie Company to continue carrying the item, the manufacturer-supplier provided the item on a consignment basis. At the end of each month, Reggie Company (the consignee) renders a report to the manufacturer on the number sold and remits cash for the cost. At the end of December 19B, Reggie Company had five of these items on hand; therefore, they were included in the physical inventory count at $1,000 each.

Required:

Begin with the $70,000 inventory amount and compute the correct amount for the ending inventory. Explain the basis for your treatment of each of the above items. (Hint: Set up three columns: Item, Amount, and Explanation.)

P7–2 Analyzing Inventory Errors

The income statements for four consecutive years for Clement Company reflected the following summarized amounts:

	19A	19B	19C	19D
Sales revenue	$50,000	$51,000	$62,000	$58,000
Cost of goods sold	32,500	35,000	43,000	37,000
Gross margin	17,500	16,000	19,000	21,000
Expenses	10,000	12,000	14,000	12,000
Pretax income	$ 7,500	$ 4,000	$ 5,000	$ 9,000

Subsequent to development of the above amounts, it has been determined that the physical inventory taken on December 31, 19B, was understated by $3,000.

Required:

1. Recast the above income statements to reflect the correct amounts, taking into consideration the inventory error.
2. Compute the gross margin ratio for each year (*a*) before the correction and (*b*) after the correction. Do the results lend confidence to your corrected amounts? Explain.
3. What effect would the error have had on the income tax expense assuming a 30% average rate?

P7–3 Analyzing and Correcting an Error in Ending Inventory

The income statement for Sherwood Company summarized for a four-year period shows the following:

	19A	19B	19C	19D
Sales revenue	$2,000,000	$2,400,000	$2,500,000	$3,000,000
Cost of goods sold	1,400,000	1,630,000	1,780,000	2,100,000
Gross margin	600,000	770,000	720,000	900,000
Expenses	450,000	500,000	520,000	550,000
Pretax income	150,000	270,000	200,000	350,000
Income tax expense (30%)	45,000	81,000	60,000	105,000
Net income	$ 105,000	$ 189,000	$ 140,000	$ 245,000

An audit revealed that in determining the above amounts, the ending inventory for 19B was overstated by $20,000. The company uses a periodic inventory system.

Required:

1. Recast the above income statements on a correct basis.
2. Did the error affect cumulative net income for the four-year period? Explain.
3. Did the error affect cash inflows or outflows? Explain.

P7–4 Using Four Alternative Inventory Methods with the Periodic System

Allsigns Company uses a periodic inventory system. At the end of the annual accounting period, December 31, 19E, the accounting records for the most popular item in inventory showed:

Transactions	Units	Unit Cost
Beginning inventory, January 1, 19E	400	$30
Transactions during 19E:		
1. Purchase, February 20	600	32
2. Sale, April 1 ($46 each)	(700)	
3. Purchase, June 30	500	36
4. Sale, August 1 ($46 each)	(100)	
5. Sales return, August 5 (related to transaction 4)	20	

Required:

Compute the amount of (*a*) goods available for sale, (*b*) ending inventory, and (*c*) cost of goods sold at December 31, 19E, under each of the following inventory costing methods (show computations and round to the nearest dollar):

1. Weighted-average cost.
2. First-in, first-out.
3. Last-in, first-out.
4. Specific identification, assuming the April 1, 19E, sale was selected one-fifth from the beginning inventory and four-fifths from the purchase of February 20, 19E. Assume the sale of August 1, 19E, was selected from the purchase of June 30, 19E.

P7–5 *Analyzing and Using Alternative Inventory Methods*

At the end of January 19B, the records at Atlanta Company showed the following for a particular item that sold at $18 per unit:

Transactions	Units	Amount
Inventory, January 1, 19B	500	$2,500
Sale, January 10	(400)	
Purchase, January 12	600	3,600
Sale, January 17	(300)	
Purchase, January 26	160	1,280
Purchase return, January 28	(10)	Out of Jan. 26 purchase

Required:

1. Assuming a periodic inventory system, prepare a summarized income statement through gross margin on sales under each method of inventory: (*a*) weighted-average cost, (*b*) FIFO, (*c*) LIFO, and (*d*) specific identification. For specific identification, assume the first sale was out of the beginning inventory and the second sale was out of the January 12 purchase. Show the inventory computations in detail.
2. Between FIFO and LIFO, which method would result in the higher pretax income? Which would result in the higher EPS?
3. Between FIFO and LIFO, which method would result in the lower income tax expense? Explain, assuming a 30% average tax rate.
4. Between FIFO and LIFO, which method would produce the more favorable cash flow? Explain.

P7–6 *Manipulating Income under the LIFO Inventory Method*

Pacific Company sells electronic test equipment that it acquires from a foreign source. During the year 19W, the inventory records reflected the following:

	Units	Unit Cost	Total Cost
Beginning inventory	15	$12,000	$180,000
Purchases	40	10,000	400,000
Sales (45 units at $25,000 each)			

The company uses the LIFO inventory costing method. On December 28, 19W, the unit cost of the test equipment was decreased to $8,000. The cost will be decreased again during the first quarter of the next year.

Required:

1. Complete the following income statement summary using the LIFO method and the periodic inventory system (show computations):

Sales revenue	$ _______
Cost of goods sold	_______
Gross margin	_______
Expenses	300,000
Pretax income	$ _______
Ending inventory	$ _______

2. The management, for various reasons, is considering buying 20 additional units before December 31, 19W, at $8,000 each. Restate the above income statement (and ending inventory) assuming this purchase is made on December 31, 19W.
3. How much did pretax income change because of the decision on December 31, 19W? Is there any evidence of income manipulation? Explain.

P7–7 Changing Inventory Method from FIFO to LIFO

Allendale Corporation reported the following summarized annual data at the end of 19X:

	(Millions)
Sales revenue	$850
Cost of goods sold*	400
Gross margin	450
Expenses	310
Pretax income	$140

*Based on ending FIFO inventory of $120 million. On a LIFO basis, this ending inventory would have been $75 million.

Before issuing the preceding statement, the company decided to change from FIFO to LIFO for 19X because "it better reflects our operating results." The company has always used FIFO.

Required:

1. Restate the summary income statement on a LIFO basis.
2. How much did pretax income change due to the LIFO decision for 19X? What caused the change in pretax income?
3. If you were a stockholder, what would be your reaction to this change? Explain.

P7–8 Comparing LIFO and FIFO When Costs Are Rising and Falling

Income is to be evaluated under four different situations as follows:

a. Prices are rising:
   1. Situation A: FIFO is used.
   2. Situation B: LIFO is used.

b. Prices are falling:
   1. Situation C: FIFO is used.
   2. Situation D: LIFO is used.

The basic data common to all four situations are sales, 500 units for $12,500; beginning inventory, 300 units; purchases, 400 units; ending inventory, 200 units; and operating expenses, $4,000. The following tabulated income statements for each situation have been set up for analytical purposes:

	Prices Rising		Prices Falling	
	Situation A FIFO	Situation B LIFO	Situation C FIFO	Situation D LIFO
Sales revenue	$12,500	$12,500	$12,500	$12,500
Cost of goods sold:				
Beginning inventory	3,600	?	?	?
Purchases	5,200	?	?	?
Goods available for sale	8,800	?	?	?
Ending inventory	2,600	?	?	?
Cost of goods sold	6,200	?	?	?
Gross margin	6,300	?	?	?
Expenses	4,000	4,000	4,000	4,000
Pretax income	2,300	?	?	?
Income tax expense (30%)	690	?	?	?
Net income	$ 1,610			

Required:

1. Complete the above tabulation for each situation. In Situations A and B (prices rising), assume the following: beginning inventory, 300 units at $12 = $3,600; and purchases, 400 units at $13 = $5,200. In Situations C and D (prices falling), assume the opposite; that is, beginning inventory, 300 units at $13 = $3,900; and purchases, 400 units at $12 = $4,800. Use periodic inventory procedures.
2. Analyze the relative effects on pretax income and on net income as demonstrated by requirement 1 when prices are rising and when prices are falling.
3. Analyze the relative effects on the cash position for each situation.
4. Would you recommend FIFO or LIFO? Explain.

P7–9 Analyzing LIFO and FIFO Based on an Actual Note to the Financial Statements

General Motors

An annual report for General Motors Corporation included the following footnote:

> Inventories are stated generally at cost, which is not in excess of market. The cost of substantially all domestic inventories was determined by the last-in, first-out (LIFO) method. If the first-in, first-out (FIFO) method of inventory valuation had been used by the Corporation for U.S. inventories, it is estimated that they would be $2,077.1 million higher at the end of this year, compared with $1,784.5 million higher at the end of last year.

For the year, GM reported net income (after taxes) of $320.5 million. At year-end, the balance of the GM retained earnings account was $15,340 million.

Required:

1. Determine the amount of net income that GM would have reported for the year if the FIFO method had been used (assume a 30% tax rate).
2. Determine the amount of retained earnings that GM would have reported at year-end if the FIFO method had always been used (assume a 30% tax rate).
3. Use of the LIFO method reduced the amount of taxes that GM had to pay for the year compared with the amount that would have been paid if FIFO had been used. Calculate the amount of this reduction (assume a 30% tax rate).

P7–10 Analyzing LIFO and FIFO When Inventory Quantities Decline Based on an Actual Note

General Electric

In a recent annual report, General Electric reported the following in their inventory footnote:

December 31 (In millions)	19B	19A
Raw materials and work in progress	$5,603	$5,515
Finished goods	2,863	2,546
Unbilled shipments	$ 246	$ 280
	8,712	8,341
Less revaluation to LIFO	(2,226)	(2,076)
LIFO value of inventories	$6,486	$6,265

They also reported a $23 million change in cost of goods sold due to "lower inventory levels."

Required:

1. Compute the increase or decrease in the pretax operating profit (loss) that would have been reported for the current year had GE employed FIFO accounting for all inventory for both years.
2. Compute the increase or decrease in pretax operating profit that would have been reported had GE employed LIFO but not reduced inventory quantities during the current year.

P7–11 *Using LCM under the Periodic Inventory System*

Smart Company prepared their annual financial statements dated December 31, 19B. The company uses a periodic inventory system and applies the FIFO inventory costing method; however, the company neglected to apply LCM to the ending inventory. The preliminary 19B income statement is summarized below:

Sales revenue		$280,000
Cost of goods sold:		
Beginning inventory	$ 30,000	
Purchases	182,000	
Goods available for sale	212,000	
Ending inventory (FIFO cost)	44,000	
Cost of goods sold		168,000
Gross margin		112,000
Operating expenses		61,000
Pretax income		51,000
Income tax expense (30%)		15,300
Net income		$ 35,700

Assume you have been asked to restate the 19B financial statements to incorporate LCM. You have developed the following data relating to the 19B ending inventory:

		Acquisition Cost		Current Replacement Unit Cost
Item	Quantity	Unit	Total	(Market)
A	3,000	$3	$ 9,000	$4
B	1,500	4	6,000	2
C	7,000	2	14,000	4
D	3,000	5	15,000	3
			$44,000	

Required:

1. Restate the above income statement to reflect LCM valuation of the 19B ending inventory. Apply LCM on an item-by-item basis and show computations.
2. Compare and explain the LCM effect on each amount that was changed in (1).
3. What is the conceptual basis for applying LCM to merchandise inventories?
4. Thought question: What effect did LCM have on the cash flow of 19B? What will be the long-term effect on cash flow?

P7–12 *Accounting for Cash Discounts by the Vendor and the Purchaser*

Assume the following summarized transactions between Company V, the vendor, and Company P, the purchaser. Assume each company uses a periodic inventory system and each uses the gross method to record sales revenue and purchases.

a. Company V sold Company P merchandise for $7,000; terms 3/10, n/30.

b. Prior to payment, Company P returned $700 (one-tenth) of the merchandise for credit because it did not meet P's specifications.

Required:

Using the numbers to the left as the date notations, give the following journal entries in parallel columns for each party:

1. The sale/purchase transaction.
2. The return transaction.
3. Payment in full assuming it was made within the discount period.
4. Payment in full assuming instead it was made after the discount period. Use a form similar to the following:

		Co. V—Vendor		Co. P—Purchaser	
Date	**Accounts**	**Debit**	**Credit**	**Debit**	**Credit**

P7–13 *Recording Sales and Purchases Using the Gross Method*

Campus Stop, Incorporated, is a student co-op. On January 1, 19X, the beginning inventory was $150,000, the Accounts Receivable balance was $4,000, and the Allowance for Doubtful Accounts had a credit balance of $800. A periodic inventory system is used, and purchases are recorded using the gross method. Ending inventory was $95,000.

The following transactions (summarized) have been selected from 19X for case purposes:

a. Merchandise sales for cash	$275,000
b. Merchandise returned by customers as unsatisfactory, for cash refund	1,600
Merchandise purchased from vendors on credit; terms 3/10, n/30:	
c. August Supply Company invoice price before deduction of cash discount	5,000
d. Other vendors, invoice price, before deduction of cash discount	122,000
e. Purchased equipment for use in store; paid cash	2,200
f. Purchased office supplies for future use in the store; paid cash	700
g. Freight on merchandise purchased; paid cash (set up a separate account for this item)	400
Accounts payable paid in full during the period as follows:	
h. August Supply Company, paid after the discount period	5,000
i. Other vendors, paid within the 3% discount period	116,400

Required:

1. Prepare journal entries for each of the above transactions.
2. Prepare a partial income statement through gross margin on sales.

P7–14 *Reporting Sales Transactions on the Financial Statements*

The transactions listed below were selected from those occurring during the month of January 19D for Dan's Store, Incorporated. A wide line of goods is offered for sale. Credit sales are extended to a few select customers; the usual credit terms are n/EOM.

a. Sales to customers:	
Cash	$228,000
On credit	72,000
b. Unsatisfactory merchandise returned by customers:	
Cash	3,000
Credit	2,000
Merchandise purchased from vendors on credit; terms 2/10, n/30:	
c. XYZ Supply Company, amount billed, before deduction of cash discount	4,000
d. From other vendors, amount billed, before deduction of cash discount	68,000
e. Freight paid on merchandise purchased; paid cash (set up a separate account for this item)	1,500
f. Collections on accounts receivable	36,000
The accounts payable were paid in full during the period as follows:	
g. XYZ Supply Company, paid after the discount period	4,000
h. Other vendors, paid within the discount period	66,640
i. Purchased two new typewriters for the office; paid cash	1,000

Required:

Prepare journal entries for the above transactions assuming a periodic inventory system is in use and record purchases using the gross method.

P7–15 *Applying the Perpetual Inventory System*

Wells Company uses a perpetual inventory system for the items it sells. The following selected data relate to Item 10, a small but high-cost item stocked during the month of January 19B.

a. Beginning inventory—quantity, 40; cost, $40 each.

b. Purchases—quantity, 100; cost, $38 each plus $200 for transportation on the purchases.

c. Sales—quantity, 110; sale price, $85 each.

d. Returns—the company accepted a return of three of the items sold in (*c*) because they were not needed by the customer and they had not been used.

e. At the end of January 19B, a physical inventory count showed 31 items remaining on hand.

Required (assume all transactions were cash):

1. Give journal entries for each of the above transactions.
2. Prepare the income statement for January 19B through gross margin on sales as it related to Item 10. What was the gross margin ratio?
3. As the responsible manager, would you investigate the inventory shrinkage? How?
4. Assume that you observe quite often that the required items are out of stock. How can a perpetual inventory system be helpful in avoiding this problem?

P7–16 *Comparing Periodic and Perpetual Inventory Systems*

During January, the following transactions relating to one product sold by Elementary Company were completed in the order given:

a. Purchased—quantity, 150; cost, $25 each.

b. Sold—quantity, 90; $55 each.

c. Purchase return—returned two of the units purchased in (*a*) because they were the wrong size.

d. Sales return—accepted three units from a customer that were sold in (*b*). The customer did not need them, and they were not damaged.

e. Inventories:
Beginning inventory, January 1—40 units at total cost of $1,000.
Ending inventory, January 31—per periodic inventory count, 101 units at $25 = $2,525.

Required:

Give the journal entries for the above transactions assuming that for Case A a perpetual inventory system is used, and for Case B a periodic inventory system is used. To do this, set up the following form (assume cash transactions):

		Amounts			
		Perpetual		Periodic	
Date	**Explanation**	**Debit**	**Credit**	**Debit**	**Credit**
a.	To record the purchase				
b.	To record the sale				
c.	To record the purchase return				
d.	To record the sales return				
e.	To record the end-of-period entries for inventories				

P7–17 Comprehensive Review Problem

The following unrelated questions deal with accounting for current assets of Jack Company.

1. The company had credit sales of $250,000 during the year. At the end of the previous year, accounts receivable were $80,000 and the allowance for bad debts was $7,000. At the end of the current year, accounts receivable were $120,000 and the allowance for bad debts was $1,200 before any adjusting entries were made. Jack Company uses the aging of accounts method and developed an estimate for bad debts of $7,000. Prepare the necessary adjusting entry to record bad debt expense.
2. The company entered into a long-term construction contract that would earn total revenue of $1,050,000 and cost $750,000. In the first year, they incurred $250,000 in cost and collected advance payments of $75,000 from the customer. How much net income can the company report on this contract in the current year, assuming they use percentage-of-completion?
3. Jack purchased $40,000 in merchandise, 2/10, n/30. Record the purchase and the subsequent payment five days later, assuming that the company uses the gross method and the periodic system.
4. The company purchased inventory on the following dates: March 1, 1,000 units at $5; June 14, 500 units at $6; and December 10, 400 units at $5.50. Beginning inventory was 800 units at $4.50. On December 31, 1,000 units remained in inventory. Determine cost of goods sold. Jack uses the LIFO method and the periodic system.
5. Jack Company determined that ending inventory had been overstated by $1,200 at the end of the previous year. What impact does the error have on cost of goods sold and ending inventory for the current year?

CASES

C7–1 An International Perspective

Grand Metropolitan

As the economy becomes more international in scope, users of financial statements may be expected to analyze companies that are not incorporated in the United States. Grand Metropolitan is a major world corporation located in London. It owns many familiar U.S. businesses such as The Pillsbury Company, Burger King, and Häagen-Dazs ice cream.

Required:

Based on the concepts presented in this book, explain the meaning of the various account classifications shown on the portion of the Grand Metropolitan annual report presented below. (Note: "Share of profits of related companies" and "Minority interests and preference dividends" pertain to topics introduced in subsequent chapters.)

GRAND METROPOLITAN
Consolidated Profit and Loss Account
For the Year Ended 30th September 19B

	Notes	19B £m	19A £m
Turnover	1	9,298	6,029
Operating costs	2	(8,349)	(5,387)
		949	642
Share of profits of related companies	3	18	12
Trading profit		967	654
Profit on sale of property		80	39
Reorganisation costs		(35)	(25)
Interest	4	(280)	(93)
Profit on ordinary activities before taxation		732	575
Taxation on profit on ordinary activities	5	(216)	(155)
Profit on ordinary activities after taxation		516	420
Minority interests and preference dividends		(8)	(8)
Profit attributable to ordinary shareholders		508	412
Extraordinary items	6	560	290
Profit for the financial year		1,068	702
Ordinary dividends	7	(167)	(129)
Transferred to reserves		901	573
Earnings per share	8	55.6p	46.9p

Dana Corporation

C7–2 Effect of a Change in Accounting for Production-Related Costs

Dana Corporation designs and manufactures component parts for the vehicular, industrial and mobile off-highway original equipment markets. In a recent annual report, Dana's inventory footnote indicated the following:

> Dana changed its method of accounting for inventories effective January 1 . . . to include in inventory certain production-related costs previously charged to expense. This change in accounting principle resulted in a better matching of costs against related revenues. The effect of this change in accounting increased inventories by $23.0 and net income by $12.9.

Required:

1. Under Dana's previous accounting method, certain production costs were recognized as expenses on the income statement in the period they were incurred. When will they be recognized under the new accounting method?
2. Explain how including these costs in inventory increased both inventories and net income for the year.

General Motors

C7–3 Analysis of the Effects of LIFO Liquidations

Several years ago, General Motors reported the following in their inventory note:

> The cost of substantially all domestic inventories was determined by the last-in, first-out (LIFO) method. If the first-in, first-out (FIFO) method of inventory valuation had been used by the Corporation for U.S. inventories, it is estimated they would be $1,886.0 million higher at December 31, [current year] compared with $2,077.1 million at December 31, [prior year]. As a result of decreases in unit sales and actions taken to reduce inventories, certain LIFO inventory quantities carried at lower costs prevailing in prior years, as compared with the costs of current purchases, were liquidated . . . These inventory adjustments favorably affected income (loss) before income taxes by approximately $305.0 million [current year].

In the current year, GM recorded a small pretax operating profit of $22 million.

Required:

1. Compute the amount of pretax operating profit (loss) that GM would have reported had they not reduced inventory quantities during the current year.
2. Compute the amount of pretax operating profit (loss) for the current year that GM would have reported had they employed FIFO accounting in both years.
3. What is the normal relationship between pretax operating profit computed using LIFO and FIFO when costs are rising? Why is this relationship not in evidence in this case?

C7–4 *Analysis of the Effect of a Change to LIFO-Based Operating Results*

Quaker Oats

A recent annual report for Quaker Oats included the following information:

> The company adopted the LIFO cost flow assumption for valuing the majority of remaining U.S. Grocery Products inventories. The Company believes that the use of the LIFO method better matches current costs with current revenues. The cumulative effect of this change on retained earnings at the beginning of the year is not determinable, nor are the pro forma effects of retroactive application of LIFO to prior years. The effect of this change on the current year was to decrease net income by $16.0 million, or $0.20 per share.

Required:

1. In addition to the reason that was cited, why did management adopt LIFO?
2. As an analyst, how would you react to the $0.20 per share decrease in income caused by the adoption of LIFO?

C7–5 *Financial Statement Analysis*

Toys "Я" Us

Refer to the financial statements of Toys "Я" Us given in Appendix B at the end of this book.

1. Estimate the amount of merchandise that was purchased by the company during the current year.
2. At what point does the company recognize revenue?
3. Cost of sales as a percentage of sales increased in the current year. What explanation is provided by management?
4. Sales revenue increased in the current year. Is this increase attributable to an increase in the number of stores or an increase in sales volume at existing stores?

C7–6 *Financial Statement Analysis*

Toys "Я" Us

Refer to the financial statements of Toys "Я" Us given in Appendix B at the end of this book.

1. What method does the company use to determine the cost of its inventory?
2. If the inventories had all been valued at FIFO, inventories would show no change at year-end. How would you explain that different accounting methods would produce the same results?
3. If the company had not reported cost of sales for each of the four quarters, how could you have estimated it?
4. If the company switched to the average cost method, would you expect the reported inventory to increase or decrease by a significant amount?

8

OPERATIONAL ASSETS—PROPERTY, PLANT, AND EQUIPMENT; NATURAL RESOURCES; AND INTANGIBLES

In the previous chapters, we discussed the current assets of a business. These assets are critical for the operations of a business but many of them do not directly produce value. A business could not survive without cash, but cash does not produce goods or services that can be sold to customers. In this chapter, we will discuss noncurrent assets that are sometimes called productive assets. Many of the noncurrent assets produce value, such as a factory that manufactures cars. These assets present some interesting accounting problems because they benefit a number of accounting periods.

LEARNING OBJECTIVES

After studying this chapter, you should be able to:

1. **Define, classify, and explain the nature of operational assets.** ***408***
2. **Apply the cost principle to measure and record operational assets.** ***408***
3. **Apply the matching principle to record and report depreciation.** ***412***
4. **Describe the financial statement impact of a change in depreciation estimates.** ***420***
5. **Account for ordinary and extraordinary repairs.** ***424***
6. **Record the disposal of operational assets.** ***426***
7. **Account for natural resources and intangible assets, including amortization.** ***427***

Management Decision Setting
DELTA AIR LINES

Managing Profits through Control of Productive Capacity

Delta Air Lines is a major air carrier providing service to 161 domestic cities in 44 states and 55 international cities in 33 foreign countries. Delta is a capital-intensive company with over $7,140,745,000 in property, plant, and equipment reported on its balance sheet. In one recent year alone, Delta took delivery of 29 new aircraft and spent $2,053,211,000 on flight equipment. Demand for air travel is seasonal, with peak demand occurring during the summer months because of vacation time. Demand is very sensitive to general economic conditions. As a result, planning for optimal productive capacity is very difficult in the airline industry.

BUSINESS BACKGROUND

One of the major challenges facing managers of most businesses is forecasting the level of productive capacity that is needed in the long term. If managers underestimate the need, the company will not be able to produce goods or services that are in demand and will miss the opportunity to earn revenue. On the other hand, if needed productive capacity is overestimated, excessive costs will be incurred which will reduce profitability.

The airline industry serves as an outstanding example of the difficulty associated with planning for and analyzing productive capacity. If an airplane takes off from Kansas City, Missouri, en route to New York City with empty seats, the economic value associated with those seats is lost forever. There is obviously no way to sell the seat to a customer after the airplane has left the gate. Unlike a manufacturer, an airline cannot "inventory" seats for the future.

Likewise, if a large number of people want to board a flight, the airline must turn away customers if seats are not available. You might be willing to buy a television set from Sears even if you are told that they are out of stock and there will be a one week delay in delivery. You probably wouldn't fly home for Thanksgiving on an airline that told you that you would have to wait one week because there were no seats available on their flights. You would simply pick another airline or use a different mode of transportation.

The asset section of the balance sheet from Delta's annual report for the fiscal year ended June 30, 1993, is shown in Exhibit 8–1. Additional information about property, plant, and equipment is contained in the 10–K report for Delta. The 10–K report shows the amount of new investment in equipment for the year, the amount of equipment that was sold or retired, and the specific number of each type of aircraft that is owned by Delta. We will discuss some of that data in this chapter.

Delta has a number of large competitors with familiar names such as American, USAir, Continental, and Southwest. The notes to the Delta annual report mention that "all domestic routes served by Delta are subject to competition from new and existing carriers, and service over virtually all of Delta's domestic routes is highly competitive. Service over most of Delta's international routes is highly competitive."

Much of the battle for passengers in the airline industry is fought in terms of property, plant, and equipment. Passengers want convenient schedules

Delta Air Lines Balance Sheet **Exhibit 8–1**

CONSOLIDATED BALANCE SHEETS
June 30, 1993 and 1992

	(In Thousands)	
Assets	**1993**	**1992**
Current Assets:		
Cash and cash equivalents	$ 1,180,364	$ 50,413
Accounts receivable, net of allowance for uncollectible accounts of $82,586 at June 30, 1993, and $67,284 at June 30, 1992	1,024,869	1,090,731
Refundable income taxes	29,936	162,959
Maintenance and operating supplies, at average cost	90,593	88,465
Deferred income taxes	173,224	—
Prepaid expenses and other	322,934	305,876
Total current assets	2,821,920	1,698,444
Property and Equipment:		
Flight equipment owned	9,042,876	8,354,331
Less: Accumulated depreciation	3,559,084	3,213,042
	5,483,792	5,141,289
Flight equipment under capital leases	173,284	173,284
Less: Accumulated amortization	128,572	112,042
	44,712	61,242
Ground property and equipment	2,372,587	2,210,887
Less: Accumulated depreciation	1,143,087	983,174
	1,229,500	1,227,713
Advance payments for equipment	382,741	663,068
	7,140,745	7,093,312
Other Assets:		
Marketable equity securities	265,124	247,571
Deferred income taxes	504,645	—
Investments in associated companies	202,176	184,474
Cost in excess of net assets acquired, net of accumulated amortization of $57,612 at June 30, 1993, and $48,886 at June 30, 1992	291,579	300,305
Leasehold and operating rights, net of accumulated amortization of $100,841 at June 30, 1993, and $36,497 at June 30, 1992	305,801	369,917
Other	339,033	267,551
	1,908,358	1,369,818
	$11,871,023	$10,161,574

(which require a large number of aircraft) and want to fly with new, modern equipment.

Because airlines have such a large investment in equipment with no opportunity to inventory unused seats, they work very hard to fill aircraft to capacity for each flight. The frequent fare wars that you read about in newspaper advertisements are caused by airlines trying to build customer demand to use their large investments in productive capacity. A note to the Delta annual report addresses this issue:

> Because airline fares are competitive and change frequently, and because passenger demand is affected by, among other factors, economic conditions, it is impossible to predict how long any particular fare structure will continue or the extent to which it will affect traffic. If fare reductions are not offset by increases in traffic or changes in the mix of traffic that improve yields, Delta's operating results will be negatively affected.

Real World Excerpt

Delta Air Lines Annual Report

As you can see from this discussion, issues surrounding property, plant, and equipment have a pervasive impact on a company in terms of strategy, pricing decisions, and profitability. Managers devote considerable time to planning for optimal levels of productive capacity, and financial analysts closely review statements to determine the impact of management decisions.

CLASSIFICATION OF OPERATIONAL ASSETS

Learning Objective 1
Define, classify, and explain the nature of operational assets.

Operational assets are tangible and intangible assets owned by a business and used in its operations.

Tangible assets are operational assets that have physical substance.

Intangible assets are operational assets that have special rights but not physical substance.

The assets that determine productive capacity are often called **operational assets**. They have different characteristics depending on the nature of the business. These assets are listed as noncurrent on the balance sheet and have the following characteristics:

1. **Tangible assets** are operational assets that have physical substance; that is, they are tangible. This classification usually is called *property, plant, and equipment*. There are three kinds of tangible assets:
   a. *Land* (held for use in operations; not subject to depreciation). As is the case with Delta, land often is not shown as a separate item on the balance sheet.
   b. *Buildings, fixtures, equipment.* For Delta, this category includes aircraft, ground equipment to service aircraft, and office space.
   c. *Natural resources.* Delta does not report any natural resources on its balance sheet.
2. **Intangible assets** are operational assets without physical substance that are held by the business because of the use rights they confer on the owner. Examples are patents, copyrights, franchises, licenses, and trademarks. Leasehold and operating rights shown on the Delta balance sheet are intangible assets.

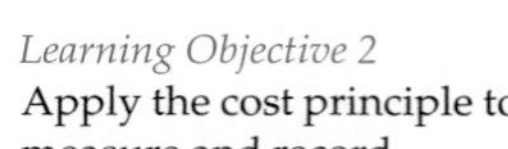

MEASURING AND RECORDING ACQUISITION COST

Learning Objective 2
Apply the cost principle to measure and record operational assets.

The **acquisition cost** is the net cash equivalent amount paid for the asset.

For the sake of illustration, let's assume that Delta purchased a single new aircraft that cost $1 million. The airplane will be used to provide commuter service to small cities. Under the cost principle, all reasonable and necessary costs incurred in acquiring an operational asset, placing it in its operational setting, and preparing it for use should be recorded in a designated asset account. These costs would be added to the $1 million purchase price of the aircraft. What types of costs would be incurred by Delta in the process of acquiring a new aircraft or any other operational asset? The three most common costs are sales taxes, transportation costs, and installation costs.

Any financing charges associated with the purchase of an operational asset should not be included in the cost of the asset but should be reported as interest expense. For example, if Cessna offered Delta a 1% discount for immediate payment for the aircraft but Delta did not take advantage of the offer, $10,000 would be reported as interest expense (1% × $1,000,000) and the cost of the aircraft would be recorded as $990,000 ($1,000,000 – $10,000). The amount recorded for the purchase is called the **acquisition cost**, which is the net cash equivalent amount paid or to be paid for the asset.

Delta would calculate the acquisition cost of a new aircraft as follows:

Invoice price of the aircraft	$1,000,000
Less: Cash discount allowed	10,000
Net cash invoice price	$ 990,000
Add: Transportation charges paid by purchaser	70,000
Installation costs paid by purchaser	40,000
Cost—amount debited to the asset account	$1,100,000

Delta would record the purchase of this aircraft with the following journal entry:

Jan. 1, 19A	Flight equipment	1,100,000	
	Interest expense	10,000	
	Cash		1,110,000

It might seem unusual for Delta to pay cash to purchase a new asset that cost over $1 million, but this is often the case. When operational assets are acquired, a company may pay with cash that was generated from operations or cash that was recently borrowed. It is also possible that the seller might finance the purchase on credit. Also, noncash consideration might be part of the transaction.

When noncash consideration is included in the purchase of an asset, the cash-equivalent cost is measured as any cash paid plus the current market value of the noncash consideration given. Alternatively, if the market value of the noncash consideration given cannot be determined, the current market value of the asset purchased is used for measurement purposes. If Delta had paid Cessna $710,000 in cash and given up 10,000 shares of Delta stock with a market value of $40 per share, the journal entry would be:

Jan. 1, 19A	Flight equipment	1,100,000	
	Interest expense	10,000	
	Cash		710,000
	Common stock, no par		400,000

In addition to purchasing buildings and equipment, a company may acquire undeveloped land, typically with the intent to build a new factory or office building. When land is purchased, all of the incidental costs paid by the purchaser, such as title fees, sales commissions, legal fees, title insurance, delinquent taxes, and surveying fees, should be included in the cost of the land. Because land is not subject to depreciation, it must be recorded as a separate operational asset.

Sometimes, an old building or used machinery is purchased for operational use in the business. Renovation and repair costs incurred by the purchaser prior to use should be included in the asset account as a part of the cost of the asset. Ordinary repair costs incurred after the asset is placed in use are normal operating expenses when incurred.

In some cases, a company may construct an asset for its own use instead of buying it from a manufacturer. For example, Delta might construct a building to support the maintenance of aircraft instead of buying an existing building. When a company constructs an asset for its own use, the cost of the asset will include all necessary costs associated with construction. In most situations, these costs will include interest that is incurred during the construction period. For example, if Delta paid $75,000 interest cost on funds that were used during the construction of a new maintenance facility, the interest would be included in the cost of the asset. The amount that is included in the cost of an asset is called **capitalized interest**. Interest on self-constructed assets should be capitalized even in cases where funds were not borrowed directly to support the construction. The amount of interest that is capitalized is based on the amount of funds that actually are invested in the construction project.

Capitalized interest represents interest expenditures included in the cost of a self-constructed asset.

Basket Purchases of Assets

When several operational assets are acquired in a single transaction and for a single lump sum, known as a **basket purchase**, the cost of each asset must be measured and recorded separately. When a building and the land on which it is located are purchased for a lump sum, two separate accounts must be

Basket purchase is an acquisition of two or more assets in a single transaction for a single lump sum.

established. One is for the building (which is subject to depreciation), and one is for the land (which is not subject to depreciation). The purchase price must be apportioned between the land and the building on a rational basis.

Relative market value of the several assets on the date of acquisition is the most logical basis on which to allocate the single lump sum. Appraisals or tax assessments often have to be used as indications of the market values. Assume Delta Air Lines paid $300,000 cash to purchase a building and the land on which the building is located. The separate, true market values of the building and land were not known; therefore, a professional appraisal was obtained. This appraisal showed the following estimated market values: building, $189,000; and land, $126,000 (apparently the buyer got a good deal). The apportionment of the $300,000 purchase price and the journal entry to record the acquisition are shown in Exhibit 8–2.

Perhaps the most common example of a basket purchase of assets occurs when one corporation buys another corporation. In this case, the basket includes all of the assets owned by the acquired corporation. We will discuss corporate acquisitions in a subsequent chapter.

NATURE OF DEPRECIATION, DEPLETION, AND AMORTIZATION

An operational asset that has a limited useful life (such as an airplane purchased by Delta Air Lines) represents the prepaid cost of a bundle of future services or benefits that will help earn future revenues. The matching principle requires that a portion of the cost of operational assets (other than land) be allocated as expense in the periods in which revenue is earned as a result of using those assets. Thus, the cost of operational assets is matched in a systematic and rational manner with the revenues that are earned by using the asset. Delta Air Lines earns revenue by flying its aircraft and incurs an expense by using up part of the limited life of its aircraft.

Three different terms are used to identify the matching of the cost of an operational asset with revenues generated by the asset:

Depreciation is the systematic and rational allocation of the cost of property, plant, and equipment (but not land) over their useful lives.

1. **Depreciation** The systematic and rational allocation of the acquisition cost of tangible operational assets, other than natural

Exhibit 8–2 Recording a Basket Purchase of Assets

Situation:
Fox Company purchased a building and the related land for $300,000 cash. Estimated current market values: Building, $189,000; and land, $126,000.

Allocation of acquisition cost:

	Appraised Value		Apportionment of Lump-Sum Acquisition Cost	
Asset	**Amount**	**Ratio**	**Computation**	**Apportioned Cost**
Building	$189,000	0.60*	$300,000 x 0.60 =	$180,000
Land	126,000	0.40†	300,000 x 0.40 =	120,000
	$315,000	1.00		$300,000

*$189,000 ÷ $315,000 = 0.60
†$126,000 ÷ $315,000 = 0.40

Entry to record the acquisition:

Plant building	180,000	
Land–plant site	120,000	
Cash		300,000

Airlines have a very significant investment in equipment as this airplane parking lot illustrates.

resources, to future periods in which the assets contribute services or benefits to help earn revenue.

Example: Depreciation of the $1.1 million cost of an aircraft acquired by Delta on January 1, 19A, over its estimated useful life of 20 years, with no remaining value at the end of the asset's life (the accounting year ends December 31):

	Adjusting entry		
Dec. 31, 19A	Depreciation expense ($1,100,000 ÷ 20 years)	55,000	
	Accumulated depreciation		55,000

2. **Depletion** The systematic and rational allocation of the acquisition cost of natural resources to future periods in which the use of those natural resources contributes to revenue.

   Example: Depletion of the $530,000 cost of a timber tract over the estimated period of cutting based on a "cutting" rate of approximately 20% per year:

	Adjusting entry		
Dec.31, 19A	Depletion expense ($530,000 × 20%)	106,000	
	Timber tract (No. 12)		106,000

   Note: A contra account such as Accumulated Depletion could be used for the credit.

Depletion is the systematic and rational allocation of the cost of a natural resource over the period of exploitation.

3. **Amortization** The systematic and rational allocation of the acquisition cost of intangible assets to future periods in which the benefits contribute to revenue.

   Example: Amortization of the $850,000 purchase cost of a patent over its estimated economic useful life to the entity of 17 years:

Amortization is the systematic and rational allocation of the acquisition cost of an intangible asset over its useful life.

	Adjusting entry		
Dec. 31, 19A	Patent expense ($850,000 ÷ 17 years)	50,000	
	Patents		50,000

   Note: A contra account such as Accumulated Patent Amortization could be used for the credit.

The three terms—*depreciation, depletion,* and *amortization*—relate to the same basic objective, the allocation of the acquisition cost of an operational asset to the future periods in which the benefits of its use contribute to earning revenue.

The amounts of depreciation, depletion, and amortization recorded during each period are reported on the income statement as expenses for the period. The amounts of depreciation, depletion, and amortization accumulated since the acquisition date are reported on the balance sheet as deductions from the assets to which they pertain. An operational asset such as the aircraft illustrated above would be reported on the balance sheet (at the end of the year in the example) as follows:

DELTA AIR LINES
Balance Sheet
At December 31, 19A

Property, plant, and equipment:		
Flight Equipment	$1,100,000	
Less: Accumulated depreciation	55,000	$1,045,000*
or		
Flight Equipment (less accumulated depreciation, $55,000)		$1,045,000*

*Called book value or carrying value.

Book (or carrying) value is the acquisition cost of an operational asset less accumulated depreciation, depletion, or amortization.

It is important to remember that the dollar amounts reported for operational assets on the balance sheet do not represent their market values at the balance sheet date. The balance sheet amounts are called book, or carrying, values. The **book value** of an operational asset is its acquisition cost, less the accumulated depreciation, depletion, or amortization from acquisition date to the date of the balance sheet. Depreciation is a process of *cost allocation*. It is not a process of determining the current market value of the asset. Under the cost principle, the cost of an operational asset is recorded at acquisition date at its current market value. The cost is not measured on a market value basis at subsequent balance sheet dates. Instead, the acquisition cost is reduced by the accumulated depreciation, depletion, or amortization.

FINANCIAL ANALYSIS

Book Value as an Approximation of Remaining Life

Some analysts compare the book value of assets to their original cost as an approximation of their remaining life. If the book value of an asset is 100% of its cost, it is a new asset; if the book value is 25% of its cost, the asset has about 25% of its estimated life remaining. In the case of Delta, the book value of its flight equipment is 61% of its original cost. This compares with 73% for Continental Airlines and 75% for Southwest Airlines. This comparison would suggest that the flight equipment used by Delta has less of its estimated life remaining than that of some other major airlines. This comparison is only a rough approximation and is influenced by some of the accounting issues discussed in the next section.

DEPRECIATION CONCEPTS

Learning Objective 3
Apply the matching principle to record and report depreciation.

The purpose of depreciation is to allocate the cost of a tangible operational asset over its useful life. The need for depreciation can be illustrated with a simple example. If you were the president of Delta in a year when it acquired a new $1.1 million aircraft, you probably would object if the accountant tried to charge the entire cost to expense in the year of acquisition. You would argue that the aircraft should produce revenue for several years, so the cost of the asset should be charged to expense over the period in which it will earn revenue. Failure to do so would understate income in the year of acquisition and overstate income in each year that the aircraft was used. This simple reason explains why accountants depreciate tangible operational assets and why depreciation is an important part of measuring the profitability of a company.

The calculation of depreciation expense requires three amounts for each asset: (1) acquisition cost, (2) estimated residual value, and (3) estimated useful life. Of these three amounts, two are estimates (residual value and useful life). Therefore, depreciation expense is an estimate. Depreciation expense for an aircraft acquired by Delta Air Lines (assuming a residual value of $100,000) may be measured as follows:

Acquisition cost	$1,100,000
Less: Estimated residual value	100,000
Amount to be depreciated over useful life	$1,000,000
Estimated useful life is 20 years	
Annual depreciation expense: $1,000,000 ÷ 20 =	$ 50,000

Residual value must be deducted from acquisition cost to compute depreciation expense.[1] It represents that part of the acquisition cost that is expected to be recovered by the user upon disposal of the asset at the end of its estimated useful life to the entity. The estimated net residual value is not necessarily the value of the asset as salvage or scrap. Rather, it may be the value to another user at the date on which the current owner intends to dispose of it. In the case of the aircraft owned by Delta Air Lines, it may be the amount they expect to receive when they sell the asset to a small regional airline that operates older equipment.

Residual value is the estimated amount to be recovered, less disposal costs, at the end of the estimated useful life of an operational asset.

Residual value is the estimated amount to be recovered less any estimated costs of dismantling, disposal, and sale. In many cases, disposal costs may approximately equal the gross residual value. Therefore, many depreciable assets are assumed to have no residual value. In the case of Delta Air Lines, the notes to their financial statements indicate that they estimate residual value to be 5% of the cost of the asset.

Estimated useful life represents the useful *economic life* to the *present owner* rather than the total economic life to all potential users. In the Delta Air Lines example, the aircraft is able to fly for more than 20 years but Delta wants to offer its customers a higher level of service by providing modern equipment. For accounting purposes, Delta uses a 20-year estimated useful life, and the subsequent owner (the regional airline) would use an estimated useful life based on its own policies.

Estimated useful life is the expected service life of an operational asset to the present owner.

The determination of estimated useful life of an operational asset must conform to the *continuity assumption*. This assumption holds that the business will continue indefinitely to pursue its commercial objectives and will not liquidate in the foreseeable future. A business should not estimate the life of an operational asset to be less than its potential life because of some conjecture that the business will liquidate in the near future.

FINANCIAL ANALYSIS

Differences in Estimated Lives within a Single Industry

Notes to actual financial statements of companies in the airline industry reveal the following estimates for lives of aircraft:

[1]Some accountants call residual value by the name *scrap*, or *salvage, value*. We prefer the term *residual value* because assets often are useful to other businesses at the end of their useful economic life to the current owner.

Company	Estimated Life
Delta	20 years
United	10 to 25 years
Continental	15 to 28 years
Southwest	15 to 20 years

The differences in estimated lives may be attributable to a number of a factors such as type of aircraft used by each company, differences in operations, and degree of management conservatism. Differences in estimated lives of assets used by specific companies can have a large impact on the comparison of the profitability of the companies. Analysts must be certain that they identify the causes for the differences in depreciable lives.

DEPRECIATION METHODS

Accountants have not been able to agree on a single, best method of depreciation because of significant differences between companies and the assets that they own. As a result, several different depreciation methods are commonly used in financial statements. The different depreciation methods are based on the same concept; each method allocates a portion of the cost of a depreciable asset to each future period in a systematic and rational manner. Nevertheless, each method allocates to each period a different portion of the cost to be depreciated. We will discuss the following depreciation methods:

1. Straight line.
2. Units of production.
3. Accelerated depreciation methods:
   a. Sum-of-the-years' digits.
   b. Declining balance.

The common set of facts and notations shown in Exhibit 8–3 will be used to illustrate these methods. This example is based on the assumption that Delta Air Lines acquired a service vehicle with an estimated life of three years.

Straight-Line Method

Straight-line (SL) depreciation is the method that allocates the cost of an operational asset in equal periodic amounts over its useful life.

More companies use **straight-line (SL) depreciation** in their financial statements than all other methods combined. Under the straight-line method, an equal portion of the acquisition cost less the estimated residual value is allocated to each accounting period during the estimated useful life of the asset. The annual depreciation expense is measured as follows (refer to Exhibit 8–3):

$$\text{Depreciation expense} = \frac{\text{Cost} - \text{Residual value}}{\text{Life in years}}$$

$$\$20{,}000 = \frac{\$62{,}500 - \$2{,}500}{3 \text{ years}}$$

Depreciation expense for Delta would be $20,000 per year if the straight-line method is used. A depreciation schedule for the entire useful life of the machine is:

Exhibit 8–3 Illustrative Data for Depreciation

Delta Air Lines	
Acquisition cost of repair truck	$62,500
Estimated residual value	2,500
Estimated life (in years)	3
Estimated life in units (miles driven)	100,000

Year	Depreciation Expense (Income Statement)	Accumulated Depreciation (Balance Sheet at Year-End)	Book Value (at Year-End)
At acquisition			$62,500
1	$20,000	$20,000	42,500
2	20,000	40,000	22,500
3	20,000	60,000	2,500

Notice that (*a*) depreciation expense is a constant amount for each year, (*b*) accumulated depreciation increases by an equal amount each year, and (*c*) book value decreases by the same amount each year. This is the reason for the designation of straight-line. Delta Air Lines uses the *straight-line* method for all of its assets and reported depreciation expense in the amount of $678,605,000, which was 5.6% of the revenues earned for the year. The straight-line method is used by most companies in the airline industry.

Units-of-Production Method

Units-of-production depreciation relates depreciable cost to the total estimated productive output. A depreciation rate per unit of production is computed as follows (refer to Exhibit 8–3):

Units-of-production depreciation is the method that allocates the cost of an operational asset over its useful life based on its periodic output related to its total estimated output.

$$\text{Depreciation rate} = \frac{\text{Cost} - \text{Residual value}}{\text{Life in units of production}}$$

$$\$0.60 = \frac{\$62{,}500 - \$2{,}500}{100{,}000 \text{ miles}}$$

For every mile that the vehicle is driven, Delta will record depreciation expense of $0.60. Depreciation expense each year is calculated as follows:

$$\text{Depreciation expense} = \text{Depreciation rate} \times \text{Units of production for the year}$$

Assume use is 30,000 miles in year 1, 50,000 miles in year 2, and 20,000 miles in year 3. Depreciation expense each year would be:

Year	Rate × Units	=	Depreciation Expense
1	$0.60 × 30,000	=	$18,000
2	0.60 × 50,000	=	30,000
3	0.60 × 20,000	=	12,000

The depreciation schedule for Delta under the units of production method is:

Year	Depreciation Expense (Income Statement)	Accumulated Depreciation (Balance Sheet at Year-End)	Book Value (at Year-End)
At acquisition			$62,500
1	$18,000	$18,000	44,500
2	30,000	48,000	14,500
3	12,000	60,000	2,500

Notice that depreciation expense, accumulated depreciation, and book value vary from period to period directly with the units produced. When the units-of-production method is used, depreciation expense is said to be a *variable expense* because it varies directly with production or use.

AMAX Gold, Inc. is in the gold exploration and mining industry. The company uses the units-of-production method:

Real World Excerpt

AMAX Gold, Inc. Annual Report

Summary of Significant Accounting Policies

Note 1: Depreciation and depletion are computed using the units of production method based on the estimated amount of gold to be recovered.

The units-of-production method is based on an estimate of the total productive capacity of an asset. As you would expect, it is very difficult to estimate future output. This is another example of the degree of subjectivity that is inherent in accounting.

Accelerated Depreciation—Concepts

Accelerated depreciation methods result in higher depreciation expense in the early years of an operational asset's life and lower expense in the later years.

Accelerated depreciation means that in the early years of the useful life of an asset, depreciation expense amounts are higher, and in the later years the amounts are correspondingly lower. Accelerated depreciation is used for the following reasons:

1. A depreciable asset produces more revenue in its early life because it is more efficient in the early years than in the later years.
2. Repair costs increase in later years; therefore, total use cost per period should include decreasing depreciation expense to offset the increasing repair expense each period.

The relationship between accelerated depreciation expense, repair expense, and total use expense can be illustrated as follows for Delta:

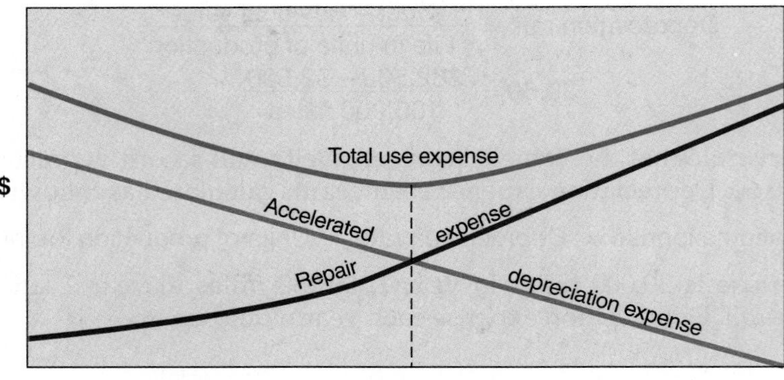

Accelerated methods are not often used for financial reporting purposes. However, the two methods used more frequently than others are the sum-of-the-years'-digits method and the declining-balance method.

Sum-of-the-Years'-Digits Method

Sum-of-the-years'-digits depreciation is the method that allocates the cost of an operational asset over its useful life based on a fraction where the denominator is the total of all of the useful years and the numerator is the year of life in inverse order.

Under the **sum-of-the-years'-digits depreciation** method, depreciation expense is computed for each accounting year by multiplying the acquisition cost, less estimated residual value, by a fraction that is determined by using as the denominator the sum of the digits that make up the estimated useful life. The numerator is the specific year of life in *inverse order*. Using the data given in Exhibit 8–3, the computations are:

1. Compute the annual depreciation fraction:

   Denominator Sum of the digits in the asset's useful life:[2] $1+2+3=6$.

[2]The denominator (i.e., the sum-of-the-years' digits) can be computed with the following formula, where n equals the number of years in the asset's useful life:

$$SYD = n\left(\frac{n+1}{2}\right)$$

For example, a five-year life would be:

$$SYD = 5\left(\frac{5+1}{2}\right) = 15$$

Numerators Digits (specific year of life) in inverse order: 3, 2, 1.
Depreciation fractions Year 1, 3/6; year 2, 2/6; year 3, 1/6 (total, 6/6).

2. Use the annual depreciation fractions as follows:

Year	Fraction	×	Cost Less Residual Value	=	Depreciation Expense
1	3/6	×	$60,000	=	$30,000
2	2/6	×	60,000	=	20,000
3	1/6	×	60,000	=	10,000

The depreciation schedule for Delta under the sum-of-the-years'-digits method is:

Year	Depreciation Expense (Income Statement)	Accumulated Depreciation (Balance Sheet at Year-End)	Book Value (at Year-End)
At acquisition			$62,500
1	$30,000	$30,000	32,500
2	20,000	50,000	12,500
3	10,000	60,000	2,500

Notice that compared to straight-line results, depreciation expense under the sum-of-the-years'-digits method is higher in the earlier years and lower in the later years. The total amount of depreciation expense over the entire life of the asset is the same under both methods. This method is used by very few companies. One company that does use this method is General Electric:

Summary of Significant Accounting Policies

Note 1. Depreciation: The cost of most of General Electric's manufacturing plant and equipment is depreciated using an accelerated method based primarily on the sum-of-the-years'-digits formula. If manufacturing plant and equipment is subject to abnormal economic conditions or obsolescence, additional depreciation is provided.

Real World Excerpt

General Electric Annual Report

Declining-Balance Method

Declining-balance depreciation is based on applying an acceleration rate to the straight-line (SL) rate. The declining-balance (DB) rate is found by (1) computing the SL rate, ignoring residual value, then (2) multiplying that SL rate by a selected acceleration rate which may not exceed 200%. Assuming a five-year estimated useful life, the SL rate, excluding residual value is:

Declining-balance (DB) depreciation is the method that allocates the cost of an operational asset over its useful life based on a multiple of the straight-line rate.

1 period of life ÷ 5 total periods = 20% per period

Computation of the DB rate for three different acceleration rates (for illustrative purposes):

SL Rate (Excluding RV)	×	Selected Acceleration Rate	=	Declining Balance Rate
Case A, 20%	×	200%	=	40%
Case B, 20%	×	175%	=	35%
Case C, 20%	×	150%	=	30%

To calculate depreciation expense under the declining-balance method, the book value of the asset is multiplied by the DB rate. Notice at this stage of the calculation, residual value is not used in the computation of depreciation expense (i.e., it is not subtracted from book value).

Computation of declining-balance depreciation expense is illustrated below using the data given in Exhibit 8–3 and assuming an acceleration rate of 200%:

1. Compute the DB rate:

$$\begin{aligned} \text{SL rate} &= 1 \text{ year} \div 3 \text{ years} \\ &= 33\ 1/3\% \\ \text{DB rate} &= \text{Acceleration rate} \times \text{SL rate} \\ &= 200\% \times 33\ 1/3\% \\ &= 66\ 2/3\% \end{aligned}$$

2. Compute depreciation expense. Use a depreciation schedule to calculate the book value that is required for computation of depreciation expense under the DB method.

   Computations:

Year	Book Value	×	DB Rate	=	Depreciation Expense
1	$62,500	×	66 2/3%	=	$41,667
2	20,833	×	66 2/3%	=	13,889
3	6,944	×	66 2/3%	=	4,629*

Year	Depreciation Expense (Income Statement)	Accumulated Depreciation (Balance Sheet at Year-End)	Book Value (at Year-End)
At acquisition			$62,500
1	$41,667	$41,667	$20,833
2	13,889	55,556	6,944
3	4,444*	60,000	2,500

*The difference between the computed depreciation expense and the amount claimed on the income statement is caused by residual value. See explanation below.

Notice that the calculated depreciation expense for year 3 ($4,629) is not the same as the amount actually reported on the income statement ($4,444). An asset should never be depreciated below its residual value. The asset owned by Delta has an estimated residual value of $2,500. If depreciation expense were recorded in the amount of $4,629, the book value of the asset would be less than $2,500. The correct depreciation expense for year 3 is $4,444 ($6,944 – $2,500) which is the amount that will reduce the book value to exactly $2,500. As you can see, it is necessary to check each year to be certain that the calculated amount of depreciation expense does not reduce the book value of the asset below its estimated residual value. In most cases where this would occur, depreciation expense is limited to the amount that reduces book value to the exact amount of the estimated residual value.

The declining-balance method is used by companies in industries that expect fairly rapid obsolescence of equipment and by many Japanese businesses. Sony is one of the companies that uses this method:

Real World Excerpt

Sony Annual Report

Summary of Significant Accounting Policies:

Note 1: Property, plant and equipment is stated at cost. Depreciation is computed on the declining balance method for the parent company and the Japanese subsidiaries and on the straight line method for foreign subsidiaries at rates based on the estimated useful life of the assets.

As this note indicates, companies may use different depreciation methods for different classes of assets. Under the consistency principle, they are expected to apply the same methods over time.

MANAGERS' SELECTION AMONG ACCOUNTING ALTERNATIVES

The 1993 edition of *Accounting Trends and Techniques* (published by the AICPA) reported the depreciation methods used by 600 companies:

Straight line	564
Declining balance	26
Sum-of-the-years' digits	12
Accelerated, but not specified	62
Units of production	47

Note that the number of methods exceeds the number of companies because some companies use more than one method.

The method used by nearly 95% of the companies for some or all of their assets is the straight-line method. Corporate managers find this method to be easy to use and to explain. During the early years of the life of an asset, the straight-line method also reports higher income compared to the accelerated methods.

Self-Study Quiz

Assume that Delta acquired new computer equipment at a cost of $240,000. The equipment has an estimated life of six years with an estimated residual value of $30,000. Determine depreciation expense for the first full year under each of the following methods:

1. Straight-line depreciation. ______________________.
2. Sum-of-the-years'-digits. ______________________.
3. 200%-declining-balance method. ______________________.

After you have completed your answers, check them with the solutions presented in the footnote at the bottom of this page.*

Depreciation and Federal Income Tax

Delta Air Lines, like most companies, maintains two sets of accounting records. One set of records is prepared under GAAP and is used for reporting to stockholders. The other set of records is prepared to determine the company's tax obligation under the Internal Revenue Code. Some people, when they first learn that companies maintain two sets of books, question the ethics or the legality of the practice. In reality, it is both legal and ethical to maintain separate records for tax accounting and financial reporting.

The reason that it is legal to maintain two sets of books is simple: the objectives of GAAP and the Internal Revenue Code are different. Financial reporting rules are designed to provide economic information about a business that is useful in projecting the future cash flows of the business. The objective of the Internal Revenue Code is to raise sufficient revenues to pay for the expenditures of the federal government. In addition, many provisions of the Internal Revenue Code are designed to encourage certain behaviors that are thought to benefit our society (e.g., contributions to charities are tax deductible to encourage people to support worthy programs).

While it is easy to understand why two sets of accounting records are permitted, perhaps the more interesting question concerns why managers elect to go to the extra cost of maintaining two sets of books. In some cases, there are differences between the Internal Revenue Code and GAAP that leave the manager no

*1. $35,000
2. $60,000
3. $70,000

choice but to have separate records. In other cases, there is an economic explanation. It is often called the *least and the latest rule.* All taxpayers want to pay the smallest amount of tax that is legally permitted and they want to pay it at the latest date possible. If you had the choice of paying $100,000 to the federal government at the end of this year or the end of next year, you would choose the end of next year. By doing so, you would be able to invest the money for an extra year and earn a significant return on the investment. By maintaining two sets of books, corporations are able to defer (delay) paying taxes in the amount of millions and sometimes billions of dollars. In the case of Delta Air Lines, the amount of deferred taxes has been as high as nearly $250 million.

Perhaps the largest dollar difference between GAAP accounting and tax accounting occurs in the area of depreciation. Some of the depreciation methods discussed in the previous section are not acceptable for federal income tax reporting. Most corporations use the Modified Accelerated Cost Recovery System (MACRS) for calculating depreciation expense for their tax statement. MACRS is similar to the declining-balance method and is applied over relatively short asset lives. It is not used for financial reporting purposes.

MACRS does not attempt to match the cost of an asset with the revenue it produces over its useful life in conformity with the matching principle. MACRS provides for rapid depreciation of an asset over a life that is usually much shorter than its estimated useful life. The intent of MACRS is to provide an incentive for corporations to invest in modern property, plant, and equipment in order to be competitive in world markets. The high depreciation expense reported under MACRS reduces a corporation's taxable income and therefore the amount it must pay in taxes. The notes to the Delta financial statements show that the excess of tax depreciation above depreciation computed according to GAAP amounted to more than $300 million during the current year.

Partial Year Depreciation

The examples that we discussed earlier in this chapter assumed that assets were acquired on the first day of the year and depreciated for the entire year. In practice, assets are purchased at various times during the year. Rather than establishing a large number of depreciation schedules based on small differences in the dates of purchase for the assets, most companies adopt a policy to cover partial year depreciation. Some typical policies are:

1. Depreciate for a full month all assets acquired before the 15th of the month. There is no depreciation for the month on assets acquired after the 15th.
2. Depreciate for a full year all assets acquired before July 1. There is no depreciation for the year on assets acquired after July 1.
3. Take one-half-year depreciation in the year of acquisition of the asset without regard to the month in which the asset was actually purchased.

CHANGES IN DEPRECIATION ESTIMATES

Learning Objective 4
Describe the financial statement impact of a change in depreciation estimates.

Depreciation is based on two estimates—useful life and residual value. These estimates are made at the time a depreciable asset is acquired. One, or both, of these initial estimates may have to be revised as experience with the asset accumulates. When it is clear that either estimate should be revised to a material degree, the undepreciated asset balance less any residual value at that date

The $4.9 billion Denver International Airport is an important resource for the airlines, but it is owned by Denver.

should be apportioned, based on the new estimate, over the remaining estimated life. This is called a change in estimate.

Assume the following for an aircraft owned by Delta:

Cost of aircraft when acquired	$1,100,000
Estimated useful life	20 years
Estimated residual value	$100,000
Accumulated depreciation through year 6 (assuming the SL method is used):	

($1,100,000 – $100,000) x 6/20 = $300,000

Shortly after the start of year 7, Delta changed the initial estimated life to 31 years. No journal entry is needed when this decision is reached. However, the adjusting entry at the end of year 7 would be:

Depreciation expense	28,000	
Accumulated depreciation		28,000

Computation:	
Acquisition cost	$1,100,000
Accumulated depreciation, years 1-6	300,000
Undepreciated balance	$ 800,000
Less: Residual value	100,000
Balance to be depreciated	$ 700,000
Annual depreciation based on remaining life:	
$700,000 ÷ (31 years – 6 years)	$ 28,000

Under GAAP, changes in accounting estimates and depreciation methods should be made only when the new estimate or accounting method "better measures" the periodic income of the business. The *comparability concept* requires that accounting information reported in the financial statements should be comparable across accounting periods and among similar entities. This principle has a significant constraint on changing depreciation estimates and methods unless the effect is to improve the measurement of depreciation expense and net income.

A recent financial statement from Delta Air Lines contained the following note:

Real World Excerpt

Delta Air Lines Annual Report

Prior to the current year, substantially all of the Company's flight equipment was being depreciated on a straight-line basis to residual values (10% of cost) over a 15-year period from the dates placed in service. As a result of a review of its fleet plan, effective this year, the Company increased the estimated useful lives of substantially all of its flight equipment. Flight equipment that was not already fully depreciated is being depreciated on a straight-line basis to residual values (5% of cost) over a 20-year period from the dates placed in service. The effect of this change was a $34.3 million decrease in depreciation expense.

Notice that Delta changed both the estimated life of its flight equipment and its estimated residual value. (At this point, you should review the previous example to see if you can compute the depreciation expense assuming the residual value is reduced also to $50,000. Hint: the correct answer is $30,000). Why would the management of Delta revise the estimates of useful life and residual value? The most likely explanation is found in other notes to the Delta financial statements. To improve financial performance, management announced a number of cost control initiatives including "a $5.4 billion reduction in planned aircraft capital expenditures." As the result of acquiring fewer new aircraft, Delta will have to get longer service from its existing equipment, and because of longer service, the equipment will have less residual value when it is eventually sold.

Financial analysts are particularly interested in changes in accounting estimates because they can have a large impact on the before tax operating income of a company. In the case of Delta, the changes added $34.3 million because of reduced depreciation expense and will add a similar amount each year over the remaining life of the aircraft. Analysts pay close attention to this number because it represents increased profitability due to an accounting adjustment.

Self-Study Quiz

Assume that Delta Air Lines owned a service truck that originally cost $100,000. When purchased, the truck had an estimated useful life of 10 years with no residual value. After operating the truck for five years, Delta determined that the remaining life was only two more years. Based on this change in estimate, what amount of depreciation should be recorded over the remaining life of the asset? Delta uses the straight-line method.

Check your answer with the footnote at the bottom of this page.*

FINANCIAL ANALYSIS

Impact of Alternative Depreciation Methods

Assume you are analyzing two companies that are exactly the same except for the fact that one uses accelerated depreciation and the other uses straight-line. Which company would you expect to report higher net income? Actually, the question is a bit tricky. The answer is that you cannot say for certain. The accelerated methods report higher depreciation during the early years of the life of an asset and therefore report lower net income. As the age of the asset increases, this effect reverses; therefore, companies that use accelerated depreciation report lower depreciation expense and higher net income during the later years of an asset's life. Exhibit 8–4 shows the pattern of depreciation over the life of an asset for the methods that were discussed in this chapter. When the curves for the accelerated methods fall below the curve for the straight-line method, the accelerated methods cause higher net income to be reported compared to straight-line.

---

*$50,000 (book value after 5 years) ÷ 2 years (remaining life) = $25,000 depreciation expense per year.

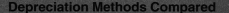

Depreciation Methods Compared **Exhibit 8–4**

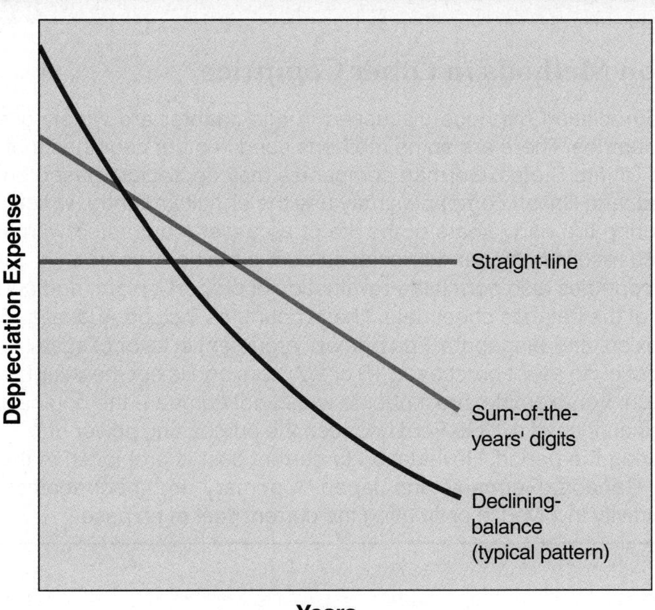

Users of financial statements must understand the impact of differences in the methods of accounting for depreciation and how the passage of time affects those differences. Significant differences in the reported net incomes of companies can be caused by differences in depreciation methods rather than by real economic differences.

DEPRECIATION AND CASH FLOWS

Depreciation expense is commonly called a noncash expense because it does not directly affect cash flows. The cash outflow associated with depreciation occurred when the related asset was acquired. Each period when depreciation is recorded, no cash payment is made (i.e., there is not a credit to cash related to recording depreciation expense). Most other expenses cause an immediate or subsequent outflow of cash. The recording of salary expense, for example, is associated with either the immediate payment of cash or a subsequent payment when salaries payable are paid.

Some analysts misinterpret the meaning of a noncash expense and often say that "cash is provided by depreciation." Depreciation is not a source of cash. Cash from operations can only be provided by selling goods and services. A company with a large amount of depreciation expense does not generate more cash compared with a company that reports a small amount of depreciation expense (assuming that they are exactly the same in every other respect). Depreciation expense reduces the amount of reported net income for a company, but it does not reduce the amount of cash generated by the company because it is a noncash expense.

While depreciation is a noncash expense, depreciation policy for tax purposes can affect cash flows for a company. Depreciation is a deductible expense for income tax purposes (i.e., taxes are based on income, or revenues minus expenses). The larger the amount of depreciation recorded by a company for tax purposes, the lower the taxable income and the taxes that must be paid. Because taxes must be paid in cash, a reduction in the tax obligation of a company results in a reduction of cash outflows for the company.

AN INTERNATIONAL PERSPECTIVE

Depreciation Methods in Other Countries

The various depreciation methods discussed in this chapter are widely used by corporations in most countries. There are some methods used in other countries that are not generally used in the United States. German companies may depreciate based on the hours that an asset is used, and British companies may use the annuity method, which results in lower depreciation during the early years of the life of an asset (contrasted with accelerated depreciation, which results in higher depreciation during the early years).

Many other countries also permit the revaluation of property, plant, and equipment to their current cost as of the balance sheet date. These countries include Australia, Brazil, England, Hong Kong, Mexico, and Singapore. The primary argument in favor of such revaluation is that the historical cost of an asset purchased 15 or 20 years ago is not meaningful because of the impact of inflation. For example, most people would not compare the original price of a 1965 Ford to the original price of a 1995 Ford because the purchasing power of the dollar changed dramatically during the period. Revaluation to current cost is prohibited in the United States (under GAAP), Canada, Germany, and Japan. A primary argument against restatement is the lack of objectivity involved in estimating the current cost of an asset.

REPAIRS, MAINTENANCE, AND ADDITIONS

Learning Objective 5
Account for ordinary and extraordinary repairs.

Most assets require substantial expenditures during their lives to maintain or enhance their productive capacity. These expenditures include ordinary repairs and maintenance, major repairs, replacements, and additions. Some unsophisticated investors assume that the terms *expenditure* and *expense* are synonymous. Such is not the case. An expenditure is the payment of money to acquire goods or services. These goods and services may be recorded as either assets or expenses depending on whether they benefit future periods or only the current period. Expenditures made after an asset is acquired are classified as follows:

Capital expenditures are recorded as increases in asset accounts, not as expenses.

Revenue expenditures are recorded as expenses.

1. **Capital expenditures**—those expenditures that provide benefits for one or more accounting periods beyond the current period; therefore, they are debited to appropriate asset accounts and depreciated, depleted, or amortized over their useful lives.
2. **Revenue expenditures**—those expenditures that provide benefits during the current accounting period only; therefore, they are debited to appropriate current expense accounts when incurred.

The following sections discuss various types of revenue and capital expenditures.

Ordinary Repairs and Maintenance

Ordinary repairs and maintenance are expenditures for normal operating upkeep of operational assets.

Ordinary repairs and maintenance are expenditures for normal maintenance and upkeep of operational assets that are necessary to keep the assets in their usual condition. These expenditures are recurring in nature, involve relatively small amounts at each occurrence, and do not directly lengthen the useful life of the asset. Ordinary repairs and maintenance are revenue expenditures. They are recorded as expense in the accounting period in which incurred.

In the case of Delta Air Lines, examples of ordinary repairs would include changing oil in engines, replacing light bulbs in the control panels, and fixing torn fabric in a passenger seat. While each expenditure for ordinary repairs is relatively small, in the aggregate these expenditures can be substantial. In a

Repairs and maintenance are an expensive but essential part of operating an airline.

recent year, Delta paid over $465 million for aircraft repairs. This amount was reported as an expense on its income statement.

Extraordinary Repairs

Extraordinary repairs are classified as capital expenditures. An extraordinary repair is debited to the related asset account and depreciated over the remaining life of that asset. **Extraordinary repairs** occur infrequently, involve large amounts of money, and increase the economic usefulness of the asset in the future because of either greater efficiency or longer life. Examples are major overhauls, complete reconditioning, and major replacements and improvements. The complete replacement of an engine on an aircraft is an example of an extraordinary repair.

Extraordinary repairs are major, high-cost, long-term repairs that increase the economic usefulness of the asset.

To illustrate the accounting for extraordinary repairs, assume Delta owns an aircraft that originally cost $1 million and is depreciating the asset on a straight-line basis over 20 years with no estimated residual value. At the beginning of the seventh year, a major reconditioning was finished that cost $130,000. As a result of this work, the estimated useful life of the asset changed from 20 years to 31 years (i.e., a change in estimate). The journal entries to record these facts are:

Extraordinary repair at the start of year 7:

	Debit	Credit
Flight equipment*	130,000	
Cash		130,000
Capital expenditure.		

*Alternatively, the debit could be made to the account for accumulated depreciation; the result would be the same.

Revised annual depreciation, years 7–31:

	Debit	Credit
Depreciation expense*	33,200	
Accumulated depreciation		33,200
Adjusting entry to record annual depreciation.		

*Computation:

Original cost	$1,000,000
Depreciation, years 1–6	300,000
Book value remaining	$ 700,000
Extraordinary repair	130,000
Balance to be depreciated over remaining life	$ 830,000

Annual depreciation: $830,000 ÷ (31 – 6 years) = $33,200.

Additions

Additions are extensions to, or enlargements of, existing assets, such as the addition of a wing to a building. These additions are capital expenditures; therefore, the cost of additions should be debited to the existing account for the asset and depreciated over the remaining life of the asset to which the cost is related. However, if the life of the addition is shorter than the life of the related asset, the addition should be depreciated over its remaining useful life (less its residual value).

To Capitalize or to Expense

In many cases, there is no clear line to distinguish between capital expenditures and revenue expenditures (expenses). In these situations, managers must exercise professional judgment and make a subjective decision. Many managers would prefer to classify an item as a capital expenditure for financial reporting because net income for the period is higher by not reporting the total amount as an expense in the current period. Of course, most managers would prefer to classify the expenditure as a deductible expense on the income tax return in order to pay lower taxes in the current period. Because these decisions are subjective, auditors closely review the items that are reported as capital and revenue expenditures.

To avoid spending too much time on classifying capital and revenue expenditures, some companies develop simple policies that govern the accounting for these expenditures. For example, one large computer company expenses all individual items that cost less than $1,000. These policies are acceptable because of the *materiality constraint.*

DISPOSAL OF OPERATIONAL ASSETS

Learning Objective 6
Record the disposal of operational assets.

In some cases, a business may decide not to hold an operational asset for its entire life. The company may drop a product from its line and no longer need the equipment that was used to produce the product, or it may want to trade in a machine for a more efficient one. These disposals are voluntary and include sale, trade-in, or retirement. Delta, when it disposes of an old aircraft, may sell it to a cargo airline or regional airline.

A business may also dispose of an asset involuntarily as a result of a casualty, such as a storm, fire, or accident. Whatever the nature of the disposal, the cost of the asset and any accumulated depreciation, depletion, or amortization must be removed from the accounts at the date of disposal. The difference between any resources received on disposal of an operational asset and the book, or carrying, value of the asset at the date of disposal is a gain or loss on disposal of operational assets. This gain (or loss) is reported on the income statement. However, it is not revenue (or expense) because it is from "peripheral or incidental" activities rather than from normal operations.

Assume that Delta Air Lines sold an aircraft that was no longer needed because of the elimination of flight service to a small city. The aircraft was sold for $350,000 cash when the account balances showed flight equipment of $1 million and accumulated depreciation of $700,000 (i.e., a book value of $300,000). The entry to record this sale is:

Account	Debit	Credit
Cash	350,000	
Accumulated depreciation	700,000	
Flight equipment		1,000,000
Gain on sale of operational asset		50,000

Gain computed:	
Sale price	$350,000
Book value at date of sale ($1,000,000 – $700,000)	300,000
Difference, gain	$ 50,000

A gain or loss on disposal occurs because (1) depreciation expense is based on estimates that may differ from actual experience and (2) depreciation is based on original cost, not current market value. Because the gain or loss on disposal is not part of the continuing operating activities of a company, it is usually shown as a separate line item on the income statement. In a recent year, Delta Air Lines sold 18 DC–9 aircraft and reported a gain of $64,843,000 as a separate item on its income statement.

Disposals of operational assets seldom occur on the last day of the accounting period. Therefore, the depreciation, depletion, or amortization must be updated to the date of disposal. The disposal of a depreciable operational asset usually requires two entries: (1) an adjusting entry to update the depreciation expense and accumulated depreciation accounts and (2) an entry to record the disposal.

Real World Excerpt
The Wall Street Journal

Managing Profits

How General Electric
Damps Fluctuations
In Its Annual Earnings

GE almost seems able to override the business cycle. How does GE do it?..."earnings management," the orchestrated timing of gains and losses to smooth out bumps and, especially, avoid a decline.

Take a hypothetical example of an aircraft nearing the end of a 15–year [life]. GE may have already written off most of the plane's cost, leaving its book value low. GE can potentially book a gain if it then sells the plane.

Howard Schilit, an accounting professor at American University in Washington, comments: "Earnings management can be very dangerous for the investor because you are creating something artificial. The numbers should reflect how the company is actually doing."

In an initial interview, GE Capital Chairman Gary Wendt said, "We do a little, not a lot."

SOURCE: *The Wall Street Journal*, November 3, 1994, p. A1.

NATURAL RESOURCES

Learning Objective 7
Account for natural resources and intangible assets, including amortization.

You are probably most familiar with large companies that are involved in manufacturing goods (Ford, Black & Decker), distribution of goods (Sears, Home Depot), or performing a service (Federal Express, Holiday Inn). There are also a number of large companies, some of which are less well known, that develop raw materials and products from **natural resources** which include mineral deposits (such as gold or iron ore), oil wells, and timber tracts. These resources are often called *wasting assets*, because they are depleted (i.e., physically used). Companies involved with natural resources are critical to the economy because they produce such essential items as lumber for construction, fuel for heating and transportation, and food for consumption. Companies involved with natural resources also attract considerable attention because of the significant effect they can have on the environment. Concerned citizens often read financial statements from companies involved in exploration for oil, coal, and various ores to determine the amount of money that is being spent to protect the environment.

Natural resources are assets that occur in nature.

When natural resources are acquired or developed, they are recorded in conformity with the *cost principle*. As a natural resource is used up, its acquisition cost, in conformity with the *matching principle*, must be apportioned among the various periods in which the resulting revenues are earned. The term *depletion* describes the process of periodic cost allocation over the economic life of a natural resource. The concept of depletion is exactly the same as depreciation. The only difference is the type of asset that is being accounted for.[3]

A *depletion rate* is computed by dividing the total acquisition and development cost (less any estimated residual value, which is rare) by the estimated units that can be withdrawn economically from the resource. The depletion rate is multiplied each period by the actual number of units withdrawn during the accounting period. This procedure is the same as the units-of-production method of calculating depreciation.

When buildings and similar improvements are acquired for the development and exploitation of a natural resource, they should be recorded in separate asset accounts and *depreciated*—not depleted. Their estimated useful lives cannot be longer than the time needed to exploit the natural resource unless they have a significant use after the source is depleted.

INTANGIBLE ASSETS

An intangible asset, like any other asset, has value because of certain rights and privileges conferred by law on the owner of the asset. However, an intangible asset has no material or physical substance as do tangible assets such as land and buildings. Intangible assets are recorded in conformity with the *cost principle* only if they are purchased. If an intangible asset is developed internally, the cost of development will normally be recorded as an expense. For example, Abbott Laboratories (a manufacturer of pharmaceutical and nutritional products) recently spent more than $772 million on research to discover new products. This amount was reported as an expense, not an asset. If Abbott Labs had spent an equivalent amount to purchase patents for new products from other drug companies, it would have recorded the expenditure as an asset. After acquisition, intangible assets are amortized (a process similar to depreciation and depletion) and are recorded at cost less accumulated amortization in conformity with the matching principle.

EXAMPLES OF INTANGIBLE ASSETS

A *patent* is an exclusive right granted by the federal government for a period of 17 years. It is typically granted to an inventor who discovers a new product or process. The patent enables the owner to use, manufacture, and sell the subject of the patent and the patent itself. Without the protection of a patent it is unlikely that inventors would be willing to search for new products. The patent prevents a competitor from simply copying a new discovery until the inventor has had a period of time to earn an economic return on the new product.

A patent that is *purchased* is recorded at cost. An *internally developed* patent is recorded at only its registration and legal cost because GAAP requires the immediate expensing of research and development costs. In conformity with the *matching principle*, the cost of a patent must be amortized over the shorter of its economic life or its remaining legal life. Amortization is usually recorded with a debit to Amortization Expense and a credit directly to the asset account instead of a contra account Accumulated Amortization.

A **copyright** is the exclusive right to publish, use, and sell a literary, musical, or artistic work.

A **copyright** gives the owner the exclusive right to publish, use, and sell a literary, musical, or artistic piece of work for a period not exceeding 50 years after the author's death. The book that you are reading has a copyright to

[3]Consistent with the procedure for recording depreciation, an Accumulated Depletion account may be used. In practice, most companies credit the asset account directly for the periodic depletion. This procedure is typically used for intangible assets, discussed in the next section.

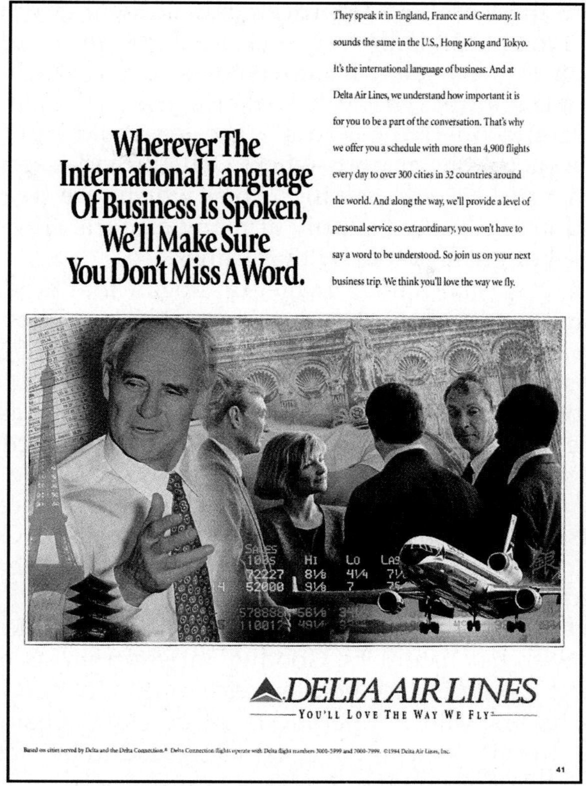

Advertising helps create goodwill by establishing customer loyalty.

protect the publisher and the authors. It would be against the law, for example, if an instructor copied several chapters from this book and handed them out in class. The same principles, guidelines, and procedures used in accounting for the cost of patents also are used for copyrights.

Franchises and licenses may be granted by either the government or other businesses for a specified period and purpose. A city may grant one company a franchise to distribute gas to homes for heating purposes, or a company may sell franchises, such as the right for a local outlet to operate a KFC restaurant. Franchise agreements are contracts that can have a variety of provisions. Franchises and licenses usually require an investment by the franchisee to acquire them; therefore, they should be accounted for as intangible assets. The life of the franchise agreement depends on the contract and may be for a single year or an indefinite period. Blockbuster Video is a popular company in the home video rental business. In order to expand rapidly, the company enters into franchise agreements with local operators. The franchise agreement requires the payment of a franchise fee and covers a period of 20 years. Blockbuster has opened over 1,100 stores under franchise agreements.

A **leasehold** is the right granted in a contract called a lease to use a specific asset. Leasing is a common type of business contract. For a consideration called *rent*, the owner (lessor) extends to another party (lessee) certain rights to use specified property. Leases may vary from simple arrangements, such as the month-to-month lease of an office or the daily rental of an automobile, to long-term leases having complex contractual arrangements.

Leaseholds are rights granted to a lessee under a lease contract.

Lessees sometimes make significant improvements to a leased property when they enter into a long-term lease agreement. A company that agrees to lease office space on a 15-year lease may install new fixtures or move walls to make the space more useful. These improvements are called *leasehold improvements* and are recorded as an asset by the lessee despite the fact that the lessor usually will own the leasehold improvements at the end of the term of the lease. The cost of leasehold improvements should be amortized over the estimated useful life of the related improvements or the remaining life of the lease, whichever is shorter. The Delta balance sheet (Exhibit 8–1) shows an asset "Leasehold and operating rights." The leasehold rights are improvements to rented space at the airports where Delta provides services. The operating rights are authorized landing slots which are regulated by the government and are in limited supply at many airports. They are intangible assets that can be bought and sold by the airlines.

A *trademark* is a special name, image, or slogan that is identified with a product or a company. Trademarks are protected by law. They are often some of the most valuable assets that a company can own. Most of us cannot imagine the Walt Disney Company without Mickey Mouse. You probably enjoy your favorite soft drink more because of the image that has been built up around its name. Many people can identify the shape of a corporate logo as quickly as they can recognize the shape of a stop sign. While trademarks are valuable assets, they are rarely seen on balance sheets. The reason is simple; intangible assets are not recorded unless they are purchased. Companies often spend millions of dollars developing trademarks but these expenditures are usually recorded as expenses and not capitalized.

Goodwill, as used by most business people, is the favorable reputation that a company has with its customers. Goodwill arises from such factors as customer confidence, reputation for good service or quality goods, and financial standing. From its first day of operations, a successful business continually builds goodwill. In this context, the goodwill is said to be *internally generated* and is not reported as an asset (i.e., it was not purchased).

For strategic purposes, one business may purchase another business as an entity. Often the purchase price of the business will exceed the fair market value of all of the assets owned by the business. Why would a company pay more for a company as a whole than it would pay if it bought the assets individually? The answer is goodwill. You could easily buy modern bottling equipment in order to sell a new cola drink but you would not make as much money as you would if you could acquire the goodwill associated with Coke or Pepsi.

For accounting purposes, **goodwill** is the excess of the purchase price of a business over the market value of the business's net assets.

For accounting purposes, **goodwill** is defined as the difference between the purchase price of a company as a whole and the fair market value of all of its assets minus the fair market value of its liabilities. It is recorded on the balance sheet after the purchase of another company. In conformity with the *cost principle,* goodwill is recorded as an intangible asset only when it actually is purchased at a measurable cost.

A number of years ago, Delta Air Lines acquired Western Air Lines, a regional carrier. Delta purchased the entire company as an entity and paid a price in excess of the fair market value of the tangible assets owned by Western. The balance sheet prepared by Delta (Exhibit 8–1) includes the individual assets from Western and an item valued at $291,579,000 called "Cost in excess of net assets acquired" (which is defined as *goodwill*). The notes to the statements include the following:

Real World Excerpt

Delta Air Lines
Annual Report

The cost in excess of net assets acquired, which is being amortized over 40 years, is related to the Company's acquisition of Western Air Lines, Inc.

Goodwill, like other intangible assets, must be amortized to expense over its estimated economic life, usually on a straight-line basis. Because it is particularly difficult to estimate the life of goodwill, GAAP (*APB Opinion 17*) requires goodwill to be amortized over a period not to exceed 40 years. Delta's income statement reports amortization of cost in excess of net assets acquired (goodwill) of $8,725,000. When Delta records amortization of goodwill, it credits the Goodwill account rather than a contra account called Accumulated Amortization. Most companies follow this practice.

Epilogue for Delta Air Lines

By the 1990s, the airline industry faced excess capacity. There were simply too many aircraft competing for a limited number of customers. Delta announced a campaign to slash $2 billion in expenses by eliminating 15,000 jobs. During the first year of the cost containment program, Delta actually achieved a 3% increase in passenger miles, to 23.7 billion, despite reducing operating capacity by 3.6%. Wall Street analysts were impressed with Delta's initial success in achieving greater productivity from its operational assets.

DEMONSTRATION CASE

(Resolve the requirements before proceeding to the suggested solution that follows.)

Diversified Industries has been operating for a number of years. It started as a residential construction company. In recent years, it expanded into heavy construction, ready-mix concrete, sand and gravel, construction supplies, and earth-moving services.

The transactions below were selected from those completed during 19D. They focus on the primary issues discussed in this chapter. Amounts have been simplified for case purposes.

19D		
Jan.	1	The management decided to buy a building that was about 10 years old. The location was excellent, and there was adequate parking space. The company bought the building and the land on which it was situated for $305,000 cash. A reliable appraiser provided the following market values: land, $126,000; and building, $174,000.
	12	Paid renovation costs on the building of $38,100.
June	19	Bought a third location for a gravel pit (designated No. 3) for $50,000 cash. The location had been carefully surveyed. It was estimated that 100,000 cubic yards of gravel could be removed from the deposit.
July	10	Paid $1,200 for ordinary repairs on the building.
Aug.	1	Paid $10,000 for costs of preparing the new gravel pit for exploitation.

December 31, 19D (end of the annual accounting period)—the following data were developed as a basis for the adjusting entries:

a. The building will be depreciated on a straight-line basis over an estimated useful life of 30 years. The estimated residual value is $35,000.

b. During 19D, 12,000 cubic yards of gravel were removed from gravel pit No. 3 and sold.

c. The company owns a patent right that is used in operations. On January 1, 19D, the patent account had a balance of $3,300. The patent has an estimated remaining useful life of six years (including 19D).

Required:

1. Give the journal entries for the five transactions completed during 19D.
2. Give the adjusting entries on December 31, 19D.
3. Show the December 31, 19D, balance sheet classification and amount for each of the following items: land, building, gravel pit, and patent.

SUGGESTED SOLUTION

1. Entries during 19D:

Jan. 1, 19D:	Land (building site)	128,100	
	Building	176,900	
	Cash		305,000

Allocation of cost (based on appraisal):

Item	Appraisal Value	Percent		Computation		Allocation
Land	$126,000	42	×	$305,000	=	$128,100
Building	174,000	58	×	305,000	=	176,900
Totals	$300,000	100				$305,000

Jan. 12, 19D:	Building	38,100	
	Cash		38,100
	Renovation costs on building prior to use.		
June 19, 19D:	Gravel pit (No. 3)	50,000	
	Cash		50,000
	Purchased gravel pit; estimated production, 100,000 cubic yards.		
July 10, 19D:	Repair expense	1,200	
	Cash		1,200
	Ordinary repairs.		
Aug. 1, 19D:	Gravel pit (No. 3)	10,000	
	Cash		10,000
	Preparation costs.		

2. Adjusting entries Dec. 31, 19D:

a. Depreciation expense, building	6,000	
Accumulated depreciation		6,000

Computation:

Cost ($176,900 + $38,100)	$215,000
Less: Residual value	35,000
Cost to be depreciated	$180,000

Annual depreciation: $180,000 ÷ 30 years = $6,000.

b. Depletion expense	7,200	
Gravel pit (No. 3)		7,200

Computation:
Cost ($50,000 + $10,000) $60,000

Depletion rate:
$60,000 ÷ 100,000 cubic yards = $0.60

Depletion expense: $0.60 x 12,000 cubic yards = $7,200

c. Patent expense	550	
Patent		550

Computations:
$3,300 ÷ 6 years = $550.

3. Balance sheet, December 31, 19D:

Assets

Operational assets:		
Land		$128,100
Building	$215,000	
Less: Accumulated depreciation	6,000	209,000
Gravel pit		52,800
Patent ($3,300 – $550)		2,750
Total operational assets		$392,650

SUMMARY

This chapter discussed accounting for operational assets. These are the noncurrent assets that a business retains for long periods of time for use in the course of normal operations rather than for sale. They include tangible assets and intangible assets. At acquisition, an operational asset is recorded at cost. Cost includes the cash equivalent purchase price plus all reasonable and necessary expenditures made to acquire and prepare the asset for its intended use.

An operational asset represents a bundle of future services and benefits that have been paid for in advance. As an operational asset is used, this bundle of services gradually is used to earn revenue. Therefore, in conformity with the matching principle, cost (less any estimated residual value) is allocated to periodic expense over the periods benefited. In this way, the expense associated with the use of operational assets is matched with the revenues earned. This allocation process is called *depreciation* in the case of property, plant, and equipment; *depletion* in the case of natural resources; and *amortization* in the case of intangibles.

Four methods of depreciation are used widely: straight line, units of production, sum-of-the-years' digits, and declining balance.

Expenditures related to operational assets are classified as follows:

1. Capital expenditures—those expenditures that provide benefits for one or more accounting periods beyond the current period. They are debited to appropriate asset accounts and depreciated, depleted, or amortized over their useful lives.
2. Revenue expenditures—those expenditures that provide benefits during the current accounting period only. They are debited to appropriate current expense accounts when incurred.

Ordinary repairs and maintenance costs are revenue expenditures. Extraordinary repairs and asset additions are capital expenditures.

Operational assets may be disposed of voluntarily by sale or retirement, or involuntarily through casualty, such as storm, fire, or accident. Upon disposal, such assets must be depreciated, depleted, or amortized up to the date of disposal. The disposal transaction is recorded by removing the cost of the old asset and the related accumulated depreciation, depletion, or amortization amount from the accounts. A gain or loss on disposal of an operational asset will result when the disposal price is different from the book value of an old asset. Special rules apply to the trade-in of an asset as all, or part, of the consideration given for another asset (trade-ins are discussed in Chapter Supplement A).

Chapter Supplement A

Trading In Assets

It is not unusual when acquiring an asset to trade in another asset. Although there may be a direct trade of two assets, the typical case involves the trading in of an old asset plus the payment of cash for any difference in the value of the assets. In such transactions, the asset acquired must be recorded in the accounts, and the old asset is removed from the accounts.

Accounting for the exchange of one asset for another asset depends on two factors:

1. Whether the two assets are similar or dissimilar.
2. Whether cash for the difference is paid or received.

The trading in of an old truck for a new truck would involve similar assets. In contrast, the trading in of a plot of land for a new truck would involve dissimilar assets.

The basic principle for recording the exchange of assets can be stated as follows: If the assets exchanged are similar, the exchange should be recorded on a book value basis because there is no completed earning process. If the assets exchanged are dissimilar, the exchange should be recorded on a market value basis because there is a completed earning process (for the old asset).

Exhibit 8–5 illustrates accounting for the acquisition of an asset when another asset is given as a trade-in. Four independent cases are illustrated:

Case	Situations
A	Similar assets are exchanged; no cash is paid.
B	Dissimilar assets are exchanged; no cash is paid.
C	Similar assets are exchanged; cash is paid.
D	Dissimilar assets are exchanged; cash is paid.

Exhibit 8–5 **Trading In Used Assets Illustrated**

Situation of Company T:

Transaction: Company T acquired Asset N and traded in Asset O. At the date of the transaction, the accounts of Company T reflected the following:

Asset O:	
Cost when acquired	$5,000
Accumulated depreciation	3,000
Estimated market value	2,200
Asset N:	
Market value	2,250

Case A—similar assets are exchanged; no cash paid.

Principle applied: The asset acquired is recorded at the book value of the asset traded in.

Asset N	2,000	
Accumulated depreciation, Asset O	3,000	
Asset O		5,000

Case B—dissimilar assets are exchanged; no cash paid.

Principle applied: The asset acquired is recorded at the market value of the asset traded in.

Asset N	2,200	
Accumulated depreciation, Asset O	3,000	
Asset O		5,000
Gain on disposal of operational asset		200

Case C—similar assets are exchanged; $60 cash is paid.

Principle applied: The asset acquired is recorded at the book value of the asset traded in plus the cash paid.

Asset N ($2,000 +$60)	2,060	
Accumulated depreciation, Asset O	3,000	
Asset O		5,000
Cash		60

Case D—dissimilar assets are exchanged; $60 cash is paid.

Principle applied: The asset acquired is recorded at the market value of the asset traded in plus the cash paid.

Asset N	2,250*	
Accumulated depreciation, Asset O	3,000	
Asset O		5,000
Cash		60
Gain on disposal of operational assets		190

*Calculation: $2,200 + $60, but this amount cannot exceed the market value of the asset acquired, $2,250.

In the illustration in Exhibit 8–5, the market value of old Asset O was $200 in excess of its book value [i.e., $2,200 – ($5,000 – $3,000)]. Therefore, in Cases B and D (relating to dissimilar assets), this amount was recorded as a gain. In contrast, if the market value of old Asset O had been $1,900 (i.e., $100 below book value), a loss of $100 would be reported in Cases B and D. A loss would be recorded for Cases A and C (similar assets), when the market value of either asset is below book value, because an acquired asset cannot be recorded at an amount greater than its market value.

KEY TERMS

Accelerated Depreciation Methods that result in higher depreciation expense in the early years of an operational asset's life and lower expense in the later years. *416*

Acquisition Cost Net cash equivalent amount paid for an asset. *408*

Amortization Systematic and rational allocation of the cost of an intangible asset over its useful life. *411*

Basket Purchase Acquisition of two or more assets in a single transaction for a single lump sum. *409*

Book (or Carrying) Value Acquisition cost of an operational asset less accumulated depreciation, depletion, or amortization. *412*

Capital Expenditures Expenditures that are debited to an asset account; the acquisition of an asset. *424*

Capitalized Interest Interest expenditures included in the cost of a self-constructed asset. *409*

Copyright Exclusive right to publish, use, and sell a literary, musical, or artistic work. *428*

Declining-Balance (DB) Depreciation The method that allocates the cost of an operational asset over its useful life based on a multiple of the SL rate. *417*

Depletion Systematic and rational allocation of the cost of a natural resource over the period of exploitation. *411*

Depreciation Systematic and rational allocation of the cost of property, plant, and equipment (but not land) over their useful lives. *410*

Estimated Useful Life Estimated service life of an operational asset to the present owner. *413*

Extraordinary Repairs Major, high-cost, long-term repairs that increase the economic usefulness of the asset. Debited to an asset account (or accumulated depreciation); a capital expenditure. *425*

Goodwill For accounting purposes, the purchase price of a business that is in excess of the market value of the other net assets of that business. *430*

Intangible Assets Operational assets that have special rights but not physical substance. *408*

Leaseholds Rights granted to a lessee under a lease contract. *429*

Natural Resources Mineral deposits, timber tracts, oil, and gas. *427*

Operational Assets Tangible and intangible assets owned by a business and used in its operations. *408*

Ordinary Repairs and Maintenance Expenditures for the normal operating upkeep of operational assets; debit expense for ordinary repairs. *424*

Residual Value Estimated amount to be recovered, less disposal costs, at the end of the estimated useful life of an operational asset. *413*

Revenue Expenditures Expenditures that are debited to an expense account; the incurrence of an expense. *424*

Straight-Line (SL) Depreciation Method that allocates the cost of an operational asset in equal periodic amounts over its useful life. *414*

Sum-of-the-Years'-Digits Depreciation Method that allocates the cost of an operational asset over its useful life based on a fraction where the denominator is the total of all of the useful years and the numerator is the year of life in inverse order. *416*

Tangible Assets Operational assets that have physical substance. *408*

Units-of-Production Depreciation Method that allocates the cost of an operational asset over its useful life based on its periodic output related to its total estimated output. *415*

QUESTIONS

1. Define operational assets. Why are they considered a "bundle of future services"?
2. What are the classifications of operational assets? Explain each.
3. Relate the cost principle to accounting for operational assets.
4. Describe the relationship between the matching principle and accounting for operational assets.
5. Define and calculate the book value of a three-year-old operational asset that cost $21,500, has an estimated residual value of $1,500, and an estimated useful life of five years. Relate book value to carrying value and market value.
6. Under the cost principle, what amounts usually should be included in the acquisition cost of an operational asset?
7. What is a basket purchase? What measurement problem does it pose?
8. Distinguish between depreciation, depletion, and amortization.
9. In computing depreciation, three values must be known or estimated; identify and explain the nature of each.
10. Estimated useful life and residual value of an operational asset relate to the current owner or user rather than all potential users. Explain this statement.
11. What kind of a depreciation-expense pattern is provided under the straight-line method? When would its use be appropriate?
12. What kind of depreciation-expense pattern emerges under the units-of-production method? When would its use be appropriate?
13. What are the arguments in favor of accelerated depreciation?
14. Explain how monthly depreciation should be computed when the sum-of-the-years'-digits method is used for an asset having a 10-year life.
15. Distinguish between capital expenditures and revenue expenditures.
16. Distinguish between ordinary and extraordinary repairs. How is each accounted for?
17. Over what period should an addition to an existing operational asset be depreciated? Explain.
18. Define an intangible asset.
19. What period should be used to amortize an intangible asset?
20. Define goodwill. When is it appropriate to record goodwill as an intangible asset?
21. Distinguish between a leasehold and a leasehold improvement.
22. Over what period should a leasehold improvement be amortized? Explain.

EXERCISES

E8–1 Recording Asset Acquisition and Straight-Line Depreciation: Basket Purchase

Lion Company bought a building and the land on which it is located for a total cash price of $178,000. Also, the company paid transfer costs of $2,000. Renovation costs on the building were $21,200. An independent appraiser provided market values of building, $158,384; and land, $50,016.

Required:

1. Apportion the cost of the property on the basis of the appraised values. Show computations.
2. Give the journal entry to record the purchase of the property, including all expenditures. Assume that all transactions were for cash and that all purchases occurred at the start of year 1.
3. Give the journal entry to record straight-line depreciation at the end of one year assuming an estimated 12-year useful life and a $14,000 estimated residual value.
4. What would be the book value of the property at the end of year 2?

E8–2 Applying Cost Principle and Recording Straight-Line Depreciation

A machine was purchased by Cooper Company on March 1, 19A, at an invoice price of $20,000. On date of delivery, March 2, 19A, the company paid $8,000 on the machine, and the balance was on credit at 12% interest. On March 3, 19A, $250 was paid for freight on the machine. On March 5, installation costs relating to the machine were paid amounting to $1,200. On October 1, 19A, the company paid the balance due on the machine plus the interest.

Required (round all amounts to the nearest dollar):

1. Give the journal entries on each of the above dates through October 19A.
2. Give the adjusting entry for straight-line depreciation at the end of 19A assuming an estimated useful life of 10 years and an estimated residual value of $3,450. Depreciate to the nearest month. The accounting period ends December 31, 19A.
3. What would be the book value of the machine at the end of 19B?

E8–3 Computing Depreciation for Four Years Using Four Different Depreciation Methods

Glenda Corporation bought a machine at a cost of $6,400. The estimated useful life was four years, and the residual value, $800. Assume that the estimated productive life of the machine is 80,000 units. Yearly production was year 1, 28,000 units; year 2, 22,000 units; year 3, 18,000 units; and year 4, 12,000 units.

Required:

1. Determine the amount for each cell in the following schedule. Show your computations, and round to the nearest dollar.

	Depreciation Expense			
	Straight-Line	**Units of Production**	**Sum-of-the-Years' Digits**	**150% Declining-Balance**
1				
2				
3				
4				
Totals				

2. Assuming the machine was used directly in the production of one of the products manufactured and sold by the company, what factors might be considered in selecting a preferable depreciation method in conformity with the matching principle?

E8–4 *Computing Depreciation and Book Value for Two Years Using Four Depreciation Methods*

Stello Company bought a machine for $65,000. The estimated useful life was five years, and the estimated residual value, $5,000. Assume the estimated useful life in productive units is 150,000. Units actually produced were 40,000 in year 1, and 45,000 in year 2.

Required:

1. Determine the appropriate amounts to complete the schedule below. Show computations, and round to the nearest dollar.

Method of Depreciation	Depreciation Expense		Book Value at End of	
	Year 1	**Year 2**	**Year 1**	**Year 2**
Straight-line				
Units of production				
Sum-of-the-years' digits				
150% declining balance				

2. Which method would result in the lowest EPS for year 1? For year 2?

E8–5 *Recording and Explaining Changes in Useful Life and Residual Value*

Moore Company owns the office building occupied by its administrative office. The office building was reflected in the accounts at the end of last year as follows:

Cost when acquired	$450,000
Accumulated depreciation (based on straight-line depreciation, an estimated life of 30 years, and a $30,000 residual value)	196,000

During January of this year, on the basis of a careful study, the management decided that the total estimated useful life should be changed to 25 years (instead of 30) and the residual value reduced to $23,000 (from $30,000). The depreciation method will not be changed.

Required:

1. Give the adjusting entry (or entries) related to depreciation at the end of the year in which the change is made. Show computations.
2. Explain the basis for the entry (or entries) that you gave in (1).

E8–6 *Identifying Capital and Revenue Expenditures*

For each item listed below, enter the correct letter to the left to show the type of expenditures. Use the following:

Type of Expenditure

A Capital expenditure
B Revenue expenditure
C Neither

Transactions

_________ (1) Paid $400 for ordinary repairs.

_________ (2) Paid $6,000 for extraordinary repairs.

_________ (3) Addition to old building; paid cash, $20,000.

_________ (4) Routine maintenance; cost, $200; on credit.

_________ (5) Purchased a machine; $7,000; gave long-term note.

_________ (6) Paid $2,000 for organization costs.

_________ (7) Paid three-year insurance premium, $900.

_________ (8) Purchased a patent, $4,300 cash.

_________ (9) Paid $10,000 for monthly salaries.

_________ (10) Paid cash dividends, $20,000.

E8–7 Recording Depreciation, Repairs, and Amortization

Donnelly Company operates a small manufacturing facility as a supplement to its regular service activities. At the beginning of 19L, an operational asset account for the company showed the following balances:

Manufacturing equipment	$80,000
Accumulated depreciation through 19K	55,000

During 19L, the following expenditures were incurred for repairs and maintenance:

Routine maintenance and repairs on the equipment	$ 850
Major overhaul of the equipment	10,500

The equipment is being depreciated on a straight-line basis over an estimated life of 15 years with a $5,000 estimated residual value. The annual accounting period ends on December 31.

Required:

1. Give the adjusting entry for depreciation on the manufacturing equipment that was made at the end of 19K. Starting with 19L, what is the remaining estimated life?
2. Give the journal entries to record the two expenditures for repairs and maintenance during 19L.
3. Give the adjusting entry that should be made at the end of 19L for depreciation of the manufacturing equipment assuming no change in the estimated life or residual value. Show computations.

E8–8 Recording Depreciation, Extraordinary Repairs, and Changes in Estimated Useful Life and Residual Value

At the end of the annual accounting period, December 31, 19C, the records of Nina Company reflected the following:

Machine A:	
Cost when acquired	$28,000
Accumulated depreciation	10,000

During January 19D, the machine was renovated, including several major improvements, at a cost of $11,000. As a result, the estimated life was increased from five years to eight years, and the residual value was increased from $3,000 to $5,000. The company uses straight-line depreciation.

Required:

1. Give the journal entry to record the renovation. How old was the machine at the end of 19C?
2. Give the adjusting entry at the end of 19D to record straight-line depreciation for the year.
3. Explain the rationale for your entries in (1) and (2).

Freeport-McMoran

E8–9 Recording Acquisition and Depletion of a Natural Resource

Freeport–McMoran is a natural resources company involved in the business of exploration, development, and extraction of natural resources. Annual revenues exceed $1 billion. Assume that in February 19A, Freeport–McMoran paid $700,000 for a mineral deposit in Wyoming. During March, $65,000 was spent in preparing the deposit for exploitation. It was estimated that 900,000 total cubic yards could be extracted economically. During 19A, 60,000 cubic yards were extracted. During January 19B, another $6,000 was spent for additional developmental work. After conclusion of the latest work, the estimated remaining recovery was increased to 1,200,000 cubic yards over the remaining life. During 19B, 50,000 cubic yards were extracted.

Required: Give the appropriate journal entry for each of the following dates:

1. February 19A, acquisition of the deposit.
2. March 19A, developmental costs.
3. Year 19A, annual depletion assuming the company uses a contra account (show computations).
4. January 19B, developmental costs.
5. Year 19B, annual depletion (show computations).

E8–10 Recording Acquisition, Amortization, and Reporting of Three Different Intangible Assets

Wyatt Company had three intangible operational assets at the end of 19F (end of the accounting year):

a. A patent purchased from R. Jay on January 1, 19H, for a cash cost of $5,640. Jay had registered the patent with the U.S. Patent Office seven years earlier on January 1, 19A. Amortize over the remaining legal life.

b. A franchise acquired from the local community to provide certain services for five years starting on January 1, 19H. The franchise cost $25,000 cash.

c. A lease on some property for a five-year term beginning January 1, 19H. The company immediately spent $7,800 cash for long-term improvements (estimated useful life, eight years; no residual value). At the termination of the lease, there will be no recovery of these improvements.

Required:

1. Give the journal entry to record the acquisition of each intangible asset. Provide a brief explanation with the entries.
2. Give the adjusting journal entry at December 31, 19H, for amortization of each intangible. Show computations. The company does not use contra accounts.
3. Show how these assets and any related expenses should be reported on the financial statements for 19H.

E8–11 Recording a Patent, Copyright, and Goodwill: Amortizing Each

Flagg Company acquired three intangible operational assets during 19F. The relevant facts were:

a. On January 1, 19F, the company purchased a patent from M. Masters for $6,000 cash. Masters had developed the patent and registered it with the Patent Office on January 1, 19A. Amortize over the remaining legal life.

b. On January 1, 19F, the company purchased a copyright for a total cash cost of $14,000, and the remaining legal life was 25 years. The company executives estimated that the copyright would have no value by the end of 20 years.

c. The company purchased another company in January 19F at a cash cost of $120,000. Included in the purchase price was $30,000 for goodwill; the balance was for plant, equipment, and fixtures (no liabilities were assumed). Amortize the goodwill over the maximum period permitted.

Required:

1. Give the journal entry to record the acquisition of each intangible asset.
2. Give the adjusting journal entry that would be required at the end of the annual accounting period, December 31, 19F, for each intangible asset. The company uses contra accounts. Include a brief explanation and show computations.
3. What would be the book (carrying) value of each intangible asset at the end of 19G?

E8–12 Recording and Amortizing Rent Paid in Advance, Leasehold Improvements, and Periodic Rent

Starbucks Coffee Company

Starbucks Coffee Company is a rapidly expanding retailer of specialty coffee. They have over 250 stores in 10 markets and are currently expanding into three new markets: Boston, New York, and Minneapolis. Assume that Starbucks planned to open a new store on Commonwealth Avenue near Boston University and the company obtained a 15-year lease, starting January 1, 19D. Although there was a serviceable building on the property, the company had to build an additional structure to be used for storage. The 15-year lease required a $12,000 cash advance payment, plus cash payments of $4,000 per month during occupancy. During January 19D, the company spent $60,000 cash building the structure. The new structure has an estimated life of 18 years with no residual value (straight-line depreciation).

Required:

1. Give the journal entries for the company to record the payment of the $12,000 advance on January 1, 19D, and the first monthly rental.
2. Give the journal entry to record the construction of the new structure.
3. Give any adjusting entries required at the end of the annual accounting period on December 31, 19D, in respect to (*a*) the advance payment and (*b*) the new structure. Show computations.
4. Compute the total amount of expense resulting from the lease for 19D.

E8–13 Recording the Disposal of an Asset at Three Different Assumed Sale Prices

Federal Express

Federal Express has developed a worldwide network that delivers over 1.7 million packages every working night. In addition to the world's largest fleet of all-cargo aircraft, the company has more than 28,000 ground vehicles that are used to pick up and deliver packages. Assume that Federal Express sold a small delivery truck that had been used in the business for three years. The records of the company reflected the following:

Delivery truck	$18,000
Accumulated depreciation	13,000

Required:

1. Give the journal entry for the disposal of the truck assuming the sales price was $5,000.
2. Give the journal entry for the disposal of the truck assuming the sales price was $5,600.
3. Give the journal entry for the disposal of the truck assuming the sales price was $4,600.
4. Summarize the effects of the disposal of the asset under the three different situations above.

E8–14 Recording the Disposal of an Operational Asset: Computing Estimated Life

Fisher-Price

Fisher-Price manufactures and markets high-quality preschool and infant toys. The company's revenues exceed $600 million. In the toy business, it is very difficult to determine the life expectancy of a product. Products that kids love one Christmas may sit on the shelf the following year. As a result, companies in the toy business often sell productive assets that are no longer needed. Assume on December 31, 19D (after adjusting entries), the records of

Fisher-Price showed the following data about a machine that was no longer needed to make a toy which was popular last year:

Machine, original cost	$52,000
Accumulated depreciation	27,500*

*Based on an eight-year estimated useful life, an $8,000 residual value, and straight-line depreciation.

On April 1, 19E, the machine was sold for $26,000 cash. The accounting period ends on December 31.

Required:

1. How old was the machine on January 1, 19E? Show computations.
2. Give the journal entry, or entries, related to the sale of the machine.

E8–15 Recording Accident and Insurance Indemnity on an Operational Asset

On September 30, 19C, a delivery truck owned by Queen Corporation was a total loss as a result of an accident. On January 1, 19C, the records showed the following:

Truck (estimated residual value, $2,000)	$12,000
Accumulated depreciation (straight-line, two years)	4,000

The truck was insured; therefore, the company collected $5,600 cash from the insurance company on October 5, 19C.

Required:

1. Based on the data given, compute the estimated useful life of the truck.
2. Give all the journal entries with respect to the truck from January 1 through October 5, 19C. Show computations.

Eastman Kodak

E8–16 Analyzing Depreciation Policy

The annual report for Eastman Kodak contained the following note:

Significant Accounting Policies
Depreciation. Depreciation expense is provided based on historical cost and the estimated useful lives of the assets. The Company generally uses the straight–line method for calculating the provision for depreciation. For assets in the United States acquired prior to January 1, 1992, the provision for depreciation is generally calculated using accelerated methods.

Required:

1. Explain the term *historical cost.* What is the meaning of "provision for depreciation"?
2. Why do you think the company changed its depreciation method for assets acquired in 1992 and subsequent years? What impact did the change have on net income?

Federal Express

E8–17 Comparing Depreciation for Tax and Financial Reporting

The annual report for Federal Express Corporation includes the following information:

For financial reporting purposes, depreciation and amortization of property and equipment is provided on a straight–line basis over the asset's service life. For income tax purposes, depreciation is generally computed using accelerated methods.

Explain why Federal Express uses different methods of depreciation for financial reporting and tax purposes.

E8–18 *Reporting Interest on Self-Constructed Assets*

Hilton Hotels

The financial statements for Hilton Hotels include the following note:

> **Summary of Significant Accounting Policies**
> *Property, Equipment and Depreciation*
> Property and equipment are stated at cost. Interest incurred during construction of facilities is capitalized and amortized over the life of the asset.

Required:

1. Why is it appropriate to capitalize interest on self-constructed assets?
2. What is the impact of this policy on the financial statements of Hilton?

PROBLEMS

P8–1 *Applying the Cost Principle to Determine the Cost of an Operational Asset*

On January 1, 19A, Tonkawa Company bought a machine for use in operations. The machine has an estimated useful life of eight years and an estimated residual value of $1,500. The expenditures given below were provided by the company:

a. Invoice price of the machine, $70,000.
b. Less: Cash discount of 2% on all cash paid by January 10.
c. Freight paid by the vendor per sales agreement, $800.
d. Installation costs, $2,000.
e. Payment of the $70,000 was made on January 15, 19A, as follows:
 (1) Tonkawa common stock, par $1; 2,000 shares (market value, $3 per share).
 (2) Note payable, $40,000, 12% due April 16, 19A (principal plus interest).
 (3) Balance of the invoice price settled with cash.

Required:

Compute the cost of the machine that the company should record. Explain the basis you used for any questionable items.

P8–2 *Basket Purchase Allocation: Record Cost and Depreciation—Three Methods*

Burton Company bought three used machines from J. Doe for a total cash price of $58,000. Transportation costs on the machines were $2,000. The machines immediately were overhauled, installed, and started operating. The machines were different; therefore, each had to be recorded separately in the accounts. An appraiser was employed to estimate their market value at date of purchase (prior to the overhaul and installation). The book values shown on Doe's books also are available. The book values, appraisal results, installation costs, and renovation expenditures were:

	Machine A	Machine B	Machine C
Book value—Doe	$8,000	$12,000	$6,000
Appraisal value	9,500	32,000	8,500
Installation costs	300	500	200
Renovation costs prior to use	2,000	400	600

Required:

1. Compute the cost of each machine by making a supportable allocation. Explain the rationale for the allocation basis used.
2. Give the journal entry to record the purchase of the three machines assuming all payments were cash. Set up a separate asset account for each machine.

3. Give the entry to record depreciation expense at the end of year 1, assuming:

	Estimates		
Machine	Life	Residual Value	Depreciation Method
A	5	$1,500	Straight-line
B	5	900	SYD
C	4	2,000	200% DB

Southwestern Bell

P8–3 Computing and Recording Depreciation Using Four Methods, and Explaining Effect of Depreciation on Cash Flow and EPS

Southwestern Bell provides telecommunication services to customers in Arkansas, Kansas, Missouri, Oklahoma and Texas. The assets of the company exceed $22 billion. As a result, depreciation is a significant item on the Southwestern Bell income statement. Assume that you are a financial analyst for Southwestern Bell and that you have been asked to determine the impact of alternative depreciation methods. For your analysis, you have been asked to compare methods based on a machine that cost $68,225. The estimated useful life is 10 years, and the estimated residual value is $2,225. The machine has an estimated useful life in productive output of 88,000 units. Actual output was 10,000 in year 1, and 8,000 in year 2.

Required:

1. Determine the appropriate amounts for the table below. Show your computations.

	Depreciation Expense		Book Value at End of	
Depreciation Method	Year 1	Year 2	Year 1	Year 2
Straight-line				
Units of production				
Sum-of-the-years' digits				
200% declining balance				

2. Give the adjusting entries for years 1 and 2 under each method.
3. In selecting a depreciation method, some companies assess the comparative effect on cash flow and EPS. Briefly comment on the depreciation methods in terms of effects on cash flow and EPS.

Reader's Digest

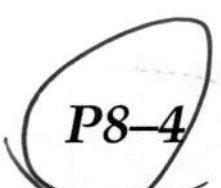

P8–4 Analyzing and Recording Entries Related to a Change in Estimated Life and Residual Value

Reader's Digest is a global publisher of magazines, books, and music and video collections, and one of the world's leading direct mail marketers. Many direct mail marketers use high-speed Didde press equipment to print their advertisements. These presses can cost over $ 1 million. Assume that Reader's Digest owns a Didde press that was acquired at an original cost of $400,000. It is being depreciated on a straight-line basis over a 20-year estimated useful life and has a $50,000 estimated residual value. At the end of 19H, the press had been depreciated for a full eight years. In January 19I, a decision was made, on the basis of improved maintenance procedures, that a total estimated useful life of 25 years, and a residual value of $73,000 would be more realistic. The accounting period ends December 31.

Required:

1. Compute (*a*) the amount of depreciation expense recorded in 19H and (*b*) the book value of the printing press at the end of 19H.
2. Compute the amount of depreciation that should be recorded in 19I. Show computations.
3. Give the adjusting entry for depreciation at December 31, 19I.

P8–5 *Computing Interest that Must Be Capitalized on an Operational Asset*

AMC Entertainment

AMC Entertainment is the second-largest motion picture exhibitor in the United States based on the number of screens that it operates. Last year, nearly 100 million people watched a movie in an AMC operated theater. The notes to a recent AMC annual report stated the following:

> Expenditures for additions (including interest during construction), major renewals and betterments are capitalized. Interest capitalized for the current year was $90,000.

To examine how AMC accounts for construction projects, assume that on January 1, 19A, AMC bought land at a cost of $130,000 and paid transfer fees of $5,000. Clearing the land and planning for the building construction was started immediately. Construction of a theater was started on April 1, 19A. The company borrowed about 75% of the funds to purchase the land and construct the theater at a 10% interest rate. The remaining cash needed was paid from company funds. Total interest cost for 19A was $25,000. The company made the following cash expenditures at the dates indicated:

January 1, 19A, down payment on the land (25%)	$ 32,500
January 1, 19A, transfer costs on the land	5,000
March 1, 19A, fees for preliminary surveys and work prior to start of construction	18,000
Progress payments to contractor for construction costs:	
May 31, 19A, No. 1	100,000
August 31, 19A, No. 2	300,000
November 30, 19A, No. 3 (end of the construction period)	200,000

Required:

1. Compute the cost of the theater with separate amounts for the land and building. Assume the construction period started on April 1, 19A. Show computations.
2. How much interest expense should be reported on the 19A income statement?

P8–6 *Recording Repairs and an Addition*

Federal Express

A recent annual report for Federal Express included the following note:

> **Property and equipment**
>
> Expenditures for major additions, improvements, flight equipment modifications and overhaul costs are capitalized. Maintenance and repairs are charged to expense as incurred.

Assume that Federal Express made extensive repairs on an existing building and added a new wing. The building is a garage and repair facility for delivery trucks that serve the Denver area. The existing building originally cost $420,000, and by the end of 19J (10 years) it was half depreciated on the basis of a 20-year estimated useful life and no residual value. During 19K, the following expenditures were made that were related to the building:

a. Ordinary repairs and maintenance expenditures for the year, $7,000 cash.

b. Extensive and major repairs to the roof of the building, $22,000 cash. These repairs were completed on June 30, 19K.

c. The new wing was completed on June 30, 19K, at a cash cost of $130,000. The wing had an estimated useful life of 10 years and no residual value.

Required:

1. Give the journal entry to record each of the 19K transactions.
2. Give the adjusting entry that would be required at the end of the annual accounting period, December 31, 19K, for the building after taking into account your entries in (1)

above. Assume straight-line depreciation. The company computes depreciation based on the nearest month.

3. Show how the assets would be reported on the December 31, 19K, balance sheet.

P8–7 *Analyzing, Recording, Adjusting Entries, and Computing Book Value Related to Five Different Intangible Assets*

Distance Company has five different intangible assets to be accounted for and reported on the financial statements. The management is concerned about the amortization of the cost of each of these intangibles. Facts about each intangible are:

a. **Patent.** The company purchased a patent at a cash cost of $54,600 on January 1, 19E. The patent had a legal life of 17 years from date of registration with the U.S. Patent Office, which was January 1, 19A. Amortize over the remaining legal life.

b. **Copyright.** On January 1, 19E, the company purchased a copyright for $22,500 cash. The legal life remaining from that date is 30 years. It is estimated that the copyrighted item will have no value by the end of 25 years.

c. **Franchise.** The company obtained a franchise from X Company to make and distribute a special item. The franchise was obtained on January 1, 19E, at a cash cost of $14,400 and covered a 12-year period.

d. **License.** On January 1, 19D, the company secured a license from the city to operate a special service for a period of five years. Total cash expended to obtain the license was $14,000.

e. **Goodwill.** The company started business in January 19C by purchasing another business for a cash lump sum of $400,000. Included in the purchase price was "Goodwill, $60,000." Company executives stated that "the goodwill is an important long-term asset to us." Amortize over the maximum period permitted.

Required:

1. Analyze each intangible asset and give the journal entry to record each of the five acquisitions.
2. Give the adjusting entry for each intangible asset that would be necessary at the end of the annual accounting period, December 31, 19E. Provide a brief explanation and show computations. If no entry is required for a particular item, explain the basis for your conclusion.
3. Give the book value of each intangible asset on January 1, 19G.

Reebok

P8–8 *Recording Purchase of a Business, Including Goodwill, Depreciation of Assets Acquired, and Amortization of Goodwill*

Reebok International is a leading worldwide designer, marketer and distributor of sport, fitness and lifestyle products, including footwear and apparel. The notes to a recent annual report from Reebok included the following:

> **Business Acquisitions**
>
> During the current year, the Company acquired the assets of Perfection Sport Fashions, Inc., a designer and marketer of performance apparel and accessories marketed under the *Tinley* brand name.

Assume that Reebok acquired Perfection Sport Fashions on January 5, 19A. Reebok acquired the name of the company and all of their assets, except cash, for $400,000 cash. The liabilities were not assumed by Reebok. The transaction was closed on January 5, 19A, at which time the balance sheet of Perfection Sport Fashions reflected the book values shown below:

PERFECTION SPORT FASHIONS
January 5, 19A

	Book Value	Market Value*
Accounts receivable (net)	$ 45,000	$ 45,000
Inventory	220,000	210,000
Operational assets (net)	32,000	60,000
Other assets	3,000	10,000
Total assets	$300,000	
Liabilities	$ 60,000	
Owners' equity	240,000	
Total liabilities and owners' equity	$300,000	

*These values for the assets purchased were provided to Reebok by an independent appraiser.

Required:

1. Give the journal entry by Reebok to record the purchase. Include goodwill. (Hint: Record the assets at market value in conformity with the cost principle.)
2. Give the adjusting entries that would be made by Reebok at the end of the annual accounting period, December 31, 19A, for:
   a. Depreciation of the operational assets (straight-line) assuming an estimated remaining useful life of 20 years and no residual value.
   b. Amortization of goodwill assuming the maximum amortization period is used.

P8–9 Recording the Disposal of Three Operational Assets

During 19K, Baldwin Company disposed of three different assets. On January 1, 19K, prior to their disposal, the accounts reflected the following:

Assets	Original Cost	Residual Value	Estimated Life	Accumulated Depreciation (Straight-Line)
Machine A	$20,000	$3,000	8 years	$12,750 (6 years)
Machine B	42,600	4,000	10 years	30,880 (8 years)
Machine C	76,200	4,200	15 years	57,600 (12 years)

The machines were disposed of in the following ways:

a. Machine A: Sold on January 1, 19K, for $8,200 cash.
b. Machine B: Sold on April 1, 19K, for $10,000; received cash, $3,000, and a $7,000 interest-bearing (12%) note receivable due at the end of 12 months.
c. Machine C: July 2, 19K, this machine suffered irreparable damage from an accident. On July 10, 19K, it was given to a salvage company at no cost. The salvage company agreed to remove the machine immediately at no cost. The machine was insured, and $18,500 cash was collected from the insurance company.

Required:

Give all journal entries related to the disposal of each machine. Explain the accounting rationale for the way that you recorded each disposal.

P8–10 Analyzing Five Transactions to Give Original Entry and Any Related Depreciation and Amortization Adjusting Entries

During the 19X5 annual accounting period, McGuire Company completed the following transactions:

a. On January 10, 19X5, paid $7,000 for a complete reconditioning of each of the following machines acquired on January 1, 19X1 (total cost, $14,000):

(1) Machine A: Original cost, $26,000; accumulated depreciation (straight-line) to December 31, 19X4 $18,400 ($3,000 residual value).

(2) Machine B: Original cost, $32,000; accumulated depreciation (straight-line) $13,000 ($6,000 residual value).

b. On July 1, 19X5, purchased a patent for $19,600 cash (estimated useful life, seven years).

c. On January 1, 19X5, purchased another business for cash $60,000 including $16,000 for goodwill. No liabilities were assumed by the company.

d. On September 1, 19X5, constructed a storage shed on some land leased from J. Doe. The cost was $10,600; the estimated useful life was five years with no residual value. The company uses straight-line depreciation. The lease will expire at the end of 19X8.

e. Total expenditures during 19X5 for ordinary repairs and maintenance were $4,800.

f. On July 1, 19X5, sold Machine A for $6,000 cash.

Required (compute depreciation to the nearest month):

1. For each of the above transactions, give the entry (or entries) that should be made during 19X5.
2. For each of the above transactions, give any adjusting entry that should be made at December 31, 19X5.

P8–11 *Chapter Supplement A: Recording the Sale of an Operational Asset under Two Assumptions—All Cash and Exchange*

Tiny Company operates a number of machines. One particular group of machines has six identical machines acquired on the same date. At the beginning of 19G, the operational asset account for the machines showed the following:

Machinery (Type A, six machines)	$360,000
Accumulated depreciation (Type A machines)	139,200*

*Based on 10-year estimated useful life and $2,000 residual value per machine and straight-line depreciation.

One of the machines (Type A) was disposed of on October 1, 19G.

Required:

1. How old were the Type A machines at January 1, 19G? Show computations.
2. What was the book value of the machine sold (at date of disposal)? Show computations. The company computes depreciation to the nearest full month.
3. Give all journal entries to record the disposal of the machine under two independent assumptions:
   a. It was sold outright for $30,000 cash.
   b. It was exchanged for a new similar machine having a list price of $57,000; however, it was determined that it could be purchased for $55,000 cash. The old machine was traded in, and $28,000 was paid in cash. Assume the machines were similar. No reasonable market value was determinable for the old machine.

P8–12 *Chapter Supplement A: Recording Exchanges of Similar and Dissimilar Machines, with and without a Cash Difference*

Ryan Company owned a particular machine (designated Machine R for case purposes) which no longer met their needs. On December 31, 19F, the records reflected the following:

Machine R:	
Original cost	$25,000
Accumulated depreciation	13,000

On January 3, 19G, the company acquired another machine (Machine S) and traded in Machine R. On this date, a reliable estimate of the market value of Machine R was $14,000.

Required:

1. Give the journal entry to record the transaction completed on January 3, 19G, for each of the following independent cases:
   a. Case A: The machines were similar, and no cash difference was paid or received.
   b. Case B: The machines were dissimilar, and no cash difference was paid or received.

   For each case, explain the underlying reasons for the amount that you recorded as the cost of Machine S.
2. Use the facts and requirements given above, except that for each case assume the company paid a $3,000 cash difference and that the market value of Machine S was $17,800.

P8–13 Analyzing an Accounting Change

Ford Motor Company

A recent annual report for Ford Motor Company included the following information:

Note 6. Net Property, Depreciation and Amortization—Automotive

Assets placed in service before January 1, 1993, are depreciated using an accelerated method. Assets placed in service beginning in 1993 will be depreciated using the straight-line method of depreciation. This change in accounting principle is being made to reflect improvements in the design and flexibility of manufacturing machinery and equipment and improvements in maintenance practices. These improvements have resulted in more uniform productive capacities and maintenance costs over the useful life of an asset. Straight-line is preferable in these circumstances. The change is expected to improve 1993 after-tax results by $80 to $100 million.

Required:

1. Prepare any journal entries that are required to reflect this accounting change.
2. What impact does this change have on cash flows for Ford?
3. Explain why "straight-line is preferable in these circumstances."
4. What other factors do you think management considered when they decided to make this accounting change?
5. As an investor, how would you react to the fact that Ford's net income will increase by $80 to $100 million as the result of this change?

CASES

C8–1 Analyzing the Age of Assets

Black & Decker

A note to a recent annual report for Black & Decker contained the following information (in $ thousands):

	Current Year	Previous Year
Land and improvements	$ 69,091	$ 20,963
Buildings	298,450	160,570
Machinery and equipment	928,151	626,453
	1,295,692	807,986
Less accumulated depreciation	468,511	404,591
	$ 827,181	$403,395

Depreciation expense (in $ thousands) charged to operations was $99,234 in the current year and $81,459 in the previous year. Depreciation is computed generally on the straight-line method for financial reporting purposes.

Required:

1. What is your best estimate of the average expected life for Black & Decker's depreciable assets?
2. What is your best estimate of the average age of Black & Decker's depreciable assets?

Eastman Kodak

C8–2 Analyzing the Sale of Assets

A recent annual report for Eastman Kodak reported that the balance of property, plant, and equipment at the end of the current year was $16,774 million. At the end of the previous year it was $15,667 million. During the current year, the company bought $2,118 million worth of new equipment. The balance of accumulated depreciation at the end of the current year was $8,146 million and at the end of the previous year was $7,654 million. Depreciation expense for the current year was $1,181 million. The annual report does not disclose any gain or loss on the disposition of property, plant, and equipment so you may assume the amount was zero. What amount of proceeds did Eastman Kodak receive when it sold property, plant, and equipment during the current year?

Amerada Hess Corporation

C8–3 Impact of the Capitalization of Interest on an Accounting Ratio

The capitalization of interest associated with self-constructed assets was discussed in this chapter. A recent annual report for Amerada Hess Corporation disclosed the following information concerning capitalization of interest:

> Interest costs related to certain long-term construction projects are capitalized to comply with FAS No. 34, "Capitalization of Interest Cost." Capitalized interest in the current year amounted to $34,897,000.

The income statement for that year disclosed that interest expense was $224,200,000. A popular accounting ratio used by some analysts is the interest coverage ratio (income ÷ interest expense). Explain why an analyst would calculate this ratio. Did Amerada Hess include the $34,897,000 in the reported interest expense of $224,200,000? If not, should an analyst include it when calculating the interest coverage ratio? Explain.

The Coca-Cola Company

C8–4 Analyzing of a Note Concerning Depreciation

A recent annual report for The Coca-Cola Company contained the following note:

> Property, plant, and equipment is stated at cost, less allowance for depreciation. Depreciation expense is determined principally by the straight-line method. The annual rates of depreciation are 2 percent to 10 percent for buildings and improvements and 7 percent to 34 percent for machinery, equipment, and containers.

Required:

1. What is the range of expected lives for buildings and improvements?
2. Explain why Coca-Cola depreciates the cost of their containers instead of including the total in cost of goods sold in the year the product is sold.

Grand Metropolitan

C8–5 Comparing Depreciation Methods in Different Countries

Grand Metropolitan is a major international company that is located in London. A recent annual report contained the following information concerning their accounting policies.

> **Fixed assets and depreciation**
>
> Fixed assets are stated at cost or at professional valuation. Cost includes interest, net of any tax relief, on capital employed in major developments.
> No depreciation is provided on freehold land. Other leaseholds are depreciated over the

unexpired period of the lease. All other buildings, plant, equipment, and vehicles are depreciated to residual values over their estimated useful lives within the following ranges:

Industrial buildings	25 to 100 years
Plant and machinery	3 to 25 years
Fixtures and fittings	3 to 17 years

Required:

Compare accounting for fixed assets and depreciation in England with procedures used in this country.

C8–6 *Financial Statement Analysis*

Toys "Я" Us

Refer to the financial statements of Toys "Я" Us given in Appendix B at the end of this book.

Required:

1. What method of depreciation is used by the company?
2. What are the amounts of accumulated depreciation and amortization at the end of the current year?
3. For depreciation purposes, what is the estimated useful life of furniture and equipment?
4. What was the original cost of buildings owned by the company at the end of the current year?
5. What amount of depreciation and amortization was reported as expense for the current year?

9

General Mills
CRISPIER
Now Better than Ever!
Better Toasted Oat Taste
Cheerios
Nestlé
ΜΕ 8 ΒΙΤΑΜΙΝΕΣ & ΣΙΔΗΡΟ
Cheerios
μέλι και αμύγδαλα
NET WT 5 LB (2.26kg)
AMERICA'S #1 FLOUR
Gold MEDAL
ALL-PURPOSE
ENRICHED • BLEACHED • PRESIFTED FLOUR
13 Quick and Easy Recipes
Betty Crocker
POP·SECRET
MICROWAVE POPCORN
ORIGINAL
Homestyle Hamburger Helper
Betty Crocker
ADD HAMBURGER
Betty Crocker
FRENCH VANILLA
VANILLE FRANÇAISE
SuperMoist
NO CHOLESTEROL
SANS CHOLESTEROL
Betty Crocker
CHEWY FRUIT SNACKS
FRUIT ROLL-UPS
CHERRY
CHURRERIA
SANTA ANA
Betty Crocker
Creamy Deluxe
FROSTING
CHOCOLATE
Yoplait
Original
BOYSENBERRY
FAT FREE
Colombo
Yoplait
LIGHT
RED RASPBERRY

MEASURING AND REPORTING LIABILITIES

In the previous chapters, we discussed business and accounting issues related to the assets held by a company. In this chapter and the next two, we will shift our focus to the other side of the balance sheet to see how managers finance the operations of their business and the acquisition of productive assets. We will discuss various types of liabilities in Chapters 9 and 10 and examine owners' equity in Chapter 11.

LEARNING OBJECTIVES

After studying this chapter you should be able to:

Management Decision Setting
GENERAL MILLS

Managing Capital Structure

Throughout the 1980s and 1990s, General Mills has been known as a leader in the food industry. The company sells a full line of familiar breakfast cereals, numerous snack foods, and the popular Betty Crocker products. General Mills also operates the Red Lobster and Olive Garden restaurants.

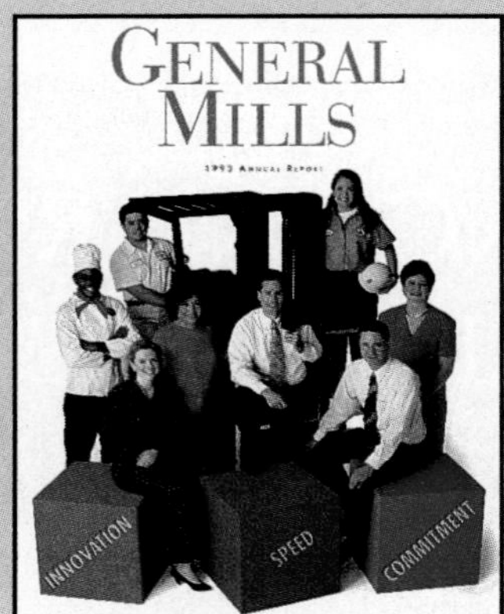

Management of General Mills has established aggressive goals for the company to meet by the year 2000. As you would expect, many of these goals involve increasing sales volume and improving operating efficiencies. We have abstracted from the annual report one of their financial goals:

> General Mills' financial goal for the 1990s is to achieve performance that places us in the top 10 percent of major American companies, ranked by the combination of growth in earnings per share and return on capital over a five-year period. Our major financial targets for top-decile performance include:
>
> * * * * *
>
> • Maintaining a Balance Sheet with a Strong "A" Bond Rating which will allow access to financing at reasonable costs.

Financial analysts consider a number of factors when they assess the strength of a balance sheet. One of the key areas they examine is how the company has financed its operations. The management of a company's liabilities is often as important as the management of a company's assets.

BUSINESS BACKGROUND

Businesses finance the acquisition of their assets from two sources: funds supplied by creditors (debt) and funds provided by owners (equity). The mixture of debt and equity used by a business is called its *capital structure*. Theoretically, managers could select virtually any capital structure for their company (e.g., 60% debt and 40% equity).

The balance sheet for General Mills (Exhibit 9–1) shows that total liabilities are approximately 74% of capital structure and equity is 26%. This compares with Kellogg Co., a principal competitor, which has a capital structure of 51% debt and 49% equity.

What factors do managers consider when they select a capital structure? The answer is a complex one that will be discussed in great detail in your finance courses. Two key factors that are taken into consideration are risk and return. Debt capital is more risky than equity because interest payments on debt are a legal obligation of the company. If a company is not able to meet a required interest payment because of a temporary cash shortage, the creditors may force the company into bankruptcy and require the sale of assets to satisfy the debt obligations. In contrast, dividend payments on stock are not a legal obligation until declared by the board of directors, which means that equity offers lower risk to the issuing corporation.

Despite the risk associated with debt, most companies include borrowed funds in their capital structure because these funds can be used to earn a higher rate of return for the stockholders. The higher rate of return can be earned whenever it is possible to borrow money at one rate (say 6%) and invest at a higher rate (say 8%). Borrowing at one rate and investing at a different rate is called *financial leverage* and is discussed in detail in the next chapter.

Companies that include debt in their capital structure must also make strategic decisions concerning the proper balance between short-term debt and long-term debt. Financial analysts calculate a number of accounting

General Mills' Balance Sheet **Exhibit 9–1**

CONSOLIDATED BALANCE SHEETS

In Millions	**May 30, 1993**	**May 31, 1992**
Assets		
Current Assets:		
Cash and cash equivalents	**$ 100.0**	$ .5
Receivables, less allowance for doubtful accounts of $4.3 in 1993 and $6.4 in 1992	**287.4**	291.9
Inventories	**439.0**	487.2
Prepaid expenses and other current assets	**108.2**	106.3
Deferred income taxes	**142.3**	148.7
Total Current Assets	**1,076.9**	1,034.6
Land, Buildings and Equipment, at cost	**2,859.6**	2,648.6
Other Assets	**714.3**	621.8
Total Assets	**$4,650.8**	$4,305.0
Liabilities and Stockholders' Equity		
Current Liabilities:		
Accounts payable	**$ 617.0**	$ 632.5
Current portion of long-term debt	**64.3**	32.6
Notes payable	**339.6**	169.3
Accrued taxes	**139.7**	127.9
Accrued payroll	**158.8**	165.0
Other current liabilities	**239.4**	244.4
Total Current Liabilities	**1,558.8**	1,371.7
Long-term Debt	**1,268.3**	920.5
Deferred Income Taxes	**262.0**	231.5
Deferred Income Taxes–Tax Leases	**195.6**	203.0
Accrued Postretirement Benefits	**72.1**	103.6
Other Liabilities	**75.5**	103.8
Total Liabilities	**3,432.3**	2,934.1
Stockholders' Equity:		
Cumulative preference stock, none issued	**—**	—
Common stock, 204.2 shares issued	**358.7**	343.6
Retained earnings	**2,284.5**	2,049.0
Less common stock in treasury, at cost, shares of 43.7 in 1993 and 38.7 in 1992	**(1,196.4)**	(802.9)
Unearned compensation and other	**(167.5)**	(172.3)
Cumulative foreign currency adjustment	**(60.8)**	(46.5)
Total Stockholders' Equity	**1,218.5**	1,370.9
Total Liabilities and Stockholders' Equity	**$4,650.8**	$4,305.0

See accompanying notes to consolidated financial statements.

ratios to evaluate a company's capital structure and the balance between short-term and long-term debt. In this chapter we will discuss both short-term and long-term debt. In the next chapter, we will discuss a special category of long-term debt, bonds payable.

LIABILITIES DEFINED AND CLASSIFIED

Learning Objective 1
Define and classify liabilities.

Most people have a reasonable understanding of the definition of the word *liability*. Accountants formally define **liabilities** as probable future sacrifices of economic benefits. Liabilities arise from present obligations of an entity to transfer assets or provide services to other entities in the future as a result of past transactions or events. As shown on the balance sheet (Exhibit 9–1), General Mills borrowed long-term debt of $1,268,300,000 at some point in the past from a group of creditors (a past transaction). The company has a current obligation to pay cash (an asset) to those creditors at some time in the future

Liabilities are probable future sacrifices of economic benefits that arise from past transactions.

based on the borrowing agreement. Because of this obligation, General Mills must record a long-term debt.

When a liability is first recorded, it is measured in terms of its current cash equivalent, which is the cash amount that a creditor would accept to settle the liability at the current time. General Mills borrowed $1,268,300,000 but will repay much more than that because the company must repay the money it borrowed plus interest that accrues on the debt. Interest that will be paid in the future is not included in the amount of the liability because interest accrues (and becomes a liability) with the passage of time.

General Mills, like most businesses, has several kinds of liabilities and a wide range of creditors. Users of financial statements rely on the statements for relevant information about the kinds and amounts of liabilities owed by the entity. The listing of liabilities on the balance sheet will be different for almost every company that you study because different operating activities will result in different types of liabilities.

Current liabilities are short-term obligations that will be paid within the current operating cycle or one year, whichever is longer.

The liability section of the General Mills report begins with the caption "current liabilities." **Current liabilities** are defined as short-term obligations that will be paid within the current operating cycle of the business or within one year of the balance sheet date, whichever is longer. Most companies have an operating cycle that is less than one year. In the majority of situations you encounter, current liabilities can be defined simply as liabilities that are due within one year. Noncurrent liabilities include all liabilities not properly classified as current liabilities.

FINANCIAL ANALYSIS

Evaluating Liquidity

Most analysts evaluate the amount of current liabilities in relation to the amount of current assets. Remember that if a company fails to meet its debt obligations, creditors can force the company into bankruptcy. Current liabilities, by definition, must be paid in the near future. As a result, analysts want to assess the probability that the company will be able to meet its current obligations.

The **current ratio** is the ratio of total current assets divided by total current liabilities.

Working capital is the dollar difference between total current assets and total current liabilities.

When evaluating the ability of a company to meet its short-term obligations, analysts often calculate the **current ratio** (current assets ÷ current liabilities). This relationship can also be expressed as a dollar amount called **working capital** (current assets – current liabilities).

The balance sheet for General Mills reports current assets of $1,076,900,000 and current liabilities of $1,558,800,000. Their current ratio is 0.69 which means that the company has 69 cents worth of current assets for every $1 of current liabilities. The current ratio for General Mills is unusually low. Most companies report a current ratio between 1.0 and 2.0. In comparison, the current ratio for the Kellogg Co. is 1.2.

A very low current ratio is not necessarily cause for concern. Other factors must be taken into consideration. General Mills generates very strong cash flows from operating activities, has $100 million in cash, and has a line of credit that gives it the right to borrow $250 million from a bank if cash is needed. For these reasons, most analysts would not be concerned about the low current ratio for General Mills.

Liabilities are very important from an analytical perspective because they affect a company's future cash flows and risk characteristics. Most analysts devote a considerable amount of time to reviewing the liabilities of a company. The easiest way for us to discuss the topic of liabilities is to review them in the same order that they are listed on most balance sheets. In this manner, you will have a better understanding of the information reported on the balance sheet. We will focus on the liabilities that you have not been exposed to in previous chapters.

CURRENT LIABILITIES

Accounts Payable

Learning Objective 2
Record and report current liabilities.

Most companies do not produce all the goods and services that they use in their basic operating activities. Instead, they purchase these goods and services from other businesses. Typically, these transactions involve credit terms with cash payments made after the goods and services have been provided. Trade accounts payable are created in the normal course of business as the result of the purchase of goods and services. The term *accounts payable* is used in accounting to mean trade accounts payable. For many companies, trade credit is a relatively inexpensive way to finance the purchase of inventory. Interest does not normally accrue on accounts payable. As an incentive to encourage more sales, some vendors offer very generous credit terms which may give the buyer the opportunity to resell merchandise and collect cash before payment must be made to the original vendor.

It may be tempting for some managers to delay payment to suppliers for as long as possible to conserve cash. This strategy normally is not advisable. Most successful companies develop positive working relationships with their suppliers. These relationships assure quality goods and services. A positive relationship can be destroyed by slow payment of debt. Financial analysts are also concerned if a business does not meet its obligations to trade creditors on a timely basis because this slowness is often an indication of financial distress.

For General Mills , the single largest current liability is accounts payable ($617 million). As you can see, trade creditors are an important source of financing for General Mills. Journal entries associated with accounts payable were discussed in Chapter 7.

General Mills is a company dedicated to helping the community and environment through employee volunteers. One such program employed the help of approximately 425 Minneapolis employees and retirees pledging over 8,000 hours of labor to build housing with Twin Cities Habitat for Humanity.

Accrued Liabilities

Accrued liabilities are expenses that have been incurred but have not yet been paid at the end of the accounting period.

In many situations, a business will incur an expense in one accounting period and make cash payment for the expense in a subsequent period. **Accrued liabilities** (also called *accrued expenses*) are recorded when expenses have been incurred before the end of an accounting period but have not yet been paid. These expenses include such items as property taxes, electricity, and salaries. Accrued liabilities are recorded as adjusting entries at year-end (because no exchange transaction has taken place). Adjusting entries were discussed in Chapter 4.

Income Taxes Payable

Corporations, like individuals, must pay taxes on income that is earned. Corporate tax rates are graduated with large corporations paying a top federal tax rate of 35%. In addition, corporations may pay state and local income taxes and in some cases, foreign income taxes. The notes to the General Mills annual report include the following information:

Real World Excerpt

General Mills Annual Report

Note Fifteen: Income Taxes
The components of earnings before taxes and the income tax thereon are as follows:

	(millions of dollars)		
	1993	**1992**	**1991**
Earnings (loss) before taxes:			
U.S.	$887.2	$818.3	$710.4
Foreign	(43.2)	26.2	55.2
Total	$844.0	$844.5	$765.6
Income taxes:			
Federal	$243.1	$254.0	$238.3
State and local	60.2	55.1	49.9
Foreign	(6.2)	16.3	12.3
Total	$297.1	$325.4	$300.5

Notice on the General Mills balance sheet (Exhibit 9–1) that the amount of accrued taxes for 1993 ($139.7 million) differs from the amount of taxes reported in the previous note. The amount of taxes reported in the note represents the tax obligation for the year. Some of that obligation was paid in cash during the year. The amount of taxes shown on the balance sheet is the amount accrued during the year but unpaid at year-end.

Payroll Liabilities

Liabilities associated with unpaid salaries may be reported as part of accrued liabilities or as a separate item, as is the case with General Mills. In addition to accruing salaries that have been earned but unpaid, companies must also accrue the cost of benefits. These benefits include retirement programs, vacation time, Social Security benefits, health insurance, and many others.

All salaries and wages are taxed. The largest deductions for most people are the following two categories of taxes:

Employee Income Taxes Federal laws (as well as many state and local laws) require the employer to deduct an appropriate amount of income tax each period from the gross earnings of each employee. The amount of income tax withheld from the employee's wages is recorded by the employer as a current liability between the date of deduction and the date the amount withheld is remitted to the government.

Employee FICA Taxes The Social Security taxes paid by the employee are called FICA taxes because they are required by the Federal Insurance Contributions Act. The funds required by the government to provide the benefits under the Social Security Act are obtained by payroll taxes, which are imposed in equal amounts on both the employee and the employer. Effective January 1, 1995, the FICA rate was 7.65% on the first $61,200 paid to each employee during the year. In addition, the 1.45% of FICA attributable to Medicare applies to income above $61,200.

To illustrate the basic accounting entry for the payment of a payroll and the accrual of liabilities for the employee deductions, assume that General Mills accumulated the following data in the detailed payroll records for the last pay period of December 19B:

Salaries and wages earned	$600,000
Income taxes withheld	120,000
FICA taxes	42,000

The entry to record the payroll and employee deductions would be:

Dec. 31, 19A:	Salary and wage expense	600,000	
	Employee benefit expense	42,000	
	Liability for income taxes withheld—employees		120,000
	FICA taxes payable—employees' share		42,000
	FICA taxes payable—employer's share		42,000
	Salaries payable		438,000

Notice that the expense for employees' services is more than the salary and wage expense. This occurs because the employer must pay Social Security taxes based on salary and wages that have been earned.

Other Payroll Liabilities

Most businesses grant employees paid vacation time based on the number of months they have worked (e.g., one vacation day for each month). Under the matching concept, the cost of vacation time must be recorded in the year that employees perform service (i.e., help generate revenue) instead of the year that they actually take vacation. If General Mills estimated the cost of accrued vacation time was $125,000, the following adjusting entry would be made:

Dec. 31, 19B:	Salary and wage expense	125,000	
	Accrued vacation liability		125,000

When the vacations were taken, the accountant would record:

Aug. 31, 19C:	Accrued vacation liability	125,000	
	Cash		125,000

Accrued vacation liabilities usually are not large relative to other liabilities but they can be substantial in amount. In a recent statement, Eastman Kodak Company reported the following information in a note:

Real World Excerpt

Eastman Kodak Company Annual Report

PAYABLES AND SHORT-TERM BORROWINGS

	(in millions)	
	1992	**1991**
Accrued payrolls	220	231
Accrued vacation pay	345	325

As you can see, the liability for accrued vacation pay is actually larger than the accrued payroll liability. The accrued vacation liability for Eastman Kodak was approximately 2% of its total liabilities. Because of the size of these liabilities, some managers try to control the amount of accrued vacation liability by requiring employees to take vacations each year. A few years ago, managers of IBM offered employees an incentive to take vacation before the end of the fiscal year in an effort to reduce the amount of the accrued vacation liability reported on the balance sheet.

General Mills does not separately disclose the amount of accrued vacation liability. Instead it is shown on the balance sheet as part of accrued payroll. Apparently, in the opinion of management, the amount of accrued vacation liability is not a material factor in the analysis of General Mills. Most analysts would probably agree.

Deferred Revenues and Service Obligations

In most business transactions, cash is paid after the product or service has been delivered. In some cases, cash is paid before delivery. You have probably paid for several magazines that you will receive at some time in the future. The publisher collects money for your subscription in advance of publishing the magazine. When a company collects cash before the related revenue has been earned, this cash is called **deferred revenues** (or *unearned revenues* or *revenues collected in advance*). Under the revenue principle, revenue cannot be recorded until it has been earned.

Deferred revenues are revenues that have been collected but not earned; liabilities until the goods or services are provided.

Deferred revenues are reported as a liability because cash has been collected but the related revenue has not been earned by the end of the accounting period. There is an obligation to provide the services or goods in the future. Accounting for deferred revenues was discussed in Chapter 6.

Another example of a liability associated with the obligation to provide a service in the future is the frequent-flyer programs offered by most major airlines. Under these programs, customers earn free tickets by flying a certain number of miles. Each year, these airlines must make an adjusting entry to record the estimated expense and related liability associated with awarding free tickets. The following note from a recent Southwest Airlines annual report illustrates this policy:

Real World Excerpt

Southwest Airlines Annual Report

Frequent flyer awards. The Company accrues the estimated incremental cost of providing free travel awards under its Company Club frequent flyer program.

Notice that the amount of the liability is the incremental cost of providing free travel and not the actual selling price of an airline ticket. Some analysts believe that the true cost of a frequent flyer program is the lost revenue associated with giving a ticket to a customer instead of selling it. These analysts believe that the liabilities reported for frequent flyer programs are severely understated. Currently GAAP permits recording these liabilities based on incremental cost because there is no accurate method to estimate the number of travelers who would have bought tickets if they had not earned a free award.

Many companies offer warranties on the products they sell. This is another form of future service obligations. The cost of providing repair work must be estimated and recorded as a liability (and expense) in the period in which the product is sold. General Mills, like most companies, quickly refunds money for any defective products that it sells. The company does not report a liability for this type of obligation because the company estimates that it is immaterial in amount.

Notes Payable

Creditors are willing to lend cash because they will earn interest to compensate them for giving up the use of their money for a period of time. This simple concept is called the **time value of money**. The word *time* is significant because the longer borrowed money is held, the larger is the total dollar amount of interest expense. There is more interest for a two-year loan, at a given interest rate, than for a one-year loan. To the *borrower*, interest is an expense; to the *creditor*, interest is a revenue.

The **time value of money** is interest that is associated with the use of money over time.

To calculate interest, three variables must be considered: (1) the principal (i.e., the cash that was borrowed), (2) the annual interest rate, and (3) the time period for the loan. The interest formula is:

$$\text{Interest} = \text{Principal} \times \text{Interest rate} \times \text{Time}$$

The basic accounting for a note is the same whether it is long term or short term. Assume that on November 1, 19A, General Mills borrowed $100,000 cash on a one-year, 12% note payable. The interest is payable on December 31 and June 30. The principal is payable at the maturity date of the note, October 31, 19B. The note is recorded in the accounts as follows:

Nov. 1, 19A:	Cash	100,000	
	Note payable, short-term		100,000

Interest is an expense of the period when the money is used. Under the matching concept, interest expense is recorded when it is incurred rather than when the cash actually is paid. When does General Mills incur interest cost associated with the note that was recorded in the previous journal entry? Because the company uses the money for two months during 19A, it should record interest expense in 19A for two months. During 19B, the company uses the money for 10 months; therefore, it should record interest expense for 10 months in 19B.

The computation of interest expense is shown below:

Interest	=	Principal	×	Interest rate	×	Time
$2,000	=	$100,000	×	12%	×	2/12

The entry to record interest expense is:

Dec. 31, 19A:	Interest expense	2,000	
	Cash		2,000

Current Portion of Long-Term Debt

Learning Objective 3
Compare current and long-term liabilities.

The distinction between current and long-term debt is an important one for both managers and analysts because current debt must be paid within the next year. The company must have sufficient cash to repay currently maturing debt. In order to provide accurate information concerning current liabilities, long-term debt within a year of its maturity date must be reclassified as a current liability. Assume that General Mills signed a five-year note payable of $500,000 on January 1, 19A. Repayment is in two installments as follows: December 31, 19D, $250,000; December 31, 19E, $250,000. The December 31, 19B, 19C, and 19D, balance sheets would report the following:

Dec. 31, 19B:
Long-term liabilities:
Note payable $500,000

December 31, 19C:	
Current liabilities:	
Current portion of long-term note	250,000
Long-term liabilities:	
Long-term note	250,000
December 31, 19D:	
Current liabilities:	
Current portion of long-term note	250,000

An example of this type of disclosure can be seen in Exhibit 9–1. Notice that General Mills reported $64.3 million as the current portion of long-term debt in 1993 which will be paid in full during the following accounting period.

FINANCIAL ANALYSIS

Refinanced Debt: Current or Noncurrent?

Many companies refinance their debt when it matures. Instead of repaying the debt from current cash that is available, the company either signs a new loan agreement with a new maturity date or borrows money from a new creditor and repays the original creditor. An interesting accounting question arises if a company intends to refinance debt and has the ability to do so: should currently maturing debt that will be refinanced be classified as a current or long-term liability? Remember that analysts are interested in the current liabilities of a company because these liabilities will generate cash outflows in the next accounting period. If the liability will not generate a cash outflow in the next accounting period, GAAP requires that it should not be classified as current. This rule can be illustrated with a note from the General Mills annual report:

Real World Excerpt
General Mills Annual Report

> We have entered into a new agreement in July 1993, which expires in July 1996. This agreement provides us with the ability to refinance short-term borrowings on a long-term basis, and therefore we have reclassified a portion of our short-term notes payable to long-term.

LONG-TERM LIABILITIES

Many companies use long-term liabilities to generate funds to purchase operational assets. Indeed, many financial analysts like to see companies maintain a reasonable balance between the expected life of an asset and the term of the financing that was used to acquire the asset. To illustrate the analysts' concern, consider what would happen if General Mills purchased equipment that had an expected life of 10 years during which time it was expected to provide a 12% return on investment. The company would create additional risk if it financed the purchase with a one-year bank loan that it intended to renew each year during the life of the asset. In the first year, interest rates might be 8% which would provide a net return on the equipment of 4% (12% – 8%). If interest rates increased in subsequent years, General Mills might experience losses on the operation of the equipment. If interest rates were 14% when the loan was renewed, the company would have a net negative return of 2% (12% – 14%). General Mills could lessen this type of risk by using long-term debt to finance the acquisition of long-lived assets.

Long-term liabilities include long-term notes payable and bonds payable which are contracts that specify the terms of the borrowing agreement (e.g., interest rate and repayment schedule). **Long-term liabilities** include all obligations of the entity not classified as current liabilities.

Long-term liabilities are all obligations of the entity that are not classified as current liabilities.

To reduce risk for creditors who are willing to lend money for a long period (which, in turn, reduces the interest rate that must be paid), some companies pledge specific assets as security for the liability. A liability supported by this type of pledge (typically a mortgage) is called *secured debt.* An *unsecured debt* is one for which the creditor relies primarily on the integrity and general earning power of the borrower.

Long-term liabilities are reported on the balance sheet immediately following current liabilities. Notice the example for General Mills in Exhibit 9–1. The accounts long-term debt, deferred income taxes, deferred income taxes—tax leases, accrued postretirement benefits, and other liabilities are all long-term liabilities despite the fact that there is no separate caption to identify them as such.

Long-Term Debt

Companies can raise long-term debt capital directly from a number of financial service organizations including banks, insurance companies, and pension plans. Raising debt from one of these organizations is known as a *private placement.* This type of debt often is called a *note payable,* which is a written promise to pay a stated sum at one or more specified future dates called the *maturity dates.*

In many cases, a company's need for debt capital will exceed the financial ability of any single creditor. In these situations, the company may issue publicly traded debt called *bonds*. The bonds can be traded in established markets that provide bondholders with liquidity. They can sell their bonds to other investors prior to maturity if they have an immediate need for cash. Notes and bonds are very similar because they are both written promises to pay a debt. Bonds will be discussed in detail in the next chapter.

AN INTERNATIONAL PERSPECTIVE

Borrowing in Foreign Currencies

Over the past years, business operations have become more global. Successful corporations market their products in many countries and locate manufacturing facilities around the world based on cost and productivity considerations. The financing of corporations has also become international, even in cases where the company does not have international operations.

Many corporations with foreign operations elect to finance those operations with foreign debt to lessen the *exchange rate risk.* This type of risk exists because the relative value of each nation's currency varies on virtually a daily basis because of various economic factors. As this book is being written, the British pound is worth approximately $1.60. A year earlier, it was worth $1.75. A U.S. company that owed debt denominated in pounds would gain from this decline in the value of the pound.

A U.S. corporation that conducts business operations in England might decide to borrow pounds to finance its operations. The profits from the business will be in pounds which can be used to pay off the debt which is in pounds. If the business earned profits in pounds but paid off debt in dollars, the company would be exposed to exchange rate risk because the relative value of the dollar and the pound fluctuate.

Foreign corporations face this same problem. A note to a recent annual report from Toyota (a Japanese company) stated:

> Earnings declined in the current year ended, as the appreciation of the yen aggravated the adverse effects of sluggish demand....The movement in exchange rates reduced operating income of the company. Losses on currency exchange thus offset most of the cost savings we achieved.

Real World Excerpt

Toyota Annual Report

Toyota has borrowed a large amount of money in the United States to lessen the exchange rate risk that it faces. The company also owns and operates many factories in this country.

While many of these packages seem familiar, notice that they are international versions of General Mills products.

Even if a company does not have international operations, it may elect to borrow in foreign markets. When a country is experiencing a recession, interest rates are often low. These situations give corporations the opportunity to borrow money at a lower cost.

Accountants must convert, or translate, foreign debt into U.S. dollars for reporting purposes. Conversion rates for all major currencies are published in most newspapers. These rates change on a daily basis due to economic factors. To illustrate foreign currency translation, assume that General Mills borrowed 1 million pounds (£). For the General Mills annual report, the accountant must use the conversion rate for the balance sheet date, which we will assume was £1.00 to $1.60. The dollar equivalent of the debt is $1,500,000 (£1,000,000 x 1.60 = $1,600,000). As you can see, the dollar equivalent of foreign debt may change if the conversion rate changes even when there are no additional borrowings or repayments.

The notes to the balance sheet for General Mills indicate that the company has borrowed money primarily in the United States and Canada. In contrast, consider the following note from the Washington Post (in thousands):

Real World Excerpt

Washington Post Annual Report

	1992	1991
10.1 percent unsecured European Currency Unit notes due in 1996	$50,442	$50,515
10.68 percent unsecured promissory notes due in 1991–1994		25,000
10.875 percent unsecured Eurodollar notes due in 1995	1,400	1,400
Less amounts included in current liabilities		(25,000)

Despite the fact that 96% of the assets owned by the Washington Post Company are located in the United States, the company borrows heavily in international markets. This is typical for most large corporations and is further justification for business executives to develop an understanding of international markets. The note above uses two terms that may not be familiar to you. *Eurodollars* are U.S. dollars that are deposited outside the U.S. banking system; in this case, in Europe. A *European Currency Unit* is an index of 10 European currencies. It is used as a basis for borrowing and lending but is not an actual currency that can be used by consumers to purchase merchandise.

Self-Study Quiz

In an earlier example, we assumed that the $100,000 note payable for General Mills required payment of interest on December 31 and June 30 of each year. Review that example and now assume that the note required the payment of interest on January 31 and July 31 of each year.

1. What adjusting entry should General Mills make at the end of their fiscal year on December 31, 19A?
2. What entry should the company make on January 31, 19B?
3. What entry should the company make on July 31, 19B?

After you have completed your answers, check them with the solutions in the footnote at the bottom of this page.*

OTHER TOPICS

There are two areas of business operations that may result in the creation of either an asset or a liability. These areas involve accounting for income taxes and employee retirement benefits. On most financial statements, you will see these items as liabilities, so we will discuss them along with other liabilities.

Deferred Taxes

Learning Objective 4
Apply deferred income tax allocation.

In previous chapters, we made simplifying assumptions concerning tax expense. We often told you the amount of tax expense (e.g., $100,000) and had you make a journal entry similar to the following:

Tax expense	100,000	
Taxes payable		100,000

Because there are separate rules governing the preparation of financial statements (GAAP) and tax returns (Internal Revenue Code), the amount of income before taxes reported on the income statement is normally different from the amount of taxable income computed on the tax return. This difference creates an interesting accounting problem: should tax expense on the income statement be based on the income that is reported on the income statement or income reported on the tax return? Accountants have resolved this issue by applying the matching concept. They determine tax expense based on the amount of income reported on the income statement because tax expense is a necessary cost associated with earning income and therefore should be recorded in the same period as the related income. This means that the amount of *tax expense* and the amount of *taxes payable* are normally different. In order to have our journal entry balance, we need a new account. This new account is called Deferred Taxes. In practice, deferred taxes can be either assets or liabilities but in most cases will be liabilities. Notice in Exhibit 9–1 that General Mills has deferred tax amounts reported as both assets and liabilities.

Deferred tax items exist because of timing differences caused by reporting revenues and expenses according to GAAP on a company's income statement and according to the Internal Revenue Code on the tax return.

Deferred tax items exist because of timing differences in reporting revenues and expenses on a company's income statement and tax return. These **temporary differences** are caused by differences in GAAP that govern financial statement preparation and the Internal Revenue Code that governs the preparation of tax returns. General Mills uses straight-line depreciation for its financial statements and accelerated depreciation for its tax return. As a result, it reports lower income on the tax return than on the income statement.

Temporary differences are timing differences that cause deferred income taxes and will reverse, or turn around, in the future.

*1.	Interest expense	2,000	
	Interest payable		2,000
2.	Interest expense	1,000	
	Interest payable	2,000	
	Cash		3,000
3.	Interest expense	6,000	
	Cash		6,000

Assume that General Mills computed taxes payable of $80,000 based on the numbers reported on the tax return and tax expense of $100,000 based on the income statement. The company would record its tax obligation as follows:

Tax expense	100,000	
Deferred taxes		20,000
Taxes payable		80,000

The deferred tax amount will be paid in the future when depreciation expense "reverses." By this we mean that at some point in the future, the accelerated depreciation recorded on the tax return will be less than the straight-line depreciation reported on the income statement (remember from Chapter 8 that accelerated depreciation causes higher depreciation expense compared to straight-line in the early years of an asset's life and lower depreciation in the later years). When a temporary difference reverses, the deferred tax amount is reduced.

The notes to the General Mills annual report contain the following information concerning the causes of its deferred taxes:

Real World Excerpt

General Mills Annual Report

Note Fifteen: Income taxes

Deferred income taxes result from timing differences in the recognition of revenue and expense for tax and financial statement purposes. The tax effects of these differences follow:

	(in millions)		
	1993	**1992**	**1991**
Depreciation	$11.5	$ 6.5	$10.8
Prepaid pensions	15.3	16.8	16.1
Accrued expenses	4.4	(1.1)	(28.0)
Other	9.6	(8.7)	2.0
Total deferred income taxes	$40.8	13.5	.9

The computation of deferred taxes involves some complexities that are discussed in advanced accounting courses. At this point, we want you to understand that deferred tax liabilities are caused by temporary differences between the income statement and the tax return and that these taxes will be paid at some future time when the difference that caused the deferred taxes is reported on the tax return.

Accrued Retirement Benefits

Learning Objective 5
Explain liabilities for retirement benefits.

Most employers provide retirement programs for their employees. In a *defined contribution* program, the employer will make cash payments to a fund that will invest the money and earn income. When employees retire, they are entitled to a portion of the fund. If the investment strategy of the fund is successful, the retirement income for the employees will be larger. If the strategy is not successful, the retirees will get less money. The employer's only obligation is to make the required annual payments to the fund, which are recorded as pension expense.

As an alternative, some employers offer *defined benefit* programs. Under these programs, employees' retirement benefits are based on a percentage of the employee's pay at retirement or a certain number of dollars for each year of employment. The employer must record pension expense each year. Basically, the amount of pension expense that must be accrued each year is the change in the current cash value of the employee's retirement package. The current cash value changes each year for a variety of reasons. For example, the current cash value changes each year (1) as the employee is closer to receiving benefits, (2) as the retirement benefits increase as the result of higher pay or longer service, or (3) if the employee's life expectancy changes. The company must report a pension liability based on any portion of the current cash value of the retirement program that has not actually been funded. For example, if the company transferred $8 million to the pension fund manager but the current cash value of the pension program was $10 million, the company would report a $2 million pension liability on its balance sheet.

The financial obligation associated with defined benefit retirement programs can be very large for many corporations, especially those with unionized work forces. A recent financial statement for Ford Motor Company disclosed the following information:

Real World Excerpt

Ford Motor Company Annual Report

Note 2: Employee Retirement Benefits
(in millions)

Accumulated Postretirement Benefit Obligation	
Retirees	$ 7,035.0
Active employees eligible to retire	2,269.6
Other active employees	5,090.6
Total accumulated obligation	$14,395.2

To put the size of this obligation in perspective, it represents an amount nearly equal to the company's total stockholders' equity. The retirement benefit expense for the year was $1.3 billion which exceeded the income earned by Ford for the previous three years.

General Mills does not have a pension liability on its balance sheet because it has made cash payments to the retirement fund that are greater than the current value of the pension benefits. The notes report:

Real World Excerpt

General Mills Annual Report

Note six: Balance Sheet Information (in millions)

	1993	1992
Other assets:		
Prepaid pension	$257.4	$217.4

This information is important to analysts who are forecasting the future cash flows of a company. Ford has a much larger obligation to transfer cash to its retirement fund than does General Mills.

In recent years, there has been a great deal of discussion concerning employer-provided health care benefits. Many large companies pay for a portion of their employees' health insurance costs. The payments are recorded as an expense in the current accounting period. Some employers agree to continue to pay for health care costs after employees retire. The cost of these future benefits must be estimated and recorded as an expense in the periods when the employees perform services. The recording of future health care costs for retired employees is an excellent example of the use of estimates in accounting. Imagine the difficulty of estimating future health care costs when you do not know how long employees will live, how healthy they will be during their lives, and how much doctors and hospitals will charge for their services in the future.

Accounting for retirement benefits is a complex topic that is discussed in detail in subsequent accounting courses. This topic is introduced at this point as another example of the application of the matching concept, which requires that expenses be recorded in the year the benefit is received. It also illustrates how accounting avoids the creation of improper incentives for managers. If the future cost of retirement benefits were not included in the period in which work was performed, managers might have the incentive to offer employees increases in their retirement benefits instead of increases in their salaries. In this manner, managers could understate the true cost of employee services and make it appear as if their companies were more profitable. Many economists argue that the local, state, and federal governments have fallen into this trap. Government officials can give large pensions to current workers without the cost being recognized until the employee retires. By doing this, governments can appear to be very efficient when in reality they are simply deferring costs to the future.

CONTINGENT LIABILITIES

Learning Objective 6
Record and report contingent liabilities.

A **contingent liability** is a potential liability that has arisen as a result of a past event; not an effective liability until some future event occurs.

Each of the liabilities that we have discussed is reported on the balance sheet with a specific dollar amount. Each of these liabilities involves the *probable* future sacrifice of economic benefits. Some transactions or events create a *potential* (but not probable) future sacrifice of economic benefits. These situations create **contingent liabilities,** which are potential liabilities that have arisen because of events or transactions that have already occurred. The conversion of a contingent liability to a recorded liability depends on one or more future events. A situation that causes a contingent liability also causes a contingent loss.

Whether a situation causes a recorded or a contingent liability depends on the probability of the future economic sacrifice and the ability of management to estimate the amount of the liability. The following chart illustrates the various possibilities:

	Probable	Reasonably Possible	Remote
Subject to Estimate	Record as liability	Disclose in note	Disclosure not required
Not Subject to Estimate	Disclose in note	Disclose in note	Disclosure not required

The probabilities of occurrence are defined in the following manner:

1. Probable—the future event or events are likely to occur.
2. Reasonably possible—the chance of the occurrence of the future event or events is more than remote but less than likely.
3. Remote—the chance of occurrence of the future event or events is slight.

When recording liabilities, a company must determine whether the amount of any liability can be reasonably estimated. The general accounting guidelines are *(a)* a liability that is *both* probable and can be reasonably estimated must be recorded and reported on the balance sheet, *(b)* a liability that is reasonably possible (whether it can be estimated or not) must be disclosed in a note in the financial statements, and *(c)* remote contingencies are not disclosed.

The notes to General Mills annual report include the following:

Real World Excerpt
General Mills Annual Report

We are contingently liable under guarantees and comfort letters for $87.9 million. The guarantees and comfort letters are issued to support borrowing arrangements primarily for our joint ventures.

The company did not have to record a liability on the balance sheet because the chance of having a loss from these guarantees was not probable. Another common contingency was disclosed by Harley-Davidson:

Notice the emphasis that General Mills has placed on low-fat products. Successful companies must respond quickly to changes in consumer preferences.

Real World Excerpt

Harley-Davidson Annual Report

Note 7. Commitments and Contingencies

A state court jury in California found the Company liable for compensatory and punitive damages of $7.2 million, including interest, in a lawsuit brought by a supplier of aftermarket exhaust systems. The Company immediately appealed the verdict.

In this case, the existence of a liability was a reasonable possibility. As a result, Harley-Davidson was required by GAAP to disclose the lawsuit. The company subsequently reached an out-of-court settlement for $5 million. At that point, the loss was probable, which required recording the loss and the related liability.

General Mills Epilogue

As this book is being written, General Mills has announced plans to spin-off their restaurant operations into a separate corporation. The company announced that its goal was to free up resources and management of two fundamentally different businesses whose strategic and operating needs did not mesh.

The news was greeted with mixed emotions on Wall Street. Some analysts expressed concern about the new restaurant company's ability to attract needed capital (e.g., borrow money) once it was separate from General Mills.

PRESENT AND FUTURE VALUE CONCEPTS

Learning Objective 7
Apply the concepts of the future and present values of a single amount.

We have discussed the account classifications that you will encounter on most of the balance sheets that you will study. Before we leave the topic of liabilities, we want to introduce you to an important concept underlying most liabilities.

In our earlier discussion of notes payable, we looked at a very basic situation. To properly analyze more complex liabilities, you will use some relatively simple mathematics called *present* and *future value concepts.* These concepts will be an important part of our discussion of bond liabilities in the next chapter.

The concepts of future value (FV) and present value (PV) focus on the time value of money. Money received today is worth more than money received one year from today (or at any other future date) because it can be used to earn interest. If you invest $1,000 today at 10%, it will increase to $1,100 in one year. In contrast, if the $1,000 is to be received one year from today, you lose the opportunity to earn the $100 interest revenue for the year. The difference between the $1,000 and $1,100 is interest that can be earned during the year.

In some business situations, you will know the dollar amount of a cash flow that occurs in the future and will need to determine its value now. This is

Present value is the current value of an amount to be received in the future; a future amount discounted for compound interest.

Future value is the sum to which an amount will increase as the result of compound interest.

known as a **present value** problem. The opposite situation occurs when you know the dollar amount of a cash flow that occurs today and need to determine its value at some point in the future. This is called a **future value** problem. The value of money changes over time because money can earn interest (in other words, a dollar today is worth more than a dollar received in the future). The following diagram illustrates the basic difference between present value and future value problems:

	Now	Future
Present value	?	$1,000
Future value	$1,000	?

In addition to the two types of business situations that you will encounter (the need to determine either a present value or a future value), there are two types of cash flows: *single payment* situations that involve one payment and *annuities* that involve a series of cash payments. This means that there are four different types of situations related to the time value of money; they are identified in Exhibit 9–2. Each type of problem is based on the interest formula that was discussed earlier in this chapter:

$$\text{Interest} = \text{Principal} \times \text{Interest rate} \times \text{Time}$$

Many inexpensive hand-held calculators are available to do the detailed arithmetic computations that are required in future value and present value problems. In subsequent courses and in all business situations, you will probably use a calculator to solve these problems. At this stage, we encourage you to solve problems using the tables (Tables A–1 through A–4 in an appendix at the end of this book) which give values for each of the four types of problems for different periods of time *(n)* and at different rates of interest *(i)*. We believe that use of the tables will give you a better understanding of how and why present and future value concepts apply to business problems.

The values given in the tables are based on payments of $1. If a problem involves payments other than $1, it is necessary to multiply the value from the table by the amount of the payment.[1] We will examine each of the four types of present value and future value problems.

FUTURE AND PRESENT VALUES OF A SINGLE AMOUNT

Future Value of a Single Amount (f)

In future value of a single amount problems, you will be asked to calculate how much money you will have in the future as the result of investing a certain amount in the present. If you received a gift of $10,000, you might decide

Exhibit 9–2 Four Types of Future and Present Value Problems

Payment or Receipt	Symbol	
	Future Value	Present Value
Single amount	f	p
Annuity (equal payments or receipts for a series of equal time periods)	F	P

[1]Present value and future value problems involve cash flows. The basic concepts are the same for cash inflows (receipts) and cash outflows (payments). There are no fundamental differences between present value and future value calculations for cash payments versus cash receipts.

to put it in a savings account and use the money as a down payment on a new house when you graduate from college. The future value computation will tell you how much money will be available when you graduate.

To solve a future value problem, you need to know three items: (1) the amount that is to be invested, (2) the interest rate *(i)* that the amount will earn, and (3) the number of periods *(n)* in which the amount will earn interest.

The future value concept is based on compound interest. Therefore, the amount of interest for each period is calculated by multiplying the principal plus any interest that accrued in prior interest periods (but was not paid out) by the interest rate.

To illustrate, assume that on January 1, 19A, you deposit $1,000 in a savings account at 10% annual interest, compounded annually. At the end of three years, the $1,000 originally deposited would increase to $1,331 as follows:

Year	Amount at Start of Year	+	Interest during the Year	=	Amount at End of Year
1	$1,000	+	$1,000 × 10% = $100	=	$1,100
2	1,100	+	1,100 × 10% = 110	=	1,210
3	1,210	+	1,210 × 10% = 121	=	1,331

We can avoid the detailed arithmetic by referring to Table A–1, Appendix A, Future Value of $1, f. For $i = 10\%$, $n = 3$, we find the value 1.331. We can compute the balance at the end of year 3 as $1,000 × 1.331 = $1,331. The increase of $331 was due to the time value of money. It is interest revenue to the owner of the savings account and interest expense to the savings institution. A convenient format to display the computations for this problem is: $1,000 × $f_{i=10\%,\, n=3}$ (Table A–1, Appendix A, 1.3310) = $1,331. Exhibit 9– 3 gives a summary of this future value concept.

Present Value of a Single Amount (p)

The present value of a single amount is what it is worth to you today to be able to receive that amount at some date in the future. You might be offered the opportunity to invest in a debt instrument that would pay you $10,000 in 10 years. You would want to determine the present value of the instrument before you decided whether to invest.

To compute the present value of an amount to be received in the future, the amount is subjected to discounting (which is the opposite of compounding) at *i* interest rate for *n* periods. In discounting, the interest is subtracted rather than added (as is the case with compounding).

To illustrate, assume today is January 1, 19A, and you have the opportunity to receive $1,000 cash on December 31, 19C (i.e., three years from now). With an interest rate of 10% per year, how much would the $1,000 be worth to you on January 1, 19A? You could set up a discounting computation, year by year, that would be the inverse to the tabulation shown above for the future value.[2] However, to facilitate the computation, we can refer to Table A–2, Appendix A, Present Value of $1, p. For $i = 10\%$, $n = 3$, we find the present value of $1 is 0.7513. The $1,000, to be received at the end of three years has a present value (today) of $1,000 × 0.7513 = $751.30. The difference (i.e., the discount) of $248.70 is interest. A convenient format to display the computations for this problem is $1,000 × $p_{i=10\%,\, n=3}$ (Table A–2, Appendix A, 0.7513) = $751.30. The concept of the present value of $1 is summarized in Exhibit 9–3.

[2]The detailed discounting would be as follows:

Periods	Interest for the Year	Present Value*
1	$1,000 – ($1,000 × 1/1.10) = $90.91	$1,000 – $90.91 = $909.09
2	$909.09 – ($909.09 × 1/1.10) = $82.65	$909.09 – $82.65 = 826.44
3	$826.44 – ($826.44 × 1/1.10) = $75.14	$826.44 – $75.14 = 751.30

*Verifiable in Table A–2.

While it is not difficult to learn how to compute a present value amount, it is more important that you understand what it means. The $751.30 is the amount that you would pay to have the right to receive $1,000 at the end of three years assuming an interest rate of 10%. Conceptually, you would be indifferent about having $751.30 today and having $1,000 in three years. You are indifferent because you can use financial institutions to convert dollars from the present to the future and vice versa. If you had $751.30 today but preferred $1,000 in three years, you could simply deposit the money in a savings account and it would grow to $1,000 in three years. Alternatively, if you had a contract that promised you $1,000 in three years, you could sell it to an investor for $751.30 cash today because it would permit the investor to earn 10% on her money.

Self-Study Quiz

1. If the interest rate in a present value problem is increased from 8% to 10%, will the present value increase or decrease?

2. What is the present value of $10,000 to be received 10 years from now if the interest rate is 5% compounded annually?

Check your answers in the footnote at the bottom of this page.*

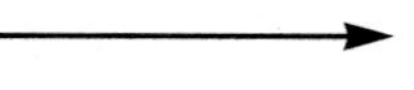

FUTURE AND PRESENT VALUES OF AN ANNUITY

An **annuity** is a series of periodic cash receipts or payments that are equal in amount each interest period.

Many business problems involve multiple cash payments over a number of periods instead of a single payment. An **annuity** is a series of consecutive payments characterized by:

1. An equal dollar amount each interest period.
2. Interest periods of equal length (year, semiannual, quarter, or month).
3. An equal interest rate each interest period.

Examples of annuities include monthly payments on an automobile or a home, yearly contributions to a savings account, and monthly retirement benefits received from a pension fund.

Future Value of an Annuity (F)

If you are saving money for some purpose, such as a new car or a trip to Europe, you might decide to deposit a fixed amount of money in a savings account each month. The future value of an annuity computation will tell you how much money will be in your savings account at some point in the future.

The future value of an annuity includes *compound interest* on each payment from the date of payment to the end of the term of the annuity. Each payment accumulates less interest than the prior payments only because the number of periods remaining to accumulate interest will be less.

Assume you deposit $1,000 cash in a savings account each year for three years at 10% interest per year (i.e., a total principal of $3,000). The first $1,000 deposit is made on December 31, 19A; the second one on December 31, 19B; and the third and last one on December 31, 19C. The first $1,000 deposit would

*1. The present value will be less.
2. $10,000 × 0.6139 = $6,139

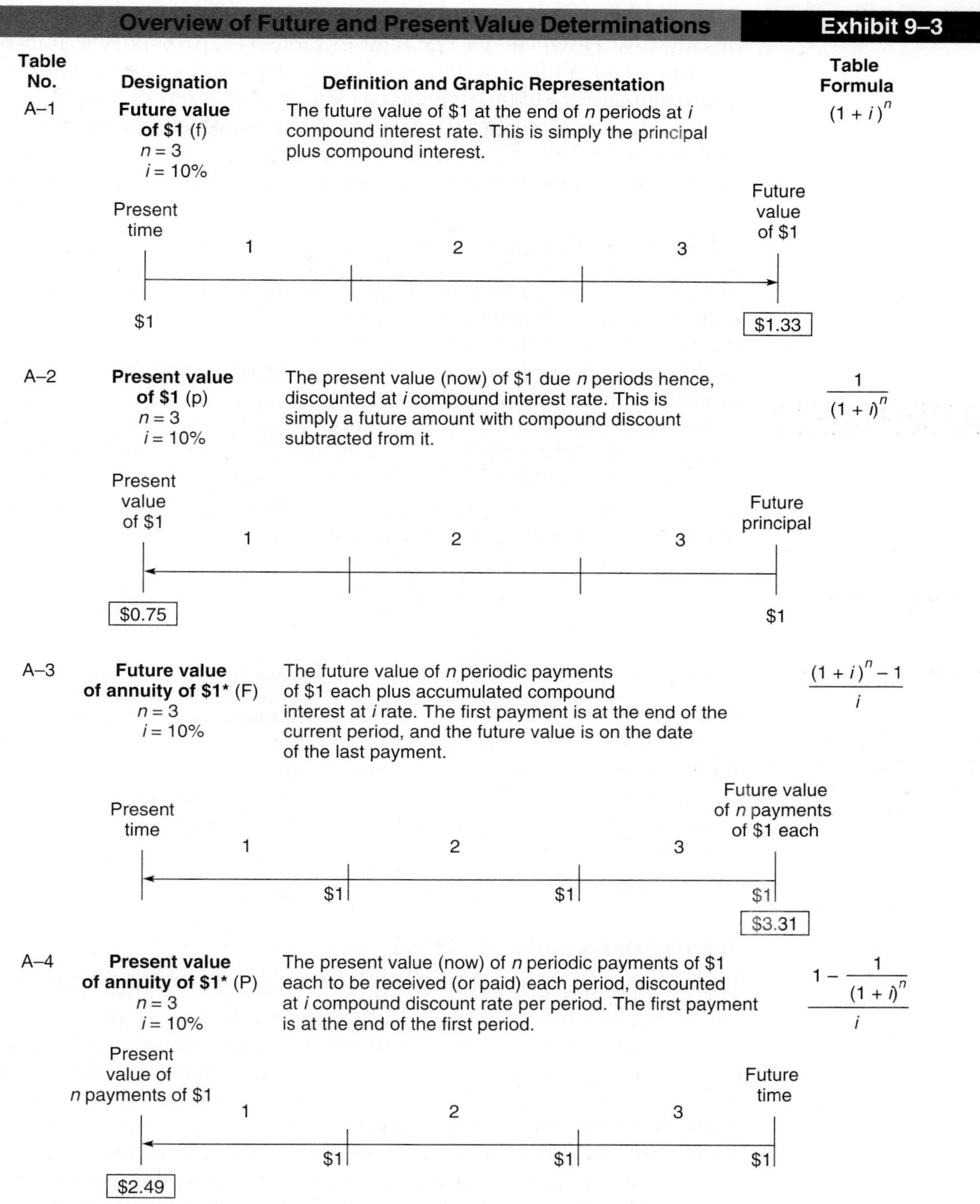

Table No.
Designation
Definition and Graphic Representation
Table Formula
A–1
Future value of $1 (f)
n = 3
i = 10%
The future value of $1 at the end of n periods at i compound interest rate. This is simply the principal plus compound interest.
$(1 + i)^n$
Present time
1
2
3
Future value of $1
$1
$1.33
A–2
Present value of $1 (p)
n = 3
i = 10%
The present value (now) of $1 due n periods hence, discounted at i compound interest rate. This is simply a future amount with compound discount subtracted from it.
$\frac{1}{(1 + i)^n}$
Present value of $1
1
2
3
Future principal
$0.75
$1
A–3
Future value of annuity of $1* (F)
n = 3
i = 10%
The future value of n periodic payments of $1 each plus accumulated compound interest at i rate. The first payment is at the end of the current period, and the future value is on the date of the last payment.
$\frac{(1 + i)^n - 1}{i}$
Present time
1
2
3
Future value of n payments of $1 each
$1
$1
$1
$3.31
A–4
Present value of annuity of $1* (P)
n = 3
i = 10%
The present value (now) of n periodic payments of $1 each to be received (or paid) each period, discounted at i compound discount rate per period. The first payment is at the end of the first period.
$\frac{1 - \frac{1}{(1 + i)^n}}{i}$
Present value of n payments of $1
1
2
3
Future time
$1
$1
$1
$2.49

Overview of Future and Present Value Determinations — **Exhibit 9–3**

*Notice that these are ordinary annuities; that is, they are often called end-of-period annuities. Thus, the table values for F, the future amount, are on the date of the last payment; and for P, the present value, are at the beginning of the period of the first payment. Annuities due assume the opposite; that is, they are "beginning-of-period" annuities. Ordinary annuity values can be converted to annuities due simply by multiplication of $(1 + i)$.

earn compound interest for two years (for a total principal and interest of $1,210); the second deposit would earn interest for one year (for a total principal and interest of $1,100); and the third deposit would earn no interest because it was made on the day that the balance is computed. Thus, the total amount in the savings account at the end of three years would be $3,310 ($1,210 + $1,100 + $1,000).

We could compute the interest on each deposit to derive the future value of this annuity. However, we can refer to Table A–3, Appendix A, Future Value of Annuity of $1 (F) for i = 10%, n = 3, to find the value 3.3100. The total of your three deposits of $1,000 each increased to $1,000 × 3.31 or $3,310, by December 31, 19C. The increase of $310 was due to interest. A convenient format for this problem is $1,000 × $F_{i=10\%,\, n=3}$ (Table A–3, Appendix A, 3.3100) = $3,310. This concept is summarized in Exhibit 9–3.

Present Value of an Annuity (P)

The present value of an annuity is the value now of a series of equal amounts to be received each period for some specified number of periods in the future. It involves discounting of each of the equal periodic amounts. A good example of this type of problem is a retirement program where the retiree is offered a monthly income for a period of time.

To illustrate, assume it is now January 1, 19A, and you are to receive $1,000 cash on each December 31, 19A, 19B, and 19C. How much would the sum of these three $1,000 future amounts be worth now, on January 1, 19A, assuming an interest rate of 10% per year? We could use Table A–2, Appendix A values to calculate the present value as follows:

Year	Amount		Value from Table A–2, Appendix A, i = 10%		Present Value
1	$1,000	×	0.9091 (n = 1)	=	$ 909.10
2	1,000	×	0.8264 (n = 2)	=	826.40
3	1,000	×	0.7513 (n = 3)	=	751.30
			Total present value	=	$2,486.80

However, the present value of this annuity can be more easily computed by using one present value amount from Table A–4, Appendix A as follows:

$1,000 × $P_{i=10\%,\, n=3}$ (Table A–4, Appendix A, 2.4869) = $2,487 (rounded)

This concept is summarized in Exhibit 9–3.

Interest Rates and Interest Periods

Notice that the preceding illustrations assumed annual periods for compounding and discounting. While interest rates almost always are quoted on an annual basis, most interest compounding periods encountered in business are less than one year (such as semiannually or quarterly). When interest periods are less than a year, the values of n and i must be restated to be consistent with the length of the interest period.

To illustrate, 12% interest compounded annually for five years requires use of n = 5 and i = 12%. If compounding is quarterly, the interest period is one quarter of a year (i.e., four periods per year), and the quarterly interest rate would be one quarter of the annual rate (i.e., 3% per quarter); therefore, 12% interest compounded quarterly for five years requires use of n = 20 and i = 3%.

ACCOUNTING APPLICATIONS OF FUTURE AND PRESENT VALUES

Learning Objective 8
Apply present value concepts to liabilities.

There are many business transactions that require the use of future and present value concepts. We will illustrate two such cases so that you can test your understanding of these concepts:

Case A On January 1, 19A, General Mills bought some new delivery trucks. The company signed a note and agreed to pay $200,000 for the trucks on

QUESTION OF ETHICS

Truth in Advertising

A number of advertisements in newspapers, magazines, and on television can be easily misinterpreted if the consumer does not understand present value concepts. We will discuss two examples.

Most car companies offer seasonal promotions with special financing incentives. A car dealer may advertise 4% interest on car loans when banks are charging 10%. Typically the lower interest rate is not a special incentive because the dealer simply charges a higher price for cars that are financed by the dealership. It may be better to borrow from the bank and "pay cash" at the dealership in order to negotiate a lower price. Customers should use the present value concepts illustrated in this chapter to compare financing alternatives.

Another misleading advertisement is seen every January and promises a chance to become an instant millionaire. The fine print discloses that the winner will receive $25,000 for 40 years, which is $1,000,000 (40 x $25,000); but the present value of this annuity at 8% is only $298,000. Most winners are happy to get the money, but they are not really millionaires.

Some consumer advocates criticize businesses that use these types of advertisements. They argue that consumers should not have to study present value concepts in order to understand advertisements. While some of these criticisms may be valid, there is no question that the quality of advertisements that include interest rates has improved during the past few years.

December 31, 19B. The market interest rate for this note was 12%. The $200,000 represents the cash equivalent price of the trucks and the interest that will be earned for two years.

1. How should the accountant record the purchase?

Answer: This case requires application of the present value of a single amount. In conformity with the cost principle, the cost of the trucks is their current cash equivalent price, which is the present value of the future payment. The present value of the $200,000 is computed as follows:

$$\$200{,}000 \times p_{i=12\%,\, n=2} \text{ (Table A–2, Appendix A, 0.7972)} = \$159{,}440$$

Therefore, the journal entry is as follows:

Jan. 1, 19A:	Delivery trucks	159,440	
	Note payable		159,440

Some companies prefer to record the following journal entry:

Jan. 1, 19A:	Delivery trucks	159,440	
	Discount on notes payable	40,560	
	Note payable		200,000

The Discount account is a contra liability account that represents the interest that will be earned on the note over its life. This account will be used extensively in the next chapter during our discussion of bonds.

2. What journal entry would be made at the end of the first and second years for interest expense?

Answer: Interest expense for each year on the amount in the Note Payable account would be recorded in an adjusting entry, as follows:

Dec. 31, 19A:	Interest expense	19,133*	
	Note payable (or, Discount on note payable)		19,133

*$159,440 × 12% = $19,133.

Dec. 31, 19B:	Interest expense	21,429*	
	Note payable (or, Discount on note payable)		21,429

*($159,440 + $19,133) × 12% = 21,429.

3. What journal entry should be made on December 31, 19B, to record payment of the debt?

Answer: At this date the amount to be paid is the balance of Note Payable, which is the same as the maturity amount on the due date. The journal entry to record full payment of the debt would be:

Dec. 31, 19B:	Note payable	200,000	
	Cash		200,000

Case B On January 1, 19A, General Mills bought new printing equipment. The company elected to finance the purchase with a note payable, to be paid off in three equal annual installments of $163,686. Each installment includes principal plus interest on the unpaid balance at 11% per year. The equal annual installments are due on December 31, 19A, 19B, and 19C.

1. What is the amount of the note?

Answer: The note is the present value of each installment payment, i = 11% and n = 3. This is an annuity because payment is made in three equal installments. The amount of the note is computed as follows:

$$\$163{,}686 \times P_{i=11\%,\, n=3} \text{ (Table A–4, Appendix A; 2.4437)} = \underline{\underline{\$400{,}000}}$$

The acquisition is recorded as follows:

Jan. 1, 19A:	Printing equipment	400,000	
	Note payable		400,000

2. What was the total amount of interest expense in dollars?

Answer:

$$\$163{,}686 \times 3 = \$491{,}058 - \$400{,}000 = \underline{\underline{\$91{,}058}}$$

3. What journal entry should be made at the end of each year to record the payment on this $400,000 note payable?

Answer:

Dec. 31, 19A:	Note payable	119,686	
	Interest expense ($400,000 × 11%)	44,000	
	Cash		163,686
	To record the first installment payment on the note.		
Dec. 31, 19B:	Note payable	132,852	
	Interest expense [($400,000 – $119,686) × 11%]	30,834	
	Cash		163,686
	To record the second installment payment on the note.		
Dec. 31, 19C:	Note payable	147,462	
	Interest expense	16,224*	
	Cash		163,686
	To record final installment payment on the note.		

*Interest: ($400,000 – $119,686 – $132,852) x 11% = $16,224 (rounded to accommodate rounding errors).

4. Prepare a debt payment schedule that shows the entry for each payment and the effect on interest expense and the unpaid amount of principal each period.

Answer:

Debt Payment Schedule

Date	Cash Payment (Credit)	Interest Expense (Prior Balance x 11%) (Debit)	Principal Decrease (Debit)	Unpaid Principal
1/1/A				$400,000
12/31/A	$163,686	$400,000 x 11% = $44,000	$119,686[a]	280,314[b]
12/31/B	163,686	280,314 x 11% = 30,834	132,852	147,462
12/31/C	163,686	147,462 x 11% = 16,224*	147,462	-0-
Total	$491,058	$91,058	$400,000	

*To accommodate rounding error.
Computations:
[a] $163,686 – $44,000 = $119,686, etc.
[b] $400,000 – $119,686 = $280,314, etc.

Notice in the debt payment schedule that for each successive payment, an increasing amount is payment on principal and a decreasing amount is interest expense. This effect occurs because the interest each period is based on a lower amount of unpaid principal. When an annuity is involved, schedules such as this one often are a useful analytical tool.

In the next chapter, we will use the present value techniques that you have just learned. As you will see, present value concepts are needed to understand how bonds function in our economy.

SUMMARY

Liabilities are obligations of either a known or estimated amount. Detailed information about the liabilities of an entity is important to many decision makers, whether internal or external to the enterprise, because liabilities represent claims against the resources of an entity. The existence and amount of liabilities sometimes are easy to conceal from outsiders. The accounting model and the verification by an independent CPA are the best assurances that all liabilities are disclosed.

Current liabilities are short-term obligations that will be paid within the coming year or within the normal operating cycle of the business, whichever is longer. All other liabilities (except contingent liabilities) are reported as long-term liabilities. A contingent liability is a potential claim due to some event or transaction that has happened, but its materialization as an effective liability is not certain because that depends on some future event or transaction. At the end of the accounting period, a contingent liability must be recorded (as a debit to a loss account and a credit to a liability account) if *(a)* it is probable that a loss will occur and *(b)* if the amount of the loss can be estimated reasonably. Contingent liabilities that are reasonably possible must be disclosed in the notes to the financial statements.

Future and present value concepts often must be applied in accounting for liabilities. These concepts focus on the time value of money (i.e., interest). Future value is the amount that a principal amount will increase to in the future due to compound interest. Present value is the amount that a future principal amount is worth today. It is computed with a process of discounting future cash flows. Future and present values are related to *(a)* a single amount or *(b)* a series of equal periodic amounts (called *annuities*). Typical applications of future and present values are to create a fund, determine the cost of an asset, account for notes payable, and account for installment debts and receivables.

Chapter Supplement A

Federal Income Tax Concepts

A business may be organized as a sole proprietorship, partnership, or corporation. Sole proprietorships and partnerships are not required to pay federal income taxes, but their owners must report and pay taxes on their personal tax returns. Corporations, as separate legal entities, are required to pay income taxes.

Corporations must prepare a U.S. Corporate Tax Return (Form 1120), which lists revenue and expenses for the year. The amount of the tax that is payable is based on the taxable income reported on the tax return. Taxable income is usually different from the income reported on the income statement because the income statement is prepared in conformity with GAAP and the tax return is prepared in conformity with the Internal Revenue Code.

Calculation of Taxes Payable

In most cases, a large corporation's tax obligation is determined by multiplying its taxable income by 35%. There are graduated rates so that very small corporations pay lower rates than large corporations. Exhibit 9–4 illustrates the calculation of taxes payable at various income levels.

Notice in Case C that a portion of the income is taxed at a rate that is actually greater than the maximum of 35%. The purpose of the 39% rate is to phase out the benefits of the lower rates that were intended to benefit only smaller corporations. The $136,000 taxes payable on taxable income of $400,000 is an effective tax rate of exactly 34%.

The 35% tax rate applies to taxable incomes greater than $10 million. There is a provision that phases out the 34% tax rate for very large corporations. The tax rate from $15,000,000 to $18,333,333 is 38%. At higher incomes, the rate re-

Exhibit 9–4 Calculation of Taxes Payable

Case A taxable income, $90,000:	
Computation:	
15% of first $50,000	$ 7,500
25% of next $25,000	6,250
34% of $15,000	5,100
Taxes payable	$ 18,850
Case B taxable income, $150,000:	
Computation:	
15% of first $50,000	$ 7,500
25% of next $25,000	6,250
34% of next $25,000	8,500
39% of $50,000 ($150,000 – $100,000)	19,500
Taxes payable	$ 41,750
Case C taxable income, $400,000:	
Computation:	
15% of first $50,000	$ 7,500
25% of next $25,000	6,250
34% of next $25,000	8,500
39% of next $235,000	91,650
34% of $65,000 ($400,000 – $335,000)	22,100
Taxes payable	$136,000

verts to 35%. This results in an effective tax rate of 35% once a corporation earns more than $18,333,333.

Revenue and Expense Recognition for Income Tax Purposes

There are several differences between GAAP and the rules that govern the preparation of the federal income tax return. Common examples are:

1. Interest revenue on state and municipal bonds is generally excluded from taxable income, although it is included in accounting income.
2. Revenue collected in advance (e.g., rent revenue) is included in taxable income when it is collected but it is included in accounting income when it is earned.
3. Proceeds from life insurance policies (e.g., "key executive" insurance) is excluded from taxable income but is included in accounting income.
4. Corporations that own less than 20% of another corporation's stock may exclude 70% of the dividends received from taxable income, although all the dividends are included in accounting income. The exclusion is 80% if the corporation owns more than 20% of the other corporation's stock.
5. Depreciation expense for tax purposes is generally based on the Accelerated Cost Recovery System (ACRS) if the assets were placed in service after 1980 and before 1987, or the Modified Accelerated Cost Recovery System (MACRS) if the assets were placed in service after 1986. These methods were discussed in Chapter 8.

Tax Minimization versus Tax Evasion

Most large corporations spend considerable time and money developing strategies that minimize the amount of federal income taxes that must be paid. There is nothing wrong with this approach because courts have stated that there is no legal obligation to pay more taxes than the law demands. Even if you do not major in accounting, you will probably want to take a course in federal income taxation because knowledge of the Internal Revenue Code is important for most executives. This knowledge offers opportunities to save significant amounts of money.

In contrast, tax evasion involves illegal means to evade paying taxes that are due. Use of accelerated depreciation is an example of tax minimization; failure to report revenue that was collected in cash is an example of tax evasion. While efforts at tax minimization represent good business practice, tax evasion is morally and legally wrong. Individuals who evade taxes run the risk of severe financial penalties including the possibility of being sent to jail.

KEY TERMS

Accrued Liabilities Expenses that have been incurred but have not yet been paid at the end of the accounting period. *458*

Annuity A series of periodic cash receipts or payments that are equal in amount each interest period. *472*

Contingent Liability Potential liability that has arisen as the result of a past event; not an effective liability until some future event occurs. *468*

Current Liabilities Short-term obligations that will be paid within the current operating cycle or one year, whichever is longer. *456*

Current Ratio The ratio of total current assets divided by total current liabilities; also known as the *working capital ratio.* *456*

Deferred Tax Items Difference between income tax expense and income tax liability; caused by temporary differences; may be a liability or an asset. *465*

Deferred Revenues Revenues that have been collected but not earned; liabilities until the goods or services are provided. *460*

Future Value The sum to which an amount will increase as the result of compound interest. *470*

Liabilities Probable future sacrifices of economic benefits that arise from past transactions. *455*

Long-Term Liabilities All obligations of the entity that are not classified as current liabilities. *462*

Present Value The current value of an amount to be received in the future; a future amount discounted for compound interest. *470*

Temporary Differences Timing differences that cause deferred income taxes and will reverse, or turn around, in the future. *465*

Time Value of Money Interest that is associated with the use of money over time. *461*

Working Capital The dollar difference between total current assets and total current liabilities. *456*

QUESTIONS

1. Define a liability. Differentiate between a current liability and a long-term liability.
2. How can external parties be informed about the liabilities of a business?
3. Liabilities are measured and reported at their current cash equivalent amount. Explain.
4. A liability is a known obligation of either a definite or estimated amount. Explain.
5. Define working capital. How is it computed?
6. What is the current ratio? How is the current ratio related to the classification of liabilities?
7. Define an accrued liability. What kind of an entry usually reflects an accrued liability?
8. Define a deferred revenue. Why is it a liability?
9. Define a note payable. Differentiate between a secured and an unsecured note.
10. Some notes are called non-interest-bearing because they do not include an explicit interest rate. Differentiate between an interest-bearing note and a non-interest-bearing note.
11. Define deferred income tax. Explain why deferred income tax "reverses, or turns around," in subsequent periods.
12. What is a contingent liability? How is a contingent liability reported?
13. Compute 19A interest expense for the following note: face, $4,000; 12% interest; date of note, April 1, 19A.
14. Explain the time value of money.
15. Explain the basic difference between future value and present value.
16. If you deposited $10,000 in a savings account that would earn 10%, how much would you have at the end of 10 years? Use a convenient format to display your computations.
17. If you hold a valid contract that will pay you $8,000 cash 10 years hence and the going rate of interest is 10%, what is its present value? Use a convenient format to display your computations.
18. What is an annuity?
19. Complete the following schedule:

		Table Values		
Concept	**Symbol**	$n = 4, i = 5\%$	$n = 7, i = 10\%$	$n = 10, i = 14\%$
FV of $1 PV of $1 FV of annuity of $1 PV of annuity of $1				

20. If you deposit $1,000 for each of 10 interest periods (ordinary annuity) that would earn 8% interest, how much would you have at the end of period 10? Use a convenient format to display your computations.
21. You purchased an XIT auto for $18,000 by making a $3,000 cash payment and six semiannual installment payments for the balance at 12% interest. Use a convenient format to display computation of the amount of each payment.

EXERCISES

E9–1 *Computing Owners' Equity, Working Capital, and Interest Expense, and Providing an Adjusting Entry*

Flair Corporation is preparing its 19B balance sheet. The company records show the following related amounts at the end of the accounting period, December 31, 19B:

Total current assets	$170,100
Total all remaining assets	525,000
Liabilities:	
Notes payable (8%, due in 5 years)	18,000
Accounts payable	60,000
Income taxes payable	12,000
Liability for withholding taxes	3,000
Rent revenue collected in advance	4,000
Bonds payable (due in 15 years)	100,000
Wages payable	7,800
Property taxes payable	2,000
Note payable (10%; due in 6 months)	10,000
Interest payable	400

Required:

1. Compute total owners' equity.
2. Compute *(a)* working capital and *(b)* the current ratio (show computations).
3. Compute the amount of interest expense for 19B on the long-term note. Assume it was dated October 1, 19B.
4. Give any adjusting entry required for the long-term note payable on December 31, 19B.

E9–2 *Accounting for and Reporting Accrued Liabilities and Deferred Revenue*

During 19B, the two transactions given below were completed by Riverside Company. The annual accounting period ends December 31.

a. Wages paid and recorded during 19B were $130,000; however, at the end of December 19B, there were three days' wages unpaid and unrecorded because the weekly payroll will not be paid until January 6, 19C. Wages for the three days were $3,600.

b. On December 10, 19B, the company collected rent revenue of $2,400 on office space that it rented to another party. The rent collected was for 30 days from December 10, 19B, to January 10, 19C, and was credited in full to Rent Revenue.

Required:

1. Give *(a)* the adjusting entry required on December 31, 19B, and *(b)* the January 6, 19C, journal entry for payment of any unpaid wages from December 19B.
2. Give *(a)* the journal entry for the collection of rent on December 10, 19B, and *(b)* the adjusting entry on December 31, 19B.
3. Show how any liabilities related to the above transactions should be reported on the company's balance sheet at December 31, 19B.

Dayton Hudson

E9–3 Accounting for a Note Payable through Its Time to Maturity

Many businesses have to borrow money during periods of increased business activity in order to finance inventory and accounts receivable. Dayton Hudson is one of America's largest general merchandise retailers. Each Christmas, Dayton Hudson builds up its inventory to meet the needs of Christmas shoppers. A large portion of Christmas sales are on credit. As a result, it is often several months after Christmas before Dayton Hudson collects cash from the sales. Assume that on November 1, 19A, Dayton Hudson borrowed $4.5 million cash from the Metropolitan Bank for working capital purposes and signed an interest-bearing note. The note was due in six months. The interest rate was 10% per annum payable at maturity. The accounting period ends December 31.

Required:

1. Give the journal entry to record the note on November 1.
2. Give any adjusting entry that would be required at the end of the annual accounting period.
3. Give the journal entry to record payment of the note and interest on the maturity date, April 30, 19B.

E9–4 Recording a Payroll, Including Deductions

Town Lake Company has completed the payroll for January 19B, reflecting the following data:

Salaries and wages earned	$82,000
Employee income taxes withheld	9,500
Union dues withheld	1,200
FICA payroll taxes*	6,013
FUTA payroll taxes†	589
State unemployment taxes	2,270

*Assessed on both employer and employee (i.e., $6,013 each).

†Unemployment taxes

Required:

1. Give the journal entry to record payment of the payroll and employee deductions.
2. Give the journal entry to record employer payroll taxes.
3. What was the amount of additional labor expense to the company due to tax laws? What was the amount of the employees' take-home pay?
4. List the liabilities, and their amounts, that are reported on the company's January 31, 19B, balance sheet.

E9–5 Accounting for Accounts Payable and a Note Payable

Bryant Company sells a wide range of goods through two retail stores that are operated in adjoining cities. Most purchases of goods for resale are on invoices. Occasionally, a short-term note payable is used to obtain cash for current use. The following transactions were selected from those occurring during 19B:

a. On January 10, 19B, purchased merchandise on credit, $18,000. The company uses a periodic inventory system.

b. On March 1, 19B, borrowed $40,000 cash from City Bank and gave an interest-bearing note payable: face amount, $40,000, due at the end of six months, with an annual interest rate of 8% payable at maturity.

Required:

1. Give the journal entry for each of the above transactions.
2. Give the journal entry for the payment of the note payable plus interest on its maturity date.

Ford Motor Company

E9–6 Identifying a Liability

The annual report for Ford Motor Company contained the following information:

> Postretirement Health Care and Life Insurance Benefits
> The company and certain of its subsidiaries sponsor unfunded plans to provide selected health care and life insurance benefits for retired employees. The company's employees may become eligible for those benefits if they retire while working for the company. However, benefits and eligibility rules may be modified from time to time.

Should Ford report a liability for these benefits on its balance sheet? Explain.

E9–7 Deferred Income Tax: One Temporary Difference

The comparative income statements of Martin Corporation at December 31, 19B, showed the following summarized pretax data:

	Year 19A	Year 19B
Sales revenue	$65,000	$72,000
Expenses (excluding income tax)	50,000	54,000
Pretax income	$15,000	$18,000

Included in the above 19B data is a $2,800 expense that was deductible only in the 19A income tax return (rather than in 19B). The average income tax rate was 30%. Taxable income from the income tax returns was 19A, $14,000; and 19B, $17,400.

Required:

1. For each year compute *(a)* income taxes payable and *(b)* deferred income tax. Is the deferred income tax a liability or an asset? Explain.
2. Give the journal entry for each year to record income taxes payable, deferred income tax, and income tax expense.
3. Show what amounts related to income taxes should be reported each year on the income statement and balance sheet. Assume income tax is paid on April 15 of the next year.

E9–8 Deferred Income Tax: One Temporary Difference

The comparative income statement for Chung Corporation at the end of December 31, 19B, provided the following summarized pretax data:

	Year 19A	Year 19B
Revenues	$80,000	$88,000
Expenses (excluding income tax)	65,000	69,000
Pretax income	$15,000	$19,000

Included in the above 19B data is a $5,000 revenue that was taxable only in the 19A income tax return (rather than in 19B). The average income tax rate was 32%. Taxable income shown in the tax returns was 19A, $13,000; and 19B, $18,500.

Required:

1. For each year compute *(a)* income taxes payable and *(b)* deferred income tax. Is the deferred income tax a liability or an asset? Explain.
2. Give the journal entry for each year to record income taxes payable, deferred income tax, and income tax expense.
3. Show what amounts related to income taxes should be reported each year on the income statement and balance sheet. Assume income tax is paid on April 15 of the next year.

E9–9 Deferred Income Tax: Depreciation

Amber Corporation reported the following summarized pretax data at the end of each year:

Income Statement at December 31	19A	19B	19C
Revenues	$170,000	$182,000	$195,000
Expenses (including depreciation)*	122,000	126,000	130,000
Pretax income	$ 48,000	$ 56,000	$ 65,000

*Depreciation expense on the income statement was straight line, on a machine purchased January 1, 19A, for $75,000. The machine has a three-year estimated life and no residual value. The company used accelerated depreciation on the income tax return as follows: 19A, $37,500; 19B, $25,000; and 19C, $12,500. The average income tax rate is 28% for the three years.

Taxable income from the income tax return was as follows: 19A, $32,000; 19B, $56,000; and 19C, $85,000.

Required:

1. For each year compute *(a)* income taxes payable and *(b)* deferred income tax. Is the deferred income tax a liability or an asset? Explain.
2. Give the journal entry for each year to record income taxes payable, deferred income tax, and income tax expense.
3. Show what amounts related to income taxes should be reported each year on the income statement and balance sheet.

Colgate-Palmolive

E9–10 Deferred Tax Accounting

The annual report for Colgate-Palmolive contains the following information (in millions):

Income Taxes

Difference between accounting for financial statement purposes and accounting for tax purposes result in taxes currently payable (lower) higher than the total provision for income taxes as follows:

	1992	1991	1990
Excess tax over book depreciation	$(18.0)	$(19.8)	$(18.9)
Other	(31.4)	76.6	(25.5)
Total	$(49.4)	$ 56.8	$(44.4)

Required:

1. Determine whether tax expense is greater or less than taxes payable for each year.
2. Explain the most likely reason for tax depreciation to be greater than book depreciation.
3. Is the deferred tax liability reported on the 1992 balance sheet $49.4 million? Explain.

E9–11 Applying the Four Kinds of Present and Future Values

On January 1, 19A, Wesley Company completed the following transactions (assume an 11% annual interest rate):

a. Deposited $12,000 in a fund (designated Fund A).

b. Established a fund (designated Fund B) by agreeing to make six annual deposits of $2,000 each. Deposits are made each December 31.

c. Established a fund (designated Fund C) by depositing a single amount that will increase to $40,000 by the end of year 7.

d. Decided to deposit a single sum in a fund (designated Fund D) that will provide 10 equal annual year-end payments of $15,000 to a retired employee (payments starting December 31, 19A).

Required (show computations and round to the nearest dollar):

1. What will be the balance of Fund A at the end of year 9?
2. What will be the balance of Fund B at the end of year 6?

3. What single amount must be deposited in Fund C on January 1, 19A?
4. What single sum must be deposited in Fund D on January 1, 19A?

E9–12 Accounting for a Savings Account: A Single Amount

On January 1, 19A, you deposited $6,000 in a savings account. The account will earn 10% annual compound interest, which will be added to the fund balance at the end of each year.

Required (round to the nearest dollar):

1. What will be the balance in the savings account at the end of 10 years?
2. What is the interest for the 10 years?
3. How much interest revenue did the fund earn in 19A? 19B?
4. Give the journal entry to record interest revenue at the end of 19A and 19B.

E9–13 Computing Deposit Required and Accounting for a Single-Sum Savings Account

On January 1, 19A, Alan King decided to deposit an amount in a savings account that will provide $80,000 four years later to send his son to college. The savings account will earn 8%, which will be added to the fund each year-end.

Required (show computations and round to the nearest dollar):

1. How much must Alan deposit on January 1, 19A?
2. Give the journal entry that Alan should make on January 1, 19A.
3. What is the interest for the four years?
4. Give the journal entry that Alan should make on *(a)* December 31, 19A, and *(b)* December 31, 19B.

E9–14 Accounting for a Savings Account with Equal Periodic Payments

On each December 31, you plan to deposit $2,000 in a savings account. The account will earn 9% annual interest, which will be added to the fund balance at year-end. The first deposit will be made December 31, 19A (end of period).

Required (show computations and round to the nearest dollar):

1. Give the required journal entry on December 31, 19A.
2. What will be the balance in the savings account at the end of the 10th year (i.e., 10 deposits)?
3. What is the interest earned on the 10 deposits?
4. How much interest revenue did the fund earn in 19B? 19C?
5. Give all required journal entries at the end of 19B and 19C.

E9–15 Accounting for a Savings Fund with Periodic Deposits

You have planned to take a trip around the world upon graduation four years from now (now is January 1, 19A). Your grandmother wants to deposit sufficient funds for this trip in a savings account for you. On the basis of a budget, you estimate the trip now would cost $15,000. To be generous, your grandmother decided to deposit $3,500 in the fund at the end of each of the next four years, starting on December 31, 19A. The savings account will earn 6% annual interest, which will be added to the savings account at each year-end.

Required (show computations and round to the nearest dollar):

1. What journal entry should your grandmother make on December 31, 19A, to record the first deposit?

2. How much money will you have for the trip at the end of year 4 (i.e., after four deposits)?
3. What is the interest for the four years?
4. How much interest revenue did the fund earn in 19A, 19B, 19C, and 19D?
5. Give the journal entries at the end of 19B, 19C, and 19D. Yes, you left on January 1, 19E.

E9–16 Valuating an Asset Based on Present Value

You have the chance to purchase the royalty interest in an oil well. Your best estimate is that the net royalty income will average $25,000 per year for five years. There will be no residual value at that time. Assume the cash inflow is at each year-end and that considering the uncertainty in your estimates, you expect to earn 15% per year on the investment.

Required (show computations and round to the nearest dollar):

1. What should you be willing to pay for this investment on January 1, 19A?
2. Give the required journal entry (cash paid in full for the royalty interest) on January 1, 19A.
3. Give the required journal entries on December 31, 19A, assuming the net cash received was equal to your estimate. Assume the cost of royalty interest is depleted on a straight-line basis.

Carnival Cruise Lines

E9–17 Determination of a Liability

Carnival Cruise Lines provides exotic vacations on board luxurious passenger ships. In 1989, the company moved its offices and included the following note in its current annual report:

> **Leases**
>
> On March 27, 1989, the Company entered into a ten-year lease for 230,000 square feet of office space located in Miami, Florida. The Company moved its operation to this location in October 1989. The total rent payable over the ten-year term of the lease is approximately $24 million.

Based on these facts, do you think the company should report this obligation on its balance sheet? Explain. If the obligation should be reported as a liability, how should the amount be measured?

PROBLEMS

P9–1 Recording and Reporting Five Current Liabilities

Curb Company completed the transactions listed below during 19B. The annual accounting period ends December 31, 19B.

Jan.	8	Purchased merchandise for resale at an invoice cost of $13,580; assume a periodic inventory system.
	17	Paid invoice of January 8.
Apr.	1	Borrowed $40,000 from the National Bank for general use; executed a 12-month, 12% interest-bearing note payable.
June	3	Purchased merchandise for resale at an invoice cost of $17,820.
July	5	Paid invoice of June 3.
Aug.	1	Rented two rooms in the building owned by the company and collected six months' rent in advance amounting to $5,100. (Record the collection in a way that will not require an adjusting entry at year-end.)
Dec.	20	Received a $100 deposit from a customer as a guarantee to return a large trailer "borrowed" for 30 days.
	31	Wages earned but not yet paid on December 31 of $6,500 (disregard payroll taxes).

Required:

1. Prepare journal entries for each of the above transactions.
2. Prepare all adjusting entries required on December 31, 19B.

3. Show how all of the liabilities arising from the above transactions would be reported on the balance sheet at December 31, 19B.

P9–2 Accounting for a Note Payable, with Adjusting Entries

Carlyle Golf Inc.

Carlyle Golf, Inc. is a small company that designs and markets high-quality golf shirts that are sold in pro shops at exclusive country clubs. Carlyle shirts are worn by many golf professionals on the PGA tour. Assume that the company purchased a computer-aided design system to permit them to shorten the design time for new golf shirts. Carlyle bought the equipment for $180,000 on April 1, 19A, with a cash down payment of $50,000. A $130,000 interest-bearing note (including a mortgage on the equipment) was given for the balance. The note specified 8% annual interest. Two payments on principal of $65,000 each, plus interest on the unpaid balance on March 31, 19B, and March 31, 19C, are required—these will be unequal cash payments. The accounting period ends December 31.

Required:

1. Give all of the related journal entries for the terms of this note.
2. Show how the liabilities should be reported on the company's 19A and 19B balance sheets.

P9–3 Analysis of Note Describing Retirement Plan

Chrysler Corporation

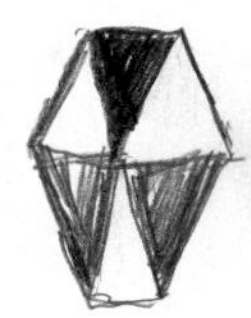

A recent annual report for Chrysler contained the following note:

Employee Retirement Plans

Noncontributory benefits are based on a fixed rate per year of service. Annual contributions to the pension trust fund are in compliance with federal law. All income accruing to the fund are used solely to pay pension benefits. Chrysler made pension fund contributions totaling $816 million in 1992, $327 million in 1991 and $776 million in 1990. The components of periodic pension cost are as follows:

in millions of dollars	1992	1991	1990
Service costs—benefits earned during the year	$171	$125	$120
Interest costs on future benefits	742	737	651
Return on plan's assets	(945)	(883)	88
Other	836	805	(338)
Net pension expense	$804	$784	$521

This note introduces many terms that were not discussed in the chapter. Based on the general discussion in the chapter and your knowledge of pension programs, explain how the yearly cost of Chrysler's pension program is determined.

P9–4 Deferred Income Tax: Two Temporary Differences

The records of Calib Corporation provided the following summarized data for 19D and 19E:

	Year-End December 31	
	19D	19E
Income statement:		
Revenues	$210,000	$218,000
Expenses (excluding income tax)	130,000	133,000
Pretax income	$ 80,000	$ 85,000

a. Income tax rate, 32%. Assume income taxes payable are paid 80% in the current year and 20% on April 15 of the next year.

b. Temporary differences:

(1) The 19E expenses include an $8,000 expense that must be deducted only in the 19D tax return.

(2) 19E revenues include a $6,000 revenue that was taxable only in 19F.

c. Taxable income shown in the tax returns was 19D, $82,000; and 19E, $85,000.

Required:

1. For each year compute *(a)* income taxes payable and *(b)* deferred income tax. Is each deferred income tax a liability or an asset? Explain.
2. Give the journal entry for each year to record income taxes payable, deferred income tax, and income tax expense.
3. Show what amounts related to income taxes should be reported each year on the income statement and balance sheet.

P9–5 Deferred Income Tax: Depreciation

At December 31, 19A, the records of Pearson Corporation provided the following information:

Income statement:	
Revenues	$160,000*
Depreciation expense (straight-line)	(11,000)†
Remaining expenses (excluding income tax)	(90,000)
Pretax income	$ 59,000

*These revenues include $20,000 interest on tax-free municipal bonds.

†Equipment depreciated—acquired January 1, 19A, cost $44,000; estimated useful life, four years and no residual value. Accelerated depreciation is used on the tax return as follows: 19A, $17,600; 19B, $13,200; 19C, $8,800; and 19D, $4,400.

a. Income tax rate, 30%. Assume 85% is paid in year incurred.

b. Taxable income from the 19A income tax return, $80,000.

Required:

1. Compute income taxes payable and deferred income tax for 19A. Is the deferred income tax a liability or asset? Explain.
2. Give the journal entry to record income taxes for 19A.
3. Show what amounts related to 19A income taxes should be reported on the income statement and balance sheet.

P9–6 Accounting for Payroll Costs

McLoyd Company completed the salary and wage payroll for March 19A. Details provided by the payroll were:

Salaries and wages earned	$230,000
Employee income taxes withheld	46,000
Union dues withheld	3,000
Insurance premiums withheld	1,200
FICA taxes*	16,445
FUTA taxes†	1,610
State unemployment taxes	6,210

*Equal amount for employer and employees.

† Federal unemployment taxes

Required:

1. Give the journal entry to record the payroll for March, including employee deductions.
2. Give the journal entry to record the employer's payroll taxes.
3. Give a combined journal entry to show the payment of amounts owed to governmental agencies and other organizations.
4. What was the total labor cost for the company? Explain. What percent of the payroll was take-home pay?

P9–7 Looking at Various Liabilities

1. Polaroid designs, manufactures and markets products primarily in instant image recording. Their annual report contained the following note: **Polaroid**

Product Warranty:

Estimated product warranty costs are accrued at the time products are sold.

Assume that estimated warranty costs for 19A were $2 million and that the warranty work was performed during 19B. Prepare the necessary journal entries based on Polaroid's policy.

2. Reader's Digest Association is a publisher of magazines, books, and music collections. The following note is from their annual report: **Reader's Digest Association**

Revenues Sales of subscriptions to magazines are recorded as unearned revenue at the time the order is received. Proportional shares of the subscription price are recognized as revenues when the subscription is fulfilled.

Assume that Reader's Digest collected $10 million in 19A for magazines that will be delivered in future years. During 19B, the company delivered $8 million worth of magazines on those subscriptions. Prepare any necessary journal entries based on Reader's Digest's policy.

3. Brunswick Corporation is a multinational company that manufactures and sells marine and recreational products. Their annual report contained the following information: **Brunswick Corporation**

Litigation

The Company is subject to certain legal proceedings and claims which have arisen in the ordinary course of its business and have not been finally adjudicated. In 1992, 1991, 1990, the Company recorded pretax provisions of $4.8 million, $38.0 million and $12.1 million respectively for litigation matters.

Prepare any journal entries required to record the results of litigation in 1992. What impact, if any, does litigation have on the financial statements of Brunswick?

4. A recent annual report for The Coca-Cola Company reported current assets of $4,247,677 and current liabilities of $5,303,222. Based on the current ratio, do you think that Coca-Cola is experiencing financial difficulty? **The Coca-Cola Company**

5. Alcoa is involved in the mining and manufacturing of aluminum. Its products can become an advanced alloy for the wing of a Boeing 777 or a common recyclable Coca–Cola can. The annual report for Alcoa stated: **Alcoa**

Environmental Expenditures. Liabilities are recorded when remedial efforts are probable and the costs can be reasonably estimated.

In your own words, explain the Alcoa accounting policy for environmental expenditures. What is the justification for this policy?

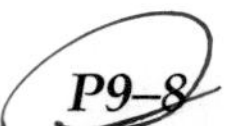

P9–8 Applying Four PV and FV Concepts

On January 1, 19A, Plymouth Company completed the following transactions (use an 8% annual interest rate for all transactions):

a. Deposited $50,000 in a debt retirement fund. Interest will be computed at six-month intervals and added to the fund at those times (i.e., semiannual compounding). (Hint: Think carefully about *n* and *i*).

b. Established a plant addition fund of $400,000 to be available at the end of year 5. A single sum will be deposited on January 1, 19A, that will grow to the $400,000.

c. Established a pension retirement fund of $500,000 to be available by the end of year 6 by making six equal annual deposits each at year-end, starting on December 31, 19A.

d. Purchased a $180,000 machine on January 1, 19A, and paid cash, $60,000. A four-year note payable is signed for the balance. The note will be paid in four equal year-end payments starting on December 31, 19A.

Required (show computations and round to the nearest dollar):

1. In transaction *a* above, what will be the balance in the fund at the end of year 4? What is the total amount of interest revenue that will be earned?
2. In transaction *b* above, what single sum amount must the company deposit on January 1, 19A? What is the total amount of interest revenue that will be earned?
3. In transaction *c* above, what is the required amount of each of the six equal annual deposits? What is the total amount of interest revenue that will be earned?
4. In transaction *d* above, what is the amount of each of the equal annual payments that will be paid on the note? What is the total amount of interest expense that will be incurred?

P9–9 Accounting for a Fund: Fund Accumulation Schedule and Entries

On January 1, 19A, Jalopy Company decided to accumulate a fund to build an addition to its plant. The company will deposit $320,000 in the fund at each year-end, starting on December 31, 19A. The fund will earn 9% interest, which will be added to the fund at each year-end. The accounting period ends December 31.

Required:

1. What will be the balance in the fund immediately after the December 31, 19C, deposit?
2. Complete the following fund accumulation schedule:

Date	Cash Payment	Interest Revenue	Fund Increase	Fund Balance
12/31/19A				
12/31/19B				
12/31/19C				
Total				

3. Give journal entries on December 31, 19A, 19B, and 19C.
4. The plant addition was completed on January 1, 19D. The total cost was $1,060,000. Give the entry assuming this amount is paid in full to the contractor.

P9–10 Accounting for a Plant Fund: A Single Amount

Texas Company will build another plant during 19C estimated to cost $800,000. At the present time, January 1, 19A, the company has excess cash, some of which will be set aside in a savings account to cover the plant cost. The savings account will earn 8% annual interest which will be added to the savings account each year-end.

Required (show computations and round to the nearest dollar):

1. What single amount must be deposited in the savings account on January 1, 19A, to create the desired amount by the end of 19C?
2. What amount of interest will be earned by the end of 19C?
3. How much interest revenue will be earned each year (19A through 19C)?
4. Give the following journal entries:
   a. Establishment of the fund.
   b. Interest earned at each year-end.
   c. Use of the fund and other cash needed to pay for the plant (completed December 31, 19C, at a cost of $825,000).

P9–11 Accounting for a Debt Retirement Fund: A Single Amount

On January 1, 19A, Athletic Company set aside a fund to provide cash to pay off the principal amount of a $100,000 long-term debt that will be due at the end of six years. The single deposit will be made with an independent trustee. The fund will earn 10% annual interest which will be added to the fund balance at each year-end.

Required (show computations and round to the nearest dollar):

1. How much must be deposited as a single sum on January 1, 19A, to pay off the debt?
2. What amount of interest will be earned during the six years?
3. How much interest revenue will the fund earn in 19A? 19B?
4. Give the journal entries for the company to record:
   a. The deposit on January 1, 19A.
   b. The interest revenue for 19A and 19B (separately).
   c. Payment of the maturing liability at the end of the sixth year.
5. Show how the effects of the fund will be reported on the 19B income statement and balance sheet.

P9–12 Accounting for a Debt Fund: Equal Periodic Deposits

On December 31, 19A, Post Company set aside, in a fund, cash to pay the principal amount of a $140,000 debt due on December 31, 19D. The company will make four equal annual deposits on each December 31, 19A, 19B, 19C, and 19D. The fund will earn 7% annual interest, which will be added to the balance of the fund at each year-end. The fund trustee will pay the loan principal (to the creditor) upon receipt of the last fund deposit. The company's accounting period ends December 31.

Required (show computations and round to the nearest dollar):

1. How much must be deposited each December 31?
2. What amount of interest will be earned?
3. How much interest revenue will the fund earn in 19A, 19B, 19C, and 19D?
4. Give journal entries for the company on the following dates:
   a. For the first deposit on December 31, 19A.
   b. For all amounts at the ends of 19B and 19C.
   c. For payment of the debt on December 31, 19D.
5. Show how the effect of the fund will be reported on the December 31, 19B, income statement and balance sheet.

P9–13 Paying Debt in Equal Installments: Debt Payment Schedule and Entries

On January 1, 19A, Idaho Company sold a new machine to U.S. Company for $80,000. A cash down payment of $30,000 was made by U.S. Company. A $50,000, 8% note was signed by U.S. Company for the balance due. The note is to be paid off in three equal installments due on December 31, 19A, 19B, and 19C. Each payment is to include principal plus interest on the unpaid balance. The purchase was recorded by U.S. as follows:

Jan. 1, 19A:	Machine	80,000	
	Cash		30,000
	Note payable		50,000

Required (show computations and round to the nearest dollar):

1. What is the amount of the equal annual payments that must be made by U.S. Company?
2. What is the interest on the note?

3. Complete the following debt payment schedule:

Date	Cash Payment	Interest Expense	Principal Decrease	Unpaid Principal
1/1/19A				
12/31/19A				
12/31/19B				
12/31/19C				
Total				

4. Give the journal entries for each of the three payments.
5. Explain why interest expense decreased in amount each year.

P9–14 *Paying for Auto in Equal Periodic Installments: Debt Payment Schedule and Entries*

On January 1, 19A, you bought a new ZS238 automobile for $22,000. You made a $5,000 cash down payment and signed a $17,000 note, payable in four equal installments on each December 31, the first payment to be made on December 31, 19A. The interest rate is 12% per year on the unpaid balance. Each payment will include payment on principal plus the interest.

Required:

1. Compute the amount of the equal payments that you must make.
2. What is the interest on the installment debt during the four years?
3. Complete a schedule using the format below:

DEBT PAYMENT SCHEDULE				
Date	Cash Payment	Interest Expense	Reduction of Principal	Unpaid Principal
1/1/A				
12/31/A				
12/31/B				
12/31/C				
12/31/D				
Totals				

4. Explain why the amount of interest expense decreases each year.
5. Give the journal entries on December 31, 19A, and 19B.

CASES

Dayton Hudson

C9–1 *Accounting for Warranty Expense and Warranty Liability: A Challenging Case*

Dayton Hudson operates a number of general merchandise stores under a variety of names including Target, Mervyn's, Marshall Field's, as well as Dayton Hudson. This case relates to CD players sold by a single electronics department in a Target store. During 19A, the department sold CD players for $220,000 cash; the related cost of goods sold was $100,000. Each CD player is guaranteed for one year for defective parts. In case of a defective part, the part is replaced and the labor cost of replacing it involves no cost to the customer. Experience by the manufacturer shows that the average cost to make good the warranty is approximately 5% of cost of goods sold. Assume that Target uses a perpetual inventory system and the accounting period ends December 31.

Actual expenditures for warranties (i.e., replacement parts and labor) during 19A were $3,400. During 19A, this amount was debited to an account called Warranty Expense and credited to Cash. CD player sales were much higher during December than in any other prior month.

Required:

1. Give the two summary journal entries for the company to record the sales of CD players during 19A.
2. Explain why the company debited the actual 19A warranty expenditures to Warranty Expense.
3. Explain the nature of any liability that the company should record at the end of 19A related to the warranties.
4. Compute the estimated amount of any warranty liability that exists at December 31, 19A.
5. Give any entry needed based on your answer to requirement 4.
6. Show how warranty expense and any warranty liability should be reported in the 19A income statement and balance sheet.

C9–2 Hidden Interest in a Real Estate Deal: PV

Many advertisements contain offers that seem too good to be true. Often these offers are not what they seem to be. A few years ago an actual newspaper ad offered "a $150,000 house with a zero interest rate mortgage" for sale. If the purchaser made monthly payments of $3,125 for four years ($150,000 ÷ 48 months), there would be no additional charge for interest. When the offer was made, mortgage interest rates were 12%. Present value for $n = 48$, and $i = 1\%$ is 37.9740.

Required:

1. Did the builder actually provide a mortgage at zero interest?
2. Estimate the true price of the home that was advertised. Assume that the monthly payment was based on an implicit interest rate of 12%.

C9–3 Accrued Liability for a Frequent Flyer Program

Southwest Airlines

Most major airlines have frequent flyer programs that permit passengers to earn free tickets based on the number of miles they have flown. A recent Southwest Airlines annual report contained the following note:

> *Frequent flyer awards* The Company accrues the estimated incremental cost to provide transportation for travel awards when earned under its Company Club frequent flyer program.

The phrase *incremental cost* means the additional expense associated with an extra passenger taking the flight (e.g., the cost of a soft drink and a snack).

Required:

1. What other measures of cost could be used by Southwest other than incremental cost?
2. What account should Southwest debit when it accrues this liability?

C9–4 Liability for Retirement Benefits

H. J. Heinz Company

Many companies provide health care benefits for employees who have retired. A recent H. J. Heinz Company annual report contained the following note:

> In addition to providing pension benefits, the company and certain of its subsidiaries provide health care and life insurance benefits for retired employees. Substantially all of the company's U.S. and Canadian employees may become eligible for these benefits.

> The cost of retiree health care and life insurance benefits is expensed as incurred. These costs were $4.9 million for the current year and $4.2 million for the previous year.

Since this annual report was issued, the FASB issued a new rule, which stated that the cost of future health care for retirees should be estimated and recorded as a current expense while employees were working rather than when they received the benefits. How would the FASB justify the new rule? What problems would you anticipate in implementing the new rule?

PepsiCo, Inc.

C 9–5 Classification of Short-Term Borrowings

PepsiCo, Inc., engages in a number of activities that are part of our daily lives. Their businesses include Pepsi-Cola, Frito-Lay, KFC, and Pizza Hut. A recent PepsiCo annual report contained the following information:

> At the end of the current year, $3.6 billion of short-term borrowings were classified as long-term, reflecting PepsiCo's intent and ability to refinance these borrowings on a long-term basis, through either long-term debt issuances or rollover of existing short-term borrowings. The significant amount of short-term borrowings classified as long-term, as compared to the end of the previous year when no such amounts were reclassified, primarily reflects the large commercial paper issuances in the current year, but also resulted from a refined analysis of amounts expected to be refinanced beyond one year.

As an analyst, comment on the company's classification of short-term borrowings as long-term liabilities. What conditions should exist to permit a company to make this type of classification?

Delta Air Lines

C 9–6 Present Value of Lease Obligations

A recent annual report for Delta Air Lines included the following note:

> At June 30, 1990, the Company's minimum rental commitments under capital leases and noncancelable operating leases with initial or remaining terms of more than one year were as follows:

Years Ending June 30	Operating Leases *(in thousands)*
1991	$ 533,891
1992	533,106
1993	523,391
1994	515,457
1995	512,897
After 1995	6,984,779
Total minimum lease payments	$9,603,521

You are a lending officer for a large commercial bank and for comparative purposes you want to compute the present values of these leases. Determine the present value of the minimum lease payments shown above as of June 30, 1990. You may assume an interest rate of 10%. Identify other assumptions that you must make.

Grand Metropolitan

C9–7 Comparing Accounting for Deferred Taxes in Different Countries

Grand Metropolitan is a major international company that is located in London. A recent annual report contained the following information concerning their accounting policies.

> **Taxation**
>
> The charge for taxation is based on the profit for the year and takes into account taxation deferred because of timing differences between the treatment of certain items for taxa-

tion and accounting purposes. However, no provision is made for taxation deferred, principally by accelerated taxation allowances on capital expenditure, if there is reasonable evidence that such deferred taxation will not be payable or recoverable in the foreseeable future.

Compare and contrast accounting for deferred taxes in England with procedures used in this country.

C9–8 Financial Statement Analysis

Toys "Я" Us

Refer to the financial statements of Toys "Я" Us given in Appendix B at the end of this book.

Required:

1. How much money does the company owe its suppliers at the end of the current year?
2. How much interest was capitalized during the current year?
3. What is the amount of federal income tax expense for the current year?
4. How much of the tax expense for the current year was deferred?
5. Compute and evaluate the current ratio.

10

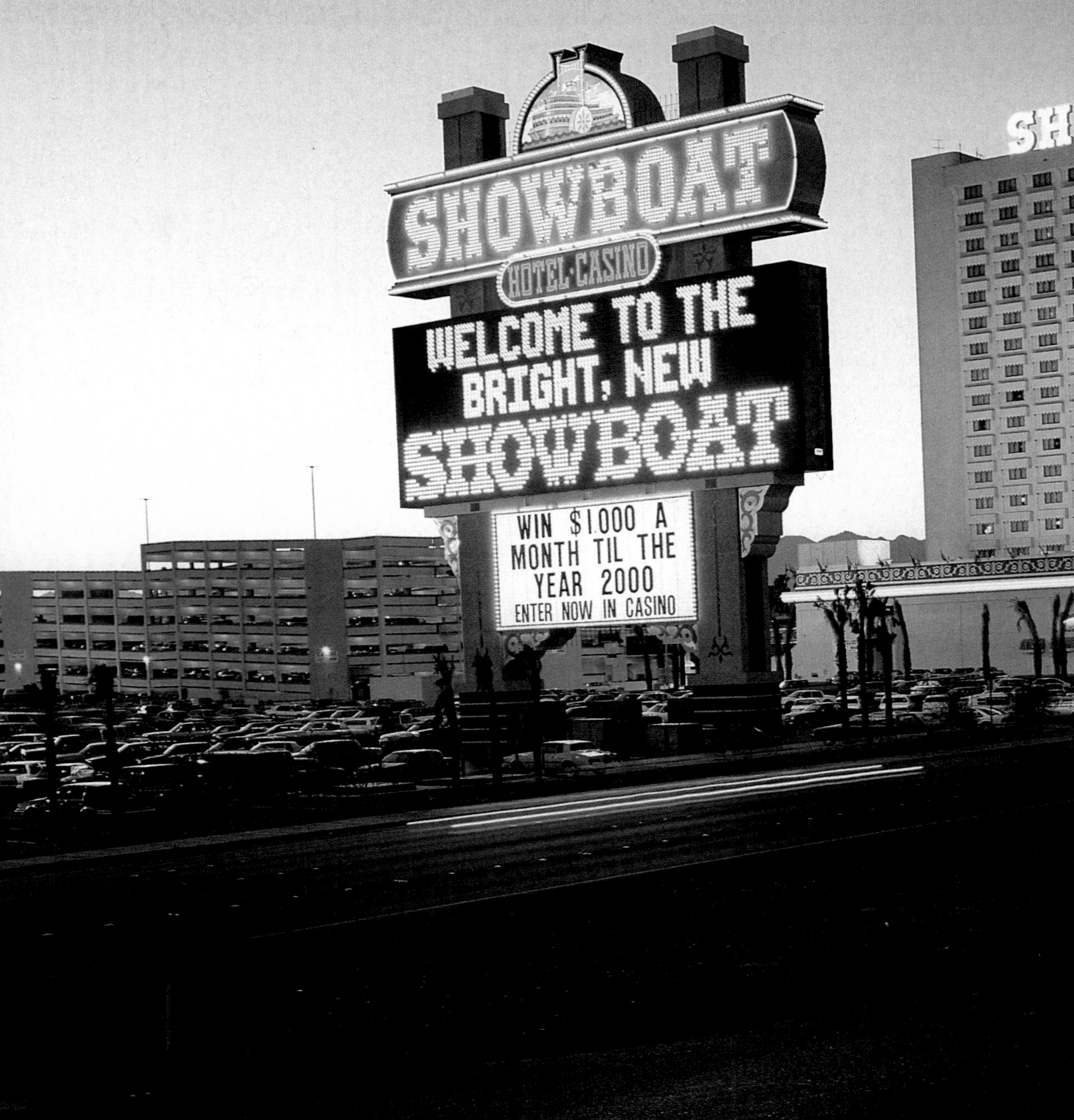
SHOWBOAT
HOTEL·CASINO
WELCOME TO THE
BRIGHT, NEW
SHOWBOAT
WIN $1000 A
MONTH TIL THE
YEAR 2000
ENTER NOW IN CASINO

MEASURING AND REPORTING BONDS

In the previous chapter, we discussed many types of liabilities that are commonly found on most balance sheets. For many companies, the largest liability classification is bonds payable. In this chapter, we will examine the business purpose and accounting treatment of bonds in considerable depth. You will use the present value concepts that were introduced in the previous chapter to determine the current value of bonds. We will also discuss bond investments.

LEARNING OBJECTIVES

After studying this chapter, you should be able to:

1. **Explain corporations' use of bonds payable.** ***498***
2. **Classify bonds payable.** ***499***
3. **Record bonds payable and interest expense.** ***502***
4. **Account for bonds sold at a discount.** ***506***
5. **Account for bonds sold at a premium.** ***508***
6. **Use the effective-interest method of amortization.** ***510***
7. **Record the early retirement of bonds.** ***513***
8. **Explain the use of bond sinking funds.** ***514***
9. **Account for bond investments held to maturity.** ***516***

Management Decision Setting
SHOWBOAT, INC.

Financing Growth with Bonds Payable

Showboat, Inc., recently issued bonds in the amount of $275 million. This money was needed because the company is actively pursuing expansion opportunities in emerging gaming (gambling) markets in the United States and internationally. Showboat currently owns gambling casinos in Atlantic City and Nevada. Gaming has become big business. The Atlantic City Showboat is a 24-story casino hotel featuring a 60,000 square foot gambling area with 2,138 slot machines and 69 table games. The parking facilities include a 14-bus depot and space for 2,500 cars.

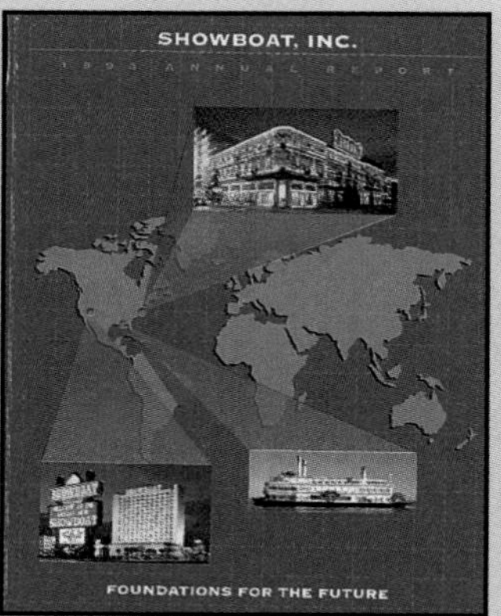

The gaming industry has become more competitive in recent years. As a result, gaming operators have been forced to expand and modernize their operations. The Atlantic City Showboat was completed in 1987 but the company has already started a $53.5 million expansion project for the hotel and casino.

Because of the company's strategy of expanding into new markets and the need to modernize existing facilities, Showboat, Inc., has been required to raise large amounts of new capital in addition to retaining a large amount of their income. Why did management decide to raise this money through the issuance of bonds? We will answer the question in this chapter.

BUSINESS BACKGROUND

Learning Objective 1
Explain corporations' use of bonds payable.

In the previous chapter, we introduced the term *capital structure,* which is the mixture of debt and equity that is used to finance a company's operations. Almost all companies employ some debt in their capital structure. Indeed, large corporations need to borrow billions of dollars, which makes it impractical for them to borrow money from individual creditors. Instead, these corporations can issue bonds to raise debt capital.

Bonds are securities that are issued by corporations and governmental units when they borrow large amounts of money. After bonds are issued, they can be traded on established exchanges such as the New York Bond Exchange. The ability to sell a bond on the bond exchange is a significant advantage for creditors because it provides them with *liquidity,* or the ability to convert their investment into cash. If you lend money directly to a corporation for 20 years, you must wait that long to have your cash investment repaid to you. If you lend money by purchasing a bond, you can sell the bond to another creditor if you need cash before the bond matures.

The liquidity that is available with publicly traded bonds offers an important advantage to corporations. Because most creditors are reluctant to lend money for long periods of time with no opportunity to receive cash prior to the maturity date of the debt, they would demand a higher interest rate to compensate them for long-term loans. The liquidity associated with bonds permits corporations to reduce the cost of borrowing money for long periods of time.

The use of bonds to raise long-term capital offers other significant advantages to corporations like Showboat:

1. Ownership and control of the company are not diluted. In contrast to stockholders, bondholders do not participate in the management (by voting) and accumulated earnings of the company.
2. Cash payments to the bondholders are limited to the specified interest payments and the principal of the debt.
3. Interest expense is a tax-deductible expense, while dividends paid to stockholders are not. The tax deductibility of interest expense

reduces the net cost of borrowing. For example, if a corporation paid $100,000 interest during the year, its taxable income would be $100,000 less. If the tax rate is 35%, the corporation would pay $35,000 less in taxes (35% × $100,000) because of the lower taxable income. Thus, the **net interest cost** is $65,000 ($100,000 – $35,000). If the corporation paid $100,000 in dividends, the net cost would be $100,000 because dividends are not tax deductible.

Net interest cost is interest cost less any income tax savings associated with interest expense.

4. It is often possible to borrow funds at a low interest rate and invest them at a higher rate, which is called positive **financial leverage.** To illustrate financial leverage, assume that Home Video, Inc., owns a video rental store. The company has stockholders' equity of $100,000 invested in the store and no debt. The company earns net income of $20,000 per year on the store (which is a 20% return on the stockholders' investment). Management plans to open a new store which will also cost $100,000 and will earn $20,000 per year. If the stockholders provide the new funds, they will still earn 20% on their investment ($40,000 ÷ $200,000), but if the company borrows $100,000 for the new store at a net after-tax interest cost of 8%, the stockholders' rate of return will actually increase. They will earn $20,000 on the first store and $12,000 on the second store ($20,000 – $8,000 interest) for a total return of $32,000. Because the company borrowed money, stockholders' equity remains at $100,000 with a rate of return of 32% ($32,000 ÷ $100,000).

Financial leverage is the use of borrowed funds to increase the rate of return on owners' equity; it occurs when the interest rate on debt is lower than the earnings rate on total assets.

Unfortunately, the issuance of bonds also has some disadvantages. The primary disadvantages are (*a*) the required interest payments must be made each interest period and (*b*) the large principal amount must be paid at the maturity date. Interest payments to bondholders are fixed charges, which increase the risk of business. Interest payments legally must be paid each period, whether the corporation earns income or incurs a loss. In contrast, dividends usually are paid to stockholders only if earnings are satisfactory. Each year, some companies go bankrupt because of their inability to make their required interest payments to creditors. Sound business practice requires maintaining an appropriate balance between debt and equity capital.

FINANCIAL ANALYSIS

Evaluating the Balance between Debt and Equity

Because of the importance of the balance between debt and equity, most analysts use the *debt-equity ratio* which, as the name implies, is computed by dividing total debt by total equity. This ratio shows how much debt a company has for each dollar of its stockholders' equity. A company with a large debt-equity ratio is called a *highly leveraged* company. These companies normally are considered to be more risky than less highly leveraged companies. Companies that are highly leveraged have a large amount of debt and, consequently, a large amount of debt payments. If they experience a difficult financial period, they may not be able to meet their obligatory payments and could face bankruptcy.

CHARACTERISTICS OF BONDS PAYABLE

Learning Objective 2
Classify bonds payable.

Different types of bonds have different characteristics. Exhibit 10–1 summarizes many of the most common features of corporate bonds. At first, it may seem perplexing to see so many different types of bonds but there is a solid economic reason. Different types of creditors have different types of risk and

Exhibit 10–1 Bond Characteristics and Classifications of Bonds

Bond Classification	Bond Characteristic
1. On the basis of collateral (assets):	
a. Unsecured bonds (often called *debentures*).	*a.* Bonds that do not include a mortgage or pledge of specific assets as a guarantee of repayment at maturity.
b. Secured bonds (often designated on the basis of the type of asset pledged, such as a real estate mortgage).	*b.* Bonds that include the pledge of specific assets as a guarantee of repayment at maturity.
2. On the basis of repayment of principal:	
a. Ordinary or single-payment bonds.	*a.* The principal is payable in full at a single specified maturity date in the future.
b. Serial bonds.	*b.* The principal is payable in installments on a series of specified maturity dates in the future.
3. On the basis of early retirement:	
a. Callable bonds.	*a.* Bonds that may be called for early retirement at the option of the *issuer.*
b. Redeemable bonds.	*b.* Bonds that may be turned in for early retirement at the option of the *bondholder.*
c. Convertible bonds.	*c.* Bonds that may be converted to other securities of the issuer (usually common stock) at the option of the *bondholder.*
4. On the basis of payment of interest:	
a. Registered bonds.	*a.* Payment of interest is made by check and mailed *directly* to the bondholder, whose name must be on file (i.e., in the bond register).
b. Coupon bonds.	*b.* Bonds with a printed coupon attached for each interest payment. The bondholder "clips" the coupon on the interest date and deposits it in a bank like a check, or mails it to the issuing company. Then the company mails the interest check directly to the person and address shown on the completed coupon. The interest rate on coupon bonds often is called the *coupon rate.*

return preferences. A retired person, for example, may be willing to receive a lower interest rate in return for having more security. This type of creditor might want a mortgage bond that would pledge a specific asset as security if the company is unable to repay the bond (called a *secured bond*). Another creditor might be willing to accept a low interest rate and an unsecured status if the company provides the opportunity to convert the bond into common stock at some point in the future if the company does very well. A bond that is not secured with the pledge of a specific asset is called a **debenture.** Companies try to design bond features that are attractive to different groups of creditors just as automobile manufacturers try to design cars that appeal to different groups of consumers.

A **debenture** is an unsecured bond; no assets are specifically pledged to guarantee repayment.

The **bond principal** is the amount payable at the maturity of the bond; face amount, on which the periodic cash interest payments are computed.

Par value is another name for bond principal, or the maturity amount of the bond.

Face amount is another name for principal, or the principal amount of the bond.

The **stated rate** is the rate of cash interest per period specified in the bond contract.

A bond usually requires the payment of interest over its life with the repayment of principal on the maturity date. The **bond principal** is the amount (*a*) payable at the maturity date and (*b*) on which the periodic cash interest payments are computed. It does not change. The principal is also called the **par value, face amount**, and *maturity value*. All bonds have a par value which is the amount that will be paid when the bond matures. For most bonds, the par value is $1,000 but it can be any amount.

A bond will always specify a **stated rate** of interest and when periodic cash interest payments must be paid—usually annually or semiannually. Each periodic interest payment is computed as principal times the stated interest rate.

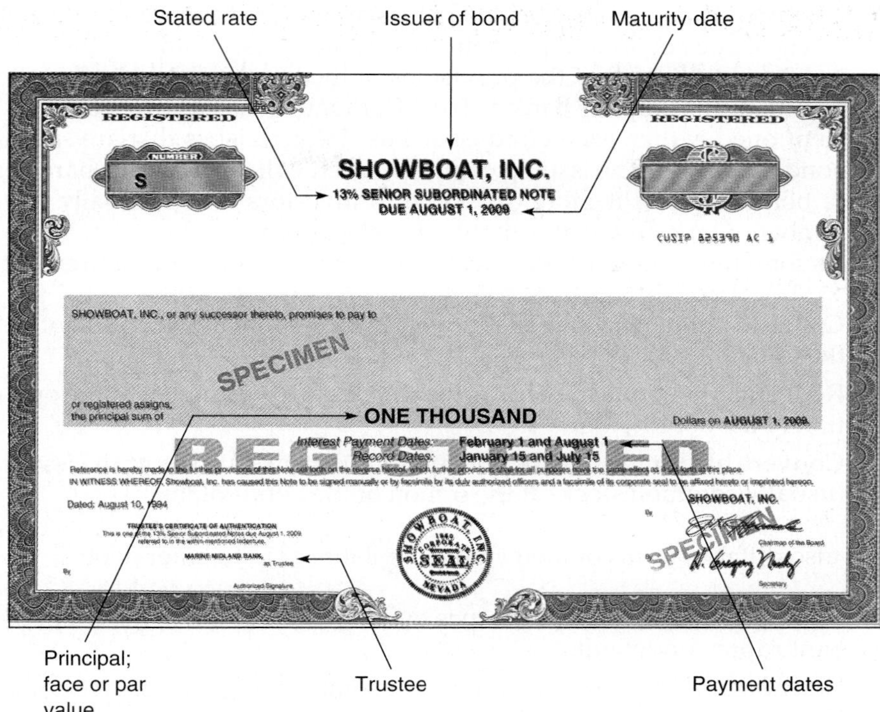

A bond certificate includes inportant information concerning the bond.

The selling price of a bond does not affect the periodic cash payment of interest. For example, a $1,000, 8% bond always pays cash interest of (*a*) $80 on an annual basis or (*b*) $40 on a semiannual basis.

When Showboat, Inc., decided to issue new bonds, it prepared a bond **indenture** (bond contract) that stated the legal provisions of the bonds. These provisions include the maturity date, rate of interest to be paid, date of each interest payment, and any conversion privileges (explained later). The indenture also contains covenants which are designed to protect the creditors. The Showboat indenture included limitations on new debt and on the amount of dividends that could be paid. Management would prefer to have the least restrictive covenants possible because they may limit future action. The creditors prefer more restrictive covenants because they lessen the risk of the investment. As in any business transaction, the final result is achieved through a process of negotiation. As we will see later in the chapter, one of the covenants included in the indenture prevented Showboat management from taking advantage of a new business opportunity. We will see what management did to overcome the restrictions in a covenant.

An **indenture** is a bond contract that specifies the legal provisions of a bond issue.

Showboat also prepared a *prospectus*, which is a legal document given to potential buyers of the bonds. The prospectus describes the company, the bonds, and how the proceeds of the bond will be used. Most companies work with an underwriter who either buys the entire issue of bonds and then resells them to individual creditors (called a *firm commitment underwriter*), or simply sells the bonds without any obligation to purchase them (called a *best efforts underwriter*). Showboat used two underwriters (on a firm commitment basis), Donaldson, Lufkin & Jenrette, and Lehman Brothers. The underwriting commission paid to these firms was $6,531,250 on a bond issue of $275 million.

When a bond is issued to the investor, the person receives a **bond certificate.** All of the bond certificates for a single bond issue are identical. The face of each certificate shows the same maturity date, interest rate, interest dates, and other provisions.

A **bond certificate** is the bond document; each bondholder receives a bond certificate.

A **trustee** is an independent party appointed to represent the bondholders.

A third party, called the **trustee,** usually is appointed to represent the bondholders. The duties of an independent trustee are to ascertain whether the issuing company fulfills all of the provisions of the bond indenture. Showboat, Inc., appointed IBJ Schroder Bank & Trust Company to act as trustee.

As mentioned earlier, each bond issue has characteristics that are specified in the bond indenture. The issuing company often will add special characteristics to a bond to make it more attractive to investors who normally have a large number of investment alternatives to select from.

Callable bonds are bonds that may be called for early retirement at the option of the issuer.

Redeemable bonds are bonds that may be turned in for early retirement at the option of the bondholder.

Convertible bonds are bonds that may be converted to other securities of the issuer (usually common stock).

Bonds sometimes offer different features with respect to early retirement:

a. **Callable bonds** may be called for early retirement at the option of the issuer.

b. **Redeemable bonds** may be turned in for early retirement at the option of the bondholder.

c. **Convertible bonds** may be converted to other securities of the issuer (usually common stock) at the option of the bondholder.

Bonds also differ in terms of their status in relationship to other debt:

a. *Senior debt* will receive preference over other creditors in the event of bankruptcy or default.

b. *Subordinated debt* will be paid off after some other group of creditors. Obviously, subordinated debt is more risky than senior debt.

Each year, corporations introduce new features that are included with their bonds. For example, The Walt Disney Company recently issued the first bond with a 100-year maturity. Despite an increase in unusual features, the basics that we discuss in this chapter will permit you to deal with most types of bonds.

MEASURING BONDS PAYABLE AND INTEREST EXPENSE

Learning Objective 3
Record bonds payable and interest expense.

When Showboat issued its bonds, it specified two types of cash payments in the bond contract:

1. *Principal.* This is usually a single payment made when the bond matures. This is also called the par, or face, value.
2. *Cash interest payments.* These payments represent an annuity and are computed by multiplying the principal amount times the interest rate, called the *contract, stated,* or **coupon rate** of interest stated in the

The **coupon rate** is the stated rate of interest on coupon bonds.

Gaming casinos must have dramatic facades to attract customers, just as bonds must have attractive features to attract investors.

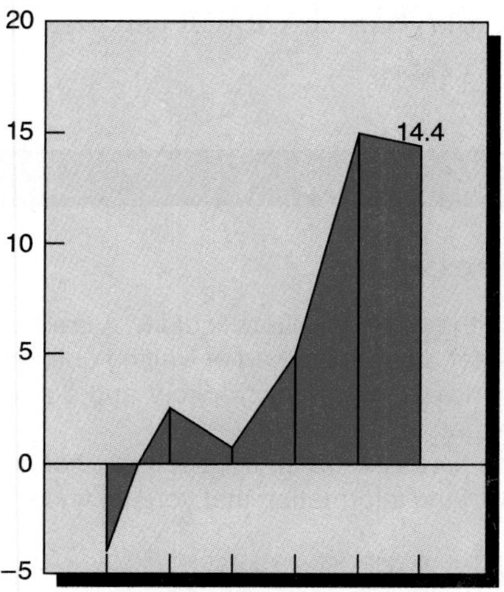

Recurring Net Income approximated the prior year. Costs associated with development in new jurisdictions was the primary cause of the $.6 million decrease.

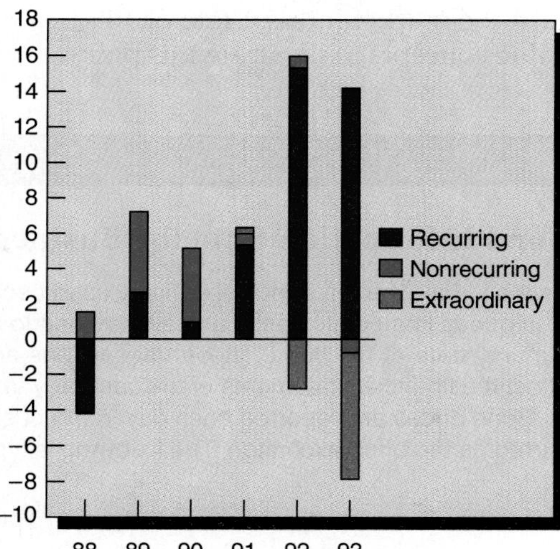

Net income decreased $5.1 million to $7.3 million primarily due to the extraordinary loss on the retirement of the 11-3/8% Mortgage-Backed Bonds and the costs associated with the development in new jurisdictions.

Costs associated with financing and developing new property can affect income.

bond contract. The bond contract will specify whether these payments are made quarterly, semiannually, or annually.

The price at which the bonds will sell is not determined by either Showboat or the underwriter. Instead, the price is determined by the market using the present value concepts that were introduced in the previous chapter. To determine the present value of the bond, you compute the present value of the principal (a single payment) and the present value of the interest payments (an annuity) and add the two amounts together.

Creditors demand a certain rate of interest to compensate them for the risks related to bonds. The interest rate demanded by these creditors is the **market interest rate** (also called the **yield**, or **effective interest rate**). The market rate is the interest rate that should be used in the computation of the present value of the bond.

Market interest rate is the current rate of interest on a debt when incurred; also called the **yield**, or **effective interest rate**.

The present value of a bond may be the same as par, above par (**bond premium**), or below par (**bond discount**). If the stated and the market interest rates are the same, a bond will sell at par; if the market rate is higher than the stated rate, a bond will sell at a discount; and if the market rate is lower than the stated rate, the bond will sell at a premium. These relationships can be understood in commonsense terms. If a bond pays an interest rate that is less than creditors demand, they will not buy the bond unless the price of the bond is reduced (i.e., a discount must be provided). If a bond pays more than creditors demand, they will be willing to pay a premium to buy the bond.

Bond premium is the difference between the selling price and par when the bond is sold for more than par.

Bond discount is the difference between the selling price and par when the bond is sold for less than par.

When a bond is issued at par, the issuer receives cash equal to the par value of the bond. When a bond is issued at a discount, the issuer receives less cash than the par value of the bond. When a bond is issued at a premium, the issuer receives more cash than the par value.

Basically, corporations and creditors do not care if a bond is issued at par, a discount, or a premium because bonds are always priced to provide the market rate of interest. To illustrate, consider a corporation that issues three separate bonds on the same day. The bonds are exactly the same except one has a stated interest of 8%, another 10%, and a third 11%. If the market rate of interest was 10%, the first would be issued at a discount, the second at par, and the third at a premium, but a creditor who bought any one of the bonds would earn the market interest rate of 10%. Later in this chapter, we will use present value concepts to illustrate this point.

FINANCIAL ANALYSIS

Bond Information from the Business Press

As mentioned earlier, bonds are widely used because they offer creditors liquidity. A creditor who needs immediate cash can sell the bond to another creditor instead of waiting until the maturity date of the bond. These transactions are between individual creditors and do not affect the financial statements of the company that issued the bonds.

Bond prices are reported each day in the business press based on transactions that occurred on the bond exchange. The following is typical of the information that you will find:

Bond	Yield	Volume	Close	Change
Safeway 9.6 04	9.6	58	100	–1/4
Sears 9 1/2 99	9.1	25	104 1/4	–3/8
Showboat 9 1/4 08	11.3	580	82 1/8	–7/8

This listing means that the Showboat bond has a coupon interest rate of 9 1/4% and will mature in the year 2008. The bond currently provides a cash yield of 11.3% with a selling price which is 82 1/8% of par or $821.13. On this particular date 580 bonds were sold and the price fell 7/8 point from the previous trading date. A point is 1%.

While analysts may study the daily price changes of bonds, remember that they do not affect the financial statements of the company. For financial reporting purposes, the company will use the interest rates that existed when the bonds were first sold to the public. Subsequent changes do not affect the company's accounting for the bonds.

Self-Study Quiz

Your study of bonds will be easier if you understand the new terminology that has been introduced in this chapter. Let's review some of those terms. Provide definitions for the following:

1. Market interest rate ____________________.
2. Synonyms for market interest rate ____________________.
3. Coupon interest rate ____________________.
4. Synonyms for coupon interest rate ____________________.
5. Bond discount ____________________.
6. Bond premium ____________________.

Check your answers in the footnote at the bottom of this page.*

*1. The market rate is the interest rate demanded by creditors. It is the rate used in the present value computations to discount future cash flows.
2. Market interest rate is also called yield or effective interest rate.
3. Coupon interest rate is the stated rate on the bonds.
4. Coupon rate is also called stated rate and contract rate.
5. A bond that sells for less than par is sold at a discount. This occurs when the coupon rate is less than the market rate.
6. A bond that sells for more than par is sold at a premium. This occurs when the coupon rate is more than the market rate.

ACCOUNTING FOR BONDS ILLUSTRATED

In this section of the chapter, we will illustrate three different cases of accounting for bonds payable: (1) bonds issued at par, (2) bonds issued at a discount, and (3) bonds issued at a premium. We will use Showboat, Inc., for our illustration, but for the sake of simplification, we will assume that the company issued bonds with a maturity value of $400,000.

Bonds Issued at Par

Bonds sell at their par value when buyers are willing to invest in them at the stated interest rate on the bond. To illustrate, let's assume that on January 1, 19A, Showboat, Inc., issued 10% bonds with a par value of $400,000 and received $400,000 in cash (which means that the bonds sold at par). The bonds were dated to start interest on January 1, 19A and will pay interest each June 30 and December 31. The bonds mature in 10 years on December 31, 19J. The entry by Showboat to record the issuance of these bonds is:

Jan. 1, 19A	Cash	400,000	
	Bonds payable		400,000

The creditors who bought the bonds did so with the expectation that they would earn interest over the life of the bond. Showboat will pay interest at 5% (i.e., 10% per year) on the par value of the bonds each June 30 and December 31 until the maturity date of the bond. The amount of interest each period will be $20,000 (5% × $400,000). The entry to record the interest payments is:

June 30, 19A	Bond interest expense	20,000	
	Cash		20,000

It is rare to have bond interest payment dates coincide with the last day of a company's fiscal year. Under the matching concept, interest expense that has been incurred but not paid must be accrued with an adjusting entry. If the Showboat fiscal year ended on May, 31 19A, the company would accrue interest for five months and record interest expense and interest payable. Adjusting entries were discussed in Chapter 4.

Notice in the previous journal entry that interest expense and cash interest paid are the same amount. This is the case whenever the effective interest rate and the stated rate are the same. When bonds are sold at a discount or a premium, this will not be the case. We will illustrate these cases later in the chapter.

The $400,000 cash that Showboat received when the bonds were sold is the present value of the future cash flows associated with the bonds. This is computed using the present value tables contained in Appendix A:

	Present Value
a. Principal: $400,000 × $p_{n=20,\ i=5\%}$ (0.3769)	$150,760
b. Interest: $20,000 × $P_{n=20,\ i=5\%}$ (12.4622)	249,240*
Issue price of Showboat bonds	$400,000

*rounded

When the effective rate of interest is equal to the stated rate of interest, the present value of the future cash flows associated with a bond *always* will equal the bond's par amount. It is important to remember that the selling price of a bond is determined by the present value of its future cash flows, not the par value. Also, bond liabilities are initially recorded at the present value of future cash flows on date of issue, not par value.

Bonds Issued at a Discount

Learning Objective 4
Account for bonds sold at a discount.

Bonds sell at a bond discount when the buyers are willing to invest in them only if they receive the market rate of interest which is *higher* than the stated interest rate on the bonds. Let's now assume the market rate of interest was 12% when Showboat sold its bonds (which have a par value of $400,000). The bonds have a stated rate of 10%, payable semiannually, which is less than the rate demanded by the market. Therefore, the bonds sold at a discount. To compute the cash issue price of the bonds requires computation of the present value, at the *market rate of interest,* of the future cash flows specified on the bond: (*a*) the principal ($n = 20, i = 6\%$) and (*b*) the cash interest paid each semiannual interest period ($n = 20, i = 6\%$). Thus, the cash issue price of the Showboat bonds is computed as follows:

	Present Value
a. Principal: $400,000 × $p_{n=20,\,i=6\%}$ (0.3118)	$124,720
b. Interest: $20,000 × $P_{n=20,\,i=6\%}$ (11.4699)	229,398
Issue (sale) price of Showboat bonds	$354,118*

*Discount: $400,000 – $354,118 = $45,882.

The cash price of the bonds issued by Showboat is $354,118. Some people refer to this price as 88.5, which means that the bonds were sold at 88.5% of their par value ($354,118/$400,000).

When a bond is sold at a discount, the Bonds Payable account is credited for the par amount and the discount is recorded as a debit to Discount on Bonds Payable. The issuance of the Showboat bonds at a discount is shown below:

Jan. 1, 19A	Cash	354,118	
	Discount on bonds payable	45,882	
	Bonds payable		400,000

This journal entry shows the discount in a separate contra liability account (Discount on Bonds Payable) as a debit. The balance sheet reports the bonds payable at their book value which is their maturity amount less any unamortized discount.

Measuring and Recording Interest on Bonds Issued at a Discount

During the 10-year term of the bonds, Showboat must make 20 semiannual cash interest payments of $20,000 (i.e., $400,000 × 5%) and at maturity pay back the $400,000 cash principal. Therefore, in addition to the cash interest, Showboat must repay more money than it received when it sold the bonds (i.e., it borrowed $354,118 and it must repay $400,000). This extra cash that must be paid is an adjustment of interest expense that will ensure that creditors earn the market rate of interest on the bonds. In order to adjust interest expense, the bond discount must be apportioned (*amortized*) to each semiannual interest period as an increase in interest expense. Therefore, the amortization of bond discount results in an increase in bond interest expense.

There are two methods for allocating the bond discount: (1) straight-line amortization and (2) effective-interest amortization. Straight-line amortization is easy to compute. The effective-interest method is discussed later in this chapter.

The **straight-line amortization** of a bond discount or premium is a simplified method that allocates an equal dollar amount to each interest period.

Straight-Line Amortization. To amortize the $45,882 bond discount over the life of the Showboat bonds on a straight-line basis, an equal dollar amount is allocated to each interest period. The Showboat bonds have 20 six-month interest periods. Therefore, the computation is $45,882 ÷ 20 periods = $2,294 amortization on each semiannual interest date. This amount is added to the

Sports betting areas in casinos require large investments in modern technology.

cash payment of interest ($20,000) to compute interest expense for the period ($22,294). The interest payments on the Showboat bonds each period are:

June 30, 19A	Bond interest expense	22,294	
	Discount on bonds payable		2,294
	Cash		20,000

Bonds payable should be reported on the balance sheet at their *book value;* that is, the maturity amount less any unamortized bond discount (or plus any unamortized bond premium). Therefore, on June 30, 19A, the book value of the Showboat bonds is $356,412 ($354,118 + $2,294).

Each succeeding interest period, the unamortized discount will decrease by $2,294; therefore, the book value of the bonds will increase each interest period by $2,294. At the maturity date of the bonds, the unamortized discount (i.e., the balance in the Discount on Bonds Payable account) will be *zero.* At that time the maturity amount of the bonds and the book value will be the same (i.e., $400,000).

A note from the annual report for Ames Department Stores effectively summarizes our discussion of this point:

Real World Excerpt

Ames Department Stores Annual Report

Debt:
Debt obligations that carried face interest rates significantly less than market were discounted to their present values using estimated market rates. The discount amount will be amortized to interest expense over the term of the related obligation. The determination of appropriate interest rates was based upon evaluation of Ames' credit standing, the nature of the collateral, if any, and other terms pertaining to the debt, and the prevailing rates for similar instruments or issues with similar credit rating.

Bonds are recorded at the present value of their future cash flows using an interest rate determined by the market on the date the bonds were sold. The accounting for the bonds is not affected by subsequent changes in the market rate of interest. This interest rate is based on the terms of the debt issue and the risk characteristics of the debt.

Zero Coupon Bonds

Some bonds do not pay periodic cash interest. These bonds are often called *zero coupon bonds* because the coupon interest rate is zero. Why would an investor buy a bond that did not pay interest? Our discussion of bond discounts has probably given you a pretty good idea of the right answer. The coupon interest rate on a bond can be virtually any amount and the price of the bond will be adjusted so that investors earn the market rate of interest. A bond with a zero coupon interest rate is simply a *deep discount bond* that will sell for substantially less than its maturity value.

Let's use the $400,000 Showboat bond to illustrate a zero coupon. Assume that instead of paying 10% cash interest, the bond paid *no* cash interest. The selling price of the bond is the present value of the maturity amount because there are no other cash payments over the life of the bond:

	Present Value
a. Principal: $400,000 × $p_{n=20,\ i=6\%}$ (0.3118)	$124,720

This zero coupon bond is recorded as follows:

Cash	124,720	
Discount on bond payable	275,280	
Bonds payable		400,000

As you can see, the accounting for the zero coupon bond is no different than any bond sold at a discount. The only difference is that the amount of the discount is much larger. The annual report for Sears, Roebuck & Co. contained the following information concerning zero coupon bonds:

Real World Excerpt

Sears, Roebuck & Co. Annual Report

Long-term debt (millions)

	1992	1993
Zero coupon bonds, $400 million face value, due 1994, effective rate 12.8%	$338.4	$299.9
Zero coupon bonds, $500 million face value, due 1998, effective rate 12.0%	267.9	239.2

The note from the Sears annual report illustrates several important points concerning zero coupon bonds. Notice that the book value of the bonds increases each year. This is because of the amortization of the bond discount. The bonds that mature in 1994 are closer to their maturity value than the bonds that mature in 1998. This occurs because amortization will cause the book value of the bonds to be exactly the same as the maturity value when the bonds mature. Also notice that despite the fact that these bonds do not pay cash interest, they have been priced to provide the investor with effective interest of either 12.8% or 12%.

Bonds Issued at a Premium

Learning Objective 5
Account for bonds sold at a premium.

Bonds sell at a bond premium when the market rate of interest is *lower* than the stated interest rate on the bonds. For example, let's assume that the market rate of interest was 8 1/2% while the Showboat bonds paid cash interest of 10%. In this case, the bonds would sell at a premium. The cash issue price for the Showboat bonds when the market rate of interest was 8 1/2% is computed as follows:

	Present Value
a. Principal: $400,000 × $p_{n=20,\ i=4\ 1/4\%}$ (0.4350)	$174,000
b. Interest: $20,000 × $P_{n=20,\ i=4\ 1/4\%}$ (13.2944)	265,888
Issue (sale) price of Showboat bonds	$439,888

When a bond is sold at a premium, the Bonds Payable account is credited for the par amount, and the premium is recorded as a credit to Premium on Bonds Payable. The issuance of the bonds of Showboat at a premium is recorded as follows:

Jan. 1, 19A	Cash	439,888	
	Premium on bonds payable		39,888
	Bonds payable		400,000

The book value of the bond is the sum of the two accounts, Premium on Bonds Payable and Bonds Payable, or $439,888.

Measuring and Recording Interest Expense on Bonds Issued at a Premium

The premium of $39,888 recorded by Showboat must be apportioned to each of the 20 interest periods. Using the straight-line method, the amortization of premium each semiannual interest period is $39,888 ÷ 20 periods = $1,994. This amount is subtracted from the cash interest payment ($20,000) to calculate interest expense ($18,006). Therefore, amortization of the bond premium decreases interest expense. The payment of interest on the bonds is recorded as follows:

June 30, 19A	Bond interest expense	18,006	
	Premium on bonds payable	1,994	
	Cash		20,000

Notice that the $20,000 cash paid each period includes $18,006 interest expense and $1,994 of premium amortization. Thus, the cash payment to the investors includes the current interest they have earned plus a return of part of the premium they paid when they bought the bonds.

The book value of the bonds is the amount in the Bonds Payable account plus any unamortized premium. On June 30, 19A, the book value of the bonds is $437,894 ($400,000 + $39,888 – $1,994).

At maturity date, after the last interest payment, the bond premium of $39,888 will be fully amortized, and the maturity amount of the bonds and the book value of the bonds will be the same (i.e., $400,000). At maturity, December 31, 19J, the bonds will be paid off in full, resulting in the same entry whether the bond was originally sold at par, a discount, or a premium.

The effect of the amortization of bond discount and bond premium on a $1,000 bond is illustrated in Exhibit 10–2.

Self-Study Quiz

Assume that Showboat issued $100,000 bonds that will mature in 10 years. The bonds pay interest twice each year at an annual rate of 9%. They were sold when the market rate was 8%. Determine the selling price of the bonds.

Check your answer with the footnote at the bottom of this page.*

ADDITIONAL TOPICS IN ACCOUNTING FOR BONDS PAYABLE

In the following sections, we will discuss four topics commonly encountered in accounting for bonds payable: (1) effective-interest amortization of bond discounts and premiums, (2) bonds sold between interest dates, (3) early retirement of debt, and (4) bond sinking funds.

* $4,500 ×	13.5903 =	$ 61,156
100,000 ×	.4564 =	45,640
		$106,796

Exhibit 10–2 **Amortization of Bond Discount and Premium Compared**

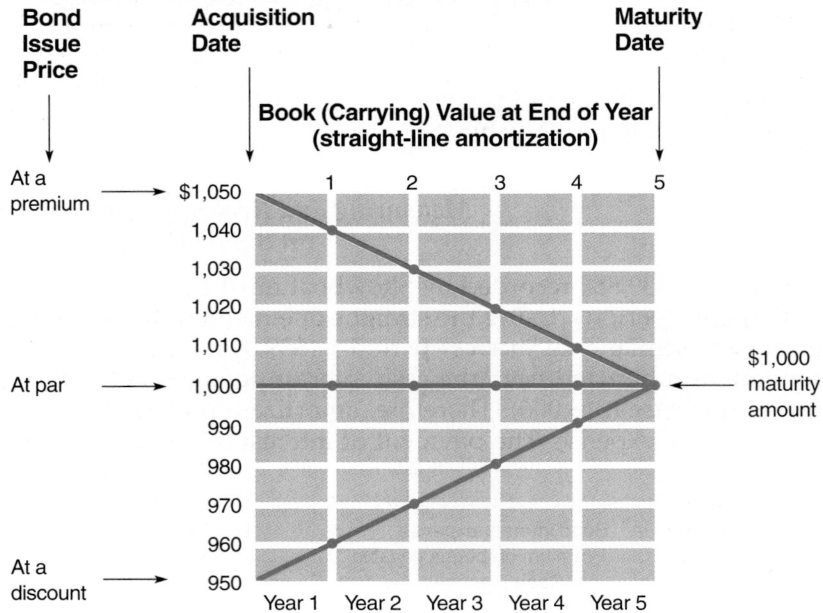

Effective-Interest Amortization of Bond Discounts and Premiums

Learning Objective 6
Use the effective-interest method of amortization.

The **effective-interest method** is the method of amortizing a bond discount or premium on the basis of the effective-interest rate; theoretically preferred method.

We introduced you to the straight-line method for amortizing a bond discount or premium earlier in this chapter. The only advantage of the straight-line method is calculational simplicity. Under GAAP, the straight-line method may be used only if the reported results are not materially different from the effective-interest method. The **effective-interest method** is conceptually superior, and we believe it provides a better basis for understanding why the amortization of a bond discount or premium is an adjustment to interest expense.

Interest expense is the cost of borrowing money. Interest expense is correctly measured by multiplying the *true* interest rate times the amount of money that was actually borrowed. What is the true interest rate? It is the rate that the market used to determine the present value of the bond. The actual amount borrowed is the cash that was received when the bond was sold, not the maturity value of the bond.

Under the effective-interest method, interest expense for a bond is computed by multiplying the current unpaid balance (i.e., the amount that was actually borrowed) times the market rate of interest that existed on the date the bonds were sold. The periodic amortization of a bond premium or discount is then calculated as the difference between interest expense and the amount of cash paid or accrued.

Earlier in this chapter, we illustrated accounting for bonds issued at a discount. Let's expand that example to see how the discount is amortized under the effective-interest method. The previous example involved 10% Showboat bonds with a par value of $400,000 that were issued when the market rate was 12%. The issue price of the bonds was $354,118. The sale was recorded with the following entry:

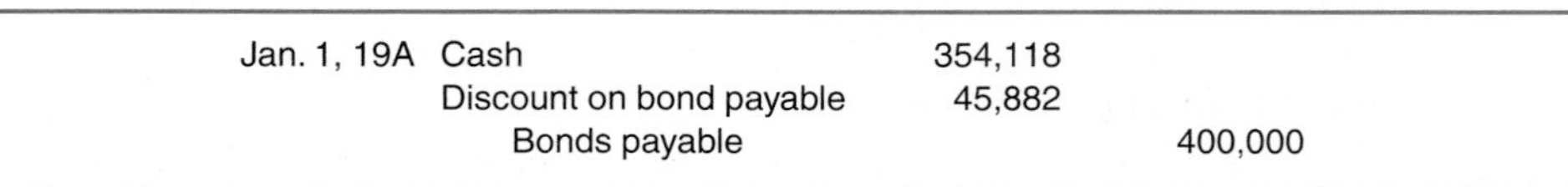

Date	Account	Debit	Credit
Jan. 1, 19A	Cash	354,118	
	Discount on bond payable	45,882	
	Bonds payable		400,000

The first interest payment on the Showboat bonds is on June 30, 19A. The interest expense at the end of the first six months is calculated by multiplying the amount that was actually borrowed by the market rate of interest for six months ($354,118 × 12% × 6/12 = $21,247). The amount of cash that is paid is calculated by multiplying the principal by the stated rate of interest for six months ($400,000 × 10% × 6/12 = $20,000). The difference between the interest expense and the cash paid (or accrued) is the amount of discount that has been amortized ($21,247 – $20,000 = $1,247). The journal entry to record interest expense on June 30, 19A is:

Interest expense	21,247	
Discount on bonds payable		1,247
Cash		20,000

The Discount on Bonds Payable account is a contra liability with a debit balance. The credit amount ($1,247) in the previous entry reduces the balance of the Discount on Bonds Payable account. A reduction of a contra liability account increases the book value of the liability, as shown below:

	January 1, 19A	June 30, 19A
Bonds payable	$400,000	$400,000
Discount on bonds payable	45,882	44,635*
Book value	$354,118	$355,365

*$45,882 – $1,247 = $44,635.

Each period, the amortization of the bond discount increases the book value (or unpaid balance) of the bond. The $1,247 amortization of bond discount can be thought of as interest that was earned by the bondholders but not paid to them. During the first six months of 19A, the bondholders earned interest of $21,247 but only $20,000 was paid in cash. The additional $1,247 was added to the principal of the bond and will be paid when the bond matures.

Interest expense for the second six months of 19A must reflect the change in the unpaid balance of bonds payable that occurred with the amortization of the bond discount. The interest expense for the second half of 19A is calculated by multiplying the unpaid balance on June 30, 19A, by the market rate of interest for six months ($355,365 × 12% × 6/12 = $21,322). The entry to record interest expense on December 31, 19A, is:

Interest expense	21,322	
Discount on bonds payable		1,322
Cash		20,000

Notice that interest expense for the second half of 19A is greater than the amount for the first six months of 19A. This is logical because Showboat effectively borrowed more money during the second half of the year (i.e., the $1,247 unpaid interest). Each year during the life of the bond, interest expense will increase because of the amortization of the bond discount.

An example that demonstrates both a bond premium and an adjusting entry to record accrued interest under the effective-interest amortization method is provided in the demonstration case at the end of this chapter.

Some companies use a bond amortization schedule to assist in the detailed computations that are required under the effective-interest amortization method. A typical schedule is shown below:

Date	*(a)* Cash Interest	*(b)* Interest Expense	*(c)* Amortization	*(d)* Unpaid Balance
1/1/19A				$354,118
6/30/19A	$20,000	$21,247	$1,247	355,365
12/31/19A	20,000	21,322	1,322	356,687

Even a simple game like bingo requires a major investment to be popular with customers.

Interest expense (column *b*) is computed by multiplying the market rate of interest by the unpaid balance at the beginning of the period (column *d*). Amortization is computed by subtracting cash interest (column *a*) from interest expense (column *b*). The unpaid balance (column *d*) is computed by adding amortization (column *c*) to the unpaid balance at the beginning of the period.

FINANCIAL ANALYSIS

Understanding Alternative Amortization Methods

While the effective-interest method is preferred conceptually, some companies use the straight-line method because of the materiality constraint. Accounting for various transactions should be in conformity with generally accepted accounting principles (GAAP) unless the amounts involved are immaterial and will not affect the decisions made by users of the statements. The straight-line method is permitted when the difference in periodic amortization between the two methods is not material in amount. Because differences are immaterial, most financial statements do not disclose which method is used by the company. An exception is Showboat, which indicates the following in its notes:

Real World Excerpt

Showboat, Inc.
Annual Report

Summary of Significant Accounting Policies
Original issue discount is amortized over the life of the related indebtedness using the effective interest method.

Compare the note for Showboat to one from Kansas City Southern Industries:

Real World Excerpt

Kansas City Southern Industries Annual Report

Note 5: Debt
Debt was issued at a discount of $1.6 million which will be amortized over the respective debt maturities on a straight line basis which is not materially different from the interest method.

Notice that in both cases, the analysts cannot quantify the impact of using one method versus the other. As a result, most analysts are not concerned about which method a company chooses.

Bonds Sold between Interest Dates

For the sake of illustration, we have assumed that bonds were sold on the first day of an interest period. In practice, bonds will be sold at a variety of dates during the interest period. Bonds that are sold between interest dates sell for their market value *plus* any interest that has accrued on them since the last interest payment.

From our previous example, if Showboat sold $400,000 worth of 10% bonds at par on April 1 instead of January 1, the investor would have to pay accrued interest (remember the bonds paid interest on June 30 and December 31). The amount of interest is computed as follows:

Accrued Interest	=	Face Value	×	Coupon Rate	×	Time
$10,000	=	$400,000	×	10%	×	3/12

To record the issuance of the bonds, Showboat would record the following:

Cash	410,000	
Bonds payable		400,000
Interest payable		10,000

When the interest is paid on June 30, 19A, Showboat would make the following entry:

Interest expense	10,000	
Interest payable	10,000	
Cash		20,000

By accounting for interest in this way, the interest expense is properly measured (i.e., Showboat records interest expense for only the three months that it actually borrowed money). This method also avoids the complication of preparing numerous different interest checks for different investors if the bonds had been sold to multiple investors at different times.

Early Retirement of Debt

Learning Objective 7
Record the early retirement of bonds.

Bonds are normally issued for long periods of time, such as 20 or 30 years. As mentioned earlier in the chapter, bondholders who need cash prior to the maturity date can simply sell the bonds to another investor. This transaction would not affect the books of the company that issued the bonds.

There are also several situations under which a corporation would like to retire a bond before its maturity date. A bond with a call feature may be called in for early retirement at the option of the issuer. Typically, the bond indenture includes a call premium if the bonds are retired before the maturity date. This call premium is often stated as a percentage of the par value of the bonds. The prospectus for the Showboat bonds included the following:

Real World Excerpt
Showboat, Inc.
Bond Prospectus

The bonds will be subject to redemption at the option of the Company, in whole or in part . . . at the redemption prices set forth below plus accrued and unpaid interest thereon:

Year	Percentage
2000	102.775%
2001	101.850%
2002	100.925%
2003 and thereafter	100.000%

Assume that in 1994, Showboat issued 10% bonds in the amount of $1 million and that the bonds sold at par. If the bonds were called in 2001 with 90 days of accrued interest, Showboat would make the following journal entry:

Bonds payable	1,000,000	
Interest expense	25,000*	
Loss on bond call	18,500	
Cash		1,043,500

*$1,000,000 × 10% × 90/360 = $25,000

The loss on bond call is the premium over par that must be paid according to the bond indenture. This premium is 1.850% (101.850% – 100.000%) which is multiplied by the par value of the bond to derive the expense of $18,500 (1.850% × $1,000,000). The loss on bond call is reported on the income statement as an extraordinary item.

Southwestern Bell recently engaged in a transaction similar to the one illustrated above and included the following description in the notes to its statements:

Real World Excerpt

Southwestern Bell Annual Report

> The Telephone Company reflected an extraordinary loss on the early extinguishment of debt as the result of refinancing $732,000,000 of long-term bonds. Expense associated with the refinancing, including a call premium of $67,500,000, totaled $129,300,000.

In other cases, a company may elect to retire debt early by purchasing it in the open market, just like an investor. This approach is necessary if the bond did not have a call feature. It might also be an attractive approach if the price of the bonds fell after the date of issue.

What factors would cause the price of a bond to fall? The most common cause is a rise in interest rates. As you may have noticed during our discussion of present value concepts earlier in this chapter, bond prices move in the opposite direction of interest rates. If interest rates go up, bond prices will fall and vice versa. When interest rates have gone up, a company that wants to retire a bond before maturity may find that it is less expensive to buy the bond in the market than to pay a call premium.

Showboat , Inc., engaged in this type of transaction as described in the notes to their statement:

Real World Excerpt

Showboat, Inc. Annual Report

> In the current and previous years, the Company purchased $12,096,000 and $18,460,000 face value, respectively, of the 11 3/8% Mortgage-Backed Bonds Due 2002 for $11,696,000 and $12,258,000, respectively. Accordingly, the Company realized an extraordinary gain in the current year of $273,000 before income taxes of $93,000, resulting in an after-tax gain of $180,000 or $.02 per share. In the previous year, the Company realized an extraordinary gain of $6,015,000 before income taxes of $2,045,000, resulting in an after-tax gain of $3,970,000 or $.35 per share.

The note illustrates three important issues. The gain or loss on the early retirement of debt is always reported separately on the income statement as an extraordinary item. The gain from this transaction is taxable, which is an important cost for managers to consider. The amount of the gain from the early retirement of debt can be substantial. The $.35 per share gain mentioned in the Showboat note was over 60% of the income reported in that year. Analysts must use caution when evaluating gains from debt retirement because these gains do not represent profits from the ongoing business activities of the company.

Learning Objective 8
Explain the use of bond sinking funds.

Bond Sinking Funds

A **bond sinking fund** is a cash fund accumulated for payment of a bond at maturity.

To reduce risk for bondholders, many bond indentures include the requirement for the company to establish a **bond sinking fund** which is a special cash fund to be used to meet the principal payment when the bond matures. This fund assures creditors that cash will be available for retirement of the bonds at their maturity date. Managers, on the other hand, would prefer not to have a sinking fund requirement. This requirement forces them to put cash in a special fund instead of investing it in productive assets related to the operations of the business.

Normally, cash contributions are made to the fund each year. The cash is often deposited with an independent trustee (a designated third party such as a bank or another financial institution). The trustee invests the cash and adds the earnings to the fund balance each year. Interest earned on a sinking fund is recorded as an increase in the fund balance (a debit) and as interest revenue (a credit). Thus, a bond sinking fund has the characteristics of a savings account. At the maturity date of the bonds, the balance of the fund is used to pay the bondholders. Any excess cash is returned to the issuing corporation, or in the case of a deficit, it is made up by the issuer.

The purpose of a sinking fund is to reduce the risk that the issuer will not be able to meet the principal payment when bonds mature. As a result, many bond indentures permit the issuing corporation to meet sinking fund requirements either by making cash payments to a fund or by redeeming outstanding bonds. A note to a recent annual report for Harrow Industries illustrates a typical disclosure concerning sinking funds:

Real World Excerpt

Harrow Industries Annual Report

> The debentures require annual sinking fund payments of $6,500,000 beginning April 15, 1995. Sinking fund payments may be deferred to the extent that debentures purchased on the open market are tendered for cancellation. The Company has repurchased debentures totalling $26,970,000 which are available for such purpose.

By repurchasing debentures, Harrow Industries is able to satisfy sinking fund requirements for nearly four years. As a result, they will not have to make deposits of $6.5 million for each of those years. This type of information is important to analysts who wish to project the future cash flows of a business.

A bond sinking fund is normally reported on the balance sheet as a noncurrent asset. This is done because the cash that is in the fund is not available for ongoing business activities or to pay current liabilities. It would be misleading for financial analysts to conclude that a bond sinking fund was part of the working capital of a company.

FINANCIAL ANALYSIS

Understanding Notes to Financial Statements

As mentioned earlier, features are included in bond indentures to make the bond issue more attractive to potential creditors. The wide variety of features that are available can make some bond contracts quite complex. Fortunately, most of the features are based on the concepts that have been discussed in this chapter. As a result, you should be able to analyze most bonds issued by corporations. To illustrate, consider the following note from the Eastman Kodak annual report:

Real World Excerpt

Eastman Kodak Annual Report

> **Bond liabilities:**
> The zero coupon convertible subordinated debentures due in 2011 ($3,680 million face value, 6.75% yield to maturity) are convertible at the option of the holder at any time prior to maturity for the Company's common stock at a conversion rate of 5.622 shares per debenture. At the option of the holder, the debenture must be purchased by the Company at October 15, 1994, 1995, 1996, 2001, and 2006 at a price equal to the issue price plus amortized discount.

This note would be impossible to understand if you had not studied the chapter but, as you can see, it includes many of the issues that we have discussed.

LONG-TERM INVESTMENTS IN BONDS

Learning Objective 9
Account for bond investments held to maturity.

Up to this point, we have discussed bonds from the perspective of the issuer. Let's change that perspective and consider bonds from the point of view of a corporation that purchases bonds from another corporation. The only reason to invest in bonds is to earn a return on funds because bonds do not permit the holder to exert influence over another company, as would be the case with an investment in common stock. Corporate bonds are more risky than government securities and savings accounts. As a result, an investment in the bonds of another corporation permits an investing corporation to earn a higher rate of return.

Bonds may be held for either short-term or long-term purposes. Short-term investments in bonds will be discussed with short-term investments in common stock in Chapter 11. In this chapter, we will discuss accounting for long-term investments in bonds.

As you saw earlier in this chapter, bonds have a fixed maturity date. This fixed maturity date offers important advantages to corporations that invest in bonds. Why would managers of a corporation invest in bonds of another corporation? A key responsibility for senior executives is cash flow management, both short-term and long-term. Just as a corporation must have cash on hand to meet its current obligations, it must plan to have cash available to meet its long-term needs, such as the maturity of debt or the replacement of productive assets. Bonds permit management of the investing corporation to plan future cash flows with a minimum of risk. Management that needs cash in five years can purchase bonds that mature in five years. Bonds will pay their face value on their maturity date which permits the creditor to effectively budget future cash flows. Prior to maturity, a bond may sell for more or less than its face value, depending on interest rates in the market. If a bond must be sold prior to maturity, there is more uncertainty concerning the amount of cash that will be available. By holding bonds to maturity, a corporation can eliminate this uncertainty.

A **held-to-maturity portfolio** is a long-term investment in bonds that management has the ability and intent to hold until maturity.

When management plans to hold a bond investment until its maturity, it is reported in an account appropriately called the **held-to-maturity portfolio**. Bonds should be listed as held-to-maturity securities if management has the intent and the ability to hold the bonds until maturity. These bonds are listed at cost (adjusted for the amortization of any bond discount or premium) and not at their fair market value. Cost is considered to be a more reasonable measure of value because, by definition, the bonds will be held to maturity, at which time they will be worth face value. Unrealized gains and losses on bonds will disappear as the bonds approach their maturity date. Therefore, it is misleading to record these gains and losses during the life of the bonds.

Showboat does not show any bond investments on its balance sheet. This is probably not surprising given the growth strategy adopted by the company. Management currently wants to invest all available cash in new facilities instead of the investing cash in the bonds of other corporations.

Halliburton Corporation includes held-to-maturity securities on its balance sheet. As the notes to the statements indicate:

Real World Excerpt
Halliburton Corporation Annual Report

Note 1: Significant accounting policies.
Investments classified as held-to-maturity are measured at amortized cost. This classification is based on the company's intent and ability to hold these securities to full maturity.

The annual report for American Brands shows investments in stock and bonds of other corporations in excess of $5.8 billion. Its largest investment is the held-to-maturity classification (which includes only bonds). This portfolio is valued in excess of $4.5 billion or 78% of their total investments. Why does

The American Brands investment strategy rely so heavily on bonds? The answer is related to the nature of its business. American Brands owns an insurance subsidiary, Franklin Life. Actuaries can predict with great accuracy the life expectancy of various groups in our society. As a result, Franklin Life can forecast when it will have to pay life insurance benefits for its policyholders. Franklin would assume a large amount of risk if it invested all of its cash in the stock market. It might have difficulty in paying benefits if stock prices were severely depressed, as was the case in the stock market crash of 1987. By investing in bonds, Franklin Life can match the maturity date of bonds with the actuarially determined date that benefits must be paid. Through this matching process, Franklin substantially reduces the market risk of its investments.

REPORTING BOND INVESTMENTS HELD TO MATURITY

At the date of purchase, a bond investment that management intends to hold to maturity is recorded in conformity with the *cost principle*. The purchase cost, including all incidental acquisition costs (such as transfer fees and broker commissions), is debited to the Held-to-Maturity account. This amount may be the same as the maturity amount (if acquired at par), less than the maturity amount (if acquired at a discount), or more than the maturity amount (if acquired at a premium). Usually the premium or discount on a bond investment is not recorded in a separate account as is done for bonds payable. The investment account shows the current book value.

When discussing the price of a bond, many analysts refer to the price as a percentage of par. *The Wall Street Journal* might report, for example, that an Exxon bond with a par value of $1,000 is selling at 82.97 which means that it would cost $829.70 (82.97% of $1,000) to buy the bond. While bond prices are traditionally quoted as a percentage of par, the determination of the price of a bond is based on the present value techniques shown earlier in this chapter. The concepts underlying accounting for bond investments are the same as accounting for bond liabilities.

Bonds Purchased at Par

To illustrate accounting for bond investments, assume that on July 1, 19F, Showboat invested $100,000 in 10-year, 8% bonds purchased in the open market. The bonds were issued originally on July 1, 19A, and mature on June 30, 19K. The 8% interest is paid each June 30 and December 31. Management of Showboat plans to hold the bonds until maturity.

When bond investors accept a rate of interest on a bond investment that is the same as the stated rate of interest on the bonds, the bonds will sell at par (i.e., at 100). The journal entry to record the purchase of the bond is:

Held-to-maturity investment	100,000	
Cash		100,000

If a bond investment was acquired at par, the book value remains constant over the life of the investment because there is no premium or discount to be amortized. In this situation, revenue earned from the investment each period is measured as the amount of cash interest collected (or accrued). The journal entry to record the receipt of interest on December 31 is:

Cash ($100,000 × 8% × 1/2)	4,000	
Interest revenue		4,000

Bonds Purchased at a Discount

If bond investors demand a rate of interest that is higher than the stated rate, bonds will sell at a *bond discount*. When a bond is purchased at a discount, the investor receives the periodic interest payments stated in the bond contract plus the maturity value, which is a greater amount than the initial cash invested. As a result, the investor will earn a return that is greater than the stated rate.

To illustrate accounting for a bond issued at a discount, assume that on July 1, 19F, Showboat bought 8% bonds with a maturity value of $250,000 and paid $240,000 cash (the bonds sold at a discount). The bonds will mature in five years (in 19K). Interest is paid each June 30 and December 31. Management of Showboat intends to hold the bonds until maturity.

The purchase of the bonds is recorded as follows:

Held-to-maturity investment	240,000	
Cash		240,000

Notice that the purchase cost is entered into the investment account. It is not necessary to record the investment at par and establish a separate bond discount account. However, it is necessary to keep track of the bond discount and amortize it over the life of the bond.

The interest earned on the bonds purchased by Showboat will be more than the total of the annual interest payments (8% × $250,000 × 5 years = $100,000). This is true because Showboat will receive $250,000 when the bonds mature but paid only $240,000 when the bonds were purchased. This extra $10,000 is additional interest revenue.

The recording of interest revenue on December 31 is as follows:

Cash ($250,000 × 8% × 6/12)	10,000	
Held-to-maturity investment	1,000	
Interest revenue		11,000

The debit to the Held-to-Maturity account represents amortization of the bond discount. The discount is amortized over the life of the bond. Most companies use the straight-line method for bond investments. In the case of the bonds purchased by Showboat, the life is five years or 10 interest periods because the bonds pay interest every six months. The bond discount is allocated with an equal amount to each period, $10,000 ÷ 10 periods, or $1,000. Interest revenue for the period is cash received (or accrued) plus the amortization of the bond discount. Some companies may use the effective-interest amortization method. The procedures are similar to the ones illustrated earlier in this chapter for bond liabilities.

When a bond is held to maturity, a portion of the bond discount will be amortized each period. Through amortization of the discount, the balance of the investment account is increased each period so that the book value will be the same as the par amount on the maturity date. In the case of a bond premium, amortization reduces the balance of the investment account so that the book value will be the same as the par value on the maturity date.

In our example, the bonds purchased by Showboat mature on June 30, 19K. At that point, the bond discount will be fully amortized and Showboat will receive the maturity value of the bonds. The journal entry to record the cash received upon maturity is:

Cash	250,000	
Held-to-maturity investment		250,000

Accounting for bond investments when bonds are purchased at a premium is based on the same concepts as accounting for bonds purchased at a discount.

Epilogue for Showboat

Showboat successfully sold $275 million of its 9 1/4% first mortgage bonds and continued its expansion efforts. Within a year, the company had new expansion opportunities and returned to the debt market to raise additional funds. Unfortunately, a restrictive debt covenant in the indenture for the 9 1/4% bonds discussed in this chapter made it difficult to sell new bonds. Management of Showboat had to contact all of the owners of the 9 1/4% bonds to ask them to agree to modify their bond indenture. The documents sent to the bondholders included the following incentive:

Real World Excerpt

Showboat, Inc.
Letter to Bondholders

> As compensation, Showboat will pay holders who consent to the proposed amendments a cash fee equal to .50% of the outstanding principal amount of the bonds held by each holder.

The bondholders agreed to modify the indenture and Showboat was able to sell a new issue of bonds. The funds were used to develop a new gaming property in Sydney, Australia.

DEMONSTRATION CASE

(Try to resolve the requirements before proceeding to the suggested solution that follows.)

To raise funds to build a new plant, the management of Reed Company issued bonds. A bond indenture was approved by the board of directors. Some provisions in the bond indenture and specified on the bond certificates were:

Par value of the bonds ($1,000 bonds) $600,000.

Date of bond issue—February 1, 19A; due in 10 years on January 31, 19K.

Interest—10% per annum, payable 5% on each July 31 and January 31.

All of the bonds were sold on February 1, 19A, at 102 1/2. The annual accounting period for Reed Company ends on December 31.

Required:

1. How much cash was received by Reed Company from the sale of the bonds payable on February 1, 19A? Show computations.
2. What was the amount of premium on the bonds payable? Over how many months should it be amortized?
3. Compute the amount of amortization of premium per month and for each six-month interest period; use straight-line amortization. Round to the nearest dollar.
4. Give the journal entry on February 1, 19A, to record the sale and issuance of the bonds payable.
5. Give the journal entry for payment of interest and amortization of premium for the first interest payment on July 31, 19A.
6. Give the adjusting entry required on December 31, 19A, at the end of the accounting period.
7. Give the journal entry to record the second interest payment and the amortization of premium on January 31, 19B.
8. Show how bond interest expense and bonds payable are reported on the financial statements at December 31, 19A.

SUGGESTED SOLUTION

1. Sale price of the bonds: $600,000 × 102.5% = $615,000
2. Premium on the bonds payable: $600,000 × 2.5% = $15,000
   Months amortized: From date of sale, February 1, 19A, to maturity date, January 31, 19K = 120 months
3. Premium amortization: $15,000 ÷ 120 months = $125 per month, or $750 each six-month interest period (straight-line).
4. February 1, 19A (issuance date):

Cash	615,000	
Premium on bonds payable		15,000
Bonds payable		600,000
To record sale of bonds payable at 102 1/2.		

5. July 31, 19A (first interest payment date):

Bond interest expense ($30,000 – $750)	29,250	
Premium on bonds payable	750	
Cash ($600,000 × 5%)		30,000
To record payment of semiannual interest.		

6. December 31, 19A (end of the accounting period):

Bond interest expense	24,375	
Premium on bonds payable ($125 × 5 months)	625	
Bond interest payable ($600,000 × 10% × 5/12)		25,000
Adjusting entry for five months' interest accrued plus amortization of premium, August 1 to December 31, 19A.		

7. January 31, 19B (second interest date):

Bond interest payable	25,000	
Premium on bonds payable	125	
Bond interest expense	4,875	
Cash		30,000
To record payment of semiannual interest.		

8. Interest expense reported on the 19A income statement should be for the period outstanding during the year (i.e., for 11 months, February 1 through December 31). Interest expense, per the above entries, is $29,250 + $24,375 = $53,625; or alternatively, ($600,000 × 10% × 11/12 = $55,000) – ($125 × 11 months = $1,375) = $53,625.

Income statement for 19A:	
Interest expense	$ 53,625
Balance sheet, December 31, 19A:	
Long-term liabilities:	
Bonds payable, 10% (due January 31, 19K)	$600,000
Add unamortized premium*	13,625
	$613,625

*$15,000 – (750 + $625) = $13,625.

SUMMARY

This chapter discussed bonds payable that represent a primary way of obtaining funds to acquire long-term assets and to expand a business. An important advantage of bonds payable is that the cost of borrowing the funds— interest expense—is deductible for income tax purposes, which reduces the interest cost of the business.

Bonds may be sold at their par amount, at a premium, or at a discount, depending on the stated interest rate on the bonds compared with the market rate of interest. In each case, bonds are recorded at the present value of their future cash flows. The price of a bond varies based on the relationship between the market rates and stated rates of interest. If the market rate is higher than the stated rate on the bond, the bonds will sell at a discount. Conversely, if the market rate is lower than the stated rate on the bond, the bonds will sell at a premium.

Discounts and premiums on bonds payable are adjustments to interest expense for the issuing company during the term of the bonds. Therefore, a discount or premium on bonds payable is amortized over the period outstanding from issue date to maturity date.

To assure that funds are available to retire bonds payable at maturity, a company may set aside cash in advance by means of periodic contributions to a bond sinking fund. Such a fund is like a savings account. The bond sinking fund usually is administered by an independent trustee. Interest earned on the fund balance is added to the fund each period. At the maturity date of the bonds, the fund is used to pay the bondholders. The fund is reported on the balance sheet under the caption "Investments and funds." Interest earned on the fund is reported on the income statement as "Interest revenue."

KEY TERMS

Bond Certificate The bond document; each bondholder receives a bond certificate. *501*

Bond Discount The difference between selling price and par when a bond is sold for less than par. *503*

Bond Premium The difference between selling price and par when a bond is sold for more than par. *503*

Bond Principal The amount payable at the maturity of the bond; face amount, on which the periodic cash interest payments are computed. *500*

Bond Sinking Fund A cash fund accumulated for payment of a bond at maturity. *514*

Callable Bonds Bonds that may be called for early retirement at the option of the issuer. *502*

Convertible Bonds Bonds that may be converted to other securities of the issuer (usually common stock). *502*

Coupon Rate The stated rate of interest on bonds. *502*

Debenture An unsecured bond; no assets are specifically pledged to guarantee repayment. *500*

Effective-Interest Amortization Method that amortizes a bond discount or premium on the basis of the effective-interest rate; theoretically preferred method. *510*

Effective-Interest Rate Another name for the market rate of interest on a bond when issued; also called the yield rate. *503*

Face Amount Another name for principal or the principal amount of a bond. *500*

Financial Leverage Use of borrowed funds to increase the rate of return on owners' equity; occurs when the interest rate on debt is lower than the earnings rate on total assets. *499*

Held-to-Maturity Portfolio A long-term investment in bonds that management has the ability and intent to hold until maturity. *516*

Indenture A bond contract that specifies the legal provisions of a bond issue. *501*

Market Interest Rate Current rate of interest on a debt when incurred; also called **yield** or **effective interest rate**. *503*

Net Interest Cost Interest cost, less any income tax savings associated with interest expense. *499*

Par Value Another name for bond principal or the maturity amount of a bond. *500*

Redeemable Bonds Bonds that may be turned in for early retirement at the option of the bondholder. *502*

Stated Rate The rate of cash interest per period specified in the bond contract. *500*

Straight-Line Amortization Simplified method of amortizing a bond discount or premium that allocates an equal dollar amount to each interest period. *506*

Trustee An independent party appointed to represent the bondholders. *502*

Yield Another name for the market rate of interest on a bond. *503*

QUESTIONS

1. What are the primary characteristics of a bond? For what purposes are bonds usually issued?
2. What is the difference between a bond indenture and a bond certificate?
3. Differentiate secured bonds from unsecured bonds.
4. Differentiate between callable, redeemable, and convertible bonds.
5. Differentiate registered bonds from coupon bonds.
6. From the perspective of the issuer, what are some advantages of issuing bonds as compared with issuing capital stock?
7. As the tax rate increases, the net cost of borrowing money decreases. Explain.
8. Explain financial leverage. Can financial leverage be negative?
9. At the date of issuance, bonds are recorded at their current cash equivalent amount. Explain.
10. What is the nature of the discount and premium on bonds payable? Explain.
11. What is the difference between the stated interest rate and the effective-interest rate on a bond?
12. Differentiate between the stated and effective rates of interest on a bond (*a*) sold at par, (*b*) sold at a discount, and (*c*) sold at a premium.
13. Why are bond discounts and premiums amortized over the outstanding life of the related bonds payable rather than the period from the date of the bonds to their maturity date?
14. What is the book value of a bond payable?
15. Why is the lender (i.e., the purchaser of a bond) charged for the accrued interest from the last interest date to the date of purchase of the bonds?
16. If a 10-year bond dated January 1, 19A, is sold on April 1, 19B, how many months are used as the period outstanding for amortizing any bond premium or discount?
17. What is a bond sinking fund? How should a bond sinking fund be reported in the financial statements?
18. Explain the basic difference between straight-line amortization and effective-interest amortization of bond discount or premium. Explain when each method should, or may, be used.
19. If management plans (and has the ability) to hold a common stock investment for the long-term, should it be reported in the held-to-maturity portfolio? Explain.

EXERCISES

E10–1 Matching Bond Characteristics with Bond Classifications

Match each bond characteristic with its related bond classification by entering the answer code in the space provided.

Bond Classification	Bond Characteristics
________ (1) Serial bonds	A. Bonds with parts attached that are turned in to receive interest.
________ (2) Unsecured bonds	B. Bonds that may be retired early on request of the issuer.
________ (3) Convertible bonds	C. The principal amount is payable at a single maturity date.
________ (4) Ordinary bonds	D. Bonds that may be turned in for early retirement at the option of the bondholders.
________ (5) Coupon bonds	E. Principal amount is payable in installments.
________ (6) Redeemable bonds	F. Do not include a mortgage on specific assets.
________ (7) Registered bonds	G. Bonds that include pledged assets to assure payment at maturity.
________ (8) Callable bonds	H. Bonds that may be exchanged for other securities at the option of the bondholder.
________ (9) Secured bonds	I. Interest payments are made by check directly to the bondholders on each interest date.

E10–2 *Computing Issue Prices of Bonds for Three Cases and Recording Bond Issuances*

Thompson Corporation is planning to issue $100,000, five-year, 8% bonds. Interest is payable semiannually each June 30 and December 31. All of the bonds will be sold on January 1, 19A. The bonds mature on December 31, 19E.

Required:

1. Compute the issue (sale) price on January 1, 19A, for each of the following three independent cases (show computations):
   a. Case A: market (yield) rate, 8%.
   b. Case B: market (yield) rate, 6%.
   c. Case C: market (yield) rate, 10%.
2. Give the journal entry to record the issuance for each case.

E10–3 *Recording Bond Issue and First Interest Payment, with Discount, and Verifying Issue Price*

On January 1, 19A, Seton Corporation sold a $200,000, 8% bond issue (9% market rate). The bonds were dated January 1, 19A, and pay interest each December 31. The bonds mature 10 years from January 1, 19A.

Required:

1. Give the journal entry to record the issuance of the bonds.
2. Give the journal entry to record the interest payment on December 31, 19A. Assume straight-line amortization.
3. Show how the bond interest expense and the bonds payable should be reported on the December 31, 19A, annual financial statements.

E10–4 *Recording Bond Issue and First Interest Payment, with Premium, Showing Reporting, and Verifying the Issue Price*

Grocery Corporation sold a $250,000, 11% bond issue on January 1, 19A, at a market rate of 8%. The bonds were dated January 1, 19A, with interest to be paid each December 31. The bonds mature 10 years from January 1, 19A.

Required:

1. Give the journal entry to record the issuance of the bonds.
2. Give the journal entry for the interest payment on December 31, 19A. Assume straight-line amortization.
3. Show how the bond interest expense and the bonds payable should be reported on the December 31, 19A, annual financial statements.

E10–5 *Analyzing Bond Issue Price and Stated Interest Rate: Entries for Issuance and Interest*

Northland Corporation had $400,000, 10-year coupon bonds outstanding on December 31, 19A (end of the accounting period). Interest is payable each December 31. The bonds were issued (sold) on January 1, 19A. The 19A annual financial statements showed the following:

Income statement:	
Bond interest expense (straight-line amortization)	$ 33,200
Balance sheet:	
Bonds payable (net liability)	389,200

Required (show computations):

1. What was the issue price of the bonds? Give the issuance entry.
2. What was the coupon rate on the bonds? Give the entry to record 19A interest.

E10–6 *Effective-Interest Amortization of a Bond Discount*

Eagle Corporation issued $10,000, 10% bonds dated April 1, 19A. The market rate of interest was 12%. Interest is paid each March 31. The bonds mature in three years on March 31, 19D. The accounting period ends each December 31.

Required:

1. Give the journal entry to record the bond issuance on April 1, 19A.
2. Give the adjusting entry required on December 31, 19A. Use effective-interest amortization.
3. Show how the bonds should be reported on the balance sheet at December 31, 19A.
4. Give the journal entry to record the first interest payment on March 31, 19B.

E10–7 *Analyzing a Bond Amortization Schedule: Reporting Bonds Payable*

Stein Corporation issued a $1,000 bond on January 1, 19A. The bond specified an interest rate of 9% payable at the end of each year. The bond matures at the end of 19C. It was sold at a market rate of 11% per year. The following schedule was completed:

	Cash	Interest	Amortization	Balance
January 1, 19A (issuance)				$ 951
End of year 19A	$90	$105	$15	966
End of year 19B	90	106	16	982
End of year 19C	90	108	18	1,000

Required:

1. What was the issue price of the bond?
2. Did the bond sell at a discount or a premium? How much was the premium or discount?
3. What amount of cash was paid each year for bond interest?
4. What amount of interest expense should be shown each year on the income statement?
5. What amount(s) should be shown on the balance sheet for bonds payable at each year-end? (For year C, show the balance just before retirement of the bond.)
6. What method of amortization was used?
7. Show how the following amounts were computed for year B: (1) $90, (2) $106, (3) $16, and (4) $982.
8. Is the method of amortization that was used preferable? Explain why.

E10–8 *Preparing a Debt Payment Schedule with Effective-Interest Amortization: Entries*

Shuttle Company issued a $10,000, three-year, 10% bond on January 1, 19A. The bond interest is paid each December 31. The bond was sold to yield 9%.

Required:

1. Complete a bond payment schedule. Use the effective-interest method.
2. Give the interest and amortization entry at the end of 19A, 19B, and 19C.

E10–9 Debt Sold at a Discount

Apple Computer

The annual report of Apple Computer, Inc., contained the following note:

> **Long-Term Debt**
> On February 10, 1994, the Company issued $300 million aggregate principal amount of its 6.5% unsecured notes. The notes were sold at 99.925% of par, for an effective yield of 6.51%. The notes pay interest semiannually and mature on February 15, 2004.

After reading this note, one student asked why Apple didn't simply sell the notes for an effective yield of 6.5% and avoid having to account for a very small discount over the next 10 years. How would you respond to the question?

E10–10 Bond Terminology

Carnival Cruise Lines

The balance sheet for Carnival Cruise Lines includes "Zero Coupon Convertible Subordinated Notes." In your own words, explain the features of this debt. The balance sheet does not report a premium or a discount associated with this debt. Do you think it is recorded at par?

E10–11 Accounting for Bonds Subsequent to Issuance

Showboat, Inc.

As this book was being written, the business press reported the following information concerning the Showboat bonds which were discussed in this chapter:

Bonds	Yield	Close
Showboat 9 1/4	10.8	86

Explain the meaning of the information that was reported. If you bought Showboat bonds with $10,000 face value, how much would you pay (based on the information reported above)? Assume the bonds were originally sold at par. Prepare any journal entries that Showboat would have to record based on the change in value reported by the business press.

E 10–12 Bonds Held to Maturity

Sears, Roebuck & Co.

Sears, Roebuck & Co. is perhaps best known for its mall-based retail stores that sell apparel, home, and automotive products. Sears also owns Allstate insurance which sells a full range of insurance products. Allstate is the second largest insurer of homes and autos in the United States.

Assume that as part of its cash management strategy, Allstate purchased bonds with $10 million face value for $10.5 million cash on July 1, 19A. The bonds pay 10% interest each June 30 and December 31, and mature in 10 years. Allstate plans to hold the bonds until maturity.

Required:

1. Record the purchase of the bonds on July 1, 19A.
2. Record the receipt of interest on December 31, 19A.
3. Should Allstate prepare a journal entry if the market value of the bonds increased to $11 million on December 31, 19A? If so, what is the entry?

E10–13 Bonds Held to Maturity

Starbucks

Starbucks is a rapidly expanding company that provides high-quality coffee products. Assume that as part of its expansion strategy, Starbucks plans to open numerous new stores in Mexico but does not plan to do so for five years. The company has $5 million to support the expansion and has decided to invest the funds in corporate bonds until the money is needed. Assume that Starbucks purchased bonds with $5 million face value for $4.5 million cash on July 1, 19A. The bonds pay 8% interest each June 30 and December 31, and mature in five years. Starbucks plans to hold the bonds until maturity.

Required:

1. Record the purchase of the bonds on July 1, 19A.
2. Record the receipt of interest on December 31, 19A.
3. Should Starbucks prepare a journal entry if the market value of the bonds decreased to $4,000,000 on December 31, 19A? If so, what is the entry?

PepsiCo, Inc.
The Walt Disney Company

E10–14 Comparing Bond Features

Assume that you have decided to invest $100,000 in corporate bonds. You have found two bonds that interest you. One is a zero coupon bond issued by PepsiCo with an effective interst rate of 9% and a maturity date of 2015. It is callable at par. The other is a Walt Disney bond that matures in 2093. It has an effective interest rate of 9.5% and is callable at 105% of par. Which bond would you chose and why? Would your answer be different if you expected that interest rates would fall significantly over the next few years? Would you prefer a different bond if you were retired?

PROBLEMS

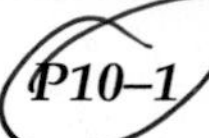

P10–1 Comparing Bonds Issued at Par, Discount, and Premium: Entries and Reporting

Sikes Corporation, whose annual accounting period ends on December 31, issued the following bonds:

Date of bonds: January 1, 19A.
Maturity amount and date: $100,000 due in 10 years (December 31, 19J).
Interest: 10% per annum payable each December 31.
Date sold: January 1, 19A.

Required:

1. Give the journal entries to record the issuance and the first two interest payments under each of the three different independent cases (assume straight-line amortization):
   a. Case A: bonds sold at par.
   b. Case B: bonds sold at 96.
   c. Case C: bonds sold at 102.
2. Provide the following amounts to be reported on the 19A financial statements:

	Case A	Case B	Case C
a. Interest expense	$	$	$
b. Bonds payable			
c. Unamortized premium or discount			
d. Net liability			
e. Stated rate of interest			
f. Cash interest paid			

3. Explain why items *a* and *f* are different in requirement 2.

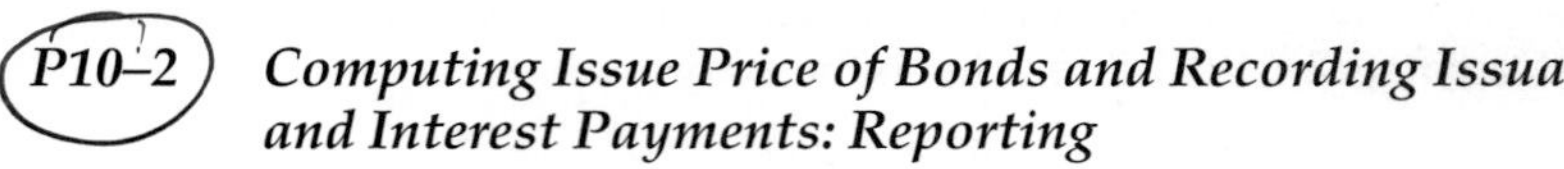

P10–2 Computing Issue Price of Bonds and Recording Issuance and Interest Payments: Reporting

West Company issued bonds with the following provisions:

Maturity value: $600,000.
Interest: 9% per annum payable semiannually each June 30 and December 31.
Terms: Bonds dated January 1, 19A, due five years from that date.

The annual accounting period ends December 31. The bonds were sold on January 1, 19A, at an 8% market rate.

Required:

1. Compute the issue (sale) price of the bonds (show computations).
2. Give the journal entry to record issuance of the bonds.
3. Give the journal entries at the following dates (use straight-line amortization): June 30, 19A; December 31, 19A; and June 30, 19B.
4. How much interest expense would be reported on the income statement for 19A? Show how the liability related to the bonds should be reported on the December 31, 19A, balance sheet.

P10–3 A Comprehensive Analysis of the Issuance of Bonds at Par, Discount, and Premium: No Entries

On January 1, 19A, Delaware Corporation sold and issued $100,000, five-year, 10% bonds. The bond interest is payable annually each December 31. Assume three separate and independent selling scenarios: Case A, at par; Case B, at 90; and Case C, at 110.

Required:

1. Complete a schedule similar to the following for each separate case assuming straight-line amortization of discount and premium. Disregard income tax. Give all dollar amounts in thousands.

	At Start of 19A	At End of 19B	At End of 19C	At End of 19D	At End of 19E	At End of 19E: Prior to Payment of Principal	At End of 19E: Payment of Principal
Case A: sold at par (100):	$	$	$	$	$	$	$
Pretax cash inflow							
Pretax cash outflow							
Interest expense on income statement							
Net liability on balance sheet							
Case B: sold at a discount (90):							
Pretax cash inflow							
Pretax cash outflow							
Interest expense on income statement							
Net liability on balance sheet							
Case C: sold at a premium (110):							
Pretax cash inflow							
Pretax cash outflow							
Interest expense on income statement							
Net liability on balance sheet							

2. For each separate case, calculate each of the following:
   a. Total pretax cash outflow.
   b. Total pretax cash inflow.
   c. Difference—net pretax cash outflow.
   d. Total pretax interest expense.

3. *a.* Explain why the net pretax cash outflows differ among the three cases.
   b. For each case, explain why the net pretax cash outflow is the same as total interest expense.

P10–4 *Analyzing Differences between Bonds Issued at Par, Discount, and Premium: Issuance and Interest Entries*

Quartz Corporation sold a $500,000, 7% bond issue on January 1, 19A. The bonds pay interest each December 31 and will mature 10 years from January 1, 19A. For comparative study and analysis, assume three separate cases. Use straight-line amortization and disregard income tax unless specifically required. Assume three independent selling scenarios: Case A, bonds sold at par; Case B, bonds sold at 98; Case C, bonds sold at 102.

Required:

1. Complete the following schedule to analyze the differences among the three cases.

	Case A (Par)	Case B (at 98)	Case C (at 102)
a. Cash inflow at issue (sale) date			
b. Total cash outflow through maturity date			
c. Difference—total interest expense			
Income statement for 19A:			
d. Bond interest expense, pretax			
Balance sheet at December 31, 19A:			
Long-term liabilities:			
e. Bonds payable, 7%			
f. Unamortized discount			
g. Unamortized premium			
h. Net liability			
i. Stated interest rate			
j. Total interest expense, net of income tax (25% tax rate)			

2. Give the journal entries for each case on January 1, 19A, and December 31, 19A (excluding closing entries).
3. For each case, explain why the amounts in items *c*, *d*, and *j* of requirement 1 are the same or different.

P10–5 *Determining the Issue Price of a Bond*

Kaizen Corporation issued a $500,000 bond that matures in 10 years. The bond has a stated interest rate of 10%. When the bond was issued, the market rate was 10%. The bond pays interest twice per year. At what price was the bond issued?

P10–6 *Determining the Issue Price of a Bond*

Imai Company issued a $1 million bond that matures in five years. The bond has a stated rate of interest of 10%. When the bond was issued, the market rate was 8%. The bond pays interest twice per year on June 30 and December 31. Record the issuance of the bond on June 30.

P10–7 *Determining the Issue Price of a Bond*

Charger Corporation issued a $150,000 bond that matures in five years. The bond has a stated interest rate of 8% and pays interest on February 1, May 1, August 1, and November 1. When the bond was issued, the market rate of interest was 12%. Record the issuance of the bond on February 1. Also record the payment of interest on May 1 and August 1. Use the straight-line method for amortization of any discount or premium.

P10–8 Effective-Interest Amortization of Bond Premium: Completion and Analysis of an Amortization Schedule

Berkley Corporation issued bonds and received cash in full for the issue price. The bonds were dated and issued on January 1, 19A. The stated interest rate was payable at the end of each year. The bonds mature at the end of four years. The following schedule has been completed:

Date	Cash	Interest	Amortization	Balance
January 1, 19A				$6,101
End of year 19A	$450	$427	$23	6,078
End of year 19B	450	?	?	6,053
End of year 19C	450	?	?	?
End of year 19D	450	?	?	6,000

Required:

1. Complete the amortization schedule.
2. What was the maturity amount of the bonds?
3. How much cash was received at date of issuance (sale) of the bonds?
4. Was there a premium or a discount? If so, which and how much?
5. How much cash will be disbursed for interest each period and in total for the full life of the bond issue?
6. What method of amortization is being used? Explain.
7. What is the stated rate of interest?
8. What is the effective rate of interest?
9. What amount of interest expense should be reported on the income statement each year?
10. Show how the bonds should be reported on the balance sheet at the end of each year (show the last year immediately before retirement of the bonds).
11. Why is the method of amortization being used preferable to other methods? When must it be used?

P10–9 Straight-Line versus Effective-Interest Methods of Amortizing Bond Discount and Premium

Dektronik Corporation manufactures electrical test equipment. The board of directors of the company authorized a bond issue on January 1, 19A, with the following terms:

Maturity (par) value: $800,000.
Interest: 8% per annum payable each December 31.
Maturity date: December 31, 19E.
The bonds were sold at an effective-interest rate of 12%.

Required:

1. Compute the bond issue price. Explain why both the stated and effective-interest rates are used in this computation.
2. Give the entry to record this bond issue.
3. Assume the company used the straight-line approach to amortize the discount on the bond issue. Compute the following amounts for each year (19A-E):
   a. Cash payment for bond interest.
   b. Amortization of bond discount or premium.
   c. Bond interest expense.
   d. Interest rate indicated (Item $c \div \$800,000$).
   e. The straight-line rate is theoretically deficient when interest expense, (*d*) above, is related to the net liability (i.e., book value of the debt). Explain.
4. Assume instead that the company used the effective-interest method to amortize the discount. Prepare an effective-interest bond amortization schedule similar to the one in

the text. The effective-interest method provides a constant interest rate when interest expense is related to the net liability. Explain by referring to the bond amortization schedule.

5. Which method should be used by the company to amortize the bond discount?

P10–10 Using the Effective-Interest Method

Carter Corporation issued $400,000 in bonds that mature in 10 years. The bonds have a stated interest rate of 6% and pay interest on March 1 and September 1. When the bonds were sold, the market rate of interest was 8%. Carter uses the effective-interest method.

Required:

1. Record the issuance of the bond on March 1, 19A.
2. Record the payment of interest on September 1, 19A.
3. Record the adjusting entry for accrued interest on December 31, 19A.

P10–11 Comprehensive Review Problem (Chapters 9 and 10)

Part A Determine which of the following situations would require the reporting of a liability. Unless otherwise stated, assume that the amount in question can be reasonably estimated.

a. Chrysler sells an automobile with a seven-year warranty.
b. Coke sells 100,000 bottles of soda and collects $0.05 per bottle deposit.
c. Action Delivery Company signs a 14-month lease on new delivery trucks.
d. Vacation Motor Inns sells special coupons during the winter that provide free rooms at their motels during the following summer. Each coupon costs 75% of the normal room rate. Vacation Motor Inns collects cash when the coupon is sold.
e. A five-year employment contract is signed with the president of the company.
f. A company accidentally dumps chemicals into a nearby river and is required to clean up the damage. At this time, it is impossible to determine the cost of the work.
g. Ace Manufacturing announces that next year it will give $1 million to the city to build a new park.
h. A timber company is clearing 500,000 acres of land and will be required to bring in new top soil and replant trees when the project is complete. This year, 300,000 acres were cleared.
i. An amusement park estimates that one out of every 500,000 customers will be seriously injured resulting in a major lawsuit. This year, 300,000 customers visit the park without any injuries.

Part B Ridge Corporation issued a $100,000 bond that matures in 10 years. The stated interest rate was 10% and the effective rate was 12%. The bond pays interest on June 30 and December 31.

a. Record the issuance of the bond on January 1st.
b. Record the payment of interest on June 30. Use the effective-interest method.
c. Record the payment of interest on December 31.

Martin Marietta Corporation

P10–12 Analyzing a Disclosure Concerning Long-Term Debt

Martin Marietta Corporation designs and manufactures systems and products in leading-edge technologies including aerospace, electronics and information management. The Martin Marietta annual report includes the following information concerning one of its debt issues:

> The 7% debentures were sold at 53.835% of their principal amount of $175,000,000 in 1981 (they mature in 2011). These debentures are carried net of original issue discount, which is being amortized by the interest method over the life of the issue. The effective interest rate is 13 1/4%. The debentures are redeemable in whole or part at the Corporation's option at any time at 100% of their principal amount.

In your own words, explain the meaning of this note.

P10–13 *The Difference between Carrying Value and Market Value*

Hilton Hotels

The name Hilton is well known in the hotel industry. The Hilton annual report contained the following information concerning long-term debt:

> *Long-term debt*
>
> The estimated current market value of long-term debt is based on the quoted market price for the same or similar issues. The current carrying value for long-term debt is $1,132.5 (million) and the current market value is $1,173.5 (million).

Explain why there is a difference between the carrying value and the current market value of the long-term debt for Hilton. Assume that Hilton decided to retire all of its long-term debt for cash (a very unlikely event). Prepare the journal entry to record the transaction.

P10–14 *Reclassification of Debt*

PepsiCo, Inc.

PepsiCo, Inc., is a $25 billion company in the beverage, snack foods, and restaurant businesses. The annual report for PepsiCo included the following note:

> At year-end, $3.5 billion of short-term borrowings were reclassified as long-term, reflecting PepsiCo's intent and ability to refinance these borrowings on a long-term basis, through either long-term debt issuances or rollover of existing short-term borrowings.

As a result of this reclassification, the current ratio for PepsiCo improved from .51 to .79. Do you think the reclassification was appropriate? Why do you think management made the reclassification? As a financial analyst, would you use the current ratio before the reclassification or after the reclassification to evaluate the liquidity of PepsiCo?

P10–15 *Early Retirement of Debt*

AMC Entertainment, Inc.

AMC Entertainment, Inc., owns and operates 243 movie theaters with 1,617 screens in 22 states. On August 12, 1992, the company sold 11 7/8% bonds in the amount of $52,720,000 and used the cash proceeds to retire bonds with a coupon rate of 13.6%. At that time the 13.6% bonds had a book value of $50,000,000.

Required:

1. Prepare the journal entry to record the early retirement of the 13.6% bonds.
2. How would AMC report any gain or loss on this transaction?
3. Why did management decide to make an early retirement of this debt?

CASES

C10–1 *Demonstration of Financial Leverage: Computation and Interpretation*

The financial statements of Cricket Corporation for 19A showed the following:

Income Statement

Revenues	$300,000
Expenses	(198,000)
Interest expense	(2,000)
Pretax income	100,000
Income tax (30%)	(30,000)
Net income	$ 70,000

Balance Sheet

Assets	$300,000	
Liabilities (average interest rate, 10%)		$ 20,000
Common stock, par $10		200,000
Retained earnings		80,000
		$300,000

Notice in the above data that the company had a debt of only $20,000 compared with common stock outstanding of $200,000. A consultant recommended the following: debt, $100,000 (at 10%) instead of $20,000 and common stock outstanding of $120,000 (12,000 shares) instead of $200,000 (20,000 shares). That is, the company should have more debt and less owner contributions to finance the business.

Required (round to nearest percent):

1. You have been asked to develop a comparison between (*a*) the actual results and (*b*) the results had the consultant's recommendation been followed. To do this you decided to develop the following schedule:

Item	Actual Results for 19A	Results with an Increase in Debt of $80,000
a. Total debt		
b. Total assets		
c. Total stockholders' equity		
d. Interest expense (total at 10%)		
e. Net income		
f. Return on total assets		
g. Earnings available to stockholders:		
(1) Amount		
(2) Per share		
(3) Return on stockholders' equity		
h. Financial leverage		

2. Based on the completed schedule in (1), provide a comparative analysis and interpretation of the actual results and the recommendation.

J.C. Penney Company

C10–2 Analyzing Zero Coupon Bonds from an Actual Company

Early in 1981, J.C. Penney Company issued zero coupon bonds with a face (maturity) value of $400 million due in 1989 (eight years after issuance). When the bonds were sold to the public, similar bonds paid 15% effective interest. An article in *Forbes* magazine (May 25, 1981) discussed the J.C. Penney bonds and stated: "It's easy to see why corporations like to sell bonds that don't pay interest. But why would anybody want to buy that kind of paper (bond)?"

Required:

1. Explain why an investor would buy a J.C. Penney bond with a zero interest rate. If investors could earn 15% on similar investments, how much should they be willing to pay for a J.C. Penney bond with a par value of $1,000 (due eight years after issuance)?
2. Assume that J.C. Penney sold the $400 million bond issue on May 1, 1981, the first day of the term (life) of the bond issue. Give the journal entry to record the sale of the bonds for cash.
3. Assume that the accounting period for J.C. Penney ends on December 31 each year. Give the journal entry required on December 31, 1981, to record accrued interest expense. If none is required, explain.
4. Give the entry on maturity date to pay the bondholders. How much cash interest was paid on the bonds? Explain.

C10–3 Bonds and Present Value Concept

Times Company issued a $100,000 bond with a stated interest rate of 8%. When the bond was issued, the market rate was 6%. The bond matures in 10 years and pays interest on December 31 each year. The bond was issued on January 1, 19A.

Required:

1. Record the issuance of the bond on January 1, 19A.
2. Compute the present value of the difference between the interest paid each year ($6,000) and the interest demanded by the market ($100,000 × 8% = $8,000). Use the market rate of interest and the 10-year life of the bond in your present value computation. Compare this amount to the bond premium recorded in requirement 1. Explain.
3. Record the payment of interest during 19A, 19B, and 19C using the effective-interest method. Why does interest expense change each year?
4. What is the book value of the bond at the end of 19C?
5. Compute the present value of the Times Company bonds, assuming they had a 7-year life instead of 10 years. Compare this amount to the book value computed in requirement 4. Explain.

C10–4 Financial Statement Analysis

Toys "Я" Us

Refer to the financial statement of Toys " Я " Us given in Appendix B at the end of this book.

Required:

1. What is the fair market value of the company's debt on January 30, 1993?
2. What is the current portion of long-term debt reported in the current year?
3. What amount of long-term debt matures in 1998?
4. The company reports debt denominated in Japanese yen and British pound sterling. In your opinion, why didn't management borrow all the needed funds in dollars?

11

MEASURING AND REPORTING OWNERS' EQUITY

In the previous two chapters, we discussed accounting and business issues related to funds provided by creditors. In this chapter, we will examine issues pertaining to funds provided by the owners of a business. We will focus primarily on the corporate form, the most prominent type of business in this country.

LEARNING OBJECTIVES

After studying this chapter, you should be able to:

Management Decision Setting

WAL-MART

Financing Corporate Growth by Selling Stock

Wal-Mart is a real American success story. Today Wal-Mart operates over 1,880 discount department stores, 256 warehouse clubs, 64 warehouse outlets, and four hypermarkets. The company sells over $56 billion worth of merchandise each year (which requires over 850,000 truck trailers to ship) and employs more than 434,000 people.

Substantially all merchandise purchases are controlled from the home office. Approximately 77% of each Wal-Mart store's merchandise is shipped from one of the 22 distribution centers operated by Wal-Mart. Centralized buying is a key component of the company's strategy. The large volume of merchandise purchased by Wal-Mart permits it to negotiate aggressively with its vendors. These cost savings permit the company to achieve its advertising slogan of "Everyday Low Price" which is critical to its large market share, rapid growth, and overall success.

Shares of Wal-Mart stock were first sold to the public in 1970 at a cost of $16.50 per share. If in 1970 you had purchased one thousand shares of Wal-Mart stock for $16,500, your investment would be worth $2,355,200 today!

Stock, like bonds, can provide many different features. Managers must identify the best mixture of features to attract investors.

BUSINESS BACKGROUND

To some people, the words *corporation* and *business* are almost synonymous terms. You've probably heard friends refer to business careers as "working in the corporate world." Equating business and corporations is understandable because corporations are the dominant form of business organization in terms of volume of operations. If you were to write the names of 50 familiar companies on a piece of paper, they probably all would be corporations.

The popularity of the corporate form can be attributed to a critical advantage that a corporation has over the sole proprietorship and the partnership: it is easiest for individuals to participate in the ownership of corporations. This ease is related to three important factors. First, it is simple for people to become part owners by purchasing shares of stock in small amounts. You could buy a single share of Wal-Mart stock for about $25 and become one of the owners of this very successful company. Second, the corporate form facilitates the transfer of separate ownership interests because stock can be transferred easily to others by selling it in established markets such as the New York Stock Exchange. Third, corporations provide the stockholder with limited liability.[1]

The corporation is the only business form that is recognized in law as a separate legal entity. As a distinct entity, the corporation enjoys a continuous existence separate and apart from its owners. It may own assets, incur liabilities, expand and contract in size, sue others, be sued, and enter into contracts independently of the stockholder owners.

Many Americans own stock, either directly or indirectly through a mutual fund or pension program. Stock ownership offers the opportunity to earn higher returns than are available through deposits to bank accounts or investments in corporate bonds. Unfortunately, stock ownership also involves

[1]In case of the insolvency of a corporation, the creditors have recourse for their claims only to the assets of the corporation. Thus, the stockholders stand to lose, as a maximum, only their equity in the corporation. In the case of a partnership or sole proprietorship, creditors have recourse to the personal assets of the owners if the assets of the business are insufficient to meet the outstanding debts of the business.

higher risk. The proper balance between risk and expected returns depends on the preferences of each individual.

Consolidated statements of shareholders' equity for Wal-Mart are shown in Exhibit 11–1 along with consolidated balance sheets. We will use this exhibit to illustrate our discussion of stockholders' equity.

Consolidated Balance Sheets and Statements of Shareholders' Equity — Exhibit 11–1

Consolidated Balance Sheets

WAL-MART STORES, INC. AND SUBSIDIARIES
(Amounts in thousands.)

	January 31, 1993	January 31, 1992
ASSETS		
Current assets:		
Cash and cash equivalents	$ 12,363	$ 30,649
Receivables	524,555	418,867
Recoverable costs from sale/leaseback	312,016	681,387
Inventories:		
At replacement cost	9,779,981	7,856,871
Less LIFO reserve	511,672	472,572
LIFO	9,268,309	7,384,299
Prepaid expenses	80,347	60,221
TOTAL CURRENT ASSETS	10,197,590	8,575,423
Property, Plant, and Equipment, at Cost:		
Land	1,692,510	1,077,658
Buildings and improvements	4,641,009	2,569,095
Fixtures and equipment	3,417,230	2,683,481
Transportation equipment	111,151	86,491
	9,861,900	6,416,725
Less accumulated depreciation	1,607,623	1,338,151
Net property, plant, and equipment	8,254,277	5,078,574
Property under capital leases	1,986,104	1,724,123
Less accumulated amortization	447,500	368,896
Net property under capital leases	1,538,604	1,355,227
Other assets and deferred charges	574,616	434,165
Total assets	$20,565,087	$15,443,389
LIABILITIES AND SHAREHOLDERS' EQUITY		
Current liabilities:		
Commercial paper	$ 1,588,825	$ 453,964
Accounts payable	3,873,331	3,453,529
Accrued liabilities	1,042,108	829,381
Accrued federal and state income taxes	190,620	226,828
Long-term debt due within one year	13,849	5,156
Obligations under capital leases due within one year	45,553	34,917
TOTAL CURRENT LIABILITIES	6,754,286	5,003,775
Long-term debt	3,072,835	1,722,022
Long-term obligations under capital leases	1,772,152	1,555,875
Deferred income taxes	206,634	172,007
Shareholders' equity:		
Preferred stock ($.10 par value; 100,000 shares authorized, none issued)		
Common stock ($.10 par value; 5,500,000 shares authorized, 2,299,638 and 1,149,028 issued and outstanding in 1993 and 1992 respectively)	229,964	114,903
Capital in excess of par value	526,647	625,669
Retained earnings	8,002,569	6,249,138
TOTAL SHAREHOLDERS' EQUITY	8,759,180	6,989,710
Total liabilities and shareholders' equity	$20,565,087	$15,443,389

See accompanying notes.

Exhibit 11–1 (concluded)

Consolidated Statements of Shareholders' Equity

WAL-MART STORES, INC. AND SUBSIDIARIES

(Amounts in thousands except per share data.)	Number of shares	Common stock	Capital in excess of par value	Retained earnings	Total
Balance—January 31, 1990	566,135	$ 56,614	$180,465	$3,728,482	$3,965,561
Net income				1,291,024	1,291,024
Cash dividends ($.07 per share)				(158,889)	(158,889)
Exercise of stock options	156	15	1,327		1,342
Other	(34)	(4)	(1,626)		(1,630)
Two-for-one stock split	566,257	56,625	(56,625)		
Exercise of stock options	506	51	2,427		2,478
Shares issued for McLane acquisition	10,366	1,037	273,659		274,696
Tax benefit from stock options			6,075		6,075
Purchase of stock	(1,000)	(100)	(819)	(24,907)	(25,826)
Walton Enterprises, Inc. stock exchange			14,000		14,000
Other	(104)	(10)	(3,297)		(3,307)
Balance—January 31, 1991	1,142,282	114,228	415,586	4,835,710	5,365,524
Net income				1,608,476	1,608,476
Cash dividends ($.09 per share)				(195,048)	(195,048)
Exercise of stock options	914	91	8,379		8,470
Shares issued for acquisition of:					
The Wholesale Club	5,190	519	161,683		162,202
Western Merchandisers	655	66	27,934		28,000
Phillips	168	17	7,983		8,000
Tax benefit from stock options			12,555		12,555
Other	(181)	(18)	(8,451)		(8,469)
Balance—January 31, 1992	1,149,028	114,903	625,669	6,249,138	6,989,710
Net Income				1,994,794	1,994,794
Cash dividends ($.11 per share)				(241,363)	(241,363)
Exercise of stock options	1,046	105	12,668		12,773
Two-for-one stock split	1,149,819	114,982	(114,982)		
Tax benefit from stock options			18,036		18,036
Other	(255)	(26)	(14,744)		(14,770)
Balance—January 31, 1993	**2,299,638**	**$229,964**	**$526,647**	**$8,002,569**	**$8,759,180**

See accompanying notes.

OWNERSHIP OF A CORPORATION

Learning Objective 1
Describe the basic nature of a corporation.

When you invest in a corporation, you are known as a *stockholder* or *shareholder.* As a stockholder, you will receive shares of capital stock (a stock certificate) that can be subsequently sold on established stock exchanges without affecting the corporation. The stock certificate states the name of the stockholder, date of purchase, type of stock, number of shares represented, and the characteristics of the stock. The back of the certificate has instructions and a form to be completed when the shares are sold or transferred to another party.

As an owner of common stock, you receive the following rights:

1. You may vote in the stockholders' meeting (or by proxy) on major issues concerning management of the corporation.[2]
2. You may participate proportionately with other stockholders in the distribution of profits of the corporation.
3. You may share proportionately with other stockholders in the distribution of corporate assets upon liquidation.

[2]A voting proxy is a written authority given by a stockholder that gives another party the right to vote the stockholder's shares in the annual meeting of the stockholders. Typically, proxies are solicited by, and given to, the president of the corporation.

4. You may purchase shares of any new issues of common stock on a pro rata basis in order to maintain your percentage of ownership.

Owners, unlike creditors, are able to vote at the annual stockholders' meeting. The following "Notice of Annual Meeting of Shareholders" was recently sent to all owners of Wal-Mart stock:

Real World Excerpt

Wal-Mart Stores, Inc. Notice of Shareholders' Meeting

> Notice is hereby given that the annual meeting of shareholders of Wal-Mart Stores, Inc., a Delaware corporation, will be held June 5 at 10:00 A.M., in Barnhill Arena, University of Arkansas, Fayetteville, Arkansas, for the following purposes:
>
> (1) To elect directors.
> (2) To consider and act upon a proposal to ratify the adoption by the Board of Directors of the Directors Deferred Compensation Plan.
> (3) To transact other business as may properly come before the meeting or any adjournment thereof.
>
> Only shareholders of record at the close of business on April 6, are entitled to notice of and to vote at the meeting.

The notice of the annual meeting contained several pages of information concerning deferred compensation plans and the people who were nominated to be members of the board of directors. Most owners do not actually attend the annual meeting. To permit those people to vote, the notice included a proxy card which is similar to an absentee ballot. Each owner may complete the proxy and mail it to the company. Their votes will then be included at the annual meeting.

To protect everyone's rights, the creation and governance of corporations are tightly regulated by law. Corporations are created by making application to a specific state government (not the federal government). Each state has different laws that govern the organization of corporations that are created within their boundaries.

To create a corporation, an application for a charter must be submitted to the appropriate state official. The application must specify the name of the corporation, the purpose (type of business), the kinds and amounts of capital stock authorized, and a minimum amount of capital that must be invested by the owners at the date of organization. Most states require a minimum of three stockholders when the corporation is formed. Upon approval of the application, the state issues a *charter,* sometimes called the *articles of incorporation*. The governing body of a corporation is the board of directors, which is elected by the stockholders.

Most corporations adopt organizational structures similar to the one shown in Exhibit 11–2. The actual structure will depend on the nature of the company's business. In the case of Wal-Mart, there are seven executive vice-presidents. One is responsible for each of the following areas: information systems, real estate and construction, finance and accounting, and each of the four operating divisions. This structure is unique to Wal-Mart because of the nature of the business. It might seem unusual to assign one of the most senior executives to real estate and construction but this area is critical for the strategy of Wal-Mart. Last year, for example, they opened more than 34.5 million square feet of new retail space.

Authorized, Issued, and Outstanding Capital Stock

When a corporation is created, the corporate charter must specify the maximum number of shares of capital stock that can be sold to the public. This maximum is called the **authorized number of shares**. In the case of Wal-Mart,

The **authorized number of shares** is the maximum number of shares of capital stock of a corporation that can be issued as specified in the charter.

Exhibit 11–2 **Typical Organizational Structure of a Corporation**

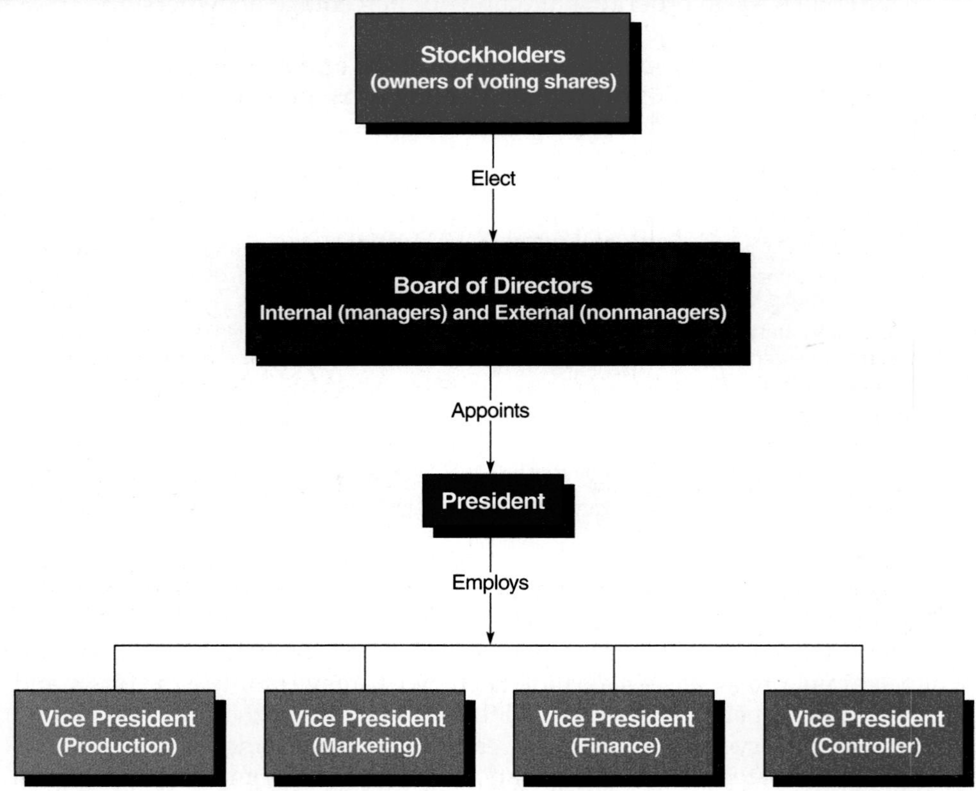

the number of authorized shares of common stock is 5,500,000,000 as shown in Exhibit 11–1. Typically, the corporate charter authorizes a larger number of shares than the corporation expects to issue initially. This strategy provides future flexibility for the issuance of additional shares without the need to amend the charter.

Issued shares are the total shares of stock that have been issued; shares outstanding plus treasury shares held.

Outstanding shares are the total shares that are owned by stockholders on any particular date.

Unissued shares are authorized shares of a corporation's stock that have never been issued.

The number of **issued shares** and the number of **outstanding shares** are determined by the stock transactions of the corporation. Authorized shares of stock that never have been sold to the public are called **unissued shares**. For Wal-Mart, the number of issued shares and the number of outstanding shares are the same. In 1993, this number was 2,299,638,000. The number of issued shares may differ from the number of outstanding shares if the company has bought back some of its shares from the owners. As you can see, Wal-Mart can issue more than 3,200,000,000 additional shares without exceeding the maximum authorized in its charter.

If a corporation needs to sell more shares than authorized in its charter, it must seek permission from the current stockholders to modify the charter. Late in 1994, Greyhound Lines Inc. faced possible bankruptcy. The company worked out an agreement with creditors under which they would trade debt for stock, but the company did not have a sufficient number of unissued shares to complete the agreement. Management was forced to ask the stockholders to approve an increase in the number of shares authorized. As *Bloomberg Business News* reported, the vote was close:

Real World Excerpt
Bloomberg Business News

Greyhound President Craig Lentzsch said 9.9 million of the company's 14 million outstanding shares voted in favor of the plan. Greyhound needed 9.7 million for the plan to be approved. A total of 10 million shares were voted.

Authorized, Issued, and Outstanding Shares — **Exhibit 11–3**

Definitions	Illustrations	
Authorized number of shares: The maximum number of shares that can be issued as specified in the charter of the corporation.	Charter specifies "authorized capital stock, 100,000 shares, par value $1 per share."	
Issued number of shares: The total cumulative number of shares that have been issued to date by the corporation.	To date, XYZ Corporation has sold and issued 30,000 shares of its capital stock.	
Unissued number of shares: The number of authorized shares that have never been issued to date.	Authorized shares	100,000
	Issued shares	30,000
	Unissued shares	70,000
Treasury stock:* Shares that have been issued to investors and then reacquired by the issuing corporation.	To date, XYZ Corporation has repurchased 1,000 shares of previously issued stock.	
Outstanding number of shares: The number of shares currently owned by stockholders; that is, the number of shares authorized minus the total number of unissued shares and minus the number of treasury shares.	Authorized shares	100,000
	Treasury stock	(1,000)
	Unissued shares	(70,000)
	Outstanding shares	29,000

*Treasury stock will be discussed later. Notice that when treasury stock is held, the number of shares issued and the number outstanding will differ by the number of shares of treasury stock held (treasury stock is included in "issued" but not in "outstanding").

Exhibit 11–3 defines and illustrates the terms usually used in respect to corporate shares.

TYPES OF CAPITAL STOCK

Learning Objective 2
Compare and contrast the various types of capital stock.

When people refer to *corporate stock,* they usually have in mind common stock, which must be issued by all corporations. Some corporations also issue preferred stock which grants preferences that the common stock does not have. Notice in Exhibit 11–1 that Wal-Mart has authorized the issuance of preferred stock but has not issued any.

In the previous chapter, we mentioned that corporations issue many different types of bonds to appeal to the risk and return preferences of individual creditors. The same is true of stock. In this chapter, we will introduce you to many features that are used to encourage investors to buy stock.

Common Stock

Common stock is the basic, normal, voting stock issued by a corporation; called *residual equity* because it ranks after preferred stock for dividend and liquidation distributions.

Common stock is the basic voting stock issued by a corporation. It is often called the *residual equity* because it ranks after the preferred stock for dividends and assets distributed upon liquidation of the corporation. The dividend rate for common stock is determined by the board of directors based on the profitability of the company, unlike the dividend rate on preferred stock which is fixed by contract. In the jargon of Wall Street, common stock has more "upside potential" than preferred stock and more "downside risk". This means that if the company is profitable, common stock dividends may grow to be more than preferred dividends and in fact, may increase each year (upside potential). When the company is not profitable, the board may cut or eliminate common stock dividends, but in most cases it cannot reduce preferred dividends. As a result, common stock dividends may be less than preferred stock dividends during troubled times (downside risk).

The fact that common stock dividends may be increased with increases in the profitability of a company helps explain why investors can make money in the stock market. Basically, you can think of the price of a share of stock as the present value of all of its future dividends. If the profitability of a company improves so that it can pay out higher dividends, the present value of its common stock increases. In this situation, you would not expect the value of the preferred stock to change significantly because preferred dividends are fixed.

Par Value and Nopar Value Stock

Par value is the nominal value per share of capital stock specified in the charter; serves as the basis for legal capital.

Par value is a nominal value per share established in the charter of the corporation. It has no relationship to the market value of the stock. Notice in Exhibit 11–1 that Wal-Mart common stock lists a par value of $0.10; the market value of the stock is several hundred times greater than its par value. Stock that is sold by the corporation to investors above par value is said to sell at a premium; whereas stock sold below par is said to sell at a discount. The initial sale of stock by the corporation to investors cannot be below par value.[3]

Most states require stock to have a par value. It was originally designed to offer protection for the creditors of a company but has little importance today to financial analysts. The concept of par value was established as protection for creditors by specifying a permanent amount of capital that could not be withdrawn by the owners as long as the corporation existed. Thus, owners could not withdraw all of their capital in anticipation of business failure and bankruptcy, and leave creditors with an empty corporate shell. This permanent amount of capital is called **legal capital**.

Legal capital is the permanent amount of capital, defined by state law, that must remain invested in the business; serves as a cushion for creditors.

Nopar value stock is capital stock that has no par value specified in the corporate charter.

Many states permit the issuance of **nopar value stock**. Nopar value stock does not have an amount per share specified in the charter. It may be issued at any price without a discount or premium. When nopar stock is issued by a corporation, the legal, or stated, capital is as defined by the state law.

The definition of legal capital varies among states, but legal capital usually is viewed as the par value of the stock outstanding. In the case of nopar stock, legal capital is viewed as either the stated value set by the company or the amount for which the stock was sold originally. Legal capital usually cannot be used as the basis for dividends, and it represents the amount of capital that must remain invested in the corporation until it is liquidated.

Preferred Stock

Preferred stock is stock that has specified rights over the common stock.

In addition to common stock some corporations issue **preferred stock**, which is stock with certain special rights. Some investors have risk and return preferences that can best be met by combining some of the features of bonds with some of the features of common stock. Preferred stock is sometimes the right choice for these investors. Preferred stock does not appeal to investors who want some control over the operations of the corporation because preferred stock usually does not convey voting rights. Indeed, this is one of the main reasons that some corporations issue preferred stock to raise equity capital. Preferred stock permits them to raise funds without diluting the common stockholders' control of the company.

Preferred stock may be nopar value, although typically it has a par value. Most preferred stock has a fixed dividend rate. For example, "6% preferred stock, par value $10 per share" would pay an annual dividend of 6% of par, or

[3]Our discussions concerning the sale of capital stock refer to the initial sale of the stock by the corporation rather than to later sales between investors. Because the sale of stock by a corporation at a discount no longer is legal in many states, no further discussion of it is included. The sale of stock among individuals is not recorded in the accounts of the corporation.

$0.60 per share. If the preferred stock is nopar value, the preferred dividend would be specified as $0.60 per share.

Generally, preferred stock is less risky than common stock because of the priority it receives on dividend payments and asset distributions. We will compare common stock dividends and preferred stock dividends later in this chapter.

The priority on distribution of assets for the preferred stock occurs if the corporation goes out of business. Preferred stock usually has a specified amount per share that must be paid upon dissolution to the preferred stockholders before any assets can be distributed to the common stockholders.

Special Features of Preferred Stock

Some corporations issue **convertible preferred stock** which provides preferred stockholders the option to exchange their preferred shares for shares of common stock of the corporation. The terms of the conversion will specify dates and a conversion ratio. The notes to the annual report for Chrysler contain typical information concerning convertible preferred stock:

Convertible preferred stock is preferred stock that is convertible to common stock at the option of the holder.

> The annual dividend on convertible preferred stock is $46.25 per share. The convertible preferred stock is convertible at a rate of 27.78 shares of common stock for each share of convertible preferred, which is equivalent to a conversion price of $18.00 per share of common stock.

Real World Excerpt

Chrysler Corporation Annual Report

Some preferred stock is callable. At the option of the issuing corporation, holders of callable preferred stock can be required to return the shares to the corporation for a specified amount of cash. The call price usually is higher than the par value. Creative Learning Products described its call feature in the following note to its annual report:

> The Company may, at its option, call all or a part of the preferred stock for redemption at $1.50 per share, plus all accrued but unpaid dividends.

Real World Excerpt

Creative Learning Products Annual Report

ACCOUNTING FOR CAPITAL STOCK

Learning Objective 3
Record transactions affecting capital stock.

Notice the stockholders' equity section of the balance sheet for Wal-Mart shown in Exhibit 11–1. There are four different stockholder equity accounts reported on the Wal-Mart balance sheet. These accounts represent the two primary sources of stockholders' equity:

1. *Contributed Capital* from the sale of stock which is the amount invested by stockholders through the purchase of shares of stock from the corporation. Contributed capital has two distinct components: *(a)* par or stated value derived from the sale of capital stock and *(b)* additional contributed capital in excess of par or stated value. This often is called *Additional Paid-In Capital.* The contributed capital accounts for Wal-Mart are preferred stock, common stock, and capital in excess of par value.
2. *Retained Earnings* generated by the profit-making activities of the company. This is the *Cumulative* amount of net income earned since the organization of the corporation less the cumulative amount of dividends paid by the corporation since organization.

Most companies generate a significant part of their stockholders' equity from retained earnings rather than from capital raised through the sale of stock. In the case of Wal-Mart, over 90% of the total stockholders' equity was generated by retained earnings.

Sale and Issuance of Capital Stock

There are two names applied to transactions involving the initial sale of a company's stock to the public. An *initial public offering*, or IPO, involves the very first sale of a company's stock to the public (i.e., when the company first goes public). A *seasoned new issue* is the subsequent sale of new stock to the public after an IPO. As was the case with bonds (discussed in the previous chapter), most companies use an underwriter to assist in the sale of stock. The underwriter is usually an investment bank that acts as an intermediary between the corporation and the investors. The underwriter advises the corporation on matters concerning the sale and is directly involved in the sale of shares to the public.

Most sales of stock to the public are cash transactions. To illustrate accounting for an initial sale of stock, assume that Wal-Mart sold 100,000 shares of its $0.10 par value stock for $22 per share. The company would record the following journal entry:

Cash (100,000 × $22)	2,200,000	
Common stock (100,000 × $0.10)		10,000
Capital in excess of par value		2,190,000

The sale of common stock would be reported on the balance sheet in the format shown in Exhibit 11–1.

Some corporations do not specify a par value for their stock. In these cases, depending on state law, common stock is recorded under one of the following two approaches:

1. The corporation must specify in its bylaws a stated value per share as legal capital. This stated value is used as a substitute for par value, and the sale of common stock is recorded in a manner similar to the previous journal entry.
2. The corporation must record the total proceeds received from each sale of nopar stock as legal capital. In this case, the total proceeds would be recorded in the Common Stock account and there would be no account called Capital in Excess of Par.

Secondary Markets

When a company sells stock to the public, the transaction is between the issuing corporation and the buyer. As a result, the company records the sale on its books in the manner shown above.

Subsequent transactions affecting the stock are between two investors and do not directly affect the accounting records of the corporation. For example, if investor Jon Drago sold 1,000 shares of Wal-Mart stock to Jennifer Lea, Wal-Mart would not record a journal entry on its books. Mr. Drago received cash for the shares he sold, and Ms. Lea received stock for the cash she paid. Wal-Mart, itself, did not receive or pay anything because of the transaction.

Each business day, *The Wall Street Journal* reports the results of thousands of transactions between investors in the secondary markets. These markets include the New York Stock Exchange (NYSE), the American Stock Exchange (AMEX) and the over-the-counter market (OTC).

Managers of corporations follow very closely the movements in the price of their company's stock. Stockholders expect to earn money on their investment because of dividends and increases in the price of the stock. There have been many instances where senior management was replaced because of poor performance of the stock in the secondary markets. While managers watch the stock price on a daily basis, it is important to remember that the transactions between investors do not directly affect the books of the company (i.e., journal entries are not prepared to record the transactions).

FINANCIAL ANALYSIS

Going Public

An initial public offering (IPO) is the first sale of stock to the public. Prior to that sale, the company is a private company. Why would a company want to go public? There are two common reasons. For a company to grow and meet consumer demand, it must expand its productive capacity. The need for new capital may be beyond the capability of the private owners. By going public, the company can raise the funds needed to expand.

In some cases, the company may not need significant funds but the current owners may want to create a market for its shares. It is often difficult to sell shares of stock if the company is not listed on a major stock exchange. By going public, a company can increase the liquidity of its shares.

Initial public offerings often create a great deal of interest among investors. There are some good opportunities to earn excellent returns by investing in growing companies. There is also substantial risk associated with many IPOs

Capital Stock Sold and Issued for Noncash Assets and/or Services

Small companies are playing an increasingly important role in the U.S. economy. A large percentage of the new jobs that have been created in the past decade were created by small companies. Many of the corporate giants of today were small start-up companies just a few years ago. Companies such as Dell Computers, Microsoft, and Apple Computers began literally as basement operations in the homes of their founders.

One feature common to all start-up companies is a shortage of cash. Because these companies often cannot afford to pay cash for needed assets and services, they sometimes issue stock to people who can supply these assets

The success of a company is dependent on meeting customer needs. Notice that this store includes printing and shipping services, a photo lab, and optical services.

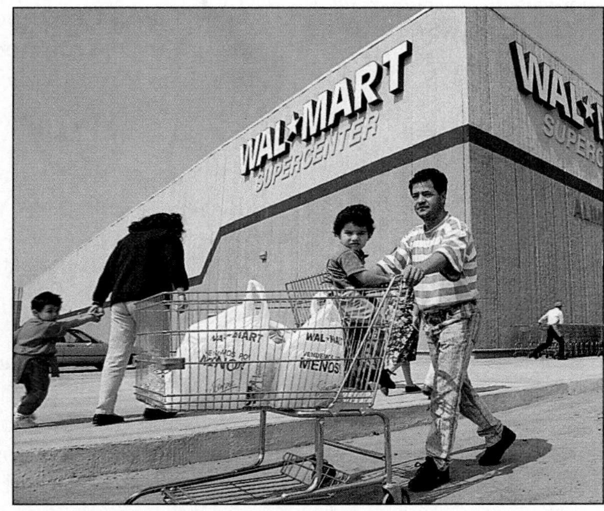

Some businesses meet customer needs by forming alliances with other businesses. This Wal-Mart includes a McDonald's restaurant.

and services. Indeed, many executives will join start-up companies for very low salaries because they also earn shares of stock. An executive who was given Apple stock during its early days would be very wealthy today.

When a company issues stock to acquire assets or services, the acquired items should be recorded at the *market value* of the stock issued at the date of the transaction in accordance with the *cost principle.* If the market value of the stock issued cannot be determined, then the market value of the consideration received should be used.

To illustrate, assume that during its early years of operations, Wal-Mart was unable to pay cash for needed legal services. The company issued 10,000 shares of stock to the Rose law firm when the stock was selling for $15 per share. At that time, the company would record the following journal entry:

Legal fees	150,000	
Common stock (10,000 × $0.10)		1,000
Capital in excess of par value		149,000

Notice that the value of the legal services received is assumed to be the same as the value of the stock that was issued. This assumption is reasonable because two independent parties usually would keep negotiating a deal until the point where the value of what is given up is equal to the value of what is received.

TREASURY STOCK

Learning Objective 4
Define and account for treasury stock.

There are a number of strategic reasons why a corporation may want to purchase its own stock. A common reason is the existence of an employee bonus plan that provides workers with shares of the company's stock as part of their compensation. Because of Securities and Exchange Commission regulations concerning newly issued shares, most companies find that it is less costly to give their employees shares of stock that were repurchased from stockholders than to issue new shares.

Treasury stock is a corporation's own stock that had been issued but was subsequently reacquired and is still being held by that corporation.

Stock that was issued to stockholders, then subsequently *reacquired* and held by that corporation is called **treasury stock**. While this stock is held by the issuing corporation, it has no voting, dividend, or other stockholder rights.

Two alternative approaches generally are used to account for treasury stock—the cost method and the par value method. We will limit our discussions to the cost method because it is more widely used. The par value method is discussed in most accounting texts at the intermediate level. The recording of the purchase of treasury stock is based on the cost of the shares that were purchased. Assume that Wal-Mart bought 100,000 shares of its stock in the open market when the stock was selling for $22 per share. Using the cost method, the company would record the following journal entry:

Treasury stock (100,000 × $22)	2,200,000	
Cash		2,200,000

Intuitively, many students expect that the treasury stock account should be reported as an asset. Such is not the case because a company cannot create an asset by investing in itself. The treasury stock account is actually a *contra equity account*, which means that it is reported as a subtraction from the total stockholders' equity. This makes sense because treasury stock is stock that is no longer outstanding and therefore, should not be included as part of stockholders' equity.

As you can see in Exhibit 11–1, Wal-Mart does not report any treasury stock on its balance sheet. The company actually purchased treasury stock but it uses a fairly unusual accounting alternative that treats the repurchase of stock as a retirement of the stock. Under this alternative, the common stock account and paid-in capital accounts are reduced. If Wal-Mart had used the cost method, its stockholders' equity section would appear as follows (numbers in thousands, based on the previous example):

WAL-MART STORES, INC.
Shareholders' Equity (summarized)

Common stock	$ 229,964,000	
Capital in excess of par	526,647,000	
Retained earnings	8,002,569,000	
Less: Treasury stock	(2,200,000)	
Total stockholders' equity		$8,756,980,000

If Wal-Mart eventually sold its treasury stock, it would not report a profit or loss on the transaction even if it sold the stock for more or less than it paid. GAAP does not permit a corporation to report income or losses from investments in its own stock because transactions with the owners are not considered to be normal profit-making activities. Based on the previous example, assume that Wal-Mart sold 10,000 shares of treasury stock for $30 per share. Remember that the company had purchased the stock for $22 per share. Wal-Mart would record the following entry:

Cash (10,000 × $30)	300,000	
Treasury stock (10,000 × $22)		220,000
Contributed capital from treasury stock transactions		80,000

If treasury stock were sold at a price below its purchase price (i.e., an economic loss), the Contributed Capital from Treasury Stock Transactions account would be debited for the amount of the loss. Retained Earnings would be debited for some or all of the amount of the economic losses only if there were an insufficient credit balance in the Contributed Capital account.

Neither the purchase nor sale of treasury stock affects the number of shares of stock that are issued or unissued. Treasury stock only affects the number of shares of outstanding stock. The basic difference between treasury stock and unissued stock is that treasury stock has been sold at least once.

Self-Study Quiz

1. Assume Applied Technology Corporation issued 10,000 shares of its common stock, par value $2, for $150,000 cash. Prepare the journal entry to record this transaction.

2. Assume Applied Technology purchased 5,000 shares of its stock in the open market for treasury stock when the stock was selling for $12 per share. Record this transaction using the cost method.

Check your answer with the one provided in the footnote at the bottom of this page.*

*1.	Cash	150,000	
	Common stock		20,000
	Contributed capital in excess of par		130,000
2.	Treasury stock	60,000	
	Cash		60,000

ACCOUNTING FOR CASH DIVIDENDS

Dividends Defined

Learning Objective 5
Account for dividends on common and preferred stock.

Investors buy common stock because they expect a return on their investment. This return can come in two forms: stock price appreciation and dividends to owners. Some investors prefer to buy stocks that pay little or no dividends. Companies that reinvest the majority of their earnings tend to increase their future earnings potential. By increasing their future earnings potential, these companies often experience increases in their stock price. Wealthy investors in high tax brackets prefer to receive their return on stock investments in the form of higher stock prices because capital gains may be taxed at a lower rate than dividend income.

Other investors, such as retired people, prefer to receive their return on an investment in the form of dividends because they have a need for steady income. These people often seek out stock that will pay very high dividends. Utility stocks are held by many retired people because they are usually conservative investments that pay high dividends.

Dividends must be approved (i.e., declared) by the board of directors before they can be paid. A corporation does not have a legal obligation to pay dividends. Creditors can force a company into bankruptcy if it does not meet required interest payments on debt, but stockholders do not have a similar right if a corporation is unable to pay dividends.

Without a qualifier, the term *dividend* means a cash dividend. Dividends can be paid in assets other than cash. Some corporations issue stock dividends, which are dividend distributions of the corporation's own stock. The most common type of dividend is a cash dividend.

While a corporation does not have a legal obligation to pay dividends, a liability is created once the board formally declares a dividend. An actual press release announcing a dividend declaration for Wal-Mart contained the following information:

Real World Excerpt

Wal-Mart Stores, Inc. Dividend Declaration

Dateline: Bentonville, Ark., June 2, 1994

The Board of Directors of Wal-Mart Stores, Inc. today declared a quarterly cash dividend on common stock of four-and-one-quarter cents ($0.0425) a share, payable July 8, 1994, to shareholders of record June 13, 1994.

This declaration creates a liability. Immediately on June 2, Wal-Mart would record the following journal entry to reflect the declaration of a cash dividend based on 2,299,638,000 shares outstanding ($\$0.0425 \times 2{,}299{,}638{,}000 = \$97{,}734{,}615$):

June 2, 1994:	Retained earnings (or Dividends declared, which is closed to Retained earnings)	97,734,615	
	Dividends payable		97,734,615

The subsequent payment of the liability on July 8, 1994, is recorded as follows:

July 8, 1994:	Dividends payable	97,734,615	
	Cash		97,734,615

Notice that the declaration and payment of a cash dividend have two impacts: they reduce assets (cash) and stockholders' equity (retained earnings) by the same amount. This observation helps us understand the two fundamental requirements for the payment of a cash dividend:

1. *Sufficient retained earnings.* The corporation must have accumulated a sufficient amount of retained earnings to cover the amount of the dividend. State incorporation laws usually place restrictions on cash dividends. For example, the state laws often limit cash dividends to the balance in retained earnings.
2. *Sufficient cash.* The corporation must have access to sufficient cash to pay the dividend and to meet the continuing operating needs of the business. The mere fact that there is a large credit in the Retained Earnings account does not mean that the board of directors can declare and pay a cash dividend. The cash generated in the past by earnings represented in the Retained Earnings account may have been expended to acquire inventory, buy operational assets, and pay liabilities. Consequently, there is no necessary relationship between the balance of retained earnings and the balance of cash on any particular date (simply, retained earnings is not cash).

Dividend Dates

Refer back to the earlier example of a dividend declaration by Wal-Mart. Notice that the declaration includes three important dates:

1. **Declaration date—June 2, 1994.** This is the date on which the board of directors officially approved the dividend. As soon as the declaration is made, a dividend liability is created.
2. **Date of record—June 13, 1994.** This date follows the declaration date. It is the date on which the corporation prepares the list of current stockholders based on the stockholder records. The dividend is payable only to those names listed on the record date. No journal entry would be made on this date.
3. **Date of payment—July 8, 1994.** This is the date on which the cash is disbursed to pay the dividend liability. It follows the date of record as specified in the dividend announcement.

The **declaration date** is the date on which the board of directors officially approved the dividend.

The **record date** is the date on which the corporation prepares the list of current stockholders as shown on its records; dividends can be paid only to the stockholders who own stock on that date.

The **payment date** is the date on which a cash dividend is paid to the stockholders of record.

For instructional purposes, the time lag between the date of declaration and the date of payment may be ignored because it does not pose any substantive issues. Also, when all three dates fall in the same accounting period, a single entry on the date of payment may be made in practice for purely practical reasons.

Dividends on Preferred Stock

Investors who purchase preferred stock give up certain advantages that are available to investors in common stock. Generally, preferred stockholders do not have the right to vote at the annual meeting and they do not share in increased earnings if the company becomes more profitable. To compensate these investors, preferred stock offers some advantages that are not available to common stockholders. Perhaps the most important advantage is dividend preference. You will frequently encounter the following dividend preferences:

1. Current dividend preference.
2. Cumulative dividend preference.

Current Dividend Preference on Preferred Stock

Current dividend preference is the basic dividend preference on preferred stock for a particular year.

Preferred stock always carries a **current dividend preference.** It requires that the current preferred dividend must be paid before any dividends can be paid on the common stock. When the current dividend preference has been met and no other preference is operative, dividends can be paid to the common stockholders.

Declared dividends must be allocated between the preferred and common stock. First, the preferences of the preferred stock must be met, then the remainder of the total dividend can be allocated to the common stock. Exhibit 11–4, Case A, illustrates the allocation of the current dividend preference under three different assumptions concerning the total amount of dividends to be paid.

Cumulative Dividend Preference on Preferred Stock

Cumulative dividend preference is the preferred stock preference that requires specified current dividends not paid in full to accumulate for every year in which they are not paid. These cumulative preferred dividends must be paid before any common dividends can be paid.

Dividends in arrears are dividends on cumulative preferred stock that have not been declared in prior years.

Cumulative preferred stock has a **cumulative dividend preference** that states if all or a part of the specified current dividend is not paid in full, the unpaid amount becomes **dividends in arrears.** The amount of any cumulative preferred dividends in arrears must be paid before any common dividends can be paid. Of course, if the preferred stock is noncumulative, dividends never can be in arrears. Therefore any dividends passed (i.e., not declared) are lost permanently by the preferred stockholders. Because preferred stockholders are not willing to accept this unfavorable feature, preferred stock is usually cumulative.

Exhibit 11–4 Dividends on Preferred Stock

Case A—Current dividend preference only:
Preferred stock outstanding, 6%, par $20; 2,000 shares = $40,000 par.
Common stock outstanding, par $10; 5,000 shares = $50,000 par.

Allocation of dividends between preferred and common stock assuming **current dividend preference** only:

Assumptions	Total Dividends Paid	Amount of Dividend Paid to Stockholders of: 6% Preferred Stock (2,000 shares at $20 par = $40,000)*	Common Stock (5,000 shares at $10 Par = $50,000)
No. 1	$ 2,000	$2,000	–0–
No. 2	3,000	2,400	$ 600
No. 3	18,000	2,400	15,600

*Preferred dividend preference, $40,000 × 6% = $2,400; or 2,000 shares × $1.20.

Case B—Cumulative dividend preference:
Preferred and common stock outstanding—same as above. Dividends in arrears for the two preceding years.

Allocation of dividends between preferred and common stock assuming **cumulative preference:**

Assumptions (dividends in arrears, 2 Years)	Total Dividends Paid	Amount of Dividend Paid to Stockholders of: 6% Preferred Stock (2,000 shares at $20 par = $40,000)*	Common Stock (5,000 shares at $10 Par = $50,000)
No. 1	$ 2,400	$2,400	–0–
No. 2	7,200	7,200	–0–
No. 3	8,000	7,200	$ 800
No. 4	30,000	7,200	22,800

*Current dividend preference, $40,000 × 6% = $2,400; dividends in arrears preference, $2,400 × 2 years = $4,800; and current dividend preference plus dividends in arrears = $7,200.

Wal-Mart operates Sam's Club stores. It was able to create this successful division because it was able to raise new capital from owners.

Dividends are never an actual liability until declared by the board of directors. Dividends in arrears would not be reported on the balance sheet but would be disclosed in the notes to the statements.

The allocation of dividends between cumulative preferred stock and common stock is illustrated in Exhibit 11–4, Case B, under four different assumptions concerning the total amount of dividends to be paid. Observe that the dividends in arrears are paid first, next the current dividend preference is paid, and, finally, the remainder is paid to the common stockholders.

FINANCIAL ANALYSIS

Impact of Dividends in Arrears

The existence of dividends in arrears is important information for analysts. This situation limits the ability of a company to pay dividends to its common stockholders and it has implications for the future cash flows of the company. The following note from Lone Star Industries is typical if a company has dividends in arrears:

Real World Excerpt

Lone Star Industries Annual Report

> The total of dividends in arrears on the $13.50 preferred stock at the end of the year was $11,670,000. The aggregate amount of such dividend must be paid before any dividends are paid on common stock.

Remember that various issues of preferred stock can offer different features. Most preferred stock has the cumulative dividend preference to provide stockholders with extra security. Companies can offer additional features to provide even more security. Many companies offer the feature described in the following note from Bally Manufacturing:

Real World Excerpt

Bally Manufacturing Annual Report

> The holders of preferred stock do not have voting rights except that the holders would have the right to elect two additional directors of Bally if dividends on the preferred stock are in arrears in an amount equal to at least six quarterly dividends.

By electing two members of the board of directors, preferred stockholders would have specific individuals to represent their interests. Bally included this feature with their preferred stock to make it more attractive to potential stockholders.

ACCOUNTING FOR STOCK DIVIDENDS AND STOCK SPLITS

Stock Dividends

Learning Objective 6
Contrast and account for stock dividends and stock splits.

A **stock dividend** is a distribution of additional shares of a corporation's capital stock to current stockholders on a pro rata basis at no cost; decreases retained earnings.

Each year, hundreds of corporations issue stock dividends. A **stock dividend** is a distribution of additional shares of a corporation's own capital stock on a pro rata basis to its stockholders at no cost. Stock dividends usually consist of common stock issued to the holders of common stock. *Pro rata basis* means that each stockholder receives additional shares equal to the percentage of shares already held. A stockholder with 10% of the outstanding shares would receive 10% of any additional shares issued as a stock dividend.

You should be careful as you read annual reports and the business press. The term *stock dividend* is sometimes ambiguous. A recent *Wall Street Journal* headline announced that a particular company had just declared a "stock dividend." A close reading of the article revealed that the company had declared a cash dividend on the stock. Just remember that a dividend paid in stock is a stock dividend and one paid in cash is a cash dividend.

There is much debate about the value of a stock dividend. In reality, there is no economic value to a stock dividend, as such. All stockholders receive a pro rata distribution of shares, which means each owns exactly the same portion of the company both before and after the stock dividend. The value of an investment is determined by the percent of the company that is owned, not the number of shares that are held. If you get change for a dollar, you do not have more wealth because you hold *four* quarters instead of only *one* dollar. Similarly, if you own 10% of a company, you do not have more wealth simply because the company declares a stock dividend and gives you (and all other stockholders) more shares of stock. At this point, you may still wonder why having extra shares of stock does not make an investor more wealthy. The reason is simple: the stock market reacts immediately when a stock dividend is issued and the stock price falls proportionally. If the stock price was $60 before a stock dividend, normally (in the absence of events affecting the company) the price will fall to $30 if the number of shares is doubled. Thus an investor could own 100 shares worth $6,000 before the stock dividend (100 × $60) and 200 shares worth $6,000 after the stock dividend (200 × $30).

In reality, the price of a stock does not fall exactly in proportion to the number of new shares that are issued. In some cases, the stock dividend makes the stock more attractive to new investors. Many investors prefer to buy stock in *round lots* which are multiples of 100 shares. An investor with $10,000 might not buy a stock selling for $150 because she cannot afford to buy 100 shares. The investor might buy the stock if the price was brought down to less than $100 as the result of a stock dividend. In other cases, stock dividends are associated with increases in cash dividends which would be attractive to some investors. A recent press release announcing a stock dividend for Alcoa contained both of these elements:

Real World Excerpt
Alcoa Stock Dividend Announcement

> The Board of Directors of Alcoa today declared a 100% stock dividend. The additional shares are being issued to encourage wider distribution of Alcoa stock.
>
> The Board also approved an increase in the company's base quarterly dividend from 40 cents per share to 45 cents per share.

Stock dividends are very common for companies that grow rapidly. Wal-Mart has issued 10 stock dividends since it went public. In January 1992 the business press reported the following story:

Real World Excerpt

Wal-Mart Stores Inc.

Wal-Mart Stores, Inc., the largest retailer in the United States, said yesterday that its board of directors had declared a stock dividend, its first since July 1990. The company will issue a 100 percent stock dividend February 25 to shareholders of record on February 2. Wal-Mart has 1,149,819,000 shares outstanding. The stock was the seventh-most-active stock on the New York Stock Exchange, with volume of nearly four million shares.

In Exhibit 11–1, notice the accounting for the stock dividend in the statement of shareholders' equity. In this statement, Wal-Mart uses the term "two-for-one stock split." This terminology is required by the Securities and Exchange Commission whenever a stock dividend is 25% or more of the outstanding shares. The notes to the Wal-Mart statements provide additional explanation:

Real World Excerpt

Wal-Mart Stores, Inc. Annual Report

On January 22, 1993, The Company announced a two-for-one stock split which has been accounted for as a 100% stock dividend.[4]

Stock dividends are classified as either large or small. A *large* stock dividend involves the distribution of additional shares that are more than 20–25% of the currently outstanding shares. A *small* stock dividend involves additional shares that are less than 20–25% of the outstanding shares. Because the Wal-Mart stock dividend was equal to 100% of the outstanding shares, it should be classified as a large dividend. The company would make the following entry to record a large stock dividend:

Retained earnings ($0.10 × 1,149,819,000)	114,981,900	
Common stock		114,981,900

Notice that this journal entry moves an amount from retained earnings to the permanent contributed capital of the company. The stock dividend did *not* change total stockholders' equity—it only changed some of the balances of the accounts that constitute stockholders' equity. This process of transferring an amount from retained earnings to contributed capital often is called *capitalizing earnings* because it reduces the amount of retained earnings available for future dividends.

The amount that was transferred from Retained Earnings to Contributed Capital was based on the par value of the shares issued as a stock dividend. Par value is used whenever the stock dividend is classified as large. In those cases where a stock dividend is small (i.e., less than 20–25%), the amount transferred should be the total market value of the shares issued.

Stock Splits

Stock splits are *not* dividends. They are similar to a stock dividend but are quite different in terms of their impact on the stockholders' equity accounts. In a **stock split**, the *total* number of authorized shares is increased by a specified amount, such as a two-for-one split. In this instance, each share held is called in, and two new shares are issued in its place. Typically, a stock split is accomplished by reducing the par or stated value per share of all authorized shares so that the total par value of all authorized shares is unchanged. If Wal-Mart executed a 2-for-1 stock split, it would reduce the par value of its stock from $0.10 to $0.05 and it would double the number of shares outstanding. In contrast to a stock dividend, a stock split does *not* result in a transfer of retained

A stock split is an increase in the total number of authorized shares by a specified ratio; does not decrease retained earnings.

[4]The method used by Wal-Mart to record its stock dividend is permitted by GAAP but it is not the method used by most companies. We will illustrate how Wal-Mart would record a stock dividend under the methods used by most companies rather than the one they actually used.

earnings to contributed capital. No transfer is needed because the reduction in the par value per share compensates for the increase in the number of shares.

In both a stock dividend and a stock split, the stockholder receives more shares of stock but does not disburse any additional assets to acquire the additional shares. A stock dividend requires a journal entry, while a stock split does not require a journal entry. A stock split would be disclosed in the notes to the financial statements.

The comparative effects of a stock dividend versus a stock split may be summarized as follows:

Stockholders' Equity

	Before	After a 100% Stock Dividend	After a Two-for-One Stock Split
Contributed capital:			
Number of shares outstanding	30,000	60,000	60,000
Par value per share	$ 10	$ 10	$ 5
Total par value outstanding	300,000	600,000	300,000
Retained earnings	650,000	350,000	650,000
Total stockholders' equity	950,000	950,000	950,000

Self-Study Quiz

Barton Corporation issued 100,000 new shares of common stock (par value $10) in a stock dividend when the market value was $30 per share.

1. Record this transaction assuming that it was a small stock dividend.
2. Record this transaction assuming that it was a large stock dividend.
3. What journal entry would be required if the transaction had been a stock split?

Check your response with the answer contained in the footnote at the bottom of this page.*

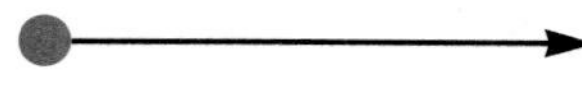

RETAINED EARNINGS

Learning Objective 7
Measure and report retained earnings.

Retained earnings represent income that has been earned less dividends that have been paid out since the first day of operations for the company. In Exhibit 11–1, you can see the changes in the Wal-Mart retained earnings that took place during 1992 ($ in thousands):

Balance–January 31, 1992	$6,249,138
Net income	1,994,794
Cash dividends	(241,363)
Balance–January 31, 1993	$8,002,569

This represents a fairly typical statement of changes in retained earnings. Under rare circumstances, you may see a statement that includes an adjustment to the beginning balance of retained earnings. This adjustment is called a

*1.	Retained earnings	3,000,000	
	Common stock		1,000,000
	Contributed capital in excess of par		2,000,000
2.	Retained earnings	1,000,000	
	Common stock		1,000,000

3. No journal entry is required in the case of a stock split.

prior period adjustment which is a correction of an accounting error that occurred in the financial statements of a prior period.

A **prior period adjustment** is an amount debited or credited directly to retained earnings to correct an accounting error of a prior period.

If an accounting error from a previous period were corrected by making an adjustment to the current income statement, net income for the current period would be improperly measured. To avoid this problem, prior period adjustments are reported as an adjustment of the beginning balance of retained earnings because the incorrect amount of net income from the earlier year was closed to retained earnings in the year the error was made. Prior period adjustments are not reported on the current income statement.

An example of an accounting error that could result in a prior period adjustment was discussed in Chapter 7. Several years ago, the financial statements of Lafayette Radio Electronics Corporation contained the following note:

Real World Excerpt

Lafayette Radio Electronics Corporation Annual Report

> Subsequent to the issuance of its financial statements the company discovered a computational error in the amount of $1,046,000 in the calculation of its year-end inventory which resulted in an overstatement of ending inventory.

The overstatement of inventory by Lafayette Radio resulted in an overstatement of pretax income by $1,046,000. If the company corrected the error in the year it was discovered, pretax income would have been understated by $1,046,000. The incorrect measurement of income for each year could mislead some users of financial statements.

Restrictions on Retained Earnings

As the result of several types of business transactions, restrictions may be placed on retained earnings to limit the ability of a company to pay dividends to its owners. The most typical example occurs when a business borrows money from a bank. For additional security, some banks include a loan covenant that limits the amount of dividends that a corporation can pay by placing a restriction on their retained earnings.

The *full-disclosure principle* requires that restrictions on retained earnings be reported in the financial statements or in a separate note to the financial statements. Analysts are particularly interested in information concerning these restrictions because of the impact they have on the dividend policy of the company.

Most companies report restrictions on retained earnings in the notes to the statements. An example of such a note from the annual report of May Department Store is shown below:

Real World Excerpt

May Department Store Annual Report

> Under the most restrictive covenants of long-term debt agreements, $1.2 billion of retained earnings was restricted as to the payment of dividends and/or common share repurchase.

This type of note would describe other restrictions that were imposed as the result of debt covenants. These restrictions often include a limit on borrowing and required minimum balances of cash or working capital. If debt covenants are violated, the creditor can demand immediate repayment of the debt. For this reason, analysts want to review these restrictions to be sure that companies are not close to violating loan agreements.

ACCOUNTING AND REPORTING FOR UNINCORPORATED BUSINESSES

Learning Objective 8
Discuss the differences between corporations, proprietorships, and partnerships.

There are three forms of business organizations: corporations, sole proprietorships (one owner), and partnerships (two or more owners). The fundamentals of accounting and reporting for unincorporated businesses are the same as for

Exhibit 11–5 **Comparative Account Structures among Types of Business Entities**

Typical Account Structure		
Corporation (Stockholders' Equity)	**Sole Proprietorship (Owner's Equity)**	**Partnership (Partners' Equity)**
Capital Stock Contributed Capital in Excess of Par	Doe, Capital	Able, Capital Baker, Capital
Retained Earnings	Not used	Not used
Dividends Paid	Doe, Drawings	Able, Drawings Baker, Drawings
Income Summary (closed to Retained Earnings)	Income Summary (closed to Doe, Capital)	Income Summary (closed to Able, Capital and Baker, Capital)
Revenues, expenses, gains, and losses	Same	Same
Assets and liabilities	Same	Same

a corporation except for owners' equity. Typical account structures for the three forms of business organizations are outlined in Exhibit 11–5.

Accounting for sole proprietorships and partnerships is discussed in Chapter Supplement A.

EPILOGUE FOR WAL-MART

In early 1995, Wal-Mart issued the following press release:

Real World Excerpt

Wal-Mart Stores, Inc.
Press Release

> Wal-Mart Stores, Inc., the nation's largest retailer, said Wednesday that it will repurchase up to $100 million of its common stock from time to time on the open market.
> "We believe that the stock is an excellent long-term value," said David Glass, President and Chief Executive.

During the 18 months preceding this announcement, Wal-Mart stock had fallen in value by more than one-third. Clearly, investments in common stock offer the opportunity to earn significant returns. Unfortunately, it is also possible to lose large amounts of money when stock prices fall. In these situations management often reacts quickly to attempt to create shareholder value.

DEMONSTRATION CASE

(Try to resolve the requirements before proceeding to the suggested solution that follows.)

This case focuses on the organization and operations for the first year of Shelly Corporation, which was organized on January 1, 19A. The laws of the state specify that the legal capital for nopar stock is the full sale amount. The corporation was organized by 10 local entrepreneurs for the purpose of operating a business to sell various supplies to hotels. The charter authorized the following capital stock:

Common stock, nopar value, 20,000 shares.

Preferred stock, 5%, $100 par value, 5,000 shares (cumulative, nonconvertible, and nonvoting; liquidation value, $110).

The following summarized transactions, selected from 19A, were completed on the dates indicated:

a. Jan. Sold a total of 7,500 shares of nopar common stock to the 10 entrepreneurs for cash at $52 per share. Credit the Nopar Common Stock account for the total issue amount.

b. Feb. Sold 1,890 shares of preferred stock at $102 per share; cash collected in full.

c. Mar. Purchased land for a store site and made full payment by issuing 100 shares of preferred stock. Early construction of the store is planned. Debit Land (store site). The preferred stock is selling at $102 per share.

d. Apr. Paid $1,980 cash for organization costs. Debit an intangible asset account called Organization Cost.

e. May Issued 10 shares of preferred stock to A. B. Cain in full payment of legal services rendered in connection with organization of the corporation. Assume the preferred stock is selling regularly at $102 per share. Debit Organization Cost.

f. June Sold 500 shares of nopar common stock for cash to C. B. Abel at $54 per share.

g. July Purchased 100 shares of preferred stock that had been sold and issued earlier. The stockholder was moving to another state and needed the money. Shelly Corporation paid the stockholder $104 per share.

h. Aug. Sold 20 shares of the preferred treasury stock at $105 per share.

i. Dec. 31 Purchased equipment for $600,000; paid cash. No depreciation expense should be recorded in 19A.

j. Dec 31 Borrowed $20,000 cash from the City Bank on a one-year, interest-bearing note. Interest is payable at a 12% rate at maturity.

k. Dec 31 Gross revenues for the year amounted to $129,300; expenses, including corporation income tax but excluding amortization of organization costs, amounted to $98,000. Assume that these summarized revenue and expense transactions involved cash. Because the equipment and the bank loan transactions were on December 31, no related adjusting entries at the end of 19A are needed.

l. Dec 31 Shelly Corporation decided that a reasonable amortization period for organization costs, starting as of January 1, 19A, would be 10 years. This intangible asset must be amortized to expense. Give the required adjusting entry for 19A.

Required:

1. Give appropriate journal entries, with a brief explanation for each of the above transactions.
2. Give appropriate closing entries at December 31, 19A.
3. Prepare a balance sheet for Shelly Corporation at December 31, 19A. Emphasize full disclosure of stockholders' equity.

SUGGESTED SOLUTION

1. Journal entries:

	Date	Account	Debit	Credit
a.	Jan. 19A	Cash	390,000	
		Nopar common stock (7,500 shares)		390,000
		Sale of nopar common stock ($52 × 7,500 shares = $390,000).		
b.	Feb. 19A	Cash	192,780	
		Preferred stock, 5% (par $100, 1,890 shares)		189,000
		Contributed capital in excess of par, preferred stock [1,890 shares × ($102 – $100)]		3,780
		Sale of preferred stock ($102 × 1,890 shares = $192,780).		
c.	March 19A	Land (store site)	10,200	
		Preferred stock, 5% (par $100, 100 shares)		10,000
		Contributed capital in excess of par, preferred stock		200
		Purchased land for future store site; paid in full by issuance of 100 shares of preferred stock. The market value is $102 × 100 shares = $10,200.		
d.	Apr. 19A	Organization cost	1,980	
		Cash		1,980
		Paid organization cost.		

	Date	Account	Debit	Credit
e.	May 19A	Organization cost	1,020	
		Preferred stock 5% (par $100, 10 shares)		1,000
		Contributed capital in excess of par, preferred stock		20
		Organization cost (legal services) paid by issuance of 10 shares of preferred stock. The implied market value is $102 × 10 shares = $1,020.		
f.	June 19A	Cash	27,000	
		Nopar common stock (500 shares)		27,000
		Sold 500 shares of the nopar common stock ($54 × 500 shares = $27,000).		
g.	July 19A	Treasury stock, preferred (100 shares at $104)	10,400	
		Cash		10,400
		Purchased 100 shares of preferred treasury stock ($104 × 100 shares = $10,400).		
h.	Aug. 19A	Cash (20 shares at $105)	2,100	
		Treasury stock, preferred (20 shares at $104)		2,080
		Contributed capital from treasury stock transactions		20
		Sold 20 shares of the preferred treasury stock at $105.		
i.	Dec. 31, 19A	Equipment	600,000	
		Cash		600,000
		Purchased equipment.		
j.	Dec. 31, 19A	Cash	20,000	
		Note payable		20,000
		Borrowed on one-year, 12% interest-bearing note.		
k.	Dec. 31, 19A	Cash	129,300	
		Revenues		129,300
		Expenses	98,000	
		Cash		98,000
		To record summarized revenues and expenses.		
l.	Dec. 31, 19A	Expenses	300	
		Organization cost		300
		Adjusting entry to amortize organization cost for one year [($1,980 + $1,020) ÷ 10 years = $300].		

2. Closing Entries:

	Date	Account	Debit	Credit
m.	Dec. 31, 19A	Revenues	129,300	
		Income summary		129,300
		Income summary	98,300	
		Expenses ($98,000 + $300)		98,300
		Income summary	31,000	
		Retained earnings		31,000
		($129,300 − $98,300 = $31,000).		

3. Balance Sheet

SHELLY CORPORATION
Balance Sheet
At December 31, 19A

Assets

Current assets:		
Cash		$50,800
Tangible assets:		
Land	$ 10,200	
Equipment (no depreciation assumed in the problem)	600,000	610,200
Intangible assets:		
Organization cost (cost, $3,000 less amortization, $300)		2,700
Total assets		$663,700

Liabilities		
Current liabilities:		
Note payable, 12%		$ 20,000
Stockholders' Equity		
Contributed capital:		
Preferred stock, 5% (par value $100; authorized 5,000 shares, issued 2,000 shares of which 80 shares are held as treasury stock)	$200,000	
Common stock (nopar value; authorized 20,000 shares, issued and outstanding 8,000 shares)	417,000	
Contributed capital in excess of par, preferred stock	4,000	
Contributed capital from treasury stock transactions	20	
Total contributed capital	621,020	
Retained earnings	31,000	
Total contributed capital and retained earnings	652,020	
Less cost of preferred treasury stock held (80 shares)	(8,320)	
Total stockholders' equity		643,700
Total liabilities and stockholders' equity		$663,700

SUMMARY

This chapter discussed accounting for owners' equity for corporations. Sole proprietorships and partnerships are discussed in Chapter Supplement A. Except for owners' equity, accounting basically is unaffected by the type of business organization. Separate accounts are kept for the two basic sources of owners' equity for a corporation, contributed capital and retained earnings. Separate accounts are kept for each type of common and preferred stock that has been issued.

Frequently a corporation purchases its own stock in the marketplace. Stock previously issued by the corporation and subsequently reacquired is known as treasury stock as long as it is held by the issuing corporation. The purchase of treasury stock reduces the amount of corporate capital, and the subsequent resale of the treasury stock increases corporate capital.

The earnings of a corporation that are not retained in the business for growth and expansion are distributed to the stockholders by means of dividends. Dividends are paid only when formally declared by the board of directors of the corporation. A cash dividend results in a decrease in assets (cash) and a commensurate decrease in stockholders' equity (retained earnings). In contrast, a stock dividend does not change assets, liabilities, or total stockholder's equity. A stock dividend results in a transfer of retained earnings to the permanent or contributed capital of the corporation by the amount of the stock dividend. Therefore, a stock dividend affects only certain account balances within stockholders' equity. A stock split affects only the par value of the stock and the number of shares outstanding; the individual equity account balances are not changed.

Chapter Supplement A

Accounting for Owners' Equity for Sole Proprietorships and Partnerships

Owner's Equity for a Sole Proprietorship

A sole proprietorship is an unincorporated business owned by one person. The only owner's equity accounts needed are (1) a capital account for the proprietor (J. Doe, Capital) and (2) a drawing (or withdrawal) account for the proprietor (J. Doe, Drawings). The capital account of a sole proprietorship is used for two purposes: to record investments by the owner and to accumulate the periodic income or loss. Thus, the Income Summary account is closed to the capital account at the end of each accounting period. The drawing account is used to record withdrawals of cash or other assets by the owner from the business. The drawing account is closed to the capital account at the end of each accounting period. The capital account reflects the cumulative total of all investments by the owner plus all earnings of the entity less all withdrawals of resources from the entity by the owner. In most respects, the accounting for a sole proprietorship is the same as for a corporation.

Exhibit 11–6 presents the recording of selected transactions and the owner's equity section of the balance sheet of Doe Retail Store to illustrate the accounting for owner's equity for a sole proprietorship.

A sole proprietorship does not pay income taxes. Therefore, the financial statements of a sole proprietorship will not reflect income tax expense or income taxes payable. The net income of a sole proprietorship is taxed when it is included on the *personal* income tax return of the owner. Also, because an em-

Exhibit 11–6 **Accounting for Owner's Equity for a Sole Proprietorship**

Selected entries during 19A:

January 1, 19A:
J. Doe started a retail store by investing $150,000 of personal savings. The journal entry for the business would be as follows:

	Debit	Credit
Cash	150,000	
J. Doe, capital		150,000
Investment by owner.		

During 19A:
Each month during the year, Doe withdrew $1,000 cash from the business for personal living costs. Accordingly, each month the following journal entry was made:

	Debit	Credit
J. Doe, drawings	1,000	
Cash		1,000
Withdrawal of cash by owner for personal use.		

Note: At December 31, 19A, after the last withdrawal, the drawings account will reflect a debit balance of $12,000.

December 31, 19A:
Usual journal entries for the year, including adjusting and closing entries for the revenue and expense accounts, resulted in an $18,000 credit balance in the Income Summary account (i.e., $18,000 net income). The next closing entry will be:

	Debit	Credit
Income summary	18,000	
J. Doe, capital		18,000
Closing entry to transfer net income for the year to the owner's equity account.		

December 31, 19A:
The journal entry required on this date to close the drawings account would be:

	Debit	Credit
J. Doe, capital	12,000	
J. Doe, drawings		12,000
Closing entry to transfer drawings for the year to the capital account		

Balance sheet December 31, 19A (partial):

Owner's equity		
J. Doe, capital, January 1, 19A	$150,000	
Add: Net income for 19A	18,000	
Total	168,000	
Less: Withdrawals for 19A	(12,000)	
J. Doe, capital, December 31, 19A		$156,000

ployer/employee contractual relationship cannot exist with only one party involved, a "salary" to the owner is not recognized as an expense of a sole proprietorship. The salary of the owner is accounted for as a distribution of profits (i.e., a withdrawal).

Owners' Equity for a Partnership

The Uniform Partnership Act, which has been adopted by most states, defines a partnership as "an association of two or more persons to carry on as co-owners of a business for profit." The partnership form of business is used by small businesses and professionals such as accountants, doctors, and lawyers. A partnership is formed by two or more persons reaching mutual agreement about the terms of the partnership. The law does not require an application for a charter as it does in the case of a corporation. The agreement between the partners constitutes a partnership contract that should be in writing. The partnership agreement should specify such matters as division of periodic income, management responsibilities, transfer or sale of partnership interests, disposition of assets upon liquidation, and procedures to be followed in case of the death of a partner. If the partnership agreement does not specify these matters, the laws of the resident state will be binding. The primary advantages of a partnership are (1) ease of formation, (2) complete control by the partners, and (3) no income taxes on the business itself. The primary disadvantage is the unlimited liability of each partner for the liabilities of the partnership. As a result of unlimited liability, creditors of the partnership can take the personal assets of the partners if there are not sufficient assets in the partnership to satisfy outstanding debt.

As with a sole proprietorship, accounting for a partnership follows the same underlying fundamentals of accounting as any other form of business organization, except for those entries that directly affect owners' equity. Accounting for partners' equity follows the same pattern as illustrated earlier for a sole proprietorship, except that separate partner capital and drawings accounts must be established for each partner. Investments by each partner are credited to the partner's capital account. Withdrawals from the partnership by each partner are debited to the respective drawings account. The net income for a partnership is divided between the partners in the profit ratio specified in the partnership agreement. The Income Summary account is closed to the respective partner capital accounts. The respective drawings accounts also are closed to the partner capital accounts. Therefore, after the closing process, the capital account of each partner reflects the cumulative total of all investments of the individual partner plus the partner's share of all partnership earnings less all withdrawals by the partner.

Exhibit 11–7 presents selected journal entries and partial financial statements for AB Partnership to illustrate the accounting for the distribution of income and partners' equity.

The financial statements of a partnership follow the same format as a corporation except (1) the income statement includes an additional section entitled "Distribution of net income," (2) the partners' equity section of the balance sheet is detailed for each partner in conformity with the full-disclosure principle, (3) there is no income tax expense because partnerships do not pay income tax (each partner must report his or her share of the partnership profits on their individual tax return), and (4) salaries paid to partners are not recorded as expense but are treated as a distribution of earnings (withdrawals).

Exhibit 11–7 Accounting for Partners' Equity

Selected entries during 19A:

January 1, 19A:
AB Partnership was organized by A. Able and B. Baker on this date. Able contributed $60,000 and Baker $40,000 cash in the partnership and agreed to divide net income (and net loss) 60% and 40%, respectively. The journal entry for the business to record the investment would be:

Cash	100,000	
A. Able, capital		60,000
B. Baker, capital		40,000
Investment to initiate a partnership.		

During 19A:
It was agreed that Able would withdraw $1,000 and Baker $650 per month in cash. Accordingly, each month the following journal entry for the withdrawals was made:

A. Able, drawings	1,000	
B. Baker, drawings	650	
Cash		1,650
Withdrawal of cash by partners for personal use.		

December 31, 19A:
Assume the normal closing entries for the revenue and expense accounts resulted in a $30,000 credit balance in the Income Summary account (i.e., $30,000 net income). The next closing entry would be:

Income summary	30,000	
A. Able, capital		18,000
B. Baker, capital		12,000

Closing entry to transfer net income to the respective capital accounts.
Net income is divided as follows:

A. Able, $30,000 × 60%	$18,000
B. Baker, $30,000 × 40%	12,000
Total	$30,000

December 31, 19A:
The journal entry required to close the drawings accounts would be:

A. Able, capital	12,000	
B. Baker, capital	7,800	
A. Able, drawings		12,000
B. Baker, drawings		7,800

Closing entry to transfer drawings for the year to the respective capital accounts.

After the closing entries the partners' accounts would reflect the following balances:

Income summary	-0-
A. Able, drawings	-0-
B. Baker, drawings	-0-
A. Able, capital	$66,000
B. Baker, capital	44,200

Reporting partners' distribution of net income and partners' equity:

Income statement for the year ended December 31, 19A:

Net income		$30,000
Distribution of net income:		
A. Able (60%)	$18,000	
B. Baker (40%)	12,000	
	$30,000	

Balance sheet December 31, 19A:

Partners' Equity

A. Able, capital	$66,000	
B. Baker, capital	44,200	
Total partners' equity		$110,200

A separate statement of partners' capital similar to the following customarily is prepared to supplement the balance sheet:

(concluded) **Exhibit 11–7**

AB PARTNERSHIP
Statement of Partners' Capital
For the Year Ended December 31, 19A

	A. Able	B. Baker	Total
Investment, January 1, 19A	$60,000	$40,000	$100,000
Add: Additional investments during the year	-0-	-0–	-0-
Net income for the year	18,000	12,000	30,000
Totals:	78,000	52,000	130,000
Less: Drawings during the year	(12,000)	(7,800)	(19,800)
Partners' equity, December 31, 19A	$66,000	$44,200	$110,200

KEY TERMS

Authorized Number of Shares Maximum number of shares of capital stock of a corporation that can be issued as specified in the charter. *539*

Common Stock The basic, normal, voting stock issued by a corporation; called *residual equity* because it ranks after preferred stock for dividend and liquidation distributions. *541*

Convertible Preferred Stock Preferred stock that is convertible to common stock at the option of the holder. *543*

Cumulative Dividend Preference Preferred stock preference that requires specified current dividends not paid in full to accumulate for every year in which they are not paid. These cumulative preferred dividends must be paid before any common dividends can be paid. *550*

Current Dividend Preference The basic dividend preference on preferred stock for a particular year. *550*

Dividend Dates:

Declaration Date Date on which the board of directors officially approves the dividend. *549*

Payment Date Date on which a cash dividend is paid to the stockholders of record. *549*

Record Date Date on which the corporation prepares the list of current stockholders as shown on its records; dividends can be paid only to the stockholders who own stock on that date. *549*

Dividends in Arrears Dividends on cumulative preferred stock that have not been declared in prior years. *550*

Issued Shares Total shares of stock that have been issued; shares outstanding plus treasury shares held. *540*

Legal Capital The permanent amount of capital defined by state law, that must remain invested in the business; provides a "cushion" for creditors. *542*

Nopar Value Stock Shares of capital stock that have no par value specified in the corporate charter. *542*

Outstanding Shares Total shares of stock that are owned by stockholders on any particular date. *540*

Par Value Nominal value per share of capital stock specified in the charter; serves as the basis for legal capital. *542*

Preferred Stock Shares of stock that have specified rights over the common stock. *542*

Prior Period Adjustment Amount debited or credited directly to retained earnings to correct an accounting error of a prior period. *555*

Stock Dividend Distribution of additional shares of a corporation's own capital stock to current stockholders on a pro rata basis at no cost; decreases retained earnings. *552*

Stock Split An increase in the total number of authorized shares by a specified ratio; does not decrease retained earnings. *552*

Treasury Stock A corporation's own stock that had been issued but was subsequently reacquired and is still being held by that corporation. *546*

Unissued Shares Authorized shares of a corporation's stock that have never been issued. *540*

QUESTIONS

1. Define a corporation and identify its primary advantages.
2. What is the charter of a corporation?
3. Explain each of the following terms: *(a)* authorized capital stock, *(b)* issued capital stock, *(c)* unissued capital stock, and *(d)* outstanding capital stock.
4. Differentiate between common stock and preferred stock.
5. Explain the distinction between par value stock and nopar value capital stock.
6. What are the usual characteristics of preferred stock?
7. What are the two basic sources of stockholders' equity? Explain each.
8. Owners' equity is accounted for by source. What is meant by source?
9. Define treasury stock. Why do corporations acquire treasury stock?
10. How is treasury stock reported on the balance sheet? How is the "gain or loss" on treasury stock that has been sold reported on the financial statements?
11. What are the two basic requirements to support a cash dividend? What are the effects of a cash dividend on assets and stockholders' equity?
12. Differentiate between cumulative and noncumulative preferred stock.
13. Define a stock dividend. How does it differ from a cash dividend?
14. What are the primary purposes of issuing a stock dividend?
15. Identify and explain the three important dates in respect to dividends.
16. Define retained earnings. What are the primary components of retained earnings at the end of each period?
17. Define prior period adjustments. How are they reported?
18. What is meant by restrictions on retained earnings?

EXERCISES

E11–1 Preparing the Stockholders' Equity Section of the Balance Sheet

Sampson Corporation was organized in 19A to operate a financial consulting business. The charter authorized the following capital stock: common stock, par value $8 per share, 12,000 shares. During the first year, the following selected transactions were completed:

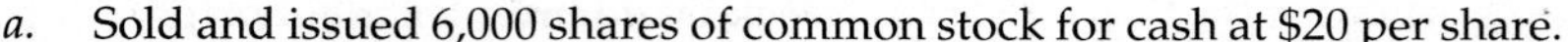

a. Sold and issued 6,000 shares of common stock for cash at $20 per share.

b. Issued 600 shares of common stock for a piece of land that will be used for a facilities site; construction began immediately. Assume the stock was selling at $22 per share at the date of issuance. Debit land.

c. Sold and issued 2,000 shares of common stock for cash at $23 per share.

d. At year-end, the Income Summary account reflected a $7,000 loss. Because a loss was incurred, no income tax expense was recorded.

Required:

1. Give the journal entry required for each of the transactions listed above.
2. Prepare the stockholders' equity section as it should be reported on the year-end balance sheet.

E11–2 Analyzing Transactions Affecting Stockholders' Equity

Shelby Corporation was organized in January 19A by 10 stockholders to operate an air conditioning sales and service business. The charter issued by the state authorized the following capital stock:

Common stock, $1 par value, 200,000 shares.

Preferred stock, $10 par value, 6%, noncumulative, 50,000 shares.

During January and February 19A, the following stock transactions were completed:

a. Collected $40,000 cash from each of the 10 organizers and issued 2,000 shares of common stock to each of them.

b. Sold 15,000 shares of preferred stock at $25 per share; collected the cash and immediately issued the stock.

Required:

1. Give the journal entries to record the above stock transactions.
2. Net income for 19A was $40,000; cash dividends declared and paid at year-end were $10,000. Prepare the stockholders' equity section of the balance sheet at December 31, 19A.

E11–3 Issuing Common and Preferred Stock

Kelly, Incorporated, was issued a charter on January 15, 19A, that authorized the following capital stock:

Common stock, nopar, 100,000 shares.

Preferred stock, 7%, par value $10 per share, 5,000 shares.

The board of directors established a stated value on the nopar common stock of $6 per share. During 19A, the following selected transactions were completed in the order given:

a. Sold and issued 20,000 shares of the nopar common stock at $18 cash per share.

b. Sold and issued 3,000 shares of preferred stock at $22 cash per share.

c. At the end of 19A, the Income Summary account had a credit balance of $38,000.

Required:

1. Give the journal entry indicated for each of the above transactions.
2. Prepare the stockholders' equity section of the balance sheet at December 31, 19A.

E11–4 Stockholders' Equity Transactions, Including Noncash Consideration

Teacher Corporation obtained a charter at the start of 19A that authorized 50,000 shares of nopar common stock and 20,000 shares of preferred stock, par value $10. The corporation was organized by four individuals who "reserved" 51% of the common stock shares for themselves. The remaining shares were to be sold to other individuals at $40 per share on a cash basis. During 19A, the following selected transactions occurred:

a. Collected $15 per share cash from three of the organizers and received two adjoining lots of land from the fourth organizer. Issued 4,000 shares of common stock to each of the four organizers and received title to the land.

b. Sold and issued 6,000 shares of common stock to an outsider at $40 cash per share.

c. Sold and issued 8,000 shares of preferred stock at $20 cash per share.

d. At the end of 19A, the Income Summary account after income taxes reflected a credit balance of $36,000.

Required:

1. Give the journal entries indicated for each of the transactions listed above.

2. Prepare the stockholders' equity section of the balance sheet at December 31, 19A.
3. Explain the basis that you used to determine the cost of the land.

E11–5 Finding Amounts Missing from the Stockholders' Equity Section

The stockholders' equity section on the December 31, 19D, balance sheet of Chemfast Corporation was:

Stockholders' Equity

Contributed capital:	
Preferred stock (par $20; authorized 10,000 shares, ? issued, of which 500 shares are held as treasury stock)	$104,000
Common stock (nopar; authorized 20,000 shares, issued and outstanding 8,000 shares)	600,000
Contributed capital in excess of par, preferred	14,300
Contributed capital, treasury stock transactions	1,500
Retained earnings	30,000
Cost of treasury stock, preferred	9,500

Required:

Complete the following statements and show your computations.

1. The number of shares of preferred stock issued was ________.
2. The number of shares of preferred stock outstanding was ________.
3. The average sale price of the preferred stock when issued was $________ per share.
4. Have the treasury stock transactions *(a)* increased corporate resources ________? or *(b)* decreased resources ________? By how much? ________.
5. The treasury stock transactions increased (decreased) stockholders' equity by ________.
6. How much did the treasury stock held cost per share? $________.
7. Total stockholders' equity is $________.
8. The average issue price of the common stock was $________.
9. Assuming one-fourth of the treasury stock is sold at $35 per share, the remaining balance in the Treasury Stock account would be $________.

PepsiCo, Inc.

E11–6 Finding Information Missing from an Annual Report

The annual report for PepsiCo, Inc. contained the following information:

a. Retained earnings at the end of 1992 were $5,439.7 million.

b. Treasury stock amounted to $667 million at the end of 1992 and $913.2 million at the end of 1993.

c. Net income for 1993 was $1,587.9 million.

d. Par value of the stock is 1 2/3 cents per share.

e. Cash dividends declared in 1993 were 61 cents per share.

f. The Common Stock, Par Value account was $14.4 million at the end of both 1992 and 1993.

Required: (Assume there is no other relevant information concerning stockholders' equity.)

1. Estimate the number of shares outstanding during 1993.
2. Estimate the amount of retained earnings at the end of 1993.
3. Did the number of shares outstanding change during 1993?

E11–7 Accounting for Treasury Stock Transactions

The balance sheet (summarized) of Italy Corporation reflected the information shown below at December 31, 19B:

ITALY CORPORATION
Balance Sheet
At December 31, 19B

Assets		**Liabilities**		
Cash	$ 76,000	Current liabilities		$ 80,000
All other assets	544,000	Long-term liabilities		92,000
		Total liabilities		172,000
		Stockholders' Equity		
		Contributed capital:		
		Common stock (par $10; authorized 40,000 shares, outstanding 36,000 shares)	360,000	
		Contributed capital in excess of par	68,000	
		Retained earnings	20,000	
		Total stockholders' equity		448,000
Total assets	$620,000	Total liabilities and stockholders' equity		$620,000

During the next year, 19C, the following selected transactions affecting stockholders' equity occurred:

Feb.	1	Purchased, in the open market, 200 shares of the company's own common stock at $22 cash per share.
July	15	Sold 100 of the shares purchased on February 1, 19C, at $24 cash per share.
Sept	1	Sold 60 more of the shares purchased on February 1, 19C, at $20 cash per share.
Dec.	15	Sold an additional 20 of the treasury shares at $15 per share.
	31	The credit balance in the Income Summary account was $32,500.

Required:

1. Give the indicated journal entries for each of the five transactions.
2. Prepare the stockholders' equity section of the balance sheet at December 31, 19C.

E11–8 Computing Shares Outstanding

Philip Morris Companies, Inc.

The annual report for Philip Morris Companies, Inc. disclosed that 4 billion shares of common stock have been authorized. At the end of 1992, 935,320,439 shares had been issued and the number of shares in treasury stock was 42,563,254. During 1993, there were no additional shares issued but 17,278,900 additional shares were purchased for treasury stock and 1,612,405 were sold from treasury stock. Determine the number of shares outstanding at the end of 1993.

E11–9 Comparing Various Types of Preferred Stock

The records of Hoffman Company reflected the following balances in the stockholders' equity accounts at December 31, 19H:

Common stock, par $12 per share, 40,000 shares outstanding.

Preferred stock, 8%, par $10 per share, 6,000 shares outstanding.

Retained earnings, $220,000.

On September 1, 19H, the board of directors was considering the distribution of a $62,000 cash dividend. No dividends were paid during 19F and 19G. You have been asked to determine the total and per share amounts that would be paid to the common stockholders and to the preferred stockholders under two independent assumptions (show computations):

a. The preferred stock is noncumulative.
b. The preferred stock is cumulative.

Required:

1. Give the journal entry to record dividends separately for preferred and common stock under each assumption.

2. Explain why the dividends per share of common stock were less for the second assumption.
3. What factor would cause a more favorable per share result to the common stockholders?

TWA

E11–10 Dividends in Arrears

The annual report for TWA contained the following note:

> Dividends were suspended in 1991 and at December 31, 1992, $29,700,000 of cumulative dividends were in arrears on the $2.25 preferred stock.

A student who read the note suggested that the TWA preferred stock would be a good investment because of the large amount of dividend income that would be earned when TWA started paying dividends again: "As the owner of the stock, I'll get dividends for the period I hold the stock plus some previous periods when I didn't even own the stock." Do you agree? Explain.

E11–11 Recording Dividends

Average Corporation has the following capital stock outstanding at the end of 19B:

Preferred stock, 6%, par $15, outstanding shares, 8,000.

Common stock, par $8, outstanding shares, 30,000.

On October 1, 19B, the board of directors declared dividends as follows:

Preferred stock: Full cash preference amount, payable December 20, 19B.

Common stock: 10% common stock dividend (i.e., one additional share for each 10 held), issuable December 20, 19B.

On December 20, 19B, the market prices were preferred stock, $40, and common stock, $32.

Required:

1. Give any required journal entry(s) to record the declaration and subsequent payment of the dividend on the preferred stock.
2. Give any required journal entry(s) to record the declaration and issuance of the stock dividend on the common stock.
3. Explain the overall effect of each of the dividends on the assets, liabilities, and stockholders' equity of the company.

Sears, Roebuck and Co.

E11–12 Recording the Payment of Dividends

A recent annual report for Sears, Roebuck and Co. disclosed that the company paid preferred dividends in the amount of $119.9 million. The company declared and paid dividends on common stock in the amount of $2 per share. During the year, Sears had 1,000,000,000 shares of common authorized; 387,514,300 shares had been issued; 41,670,000 shares were in treasury stock. Prepare a journal entry to record the declaration and payment of dividends. Assume the transaction occurred on July 15.

E11–13 Analyzing Stock Dividends

On December 31, 19E, the stockholders' equity section of the balance sheet of R & B Corporation reflected the following:

Common stock (par $10; authorized 60,000 shares, outstanding 25,000 shares)	$250,000
Contributed capital in excess of par	12,000
Retained earnings	75,000

On February 1, 19F, the board of directors declared a 12% stock dividend to be issued April 30, 19F. The market value of the stock on February 1, 19F, was $18 per share. The market value will be capitalized.

Required:

1. Give any required journal entry(s) to record the declaration and issuance of the stock dividend.
2. For comparative purposes, prepare the stockholders' equity section of the balance sheet *(a)* immediately before the stock dividend and *(b)* immediately after the stock dividend. (Hint: Use two amount columns for this requirement.)
3. Explain the effects of this stock dividend on the assets, liabilities, and stockholders' equity.

E11–14 Repurchasing Stock

Apple Computer

A recent annual report for Apple Computer contained the following note:

> **Stock Repurchase Programs**
>
> In November 1992, the Board of Directors authorized the purchase of up to 10 million shares of the Company's common stock in the open market. No shares were repurchased in the current year, while 3.4 million shares were repurchased in 1993.

Required:

1. Prepare the journal entry, if any is required, to record the authorization to purchase the 10 million shares.
2. Prepare the journal entry, if any is required, to record the purchase of the 3.4 million shares. Apple stock has no par value and it was selling for $38 per share when the stock was repurchased.
3. What impact will this purchase have on future dividend obligations for Apple?

E11–15 Preparing a Statement of Retained Earnings

The following account balances were selected from the records of Blake Corporation at December 31, 19E, after all adjusting entries were completed:

Common stock (par $15; authorized 100,000 shares, issued 35,000 shares, of which 1,000 shares are held as treasury stock)	$525,000
Contributed capital in excess of par	180,000
Bond sinking fund	90,000
Dividends declared and paid in 19E	18,000
Retained earnings, January 1, 19E	76,000
Correction of prior period accounting error (a debit, net of income tax)	8,000
Treasury stock at cost (1,000 shares)	20,000
Income summary for 19E (credit balance)	28,000

Restriction on retained earnings equal to the cost of treasury stock held is required by law in this state.

Required:

1. Prepare the statement of retained earnings for 19E.
2. Prepare the stockholders' equity section of the balance sheet at December 31, 19E.

E11–16 Preparing the Statement of Retained Earnings

The data given below were selected from the records of Crosby Corporation at December 31, 19B.

Common stock (par \$5; authorized 500,000 shares, issued 125,000 shares of which 500 are held as treasury stock [purchased at \$12 per share])	\$625,000
Preferred stock, 8% (par \$10; authorized 30,000 shares, issued and outstanding 12,000 shares)	120,000
Contributed capital in excess of par:	
Common stock	170,000
Preferred stock	95,000
Dividends declared and paid during 19B	14,000
Net income for 19B	76,000
Retained earnings balance, January 1, 19B	120,000
Prior period adjustment (gain, net of income tax)	15,000
Extraordinary loss (unusual and infrequent, net of income tax)	30,000

Required:

1. Prepare a statement of retained earnings for the year ended December 31, 19B.
2. Prepare the stockholders' equity section of the balance sheet dated December 31, 19B.

Carnival Cruise Lines

E11–17 Declaring and Paying Dividends

The annual report for Carnival Cruise Lines contained the following note:

> **Note 6—Shareholders' Equity**
>
> On January 15, 1993, the Company declared a cash dividend of \$.14 per share payable on March 15, 1993, to shareholders of record on March 1, 1993.

At this time, Carnival had 399,500,000 shares authorized, and 113,590,000 issued and outstanding. The par value for Carnival stock is \$.01 per share.

Required:

Prepare journal entries as appropriate for each of the dates mentioned in the note.

E11–18 Comparing Stock Dividends and Splits

On July 1, 19B, Jones Corporation had the following capital structure:

Common stock (par \$1, authorized shares)	\$200,000
Common stock (par \$1, unissued shares)	50,000
Contributed capital in excess of par	88,000
Retained earnings	72,000
Treasury stock, none.	

Required:

1. The number of issued shares is ________.
2. The number of outstanding shares is ________.
3. Total stockholders' equity is ________.
4. Assume the board of directors declared and issued a 10% stock dividend when the stock was selling at \$4 per share. Give any required journal entry(s). If none is required, explain why.
5. Disregard the stock dividend in (4) above. Assume that the board of directors voted a six-to-five stock split (i.e., a 20% increase in the number of shares). The market price prior to the split was \$4 per share. Give any required journal entry(s). If none is required, explain why.
6. Complete the following comparative tabulation followed by comments on the comparative effects:

Items	Before Dividend and Split	After Stock Dividend	After Stock Split
Common stock account	$	$	$
Par per share	$1	$	$
Shares outstanding	#	#	#
Contributed capital in excess of par	$88,000	$	$
Retained earnings	$72,000	$	$
Total stockholders' equity	$	$	$

E11–19 Paying Cash Dividends

Sizzler

Sizzler is a chain of popular family restaurants. As the annual report noted "closing the books on fiscal 1993 marks the end of a challenging year." In 1993, Sizzler lost $9,482,000. Nevertheless, the Company declared and paid dividends in the amount of $4,666,000.

Required:

1. Prepare the journal to record the payment of dividends by Sizzler, recognizing that the company experienced a loss.
2. Explain why Sizzler can pay dividends despite its loss in 1993.
3. What factors did the board of directors consider when it declared the dividends?

PROBLEMS

P11–1 Preparing the Stockholders' Equity Section of the Balance Sheet

Skyhawk Corporation received its charter during January 19A. The charter authorized the following capital stock:

Preferred stock: 8%, par $10, authorized 20,000 shares.

Common stock: par $8, authorized 50,000 shares.

During 19A, the following transactions occurred in the order given:

a. Issued a total of 40,000 shares of the common stock to the four organizers at $11 per share. The company collected cash in full from three of the organizers and received legal services from the other organizer in full payment for the shares. The stock was issued immediately.

b. Sold 5,000 shares of the preferred stock at $18 per share. Collected the cash and issued the stock immediately.

c. Sold 3,000 shares of the common stock at $14 per share and 1,000 shares of the preferred stock at $28. Collected the cash and issued the stock immediately.

d. Total revenues for 19A were $310,000 and total expenses (including income tax) were $262,000.

Required:

1. Give all the journal entries required for the above items including closing entries.
2. Prepare the stockholders' equity section of the balance sheet at December 31, 19A.
3. What was the average issue price of the common stock?
4. Explain the basis you used to value the legal services in the first journal entry.

P11–2 Analyzing Transactions Affecting Stockholders' Equity

Kerr Corporation began operations in January 19A. The charter authorized the following capital stock:

Preferred stock: 9%, $10 par, authorized 40,000 shares.

Common stock: Nopar, authorized 80,000 shares. The corporation, in conformity with state laws, established a stated value per share of $5 for the nopar common stock.

During 19A, the following transactions occurred in the order given:

a. Issued 20,000 shares of the nopar common stock to each of the three organizers. Collected $9 cash per share from two of the organizers and received a plot of land, with a small building thereon, in full payment for the shares of the third organizer and issued the stock immediately. Assume that 30% of the noncash payment received applies to the building.

b. Sold 6,000 shares of the preferred stock at $18 per share. Collected the cash and issued the stock immediately.

c. Sold 500 shares of the preferred stock at $20 and 1,000 shares of the nopar common stock at $12 per share. Collected the cash and issued the stock immediately.

d. Operating results at the end of 19A were as follows:

Revenue accounts	$220,000
Expense accounts, including income taxes	160,000

Required:

1. Give the journal entries indicated (including closing entries) for each of the above transactions.
2. Prepare the stockholders' equity section of the balance sheet at December 31, 19A.
3. Explain what you used to determine the cost of the land and the building in the first journal entry.

P11–3 Comparing Par and Nopar Stock

McNally Company was issued a charter in January 19A, which authorized 100,000 shares of common stock. During 19A, the following selected transactions occurred in the order given:

a. Sold 9,000 shares of the stock for cash at $60 per share. Collected the cash and issued the stock immediately.

b. Acquired land to be used as a future plant site; made payment in full by issuing 600 shares of stock. Assume a market value per share of $66.

c. At the end of 19A, the Income Summary account reflected a credit balance of $48,000.

Three independent cases are assumed as follows for comparative study purposes:

Case A Assume the common stock was $25 par value per share. The state law specifies that par value is legal capital.

Case B Assume the common stock was nopar and that the total sale price is credited to the Common Stock, Nopar, account because the state law specifies this amount as legal capital.

Case C Assume the common stock is nopar with a stated value, specified by the board of directors, of $15 per share.

Required:

1. Give the journal entries for each of the three transactions.
2. Prepare the stockholders' equity section of the balance sheet at December 31, 19A.
3. Should total stockholders' equity be the same amount among the three independent cases? Explain.
4. Should the noncash asset (land) be recorded at the same cost under each of the three independent cases? Explain.

P11–4 Analyzing Stockholders' Equity Transactions

Worldwide Company obtained a charter from the state in January 19A, which authorized 200,000 shares of common stock, $10 par value. The stockholders comprised 30 local citizens. During the first year, the following selected transactions occurred in the order given:

a. Sold 60,000 shares of the common stock to the 30 stockholders at $12 per share. Collected the cash and issued the stock.

b. During the year, one of the 30 stockholders needed cash and wanted to sell the stock back to the company. Accordingly, the company purchased the investor's 2,000 shares at $15 cash per share.

c. Two months later, 1,000 of the shares of the treasury stock purchased in (*b*) were resold to another individual at $18 cash per share.

d. An additional 500 shares of the treasury stock were sold at $14 cash per share.

e. On December 31, 19A, the end of the first year of business, the Income Summary account reflected a credit balance of $38,200.

Required:

1. Give the indicated journal entry for each of the above items.
2. Prepare the stockholders' equity section of the balance sheet at December 31, 19A.
3. What dollar effect did the treasury stock transactions have on the assets, liabilities, and stockholders' equity of the company? Explain.

P11–5 *Analyzing Stockholder Transactions, Including Noncash Consideration*

Arnold Company was granted a charter that authorized the following capital stock:

Common stock: Nopar, 100,000 shares. Assume the nopar stock is not assigned a stated value per share.

Preferred stock: 8%, par $5, 20,000 shares.

During the first year, 19A, the following selected transactions occurred in the order given:

a. Sold 30,000 shares of the nopar common stock at $40 cash per share and 5,000 shares of the preferred stock at $26 cash per share. Collected cash and issued the stock immediately. For the nopar stock, credit the full selling price to the common stock account.

b. Issued 2,000 shares of preferred stock as full payment for a plot of land to be used as a future plant site. Assume the stock was selling at $26.

c. Purchased 3,000 shares of the nopar common stock sold earlier; paid cash, $38 per share.

d. Sold all of the treasury stock (common) purchased in (*c*). The sale price was $39 per share.

e. Purchased 1,000 shares of the company's own preferred stock at $28 cash per share.

f. At December 31, 19A, the Income Summary account reflected a credit balance of $33,500.

Required:

1. Give the journal entries indicated for each of the above transactions.
2. Prepare the stockholders' equity section of the balance sheet at December 31, 19A, end of the annual accounting period.

P11–6 *Comparing Stock and Cash Dividends*

Water Tower Company had the following stock outstanding and retained earnings at December 31, 19E:

Common stock (par $8; outstanding, 30,000 shares)	$240,000
Preferred stock, 7% (par $10; outstanding, 6,000 shares)	60,000
Retained earnings	280,000

The board of directors is considering the distribution of a cash dividend to the two groups of stockholders. No dividends were declared during 19C or 19D. Three independent cases are assumed:

Case A The preferred stock is noncumulative; the total amount of dividends is $30,000.

Case B The preferred stock is cumulative; the total amount of dividends is $12,600.

Case C Same as Case B, except the amount is $66,000.

Required:

1. Compute the amount of dividends, in total and per share, that would be payable to each class of stockholders for each case. Show computations.
2. Give the journal entry to record the cash dividends declared and paid in 19E for Case C only. Assume that the declaration and payment occurred simultaneously on December 31, 19E.
3. Give the required journal entry assuming, instead of a cash dividend, the declaration and issuance of a 10% common stock dividend on the outstanding common stock. Assume the market value per share of common stock was $24.
4. Complete the following comparative schedule including explanation of the comparative differences.

Item	Amount of Dollar Increase (Decrease) — Cash Dividend—Case C	Amount of Dollar Increase (Decrease) — Stock Dividend
Assets	$	$
Liabilities	$	$
Stockholders' equity	$	$

Capital Cities/ ABC, Inc.

P11–7 Dividend Policy

Capital Cities/ABC, Inc. is a diversified communications company that owns television and radio stations, newspapers, publishing companies, and the ABC and ESPN networks. The company's annual report contains the following information:

> **Common Stock and Stockholder Information**
>
> As of February 26, 1993, the approximate number of holders of common stock was 9,150. Dividends of $.05 per share have been paid for each quarter of 1992 and 1991. The common stock is traded on the New York and Pacific Stock Exchanges. The high price of the stock during the previous year was $521 and the low price was $410.

At the time this report was issued, Capital Cities stock was the second most expensive stock traded on the New York Stock Exchange. If you were an advisor to the board of directors, would you recommend they consider announcing a stock split or stock dividend? Justify your position.

P11–8 Recording Dividends

Lynn Company has outstanding 60,000 shares of $10 par value common stock and 25,000 shares of $20 par value preferred stock (8%). On December 1, 19B, the board of directors voted an 8% cash dividend on the preferred stock and a 10% common stock dividend on the common stock. At the date of declaration, the common stock was selling at $35 and the preferred at $20 per share. The dividends are to be paid, or issued, on February 15, 19C. The annual accounting period ends December 31.

Required:

1. Give any journal entry(s) required to record the declaration and payment of the cash dividend.
2. Give any journal entry(s) required to record the declaration and issuance of the stock dividend.
3. Explain the comparative effects of the two dividends on the assets, liabilities, and stockholders' equity (*a*) through December 31, 19B; (*b*) on February 15, 19C; and (*c*) the

overall effects from December 1, 19B, through February 15, 19C. A schedule similar to the following might be helpful:

	Comparative Effects Explained	
Item	**Cash Dividend on Preferred**	**Stock Dividend on Common**
1. Through December 31, 19B:		
Assets etc.		

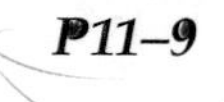

P11–9 *Analyzing Stockholders' Equity Transactions, Including Treasury Stock*

The accounts of Quarry Corporation reflected the following balances on January 1, 19C:

Preferred stock, 8% (par $100; cumulative, authorized 5,000 shares, issued and outstanding 1,500 shares)	$150,000
Common stock (par $10; authorized 100,000 shares, outstanding 40,000 shares)	400,000
Contributed capital in excess of par, preferred	3,000
Contributed capital in excess of par, common	46,000
Retained earnings	380,000
Total stockholders' equity	$979,000

The transactions during 19C relating to the stockholders' equity are listed below in order:

a. Purchased 100 shares of preferred treasury stock at $125 per share.

b. The board of directors declared and paid a cash dividend to the preferred stockholders only. No dividends were declared during 19A or 19B. The dividend was sufficient to pay the arrears plus the dividend for the current year.

c. The board of directors declared a 15% common stock dividend on the outstanding common stock. Market value of $28 per share is to be capitalized.

d. Net income for the year was $81,000.

Required:

1. Give the journal entry for each of the above transactions, including the closing entries. Show computations.
2. Prepare a statement of retained earnings for 19C and the stockholders' equity section of the balance sheet at December 31, 19C.
3. Explain the comparative effects on assets and stockholders' equity of (*a*) the cash dividend and (*b*) the stock dividend.

P11–10 *Preparing the Stockholders' Equity Section of the Balance Sheet*

Fulbright Company is completing its year-end accounting, including the preparation of the annual financial statements, at December 31, 19E. The stockholders' equity accounts reflected the following balances at the end of the year, 19E:

Common stock (par $20; shares outstanding, 40,000)	$800,000
Contributed capital in excess of par	70,000
Retained earnings, January 1, 19E (credit)	175,000
Cash dividends declared and paid during 19E (debit)	50,000
Income summary account for 19E (credit balance; after tax)	48,000

The following selected transactions occurred near the end of 19E; they are not included in the above amounts:

a. During 19D, the company was sued for $30,000, and it was clear that the suit would be lost. Therefore, in 19D, the company should have debited a loss and credited a liability for this amount. This journal entry was not made and the accounting error was found in 19E. (Hint: credit Liability for Damages.) Disregard any income tax effects.

b. The board of directors voted a voluntary restriction of $125,000 on retained earnings. It is to be designated "earnings appropriated for plant expansion" effective for the 19E financial statements.

Required:

1. Give the appropriate journal entries for the events listed immediately above. If no entry is given, explain.
2. Prepare a statement of retained earnings for 19E and the stockholders' equity section of the balance sheet at December 31, 19E.

P11–11 Preparing the Statement of Retained Earnings

Dixon Company has completed all of the annual information processing at December 31, 19D, except for preparation of the financial statements. The following account balances were reflected at that date:

DIXON COMPANY
Adjusted Trial Balance
December 31, 19D

	Debit	Credit
Cash	$ 56,000	
Accounts receivable (net)	42,000	
Merchandise inventory, December 31, 19D	110,000	
Long-term investment in Company Y	30,000	
Bond sinking fund	60,000	
Land	25,000	
Buildings and equipment (net)	815,000	
Other assets	21,000	
Accounts payable		$ 42,000
Income taxes payable		9,000
Bonds payable (9%, payable December 31)		150,000
Preferred stock (par $10, authorized 60,000 shares)		200,000
Common stock (par $5, authorized 300,000 shares)		625,000
Contributed capital in excess of par, preferred		7,200
Contributed capital in excess of par, common		20,100
Treasury stock, preferred, 20 shares at cost	2,300	
Retained earnings, January 1, 19D		152,000
19D net income		66,000
19D cash dividends on preferred	12,000	
19D common stock dividends distributed (11,000 shares)	88,000	
19D, discovered an accounting error made in 19A in recording a purchase of land (the correction required a net credit to land of $10,000)	10,000	
	$1,271,300	$1,271,300

Note: Retained earnings is restricted in an amount equal to the bond sinking fund per the provisions of the bond indenture.

Required:

Prepare a statement of retained earnings for 19D and a classified balance sheet at December 31, 19D.

Charles Schwab Corp.

P11–12 Recording Dividends

The business press reported the following story about a well-known stock brokerage firm:

January 17, 1995

Charles Schwab Corp. said today that it raised its quarterly dividend to $0.09 a share from $0.07 a share and declared a 50 per cent stock dividend. It said the cash dividend is payable February 15, 1995, to holders of record on February 1, 1995. The 50 per cent stock dividend is payable March 1, 1995, to shareholders of record February 1, 1995.

Required:

1. Prepare any journal entries that should be made by Schwab as the result of information contained above. Assume that the company has 2 million shares outstanding, the par value is $0.10 per share and the market value is $40 per share.
2. What do you think happened to the company's stock price after the January 17 announcement?
3. What factors did the board of directors consider in making this decision?

P11–13 Recording Stockholders' Equity Transactions

Kmart

The annual report for Kmart described the following transactions that affected stockholders' equity:

a. Cash dividends of $0.92 per share were declared. Total dividends were $374 million.

b. Series B convertible preferred stock (nopar) was sold in the amount of $157 million.

c. Treasury stock was sold for $10 million. Its original cost was $8 million.

d. A 100% stock dividend on common stock was issued. The par value of this stock was $206 million and the market value was $784 million.

Required

Prepare journal entries to record each of these transactions.

P11–14 Chapter Supplement A: Comparing Stockholders' Equity Sections for Alternative Forms of Organization

Assume for each of the three independent cases below that the annual accounting period ends on December 31, 19W, and that the Income Summary account at that date reflected a debit balance (loss) of $20,000.

Case A Assume that the company is a sole proprietorship owned by Proprietor A. Prior to the closing entries, the capital account reflected a credit balance of $50,000 and the drawings account a balance of $8,000.

Case B Assume that the company is a *partnership* owned by Partner A and Partner B. Prior to the closing entries, the owners' equity accounts reflected the following balances: A, Capital, $40,000; B, Capital, $38,000; A, Drawings, $5,000; and B, Drawings, $9,000. Profits and losses are divided equally.

Case C Assume that the company is a *corporation*. Prior to the closing entries, the stockholders' equity accounts showed the following: Capital Stock, par $10, authorized 30,000 shares, outstanding 15,000 shares; Contributed Capital in Excess of Par, $5,000; and Retained Earnings, $65,000.

Required:

1. Give all the closing entries indicated at December 31, 19W, for each of the separate cases.
2. Show how the owners' equity section of the balance sheet would appear at December 31, 19W, for each case.

CASES

C11–1 Finding Missing Amounts

At December 31, 19E, the records of Nortech Corporation provided the following selected and incomplete data:

Common stock (par $10; no changes during 19E):
  Shares authorized, 200,000.
  Shares issued, ____?_____; issue price $17 per share; cash collected in full, $2,125,000.
  Shares held as treasury stock, 3,000 shares, cost $20 per share.
Net income for 19E, $118,000.
Dividends declared and paid during 19E, $73,200.
Bond sinking fund balance, $40,000.
Prior period adjustment, correction of 19B accounting error, $9,000 (a credit, net of income tax).
Retained earnings balance, January 1, 19E, $155,000.
State law places a restriction on retained earnings equal to the cost of treasury stock held.
The treasury stock was acquired after the stock dividend was issued. Extraordinary gain (net of income tax), $12,000.

Required:

1. Complete the following tabulation:
   Shares authorized ________.
   Shares issued ________.
   Shares outstanding ________.
2. The balance in the Contributed Capital in Excess of Par account appears to be $________.
3. EPS on net income is $________.
4. Dividend paid per share of common stock is $________.
5. The bond sinking fund should be reported on the balance sheet under the classification ________.
6. Net income before extraordinary items was $________.
7. The prior period adjustment should be reported on the ________ as an addition ________ or a deduction ________.
8. Treasury stock should be reported on the balance sheet under the major caption ________ in the amount of $________.
9. The amount of retained earnings available for dividends on January 1, 19E, was $________.
10. Assume the board of directors voted a 100% stock split (the number of shares will double). After the stock split, the par value per share will be $________ and the number of outstanding shares will be ________.
11. Assuming the stock split given in (10) above, give any journal entry that should be made. If none, explain why.
12. Disregard the stock split (assumed in [10] and [11] above). Assume instead that a 10% stock dividend was declared and issued when the market price of the common stock was $21. Give any journal entry that should be made.

C11–2 *Computing Dividends for an Actual Company*

Halliburton Company

A recent annual report for Halliburton Company contained the following information (in $ millions):

Stockholders' Equity	Current Year	Previous Year
Common stock, par value $2.50, authorized 2,000 shares	$ 298.3	$ 298.4
Paid-in capital in excess of par	130.5	129.9
Retained earnings	2,080.8	2,052.3
Less 12.8 and 13.0 treasury stock, at cost	382.2	384.7

In the current year, Halliburton declared and paid cash dividends of $1 per share. What would be the total amount of dividends declared and paid if they had been based on the amount of stock outstanding at the end of the year?

C 11–3 Financial Statement Analysis

Toys "Я" Us

Refer to the financial statements of Toys "Я" Us given in Appendix B at the end of this book.

Required:

1. What is the par value of the company's stock?
2. What was the average price paid per share for treasury stock at the end of the current year?
3. What amount of dividends was paid in 1994?
4. How many stockholders have invested in this company?
5. What was the amount of earnings per share for the current year?

12

ORDER FORM
October 1995
ACCO
#1 WORLD BRAND™
100 Paper Clips
An ACCO World Product
JUMBO WORLD BRAND™
100 Paper Clips
An ACCO World Product
ACCO
JUMBO WORLD BRAND™
100 Paper Clips

MEASURING AND REPORTING INVESTMENTS IN OTHER CORPORATIONS

Corporations invest in the securities of other corporations for a variety of reasons. Often the investment is for a short term, designed to earn a return on idle funds. Other investments are for the long term. The latter may be designed to provide the investing corporation with significant influence or control over the other corporation. In this chapter, we will discuss different methods of accounting for these different types of investments.

LEARNING OBJECTIVES

After studying this chapter, you should be able to:

1. **Discuss why corporations invest in each other.** ***582***
2. **Compare the available-for-sale and trading securities portfolios.** ***585***
3. **Use the market value method.** ***585***
4. **Record the sale of investments.** ***590***
5. **Use the equity method.** ***592***
6. **Explain the purpose of consolidated statements.** ***596***
7. **Apply the pooling and purchase methods and prepare elimination entries.** ***597***
8. **Prepare consolidated statements in years after the year of acquisition.** ***604***

Management Decision Setting

AMERICAN BRANDS, INC.

Diversification as a Business Strategy

American Brands, Inc., is a global consumer products holding company (which means it is a company that has bought and holds stock in other companies). Its businesses include tobacco, distilled spirits, life insurance, hardware and home improvement products, office products, and specialty businesses. You are probably familiar with many of its brands. It manufactures and sells such items as Lucky Strike cigarettes, Sears Craftsman brand tools, Titleist golf equipment, Master Lock security devices, and Jim Beam whiskey. The company also provides insurance under the name Franklin Life Insurance.

The reason that the management of American Brands has pursued a strategy of acquiring businesses in a variety of fields is clearly stated in the company's SEC Form 10-K report:

> In recent years, the company has engaged in a program of seeking to enhance the operations of its subsidiaries in certain core businesses and the development of other core businesses. Pursuant to such programs, the company has since 1986 made major acquisitions in the distilled spirits business, the office products business and the hardware and home improvement business.

When most people think of a company following a growth strategy, they think in terms of direct investments in new productive assets. If Ford Motor Company wanted to produce and sell more cars, it might invest in a new factory. As the previous note indicates, some companies seek growth by investing in the stock of existing companies. In the following section, we will discuss some reasons that motivate business managers to invest in securities instead of productive assets.

BUSINESS BACKGROUND

Learning Objective 1
Discuss why corporations invest in each other.

There are many strategic reasons that motivate managers to invest in securities. It is easier to understand the business purpose of an investment if you first classify it in one of three categories:

1. *Short-term investment* These investments are made with the purpose of earning a high rate of return on funds that may be needed for operating purposes in the future. Instead of leaving cash in a checking account that does not earn interest, many companies buy securities that provide a higher return. Some companies can be very aggressive with these investments and will actively trade the securities on established exchanges in an effort to maximize return. However, most companies invest in very low-risk securities. These investments typically include stocks, bonds, Treasury bills (short-term debt issued by the federal government), and commercial paper (short-term debt issued by corporations).
2. *Long-term investments made with no intent of exerting influence over another corporation* The purpose of these investments is similar to the purpose of short-term investments. In this case, management invests funds that are not needed for operating purposes but may be needed for some long-term purpose. During the 1980s, there was a depression in the oil industry which significantly slowed business activity. McDermott Corporation is a manufacturer of oil well equipment. Because of the business slowdown during that period, McDermott placed nearly $1 billion in long-term investments with the

intent of using the funds to buy new equipment when oil drilling activity resumed. Long-term investments include stocks, bonds, and Treasury notes.

3. *Long-term investments made with the intent of influencing another corporation* By being active in the management of another corporation, an investor may be able to earn a higher return on the investment. In some cases, it may be possible to achieve synergy between two or more companies where the combined effectiveness of their operations is more than the sum of their individual activities. In other cases, the investing corporation may intend to exert an absolute minimum of influence. These investments can achieve diversification so that a company is not dependent on the economic fortunes of a single area of business. American Brands has purchased a controlling influence in several consumer product companies to lessen the risk of being too dependent on the tobacco industry. This category of investments includes only common stock (with voting rights) of another corporation.

In Chapter 10, we discussed investments in bonds. In this chapter, we will focus on investments in stock. When one corporation acquires common stock of another corporation, it usually purchases outstanding shares from other stockholders for cash or exchanges some of its own stock for outstanding stock of the other corporation. A transaction between the acquiring corporation and the stockholders of the acquired corporation affects only the acquiring corporation's accounting records. The transaction has no effect on the accounting records of the acquired corporation. The diagram below illustrates a typical transaction.

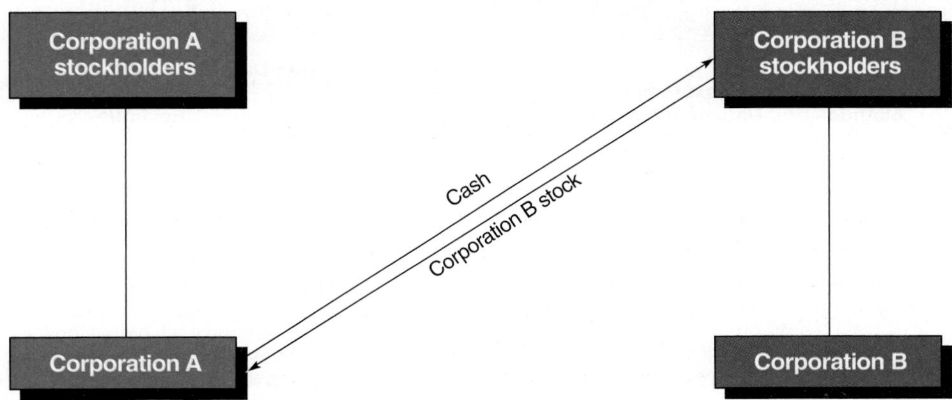

ACCOUNTING FOR INVESTMENTS IN SECURITIES

The accounting methods that are used to record investments are directly related to the purpose of the investment. A critical feature that determines the appropriate accounting method is the nature of the relationship between the investor corporation and the investee. This relationship can be characterized based on the degree of influence and control the investor corporation can exert over the investee. Significant influence and control are defined as follows:

Significant influence is the ability of an investor company to have an important impact on the operating and financing policies of another company.

1. **Significant influence** The ability of the investing company to have an *important impact* on the operating and financing policies of another company in which it owns shares of voting stock. Significant influence

may be indicated by (*a*) membership on the board of directors of the other company, (*b*) participation in the policy-making processes, (*c*) material transactions between the two companies, (*d*) interchange of management personnel, or (*e*) technological dependency. In the absence of a clear-cut distinction based on these factors, significant influence is presumed if the investing company owns at least 20%, but not more than 50% of the outstanding voting shares of the other company.

Control is the ability of the investing company to determine the operating and financing policies of another company in which it owns shares of the voting stock.

2. **Control** The ability of the investing company to *determine* the operating and financing policies of another company in which it owns shares of the voting stock. For all practical purposes, control is presumed when the investing company owns more than 50% of the outstanding voting stock of the other company.

Once you have determined the purpose of the investment in terms of significant influence or control, it is easy to determine the appropriate accounting method to use for the investment. The three basic approaches are:

Level of Ownership	Measuring and Reporting Method
1. Neither significant influence nor control	Market value method
2. Significant influence but not control	Equity method
3. Control	Consolidated statement method

Each of these approaches is outlined in Exhibit 12–1. The following note from a recent Chiquita Brands annual report is a good example of how many companies describe their use of the market value and equity methods:

Exhibit 12–1 **Measuring and Reporting Long-Term Investments in Voting Stock of Another Company**

			Measurement after Date of Acquisition	
Status of Ownership	**Method**	**Measurement at Date of Acquisition**	**Investment**	**Revenue**
1. **Investor can exercise no significant influence or control.** Presumed if investor owns less than 20% of the outstanding voting stock of the investee company.	Market value method	Investor records the investment at cost. Cost is the total outlay made to acquire the shares.	Investor reports the investment on the balance sheet at market value.	Investor recognizes revenue each period when dividends are declared by the investee company. An unrealized gain or loss is recorded each accounting period.
2. **Investor can exercise significant influence, but not control,** over the operating and financing policies of the investee company. Presumed if the investor owns at least 20%, but not more than 50%, of the outstanding voting shares of the investee company.	Equity method	Same as above	Investor measures and reports the investment at cost **plus** the investor's share of the earnings (or less the losses) and **minus** the dividends received from (i.e., declared by) the other company.	Investor recognizes as revenue each period the investor's proportionate share of the earnings (or losses) reported each period by the investee company. A realized gain or loss is recognized when the investment is sold.
			(Dividends received are not considered revenue. To recognize dividends as revenue, rather than as a reduction in the investment, would involve double counting.)	
3. **Investor can exercise control** over the operating and financing policies of the investee company. Control is presumed if the investor owns more than 50% of the outstanding voting stock of the investee company.	Consolidated financial statement method	Same as above	Consolidated financial statements required each period .	

Real World Excerpt

Chiquita Brands Annual Report

> Investments representing minority interests are accounted for by the equity method when Chiquita has the ability to exercise significant influence in the investees' operations; otherwise, they are accounted for by the market value method.

MARKET VALUE METHOD

Learning Objective 2
Compare the trading securities and available-for-sale portfolios.

Market value method records securities at their current market value.

The **market value method** of accounting reports securities at their current market value. It must be used when the number of shares of stock held does not give the investing corporation the ability to exercise significant influence or control. An investment in stock with voting rights is accounted for under the market value method if less than 20% of the outstanding stock is held. All nonvoting stock is accounted for under the market value method without regard to the level of ownership.

Investments in stock accounted for under the market value method are classified in one of the following two categories:

Trading securities are all investments in stocks or bonds that are held primarily for the purpose of selling them in the near future.

Available-for-sale securities are all investments other than trading securities that are accounted for under the market value method.

1. **Trading securities**, which are shares held primarily for the purpose of selling them in the near future. The trading securities portfolio is managed with the objective of generating profits on short-term differences in the price of the securities. The management philosophy for this portfolio is similar to the approach taken by many mutual funds. The portfolio manager actively seeks opportunities to buy and sell securities. This portfolio may include both stocks and bonds.
2. **Available-for-sale securities**, which include all other investments in stocks or bonds accounted for under the market value method. This portfolio is not as actively traded as the trading securities portfolio. The purpose of this portfolio is to earn a return on funds that may be required for operating purposes in the future.

The trading securities portfolio is always reported on the balance sheet as a current asset. The available-for-sale securities portfolio may be reported as either a current asset or a noncurrent asset depending on the intent of management. If management intends to sell securities within the next year, they should be classified as current. Otherwise, the securities should be classified as noncurrent.

The notes to the annual report for American Brands contain the following information concerning its investment portfolios:

Real World Excerpt

American Brands, Inc. Annual Report

> *Valuation of Investments*
>
> Trading securities, primarily equity securities purchased with the intent of selling in the near term, are carried at fair value with unrealized gains and losses included in income. Available-for-sale securities are carried at fair value with unrealized gains and losses included directly in common stockholders' equity.

In the following sections, we will examine the accounting procedures described in this note.

Recording Investments at Market Value

Learning Objective 3
Use the market value method.

Accounting for investments under the market value method represents an important departure from the *cost principle* that governs the reporting of all other assets. Under the cost principle, assets are reported on the balance sheet based on their cost, not on their current fair market value. An exception is made for

American Brands bought shares of the Jim Beam Company and the American Tobacco Company for strategic purposes, not to earn a return on idle funds.

investments held in the trading securities portfolio and the available-for-sale portfolio. These securities are reported on the balance sheet in terms of their current market value as of the date of the balance sheet.

Before we discuss the specific accounting for investments, we should consider an important question: why are investments accounted for under the market value method the only assets that are reported at fair market value on the balance sheet? There are two primary factors that answer this question:

1. *Relevance* Analysts who study financial statements often attempt to forecast the future cash flows of a company. They want to know how a company can generate cash for such purposes as expansion of the business, payment of dividends, or survival during a prolonged economic downturn. One source of cash is the sale of stock from the trading securities portfolio or the available-for-sale portfolio. The best estimate of the cash that could be generated by the sale of these securities is their current market value. Notice that these investments are different from most assets held by the company. In the normal course of business, a company will use and not sell productive assets such as manufacturing equipment or office buildings. Investments do not serve that same purpose. They cannot produce goods or services. Their only value comes from an ability to convert them into cash.
2. *Measurability* Accountants can record only items that can be measured in dollar terms with a high degree of reliability (an unbiased, and verifiable measurement). It is very difficult to determine the fair market value of most assets because they are not actively traded. The John Hancock building is an important part of the Boston skyline. The balance sheet of John Hancock reports the building in terms of its original cost, in part, because of the difficulty of determining an objective value for the building. Contrast the difficulty of determining the value of a building with the ease of determining the value of securities that John Hancock may own. It is relatively easy to use *The Wall Street Journal* to determine the current price of IBM or Exxon stock because these securities are traded each day on established stock exchanges.

Holding Gains and Losses

At this point in our discussion, you may have anticipated another important issue concerning investments. Under the double entry method of accounting, every journal entry affects at least two accounts. If accountants adjust the value of the investment account to reflect changes in fair market value, what other account will be impacted when the asset account is increased or decreased? The answer is that **unrealized holding gains and losses** (which are gains and losses associated with price changes of securities that are currently held) are recorded whenever there is a change in the fair market value of investments. If the value of the investments increased by $100,000 during the year, a journal entry would record the increase in the asset account and an unrealized holding gain for $100,000. If the value of the investments decreased by $75,000 during the year, a journal entry would record the decrease in the asset and an unrealized holding loss.

Unrealized holding gains and losses are associated with price changes of securities that are currently held.

The recording of an unrealized holding gain is a departure from the revenue principle that states that revenues and gains should be recorded when the company has completed the earnings process that generated the revenue or gain. Recording of revenues and gains normally takes place at the point of sale. The word *unrealized* in the name unrealized holding gain (or loss) is intended to emphasize that the gain (or loss) did not occur as the result of a sale but instead was recorded as part of an adjusting entry to reflect the fair market value of the investments in securities account.

The accounting impact of unrealized holding gains or losses is dependent on the classification of the investment:

1. Trading securities Unrealized holding gains and losses are included on the income statement and are included in the computation of net income. In other words, holding gains increase net income, and holding losses decrease net income.
2. Available-for-sale Unrealized holding gains and losses are reported as a separate component of stockholders' equity. They are not reported on the income statement and do not affect net income.

Based on our discussion of accounting for investments, let's examine the journal entries that would be recorded over the life of an investment. Assume American Brands purchased 10,000 shares of Kmart stock at a price of $25 per share on February 1, 19A. Management intends to hold these securities for a long period of time as a cushion against a future business downturn. This investment would be recorded as follows:

Feb. 1, 19A	Available-for-sale securities	250,000	
	Cash		250,000

If management had purchased these securities as part of their portfolio of trading securities, the debit in the previous entry would have been to Trading Securities. The initial recording of the investment is the same for either portfolio. It would be very unusual for a company to have just a single security as an investment. It is much less risky to own a portfolio of securities. We will illustrate our discussion with a single security because we have found that it is easier for you to see the impact of the accounting procedures without the burden of additional details. Just remember that the procedures apply to the total value of the portfolio without regard to the number of securities in the portfolio.

Investments in securities earn a return from two sources: price appreciation and dividend income. To illustrate the recording of dividend income, assume that on November 30, 19A, the board of directors declared and paid a $0.50 per share dividend on Kmart stock. The receipt of the dividend is recorded by American Brands as follows:

Nov. 30, 19A	Cash ($0.50 × 10,000 shares)	5,000	
	Revenue from investments		5,000

Revenue from investments is reported on the income statement and is included in the computation of net income for the period. This account is the same for dividend income received for shares in both the trading securities and available-for-sale portfolios.

At the end of each accounting period, the value of the investment portfolios must be determined and any unrealized holding gain or loss must be computed. The unrealized holding gain or loss can be determined by comparing the market value of the portfolio at the end of the period with the market value at the beginning, adjusted for the purchase or sale of securities during the year. To illustrate, assume the value of the Kmart stock purchased by American Brands was $275,000 on December 31, 19A. The stock was purchased during 19A at a cost of $250,000. Therefore, American Brands would record an unrealized holding gain:

Dec. 31, 19A	Allowance to adjust to market	25,000	
	Unrealized holding gain		25,000

The debit in the previous journal entry is made to a special asset adjustment account instead of directly to the asset account. This account is reported on the balance sheet as an adjustment in the carrying value of the investment, which means that the available-for-sale securities would be reported at $275,000 (cost plus the allowance). The use of this account facilitates accounting for the investment. In subsequent years, the cost of the securities in the portfolio can be compared to their market value and this difference then can be compared to the balance in the Allowance to adjust to market. The unrealized holding gain or loss is simply the amount needed to change the balance in the Allowance account to the amount of the difference between the total cost and the total market.

To illustrate, assume that in 19B the market value of Kmart stock had fallen to $200,000. What is the amount of the holding loss? Some people might be tempted to say that the loss was $50,000 (American Brands paid $250,000 for stock that was now worth $200,000, for a loss of $50,000). This answer would be wrong. The unrealized loss is $75,000 which is the difference between the value of the portfolio at the beginning of the year ($275,000) and the value at the end of the year ($200,000). This answer makes good economic sense because management could have sold the Kmart stock for $275,000 in cash at the end of 19A. Instead, they held the stock for an extra year and can now sell it for only $200,000. Clearly, there was an economic loss of $75,000.

Notice how the use of the Allowance account facilitates computation of the unrealized holding loss. At the beginning of 19B, the account had a debit balance (that increased the carrying value of the portfolio). At the end of 19B, it should have a credit balance of $50,000 to reduce the $250,000 cost to a $200,000 carrying value. Accordingly, a $75,000 credit should be made to the Allowance account, which is the amount of the holding loss. American Brands would make the following journal entry to record the holding loss:

Dec. 31, 19B	Unrealized holding loss	75,000	
	Allowance to adjust to market		75,000

The Allowance to adjust to market (with a $50,000 credit balance) would be subtracted from the Investment account that is reported on the balance sheet. The net result is a carrying value of $200,000, which is the current market value of the securities.

The recording of holding gains and losses is essentially the same for both the trading securities and available-for-sale portfolios. The primary difference is the impact of the recorded unrealized holding gain or loss. In the case of trading securities, it is reported on the income statement. In the case of available-for-sale securities, it is a component of stockholders' equity.

The actual unrealized holding gain on the available-for-sale portfolio for American Brands at the end of 1993 was $5.3 million. The reporting of this amount in the stockholders' equity section of the American Brands balance sheet is shown in Exhibit 12–2. American Brands also reported an unrealized gain of $2.6 million on the trading portfolio. This amount was included in net income but it was not separately identified on its income statement.

The asset section of the balance sheet for American Brands reports that the total amount of its investments is $5,808.8 million. Additional details concerning the composition of those investments is provided in the note reproduced in Exhibit 12–3. Investments represent over one-third of the total assets for American Brands, which is a higher percent than would be the case for most compa-

Unrealized Holding Gain on American Brands Balance Sheet **Exhibit 12–2**

	December 31	
	1993	1992
LIABILITIES AND STOCKHOLDERS' EQUITY		
Consumer products and corporate		
Current liabilities		
Notes payable to banks	$ 298.9	$ 247.1
Commercial paper	711.3	433.4
Accounts payable	454.1	339.6
Accrued excise and other taxes	726.3	884.0
Accrued expenses and other liabilities	794.4	740.4
Current portion of long-term debt	172.7	144.2
Total consumer products and corporate current liabilities	3,157.7	2,788.7
Long-term debt	2,492.4	2,406.8
Deferred income taxes	124.7	195.2
Postretirement and other liabilities	520.3	176.5
Total consumer products and corporate liabilities	6,295.1	5,567.2
Life insurance		
Policy reserves and claims	2,553.4	2,401.2
Investment-type contract deposits	2,732.3	2,265.9
Other policyholders' funds	238.1	217.1
Other liabilities	248.7	166.7
Total life insurance liabilities	5,772.5	5,050.9
Convertible preferred stock-redeemable at Company's option		
$2.67 convertible preferred stock, without par value, stated value $30.50 per share	17.1	19.1
Common stockholders' equity		
Common stock, par value $3.125 per share, 229.6 shares issued	717.4	717.4
Paid-in capital	173.3	177.9
Unrealized appreciation on investments	5.3	10.5
Foreign currency adjustments	(317.4)	(260.9)
Retained earnings	4,393.4	4,322.7
Treasury stock, at cost	(717.7)	(685.1)
Total common stockholders' equity	4,254.3	4,282.5
Total liabilities and stockholders' equity	$16,339.9	$14,919.7

Exhibit 12–3 **Note to American Brands Financial Statements**

Valuation of Investments

At December 31,1993, held-to-maturity securities, which are fixed maturity securities that Franklin has the ability and intent to hold until maturity, are carried at amortized cost. Trading securities, principally equity securities that Franklin purchased with the intent of selling in the near term, are carried at fair value with unrealized gains and losses included in income. Available-for-sale securities, representing fixed maturity securities not elsewhere classified, are carried at fair value with unrealized gains and losses included directly in Common stockholders' equity, net of applicable deferred federal income taxes.

Prior to December 31, 1993, all fixed maturity securities were valued at amortized cost. Unrealized appreciation and depreciation on marketable equity securities (including Invergordon through November 1993) were included directly in Common stockholders' equity, net of applicable deferred federal income taxes.

Investment income is recognized as revenue when earned. Realized gains and losses on disposals of investments are determined on a specific identification basis and are included in income.

nies. Why does American Brands have such a large percentage of its funds invested in securities? To answer this type of question, you must analyze a company's business operations and strategy. American Brands owns a number of subsidiaries, one of which is in the insurance business. Companies in the insurance business collect policy premiums (cash) from their customers and pay out cash in the future when some event occurs, such as a fire or a car accident. Insurance companies are able to earn significant profits by investing this cash before it must be paid out to meet the claims of policyholders. The balance sheets for all insurance companies show a large amount of investments.

FINANCIAL ANALYSIS

The Market Value Method and Cash Flows

Notice that the recording of an unrealized holding gain or loss in the trading securities portfolio affects net income but it does not affect cash flows. Cash flows are affected when the securities are bought or sold, not when unrealized gains or losses are recorded.

Despite the fact that unrealized gains and losses do not affect current cash flows, analysts are interested in these items because they may be useful in predicting future cash flows. A company that has large unrealized gains will have more cash when it sells securities than a company with large unrealized losses, assuming the same initial investment.

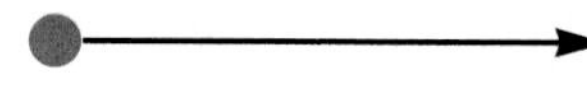

SALE OF AN INVESTMENT

Learning Objective 4
Record the sale of investments.

Because accounting methods for each investment portfolio differ, there are different procedures for recording the sale of securities from the different portfolios. In the following section, we will discuss the various methods. We will not discuss the sale of securities accounted for under the equity method. These sales are fairly rare because of the strategic purpose of this type of investment (i.e., to achieve influence over another corporation).

Securities Sold from the Trading Portfolio

To illustrate accounting for the sale of stock from the trading portfolio, assume that American Brands sold stock on January 15, 19C, for $209,000. The stock was purchased during 19B at a cost of $200,000. On December 31, 19B, the fair market value of the stock was $205,000. On that date, an unrealized holding gain of $5,000 was recorded. American Brands would record the following entry on the date of sale:

Jan. 15, 19C	Cash	209,000	
	Trading securities		200,000
	Gain on sale of trading securities		9,000

Notice that the gain is not affected by the previous recording of unrealized gains. At this point there is an obvious double counting of a portion of the gain (once when the adjusting entry was recorded and a second time when the securities were sold). This double counting is corrected at the end of the accounting period when the trading security portfolio is reviewed. Remember, at the end of each accounting period the market value of the portfolio is compared to its cost and the Allowance account is adjusted to reflect this difference. Because American Brands sold the stock during 19C, there is no difference between cost and market for the securities at year-end. The records of American Brands would still show a $5,000 balance in the Allowance to Adjust to Market entry related to the entry that was made at the end of 19B to record an unrealized holding gain. As a result, American Brands must make the following adjusting entry at the end of 19C:

Dec. 31, 19C	Adjustment for unrealized gain	5,000	
	Allowance to adjust to market		5,000

The adjustment for the unrealized gain would be reported on the income statement as a deduction from the gain associated with the sale on January 15, 19C. This adjustment avoids double counting part of the gain. In most cases, there would be many securities in the portfolio at year-end. The adjusting entry would normally cause an unrealized gain or loss to be recorded (rather than an adjustment for unrealized gain that was recorded because American Brands sold the last security in the portfolio).

Securities Sold from the Available-for-Sale Portfolio

To illustrate the sale of stock from the available-for-sale portfolio, let's use the same assumptions as for our previous example of a sale from the trading portfolio. Assume that American Brands sold stock on January 15, 19C, for $209,000. The stock was purchased during 19B at a cost of $200,000. On December 31, 19B, the fair market value of the stock was $205,000. On that date, an unrealized holding gain of $5,000 was recorded. To record the sale, American Brands would make the following entries:

Jan. 15, 19C	Cash	209,000	
	Available-for-sale securities		200,000
	Gain on sale of investment		9,000
Dec. 31, 19C	Unrealized gains on investment	5,000	
	Allowance to adjust to market		5,000

The Unrealized Gains on Investment account is a stockholders' equity account. The balance represents previously recorded unrealized gains. The debit is made to this account to reduce the balance because the security related to the gain is being sold. This debit does not affect the income statement. The amount of the Gain on the Sale of Investment is the difference between the selling price ($209,000) and the purchase price ($200,000). The full amount of the gain is reported in the year of sale because the previously recorded unrealized gains were reflected in a stockholders' equity account and were not reported on the income statement.

Some companies invest in others to gain better control of the flow of merchandise through distribution channels.

EQUITY METHOD

Learning Objective 5
Use the equity method.

When American Brands invests cash in various securities reported on its balance sheet, it is a passive investor. American Brands seeks to earn a high rate of return on these investments. It does not become involved in exerting influence over the financing and operating activities of the companies in which it invests. Accountants presume that investors are passive whenever they purchase less than 20% of the outstanding stock of another company, that is, when the market value method is used.

In many other situations, an investor may want to be able to exert influence without becoming the majority owner (i.e., an investment in 20% to 50% of the outstanding stock). A company may want to exert influence over another company for a variety of strategic reasons. For example, a retailer may want to influence a manufacturer to be sure that it can get certain products designed to its specifications; a manufacturer may want to influence a computer consulting firm to ensure that it can incorporate cutting-edge technology in its manufacturing processes; a furniture manufacturer may recognize that a service company lacks experienced management and could prosper with additional managerial support. As shown in Exhibit 12–1, the **equity method** is used when an investor can exert significant influence over an investee. This method permits the investor to report its share of the investee's income.

Equity method permits recording of investor's share of investee's income.

Under the equity method, there is a presumption that the investment was made for a long-term strategic purpose. *In contrast,* the market value method is based on the presumption that the investment was made to earn a return on cash that was not currently needed for operating purposes. Earlier in the chapter, we discussed the fact that investments under the market value method are reported at their fair market value because there is an intent to convert them to cash at some future time. Investments under the equity method are *not* reported at fair market value because they are made for long-term strategic purposes.

The equity method recognizes that the investing company has the ability to exert influence over the investee company and may, therefore, be involved in the operations of the investee. As a result, the investing corporation reports income on the investment based on the income earned by the investee company instead of the dividends paid by the investee company.

To illustrate the equity method, assume American Brands bought 3,000 shares of Davis Corporation stock at $120 per share on January 15, 19A. This represents 30% of the outstanding stock of Davis. The initial recording of an investment in stock is similar under the market value method and the equity method. American Brands would record the investment under the equity method as follows:

Jan. 15, 19A	Long-term investment	360,000	
	Cash ($120 × 3,000 shares)		360,000

Subsequent to the initial recording of an investment, there are significant differences between the market value method and the equity method. When dividends are paid on stock that is accounted for under the equity method, the dividend is treated as a return of part of the investment. Therefore, under the equity method, dividends reduce the carrying value of the investment. Assume Davis Corporation declared and paid a $1 per share dividend on June 14, 19A. American Brands would record the dividend as follows:

June 14, 19A	Cash ($1 × 3,000 shares)	3,000	
	Long-term investment		3,000

Notice that the dividend does not affect the income reported by American Brands (as it would if the market value method were used). There is an important reason for this accounting treatment. Because American Brands can exert significant influence over Davis, it is able to affect the dividend policy of Davis. If investment income were based on the amount of dividends paid, it would be possible for the investor to manipulate its income when significant influence existed.

With equity investments, the investor often is actively involved in significant operating and financing decisions affecting the investee company. Because the investor participates in the process of earning income for the investee company, it is appropriate to base the investment income on the earnings of the investee company instead of the dividends paid by them. To illustrate, assume on December 31, 19A, Davis Corporation reported net income of $40,000. American Brands owns 30% of Davis; therefore, its proportionate share of income is $12,000 ($40,000 × 30%). American Brands would make the following entry to record its share of the income reported by Davis:[1]

Dec. 31, 19A	Long-term investment	12,000	
	Revenue from investments*		12,000

*Sometimes called Equity in Earnings of Affiliated Company.

Based on the two previous journal entries, you can see that the Long-Term Investment account reported on the balance sheet does not reflect either cost or market. The investment account is increased for the cost of shares that were purchased and the proportionate share of the investee company's income. The account is reduced by the amount of dividends received from the investee company. At the end of the accounting period, accountants do not adjust the investment account to reflect changes of the fair market value of the securities that are held.

Under the equity method, an investor also must report its share of any loss incurred by the investee corporation. The proportionate share of the loss is recorded with a debit to a Loss on Investment account and a credit to Long-Term Investment.

FINANCIAL ANALYSIS

Managers' Selection of Accounting Alternatives

The market value and equity methods are two alternative methods of accounting for investments. The selection of a specific method is determined by the facts surrounding the investment and not by management discretion. Managers can freely choose between LIFO and

[1]In this example, we assume that the investment was purchased at book value. More complex situations will be discussed in advanced accounting courses.

FIFO or accelerated depreciation and straight-line depreciation. In the case of investments, managers may not simply choose either the market value or equity methods. Investments in less than 20% of the outstanding stock of a company are accounted for under the market value method and investments in 20% to 50% are recorded under the equity method.

In some cases, managers may be able to structure the acquisition of stock in a manner that permits them to use the accounting method that they prefer. For example, a company that wants to use the market value method could purchase only 19.9% of the outstanding stock of another company. Why would managers want to be able to avoid using the market value method or the equity method? A typical explanation has to do with the volatility of earnings. Most managers prefer to minimize variations in reported earnings. If a company was going to buy stock in a company that reported large earnings in some years and large losses in others, they might want to use the market value method. In this way, they would not have to report their share of the investee company's earnings and losses. Likewise, an investor may want to use the equity method if the investee company had relatively stable earnings but more significant variations in its stock price. By using the equity method, the investor would not have to report unrealized gains and losses on the investment.

Analysts who compare several companies must understand how differences in the market value and equity methods can affect earnings associated with similar investments. Analysts also should examine how management may affect reported earnings through the level of ownership that is acquired.

Self-Study Quiz

Assume that the Belverd Company was an investor in the Needles Corporation. On August 15, 19A, Needles paid total dividends of $500,000 and on December 31, 19A, it reported net income of $2,500,000. Prepare journal entries to record each of these events.

Case A Assume that Belverd owned 10% of Needles.

Case B Assume that Belverd owned 40% of Needles.

Check your response with the answer provided in the footnote at the bottom of this page.*

INVESTING TO ACHIEVE A CONTROLLING INTEREST

Earlier in this chapter, we discussed a number of strategic reasons for corporations to invest in other companies at a level that did not permit control (i.e., less than 50% ownership of the outstanding voting stock). Before we discuss accounting procedures for situations where a company owns 50% or more of the outstanding common stock of another corporation, we should consider the management reasons for acquiring this level of ownership.

Some of the reasons for acquiring control of another corporation are

1. Vertical integration In this type of acquisition, a company acquires another at a different level in the channels of distribution. For exam-

*Case A:

Aug. 15, 19A	Cash	50,000	
	Dividend income		50,000
Dec. 31, 19A	No entry		

Case B:

Aug. 15, 19A	Cash	200,000	
	Long-term investment		200,000
Dec. 31, 19A	Long-term investment	1,000,000	
	Revenue from investments		1,000,000

QUESTION OF ETHICS

Improper Influence

A key underlying assumption in accounting is that all transactions occur at "arm's length," where each party to the transaction is acting in his or her own self-interest. When one corporation is able to exert a significant influence over another (i.e., it owns 20% to 50% of the common stock), it is unreasonable to assume that transactions between the corporations are at arm's length. The equity method is designed to overcome this problem.

Consider what might happen if an investor corporation could affect the dividend policy of an investee corporation. If dividends paid by the investee corporation could be reported by the investor as dividend income, the investor corporation could manipulate its income by influencing the dividend policy of the other company. In a bad year, the investor might request large dividend payments to bolster its income. In a good year, it might try to cut dividend payments in order to build up the retained earnings of the investee company to support large dividends in the future when needed.

The equity method prevents this type of manipulation by not recognizing dividends as income. Instead, income from an investment in another company is based on a percentage of the affiliated company's reported net income.

The equity method is a good example of how accounting methods can affect the appearance and the reality of integrity in financial reporting.

ple, a retailer may purchase a manufacturer. At one time, the large retailer Sears followed this strategy. By doing so, Sears was able to assure the quality, quantity, and price of the products that it sold.

2. Horizontal growth These acquisitions involve companies at the same level in the channels of distribution. In this case, a retailer may acquire another retailer. Many regional companies have captured national markets by acquiring other regional companies.
3. Synergy The operation of two companies together may be more profitable than the combined profitability of the companies as separate entities. By merging and sharing production facilities, a lawn mower manufacturer with heavy summer demand and a snow blower manufacturer with heavy winter demand may create more profits than separate operations.
4. Diversification American Brands, which at one point derived most of its profits from the tobacco industry, has acquired numerous companies in other fields to lessen its dependency on a single product. In this way, it has sought to reduce the risk of its operations.
5. Special assets Some companies are acquired because they own needed assets. These could include cash, significant raw materials, patents, and key employees.
6. Undervalued opportunities Some companies have great potential but are on the verge of bankruptcy because of inadequate capital or management talent. Another company that has the needed resources may be able to acquire this type of company and operate it in a profitable manner.

Understanding why one company has invested in other companies is a key factor in understanding the company's overall business strategy. Analysts often study recent acquisitions in an effort to predict future acquisitions. For example, if a retail company acquires regional retailers in every region of the country except New England, it might be reasonable to assume that it will seek to acquire a New England-based company.

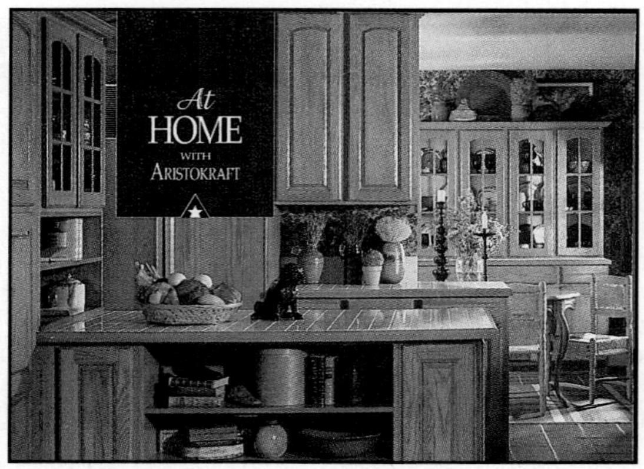

American Brands has followed a diversification strategy acquiring companies in the home improvement industry, such as Aristokraft, Moen, Master Lock, and Waterloo.

WHAT ARE CONSOLIDATED STATEMENTS?

Learning Objective 6
Explain the purpose of consolidated statements.

Parent is the company that gains a controlling influence over another company.

Subsidiary is the company that is acquired by the parent.

Consolidated financial statements are the financial statements of two or more companies that have been combined into a single set of financial statements.

In any corporate acquisition, there are two companies. The **parent** is the company that gains a controlling influence over another company. The **subsidiary** is the company that is acquired by the parent.

When a company acquires a controlling influence in another, accountants must prepare **consolidated financial statements** which combine the operations of two or more companies into a single set of statements. Basically, consolidated statements can be thought of as the adding together of the separate financial statements for two or more companies to make it appear as if there is a single company. Thus, the cash accounts for each company are added together as are the inventory accounts, land accounts, and others.

The notes to the American Brands annual report simply indicate that consolidated statements have been prepared. Most notes provide some additional detail. For example, the notes to the Delta Air Lines annual report state:

Real World Excerpt
Delta Air Lines Annual Report

Basis of Presentation The consolidated financial statements include the accounts of Delta Air Lines, Inc., and its wholly-owned subsidiaries. All significant intercompany accounts and transactions have been eliminated.

As the Delta note indicates, it is necessary to eliminate any *intercompany* items when consolidated statements are prepared. Remember that consolidated statements make it appear as if a single company exists when in fact there are two or more separate legal entities. Intercompany items would not exist if there were only a single corporation. For example, a debt owed by Delta (the parent) to one of its subsidiaries would not be reported on a consolidated statement because a company cannot owe itself money.

Before we discuss the specific process of consolidation, let's examine different methods that a company can use to acquire a controlling influence in another company.

METHODS OF ACQUIRING A CONTROLLING INTEREST

From an accounting perspective, there are two methods of acquiring a controlling interest. In some cases, the stock of one company, such as Gallaher Tobacco (the subsidiary), is acquired by exchanging shares for shares of another company, such as American Tobacco (the parent). Before the merger, the owners of Gallaher Tobacco held shares in that company. After the merger, they hold shares in American Tobacco. If certain additional criteria are met, this type of acquisition is called a **pooling of interests.** To be accounted for as a pooling of interests, a transaction must meet a rigid list of criteria (discussed in advanced accounting courses). Basically, a pooling occurs when there is a stock-for-stock swap.

A **pooling of interests** is an acquisition that is completed by exchanging parent company stock for subsidiary voting capital stock.

As an alternative, American Tobacco could offer cash to the owners of Gallaher Tobacco. In that case, after the merger the former owners of Gallaher Tobacco would hold cash and no stock in either company. This type of acquisition is known as a combination by **purchase.**

A **purchase** is an acquisition that is completed by purchasing subsidiary company voting capital stock for cash.

We will discuss both the purchase and pooling methods of consolidation. To facilitate your comparison of these two methods, we will use a continuing example in this chapter to illustrate the consolidation process. We have found that discussions of consolidation procedure can become complex. To make the discussion a little easier, we will use simplified data for two hypothetical companies; information for Company P (the parent) and Company S (the acquired subsidiary) is shown in Exhibit 12–4.

Pooling of Interests Method

Learning Objective 7
Apply the pooling and purchase methods and prepare the related elimination entries.

Under the pooling of interests method, the acquisition of a subsidiary is recorded in terms of the book value of the assets that are acquired, not their fair market value. Accountants view this type of transaction as a joining of ownership interests and not a normal purchase/sale transaction. To illustrate, assume Company P (the parent) acquired 100% of the voting stock of Company S (the subsidiary) on January 2, 19A, immediately after the financial statements shown in Exhibit 12–4 were prepared. Company P would record the exchange of stock as follows:

Illustrative Data for Consolidation — **Exhibit 12–4**

COMPANY P AND COMPANY S
Separate Balance Sheets
January 1, 19A, Immediately before Acquisition

Assets	**Company P**	**Company S**
Cash	$205,000	$ 35,000
Accounts receivable (net)*	15,000	30,000
Receivable from Company S	10,000	
Inventories	170,000	70,000
Plant and equipment (net)*	100,000	45,000
Total assets	$500,000	$180,000
Liabilities and Stockholders' Equity		
Liabilities:		
Accounts payable	$ 60,000	$ 20,000
Payable to Company P		10,000
Stockholders' equity:		
Company stock, Company P (par $6)	300,000	
Common stock, Company S (par $10)		100,000
Retained earnings	140,000	50,000
Total liabilities and stockholders' equity	$500,000	$180,000

*Accounts receivable, less the allowance for doubtful accounts; and plant and equipment, less accumulated depreciation. The net amounts are used to simplify the example. The end results will be the same as they would have been had the separate control accounts been used.

Jan. 2, 19A	Investment in Company S	150,000	
	Common stock		60,000
	Contributed capital		90,000

The transaction was an exchange of stock between Company P and the *stockholders* of Company S. Therefore, Company S does not record the transaction. After this journal entry is posted to the accounts, the balance sheets for each company would appear as shown in Exhibit 12–5.

Notice that the investment in Company S is recorded at the book value of the stock that was acquired (common stock, $100,000 + retained earnings, $50,000) and not the fair market value of the stock. Consolidated financial statements under the pooling of interests method reflect book values, not market values, that existed on the date that the subsidiary was acquired.

To illustrate the consolidation process, we will combine the two separate balance sheets shown in Exhibit 12–5 into a single consolidated balance sheet. Remember, the result of the consolidation is the set of financial statements that would appear if there were a *single entity.* Basically, consolidation involves adding together the individual items reported on each company's financial statements. For example, when the parent company consolidates the balance sheets shown in Exhibit 12–5, the consolidated cash balance will be $240,000 (i.e., $205,000 + $35,000).

During consolidation, some accounts are *eliminated* (or adjusted) to avoid including amounts that would not be reported if only a single entity existed. For example, the balance sheet of Company P shows a receivable from Company S of $10,000, and the balance sheet of Company S shows a payable to Company P of $10,000. It is impossible for an entity to owe itself money. Therefore, during consolidation, these accounts must be eliminated, which means that they will not be reported on the consolidated balance sheet.

Exhibit 12–5 **Balance Sheets Immediately after Acquisition (Pooling of Interests Method)**

COMPANY P AND COMPANY S
Separate Balance Sheets (Pooling of Interests Method)
January 2, 19A, Immediately after Acquisition

Assets	**Company P**	**Company S**
Cash	$205,000	$ 35,000
Accounts receivable (net)	15,000	30,000
Receivable from Company S	10,000	
Inventories	170,000	70,000
Investment in Company S (100%)	150,000*	
Plant and equipment (net)	100,000	45,000
Total assets	$650,000	$180,000
Liabilities and Stockholders' Equity		
Accounts payable	$ 60,000	$ 20,000
Payable to Company P		10,000
Common stock, Company P (par $6)	360,000*	
Common stock, Company S (par $10)		100,000
Contributed capital	90,000*	
Retained earnings, Company P	140,000	
Retained earnings, Company S		50,000
Total liabilities and stockholders' equity	$650,000	$180,000

*Amounts changed from pre-acquisition balance sheets given in Exhibit 12–4. Notice the transaction does not affect Company S.

The entries to eliminate and adjust accounts are not entered into the records of either the parent or the subsidiary. Instead, consolidated statements are prepared using a worksheet. We will illustrate the elimination and adjustment of several accounts by using the journal entry format with which you are familiar. We will also show whether the adjustment is an increase or decrease in the account and record the entries on the worksheet in terms of an increase or decrease.

Two items must be eliminated when the balance sheets shown in Exhibit 12–5 are consolidated under the pooling of interests method:

1. Company P shows a receivable of $10,000 from Company S, and the accounts of Company S show this as a payable to Company P. This amount is called an *intercompany debt.* When the two balance sheets are combined into a single consolidated balance sheet, intercompany debt must be eliminated because there is no external debt or receivable for the combined entity. Thus, the following elimination must be made when the two balance sheets are combined:

(a) Payable to Company P (decrease)	10,000	
Receivable from Company S (decrease)		10,000

2. The Investment in Company S account represents Company P's investment in the assets of Company S. These specific assets will be included on the consolidated balance sheet. To prevent a double counting of assets and the investment in the assets, the investment account must be eliminated. Related to this elimination is the reduction of stockholders' equity. The credit balance of $100,000 in the Company S common stock account is owned by Company P. Because it is impossible for a company to invest in itself, the Company S stock held by Company P must be eliminated from the consolidated balance sheet. Finally, the difference between the balances in the investment account and the common stock account of Company S ($150,000 – $100,000 = $50,000) must be eliminated from Contributed

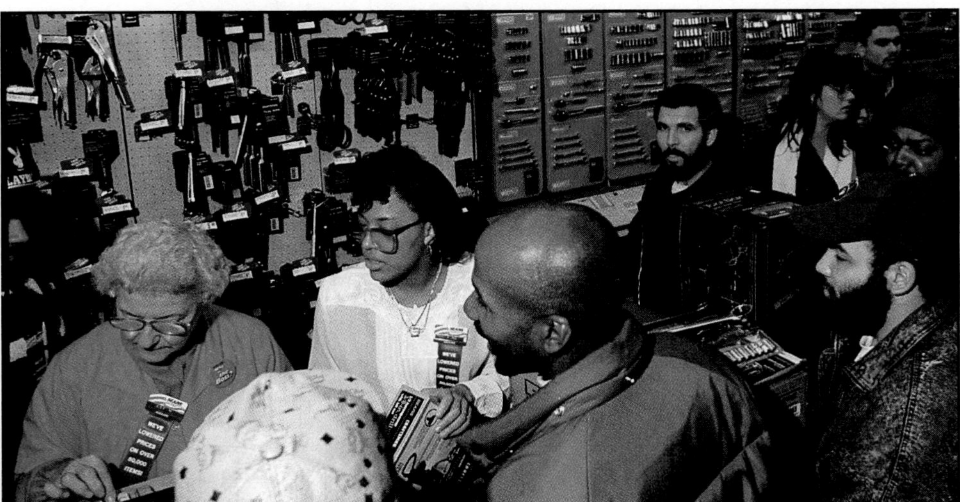

Intercompany ownership can provide some surprises. The company that manufactures the well-known Sears Craftsman tools is owned by American Brands.

Capital (on Company P's books). The elimination can be summarized as follows:

(b) Common stock, Company S (decrease)	100,000	
Contributed capital (decrease)	50,000	
Investment account (decrease)		150,000

The balance sheets of Company P and Company S are shown separately in Exhibit 12–6. The eliminations and adjustments are shown in the next column. In the last column, the balance sheets are combined on a line-by-line basis, after deducting the eliminations, to develop the consolidated balance sheet amounts. In an external consolidated financial statement, only the last column would be reported. The amount reported on the consolidated balance sheet is the sum of the account balances from each of the separate companies adjusted for any intercompany items.

Purchase Method

Under the purchase method, the stockholders of the acquired company receive cash for the shares of stock they sell and are no longer owners of either the parent or the subsidiary. Accountants view this as a purchase/sale transaction. As you saw in earlier chapters, assets that are purchased should be recorded in terms of their cost. Thus, there is no conceptual difference between the direct purchase of a building that is worth $500,000 and the purchase of a company that has a single asset which is a building worth $500,000. On the acquisition date, the investment account reflects the *market value* of the acquired

Exhibit 12–6 **Preparation of Consolidated Balance Sheet (Pooling of Interests Method)**

COMPANY P and Its Subsidiary, COMPANY S (100% Owned)
Consolidated Balance Sheet (Pooling of Interests Method)
At January 2, 19A, Immediately after Acquisition

	Separate Balance Sheets			
Assets	**Company P**	**Company S**	**Elimination***	**Consolidated Balance Sheet**
Cash	$205,000	$ 35,000		$240,000
Accounts receivable (net)	15,000	30,000		45,000
Receivable from Company S	10,000		*(a)* –$ 10,000	-0-
Inventories	170,000	70,000		240,000
Investment in Company S	150,000		*(b)* – 150,000	-0-
Plant and equipment (net)	100,000	45,000		145,000
Total assets	$650,000	$180,000		$670,000
Liabilities				
Accounts payable	$ 60,000	$ 20,000		$ 80,000
Payable to Company P		10,000	*(a)* – 10,000	-0-
Stockholders' Equity				
Common stock, Company P	360,000			360,000
Common stock, Company S		100,000	*(b)* – 100,000	-0-
Contributed capital	90,000		*(b)* – 50,000	40,000
Retained earnings, Company P	140,000			190,000
Retained earnings, Company S		50,000		
Total liabilities and stockholders' equity	$650,000	$180,000		$670,000

*Usually a formal worksheet (with debit-credit columns) is used to prepare consolidated statements.

shares and not the book value of the acquired assets (as was the case in the pooling of interests).

To illustrate the purchase method, we will use the same data that were used for our previous illustration (the balance sheets of Companies P and S are shown in Exhibit 12–4). Assume that on January 2, 19A, Company P purchased from stockholders 100% of the outstanding voting stock of Company S for $165,000 and paid cash. On this date, Company P would make the following journal entry in its accounts:

Jan. 2, 19A:	Investment in stock of Company S	165,000	
	Cash		165,000

Notice that Company P paid $165,000 cash to buy all the stock of Company S, although the total *book value* of the stockholders' equity of Company S was only $150,000. Thus, Company P paid $15,000 more than book value. Why would Company P pay more than book value for the investment? Actually, the answer is a simple one: remember that the book value of an asset is not the same as its fair market value. Company P had to pay fair market value to acquire Company S. The former owners would not have been willing to sell their stock for only book value. An analysis of Company B's assets revealed the following facts: (1) the plant and equipment owned by Company S had a market value of $50,000 at the acquisition date (compared with the book value of $45,000 reported by Company S), and (2) Company S had developed a good reputation with its customers, which increased the overall value of Company S. For these reasons, Company P was willing to pay $15,000 more than book value to acquire the stock of Company S.

After the journal entry to record the purchase of Company S is posted to the books, the balance sheets of Company P and Company S would appear as shown in the first two columns of Exhibit 12–7.

Preparation of Consolidated Balance Sheet (Purchase Method) — Exhibit 12–7

COMPANY P and Its Subsidiary, COMPANY S (100% Owned)
Consolidated Balance Sheet (Purchase Method)
At January 2, 19A, Immediately after Acquisition

	Separate Balance Sheets				Consolidated
Assets	**Company P**	**Company S**		**Elimination**	**Balance Sheet**
Cash	$ 40,000	$ 35,000			$ 75,000
Accounts receivable (net)	15,000	30,000			45,000
Receivable from Company S	10,000		*(a)*	–$ 10,000	-0-
Inventories	170,000	70,000			240,000
Investment in Company S	165,000		*(b)*	– 165,000	-0-
Plant and equipment (net)	100,000	45,000	*(b)*	+ 5,000	150,000
Goodwill			*(b)*	+ 10,000	10,000
Total assets	$500,000	$180,000			$520,000
Liabilities					
Accounts payable	$ 60,000	$ 20,000			$ 80,000
Payable to Company P		10,000	*(a)*	– 10,000	-0-
Stockholders' Equity					
Common stock, Company P	300,000				300,000
Common stock, Company S		100,000	*(b)*	– 100,000	-0-
Retained earnings, Company P	140,000				140,000
Retained earnings, Company S		50,000	*(b)*	– 50,000	-0-
Total liabilities and stockholders' equity	$500,000	$180,000			$520,000

The basic process for consolidation under the purchase method is similar to the process for consolidation under a pooling of interests (as illustrated in Exhibit 12–6). In our example, there are two intercompany items that must be eliminated.

1. The intercompany debt must be eliminated for the reasons discussed under the pooling of interests. This elimination is as follows:

(a) Payable to Company P (decrease)	10,000	
Receivable from Company S (decrease)		10,000

2. The investment account must be eliminated. Under the purchase method, this elimination differs significantly from the one that was made under the pooling method. The eliminations differ because the investment account is based on fair market value under the purchase method and book value under the pooling method. The investment account balance of $165,000 on Company P's books represents market value at the date of acquisition. It must be eliminated against the stockholders' equity of Company S, which is at *book value*. Remember that there were two reasons why Company P paid $15,000 more than book value to acquire Company S: (1) the plant and equipment owned by Company S had a market value of $50,000 at acquisition (compared with its book value of $45,000), and (2) Company S had developed a good reputation with its customers, which increased its overall value. The difference between the purchase cost and the book value of the investment may be analyzed as follows:

Purchase price for 100% interest in Company S		$165,000
Net assets purchased, valued at market:		
Book value, $180,000, plus market value increment of plant and equipment, $5,000	$185,000	
Less: liabilities assumed	30,000	
Total market value purchased		(155,000)
Goodwill purchased		$ 10,000

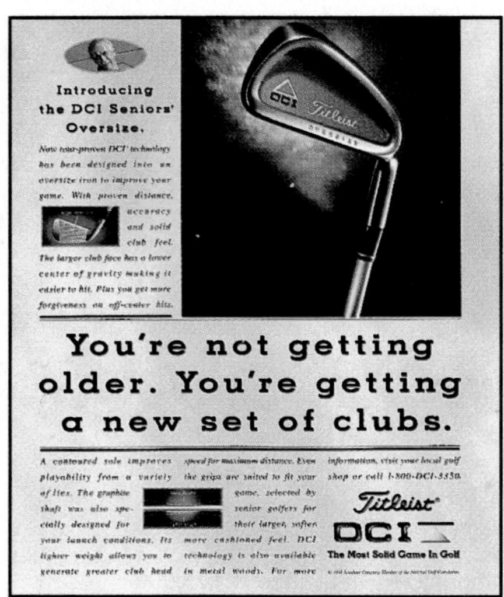

Goodwill is often enhanced with effective advertising. Titleist is an American Brands company.

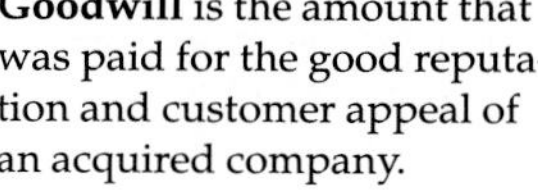

Goodwill is defined by accountants as the difference between the purchase price of a company and the fair market value of the net assets (assets minus liabilities) that were acquired. The following note from the Lands' End annual report provides a good definition of goodwill:

Goodwill is the amount that was paid for the good reputation and customer appeal of an acquired company.

Real World Excerpt

Lands' End Annual Report

> Intangible assets consist primarily of goodwill which is the excess cost over the fair market value of net assets of businesses purchased.

Goodwill is created by a number of factors such as a good reputation, customer appeal, and general acceptance of the business. All successful companies have some amount of goodwill but it can be reported on the balance sheet only if it is acquired in a purchase transaction. Goodwill is never recorded in a pooling of interests. The balance sheet for American Brands includes goodwill in Other Assets. Some companies identify goodwill separately on the balance sheet.

To eliminate the Company P investment account and the owners' equity accounts of Company S, the following five steps must be completed:

1. Increase the plant and equipment of Company S from the book value of $45,000 to market value of $50,000; the increase is $5,000.
2. Recognize the $10,000 goodwill purchased as an asset.
3. Eliminate the investment account balance of $165,000.
4. Eliminate the Company S common stock balance of $100,000.
5. Eliminate the Company S retained earnings balance of $50,000.

When the purchase method is used, the balance of Retained Earnings for the subsidiary at acquisition is eliminated. In contrast, under the pooling of interests method, retained earnings is not eliminated. This elimination is made with the purchase method because the retained earnings of the subsidiary were, in effect, paid to the former stockholders of Company S when they were bought out for cash.

These five steps are implemented in the following journal entry:

(b) Common stock Company S (decrease)	100,000	
Retained earnings Company S (decrease)	50,000	
Plant and equipment (increase)	5,000	
Goodwill (increase)	10,000	
Investment (decrease)		165,000

The two separate Balance Sheet columns are shown in Exhibit 12–7. After eliminations, they are combined on a line-by-line basis to develop the Consolidated Balance Sheet amounts shown in the last column. In an external consolidated financial statement, only the consolidated balance sheet entries shown in the last column (and not the separate balance sheet entries) would be reported.

AN INTERNATIONAL PERSPECTIVE

Alternative Methods of Accounting for Corporate Acquisitions

Most countries require the preparation of consolidated financial statements when a parent company acquires a controlling influence in a subsidiary. All countries permit the purchase method to be used in the consolidation, but a small number of countries, such as France, Mexico and Spain, do not permit the use of the pooling of interests method. Generally, all subsidiaries in which the parent holds 50% of the voting stock will be consolidated, but there are exceptions. In Japan, consolidation is not required if the subsidiary amounts to less than 10% of the consolidated entity's assets. In Canada and Mexico, a subsidiary with a financial structure significantly different from the parent's is not consolidated (e.g., a manufacturer and a finance company).

In addition, considerable controversy exists internationally concerning accounting for goodwill. In the United States, goodwill that is acquired in a purchase transaction is recorded as an asset and amortized over its estimated life, which may not exceed 40 years. Similar rules exist in many countries, but the maximum amortization period is different. Some examples: Australia, where the maximum is 20 years; Italy, 10 years; Japan, generally 5 years; and Mexico, no maximum is required. In several other countries, purchased goodwill is not recorded as an asset. In England, for example, goodwill may be deducted from retained earnings.

Each year, financial markets become more international in scope. Investors and creditors who provide funds to corporations around the world must be sensitive to the range of accounting alternatives that are required in different countries.

CONSOLIDATION IN SUBSEQUENT ACCOUNTING PERIODS

Learning Objective 8
Prepare consolidated statements in years after year of acquisition.

The revaluation of assets and the creation of goodwill have implications for future accounting periods. In future years, these assets must be depreciated and amortized, respectively. The original cost of the plant and equipment is depreciated on the books of Company P and Company S. As a result, it is not necessary to make a special entry during consolidation to record depreciation on this amount. It is necessary, however, to record depreciation on the market value increment that is created during consolidation. If we assume that there are five years remaining to the life of the plant and equipment \$1,000 of *additional* depreciation should be recorded during consolidation (\$5,000 ÷ 5 years):

Depreciation expense	1,000	
Accumulated depreciation		1,000

Likewise, it is necessary to record amortization of goodwill as part of the consolidation process. Goodwill is created during consolidation and is not recorded on the books of either Company P or S. As a result, it is necessary to record the full amortization of goodwill as part of consolidation. It is very difficult to estimate the expected life of goodwill. For some companies, it may have economic value for an extremely long period of time. For others, goodwill may exist for a very short time. Because of the difficulty in estimating the life of goodwill, GAAP requires that goodwill must be amortized over a realistic period not longer than 40 years. Assume that Company P decided to use a 20-year life to amortize the \$10,000 goodwill which was recognized. This amount must be amortized each period with the following entry on the worksheet:

Amortization expense (goodwill)	500	
Goodwill		500

\$10,000 ÷ 20 years = \$500.

You will encounter a variety of amortization periods for goodwill, as the following sample of notes from financial statements illustrates:

Real World Excerpt

Lands' End Annual Report

Mattel Annual Report

LANDS' END
Goodwill is being amortized over 40 years on a straight-line basis.

MATTEL
In 1992, the amortization period for goodwill arising from certain transactions was changed from 10 years to 20 years to better reflect the estimated periods over which benefits will be realized.

Real World Excerpt

Snap On Tools Annual Report

SNAP ON TOOLS
Goodwill is amortized over a period of 20 years.

Nike Annual Report

NIKE
Goodwill is being amortized on a straight-line basis primarily over 25 to 40 years.

The period over which goodwill is amortized is an important factor for analysts to consider. For some companies, goodwill can be a large portion of their assets. The decision to amortize goodwill over 40 years instead of 20 years can have a significant impact on reported earnings. Because the amortization of goodwill is a noncash expense, decisions concerning amortization periods will have no impact on cash flows.

Self-Study Quiz

The Lexis Corporation owns 100% of Nexis Company and reports on a consolidated basis. There is an intercompany account payable/receivable of $150,000.

a. Prepare the elimination entry for the intercompany accounts assuming that the purchase method is used.

b. Prepare the elimination entry for the intercompany accounts assuming the pooling method is used.

c. Assume that goodwill was reported on the consolidated balance sheet. Which consolidation method was used?

Check your responses with the answers in the footnote at the bottom of this page.*

FINANCIAL ANALYSIS

Impact of Pooling and Purchase on Ratio Analysis

Nearly all large corporations prepare consolidated financial statements. Analysts must understand the consolidation process because the majority of the statements they work with are prepared on a consolidated basis.

The pooling of interests and purchase methods have significantly different effects on consolidated statements. Analysts must be aware of these differences to properly use consolidated statements. Some analysts use the return-on-investment (ROI) ratio to evaluate the effectiveness of the management of a company. The ratio is calculated as follows:

$$\text{ROI} = \frac{\text{Net income}}{\text{Total assets}}$$

The use of pooling of interests versus purchase can have a dramatic effect on the ROI ratio. Under pooling of interests, net income is normally higher because there is no additional depreciation expense associated with the increased asset values reported under the purchase method. Also under pooling of interests, the amount of total assets reported is normally lower because of the use of book values for the assets of the subsidiary. As a

---

**a.*	Account payable	150,000	
	Account receivable		150,000
b.	Account payable	150,000	
	Account receivable		150,000

c. The purchase method.

result of the higher numerator for the ratio (net income) and the lower denominator (total assets), ROI for companies that use pooling is often significantly higher than ROI for companies that use the purchase method. Analysts must understand consolidation to be sure they identify real economic differences between companies, not differences created by accounting alternatives.

EPILOGUE FOR AMERICAN BRANDS

Throughout the 1980s, American Brands followed an investment strategy that emphasized diversification. That strategy changed in the mid 1990s. On January 31, 1995, American Brands sold its life insurance subsidiary, Franklin Life, to American General for $1.17 billion in cash. The previous month, the company sold its domestic tobacco subsidiary, the American Tobacco Company. The American Brands chairman and chief executive officer, Thomas G. Hay, announced that the "new" American Brands is a focused consumer product company with powerful brands and leading market positions. As a result of this change in strategy, American Brands is a different company. Financial analysts must understand accounting for investments in order to evaluate companies like American Brands that conduct major acquisitions and divestitures.

DEMONSTRATION CASE

(Try to resolve the requirements before proceeding to the suggested solution that follows.)

Case A: Howell Equipment Corporation sells and services a major line of farm equipment. Both sales and service operations have been profitable. The following transactions affected the company during 19S:

a. Jan. 1 Purchased 2,000 shares of common stock of Dear Company at $40 per share. This was 1% of the shares outstanding. Management intends to actively trade these shares.

b. Dec. 28 Received $4,000 cash dividend on the Dear Company stock.

c. Dec. 31 The current market price of the Dear stock is $39.

Required:

Give the journal entry for each of the above transactions.

SUGGESTED SOLUTION

	Date	Account	Debit	Credit
a.	Jan. 1, 19S:	Trading securities	80,000	
		Cash		80,000
		Purchased 2,000 shares Dear Company common stock at $40 per share.		
b.	Dec. 28, 19S:	Cash	4,000	
		Revenue from investments		4,000
		Received dividend on Dear Company stock.		
c.	Dec. 31, 19S:	Unrealized loss on trading securities	2,000	
		Allowance to adjust to market		2,000
		To record unrealized loss on Dear stock: 2,000 shares × $1 ($40 – $39) = $2,000.		

Case B: On January 1, 19A, Connaught Company purchased 100% of the outstanding voting shares of London Company in the open market for $85,000 cash. On the date of acquisition, the market value of the operational assets of London Company was $79,000.

Required:

1. Was this combination by pooling of interests or by purchase? Explain.
2. Give the journal entry that should be made by Connaught Company at date of acquisition. If none is required, explain why.
3. Give the journal entry that should be made by London Company at date of acquisition. If none is required, explain why.
4. Analyze the acquisition to determine the amount of goodwill purchased.
5. Should the assets of London Company be included on the consolidated balance sheet at book value or market value? Explain.

SUGGESTED SOLUTION

1. The purchase method should be used because the stock of the subsidiary was acquired for cash.
2.

Jan. 1, 19A:	Investment in subsidiary	85,000	
	Cash		85,000

3. London Company would not record a journal entry related to the purchase of stock by Connaught Company. The transaction was between Connaught and the stockholders of London Company. The transaction did not directly involve the London Company.
4.

Purchase price for London Company	$85,000
Market value of net assets purchased	79,000
Goodwill	$ 6,000

5. Under the purchase method, the assets of London Company should be included on the consolidated balance sheet at their market values as of the date of acquisition. The cost principle applies because a purchase/sale transaction is assumed when the combination is accounted for as a purchase. When the pooling of interests method is used, the assets of the subsidiary are reported on the consolidated balance sheet at their book value.

SUMMARY

The measuring and reporting of long-term investments in the capital stock of another company are determined by the percentage of shares owned in relation to the total number of shares outstanding. If the ownership level of *voting* shares is less than 20%, or if the ownership is of nonvoting stock, the market value method must be used. Under this method, the investment amount for common stock reported by the investor is based on the current market value of the stock.

Investments in equity securities accounted for under the market value method are reported on the balance sheet in either the trading securities portfolio or the available-for-sale portfolio. Unrealized holding gains and losses are recorded on investments held in both the trading securities and the available-for-sale portfolios. Unrealized gains and losses on securities in the trading portfolio are reported on the income statement, while unrealized gains and losses on securities in the available-for-sale portfolio are reported as a component of stockholders' equity.

If the ownership is at least 20% but not more than 50%, the equity method must be used. Under this method, the investment is recorded at cost by the investor at the date of acquisition. Each period thereafter, the investment amount is increased (or decreased) by the proportionate interest in the income (or loss) reported by the investee corporation and decreased by the proportionate share of the dividends declared by the investee corporation. Each period, the investor recognizes as revenue its proportionate share of the income (or loss) reported by the investee company.

Consolidated financial statements are required in most situations when one corporation owns more than 50% of the outstanding voting stock of another corporation. The concept of consolidation is based on the view that a parent company and its subsidiaries constitute one economic entity. Therefore, the separate income statements, balance sheets, and statements of cash flows should be combined each period on an item-by-item basis as a single set of consolidated financial statements.

Ownership of a controlling interest of another corporation may be accounted for as either a pooling of interests or combination by purchase. The measurement of amounts reported on the consolidated financial statements is influenced by these two different accounting methods.

The pooling of interests method usually is used when the parent company exchanges shares of its own voting stock for a controlling interest in the voting shares of the subsidiary. In this situation, there is no purchase/sale (exchange) transaction. Rather, there is a joining of interests by exchanging stock and the cost principle is not applied. Therefore, in preparing consolidated statements under the pooling of interests method, the book values of each related company are added together. Acquisition market values are disregarded.

Under the purchase method, the parent company usually pays cash and/or incurs debt to acquire the voting shares of the subsidiary. In these circumstances, a purchase/sale transaction has been completed, and the acquisition is accounted for in conformity with the cost principle. Therefore, the assets of the subsidiary must be measured at their acquisition market values when combined with the statements of the parent company.

KEY TERMS

Available-for-Sale Securities All investments, other than trading securities, that are accounted for under the market value method. *585*

Consolidated Financial Statements The financial statements of two or more companies that have been combined into a single set of financial statements. *596*

Control The ability of the investing company to determine the operating and financing policies of another company in which it owns shares of the voting stock; presumed to exist when more than 50% of the voting stock of an entity is owned by one investor. *584*

Equity Method Method used by investor if 20% to 50% of the voting stock of the investee company is owned by the investor. It permits recording of investor's share of investee's income. *592*

Goodwill The amount that was paid for the good reputation and customer appeal of an acquired company. *603*

Market Value Method Method used by investor if less than 20% of the voting stock of the investee company is owned by the investor; unrealized gains and losses are recorded based on changes in the prices of securities that are held. *585*

Parent The company that has a significant investment in a subsidiary company. *596*

Pooling of Interests An acquisition that is completed by exchanging parent company stock for subsidiary voting capital stock. *597*

Purchase An acquisition that is completed by purchasing subsidiary company voting capital stock for cash. *597*

Significant Influence The ability of an investor company to have an important impact on the operating and financing policies of another company (the investee). *583*

Subsidiary The company that is owned by a parent company as evidenced by more than 50% of the voting capital stock. *596*

Trading Securities All investments in stocks or bonds that are held primarily for the purpose of selling them in the near future; accounted for under the market value method. *585*

Unrealized Holding Gains and Losses Amounts recorded when there is a price change for securities which are currently held. *587*

QUESTIONS

1. Explain the difference between a short-term investment and a long-term investment.
2. Match the following:

   Measurement method:

   ________ Market value method.
   ________ Equity method.
   ________ Consolidation.

   Level of ownership of the voting capital stock:

   a. More than 50% ownership.
   b. Less than 20% ownership.
   c. At least 20% but not more than 50% ownership.
3. Explain the application of the cost principle to the purchase of capital stock in another company.
4. Under the market value method, when and how is revenue measured by the investor company?
5. Under the equity method, why is revenue measured on a proportionate basis by the investor company when income is reported by the other company rather than when dividends are declared?
6. Under the equity method, dividends received from the investee company are not recorded as revenue. To record dividends as revenue would involve double counting. Explain.
7. Match the following items that relate to the long-term investment amount reported on the balance sheet of the investor company:

   Measurement method:

   ________ Market value method.
   ________ Equity method.

   Explanation of balance in the investment account:

   a. Market value.
   b. Original cost plus proportionate part of the income of the investee, less proportionate part of the dividends declared by investee.
8. What is a parent-subsidiary relationship?
9. Explain the basic concept underlying consolidated statements.
10. What is the basic element that must be present before consolidated statements are appropriate?
11. What is pooling of interests?
12. What is a combination by purchase?
13. The investing corporation debits a long-term investment account when it acquires a controlling influence in another corporation. In the case of a pooling of interests, describe how to determine the amount that is debited to the investment account.
14. What are intercompany eliminations?
15. Explain why the investment account must be eliminated against stockholders' equity when consolidated statements are prepared.
16. Explain why the book values of the parent and subsidiary are aggregated on consolidated statements when there is a pooling of interests, but acquisition market values of the subsidiary assets are used when the combination is by purchase.
17. Why is goodwill not recognized in a pooling of interests? Why is it recognized in a combination by purchase?
18. Explain why additional depreciation expense usually must be recognized on consolidation when the combination was by purchase.
19. What is goodwill?
20. Explain why the management of a company might prefer to account for a consolidation using pooling instead of the purchase method.

21. Explain the basis for each of the following statements:
    a. Pooling of interests, given the same situation, reports a higher net income than combination by purchase.
    b. The cash position, other things being equal, usually is better when the combination is by pooling of interests than when the combination is by purchase.
    c. Pooling of interests, other things being equal, reports a higher amount of retained earnings than does combination by purchase.

EXERCISES

E12–1 Comparing Primary Characteristics of Market Value and Equity Methods

Company A purchased a certain number of the outstanding voting shares of Company B at $18 per share as a long-term investment. Company B had outstanding 20,000 shares of $10 par value stock. On a separate sheet complete the following matrix relating to the measurement and reporting by Company A after acquisition of the shares of Company B stock.

Questions	Market Value Method	Equity Method
a. What is the applicable level of ownership by Company A of Company B to apply the method?	Percent	Percent
For (*b*), (*e*), (*f*), and (*g*) that follow, assume:		
Number of shares acquired of Company B stock	1,500	5,000
Net income reported by Company B in the first year	$60,000	$60,000
Dividends declared by Company B in the first year	$15,000	$15,000
Market price at end of first year, Company B stock, $15		
b. At acquisition, the investment account on the books of Company A should be debited at what amount?	$	$
c. On what basis should Company A recognize revenue earned on the stock of Company B? Explanation required.		
d. After acquisition date, on what basis should Company A change the balance of the investment account in respect to the stock of Company B owned (other than for disposal of the investment)? Explanation required.		
e. What would be the balance in the investment account on the books of Company A at the end of the first year?	$	$
f. What amount of revenue from the investment in Company B should Company A report at the end of the first year?	$	$
g. What amount of unrealized loss should Company A report at the end of the first year?	$	$

E12–2 Identifying and Using the Proper Method to Account for a Long-Term Investment in Equity Securities

During 19B, Princeton Company acquired some of the 50,000 outstanding shares of the common stock, par $10, of Cox Corporation as a long-term investment. The accounting period for both companies ends December 31. The following transactions occurred during 19B:

July	2	Purchased 8,000 shares of Cox common stock at $28 per share.
Dec.	31	Received the 19B annual financial statement of Cox Corporation that reported net income of $52,000.
	31	Cox Corporation declared and paid a cash dividend of $2 per share.
	31	Market price of Cox stock was $25 per share.

Required:

1. What accounting method should the company use? Why?
2. Give the journal entries for each of the above transactions. If no entry is required, explain why.
3. Show how the long-term investment and the related revenue should be reported on the 19B financial statements of the company.

E12–3 *Recording and Reporting a Long-Term Investment in an Equity Security*

Felicia Company acquired some of the 60,000 shares of outstanding common stock (nopar) of Nueces Corporation during 19E as a long-term investment. The annual accounting period for both companies ends December 31. The following transactions occurred during 19E:

Jan.	10	Purchased 21,000 shares of Nueces common stock at $12 per share.
Dec.	31	Received the 19E financial statement of Nueces Corporation, which reported net income of $90,000.
	31	Nueces Corporation declared and paid a cash dividend of $0.60 per share.
	31	Market price of Nueces stock was $11 per share.

Required:

1. What accounting method should the company use? Why?
2. Give the journal entries for each of the above transactions. If no entry is required, explain why.
3. Show how the long-term investment and the related revenue should be reported on the 19E financial statements of the company.

E12–4 *Identifying and Using the Proper Method to Account for a Long-Term Investment in an Equity Security*

During 19H, Russell Company purchased some of the 90,000 shares of common stock, par $8, of Sea Tuna, Inc., as a long-term investment. The annual accounting period for each company ends December 31. The following transactions occurred during 19H:

Jan.	7	Purchased 9,000 shares of Sea Tuna common stock at $32 per share.
Dec.	31	Received the 19H financial statement of Sea Tuna, which reported net income of $200,000.
	31	Sea Tuna declared and paid a cash dividend of $3 per share.
	31	Market price of Sea Tuna stock was $40 per share.

Required:

1. What accounting method should the company use? Why?
2. Give the journal entries for each of the above transactions. If no entry is required, explain why.
3. Show how the long-term investment and the related revenue should be reported on the 19H financial statements of the company.

E12–5 *Identifying and Using the Proper Method to Account for a Long-Term Investment in an Equity Security*

Use the same situation for Russell Company and the data given in Exercise 12–4, except for the January 7, 19H, transaction. Assume it was as follows:

Jan.	7	Purchased 40,500 shares of Sea Tuna stock at $32 per share.

(The data for December 31 are unchanged.)

Required:

1. What accounting method should the company use? Why?
2. Give the journal entries for each transaction (refer also to transactions given in Exercise 12–4). If no entry is required, explain why.
3. Show how the long-term investment and the related revenue should be reported on the 19H financial statements of the company.

E12–6 Recording Gains and Losses in the Trading Security Portfolio

On June 30, 19A, MetroMedia, Inc., purchased 10,000 shares of Mitek stock for $20 per share. Management purchased the stock for speculative purposes and recorded the stock in the trading security portfolio. The following information pertains to the price per share of Mitek stock:

	Price
12/31/19A	$24
12/31/19B	31
12/31/19C	25

MetroMedia sold all of the Mitek stock on February 14, 19D, at a price of $23 per share. Prepare any journal entries that are required by the facts presented in this case.

E12–7 Recording Gains and Losses in the Available-for-Sale Portfolio

Using the data in the previous exercise, assume that management of MetroMedia purchased the Mitek stock for the available-for-sale portfolio instead of the trading securities portfolio. Prepare any journal entries that are required by the facts presented in the case.

E12–8 Recording Gains and Losses in the Trading Security Portfolio

On March 10, 19B, General Solutions, Inc., purchased 5,000 shares of MicroTech stock for $50 per share. Management purchased the stock for speculative purposes and recorded the stock in the trading security portfolio. The following information pertains to the price per share of MicroTech stock:

	Price
12/31/19B	$55
12/31/19C	40
12/31/19D	42

General Solutions sold all of the MicroTech stock on September 12, 19E, at a price of $39 per share. Prepare any journal entries that are required by the facts presented in this case.

E12–9 Recording Gains and Losses in the Available-for-Sale Portfolio

Using the data in the previous exercise, assume that management of General Solutions purchased the MicroTech stock for the available-for-sale portfolio instead of the trading securities portfolio. Prepare any journal entries that are required by the facts presented in the case.

E12–10 Preparing a Consolidated Balance Sheet

On January 2, 19A, Company P acquired all of the outstanding voting stock of Company S by exchanging, on a share-for-share basis, its own unissued stock for the stock of Company S. Immediately after the acquisition of Company S, the separate balance sheets showed the following:

	Balances, January 2, 19A, Immediately after Acquisition	
	Company P	**Company S**
Cash	$ 25,000	$17,000
Receivable from Company S	6,000	
Inventory	42,000	11,000
Investment in Company S (100%)	50,000	
Operational assets (net of accumulated depreciation)	65,000	36,000
Total assets	$188,000	$64,000
Liabilities	$ 44,000	$ 8,000
Payable to Company P		6,000
Common stock (Company P, par $5; Company S, par $5)	100,000	38,000
Contributed capital from pooling of interests	12,000	
Retained earnings	32,000	12,000
Total liabilities and stockholders' equity	$188,000	$64,000

Required:

1. Is this a pooling of interests or a combination by purchase? Explain why.
2. Give the journal entry that was made by Company P to record the acquisition.
3. Prepare a consolidated balance sheet immediately after the acquisition.
4. On the consolidated balance sheet, were the assets of the subsidiary added to those of the parent at book value or at market value? Explain why.
5. What were the balances in the accounts of Company P immediately prior to the acquisition for (*a*) investment and (*b*) common stock? Were any other account balances for either Company P or Company S changed by the acquisition? Explain.

E12–11 Comparison of the Pooling of Interests and the Purchase Methods

On January 1, 19A, Company P acquired 100% of the outstanding common stock of Company S. At date of acquisition, the balance sheet of Company S reflected the following book values (summarized):

Total assets (market value, $310,000)*	$290,000
Total liabilities	70,000
Stockholders' equity:	
Common stock, par $10	160,000
Retained earnings	60,000

*One half subject to depreciation; 10-year remaining life and no residual value.

Two separate and independent cases are given below that indicate how Company P acquired 100% of the outstanding stock of Company S.

Case A Exchanged three shares of its own common stock (par $1) for each share of Company S stock.

Case B Paid $16 per share for the stock of Company S.

Required:

For each case, answer the following:

1. Was this a combination by pooling of interests or by purchase? Explain.
2. Give the journal entry that Company P should make to record the acquisition. If none, explain why.
3. Give the journal entry in the accounts of Company S to record the acquisition. If none, explain why.
4. Analyze the transaction to determine the amount of goodwill purchased. If no goodwill was purchased, explain why.
5. In preparing a consolidated balance sheet, should the subsidiary's assets be included at book value or market value? Explain.

E12–12 *Identifying the Appropriate Consolidation Method*

On January 1, 19A, Company P purchased 100% of the outstanding voting shares of Company S in the open market for $80,000 cash. On that date (prior to the acquisition), the separate balance sheets (summarized) of the two companies reported the following book values:

	Prior to Acquisition	
	Company P	**Company S**
Cash	$ 92,000	$14,000
Receivable from Company P		4,000
Operational assets (net)	48,000	42,000
Total assets	$140,000	$60,000
Liabilities	$ 36,000	$ 9,000
Payable to Company S	4,000	
Common stock:		
Company P (nopar)	90,000	
Company S (par $10)		40,000
Retained earnings	10,000	11,000
Total liabilities and stockholders' equity	$140,000	$60,000

It was determined on the date of acquisition that the market value of the operational assets of Company S was $56,000.

Required:

1. Was this a combination by pooling of interests or by purchase? Explain why.
2. Give the journal entry that should be made by Company P at date of acquisition. If none is required, explain why.
3. Give the journal entry that should be made by Company S at date of acquisition. If none is required, explain why.
4. Analyze the acquisition to determine the amount of goodwill purchased.
5. Should the assets of Company S be included on the consolidated balance sheet at book value or market value? Explain.
6. Prepare a consolidated balance sheet immediately after acquisition.

E12–13 *Preparing a Consolidated Balance Sheet after Acquisition*

On January 4, 19A, Company P acquired all of the outstanding stock of Company S for $12 cash per share. At the date of acquisition, the balance sheet of Company S reflected the following:

Common stock (par $5)	$40,000
Retained earnings	36,000

Immediately after the acquisition, the balance sheets reflected the following:

	Balances, Jan. 4, 19A, Immediately after Acquisition	
	Company P	**Company S**
Cash	$ 22,000	$14,000
Receivable from Company P		9,000
Investment in Company S (100%), at cost	96,000	
Operational assets (net)	132,000	65,000*
Total assets	$250,000	$88,000
Liabilities	$ 18,000	$12,000
Payable to Company S	9,000	
Common stock (par $5)	120,000	40,000
Retained earnings	103,000	36,000
Total liabilities and stockholders' equity	$250,000	$88,000

*Determined by Company P to have a market value of $72,000 at date of acquisition.

Required:

1. Was this a combination by pooling of interests or by purchase? Explain why.
2. Give the journal entry that should be made by Company P to record the acquisition.
3. Analyze the acquisition to determine the amount of goodwill purchased.
4. Should the assets of Company S be included on the consolidated balance sheet at book value or market value? Explain.
5. Prepare a consolidated balance sheet immediately after acquisition.

E12–14 *Completing a Consolidation Worksheet*

On January 1, 19A, Company P acquired all of the outstanding voting stock of Company S by exchanging one share of its own stock for each share of Company S stock. At the date of the exchange, the balance sheet of Company S showed the following:

Common stock (par $10)	$50,000
Retained earnings	12,000

One year after acquisition the two companies prepared their separate financial statements as shown on the following worksheet:

COMPANY P and Its Subsidiary, COMPANY S (100% Owned)
Consolidated Balance Sheet and Income Statement
December 31, 19A

Items	Separate Statements: Company P	Separate Statements: Company S	Eliminations	Consolidated Statements
Income statement (for 19A):				
Sales revenue	130,000	36,000		
Cost of goods sold	(80,000)	(20,000)		
Expenses (not detailed)	(22,000)	(9,000)		
Net income	28,000	7,000		
Balance sheet (at December 31, 19A):				
Cash	32,000	28,000		
Receivable from Company P		3,000		
Investment in Company S (100%)	62,000			
Operational assets (net)	70,000	45,000		
Totals	164,000	76,000		
Liabilities	24,000	7,000		
Payable to Company S	3,000			
Common stock, Company P (par $10)	65,000			
Contributed capital	12,000			
Common stock, Company S (par $10)		50,000		
Beginning retained earnings, Company P	32,000			
Beginning retained earnings, Company S		12,000		
Net income, 19A (from above)	28,000	7,000		
Totals	164,000	76,000		

Required:

1. Give the journal entry that was made by Company P to record the pooling of interests on January 1, 19A.
2. Complete the Eliminations column in the above worksheet, then combine the two sets of statements in the last column to develop the consolidated income statement and balance sheet.

E12–15 Analyzing a Consolidation Worksheet

On January 1, 19A, Company P purchased all the outstanding voting stock of Company S at $4.50 per share. At that date the balance sheet of Company S reflected the following:

Common stock (par $1)	$10,000
Retained earnings	15,000

One year after acquisition each company prepared its own separate financial statements and Company P set up the following consolidation worksheet (partially completed):

	Separate Statements		Intercompany Eliminations		
Items	**Company P**	**Company S**	**Debit**	**Credit**	**Consolidated Balances**
Income statement (for 19A):					
Sales revenue	175,000	82,000			
Expenses (not detailed)	(121,000)	(66,000)			
Depreciation expense	(10,000)	(4,000)	(c) 900		
Amortization expense (goodwill)			(d) 550		
Net income	44,000	12,000			
Balance sheet (at Dec. 31, 19A):					
Cash	32,000	8,000			
Receivable from Co. P		5,000		(b) 5,000	
Investment in Co. S	45,000			(a) 45,000	
Operational assets (net)	80,000	42,000*	(a) 9,000	(c) 900	
Goodwill (amortize over 20 years)			(a) 11,000	(d) 550	
Totals	157,000	55,000			
Liabilities	16,000	18,000			
Payable to Co. S	5,000		(b) 5,000		
Common stock, Co. P	70,000				
Common stock, Co. S		10,000	(a) 10,000		
Beginning retained earnings, Co. P	22,000				
Beginning retained earnings, Co. S		15,000	(a) 15,000		
Net income, 19A (per above)	44,000†	12,000†			
Totals	157,000	55,000	51,450	51,450	

*Market value of the operational assets at acquisition was $9,000 above book value and their remaining useful life was 10 years.
†Carried down.

Required:

1. Give the journal entry made by Company P on January 1, 19A, to record the purchase of Company S stock.
2. Show how the $11,000 of goodwill was computed.
3. Complete the last column of the worksheet (note that under "Eliminations" debit/credit instead of +/– were used).
4. Give a brief explanation of eliminations (*c*) and (*d*).

Chrysler Corporation

E12–16 Explaining Consolidation Policy

The annual report for Chrysler includes the statement that "intercompany accounts and transactions have been eliminated in consolidation." In your own words, explain the meaning of this statement. Why is it necessary to eliminate all intercompany accounts and transactions in consolidation?

Maytag

E12–17 Explaining Consolidation Policy

The annual report for Maytag includes the following note:

> **Principles of Consolidation:** The consolidated financial statements include the accounts and transactions of the Company and its wholly owned subsidiaries. Subsidiaries located outside the United States are consolidated as of one month earlier than subsidiaries in the United States.

While this issue was not discussed directly in the chapter, why do you suppose foreign affiliates are consolidated as of one month earlier than US affiliates?

E12–18 Interpreting Accounting Policy

Martin Marietta Corporation

Martin Marietta Corporation is involved in the manufacture of leading edge technologies. The company's annual report states "costs in excess of net assets acquired are amortized ratably over appropriate periods ranging from 20 to 40 years." Based on the discussion in this chapter, express this policy in your own words.

E12–19 Analyzing an Acquisition

Colgate-Palmolive

The notes to the financial statements of Colgate-Palmolive contained the following information:

> **2. Acquisitions**
> In March 1992, the Company acquired the Menner Company for an aggregate price of $670 million paid with 11.6 million shares of the Company's common stock and $127 million in cash.

Should Colgate-Palmolive account for this transaction as a purchase or a pooling? Explain.

E12–20 Analysis of Goodwill

Capital Cities, Inc.

Capital Cities, Inc. owns television and radio stations, newspapers, and television networks, including ABC and ESPN. The Capital Cities balance sheet reports goodwill in the amount of $2,047,191 which is more than 30% of the company's total assets. This percentage is very large compared to most companies. Explain why you think Capitol Cities has such a large amount of goodwill reported on its balance sheet.

PROBLEMS

P12–1 Recording Investments

On August 4, 19A, Coffman Corporation purchased 1,000 shares of Wefald Company for $45,000. The following information applies to the stock price of Wefald Company:

12/31/19A	$52
12/31/19B	47
12/31/19C	38

The Wefald Company declares and pays cash dividends of $2 per share on June 1 of each year.

Required:

1. Prepare journal entries to record the facts in the case assuming that Coffman purchased the shares for the trading portfolio.
2. Prepare journal entries to record the facts in the case assuming that Coffman purchased the shares for the available-for-sale portfolio.
3. Prepare journal entries to record the facts in the case assuming that Coffman used the equity method to account for the investment. Coffman owns 30% of Wefald and Wefald reported $50,000 in income each year.

P12–2 Recording Investments

On March 1, 19A, HiTech Industries purchased 10,000 shares of Integrated Services Company for $20 per share. The following information applies to the stock price of Integrated Services:

12/31/19A	$18
12/31/19B	24
12/31/19C	30

Required:

1. Prepare journal entries to record the facts in the case assuming that HiTech purchased the shares for the trading portfolio.
2. Prepare journal entries to record the facts in the case assuming that HiTech purchased the shares for the available-for-sale portfolio.

P12–3 Recording Investments

On September 15, 19A, James Media Corporation purchased 5,000 shares of Community Broadcasting Company for $30 per share. The following information applies to the stock price of Community Broadcasting:

12/31/19A	$32
12/31/19B	24
12/31/19C	20

Required:

1. Prepare journal entries to record the facts in the case assuming that James Media purchased the shares for the trading portfolio.
2. Prepare journal entries to record the facts in the case assuming that James Media purchased the shares for the available-for-sale portfolio.

P12–4 Identifying, Recording, and Reporting Using the Proper Method to Account for an Equity Investment

During January 19A, Hexagon Company purchased 12,000 shares of the 200,000 outstanding common shares (nopar value) of Seven Corporation at $30 per share. This block of stock was purchased as a long-term investment. Assume the accounting period for each company ends December 31.

Subsequent to acquisition, the following data were available:

	19A	19B
Income reported by Seven Corporation at December 31	$40,000	$60,000
Cash dividends declared and paid by Seven Corporation during the year	60,000	80,000
Market price per share of Seven common stock on December 31	28	29

Required:

1. What accounting method should be used by the company? Why?
2. Give the journal entries for the company for each year (use parallel columns) for the following (if none, explain why):
   a. Acquisition of Seven Corporation stock.
   b. Net income reported by Seven Corporation.
   c. Dividends received from Seven Corporation.
   d. Market value effects at year-end.
3. Show how the following amounts should be reported on the financial statements for each year:
   a Long-term investment.
   b. Stockholders' equity—unrealized loss.
   c. Revenues.

P12–5 *Identifying, Recording, and Reporting Using the Proper Method to Account for Two Different Equity Investments*

During January 19A, Crystal Company purchased the shares listed below as a long-term investment:

Stock	Number of Shares Outstanding	Purchase	Cost per Share
Q Corporation Common (nopar)	90,000	12,600	$ 5
R Corporation Preferred, nonvoting (par $10)	20,000	12,000	$30

Subsequent to acquisition, the following data were available:

	19A	19B
Net income reported at December 31:		
Q Corporation	$30,000	$36,000
R Corporation	40,000	48,000
Dividends declared and paid per share during the year:		
Q Corporation common stock	$0.80	$0.85
R Corporation preferred stock	0.90	0.90
Market value per share at December 31:		
Q Corporation common stock	4.00	4.00
R Corporation preferred stock	29.00	30.00

Required:

1. What accounting method should be used for the investment in Q common stock? R preferred stock? Why?
2. Give the journal entries for the company for each year in parallel columns (if none, explain why) for each of the following:
   a. Purchase of the investments.
   b. Income reported by Q and R Corporations.
   c. Dividends received from Q and R Corporations.
   d. Market value effects at year-end.
3. For each year, show how the following amounts should be reported on the financial statements for 19A:
   a. Long-term investment.
   b. Stockholders' equity—unrealized loss.
   c. Revenues.

P12–6 *Comparing Methods to Account for Various Levels of Ownership of Voting Stock*

Company C had outstanding 30,000 shares of common stock, par value $10 per share. On January 1, 19B, Company D purchased some of these shares at $25 per share. At the end of 19B, Company C reported the following: income, $50,000; and cash dividends declared and paid during the year, $25,500. The market value of Company C stock at the end of 19B was $22 per share.

Required:

1. For each case given below (in the tabulation), identify the method of accounting that should be used by Company D. Explain why.
2. Give the journal entries for Company D at the dates indicated below for each of the two independent cases. If no entry is required, explain why. Use the following format:

Tabulation of Items	Case A 3,600 Shares Purchased	Case B 10,500 Shares Purchased
a. Entry to record the acquisition at January 1, 19B.		
b. Entry to recognize the income reported by Company C for 19B.		
c. Entry to recognize the dividends declared and paid by Company C.		
d. Entry to recognize market value effect at end of 19B.		

3. Complete the following schedule to show the separate amounts that should be reported on the 19B financial statements of Company D:

	Dollar Amounts	
	Case A	Case B
Balance sheet:		
Investments and funds		
Stockholders' equity		
Income statement:		
Revenue from investments		

4. Explain why assets, stockholders' equity, and revenues are different between the two cases.

P12–7 Comparing the Market Value and Equity Methods

Packer Company purchased, as a long-term investment, some of the 200,000 shares of the outstanding common stock of Boston Corporation. The annual accounting period for each company ends December 31. The following transactions occurred during 19E:

Jan	10	Purchased shares of common stock of Boston at $15 per share as follows: Case A—30,000 shares. Case B—80,000 shares.
Dec	31	Received the 19E financial statements of Boston Corporation; the reported net income was $90,000.
	31	Received a cash dividend of $0.60 per share from Boston Corporation.
	31	Market price of Boston stock, $9 per share.

Required:

1. For each case, identify the accounting method that should be used by the company. Explain why.
2. Give the journal entries for each case for the above transactions. If no entry is required, explain why. (Hint: Use parallel columns for Case A and Case B.)
3. Give the amounts for each case that should be reported on the 19E financial statements. Use the following format:

	Case A	Case B
Balance sheet (partial):		
Investments and funds:		
Investments in common stock, Boston Corporation		
Stockholders' equity:		
Unrealized loss		
Income statement (partial):		
Revenue from investments		

P12–8 Comparing the Market Value and Equity Methods

Ship Corporation had outstanding 100,000 shares of nopar common stock. On January 10, 19B, Shore Company purchased a block of these shares in the open market at $20 per share. At the end of 19B, Ship Corporation reported net income of $300,000 and cash dividends of $.60 per share. At December 31, 19B, the Ship stock was selling at $18 per share. This problem involves two separate cases:

Case A 10,000 shares of Ship common stock were purchased.

Case B 40,000 shares of Ship common stock were purchased.

Required:

1. For each case, identify the accounting method that should be used by the company. Explain why.
2. For each case, in parallel columns, give the journal entries for each of the following (if no entry is required, explain why):
   a. Acquisition.
   b. Revenue recognition.
   c. Dividends received.
   d. Market value effects.
3. For each case show how the following should be reported on the 19B financial statements:
   a. Long-term investments.
   b. Market effects.
   c. Revenues.
4. Explain why the amounts reported in requirement 3 are different between the two cases.

P12–9 Comparing Accounting for Equity Securities with Accounting for Debt Securities

(Hint: You may want to review material in Chapter 10.)

On January 1, 19B, Duplex Company purchased $80,000, 12% bonds of Quatro Company as a long-term investment, at 100 (plus any accrued interest). Interest is payable annually on December 31. The bonds have six years to maturity from December 31, 19A. The company's annual accounting period ends December 31. In addition, on January 2, 19B, the company purchased in the market 10% of the 20,000 shares of outstanding common stock of Quatro Company at $50 per share.

Required:

1. Give the journal entry to record the purchase of the bonds on January 1, 19B. The company intends to hold the bonds until maturity.
2. Give the journal entry to record the purchase of the common stock on January 2, 19B.
3. Give the journal entry assuming a cash dividend of $3 per share was declared and received on the Quatro stock on December 28, 19B.
4. Give the required journal entries for December 31, 19B.
5. Show how the long-term investments and the related revenues should be reported on the 19B annual financial statements. Market price of Quatro stock was $55 at the end of 19B.

P12–10 Analyzing an Acquisition and Preparing a Consolidated Balance Sheet

During January 19A, Company P acquired all of the outstanding voting shares of Company S by exchanging one share of its own unissued voting common stock for two shares of Company S stock. Immediately prior to acquisition, the separate balance sheets of the two companies reflected the following:

	Balances Immediately prior to Acquisition	
	Company P	**Company S**
Cash	$250,000	$ 38,000
Receivable from Company P		6,000
Inventory	60,000	12,000
Operational assets (net of accumulated depreciation)	80,000	58,000
Total assets	$390,000	$114,000
Liabilities	$ 52,000	$ 20,000
Payable to Company S	6,000	
Common stock, Company P (par $8)	176,000	
Common stock, Company S (par $10)		80,000
Contributed capital from pooling		
Retained earnings	156,000	14,000
Total liabilities and stockholders' equity	$390,000	$114,000

Additional Data:

a. At the date of acquisition, the market price of Company S stock was $18 per share; there was no established market for Company P stock.

b. The operational assets of Company S were appraised independently at the date of acquisition at $96,000.

Required:

1. Is this a purchase or a pooling of interests? Explain why.
2. What account balances on each of the above balance sheets would be changed by the exchange of shares? List each account and amount.
3. Give the journal entry that should be made by each company to record the exchange; if no entry is required, explain why.
4. How much goodwill should be recognized? Why?
5. Prepare a consolidated balance sheet immediately after the acquisition.
6. Did you use any market values in solving the above requirements? Explain why.

P12–11 *Analyzing an Acquisition and Preparing a Consolidated Balance Sheet*

Assume the same facts given in problem 12–10 except that instead of an exchange of shares of stock, Company P purchased from the stockholders 100% of the outstanding voting shares of Company S at a cash price of $144,000.

Required:

1. Is this a purchase or a pooling of interests? Explain why.
2. What account balances on each of the balance sheets would be changed by the purchase of the shares? List each account and amount.
3. Give the journal entry that should be made by each company to record the exchange; if no entry is required, explain why.
4. How much goodwill should be recognized? Why?
5. Prepare a consolidated balance sheet immediately after acquisition.
6. Did you use any market values in solving the above requirements? Explain why.

P12–12 *Analyzing Entry to Record an Acquisition and Preparing a Consolidated Balance Sheet*

On January 1, 19A, the separate balance sheets of two corporations showed the following:

	Balances, Jan. 1, 19A	
	Company P	Company S
Cash	$ 18,000	$11,000
Receivable from Company P		2,000
Operational assets (net)	92,000	27,000
Total assets	$110,000	$40,000
Accounts payable	$ 20,000	$ 8,000
Payable to Company S	2,000	
Common stock (par $10)	50,000	20,000
Retained earnings	38,000	12,000
Total liabilities and stockholders' equity	$110,000	$40,000

On January 3, 19A, Company P acquired all of the outstanding voting shares of Company S by exchanging one share of its own stock for two shares of Company S stock.

Required:

1. Was this a combination by pooling of interests or by purchase? Explain why.
2. Company P made the following journal entry on its books, at the date of acquisition, to record the investment:

Jan. 3, 19A:	Investment in Co. S.	32,000	
	Common stock		10,000
	Contributed capital from pooling of interests		22,000

   Explain the basis for each of the three amounts in this entry.
3. Should any goodwill be recognized on the consolidated balance sheet? Explain why.
4. Prepare a consolidated balance sheet immediately after the acquisition.

P12–13 *Analyzing Consolidation Method and Preparing a Consolidated Balance Sheet*

On January 2, 19A, Company P acquired all the outstanding stock of Company S by exchanging its own stock for the stock of Company S. One share of Company P stock was exchanged for two shares of Company S stock. Immediately after the acquisition was recorded by Company P, the balance sheets showed the following:

	Balances, Jan. 2, 19A, Immediately after Acquisition	
	Company P	Company S
Cash	$ 42,000	$24,000
Receivable from Company S	7,000	
Inventory	58,000	18,000
Investment in Company S (100%)	78,000	
Operational assets (net)	70,000	40,000
Other assets	4,000	12,000
Total assets	$259,000	$94,000
Liabilities	$ 31,000	$ 9,000
Payable to Company P		7,000
Common stock (par $4)	100,000	48,000
Contributed capital from pooling of interests	54,000	
Retained earnings	74,000	30,000
Total liabilities and stockholders' equity	$259,000	$94,000

Required:

1. Was this a combination by pooling of interests or by purchase? Explain why.

2. Give the journal entry that was made by Company P to record the acquisition on January 2, 19A. Explain the basis for each amount included in the entry.
3. Should the assets of Company S be included on the consolidated balance sheet at book value or market value? Explain.
4. Will any goodwill be recognized on the consolidated balance sheet? Explain why.
5. Prepare a consolidated balance sheet immediately after acquisition.

P12–14 *Analyzing Goodwill and Preparing a Consolidated Balance Sheet*

On January 5, 19A, Company P purchased all the outstanding stock of Company S for $80,000 cash. Immediately after the acquisition the separate balance sheets of the two companies showed the following:

	Jan. 5, 19A, Immediately after Acquisition	
	Company P	**Company S**
Cash	$ 18,000	$ 7,000
Accounts receivable (net)	12,000	5,000
Receivable from Company S	3,000	
Inventory	40,000	22,000
Investment in Company S (at cost)	80,000	
Operational assets (net)	128,000	54,000
Other assets	10,000	2,000
Total assets	$291,000	$90,000
Accounts payable	$ 15,000	$23,000
Payable to Company P		3,000
Bonds payable	70,000	
Common stock (par $10)	160,000	50,000
Contributed capital in excess of par	16,000	
Retained earnings	30,000	14,000
Total liabilities and stockholders' equity	$291,000	$90,000

The operational assets of Company S were estimated to have a market value at date of acquisition of $62,000.

Required:

1. Was this a combination by pooling of interests or by purchase? Explain why.
2. Give the journal entry that Company P should make at the date of acquisition.
3. Analyze the acquisition to determine the amount of goodwill purchased.
4. Should the assets of Company S be included on the consolidated balance sheet at book value or market value? Explain.
5. Prepare a consolidated balance sheet immediately after acquisition.

CASES

C12–1 *Analyzing the Financial Effects of the Market Value and Equity Methods*

On January 1, 19B, Woodrow Company purchased 30% of the outstanding common stock of Trevor Corporation at a total cost of $560,000. Management intends to hold the stock for the long term. On the December 31, 19B, balance sheet, the investment in Trevor Corporation was $720,000, but no additional Trevor stock was purchased. The company received $80,000 in cash dividends from Trevor. The dividends were declared and paid during 19B. The company used the equity method to account for its investment in Trevor. The market price of Trevor stock increased during 19B to a total value of $600,000.

Required:

1. Explain why the investment account balance increased from $560,000 to $720,000 during 19B.
2. What amount of revenue from the investment was reported during 19B?
3. If Woodrow used the market value method, what amount of revenue from the investment should have been reported in 19B?
4. If the market value method was used, what amount would be reported as the investment in Trevor Corporation on the December 31, 19B, balance sheet?

C12–2 Comparing the Pooling of Interests and the Purchase Methods

Some analysts believe that management would prefer to account for an acquisition under the pooling of interests method instead of the purchase method. Accounting rules do not permit management to select the method, but these analysts believe that management will structure the transaction so that it will be accounted for as a pooling. One of the alleged benefits of the pooling of interests method for management is that return on investment (net income/total assets) is usually higher under pooling. Why would you expect return on investment to be higher under pooling?

C12–3 An International Perspective

Grand Metropolitan

Grand Metropolitan is a major international company that is located in London. A recent annual report contained the following information concerning their accounting policies.

> **Acquisitions** On the acquisition of a business, including an interest in a related company, fair values are attributed to the group's share of net tangible assets and significant owned brands acquired. Where the cost of acquisition exceeds the values attributable to such net assets, the difference is treated as goodwill and is written off directly to reserves in the year of acquisition.
>
> **Intangible assets** Significant owned brands, acquired after 1st January 1985, the value of which is not expected to diminish in the foreseeable future, are recorded in the balance sheet as fixed intangible assets. No amortisation is provided on these assets but their value is reviewed annually by the directors and the cost written down as an exceptional item where permanent diminution in value has occurred.

The word *reserves* is used by Grand Metropolitan to mean retained earnings. Discuss how this accounting treatment compares to procedures used in this country.

C12–4 Financial Statement Analysis

Toys "Я" Us

Refer to the financial statement of Toys "Я" Us given in Appendix B at the end of this book.

Required:

The notes indicate that the company eliminates all intercompany balances and transactions during consolidation. Explain.

13

HOME SHOPPING CLUB'S PREFERRED MEMBER MAGAZINE • MARCH/APRIL 1995 • $2.75

Bargaineer

Garden Solutions & Troy-Bilt: We're how America grows

How F
Hayn
made his m
in Beverly

Plus a rainbow of springtime fashions & jewelry!

STATEMENT OF CASH FLOWS

Each year, many companies report healthy profits but file for bankruptcy nevertheless. Some investors consider such a situation to be a strange paradox, but sophisticated analysts understand how this situation can occur. These analysts recognize that the income statement is prepared under the accrual concept (revenue is reported when earned and the related expense is matched with the revenue). The income statement does not report cash collections and cash payments. Troubled companies usually file for bankruptcy because they cannot meet their cash obligations (e.g., they cannot pay their suppliers or meet their required interest payments). The income statement does not help analysts assess the cash flows of a company. The statement of cash flows (SCF) is designed to help statement users evaluate a company's cash inflows and outflows.

LEARNING OBJECTIVES

After studying this chapter, you should be able to:

Management Decision Setting
HOME SHOPPING NETWORK

Technology Brings Shopping to the Home

The retail industry is extremely competitive. Merchants constantly seek new ways to meet customer needs at lower costs. Home shopping is a rapidly growing segment of the retail industry as more families rely on two incomes. Consumers spend more than $80 billion each year buying merchandise from catalogues. There are now two cable networks that permit shoppers to view merchandise on television and purchase it with a simple telephone call. Cable home shopping generates over $2 billion in sales each year.

Home Shopping Network, Inc. 1993 Annual Report
click!
Tuning Into Our Customers.

The Home Shopping Network (HSN) produces three separate retail sales programs that are available on cable and broadcast channels across the country. Profitability for HSN has shown a great deal of variability, ranging from an $8.9 million loss in one year to a $37.2 million profit in the next. Despite this variability, cash flows for HSN have remained strong. As the chairman of the board, Roy Speer, noted in a recent letter to shareholders:

> As demonstrated in previous years, HSN's cash flows from operations continue to show strength. Throughout the year HSN used improved cash flow to enhance HSN's technologically–based infrastructure and retire $4.1 million in debt as attractive market opportunities became available. As a continuation of this program, on October 15, 1992, HSN retired an additional $37.5 million of its 11 3/4% Senior Notes due in 1996, as permitted under the note indenture, funded primarily from internally generated cash.

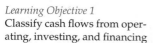

BUSINESS BACKGROUND

Clearly, net income is an important number, but as Mr. Speer's letter implies, cash flow is critical. Cash flow permits a company to expand its operations, replace needed assets, take advantage of market opportunities, and pay dividends to its owners. Some Wall Street analysts go as far as saying "cash flow is king". Both managers and analysts need to understand the various sources and uses of cash that are associated with business activity. There are three main categories of activities that generate and use cash: activity related to operating the business, activity related to financing the business, and activity related to investments in productive assets. The statement of cash flows (SCF) is designed to provide managers and analysts with information concerning these important activities. The SCF for the Home Shopping Network is shown in Exhibit 13–1. We will now discuss the information that is provided on this required statement.

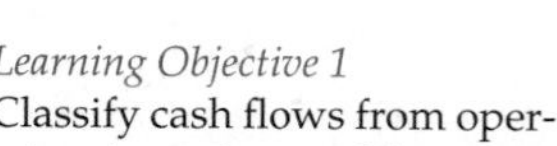

CLASSIFICATIONS ON THE SCF

Learning Objective 1
Classify cash flows from operating, investing, and financing activities.

A **cash equivalent** is a short-term, highly liquid investment with an original maturity of less than three months.

Basically, the SCF explains how the cash balance at the beginning of the year became the cash balance at the end of the year. For purposes of the SCF, the definition of cash includes cash and cash equivalents. **Cash equivalents** are defined as short-term, highly liquid investments that are both:

a. Readily convertible to known amounts of cash.
b. So near their maturity that they present insignificant risk of changes in value because of changes in interest rates.

Generally, only investments with original maturities of less than three months qualify as a cash equivalent under this definition.[1] Examples of cash equivalents are Treasury bills, money market funds, and commercial paper.

[1] Original maturity means original maturity to the entity holding the investment. For example, both a three-month Treasury bill and a three-year Treasury note purchased three months from maturity qualify as cash equivalents. However, a Treasury note purchased three years ago does not become a cash equivalent when its remaining maturity is three months.

Consolidated Statements of Cash Flows **Exhibit 13–1**

Home Shopping Network, Inc. and Subsidiaries

	Years Ended August 31,		
	1992	**1991**	**1990**
		(In thousands)	
Cash flows from operating activities:			
Net earnings (loss)	**$37,293**	$ (8,945)	$38,754
Adjustments to reconcile net earnings (loss) to net cash provided by operating activities:			
Depreciation and amortization	**46,894**	51,240	46,647
Provision for losses on accounts and notes receivable	**34**	6,893	(236)
Loss on sale of assets	**124**	411	255
Noncash interest income	**(968)**	—	—
Loss (gain) on retirement of long-term obligations	**194**	(1,105)	(10,346)
Deferred income taxes	**11,902**	(18,771)	3,024
Common stock issued for services provided	**3,463**	2,857	152
Equity in losses of unconsolidated affiliates	**99**	—	—
Change in current assets and liabilities:			
Increase in accounts receivable	**(11,529)**	(2,756)	(2,802)
Decrease in income tax receivable	—	—	2,158
(Increase) decrease in inventories	**(296)**	26,686	(26,634)
(Increase) decrease in other current assets	**1,840**	(5,819)	(1,326)
Increase (decrease) in accounts payable	**(17,362)**	(7,622)	28,140
Increase (decrease) in sales taxes payable	**(366)**	304	1,274
Increase (decrease) in accrued liabilities	**(26,217)**	48,403	10,414
Net cash provided by operating activities	**45,105**	91,776	89,474
Cash flows from investing activities:			
Capital expenditures	**(35,973)**	(52,936)	(34,741)
Proceeds from sale of assets	**410**	497	730
Increase in intangible assets	**(1,830)**	(6,439)	(8,833)
Increase in long-term investments	**(5,710)**	—	(45)
Increase in notes receivable and other	**(3,432)**	(3,854)	(4,490)
Proceeds from long-term notes receivable	**2,231**	—	—
Net cash used in investing activities	**(44,304)**	(62,732)	(47,379)
Cash flows from financing activities:			
Principal payments on and redemptions of long-term obligations	**(7,432)**	(16,230)	(49,731)
Proceeds from issuance of common stock	**3,561**	256	2,603
Purchase of treasury stock	—	(10,109)	(3,918)
Cash portion of dividend	**(4,971)**	—	—
Net cash used in financing activities	**(8,842)**	(26,083)	(51,046)
Net increase (decrease) in cash and cash equivalents	**(8,041)**	2,961	(8,951)
Cash and cash equivalents at beginning of year	**61,589**	58,628	67,579
Cash and cash equivalents at end of year	**$53,548**	$61,589	$58,628

The accompanying Notes to Consolidated Financial Statements are an integral part of these statements.

As you can see in Exhibit 13–1, the SCF reports cash inflows and outflows based on three broad categories: (1) operating activities, (2) investing activities, and (3) financing activities. To improve comparability, *FASB Statement 95* defines each category included in the required SCF. These definitions (with explanations) are as follows:

A. **Cash flows from operating activities.** This classification reports both the cash inflows and cash outflows that are directly related to income from normal operations reported on the income statement. Under this classification, the usual cash flows are:

Cash flows from operating activities are cash inflows and outflows directly related to earnings from normal operations.

Inflows Cash Received from	*Outflows* Cash Paid for
Customers.	Purchase of goods for resale.
Interest on receivables.	Interest on liabilities.
Dividends.	Income taxes.
	Salaries and wages.

The difference between the above inflows and outflows is called the net cash inflow (outflow) from operating activities. For Home Shopping Network, this amount was an inflow of $45,105,000 for 1992.

Cash flows from investing activities are cash inflows and outflows related to the acquisition or sale of productive facilities and the making or collecting of loans.

B. **Cash flows from investing activities.** This classification reports cash inflows and outflows that are related to the acquisition of productive facilities used by the company and other noncash assets. Under this classification, the cash outflows represent the "investments" of cash by the entity to acquire its noncash assets; and the cash inflows occur only when cash is received from the prior investments. Typical cash flows from investing activities are:

Inflows Cash Received from	*Outflows* Cash Paid for
Disposal of property, plant, and equipment.	Property, plant, and equipment.
Disposal of investments in securities.	Purchase of long-term investments.
Collection of a loan (excluding interest, which is an operating activity).	Lending to other parties.
Disposal of other assets used in productive activities (excluding inventories which is an operating activity).	Other assets used in productive activities (excluding inventories).

The difference between the above cash inflows and outflows is called net cash inflow (outflow) from investing activities. For Home Shopping Network, this amount was an outflow of $44,304,000 for 1992.

Cash flows from financing activities are cash inflows and outflows related to how cash was obtained to finance the enterprise.

C. **Cash flows from financing activities.** This classification represents both cash inflows and outflows that are related to how cash was obtained to finance the enterprise (including its operations). Under this classification, the cash inflows represent the financing activities used to obtain cash for the entity. The cash outflows occur only when cash is paid back to the owners and creditors for their prior cash-providing activities. Usual cash flows from financing activities are:

Inflows Cash Received from	*Outflows* Cash Paid for
Owners (issuing equity securities).	Dividends (to owners).
Borrowing on notes, mortgages, bonds, etc.	Payment of principal amounts borrowed - (excluding interest, which is an operating activity).
Owners for treasury stock sold.	

The difference between the above cash inflows and outflows is called net cash inflow (outflow) from financing activities. For Home Shopping Network, this amount was an outflow of $8,842,000 for 1992.

Noncash investing and financing activities are transactions that do not have direct cash flow effects; reported on the SCF in narrative or schedule form.

D. **Noncash investing and financing activities.** These activities are the investing and financing transactions that involve noncash effects. An example is the purchase of a building where there is no cash down payment and the seller provides the mortgage. In this case, there is an investing activity that did not cause a cash outflow and a financing activity that did not cause a cash inflow. Noncash activities must be reported in a separate schedule or set out separately in the disclosure notes. Home Shopping Network did not report any noncash investing and financing activities.

A CLOSER LOOK AT THE SCF

The operating activities section of the SCF describes cash flows related to the profit-making activities of a business. Notice in Exhibit 13–1 that in 1991, Home Shopping Network lost $8,945,000 but generated positive cash flows of $91,776,000. The cash flows from operating activities were actually larger in 1991 than in 1992 when the company earned a profit of $37,293,000! The SCF helps the analyst understand the causes of changes in the cash flows of a business.

First, let's review why the income of a company and its cash flows from operating activities should be so different. Remember that the income statement is prepared under the accrual concept. Revenues are recorded when earned without regard to when the related cash flows occur. Expenses are matched with revenues and recorded in the same period as the revenues without regard to when the related cash flows occur. The statement of cash flows starts with the income number computed under the accrual concept and adjusts it to a cash basis.

Notice in Exhibit 13–1 that the SCF for Home Shopping Network starts with net earnings for 1992 of $37,293,000 and adds depreciation and amortization. As you know, depreciation and amortization are noncash expenses which were subtracted from revenue on the income statement. By adding them back, we begin the process of converting accrual income to a cash basis.

The SCF for the Home Shopping Network also reports an increase in accounts receivable during 1992 in the amount of $11,259,000 which was subtracted from net earnings. Why is an increase in accounts receivable subtracted from net earnings? Remember that an account receivable is a sale that took place on credit and, therefore, did not generate cash. The increase in accounts receivable represents noncash revenues that must be subtracted from net earnings to convert that figure to a cash basis. We will discuss other adjustments later in this chapter.

By reviewing the operating activities section of the SCF, you can determine the specific reasons why cash flows from operating activities were stronger in 1991 than 1992. The single biggest factor was the large increase in accrued liabilities (which meant that certain accrued expenses were not paid in cash during 1991) followed by a reduction in accrued liabilities in 1992 (which required a cash outflow).

The investing activities section of the SCF shows the long-term investment strategy for Home Shopping Network. The letter from the chairman of the board indicated that the company was investing in technologically based infrastructure. The SCF reports that the company had nearly $125 million in capital expenditures during a three-year period.

The financing activities section of the SCF shows that Home Shopping Network has generated none of its financial resources from owners and creditors. Indeed during the past three years, the company has paid out more to owners and creditors than it has received. This is further evidence of the strong cash flows that HSN can generate from operating activities.

To give you a better understanding of the SCF, we will now discuss the preparation of this statement. There are two alternative approaches for preparing the operating activities section of the SCF:

1. The **indirect method,** which adjusts net income to compute net cash inflow (outflow) from operating activities. This is the method used by the Home Shopping Network and most other companies. According to *Accounting Trends & Techniques,*[2] 97 percent of the companies that were surveyed use the indirect method. Because of the extensive use of this method in actual financial reporting, we will emphasize it in our discussions.

The **indirect method** of preparing the operating activities section of the SCF adjusts net income to compute net cash inflow (outflow) from operating activities.

2. The **direct method,** which reports the components of cash flows from operating activities as gross receipts and gross payments, such as total cash receipts from customers and total cash payments to employees. This method starts with cash revenues and cash expenses

The **direct method** of preparing the operating activities section of the SCF reports components of cash flows from operating activities as gross receipts and gross payments.

[2]*Accounting Trends & Techniques* (New York: American Institute of CPAs, 1993), p. 452.

The Home Shopping Network utilizes state-of-the-art technology, but it is still necessary to have people answer the telephone calls from customers.

to compute net cash inflow (outflow) from operating activities. This method will be illustrated in Supplement A to this chapter. You can see an actual SCF prepared under the direct method in Exhibit 13–7, in Supplement A. The direct method was recommended by the FASB but it is rarely seen in practice. Many financial executives have reported that they do not use the direct method because it is more expensive to implement than the indirect method.

PREPARATION OF THE SCF, INDIRECT METHOD

In the previous chapters, you made a number of journal entries to record transactions. These amounts were posted to T-accounts which were used to prepare the income statement and the balance sheet. You cannot prepare the SCF by using amounts recorded in T-accounts because these amounts are based on accrual accounting. Instead, you must analyze numbers recorded under the accrual method and adjust them to a cash basis. To prepare the SCF, you need the following data:

1. A complete income statement, used primarily in preparing cash flows from operating activities.
2. Comparative balance sheets, used in preparing the cash flows from all activities (operating, investing, and financing).
3. Additional details concerning selected accounts that reflect several different kinds of transactions and events. Analysis of individual accounts is necessary because the total change amount in an account balance during the year often does not reveal the underlying nature of the cash flows.

Because of the complexity of the SCF for the Home Shopping Network, we will use a simplified case to illustrate the procedures for preparing the SCF. Information for the UTEX Company is shown in Exhibit 13–2. We will also make frequent reference to the SCF for Home Shopping Network so that you can see how these procedures affect an actual company.

To prepare the SCF, you will analyze the balance sheet and income statement accounts to prepare the three sections of the statement:

1. *Cash flow from operating activities* You should analyze accounts that are related to earning income. This will include all income statement accounts and the balance sheet accounts that are related to income statement accounts. The following relationships are the ones that you will encounter most frequently when preparing the SCF:

Income Statement Account	Related Balance Sheet Account	Impact on the SCF
Sales Revenue	Accounts Receivable	Cash collected from customers
Cost of Goods Sold	Inventory and Accounts Payable	Cash payments to suppliers
Operating Expenses	Prepaid Expenses and Accrued Liabilities	Cash payments for operating expenses
Depreciation Expense	Accumulated Depreciation	No cash flow

2. *Cash flow from investing activities* To prepare this section, you will analyze changes in *long-term asset* accounts such as the purchase or sale of property, plant, and equipment.

UTEX Company: Current Income Statement and Comparative Balance Sheet (in thousands) **Exhibit 13–2**

A. Income statement for the year ended December 31,19B:

Sales revenue	$ 66
Salaries expense	(20)
Cost of goods sold	(8)
Depreciation expense	(4)
Administrative and selling expense (excluding salaries)	(12)
Net income	$ 22

B. Comparative balance sheet, December 31, 19B:

Items	12/31/19A	12/31/19B
Cash (no cash equivalents)	$ 42	$ 76
Accounts receivable	21	27
Inventory	10	12
Plant assets	82	81
Less: Accumulated depreciation	(20)	(14)
Total assets	$135	$182
Salaries payable	$ 3	$ 5
Note payable, long-term	46	40
Common stock (par $10)	61	101
Contributed capital in excess of par	9	17
Retained earnings	16	19
Total liabilities and stockholders' equity	$135	$182

C. Analysis of individual accounts to identify cash flows (source—accounting records):

a. Plant Assets account:
   (1) Purchased plant assets for cash, $30
   (2) Sold old plant assets for cash, $21; recorded as follows (at book value):

Cash	21	
Accumulated depreciation	10	
Plant assets		31

b. Long-Term Note Payable account:
   Payments on note principal, $6

c. Statement of retained earnings:

Balance, December 31, 19A	$ 16
Net income for 19B	22
Cash dividend paid in cash at end of 19B	(19)
Balance, December 31, 19B	$ 19

d. Issued common stock for $48 cash.

3. *Cash flow from financing activities* This section reflects changes in long-term liability and owners' equity accounts such as the issuance of new debt and the payment of dividends.

Computing Cash Flow from Operating Activities

Converting Revenues to a Cash Basis

Learning Objective 2
Compute cash flow from operating activities.

Accrual basis sales revenue often includes sales that did not generate cash. These *noncash* amounts cause changes in the balance of accounts receivable. If less cash is collected from customers than the amount of revenue recognized on the accrual basis, the balance of accounts receivable will increase. We can see an example of this when we analyze the accounts receivable for UTEX. It is helpful to use a T-account to analyze changes in account balances (in thousands):

Accounts Receivable			
Beg. bal.	21		
Sales	66	Collections	60
End. bal.	27		

By entering the amount of sales revenue from the income statement and the beginning and ending balance of accounts receivable from the balance sheet, we can compute the cash collected from sales as $60 because it is the amount needed to balance the T-account. From our UTEX example, we can generalize a rule: *When there is an increase in accounts receivable, cash collected from customers is always less than accrual revenue; when there is a decrease in accounts receivable, cash collected from customers is always more than accrual revenue.* This rule can be summarized with the following formula to convert amounts from the accrual basis to the cash basis for all revenues:

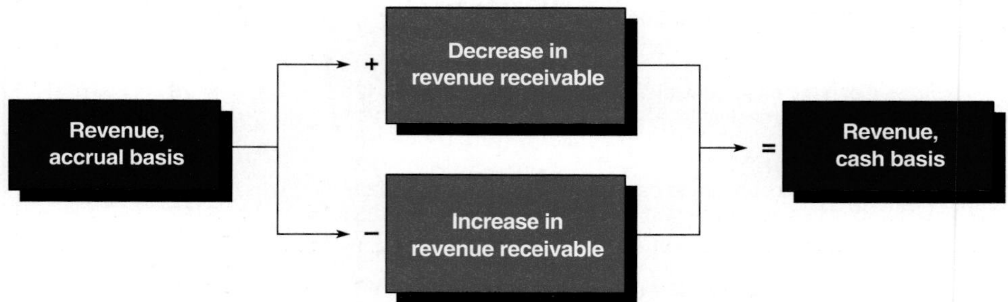

This formula applies to all revenues, without regard to the source. You may use the formula for revenue from the sale of merchandise, service, interest, dividends, royalty, rent, and so on.

The following cases illustrate use of this formula (in thousands):

Case	Accounts Receivable	Revenue (Accrual Basis)	Change A	Change B	Change C	Cash Basis (Inflow)
A	No change	$66	—			$66
B	Increase, $6	66		− $6		60
C	Decrease, $6	66			+ $6	72

The income statement for UTEX Company (Exhibit 13–2) reported revenue of $66, but $6 of the sales were on credit and not collected in cash. This amount can be computed by either analyzing the Accounts Receivable T-account or by using the conversion formula. To prepare the SCF under the indirect method, $6 of noncash revenue is subtracted from net income to convert income to cash flow from operating activities.

UTEX Company: Schedules to Prepare the SCF, Indirect Method (in thousands) **Exhibit 13–3**

Schedule A, Indirect Method Computation of net cash flow from operating activities (conversion of net income to net cash flow):

Items (Exhibit 13–2)	Amount	Explanation
Net income, accrual basis	$22	From income statement.
Add (subtract) to convert to cash basis:		
Accounts receivable increase	− 6	Subtract because cash inflow from sales transactions is less than accrual basis revenues.
Salaries payable increase	+ 2	Add because cash payments to employees are less than accrual basis salary expense.
Inventory increase	− 2	Subtract because cash payments to suppliers are more than accrual basis of cost of goods sold.
Depreciation expense	+ 4	Add because depreciation expense is a noncash expense.
Net cash inflow from operating activities	$20	Reported on the SCF.

Schedule B, Computation of net cash flows from investing activities (analysis of comparative balance sheet and individual accounts):

Items from Balance Sheet and Account Analysis	Cash Inflow (Outflows)	Explanation
Purchase of plant assets	$(30)	Payment in full for noncash asset.
Sale of plant assets	21	Total cash received from sale of noncash asset.
Net cash inflow (outflow) from investing activities	$ (9)	Reported on the SCF.

Schedule C, Computation of net cash flows from financing activities:

Items from Balance Sheet and Account Analysis	Cash Inflows (Outflows)	Explanation
Issuance of common stock	$ 48	From Common Stock account.
Payments on long-term note	(6)	From Long-Term Note Payable account.
Paid cash dividend	(19)	From Statement of Retained Earnings.
Net cash inflow (outflow) from financing activities	$ 23	Reported on the SCF.

To keep track of all the adjustments that are made to convert the income statement to the SCF, it is useful to set up a schedule to record the computations. An example for UTEX is shown in Exhibit 13–3. Notice that it is the $6 of noncash revenue that is subtracted from net income to compensate for the fact that the full $66 of revenue was included in the original computation of net income.

As you can see in the SCF for Home Shopping Network (Exhibit 13–1), the company's accounts receivable increased by $11,529,000 during 1992. This increase represents sales on credit that did not generate cash. As a result, HSN subtracted the increase in accounts receivable to convert its net earnings to a cash basis.

FINANCIAL ANALYSIS

Managing Cash Flows

The SCF highlights important information for both managers and analysts. Normally, a large increase in sales volume is viewed as a positive indication. In some cases, it might not be. If managers use risky or uneconomical methods to generate sales, a large increase in volume might be a negative.

Consider a company that manufactures personal computers. Near the end of the year, management recognizes that it overestimated demand for computers and the company will be stuck with a large amount of inventory to report on its balance sheet. To solve this problem, the company offers its customers (retail stores) a special incentive; if a retail store increases its normal orders by 100%, the manufacturer will not require payment until the computers are sold to individual consumers. This type of incentive might produce a large increase in sales revenue but it would not improve cash flows as reported on the SCF. Most analysts would want to review this situation very closely because it might cause serious cash problems for the manufacturer if these computers do not sell for some time. Also, the manufacturer might experience reduced sales volume in the subsequent year as the retail stores work off the big buildup in inventory.

Converting Expenses

Under accrual accounting, the total amount of an expense may be different from the cash outflow associated with that activity. This situation can be easily identified by analyzing the changes in the balance sheet accounts that are directly related to an expense account (e.g., prepaid rent and accrued rent payable for rent expense). In the case of UTEX, salary expense of $20 was reported on the income statement. The related balance sheet account is Salaries Payable:

Salaries Payable			
		Beg. bal.	3
Cash paid	18	Salary exp.	20
		End. bal.	5

By entering amounts from the balance sheet and income statement for UTEX, we see that the amount of cash paid for salaries was $18 which is less than the salary expense. From this situation, we can generalize another rule: *When there is an increase in an expense payable, cash paid for the expense is always less than the accrued expense; when there is a decrease in an expense payable, cash paid for the expense is always more than the accrued expense.* This rule can be summarized with the following formula to convert amounts from the accrual basis to the cash basis for all expenses:

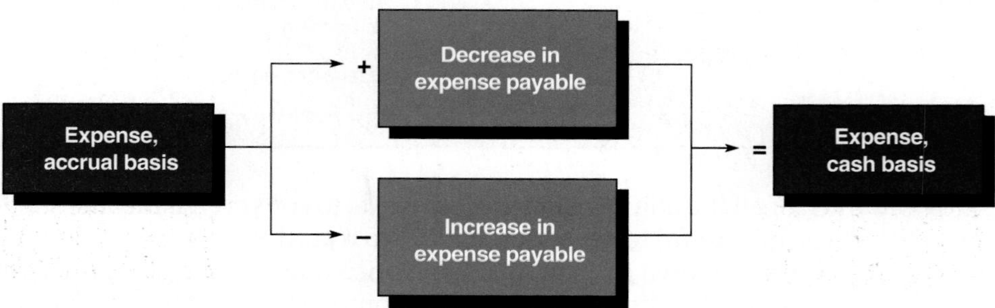

This formula applies for all expenses without regard to the type of expense. The following cases illustrate use of this formula (in thousands):

Case	Salaries Payable	Salaries Expense (Accrual Basis)	Change A	Change B	Change C	Cash Basis (Outflow)
A	No change	$20	—			$20
B	Increase, $2	20		− $2		18
C	Decrease, $2	20			+ $2	22

For UTEX, the cash payments for salaries were $18, or $2 less than the reported salary expense. This adjustment was entered on the schedule shown in Exhibit 13–3. There are two other expense items for UTEX that we should analyze:

1. *Cost of goods sold* In addition to purchasing the merchandise that was sold ($8), UTEX purchased $2 of additional inventory ($12 – $10). The company, therefore, paid $10 in cash to purchase merchandise but the income statement only reflects the $8 that was paid for the merchandise that was sold. The $2 of additional cash outflow must be subtracted from net income to convert it to cash from operating activities. This computation is more complex if the company also has a balance in accounts payable. We will discuss this type situation in the next section of this chapter.
2. *Administrative and selling expense* There are no balance sheet accounts related to administrative and selling expense for UTEX. This means that there were no administrative and selling expenses that were accrued or prepaid. In other words, the accrual amount for administrative and selling expense is the same as the amount of cash paid for these items. Therefore, no adjustment to net income is required.

Converting Cost of Goods Sold to a Cash Basis

Cost of goods sold represents the cost of merchandise sold during the accounting period. It may be more or less than the amount of cash paid to suppliers during the period. In the case of UTEX Company, inventory increased during the year. The company bought more merchandise from its suppliers than it sold to its customers. Therefore, UTEX Company paid more cash to its suppliers than the amount of cost of goods sold.

Typically, companies owe their suppliers money (i.e., there will be an accounts payable balance reported on the balance sheet). In these cases, the calculation of cash payments to suppliers is more complex. To convert cost of goods sold, two accounts must be considered—Inventory and Accounts Payable. Cash is required to increase inventory or to decrease accounts payable. Conversely, a decrease in inventory or an increase in accounts payable reduces cash requirements.

Cost of goods sold can be converted to a cash basis in the following manner:

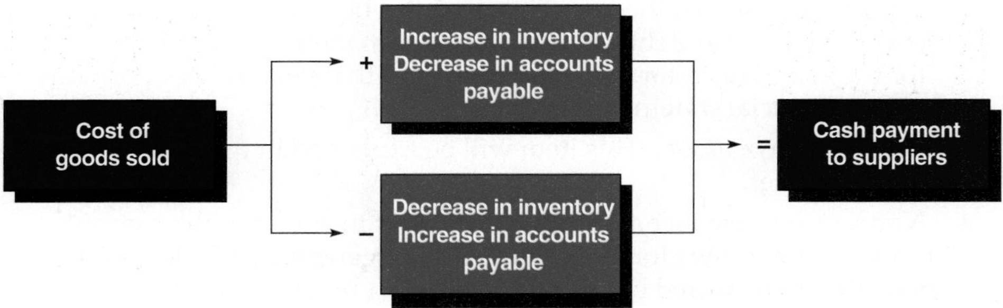

The following cases illustrate this conversion:

Case	Cost of Goods Sold (Accrual Basis)	Inventory Change Increase (Decrease)	Accounts Payable Change Increase (Decrease)	Cash Payments to Suppliers
A	$42	—	—	$42
B	42	$7	—	49
C	42	(7)	—	35
D	42	—	$4	38
E	42	—	(4)	46
F	42	7	(4)	53
G	42	(7)	(4)	39

Noncash Expenses

Learning Objective 3
Define noncash expenses.

Noncash expenses are expenses that do not cause an immediate cash outflow; for example, depreciation expense.

Noncash expenses, such as bad debt expense and depreciation, are reported on most income statements. The recording of noncash expenses does not involve either a credit or debit to cash. Since noncash expenses have been subtracted from revenue to determine net income, you always add them to income to convert it to a cash basis. In the case of UTEX, you should add depreciation expense of $4 to net income to convert it to a cash basis (see Exhibit 13–3).

We can summarize the typical adjustments that are required to reconcile net income with cash flow from operating activities as follows:

	Plus and Minus Adjustments to Net Income	
Item	**When Item Increases**	**When Item Decreases**
Accounts receivable (trade)	–	+
Accounts payable (trade)	+	–
Accrued liabilities	+	–
Prepaid assets	–	+
Inventory	–	+
Depreciation, depletion, and amortization	+	

Notice in this table that adjustments that are recorded as debits (e.g., an increase in accounts receivable or a decrease in accounts payable) are always *subtracted* to reconcile net income to a cash basis. Adjustments that are recorded as credits (e.g., a decrease in inventory or an increase in accrued liabilities) are always *added* to reconcile net income to a cash basis.

The SCF for Home Shopping Network (Exhibit 13–1) shows numerous adjustments to net income to convert it to a cash basis:

1. Depreciation and amortization. Because this is a noncash expense, it is added to net income. Notice that it is the single largest adjustment on the HSN statement of cash flows.
2. Provision for losses on accounts and notes receivable. Typically, this item is a noncash expense that must be added to net income to convert it to a cash basis. Notice in 1990 that the provision was subtracted from net income. This occurred because HSN actually recovered more bad debts than the amount of their bad debt expense for the year. This is an unusual occurrence that you will not normally see on financial statements.
3. Loss on sale of assets. This item will be explained in the next section of the chapter.
4. Noncash interest income. This income was included in the computation of net earnings for HSN but it did not generate cash. Therefore, it must be subtracted on the SCF.
5. Deferred income taxes. Deferred taxes result from timing differences that exist between GAAP used for financial reporting and U.S. tax law that governs preparation of tax returns. An increase in a deferred tax liability is associated with an expense in the current period even though it will not cause a cash outflow until some future accounting period. Because an increase in a deferred tax liability does not cause a cash outflow in the current period, it is added to net income on the SCF. Deferred taxes always reverse at some point in the future and cause a cash outflow. When they do, they must be subtracted from net income on the SCF. Notice that this occurred for HSN in 1991.

HSN offers the consumer the convenience of in-home shopping plus the ability to see the product before it is bought.

6. Common stock issued for services provided. Instead of paying cash for services that were used to generate income, HSN issued common stock to the supplier of the service. As a result, this service expense did not generate a cash outflow.
7. Equity in losses of unconsolidated affiliates. When the equity method is used to account for an intercorporate investment, the investor must record its share of any profits or losses generated by the affiliate. This share of profit or loss does not affect cash flows. Therefore, equity profits must be subtracted from net income because there is no cash inflow and equity losses must be added back because there is no cash outflow.
8. Change in current assets and liabilities. Notice each of these accounts is related to an income statement item. For example, accounts receivable is related to revenue and inventories are related to cost of goods sold. These adjustments are based on the same logic that we illustrated with the UTEX Company.

A Comparison of the Direct and Indirect Methods

Learning Objective 4
Compare the direct and indirect methods.

The indirect method of reporting cash flows from operating activities starts with net income and makes adjustments to compute net cash inflow or outflow. In contrast, the direct method makes adjustments to each income statement item to convert it to a cash basis. The net cash inflow or outflow is the same regardless of whether the direct or indirect method is used and the analytical approach for each method is the same. The two methods differ only in terms of the details that are reported on the SCF. To illustrate, let's prepare the operating activities section of the SCF under both the direct and indirect methods based on the data in Exhibit 13–3.

In the case of the indirect method, each of the adjustments shown in Exhibit 13–3 is reported as an adjustment of net income. Under the direct method, these adjustments are made to the related income statement accounts. Exhibit 13–4 shows a comparison of these two reporting alternatives.

Exhibit 13–4 **Comparison of Direct and Indirect Methods**

Operating Activities Section of the SCF under the Indirect Method

UTEX COMPANY
Statement of Cash Flows—Indirect Method
(in thousands)

Cash flows from operating activities:		
Net income.	$22	
Adjustments to reconcile net income to net cash flow:		
Accounts receivable increase	(6)	
Inventory increase	(2)	
Depreciation expense	4	
Salaries payable increase	2	
Net cash inflow from operating activities		$20

Operating Activities Section of the SCF under the Direct Method

UTEX COMPANY
Statement of Cash Flows—Direct Method
(in thousands)

Cash flows from operating activities:		
Cash collected from customers	$60	
Cash payments to suppliers	(10)	
Cash payment to employees	(18)	
Cash payments for administrative and selling expense	(12)	
Net cash inflow from operating activities		$20

Computations under the direct method:

Item	Accrual Basis from Income Statement	Adjustment from Exhibit 3	Cash Basis
Sales revenue	$66	$(6)	$60
Cost of goods sold	(8)	(2)	(10)
Salaries expense	(20)	2	(18)
Administrative and selling expense	(12)		(12)

Self-Study Quiz

Use the T-account approach to compute the cash outflow associated with cost of goods sold for UTEX.

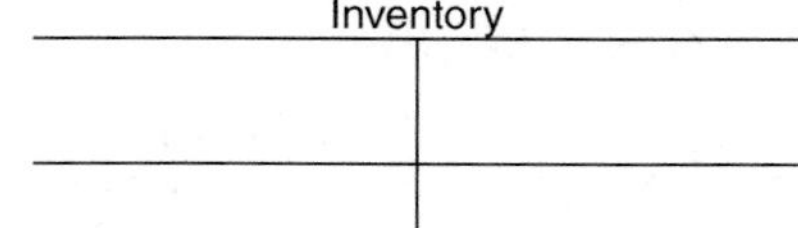

Check your answer with the footnote at the bottom of this page.*

Adjustment for Gains and Losses

As seen in the case of HSN (Exhibit 13–1), the operating activities section of the SCF may include an adjustment for gains and losses reported on the income statement. The transactions that cause gains and losses should be classified on the SCF as operating, investing, or financing activities, depending on their dominant characteristics. For example, if the sale of a productive asset (e.g., a delivery truck) produced a gain, it would be classified as an investing activity.

---

*

Inventory			
Beg. bal.	10	Cost of	
Purch.	10	goods sold	8
End.bal.	12		

An adjustment must be made in the operating activities section to avoid a double counting of the gain or loss. To illustrate, consider the following entry for Home Shopping Network to record the disposal of a television camera:

Cash	8,000	
Accumulated depreciation	4,000	
Operational assets		10,000
Gain on disposal		2,000

The inflow of cash was $8,000, but only the reported gain of $2,000 was shown on the income statement. This transaction should be reported on the SCF as an investing activity with a cash inflow of $8,000. Because the gain was included in the computation of income, it is necessary to remove the $2,000 gain from the operating activities section of the SCF to avoid double counting. If we avoided the double counting by reporting only $6,000 cash inflow from investing activities, we would misstate the actual effects of the transaction.

When a loss is reported on the income statement, it must also be removed when preparing the SCF. Consider the following entry for HSN to record the sale of assets:

Cash	410,000	
Accumulated depreciation	150,000	
Loss	124,000	
Operational assets		684,000

To prepare the SCF, the loss of $124,000 must be removed from operating activities and the total cash collected of $410,000 must be shown in the investing activities section of the statement.

Notice the actual SCF for Home Shopping Network in Exhibit 13–1. The cash flow from operating activities section shows a loss on the sale of assets of $124,000 for 1992, which is added back to net income. In the investing activities section, the proceeds from the sale of the assets is reported as $410,000, which is the actual cash received from the sale.

Computing Cash Flow from Investing Activities

Learning Objective 5
Compute cash flows from investing activities.

Investing activities include the acquisition or sale of long-term assets. In the case of UTEX Company, the analysis (shown in Exhibit 13–2) found that the only investing activities involved plant assets. The company purchased new plant assets for cash in the amount of $30 and sold other plant assets for cash in the amount of $21. Both of these activities are investing activities; the former is a cash outflow, and the latter is a cash inflow. Each is listed separately on the schedule shown in Exhibit 13–3 and on the SCF. The net cash outflow from investing activities is $9.

As you would expect, the investing activities for an actual company are quite complex and diverse. In the case of Home Shopping Network (Exhibit 13–1), the SCF identifies several investing activities with additional information provided in the notes to the statements:

1. Capital expenditures that include the acquisition of tangible productive assets such as buildings and equipment.
2. Proceeds from the sale of assets. This is the amount of cash that was received from the sale of assets that are no longer needed in the operation of HSN.

3. Increase in intangible assets. During the year, HSN paid cash to acquire mailing lists and Federal Communication Commission licenses which are recorded as intangible assets.
4. Increase in long-term investments. HSN purchased, for cash, preferred stock in another company which is recorded as a long-term investment.
5. Increase in notes receivable and other. This increase represents cash that is invested in long-term notes.
6. Proceeds from long-term notes receivable. This is a cash inflow from the scheduled collection of principal payments on long-term notes or the sale of the notes to another party. The footnotes to the HSN financial statements do not provide any specific information concerning these notes. Cash interest received on these notes is included as a cash flow from operating activities.

FINANCIAL ANALYSIS

Investing Cash for Future Profitability

The investing activities section of the SCF reveals important information about a company's strategy. Investments made in the current period will determine productive capacity in future periods. Decisions made today concerning investments in specific technologies or business segments will have an important impact on future profitability.

Mr. Roy M. Speer, the chief executive officer for HSN, states in the annual report that "as always, HSN continues to develop strategic plans which utilize its technological infrastructure and focus on HSN's future role in the burgeoning world of interactive technologies." An analyst can test the statement by reviewing the capital investments made by HSN and reported on the SCF (Exhibit 13–1). As you can see, HSN has made capital expenditures of nearly $125 million during the three-year period covered by the SCF. As a comparison, this investment is nearly twice the amount of income during the period. Clearly, HSN is making significant investments to support future profitability.

Computing Cash Flows from Financing Activities

Learning Objective 6
Compute cash flows from financing activities.

Financing activities are associated with generating capital from creditors and owners. To compute cash flows from financing activities, you should review debt and stockholders' equity accounts. For UTEX Company, there were three transactions that affected cash flows from financing activities. The issuance of common stock resulted in a cash inflow of $48. Both the payments on debt ($6) and the cash dividends ($19) were cash outflows. All three of these transactions are shown on the schedule in Exhibit 13–3 and the SCF. The net cash inflow from financing activities was $23.

In the case of Home Shopping Network, there were four financing activities which were quite similar to our simplified example:

1. Principal payments on and redemptions of long-term debt. Notice that cash outflows associated with debt include the periodic repayment of principal as well as the early retirement of debt. As you saw in previous chapters, most debt requires periodic payments of both principal and accrued interest. The portion of the cash payment that is associated with principal is listed as a cash flow from financing activities. The portion that is associated with interest is a cash flow from operating activities.

2. Proceeds from the issuance of common stock. This represents cash received from the sale of common stock to investors.
3. Purchase of treasury stock. Notice that during 1992, HSN did not purchase any new treasury stock. This item is listed on the SCF because the company did purchase treasury stock in 1990 and 1991, which are shown for comparative purposes.
4. Cash portion of dividends. This is the amount of cash dividends paid to owners during the year. Some students wonder why cash payments made to creditors (interest) are shown as an operating activity while cash payments to owners (dividends) are shown as a financing activity. Remember that interest is reported on the income statement and is, therefore, directly associated with earning income (i.e., it is an operating activity). Dividend payments are not reported on the income statement because they represent a distribution of income. Dividends are more appropriately shown as a financing activity.

FINANCIAL ANALYSIS

Financing Growth

The long-term growth of a company is normally financed from three sources: internally generated funds (cash from operating activities), the issuance of stock, and borrowing money on a long-term basis. As we discussed in Chapter 10, companies can adopt a number of different capital structures (the balance of debt and equity). The funding sources that management uses to fund growth will have an important impact on the risk and return characteristics of the firm. The SCF shows how management has elected to fund its growth. This information is used by analysts who wish to evaluate the capital structure and growth potential of a business.

Noncash Investing and Financing Activities

Learning Objective 7
Explain the impact of noncash financing and investing activities.

Certain transactions are important investing and financing activities, but they do not have any cash flow effects. For example, the purchase of a $100,000 building with a $100,000 mortgage does not cause either the inflow or the outflow of cash. *FASB Statement 95* requires disclosure of these transactions in either narrative or schedule form. The SCF for Home Shopping Network does not list any noncash investing and financing activities. The following schedule from the annual report of USAir illustrates the significance and diversity of these noncash transactions.

Real World Excerpt
USAir
Annual Report

	(in thousands)		
	1992	**1991**	**1990**
Issuance of debt for aircraft acquisition	$218,611	$132,455	$404,092
Issuance of debt for additions to other property		4,200	
Issuance of debt for materials	909		

Preparation of the SCF

The formal SCF for UTEX Company is shown in Exhibit 13-5. As you can see, it is a simple matter to prepare the SCF after the detailed analysis of the

Exhibit 13–5 **Indirect Method, Statement of Cash Flows**

UTEX COMPANY
Statement of Cash Flows—Indirect Method
For the Year Ended December 31, 19B
(in thousands)

A. Cash flows from operating activities		
Net income (from the income statement)	$22	
Add (deduct) to reconcile net income to net cash inflow:		
Accounts receivable increase	(6)	
Inventory increase	(2)	
Depreciation expense	4	
Salaries payable increase	2	
Net cash inflow from operating activities		$20
B. Cash flows from investing activities:		
Cash inflows:		
Cash received from sale of plant assets	21	
Cash outflows:		
Cash paid for acquisition of plant assets	(30)	
Net cash outflow from investing activities		(9)
C. Cash flows from financing activities:		
Cash inflows:		
Cash received from sale of common stock	48	
Cash outflows:		
Cash paid on long-term debt (principal only)	(6)	
Cash paid for dividends	(19)	
Net cash inflow from financing activities		23
D. Net increase (decrease) in cash during 19B		$34
Cash balance, January 1, 19B		42
Cash balance, December 31, 19B		$76

accounts and transactions has been completed (as shown in Exhibit 13–3). As you would expect, the preparation of the SCF for a large company with millions of transactions is more difficult than was the case for our simplified example. Despite the added complexity, the preparation of the SCF for a large company is based on the same analytical approach that we have just discussed. In the next section of this chapter, we will show you some methods of dealing with the added complexity associated with a larger company.

Self-Study Quiz

The financial statements for Oxford Corporation reported the following information:

	19A	19B
Inventory	$100,000	$175,000
Accounts receivable	80,000	60,000
Accounts payable	40,000	30,000
Cost of goods sold	250,000	300,000

Determine the amount of cash that Oxford paid to suppliers. Check your answer with the one contained in the footnote at the bottom of this page.*

*	Cost of goods Sold (19B)	+	Increase in inventory	+	Decrease in accounts payable	=	Cash paid to suppliers
	$300,000	+	$75,000	+	$10,000	=	$385,000

Well-known celebrities, such as Suzanne Somers, enhance the entertainment value of HSN programming.

SPREADSHEET APPROACH—SCF, INDIRECT METHOD

Learning Objective 8
Use a spreadsheet to prepare the SCF.

As situations become more complex, the analytical approach that we used to prepare the SCF for UTEX Company becomes cumbersome and inefficient. In actual practice, most companies use a spreadsheet approach to prepare the SCF. The spreadsheet is based on the same logic that we used in our previous illustration. The primary advantage of the spreadsheet is that it offers a more systematic way to keep track of data. You may find it useful even in simple situations because it minimizes the possibility of errors.

Exhibit 13–6 shows the spreadsheet for UTEX Company. The spreadsheet is organized as follows:

1. Four columns to record dollar amounts are established. The first column is for the beginning balances for items reported on the balance sheet; the next two columns reflect debit and credit changes to those balances; the final column contains the ending balances for the balance sheet accounts.
2. On the far left of the top half of the spreadsheet, each account name from the balance sheet is entered.
3. On the far left of the bottom half of the spreadsheet, the name of each item that will be reported on the SCF is entered.

Changes in the various balance sheet accounts are analyzed in terms of debits and credits in the top half of the spreadsheet with the offsetting debits and credits being recorded in the bottom half of the spreadsheet in terms of their impact on cash flows. To illustrate, let's examine each of the entries on the spreadsheet for UTEX Company shown in Exhibit 13–6. For convenience, these entries are reproduced below in journal entry format with explanations.

		Debit	Credit
Entry *a*	Net income	22	
	Retained earnings		22
	To record net income		

This entry is used to start the reconciliation; net income is shown as an inflow to be reconciled by the noncash reconciling entries. The credit to Retained Earnings reflects the effects of the original closing entry. This is the starting point for the reconciliation.

Exhibit 13–6 **Spreadsheet to Prepare SCF, Indirect Method, UTEX Company, December 31, 19B (in thousands)**

	Beginning Balances, 12/31/19A	Analysis of Changes				Ending Balances 12/31/19B
		Debit		Credit		
Items from balance sheet:						
Cash	42	(*k*)	34			76
Accounts receivable	21	(*b*)	6			27
Inventory	10	(*d*)	2			12
Plant assets	82	(*g*)	30	(*f*)	31	81
Accumulated depreciation	(20)	(*f*)	10	(*e*)	4	(14)
Salaries payable	3			(*c*)	2	5
Note payable, long-term	46	(*i*)	6			40
Common stock (par $10)	61			(*h*)	40	101
Contributed capital in excess of par	9			(*h*)	8	17
Retained earnings	16	(*j*)	19	(*a*)	22	19
		Inflows		**Outflows**		**Subtotals**
Statement of cash flows:						
Reconciliation of net income to cash flow from operating activities:						
Net income		(*a*)	22			
Accounts receivable increase				(*b*)	6	20
Salaries payable increase		(*c*)	2			
Inventory increase				(*d*)	2	
Depreciation expense		(*e*)	4			
Cash flows from investing activities:						
Sale of plant assets		(*f*)	21			
Purchase of plant assets				(*g*)	30	(9)
Cash flows from financing activities:						
Issuance of common stock		(*h*)	48			
Payments on long-term note				(*i*)	6	23
Paid cash dividend				(*j*)	19	
Net increase (decrease) during the year				(*k*)	34	
Totals			204		204	34

Entry *b*	Accounts receivable	6	
	Reconciling amount (deduct from net income)		6
	Increase in accounts receivable		

This entry reconciles the change in accounts receivable during the period with net income. It is deducted from net income because cash collections from customers were less than sales revenue.

Entry *c*	Reconciling amount (add to net income)	2	
	Salaries payable		2
	Salaries payable increase		

This entry reconciles the change in salaries payable with net income. It is added to net income because payments to employees were less than the accrual basis salary expense.

Entry *d*	Inventory	2	
	Reconciling amount (deduct from net income)		2
	Inventory increase		

This is a deduction because cash outflow for inventory was more than accrual basis cost of goods sold.

Entry *e*	Reconciling amount (add to net income)	4	
	Accumulated depreciation		4
	Depreciation expense		

Depreciation expense is a noncash expense. It is added back to net income because this type of expense does not cause a cash outflow when it is recorded.

There were two transactions in the Plant Assets account that affected cash flows:

1. Purchased plant assets for cash, $30.
2. Sold old plant assets for cash, $21; recorded as follows (at book value):

Cash	21	
Accumulated depreciation	10	
Plant assets		31

The related spreadsheet entries are shown below.

Entry *f*	Investing activities	21	
	Accumulated depreciation (to remove)	10	
	Plant assets (to remove)		31
	Sale of old plant assets		

This is a cash inflow, because assets were sold for cash.

Entry *g*	Plant assets	30	
	Investing activities		30
	Purchase of plant assets		

This is the cash outflow, because assets were bought for cash.

Entry *h*	Financing activities	48	
	Common stock (par $10)		40
	Contributed capital in excess of par		8
	Issuance of common stock		

This entry recognizes the issuance of common stock which is a financing activity. It is a cash inflow.

Entry *i*	Note payable	6	
	Financing activities		6
	Payment of long-term note payable		

This is a cash outflow for the payment of debt.

Entry *j*	Retained earnings	19	
	Financing activities		19
	Payment of cash dividends		

This is a cash outflow that is associated with a financing activity.

Entry *k*	Cash	34	
	Net increase during the year		34
	For balancing purposes		

The net increase or decrease reported on the SCF is the same as the change in the cash balance during the year.

The preceding entries complete the spreadsheet analysis because all accounts are reconciled. The accuracy of the analysis can be checked by adding the two analysis columns to verify that Debits = Credits. The formal SCF can be prepared directly from the spreadsheet.

The preparation of an SCF is more difficult than preparing an income statement or a balance sheet. To develop the SCF it is necessary to analyze changes in various accounts to determine the cash flow effects. The other statements can be easily prepared by taking the balances from various accounts in the ledger.

The analytical technique that you have learned for preparing the SCF will help you deal with other significant business problems. For example, this type of analysis is useful for developing cash budgets for a business. Many small businesses that experience rapid sales growth get into serious financial difficulties because they did not forecast the cash flow effects associated with credit sales and large increases in inventory.

DEMONSTRATION CASE

(Try to resolve the requirements before proceeding to the suggested solution that follows.)

The following information pertains to the Gomez Corporation:

Sales		$200,000
Expenses:		
Cost of goods sold	$120,000	
Depreciation expense	12,000	
Salary expense	42,000	174,000
Net income		$ 26,000
Accounts receivable decrease		$ 4,000
Merchandise inventory increase		10,000
Accounts payable increase		400
Salaries payable decrease		800

Required:

Prepare the cash flows from operating activities section of the SCF for Gomez Corporation using the indirect method.

SUGGESTED SOLUTION

Cash flows from operating activities, indirect method:

Net income	$26,000
Adjustments to reconcile net income to net cash provided by operating activities:	
Decrease in accounts receivable	4,000
Increase in merchandise inventory	(10,000)
Increase in accounts payable	400
Depreciation expense	12,000
Decrease in salaries payable	(800)
Net cash provided by operating activities	$31,600

SUMMARY

The SCF is one of the required financial statements. Its primary purpose is to provide cash flow information in a manner that maximizes its usefulness to investors, creditors, and others in projecting future cash flows related to the enterprise.

The SCF has three main sections: cash flows from operating activities which are related to earning income from normal operations; cash flow from investing activities which are related to the acquisition and sale of productive assets; and cash flows from financing activities which are related to financing the enterprise. The net cash inflow or outflow for the year is the same amount as the increase or decrease in cash and cash equivalents for the year. Cash equivalents are highly liquid investments with original maturities of less than three months.

Two different methods for reporting cash flows from operating activities are permitted. They are called the direct and indirect methods. Investing and financing activities are reported in exactly the same way under both methods. The direct method reports the cash flows from the main classifications of revenues and expenses. In contrast, the indirect method reports operating activities by showing a reconciliation of net income with net cash flow from operating activities.

Two approaches are available for developing the SCF—the schedule approach and the spreadsheet approach. Both approaches are efficient; however, the spreadsheet approach is preferable in complex cases because it is a coordinated and self-checking approach.

Chapter Supplement A

Spreadsheet Approach to Develop an SCF, Direct Method

Under the direct method, the cash flows from operating activities section of the SCF reports the actual cash flows from each activity. For example, the statement shows cash collected from customers, cash paid to employees, and cash paid to suppliers. An actual SCF prepared under the direct method for Pep Boys is shown in Exhibit 13–7. Pep Boys operates large warehouse-style units that provide service and merchandise for "do-it-yourself" car mechanics.

The preparation of the SCF under the direct method is based on the same logic as the analysis you performed with the indirect method. Earlier in this chapter, you saw that changes in various balance sheet accounts can be used to convert net income to cash flow from operating activities. Under the direct method, you will use these changes to convert each separate item on the income statement to a cash basis. For example, a decrease in accounts receivable should be added to sales revenue to compute cash collected from customers.

Exhibit 13–8 shows a completed spreadsheet for UTEX Company using the direct method. Notice the following features: (*a*) it starts with the income statement and balance sheet, (*b*) it analyzes all changes between the beginning and ending balances by using a series of straightforward debit-credit entries, (*c*) it provides all of the information for the SCF, and (*d*) it balances throughout.

The SCF spreadsheet is easy to prepare by using the following organized approach:

Step 1. Set up the four money columns with the standard headings shown in Exhibit 13–8.

Step 2. Copy the income statement (amounts in the two middle columns) and the balance sheet (amounts in the first and last money columns) as shown in Exhibit 13–8.

Step 3. Immediately below the income statement and the balance sheet data, write the following side captions, leaving adequate space below each of the captions: statement of cash flows, cash flows from operating activities, cash flows from investing activities, cash flows from financing activities, net increase (decrease) during the year, and totals.

Step 4. Make debit-credit analytical entries under the two Analysis of Changes columns. The spreadsheet is complete when the changes between the beginning and ending balances on each line are accounted for by the analytical entries.

Exhibit 13–7 **Consolidated Statements of Cash Flows (dollar amounts in thousands)**

The Pep Boys—Manny, Moe & Jack and Subsidiaries

Year Ended	January 30, 1993	February 1, 1992	February 2, 1991
Cash Flows from Operating Activities:			
Cash received from customers	**$1,155,004**	$1,001,892	$883,793
Cash paid to suppliers and employees	**(1,034,425)**	(867,877)	(832,603)
Income taxes paid	**(28,531)**	(18,855)	(20,579)
Interest paid	**(18,915)**	(21,687)	(20,117)
Interest and other income received	**3,281**	1,867	1,958
Net Cash Provided by Operating Activities	**76,414**	95,340	12,452
Cash Flows from Investing Activities:			
Capital expenditures	**(78,025)**	(65,801)	(105,826)
Net sales and maturities of marketable securities	**3,286**	2,340	3,196
Proceeds from sale of property and equipment	**738**	1,076	1,134
Other, net	**(1,993)**	621	288
Net Cash Used in Investing Activities	**(75,994)**	(61,764)	(101,208)
Cash Flows from Financing Activities:			
Net borrowings (payments) under line of credit agreements	**18,301**	(148,869)	93,400
Reduction of long-term debt	**(16,177)**	(1,168)	(1,305)
Dividends paid	**(8,173)**	(7,097)	(6,530)
Proceeds from exercise of stock options	**6,252**	1,487	929
Contributions to employees' savings plan	**(291)**	(83)	560
Proceeds from dividend reinvestment plan	**279**	195	145
Net proceeds from sale of 8 7/8% notes	—	123,596	—
Net Cash Provided by (Used in) Financing Activities	**191**	(31,939)	87,199
Net Increase (Decrease) in Cash	**611**	1,637	(1,557)
Cash at Beginning of Year	**11,033**	9,396	10,953
Cash at End of Year	**$ 11,644**	$ 11,033	$ 9,396
Reconciliation of Net Earnings to Net Cash Provided by Operating Activities:			
Net Earnings	**$ 54,579**	$ 38,872	$ 37,530
Adjustments to Reconcile Net Earnings to Net Cash Provided by Operating Activities:			
Depreciation and amortization	**36,674**	33,439	27,838
Increase in payable to banks, accounts payable and accrued expenses	**49,540**	27,262	17,587
(Increase) in accounts receivable and other	**(2,865)**	(10,746)	(793)
(Increase) decrease in merchandise inventories	**(64,285)**	3,794	(70,839)
Increase (decrease) in income taxes payable	**4,771**	(783)	56
Loss (gain) on sale of property and equipment	**266**	(66)	461
(Decrease) increase in deferred income taxes	**(2,266)**	3,568	612
Total Adjustments	**21,835**	56,468	(25,078)
Net Cash Provided by Operating Activities	**$ 76,414**	$ 95,340	$ 12,452
Supplemental Disclosure of Noncash Financing Activities:			
Conversion of 6% convertible subordinated debentures into equity	**$ 74,763**		

See notes to consolidated financial statements.

Explanation of Spreadsheet Entries

It is preferable to start with the first item on the income statement and continue in order until all entries are made. The rationale for each entry is given below. For instructional convenience the following abbreviations are used: OA = operating activities, IA = investing activities, and FA = financing activities. Also, entries on the worksheet are coded as (*a*), (*b*), (*c*), and so on for reference purposes.

Spreadsheet to Prepare SCF, Direct Method; UTEX Company, December 31, 19B — Exhibit 13–8

Items from Financial Statements	Beginning Balances, 12/31/19A	Analysis of Changes: Debit	Analysis of Changes: Credit	Ending Balances 12/31/19B
Phase A—analysis of income statement:				
Revenues:				
Sales			(*a*) 66	
Expenses:				
Salaries		(*b*) 20		
Cost of goods sold		(*c*) 8		
Depreciation		(*d*) 4		
Administrative and selling (including interest)		(*e*) 12		
Net income (to retained earnings)		(*f*) 22		
Phase B—analysis of balance sheet:				
Cash	42	(*o*) 34		76
Accounts receivable	21	(*g*) 6		27
Inventory	10	(*h*) 2		12
Plant assets (analysis needed)	82	(*j*) 30	(*i*) 31	81
Less: Accumulated depreciation	(20)	(*i*) 10	(*d*) 4	(14)
Total assets	135			182
Salaries payable	3		(*k*) 2	5
Note payable, long-term	46	(*l*) 6		40
Common stock (par $10)	61		(*m*) 40	101
Contributed capital in excess of par	9		(*m*) 8	17
Retained earnings	16	(*n*) 19	(*f*) 22	19
Total liabilities and stockholders' equity	135			182
		Inflows	**Outflows**	**Subtotals**
Statement of cash flows:				
Cash flows from operating activities:				
From customers—sales		(*a*) 66		60
Accounts receivable increase			(*g*) 6	
Paid to employees—salaries			(*b*) 20	
Salaries payable increase		(*k*) 2		(40)
Paid to suppliers—cost of goods sold			(*c*) 8	20
Inventory increase			(*h*) 2	
Administrative and selling expense			(*e*) 12	
Cash flows from investing activities:				
Sale of plant assets		(*i*) 21		
Purchase of plant assets			(*j*) 30	(9)
Cash flows from financing activities:				
Issuance of common stock		(*m*) 48		
Payments on long-term note			(*l*) 6	23
Paid cash dividend			(*n*) 19	
Net increase (decrease) during the year			(*o*) 34	
Totals (to verify)		310	310	34

Enter the income statement amounts as follows:

		Debit	Credit
Entry *a*	OA—from customers (a debit to cash flow)*	66	
	Sales (to record)		66
	Revenues		

*This amount is adjusted in Entry *g* for the effects of changes in accounts receivable.

		Debit	Credit
Entry *b*	Salaries expense (to record)	20	
	OA—paid to employees (a credit to cash outflow)		20
	Expenses that require cash		
Entry *c*	Cost of goods sold	8	
	OA—paid to suppliers (a credit to cash outflow)		8
	Expenses that require cash		

Entry *d*	Depreciation	4	
	Accumulated depreciation (on the balance sheet)*		4
	Noncash expenses; no effect on cash flows		

*Noncash expenses are not reported on SCF, direct method; no OA, IA, or FA effects.

Entry *e*	Administrative and selling expense (to record)	12	
	OA—Paid to employees (a credit to cash outflow)*		12
	Expenses that require cash		

*This amount is all cash because there were no related accruals or deferrals.

Entry *f*	Net income (i.e., income summary)	22	
	Retained earnings*		22
	Transfer net income to retained earnings		

*A noncash transfer, no OA, IA, or FA effects.

After the above entries are made on the spreadsheet, all of the income statement accounts and some of the balance sheet accounts have been reconciled. Those reconciled accounts can be checked off because no additional entries will be made to them. Spreadsheet entries classify the cash flow effects for the remaining changes in the account balances reported on the balance sheet. Each entry that follows classifies cash flows as either OA, IA, or FA. These spreadsheet entries can be made in any order; however, for instructional convenience they follow the worksheet order. Therefore, we start with accounts receivable.

Entry *g*	Accounts receivable (check off; this account is now reconciled)	6	
	OA—from customers*		6
	Record the increase in accounts receivable		

*This adjusted the $66 sales revenue amount to the cash basis, $60. Notice that entry *a* could have been made to include the entry as follows:

	OA—from customers ($66 – $6)	60	
	Accounts receivable	6	
	Sales		66
Entry *h*	Inventory	2	
	OA—paid to suppliers		2
	Record the increase in inventory		
Entry *i*	IA—sale of plant assets*	21	
	Accumulated depreciation (to remove)	10	
	Plant assets (to remove)		31
	Sale of old plant assets		

*This is the cash inflow; see analysis of plant assets, Exhibit 13–2.

Entry *j*	Plant assets	30	
	IA—purchase of plant assets*		30
	Purchase of plant assets		

*This is the cash outflow for this transaction; see analysis of plant assets, Exhibit 13–2.

Notice that after spreadsheet Entries *i* and *j* are made, plant assets and accumulated depreciation are fully reconciled.

Entry *k*	OA—paid to employees*	2	
	Salaries payable (increase during year)		2
	Increase in salaries payable		

*This entry is an adjustment of salaries expense Entry *b*, from the accrual to cash basis. Entry *b* could have included this entry.

Entry *l*	Note payable	6	
	FA—payment on note*		6
	Payment of long-term note payable		

*This is the cash outflow; see analysis of note payable, Exhibit 13–2.

Entry *m*	FA—issuance of common stock	48	
	Common stock (par $10)		40
	Contributed capital in excess of par		8
	Issuance of common stock		

Entry *n*	Retained earnings*	19	
	FA—payment of dividend		19
	Cash dividend paid		

*Check off retained earning because it is reconciled (i.e., $16 + $22 – $19 = $19).

Entry *o*	Cash	34	
	Net increase during the year (to balance)		34
	Enter, for balancing purposes only, the key check figure which is the change in cash during the period		

*This fully reconciles the beginning and ending cash balances ($42 + $34 = $76). This is an optional entry on the spreadsheet.

The above entries complete the spreadsheet analysis because all accounts are reconciled. Finally, add the two analysis columns to verify that Debits = Credits. The SCF can now be prepared by using only the bottom part of the spreadsheet. The subtotals in the lower right column of the spreadsheet tie in directly with the SCF. The SCF for UTEX prepared under the direct method is shown in Exhibit 13–9.

Direct Method, Statement of Cash Flows **Exhibit 13–9**

UTEX COMPANY
Statement of Cash Flows—Direct Method
For the Year Ended December 31, 19B
(in thousands)

A. Cash flows from operating activities:		
Cash inflows:		
From customers	$60	
Cash outflows:		
Payments to employees	(18)	
Payments to suppliers	(10)	
Administrative and selling expense	(12)	
Net cash inflow from operating activities		$20
B. Cash flows from investing activities:		
Cash inflows:		
Cash received from sale of plant assets	21	
Cash outflows:		
Cash paid for acquisition of plant assets	(30)	
Net cash outflow from investing activities		(9)
C. Cash flows from financing activities:		
Cash inflows:		
Cash received from sale of common stock	48	
Cash outflows:		
Cash paid on long-term debt (principal only)	(6)	
Cash paid for dividends	(19)	
Net cash inflow from financing activities		23
D. Net increase (decrease) in cash during 19B		34
Cash balance, January 1, 19B		42
Cash balance, December 31, 19B		$76

KEY TERMS

Cash Equivalent A short-term highly liquid investment with original maturity of less than three months. SCF reports changes in cash and cash equivalents. *628*

Cash Flows from Financing Activities Cash inflows and outflows related to how cash was obtained to finance the enterprise. *630*

Cash Flows from Investing Activities Cash inflows and outflows related to the acquisition or sale of productive facilities and the making or collecting of loans. *630*

Cash Flows from Operating Activities Cash inflows and outflows directly related to earnings from normal operations. *629*

Direct Method Reports components of cash flows from operating activities as gross receipts and gross payments. *631*

Indirect Method The method of preparing the operating section of the SCF that adjusts net income to compute cash flows from operating activities. *631*

Noncash Expenses Expenses that do not cause an immediate cash outflow; for example, depreciation expense. *638*

Noncash Investing and Financing Activities Transactions that do not have direct cash flow effects; reported on the SCF in narrative or schedule form. *630*

QUESTIONS

1. Compare the purposes of the income statement, the balance sheet, and the SCF.
2. What information does the SCF report that is not reported on the other required financial statements? How do investors and creditors use that information?
3. What are the major categories of business activities reported on the SCF? Define each of these activities.
4. What are the typical cash inflows from operating activities? What are the typical cash outflows from operating activities?
5. What are the typical cash inflows from investing activities? What are the typical cash outflows from investing activities?
6. What are the typical cash inflows from financing activities? What are the typical cash outflows from financing activities?
7. What are noncash investing and financing activities? Give two examples. How are they reported on the SCF?
8. What are cash equivalents? How are purchases and sales of cash equivalents reported on the SCF?
9. If a business purchases a Treasury bill that matures in six months, is the Treasury bill considered a cash equivalent? Will that Treasury bill be considered a cash equivalent when it has only three months remaining to maturity?
10. How is the sale of equipment reported on the SCF using the direct method?
11. Compare the two methods of reporting cash flows from operating activities in the SCF.
12. Under the indirect method, depreciation expense is added to net income to report cash flows from operating activities. Does depreciation cause an inflow of cash?
13. How is depreciation expense handled when preparing an SCF using the direct method? Using the indirect method? What other expenses are handled similarly to depreciation?
14. Assume you are preparing an SCF and are trying to determine if there were any investing activities. Where would you find this information?
15. Assume you are preparing an SCF and are trying to determine if there were any financing activities. Where would you find this information?

16. Explain why cash paid during the period for purchases and for salaries is not specifically reported on the SCF, indirect method, as cash outflows.
17. Explain why a $50,000 increase in inventory during the year must be included in developing cash flows for operating activities under both the direct and indirect methods.

EXERCISES

E13–1 *Reporting Noncash Transactions on the SCF*

An analysis of Martin Corporation's operational asset accounts provided the following information:

a. Martin acquired a large machine that cost $26,000. Martin paid for the machine by giving a $15,000, 12% interest-bearing note due at the end of two years and 500 shares of its common stock, with a par value of $10 per share and a market value of $22 per share.

b. Martin acquired a small machine that cost $8,700. Full payment was made by transferring a tract of land that had a book value of $8,700.

Required:

Show how this information should be reported on the SCF.

E13–2 *Calculating Cash Receipts from Customers*

For each independent case listed in the following schedule, calculate cash receipts from customers.

	Case A	Case B	Case C
Sales revenue	$400,000	$200,000	$500,000
Beginning accounts receivable	14,000	21,000	28,000
Ending accounts receivable	20,000	17,000	28,000
Cash receipts from customers			

E13–3 *Determining Cash Flows from the Sale of an Asset*

During 19F, English Company sold some excess equipment at a loss. The following information was collected from the company's accounting records:

From the income statement:	
Depreciation expense	$ 700
Loss on sale of equipment	3,000
From the balance sheet:	
Beginning equipment	12,500
Ending equipment	8,000
Beginning accumulated depreciation	2,000
Ending accumulated depreciation	2,400

No new equipment was bought during 19F.

Required:

For the equipment that was sold, determine the original cost, the accumulated depreciation on the equipment, and the cash received from the sale.

E13–4 *Calculating Cash Flows from Operating Activities, Indirect Method*

The following information pertains to Day Company:

Sales		$80,000
Expenses:		
Cost of goods sold	$50,000	
Depreciation expense	6,000	
Salaries expense	12,000	68,000
Net income		$12,000
Accounts receivable increase	$ 5,000	
Merchandise inventory decrease	8,000	
Salaries payable increase	500	

Required:

Prepare the operating activities section of the SCF for Day Company using the indirect method.

E13–5 *Preparing the Operating Activities Section of the SCF, Indirect Method*

The following information pertains to Night Company:

Sales		$80,000
Expenses:		
Cost of goods sold	$50,000	
Depreciation expense	6,000	
Salaries expense	12,000	68,000
Net income		$12,000
Accounts receivable decrease	$ 5,000	
Merchandise inventory increase	8,000	
Salaries payable decrease	500	

Required:

Prepare the operating activities section of the SCF for Night Company using the indirect method.

E13–6 *Calculating Cash Flows from Operating Activities under the Indirect Method*

The Kane Company completed its income statement and balance sheet for 19D and provided the following information:

Service revenue		$50,000
Expenses:		
Salaries	$42,000	
Depreciation	7,000	
Amortization of copyrights	300	
Utilities	7,000	
Other expenses	1,700	58,000
Net loss		$ (8,000)
Decrease in accounts receivable	$12,000	
Bought a small service machine	5,000	
Increase in salaries payable	9,000	
Decrease in service revenue collected in advance	4,000	

Required:

Prepare the operating activities section of the SCF for Kane Company using the indirect method.

E13–7 *Preparing the SCF, Direct Method*

Langley Company completed its income statement and comparative balance sheet at December 31, 19B, and has provided the following data:

Beginning cash balance	$ 60,000
Sales revenue	300,000
Depreciation expense	4,000
Cost of goods sold	240,000
Other expenses	32,000
Sales of long-term investments (sold at book value for $5,000 cash)	5,000
Inventory increase during the period	6,000
Declared and paid cash dividends during the period	10,000
Borrowed on short-term note	15,000
Payment of long-term note	25,000
Acquired land for future use; issued capital stock in payment	30,000
Ending cash balance	67,000

Required:

Prepare an SCF for Langley Company using the direct method.

E13–8 *Preparing the SCF, Direct Method*

Price Corporation completed its income statement and balance sheet on December 31, 19B, and provided the following information:

Beginning cash balance	$ 18,000
Depreciation expense	8,000
Bought treasury stock	6,500
Sold a long-term investment at book value	12,000
Service revenue	150,000
Declared and paid cash dividends	8,000
Salaries expense	60,000
Net income	20,000
Salaries recorded but unpaid on December 31, 19A*	2,000
Service revenue recorded but uncollected on December 31, 19A*	4,000
Issued 200 shares of common stock	1,500
Purchased operational assets for cash	40,000
Other operating expenses	9,000
Ending cash balance	60,000

*Paid or collected in 19B.

Required:

Prepare the 19B SCF for Price Corporation using the direct method.

E13–9 *SCF, Direct Method: Complete Spreadsheet*

Analysis of accounts: (*a*) purchased an operational asset, $20,000, issued capital stock in full payment; (*b*) purchased a long-term investment for cash, $15,000; (*c*) paid cash dividend, $12,000; (*d*) sold operational asset for $6,000 cash (cost, $21,000, accumulated depreciation, $19,000); and (*e*) sold capital stock, 500 shares at $12 per share cash.

	Beginning Balances, 12/31/19A	Analysis of Changes Debit	Analysis of Changes Credit	Ending Balances, 12/31/19B
Income statement items:				
Sales			$140,000	
Cost of goods sold		$59,000		
Depreciation		7,000		
Wage expense		28,000		
Income tax expense		9,000		
Interest expense		5,000		
Remaining expenses		15,800		
Gain on sale of operational asset			4,000	
Net income		20,200		
Balance sheet items:				
Cash	$ 20,500			$ 19,200
Accounts receivable	22,000			22,000
Merchandise inventory	68,000			75,000
Investments, long-term				15,000
Operational assets	114,500			113,500
Total debits	$225,000			$244,700
Accumulated depreciation	$ 32,000			$ 20,000
Accounts payable	17,000			14,000
Wages payable	2,500			1,500
Income taxes payable	3,000			4,500
Bonds payable	54,000			54,000
Common stock, nopar	100,000			126,000
Retained earnings	16,500			24,700
Total credits	$225,000			$244,700
		Inflows	**Outflows**	
Statement of cash flows:				
Cash flows from operating activities:				
Cash flows from investing activities:				
Cash flows from financing activities:				
Net increase (decrease) in cash				
Totals				

Required:

Complete the spreadsheet for the SCF, direct method.

E13–10 SCF: Cash Flow Analysis of Cost of Goods Sold

The records of Johnny Company showed cost of goods sold (on the income statement) of $30,000 and a change in the inventory and accounts payable balances. To demonstrate the effect of these changes on cash outflow for cost of goods sold (i.e., payments to suppliers), eight independent cases are used. Complete the following tabulation for each case:

Case	Cost of Goods Sold	Inventory Increase (Decrease)	Accounts Payable Increase (Decrease)	Computations	Outflow*
A	$30,000	—	—		
B	30,000	$5,000	—		
C	30,000	(5,000)	—		
D	30,000	—	$2,000		
E	30,000	—	(2,000)		
F	30,000	5,000	2,000		
G	30,000	(5,000)	(2,000)		
H	30,000	(5,000)	(5,000)		

*This is the amount of cash paid during the current period for past and current purchases.

E13–11 Calculating Cash Payments to Suppliers

For each independent case listed in the following schedule, calculate cash payments to suppliers.

	Case A	Case B	Case C	Case D
Cost of goods sold	$30,000	$50,000	$40,000	$40,000
Beginning inventory	25,000	10,000	20,000	25,000
Ending inventory	20,000	10,000	25,000	25,000
Beginning accounts payable	6,000	6,000	8,000	5,000
Ending accounts payable	5,000	7,000	8,000	5,000
Cash payments to suppliers				

E13–12 Comparing the Direct and Indirect Methods

To compare SCF reporting under the direct and indirect methods, enter check marks to indicate which items are used with each method.

Cash Flows (and Related Changes)	SCF Method Direct	SCF Method Indirect
1. Revenues from customers		
2. Accounts receivable increase or decrease		
3. Payments to suppliers		
4. Inventory increase or decrease		
5. Accounts payable increase or decrease		
6. Payments to employees		
7. Wages payable, increase or decrease		
8. Depreciation expense		
9. Net income		
10. Cash flows from operating activities		
11. Cash flows from investing activities		
12. Cash flows from financing activities		
13. Net increase or decrease in cash during the period		

E13–13 SCF, Indirect Method: Preparing the Reconciliation for Operating Activities

The data given below were provided by the accounting records of McDonald Company. Prepare the reconciliation of net income with cash flow from operating activities for inclusion in the SCF, indirect method.

Net income (accrual basis),	$70,000
Depreciation expense,	8,200
Decrease in wages payable,	1,500
Decrease in accounts receivable,	2,100
Increase in inventory,	4,000
Increase in long-term liabilities,	20,000
Sale of capital stock for cash,	35,000
Accounts payable increase,	5,000
Dividend paid,	12,000

E13–14 SCF, Indirect Method: Complete Spreadsheet

The data used in this exercise are given in Exercise 13–9.

Required:

Complete the SCF, indirect method, spreadsheet given below.

Items	Beginning Balances, 12/31/19A	Analysis of Changes Debit	Credit	Ending Balances, 12/31/19B
Cash plus short-term investments	$ 20,500			$ 19,200
Accounts receivable	22,000			22,000
Merchandise inventory	68,000			75,000
Investments, long-term				15,000
Operational assets	114,500			113,500
Totals	$225,000			$244,700
Accumulated depreciation	$ 32,000			$ 20,000
Accounts payable	17,000			14,000
Wages payable	2,500			1,500
Income taxes payable	3,000			4,500
Bonds payable	54,000			54,000
Common stock, nopar	100,000			126,000
Retained earnings	16,500			24,700
Totals	$225,000			$244,700
Statement of cash flows:				
Conversion of net income to cash flows from operating activities:				
Cash flows from investing activities:				
Cash flows from financing activities:				
Net increase (decrease) in cash				
Totals				

PepsiCo

E13–15 Computing Cash Flows from Operating Activities (indirect method)

The annual report for PepsiCo contained the following information for 1993 (in millions):

Net income	$1,587.9
Depreciation and amortization	1,444.2
Increase in accounts receivable	161.0
Increase in inventory	89.5
Decrease in prepaid expense	3.3
Increase in accounts payable	143.2
Decrease in taxes payable	125.1
Decrease in other current liabilities	96.7
Cash dividends paid	461.6
Treasury stock purchased	463.5

Required:

Compute cash flows from operating activities for PepsiCo using the indirect method.

Colgate-Palmolive

E13–16 Analysis of Adjustments under the Indirect Method

The SCF for Colgate-Palmolive reported the following information (in millions):

Operating Activities	1992
Net income	$477.0
Depreciation	192.5
Cash effect of changes in:	
Receivables	(38.0)
Inventories	28.4
Other current assets	10.6
Payables	(10.0)
Other	(117.8)
Net cash provided by operations	$542.7

Required:

Based on the information reported on the SCF for Colgate-Palmolive, determine whether the following accounts increased or decreased during 1992: receivables, inventories, other current assets, and payables.

E13–17 Analyzing Adjustments under the Indirect Method

Apple Computers, Inc.

The SCF for Apple Computers contained the following information (in thousands);

Operations	1994
Net income	$310,178
Depreciation	167,958
Changes in assets and liabilities:	
Accounts receivable	(199,401)
Inventories	418,204
Other current assets	33,616
Accounts payable	139,095
Income taxes payable	50,045
Other current liabilities	39,991
Other adjustments	(222,691)
Cash generated by operations	736,995

Required:

For each of the asset and liability accounts listed on the SCF, determine whether the account balances increased or decreased during 1994.

E13–18 Computing Cash Flow from Operating Activities (Indirect Method)

Sizzler International, Inc.

Sizzler International, Inc. operates 700 family restaurants around the world. The company's annual report contained the following information (in thousands):

	1993
Net loss	$(9,482)
Depreciation and amortization	33,305
Increase in receivables	170
Decrease in inventories	643
Increase in prepaid expenses	664
Decrease in accounts payable	2,282
Decrease in accrued liabilities	719
Increase in income taxes payable	1,861
Reduction of long-term debt	12,691
Additions to equipment	29,073

Required:

Based on this information, compute cash flow from operating activities using the indirect method.

E13–19 Analyzing Noncash Expenses

QuickServe, a chain of convenience stores, was experiencing some serious cash flow difficulties because of rapid growth. The company did not generate sufficient cash from operating activities to finance its new stores and creditors were not willing to lend money because the company had not produced any income for the previous three years. The new controller for QuickServe proposed a reduction in the estimated life of store equipment to increase depreciation expense, thus "we can improve cash flows from operating activities because depreciation expense is added back on the SCF." Other executives were not sure that this was a good idea because the increase in depreciation would make it more difficult to have positive earnings: "without income, the bank will never lend us money."

What action would you recommend for QuickServe? Why?

E13–20 Sale of Property

AMC Entertainment

AMC Entertainment is the second-largest motion picture exhibitor in the United States. The following was abstracted from the company's SCF (in thousands):

	1993	1992	1991
Cash flows from operating activities:			
Gain on sale of property	(9,638)	(7,314)	
Cash flows from investing activities:			
Proceeds from disposition of property	14,768	11,623	1,797

Required:

Determine the cash flow from the sale of property for each year for AMC.

PROBLEMS

P13–1 Calculating Cash Flows: Preparing Schedule to Reconcile Net Income with Cash Flows

The income statement of Frank Corporation is given below.

FRANK CORPORATION
Income Statement
For the Year Ended December 31, 19C
Accrual Basis

			Cash Flow
Sales revenue (one-fourth on credit; accounts receivable year's end 19A, $12,000; 19B, $17,000)		$400,000	$ ______
Cost of goods sold (one-third on credit; accounts payable year's end 19A, $10,000; 19B, $7,000; inventory at year's end—19A, $60,000; 19B, $52,000)		268,000	______
Expenses:			
Salaries and wages (including accrued wages payable at year's end—19A, $1,000; 19B, $800)	$51,000		______
Depreciation expense	9,200		______
Rent expense (no accruals)	5,800		______
Remaining expenses (no accruals)	12,200		______
Income tax expense (income taxes payable at year's end—19A, $3,000; 19B, $5,000)	11,800		______
Total expenses		90,000	______
Net income		$ 42,000	______
Cash flow from operating activities			$ ______

Required:

1. Provide the cash flow amounts in the blanks given to the right.
2. Prepare a schedule to reconcile net income to net cash provided by operating activities.

P13–2 Preparing SCF Spreadsheet and SCF Using Direct Method

Riverview Company is developing its annual financial statements at December 31, 19B. The income statement and balance sheet are finished, and the SCF is being developed. The income statement and comparative balance sheet are summarized below.

	19A	19B
Balance sheet at December 31:		
Cash	$11,600	$10,600
Accounts receivable	8,000	9,000
Merchandise inventory	7,400	6,000
Operational assets (net)	30,000	36,000
Patent	16,000	14,400
Total assets	$73,000	$76,000
Accounts payable	$12,000	$ 4,000
Income taxes payable	500	800
Note payable, long-term	20,000	12,000
Common stock (nopar)	31,000	43,700
Retained earnings	9,500	15,500
Total liabilities and stockholders' equity	$73,000	$76,000

Income statement for 19B:	
Sales revenue	$80,000
Cost of goods sold	54,000
Gross margin	26,000
Expenses (including depreciation, $5,000; patent amortization, $1,600; income tax expense, $4,000; and other expenses, $4,400)	15,000
Net income	$11,000

Additional Data for 19B:

Purchased operational assets for cash, $11,000. Paid $8,000 on long-term note payable. Sold and issued common stock for $12,700 cash. Declared and paid a $5,000 cash dividend on capital stock during 19B.

Required:

1. Prepare an SCF spreadsheet using the direct method to report cash flows from operating activities.
2. Prepare the SCF.
3. Prepare a schedule of noncash investing and financing activities if necessary.

P13–3 Preparing SCF Spreadsheet and SCF Using Direct Method

Hunter Company is developing the annual financial statements at December 31, 19B. The statements are complete except for the SCF. The completed comparative balance sheets and income statement are summarized below:

	19A	19B
Balance sheet at December 31:		
Cash	$ 18,000	$ 44,000
Accounts receivable	29,000	27,000
Merchandise inventory	36,000	30,000
Operational assets (net)	72,000	75,000
	$155,000	$176,000
Accounts payable	$ 22,000	$ 25,000
Wages payable	1,000	800
Note payable, long-term	48,000	38,000
Common stock, nopar	60,000	80,000
Retained earnings	24,000	32,200
	$155,000	$176,000
Income statement for 19B:		
Sales		$100,000
Cost of goods sold		(61,000)
Expenses		(27,000)
Net income		$ 12,000

Additional Data:

Bought operational assets for cash, $9,000. Paid $10,000 on the long-term note payable. Sold unissued common stock for $20,000 cash. Declared and paid a $3,800 cash dividend. Expenses included depreciation, $6,000; wages, $10,000; taxes, $3,000; other, $8,000.

Required:

1. Prepare an SCF spreadsheet using the direct method to report cash flows from operating activities.
2. Prepare the SCF.
3. Prepare a schedule of noncash investing and financing activities if necessary.

P13–4 *Preparing SCF Spreadsheet and SCF Using Direct Method: Includes Noncash Investing and Financing Activity and the Sale of an Asset at Book Value*

Ellington Company is developing the 19B annual report. The following information is provided:

	19A	19B
Cash	$21,000	$22,400
Accounts receivable	18,000	21,000
Inventory	35,000	32,000
Prepaid insurance	2,400	1,400
Investments, long-term	12,500	9,300
Operational assets (net)	31,100	59,600
Patent	2,000	1,500
Accounts payable	27,000	15,000
Wages payable	4,000	1,000
Income taxes payable	2,000	2,200
Note payable, long-term	20,000	10,000
Common stock ($10 par)	50,000	80,000
Contributed capital in excess of par	3,000	6,000
Retained earnings	16,000	33,000

Other Information

Sold long-term investment at book value, $3,200. Purchased operational assets by issuing 3,000 shares of common stock, market value of common stock, $11 per share.

Revenues, $150,000.

Expenses: depreciation, $4,500; patent amortization, $500; insurance $2,000; wages, $48,500; income taxes, $7,000; and cost of goods sold, $62,000.

Required:

1. Prepare an SCF spreadsheet using the direct method to report cash flows from operating activities.
2. Prepare the SCF.
3. Prepare a schedule of noncash investing and financing activities.

P13–5 *Preparing SCF Using Direct Method; Includes a Noncash Investing and Financing Activity, and Gain on Disposal of a Machine*

Oklaco Company has prepared its 19B financial statements, which include the following information:

	Comparative	
	19A	19B
Balance sheet:		
Cash	$ 30,000	$ 79,000
Inventory	45,000	53,000
Accounts receivable	15,000	12,000
Long-term investment stock Co. A	20,000	8,000
Machinery and equipment (net)	75,000	68,000
	$185,000	$220,000
Accounts payable	$ 16,000	$ 13,000
Income taxes payable	5,000	12,000
Note payable, long-term	25,000	20,000
Bonds payable	20,000	10,000
Common stock (par $10)	110,000	120,000
Contributed capital in excess of par	7,000	8,000
Retained earnings	2,000	37,000
	$185,000	$220,000

Income statement:	
Revenue	$180,000
Cost of goods sold	(89,000)
Depreciation expense	(10,000)
Remaining operating expenses	(32,000)
Income tax expense	(8,000)
Gain on disposal of machine (net of tax)	3,000
Net income	$ 44,000

Additional Data for 19B:

a. Machinery that had a book value of $8,000 was sold for $11,000 cash.

b. Long-term investment (shares of Company A stock) was sold for $12,000 cash; carrying value was $12,000.

c. Equipment was acquired, and payment in full was made by issuing 1,000 shares of capital stock that had a market value of $11 per share.

d. Payment on debt; long-term note, $5,000; bonds payable, $10,000.

e. Declared and paid a cash dividend, $9,000.

Required:

1. Prepare an SCF spreadsheet using the direct method to report cash flows from operating activities.
2. Prepare an SCF.
3. Prepare a schedule of noncash investing and financing activities.

P13–6 Preparing SCF Spreadsheet, Using Direct Method: Includes a Noncash Investing and Financing Activity

Ironside Company is preparing the annual financial statements, including an SCF at December 31, 19B. The 19B comparative balance sheet and the income statement and some additional data are summarized below:

	19A	19B
Balance sheet at December 31:		
Cash	$ 21,000	$ 26,500
Accounts receivable	30,000	32,000
Merchandise inventory	32,000	37,000
Prepaid insurance	800	500
Investment, long-term (S Corp. stock)		7,000
Operational assets (net)	118,000	309,000
Patent (net)		30,000
Total assets	$201,800	$442,000
Accounts payable	$ 17,000	$ 22,000
Note payable, short-term (nontrade)	14,000	10,000
Wages payable	2,000	1,600
Income taxes payable	400	1,000
Note payable, long-term	25,000	15,000
Bonds payable		200,000
Common stock (par $10)	120,000	160,000
Contributed capital in excess of par	3,400	5,400
Retained earnings	20,000	27,000
Total liabilities and stockholders' equity	$201,800	$442,000
Income statement for 19B:		
Sales revenue		$300,000
Cost of goods sold		(211,000)
Expenses (not detailed)		(56,000)
Depreciation expense		(9,000)
Amortization of patent		(2,000)
Income tax expense		(10,000)
Net income		$ 12,000

Additional Data for 19B:

a. Bought patent on January 1, 19B, for $32,000 cash.
b. Bought stock of S Corporation as a long-term investment for $7,000 cash.
c. Paid $10,000 on the long-term note payable.
d. Sold and issued 4,000 shares of common stock for $42,000 cash.
e. Declared and paid a $5,000 cash dividend.
f. Acquired a building (an operational asset) and paid for it by issuing $200,000 bonds payable at par to the former owner—date of transaction was December 30, 19B.

Required:

1. Prepare an SCF spreadsheet using the direct method to report cash flows from operating activities.
2. Prepare the SCF.
3. Prepare a schedule of noncash investing and financing activities.

P13–7 *Preparing SCF Using Direct Method: Includes Gain on Sale of Equipment*

The income statement, comparative balance sheet, and additional information for Edgar Corporation for 19B appear below (in thousands):

Income Statement

Revenues:		
Sales	$1,400	
Gain on sale of equipment	30	$1,430
Expenses:		
Cost of goods sold	800	
Advertising expense	50	
Depreciation expense	70	
Rent expense	40	
Wages expense	110	
Income tax expense	72	
Interest expense on bonds	14	1,156
		$ 274

Comparative Balance Sheet

	19A	19B
Cash	$ 75	$282
Accounts receivable	32	67
Merchandise inventory	62	187
Prepaid rent	6	16
Equipment	181	201
Accumulated depreciation	(16)	(51)
Totals	$340	$702
Income taxes payable	$ 60	$ 68
Accounts payable	15	105
Wages payable	20	30
Bonds payable	125	125
Common stock	100	100
Retained earnings	20	274
Totals	$340	$702

Other Data:

a. Equipment with an original cost of $70 and accumulated depreciation of $35 was sold for $65.
b. Additional equipment was purchased for cash.
c. No additional bonds were issued or retired during the year.
d. Cash dividends were declared and paid during the year.

Required:

1. Prepare an SCF spreadsheet using the direct method to report cash flows from operating activities.
2. Prepare the SCF.

P13–8 Preparing SCF Using Direct Method: Includes a Noncash Investing and Financing Activity, Sale of Equipment at a Loss, and a Net Loss

The income statement, comparative balance sheet, and additional information for Elich Corporation for 19D appear below (in thousands):

Income Statement

Revenues:		
Sales		$1,200
Expenses:		
Cost of goods sold	$600	
Depreciation expense	40	
Rent expense	310	
Wage expense	180	
Other operating expenses	110	
Interest expense	6	
Loss on sale of equipment	4	1,250
Net loss		$ (50)

Comparative Balance Sheet

	19C	19D
Cash	$ 60	$ 25
Accounts receivable	103	78
Merchandise inventory	40	160
Prepaid rent	4	44
Equipment	190	280
Accumulated depreciation	(38)	(66)
Total assets	$359	$521
Accounts payable	$ 12	$ 4
Wages payable	16	12
Notes payable	0	0
Interest payable	0	4
Bonds payable	0	100
Common stock, nopar value	70	190
Retained earnings	261	211
Totals	$359	$521

Other Data:

a. Equipment was purchased during the year by issuing $120 of common stock.
b. Equipment with an original cost of $30 and accumulated depreciation of $12 was sold for $14.
c. Bonds were issued at face value during the year. Interest of $4 was accrued at year-end.
d. $40 was borrowed on a short-term note payable. The note and $2 of interest was repaid.

Required:

1. Prepare an SCF spreadsheet using the direct method to report cash flows from operating activities.
2. Prepare the SCF.
3. Prepare a schedule of noncash investing and financing activities.

P13–9 *Preparing SCF Using Direct Method: Includes a Noncash Investing and Financing Activity, the Sale of an Asset at a Gain, and a Net Loss*

The income statement, comparative balance sheet, and additional information for Robert Corporation appear below (in thousands):

Income Statement

Revenues:		
Sales	$900	
Gain on sale of equipment	50	$950
Expenses:		
Cost of goods sold	$700	
Salaries expense	50	
Rent expense	40	
Office supplies expense	20	
Patent amortization expense	30	
Depreciation expense	70	
Interest expense on bonds	87	997
Net loss		$ (47)

Comparative Balance Sheet

	19B	19C
Cash	$ 185	$ 113
Accounts receivable	50	170
Merchandise inventory	500	200
Office supplies	15	18
Long-term investments	60	90
Operational assets	1,500	2,950
Accumulated depreciation	(450)	(440)
Patent	300	270
Totals	$2,160	$3,371
Accounts payable	$ 85	$ 68
Rent payable	25	40
Bonds payable	0	500
Common stock ($1 par)	300	410
Contributed capital	800	1,590
Retained earnings	950	903
Treasury stock	-0-	(140)
Totals	$2,160	$3,371

Other Information:

a. Equipment with an original cost of $200 and accumulated depreciation of $80 was sold for $170. Equipment costing $750 was purchased for cash.

b. Land and building valued at $900 were acquired by issuing 110 shares of common stock.

c. Bonds payable were issued during the year.

d. Long-term investments were purchased during the year.

e. Treasury stock was purchased during the year.

Required:

1. Prepare an SCF spreadsheet using the direct method to report cash flows from operating activities.
2. Prepare the SCF.
3. Prepare a schedule of noncash investing and financing activities.

P13–10 *Preparing SCF, Indirect Method: Use Schedule Approach to Prepare the Statement*

Stonewall Company was organized on January 1, 19A. During the year ended December 31, 19A, the company provided the following data:

Income statement:	
Sales revenue	$ 80,000
Cost of goods sold	(35,000)
Depreciation expense	(4,000)
Remaining expenses	(32,000)
Net income	$ 9,000
Balance sheet:	
Cash	$ 48,000
Accounts receivable	18,000
Merchandise inventory	15,000
Machinery (net)	25,000
Total assets	$106,000
Accounts payable	$ 10,000
Accrued expenses payable	21,000
Dividends payable	2,000
Note payable, short-term	15,000
Common stock	54,000
Retained earnings	4,000
Total liabilities and stockholders' equity	$106,000

Analysis of Selected Accounts and Transactions:

a. Sold 3,000 shares of common stock, par $10, at $18 per share; collected cash.

b. Borrowed $15,000 on a one-year, 8% interest-bearing note; the note was dated June 1, 19A.

c. During 19A, purchased machinery; paid $29,000.

d. Purchased merchandise for resale at a cost of $50,000 (debited Inventory because the perpetual system is used); paid $40,000 cash, balance credited to Accounts Payable.

e. At December 31, 19A, declared a cash dividend of $5,000; paid $3,000 in December 19A; the balance will be paid March 1, 19B.

Required:

Prepare an SCF, indirect method, using the schedule approach.

P13–11 *Preparing SCF Spreadsheet, SCF, and Schedules Using Indirect Method: Includes a Noncash Investing and Financing Activity, and a Sale of an Asset at a Loss*

Mopac Company is preparing its 19B financial statements. The following information is given by the completed 19B comparative balance sheet and income statement:

	19A	19B
Balance sheet:		
Cash	$ 12,000	$ 6,000
Accounts receivable	18,600	32,000
Inventory	14,000	29,000
Prepaid expense	2,400	1,400
Operational assets (net)	62,000	65,000
Plant site		15,000
Long-term investment	21,000	9,000
Total assets	$130,000	$157,400
Accounts payable	$ 9,000	$ 15,000
Wages payable	3,000	3,200
Short-term note payable (interest, December 31)	8,000	4,000
Long-term note payable (interest, December 31)	12,000	6,000
Bonds payable (interest, December 31)	25,000	40,000
Common stock (par $10)	65,000	65,750
Contributed capital in excess of par	5,000	5,450
Retained earnings	3,000	18,000
Total liabilities and stockholders' equity	$130,000	$157,400

Income statement:	
Revenues	$150,000
Depreciation expense	(20,000)
Remaining expenses	(101,000)
Loss on sale of long-term investment	(4,000)
Net income	$ 25,000

Additional Data:

a. Purchased operational asset for cash, $23,000.
b. Sold long-term investment for $8,000 cash; carrying value, $12,000.
c. Sold 75 shares of common stock at $16 cash per share.
d. Declared and paid a cash dividend of $10,000.
e. Payment on short-term note, $4,000.
f. Payment on a long-term note, $6,000.
g. Acquired plant site and issued bonds, $15,000 for full purchase price (the bonds were selling at par).

Required:

1. Prepare an SCF spreadsheet using the indirect method to report cash flows from operating activities.
2. Prepare an SCF.
3. Prepare a schedule of noncash investing and financing activities.

P13–12 Comparing Cash Flows from Operating Activities Using Direct and Indirect Methods

The accountants for Beta Company just completed the income statement and balance sheet for the year and have provided the following information (in thousands):

Income Statement

Sales revenue	$20,600	
Expenses:		
Cost of goods sold	$9,000	
Depreciation expense	2,000	
Salaries expense	5,000	
Rent expense	2,500	
Insurance expense	800	
Utilities expense	700	
Interest expense on bonds	600	
Loss on sale of investments	400	21,000
Net loss		$ (400)

Selected Balance Sheet Accounts

	19A	19B
Merchandise inventory	$ 60	$ 82
Accounts receivable	450	380
Accounts payable	210	240
Salaries payable	20	29
Rent payable	6	2
Prepaid rent	7	2
Prepaid insurance	5	14

Other Data:

The company issued $20,000, 8% bonds payable during the year.

Required:

1. Prepare the cash flows from operating activities section of the SCF using the direct method.
2. Prepare the cash flows from operating activities section of the SCF using the indirect method.

P13–13 Prepare SCF Spreadsheet, SCF, and Schedules Using Indirect Method

Required (use information from problem 13–3):

1. Prepare an SCF spreadsheet using the indirect method to report cash flows from operating activities.
2. Prepare the SCF.
3. Prepare a schedule of noncash investing and financing activities if necessary.

P13–14 Preparing SCF Spreadsheet and SCF Using Indirect Method: Includes Noncash Investing and Financing Activity and Sale of an Asset at Book Value

Required (use information from problem 13–4):

1. Prepare an SCF spreadsheet using the indirect method to report cash flows from operating activities.
2. Prepare the SCF.
3. Prepare a schedule of noncash investing and financing activities.

P13–15 Preparing SCF Using Indirect Method: Includes a Noncash Investing and Financing Activity, and Gain on Disposal of a Machine

Required (use information from problem 13–5):

1. Prepare an SCF spreadsheet using the indirect method to report cash flows from operating activities.
2. Prepare the SCF.
3. Prepare a schedule of noncash investing and financing activities.

P13–16 Preparing SCF Spreadsheet, Using Indirect Method: Includes a Noncash Investing and Financing Activity

Required (use information from problem 13–6):

1. Prepare an SCF spreadsheet using the indirect method to report cash flows from operating activities.
2. Prepare the SCF.
3. Prepare a schedule of noncash investing and financing activities.

CASES

C13–1 Cash Flow Analysis

Carlyle Golf, Inc.

Carlyle Golf, Inc., was formed in September 1992. The company designs, contracts for the manufacture of, and markets a line of men's golf apparel. A portion of the SCF for Carlyle is shown below:

	1993
Cash Flows from Operating Activities:	
Net income	$(460,089)
Depreciation	3,554
Noncash compensation (stock)	254,464
Deposits with suppliers	(404,934)
Increase in prepaid assets	(42,260)
Increase in accounts payable	81,765
Increase in accrued liabilities	24,495
Net cash flows	$(543,005)

Management expects a solid increase in sales in the near future. To support the increase in sales, they plan to add $2.2 million to their inventory. The company did not disclose a sales forecast. At the end of 1993, Carlyle had less than $1,000 in cash. It is not unusual for a new company to experience a loss and negative cash flows during its start-up phase. Evaluate the problems facing Carlyle.

Toys "Я" Us

C13–2 Financial Statement Analysis

Refer to the financial statements of Toys "Я" Us given in Appendix B at the end of this book.

Required:

1. Which of the two basic reporting approaches for the SCF was adopted by the company?
2. What amount of tax payments was made during the current year?
3. Short-term borrowings are shown in the financing activity section. Does this amount include interest payments on this debt? Explain.
4. Cash from operating activities was greater than net income in 1994 but less than net income in the current year. Evaluate this difference.
5. The company has not paid cash dividends for a number of years. Use the SCF to explain why.

14

The DEPOT Diner

THE HOME DEPOT

BURGER KING

Enjoy Coca-Cola

USING AND INTERPRETING FINANCIAL STATEMENTS

Throughout the preceding chapters, we emphasized the conceptual basis of accounting. An understanding of the rationale underlying accounting is important for both preparers and users of financial statements. In this chapter, we introduce the use and analysis of financial statements. Many widely used analytical techniques are discussed and illustrated. As you study this chapter, you will see that an understanding of accounting rules and concepts is essential for effective analysis of financial statements.

LEARNING OBJECTIVES

After studying this chapter, you should be able to:

Management Decision Setting

HOME DEPOT

Financial Analysis: Bringing It All Together

The history of Home Depot is an unusual success story. Founded in 1978 in Atlanta, Home Depot has grown to be America's largest home improvement retailer and, according to *Fortune* magazine, ranks among the nation's 30 largest retailers. Financial statements for Home Depot are shown in Exhibit 14–1.

As you can see, Home Depot is continuing its rapid growth. Sales revenue for the year ended January 31, 1993 was

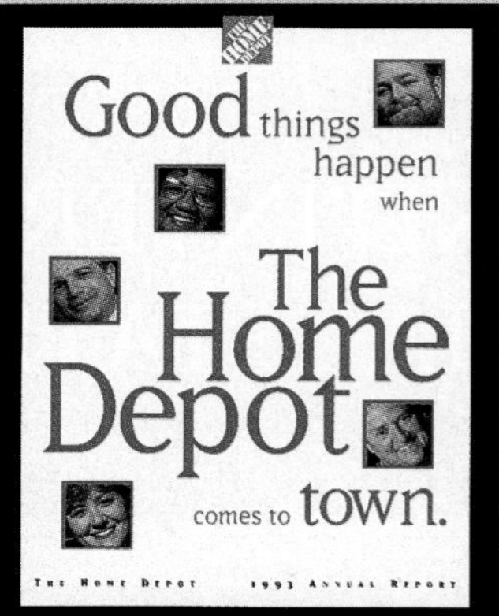

nearly 40% higher than 1992 and the company's net earnings increased by more than 45%. If you were an investor, would you want to buy Home Depot stock? To make a rational decision, you would want to consider more factors than just its rapid growth in profitability. Indeed, you would want to consider more information than what is reported in its annual report.

BUSINESS BACKGROUND

Learning Objective 1
Identify the major users of financial statements and explain how they use statements.

In the United States, billions of dollars are spent each year preparing, auditing and publishing financial statements. This money is spent because financial statements provide information that helps people make better economic decisions. There are two broad groups of people who use financial statements. One group is the management of the business, who rely on accounting data to make important operating decisions, such as the pricing of their products, or expansion of productive capacity. The second group is external decision makers. This group consists primarily of investors (both present and potential owners), investment analysts, creditors, government, labor organizations, and the public. Financial statements serve a diverse group of decision makers with different information needs.

Users of financial statements are interested in three types of information:

1. *Information about past performance.* Information concerning such items as income, sales volume, cash flows, and return earned on the investment helps assess the success of the business and the effectiveness of the management. Such information also helps the decision maker compare one company with others.
2. *Information about the present condition of a business.* This type of information helps answer such questions as: What types of assets are owned? How much debt does the business owe, and when is it due? What is the cash position? What are the EPS, return-on-investment, and debt/equity ratios? What is the inventory position? Answers to these and similar questions help people assess the successes and failures of the past; but, more importantly, they provide useful information in assessing the cash flow and profit potentials of the business.
3. *Information about the future performance of the business.* Decision makers select from among several alternative courses of action. All decisions are future oriented. As you know, financial statements report on the past and cannot predict the future. Nevertheless, reliable measurements of what has happened in the past are an important part of predicting what will happen in the future. For example, the re-

Home Depot Financial Statements — Exhibit 14–1

CONSOLIDATED BALANCE SHEETS

THE HOME DEPOT, INC. AND SUBSIDIARIES
Amounts in thousands, except share data

	January 31, 1993	February 2, 1992
ASSETS		
CURRENT ASSETS:		
Cash and Cash Equivalents	$ 121,744	$ 218,549
Short-term Investments, including current maturities of long-term investments (note 7)	292,451	176,650
Accounts Receivable, Net	177,502	79,472
Mechandise Inventories	939,824	662,257
Other Current Assets	30,452	21,320
Total Current Assets	1,561,973	1,158,248
PROPERTY AND EQUIPMENT, at cost:	694,276	64,268
Land	514,468	386,453
Buildings	619,909	444,249
Furniture, Fixtures and Equipment	344,139	253,831
Leasehold Improvements	212,196	178,460
Construction in Progress	101,064	120,390
	1,791,776	1,383,383
Less Accumulated Depreciation and Amortization	183,792	128,609
Net Property and Equipment	1,607,984	1,254,774
LONG-TERM INVESTMENTS (note 7)	694,276	64,268
COST IN EXCESS OF THE FAIR VALUE OF NET ASSETS ACQUIRED, net of accumulated amortization of $5,155 at January 31, 1993 and $4,523 at February 2, 1992	20,136	20,768
OTHER	47,421	12,234
	$3,931,790	$2,510,292
LIABILITIES AND STOCKHOLDERS' EQUITY		
CURRENT LIABILITIES:		
Accounts Payable	$ 420,318	$ 293,958
Accrued Salaries and Related Expenses	127,133	92,531
Sales Taxes Payable	46,320	34,387
Other Accrued Expenses	135,478	89,305
Income Taxes Payable	23,868	22,288
Current Installments of Long-term Debt (note 2)	1,828	1,842
Total Current Liabilities	754,945	534,311
LONG-TERM DEBT, excluding current installments (notes 2 and 6)	843,672	270,575
OTHER LONG-TERM LIABILITIES	12,968	7,126
DEFERRED INCOME TAXES (note 3)	16,124	7,068
STOCKHOLDERS' EQUITY (notes 2 and 4):		
Common stock, par value $.05. Authorized: 1,000,000,000 shares; issued and outstanding-443,585,000 shares at January 31, 1993 and 422,224,000 shares at February 2, 1992	22,179	21,111
Paid-in Capital	1,339,821	1,022,043
Retained Earnings	993,517	666,471
	2,355,517	1,709,625
Less Notes Receivable From ESOP (note 6)	51,436	18,413
Total Stockholders' Equity	2,304,081	1,691,212
COMMITMENTS AND CONTINGENCIES (notes 5 and 8)		
	$3,931,790	$2,510,292

See accompanying notes to consolidated financial statements.

Exhibit 14–1 *(concluded)*

CONSOLIDATED STATEMENTS OF EARNINGS

THE HOME DEPOT, INC. AND SUBSIDIARIES
Amounts in thousands, except per share data

	Fiscal Year Ended		
	January 31, 1993 (52 weeks)	February 2, 1992 (52 weeks)	February 3, 1991 (53 weeks)
NET SALES	$7,148,436	$5,136,674	$3,815,356
COST OF MERCHANDISE SOLD	5,179,368	3,692,337	2,751,085
GROSS PROFIT	1,969,068	1,444,337	1,064,271
OPERATING EXPENSES:			
Selling and Store Operating	1,245,608	928,928	693,657
Pre-Opening	26,959	17,668	13,315
General and Administrative	147,080	116,063	91,664
TOTAL OPERATING EXPENSES	1,419,647	1,062,659	798,636
OPERATING INCOME	549,421	381,678	265,635
INTEREST INCOME (EXPENSE):			
Interest Income	67,562	26,790	17,579
Interest Expense (note 2)	(41,010)	(12,348)	(23,386)
INTEREST, NET	26,552	14,442	(5,807)
EARNINGS BEFORE INCOME TAXES	575,973	396,120	259,828
INCOME TAXES (note 3)	213,110	146,970	96,400
NET EARNINGS	$ 362,863	$ 249,150	$ 163,428
EARNINGS PER COMMON AND COMMON EQUIVALENT SHARE	$ .82	$ .60	$ .45
WEIGHTED AVERAGE NUMBER OF COMMON AND COMMON EQUIVALENT SHARES (note 4)	444,989	415,997	362,505

See accompanying notes to consolidated financial statements.

cent sales and earnings trends of a business are good indicators of what might be expected in the future. In other words, you must know where you are in order to plan where you are able to go.

The Investment Decision

Perhaps the single largest group of people who use financial statements is investors including current owners, potential owners, and investment analysts (because they advise investors). Investors purchase stock with the expectation of earning a return on their investment. The return on a stock investment has two components: (1) dividend revenue during the investment period and (2) increases in the market value of the shares owned.

When considering a stock investment, the investor should evaluate the future income and growth potential of the business on the basis of three factors:

1. *Economywide factors.* Often the overall health of the economy will have a direct impact on the performance of an individual business. Investors should consider such data as the gross national product, productivity, unemployment rate, general inflation rate, and changes in interest rates. For example, increases in interest rates often slow

economic growth because consumers are less willing to buy merchandise on credit when interest rates are high.

2. *Industry factors.* Certain events have a major impact on each company within an industry, but have only a minor impact on other companies. For example, a major drought may be devastating for food-related industries but have no effect on the electronics industry.
3. *Individual company factors.* To properly analyze a company, you should get to know as much as you can about it. Good analysts do not rely only on the information contained in the financial statements. They visit the company, buy its products, and read about the company in the business press. If you evaluate McDonald's, it is equally important to assess the quality of their balance sheet and the quality of their Big Mac. The importance of nonquantitative information can be illustrated by a research report on Home Depot written by Salomon Brothers, a large investment banking firm:

> We believe that the company's strong culture—which focuses on employee empowerment and customer service—is the key reason that it has become the nation's largest home center chain in only 12 years and that it will be able to dramatically expand its national market share over the next several years, as it expands its presence across the country and around the world.

Real World Excerpt

Home Depot
Salomon Brothers
Research Report

UNDERSTANDING A COMPANY'S STRATEGY

Financial statement analysis is more than just "crunching numbers." Before you start looking at numbers, you should know what you are looking for. The best place to start is with a solid understanding of the company's business strategy. In order to evaluate how a company is doing, you must know what they are trying to do. You can learn a great deal about a company's strategy by reading the complete annual report, especially the letter from the president. It is also useful to read articles about the company in the business press.

Home Depot's business strategy is described by Salomon Brothers as follows:

> The Home Depot successful formula combines the low everyday prices of a large store, "category killer" retailer, with the service usually found only in a small, local hardware store. Few if any of its competitors are able to duplicate both of these customer driven strategies.

Real World Excerpt

Home Depot
Salomon Brothers
Research Report

This strategy has several implications for our analysis of Home Depot. For example,

1. Cost control is critical. Home Depot must be able to purchase merchandise at low prices to beat competitors.
2. Stores must be able to generate high volume to cover the cost of operating large stores.
3. Employee compensation and training costs will be higher than competitors' costs in these areas in order to offer a high level of service. This will put greater pressure on Home Depot to control costs in other areas.

By understanding the strategy of a company, the analyst is able to attach more meaning to the information contained in the financial statements.

ANALYSIS OF FINANCIAL STATEMENTS

Financial statements include a large volume of quantitative data supplemented by disclosure notes. It is impossible to analyze financial data without a basis of comparison. For example, would you be impressed with a company that earned $1 million last year? You probably answered the question by thinking "it depends." A profit of $1 million might be very good for a company that lost money the year before but not good for a company that made $500 million during the previous year; it might be good for a small company but not good for a very large company; it might be good if all the other companies in the industry lost money but not good if they all earned much larger profits. As you can see from this simple example, financial results cannot be evaluated in isolation. You must develop appropriate comparisons to properly analyze the information reported in financial statements. Finding an appropriate benchmark requires judgment and is not always an easy task. For this reason, financial analysis is a sophisticated skill instead of a mechanical process.

There are two types of benchmarks for making financial comparisons:

1. *Time series analysis.* In this type of analysis, information for a single company is compared over time. For example, a company may have a current ratio (current assets divided by current liabilities) of 1.2. Without additional information, this ratio does not tell us very much. Time series analysis might tell you that the ratio had declined each year for the past five years, from a high of 2. This time series information might cause you to do further study concerning the factors that had caused a steady deterioration of this ratio in the recent past.
2. *Comparison with similar companies.* Financial results are often affected by industry and economywide factors. By comparing a company with another one in the same line of business, the analyst can get better insights concerning company specific performance. An analyst would be concerned if General Motors sales revenue fell by 2% in a given year. The analyst might be less concerned if for the same period Ford experienced a 10% decline and Chrysler had a 16% decline. This comparison would indicate that the entire automobile industry had a bad year but that General Motors had done well compared to its major domestic competitors.

Finding comparable companies is often very difficult. In a previous chapter, we discussed American Brands which is involved in tobacco, distilled spirits, life insurance, home improvement products, office products, and golf equipment. No other company sells exactly that group of products. Care must be exercised when selecting comparable companies from the same basic industry. Days Inn, La Quinta, Hilton, Four Seasons, Mariott, and Mirage Resorts are all in the hotel industry but not all could be considered comparable companies for purposes of financial analysis.

The federal government has established standard industrial classification codes that are used to report economic data. These four-digit codes are often used by analysts to identify industry comparisons for various companies. Financial information services, such as Robert Morris Associates, provide averages for many common accounting ratios for various industries as defined by the standard industrial classification codes. Because of the diversity of companies included in each industry classification, you should use these data with great care. Some analysts prefer to compare two companies that are very similar instead of using industrywide comparisons.

RATIO AND PERCENTAGE ANALYSES

Learning Objective 2
Explain the objectives of ratio analysis.

All financial analysts use **ratio analysis**, or **percentage analysis**, when they review companies. A ratio or percent expresses the proportionate relationship between two different amounts. A ratio or percent is computed by dividing one quantity by another quantity. For example, the fact that a company earned net income of $500,000 assumes greater significance when net income is compared with the stockholders' investment in the company. Assuming that stockholders' equity is $5 million, the relationship of earnings to stockholder investment is $500,000 ÷ $5,000,000 = 10%. This measure indicates a different level of performance than would be the case if stockholders' equity were $50 million. Ratio analysis helps decision makers identify significant relationships and compare companies more realistically than if only single amounts were analyzed.

Ratio (percentage) analysis is an analytical tool designed to identify significant relationships; it measures the proportional relationship between two financial statement amounts.

Ratios may be computed using amounts within one statement, such as the income statement, or between different statements, such as the income statement and the balance sheet. The current ratio (current assets divided by current liabilities) is based on information from a single statement. Return on assets (net income divided by total assets) is based on information from the income statement and the balance sheet.

Financial statement analysis is a judgmental process. No single ratio can be identified as appropriate to all situations. Each analytical situation may require the calculation of several ratios. We will discuss several ratios that are appropriate to many situations.

Component Percentages

Component percentages are used to express each item on a particular statement as a percentage of a single *base amount*, the denominator of the ratio. To compute component percentages for the income statement, the base amount is net sales revenue. Each expense is expressed as a percentage of net sales revenue. On the balance sheet, the base amount is total assets. The percentages are derived by dividing each balance sheet account by total assets.

A **component percentage** is a percentage that expresses each item on a particular financial statement as a percentage of a single base amount.

It is difficult to discern important relationships and trends in the Home Depot income statement shown in Exhibit 14–1 without using component percentages. Income more than doubled between 1991 and 1993, which is obviously very good, but it would be difficult for an analyst to evaluate the operating efficiency of Home Depot based on the reported numbers on the income statement.

Exhibit 14–2 shows a component analysis for Home Depot's income statement (from Exhibit 14–1). Notice how several important issues become much more apparent. For example:

1. The majority of the increase in net income can be attributed to an increase in sales revenue, but another important factor was the increase in profitability per dollar of sales. In 1991, profit was 4.3% of sales; by 1993, it grew to 5.1% of sales.
2. The increase in profit as a percentage of sales was due to improvements in operating efficiency. Selling and store operating costs fell from 18.2% of sales to 17.4%, while general and administrative costs fell from 2.4% to 2.1%.
3. Cost of goods sold as a percentage of sales declined between 1991 and 1992 but increased significantly in 1993. This may be an indication that increased competition is forcing Home Depot to cut

Exhibit 14–2 Component Percentages for Home Depot

Income Statement	Component Percentages 1993	1992	1991
Net sales	100.0%	100.0%	100.0%
Cost of merchandise sold	72.5	71.9	72.1
Gross profit	27.5	28.1	27.9
Operating expenses:			
Selling and store operating	17.4	18.1	18.2
Preopening	.4	.3	.3
General and administrative	2.1	2.3	2.4
Total operating expenses	19.9	20.7	20.9
Operating income	7.7	7.4	7.0
Interest income	.9	.5	.5
Interest expense	(.6)	(.2)	(.6)
Interest, net	.4	.3	(.2)
Earnings, before taxes	8.1	7.7	6.8
Income taxes	3.0	2.9	2.5
Net earnings	5.1	4.9	4.3

its selling prices. An analyst would want to gather more information concerning this important issue.

4. There is significant stability in all of the income statement relationships which would indicate a well-run company. Notice that all of the individual income statement items changed by less than one percentage point over a three-year period.
5. Preopening costs doubled between 1991 and 1993. This increase seems less important when the analysis reveals that the costs have remained relatively constant as a percentage of sales.

COMMONLY USED RATIOS

Learning Objective 3
List five categories of accounting ratios.

In addition to component percentages, analysts use a large number of ratios that compare related items from the financial statements. You have been exposed to many of these ratios earlier in this book. For example, the current ratio compares current assets and current liabilities. This comparison is widely used as a measure of solvency, or the ability of a company to pay its short-term debt. The comparison makes sense because current liabilities may be paid with current assets.

Numerous ratios can be computed from a single set of financial statements, but only a selected number may be useful in a given situation. It would never be useful to compare cost of goods sold to property, plant, and equipment because these items have no natural relationship. A common approach is to compute certain widely used ratios and then decide which additional ratios are relevant to the particular decision. For example, research and development costs as a percentage of sales is not a common ratio but it would be useful in some special situations. You would want to look at that ratio if you were evaluating companies that depended on new products, such as manufacturers of drugs or computers.

When you compute ratios, it is important to remember a basic fact about financial statements. Balance sheet amounts relate to one instant in time, and income statement amounts relate to a period of time. Therefore, when an income statement account is compared with a balance sheet amount, a balance sheet

Widely Used Accounting Ratios — **Exhibit 14–3**

Ratio	Basic Computation
Tests of profitability:	
1. Return on owners' investment (ROI_O)	$\frac{\text{Income}}{\text{Average owners' equity}}$
2. Return on total investment (ROI_t)	$\frac{\text{Income + Interest expense (net of tax)}}{\text{Average total assets}}$
3. Financial leverage ($ROI_O - ROI_t$)	Return on owners' investment − Return on total investment
4. Earnings per share	$\frac{\text{Income}}{\text{Average number of shares of common stock outstanding}}$
5. Profit margin	$\frac{\text{Income (before extraordinary items)}}{\text{Net sales revenue}}$
Tests of liquidity:	
6. Current ratio	$\frac{\text{Current assets}}{\text{Current liabilities}}$
7. Quick ratio	$\frac{\text{Quick assets}}{\text{Current liabilities}}$
8. Receivable turnover	$\frac{\text{Net credit sales}}{\text{Average net trade receivables}}$
9. Inventory turnover	$\frac{\text{Cost of goods sold}}{\text{Average inventory}}$
Test of solvency and equity position:	
10. Debt/equity ratio	$\frac{\text{Total liabilities}}{\text{Owners' equity}}$
Market tests:	
11. Price/earnings ratio	$\frac{\text{Current market price per share}}{\text{Earnings per share}}$
12. Dividend yield ratio	$\frac{\text{Dividends per share}}{\text{Market price per share}}$
Miscellaneous ratio:	
13. Book value per share	$\frac{\text{Common stock equity}}{\text{Number of shares of common stock outstanding}}$

average amount should be used to reflect changes in the balance sheet amounts. The selected balance sheet amount usually is computed as the average of the amounts shown on the beginning and ending balance sheets.

Commonly used financial ratios can be grouped into the five categories shown in Exhibit 14–3.

TESTS OF PROFITABILITY

Learning Objective 4
Identify and compute 13 widely used accounting ratios.

Profitability is a primary measure of the overall success of a company. Indeed, it is a necessary condition for survival. Investors and creditors would prefer a single measure of profitability that would be meaningful in all situations. Unfortunately, no single measure can be devised to meet this comprehensive need. Tests of profitability focus on measuring the adequacy of income by comparing it with one or more primary activities or factors that are measured in the financial statements. Five different tests of profitability are commonly used.

1. Return on Owners' Investment (ROI_O)

This ratio is a fundamental test of profitability. It relates income to the investment that was made by the owners to earn income. It reflects the simple fact that investors expect to earn more money if they invest more money. Two investments that offer a return of $10,000 are not comparable if one requires a $100,000 investment and the other requires a $250,000 investment. The return on owners' investment ratio is computed as follows:[1]

$$\text{Return on owners' investment} = \frac{\text{Income}^*}{\text{Average owners' equity}^\dagger}$$

$$\text{Home Depot 1993} = \frac{\$362{,}863^*}{\$1{,}997{,}646^\dagger} = 18.2\%$$

*Income **before** extraordinary items should be used.
†Average owners' equity is preferable when available. For Home Depot, it is computed as: ($2,304,081 + $1,691,212) ÷ 2 = $1,997,646.

Home Depot earned 18.2%, after income taxes, on the investment provided by the owners. Is this return good or bad? The question can be answered only by making comparisons with similar companies. The return on owners' investment for three of Home Depot's competitors is shown below:

Lowe's	11.6%
Hechinger	6.5
Grossman's	3.9
Home Depot	18.2

Clearly, this comparison indicates that Home Depot is doing very well.

2. Return on Total Investment (ROI_t)

Another view of the return on investment concept relates income to total assets (i.e., total investment) used to earn income. Many analysts consider this ratio to be a better measure of management's ability to effectively utilize assets independent of how the assets were financed. The return on owners' investment could be very large for a company that was highly leveraged (i.e., employed a large amount of debt) even though management earned a low rate of return on total assets. Return on total investment is computed as follows:

$$\text{Return on total investment} = \frac{\text{Income}^* + \text{Interest expense (net of tax)}}{\text{Average total assets}^\dagger}$$

$$\text{Home Depot 1993} = \frac{\$362{,}863 + (\$41{,}010 \times 66\%)}{\$3{,}221{,}041} = 12.5\%$$

*Income before extraordinary items should be used. This illustration uses a corporate tax rate of 34%.
†Average total assets should be used. For Home Depot that is ($3,931,790 + $2,510,292) ÷ 2 = $3,221,041.

Home Depot earned 12.5% on the total resources it used during the year. Under this concept, investment is the amount of resources provided by both owners and creditors. Notice that the measure of return includes the return to both owners and creditors. To compute return on total investment, interest expense (net of income tax) is added back to income because interest is the return on the creditors' investment. It must be added back because it was previously deducted to compute net income. The denominator represents

[1]The figures for Home Depot used throughout the following 13 ratio examples are taken from the financial statements in Exhibit 14–1.

Home Depot achieves exceptional profitability by meeting customer needs. It is possible to have a good fast-food meal without leaving the store.

total investment; therefore, the numerator (income) must include the total return that was available to the suppliers of funds. Interest expense is measured net of income tax because it represents the net cost to the corporation for the funds provided by creditors.

As you would expect, return on total investment is usually smaller than return on owners' investment. The return on total investment for Home Depot's competitors is shown below. Each of these ratios is less than the return on owners' investment ratio that was shown earlier.

Lowe's	5.3%
Hechinger	2.9
Grossman's	2.0
Home Depot	12.5

3. Financial Leverage

Financial leverage is the advantage, or disadvantage, that occurs as the result of earning a return on owners' investment that is different from the return earned on total investment (i.e., ROI_O - ROI_t). Most companies have positive leverage. Positive leverage occurs when the rate of return on a company's investments is higher than the average aftertax interest rate on borrowed funds. Basically, the company borrows at one rate and invests at a higher rate of return.

Financial leverage can be measured by comparing the two return-on-investment ratios as follows:

Financial leverage	=	Return on owners' investment	–	Return on total investment		(positive leverage)
Home Depot 1993	=	18.2%	–	12.5%	=	5.7%

When a company is able to borrow funds at an aftertax interest rate and invest those funds to earn a higher aftertax rate of return, the difference accrues to the benefit of the owners. The notes to the Home Depot annual report indicate that the company has borrowed money at rates ranging from 4.5% to

11.5% and invested this money in assets earning 18.2%. The difference between the money that the company earns and the amount that it pays out in interest to creditors is available for the owners of Home Depot. Financial leverage is the primary reason that most companies obtain a significant amount of resources from creditors rather than obtaining resources only from the sale of their capital stock.

4. Earnings per Share (EPS)

Some analysts are critical of the return-on-investment ratios because they are based on historical cost data. The amount of owners' investment represents their original investment plus retained earnings, not the current market value of that investment. The same concern applies to the return on total assets.

Earnings per share is based on the number of shares outstanding instead of dollar amounts reported on the balance sheet. Investors can easily interpret EPS in terms of their personal circumstances. An investor with 1,000 shares of stock can quickly compute the return on his or her investment using EPS. The investor would not be able to compute his or her return with only the information that the company had earned 18.2% on owners' equity. Basically, EPS is computed as follows:

$$\text{Earnings per share} = \frac{\text{Income}}{\text{Average number of shares of common stock outstanding}}$$

$$\text{Home Depot 1993} = \frac{\$362{,}863}{432{,}905^{*}} = \$.84 \text{ per share}$$

*Average number of shares is (443,585 + 422,224) ÷ 2 = 432,905

Notice that our computation of EPS ($.84) is different from the amount actually reported on the income statement for Home Depot shown in Exhibit 14–1 ($.82). This difference is caused by some additional complexities in the computation of EPS that will be discussed in advanced accounting courses. In practice, EPS is based on the average number of common shares outstanding plus any securities whose value is determined primarily from their ability to be converted into common stock. These securities are called common stock equivalents. A good example of a common stock equivalent is a stock option which permits you to buy common stock at a fixed price. The only reason to buy a stock option is because it can be converted into common stock. Therefore, it is a common stock equivalent. Home Depot included stock options in their computation of earnings per share which explains the difference between its reported number and the one we computed above.

EPS usually is computed on three amounts if extraordinary items are reported on the income statement: (1) income before extraordinary items (required), (2) extraordinary items (optional), and (3) net income (required). Of the three EPS amounts, the first one is considered the most relevant because extraordinary items are unusual and do not recur.

Earnings per share is probably the single most widely watched ratio. When companies announce their EPS each quarter during the fiscal year, it is normally reported in the business press. The following report concerning Home Depot appeared in Reuters News Service in early 1995:

Real World Excerpt

Home Depot EPS Announcement in Reuters News Service

Home Depot stock fell sharply on the New York Stock Exchange where shares lost $2 1/2 to stand at $46 in late morning trading. Fourth-quarter earnings per share of $0.32 were $.01 less than Wall Street consensus expectations.

5. Profit Margin

This percent is based on two income statement amounts. It is computed as follows:

$$\text{Profit margin} = \frac{\text{Income (before extraordinary items)}}{\text{Net sales}}$$

$$\text{Home Depot 1993} = \frac{\$362,863}{\$7,148,436} = 5.1\%$$

This profitability measurement represents the percentage of each sales dollar, on the average, that is profit. For Home Depot, each dollar of sales generated 5.1 cents of profit. Care must be used in analyzing the profit margin because it does not consider the amount of resources employed (i.e., total investment) to earn income. For example, the hypothetical income statements of Home Depot and Hechinger might show the following:

		Home Depot	Hechinger
a.	Sales revenue	$100,000	$150,000
b.	Income	$ 5,000	$ 7,500
c.	Profit margin (*b*) ÷ (*a*)	5%	5%
d.	Total investment	$ 50,000	$125,000
e.	Return on total investment* (*b*) ÷ (*d*)	10%	6%

*Assuming no interest expense.

In this example, both companies reported the same profit margin (5%). Home Depot, however, appears to be performing much better because it is earning a 10% return on the total investment versus the 6% earned by Hechinger. The profit margin percentages do not reflect the effect of the $50,000 total investment in Home Depot compared to the $125,000 total investment in Hechinger. The effect of the different amounts of investment in each company is reflected in the return-on-investment (ROI) percentages. Thus, the profit margin omits one of the two important factors that should be used in evaluating return on the investment.

Comparing profit margins for companies in different industries is difficult. For example, profit margins in the food industry are low while profit margins in the jewelry business are large. Both types of businesses can be quite profitable because they differ in terms of the sales volume that can be generated from a given level of investment. Grocery stores have small margins but generate a large sales volume from relatively inexpensive stores and inventory. Jewelry stores earn more profit from each sales dollar but require a large investment in luxury stores and very expensive inventory. This relationship between profit margin and sales volume can be stated in very simple terms; would you prefer to have 5% of $1,000,000 or 10% of $100,000? As you can see, a larger percent is not always better.

The operating strength of Home Depot comes into clearer focus when you compare its profit margin with that of major competitors:

Lowe's	2.2%
Hechinger	1.7
Grossman's	.7
Home Depot	5.1

Self-Study Quiz

Show how to compute the following ratios:

1. Return on owners' investment = ________________

2. Return on total investment = ______________________

3. Profit margin = ______________________

Check your answers with the solution in the footnote at the bottom of this page.*

TESTS OF LIQUIDITY

Tests of liquidity are ratios that measure a company's ability to meet its currently maturing obligations.

Liquidity refers to a company's ability to meet its currently maturing debts. **Tests of liquidity** focus on the relationship between current assets and current liabilities. The ability of a company to pay its current liabilities is an important factor in evaluating short-term financial strength. For example, a company that does not have cash available to pay for purchases on a timely basis will lose its cash discounts and run the risk of discontinued credit by vendors. Two ratios are used to measure liquidity: the current ratio and the quick ratio. Recall that working capital is the dollar difference between total current assets and total current liabilities.

6. Current Ratio

This ratio measures the relationship between total current assets and total current liabilities at a specific date. It is computed as follows:

$$\text{Current ratio} = \frac{\text{Current assets}}{\text{Current liabilities}}$$

$$\text{Home Depot 1993} = \frac{\$1{,}561{,}973}{\$754{,}945} = 2.1 \text{ to } 1$$

At year-end, current assets for Home Depot were 2.1 times current liabilities or, alternatively, for each $1 of current liabilities there were $2.10 of current assets. The current ratio measures the cushion of working capital maintained to allow for the inevitable unevenness in the flow of funds through the working capital accounts. Because the current ratio measures the adequacy of working capital, it is sometimes called the *working capital ratio*.

Analysts would consider a current ratio of 2 to be conservative. Indeed, most companies have current ratios that are less than 2. The optimal level for a current ratio depends on the business environment in which a company operates. If cash flows are predictable and stable (a utility company, for example), the current ratio can be just a little greater than 1. For a business with highly variable cash flows (such as an airline), a current ratio closer to 2 may be desirable.

It is possible to have a current ratio that is too high. It is normally considered to be inefficient to tie up too much money in inventory or accounts receivable. If a Home Depot store sells 100 hammers a month, there is no reason to have 1,000 in stock. A very high current ratio may be an indication of serious operating difficulties.

---

*1. $\dfrac{\text{Income}}{\text{Average owners' equity}}$

2. $\dfrac{\text{Income + Interest expense (net of tax)}}{\text{Average total assets}}$

3. $\dfrac{\text{Income (before extraordinary items)}}{\text{Net sales}}$

7. Quick Ratio (Acid Test)

This ratio is similar to the current ratio except that it is a more stringent test of short-term liquidity. It is computed as follows:

$$\text{Quick ratio} = \frac{\text{Quick assets}}{\text{Current liabilities}}$$

$$\text{Home Depot 1993} = \frac{\$591{,}697}{\$754{,}945} = 0.78 \text{ to } 1$$

Quick assets are readily convertible into cash at approximately their book values. Quick assets include cash, short-term investments, and accounts receivable (net of the allowance for doubtful accounts). Inventories usually are omitted from quick assets because of the uncertainty of when cash will be received from the sale of inventory in the future. Thus, the quick, or acid test, ratio is a more severe test of liquidity than is the current ratio.

8. Receivable Turnover

Short-term liquidity and operating efficiency can be measured in terms of *turnover* of certain current assets. Two additional ratios that measure nearness to cash are receivable turnover and inventory turnover.

Receivable turnover is computed as follows:

$$\text{Receivable turnover} = \frac{\text{Net credit sales*}}{\text{Average net trade receivables}}$$

$$\text{Home Depot 1993} = \frac{\$7{,}148{,}436}{\$128{,}487^{\dagger}} = 55.6 \text{ times}$$

*When the amount of credit sales is not known, total sales may be used as a rough approximation.
†($177,502 + $79,472) ÷ 2 = $128,487

This ratio is called a turnover because it reflects how many times the trade receivables were recorded, collected, then recorded again during the period (i.e., "turnover"). Receivable turnover expresses the relationship of the average balance in Accounts Receivable to the transactions (i.e., credit sales) that created those receivables. This ratio measures the effectiveness of the credit-granting and collection activities of the company. A high receivable turnover ratio suggests effective collection activities. Granting credit to poor credit risks and ineffective collection efforts will cause this ratio to be low. A very low ratio is obviously a problem, but a very high ratio can also be a problem. A very high ratio may indicate an overly stringent credit policy that would cause lost sales and profits.

The receivable turnover ratio often is converted to a time basis known as the *average age of receivables*. The computation is as follows:

$$\text{Average age of trade receivables} = \frac{\text{Days in year}}{\text{Receivable turnover}}$$

$$\text{Home Depot 1993} = \frac{365}{55.6} = 6.6 \text{ average days to collect}$$

The effectiveness of credit and collection activities sometimes is judged by the rule of thumb that the average days to collect should not exceed 1 1/2 times the credit terms. For example, if the credit terms require payment in 30 days, the average days to collect should not exceed 45 days (i.e., not more than 15 days past due). Like all rules of thumb, this one has many exceptions.

When you evaluate financial statements, you should always think about the reasonableness of the numbers you compute. We computed the average age of

A key to rapid growth is effective marketing. Home Depot signed on as a sponsor of the Olympic Games in Atlanta.

receivables for Home Depot as 6.6 days. Is that number reasonable? Probably not. It is very unlikely that Home Depot collects cash from its credit customers on average in just 6.6 days. Remember that we do not know the amount of credit sales for Home Depot and had to use total sales as an approximation. In reality, Home Depot grants very little credit under its own name. Instead, it utilizes major credit cards such as Mastercard and Visa which are recorded virtually the same as cash from the perspective of the seller. As a result, the accounts receivable turnover ratio is not meaningful for Home Depot.

9. Inventory Turnover

Inventory turnover measures the liquidity of the inventory. It reflects the relationship of the inventory to the volume of goods sold during the period. The computation is as follows:

$$\text{Inventory turnover} = \frac{\text{Cost of goods sold}}{\text{Average inventory}}$$

$$\text{Home Depot 1993} = \frac{\$5,179,368}{\$801,040^{*}} = 6.5 \text{ times}$$

* ($939,824 + $662,257) ÷ 2 = $801,040

The inventory for Home Depot "turned over" 6.5 times during the year. Because profit normally is realized each time the inventory is sold (i.e., turned over), an increase in the ratio is usually favorable. However, if the ratio is too high, sales may be lost because of items that are out of stock.

Home Depot must maintain an inventory of a large variety of home improvement items.

The inventory turnover ratio is critical for a company that has adopted the Home Depot strategy. They want to be able to offer the customer the right product when it is needed at a price that beats the competition. If they do not effectively manage their inventory levels, they will incur extra costs that must be passed on to the customer. Let's compare the Home Depot inventory turnover to the company's major competitors:

Lowe's	6.0
Hechinger	5.2
Grossman's	6.1
Home Depot	6.5

As you can see, Home Depot has the highest turnover among the peer group but there is not a very significant difference between the companies. Home Depot has recently spent $9 million to upgrade computer systems in all of its stores and is now transmitting data via satellite. One of the announced goals of this investment is to increase inventory turnover.

The turnover ratio often is converted to a time-basis expression called the average days' supply in inventory. The computation is:

$$\text{Average days' supply in inventory} = \frac{\text{Days in year}}{\text{Inventory turnover}}$$

$$\text{Home Depot 1993} = \frac{365}{6.5}$$

$$= \text{56 average days' supply in inventory}$$

Turnover ratios vary significantly by industry classification. Companies in the food industry (grocery stores and restaurants) have high inventory turnover ratios because their inventory is subject to rapid deterioration in quality. Companies that sell expensive merchandise (automobile dealers and high-fashion clothes) have much lower ratios because sales of these items are infrequent but customers want to have a selection to choose from when they do buy.

TESTS OF SOLVENCY AND EQUITY POSITION

Solvency refers to the ability of a company to meet its long-term obligations on a continuing basis, and **tests of solvency** measure a company's ability to meet these obligations. Certain critical relationships can be identified by analyzing how a company has financed its assets and activities. The relative amount of resources provided by creditors and owners is known as a company's *equity position*. The debt/equity ratio is used to reflect the equity position of a company.

Tests of solvency are ratios that measure a company's ability to meet its long-term obligations.

10. Debt/Equity Ratio

This ratio expresses the proportion between debt and owners' equity.[2] It is computed as follows:

[2]The relationship between debt and owners' equity alternatively may be calculated with the following two ratios:

$$\text{Owners' equity to total equities} = \frac{\text{Owners' equity}}{\text{Total equities}}$$

$$\text{Home Depot 1993} = \frac{\$2,304,081}{\$3,931,790} = 58.6\%$$

$$\text{Creditors' equity to total equities} = \frac{\text{Creditors' equity}}{\text{Total equities}}$$

$$\text{Home Depot 1993} = \frac{\$1,627,709}{\$3,931,790} = 41.4\%$$

$$\text{Debt/equity ratio} = \frac{\text{Total liabilities (i.e., creditors' equity)}}{\text{Owners' equity}}$$

$$\text{Home Depot 1993} = \frac{\$1,627,709}{\$2,304,081} = 0.71 \text{ (or 71\%)}$$

This ratio means that for each $1 of owners' equity, there were 71 cents of liabilities. Debt is risky for a company because it imposes important contractual obligations. There are (*a*) specific maturity dates for the principal amounts and (*b*) specific interest payments that must be made. Debt obligations are enforceable by law and do not depend on the earnings of the company. In contrast, dividends for stockholders are always at the discretion of the company and are not legally enforceable until declared by the board of directors. Owners' equity is "permanent" capital that does not have a maturity date. Thus, equity capital usually is seen as much less risky than debt for a company.

Despite the risk associated with debt, most companies get significant amounts of resources from creditors because of the advantages of financial leverage which were discussed earlier in this chapter. In addition, interest expense is a deductible expense on the income tax return. When selecting a capital structure, a company must balance the higher returns that are available with leverage against the higher risk associated with debt. Because of the importance of this risk and return relationship, most analysts consider the debt/equity ratio to be a key part of any company evaluation.

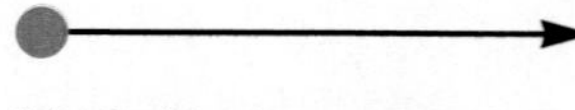

MARKET TESTS

Market tests are ratios that tend to measure the market worth of a share of stock.

Several ratios measure the "market worth" of a share of stock. These **market tests** relate the current market price of a share of stock to an indicator of the return that might accrue to the investor. The tests focus on the current market price of the stock because that is the amount the buyer would invest. Two market test ratios used by analysts and investors are the price/earnings ratio and the dividend yield ratio.

11. Price/Earnings (P/E) Ratio

This ratio measures the relationship between the current market price of the stock and its earnings per share. A recent price for Home Depot stock was $44 per share. The EPS for Home Depot calculated earlier was $0.84. The P/E ratio for the company is computed as follows:

$$\text{Price/earnings ratio} = \frac{\text{Current market price per share}}{\text{Earnings per share}}$$

$$\text{Home Depot 1993} = \frac{\$44}{\$0.84} = 52.4$$

Home Depot stock was selling at 52.4 times the EPS. The P/E ratio often is referred to as the *multiple*, as in price/earnings multiple. The P/E ratio is used as an indicator of the future performance of the stock. A high price/earnings multiple indicates that the market expects earnings to grow rapidly. The P/E ratio for Home Depot is very high compared to its major competitors:

Lowe's	33.1
Hechinger	12.8
Grossman's	12.5
Home Depot	52.4

The analysts at Salomon Brothers noted this very high multiple and said the following:

Real World Excerpt

Salomon Brothers Research Report

> The stock appears to be rather expensive relative to that of its direct competitors because the stock trades at a significantly higher multiple. However, given Home Depot's above-average financial performance, we believe that the stock's premium is entirely warranted. Based on an estimated growth rate of 28–32% annually over the next three to five years, we continue to recommend the stock.

Sometimes the components of the P/E ratio are inverted, giving the capitalization rate. This is the rate at which the stock market apparently is capitalizing the current earnings. Computation of the capitalization rate on current earnings per share for Home Depot would be $0.84 ÷ $44 = 1.9%.

12. Dividend Yield Ratio

When investors buy stock, they expect returns from two sources: price appreciation and dividend income. The dividend yield ratio measures the relationship between the dividends per share paid and the current market price of the stock. Home Depot paid dividends of 55 cents per share when the market price per share was $44. The dividend yield ratio for Home Depot is computed as follows:

$$\text{Dividend yield ratio} = \frac{\text{Dividend per share}}{\text{Market price per share}}$$

$$\text{Home Depot 1993} = \frac{\$0.55}{\$44} = 1.25\%$$

Dividend yields for most stocks are not very high compared to alternative investments. A regular savings account, for example, would pay an investor much more than 1.25%. Investors are willing to accept low dividend yields when they expect that the price of the stock will increase while they own it. Stocks with low growth potential often offer much higher dividend yields than stocks with high growth potential. These stocks often appeal to investors who are retired and need current income rather than future growth potential.

MISCELLANEOUS RATIO

13. Book Value per Share

The book value per share of stock measures the owners' equity in terms of each share of common stock outstanding. In the case of a simple capital structure, with *only* common stock outstanding, the computation of book value per share is not difficult. The computation of book value per share is:

$$\text{Book value per common share} = \frac{\text{Total owners' equity (applicable to common shares)}}{\text{Common shares outstanding}}$$

$$\text{Home Depot 1993} = \frac{\$2,304,081}{443,585 \text{ shares}} = \$5.19$$

Notice that book value per share has no relationship to market value. The book value of a share of Home Depot stock was $5.19 when the market value was $44. For most companies, book value per share will be less than the market value. Some analysts compute a price/book value ratio which compares the current market value of the stock (i.e., selling price) with the book value. The price/book ratio for Home Depot is $44 ÷ $5.19 = 8.5. Over the past five years, this ratio has ranged from a low of 2.9 to a high of 12. A high ratio is an indication of a company with good growth potential.

Self-Study Quiz

Show how to compute the following ratios:

1. Current ratio = ______________________
2. Inventory turnover = ______________________
3. Price/earnings ratio = ______________________

Check your answers with the solution shown in the footnote at the bottom of this page.*

OTHER ANALYTICAL CONSIDERATIONS

The ratios that we have discussed so far are general purpose ratios that are useful in most analytical considerations. Each company is different and your evaluation of each company should be different.

To illustrate, let's look at some special factors that might affect our analysis of Home Depot.

1. *Rapid growth* In some cases, a company that opens many new stores each year may obscure the fact that existing stores are not meeting customer needs and are experiencing declining sales. In other words, growth in total sales volume does not always indicate that a company is successful. A family pizza chain called Chuck-E-Cheese reported rapid growth in total sales revenue for a number of years but it was generated by opening new stores. New stores initially generated very large sales volumes because they were very popular with young children. Unfortunately, the novelty of the Chuck-E-Cheese stores proved to be short-lived fads and same-store sales volume fell quickly. The company was forced to reorganize. In contrast, the annual report for Home Depot shows that the company has had same-store sales increases above 10% in each of the previous five years which indicates that they are able to generate increases in sales volume from both new and existing stores.
2. *Uneconomical expansion* Some growth oriented companies open stores in less desirable locations once all the good locations have been taken. These poor locations can cause the average productivity of the stores to decline. One measure of productivity in the retail industry is sales volume per square foot of selling space. For Home Depot, productivity is increasing each year:

---

*1. $\dfrac{\text{Current assets}}{\text{Current liabilities}}$

2. $\dfrac{\text{Cost of goods sold}}{\text{Average inventory}}$

3. $\dfrac{\text{Current market price per share}}{\text{Earnings per share}}$

Year	Sales per Sq. Ft.
1993	$387
1992	348
1991	322
1990	303
1989	282

3. *Subjective factors* It is important to remember that there is vital information about a company that is not contained in the annual report. We discussed earlier that a strategy of Home Depot is to be a price leader. The best way to evaluate that strategy is to visit the stores of Home Depot and several competitors. The analyst who studied Home Depot for Salomon Brothers did exactly that:

> On July 15, 1993, we surveyed the Boca Raton, Florida market. The Home Depot store is about two years old and was particularly impressive with respect to its in-stock position, customer service and total store presentation. We were able to compare Home Depot's pricing on 20 sample items. Our price analysis revealed that Home Depot is the price leader in the market by an average of 11% below the average total price of our 20-item market basket. Given the Home Depot's low cost structure, we believe that it will remain the price leader in this important market.

Real World Excerpt
Home Depot
Salomon Brothers
Research Report

As these examples illustrate, there is no single approach that can be used to analyze all companies. Furthermore, effective analysis requires going beyond the information contained in an annual report.

INTERPRETING RATIOS

Learning Objective 5
Interpret accounting ratios.

The computation of any particular ratio is not standardized. Neither the accounting profession nor security analysts have prescribed the manner in which a ratio must be computed (except for earnings per share). Thus, users of financial statements should compute the various ratios in accordance with their decision objectives. Before using ratios computed by others, the analyst should determine the computational approach that was used.

To interpret a ratio, it should be compared with some standard that represents an optimal or desirable value. For example, the return-on-investment ratio may be compared with alternative investment opportunities. Some ratios, by their characteristics, are unfavorable if they are either too high or too low. For example, analysis may indicate that a current ratio of approximately 2:1 may be considered optimal for a company. In this situation, a ratio of 1:1 may indicate a danger of being unable to meet maturing debts. A ratio of 3:1 may indicate that excess funds are being left idle rather than being employed

Home Depot was able to speed up its expansion in Canada by acquiring Aikenhead's, a chain of home improvement stores.

Exhibit 14–4 Selected Financial Ratios for Braniff International

	Years before Bankruptcy				
	5	4	3	2	1
Current ratio	1.20	0.91	0.74	0.60	0.49
Debt/equity ratio	2.03	2.45	4.88	15.67	N/A*

*In the year before bankruptcy, Braniff reported negative owners' equity as the result of a large net loss that produced a negative balance in retained earnings. Creditors' equity exceeded total equities.

profitably. Furthermore, an optimal ratio for one company often is not the optimal ratio for another company. Comparisons of ratios for different companies are appropriate only if the companies are indeed comparable. Noteworthy differences in industry, nature of operations, size, and accounting policies can make the value of many comparisons questionable.

Most ratios represent averages. Therefore, they may obscure underlying factors that are of interest to the analyst. To illustrate, a current ratio of 2:1 may be considered optimal in a given industry. But even an optimal current ratio may obscure a short-term liquidity problem if the company has a very large amount of inventory and a minimal amount of cash with which to pay debts as they mature. Careful analysis can uncover this liquidity problem. In other cases, careful analysis cannot uncover obscured problems. For example, consolidated statements include financial information about the parent and its subsidiaries. The parent company may have a high current ratio and the subsidiary a low ratio. When the statements are consolidated, the current ratio (in effect, an average of the parent and the subsidiary) may be within an acceptable range. Obscured is the fact that the subsidiary may have a serious liquidity problem.

Despite limitations, ratio analysis is a useful analytical tool. Financial ratios are effective for predicting bankruptcy. Exhibit 14–4 gives the current and debt/equity ratios for Braniff International Corporation for each year before it filed for bankruptcy. Notice the deterioration of these ratios each year. Analysts who studied the financial ratios probably were not surprised by the bankruptcy of Braniff. After selling many of its assets and undergoing a complete financial restructuring, Braniff was able to resume limited flight operations but was forced to file for bankruptcy for a second time after additional financial difficulty.

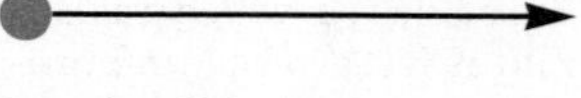

IMPACT OF ACCOUNTING ALTERNATIVES ON RATIO ANALYSIS

Learning Objective 6
Describe how accounting alternatives affect ratio analysis.

Financial statements provide information for the average investor. Users who understand basic accounting are able to more effectively analyze the information contained in financial statements. While studying this book, you have developed an understanding of the accounting vocabulary. A knowledge of this vocabulary is necessary to understand financial statements.

Also, familiarity with the underlying accounting concepts is essential for proper analysis of statements. Some unsophisticated users do not understand the cost principle and believe that assets are reported on the balance sheet at their fair market value. We have stressed accounting concepts throughout the book because it is impossible to interpret accounting numbers without an understanding of the concepts that were used to develop the numbers.

When comparing companies, you will find that they rarely use exactly the same accounting policies. If the comparisons are to be useful, the analyst must understand the impact of various accounting alternatives. One company may

QUESTION OF ETHICS

Insider Information

Financial statements are an important source of information for investors. Announcement of an unexpected earnings increase or decrease can cause a substantial movement in the price of a company's stock.

Accountants for a company may become aware of important financial information before it is made available to the public. This type of data is called *insider information.* It might be tempting for some people to buy or sell stock based on insider information, but to do so is a serious criminal offense. The Securities and Exchange Commission has brought a number of cases against individuals who traded on insider information, which resulted in large fines and time in jail.

In some cases, it may be difficult to decide if something is insider information. An individual may simply overhear a comment made in the company elevator by two executives. A well-respected Wall Street investment banker gave good advice: "If you are not sure if something is right or wrong, apply the newspaper headline test. Ask yourself how you would feel to have your family and friends read about what you had done in the newspaper." Interestingly, many people who spent time in jail and lost small fortunes in fines because of insider trading convictions say that the most difficult part of the process was telling their families.

In order to uphold the highest ethical standard, many public accounting firms have rules that prevent members of their professional staff from investing in companies that the firm audits. These rules are designed to ensure that there can be no temptation for the company's auditors to engage in insider trading.

use conservative accounting alternatives such as accelerated depreciation and LIFO, while another may use income-maximizing alternatives such as straight-line depreciation and FIFO. Users who do not understand the effects of accounting methods may misinterpret financial results. Perhaps the most important first step in analyzing financial statements is a review of the accounting policies that the company has selected. This information must be disclosed in a note to the statements. An example of this disclosure is shown in the annual report in the appendix preceding the index.

Information in an Efficient Market

There has been considerable research performed to study how the stock markets react to new information. Much of this evidence supports the view that the markets react very quickly to new information in an unbiased manner (the market does not systematically overreact or underreact to new information). A market that reacts to information in this manner is called an **efficient market**. In an efficient market, the price of a security fully reflects all available information.

Efficient markets are securities markets in which prices fully reflect available information.

It is not surprising that the stock markets react quickly to new information. Many professional investors manage portfolios of stock that are valued in the hundreds of millions of dollars. These investors have a large financial incentive to find new, relevant information about a company and to trade quickly based on that information.

The research on efficient markets has important implications for financial analysis. It probably is not beneficial to study old information (say an annual report that was released six months earlier) to identify a stock that has been undervalued by the market. In an efficient market, the price of the stock would reflect all of the information contained in the report shortly after it was released.

In an efficient market, we would expect that it would not be possible for a company to manipulate the price of its stock by manipulating accounting policy. The market should be able to differentiate a company with increasing earnings due to improved productivity from one that has increased earnings by changing from conservative to liberal accounting policies.

SUMMARY

Interpretation of amounts reported on financial statements may be enhanced by expressing certain relationships as ratios or percents. Although many ratios can be calculated, only a few will be useful for a given decision. Having selected the relevant ratios, the analyst has the problem of evaluating the results. This evaluation involves the task of selecting one or more realistic standards with which to compare the results. Four types of standards are used: (1) historical standards, (2) external standards, (3) experience, and (4) planned standards. The interpretation of ratios may suggest strengths and weaknesses in the operations and/or the financial position of the company that should be accorded in-depth investigation and evaluation.

KEY TERMS

Component Percentage A percentage that expresses each item on a particular financial statement as a percentage of a single base amount. *681*

Efficient Markets A securities market in which prices fully reflect available information. *697*

Market Tests Ratios that tend to measure the market worth of a share of stock. *692*

Ratio (Percentage) Analysis An analytical tool designed to identify significant relationships; measures proportional relationship between two financial statement amounts. *681*

Tests of Liquidity Ratios that measure a company's ability to meet its currently maturing obligations. *688*

Tests of Solvency Ratios that measure a company's ability to meet its long-term obligations. *691*

QUESTIONS

1. What are three fundamental uses of external financial statements by decision makers?
2. What are some of the primary items on financial statements about which creditors usually are concerned?
3. Explain why the notes to the financial statements are important to decision makers.
4. What is the primary purpose of comparative financial statements?
5. Why are statement users interested in financial summaries covering several years? What is the primary limitation of long-term summaries?
6. What is ratio analysis? Why is ratio analysis useful?
7. What are component percentages? Why are component percentages useful?
8. Explain the two concepts of return on investment.
9. What is financial leverage? How is financial leverage measured?
10. Is profit margin a useful measure of profitability? Explain.
11. Compare and contrast the current ratio and the quick ratio.
12. What does the debt/equity ratio reflect?
13. What are market tests?
14. Identify two factors that limit the effectiveness of ratio analysis.

EXERCISES

E14–1 Analyzing Comparative Financial Statements Using Percentages

The comparative financial statements prepared at December 31, 19B, for Goldfish Company showed the following summarized data:

	19B	19A
Income statement:		
Sales revenue	$180,000*	$165,000*
Cost of goods sold	110,000	100,000
Gross margin	70,000	65,000
Operating expenses and interest expense	56,000	53,000
Pretax income	14,000	12,000
Income tax	4,000	3,000
Net income	$ 10,000	$ 9,000
Balance sheet:		
Cash	$ 4,000	$ 8,000
Accounts receivable (net)	14,000	18,000
Inventory	40,000	35,000
Operational assets (net)	45,000	38,000
	$103,000	$ 99,000
Current liabilities (no interest)	$ 16,000	$ 19,000
Long-term liabilities (10% interest)	45,000	45,000
Common stock (par $5)	30,000	30,000
Retained earnings†	12,000	5,000
	$103,000	$ 99,000

*One-third were credit sales.

†During 19B, cash dividends amounting to $9,000 were declared and paid.

Required:

1. Complete the following columns for each item in the above comparative financial statements:

Increase (Decrease) 19B over 19A	
Amount	**Percent**

2. Answer the following questions:
   a. Compute the percentage increase in sales revenue, net income, cash, inventory, liabilities, and owners' equity.
   b. By what amount did working capital change?
   c. What was the percentage change in the average income tax rate?
   d. What was the amount of cash inflow from revenues for 19B?
   e. By what percent did the average markup realized on goods sold change?
   f. How much did the book value per share change?

E14–2 Analyzing a Financial Statement Using Component Percentages and Selected Ratios

Use the data given in Exercise 14–1 for Goldfish Company.

Required:

1. Present component percentages for 19B only.
2. Answer the following questions for 19B:
   a. What was the average percentage markup on sales?
   b. What was the average income tax rate?
   c. Compute the profit margin. Was it a good or poor indicator of performance? Explain.
   d. What percentage of total resources was invested in operational assets?
   e. Compute the debt/equity ratio. Does it look good or bad? Explain.

f. What was the return on owners' investment?
g. What was the return on total investment?
h. Compute the financial leverage percent. Was it positive or negative? Explain.
i. What was the book value per share of common stock?

E14–3 *Analyzing a Financial Statement Using Each Ratio Discussed in the Chapter*

Use the data given in Exercise 14–1 for Goldfish Company. Use a separate sheet and complete the following tabulation for 19B only (assume a common stock price of $28 per share); compute the ratios that usually are included under each category:

Name and Computation of the Ratio (Show Computations)	Brief Explanation of the Ratio
A. Tests of profitability:	
1. Return on owners' investment	
2. Etc.	
B. Tests of liquidity:	
1. Current ratio	
2. Etc.	
C. Tests of solvency and equity position:	
1. Debt/equity ratio	
2. Etc.	
D. Market tests:	
1. Price/earnings ratio	
2. Etc.	
E. Miscellaneous ratio:	
1. Book value per share	

E14–4 *Matching Each Ratio with Its Computational Definition*

Match each computation with its related ratio or percentage by entering the appropriate letters in the blanks.

Ratios or Percentages

________ (1) Profit margin
________ (2) Inventory turnover ratio
________ (3) Average collection period
________ (4) Creditors' equity to total equities
________ (5) Dividend yield ratio
________ (6) Return on owners' investment
________ (7) Current ratio
________ (8) Debt/equity ratio
________ (9) Price/earnings ratio
________ (10) Financial leverage
________ (11) Receivable turnover ratio
________ (12) Average days' supply of inventory
________ (13) Owners' equity to total equities
________ (14) Earnings per share
________ (15) Return on total investment
________ (16) Quick ratio
________ (17) Book value per share

Definitions

A. Income (before extraordinary items) ÷ Net sales.
B. Days in year ÷ Receivable turnover.
C. Income ÷ Average owners' equity.
D. Income ÷ Average number of shares of common stock outstanding.
E. Return on owners' investment – Return on total investment.
F. Quick assets ÷ Current liabilities.
G. Current assets ÷ Current liabilities.
H. Cost of goods sold ÷ Average inventory.
I. Net credit sales ÷ Average net trade receivables.
J. Creditors' equity (debt) ÷Total equities.
K. Days in year ÷ Inventory turnover.
L. Total liabilities ÷ Owners' equity.
M. Dividends per share ÷ Market price per share.
N. Owners' equity ÷ Total equities.
O. Current market price per share ÷ Earnings per share.
P. Owners' equity ÷ Shares outstanding.
Q. Income + Interest expense (net of tax) ÷ Total assets.

E14–5 *Analyzing the Impact of Selected Transactions on the Current Ratio, Accounts Receivable and Inventory Turnover, and Financial Leverage*

Case A Current assets totaled $54,000, and the current ratio was 1.8. Assume the following transactions were completed: (1) purchased merchandise for $6,000 on short-term credit and (2) purchased a delivery truck for $10,000, paid $1,000 cash, and signed a two-year interest-bearing note for the balance. Compute the cumulative current ratio after each transaction.

Case B Sales for the year were $400,000 of which one-half was on credit. The average gross margin rate was 30% on sales. Account balances were:

	Beginning	Ending
Accounts receivable (net)	$25,000	$15,000
Inventory	24,000	18,000

Compute the turnover for the accounts receivable and inventory, the average age of receivables, and the average days' supply of inventory.

Case C The financial statements reported the following at year-end:

Total assets	$150,000
Total debt (10% interest)	80,000
Net income (average tax rate 30%)	25,000

Compute the financial leverage. Was it positive or negative?

E14–6 *Analyzing a Financial Statement Using Ratios and Percentage Changes*

Taber Company has just prepared the comparative annual financial statements for 19B given below.

TABER COMPANY
Comparative Income Statement
For the Years Ended December 31, 19B, and 19A

	For the Year Ended			
	19B		19A	
Sales revenue (one half on credit)		$110,000		$99,000
Cost of goods sold		52,000		48,000
Gross margin		58,000		51,000
Expenses (including $4,000 interest expense each year)		40,000		37,000
Pretax income		18,000		14,000
Income tax on operations (30%)		5,400		4,200
Income before extraordinary items		12,600		9,800
Extraordinary loss	$2,000			
Less income tax saved	600	1,400		
Extraordinary gain			$3,000	
Applicable income tax			900	2,100
Net income		$ 11,200		$11,900

TABER COMPANY
Comparative Balance Sheet
At December 31, 19B, and 19A

Assets	**19B**	**19A**
Cash	$ 49,500	$ 18,000
Accounts receivable (net; terms 1/10, n/30)	37,000	32,000
Inventory	25,000	38,000
Operational assets (net)	95,000	105,000
Total assets	$206,500	$193,000
Liabilities		
Accounts payable	$ 42,000	$ 35,000
Income taxes payable	1,000	500
Note payable, long-term	40,000	40,000
Stockholders' Equity		
Capital stock (par $10)	90,000	90,000
Retained earnings	33,500	27,500
Total liabilities and stockholders' equity	$206,500	$193,000

Required (round percents and ratios to two decimal places):

1. For 19B, compute the tests of (*a*) profitability, (*b*) liquidity, (*c*) solvency, and (*d*) market. Assume the quoted price of the stock was $23 for 19B. Dividends declared and paid during 19B were $6,750.
2. Respond to the following for 19B:
   a. Compute the percent changes in sales, income before extraordinary items, net income, cash, inventory, and debt.
   b. What appears to be the pretax interest rate on the note payable?
3. Identify at least two problems facing the company that are suggested by your responses to (*a*) and (*b*).

E14–7 Using Financial Information to Identify Mystery Companies

The following selected financial data pertain to four unidentified companies:

	Companies			
	1	**2**	**3**	**4**
Balance sheet data (component percentage)				
Cash	3.5	4.7	8.2	11.7
Accounts receivable	16.9	28.9	16.8	51.9
Inventory	46.8	35.6	57.3	4.8
Property and equipment	18.3	21.7	7.6	18.7
Income statement data (component percentage)				
Gross profit	22.0	22.5	44.8	N/A*
Profit before taxes	2.1	.7	1.2	3.2
Selected ratios				
Current ratio	1.3	1.5	1.6	1.2
Inventory turnover	3.6	9.8	1.5	N/A
Debt/equity	2.6	2.6	3.2	3.2

*N/A = Not applicable

The financial information shown above pertains to the following companies:

A. Retail fur store
B. Advertising agency

C. Wholesale candy company
D. Car manufacturer

Match each company with its financial information.

E14–8 Using Financial Information to Identify Mystery Companies

The following selected financial data pertain to four unidentified companies:

	Companies			
	1	2	3	4
Balance sheet data				
(component percentage)				
Cash	7.3	21.6	6.1	11.3
Accounts receivable	28.2	39.7	3.2	22.9
Inventory	21.6	.6	1.8	27.5
Property and equipment	32.1	18.0	74.6	25.1
Income statement data				
(component percentage)				
Gross profit	15.3	N/A*	N/A	43.4
Profit before taxes	1.7	3.2	2.4	6.9
Selected ratios				
Current ratio	1.5	1.2	.6	1.9
Inventory turnover	27.4	N/A	N/A	3.3
Debt/equity	1.7	2.2	5.7	1.3

*N/A = Not applicable

The financial information shown above pertains to the following companies:

A. Travel agency
B. Hotel
C. Meat packer
D. Drug company

Match each company with its financial information.

E14–9 Using Financial Information to Identify Mystery Companies

The following selected financial data pertain to four unidentified companies:

	Companies			
	1	2	3	4
Balance sheet data				
(component percentage)				
Cash	5.1	8.8	6.3	10.4
Accounts receivable	13.1	41.5	13.8	4.9
Inventory	4.6	3.6	65.1	35.8
Property and equipment	53.1	23.0	8.8	35.7
Income statement data				
(component percentage)				
Gross profit	N/A*	N/A	45.2	22.5
Profit before taxes	.3	16.0	3.9	1.5
Selected ratios				
Current ratio	.7	2.2	1.9	1.4
Inventory turnover	N/A	N/A	1.4	15.5
Debt/equity	2.5	.9	1.7	2.3

*N/A = Not applicable

The financial information shown above pertains to the following companies:

A. Cable TV company
B. Grocery store
C. Accounting firm
D. Retail jewelry store

Match each company with its financial information.

E14–10 Using Financial Information to Identify Mystery Companies

The following selected financial data pertain to four unidentified companies:

	Companies			
	1	2	3	4
Balance sheet data (component percentage)				
Cash	11.6	6.6	5.4	7.1
Accounts receivable	4.6	18.9	8.8	35.6
Inventory	7.0	45.8	65.7	26.0
Property and equipment	56.0	20.3	10.1	21.9
Income statement data (component percentage)				
Gross profit	56.7	36.4	14.1	15.8
Profit before taxes	2.7	1.4	1.1	.9
Selected ratios				
Current ratio	.7	2.1	1.2	1.3
Inventory turnover	30.0	3.5	5.6	16.7
Debt/equity	3.3	1.8	3.8	3.1

The financial information shown above pertains to the following companies:

A. Full-line department store
B. Wholesale fish company
C. Automobile dealer (both new and used cars)
D. Restaurant

Match each of the companies with its financial information.

PROBLEMS

P14–1 Analyzing a Financial Statement Using All of the Ratios

Summer Corporation has just completed its comparative statements for the year ended December 31, 19B. At this point, certain analytical and interpretive procedures are to be undertaken. The completed statements (summarized) are as follows:

	19B	19A
Income statement		
Sales revenue	$450,000*	$420,000*
Cost of goods sold	250,000	230,000
Gross margin	200,000	190,000
Operating expenses (including interest on bonds)	167,000	168,000
Pretax income	33,000	22,000
Income tax	10,000	6,000
Net income	$ 23,000	$ 16,000

Balance sheet		
Cash	$ 6,800	$ 3,900
Accounts receivable (net)	42,000	28,000
Merchandise inventory	25,000	20,000
Prepaid expenses	200	100
Operational assets (net)	130,000	120,000
	$204,000	$172,000
Accounts payable	$ 17,000	$ 18,000
Income taxes payable	1,000	2,000
Bonds payable (10% interest rate)	70,000	50,000
Common stock (par $5)	100,000†	100,000
Retained earnings	16,000‡	2,000
	$204,000	$172,000

*Credit sales totaled 40%.

†The market price of the stock at the end of 19B was $18 per share.

‡During 19B, the company declared and paid a cash dividend of $40,000.

Required:

1. Complete a table similar to the following (show computations; round percentages and ratios to two places):

Name and Computation of the 19B Ratio	Brief Explanation of the Ratio
Tests of profitability:	
1. Return on owners' investment.	
2. Etc.	
Tests of liquidity:	
1. Current ratio.	
2. Etc.	
Tests of solvency and equity position:	
1. Debt/equity ratio.	
2. Etc.	
Market tests:	
1. Price/earnings ratio.	
2. Etc.	

2. Answer the following questions for 19B:
   a. Evaluate the financial leverage. Explain its meaning using the computed amount(s).
   b. Evaluate the profit margin amount and explain how a stockholder might use it.
   c. Explain to a stockholder why the current ratio and the quick ratio are different. Do you observe any liquidity problems? Explain.
   d. Assuming credit terms are 1/10, n/30, do you perceive an unfavorable situation for the company related to credit sales? Explain.

P14–2 *Using Ratios to Analyze Several Years of Financial Data, Identify Favorable and Unfavorable Factors, and Give Recommendations to Improve Operations*

The following information was contained in the annual financial statements of Pine Company, which started business January 1, 19A (assume account balances only in Cash and Capital Stock on this date; all amounts are in thousands of dollars).

	19A	19B	19C	19D
Accounts receivable (net; terms n/30)	$11	$12	$18	$ 24
Merchandise inventory	12	14	20	30
Net sales (3/4 on credit)	44	66	80	100
Cost of goods sold	28	40	55	62
Net income (loss)	(8)	5	12	11

Required (Show computations and round to two decimal places):

1. Complete the tabulation given below.
2. Evaluate the results of the related ratios *a*, *b*, and *c* to identify the favorable or unfavorable factors. Give your recommendations to improve the company's operations.
3. Evaluate the results of the last four ratios (*d*, *e*, *f*, and *g*) and identify any favorable or unfavorable factors. Give your recommendations to improve the company's operations.

Items	19A	19B	19C	19D
a. Profit margin—percent				
b. Gross margin—ratio				
c. Expenses as percent of sales, excluding cost of goods sold				
d. Inventory turnover				
e. Days' supply in inventory				
f. Receivable turnover				
g. Average days to collect				

P14–3 Comparing Alternative Investment Opportunities Using All of the Ratios Discussed in the Chapter: Prepare Investment Recommendations

The 19B financial statements for Armstrong and Blair companies are summarized below:

		Armstrong Company		Blair Company
Balance sheet				
Cash		$ 35,000		$ 22,000
Accounts receivable (net)		40,000		30,000
Inventory		100,000		40,000
Operational assets (net)		140,000		400,000
Other assets		85,000		308,000
Total assets		$400,000		$800,000
Current liabilities		$100,000		$ 50,000
Long-term debt (10%)		60,000		70,000
Capital stock (par $10)		150,000		500,000
Contributed capital in excess of par		30,000		110,000
Retained earnings		60,000		70,000
Total liabilities and stockholders' equity		$400,000		$800,000
Income statement				
Sales revenue (on credit)	(1/3)	$450,000	(1/3)	$810,000
Cost of goods sold		(245,000)		(405,000)
Expenses (including interest and income tax)		(160,000)		(315,000)
Net income		$ 45,000		$ 90,000
Selected data from the 19A statements				
Accounts receivable (net)		$ 20,000		$ 38,000
Inventory		92,000		45,000
Long-term debt		60,000		70,000
Other data				
Per share price at end of 19B (offering price)		$ 18		$ 15
Average income tax rate		30%		30%
Dividends declared and paid in 19B		$ 36,000		$150,000

The companies are in the same line of business and are direct competitors in a large metropolitan area. Both have been in business approximately 10 years, and each has had steady growth. The two managements have different viewpoints in many respects; however, Blair is more conservative, and as the president said, "We avoid what we consider to be undue risk." Neither company is publicly held. Armstrong Company has an annual audit by a CPA but Blair Company does not.

Required:

1. Complete a schedule that reflects a ratio analysis of each company. Compute the ratios discussed in the chapter.
2. A client of yours has the opportunity to buy 10% of the shares in one or the other company at the per share prices given above. Your client has decided to invest in one of the companies. Based on the data given, prepare a comparative evaluation of the ratio analyses (and any other available information) and give your recommended choice with the supporting explanation.

P14–4 *Comparing Loan Requests from Two Companies Using All of the Ratios Discussed in the Chapter*

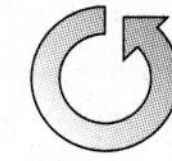

The 19B financial statements for Rand and Tand companies are summarized below:

	Rand Company	Tand Company
Balance sheet:		
Cash	$ 25,000	$ 45,000
Accounts receivable (net)	55,000	5,000
Inventory	110,000	25,000
Operational assets (net)	550,000	160,000
Other assets	140,000	57,000
Total assets	$880,000	$292,000
Current liabilities	$120,000	$ 15,000
Long-term debt (12%)	190,000	55,000
Capital stock (par $20)	480,000	210,000
Contributed capital in excess of par	50,000	4,000
Retained earnings	40,000	8,000
Total liabilities and stockholders' equity	$880,000	$292,000
Income statement:		
Sales revenue (on credit)	(1/2) $800,000	(1/4) $280,000
Cost of goods sold	(480,000)	(150,000)
Expenses (including interest and income tax)	(240,000)	(95,000)
Net income	$ 80,000	$ 35,000
Selected data from the 19A statements:		
Accounts receivable, net	$ 47,000	$ 11,000
Long-term debt (12%)	190,000	55,000
Inventory	95,000	38,000
Other data:		
Per share price at end of 19B	$ 14.00	$ 11.00
Average income tax rate	30%	30%
Dividends declared and paid in 19B	$ 20,000	$ 9,000

These two companies are in the same line of business and in the same state but in different cities. Each company has been in operation for about 10 years. Rand Company is audited by one of the national accounting firms, and Tand Company is audited by a local accounting firm. Both companies received an unqualified opinion (i.e., the independent auditors found nothing wrong) on the financial statements. Rand Company wants to borrow $75,000 cash, and Tand Company needs $30,000. The loans will be for a two-year period and are needed for "working capital purposes."

Required:

1. Complete a schedule that reflects a ratio analysis of each company. Compute the ratios discussed in the chapter.
2. Assume you work in the loan department of a local bank. You have been asked to analyze the situation and recommend which loan is preferable. Based on the data given, your analysis prepared in (1), and any other information, give your choice and the supporting explanation.

P14–5 *Assessing the Solvency of an Actual Company Using Selected Ratios*

The following information was contained in the actual financial statements of a large manufacturing company that currently is listed on The New York Stock Exchange.

Balance Sheet

	December 31 (millions of dollars)	
	19B	**19A**
Assets		
Current assets:		
Cash	$ 188.2	$ 123.2
Time deposits	120.8	248.8
Marketable securities	165.3	150.8
Accounts receivable (less allowance for doubtful accounts: 19B—$34.9 million; 19A—$16.7 million)	610.3	848.0
Inventories—at the lower of cost (substantially FIFO) or market	1,873.8	1,980.8
Prepaid insurance, taxes, and other expenses	162.3	210.2
Total current assets	3,120.7	3,561.8
Total investments and other assets	1,183.5	1,396.5
Property, plant, and equipment:		
Land, buildings, machinery, and equipment	3,733.1	3,391.3
Less accumulated depreciation	2,097.1	1,963.9
	1,636.0	1,427.4
Special tools	712.9	595.5
Net property, plant, and equipment	2,348.9	2,022.9
Total assets	$6,653.1	$6,981.2

	December 31 (millions of dollars)	
	19B	**19A**
Liabilities and Stockholders' Investment		
Current liabilities:		
Accounts payable	$1,530.4	$1,725.0
Accrued expenses	807.9	698.0
Short-term debt	600.9	49.2
Payment due within one year on long-term debt	275.6	12.4
Taxes on income	16.8	1.2
Total current liabilities	3,231.6	2,485.8
Total long-term debt and other liabilities	1,559.1	1,564.1
Minority interest in consolidated subsidiaries	38.3	4.8
Preferred stock—nopar value	218.7	217.0
Common stock—par value $6.25 per share	416.9	397.7
Additional paid-in capital	692.2	683.1
Net earnings retained	496.3	1,628.7
Total liabilities and stockholders' investment	$6,653.1	$6,981.2

Income Statement

	Year-End December 31 (millions of dollars)	
	19B	**19A**
Net sales	$12,004.3	$13,669.8
Cost of goods sold	11,631.5	12,640.1
Depreciation of plant and equipment	180.6	154.0
Amortization of special tools	220.0	198.2
Selling and administrative expenses	598.5	572.1
Pension plans	260.6	262.3
Interest expense	215.4	128.9
	13,106.6	13,955.6
Loss before taxes on income	(1,102.3)	(285.8)
Taxes on income (credit)	(5.0)	(81.2)
Net loss	$ (1,097.3)	$ (204.6)

Required:

1. Calculate the following ratios:
   a. Return on owners' investment.
   b. Return on total investment. (For purposes of this case, assume that the interest expense reported on the income statement is net of income taxes.)
   c. Financial leverage.
   d. Earnings per share.
   e. Current ratio.
   f. Quick ratio.
   g. Inventory turnover.
   h. Debt/equity ratio.
2. Based on your analysis of the ratios that you calculated in requirement 1, do you think that this company will be able to continue in existence? Explain. Would you be willing to invest in this company? Explain.

P14–6 Analyzing the Impact of Alternative Inventory Methods on Selected Ratios

Company A uses the FIFO method to cost inventory, and Company B uses the LIFO method. The two companies are exactly alike except for the difference in inventory costing methods. Costs of inventory items for both companies have been rising steadily in recent years, and each company has increased its inventory each year. Each company has paid its tax liability in full for the current year (and all previous years), and each company uses the same accounting methods for both financial reporting and income tax reporting.

Required:

Identify which company will report the higher amount for each of the following ratios. If it is not possible, explain why.

1. Current ratio.
2. Quick ratio.
3. Debt/equity ratio.
4. Return on owners' investment.
5. Earnings per share.

CASES

C14–1 Analyzing the Impact of Alternative Depreciation Methods on Ratio Analysis

Speedy Company uses the sum-of-years'-digits methods to depreciate its property, plant, and equipment, and Turtle Company uses the straight-line method. Both companies use 175% declining-balance depreciation for income tax purposes. The two companies are exactly alike except for the difference in depreciation methods.

Required:

1. Identify the financial ratios discussed in this chapter that are likely to be affected by the difference in depreciation methods.
2. Which company will report the higher amount for each ratio that you have identified? If you cannot be certain, explain why.

C14–2 Analyzing the Impact of Business Transactions on Ratio Analysis

Almost Short Company requested a sizable loan from First Federal Bank in order to acquire a large tract of land for future expansion. Almost Short reported current assets of $1,900,000

($430,000 in cash) and current liabilities of $1,075,000. First Federal denied the loan request for a number of reasons, including the fact that the current ratio was below 2:1. When Almost Short was informed of the loan denial, the comptroller of the company immediately paid $420,000 that was owed to several trade creditors. The comptroller then asked First Federal to reconsider the loan application. Based on these abbreviated facts, would you recommend that First Federal approve the loan request? Why?

Toys "Я" Us

C14–3 Financial Statement Analysis

Refer to the financial statement of Toys "Я" Us given in Appendix B at the end of this book.

Required:

Compute each of the 13 accounting ratios (for 1994) discussed in this chapter. Assume that the tax rate is 35% and that the current market price per share of common stock is $40.

APPENDIX A

Future Value of \$1, f = (1 + i)n — Table A–1

Periods	2%	3%	3.75%	4%	4.25%	5%	6%	7%	8%
0	1.	1.	1.	1.	1.	1.	1.	1.	1.
1	1.02	1.03	1.0375	1.04	1.0425	1.05	1.06	1.07	1.08
2	1.0404	1.0609	1.0764	1.0816	1.0868	1.1025	1.1236	1.1449	1.1664
3	1.0612	1.0927	1.1168	1.1249	1.1330	1.1576	1.1910	1.2250	1.2597
4	1.0824	1.1255	1.1587	1.1699	1.1811	1.2155	1.2625	1.3108	1.3605
5	1.1041	1.1593	1.2021	1.2167	1.2313	1.2763	1.3382	1.4026	1.4693
6	1.1262	1.1941	1.2472	1.2653	1.2837	1.3401	1.4185	1.5007	1.5869
7	1.1487	1.2299	1.2939	1.3159	1.3382	1.4071	1.5036	1.6058	1.7138
8	1.1717	1.2668	1.3425	1.3686	1.3951	1.4775	1.5938	1.7182	1.8509
9	1.1951	1.3048	1.3928	1.4233	1.4544	1.5513	1.6895	1.8385	1.9990
10	1.2190	1.3439	1.4450	1.4802	1.5162	1.6289	1.7908	1.9672	2.1589
20	1.4859	1.8061	2.0882	2.1911	2.2989	2.6533	3.2071	3.8697	4.6610

Periods	9%	10%	11%	12%	13%	14%	15%	20%	25%
0	1.	1.	1.	1.	1.	1.	1.	1.	1.
1	1.09	1.10	1.11	1.12	1.13	1.14	1.15	1.20	1.25
2	1.1881	1.2100	1.2321	1.2544	1.2769	1.2996	1.3225	1.4400	1.5625
3	1.2950	1.3310	1.3676	1.4049	1.4429	1.4815	1.5209	1.7280	1.9531
4	1.4116	1.4641	1.5181	1.5735	1.6305	1.6890	1.7490	2.0736	2.4414
5	1.5386	1.6105	1.6851	1.7623	1.8424	1.9254	2.0114	2.4883	3.0518
6	1.6771	1.7716	1.8704	1.9738	2.0820	2.1950	2.3131	2.9860	3.8147
7	1.8280	1.9487	2.0762	2.2107	2.3526	2.5023	2.6600	3.5832	4.7684
8	1.9926	2.1436	2.3045	2.4760	2.6584	2.8526	3.0590	4.2998	5.9605
9	2.1719	2.3579	2.5580	2.7731	3.0040	3.2519	3.5179	5.1598	7.4506
10	2.3674	2.5937	2.8394	3.10589	3.3946	3.7072	4.0456	6.1917	9.3132
20	5.6044	6.7275	8.0623	6463	11.5231	13.7435	16.3665	38.3376	86.7362

Present Value of \$1, $p = 1/(1 + i)^n$ — Table A–2

Periods	2%	3%	3.75%	4%	4.25%	5%	6%	7%	8%
1	0.9804	0.9703	0.9639	0.9615	0.9592	0.9524	0.9434	0.9346	0.9259
2	0.9612	0.9426	0.9290	0.9246	0.9201	0.9070	0.8900	0.8734	0.8573
3	0.9423	0.9151	0.8954	0.8890	0.8826	0.8638	0.8396	0.8163	0.7938
4	0.9238	0.8885	0.8631	0.8548	0.8466	0.8227	0.7921	0.7629	0.7350
5	0.9057	0.8626	0.8319	0.8219	0.8121	0.7835	0.7473	0.7130	0.6806
6	0.8880	0.8375	0.8018	0.7903	0.7790	0.7462	0.7050	0.6663	0.6302
7	0.8706	0.8131	0.7728	0.7599	0.7473	0.7107	0.6651	0.6227	0.5835
8	0.8535	0.7894	0.7449	0.7307	0.7168	0.6768	0.6274	0.5820	0.5403
9	0.8368	0.7664	0.7180	0.7026	0.6876	0.6446	0.5919	0.5439	0.5002
10	0.8203	0.7441	0.6920	0.6756	0.6595	0.6139	0.5584	0.5083	0.4632
20	0.6730	0.5534	0.4789	0.4564	0.4350	0.3769	0.3118	0.2584	0.2145

Periods	9%	10%	11%	12%	13%	14%	15%	20%	25%
1	0.9174	0.9091	0.9009	0.8929	0.8850	0.8772	0.8696	0.8333	0.8000
2	0.8417	0.8264	0.8116	0.7972	0.7831	0.7695	0.7561	0.6944	0.6400
3	0.7722	0.7513	0.7312	.7118	0.6931	0.6750	0.6575	0.5787	0.5120
4	0.7084	0.6830	0.6587	0.6355	0.6133	0.5921	0.5718	0.4823	0.4096
5	0.6499	0.6209	0.5935	0.5674	0.5428	0.5194	0.4972	0.4019	0.3277
6	0.5963	0.5645	0.5346	0.5066	0.4803	0.4556	0.4323	0.3349	0.2621
7	0.5470	0.5132	0.4817	0.4523	0.4251	0.3996	0.3759	0.2791	0.2097
8	0.5019	0.4665	0.4339	0.4039	0.3762	0.3506	0.3269	0.2326	0.1678
9	0.4604	0.4241	0.3909	0.3606	0.3329	0.3075	0.2843	0.1938	0.1342
10	0.4224	0.3855	0.3522	0.3220	0.2946	0.2697	0.2472	0.1615	0.1074
20	0.1784	0.1486	0.1240	0.1037	0.0868	0.0728	0.0611	0.0261	0.0115

Table A–3 Future Value of Annuity of $1 (ordinary), $F = (1 + i)^n - 1 / i$

Periods*	2%	3%	3.75%	4%	4.25%	5%	6%	7%	8%
1	1.	1.	1.	1.	1.	1.	1.	1.	1.
2	2.02	2.03	2.0375	2.04	2.0425	2.05	2.06	2.07	2.08
3	3.0604	3.0909	3.1139	3.1216	3.1293	3.1525	3.1836	3.2149	3.2464
4	4.1216	4.1836	4.2307	4.2465	4.2623	4.3101	4.3746	4.4399	4.5061
5	5.2040	5.3091	5.3893	5.4163	5.4434	5.5256	5.6371	5.7507	5.8666
6	6.3081	6.4684	6.5914	6.6330	6.6748	6.8019	6.9753	7.1533	7.3359
7	7.4343	7.6625	7.8386	7.8983	7.9585	8.1420	8.3938	8.6540	8.9228
8	8.5830	8.8923	9.1326	9.2142	9.2967	9.5491	9.8975	10.2598	10.6366
9	9.7546	10.1591	10.4750	10.5828	10.6918	11.0266	11.4913	11.9780	12.4876
10	10.9497	11.4639	11.8678	12.0061	12.1462	12.5779	13.1808	13.8164	14.4866
20	24.2974	26.8704	29.0174	29.7781	30.5625	33.0660	36.7856	40.9955	45.7620

Periods*	9%	10%	11%	12%	13%	14%	15%	20%	25%
1	1.	1.	1.	1.	1.	1.	1.	1.	1.
2	2.09	2.10	2.11	2.12	2.13	2.14	2.15	2.20	2.25
3	3.2781	3.3100	3.3421	3.3744	3.4069	3.4396	3.4725	3.6400	3.8125
4	4.5731	4.6410	4.7097	4.7793	4.8498	4.9211	4.9934	5.3680	5.7656
5	5.9847	6.1051	6.2278	6.3528	6.4803	6.6101	6.7424	7.4416	8.2070
6	7.5233	7.7156	7.9129	8.1152	8.3227	8.5355	8.7537	9.9299	11.2588
7	9.2004	9.4872	9.7833	10.0890	10.4047	10.7305	11.0668	12.9159	15.0735
8	11.0285	11.4359	11.8594	12.2997	12.7573	13.2328	13.7268	16.4991	19.8419
9	13.0210	13.5975	14.1640	14.7757	15.4157	16.0853	16.7858	20.7989	25.8023
10	15.1929	15.9374	16.7220	17.5487	18.4197	19.3373	20.3037	25.9587	33.2529
20	51.1601	57.2750	64.2028	72.0524	80.9468	91.0249	102.4436	186.6880	342.9447

*There is one payment each period.

Table A–4 Present Value of Annuity of $1, $P = 1 - 1/(1 + i)^n / i$

Periods*	2%	3%	3.75%	4%	4.25%	5%	6%	7%	8%
1	0.9804	0.9709	0.9639	0.9615	0.9592	0.9524	0.9434	0.9346	0.9259
2	1.9416	1.9135	1.8929	1.8861	1.8794	1.8594	1.8334	1.8080	1.7833
3	2.8839	2.8286	2.7883	2.7751	2.7620	2.7232	2.6730	2.6243	2.5771
4	3.8077	3.7171	3.6514	3.6299	3.6086	3.5460	3.4651	3.3872	3.3121
5	4.7135	4.5797	4.4833	4.4518	4.4207	4.3295	4.2124	4.1002	3.9927
6	5.6014	5.4172	5.2851	5.2421	5.1997	5.0757	4.9173	4.7665	4.6229
7	6.4720	6.2303	6.0579	6.0021	5.9470	5.7864	5.5824	5.3893	5.2064
8	7.3255	7.0197	6.8028	6.7327	6.6638	6.4632	6.2098	5.9713	5.7466
9	8.1622	7.7861	7.5208	7.4353	7.3513	7.1078	6.8017	6.5152	6.2469
10	8.9826	8.5302	8.2128	8.1109	8.0109	7.7217	7.3601	7.0236	6.7101
20	16.3514	14.8775	13.8962	13.5903	13.2944	12.4622	11.4699	10.5940	9.8181

Periods*	9%	10%	11%	12%	13%	14%	15%	20%	25%
1	0.9174	0.9091	0.9009	0.8929	0.8850	0.8772	0.8696	0.8333	0.8000
2	1.7591	1.7355	1.7125	1.6901	1.6681	1.6467	1.6257	1.5278	1.4400
3	2.5313	2.4869	2.4437	2.4018	2.3612	2.3216	2.2832	2.1065	1.9520
4	3.2397	3.1699	3.1024	3.0373	2.9745	2.9137	2.8550	2.5887	2.3616
5	3.8897	3.7908	3.6959	3.6048	3.5172	3.4331	3.3522	2.9906	2.6893
6	4.4859	4.3553	4.2305	4.1114	3.9975	3.8887	3.7845	3.3255	2.9514
7	5.0330	4.8684	4.7122	4.5638	4.4226	4.2883	4.1604	3.6046	3.1611
8	5.5348	5.3349	5.1461	4.9676	4.7988	4.6389	4.4873	3.8372	3.3289
9	5.9952	5.7590	5.5370	5.3282	5.1317	4.9464	4.7716	4.0310	3.4631
10	6.4177	6.1446	5.8892	5.6502	5.4262	5.2161	5.0188	4.1925	3.5705
20	9.1285	8.5136	7.9633	7.4694	7.0248	6.6231	6.2593	4.8696	3.9539

*There is one payment each period.

APPENDIX B
Toys "Я" Us 1994 Annual Report

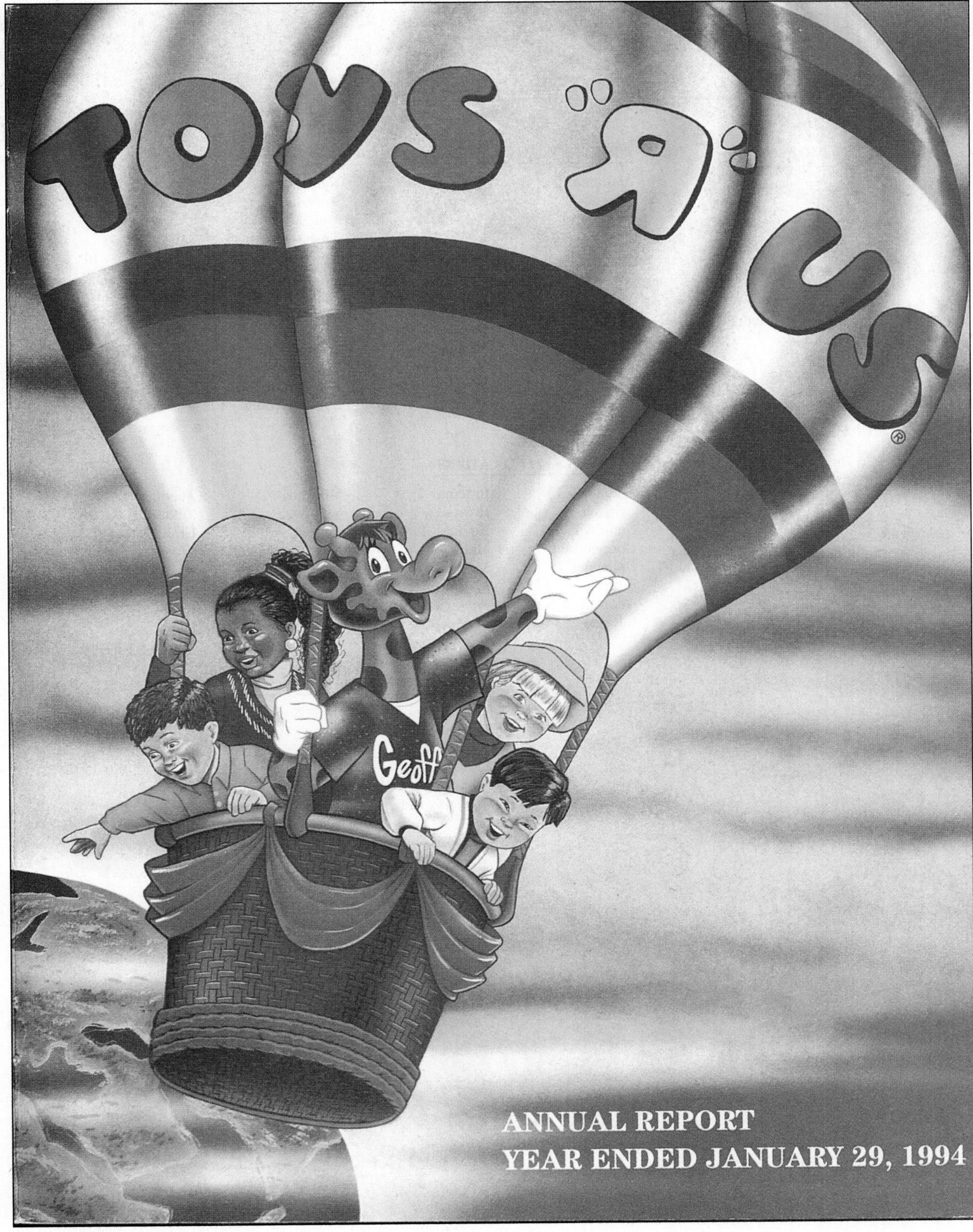
TOYS "Я" US®
Geoff
ANNUAL REPORT
YEAR ENDED JANUARY 29, 1994

TABLE OF CONTENTS

Toys "R" Us is the world's largest and fastest growing children's specialty retail chain in terms of both sales and earnings. At January 29, 1994, the Company operated 581 toy stores in the United States, 234 international toy stores and 217 Kids "R" Us children's clothing stores.

STORE LOCATIONS

TOYS "R" US UNITED STATES - 581 LOCATIONS

Alabama - 7
Alaska - 1
Arizona - 10
Arkansas - 2
California - 74
Colorado - 9
Connecticut - 8
Delaware - 2
Florida - 36
Georgia - 14
Hawaii - 1
Idaho - 1
Illinois - 33
Indiana - 12
Iowa - 6
Kansas - 4
Kentucky - 7
Louisiana - 8
Maine - 2
Maryland - 16
Massachusetts - 16
Michigan - 23
Minnesota - 11
Mississippi - 3
Missouri - 12
Montana - 1
Nebraska - 3
Nevada - 3
New Hampshire - 5
New Jersey - 21
New Mexico - 3
New York - 36
North Carolina - 15
Ohio - 27
Oklahoma - 4
Oregon - 5
Pennsylvania - 27
Rhode Island - 1
South Carolina - 8
Tennessee - 11
Texas - 43
Utah - 5
Virginia - 17
Washington - 10
West Virginia - 3
Wisconsin - 11

Puerto Rico - 4

KIDS "R" US - 217 LOCATIONS

Alabama - 1
Arizona - 4
California - 31
Connecticut - 6
Delaware - 1
Florida - 7
Georgia - 4
Illinois - 21
Indiana - 7
Iowa - 1
Kansas - 1
Maine - 2
Maryland - 8
Massachusetts - 4
Michigan - 13
Minnesota - 6
Missouri - 4
Nebraska - 1
New Hampshire - 2
New Jersey - 17
New York - 20
Ohio - 19
Pennsylvania - 14
Rhode Island - 1
Tennessee - 1
Texas - 5
Utah - 3
Virginia - 7
Wisconsin - 3

Puerto Rico - 3

TOYS "R" US INTERNATIONAL - 234 LOCATIONS

Australia - 7
Austria - 5
Belgium - 2
Canada - 50
France - 25
Germany - 44
Hong Kong - 4
Japan - 16
Malaysia - 2
Netherlands - 5
Portugal - 2
Singapore - 3
Spain - 17
Switzerland - 4
Taiwan - 3
United Kingdom - 45

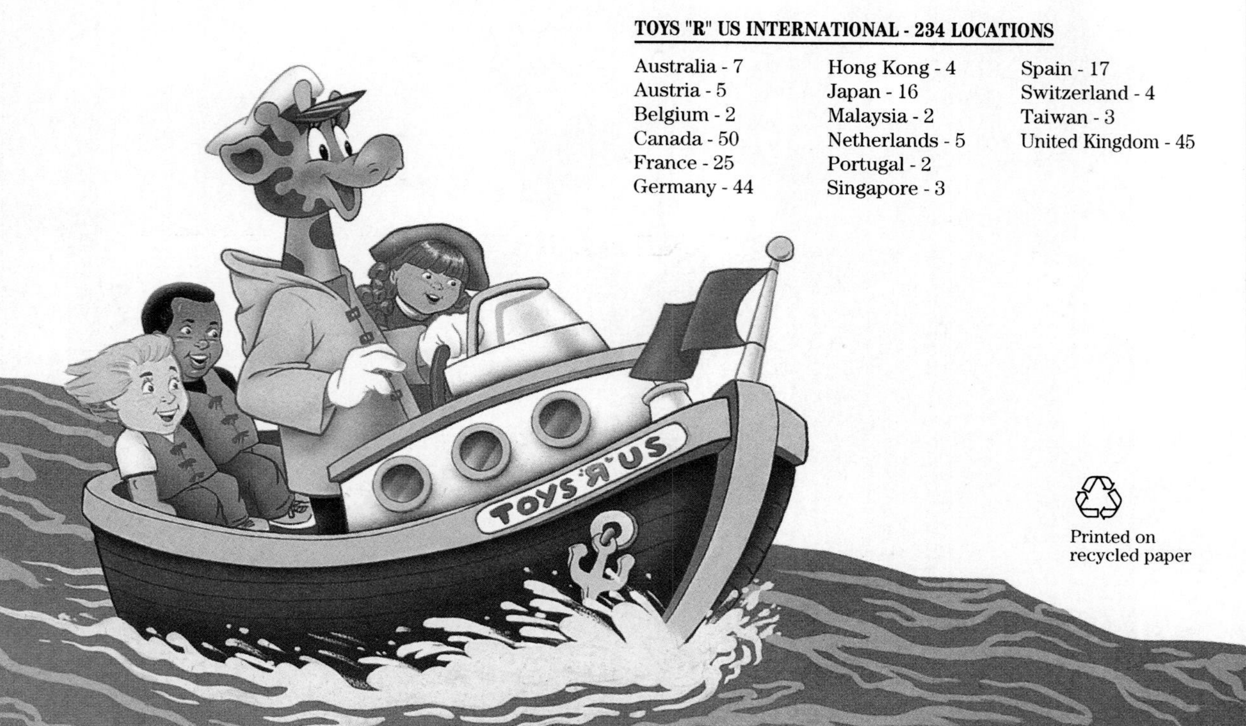

Printed on recycled paper

TOYS"R"US, INC. AND SUBSIDIARIES

FINANCIAL HIGHLIGHTS

(Dollars in millions except per share information) *Fiscal Year Ended*

	Jan 29, 1994	Jan. 30, 1993	Feb. 1, 1992	Feb. 2, 1991	Jan. 28, 1990	Jan. 29, 1989	Jan. 31, 1988	Feb. 1, 1987	Feb. 2, 1986	Feb. 3, 1985
OPERATIONS:										
Net Sales	$ 7,946	$ 7,169	$ 6,124	$ 5,510	$ 4,788	$ 4,000	$ 3,137	$ 2,445	$ 1,976	$ 1,702
Net Earnings	483	438	340	326	321	268	204	152	120	111
Earnings Per Share	1.63	1.47	1.15	1.11	1.09	.91	.69	.52	.41	.39
FINANCIAL POSITION AT YEAR END:										
Working Capital	633	797	328	177	238	255	225	155	181	222
Real Estate-Net	2,040	1,877	1,751	1,433	1,142	952	762	601	423	279
Total Assets	6,150	5,323	4,583	3,582	3,075	2,555	2,027	1,523	1,226	1,099
Long-Term Obligations	724	671	391	195	173	174	177	85	88	88
Stockholders' Equity	3,148	2,889	2,426	2,046	1,705	1,424	1,135	901	717	579
NUMBER OF STORES AT YEAR END:										
Toys"R"Us - United States	581	540	497	451	404	358	313	271	233	198
Toys"R"Us - International	234	167	126	97	74	52	37	24	13	5
Kids"R"Us	217	211	189	164	137	112	74	43	23	10

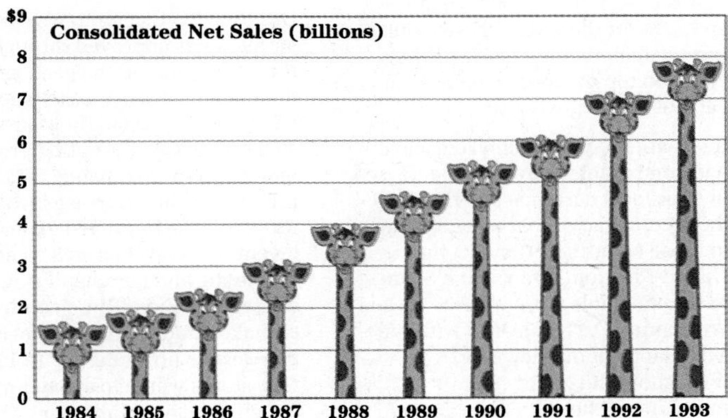

TO OUR STOCKHOLDERS

FINANCIAL HIGHLIGHTS

We are pleased to report another excellent year for Toys "R" Us. In 1993, we once again achieved record sales and earnings as well as significant market share gains. Since Toys "R" Us became a public company, we have reported 15 consecutive years of sales and earnings increases, with an annual compounded growth rate over that period of 25%.

Our sales reached $7.9 billion, an 11% increase over the $7.2 billion reported in the previous year. Pre-tax earnings increased 12% while net earnings rose to $483 million, a 10% increase over the $438 million in 1992. Earnings per share were $1.63 compared to $1.47 a year ago. Our stockholders' equity increased to $3.1 billion by the end of 1993.

Robert C. Nakasone, President and Chief Operating Officer and Michael Goldstein, Vice Chairman and Chief Executive Officer.

We achieved these outstanding results by having the best selection of merchandise, being stocked in depth, and by being competitive with our everyday low prices. Our strong performance also reflects several new marketing and merchandising initiatives implemented this year; including the wider distribution of our Holiday Toy Catalog, the expansion of Books "R" Us shops within our U.S.A. toy stores and increased customer service initiatives.

Our existing and new strategies contributed to comparable store sales increases in our U.S.A. toy stores of 6.5% in the fourth quarter and 3.3% for the year. These results are particularly impressive as they come on top of strong increases in each of the last two years.

Internationally, Germany and Japan had comparable store sales decreases in their local currencies, reflecting the recessionary economic conditions in those countries. Canada, the United Kingdom, France and Spain had comparable store sales increases. We continue to be pleased with the acceptance of our new stores throughout the world. Our International division once again, demonstrated its ability to improve inventory management and increase labor and distribution productivity in spite of the difficult economic environment in Europe and Japan.

We have created a franchising division that will enable us to bring additional countries into the Toys "R" Us family on an accelerated basis, and provide for the opening of stores in additional parts of the world. We have already signed two franchise agreements which allow for the opening of Toys "R" Us stores in the Middle East commencing in 1994. We will receive royalty and other related franchise service fees providing meaningful cash flow and earnings for our International division.

Our Kids "R" Us children's clothing stores' sales improved throughout the second half of the year, and despite a difficult apparel sales environment, ended the year with a slight increase. Operating profits increased approximately 25% following a 50% increase in 1992 reflecting the improved expense and inventory control as well as new marketing and merchandising strategies. Kids "R" Us continues to make strategic improvements to increase its profitability. In 1993, four stores were closed and we anticipate closing another 15 to 20 stores which are not meeting expectations.

Lastly, we announced a plan to buy back $1 billion of our common stock over the next several years. Even with our aggressive expansion, Toys "R" Us expects to generate excess cash flow. We believe that in addition to investing in our ongoing business, the repurchase of Toys "R" Us common stock will increase shareholder value.

OPERATIONAL HIGHLIGHTS

We are proud of our ability to provide our customers with the best selection of merchandise, stocked in depth with everyday low prices, while maintaining one of the lowest expense structures in the industry. The following highlights some 1993 accomplishments along with our plans for 1994.

In 1993, we significantly expanded the distribution of our Holiday Toy Catalog providing our customers with even more coupons than in prior years. The catalog was very successful and allowed us to highlight the broad selection of merchandise that can be found at Toys "R" Us. Customers used the catalog as a shopping aid throughout the Holiday season.

We have continued testing various "specialty shops" within our stores: the most notable being "Books "R" Us".

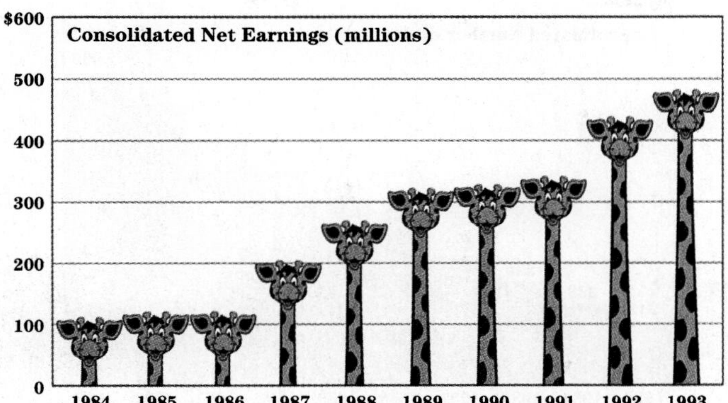

The Books "R" Us shops offer a broad selection of children's books and encourage children to read. In 1993, we added about 160 "Books "R" Us" shops and plan to have over 300 shops by the end of 1994. We have also been experimenting with other shops such as construction toys, large outdoor playsets and stuffed animals. We believe that these shops help distinguish Toys "R" Us from our competitors.

Enhancing customer service continues to be a primary focus for Toys "R" Us. In 1993, we expanded our successful "Geoffrey Helper" program in both the U.S.A. and International toy stores. In 1994, we will install customer friendly in-aisle price scanners and other service oriented technology to assist our customers who are our number one priority.

In 1990, we began remodeling about fifteen of our older U.S.A. toy stores each year. The remodeled stores enhance the customers' shopping experience while increasing in-store productivity. In 1993, we accelerated this program to about 25 stores and expect to remodel another 25 to 30 stores in 1994.

The use of technology to control expenses is a priority at Toys "R" Us. We again increased productivity and improved our ability to replenish stores by building an automated state-of-the-art distribution facility in southern Germany and retrofitting an existing facility in California with our new automated systems. In 1994, we plan to replace four U.S.A. toy distribution centers with two automated facilities in Missouri and Florida. Distribution facilities in France, Germany and Spain will also be retrofitted with new automated systems.

All U.S.A. toy stores were provided with laser radio terminal (LRT) technology in 1993, which takes advantage of wireless radio frequency communications within our stores. This equipment enhances shelf replenishment and improves employee productivity.

We installed satellite technology in North America. This technology instantaneously links our stores with our headquarters' computer databases as well as our customer transaction authorization networks in a more cost effective manner. We have also been able to utilize business television in our North American stores.

STORE GROWTH

In 1993, we opened 41 toy stores in the United States. Internationally, 67 stores opened in 11 countries, including our first stores in Australia, Portugal, Belgium, Switzerland and the Netherlands. For the first time, our International division opened more toy stores than the United States division. We also opened 10 Kids "R" Us stores. At the end of 1993, we had 815 toy stores operating in 46 states and Puerto Rico, Canada; Europe - the United Kingdom, Germany, France, Spain, Austria, Switzerland, the Netherlands, Belgium and Portugal; Asia - Japan, Hong Kong, Singapore, Malaysia and Taiwan; and Australia. We also had 217 Kids "R" Us stores operating in 29 states.

In 1994, we plan to open 40 to 45 toy stores in the U.S.A. and 65 to 70 stores internationally, including our first stores in Scandinavia. The new Scandinavian stores will be serviced from the United Kingdom. Once again, our anticipated opening of international stores will exceed the openings in the U.S.A. The international stores will capitalize on the existing infrastructure thereby enhancing the profitability of new

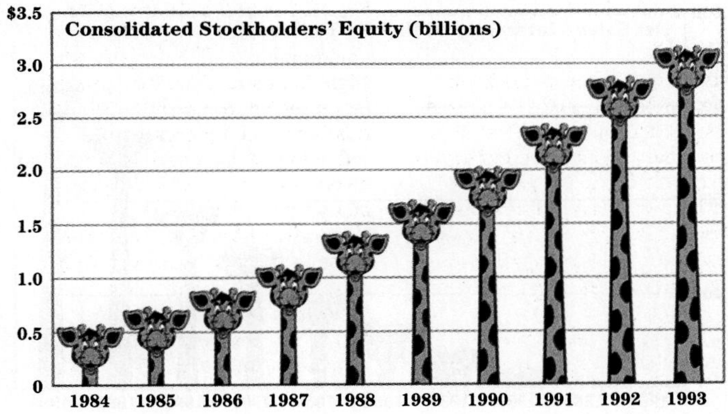

and existing stores. We plan to open about 10 new Kids "R" Us stores.

With our financial strength, we intend to capitalize on our strong competitive position throughout the world, by continued expansion to achieve greater sales, earnings and market share gains.

CORPORATE CITIZENSHIP

Toys "R" Us maintains a corporate-wide giving program focusing on improving the health care needs of children by supporting many national and regional children's health care organizations. In 1993, we contributed funds to more than 10 new children's health care organizations. We expanded our Hospital Playroom Program in 1993 by opening 4 additional playrooms bringing the total to 18. This program fixtures and equips quality children's play centers in hospitals. We expect to expand our program into eight additional hospitals in 1994.

Once again we were very involved in assisting those in need in the aftermath of the floods in the Midwest and the Southern California earthquake by providing free diapers and other basic consumables.

Toys "R" Us is a signatory to a Fair Share Agreement with the NAACP and has taken steps to support women and other minorities in the workplace. We are the leading purchaser of products from several minority-owned toy companies.

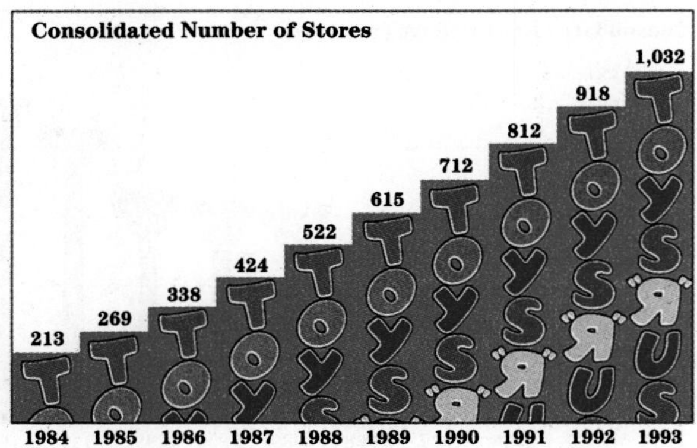

Toys "R" Us continues to have a strong toy safety program which includes the inspection of directly imported toys. Furthermore, we continue to take numerous pro-active initiatives, including a leadership position in eliminating the sale of look-a-like toy guns.

Through our new Books "R" Us shops, we are promoting literacy by demonstrating to children that reading is fun. We introduced a reading initiative called Geoffrey's Reading Railroad which offers a free reading kit with prize incentives for reading up to nine books. In conjunction with the opening of Books "R" Us shops, Toys "R" Us reached out to the community and selected Reading Is Fundamental (RIF) as the recipient of a grant. Part of this grant went towards RIF's Project Open Book, a program that provides books to children in homeless shelters.

HUMAN RESOURCES

The excellence of our management team and associates enables Toys "R" Us to expand aggressively and profitably.

We have made the following important promotions and additions to our executive ranks:

Corporate and Administrative:

Michael J. Corrigan, Vice President - Compensation and Benefits

Toys "R" Us, United States:

Lee Richardson, Vice President - Advertising

Karl S. Taylor, Vice President - Merchandise Planning and Allocation

Toys "R" Us, International:

Ken Bonning, Vice President - Logistics

Keith C. Spurgeon, Vice President - Toys "R" Us, Asia/Australia

Kids "R" Us:

Virginia Harris, Senior Vice President- General Merchandise Manager

Lorna E. Nagler, Vice President - Divisional Merchandise Manager

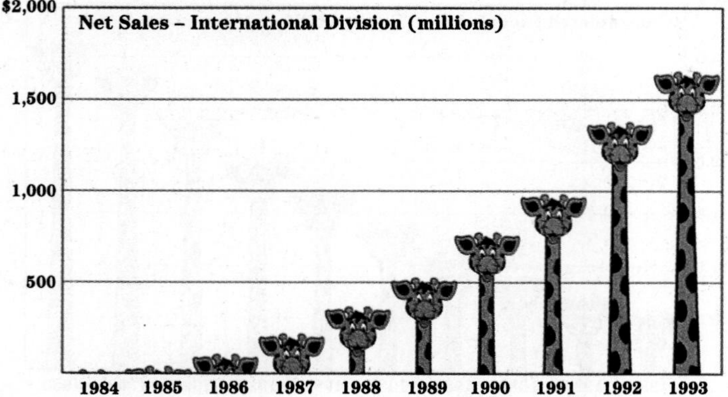

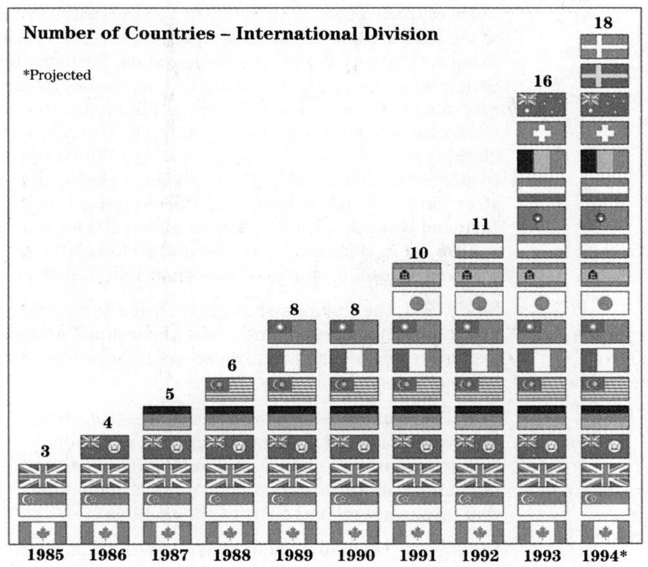

Charles Lazarus, Chairman of the Board

SUMMARY

The exciting world of Toys "R" Us continues to expand. We look forward to a strong year in 1994, with profit improvement in all three divisions. We will work hard to continue being the most trusted store in town.

We value our excellent relationships with our innovative suppliers and commend them for their products, which create excitement in our stores. Our assessment of the February New York Toy Fair indicates an exciting year in basic categories such as crafts, construction, action figures, preschool and dolls with reasonably priced quality product.

We recognize the dedication and quality work of our associates around the world who have made this another record year. Our appreciation is also extended to you, our stockholders, for your commitment and loyalty to Toys "R" Us.

Finally, we would like to thank Charles Lazarus, our founder and the Chairman of the Board for his confidence in us and the rest of the Toys "R" Us team. He has created an impressive organization and a great legacy. We intend to fully meet his expectations and live up to the standards he set.

Sincerely,

Michael Goldstein
Vice Chairman and
Chief Executive Officer

Robert C. Nakasone
President and
Chief Operating Officer

March 30, 1994

LETTER FROM THE CHAIRMAN

Over the past 46 years since I opened my first toy store in Washington, D.C., I have seen Toys "R" Us grow to become a sophisticated, multinational company with stores throughout the world. Many people have contributed to the success of our company, none more than Mike Goldstein, our new Vice Chairman and Chief Executive Officer, and Bob Nakasone, our new President and Chief Operating Officer. These appointments are an integral part of our succession planning process and give added responsibilities to our two most senior executives.

In my new role, I will continue to be significantly involved with Toys "R" Us in a variety of ways. First and foremost, I will ensure that the vision of Toys "R" Us remains intact by visiting our U.S.A. and International operations. I will also be providing guidance in the development of new merchandising and marketing concepts. Lastly, I will be working with governmental officials throughout the world to ensure that Toys "R" Us is able to continue its global expansion.

I look forward to my new role and remain as excited about the future prospects of Toys "R" Us today, as I first did more than four decades ago.

Charles Lazarus
Chairman of the Board

MANAGEMENT'S DISCUSSION-RESULTS OF OPERATIONS AND FINANCIAL CONDITION

RESULTS OF OPERATIONS*

The Company has experienced sales growth in each of its last three years; sales were up 10.8% in 1993, 17.1% in 1992 and 11.1% in 1991. Part of the growth is attributable to the opening of 130 new U.S.A. toy stores, 137 international toy stores and 57 children's clothing stores during the three year period, and a portion of the increase is due to comparable U.S.A. toy store sales increases of 3.3%, 6.9% and 2.4% in 1993, 1992 and 1991, respectively.

Cost of sales as a percentage of sales decreased to 69.2% in 1993 from 69.3% in 1992 and from 70.0% in 1991 due to a more favorable merchandise mix.

Selling, advertising, general and administrative expenses as a percentage of sales increased to 18.8% in 1993 from 18.7% in 1992 primarily as a result of start-up costs for the opening of our new market in Australia. These expenses decreased in 1992 from 18.8% in 1991 as a result of labor productivity gains and other cost cutting measures.

Interest expense increased in 1993 and 1992 compared to 1991 due to increased average borrowings, the mix between short-term and long-term borrowings and the mix between countries, partially offset by lower short-term interest rates. Short-term interest income increased during these periods due to an increase in cash available for investment.

The effective tax rate increased to 37.5% in 1993 from 36.5% in 1992, due to a 1% increase in the U.S. Federal corporate income tax rate and an adjustment for the retroactive impact of this tax change. The effective tax rate decreased to 36.5% in 1992 from 37.0% in 1991, due to a change in the mix of foreign earnings and certain foreign tax benefits. The Company believes its deferred tax assets, as reported, are fully realizable.

The Company believes that its risks attendant to foreign operations are minimal as it operates in sixteen different countries which are politically stable. International sales and operating earnings were unfavorably impacted by the translation of local currency results into U.S. dollars at lower average exchange rates in 1993 than in 1992. However, the strong dollar had a favorable impact on the cost of international capital investment in 1993.

Inflation has had little effect on the Company's operations in the last three years.

LIQUIDITY AND CAPITAL RESOURCES

The Company continues to maintain a strong financial position as evidenced by its working capital of $633 million at January 29, 1994 and $797 million at January 30, 1993. The long-term debt to equity percentage is 23.0% at January 29, 1994 as compared to 23.2% at January 30, 1993.

The Company plans to open 105 to 115 toy stores in 1994 in the United States, Australia, Austria, Belgium, Canada, France, Germany, Japan, the Netherlands, Portugal, Spain, Switzerland and the United Kingdom, as well as the new markets of Denmark and Sweden. Additionally, the Company plans to open about 10 Kids "R" Us children's clothing stores and close approximately 15 to 20 stores (4 stores closed in 1993). The Company believes that the store closings will not have a significant impact on its financial position. The Company opened 108 toy stores in 1993, 84 in 1992 and 75 in 1991 and 10 Kids "R" Us children's clothing stores in 1993, 23 in 1992 and 25 in 1991.

Since 1981, the Company has purchased a significant portion of its real estate and plans to continue this policy. Generally, real estate acquisitions are financed through internally generated funds.

For 1994, capital requirements for real estate, store and warehouse fixtures and equipment, leasehold improvements and other additions to property and equipment are estimated at $650 million (including real estate and related costs of $400 million).

In 1993, the Company completed its five million share repurchase program and announced a new one billion dollar share repurchase program which will occur over the next several years. During the three years ended January 29, 1994, the Company repurchased 5,648,000 shares of its common stock for $210,477,000 pursuant to these programs. The repurchase of shares during 1994 is anticipated to be financed by internally generated funds.

The seasonal nature of the business (approximately 49% of sales take place in the fourth quarter) typically causes cash to decline from the beginning of the year through October as inventory increases for the Christmas season and funds are used for land purchases and construction of new stores, which usually open in the first ten months of the year. Therefore, the Company has commitments and backup lines from numerous financial institutions to adequately support its short-term financing needs. Management expects that seasonal cash requirements will continue to be met primarily through operations, issuance of short-term commercial paper and bank borrowings for its foreign subsidiaries.

Where appropriate, the Company may convert short-term borrowings to long-term debt to achieve a balance between fixed and variable interest rates. In this regard, during 1993 the Company's Japanese subsidiary borrowed 4 billion yen (approximately $36 million) at various interest rates with a third party in Japan.

* References to 1993, 1992 and 1991 are for the 52 weeks ended January 29, 1994, January 30, 1993 and February 1, 1992, respectively.

TOYS"R"US, INC. AND SUBSIDIARIES

CONSOLIDATED STATEMENTS OF EARNINGS

(In thousands except per share information)		*Year Ended*	
	January 29, 1994	*January 30, 1993*	*February 1, 1992*
Net sales	$ 7,946,067	$ 7,169,290	$ 6,124,209
Costs and expenses:			
Cost of sales	5,494,766	4,968,555	4,286,639
Selling, advertising, general and administrative	1,497,011	1,342,262	1,153,576
Depreciation and amortization	133,370	119,034	100,701
Interest expense	72,283	69,134	57,885
Interest and other income	(24,116)	(18,719)	(13,521)
	7,173,314	6,480,266	5,585,280
Earnings before taxes on income	772,753	689,024	538,929
Taxes on income	289,800	251,500	199,400
Net earnings	$ 482,953	$ 437,524	$ 339,529
Earnings per share	$ 1.63	$ 1.47	$ 1.15

See notes to consolidated financial statements.

TOYS"R"US, INC. AND SUBSIDIARIES

CONSOLIDATED BALANCE SHEETS

(In thousands)

	January 29, 1994	*January 30, 1993*
ASSETS		
Current Assets:		
Cash and cash equivalents	$ 791,893	$ 763,721
Accounts and other receivables	98,534	69,385
Merchandise inventories	1,777,569	1,498,671
Prepaid expenses and other	40,400	52,731
Total Current Assets	2,708,396	2,384,508
Property and Equipment:		
Real estate, net	2,035,673	1,876,835
Other, net	1,148,794	926,715
Total Property and Equipment	3,184,467	2,803,550
Other Assets	256,746	134,794
	$ 6,149,609	$ 5,322,852
LIABILITIES AND STOCKHOLDERS' EQUITY		
Current Liabilities:		
Short-term borrowings	$ 239,862	$ 120,772
Accounts payable	1,156,411	941,375
Accrued expenses and other current liabilities	471,782	361,661
Income taxes payable	206,996	163,841
Total Current Liabilities	2,075,051	1,587,649
Deferred Income Taxes	202,663	175,430
Long-Term Debt	710,365	660,488
Obligations Under Capital Leases	13,248	10,264
Stockholders' Equity:		
Common stock	29,794	29,794
Additional paid-in capital	454,061	465,494
Retained earnings	3,012,806	2,529,853
Foreign currency translation adjustments	(56,021)	14,317
Treasury shares, at cost	(292,358)	(150,437)
	3,148,282	2,889,021
	$ 6,149,609	$ 5,322,852

See notes to consolidated financial statements.

TOYS"R"US, INC. AND SUBSIDIARIES

CONSOLIDATED STATEMENTS OF CASH FLOWS

(In thousands)	Year Ended		
	January 29, 1994	*January 30, 1993*	*February 1, 1992*
CASH FLOWS FROM OPERATING ACTIVITIES			
Net earnings	$ 482,953	$ 437,524	$ 339,529
Adjustments to reconcile net earnings to net cash provided by operating activities:			
Depreciation and amortization	133,370	119,034	100,701
Deferred income taxes	36,534	13,998	15,817
Changes in operating assets and liabilities:			
Accounts and other receivables	(29,149)	(5,307)	9,092
Merchandise inventories	(278,898)	(108,066)	(115,436)
Prepaid expenses and other operating assets	(39,448)	(36,249)	(16,176)
Accounts payable, accrued expenses and other liabilities	325,165	112,232	462,152
Income taxes payable	26,588	40,091	7,071
Total adjustments	174,162	135,733	463,221
Net cash provided by operating activities	657,115	573,257	802,750
CASH FLOWS FROM INVESTING ACTIVITIES			
Capital expenditures, net	(555,258)	(421,564)	(548,538)
Other assets	(58,383)	(22,175)	(17,110)
Net cash used in investing activities	(613,641)	(443,739)	(565,648)
CASH FLOWS FROM FINANCING ACTIVITIES			
Short-term borrowings, net	119,090	(170,887)	(94,811)
Long-term borrowings	40,576	318,035	197,802
Long-term debt repayments	(1,335)	(7,926)	(1,590)
Exercise of stock options	29,879	86,323	32,707
Share repurchase program	(183,233)	(27,244)	--
Net cash provided by financing activities	4,977	198,301	134,108
Effect of exchange rate changes on cash and cash equivalents	(20,279)	(8,691)	38,378
CASH AND CASH EQUIVALENTS			
Increase during year	28,172	319,128	409,588
Beginning of year	763,721	444,593	35,005
End of year	$ 791,893	$ 763,721	$ 444,593

SUPPLEMENTAL DISCLOSURES OF CASH FLOW INFORMATION

The Company considers its highly liquid investments purchased as part of its daily cash management activities to be cash equivalents. During the years ended January 29, 1994, January 30, 1993 and February 1, 1992, the Company made income tax payments of $220,229, $151,722 and $155,469 and interest payments (net of amounts capitalized) of $104,281, $83,584 and $46,763, respectively.

See notes to consolidated financial statements.

TOYS"R"US, INC. AND SUBSIDIARIES

CONSOLIDATED STATEMENTS OF STOCKHOLDERS' EQUITY

	Common Stock				
	Issued		In Treasury	Additional	
(In thousands)	*Shares*	*Amount*	*Amount*	*paid-in capital*	*Retained earnings*
Balance, February 2, 1991	297,938	$ 29,794	$ (129,340)	$ 353,924	$ 1,752,800
Net earnings for the year	–	–	–	–	339,529
Exercise of stock options (1,640 Treasury shares)	–	–	1,623	15,259	–
Tax benefit from exercise of stock options	–	–	–	15,620	–
Balance, February 1, 1992	297,938	29,794	(127,717)	384,803	2,092,329
Net earnings for the year	–	–	–	–	437,524
Share repurchase program (708 Treasury shares)	–	–	(27,244)	–	–
Exercise of stock options (4,479 Treasury shares)	–	–	4,524	35,301	–
Tax benefit from exercise of stock options	–	–	–	45,390	–
Balance, January 30, 1993	297,938	29,794	(150,437)	465,494	2,529,853
Net earnings for the year	–	–	–	–	482,953
Share repurchase program (4,940 Treasury shares)	–	–	(183,233)	–	–
Exercise of stock options (1,394 Treasury shares)	–	–	41,312	(21,464)	–
Tax benefit from exercise of stock options	–	–	–	10,031	–
Balance, January 29, 1994	297,938	$ 29,794	$ (292,358)	$ 454,061	$ 3,012,806

See notes to consolidated financial statements.

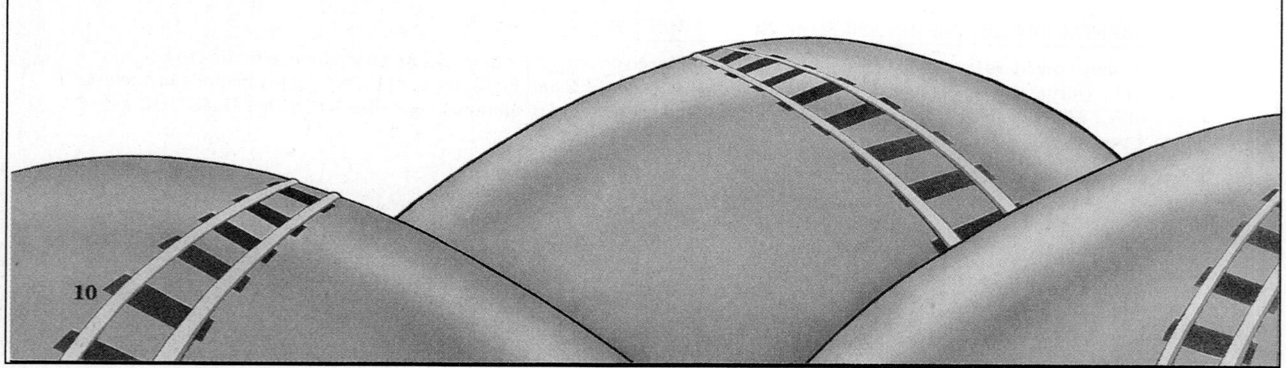

TOYS"R"US, INC. AND SUBSIDIARIES

NOTES TO CONSOLIDATED FINANCIAL STATEMENTS

SUMMARY OF SIGNIFICANT ACCOUNTING POLICIES

Fiscal Year

The Company's fiscal year ends on the Saturday nearest to January 31. References to 1993, 1992 and 1991 are for the 52 weeks ended January 29, 1994, January 30, 1993 and February 1, 1992, respectively.

Principles of Consolidation

The consolidated financial statements include the accounts of the Company and its subsidiaries. All material intercompany balances and transactions have been eliminated. Assets and liabilities of foreign operations are translated at current rates of exchange at the balance sheet date while results of operations are translated at average rates in effect for the period. Translation gains or losses are shown as a separate component of stockholders' equity. The increase (decrease) in the foreign currency translation adjustment was ($70,338,000), ($33,650,000), and $7,539,000 for 1993, 1992 and 1991, respectively.

Merchandise Inventories

Merchandise inventories for the U.S.A. toy store operations, which represent over 66% of total inventories, are stated at the lower of LIFO (last-in, first-out) cost or market as determined by the retail inventory method. If inventories had been valued at the lower of FIFO (first-in, first-out) cost or market, inventories would show no change at January 29, 1994 or January 30, 1993. All other merchandise inventories are stated at the lower of FIFO cost or market as determined by the retail inventory method.

Property and Equipment

Property and equipment are recorded at cost. Depreciation and amortization are provided using the straight-line method over the estimated useful lives of the assets or, where applicable, the terms of the respective leases, whichever is shorter.

Preopening Costs

Preopening costs, which consist primarily of advertising, occupancy and payroll expenses, are amortized over expected sales to the end of the fiscal year in which the store opens.

Capitalized Interest

Interest on borrowed funds is capitalized during construction of property and is amortized by charges to earnings over the depreciable lives of the related assets. Interest of $7,300,000, $8,403,000 and $12,237,000 was capitalized during 1993, 1992 and 1991, respectively.

Financial Instruments

The carrying amounts reported in the balance sheets for cash and cash equivalents and short-term borrowings approximate their fair market values.

Forward Foreign Exchange Contracts

The Company enters into forward foreign exchange contracts to eliminate currency movement relating to certain transactions denominated in foreign currency. Gains and losses which offset the movement in the underlying transactions are recognized as part of such transactions. As of January 29, 1994, the Company had $290,000,000 of outstanding forward contracts maturing in 1994. There were no open contracts at January 30, 1993. The Company does not expect to incur any losses as a result of counterparty defaults.

PROPERTY AND EQUIPMENT

(In thousands)	*Useful Life (in years)*	*January 29, 1994*	*January 30, 1993*
Land		$ 693,737	$ 642,368
Buildings	45-50	1,446,277	1,280,850
Furniture and equipment	5-20	953,360	809,772
Leaseholds and leasehold improvements	12 1/2-50	658,191	510,780
Construction in progress		41,855	72,895
Leased property under capital leases		24,360	20,193
		3,817,780	3,336,858
Less accumulated depreciation and amortization		633,313	533,308
		$ 3,184,467	$ 2,803,550

LONG - TERM DEBT

(In thousands)	*January 29, 1994*	*January 30, 1993*
Industrial revenue bonds, net of expenses (a)	$ 74,208	$ 74,174
Mortgage notes payable at annual interest rates from 7 1/8% to 11% (b)	13,318	13,708
Japanese yen loans payable at annual interest rates from 3.85% to 6.46%, due in varying amounts through 2012	142,688	93,904
British pound sterling 11% Stepped Coupon Guaranteed Bonds, due 2017	194,415	193,180
8 1/4% sinking fund debentures, due 2017, net of discounts	88,117	88,013
8 3/4% debentures, due 2021, net of expenses	197,978	197,906
	710,724	660,885
Less current portion	359	397
	$ 710,365	$ 660,488

(a) Bank letters of credit of $57,135,000, expiring in 1995, support certain industrial revenue bonds. The Company expects the bank letters of credit expiring in 1995 will be renewed. The bonds have fixed or variable interest rates with an average of 2.5% at January 29, 1994.

(b) Mortgage notes payable are collateralized by property and equipment with an aggregate carrying value of $18,628,000 at January 29, 1994.

The fair market value of the Company's long-term debt at January 29, 1994 is approximately $846,000,000. The fair market value was estimated using quoted market rates for publicly traded debt and estimated current interest rates for non-public debt.

The annual maturities of long-term debt at January 29, 1994 are as follows:

Year ending in	*(In thousands)*
1995	$ 359
1996	1,655
1997	3,045
1998	4,360
1999	5,310
2000 and subsequent	695,995
	$ 710,724

LEASES

The Company leases a portion of the real estate used in its operations. Most leases require the Company to pay real estate taxes and other expenses; some require additional amounts based on percentages of sales.

Obligations under capital leases require minimum payments as follows:

Year ending in	*(In thousands)*
1995	$ 2,582
1996	2,630
1997	2,475
1998	2,255
1999	1,996
2000 and subsequent	12,451
Total minimum lease payments	24,389
Less amount representing interest	9,957
Obligations under capital leases	14,432
Less current portion	1,184
	$ 13,248

Minimum rental commitments under noncancellable operating leases having a term of more than one year as of January 29, 1994 were as follows:

(In thousands) *Year ending in*	*Gross minimum rentals*	*Sublease income*	*Net minimum rentals*
1995	$ 207,664	$ 7,139	$ 200,525
1996	207,462	6,593	200,869
1997	204,867	5,754	199,113
1998	204,730	5,587	199,143
1999	203,461	4,688	198,773
2000 and subsequent	2,770,005	31,359	2,738,646
	$ 3,798,189	$ 61,120	$ 3,737,069

Total rental expense was as follows:

		Year ended	
(In thousands)	*January 29, 1994*	*January 30, 1993*	*February 1, 1992*
Minimum rentals	$ 180,118	$ 149,027	$ 118,583
Additional amounts computed as percentages of sales	5,604	5,447	5,140
	185,722	154,474	123,723
Less sublease income	7,935	5,788	2,629
	$ 177,787	$ 148,686	$ 121,094

STOCKHOLDERS' EQUITY

The common shares of the Company, par value $.10 per share, were as follows:

(In thousands)	*January 29, 1994*	*January 30, 1993*
Authorized shares	550,000	550,000
Issued shares	297,938	297,938
Treasury shares	8,416	4,870

Earnings per share is computed by dividing net earnings by the weighted average number of common shares outstanding after reduction for treasury shares and assuming exercise of dilutive stock options computed by the treasury stock method using the average market price during the year.

Weighted average numbers of shares used in computing earnings per share were as follows:

(In thousands)	*Year ended January 29, 1994*	*January 30, 1993*	*February 1, 1992*
Common and common equivalent shares	296,463	297,718	296,139

TAXES ON INCOME

The provisions for income taxes consist of the following:

(In thousands)	*Year ended January 29, 1994*	*January 30, 1993*	*February 1, 1992*
Current:			
Federal	$ 200,303	$ 186,013	$ 138,779
Foreign	17,259	15,605	15,378
State	35,704	35,884	29,426
	253,266	237,502	183,583
Deferred:			
Federal	49,961	17,187	19,545
Foreign	(16,186)	(6,705)	(7,678)
State	2,759	3,516	3,950
	36,534	13,998	15,817
Total	$ 289,800	$ 251,500	$ 199,400

Deferred tax liabilities and deferred tax assets reflect the net tax effects of temporary differences between the carrying amounts of assets and liabilities for financial reporting purposes and the amounts used for income tax purposes. The Company has gross deferred tax liabilities of $251.7 million at January 29, 1994 and $190.4 million at January 30, 1993 which consist primarily of temporary differences related to fixed assets of $194.0 million and $171.9 million, respectively. The Company had gross deferred tax assets of $92.8 million at January 29, 1994 and $63.8 million at January 30, 1993, which consist primarily of net operating losses of foreign start-up operations of $60.4 million and $38.5 million, and operating costs not currently deductible for tax purposes of $23.2 million and $18.6 million, respectively. Valuation allowances are not significant.

A reconciliation of the federal statutory tax rate with the effective tax rate follows:

(In thousands)	*Year ended January 29, 1994*	*January 30, 1993*	*February 1, 1992*
Statutory tax rate	35.0%	34.0%	34.0%
State income taxes, net of federal income tax benefit	3.2	4.0	4.1
Foreign	(0.5)	(1.2)	(0.5)
Other, net	(0.2)	(0.3)	(0.6)
	37.5%	36.5%	37.0%

Deferred income taxes were not provided on unremitted earnings of foreign subsidiaries that are intended to be indefinitely invested. Unremitted earnings were approximately $101 million at January 29, 1994, exclusive of amounts that if remitted would result in little or no tax under current U.S. tax laws. Net income taxes of approximately $35 million would be due if these earnings were to be remitted.

PROFIT SHARING PLAN

The Company has a profit sharing plan with a 401(k) salary deferral feature for eligible domestic employees. The terms of the plan call for annual contributions by the Company as determined by the Board of Directors, subject to certain limitations. The profit sharing plan may be terminated at the Company's discretion. Provisions of $29,961,000, $29,824,000 and $15,513,000 have been charged to operations in 1993, 1992 and 1991, respectively.

STOCK OPTIONS

The Company has Stock Option Plans (the "Plans"), including a new plan subject to shareholder approval, which provide for the granting of options to purchase the Company's common stock to substantially all employees and non-employee directors of the Company. The Plans provide for the issuance of non-qualified options, incentive stock options, performance share options, performance units, stock appreciation rights, restricted shares and unrestricted shares. The majority of the options become exercisable four years and nine months from the date of grant. Certain non-qualified options become exercisable nine years from the date of grant, however the exercise date of all or a portion of such options may be accelerated if the price of the Company's common stock reaches certain target amounts. The options granted to non-employee directors are exercisable 20% each year on a cumulative basis commencing one year from the date of grant.

In addition to the aforementioned Plans, stock options aggregating 6,659,375 shares were granted to certain senior executives during the period from 1984 to 1993 pursuant to individual plans. These options are exercisable 20% each year on a cumulative basis commencing one year from the date of grant.

The exercise price per share of all options granted has been the market price of the Company's common stock on the date of grant. Outstanding options must be exercised within ten years from the date of grant.

At January 29, 1994, 13,327,781 shares were available for future grants under the Plans and 4,807,607 options were exercisable. All outstanding options expire at dates varying from May 1994 to December 2003.

At January 29, 1994, an aggregate of 30,574,872 shares of authorized common stock was reserved for all of the Plans noted above.

Stock option transactions are summarized as follows:

	Shares Under Option		
(In thousands except price range)	*Incentive*	*Non-Qualified*	*Price Range*
Outstanding January 30, 1993	752	13,201	$ 7.03 - 39.63
Granted	--	5,645	36.44 - 40.94
Exercised	(224)	(1,170)	7.03 - 36.94
Cancelled	(1)	(956)	9.74 - 39.88
Outstanding January 29, 1994	527	16,720	$ 7.68 - 40.94

The exercise of non-qualified stock options results in state and federal income tax benefits to the Company related to the difference between the market price at the date of exercise and the option price. During 1993, 1992 and 1991, $10,031,000, $45,390,000 and $15,620,000, respectively, was credited to additional paid-in capital.

FOREIGN OPERATIONS

Certain information relating to the Company's foreign operations is set forth below. Corporate assets include all cash and cash equivalents and other related assets.

	Year ended		
(In thousands)	*January 29, 1994*	*January 30, 1993*	*February 1, 1992*
Sales			
Domestic	$ 6,278,591	$ 5,795,119	$ 5,154,215
Foreign	1,667,476	1,374,171	969,994
Total	$ 7,946,067	$ 7,169,290	$ 6,124,209
Operating Profit			
Domestic	$ 724,818	$ 647,640	$ 527,695
Foreign	102,923	101,132	62,846
General corporate expenses	(6,821)	(9,333)	(7,248)
Interest expense, net	(48,167)	(50,415)	(44,364)
Earnings before taxes on income	$ 772,753	$ 689,024	$ 538,929
Identifiable Assets			
Domestic	$ 3,630,921	$ 3,277,527	$ 3,095,178
Foreign	1,694,565	1,248,827	1,009,455
Corporate	824,123	796,498	477,975
Total	$ 6,149,609	$ 5,322,852	$ 4,582,608

QUARTERLY FINANCIAL DATA

The following table sets forth certain unaudited quarterly financial information.

(In thousands except per share information)	*First Quarter*	*Second Quarter*	*Third Quarter*	*Fourth Quarter*
YEAR ENDED JANUARY 29, 1994				
Net Sales	$ 1,286,479	$ 1,317,012	$ 1,449,118	$ 3,893,458
Cost of Sales	882,876	902,414	982,151	2,727,325
Net Earnings	35,436	35,505	37,457	374,555
Earnings per Share	$ .12	$ .12	$ .13	$1.27
YEAR ENDED JANUARY 30, 1993				
Net Sales	$ 1,172,476	$ 1,249,144	$ 1,345,835	$ 3,401,835
Cost of Sales	809,929	864,511	922,619	2,371,496
Net Earnings	28,304	32,709	36,796	339,715
Earnings per Share	$ .10	$ .11	$ .12	$1.14

REPORT OF MANAGEMENT

Responsibility for the integrity and objectivity of the financial information presented in this Annual Report rests with Toys "R" Us management. The accompanying financial statements have been prepared from accounting records which management believes fairly and accurately reflect the operations and financial position of the Company. Management has established a system of internal controls to provide reasonable assurance that assets are maintained and accounted for in accordance with its policies and that transactions are recorded accurately on the Company's books and records.

The Company's comprehensive internal audit program provides for constant evaluation of the adequacy of the adherence to management's established policies and procedures. The Company has distributed to key employees its policies for conducting business affairs in a lawful and ethical manner.

The 1993 and 1992 financial statements of the Company have been audited by Ernst & Young, independent auditors, in accordance with generally accepted auditing standards, including a review of financial reporting matters and internal controls to the extent necessary to express an opinion on the consolidated financial statements.

Michael Goldstein Vice Chairman and Chief Executive Officer	Louis Lipschitz Senior Vice President-Finance and Chief Financial Officer

MARKET INFORMATION

The Company's common stock is listed on the New York Stock Exchange. The following table reflects the high and low prices (rounded to the nearest one-eighth) based on New York Stock Exchange trading since February 1, 1992.

The Company has not paid any cash dividends and a change in this policy is not under consideration by the Board of Directors.

The number of stockholders of record of common stock on March 9, 1994 was approximately 25,500.

	High	*Low*
1992		
1st Quarter	38 5/8	30 3/8
2nd Quarter	37 1/8	31
3rd Quarter	41	34 3/4
4th Quarter	41 1/4	35 5/8
1993		
1st Quarter	42 3/8	36 5/8
2nd Quarter	39 3/4	32 3/8
3rd Quarter	40 3/8	33 3/4
4th Quarter	42 7/8	36

REPORT OF INDEPENDENT AUDITORS

The Board of Directors and Stockholders
Toys "R" Us, Inc.

We have audited the accompanying consolidated balance sheets of Toys "R" Us, Inc. and subsidiaries, as of January 29, 1994 and January 30, 1993, and the related consolidated statements of earnings, stockholders' equity and cash flows for the years then ended. These financial statements are the responsibility of the Company's management. Our responsibility is to express an opinion on these financial statements based on our audit. The consolidated statements of earnings, stockholders' equity and cash flows of Toys "R" Us, Inc. and subsidiaries for the year ended February 1, 1992 were audited by other auditors whose report dated March 11, 1992, expressed an unqualified opinion on those statements.

We conducted our audits in accordance with generally accepted auditing standards. Those standards require that we plan and perform the audit to obtain reasonable assurance about whether the financial statements are free of material misstatement. An audit includes examining, on a test basis, evidence supporting the amounts and disclosures in the financial statements. An audit also includes assessing the accounting principles used and significant estimates made by management, as well as evaluating the overall financial statement presentation. We believe that our audits provide a reasonable basis for our opinion.

In our opinion, the 1993 and 1992 financial statements referred to above present fairly, in all material respects, the consolidated financial position of Toys "R" Us, Inc. and subsidiaries at January 29, 1994 and January 30, 1993 and the consolidated results of their operations and their cash flows for the years then ended in conformity with generally accepted accounting principles.

Ernst + Young

New York, New York
March 9, 1994

DIRECTORS AND OFFICERS

DIRECTORS

Charles Lazarus
Chairman of the Board of the Company

Robert A. Bernhard
Real Estate Developer

Michael Goldstein
Vice Chairman and Chief Executive Officer of the Company

Milton S. Gould
Attorney-at-law; Partner - Shea & Gould

Shirley Strum Kenny
President, Queens College of The City University of New York

Reuben Mark
Chairman and CEO Colgate-Palmolive Company

Howard W. Moore
Former Executive Vice President-General Merchandise Manager of the Company; Consultant

Robert C. Nakasone
President and Chief Operating Officer of the Company

Norman M. Schneider
Former Chairman, Leisure Products Division of Beatrice Foods Company; Consultant

Harold M. Wit
Managing Director, Allen & Company Incorporated; Investment Bankers

OFFICERS - CORPORATE AND ADMINISTRATIVE

Michael Goldstein
Vice Chairman and Chief Executive Officer

Robert C. Nakasone
President and Chief Operating Officer

Dennis Healey
Senior Vice President - Management Information Systems

Louis Lipschitz
Senior Vice President - Finance and Chief Financial Officer

Michael P. Miller
Senior Vice President - Real Estate

Jeffrey S. Wells
Senior Vice President - Human Resources

Gayle C. Aertker
Vice President - Real Estate

Michael J. Corrigan
Vice President - Compensation and Benefits

Jonathan M. Friedman
Vice President - Controller

Eileen C. Gabriel
Vice President - Information Systems

Jon W. Kimmins
Vice President - Treasurer

Matthew J. Lombardi
Vice President - Information Technology

Eric A. Swartwood
Vice President - Architecture and Construction

Michael L. Tumolo
Vice President - Real Estate Counsel

Peter W. Weiss
Vice President - Taxes

Andre Weiss
Secretary - Attorney-at-law; Partner-Schulte Roth & Zabel

TOYS "R" US UNITED STATES - OFFICERS AND GENERAL MANAGERS

Roger V. Goddu
Executive Vice President - General Merchandise Manager

Van H. Butler
Senior Vice President - Marketing and Divisional Merchandise Manager

Bruce C. Hall
Senior Vice President - Store Operations and Support Services

Michael J. Madden
Senior Vice President - Distribution

Thomas J. Reinebach
Senior Vice President - Chief Financial Officer

Ernest V. Speranza
Senior Vice President - Advertising/Marketing

Robert J. Weinberg
Senior Vice President - Divisional Merchandise Manager

Kristopher M. Brown
Vice President - Distribution Operations

Richard N. Cudrin
Vice President - Employee and Labor Relations

Harvey J. Finkel
Vice President - Operations

Martin Fogelman
Vice President - Divisional Merchandise Manager

Lee Richardson
Vice President - Advertising

John P. Sullivan
Vice President - Divisional Merchandise Manager

Karl S. Taylor
Vice President - Merchandise Planning and Allocation

GENERAL MANAGERS

Robert F. Price
Vice President New York/Northern New Jersey

Larry D. Gardner
Pacific Northwest/Alaska

Michael A. Gerety
Georgia/South Carolina/Tennessee/Alabama

Gary H. Gilliard
Colorado/Utah/New Mexico/Montana

Mark H. Haag
Southern California/Arizona/Nevada/Hawaii

Daniel D. Hlavaty
Central Ohio/Indiana/Kentucky

Debra M. Kachurak
New England

Richard A. Moyer
S. Texas/Louisiana/Mississippi

Gerald S. Parker
Northern California

John J. Prawlocki
Florida/Puerto Rico

J. Michael Roberts
Pennsylvania/Delaware/Southern New Jersey

Edward F. Siegler
Kansas/Missouri/Iowa/Nebraska

Carl P. Spaulding
N.E. Ohio/W. Pennsylvania/N. New York

William A. Stephenson
Illinois/Wisconsin/Minnesota

John P. Suozzo
Maryland/Virginia/North Carolina

Brian L. Voorhees
N. Texas/Oklahoma/Arkansas

Dennis J. Williams
Michigan/N.W. Ohio

KIDS "R" US - OFFICERS

Richard L. Markee
President

Virginia Harris
Senior Vice President - General Merchandise Manager

James L. Easton
Vice President - Divisional Merchandise Manager

Jerel G. Hollens
Vice President - Merchandise Planning and Management Information Systems

Debra G. Hyman
Vice President - Divisional Merchandise Manager

Elizabeth S. Jordan
Vice President - Human Resources

Lorna E. Nagler
Vice President - Divisional Merchandise Manager

James G. Parros
Vice President - Stores and Physical Distribution

TOYS "R" US INTERNATIONAL - OFFICERS AND COUNTRY MANAGEMENT

Larry D. Bouts
President

Gregory R. Staley
Senior Vice President - General Merchandise Manager

Lawrence H. Meyer
Vice President - Chief Financial Officer

Philip Bloom
Vice President - General Merchandise Manager

Ken Bonning
Vice President-Logistics

Joseph Giamelli
Vice President - Information Systems

Adam Szopinski
Vice President - Operations

Keith Van Beek
Vice President - Development

COUNTRY MANAGEMENT

David Rurka
President - Toys "R" Us Europe
Managing Director - Toys "R" Us Holdings PLC (United Kingdom)

Arnt Klöser
President - Toys "R" Us Central Europe
Managing Director - TRU A.G. (Switzerland)

Jacques Le Foll
President - Toys "R" Us S.A.R.L. (France)

Carl Olsen
Managing Director - Toys "R" Us (Australia) Pty. Ltd.

Guillermo Porrati
Managing Director - Toys "R" Us Iberia, S.A. (Spain)

Manabu Tazaki
President - Toys "R" Us Japan, Ltd.

Elliott Wahle
President - Toys "R" Us (Canada) Ltd.

Keith C. Spurgeon
Vice President -Asia/Australia

Scott Chen
General Manager - Toys "R" Us Lifung Taiwan Limited

Michael Yeo
General Manager - Toys "R" Us Metro Pte. Ltd. (Singapore)

CORPORATE DATA

ANNUAL MEETING

The Annual Meeting of the Stockholders of Toys "R" Us will be held at the offices of the Company, 461 From Road, Paramus, New Jersey on Wednesday, June 8, 1994 at 10:00 a.m.

STOCKHOLDER INFORMATION

The Company will supply to any owner of Common Stock, upon written request to Mr. Louis Lipschitz of the Company at the address set forth below, and without charge, a copy of the Annual Report on Form 10-K for the year ended January 29, 1994, which has been filed with the Securities and Exchange Commission.

COMMON STOCK LISTED

New York Stock Exchange, Symbol: TOY

THE OFFICE OF THE COMPANY IS LOCATED AT

461 From Road
Paramus, New Jersey 07652
Telephone: 201-262-7800

GENERAL COUNSEL

Schulte Roth & Zabel
900 Third Avenue
New York, New York 10022

INDEPENDENT AUDITORS

Ernst & Young
787 Seventh Avenue
New York, New York 10019

REGISTRAR AND TRANSFER AGENT

American Stock Transfer and Trust Company
40 Wall Street
New York, New York 10005
Telephone: 718-921-8200

Printed on recycled paper

GLOSSARY

Accelerated Depreciation Methods that result in higher depreciation expense in the early years of an operational asset's life and lower expense in the later years. 416

Account A standardized format used by organizations to accumulate the dollar effects of transactions on each financial statement item. 59

Accounting A system that collects and processes (analyzes, measures, and records) financial information about an organization and reports that information to decision makers. 6

Accounting Cycle The recordkeeping process used during and at the end of the accounting period that results in the preparation of financial statements. 116

Accounting Entity The organization for which financial data are to be collected (separate and distinct from its owners). 8

Accounting Period The time period covered by the financial statements. 13

Accounts Receivable (**trade receivables** or **receivables**) Open accounts owed to the business by trade customers. 308

Accruals Revenues that have been earned and expenses that have been incurred by the end of the current accounting period but that will not be collected or paid until a future accounting period. 170

Accrual Basis Accounting Revenues are recorded when earned and expenses when incurred, regardless of when the related cash is received or paid. 111

Accrued Liabilities Expenses that have been incurred but have not yet been paid at the end of the accounting period. 458

Acquisition Cost Net cash equivalent amount paid for an asset. 408

Adjusting Entries End-of-period entries necessary to measure income properly, correct errors, and provide for adequate valuation of balance sheet accounts. 170

Aging of Accounts Receivable Method Estimates uncollectible accounts based on the age of each account receivable. 314

Allowance for Doubtful Accounts Contra asset account containing the estimated uncollectible accounts receivable; also called allowance for bad debts or allowance for uncollectible accounts. 309

Allowance Method Method that bases bad debt expense on an estimate of uncollectible accounts. 309

Amortization Systematic and rational allocation of the cost of an intangible asset over its useful life. 411

Annuity A series of periodic cash receipts or payments that are equal in amount each interest period. 472

Assets Probable future economic benefits owned by the entity as a result of past transactions. 55

Audit An examination of the financial reports to assure that they represent what they claim and conform with generally accepted accounting principles. 26

Audit Trail The referencing system with sufficiently detailed explanations necessary for tracing an entry back to its source documents. 197

Authorized Number of Shares Maxi-mum number of shares of capital stock of a corporation that can be issued as specified in the charter. 539

Available-for-Sale Securities All investments, other than trading securities, that are accounted for under the market value method. 585

Bad Debt Expense (**doubtful accounts expense, uncollectible accounts expense**, or **provision for uncollectible accounts**) Expense associated with estimated uncollectible accounts receivable. 309

Balance Sheet (Statement of Financial Position) A statement that reports the financial position (assets, liabilities, and stockholders' equity) of an accounting entity at a point in time. 8

Bank Reconciliation Process of verifying the accuracy of both the bank statement and the cash accounts of the business. 325

Bank Statement Monthly report from a bank that shows deposits recorded, checks cleared, other debits and credits, and a running bank balance. 324

Basket Purchase Acquisition of two or more assets in a single transaction for a single lump sum. 409

Basic Accounting Equation (Balance Sheet Equation) Assets = Liabilities + Stockholders' Equity. 10

Bond Certificate The bond document; each bondholder receives a bond certificate. 501

Bond Discount The difference between selling price and par when a bond is sold for less than par. 503

Bond Premium The difference between selling price and par when a bond is sold for more than par. 503

Bond Principal The amount payable at the maturity of the bond; face amount, on which the periodic cash interest payments are computed. 500

Bond Sinking Fund A cash fund accumulated for payment of a bond at maturity. 514

Book Value (Net Book Value, Carrying Value) The difference between an asset's acquisition cost and accumulated depreciation, its related contra account. 169

Book (or Carrying) Value Acquisition cost of an operational asset less accumulated depreciation, depletion, or amortization. 412

Callable Bonds Bonds that may be called for early retirement at the option of the issuer. 502

Capital Expenditures Expenditures that are debited to an asset account; the acquisition of an asset. 424

Capitalized Interest Interest expenditures included in the cost of a self-constructed asset. 409

Cash Money and any instrument that banks will accept for deposit and immediate credit to the depositor's account, such as a check, money order, or bank draft. 320

Cash Basis Accounting Revenues are recorded when cash is received and expenses are recorded when cash is paid, regardless of when the revenues are earned or expenses are incurred. Cash basis accounting is not appropriate for preparing financial statements for external users. 111

Cash Equivalent A short-term highly liquid investment with original maturity of less than three months. SCF reports changes in cash and cash equivalents. 628

Cash Equivalents Short-term investments with original maturities of three months or less that are readily convertible to cash and whose value is unlikely to change. 320

Cash Flows from Financing Activities Cash inflows and outflows related to how cash was obtained to finance the enterprise. 630

Cash Flows from Investing Activities Cash inflows and outflows related to the acquisition or sale of productive facilities and the making or collecting of loans. 630

Cash Flows from Operating Activities Cash inflows and outflows directly related to earnings from normal operations. 629

Closing Entries Made at the end of the accounting period to transfer net income or loss and dividends declared to retained earnings and to establish a zero balance in each of the temporary accounts. 188

Common Stock The basic, normal, voting stock issued by a corporation; called residual equity because it ranks after preferred stock for dividend and liquidation distributions. 541

Comparable Information Information that can be compared across businesses. 252

Completed-Contract Method Records revenue when the completed product is delivered to the customer. 318

Component Percentage A percentage that expresses each item on a particular financial statement as a percentage of a single base amount. 681

Conservatism Care should be taken not to overstate assets and revenues or understate liabilities and expenses. 254

Consistent Information Information that can be compared over time. 252

Consolidated Financial Statements The financial statements of two or more companies that have been combined into a single set of financial statements. 596

Contingent Liability Potential liability that has arisen as the result of a past event; not an effective liability until some future event occurs. 468

Continuity Assumption Businesses are assumed to continue to operate into the foreseeable future. 53

Contra Account An account that is an offset to, or reduction of, the primary account. 169

Contributed Capital Results from owners providing cash (and sometimes other assets) to the business. 55

Control The ability of the investing company to determine the operating and financing policies of another company in which it owns shares of the voting stock; presumed to exist when more than 50% of the voting stock of an entity is owned by one investor. 584

Convertible Bonds Bonds that may be converted to other securities of the issuer (usually common stock). 502

Convertible Preferred Stock Preferred stock that is convertible to common stock at the option of the holder. 543

Copyright Exclusive right to publish, use, and sell a literary, musical, or artistic work. 428

Cost-Benefit Constraint The benefits of accounting for and reporting information should outweigh the costs. 254

Cost of Goods Sold Equation BI + P – EI = CGS 358

Cost Principle An accounting assumption that requires assets to be recorded at the cash-equivalent cost, which on the date of the transaction is cash paid plus the current dollar value of all noncash considerations also given in the exchange. 57

Coupon Rate The stated rate of interest on bonds. 502

Credit Card Discount Fee charged by the credit card company for services. 303

Cumulative Dividend Preference Preferred stock preference that requires specified current dividends not paid in full to accumulate for every year in which they are not paid. These cumulative preferred dividends must be paid before any common dividends can be paid. 550

Cumulative Effects of Changes in Accounting Methods Amount reflected on the income statement for adjustments made to balance sheet accounts when applying different accounting principles. 265

Current Assets Assets that will be turned into cash or expire (be used up) within the longer of one year or the operating cycle. 256

Current Dividend Preference The basic dividend preference on preferred stock for a particular year. 550

Current Liabilities Obligations to be paid with current assets normally within one year. 256

Current Liabilities Short-term obligations that will be paid within the current operating cycle or one year, whichever is longer. 456

Current Ratio The ratio of total current assets divided by total current liabilities; also known as the working capital ratio. 456

Debits and Credits Debit is the name for the left side of an account. Debits represent increases in assets and decreases in liabilities and stockholders' equity. Credit is the name for the right side of an account. Credits represent decreases in assets and increases in liabilities and stockholders' equity. 67

Debenture An unsecured bond; no assets are specifically pledged to guarantee repayment. 500

Declining-Balance (DB) Depreciation The method that allocates the cost of an operational asset over its useful life based on a multiple of the SL rate. 417

Deferrals Previously recorded assets, liabilities, revenues, or expenses that need to be adjusted at the end of the period to reflect earned revenues or incurred expenses. 170

Deferred Revenues Revenues that have been collected but not earned; liabilities until the goods or services are provided. 460

Deferred Tax Items Difference between income tax expense and income tax liability; caused by temporary differences; may be a liability or an asset. 465

Depletion Systematic and rational allocation of the cost of a natural resource over the period of exploitation. 411

Depreciation Systematic and rational allocation of the cost of property, plant, and equipment (but not land) over their useful lives. 410

Direct Labor The earnings of employees who work directly on the products being manufactured. 357

Direct Method Reports components of cash flows from operating activities as gross receipts and gross payments. 631

Discontinued Operations Results from the disposal of a major segment of the business; reported net of income tax effects. 264

Dividend Dates:

Declaration Date Date on which the board of directors officially approves the dividend. 549

Payment Date Date on which a cash dividend is paid to the stockholders of record. 549

Record Date Date on which the corporation prepares the list of current stockholders as shown on its records; dividends can be paid only to the stockholders who own stock on that date. 549

Dividends in Arrears Dividends on cumulative preferred stock that have not been declared in prior years. 550

Earnings Forecasts Predictions of earnings for future accounting periods. 247

Effective-Interest Amortization Method that amortizes a bond discount or premium on the basis of the effective-interest rate; theoretically preferred method. 510

Effective-Interest Rate Another name for the market rate of interest on a bond when issued; also called the yield rate. 503

Efficient Markets A securities market in which prices fully reflect available information. 697

Equity Method Method used by investor if 20% to 50% of the voting stock of the investee company is owned by the investor. It permits recording of investor's share of investee's income. 592

Estimated Useful Life Estimated service life of an operational asset to the present owner. 413

Expenses Expenses are outflows of net assets (decreases in assets and/or increases in liabilities) from ongoing operations. 107

Extraordinary Items Gains and losses that are both unusual in nature and infrequent in occurrence; they are reported net of tax on the income statement. 265

Extraordinary Repairs Major, high-cost, long-term repairs that increase the economic usefulness of the asset. Debited to an asset account (or accumulated depreciation); a capital expenditure. 425

Face Amount Another name for principal or the principal amount of a bond. 500

Factory Overhead Manufacturing costs that are not raw material or direct labor costs. 357

Financial Accounting Standards Board (FASB) The private sector body given the primary responsibility to work out the detailed rules that become generally accepted accounting principles. 22

Financial Leverage Use of borrowed funds to increase the rate of return on owners' equity; occurs when the interest rate on debt is lower than the earnings rate on total assets. 499

Finished Goods Inventory Manufactured goods that are completed and ready for sale. 355

First-In, First-Out (FIFO) Method Inventory costing method that assumes the oldest units are the first units sold. 362

Footnotes (Notes) Supplemental information about the financial condition of a company, without which the financial statements cannot be fully understood. 19

Form 8-K The report used by publicly traded companies to disclose any material event not previously reported that is important to investors. 275

Form 10-K The annual report that publicly traded companies must file with the SEC. 274

Form 10-Q The quarterly report that publicly traded companies must file with the SEC. 275

Full-Disclosure Principle The requirement to disclose all relevant economic information of the business. 252

Future Value The sum to which an amount will increase as the result of compound interest. 470

Gains Gains are inflows of net assets (total assets minus total liabilities) from peripheral transactions. 108

Generally Accepted Accounting Principles (GAAP) The measurement rules used to develop the information in financial statements. 21

Goods Available for Sale The sum of beginning inventory and purchases (or transfers to finished goods) for the period. 358

Goodwill The amount that was paid for the good reputation and customer appeal of an acquired company. 603

Goodwill For accounting purposes, the purchase price of a business that is in excess of the market value of the other net assets of that business. 430

Gross Margin (gross profit) Net sales less cost of goods sold. 263

Held-to-Maturity Portfolio A long-term investment in bonds that management has the ability and intent to hold until maturity. 516

Income before Income Taxes (Pretax Earnings) Revenues less all expenses except income tax expense. 264

Income from Operations (Operating Income) Net sales less cost of goods sold and other operating expenses. 263

Income Statement (Statement of Income, Statement of Earnings, or Statement of Operations) A statement that reports the revenues less the expenses of the accounting period. 13

Income Summary A temporary account used only during the closing process to facilitate the closing of revenues and expenses; it is closed to Retained Earnings. 189

Indenture A bond contract that specifies the legal provisions of a bond issue. 501

Indirect Method The method of preparing the operating section of the SCF that adjusts net income to compute cash flows from operating activities. 631

Installment Method Recognizes revenue on the basis of cash collection after the delivery of goods. 318

Institutional Investors Managers of pension, mutual, endowment, and other funds that invest on the behalf of others. 250

Intangible Assets Operational assets that have special rights but not physical substance. 408

Internal Controls Policies and procedures designed to safeguard the assets of the business and ensure the accuracy of financial records. 321

Inventory Tangible property that is held for sale in the normal course of business or will be used in producing goods or services for sale. 354

Issued Shares Total shares of stock that have been issued; shares outstanding plus treasury shares held. 540

Journal A record that lists chronologically the effects of transactions; the book of original entry. 197

Journal Entry An accounting method for expressing the effects of a transaction on accounts in a debits-equal-credits format. 68

Last-In, First-Out (LIFO) Method Inventory costing method that assumes the most recently acquired units are sold first. 363

Leaseholds Rights granted to a lessee under a lease contract. 429

Ledger Contains all of the individual accounts for revenues, expenses, assets, liabilities, and stockholders' equity; the book of final entry. 198

Legal Capital The permanent amount of capital defined by state law, that must remain invested in the business; provides a "cushion" for creditors. 542

Lenders (Creditors) Suppliers and financial institutions that lend money to companies. 251

Liabilities Probable debts or obligations of the entity as a result of past transactions which will be paid with assets or services. 55

Liabilities Probable future sacrifices of economic benefits that arise from past transactions. 455

LIFO Liquidation A sale of a lower-cost inventory item from beginning LIFO inventory. 370

LIFO Reserve A contra-asset for the excess of FIFO over LIFO inventory. 368

Long-Term Liabilities All obligations of the entity that are not classified as current liabilities. 462

Losses Losses are outflows of net assets from peripheral transactions. 108

Lower of Cost or Market (LCM) Valuation method departing from cost principle that serves to recognize a loss when replacement cost or net realizable value drops below cost. 373

Market Interest Rate Current rate of interest on a debt when incurred; also called **yield** or **effective interest rate**. 503

Market Tests Ratios that tend to measure the market worth of a share of stock. 692

Market Value Method Method used by investor if less than 20% of the voting stock of the investee company is owned by the investor; unrealized gains and losses are recorded based on changes in the prices of securities that are held. 585

Matching Principle Expenses are recognized (recorded) when incurred in earning revenue. 112

Material Amounts Amounts large enough to influence a user's decision. 254

Merchandise Inventory Goods held for resale in the ordinary course of business. 354

Natural Resources Mineral deposits, timber tracts, oil, and gas. 427

Net Interest Cost Interest cost, less any income tax savings associated with interest expense. 499

Net Realizable Value The expected sales price less selling costs (e.g., repair and disposal costs). 374

Noncash Expenses Expenses that do not cause an immediate cash outflow; for example, depreciation expense. 638

Noncash Investing and Financing Activities Transactions that do not have direct cash flow effects; reported on the SCF in narrative or schedule form. 630

Nopar Value Stock Shares of capital stock that have no par value specified in the corporate charter. 542

Note Receivable A written promise that requires another party to pay the business under specified conditions (amount, time, interest). 308

Operating Cycle The time it takes for a company to purchase goods or services from suppliers, sell goods or services to customers, and collect cash from customers. It is also known as the cash-to-cash cycle. 109

Operational Assets Tangible and intangible assets owned by a business and used in its operations. 408

Ordinary Repairs and Maintenance Expenditures for the normal operating upkeep of operational assets; debit expense for ordinary repairs. 424

Outstanding Shares Total shares of stock that are owned by stockholders on any particular date. 540

Par Value A legal amount per share established by the board of directors; it establishes the minimum amount a stockholder must contribute and has no relationship to the market price of the stock. 259

Par Value Another name for bond principal or the maturity amount of a bond. 500

Par Value Nominal value per share of capital stock specified in the charter; serves as the basis for legal capital. 542

Parent The company that has a significant investment in a subsidiary company. 596

Percentage-of-Completion Method Records revenue based on the percentage of work completed during the accounting period. 318

Percentage of Credit Sales Method Bases bad debt expense on the historical percentage of credit sales that result in bad debts. 313

Periodic Inventory System Ending inventory and cost of goods sold are determined at the end of the accounting period based on a physical inventory count. 375

Permanent (Real) Accounts The balance sheet accounts that carry their ending balances into the next accounting period. Permanent accounts are not closed at the end of the period. 188

Perpetual Inventory System A detailed inventory record is maintained recording each purchase and sale during the accounting period. 376

Present Value The current value of an amount to be received in the future; a future amount discounted for compound interest. 470

Pooling of Interests An acquisition that is completed by exchanging parent company stock for subsidiary voting capital stock. 597

Post-Closing Trial Balance Should be prepared as the last step in the accounting cycle to check that debits equal credits and all temporary accounts have been closed. 190

Preferred Stock Shares of stock that have specified rights over the common stock. 542

Press Release A written public news announcement that is normally distributed to major news services. 270

Primary Objective of External Financial Reporting To provide useful economic information about a business to help external parties make sound financial decisions. 53

Prior Period Adjustment Amount debited or credited directly to retained earnings to correct an accounting error of a prior period. 555

Private Investors Individuals who purchase shares in companies. 251

Purchase An acquisition that is completed by purchasing subsidiary company voting capital stock for cash. 597

Purchase Discount Cash discount received for prompt payment of an account payable. 378

Purchase Discounts Account A deduction from the cost of purchases in the calculation of cost of goods sold for discounts taken. 379

Purchase Returns and Allowances A deduction from the cost of purchases associated with unsatisfactory goods. 378

Ratio (Percentage) Analysis An analytical tool designed to identify significant relationships; measures proportional relationship between two financial statement amounts. 681

Raw Materials Inventory Items acquired for the purpose of processing into finished goods. 354

Redeemable Bonds Bonds that may be turned in for early retirement at the option of the bondholder. 502

Replacement Cost The current purchase price for identical goods. 373

Relevant Information Information that can influence a decision; it is timely and has predictive and/or feedback value. 252

Reliable Information Information that is accurate, unbiased, and verifiable. 252

Report and Account Forms These are two common balance sheet preparation forms. The report form lists assets on the top and liabilities and stockholders' equity on the bottom. The account form list assets on the left side and liabilities and stockholders' equity accounts on the right side. 78

Report of Independent Accountants (Audit Report) A report that describes the auditors' opinion of the fairness of the financial statement presentations and the evidence gathered to support that opinion. 26

Report of Management A report that indicates management's primary responsibility for financial statement information and the steps taken to ensure the accuracy of the company's records. 25

Residual Value Estimated amount to be recovered, less disposal costs, at the end of the estimated useful life of an operational asset. 413

Retained Earnings Cumulative earnings of a company that are not distributed to the owners and are reinvested in the business. 56

Revenues Revenues are inflows of net assets (increases in assets and/or reductions of liabilities) from ongoing operations. 107

Revenue Expenditures Expenditures that are debited to an expense account; the incurrence of an expense. 424

Revenue Principle Revenues are recognized (recorded) when the earnings process is nearly complete, an exchange has taken place, and collection is probable. 111

Reversing Entries Optional entries made at the start of the next accounting period to reverse the effects of certain adjusting entries; facilitates subsequent entries and simplifies the bookkeeping function. 203

Sales (or **Cash) Discount** Cash discount offered to encourage prompt payment of an account receivable. 304

Sales Returns and Allowances A contra revenue account used to record return of or allowances for unsatisfactory goods. 305

Securities and Exchange Commission (SEC) The U.S. government agency that determines the financial statements that public companies must provide to stockholders and the measurement rules that must be used in producing those statements. 22

Separate-Entity Assumption Business transactions are separate from the transactions of the owners. 53

Significant Influence The ability of an investor company to have an important impact on the operating and financing policies of another company (the investee). 583

Specific Identification Method Inventory costing method that identifies the cost of the specific item that was sold. 364

Stated Rate The rate of cash interest per period specified in the bond contract. 500

Statement of Cash Flows A statement that reports inflows and outflows of cash during the accounting period in the categories of operations, investing, and financing. 17

Statement of Retained Earnings A statement that reports how net income and the distribution of dividends affected the financial position of the company during the accounting period. 16

Stockholders' Equity (Owners' Equity or Shareholders' Equity) The financing provided by the owners and the operations of the business. 55

Straight-Line Amortization Simplified method of amortizing a bond discount or premium that allocates an equal dollar amount to each interest period. 506

Straight-Line (SL) Depreciation Method that allocates the cost of an operational asset in equal periodic amounts over its useful life. 414

Stock Dividend Distribution of additional shares of a corporation's own capital stock to current stockholders on a pro rata basis at no cost; decreases retained earnings. 552

Stock Split An increase in the total number of authorized shares by a specified ratio; does not decrease retained earnings. 552

Subsidiary The company that is owned by a parent company as evidenced by more than 50% of the voting capital stock. 596

Sum-of-the-Years'-Digits Depreciation Method that allocates the cost of an operational asset over its useful life based on a fraction where the denominator is the total of all of the useful years and the numerator is the year of life in inverse order. 416

T-accounts An analytical tool for summarizing transaction effects for each account, determining balances for financial statement preparation, and drawing inferences about a company's activities. 69

Tangible Assets Operational assets that have physical substance. 408

Temporary (Nominal) Accounts Income statement and dividends declared accounts that are closed at the end of the accounting period. 188

Temporary Differences Timing differences that cause deferred income taxes and will reverse, or turn around, in the future. 465

Tests of Liquidity Ratios that measure a company's ability to meet its currently maturing obligations. 688

Tests of Solvency Ratios that measure a company's ability to meet its long-term obligations. 691

Time Value of Money Interest that is associated with the use of money over time. 461

Trade Discount A discount that is deducted from list price to derive the actual sales price. 305

Trading Securities All investments in stocks or bonds that are held primarily for the purpose of selling them in the near future; accounted for under the market value method. 585

Transaction (1) An exchange between a business and one or more external parties, such as borrowing money from a bank, or (2) a measurable event internal to a business, such as adjustments for the use of assets in operations. 57

Transaction Analysis The process of studying a transaction to determine its economic effect on the business in terms of the accounting equation: Assets = Liabilities + Stockholders' Equity. 60

Treasury Stock A corporation's own stock that had been issued but was subsequently reacquired and is still being held by that corporation. 546

Trial Balance A listing of all accounts with their balances to provide a check on the equality of the debits and credits. The unadjusted trial balance does not include the effects of the adjusting entries. 168

Time-Period Assumption The long life of a company can be reported in shorter time periods, usually months, quarters, and years. 105

Timeline A visual representation of a series of business activities, listing dates and amounts over time. 113

Trustee An independent party appointed to represent the bondholders. 502

Unit-of-Measure Assumption Accounting information will be measured and reported in the national monetary unit. 53

Units-of-Production Depreciation Method that allocates the cost of an operational asset over its useful life based on its periodic output related to its total estimated output. 415

Unissued Shares Authorized shares of a corporation's stock that have never been issued. 540

Unqualified Audit Opinion (Clean Audit Opinion) Auditors' statement that the financial statements are fair presentations in all material respects in conformity with GAAP. 246

Unrealized Holding Gains and Losses Amounts recorded when there is a price change for securities which are currently held. 587

Weighted-Average Method Inventory costing method that uses the weighted-average unit cost of the goods available for sale for both cost of goods sold and ending inventory. 363

Work in Process Inventory Goods in the process of being manufactured. 355

Working Capital The dollar difference between total current assets and total current liabilities. 456

Yield Another name for the market rate of interest on a bond. 503

Illustration Credits

Chapter 1

Photos/ads: Photo 1-1, p. 2 , Tony Stone Images; Photo 1-2, p. 4 , Maxidrive annual report cover, designed by Larry Cope, Richard D. Irwin, Inc., Photo 1-3, 7 , Tony Stone Images, Photo 1-4, p. 23 , Anthony James Dugal Photography.

Chapter 2

Photos/ads: Photo 2-1, p. 50 , James McGoon Photography; Photo 2-2, p. 52 , Courtesy Sbarro, Inc.; Photo 2-3, p. 55 , Courtesy Sbarro, Inc.; Photo 2-4, p. 60 , Courtesy Sbarro, Inc.

Chapter 3

Photos/ads: Photo 3-1, p. 102, Courtesy Sbarro, Inc.; Photo 3-2, p. 104, Courtesy Sbarro, Inc.; Photo 3-3, p. 107, Courtesy Sbarro, Inc.; Photo 3-4, p. 107, Courtesy Sbarro, Inc.; Photo 3-5, p. 107, Courtesy Sbarro, Inc.

Chapter 4

Photos/ads: Photo 4-1, p. 164, Courtesy Sbarro, Inc.; Photo 4-2, p. 166, Courtesy Sbarro, Inc.; Photo 4-3, p. 175, Courtesy Sbarro, Inc.

Chapter 5

Photos/ads: Photo 5-1, p. 242, Sports Illustrated; Photo 5-2, p. 244, Courtesy Callaway Golf; Photo 5-3, p. 251, Courtesy Callaway Golf; Photo 5-4, p. 259, Courtesy Callaway Golf 1994 annual report; Photo 5-5, p. 272, Courtesy Callaway Golf.

Chapter 6

Photos/ads: Photo 6-1, p. 298, Courtesy The Timberland Co.; Photo 6-2, p. 300, Courtesy The Timberland Co.; Photo 6-3, p. 303, John Thoeming Photography; Photo 6-4, p. 321, Courtesy The Timberland Co.; Photo 6-5, p. 321, Courtesy The Timberland Co.; Photo 6-6, p. 312, Chicago Magazine.

Chapter 7

Photos/ads: Photo 7-1, p. 350, Blair Seitz Photography; Photo 7-2, p. 352, Courtesy Harley-Davidson Motor Co.; Photo 7-3, p. 355, James Schnepf Photography; Photo 7-4, p. 373, James Schnepf Photography.

Chapter 8

Photos/ads: Photo 8-1, p. 404, Tony Stone Images; Photo 8-2, p. 406, Courtesy Delta Airlines Inc.; Photo 8-3, p. 411, Tony Stone Images; Photo 8-4, p. 425, David Gikley Photography; Photo 8-5, p. 429, Courtesy Delta Airlines, Inc.; Photo 8-6, p. 421, Courtesy Delta Airlines, Inc.

Chapter 9

Photos/ads: Photo 9-1, p. 452, Courtesy General Mills, Inc.; Photo 9-2, p. 454, Courtesy General Mills, Inc.; Photo 9-3, p. 457, Courtesy General Mills, Inc.; Photo 9-4, p. 464, Courtesy General Mills, Inc.; Photo 9-5, p. 469, Steve Niedorf Photography.

Chapter 10

Photos/ads: Photo 10-1, p. 496, Courtesy Showboat, Inc.; Photo 10-2, p. 498, Courtesy Showboat, Inc.; Photo 10-3, p. 501, Courtesy Showboat, Inc.; Photo 10-4, p. 502, Courtesy Showboat, Inc.; Photo 10-6, p. 507, Courtesy Showboat, Inc.; Photo 10-7, p. 512, Courtesy Showboat, Inc.

Chapter 11

Photos/ads: Photo 11-1, p. 534, Sygma; Photo 11-2, p. 536, Courtesy Wal-Mart, Inc.; Photo 11-3, p. 545, Sygma; Photo 11-4, p. 545, Gamma Liaison; Photo 11-5, p. 551, Sygma.

Chapter 12

Photos/ads: Photo 12-1, p. 580, John Thoeming Photography; Photo 12-2, p. 582, Courtesy American Brands, Inc.; Photo 12-3, p. 586, John Thoeming Photography; Photo 12-4, p. 586, John Thoeming Photography; Photo 12-5, p. 592, Tony Stone Images; Photo 12-6, p. 599, Courtesy American Brands, Inc.; Photo 12-7, p. 602, Gamma Liaison; Photo 12-8, p. 596, Courtesy American Brands, Inc.

Chapter 13

Photos/ads: Photo 13-1, p. 626, Courtesy Bargaineer Magazine/Home Shopping Network; Photo 13-2, p. 628, Courtesy Home Shopping Network; Photo 13-3, p. 632, Courtesy Home Shopping Network; Photo 13-4, p. 639, Courtesy Home Shopping Network; Photo 13-5, p. 645, Courtesy Home Shopping Network.

Chapter 14

Photos/ads: Photo 14-1, p. 674, Courtesy Home Depot, Photo 14-2, p. 676, Courtesy Home Depot; Photo 14-3, p. 685, Courtesy Home Depot; Photo 14-4, p. 690, Courtesy Home Depot; Photo 14-5, p. 690, Courtesy Home Depot; Photo 14-6, p. 695, Courtesy Home Depot.

BUSINESS INDEX

SUBJECT INDEX

M

N

O

P